THE CAMBRIDGE HISTORY
OF THE BRITISH EMPIRE

VOLUME SIX

Cambridge University Press
Fetter Lane, London

New York
Bombay, Calcutta, Madras
Toronto
Macmillan

Tokyo
Maruzen Company, Ltd

THE
CAMBRIDGE HISTORY
OF THE
BRITISH EMPIRE

General Editors

J. HOLLAND ROSE, M.A., Litt.D.

Vere Harmsworth Professor of Naval History in the University of Cambridge; Fellow of Christ's College, Cambridge

A. P. NEWTON, M.A., D.Lit.

Rhodes Professor of Imperial History in the University of London; Fellow of King's College, London

E. A. BENIANS, M.A.

Fellow and Senior Tutor of St John's College, Cambridge

Advisor for the Dominion of Canada

W. P. M. KENNEDY, M.A., Litt.D.

Professor of Law in the University of Toronto

VOLUME VI
CANADA
and
NEWFOUNDLAND

CAMBRIDGE
AT THE UNIVERSITY PRESS
1930

PREFACE

AN infant colony whose growth was stunted by a severe climate and feudal customs, a long colonial conflict marked by wearing border forays, a conquest leading on to racial discords and lengthy constitutional struggles, finally the oncoming of a levelling tide of somewhat prosaic prosperity—such, on a casual survey, may seem to be the outstanding features of the history of Canada. Any such summary would miss half of the truth. A more thoughtful study will reveal the working of forces which invest her annals with dignity, significance and an inner unity. To hazard here a few comments—we note that the unending struggles of Canadians with difficulties, both physical and political, have, in that invigorating climate, built up a virile population, for which every obstacle has been a challenge and every success a stimulus to greater effort. From the start the early French settlers underwent a hard but salutary schooling. Cut off by ice from the homeland during nearly half the year, and hindered in their western expansion by the tangled Laurentian uplands, they developed qualities of self-reliance that long defied Indian attacks, conquest by New Englanders and the numbing defects of the rule of Old France; and when finally they were conquered, it was by the stranglehold of sea power and the weight of numbers.

The conquest of 1760 did not end the struggle with the English, but merely transferred it from the sphere of arms to that of law, with results highly significant to students of psychology and constitutional history. Intent on incorporating the French Canadians in the British Empire, our statesmen and governors devised ways and means which invite comparison with those of ancient Rome in Greece and Gaul. The modern problem was more baffling than that which faced the Caesars; for religion and nationality now infused into it their potent influence. Consequently, the Canadians, surpassing Greeks and Gauls in national self-consciousness and therefore in political tenacity, defied both assimilation and coercion. In truth neither of these expedients was seriously contemplated by British statesmen, whose guiding principle in the Quebec Act of 1774 and the Canada Constitutional Act of 1791 was the conciliation of the French. But the rise of constitutional and other questions vital to the welfare of the growing English population complicated this problem, and a satisfactory solution was long deferred. Indeed, the facts set forth in this volume disprove the oft-repeated claim that the American Revolution forthwith endowed our imperial legislators with sagacity and foresight. On the contrary, they found the true line of advance only when the protracted ferment in both the Canadas, the strenuous

efforts of reformers in Nova Scotia, and the unanswerable arguments
of Lord Durham had closed every other avenue. From the downfall
of the Old Empire fully sixty years elapsed before the resolves of the
colonists and the bold counsel of that master-builder blazed the trail
for the New Empire.

Just as those long constitutional conflicts provided stiff training
both for Canadians and British statesmen, so too the crucial mid-
decades of the nineteenth century tested the mettle of the colonists
(now alive to the call of the West), and further revealed their sense
of the value of the British connection. The task of extending the thin
ribbon of population towards the Pacific and of holding all together
demanded both the alert resourcefulness of the pioneer and the
strategic daring and tactical caution of the true statesman. All these
qualities were forthcoming. Further, at the crisis of 1866 the ever
growing pressure exerted by the powerful southern neighbour urged
the still isolated and struggling provinces towards confederation as
the only means of both preserving their individuality and assuring
their prosperity. Certainly in the annals of political architecture the
formation of the Dominion of Canada deserves a foremost place.
Arising out of hard necessities, that achievement brought a mighty
harvest of results, both in Canada, which it extended from "the river
to the ends of the earth", and in the Empire at large, where it
beckoned Australia and South Africa to the like fruitful experiments.
Almost alone among great nation-builders, the Fathers of Confederation shed no blood, squandered no resources and bequeathed to the
future no heritage of hate, but rather pointed mankind forward to
an era of wider unions and more assured peace and prosperity.

By one of the inner harmonies of history it was reserved for a
French-Canadian statesman, Sir Wilfrid Laurier, with equal vivid-
ness and truth, to picture the future of the British Empire as that of
"a galaxy of nations under the British Crown", thus giving a wider
meaning to the vision of young nationhood seen dimly, but none the
less seen, by Sir John A. Macdonald at the dawn of confederation. And
when, seven years after Laurier spoke, the German challenge came,
Canada gallantly and without question shouldered her imperial
responsibilities. So, too, did Newfoundland. The action of the great
Dominion and of the self-contained island-colony alike refuted
Turgot's tempting simile that colonies, like fruit, were destined to
drop off when ripe. The British colonies proved rather to be like the
stout supports thrown out by the banyan tree in its maturity.

The simile is applicable also to the post-war changes in the imperial
system which are described in Chapter xxx. Resulting largely from
the bold progressiveness of Canadian statesmen, they have gone far
towards transforming the British Empire into a British Commonwealth of Nations, and thus supply one more illustration of the
adaptability of our constitution to the changing needs of the new age.

As in the sphere of imperial relations, so too in her own expansion Canada has displayed an inexhaustible resourcefulness. May we not ascribe that quality to a dauntless struggle with a seemingly hopeless configuration? Where Goldwin Smith tamely advocated "safety first" by annexation to the United States, she discerned a new call to adventure. "Fighting geography" along the border belt of plain and mountain between the Great Lakes and the Pacific, she found new sources of perennial vigour in the West and North.

The plan of this volume has in general been arranged on a chronological and unitary basis, and provincial history has designedly been subordinated to the story of developments which have made for wider union. At several points also we refer the reader to the general history of the Empire, which is the subject of the first three volumes of this series. In those earlier volumes the guiding purpose is to describe British expansion and questions of policy from the point of view of the Empire as a whole, while each Dominion volume deals with them only so far as they affect the fortunes of the Dominion concerned. For example, such matters as colonial conflicts with other Powers, trade relations, emigration, the disposal of public lands, defence and other questions of general concern are dealt with in their broader aspects in vols. i–iii; and in this volume only in their bearings on the history of Canada. In short, our aim in the general volumes is to show the outlook of the mother country on imperial problems, in the Dominion volumes the outlook of each Dominion. The addition of exact references in footnotes and of a selected Bibliography will, we trust, enhance the value of the work for students, while the requirements of the general reader have been consulted in the narrative.

It remains to express our special thanks to our twenty-eight Canadian and five British colleagues, without whose loyal and untiring co-operation the accomplishment of this work would have been impossible; to Professor W. P. M. Kennedy, for valuable advice and assistance at every stage both in the planning and execution of the volume; to Sir Robert A. Falconer, K.C.M.G., President of the University of Toronto, to the Hon. and Rev. Dr H. J. Cody and Professor H. A. Innis, also of that University, for generous assistance and counsel; to Dr A. G. Doughty, C.M.G., M.A., Litt.D., LL.D., Dominion Archivist and Deputy Minister, Ottawa, for his zeal in facilitating the researches of our contributors in the Canadian Archives and to Professor R. G. Trotter, Queen's University, for his long and valued services in connection with the Bibliography and Index.

J. H. R.
A. P. N.
E. A. B.

CAMBRIDGE
January, 1930

ABBREVIATIONS OF WORKS AND SOURCES
QUOTED IN THIS VOLUME

Am. H.R.	American Historical Review.
A.P.C. Col.	Acts of the Privy Council, Colonial.
B.M. Add. MSS.	Additional MSS. in the Department of Manuscripts, British Museum.
B.T.	Documents in the Archives of the Board of Trade, Public Record Office, London.
Cal. St. Pap. Col. Cal. St. Pap. Am. and W.I. Cal. St. Pap. Dom. Cal. St. Pap. For.	Calendars of State Papers, Colonial, America and West Indies, Domestic, Foreign, in P.R.O., London.
Can. Arch. MSS.	MSS. in the Public Archives of Canada, Ottawa.
Chatham MSS.	MSS. of Earl of Chatham and the younger Pitt in P.R.O., London.
C.H.B.F.P.	Cambridge History of British Foreign Policy.
C.H.R.	Canadian Historical Review.
C.J.	Journals of the British House of Commons.
C.M.H.	Cambridge Modern History.
C.O.	Documents in the Archives of the Colonial Office, P.R.O., London.–
E.H.R.	English Historical Review.
Hist. MSS. Comm.	Reports of the Historical MSS. Commission, London.
L.J.	Journals of the House of Lords.
N.R.S.	Publications of the Navy Records Society, London.
N.Y. Col. Doc.	Documents relating to the Colonial History of New York, ed. E. O'Callaghan.
P.R.O.	H.M. Public Record Office, London.
Pub. Arch. Can.	Public Archives of Canada, Ottawa.
T.O.	Transcripts preserved in the Archives of Canada.
T.pt.O.	Transcripts preserved in part in the Archives of Canada.

TABLE OF CONTENTS

CHAPTER I

THE GEOGRAPHICAL AND ETHNICAL BACKGROUND

By A. P. COLEMAN, Ph.D., D.Sc., LL.D., F.R.S., Professor Emeritus of Geology, the University of Toronto, and D. JENNESS, M.A., Victoria Memorial Museum, Ottawa.

CHAPTER II

THE FOUNDING OF ACADIA AND CANADA

By G. LANCTOT, Litt.D., The Public Archives, Ottawa.

CHAPTER III

THE OLD REGIME

By the Hon. T. CHAPAIS, Litt.D., LL.D., Senator of Canada, Professor of History, Laval University.

CHAPTER IV

THE STRUGGLE FOR SUPREMACY IN AMERICA

(I) 1682–1748

By J. HOLLAND ROSE, Litt.D., Vere Harmsworth Professor of Naval
History in the University of Cambridge, Fellow of Christ's
College, Cambridge.

(II) 1749–1760

By C. T. ATKINSON, M.A., Fellow and Lecturer in Modern
History, Exeter College, Oxford.

CHAPTER V

NEWFOUNDLAND, TO 1783

By A. P. NEWTON, D.Lit., F.S.A., Rhodes Professor of Imperial
History in the University of London, Fellow of King's College,
London.

CONTENTS

CHAPTER VI

THE PROBLEM OF GOVERNMENT, 1760–1774

By A. L. BURT, M.A., Professor of History, University of Alberta.

CHAPTER VII

BRITISH NORTH AMERICA AND THE AMERICAN REVOLUTION, 1774–1791

By DUNCAN A. McARTHUR, M.A., Douglas Professor of Colonial and Canadian History, Queen's University, Kingston.

CHAPTER VIII

BRITISH NORTH AMERICA UNDER REPRE-
SENTATIVE GOVERNMENT, 1791–1812

By Duncan A. McArthur, M.A.

CHAPTER IX

THE WAR OF 1812

By Duncan A. McArthur, M.A.

CHAPTER X

BRITISH NORTH AMERICA UNDER REPRE-
SENTATIVE GOVERNMENT

(A) LOWER CANADA (1815–1837)

By C. E. Fryer, M.A., Ph.D., Professor of Modern History, McGill University.

CONTENTS

CHAPTER XIII

CANADA UNDER RESPONSIBLE GOVERNMENT, 1854–1867

By Oscar D. Skelton, M.A., Ph.D., LL.D.

CHAPTER XIV

THE MARITIME PROVINCES, 1840–1867

By Chester Martin, M.A., LL.D.

CHAPTER XV

THE FINANCIAL DEVELOPMENT OF BRITISH NORTH AMERICA, 1840–1867

By Adam Shortt, C.M.G., Ph.D., LL.D., The Public Archives, Ottawa.

CHAPTER XVI

THE OPENING OF THE WEST

By L. J. BURPEE, Secretary to the International Joint
Commission, Ottawa.

CHAPTER XVII

NEWFOUNDLAND, 1783 TO 1867

By Sir C. ALEXANDER HARRIS, K.C.M.G., C.B., C.V.O., formerly
Governor of Newfoundland, and sometime Scholar of Christ's
College, Cambridge.

CHAPTER XVIII

THE COMING OF CONFEDERATION

By R. G. TROTTER, M.A., Ph.D., Professor of History, Queen's
University, Kingston.

CHAPTER XIX

EXPANSION OF THE DOMINION, TO 1880

By R. G. TROTTER, M.A., Ph.D.

CHAPTER XX

POLITICAL PARTIES AND RAILWAY POLICY, 1867–1885

By W. STEWART WALLACE, M.A., Librarian of the University of Toronto.

CHAPTER XXI

THE CONSERVATIVE AND LIBERAL ADMINISTRATIONS, 1885–1911

By W. STEWART WALLACE, M.A.

CHAPTER XXII

THE SETTLEMENT OF THE PRAIRIES, 1867–1914

By E. H. OLIVER, Ph.D., Principal of St Andrew's College, Saskatoon.

CHAPTER XXIII

THE SETTLEMENT AND PROGRESS OF BRITISH COLUMBIA, 1871–1914

By His Honour, Judge F. W. HOWAY, LL.B.

CHAPTER XXIV

THE PIONEERING SPIRIT

By Sir ROBERT A. FALCONER, K.C.M.G., M.A., D.Litt., LL.D., D.C.L., President of the University of Toronto.

CHAPTER XXV

THE ECONOMIC DEVELOPMENT OF CANADA,
1867–1921

(I) COMMUNICATIONS

By W. T. JACKMAN, M.A., Professor of Economics,
University of Toronto.

(II) AGRICULTURE

By J. COKE, B.S.A., M.F., Associate Professor of Agricultural
Economics, the Ontario Agricultural College.

(III) INDUSTRIAL DEVELOPMENT

By A. BRADY, M.A., Ph.D., Assistant Professor of Political Science,
University of Toronto.

CHAPTER XXVI

THE ECONOMIC DEVELOPMENT OF CANADA,
1867–1921 (*continued*)

(I) FINANCE AND BANKING

By A. J. GLAZEBROOK, Special Lecturer in Banking and Finance,
University of Toronto.

(II) COMMERCIAL POLICY AND THE DEVELOPMENT OF COMMERCE

By S. A. CUDMORE, M.A., Department of Statistics, Ottawa.

CHAPTER XXVII

THE ECONOMIC DEVELOPMENT OF CANADA, 1867–1921 (continued)

THE MARITIME PROVINCES

By C. R. FAY, M.A., Professor of Economics, University of Toronto, formerly Fellow of Christ's College, Cambridge; and H. A. INNIS, M.A., Ph.D., Associate Professor of Economics, University of Toronto.

CHAPTER XXVIII

NEWFOUNDLAND, 1867–1921

By Sir C. A. HARRIS, K.C.M.G., C.B., C.V.O.

CHAPTER XXIX

THE CONSTITUTION AND ITS WORKING,
1867–1921

By W. P. M. KENNEDY, M.A., Litt.D., Professor of Law,
University of Toronto.

CHAPTER XXX

CANADA AND THE EMPIRE, 1884–1921

By the Hon. N. W. ROWELL, K.C., LL.D.

CHAPTER XXXI

CANADA IN THE WORLD WAR, 1914–1918

By Lieutenant-Colonel WILLIAM WOOD.

CHAPTER XXXII

CANADA IN 1918–1921

By W. Stewart Wallace, M.A.

CHAPTER XXXIII

CULTURAL DEVELOPMENT

(A) FRENCH

By R. La Roque de Roquebrune and E. Montpetit, K.C., LL.D., Litt.D., Professor of Economics, University of Montreal.

(B) ENGLISH

By Sir Robert Falconer, K.C.M.G., D.Litt., LL.D., D.C.L.

ERRATA

p. 222 *For* Teppecanoe *read* Tippecanoe.

p. 237 *For* Sir George Drummond *read* Sir Gordon Drummond.

p. 275 *For* Reedy *read* Ready.

p. 343 *For* L. J. Drummond *read* L. T. Drummond.

p. 353 *For* Scobie *read* Scoble.

p. 813 *For* G.M.G. *read* C.M.G.

p. 877 *For* pp. 880–5 *read* p. 865.

Add to Index:

CHAPTER I

THE GEOGRAPHICAL AND ETHNICAL BACKGROUND

(A) THE GEOGRAPHICAL BACKGROUND

IT was a great adventure for a handful of French and English-speaking people to explore and take possession of half of North America, a territory nearly as large as Europe and extending from the latitude of Rome to that of Spitzbergen; and it is astonishing, even at the present time, that a population of only 9,000,000 should be in occupation of so vast a territory. That this should be possible depends partly on the character of the inhabitants but largely on the physical features of the region. The history of this great accomplishment by a small people will be given in later pages, and this first chapter will be devoted to a consideration of the geographical and ethnical background which made such a feat possible.

The mainland of Canada reaches from the north shore of Lake Erie in lat. 42° to the Arctic Ocean in lat. 74°; while to the north a great group of islands ends with Ellesmere Land in lat. 83°. The breadth of the country from east to west is 3000 miles; and the area is estimated at 3,603,910 square miles, which is greater than that of the United States including its dependency, Alaska. North America as a whole has the shape of a shallow trough narrowing southwards. The eastern rim of the trough is formed by the Appalachian Mountains toward the south and the elevated margin of the Laurentian table-land toward the north. The western rim consists of the Cordillera, which in Canada includes four chains of mountains, the Rocky Mountains proper, the Selkirks and Gold Ranges, the Coast Range, and a partially submerged range represented by Vancouver Island and the Queen Charlotte Islands. In Canada the broad middle of the trough is occupied by Hudson and James Bays and the western plains.

The physical features just outlined are accounted for by the geological history of the country, which may be very briefly sketched. Nearly half of Canada consists of ancient crystalline rocks, mostly Laurentian granite and gneiss, and it is often called the Laurentian Shield, but is better referred to as the pre-Cambrian Shield, since many areas of older and also of younger rocks are included in it. In very early times this area was occupied by great ranges of mountains which were cut down to mere stumps, forming a peneplain, before the beginning of the Palaeozoic. Some of the ancient rocks resisted erosion better than others and have remained as low hills to the present day, thus determining routes of travel and the distribution of economic materials. Resting on the upturned edges of the crystalline rocks toward the south and the west there are Palaeozoic and later sediments widely spread as nearly horizontal beds, providing excellent soils for the farmer. In the north climatic conditions have prevented the utilisation of such areas, and toward the north-east the belt of sedimentary rocks is lacking. The flat-lying sediments of the Palaeozoic and Mesozoic have been thrust up to form the Cordillera on the western side of the continent, while on the south-east the Appalachians were built toward the end of the Palaeozoic. In each case the mountains were formed by a thrust of the sea bottom against the solid pre-Cambrian nucleus of the continent.

The final shaping of the country was accomplished in the Glacial period, when almost all of Canada was buried under great ice sheets which smoothed down the hills and blocked most of the valleys with morainic deposits. In this way the pre-Glacial river systems were broken up, and on the retreat of the ice new channels were formed giving rise to the lakes and waterfalls so characteristic of the country. The history just suggested accounts for the extraordinary mingling of very ancient geological features with a very modern hydrography, which makes Canada, from the point of view of the physiographer, both the oldest and the youngest of countries. It combines the largest area of very ancient pre-Cambrian rocks with the most youthful arrangement of rivers to be found in any continent, and the number of lakes and waterfalls probably exceeds that of the rest of the world. These peculiarities in its geography largely account for its existence as a separate country from the United States, as will be shown later.

The southern part of North America, unlike Europe, is not deeply penetrated by arms of the sea; but the northern part belonging to Canada has two great inlets which extend westward from the Atlantic, forming Hudson Bay in the north and the St Lawrence system of waters in the south. The history of Canada has been strongly influenced by these inlets of the sea permitting easy access from Europe, though the northern one, for climatic reasons, has played only a minor part in the development of the country. The southern route has been of immense importance, and it is no exaggeration to describe Canada as the child of the St Lawrence. Both of these routes to the interior are due to the dropping of great blocks of the earth's crust, permitting the sea to enter far into the continent.

In discussing the relation of geography to the growth of Canada it will be convenient to refer to five physiographic regions, beginning at the east and working toward the west, thus following the actual direction of the opening up of the country. Dr G. M. Dawson, one of the early directors of the Canadian Geological Survey, first defined them, naming them the Acadian region, the lowlands of the St

Lawrence, the Laurentian Plateau, the Interior Continental Plain, and the Cordillera. Some would distinguish also the Arctic Archipelago, but this has played only an infinitesimal part in the history of Canada up to the present and may be neglected for our purpose. In area these physiographic regions are very unequal, the first two being small, the last two very large, and the Laurentian Plateau enormous, covering as great an area as the others put together; though hitherto it has been of relatively little importance from the human point of view.

The Acadian Region. The historic Acadia consisted of the Maritime Provinces, Nova Scotia, New Brunswick and Prince Edward Island, but, as the term is used here, it includes the whole of the region about the Gulf of St Lawrence where Palaeozoic sediments were upturned in the building of the Appalachian Mountains. The south-eastern corner of Quebec and also the independent Dominion of Newfoundland belong to it according to this definition.

In general the region consists of low mountains and tablelands with subordinate valleys and plains. The outlines of the land are broken by innumerable bays and sounds and no part of it is far from salt water. The largest inlet is the Bay of Fundy, between Nova Scotia and New Brunswick, noted for its powerful tides which in places rise fifty or sixty feet; and the broadest strait is that named Cabot between Nova Scotia and Newfoundland. The higher tablelands and mountains are uninhabited, and the highest of all, the Shickshocks in eastern Quebec, reaching from 3000 to 4500 feet above sea level, rise above timber-line and make a serious barrier between Quebec and New Brunswick. They have only recently been fully explored and are not yet completely mapped.

In Cainozoic times the mountains were 2000 feet higher than now and the mainland reached farther east, including Newfoundland and extending past Nova Scotia to the edge of the continental shelf. The foundering of this eastern border of Canada half submerged the Acadian region, flooded the St Lawrence valley as far as Quebec city, and provided the numberless harbours of Newfoundland and the Maritime Provinces. Almost every village has anchorage for fishing craft; while Saint John in New Brunswick, Halifax in Nova Scotia, and St John's in Newfoundland are important seaports. The sinking of the land provided also the celebrated fishing banks by drowning the lower tablelands and admitting the ice-laden Labrador current, thus giving the cool, shallow waters which suit the most valuable of fish, the cod. The landfalls of the early navigators were naturally in the part of America nearest to Europe, and the inexhaustible supply of fish gave an incentive for the exploration of the region and for the foundation of some of the first settlements. The cod and other fish still form the most important resource of the Maritime region.

There is fertile soil in many parts of the Maritime Provinces, suitable for farming and fruit growing, but much of the surface is rugged and barren, of value mainly for its forests which supply raw material for the lumber and pulp industries. Among the contorted mountain structures ores of gold and other metals have been worked to some extent, and gypsum and salt are quarried, but the only great mining industry is that of coal in Nova Scotia, where carboniferous basins are followed for miles beneath the sea and supply fuel to smelt the hematite ores of Bell Island in Newfoundland, making possible also the great steel industry of Sydney in Cape Breton Island. From the historic point of view the Acadian region has special significance as the gateway to the Gulf of St Lawrence and the starting point of the early French colonists and explorers, who ultimately saved Canada for the British.

The Lowlands of the St Lawrence. The Gulf of St Lawrence, the great highway to the interior of North America, is wholly within Canadian territory and leads up to the splendid chain of navigable lakes and rivers extending half-way across the continent. The Gulf extends between the mountainous Acadian region and the almost equally elevated south-eastern boundary of the pre-Cambrian Shield, with little cultivable land on either side; but at Quebec, where it narrows to the St Lawrence River, the lowlands of the St Lawrence begin. They consist of almost undisturbed beds of nearly horizontal Palaeozoic rocks extending 600 miles to Lake Huron, except for a short stretch of Laurentian at the Thousand Islands near the outlet of Lake Ontario.

This comparatively small area of about 35,000 square miles is largely covered with boulder clay or with deposits laid down in a post-Glacial extension of the gulf or in great glacial lakes; and possesses a very fertile soil. Its latitude and the influence of the Great Lakes give it a much milder climate than the country to the north, so that it was one of the first parts of Canada to attract settlers and at present contains sixty per cent. of the population, including the two largest cities, Montreal and Toronto. Ships of any size can reach Quebec, 650 miles from Cabot Strait, and all but the largest can go on to Montreal 150 miles above Quebec. Here rapids begin, making canals necessary, so that no ships drawing more than 14 feet of water can ascend to Lake Ontario (246 feet above the sea). The first of the rapids was significantly called Lachine by the early French explorers seeking a route to Asia.

Between Lake Ontario and Lake Erie (575 feet) comes the Niagara escarpment whose cliffs are the cause of Niagara Falls. A small part of the water of the falls generates most of the power required in the south-west peninsula of Ontario, and the proximity of this and several other falls, as well as convenient inland navigation, has helped to make the lowlands of the St Lawrence much the most important manufacturing district of Canada. Favourable climatic conditions account for the value of the southern part as a fruit-growing region, the Niagara peninsula being well known for its vineyards and peach orchards. The St Lawrence waters have their main source in Lake Superior (602 feet) and ships of 10,000 tons burthen can navigate from Lake Erie through Detroit River, Lake St Clair, and Lake Huron to the Sault Ste Marie where ship canals give access to Lake Superior. Long before canals were thought of, this route and another by the Ottawa River were used by canoes to bring the north-western furs to Montreal, giving prosperity to the French settlements and preventing Canada from joining the British colonies which have since become the United States. The French names distributed along the waterways are suggestive in this respect.

The Laurentian Region. The area of the Laurentian, or better, the pre-Cambrian region, has been estimated at 1,825,000 square miles, fully half of Canada, but it is the least populous of the five physiographic regions and considerable portions in the north are almost unexplored, so that for our present purpose only a brief description is required. It is often called the Laurentian Plateau, but this term is applicable only to the outer margin which rises in many places as tablelands. Probably half of it is less than 1000 feet above the sea, and the word basin is more nearly correct, since there is a broad depression in the interior centred about Hudson Bay. This great sheet of water is a North American Mediterranean into which many rivers flow from various directions. Its rigorous climate greatly diminishes its value to Canada, though some early explorers and the Hudson's Bay Company made use of it.

The surface of the region consists usually of rocky hills of no great height separated by shallow valleys occupied by innumerable lakes, which are connected by spillways rather than rivers, having many waterfalls and rapids. The southern part, where not burnt over, is covered with valuable forests of pine, spruce and hardwoods. In the central portions the forest becomes scrubby, and toward the north tree-line is reached, beyond which no timber grows. The so-called "barren lands" are often covered with grass and low bushes which in autumn provide great quantities of berries in the lower parts, while "reindeer moss", a pale grey lichen, grows on the hills. Large areas of flat ground toward James and Hudson Bays are covered, however, with the hopeless peat bogs usually called muskegs. In summer one can traverse the region in all directions with canoes which are portaged from lake to lake; and in winter dog teams and toboggans or sleds may be used. In these ways the furs, which are practically the only valuable products of the central and northern parts, are transported south to the nearest railway. In earlier days many of the furs were sent to England by ships on Hudson Bay.

The only portion of the pre-Cambrian region suitable for agriculture on the large scale is the "clay belt" of Ontario and Quebec, where an ancient glacial lake covered the rocks with stratified clay, making an excellent soil. Along the Canadian National Railway, which traverses the clay belt from east to west, many farms are being cleared and some parts are already in good cultivation. Before the building of the northern railways the wilderness of uninhabited pre-Cambrian territory practically cut Canada in two, there being no real connection between the farming and manufacturing communities of the east and the fertile prairies of the west except the Canadian Pacific Railway, which skirted the rocky north shore of Lake Superior. Of late years the development of great mining regions at Sudbury, Cobalt and Porcupine has been filling up this serious gap. The most important nickel mines in the world are at Sudbury; a great silver mining district is at Cobalt; and beyond the Hudson Bay watershed to the north there are many gold mines, including the Hollinger mine at Porcupine, which is one of the world's greatest producers of gold. Cities are growing up about the mines, farming communities are prospering near them, and large pulp and paper mills are operating in the region. Gold and copper mines are being developed farther west and also in Quebec to the east, and the dangerously narrow belt of civilisation fringing the Upper Lakes is rapidly widening as pre-Cambrian ore deposits are discovered and opened up.

The Interior Continental Plain. Toward the west the low hills of pre-Cambrian rock sink gently beneath flat-lying sediments, first of Palaeozoic, then of Cretaceous and later ages; and thus the transition is made to the plains. Along the International Boundary on the 49th parallel of latitude the region is typical prairie, devoid of trees except in the river valleys, and prairie extends far to the north-west, but toward the north-east clumps of trees appear and at length one enters the sub-arctic evergreen forest which runs from south-east to north-west across the continent. As settlement proceeds the prairie changes its character and most of the farm houses are now surrounded by groves of thrifty trees planted for the purpose of shelter and ornament. The flattest and richest prairie is found where ancient glacial lakes deposited silt, as near Winnipeg in Manitoba, and some of the most productive wheat fields in the world occur under these conditions; but other parts are more or less rolling and consist of morainic material, while in a few cases low tablelands, locally called mountains, rise above the general level. The prairie rises westwards from 750 feet at Winnipeg to 3500 feet at Calgary near the foot hills of the Rockies, but sinks toward the north, merging into the broad, low valley of Mackenzie River before the Arctic Ocean is reached.

The south-western part of Alberta is richly supplied with coal, some of it bituminous or semi-anthracite, while Saskatchewan, the central prairie province, has large deposits of lignite. The climate is typically continental with severe winters and warm summers, and the isotherms run north-west under the influence of the warm Pacific winds, so that spring comes nearly at the same time from Winnipeg to the Peace River, which is six degrees farther north. In the southern prairie precipitation diminishes from east to west, Saskatchewan having less moisture than Manitoba, and south-western Alberta being semi-arid, requiring irrigation to give the best results in farming. Warm and dry westerly winds called Chinooks often remove the snow in winter from southern Alberta so that horses and cattle can graze all the year round. The ranch country is subject to very rapid changes of temperature from this cause.

Except along its north-eastern edge there are few lakes on the plain, and the rivers which flow into the Arctic Ocean or Hudson Bay allow only limited navigation, so that canoe travel was not of importance in opening up the country. The Indian pony provided the best means of transport in early days, and since settlement began the railway has spread easily and rapidly over the plains, forming almost a network in the wheat-producing regions. In most respects except the cold of winter the plains present a strong contrast with the pre-Cambrian region. Bed rock is seldom exposed, the soil and the summer climate permit the growing of the finest wheat, mining is of no importance except in the Albertan coal districts, and forest products are of little account. The resources of the plains are the exact opposite to those of the pre-Cambrian region to the east; and the ease of railway construction and the lack of waterways complete the contrast.

The Cordillera. The crossing of the flat prairie makes an admirable preparation for the first view of the well-named Rocky Mountains. Foot hills give a narrow transition between the undisturbed beds of the plains and the serrated ridge of tilted strata which rises to from 7000 to 9000 feet as bare cliffs in the front range of the Cordillera. The inner ranges reach from 10,000 to 12,500 feet and their higher levels are snowy and send many glaciers into the valleys. The central dome of snow, called the Columbia Ice Field, covers 150 square miles and flows out on all sides as valley glaciers. It is remarkable as sending its waters through the Saskatchewan to Hudson Bay, through the Athabaska and Mackenzie Rivers to the Arctic Ocean, and through the Columbia into the Pacific.

A great valley hundreds of miles long separates the Rocky Mountains from the slightly lower but very snowy Selkirks and Gold Ranges; beyond which comes the Interior Plateau, followed by the Coast Range, which sometimes reaches 13,000 feet, and bears many glaciers because of its proximity to the Pacific. A half submerged chain of mountains runs through Vancouver Island and the Queen Charlotte Islands. At the north-west end of the Cordillera, where

Yukon Territory joins Alaska, there is a much higher group of mountains, including Mt St Elias (18,000 feet) and the recently climbed Mt Logan (19,850 feet), the loftiest summit in Canada. There are many profound valleys in the Cordillera, but comparatively little level farm land, so that British Columbia is not likely to become an agricultural region, though some of the broader southern valleys are excellently adapted for fruit growing. The climates of the Cordilleran region present the most striking variations found in any part of Canada, sometimes ranging within a few miles from arctic cold and snow on mountain tops to sheltered valleys having much milder winters than southern Ontario, though in a latitude seven degrees farther north. The precipitation, also, varies widely—from more than 100 inches of rain on the Pacific side of the Coast Range to desert conditions at Kamloops 170 miles to the east.

The western ranges of mountains consist largely of granitoid rocks which have penetrated older sediments, giving rise to deposits of gold, silver, copper, lead and zinc ores, the seat of great mining and smelting industries; and there are also supplies of coal in several valleys, some mines on Vancouver Island being worked beneath the sea as they are in Cape Breton Island on the Atlantic coast. The moister valleys of the mainland, the Pacific slope of the Coast Range, and Vancouver Island are covered with magnificent forest, trees sometimes reaching a height of over 200 feet and supplying fine timber. Sea fisheries off the coast and the run of salmon in the rivers make a third industry of much importance to the comparatively small population of British Columbia, and the well sheltered harbour of Vancouver, the fourth city in Canada, provides one of the best seaports on the Pacific.

The opening up of the Canadian portion of the Cordillera began from the Pacific side with the working of placer gold mines in the 'sixties, but did not progress rapidly until about twenty-five years later when the finding of passes through the mountains made possible the construction of the Canadian Pacific Railway, which brought in settlers from eastern Canada and England. The early French explorers sought in vain for a route to China by the St Lawrence, but at a far later time the building of transcontinental railways and the development of a great seaport at Vancouver have opened up an important route between Europe and the Far East.

That Canada has remained a part of the British Empire may be attributed largely to two causes, one geographical and the other racial. The highway of the Gulf and River St Lawrence allowed the French explorers and fur-traders to penetrate far into the interior of North America, even reaching the prairies with their brigades of canoes. They took possession of the country for France and completely outstripped the inland explorations of the English-speaking colonies to the south, which were halted by the forest-covered Appalachian

Mountains. The rights acquired by the French colonists through their discovery and occupation of the interior descended to the British Government on the conquest of Canada. The liberal policy of the British authorities toward the French settlers and the dread the latter had of losing their language and religion if they joined the English-speaking and mainly Protestant colonies to the south kept Canada a separate country.

When through immigration the country became predominantly English-speaking, the building of canals and east and west railways tended to consolidate the widely separated parts so different in interests and resources, and enabled Canada to resist the powerful attraction of the great nation to the south. A long and greatly varied geological preparation supplied the physical and geographical requisites for Canada's existence as a country separate from the rest of the continent; and the geological preparation of vast stretches of good soil and the storage in the rocks of great mineral resources place the future development of the Dominion on a solid foundation. In addition, shiftings of level on the Atlantic and the Pacific have opened up waterways and safe harbours on the two greatest oceans, pathways for commerce to Europe and Asia. From the physiographic point of view Canada has all that is necessary to build a great nation.

(B) THE ETHNICAL BACKGROUND

The first Europeans who landed on the Atlantic shore of Canada discovered, not a wilderness tenanted by wild beasts, but a well-peopled coastline dotted with the dwellings of aborigines very unlike the dark-skinned natives of the East Indies or the yellow inhabitants of Cathay for whom they sought. Although no old-world mariner had set eyes on these aborigines before (save perhaps a few adventurous Norsemen in the eleventh century of our era), they were not autochthonous, not a new branch of the human race that had developed independently of man in Asia and Europe. Neither in Canada, nor in the rest of the American continent, have there been discovered any certain traces of man in Pleistocene times, when our forefathers sheltered themselves in the caves and overhanging cliffs of France and Moravia, or built their flimsy dwellings along the river banks of Europe and Asia. Nevertheless, there are remains, in the east and west of Canada, even on remote islands in the Arctic sea, bearing evidences of an antiquity that must be reckoned by centuries, perhaps even millennia. The natives had a long history behind them before Europeans arrived on the scene, a history that had left its stamp on every phase of their lives. The Roman who boasted an ancestry to *pius Aeneas*, and the Viking who scoured the coasts of western Europe chanting the war-cry of Sigurd, had no greater pride of birth or nobler heritage than many an Iroquois chieftain in

Ontario, or a Haida of the Queen Charlotte Islands in British Columbia.

Physical appearance distinguishes at least one group of the Canadian aborigines from the rest, the Eskimo of the north. How many other groups there may be, and what blendings have occurred in them, is still the subject of controversy. Most authorities class them all under one racial stock, the Mongoloid, and deduce their origin from north-east Asia about the close of the Pleistocene period, some 13,000 to 25,000 years ago; not from a single migration, but from a series of migrations hundreds or even thousands of years apart. A wash of brownish-red pigment has suffused their skin since their occupation of America, and minor variations have occurred in the proportions of their faces and limbs, but in the main they have preserved their ancestral type with little change.

Language, however, was less stable than race. Nine, possibly ten, linguistic stocks have been distinguished in Canada alone, no one of which has been proved genetically related to any language outside America. It is true that the Eskimo language in the north has been affiliated with Finno-Ugric, and the Athabaskan tongues that centre geographically in the Mackenzie River valley with the Sinitic languages of eastern Asia; but the proofs still linger. Of the nine (or ten) linguistic stocks in Canada five appear in British Columbia alone, and one, Algonkian, stretched from the Atlantic Ocean to the Cordilleras long before the discovery. Yet in a history of modern Canada it would be entirely misleading to group the aborigines by their languages alone, because tribes speaking the same tongue often had different modes of life, and reacted differently to the European invasion; while conversely, tribes of diverse languages possessed at times the same culture and banded together against the common foe.

The most natural division follows rather closely the physiographic regions, which so largely determined the mode of life. All Acadia, together with the Laurentian portions of Quebec and Ontario, regions of splendid waterways and forests rich in animal life, harboured migratory tribes of Algonkian speech who wandered up and down the rivers in a never-ending quest of game. More sedentary tribes speaking Iroquoian dialects held the lowlands of the St Lawrence, having their easternmost village at Stadacona, now a part of the city of Quebec. The prairie portion of the continental plain was the home of roving buffalo hunters using three different tongues, Algonkian, Siouan and Athabaskan. On the same plain, but in the sub-arctic forest from the Peace and Nelson Rivers northward, more primitive hunters of Athabaskan speech strove always to press southward into the prairies where the buffalo abounded, or westward through the Cordilleras toward the Pacific coast. The Pacific coast itself was a cul-de-sac where tribes from north, east and south commingled and wrestled for the supremacy. Last of all, the Eskimos, distinct in appearance, language and culture, held a narrow fringe all along the northern coastline from Alaska to the north shore of the Gulf of St Lawrence opposite Anticosti, with the single exception of James Bay.

Of all these tribes none had progressed beyond the neolithic stage of culture. They knew but one metal, copper, which, found in a pure state, they treated as a malleable stone. Agriculture was practised only in the St Lawrence valley, where the Iroquois introduced from the south the cultivation of maize, kidney beans, sun-flowers and squash; but tobacco was grown from the prairies eastward, and, smoked in a pipe of clay or stone, played an important rôle in cere-monial life. The people lived a migratory life, dependent on the chase and on fishing, on wild roots, berries, and fruits. Only in two regions were there permanent villages inhabited all or most of the year: in the lowlands of the St Lawrence, where the cultivation of maize and squash made the Iroquois a more sedentary people than the surrounding tribes; and west of the Rocky Mountains, where the abundance of salmon in the rivers, of shell-fish along the coast, and of seals, whales and other large mammals in the sea, supplied food for every season of the year. Dwellings varied greatly in different regions; there were houses of snow or stone among the Eskimos, bark-covered huts in eastern Canada, semi-underground houses built of rafters and turf in the interior of British Columbia, and, on the Pacific coast, enormous dwellings of hewn planks that housed as many as two score families. Tents of skin for the summer months were universal, and were, indeed, the only dwellings on the treeless plains. Crude pottery prevailed ιrom the Atlantic coast to Manitoba; else-where cooking vessels were of skin, bark, wood, and, among the Eskimos, of stone. Climate demanded clothing made from skins, everywhere tailored, although on the North Pacific coast the natives sometimes wove their garments of goats' wool and rabbit fur. The weapons for war and the chase included the bow, the club, the spear and the harpoon. Only one animal was domesticated, the dog, which, harnessed to the sled or toboggan, served for winter transport in the north; on the prairies it dragged the curious *travois*. Boats were used everywhere except on the prairies, the bark canoe prevailing in the east and north, the skin boat in the Arctic, and the large dug-out on the Pacific coast. Broadly speaking, therefore, life on its material side differed but slightly from that of man in northern Europe two or three millennia before the Christian era.

The migratory existence of nearly all the tribes, the inefficiency of their weapons, and the precariousness of the food supply, precluded any specialisation in labour or the growth of complex societies. Every man was at once a hunter and a fisherman, the builder of his own home and the manufacturer of his tools and weapons. The typical unit of society was the band, a group of families knit together by ties of kinship, and united by looser bonds with neighbouring bands to form a tribe. Only in the regions of permanent habitations, in the St Lawrence valley and on the Pacific coast, had society progressed beyond this elementary stage. There individuals were graded according to rank, and rank, with its accompanying titles and crests, was hereditary, sometimes, as in Europe, in the male line, more often in the female. The Pacific coast tribes blended slavery with their system, and enriched their social life with elaborate festivals and the cultivation of sculpture and the drama. But the Iroquois of the St Lawrence and Ohio valleys, lesser artists, it may be, but guided by a keener political sense, organised their tribes into nations and sought to establish an hegemony over the peoples around them. The advent of the white man first stimulated, then arrested their venture, but not before they had shown promise of creating a powerful empire stretching from the Ohio River and the Great Lakes to the Atlantic, an empire pregnant with immense possibilities for the development of a new, though retarded, civilisation.

The religion of the Indians varied as much as their social organisation. Nevertheless, there prevailed everywhere a belief in supernatural powers that pervaded or were inherent in the phenomena of nature—in the sky, the winds and the thunder, in the forests, the lakes and the hills, in the species of birds and animals. The Indian sought to enlist these powers into his service by various rituals, principally by fasting and dreaming in early youth. No tribe, it would seem, had evolved the idea of a single Deity supreme over all the lesser powers; but this doctrine, seized with avidity from the earliest missionaries, spread westward with amazing rapidity and penetrated deep into the everyday life. Fragments of Christian teachings, indeed, combined with the ancient beliefs of the natives themselves, produced in certain regions Messianistic crazes that greatly stiffened the resistance of the tribes to European encroachment, and even to-day have their repercussions in remote valleys.

It is impossible to estimate with any approach to accuracy the numbers of the Indians at the time of the discovery. Wars, alcohol and disease devastated them in the three centuries following, and the survivors, losing their virility, often failed to accommodate themselves to their changed economic condition. One authority[1] estimates the aboriginal population at that time at about 220,000, twice its number to-day; but we have no means of checking the figure. As among primitive peoples elsewhere, the group instinct was all-powerful, personality but little developed. So there were no great leaders (except among the Iroquoian tribes) to direct the Indians in their struggles against the whites, or, when that struggle failed, to waken them from their apathy and divert their energies into new channels.

The invasion of the whites did not press with equal weight on

[1] Mooney, J., *Bulletin* 30, *Bureau of Amer. Ethnology*, Pt II, 1910.

every tribe. European settlement progressed slowly, and even now has left some regions almost untouched. Wherever fur-bearing animals abounded and the land was ill-suited to agriculture—as in Labrador and the basin of the Mackenzie River—the natives changed comparatively slowly, for trapping and hunting require the same mode of life. Such changes as did arise in these places resulted largely from the introduction of firearms, which evoked a spirit of aggression in the tribes that first obtained them and caused widespread unrest; thus the Crees, a relatively insignificant tribe living around the shores of James Bay, no sooner obtained firearms than they marched adventurously westward, out to the prairies, up the Nelson, the Athabaska and the Peace Rivers to the Rocky Mountains, and down the Mackenzie River to the Arctic circle; and wherever they marched they drove alien tribes in front of them, blazing a trail into the west and north-west that the fur-traders followed later. But the tribes living in the more southern parts of Canada, where agriculture and industry could prosper, either amalgamated with the invading whites or were rapidly pushed to one side.

Perhaps the most fortunate Indians were those of Eastern Canada, who bore the brunt of the first invasion from the Old World, when the steam engine was still unknown and the simplicity of European life had not been undermined by a wealth of mechanical inventions. The migratory tribes of Algonkian speech—the Micmacs and Malecites of Nova Scotia and New Brunswick, the Montagnais, Ojibwa and Cree (to name only the most prominent) of Quebec and Ontario—wandered in family bands, too weakly organised to offer any effective resistance. The *wanderlust* was in their blood; their birch-bark canoes were their second homes. They knew every lake, every river, in their territory; and they read the secrets of the woods like an open book. The early fur-traders and settlers adopted their canoes, snow-shoes and toboggans, learned their woodcraft and followed their routes of war and trade. Many daughters of the Indians became their wives, and half-breeds served as guides, boatmen and interpreters throughout the eastern woodlands. Their descendants, during two centuries of close contact with European civilisation, lost most of their old customs and beliefs, so that to-day the only primitive Indians in this section of Canada are some Montagnais and Naskapi groups who roam the wildernesses of the Labrador peninsula.

The Iroquoian tribes also prospered, but for a wholly different reason. Their genius for combining into compact political units made them formidable friends or foes to the party they espoused or rejected. The English gained their adherence from the outset, and when the wars of the colonists ended, rewarded their allies with a liberal grant of territory, and semi-autonomy. The Iroquois, long familiar with agriculture, then settled down as farmers like the colonists around them, with whom they gradually mingled their blood. Many of the more enterprising, however, entered the service of the fur-traders; being better disciplined, and therefore more reliable, than their Algonkian-speaking neighbours, they manned the big trade canoes that journeyed to the far west, to the upper waters of the Mackenzie River, and even to British Columbia.

The migratory prairie tribes, Blackfoot, Sarcee and Assinaboine, with a few Sioux who had entered Canada from the south, and some Crees who had been drawn out to the plains by the lure of the buffalo hunt, were as formidable to the early explorers as the Iroquois. Long before they acquired horses and firearms they had developed the game of war as a national sport. The horse, coming north from Mexico, accentuated this spirit, increasing the rapidity of movement. The Indians could break camp at a moment's notice, pack their tents and belongings on poles (*travois*) behind their horses, strike a blow at their foes before sunset, and be thirty miles away at dawn. A belief that amulets gave them protection in battle inspired them with fanatical courage. The early fur-traders passed them by; the grain fields of the future lay undreamed of, and the fur-bearing animals lived to the northward. More potent than the force of the traders, or the peace-doctrines of the missionaries, was the smallpox, which destroyed three-fourths of the population. Even then the prairie tribes might have recovered sufficiently to check for a little longer the settlers pushing westward, if their staff of life had not been suddenly taken from them. On the buffalo they flourished, and with the buffalo they fell. Fire-arms, and the transcontinental railways that cut across their migration routes, destroyed the herds; and the prairie Indians, reduced to starvation, gloomily submitted to permanent confinement on narrow reserves while their lands passed into the hands of strangers.

The Indians of British Columbia remained until the nineteenth century almost untouched by European civilisation, when it assailed them simultaneously from both east and west. Crushed by superior force, and unable to comprehend the new civilisation, they could neither adapt themselves to their altered environment nor contribute to the opening-up of their country. The fabric of their social organisation was too complex, and too weakly bound together, to withstand an assault from without; and with the breaking-down of that organisation they lost every power of recovery. Their dramatic festivals, which long formed their chief bulwark against the new order of things, fell under the ban of the law, and their highly conventional art was commercialised and degraded to satisfy the whim of the curiosity-seeker. Helpless, like the Indians of the prairies, they were relentlessly brushed aside by a civilisation in which only a few could find a place. Chinese and Japanese immigrants have begun to supplant them in the canneries where for a time they held their own, and in the fur-bearing districts of the interior white trappers are driving them from every stream and river. The Kwakiutl and Nootka tribes of Vancouver Island are vanishing fast. So, too, are the Haidas of the Queen Charlotte Islands, who once scoured the coasts of the mainland in huge sea-going canoes carved from single trunks of the cedar. On the mainland the Salish and Kootenay tribes in the south have dwindled to a mere handful. Farther north, the Tsimshian of the Skeena and Nass Rivers still beat against the bars, and dream of the day when they will drive the white man back to "Boston"; but in their hearts they know the struggle is futile, and the majority, like their neighbours to the south, and the Carrier and Nahani tribes behind them, have already resigned themselves to slow but certain extinction.

Mackenzie, Richardson and other early explorers have recorded the names of the principal Athabaskan-speaking tribes; to north there dwelt successively Chipewyans, Slaves, Dog-Ribs, Yellow-Knives, Hares and Loucheux, with various bands of Nahani Indians frequenting the slopes of the Rockies. Although more primitive than the Indians to the south, these Athabaskan tribes were peculiarly favoured for survival by the high latitude of their home. The severe climate precluded agriculture, and mineral wealth that would attract a large, if transient, population has never been discovered. Indeed this section of Canada has yielded little but furs, and as a trapper the Indian was unsurpassed. But the Athabaskan Indians were weak in character, morose, improvident, and self-indulgent. They speedily became addicted to spirituous liquors, and suffered all the diseases that followed in the wake of the traders. Unreliable as boatmen and packers, they lost their efficiency even as trappers. To-day the miserable bands that idle around the trading posts in summer are tainted through and through with tuberculosis, and are probably doomed to extinction within three or four generations.

The Eskimos of the Arctic coast differed greatly in temperament from their Indian neighbours, with whom they were generally at enmity. They were hardy and energetic, cheerful even in times of starvation, and gifted with great resourcefulness and mechanical ability. Furthermore, they had mastered the technique of living in an isolated region that Europeans consider a wilderness. From the earliest days they cheerfully accepted the leadership of the white man, and as guides, hunters and sled-drivers, they hold an honourable place in the history of Arctic exploration. The whalers adopted and modified their harpoon, the explorers their dog-sled. Diseases have swept them in some regions; in others the game supply, always precarious, has diminished alarmingly; but with courage and vitality unimpaired the Eskimos cling to their Arctic home, hunting and fishing during the brief summer months, hunting and trapping during the long cold winter. Every year they export thousands of beautiful white fox-skins to grace a civilisation of which they have no knowledge. They have already contributed nobly to the development of their far-away home; and in them, and their descendants, lies its greatest hope of future progress.

The aborigines of Canada illustrate very clearly the fate of peoples suddenly confronted with a civilisation totally alien and incomparably more powerful. Europe had moved forward 5000 years when it knocked at Canada's door, and the Indians could not bridge that interval in a century. During the first period of exploration and adventure they could sometimes aid through their knowledge of the country and familiarity with its resources and natural highways. They bequeathed us then the snow-shoe and the toboggan, the canoe and the dog-sled. But when that period ended, and colonisation commenced, the road became too long for them to traverse; the great majority lost heart and fell by the wayside, despite the help they received from a government that honestly sought their welfare. Only in the extreme north the Eskimos, a peculiar people living in a peculiar environment, show promise of winning for themselves a place in the new Canada, provided they are granted a reasonable opportunity.

CHAPTER II

THE FOUNDING OF ACADIA AND CANADA

IT seems almost beyond doubt that in the year 1000 Norsemen from Iceland discovered and visited the shores of Canada, though their landfall has not yet been definitely ascertained. Their attempt at colonisation having failed, they departed never to return, and for centuries the western continent remained enshrouded in distance and mystery. But documentary evidence exists which points to the presence of Breton fishermen in quest of cod on the Grand Banks about the latter part of the fifteenth century. In 1511, when Queen Joanna of Spain planned to send two vessels to the northern land, she expressly stipulated that the pilots should be *Bretons who had been there*. As early as 1514, the monks of Beaufort in Brittany claimed that the fishermen of Bréhat had been paying them, for sixty years, the tithes on fish caught on the coasts of Iceland and Newfoundland. Again a Portuguese portolano, probably of 1514, reproduced by Kuntsmann, already displayed a Canadian coastline with the words "Land which was discovered by the Bretons". In 1565 the Queen of France, Catherine de Médicis, wrote to Forquevaulx, her ambassador in Spain, that the country and coast of the Bretons "had been discovered by French fishermen" over one hundred years ago. But the fishermen, who were not interested in territorial expansion, precious metal, or oriental spices, kept their knowledge and modest profits to themselves, which explains why no individual name has survived or any benefit accrued to the outside world from their many trips. In 1472, twenty years before Columbus' first voyage, took place the expedition, still imperfectly elucidated, of John Scolp, a Dane, the first man from the European mainland to reach Canadian territory in the region of Labrador—an expedition which is the more remarkable as it was undertaken with the idea of finding a short route to the Indies.[1]

The great explorer of the period, the one whose achievement opened the way to many followers, was Giovanni Caboto, of Genoa, who sailed under the English flag. Bearing letters patent of Henry VII, he steered out of Bristol on a small ship, the *Matthew*, carrying a crew of eighteen men, in the beginning of May 1497. After several weeks of navigation, they sighted land, most probably the Labrador coast. Cabot went ashore, and, taking possession of the country in the name of King Henry VII, erected a large cross with the banners of England and St Mark. On the strength of his success, a second expedition was organised in the summer of 1498, consisting

[1] Larsen, S., "La découverte de l'Amérique vingt ans avant Christophe Colomb", *Journal des Américanistes de Paris*, t. XVIII, 75–89.

of five vessels. From the meagre material available, it seems that Cabot sailed northward to the region of icebergs and then, putting his ship about, ranged the coast southwards possibly as far as the Carolinas, whence scarcity of stores forced him to return home.

The next explorer to reach the northern lands was a wealthy Portuguese, Gaspar Corte-Real. Sailing from Terceira in May 1500 he steered a north-west course, and finally sighted land, perhaps Labrador, but more probably the coast of Newfoundland.[1] Thence he returned home. The following year, on 15 May, he set out on a new expedition with three ships. This time he explored the bays of Newfoundland, and, sending home two of his ships, he sailed north up the Labrador coast, never to return. In 1502 his brother Miguel equipped an expedition in search of the explorer, but a similar fate overtook him. About that time the knowledge of the Newfoundland fisheries had spread from the Breton to the Norman ports, and in 1504 fishermen from Normandy were noticed on the Banks. A voyage made in 1506 by Jean Denis of Honfleur and the pilot Gamart was duly recorded, and in 1508 the vessel *La Pensée* from Dieppe, under Thomas Aubert, made a trip to the new lands, while in 1509 a Norman vessel brought back to Rouen a certain number of Indians from the same region.

The first attempt to settle a colony in Canadian territory was made by the French Baron de Léry, who took over men and stock in 1518. Detained for months at sea by adverse winds and storms, he reached the Nova Scotian shores too late in the season to start a settlement. Landing his cattle on Sable Island, with the idea of returning for them, he sailed to France, but never came back. Two years later, a Portuguese, Joam Alvarez Fagundez, with letters patent of King Manoel of Portugal, reached the mainland of Nova Scotia. Skirting Cape Breton Island, he crossed over to Cape Ray and ranged the southern coast of Newfoundland. On his return home, he was granted seigneurial rights over the lands he had discovered, but failed to carry his plan any further.

Thus far, France was the only country which had not sent out any official expedition in search of new lands, though her fishermen were possibly the first Europeans to have visited North American waters since the Norsemen. In 1523, however, probably incited partly by a desire to outdo his personal rival, Charles V of Spain, and partly by the need of finding new sources of finance in his struggle for European hegemony, Francis I commissioned a Florentine pilot, Giovanni da Verazzano, to lead an expedition in search of new countries and a sea route to Cathay. Sailing on 17 January 1524, Verazzano sighted the American continent in the region of Carolina. Turning northward, he ranged the coast, landing at several points, until he reached the latitude of Newfoundland. Giving the

---

[1] See chapter v.

new land the name of Nova Francia or New France, he sailed back to Dieppe. His voyage aroused deep interest, but Francis I was in the grip of a deadly war, which ended the following year in his being captured at the battle of Pavia. Accordingly, nothing came of this expedition.

Suddenly Spain, whose ships had never visited the ice-bearing region, appeared off the Canadian coast. The suspicion was strong that Charles V was trying to intercept the French ships of his rival, for the commission of Gomez is as much like letters of marque as instructions to search for new lands. Be that as it may, Gomez sailed in the summer of 1524 in a caravel of fifty tons and came in sight of Newfoundland. Then turning southward, he ranged the coast of Cape Breton and Nova Scotia, penetrated into the Bay of Fundy and skirted the American shore southwards to Cape Cod. He then returned home by way of Cuba. It looked very much like searching the coast more for enemies than information.

In June 1527, thanks to Henry VIII's endeavour, two ships, the *Samson* and the *Mary of Guilford*, left Plymouth in search of a northwest passage to the East. On the voyage, the vessels became separated and the *Samson* was never seen again. The *Mary of Guilford* sailed northwards till stopped by ice fields. Casting about to the southwest, she sighted Labrador where a landing was effected. Setting sail again, she skirted the coast without meeting the *Samson*, and then returned to England.

The year 1534 marks the birth of Canada. France had been enjoying peace for five years. Francis I, seeking for alliances in Europe, went back to his former plan of looking to America for resources. He consequently welcomed the proposal of his admiral, Philippe de Chabot, to send an expedition in search of the land discovered by Verazzano and of a route to the Indies. For such an enterprise, he provided 6000 livres tournois. On 20 April 1534, two vessels sailed from St Malo under Jacques Cartier, a well-known Breton captain and experienced navigator. They soon reached Newfoundland, and, passing through the Straits of Belle Isle, entered the Gulf of St Lawrence, so far only known as a great bay occasionally visited by fishing vessels hugging its northern shores. After ranging part of the south Labrador coast, Cartier skirted the west coast of Newfoundland and part of Prince Edward Island and New Brunswick. After visiting Chaleur Bay, he landed at Gaspé and there, on 24 July, erecting a large cross with the arms of France, he took official possession of the country in the name of Francis I. Taking on board two young Indians of the district, he sailed back to St Malo.

The expedition had proved a complete success. First of a long line of explorers, Cartier had succeeded in breaking through the wall of fog, rock and mystery that surrounded Labrador, to reach a warm and fine country, covered with wild wheat, fruits, shrubs and many herbs of pleasant odour. To a man of the time, the conclusion at once presented itself that such a country must be the eastern extremity of Asia. Elated with the result, Francis ordered a second voyage for the completion of the discovery. Cartier departed again on 19 May 1535 with three vessels and reached the Gulf. He was the first European to sail the great river of Canada. Proceeding cautiously, he came up and dropped anchor below the rock of Quebec, where stood the Indian village of Stadacona. After entering into relations with its inhabitants, Cartier left behind two of his ships, and sailed with the smallest one up the river to explore the country. On the present site of Montreal, he came upon a large and well-fortified Indian village, named Hochelaga. Enthusiastically welcomed as supernatural beings, Cartier and his companions were shown the surrounding country from the top of a neighbouring mountain, with two great rivers, the present St Lawrence and Ottawa, flowing one from the south-west and the other from the north-west. At the same time, they were told by the natives that gold and silver were to be found in the country further west, while copper came from the Saguenay region, placed by them in a north-east direction. In possession of that invaluable information, Cartier returned to Quebec, where he spent a troublesome winter, his crews stricken with scurvy and the surrounding Indians becoming hostile. Early in the spring he took his departure, reaching St Malo in July 1536.

Once again France was at war, and peace came only in 1538. There was no more royal money for a new expedition. It had to be financed by private resources in exchange for special advantages. To a favourite, François de la Rocque, seigneur of Roberval, was entrusted the enterprise of founding a French colony in Canada, with the object of finding the route to the Indies and converting the Indian population. Volunteer colonists were to be recruited and, if necessary, prisoners taken over as settlers. To compensate him for his expenditure, Roberval was granted seigneurial ownership of the new territory with supreme authority and the title of lieutenant-general of His Majesty. Cartier was commissioned captain-general and master pilot in charge of the fleet. First to be ready, Cartier sailed in advance in May 1541. On reaching the St Lawrence, he established his people at Cap Rouge, four leagues above Quebec, where several buildings were erected with a view to permanent occupation. The place was called Charlesbourg-Royal. While the work was going on, Cartier sailed up the river to explore, but, having no guides, proceeded only a short distance above Montreal Island. With scanty provisions and the Indians hostile, the winter at Charlesbourg was unpleasant. After vainly waiting for Roberval, Cartier re-embarked his people in the spring and left for France. Roberval had not sailed till April 1542, his three ships carrying on board a few noblemen, a number of soldiers, sailors and colonists, a part of whom were convicts. The two fleets met later in a Newfoundland harbour, but in spite of Roberval's order to return with him, Cartier stole away by night for France.

Resuming his journey, Roberval entered the St Lawrence and occupied Cartier's post which he renamed France-Roy. There he constructed two forts, one on the river as a depôt for provisions and the other on the hill above, with an enclosure containing two houses, a mill, an oven and a well, so that before winter set in, the little colony was securely settled in its quarters. In the meantime, Roberval went on a reconnoitring trip up the St Lawrence, while he sent his pilot, Jean Alphonse, to explore the north coast from Quebec to Belle Isle. Having failed to find the opening that would lead to the western seas, Roberval, in June 1543, decided to ascend the Saguenay in hopes of finding the passage to the Orient, but without success. No supplies or reinforcements having arrived from France, he gave up the enterprise and left with all his company. Thus ended in failure the first attempt to plant a French colony in Canada.

For forty years, the upper St Lawrence was no more visited by Europeans. But from England, France, Spain, Portugal and Holland, fishing vessels, the number of which was continuously increasing, came to the Banks and the Gulf for cod and whale fishing. In the course of drying fish on the beach, the fishermen came in contact with the natives, and soon took to bartering furs for European goods. Year after year this trade slowly developed, specially with French ports. In order to secure a monopoly of it, France returned to her plan of founding a colony in Canada. In 1577 the Marquis de la Roche was commissioned to occupy territories and establish a settlement. He made his first attempt in 1584 when his largest ship was wrecked in sight of the French coast. Undaunted, he organised a second expedition, for which, as he could not secure voluntary colonists, he was authorised to embark prisoners. With a number of them on board, he sailed to Canada and landed sixty of his contingent on Sable Island with the idea of returning for them after a suitable location had been found for the colony. But his small ship was swept by a violent storm all the way back to France, the poor prisoners not being rescued until five years later. Thus for the second time the French failed in the attempt to colonise New France.

In 1588 the first fur-trade monopoly was granted by Henri III to Jacques Nouel and la Jaunaye, two nephews of Jacques Cartier, but on account of the protests of the St Malo merchants it was soon cancelled. In 1599 a new monopoly was obtained from Henri IV by the Huguenot, Pierre Chauvin, on condition that he should take out fifty colonists to Canada every year. But except for sixteen men left during the first winter at Tadousac and repatriated the following year, the condition was entirely disregarded, Chauvin devoting his whole industry to fur-trading along the St Lawrence. On his death, in 1603, Commander de Chastes succeeded him, being in partnership with Rouen and St Malo merchants. Before his two lieutenants, du Pont-Gravé and Champlain, returned from their trading and exploration, de Chastes had died in France.

Henceforth the leading spirit in colonial activities was Samuel Champlain, an able navigator and staunch Catholic, a man of unflinching purpose and broad vision, to whom more than to anyone France owed her Canadian empire. On the first trip he was deeply struck by the possibilities of the country as a field for commercial expansion and evangelisation. Having visited the isthmus of Panama, he conceived the notion that by pushing inland he would reach the Pacific Ocean and an open road to China. Unfortunately, on his return to France he found his chief, de Chastes, already dead. Meeting de Monts, one of his associates, Champlain won him over to his plan of a settlement in America. De Monts, who was a loyal partisan of Henri IV, experienced no difficulty in securing a royal patent for planting a colony overseas, coupled with a trade monopoly for ten years. In return for the monopoly de Monts and his company of seaport merchants were obliged to send out five ships and sixty settlers a year.

In May 1604 two ships assigned to the trading operations left Hâvre-de-Grâce, while the other two, under de Monts, steered for Acadia having on board Champlain, Poutrincourt, a nobleman desirous of settling in the New World, some priests and clergymen and 120 colonists and soldiers, both Catholic and Protestant. Skirting the coast, the ships explored the Bay of Fundy, visited Port Royal, now Annapolis, which de Monts granted to Poutrincourt, and the entrance of the St John River. Finally, de Monts selected for the site of the settlement the small island of Ste Croix, at the mouth of the river of that name, on the present coast of Maine. The choice proved most inappropriate, the island possessing no fresh water and very little wood. During the winter, which was very severe, scurvy set in, carrying off thirty-five colonists. With the summer of 1605 came new settlers and supplies from France, and Champlain explored the American coast as far as Nansett Harbour for a more suitable site. On his return, the whole colony was moved across the Bay of Fundy to Port Royal, where a settlement was established. De Monts returned to France with Poutrincourt, and du Pont-Gravé and Champlain were left in charge of the post. The next summer Poutrincourt came back with men and supplies, just in time to prevent the colonists from returning to France owing to lack of provisions. For the first time, the men were set to work to clear and sow the land. But the affairs of the company were far from prosperous. Its monopoly was continuously violated by interlopers, who often took away the best portion of the year's furs, while, on the other hand, independent merchants were clamouring for freedom of trade. Sully, the finance minister, who was opposed to colonial ventures, suddenly cancelled de Monts' privilege at the end of the third year. In the spring of 1607, after a rather pleasant winter, the Port Royal colonists were informed of the fact, whereupon they all returned to France, leaving the post a deserted place in charge of Chief Membertou and his Indians.

Undeterred, Poutrincourt appealed to Henri IV, by whom he was held in great esteem, and obtained from him a grant of Port Royal on condition of developing the place at his own expense and promoting the conversion of the Indians. For lack of financial support, not secured for three years, Poutrincourt did not return to Acadia till February 1610, when he came with his own son Charles de Biencourt, the Abbé Fléché, Claude de la Tour, his son Charles and a number of colonists. At Port Royal the buildings still in good condition were reoccupied. Early in the summer, twenty-one Indians were baptised, the first converts to the Christian faith. The following year arrived from France two Jesuits, Fathers Biard and Massé, sent by the devout Madame de Guercheville, a partner in the Port Royal enterprise. Scarcity of food nearly ruined the settlement, the colonists being forced to live by hunting in the woods. Leaving Biencourt in charge, Poutrincourt hastened back to France in July 1611 to secure new financial assistance. But the mother country was torn by civil war. Meeting with no official sympathy, Poutrincourt turned to Madame de Guercheville and with her help, on condition of a share in the benefits, a ship loaded with provisions was despatched to Port Royal in 1612. But the young Biencourt quarrelled with Biard, and Madame de Guercheville, informed of the situation, secured the grant of a territory south-west of the Bay of Fundy for a Jesuit mission. In 1613 a ship sent by her, and carrying forty-eight persons, landed its passengers and Biard and Massé in the island of Mount Desert. The new establishment, called St Sauveur, was busy with house-building, when in June an English ship, under Samuel Argall, hove in sight. Argall was on his way from Jamestown, where the Virginia Company had in 1607 established an English settlement. Although France and England were at peace, Argall, under the fictitious pretext that the French had invaded lands within the limits of the territory granted by James I, attacked and captured the unsuspecting French ship, devastated the infant settlement and carried some of the settlers prisoners to Jamestown. His action was hardly better than piracy. In October Argall sailed to Port Royal, and, finding the colonists absent in the field, plundered and burned the settlement.[1] Unaware of these events, Poutrincourt returned in 1614, and, undaunted, restored his settlement as best he could. Again visiting France to assemble men and material, he took part in the civil war

[1] Garneau, *Hist. du Canada*, 1, 67–9; also see *Cal. St. Pap., Am. and W.I.* 1574–1660, pp. 26, 119.

and was killed in December 1615, while defending the town of Méry for the King. His son Biencourt, now the owner of Port Royal, was reduced to roam the peninsula, bartering furs with passing ships. In spite of his earnest appeals, France, torn by religious dissensions, paid no attention to the Acadian colony, while the seaport towns were concerned only with securing the freedom of the fur trade. About 1624 Biencourt died leaving only a name and the deserted seigneury of Port Royal.

In the meantime, French colonial activities centred in the valley of the St Lawrence. De Monts, on returning to France with Champlain, after the suppression of his monopoly, had practically made up his mind to sever his connection with Canada. But Champlain pleaded so earnestly with him that he decided to turn his attention to the St Lawrence. This shifting of Champlain's plan from Acadia to Canada, from the seaboard to the hinterland, may have been actuated by two motives; first, the greater facility of controlling an inland fur monopoly, and secondly, the undying hope of finding somewhere to the west of the land the route to the Western Sea and the Spice Islands. In any case, de Monts was so well convinced of the soundness of this plan that he applied to Henri IV, who granted him a one year trade monopoly along the St Lawrence without imposing any condition even as to settlement. A new company was formed, which sent out two vessels to the St Lawrence in the spring of 1608. While du Pont-Gravé stopped at Tadousac for the annual fur barter, Champlain, in a small barque, went up the river looking for a suitable location for a post. He found it at the narrows called by the Indians "the point of Quebec". On 3 July he landed his men and started the building of an "abitation". By September it was completed and there Champlain wintered with twenty-seven men. Thus Quebec was founded.

Unfortunately, in January 1609, the stubborn Sully refused to renew de Monts' yearly monopoly. Exclusive seigneurial ownership and trade monopoly, so far considered as essential to colonial enterprise, were thus discarded. Having failed to achieve any permanent result, they were brushed aside and freedom of trade was introduced. Nevertheless, having reaped very substantial profits, de Monts and his associates decided to maintain the Quebec post, which seemed to assure them a preference in the rich inland fur trade. Consequently, a ship was again despatched to the St Lawrence with provisions and men for Champlain. The latter, who had befriended the Montagnais Indians and promised them his help against their enemies the Iroquois, left Quebec on an exploration trip combined with an expedition of his allies. In July 1609 Champlain and his party, reinforced by Hurons and Algonkins, entered the Richelieu River and discovered Lakes Champlain and George. On the way back, near Crown Point, on the first lake, they came across a large band of Iroquois. In the battle that ensued next morning, the firearms of Champlain and of his two companions so astounded and frightened the enemy that they soon broke and ran away. For the allies this victory was a great triumph which linked them for ever to the French, but it entailed a century-long enmity of the Iroquois, an enmity which proved to be a scourge and nearly swept the new-born colony out of existence. For such interference in inter-tribal wars Champlain has been blamed by some, while warmly defended by others. A careful examination of the facts known to Champlain leads perhaps to the conclusion that the usually reflective leader was a little short-sighted in his decision. He cannot be blamed for being ignorant of the Iroquois' superior strength and organisation, but to maintain his excellent relations with the Laurentian Indians, was it necessary for him to fight their wars? Could he not see that such wars would result in paralysing trade, blocking exploration and restricting evangelisation?

Back from France, with the Company's promise to keep up the post at Quebec, Champlain in 1610 took part in a second expedition of his allies against the Iroquois who were again defeated. But barter was far from being as good as the year before, for, as trade was now free, the Company was confronted with independent traders even above Quebec. Returning from France in 1611, Champlain pushed his way up to the Lachine Rapids, here again followed by the rival traders, anxious to benefit by his friendship with the Indians. In spite of a more successful bartering, Champlain, on reaching France, found de Monts' associates dissatisfied with the returns of the last two years; the factory at Quebec was a drain on their finances with no adequate benefit, as the rival ships coming in the spring could compete against them with an equal chance. To save the post, de Monts had to buy his partners out.

Champlain realised that something must be done to ensure the permanence of the young colony. In those days of autocracy and favouritism, he conceived the plan of securing for a company the protection of some great noble, influential at court, who for a substantial consideration would cede to it his trading privileges. As a result of negotiations, the Comte de Soissons was appointed by Louis XIII lieutenant-general in New France, with full powers of governing the country and distributing land grants. At the same time, the monopoly of the trade was granted to him. Soissons made Champlain his representative and commander at Quebec. But sudden death carried him off, and his post was transferred to his cousin the Prince of Condé, who, in turn, retained Champlain's services as lieutenant. Armed with this new commission, Champlain did not tarry at Quebec, but explored the Ottawa River to the Lake Allumette from which he brought the Algonkins to barter with the French. Back in France, he organised under Condé a company of merchants of Rouen and St Malo, known as Champlain's Company, who agreed to pay the lieutenant-general an annual sum of 3000 livres and take out six families a year. Full of hope, Champlain returned to Quebec in 1615 with missionaries of the Recollet (reformed Franciscan) Order. Always anxious to gain a fuller knowledge of the still mysterious West, he accompanied a party of Hurons up the Ottawa River and by the Mattawa and Lake Nipissing reached Lake Huron. An expedition against the Iroquois ended in failure and with a wound for Champlain. After spending the winter with a missionary and twelve Frenchmen in the Huron country, between Lakes Simcoe and Huron, which he explored, the indefatigable leader returned by way of Lake Ontario. Thanks mostly to the furs of his Indian party, the yearly trade proved profitable.

On his return to France, Champlain found that Condé had been put in prison during the troubles of the King's minority, but the only noteworthy result of the disputes that ensued was that the Company was forced by public opinion to make an attempt at colonisation. Eight years had passed since the foundation of Quebec; the fur trade was extending its limits, the country had been explored as far as Lake Huron, alliances contracted with the Montagnais, Algonkins and Hurons, and missionaries were evangelising them, but not one *bona fide* colonist had set foot in Canada, though some employees of the Company were in the habit of wintering at Quebec. Except to Champlain and the missionaries, the only end in view was trade. Now in exchange for new privileges, the company agreed to take out real colonists: one Louis Hébert, a Parisian apothecary, offered to go to Canada with his family, but the Company, who did not really want colonists, forced him to sign an agreement that made him their servant without liberty to till the land except with their consent. Such treatment was no inducement to cross the ocean and colonists did not come. At the factory, in spite of Champlain's entreaties, nobody would even attempt any cultivation: trade was all that was wanted. In 1618 he tried vainly to interest France in the great opportunities of the country, asking only a few soldiers and settlers. The Company's mercantile members remained obdurate, claiming that the insecurity of their monopoly prevented them from burdening themselves with the luxury of colonists, that their privilege was not even protected against interlopers. So the Company continued to treat the settlers in such a way that would-be emigrants were absolutely discouraged. Champlain having reported such treatment to the King, the Company replaced him at Quebec by du Pont-Gravé.

Luckily a change took place. Condé, when out of prison, sold his commission to the Duc de Montmorency, who instructed his confidant, Dolu, to enquire into the situation of New France. The report was that, outside its trading, the Company had done nothing: no colonists had been sent out, no fortifications erected, no cultivation undertaken. Dolu warned the associates that, unless they carried out their engagements, the monopoly would be suppressed. In this year, 1620, Champlain went out and sent back word to Dolu that the Company had not improved its ways. With still five years to run, the monopoly was immediately cancelled. Thus monopoly and trading companies had failed to answer expectations. Yet, untaught by such experience, the Governor-General proceeded at once, under Dolu's influence, to form a new monopolistic company, called by some the Montmorency Company, and by others the de Caen Company, because the most influential members were two Huguenots, William de Caen and his nephew Emery. The conditions were practically those of the former Company: in compensation for a monopoly of eleven years, the Company agreed to pay the Viceroy one thousand crowns a year and Champlain two hundred crowns, with the services of ten men to be employed in exploration, expedition or any kind of work. Besides maintaining six Recollets at Quebec and among the Indians, the Company was to bring out six families a year. As a matter of fact, after some legal difficulties, the old and new companies were united in 1622 under the name of the Merchants' Company.

Champlain, appointed by Montmorency his lieutenant in New France, left in March 1620 for Quebec with his young wife. For four years he remained in the country, superintending the annual fur barter, dispensing fair justice to the Indian hunters, befriending the natives, sending out interpreters and missionaries, inviting new tribes to visit his post, and always seeking more information about the inland territories. At Quebec he erected a new factory and a small fort on the rock overlooking the river. New tribes were now coming to the annual mart, even the Iroquois came up with furs, and between them and the Hurons a peace was arranged. When Champlain left in 1624, the population numbered about sixty persons, of whom some twenty were regular settlers, the rest being made up of clerks, interpreters and missionaries.

In January 1625 Montmorency resigned his viceroyalty to Henri de Lévis, Duc de Ventadour, who continued Champlain as his lieutenant. In this same year, at the request of the Recollets, the Jesuits accepted the invitation to send missionaries to Canada. Connected as they were with influential and wealthy protectors, their presence meant more extensive work in the religious field as well as greater influence at court for the good of the colony. Their establishments in and around Quebec with servants and workmen were also most beneficial. During Champlain's absence, disputes between Catholics and Huguenots often broke out, while difficulties arose even between the Company's shareholders of different faiths. On his return, in 1626, Champlain found that nothing had been attended to except

trade. He at once set to work, completing the factory and reinforcing the small fort. A farm for imported cattle was established
at Cape Tourmente, and the workmen of the Jesuits started the construction of their college. Barter with the Indians was exceptionally
good that year.

In the meantime, Acadia was slowly drifting into insignificance.
After Biencourt's death, his companion, the younger la Tour, became leader of the French in the peninsula. He had erected a fort at
Cape Sable, where he lived by hunting and fur-trading, while French
ships would also call at the River St John and other points on the coast
to barter with the Indians. At this time there appeared on the scene
a foreign rival. Moved by reports of trading posts flourishing along
the coast of America, a Scotch nobleman, Sir William Alexander,
obtained from James I, in September 1621, without regard to the
superior French title based on actual occupation, the grant of a vast
territory stretching from Cape Breton to Gaspé, including what is now
Nova Scotia, New Brunswick and the Gaspé peninsula. From this
grant, however, Prince Edward Island and Cape Breton were, a few
days later, detached and transferred to Robert Gordon of Lochinvar,
under the title of the Barony of Galloway. In 1622 Alexander
despatched a vessel carrying colonists, and a second one was sent
the following year. But nothing was effected, except the reconnoitring of the Nova Scotia coast. Short of funds after these
unsuccessful ventures, Alexander resorted to the plan of creating ten
baronetcies of Nova Scotia, each of which carried a hereditary title
and a grant of land extending three miles along the coast and ten
miles inland. The would-be holder had to pay Alexander 3000 marks
and take out six colonists.[1] On the amount being reduced to 1000
marks, eight baronetcies were sold. In January 1627 four ships
sailed with seventy settlers and took possession of Poutrincourt's
former site of Port Royal, where they built Scott's Fort, also called
Charles' Fort, and settled down to trade and cultivation.

In Canada things were slowly improving, when the Indian peace
was broken by some crack-brained young Montagnais who made an
expedition against the Iroquois. Yet, in face of approaching hostility,
de Caen was adverse to any work on fortifications, and what was
worse, the colony was left every year with only sufficient supplies to
last the winter. Champlain's strong protests and the complaints
of the Jesuits, which reached Richelieu in the midst of a civil war
against the Huguenots, were more than enough to settle the case
against de Caen. The Cardinal, who was planning to develop the
whole trade of France by the creation of commercial companies,
decided to establish his own company in Canada. After buying
up the viceroyalty of Ventadour, he cancelled the monopoly of
de Caen and his associates on the ground that they had entirely

[1] See vol. 1, pp. 153-5.

neglected colonisation. In April 1627 he formed the Company of New France, composed of one hundred associates, to whom was granted the whole of New France in full seigneurial ownership, with perpetual fur monopoly and an additional monopoly of all trade for fifteen years. On its side, the Company agreed to send out 300 colonists the first year and later such number as to reach a total of 4000 by the year 1643. Protestant settlers were barred from the colony; for France was then fighting against the Huguenots of la Rochelle. On 6 May 1628 the King ratified this agreement by letters patent. Meanwhile, late in 1626, Charles I of England had issued letters of marque against French shipping.[1]

In spite of civil war at home and British ships at large, in April 1628 the new Company imprudently sent out a fleet of four vessels carrying 400 settlers, with provisions, cattle and building material. Meanwhile, about a month before, a British fleet of three ships had sailed from England, under the command of David Kirke. Entering the St Lawrence, the fleet stopped at Tadousac, whence Kirke despatched his brother Lewis to Quebec with a demand for surrender. Champlain, though in dire straits, courageously refused to lower his flag, and Kirke decided to starve the place into surrender. Posting his ships down the river, he attacked the Company's vessels under de Roquement. After a fight of several hours, the French vessels, encumbered with stores and non-combatants, had to surrender to the English men-of-war. Burning some of his earlier captures, Kirke sent his prisoners to France and returned to England with six prizes.

The news of the disaster was a hard blow to the One Hundred Associates, who, however, fitted out a new fleet in 1629, for which the King ordered six vessels to act as convoy. But on 24 April England and France signed the Treaty of Susa, by which it was stipulated that all places and goods captured after the conclusion of peace should be restored. Consequently, the men-of-war were withdrawn and the fleet sailed out to Canada without convoy. In England, Kirke's success had raised the ambition of Alexander, who claimed that his rights had been infringed by the last expedition. After some negotiations, Alexander and Kirke decided to unite their resources, and formed the Scottish and English Company trading in Canada, with a fur monopoly in New France. Early in the spring Kirke returned to Tadousac and again sent his brother Lewis to Quebec with three ships. After a winter of privation, during which the garrison had to live on roots and wild berries, Champlain, with the English in the river, was forced to yield and surrendered Quebec on 26 July 1629. In the meantime, the French Company's vessels had sailed, but one was wrecked on the Acadian coast, another was captured by Kirke, while a third returned to France. Champlain and his men were carried to England, where, on learning that peace

[1] See vol. 1, p. 155.

had been signed, Champlain made his way to the French ambassador and urged him to press for the restoration of New France. Negotiations which were to drag on for three years were immediately begun.

While Kirke was operating against Quebec, Alexander's son sailed in 1629 in charge of the fleet for Nova Scotia. On board was Claude de la Tour who, having been captured at sea the year before by the English, agreed to change his allegiance and received from them a grant of Acadian territory. He called on his son at Cape Sable to engage him to follow his example and hand his fort over to the English, but young la Tour absolutely refused, declaring himself ready to defend his fort, and the fleet therefore proceeded to Port Royal. Before stopping at Cape Sable, Alexander had left at Cape Breton James Stewart, Lord Ochiltree, and fifty colonists. Ochiltree built a fort at Port-aux-Baleines and forced the fishermen operating in the vicinity to hand over a duty of one-tenth of their fish. But two vessels of the French company under Captain Daniel, destined for Acadia, on reaching Cape Breton heard from the infuriated fishermen of Ochiltree's new post and his levy on fishing vessels. Assisted by the fishermen, Daniel attacked the place, captured it without difficulty on 8 September, and razed all the buildings. Then moving away along the coast, he constructed a fort at Grand Cibou, where he left a garrison before sailing home. Thus at the end of 1629 France retained only the two posts of Cape Sable and Grand Cibou. Informed by Daniel, the One Hundred Associates the following year despatched ships with reinforcements of which two went to Latour with arms and provisions for the building of a stronger fort. At Cape Sable, it was decided to build a new fort at the mouth of the St John River. The other two vessels revictualled and regarrisoned Grand Cibou. The next year, 1631, the fort at St John was built and the French secured part of the fur trade. But up to 1632 the Scottish and English Company enjoyed the monopoly of the barter in the St Lawrence, which brought them, in one year only, about 300,000 livres. In Europe, negotiations for peace were slowly proceeding, and at last, in March 1632, the Treaty of St Germain-en-Laye was signed which restored to France, not only Quebec, but also Port Royal, though it had been occupied before peace was concluded.[1]

Thus ended the first period of French colonisation which extended from Francis I to Louis XIII, from Roberval to de Caen— a period of apathy, disorganisation and failure. Except in the case of Verazzano and Cartier, the King took hardly any interest in colonial ventures and gave no financial help. As a substitute for royal initiative personal enterprise showed itself incompetent and blind to opportunities. Roberval was in quest of a route to China and wealth; the successive viceroys and companies cared for nothing but the fur trade. Influenced by the Cathay myth,

[1] See vol. I, p. 155.

winter-frozen country was selected which proved a formidable handicap; the choice of vagabonds and prisoners as the first colonists was an invitation to failure; and the gratuitous attack on the Iroquois must be rated a serious blunder. Except for Champlain, nobody wanted the tilling of the soil, and he was without money and power. It is inaccurate to say that the French would not emigrate; whether Catholic or Huguenot, they were not permitted to do so by the companies. The blame for the failure lay with the King as well as with the trading companies.

At this stage came Richelieu and his Company of New France. On 13 July 1632, the French, under Emery de Caen, reoccupied Quebec, and the fleur-de-lys floated over the whole of Canada. But the Company had been ruined through the capture of its fleets by Kirke, and the loss of the whole of its capital of 300,000 livres. Unable to raise new funds, the members, in December 1632, let out for five years their trade monopoly to a group of their associates in consideration of an early payment of 10,000 livres and one-third interest in the association. Those 10,000 livres represented the administrative expenditure of the colony, salaries of the Governor and officers, the cost of garrisons and of the maintenance of the post, the allowance to the clergy and missions. In 1633, under this arrangement, which lasted five years, a fleet of three vessels brought to Quebec Champlain, who had been reappointed Governor, and some colonists. Champlain set out at once to organise the whole colony. He repaired the factory, erected a chapel and began sowing. He reopened friendly relations with the Montagnais and the Algonkins, and induced them to come and barter at Quebec. In order to intercept trade and ward off the Iroquois, who had already killed two Frenchmen, he built a small post in an inlet off the mouth of the Richelieu River. The following year he ordered La Violette to build a strong post at Three Rivers, which soon became the fur centre of the colony. At the same time, missionaries were sent out to the Montagnais and Huron countries. With trade flourishing, emigrants landing from France with their families, and houses being built, Quebec assumed an air of activity and of progress never seen before. For the first time, Quebec ceased to be a mere trading post, and became the cradle of New France. With this picture before him, for which he had toiled undespairingly for thirty years, Champlain died on 25 December 1635. A bold explorer and faithful writer, religious propagandist and the Indians' best friend, the man with a vision who forced on France the founding of New France and left her the prospective heir to a continent, he is perhaps the greatest figure of all Canadian history.

Under the next Governor, de Montmagny (1636–48), a brave soldier and wise administrator, the Company of New France, after all its ill-success, attempted to carry out its programme. Once trade was established, the country protected, and the necessary elements of civil and religious life created, the great need was to secure real settlers. Lacking the necessary funds to take them out, the Company resorted to the plan of making large grants of land, with seigneurial rights, to persons undertaking to settle them with colonists. The first concession is dated 15 January 1634, and was made to Robert Giffard, who brought over a number of settlers from Perche, and by 1640 about fifteen grants had been distributed, several of them to religious communities, who proved to be the most active and enterprising seigneurs. Every year a few more colonists came and took up land on both sides of the St Lawrence between Quebec and Three Rivers. By 1643 the colony could boast a population of about 300 souls.

If France was indifferent to emigration, she was not to evangelisation. It must be said in her praise that no country ever treated native races as generously as she did. From the day they landed in Canada with Cartier, the French befriended the Indian, made alliance with him and treated him on a footing of human equality. They tried to educate and convert him, and even offered him the full privileges of French citizenship. But the main purpose was to make him a Christian. With the money devoted to missions, France could have taken out to Canada enough people to increase her population to several thousands. In carrying out this fine programme of humanity and civilisation, the best agents France had were the Jesuits. They came to Canada in 1625, and as early as 1637 there were twenty-nine in the country with missions at Three Rivers and Miscou, and a few missionaries attached to the Montagnais and the Hurons. They had come to stay, for in Canada, with its large native population, they saw, with a broad vision, an immense field for apostolic labours and conquests. Undaunted by physical discomforts, continuous hardships and the prospect of atrocious deaths, self-sacrificing and inspired, they set themselves the noble task of christianising and civilising the Indians. This work they planned to effect in two ways. The first was to change the Indians into French citizens in accordance with the royal instructions in the Company's charter. For that purpose schools were opened for children, one for boys in 1634, at Notre Dame des Anges, the other for girls by the Ursulines in 1639. Moreover, in 1637, through the generosity of Brulart de Sillery, a village was created, a few miles out of Quebec, where a number of Algonkins, and later of Abenakis, were gathered. After learning their language, the Jesuits began to teach them the Christian message. At the same time, they gave lessons to the children, also teaching them and their parents various trades. The village included 167 Indians in 1645, while a second village at Three Rivers, begun in 1640, numbered eighty Indians in the following year.

But, as only a few Indians could be reached by that system, the Jesuits unhesitatingly adopted the second plan of going to live with the tribes on their hunting grounds far inland up the Saguenay and round the Great Lakes. Armed only with a cross and a breviary, they attached themselves to the tribes. They daily endured the discomforts of Indian life—cold, dirt, scanty and bad food, and sleeping on the earth. Always in the background, amidst daily threats, stalked the shadow of death at the hands of excitable and superstitious natives or from the blow of a lurking Iroquois. In 1640 the Jesuits had a mission at Tadousac for Montagnais and Algonkins. In 1641 they visited the Ojibwa at Sault Ste Marie, in 1651 the Attikamegue, north of Three Rivers, and in 1646 the Abenakis on the Kennebeck. They even visited the hostile Iroquois, but centred their main activities in the Huron country. In 1634 three missionaries took up residence at Ihonatiria, on Penetanguishene Bay. In 1640 they moved their quarters to St Mary on the right bank of the Wye, whence they could visit various tribes, Huron, Algonkin, Neutral and Tobacco.

Meanwhile the Company of New France was not prospering. The sub-company of 1632 had dissolved in 1637, with a handsome profit of 300,000 livres, of which the head Company received 60,000. But the new sub-company, formed for four years, did so poorly that the Company of New France lost 70,000 livres as its share. In 1641 the associates subscribed 103,500 livres to carry on the trade and administration of the colony, and met with such success that by 1645 they had realised 85,000 livres. In spite of these occasional profits, the Company was still hopelessly in debt owing to past losses, and just managed to pay the administrative charges of the country. France, absorbed by her struggle against Spain, had no concern or money for colonial ventures. Therefore the colony fared badly, few emigrants coming in, while the Iroquois were more and more menacing. In this predicament, New France was probably saved from disruption and ruin by the Jesuits' *Relations*. These were annual pamphlets of a score of pages, narrating the story of the colony, especially its religious life and progress. In an age, when few could travel and faith was fervent, they were so widely circulated that Canada was kept in the foreground of public interest. Describing the beauty and fertility of the land and the freedom of its life, they certainly suggested to many the idea of emigration, while the narratives of evangelising the Indians elicited religious vocations and impelled zealous and wealthy people to contributions in favour of far distant colonists and heathen Indians. Moreover, from this propaganda resulted nearly all the public institutions of the colony. In 1635 a rich benefactor founded in Quebec the Jesuits' College, the first educational institution in America north of Mexico. In 1639, moved by the same influence, a niece of Richelieu, the Duchesse d'Aiguillon, was responsible for the construction of the Hôtel-Dieu, while another devout lady, Madame de la Peltrie, with the assistance of Mother Marie de l'Incarnation, established a convent for girls also at Quebec.

To the Jesuits' propaganda was due the foundation of the Montreal settlement, the importance of which cannot be exaggerated, as Montreal soon proved itself a constantly growing centre and the best rampart of the colony against the Iroquois. Remarkable it certainly was for the high-spirited motives of its founders and the splendid organisation of its recruiting and maintenance. It was founded by an association of priests and laymen to be an outpost for the propagation of the Gospel among the Indians. In 1642 under the leadership of Paul de Chomedey, sieur de Maisonneuve, sixty colonists, including soldiers, artisans and farmers, were at work clearing the land and building a fort and houses, surrounded by a palisade. The following year, forty new colonists came from France and began sowing. From the start, Montreal was a strong post and a progressive settlement. Charitable and educational institutions were soon opened, for Mademoiselle Mance, with the financial help of Madame de Bullion, built a hospital, while a few years later Marguérite Bourgeoys opened a school. In 1653 the settlement had already a population of about two hundred persons, thus almost doubling the population of the colony.

On the Atlantic seaboard, it was Isaac de Razilly, appointed lieutenant-general in Acadia, to whom the country was restored by the English in 1632. He had founded a company of four persons for the resettling of the peninsula. Sailing in July of that year, with three hundred colonists from Touraine and Brittany, he landed his people at La Hève, where he built the fort of Ste Marie-de-Grâce. Pentagoët and Port Royal were also reoccupied by the French. From the latter place the English garrison returned to England, leaving behind thirty settlers, who were absorbed in the French settlement. Razilly set to work to organise his post, granting land lots and encouraging cultivation. In a neighbouring harbour, called Rossignol, Nicolas Denys built a saw-mill and prepared timber for exportation. Unfortunately Razilly died early in 1635.

Two men were left to divide his succession, Charles de la Tour and Charles de Menou, sieur d'Aulnay-Charnisay. Both ambitious, they soon quarrelled about jurisdiction. The King had to interfere in 1638, but did so with little discretion. La Tour was made lieutenant-general of the territory from Chignecto to Canso with the exception of La Hève and Port Royal, the latter place being d'Aulnay's residence, while d'Aulnay was created lieutenant-general of all the country from Chignecto to the Kennebeck, including Pentagoët, with the exception of Cape Sable and Fort St John, the residence of la Tour. Thus the residence of each was in the territory of his rival.

Trade rivalry and land ambition soon caused a clash between the two commanders, which degenerated into open warfare. In 1640 la Tour tried to surprise Port Royal but was captured by d'Aulnay, who soon after set him free. The following year, the King summoned la Tour to France and appointed d'Aulnay Governor for the whole of Acadia. Then in 1641 la Tour entered into negotiations with the Boston merchants which caused the French court to order his arrest, and d'Aulnay besieged him without success in his fort of St John. In April 1645 d'Aulnay again laid siege to the fort, which Madame la Tour, in her husband's absence, vigorously defended, but the place was stormed and captured. Broken in health and fortune, she died three weeks later. Unable to raise either men or money, la Tour left Acadia to his rival and took refuge at Quebec in August 1646. In spite of these internal quarrels, d'Aulnay, who had removed his quarters from La Hève to Port Royal, industriously improved his settlement. Settlers were brought out, seigneurial lots granted, cultivation developed, cattle reared, timber prepared and fur-trading carried on. Capuchins attended to the spiritual needs of the colonists and preached to the Indians. Port Royal, La Hève and Pentagoët were also reinforced. As a reward for his services, d'Aulnay received from the King the feudal ownership of Acadia, but was unfortunately drowned on 24 May 1650.

Another establishment was also making rapid progress. Nicolas Denys, who had received from the Company of New France the governorship of the territory extending from Cape Canso to Cape Rosiers, had founded a post at Miscou, in 1645, carrying on fishing and trading, as well as cultivation. D'Aulnay had come and seized the property, as encroaching on his jurisdiction, but was forced to recognise Denys' rights and to compensate him for his losses. Arrested in 1651, by Madame d'Aulnay, Denys once more succeeded in asserting his rights and, undaunted, resumed his various activities.

In the Laurentian colony, 1640 may be said to mark the beginning of the Iroquois hostilities against the French. The Five Nations, as they were also called, had never forgotten, still less forgiven, Champlain's interference in their struggle against the Hurons. In 1633 they had killed two Frenchmen, in an accidental encounter. Three Rivers, and Quebec especially, were too far out of their tactical line of offensive and too well fortified against the bows and arrows with which they were then still armed. But in 1640 they were actively bartering furs against muskets and powder with the Dutch on the Hudson, and could attack the white men on a footing of equality. That year they captured two Frenchmen, and the following year, on being refused by Montmagny a peace that did not include the Algonkins, they unsuccessfully attacked Three Rivers. In 1642 they captured Father Jogues and two companions. On the way back, they assailed the soldiers working on the fort that Montmagny was erecting at the mouth of the Richelieu River, which was their route to invade the colony. In 1643 they massacred two more Frenchmen at Montreal. Availing himself of the possession of Iroquois prisoners, Montmagny signed a peace with them in September 1645, but it was broken the following year when the Iroquois, in cold blood, massacred Father Jogues and his companion Lalande. Once more the country was in a state of war, with Iroquois bands roving through the colony, waiting for an opportunity to kill and scalp isolated settlers.

So far the life of the little colony had run, on the whole, peaceably. The few Iroquois raids, however annoying and distressing they were, had not yet proved damaging or dangerous. The forts at Quebec, Montreal and Three Rivers had been strengthened. The Governor-General resided at Quebec, but the other two posts had their own Governors, who really were not more than town-majors, administering the place. There was as yet no judicial organisation, except the Governor's tribunal which settled any difficulty without further appeal. The whole administrative budget did not exceed 10,000 livres, covering the salaries of the Governors and their garrisons, the maintenance of the clergy and charitable institutions. Religious, educational and hospital requirements were well provided for, such advantages being extended to the Indians. The population was small, increasing very slowly, and not exceeding three hundred persons in 1645, but each man was a staunch colonist ready to fight with his own gun. The worst difficulty was that the crops of the colony were still insufficient to feed its people, who had to rely on the annual ships from France. The fur trade was the great resource, almost the *raison d'être* of the settlement. Its monopoly had gone back in 1641 to the Company of New France, which, though hopelessly in debt, was now reaping handsome profits for the first time.

These benefits disturbed the peace of mind of a few men in the colony, among others, de Repentigny, Godefroy, Des Chatelets, Giffard and Boulard. With the purpose of sharing in such benefits, they conceived the idea of forming a company among themselves to exploit the fur monopoly, as previously conceded by the Company of New France to sub-companies. In the autumn of 1644, accompanied by Godefroy, de Repentigny went to France and pleaded his case both in and out of the court. He cleverly represented himself as voicing the sentiments of the whole colony, whose total ruin could be prevented only by the handing over of the monopoly to all the inhabitants formed in a company. As a result of negotiations, an agreement was signed by the Company of New France and the colony's delegate, which was ratified by the King's Council on 6 March 1645. Under the Order-in-Council, the Company reserved to itself the seigneurial ownership of the colony with the feudal dues thereto attached, as well as all appointments of the colonial officers. The fur monopoly was transferred to the inhabitants of New France, such monopoly not including Nova Scotia. On the other hand, the inhabitants agreed to discharge all the obligations and administrative expenditure of the Company, which implied the maintenance of the colonial clergy and Indian missions and the payment of the salaries of the Governors, officers and garrisons, which were to number at least one hundred men. They were also obliged to take out twenty colonists a year and to pay the Company one thousand beaver skins.

The new organisation known as the *Compagnie des Habitants* took charge of the trade, which in 1645 proved very profitable, yielding 320,000 livres. This prosperity occasioned disputes between the associates as to how profits should be divided and business administered, while outsiders, who had refused to come in, were displeased with the result. Some of the directors sought to have their salaries increased and special allowances granted. Complaints soon reached the court, which appointed commissaries to investigate the facts. As a result, the King issued on 27 March 1647 a new set of regulations governing the fur monopoly. But as the Company enjoying the monopoly also received the financial and commercial administration of the colony, the new edict acquired special importance as the first political constitution of Canada into which an element of the principle of representation enters. It marked also the beginning of a certain control of the colony by the King.

By this edict, a Council was created, composed of the Governor, the Superior of the Jesuits or the bishop, when there should be one, and the Governor of Montreal. The Council with its secretary was to meet at Quebec, and it was empowered to appoint by a majority vote, all the ship officers and trade clerks, who were obliged to account to it for their management and were appointed for three years only. Essentially a board of directors, the Council decided on all matters relating to fur trade, appointments, salaries and expenditure. No officers or clerks could claim anything from the Company— bonus, allowance or provisions—outside of their salaries. The Council, however, was more than a board of directors. For, besides having the financial administration of the colony, it was authorised to deal with "all matters necessary for the good of the country". In fact, therefore, it governed the country in all matters of finance, fur trade and general policy.

Another noteworthy feature of the system was that, besides the officer commanding the Company's ships, the syndics or representatives of Quebec, Montreal and Three Rivers, were entitled to attend the Council and take part in its deliberations in order to express the sentiments of those communities. These syndics were to be elected by ballot. Here, however faint, is the first vestige of popular representation. At the same time, trade with the Indians was declared free to all colonists on condition of bringing their furs to the Company's stores. The main items of the colony's budget, substantially increased since 1635, were as follows: 25,000 livres to the Governor for his salary, and pay, subsistence and arms of the Quebec and Three Rivers officers and garrisons of at least seventy men; 10,000 livres to the Governor of Montreal for his salary, and pay, subsistence and arms of a garrison of at least thirty men; 5000 livres to Indian missions. The secretary of the Council was directed to send to France a copy of all the proceedings of the Council, as well as a general yearly statement of the colony's situation. Members of the King's Council were appointed as special commissioners for the affairs of New France.

The new regulations much displeased the leading families who so far had controlled the colony's trade and affairs. In the Governor, Montmagny, they found a man who would not ignore law or serve their ends. The Governor of Three Rivers, d'Ailleboust, and Des Chatelets went to France and petitioned the King for a change of the edict of 1647, as insufficiently meeting the needs of the country under the daily menace of the Iroquois. As a result, a new edict, dated 5 March 1648, was issued under which the colony was governed until 1663. Among other changes, the new edict ruled that, in future, governors would be nominated for three years only. The Council was to consist of the Governor, the Superior of the Jesuits or the bishop, and the former Governor, and also of two more persons, elected for three years by the appointed members of the Council, the syndics of Quebec, Montreal and Three Rivers being called to attend the election meeting. For the first Council, the King nominated the three additional members, François de Chavigny, Paul Godefroy and Robert Giffard. The budget of the colony was rearranged as follows: 10,000 livres to the Governor for his salary and a garrison of twelve soldiers at Quebec; 3000 livres to the Governor of Montreal and a garrison of twelve soldiers; 3000 livres to the Governor of Three Rivers and a garrison of six soldiers; 19,000 livres for the maintenance of a flying detachment of forty soldiers. This new constitution was a step nearer to representative government, as representatives of the people appeared for the first time in the colony's Council.

Meanwhile, in the Huron country missionaries were patiently preaching to the Indians. Eleven missions had been founded, but the results were slow and meagre. After thirteen years, the Christian Indians hardly numbered a few hundreds. The main obstacles to conversion were their lax standards of sex morality, while their superstitions were part of their economic and family system. But suddenly a blow fell on the Huron nation. The Iroquois launched an irresistible offensive against them. Situated on the south of Lake Ontario, the Five Nations of the Iroquois had banded themselves under a kind of federal union, aiming at supremacy over the land. Not superior in numbers or courage, they nevertheless triumphed over their enemies through organisation, discipline and strategy.

Their plan was to attack the weakest nation first and always to make the attack a surprise. Now they overwhelmed the Hurons with a series of thunderbolt raids. In July 1648, while the Hurons were away hunting, they destroyed the village of St Joseph, killing Father Daniel. In March 1649 the bourgades of St Ignace and St Louis were also ruined and the Jesuits Brébeuf and Lalement were tortured to death, and in December St John was destroyed and Father Garnier murdered. Discouraged, the Hurons abandoned the country—part went west, while the others, under French escort, in the spring of 1650 took refuge at Quebec. In 1650–1 the Iroquois destroyed the powerful tribe of the Neutrals.

In Acadia the death of d'Aulnay brought much confusion and trouble. On hearing of it la Tour returned to France and succeeded in explaining away his attacks against d'Aulnay and his meddling with the Bostonians with such amazing success, that, on 27 February 1651, he was appointed Governor of Acadia by the court which had eight years before ordered his arrest. Armed with his commission, he obtained from Madame d'Aulnay the retrocession of Forts St John and Latour. Two years later he married the widow of his rival. But a creditor of d'Aulnay, Emmanuel le Borgne, arrived in Nova Scotia, claiming the whole country as his property. Making Nicolas Denys a prisoner at Nepisiguit, he went next to Port Royal in August 1653 and took possession of all d'Aulnay's properties. Going to France, Denys forced le Borgne to a restitution and secured for himself a royal appointment as Governor of his former territory from Cape Canso to Cape Rosiers, with a fur monopoly and fishing privileges.

But while Acadia was being torn by rival factions, an English expedition under Robert Sedgwick, with four vessels and 500 men, hove in sight. It was inspired by the Boston merchants, anxious to annex the French colony while divided against itself. Though England and France were at peace, Sedgwick, in August 1654, attacked Pentagoët, which was given up without resistance. On the appearance of the fleet at Fort St John, la Tour surrendered without firing a shot, claiming he was a British subject. At Port Royal, le Borgne defended himself as best he could, but capitulated on 16 August with the honours of war. La Tour proceeded to London in 1655, and on 18 September 1656 he was, with William Crowne and Sir Thomas Temple, heir to Sir William Alexander, granted the whole of Nova Scotia. In that month he sold his share to his associates for the twentieth part of the products of the country and returned to Acadia, where he lived until his death in 1663. With the exception of Denys' territory, Acadia remained under British rule, with garrisons at Port Royal and Fort St John. The few French families in the country, about sixty in all, applied themselves to the cultivation of the soil, while the English merchants were

reaping the benefits of the fur trade. France, which had never ac-
cepted the surprise conquest in peace-time, soon appealed to England.
But her claim was not recognised until 31 July 1667, when by the
Treaty of Breda Charles II restored Acadia to its owners.

On the introduction of the Council of 1648, Montmagny departed and was succeeded by d'Ailleboust (1648–51). The new
Governor was soon faced with the difficult situation created by
the Iroquois raids. For the Five Nations, having dispersed the
Hurons and dispelled any danger of a flank attack, now took the
offensive against the European colony. Their bands roved up
and down the St Lawrence lurking round the French posts. There
was no security outside the forts; no settler would venture to
his field without his musket. In March 1650 the Iroquois burnt
many houses and killed several isolated workers. D'Ailleboust did
what he could with his feeble resources: a flying detachment was
kept patrolling the river, and fortified houses of refuge were built at
several places. Delegates were sent to France to ask for reinforcements.

In order the better to check their enemies, the Governor and his
Council decided to form an alliance with the New England colonies,
as the Iroquois raids against the Abenakis also interfered with the
prosperity of the Boston fur trade. As early as 1647, the Massachusetts colony had proposed to New France free trade between the
two countries. Negotiations were carried on without any result, for
to the French a commercial convention appeared as a benefit only
to the British colonies and they wanted therefore to attach to it a
treaty of alliance against the Iroquois, which did not appeal to New
England. This time d'Ailleboust decided to take the initiative. Father
Druillettes, a Jesuit, was sent to Boston in September 1650, where he
was received by Governor Dudley and the colonies' Commissioners.
On his return to Quebec, the Council, in June 1651, after hearing
his report, appointed him and Jean Godefroy ambassadors to New
England, with power to sign a treaty of commerce and alliance.
But on their reaching Boston, the proposal was declined by the
English colonies, which were unwilling to bring upon themselves a
war with the Iroquois.

This same year, a new Governor, Jean de Lauzon (1651–6),
arrived in Canada with a number of new officials. He had been
instructed by the Company of New France to establish a regular
system of justice. So far, owing to the small population, the Governor
was the only and supreme tribunal, and the two local Governors of
Montreal and Three Rivers settled any disputes that might arise in
their posts. Now the administration of justice was placed under the
Great Seneschalship of New France, a purely honorary title, held by
de Lauzon's own son. A lieutenant-general, with civil and criminal
jurisdiction, was appointed at Quebec with an assistant, and from

his court an appeal lay to the Governor. At Three Rivers, there was
also a lieutenant-general. These tribunals were seigneurial courts, as
the officials were appointed by the Company of New France. At
Montreal, the Governor's tribunal still remained the only court.

Being a member of the Company of New France, de Lauzon was
greatly interested in the development of the country, the more so
as he had obtained large tracts of land for several members of his
family. From 1640 to 1651 only about ten seigneuries had been
granted in eleven years, most of them to settlers in the country
or to existing seigneurs, for hardly any colonists were coming
in. Under de Lauzon, more activity prevailed. During the five
years of his regime, more seigneuries were granted than in the preceding period. The best land between Montreal and Quebec was
being divided and distributed in such a way that by 1663 about sixty
seigneuries had been allotted. At the same time, groups of colonists
began to enter the country. In 1653 Maisonneuve brought with him
one hundred men for Montreal. The following year the Queen sent
out a certain number of "honest girls". In 1659 another convoy
of one hundred men and women went to Montreal. Almost every
year a few isolated emigrants would come in, servants, farm hands
or artisans. With the natural growth of the population, the colony
now neared two thousand.

From the mother country Canada naturally received the feudal
system of land tenure obtaining there. But, owing to the almost complete absence of any titled estates in Canada, where only seigneuries
were found, the name of seigneurial system was preferred. Furthermore, the system as introduced in the colony was much less burdensome to the tenants than the French system, and the Intendant, after
1665, always stood as the protector of the *censitaires* against any encroachments by the seigneurs. The system was simple in its details.
The tracts of land given out to feudal grantees were called seigneuries
and varied greatly in size, some covering but a few acres, while
others enclosed several thousand square miles. In the beginning, for
the convenience of communication in a wood-covered country, they
all possessed a river frontage. Except in a very few specified cases,
those seigneurial grants did not confer nobility. A few important
obligations were imposed on the seigneur. He vowed fealty and
homage to his suzerain, either to the King or the feudal Company.
He was also obliged to hand in his *aveu* and *dénombrement*, that is a
declaration and enumeration of the extent of his estate and number
and names of his tenants. At every transfer of the seigneury, except
by direct descent, he had to pay to the overlord one year of the
seigneurial revenue. Under the King, after 1663, he had to pay the
Quint or a fifth of the price of sale. The Company, and later on the
King, made certain reservations for public interest. Any seigneurial
land could be used freely for the purpose of fortification and for laying

high roads. Later on, the King reserved to himself certain rights in mines and minerals and the privilege of cutting timber for his navy.

Once in possession of his seigneury, the owner would first reserve for himself a tract of land for his manor and his own farming and then proceed to divide the rest into lots, which he would grant to prospective settlers. A lot would usually be three arpents wide and forty deep, an arpent measuring about two hundred feet. The settler, or *censitaire* as he was called, was really the owner of his piece of land, but subject to various obligations, of which the most important were the following: (*a*) the *cens et rentes*: *cens* was an annual due of one *cent* per arpent of frontage, and *rentes* an annual due of one *sol* per square arpent, both dues making a sum of 123 *sols* per year; (*b*) the *lods et ventes* were a due of a twelfth of the price of sale at each change of ownership through a sale; (*c*) dues in kind: a fat chicken for each arpent of frontage, and a bushel and a half of wheat. The *censitaire* was obliged to do one or two days' work for the seigneur, who also reserved to himself all mining rights. The *censitaire* was also under obligation (*banalité*) to have his wheat ground at the seigneurial grist mill at the fixed rate of the fourteenth part to the seigneur.

In spite of the taking up of new seigneuries and the coming in of new settlers, the fur trade still remained the great industry and resource of the colony. Unfortunately, the dispersion of the Hurons had ruined the country's best supply of furs. Instead of the average sale of 250,000 livres, the Company of the Habitants in 1652 realised only 65,000 livres. Moreover it had been in the habit of levying a duty of half the beaver brought by the settlers to its store, and this duty (the first ever levied on Canadian citizens) was earmarked to pay the colony's administrative expenses. But as the fur supply grew smaller, the colonists became more reluctant to bear so heavy a duty, as it left them with hardly enough furs to eke out a living. They made strong representations through their syndic, and the Council, in May 1663, reduced the duty to a quarter of the beaver.

The decrease of the fur supply brought about another result. Always attentive to his own gain, de Lauzon grew alarmed lest the duty on beaver should become insufficient to meet the colonial expenditures, which included his salary. To protect himself, he granted to a special company the Tadousac trade, with the condition that, out of the proceeds, would first be paid the salaries of the Governor and officials, the cost of the garrisons and the grants to the clergy, amounting in all to about 40,000 livres. At the same time, de Lauzon stopped the annual payment of one thousand beavers to the Company of New France. The latter strongly complained to the King, who issued new regulations which proved more or less futile. On further representations that the colony's Council was under the control of a small clique, Louis XIV took a very bold step for the time: by a decree of March 1657[1] he made the Council elective. The Council was now composed of the Governor, a fur-trade director, appointed for three years by the Company of New France, and four councillors, two of whom were elected by the citizens of Quebec and one each by the towns of Montreal and Three Rivers. Two were changed every two years. The colonial attorney was admitted to the Council to see that the regulations were followed. All matters relating to the fur trade and the use of the beaver-duty money, as well as all ordinary and extraordinary expenditures were settled by a majority vote. All public accounts had to be submitted to the Council.

In spite of these changes in management, trade continued to decline. Prices of goods were high and the price of beaver very low. The Indians brought fewer furs and asked more goods in return. More furs would have righted the situation, but the Iroquois raids prevented many tribes from coming down to Quebec and the French from going inland for barter. In spite of occasionally good returns, the Iroquois were slowly starving the colony's trade. In 1660 the Company of the Habitants was so much in debt that the members had to cede to the Company of Normandy the whole trade of the country against a payment of 10,000 livres to its own creditors and 50,000 livres for the beaver duty.

The Iroquois menace not only paralysed trade, but threatened the very life of the colony. Availing themselves of the protection of the forest, which covered the whole country, they could rove everywhere unperceived and wait for days for an opportunity to kill isolated settlers. It was next to impossible to stop this guerrilla warfare. In 1651 they launched several raids against Montreal, forcing the farmers to take constant refuge in the fort. They attacked Three Rivers, and the Governor, Duplessis-Bochard, imprudently sallying out, was killed with fifteen men. Badly repulsed at Montreal, in 1652, the Iroquois offered the next year a peace which was ratified in 1654, probably because they heard of a reinforcement of one hundred men reaching Montreal. They now asked for missionaries and a French garrison, but their only idea was to use them as hostages. Nevertheless, two missionaries and fifty Frenchmen took quarters among the Five Nations. But in 1657 the Iroquois killed three Montrealers and planned the massacre of the French garrison, who, however, succeeded in escaping by a stratagem. In May 1660 the Iroquois came down for a mass attack on the colony. About the same time, Dollard, a young Frenchman, with sixteen companions, some Hurons and Algonkins, planned to carry the war into the enemy's country. They had just taken position in a small palisaded fort, at the foot of the Long Sault Rapids, on the Ottawa, when they were attacked by two hundred Iroquois. For five days, they drove

[1] *Canadian Archives*, Correspond. officielle, II série, I vol. Arrêt du Conseil d'État... 7 mars 1657, p. 212.

the enemy back with heavy loss. Then reinforced by seven hundred warriors, the assailants hurled themselves against the fort. Though deserted by the Hurons, the French and the Algonkins fought desperately for three more days, when the besiegers succeeded in storming the palisade, and, after a deadly hand-to-hand fight, shot down the defenders. But the wonderful resistance of the French band saved the colony. If seventeen Frenchmen in a small stockade could resist hundreds of Iroquois, it was useless to attack the stone forts of Quebec and Montreal. The Iroquois consequently reverted to their guerrilla tactics, attacking isolated houses and surprising small groups of settlers. Every year a certain number of colonists were thus ambushed and killed by invisible enemies. The colony, short of defenders, could do nothing but offer a stout resistance, with un-flinching courage, though losing, at each new raid, what it could least afford—some brave soldier or hard-working settler. Unable to stand alone against the Iroquois, New France turned to the throne for help and assistance.

Though greatly distracted by the Indian raids, the colony had extended its activities beyond its immediate territories. Fond of ad-ventures, the French were always anxious to push forward to un-known lands. In 1634 Jean Nicolet was exploring the region of Lake Michigan, being the first white man to reach it. Then for a time the onward march was at a standstill, but in 1654 two young Frenchmen visited several Indian nations round Lake Michigan. In 1658 two bold adventurers, Radisson and Groseilliers, went on a fur-trading and exploring trip west of Lake Superior, reaching perhaps the Upper Mississippi in 1659 and mixing with the Crees and the Sioux of the plains. In 1661 they returned to the same region and, guided by Crees, are believed to have reached the Bay of the North, most probably James Bay, returning to Quebec in 1663. Thus the limits of Canada were continuously extending north and west.

In the colony itself things did not run too smoothly. To the old and feeble de Lauzon had succeeded the Vicomte d'Argenson (1657–61) who found the country overrun by the Iroquois and despondent over poor trade. The following year, Canada received its first bishop, Mgr de Laval, a favourite and disciple of the Jesuits, a man of great virtue and unbounded energy, self-sacrificing and burning with apostolic zeal, impelled by the highest spiritual motives, but domi-neering, unbending and undiplomatic. He had but one end in view, the salvation of souls; nothing else mattered. For him Canada was not so much a French colony, as a Catholic outpost devoted to the conversion of the natives. Consequently, religious ideals and standards must take precedence over practical and political ideas. To the Church's representatives must be left the decision in the con-flict of such divergent interests. With this state of mind, the bishop soon ran counter to d'Argenson, who though religious and well disposed, was unwilling to be led except by his instructions. De Laval first irritated him by denying the ordinary honours to which he was entitled in church ceremonies and by grudging him his right of precedence—bickerings which created an atmosphere of hostility. A most important dispute soon arose between the two leaders. The bishop had promptly noticed the evil effects of liquor on the Indians. To get it they would sell anything they possessed, furs, arms, clothes, even wife and children. When intoxicated, they became uncontrollable wild beasts, fighting, biting and murdering. Unscrupulous traders often played upon their desire to secure furs for next to nothing. De Laval decided to stamp out the evil and in May 1660 forbade from the pulpit the sale of liquor under pain of excommunication. But d'Argenson was opposed to such an extreme policy, and from the division of the two colonial leaders resulted a state of confusion. Already displeased with his own situation, d'Argenson asked to be relieved. He was replaced by a blunt and straightforward soldier, Baron d'Avaugour (1661–3).

A man of vision, the new Governor was struck with the fine situation of the country and its possibilities. He sedulously applied himself to its improvement. In order better to obtain the King's attention, he despatched to France Boucher, Governor of Three Rivers, to set forth the state of the colony and demand royal assistance. In the meantime, the liquor excommunication was totally disobeyed, and such a state of religious confusion prevailed that the interdict was lifted in October 1661. D'Avaugour at first supported the bishop's policy to the point of having men shot for selling brandy to the Indians.[1] But he became uneasy about its consequences: the Indians were discontented and the French undisciplined. At the same time, the bishop's imperious manners displeased the old soldier for whom the King went before the Church. An occasion presenting itself, he made use of it. A woman having been imprisoned for trading in brandy, the Jesuits intervened with the Governor for a pardon. This inconsistency irritated d'Avaugour who took his opportunity. Since the law must not apply to her, it should apply to nobody and the legal prohibition was removed. The brandy trade was now resumed. De Laval reiterated his episcopal interdict. The worst confusion ensued, rending the country into two factions. The bishop sailed for France in 1662 to lay his complaints before the King.

In France Boucher had obtained great success. Informed by him of the colonial situation, Louis XIV, who had recently resolved to govern by himself, decided to come to the rescue of the colony. In 1662 a special commissioner, Dumont, charged with the mission of reporting on the state and needs of Canada, landed at Quebec with one hundred soldiers, the vanguard of a larger detachment. Other vessels brought in two hundred colonists. The country was astir with

[1] *Journal des Jésuites*, p. 303.

excitement, activity and hope. In 1663, yielding to de Laval's demands, Louis XIV replaced d'Avaugour by de Mézy, a friend of the bishop, while on Dumont's report he cancelled the charter of the Company of New France. Annexed to the royal domain, Canada became a royal province under the King's care and administration.

The year 1663 marked a new era in the history of New France. During half a century, trading companies had owned and ruled with full authority. They had undertaken to people and develop the country. But in 1663, when their regime was brought to an end, the country was terrorised by the Iroquois, trade was so low that it did not cover the administrative expenditure, cultivation was so backward that the colony was still fed by France, while civil and religious authorities were stubbornly opposing each other. In half a century, the colony numbered only 2500 souls. The regime of the trading companies had been an utter failure.

Nevertheless, during those years France had not striven in vain. Canada had been explored from Cape Breton to Lake Superior, from Lake Champlain to Hudson Bay. Her traders roamed along the Atlantic seaboard, the Labrador coast, and inland from the Gulf of St Lawrence to the western plains. Still more daring and more active, her missionaries had visited scores of Indian tribes, Abenakis, Betiamites, Montagnais, Papinachois, Algonkins, Hurons, Iroquois, Neutrals, Tobaccos, Ottawas. Generously New France had befriended all Indians, offering trade and friendship, education and domestic arts, religion and civilisation, with the full rights of French citizenship. In the valley of the St Lawrence, the French had opened about sixty seigneuries and introduced to the country European seeds and cattle. In and around the three posts of Quebec, Montreal and Three Rivers, they had established 2500 colonists, drawn mainly from the western provinces of Normandy, Perche, Anjou and Poitou. Originating from a hardy and healthy stock, with a touch of adventurous spirit, they were hard-working, religious and brave to the point of death. Carefully selected, they lived under strong moral discipline and reared a numerous progeny of sons and daughters. Though few in numbers, they possessed in the colony all the elements of a future nation—religion, education, administration, trade, agriculture and craftsmanship. From Cartier to d'Avaugour, France had planted in Canada the seeds of a new people. Still dreaming of Indian evangelisation and a way to the Western Sea, New France was now about to become, under royal guidance, a self-supporting country.

CHAPTER III

THE OLD REGIME
(1663–1760)

FOR the purpose of the present work, the Old Regime means the historical period which, beginning in 1663, when the administration of New France was withdrawn from the hands of the Company of New France (known as the One Hundred Associates) and taken back by the King, lasted till the fall of the French colony in 1760. In 1663 a system of colonial government was framed for Canada. With a few changes and modifications, it was in existence for nearly one century. Under it, the colony slowly grew, its religious and social institutions laboriously yet steadily progressed, its boundaries expanded, its population increased, its national life followed a course often checkered and stormy, sometimes peaceful and happy. During that period a French-Canadian community planted its roots deep in the shores of the St Lawrence and farther. At the end of that period, when the fortune of war snatched New France from Old France, that government became a thing of the past. In the following pages, our aim will be to survey the political, administrative, religious, social and economic aspects of the Old Regime in Canada.

In 1663 the French colony founded by Champlain in 1608 had been in existence for over a half century. During all this time Canada had been merely struggling for life. To the shackles of commercial greed and neglect, to the forgetfulness of the mother country, had been added the curse of Indian wars. During twenty-five years, the daring and ferocious Iroquois had been the constant scourge of the handful of settlers, traders and missionaries. Champlain's successors had no military force adequate to the task of crushing these formidable foes. To make things worse, internal dissension exercised its baneful influence. A fierce contention arrayed against one another the leaders of the colony over the vexed question of the liquor traffic. Under such disheartening conditions how could New France be kept alive at all? The climax seemed to have been reached in 1663. In desperation, the spiritual and civil authorities, Governor and bishop, Jesuits and traders, all united in petitioning for assistance.

Fortunately, the moment was auspicious. France had just emerged victorious and powerful from the prolonged struggle of the Thirty Years' War and of the war with Spain. After the death of the able successor of Richelieu, Cardinal Mazarin, the young, ambitious and eager Louis XIV had taken in his own hands the reins of administration; and he had the luck of finding in the person of Jean-Baptiste

Colbert, who had been Mazarin's right-hand man, one of the greatest ministers whom France has ever known. Together, the King and the minister set to work to reorganise the different public departments, to restore the finances, to revive the navy, to encourage trade and industry, to protect agriculture, in a word, to give a fresh impetus to all the activities of the nation. It was at this most favourable hour, that the entreaties and representations of the leaders of New France were laid before the King. He carefully studied the situation and instructed Colbert to attend to it. The result was an unprecedented effort to defend and strengthen the colony and to raise it from its state of depression.

One of the first steps was to put an end to the privilege of the One Hundred Associates. This was done in the early part of the year 1663. Anticipating the King's will, the Company surrendered its charter,[1] and a new system of government was inaugurated. The old Council of Quebec, formed in 1648, was reorganised under the name of the Sovereign Council. This important body was to be composed of the Governor, the bishop, the Intendant, five councillors, an attorney-general, and a secretary or recording clerk.[2] It was invested with a rather wide jurisdiction. It had the power of hearing all civil and criminal cases, of giving judgment in the last resort, according to the laws and ordinances of the realm, and, as far as possible, in the form and manner followed in the Parlement of Paris. It could also issue ordinances in all matters of police, finance, trade and commerce. As may be seen, this Council was at once, in some degree, a judicial, an administrative and a legislative body. After a few years, the name of the Sovereign Council was changed into that of Superior Council. The number of councillors was increased from five to seven in 1675, and from seven to twelve in 1703.[3] At first, the nomination of councillors was entrusted jointly to the Governor and to the bishop. But later on, such appointment was reserved to the King himself. An ecclesiastical councillor named the conseiller-clerc was also added, and, during the last period of the French domination, two conseillers-assesseurs were named, with a deliberative voice in cases where they acted as rapporteurs and a consultative voice only in all other cases. The Superior Council of Quebec was no small part in the machinery of the Canadian administration.

The three most conspicuous members of the Council were, of course, the Governor, the bishop and the Intendant. The Governor was the political and the military head of the colony. He represented the King and held a great and effective power. The bishop was the spiritual head of the colony. He represented the Church and had a real influence even in civil matters. The Intendant was a new public

---

[1] Édits et Ordonnances, I, 31.
[2] Ibid. I, 38.   [3] Ibid. I, 83–99.

officer in Canada, and in the mother country too was of rather recent creation, dating from the time of Richelieu. The new officer soon became one of the main instruments of the royal administration in the French provinces, his title (Intendant of justice, police and finance) indicating the scope of his functions.[1] When the Sovereign Council of Quebec began its career in 1663, no Intendant was present to take his seat. Robert, who had been appointed to that office, never came to Canada, for some unknown reason. The celebrated Intendant Talon was the first to exercise these functions in the colony.

The beginnings were unpropitious. De Mézy, the Governor appointed by the King to replace Baron d'Avaugour, had followed a military career. He had fair qualities, but they were marred by a fiery temper and a terrible stubbornness. His former relations in France with Mgr de Laval, the Vicar Apostolic, had been most amicable, and it was stated that this had something to do with his appointment.[2] Unfortunately, after a while there was a clash between them. Under the King's edict, the Governor and the bishop had appointed jointly the members of the Sovereign Council, and naturally, from his previous knowledge and connections, Mgr de Laval, who had been in Canada since 1659, was instrumental in making the selection. De Mézy, at first acquiescent, afterwards felt that as a grievance. The members of the new Council were Rouer de Villeray, Juchereau de la Ferté, Ruette d'Auteuil, le Gardeur de Tilly, and Mathieu Damours. Jean Bourdon was attorney-general and Peuvret de Mesnu, secretary. Villeray, Auteuil and Bourdon soon became obnoxious to the Governor. He deemed that they were too subservient to the bishop's views and stated in a written document that they "wished to make themselves masters in the Council and had acted in divers ways against the interest of the King and the public for the promotion of personal and private ends, and had formed and fomented cabals".[3] He wanted, therefore, to dismiss them and for that purpose asked the bishop's assent, though he could not well expect that Mgr de Laval would comply. A deadlock ensued. De Mézy's proposal was that a meeting of the people should choose the successors of the councillors whom he wished removed. This was a serious blunder, for he should have known that such an election could not fail to hurt the feelings and principles of the King.

The strife went on and was marked by many strange incidents. At the end of a year, the membership of the Council had to be renewed and, as previously, that should be done by the joint act of the Governor and the bishop. Mgr de Laval wanted to appoint the same councillors. De Mézy would not agree, and he proceeded alone to the

---

[1] Clément, P., *Hist. de Colbert*, II, 9.
[2] Parkman, F., *The Old Régime in Canada*, chap. xi, p. 147.
[3] *Régistres du Conseil supérieur*, 3 Feb. 1664.

reconstruction of the Council, retaining only Tilly and Damours, and replacing Villeray, Auteuil, and la Ferté by Denis, la Tesserie and Peronne de Maze.[1] There were protests against these illegal nominations. But de Mézy went further. He decreed the expulsion of Villeray and Bourdon from the colony and sent them to France, whither they went and laid their complaints and those of the bishop before Louis XIV. Undoubtedly, the Governor had abused the King's authority, and he was recalled. But he was soon to render his accounts to a higher master; seized by a dangerous illness in the spring of 1665, he breathed his last on 6 May, leaving the colony in a state of turmoil.

Fortunately, better days were near at hand. At the end of the year 1663, the King had appointed de Tracy his lieutenant-general for South and North America.[2] This nobleman was invested with wide powers. He had left France in February 1664, had taken possession of Cayenne, which, for some time, had been in the hands of the Dutch, had restored order in Martinique and Guadeloupe, and now he came to Canada for a similar purpose, arriving at Quebec on 30 June 1665, with a staff of military officers and four companies of soldiers. During the summer, ships laden with soldiers, mechanics, settlers, young women for wives, necessaries of all kinds, arms, ammunition and horses, reached Quebec in succession.[3] Never before had the staggering colony received such reinforcements. Louis XIV and Colbert were evidently in earnest. On 12 September a new Governor, sieur Daniel Rémy de Courcelle, and an Intendant, sieur Jean Talon, arrived to take charge of their respective functions, under the superior authority of de Tracy. Both were clever and well qualified for the work.

The most urgent task was that of striking a decisive blow against the bold and barbarous foe, whose bloody raids were a daily menace to New France. It was for that purpose that a full regiment of trained soldiers—the regiment of Carignan-Salières—had been sent to Canada. De Tracy, almost immediately after his arrival, gave orders for the building of three forts along the River Richelieu and two other forts were to be built a year after. It was deemed advisable to wait till the following spring for the great expedition against the enemy. But de Courcelle, thinking that a first stroke could be dealt beforehand, attempted a rash winter raid into the territory of the Mohawks. It was too bold a move. The European soldiers were not prepared for such exertions in a frosty climate and a great many were frozen to death. The expedition failed,[4] but it made nevertheless

---

[1] *Jugements et délibérations du Conseil Souverain de la Nouvelle-France*, I, 278–80.
[2] *Édits et Ords.* IV, 27 ff.
[3] *Journ. des Jésuites*, pp. 332–4; *Rel. des Jés.* (1665).
[4] Dollier de Casson, *Histoire de Montréal*, pp. 180–1; *Rel. des Jés.* (1666), pp. 6, 7; *Docs. relating to the Col. Hist. of New York*, III.

an impression on the minds of the Iroquois and they sued for peace. Yet more than one treacherous deed on their part convinced the leaders of the colony that a conclusive proof of strength and military power could alone subdue them. During the summer of 1666 great preparations were made and, in September, de Tracy and de Courcelle, at the head of 600 soldiers, 600 Canadians, and 100 Indians, ascended the Richelieu River and Lakes Champlain and St Sacrement (Lake George), proceeding through 100 miles of forest, mountains, rivers and swamps. Heavily laden with arms, provisions and ammunition strapped on their backs, French and Canadians marched through the great woods whose autumnal glories were vanishing fast under the gusts of the chilly October winds. After many days of painful exertion, the army reached the Mohawk towns. Despairing of holding them against the invading host, the Iroquois had fled and deserted their forts. One after another, their five main towns were destroyed. The palisades, the dwellings, the bastions, the stores of grain and provisions, except what was needed by the victors, the standing crops, all were set on fire.[1] And the tremendous blaze told the Indians that at last New France had asserted her power. De Tracy's expedition was fruitful indeed. The panic-stricken Mohawks had been taught a lesson. They had learned that distance and natural impediments were no protection against the French, and the other Iroquois tribes were apt to understand such a warning. They sent delegates to Quebec, and, after some delays and pourparlers, they freed their prisoners, left in the hands of the French a number of hostages and begged for missionaries to reside in their country. In July 1667 the war hatchet was buried.[2] Peace was to endure for over eighteen years. At last New France breathed freely.

The rulers of the colony could now give all their care to the internal work of reorganisation and settlement. They had reconstructed the Sovereign Council, calling back to its fold Villeray, la Ferté, Auteuil, with Jean Bourdon and Peuvret de Mesnu as attorney-general and secretary; and that body began again to attend regularly to its functions. The Intendant, Jean Talon, devoted his talents and energy to the progress of the colony. He founded villages in the vicinity of Quebec. He encouraged the disbanded soldiers to become settlers and to till the soil, and favoured the forming of homes and families by granting bounties for that purpose. With every means at his disposal, he endeavoured to promote colonisation, agriculture, shipbuilding, trade and industry, to increase the population and to foster generally the prosperity of New France.[3] His administration as Intendant lasted seven years, with an interval of nineteen months,

[1] *Lettres de la Mère Marie de l'Incarnation*, ii, 330–5; *Rel. des Jés.* (1666), p. 8.
[2] *Rel. des Jés.* (1667), p. 28.
[3] Chapais, T., *Jean Talon, Intendant de la Nouvelle-France*, chap. xiii; Salone, E., *La Colonisation de la Nouvelle-France*, pp. 143–205.

from 1668 to 1670, when he was replaced, during his absence in France, by Intendant de Bouteroue. De Tracy, having completed his mission, had left in 1667; de Courcelle remained as governor until 1672.

That period of peaceful activity was the most happy and the most prosperous that the French colony ever knew. Louis XIV and Colbert were deeply interested in the progress of Canada. Talon enjoyed their confidence and made the most of it. Year after year, reinforcements of varied descriptions were sent from the mother country. From 1665 to 1671 there was an uninterrupted influx of settlers. During Talon's intendancy there were in all 1828 state-aided immigrants.[1] The young women were carefully selected, and it was the King's wish that they should marry promptly. Every incentive to that end was brought to bear. The Intendant gave 50 livres in household supplies and some provisions to each woman who contracted marriage. This matrimonial zeal did not exclude noblemen and officers. During the years 1665–8, 6000 livres were expended to aid the marriage of young gentlewomen without means, and 6000 to enable four captains, three lieutenants, five ensigns, and a few minor officers to settle and marry in the colony.[2]

A word must be said about the character of the young women. Some writers have cast unfair aspersions upon the girls sent out from France to marry in Canada. A great number of these were orphans reared in charitable institutions under the King's protection; they were called *les Filles du Roi*. The rest belonged to honest families, and their parents, overburdened with children, were willing to send them to a new country where they would be well provided for. In 1670 Colbert wrote to the Archbishop of Rouen: "As in the parishes about Rouen fifty or sixty girls might be found who would be very glad to go to Canada to be married, I beg you to employ your credit and your authority with the curés of thirty or forty of these parishes to find in each of them one or two girls disposed to go voluntarily for the sake of settlement in life".[3] Such was the quality of feminine emigration to Canada.

The result of these efforts was soon apparent. In 1666 Talon had taken a census—the first Canadian census—of the population of Canada. The number of souls was 3215, and the number of families 533. In 1668 the population was 6282, and the families were 1139.[4] The one had nearly, and the other had more than, doubled in less than two years. Also during this period, domestic animals, whose need was acutely felt, were sent to Canada under the King's orders. Before 1665, one solitary horse—a gift to Governor Montmagny—had

---

[1] *Lettres de la Mère Marie*, II, 313–52, 446; *Journ. des Jés.* p. 335; *Lettres, Instructions et Mémoires de Colbert.*

[2] Chapais, T., *The great Intendant*, p. 54.

[3] *Ibid.* p. 54; *Lettres, Instructions et Mémoires de Colbert*, I, 3, II, 476.

[4] *Can. Census*, 1870, IV, 2, 8.

seen the shores of St Lawrence. From that year to 1672 nearly 80
horses—stallions and mares—were received and allotted in the
settlements; and 129 sheep were also sent.[1] The activities of the
great Intendant were manifold. He caused ships to be built for
the extension of the colony's trade. One of his schemes was to
establish regular commercial intercourse between Canada, the West
Indies and France. The ships of la Rochelle and le Havre, after unloading at Quebec, would carry Canadian products to the West
Indies, where they would load cargoes of sugar for France. Those
Canadian products would be mainly fish, peas, staves, fish oil, planks
and masts much needed in the islands.[2]

One of the greatest services of Talon was the ending of the trade
monopoly of the West India Company. That big commercial society
had been founded, at the instigation of Colbert, in 1664.[3] And,
singularly enough, one year after having removed the colony from
the hands of the One Hundred Associates, the King conceded again
the fief of Canada to this new company, which he invested with
the widest powers. The result was a very peculiar situation. In
accordance with its charter, the Company held the ownership and
government of the country *de jure*. But, in point of fact, the King
wielded the government, thus taking back with one hand what he
had given with the other. This strange state of things lasted ten years,
until the West India Company's charter was revoked in 1674. From
the first, Talon had fought the privileges of the Company. In 1669
he succeeded in suppressing one of the most invidious, the monopoly
by virtue of which they alone could control the whole trade and
navigation. The King granted freedom of trade to Canada, so that
the colony could thereafter receive more easily the provisions and
supplies needed. This was for Talon and for New France a signal
victory.[4] The scope of Talon's endeavours included also the discovery
and development of mines, the fabrication of potash and tar, the
cultivation of hemp, the making of homespun cloth, and so on. It
is no exaggeration to say that, during these seven years, New France
was actually made. Talon was a colonial Colbert. What the latter
did in a wide sphere and with ample means, the former tried to do
on a small scale, and with limited resources. He surely deserves to
be called one of the makers of Canada.

This fruitful period ended in 1672. The pride and ambition of
Louis XIV involved the mother country in a war with Holland, and
soon after, with a strong European coalition; and, in that way, the
resources of France were diverted from colonial progress. Never again
would Canada feel, as it did under de Tracy, de Courcelle and Talon,

---

[1] C. II, III, *Observations faites par Talon*, 1668.
[2] Chapais, T., *Jean Talon*, p. 392.
[3] *Édits et Ords*. I, 40.
[4] *Lettres...de Colbert*, I, 2, II, 449.

the powerful help and beneficial care of the mother country. In 1672 Courcelle and Talon left Canada. Louis de Buade, Comte de Frontenac, appointed Governor of New France, began his administration on 12 September. He was a strong and clever man, conspicuous for his undaunted courage, his boldness and earnestness of purpose, his foresight and breadth of view. On the other hand, he had his failings: vindictiveness, obstinacy, irascibility, haughtiness, self-conceit. These were specially apparent during his first administration; for he was twice Governor of Canada. During his second term, his best qualities and eminent gifts were instrumental in saving the colony and in giving him one of the foremost places in the ranks of Canadian Governors.

Until 1675 no Intendant was appointed in Talon's stead and Governor Frontenac exercised the powers of both offices. This was unfortunate, because he got used to that undivided authority, and could not see without chagrin the narrowing of his jurisdiction when Jacques Duchesneau was sent to Quebec as Intendant. These two men were evidently not meant to act and work peacefully together. In fact, during the whole French regime, very seldom did the two high officers, Governor and Intendant, unite their efforts harmoniously to further the progress of Canada. Frontenac and Duchesneau were soon at loggerheads. Before the latter's arrival the Governor had been involved in a quarrel with Jean-Marie Perrot, Governor of Montreal, and also with a Sulpician priest, Abbé de Fénelon, who had imprudently interfered in the feud. These clashes caused endless and tiresome discussions and deadlocks in the Superior Council, where the cases of Perrot and Abbé de Fénelon were brought. Finally, the whole was referred to the King's Council of State in France.[1]

Now another squabble began. It was the question of the rank and title of the Governor and the Intendant in the Council which gave rise to it. Both officers stuck pertinaciously to their respective pretensions.[2] Then (as has already been related) the old dispute about the liquor traffic embittered the misunderstanding. Finally new prohibitive ordinances were enacted and were maintained until 1668. In that year there was a reversal of policy. The influence of Talon was surely instrumental in the adoption of an ordinance, on 10 November 1668, permitting the obnoxious traffic. Disorder and demoralisation again increased, and the bishop renewed his complaints. Frontenac took the other side and strenuously fought Mgr de Laval's strong views on the subject. But Duchesneau supported the bishop and this added new bitterness to the strife.

[1] *Jugements et Délibérations du Conseil Souverain*, I, 805, 860; Lorin, H., *Le Comte de Frontenac*, pp. 103–14; Faillon, *Histoire de la Colonie Française*, III, 474, 525.
[2] *Jugements*, etc. II, 279, 319; Lorin, *Le Comte de Frontenac*, pp. 148, 153.

The arguments put forward by the supporters of the trade were the following. To refuse brandy to the Indians was to let the English monopolise the profitable fur trade, and therefore to check the development of New France. The fur trade provided an abundance of beaver skins, which were a very convenient medium of exchange. The possession of these gave an impetus to commerce and brought to Canada many merchants and others who were consumers of natural products and money spenders. Moreover, in Canada furs were the main article of exportation. Their abundance swelled the public revenue—on account of the duties levied—and increased the number of ships employed in the Canadian trade. And last, to use arguments of a higher order, the brandy traffic, in fostering trade with the Indian tribes, kept them in the bonds of an alliance, strengthened the political position of France in North America, and, as an ultimate consequence, could favour the progress of the Catholic faith among the Indian tribes. Such indeed were the arguments used by the traders, finally accepted by Talon, developed by Frontenac, and approved by Colbert on many occasions.

To those arguments, Mgr de Laval, the clergy and many laymen interested in the public welfare had a double answer. First, there was at stake a question of principle important enough to be the sole ground of decision. Was it right, for the purpose of loading with furs the Quebec stores and the la Rochelle ships, to instil into the Indian veins the accursed poison which inflamed them to all the frightful frenzy of bestial passion? On the other hand, the prohibition of the brandy traffic was not as detrimental to the material development of the colony, as was contended. It was possible to trade with the Ottawas, the Algonkins, the Iroquois, without the allurement of brandy. The Indians themselves acknowledged that strong liquor ruined them. There were many articles besides brandy that were needed by them and for which they were obliged to barter their furs. As for the English competition, could not an agreement be concluded with the New England authorities? Had they not themselves once proposed to the French a joint prohibition of the sale of brandy to the Indians, and had they not even passed an ordinance to that effect? But, assuming that prohibition would have caused a decrease in the fur trade, would the evil be so great? Fewer colonists would be diverted from agriculture. As it was, the exodus from the settlements of *coureurs des bois* in search of furs was a source of weakness, and the flower of Canadian youth disappeared every year in the wilderness. The suppression, or at least the restraint, of the liquor traffic could help to lessen that drain of national vitality.[1]

Such was the controversy. Frontenac took part in it with all the

---

[1] See Ferland, *Cours d'histoire du Canada*, ii, 105; *Rapport sur les Archives canadiennes*, 1885, p. 48; *Can. Archives*, F. 3, vol. iii—Colbert à Duchesneau, 1 mai, 18 mai, 1678, Colbert à Frontenac, 16 mai 1678.

impetuosity of his temper, and the fact that Duchesneau declared himself a champion of prohibition did not smooth their relations. Their heated misunderstanding extended to other matters, for instance, to the question of the bushrangers who went to trade with the Indians in the woods, which was forbidden. Duchesneau accused Frontenac of protecting these delinquents, because he was interested in their traffic. Frontenac hurled back at the Intendant the accusation of illicit trading. At last it became evident that they could not be maintained in office without great public detriment, and both were recalled in 1682. It was to be regretted that Frontenac's abuses of power should have made his removal a necessity. He had good parts as an administrator, and as the military head of the colony he was a tower of strength. The Indians had learned to respect and fear him, and his absence was soon to be felt.

In 1677 the tribunal called *la Prévôté de Quebec* was formally established. It had been in existence previously for ten years, and had been abolished in 1674. It was now to be composed of a lieutenant-general for civil and criminal cases, of a King's attorney (*procureur du Roi*), and of a clerk (*greffier*). A sketch of the judicial system is here advisable. There was first the seigneurial jurisdiction. The Canadian seigneur was granted the right of high, middle and low justice. But, in fact, he never exercised more than the last one, in minor cases where the matter involved did not exceed fifty *sous*, or where the fine to be imposed did not exceed ten *sous*; and that exercise was far from general. Seigneurial judges existed in some of the seigneuries only. There was an appeal from these low courts to the lieutenant-general's court or *la Prévôté*. This last court was therefore a court of appeal for some minor cases, and a court of first instance for the more important ones. At Quebec, its official name was *la Prévôté*. At Three Rivers and Montreal there were similar courts called *Juridiction Royale*, composed also of a lieutenant-general, of a King's attorney, and of a clerk. These had the same powers as the *Prévôté* of Quebec. The Superior Council was mainly a court of appeal from the inferior jurisdictions. The *Prévôté* and the royal jurisdiction courts used to sit twice a week, on Tuesdays and Fridays. The Superior Council sat every Monday with the exception of the holidays. In all these courts there could be extraordinary sittings. The Intendant could also sit alone as a judge and hear all civil, criminal and police cases, and specially all cases between litigant seigneurs and between seigneurs and *censitaires*.[1] During the eighteenth century, a court of admiralty was created. Such was the system under which justice was administered in Canada during the Old Regime.

The successor of Frontenac was Le Febvre de la Barre. The choice was not a happy one. He was a naval officer and had served with

[1] Cugnet, F. J., *Traité de la Loi des Fiefs*, pp. 55, 69.

distinction in the West Indies; but he lacked the quickness of perception, the spirit of determination and the steadfastness that were needed. Ominous signs were already apparent. After a long period of peace, the Iroquois were becoming ill-disposed towards the French and their Indian allies. The very active Colonel Dongan, Governor of New York, desirous of securing for his colony trading advantages, was supposed to encourage in underhand ways their warlike dispositions.[1] Filled with anxious forebodings, de la Barre asked for military reinforcements; and he sent envoys to the Iroquois in order to dissuade them from raising the hatchet against New France's allies.[2] The astute Iroquois seemed to agree. But soon afterwards they suddenly fell on the Ottawas and the Illinois; and it was reported that the colony itself would before long see a renewal of their bloody raids. Heeding those warnings, de la Barre insisted on reinforcements; and he made preparations for an expedition, resuming, in the meantime, his entreaties to the Iroquois. They were keen enough to perceive that the new Governor was not a man of iron like Frontenac. Their arrogance and audacity increased. However, as they wanted to gain time, they sent delegates to meet de la Barre and give assurance of their good dispositions. The Governor was easily deceived and thought that peace was secured. Ere long he was to experience a rude awakening. The news came that the Iroquois had attacked a French fort in the west, and that they were on the eve of invading Canada. The Governor, at last realising the situation, deemed it advisable to strike first. That would have been a wise move if quickness of action had followed; but it was quite the reverse. An army of about seven hundred Canadians, one hundred and thirty soldiers, and two hundred Indians was gathered at Montreal.[3] Instead of marching immediately, the Governor, losing precious time, sent an envoy to Colonel Dongan, in order to win his concurrence or, at least, his compliance.[4] This was of no avail, as could have been foreseen. Proceeding then to Cataraqui, de la Barre wasted two weeks more. At last he crossed Lake Ontario and established a camp near the Oswego River, at a place afterwards appropriately called Famine Cove (*l'Anse de la Famine*). But those delays had been disastrous. Provisions ran short and, moreover, their bad quality spread disease in the army. The unlucky expedition was evidently doomed to failure. At that inauspicious moment delegates from the Iroquois arrived to make peace propositions. They soon noticed the dreadful condition of de la Barre and his troops. Full of pride and arrogance they now dictated

[1] M. de la Barre au Ministre, 7 oct. 1684.
[2] *Can. Archives*, C. 11, La Barre au Roi, 20 mai 1693, La Barre au Ministre, 3 nov. 1683, 6 juin 1684, La Barre au Roi, juillet 1684.
[3] La Barre au Roi, 9 juillet 1684.
[4] Instructions données au sieur de Salvaye envoyé par M. de la Barre au Colonel Dongan, 24 juillet 1684.

instead of being granted terms, haughtily refusing to include in the treaty the Illinois, who were allies of the French, and they insisted on an immediate retreat. The Governor acquiesced in those humiliating conditions, and the disheartened and murmuring army had to retrace its steps without having fired a shot. Such was the end of this shameful expedition. French prestige had received a death-blow in the minds not only of the Iroquois, but of all the other tribes.[1] This pitiful failure sealed the fate of de la Barre. The new Intendant, de Meulles, who had replaced Duchesneau, did not lessen the King's dissatisfaction: his letters to the court were most disparaging. De Meulles was a clever man, an active and progressive administrator, but he could be easily prejudiced and he was bitter in his displeasure. Of course, his complaints against de la Barre were not without foundation. The unlucky Governor was recalled in 1685.

The Marquis de Denonville, appointed in his stead, was a military officer of good repute. He arrived at Quebec in the summer of 1685. His administration, lasting four years, was neither happy nor successful. After studying the situation, he was soon convinced that the peace concluded by de la Barre was a very precarious one, and that hostilities were to be renewed.[2] In fact the Iroquois never ceased to attack the Ottawas, the Miamis and other allies of the French. They probably interfered with the Canadian traders, assailing their canoes and plundering their furs. Denonville wrote to the court that the old foes of New France had to be taught a new lesson, and he pointed to the urgency of reinforcements. He also proposed the building of a fort at Niagara, which would be a means of checking the Five Nations. It was only in the spring of 1687 that the soldiers asked for were sent to Canada. Great preparations were made. De Meulles had been replaced as Intendant in 1686 by Jean Bochart de Champigny,[3] an active and painstaking man who worked in perfect harmony with the Governor, a very unusual state of affairs. In June an army of over 2000 men was mustered at Montreal for an expedition against the Senecas, now one of the most aggressive of the Iroquois nations.[4] During that campaign a most untoward incident took place. A number of Iroquois chiefs had been convened to meet the Governor at Fort Frontenac (Cataraqui) and discuss with him the conditions of peace. On arriving at this fort, they were seized, chained and later on sent to France as prisoners and slaves to serve on the King's galleys. Historians do not agree as to the responsibility for this treacherous act. Charlevoix states that the Intendant, Champigny, who had gone to

[1] De Meulles au Ministre, 10 oct. 1684; de la Barre au Ministre, 7 oct. 1684; Parkman, *Frontenac and New France under Louis XIV*, chap. vi; *N.Y. Col. Doc.* vol. ix.
[2] *Can. Archives*, C. 11, Denonville au Ministre, 13 nov. 1685.
[3] *Édits et Ords.* iii, 50.
[4] *Can. Archives*, F. 3, Champigny au Ministre, 16 juillet 1687.

Cataraqui with the vanguard was the guilty party.[1] At all events, such an outrage cannot be condoned. Louis XIV, when he became cognisant of it, ordered the prisoners to be sent back to their country.[2] The expedition which followed that hateful beginning was only partially successful. The country of the Senecas was invaded. They were overpowered and defeated in a bloody fight, where they lost many warriors. Their villages were devastated, and their stores and crops were burnt.[3] But Denonville did not complete his work in inflicting the same treatment on the other Iroquois tribes and the desired result was not obtained. The Iroquois were infuriated and not daunted. Their hate against the French was increased. Their murderous incursions were continued. However, they made some pretence of negotiations during the summer of 1688, but nothing was concluded, and a state of war kept the colony on the alert. The following year was gloomy in her annals. The Iroquois executed the most daring and barbarous of their accursed deeds. On 25 August 1689, in the depth of night, 1400 of their warriors, crossing Lake St Louis during a hailstorm, disembarked at the upper end of the Island of Montreal, at the place called Lachine. Then an awful scene of murder and destruction ensued. The blood-thirsty Indians broke in on the slumbering households and butchered all human beings, men, women and children. Not satisfied with killing, they inflicted the most atrocious tortures. The Governor, who was at Montreal, could not dispose, it was said, of a military strength equal to the task of repelling the Iroquois and of stopping the horrible slaughter.[4] The appalling news spread grief and consternation in every Canadian home.

Denonville's administration was ending under that red cloud. The King had recalled him for military service in Europe, and he had decided to send again as governor Frontenac, who was known as a man of strong will and unflinching determination. His arrival at such a critical moment was welcomed by the whole population and the hopes aroused by his return were not disappointed. After having surveyed the situation, he convinced himself that a bold offensive was the best means of protecting Canada. France and England were now at war in Europe; but the hostilities in America are described in a later chapter of this volume.

The Iroquois raids, though often checked and punished, were a

[1] Charlevoix, *Histoire de la Nouvelle-France*, 1, 509; La Hontan, *Nouveau voyage dans l'Amérique Septentrionale*, 1709, 1, 93, 95; Denonville au Ministre, 25 août 1687; Champigny au Ministre, 16 juillet 1687.

[2] *Can. Archives*, B, vol. xv, Mémoire du Roi à MM. Denonville et Champigny, 1er mai 1689.

[3] Abbé de Belmont, *Histoire du Canada*, pp. 20–6 (*Collection de Méms. et de Docs. sur l'hist. ancienne du Canada*, 1840). *Recueil de ce qui s'est passé au Canada au sujet de la guerre...depuis l'année 1682*, pp. 13–17; Denonville au Ministre, 25 août 1667.

[4] *Recueil de ce qui s'est passé au Canada*, 22–5; Belmont, *Histoire du Canada*, 39–41; *Can. Archives*, C. 11, Champigny au Ministre, 16 nov. 1689; Mémoires de M. de Callières, 18 nov. 1689; La Hontan, 1, 143.

standing menace, and, specially in the Montreal district, made farming perilous and almost impossible. Frontenac, as soon as he was assured that the colony had nothing to fear from an English invasion, decided to make the Five Nations feel once more the strength of "Onontio's" arm.[1] In the summer of 1696 he marched against them at the head of 800 soldiers, 1000 Canadians and 500 Indians. This army, reaching Fort Frontenac at the head of Lake Ontario on 19 July, crossed the lake on the 26th, then worked its way up the Oswego River and through Lake Onondaga to the country beyond (1 August). The Onondagas having decided not to face Frontenac, the French found the smoking remnants of the Indian towns and burnt the crops. The town and country of the adjoining tribe, the Oneidas, were similarly devastated, and a number of chiefs were taken as hostages.[2] The Governor did not deem it advisable to go further. He had attained his object. The Iroquois and all the Indian tribes had learned anew to fear the military power of New France. And the lesson was soon to prove fruitful.

One year after, in 1697, the Treaty of Ryswick put an end to the war between the two Crowns. The welcome news was received at Quebec only in the spring of the following year. A few months later, 28 November 1698, Frontenac died, at the age of seventy-eight, leaving the fame of a strong governor and of a great leader of men, notwithstanding his admitted failings. The Chevalier de Callières, Governor of Montreal, a clever and energetic man, succeeded him. His administration was very short, but was marked by a great event, the peace concluded at last with the Iroquois Confederation and the other Indian tribes. On 4 August 1701 the memorable treaty was signed at Montreal, with all the pomp and ceremonial fitting the occasion.[3] It was a momentous day for Canada, which, hereafter, would be freed from the Iroquois scourge. "The chief objects of the late Governor were gained. The power of the Iroquois was so far broken that they were never again very formidable to the French. Canada had confirmed her Indian alliances and rebutted the English claims to sovereignty over the five tribes, with all the consequences that hung upon it".[4] De Callières did not long survive that auspicious achievement. He died on 26 May 1703.

Meanwhile, during twenty-five years, the colony had somewhat progressed. In 1673, a year after the end of Talon's administration, the population of Canada was 6705. In 1698, the year

[1] "Onontio" was the name given to the Governors of Canada by the Indians since the time of de Montmagny, because they had been told that his name meant "Great Mountain" (Mons magnus), which, in the Indian language, was equivalent to "Onontio".

[2] Can. Archives, C. 11, Frontenac au Ministre, 25 oct. 1696, Relation de ce qui s'est passé de plus remarquable en Canada, 1695–6; La Potherie, Hist. de l'Amérique Septentrionale, III, 270–82; N.Y. Col. Doc. IV, 242.

[3] Callières et Champigny au Ministre, 5 oct. 1901; N.Y. Col. Doc. vol. IX; La Potherie, vol. IV.   [4] Parkman, op. cit. p. 452.

of Frontenac's death, it was 15,255; an increase of 8650, or more than double, though immigration from France had almost completely ceased. Quebec had 1988 inhabitants, and Montreal 1185. The colony counted 2310 dwellings, 62 churches, 43 grist mills, 37,683 acres under culture or in pasture. It had grown 160,000 bushels of wheat; 21,000 bushels of oats; 10,000 bushels of corn; 23,000 bushels of other grains. It owned 684 horses; 10,209 head of cattle; 994 sheep; 5147 swine. Eight years later, in 1706, the figures showed still a steady increase. The population was 16,417; the number of cultivated acres was 43,671, of horses 1872, of cattle 14,191, of sheep 1820.[1]

Under the Treaty of Ryswick, the French Crown had retained Acadia; it was then a very weak colony, exposed to incessant raids from pirates or from the colonists of New England. A census taken in 1701 gives the following figures for the Acadian population: Port Royal, 456; Beaubassin, 188; les Mines, 490; a total of 1134. They had 1136 acres under culture; 1807 head of cattle; 1796 sheep; 1173 swine.[2] At that time the French governor was de Brouillan, successor of de Villebon, who, from 1690 to 1701, had displayed courage and steadiness during the stormy years of the war.

After the death of de Callières, de Vaudreuil, Governor of Montreal, was appointed Governor-General of Canada. He had married a lady born in the colony and was very popular. De Ramezay, formerly governor of Three Rivers, became Governor of Montreal, and de Crisacy, Governor of Three Rivers. Intendant Champigny, promoted to le Havre, in France, in 1702, had been replaced by François de Beauharnais, who filled this office at Quebec for a little less than three years. Two Intendants were jointly appointed in his stead in 1705: Jacques Raudot and Antoine Denis Raudot, his son. The father took under his special charge all matters of justice and police, and the son all matters of trade and finance.

The head of the Canadian Church in 1700 was Mgr de Saint-Vallier, who had been made bishop of Quebec in 1682, when, owing to age and illness, Mgr de Laval resigned. The ex-bishop, after having remained some time in France, came back to Canada and lived there till his death, in 1708. His presence was a great comfort to his church, as he could discharge the necessary episcopal functions during the protracted absence of his successor, who, after having been detained in France many years, on account of certain difficulties, was made a prisoner when the ship, la Seine, was captured by the English in 1705. Mgr de Saint-Vallier was endowed with great qualities. He did not entertain exactly the same views as the first bishop of Quebec on some points of diocesan organisation; but on public questions he was guided by the same principles, which brought him into serious conflict with Frontenac.

[1] Can. Census, 1665 to 1871, IV, pp. xvii, 39, 41–8. [2] Ibid. p. 45.

He enacted the statutes of the Catholic ecclesiastical discipline, and laid down the rules which, as a whole, have been followed by the Canadian clergy to the present day.[1]

Apart from the secular clergy, two religious orders ministered also to the population and were, besides, entrusted with the missionary work. They were the Jesuits and the Franciscans, the latter commonly called "Recollets". Their main houses were in Quebec, but both had convents in Montreal. The Jesuits had a college at Quebec, wherein the young Canadian could follow a course of classical education. The pupils of the Quebec Seminary, founded by Mgr de Laval in 1668, were regular attendants at this college, though living and being cared for in the former institution. The Ursulines gave instruction and education to the girls in the monastery founded at Quebec, by the celebrated Mother Marie de l'Incarnation, in 1639. Three Rivers had also an Ursuline convent devoted to similar duties. Montreal had the sisters of the Congregation, whose foundress was Marguérite Bourgeoys. They fulfilled the same educational task in that town, and, after a while, in some other places throughout the colony. The priests of Saint-Sulpice, to whom had been granted the seigneury of the island of Montreal, had opened schools for the benefit of their *censitaires'* families. Technical and scientific instruction was not altogether ignored. Mgr de Laval had started an industrial school at Saint Joachim, wherein good mechanics were trained. And there was at Quebec a school of hydrography and surveying, whose teacher was paid by the King.[2] The sick and the poor were cared for at Quebec in such institutions as the Hôtel-Dieu, founded in 1639 by the Duchesse d'Aiguillon, and the Hospital-General, founded by Mgr de Saint-Vallier in 1693; and in Montreal, in the Hôtel-Dieu, founded in 1644 by Jeanne Mance and Madame de Bullion.

In 1702 there broke out in Europe the War of the Spanish Succession. As England and France were once more at war with each other, their colonies in North America were naturally involved in the struggle. Fortunately for New France, it was to be hoped that her old foes, the Iroquois, would abide by the treaty signed at Montreal and remain neutral. But could the same dispositions be expected from New York and New England? At one moment it seemed possible to conclude an agreement with those provinces to take no part in the hostilities. Unhappily, that propitious prospect soon vanished. De Vaudreuil was perhaps too hasty when, in the summer of 1702, he sent a band of Abenakis and Canadians to lay waste the coast of Maine. This brought bloody reprisals on those Indian allies of the French. They asked for help, and help was proffered. Hence the hostilities between the French and English colonies, described

[1] Gosselin, A., *Vie de Mgr. de Laval*, 2 vols.; *Vie de Saint-Vallier*.
[2] Gosselin, A., *L'Instruction au Canada sous le régime français*.

in the next chapter; the expeditions against Deerfield and Haverhill in 1704 and 1708; the siege and capture of Port Royal in 1710; and then the mighty attempt to conquer Canada in 1711, the frustration of which evoked such earnest thanksgivings in all the churches and convents in New France. At last in 1713, thanks to Villars' victory at Denain, Louis XIV could sign at Utrecht a treaty less damaging than it would have been two or three years before. His grandson retained the crown of Spain. But in America France lost Acadia and Plaisance (Placentia) in Newfoundland, as well as the Island of St Christopher and the forts of Hudson Bay. She kept Isle-Royale, subsequently known as Cape Breton.

The peaceful period which followed was one of the happiest in the history of New France. From 1713 to 1744 there were at times distant expeditions and Indian wars on the western borders. But the St Lawrence colony enjoyed a security, a restful quietness and consequent progress unknown since thirty years. We shall now try to survey the main factors of its life during the administration of de Vaudreuil, who died in 1725, and of his successor, de Beauharnais, who was replaced by de la Galissonnière in 1747.

One of its special features is the seigneurial system, which obtained in Canada for more than two centuries. As has appeared in the previous chapter, the system was introduced very early in the French colony. When the government of Canada was reorganised in 1663 and in the following years, and when de Tracy's expedition had secured a term of peace, it was deemed timely to give a new start to the seigneurial institution. This was one of the last administrative acts of Talon. During the fall of 1672, from 10 October to 8 November, he made about sixty grants of seigneuries.[1] If he was not the originator, he may be said to have been the organiser of the seigneurial tenure in Canada. He had a dual object in his mind. First, he aimed at protecting Canada by the creation of seigneurial establishments in the River Richelieu district. The grants to de Sorel, de Chambly, de Varennes, de Contrecœur, de Saint-Ours, officers in the regiment of Carignan, were intended to become as many small military colonies, whose inhabitants would be disbanded soldiers forming a barrier against future Indian raids. In the second place, Talon had in view a more active and speedy progress in colonisation. In granting fiefs to a great many seigneurs with the stipulated condition that they should keep *feu et lieu*, that is to say that they would be residing landlords, and further, that they would grant land to would-be farmers under the same condition, Talon was hoping to promote the settlement of the country on both sides of the St Lawrence. The seigneur would feel that, in his own interest, he should try to draw as many settlers as possible to his fief, in order to increase the revenue of his rents and other feudal rights. In that

[1] *Pièces et documents relatifs à la tenure seigneuriale* (1852).

way each seigneur would become a real agent of colonisation. Talon's hopes, though not completely, were to some extent realised. The seigneurial system in Canada was undoubtedly instrumental in fostering the settlement of the country.[1]

The bond which linked the *censitaire* with the seigneur was neither oppressive nor burdensome. The former was given possession of his farm gratuitously. His yearly dues were paltry. In the fall, at Saint Martin's day, which was the appointed date, he came to the manor house with his cackling capons and his few dozen of copper coin, and he went back home a free man. He was not wealthy, but the soil, the neighbouring forest, the river and the lakes yielded ample food, and his wife and daughters were apt suppliers of the homespun clothes which would protect him against the severities of the climate. The concessions of farms were usually made along the rivers which, for a long time, were the only highways. They covered from three to four arpents in front by forty arpents in depth. The house, stable and barn were erected not far from the water's edge, for the obvious reason that the streams acted the part of roads for travel and transportation. In time these long and narrow strips of land divided by wooden fences and brightened by the whitewashed buildings offered a picturesque and lively sight.

In 1712 there were about ninety-one seigneuries in Canada. On their state and condition at that moment we have a document of capital importance—a very accurate and detailed report, made by a clever French engineer and surveyor, Gédéon de Catalogne. He had been entrusted by Intendant Raudot with the task of making a complete survey of all the Canadian seigneuries. And he did it with the greatest care.[2] For the student of Canadian history, the seigneury and the parish are intimately connected. Very often they covered almost the same territory. They had a common life, common interests and common prospects. As soon as the seigneur had succeeded in bringing on his fief a certain number of settlers, he was faced with the duty of giving them or securing for them all the needed help. From the material standpoint, the first move would be the building of a grinding mill, and from the spiritual, the erection of a chapel or church.

As soon as their limited means would enable them to make such outlay, the seigneurs endeavoured to supply their *censitaires* with that most urgent accommodation, a mill to grind their wheat and provide the daily bread. Sometimes they were lucky enough to have on their domain a convenient stream whence they got water power. Very often they had to rely on wind power. Hence, the great number of wind mills which could be seen in bygone days all over the province

[1] Munro, W.B., *The Seignorial System in Canada*; Chapais, T., *The great Intendant*, pp. 127–8; Rameau, E., *La France aux colonies*, pp. 111–12.

[2] *Can. Archives*, C. 11, Mémoire sur les plans des seigneuries de Québec, des Trois-Rivières et de Montréal, M. de Catalogne.

of Quebec, and which gave to the scenery a Dutch-like appearance. Those mills, though sometimes crude and imperfect in their machinery, were relatively expensive, and many seigneurs neglected their duty and delayed the expected construction. So it was that, in 1686, the King's Council of State gave an order whereby all seigneurs should be obliged to build a mill on their grant within one year, failing which, anybody should be free to erect one and enjoy hereafter the right of *banalité* in the landlord's stead.[1] In the year 1734, there were 118 grist mills in New France.[2]

The erection of churches was more belated. The seigneurs were not under the obligation of building them and of bearing this greater expense. Of course, they would be desirous of seeing the sacred edifice standing in the midst of their concessions as a rallying point and an inducement to incoming settlers. They would help, in granting the necessary ground, and, in some cases, they would even become pecuniary contributors. But the spiritual authorities were the persons primarily interested in the matter. And with them also, the lack of means was a deterring agent. In fact, the birth of the parish preceded almost always the building of the church. For years the spiritual care of the incipient settlements was purely missionary work. From Quebec, Three Rivers and Montreal priests would go paddling their canoes up or down the St Lawrence in summer, or tramping on snow-shoes through the dense bush in winter, to visit the scattered establishments, to baptise, hear confessions, absolve, marry, celebrate mass and give holy communion to the poor and hardy pioneers of civilisation. After a while, with the increase of population and the widening of the cultivated areas, the creation of parishes became a possibility. When Mgr de Saint-Vallier came to Canada and made his first episcopal survey, he found about thirty-six parishes.[3] In many places there was no church, and in many others there was only a kind of crumbling shed.[4] But, with the lapse of time and in more auspicious conditions, a marked improvement was felt. In 1721, under the united and co-operative authority of the Bishop, the Governor and the Intendant, Attorney-General Collet was entrusted with the task of making an enquiry on the parochial situation, for the purpose of defining limits and boundaries, or of changing them if necessary by dividing, contracting or enlarging as the case might be. The result was a very important report, which led to the adoption of an ordinance determining for years to come the official status of the parochial districts.[5] There were at that date eighty-two parishes. In some instances, one curé had two under his

---

[1] *Édits et Ords.* I, 255.   [2] *Can. Census*, IV, 57.

[3] *Can. Archives*, F. 3, État présent des cures et missions du Canada, 1683; Rôle des Cures du Canada, pourvu de curés, 2 mars, État résumé des cures du Canada (36 cures), 1686.

[4] *État présent de l'Église du Canada*, Mgr de Saint-Vallier, 1685.

[5] *Can. Archives*, C. 11, Règlement des districts de paroisses de la Nouvelle-France, 20 sept. 1721; Arrêt du Conseil d'État, 3 mars 1722.

charge, owing to the lack of priests. Almost everywhere there was a decent church or chapel. As a rule the curés were named during pleasure, notwithstanding the repeated entreaties of the King and ministers. The home authorities insisted on what they called a *fixation des cures*. On the other hand, it was represented that in a young country like Canada, special conditions were adverse to that system. The curés were supported partly by the tithes which had been first fixed at one thirteenth of all agricultural products, but later on were reduced to one twenty-sixth and restricted to grain alone. For a long while, this was not sufficient to give the parish priest a living, and the King had to supply the deficiency. It was stated that the Canadian curé to sustain himself should have an income of four or five hundred francs.

The parish was created and delimited; the church was built, the curé was appointed; the official registration of births, marriages and burials began to be kept; churchwardens were elected by the habitants to act with the curé in the administration of their temporalities. And the parochial life, once started, followed its peaceful course. The seigneur and the curé were the two heads of the little community. Sometimes there was also a *juge-bailli*. When the Canadian militia received some form of organisation, a new public officer made his appearance in the person of the captain (*le capitaine de la côte*), to whom was entrusted occasional duties. In some parishes, there were resident notaries, and, in certain districts, travelling ones who went from settlement to settlement, receiving deeds of sale, of donation, of rent, marriage contracts, and so on.

Once in a while the Bishop of Quebec would undertake a touring visit of his wide diocese. It was a great day for the parish when the head of the Canadian Church arrived in the midst of the pious flock. *Benedictus qui venit in nomine Domini*. The whole community, men, women and children, gathered in the church and listened in silent reverence to his paternal advice and exhortations. The prelate preached, celebrated mass with great solemnity, administered confirmation to the children, and, after having given to the faithful a last benediction, set out for the next parish, leaving behind him a deep and fruitful impression. Each of these small aggregations was a little world in itself. Year by year the Canadian parish slowly progressed, increasing its population, widening its cultivated area through successful inroads on the mighty forest, opening public highways, in a word, improving quietly but steadily its general condition. Very humble and uninteresting indeed would have appeared the poor Canadian parish to a superficial observer. Nevertheless, therein were elaborated all the imperishable elements of a nationality which would survive defeat and hopeless severance from the old mother nation.

Thus during the administrations of Vaudreuil and Beauharnais—

a period of thirty years—the French colony felt the beneficent influence of peace and external security. The statistical documents give us an idea of the progress then realised. In 1706, we have seen that the population of Canada was 16,417. Fifteen years later, 1721, it was 24,951, and in 1734, it was 37,716. So that, in twenty-eight years, the population had more than doubled. In the following years the increase was about one thousand per annum, the figure given for 1739 being 42,701. Further, in 1706, there were 43,671 arpents under culture; in 1721, 74,384, and in 1734, 180,768, an increase of 137,097. In 1734, the number of churches in New France was 77; the number of grist mills 118, the number of saw-mills 52. The colony had grown 737,892 bushels of wheat, 163,988 bushels of oats, 63,549 bushels of peas, 5223 bushels of corn, 3462 bushels of barley, 92,246 pounds of flax, 2221 pounds of hemp, 166,054 pounds of tobacco. There were 33,179 head of horn cattle, 19,815 sheep, 23,646 swine, 5056 horses.[1] These figures could have been much more satisfactory if the Canadian farmer had followed better methods.

Industry also made some headway during this period. Special mention may be made of the domestic industry. In a sense, the wars between France and England had a happy result. The superiority of the English navy asserted itself in stopping or curtailing sharply the usual supply of manufactured goods from France. Sometimes the English squadrons barred the waterway and prevented the French vessels from reaching the St Lawrence. Sometimes they captured them and brought the crews and prizes into English ports. This was the case in 1705, when the French ship, *la Seine*, was taken with a cargo worth one million francs.[2] Mgr de Saint-Vallier was on board. The loss of goods, including cloth and fabrics of varied description induced a Canadian lady, Madame de Repentigny, to start the manufacture of home cloth. Three years later, she could write to the minister, Pontchartrain, that a great number of looms were at work in the colony. Later on, Intendant Bégon, who had succeeded Jacques Raudot in 1712, stated that the high price of goods had made the habitants more industrious; that they had taken to weaving druggets with home wool or hemp; that, in Montreal, there were twenty-five looms in operation, making cloth and linen; that the sisters of the Congregation had shown him cloth made by themselves for their own dress, as good as that which was made in France, and that black cloth for the priests' cassocks and blue cloth for the boys at college were also made in the country.[3]

In 1737, iron works were started near Three Rivers, on the Saint-Maurice, in the vicinity of which iron ore had been discovered.[4] When the celebrated Peter Kalm, a Swedish naturalist, visited

---

[1] *Can. Census*, 1665–1871, IV, 48, 53, 57.
[2] *Can. Archives*, C. 11, Vaudreuil et Beauharnais au Ministre, 19 août 1705.
[3] Bégon au Ministre, 12 nov. 1714.
[4] Hocquart au Ministre, 12 oct. 1737; Fauteux, *Essai sur l'Industrie au Canada*.

Canada in 1749, he stated that the Canadian iron was of an excellent quality, and produced a variety of manufactured goods, from guns and mortars to stoves and kettles. The building of ships was specially active under Beauharnais and Hocquart. A shipbuilding yard was established at Quebec, and many men-of-war were launched there-from, as well as a good number of smaller craft intended for trade.[1]

The commerce of Canada showed a marked increase. The Canadian merchants, though handicapped in many ways, were not lacking in boldness or forwardness. Thus, in 1682, a group of tradesmen of Quebec, headed by a very intelligent man named Charles Aubert de la Chesnaye, formed a company to carry on the fur trade in the Hudson Bay territory. This company was known under the name of the *Compagnie de la Baie d'Hudson*, or of *La Compagnie du Nord*. The members subscribed a fairly big capital for the time. They chartered ships and organised expeditions to the great northern Bay, where under the famous d'Iberville they had to fight the English Company. The Treaty of Utrecht in 1713 was their death warrant. The importance of the Canadian association may be judged by the fact that the shares of one of its members, Aubert de la Chesnaye, represented an amount of nearly 100,000 francs.[2]

Another proof of the progressive spirit of the Canadian merchants was the other association which they organised in 1700, to farm out the King's duties and take up the beaver trade.[3] Later on, when Louisbourg was founded by the French government on the Île-Royale (Cape Breton), it soon became a convenient meeting point for the trade between France and the West Indies, France and Canada, and the West Indies and Canada. In 1735, Hocquart could write that the Canadian merchants had thirteen vessels owned by them which "were engaged in the fisheries of the lower St Lawrence, that twelve had gone to Louisbourg with flour, biscuit, lumber and beef, while six had gone as far as the West Indies with lumber, dry cod and peas". In 1741, probably for the first and only time during the Old Regime, the balance of trade was in favour of New France, her exports being greater than her imports.[4]

For some time, one important export was the plant called "ginseng". It was supposed to grow almost exclusively in Korea and Tartary. The Chinese were extraordinarily fond of it and provided for it a great and profitable market. In 1715 a Jesuit father, named Lafitau, discovered it in Canada, on the information given to him by some Iroquois. As soon as the merchants in France heard of the dis-covery, they gave big orders for the plant, in the hope of improving their trade relations with the Far East. Gathering and preparing

[1] Hocquart au Ministre, 30 sept. 1731, 2 et 15 oct. 1733, 7 oct. 1734, 13 oct. 1735, 8 oct. 1737, 5 juillet 1740, 2 oct. 1746.
[2] "La Compagnie du Nord", by "Ignotus", in *La Presse*, Montreal, 18 nov. 1899.
[3] *Can. Archives*, F. 3, vol. VI.   [4] *Canada and its Provinces*, II, 511.

ginseng for commerce became then a paying operation. At one time, the *Compagnie des Indes* paid thirty-three francs for a pound. In 1752, it is stated that Canada's exportation of ginseng amounted to 500,000 francs. Unfortunately, greed and inexperience spoiled that branch of commerce. Instead of picking the plant in September and leaving it to dry slowly for one year, it was picked in May and dried imperfectly in the oven, so that it could be gathered, sold and exported the same year.[1] In those conditions, the Canadian ginseng was soon decried and lost its commercial value.

The products of the fisheries were always one of the main supplies of Canadian trade. Salt and dried fish were usual articles of exportation, as well as fish oil. During the eighteenth century, an important branch of the fisheries industry was the porpoise-fishing, which was conducted in many places with success. One of these porpoise fisheries, the most considerable, established at Rivière-Ouelle, eighty miles below Quebec, on the south shore of the St Lawrence, has been in existence for more than two centuries and is still flourishing.[2]

The opening of the highways has been already mentioned. In early days the rivers and streams were the only roads in the French colony. "Les rivières sont des chemins qui marchent". But, later on, with the settlement of the country, the need of highways became pressing. An officer named the *grand voyer* (road overseer) was appointed as early as 1657. His name was René Robineau de Bécancourt. At first his duties were not exacting. His son and successor was kept more busy. In the seigneuries and parishes, on both sides of the great river, roads had to be opened to facilitate communications and mutual intercourse between the settlements. At an appointed date, after due notice given through the *capitaine de la côte*, the *grand voyer*, or his deputy, would arrive in the parish. The *habitants* were bound to meet him, bringing their axes and other tools, and they proceeded, under the direction of the road officer, to the felling of trees, the levelling of the ground, the digging of ditches, along the lines determined beforehand. The third *grand voyer* of New France, Lanoullier de Boisclerc, had a very active term of office. He had the honour of opening, in 1734, the first continuous road between Quebec and Montreal.[3] Previously, he had been connected with the first establishment of a postal and transportation service in Canada. This took place in 1721. Up to that time, the letters which were sent from Quebec to Three Rivers and from this last place to Montreal, and *vice versa*, were conveyed by canoes occasionally or on a special trip. But there was no official organisation or service for that purpose—a state of things causing expenses and delays very damaging to trade. In January 1721 Vaudreuil

---

[1] *Considérations sur l'état présent du Canada*, pp. 14, 15 (*Collection de Mémoires et relations sur l'histoire ancienne du Canada*, 1840).　　　　[2] *Édits et Ords.* III, 419, C. 11.
[3] *Can. Archives*, Hocquart au Ministre, 14 oct. 1734, Lanoullier de Boisclerc au Ministre, 10 oct. 1734.

and Bégon promulgated an ordinance in which they stated that Lanoullier de Boisclerc had offered to undertake a postal and transportation service if he was granted a privilege of twenty years, in consideration of which he would set up on the streams between Montreal and Quebec a system of ferry-boats large enough for the crossing of cattle, horses, and vehicles, the tolls to be paid to him according to a tariff fixed by the Governor and the Intendant. The two high officials granted the privilege,[1] and thus the date 27 January 1721 marks the inauguration of the postal service in Canada.

In regard to taxation the Canadian people were not heavily burdened. The government levied dues of one-fourth on all beaver skins and one-tenth on moose skins, and a tax of ten per cent. on wine, brandy and tobacco. The King retained also the monopoly of trade at Tadousac, that is to say, on the territory called "Le Domaine du Roi", which consisted of ninety leagues on the north shore of the Saint Lawrence, with a depth extending to the highlands.[2] These dues and trading privileges were usually farmed out for a fixed price. In the last period of the Old Regime, new duties were decreed. The taxes on wine and liquors were increased, and an excise and import tariff were enacted.[3] The revenues yielded by all these different sources were always unequal to the expense incurred by the Home Government to maintain the colonial administration, which caused yearly complaints and warnings from the ministers in their letters to the Governors and Intendants. They seemed to ignore entirely the fact that their European politics and wars were the real root of the evil.

The monetary system of Canada was peculiar. Until 1685 the colony had no currency of its own. The French silver and copper coins were used for sales and payment in the general trade, with some fluctuation in their regulated value. When it was felt that such currency was not abundant enough to meet the necessities of commerce, barter came to the rescue to supplement the deficiency. Beaver pelts were deemed a very good medium of exchange. The stringency in the available currency was sometimes most embarrassing. Intendant de Meulles felt it very acutely in the spring of 1685. He had no funds for the payment of the troops. After having borrowed as much money as he could, he resorted at last to the issuing of a card money redeemable in a short time. It consisted simply of playing cards cut in four, and signed by the Intendant.[4] This expedient incurred the disapproval of the home authorities. But necessity knows no law, and recurring difficulties made new card money issues unavoidable. This special kind of currency provided an easy

[1] *Édits et Ords.* ii, 361.   [2] *Ibid.* ii, 361.
[3] *Considérations sur l'état présent du Canada*, p. 24.
[4] Shortt, A., *Documents relating to Canadian currency exchange and finance during the French Period*, i, 74.

means of exchange and supplemented the deficiency of specie. At the end of the Spanish Succession War, the card money in circulation amounted to 1,600,000 francs. In 1717, the Council of Marine in France issued an order for the redemption and destruction of all card money,[1] which was accordingly carried out. However, after a lapse of twelve years, representations were made to the Home Government as to the desirability of authorising this useful currency. Owing to the pressure of financial stringency the request was granted; and, in 1729, a regular issue of 400,000 francs was allowed.[2] The card money had won the day and remained in existence to the end of the Old Regime.

Another kind of paper money was the *ordonnances* which were a sort of treasury notes issued by the Intendant and redeemable by means of bills of exchange drawn on the general treasurer in France. At the end of the French administration, an officer of Montcalm's army wrote the following summary, which gives a good idea of the Canadian financial system: "The Intendant issues, so far as he deems necessary, currency notes"—that is to say: *ordonnances*—"which are the money of the country. They are of forty-eight, twenty-four, twelve, and three livres, thirty-six and twenty sols, and for a year past, there have been some of ninety-six and one thousand livres. In addition, there are cards which are of twelve, six, and three livres, and of thirty and fifteen sols. In the month of October, all those who hold such notes, or cards, bring them to the treasurer, who gives them receipts for their total amount, and at the end of the period, which is towards October 25, the treasurer accepts no more. Bills of exchange are then sent to those who hold the receipts".[3] Another kind of paper money should also be mentioned, the *récépissés* of beaver skins, signed by the Compagnie des Indes, which were highly valued. Card money, *ordonnances*, *récépissés*—such was the currency of Canada, at the end of the Old Regime. Of course, this was only for internal use. It was worth nothing outside of the colony. As a contemporary writer puts it, card money had no signification as representing money, "it was the sign of a sign".[4] It was a means of internal exchange. Its external usefulness could begin only when it was commuted in drafts on France.

During the dying days of the French domination, the great expenses incurred on account of the war, the dreadful leakage which took place and the laxity of the financial administration under the infamous Intendant Bigot, caused an enormous inflation. It was stated that the *ordonnances* alone amounted to 30,000,000 francs. A few years before the final wreck, the Home Government resorted to a dilatory process and began to pay the bills of exchange in three instalments; and, in 1759, payment was completely suspended.

---

[1] Shortt, I, 398–400. [2] *Édits et Ords.* I, 522.
[3] Shortt, II, 925. [4] *Considérations sur l'état présent du Canada*, p. 21.

The paper became discredited. And after the fall of New France, the situation gave rise to speculation. Some sharks bought great quantities of the paper money at a very low price. Though the Home Government was very far from redeeming it at its face value and made a partial bankruptcy, the speculators realised a goodly profit, whilst the original Canadian creditors lost heavily.[1]

During the administrations of Vaudreuil and Beauharnais, three Intendants were successively in office—Michel Bégon, from 1712 to 1726; Claude-Thomas Dupuy, from 1726 to 1728; Gilles Hocquart, from 1729 to 1748. Bégon was active and intelligent, but having lost about 50,000 francs in the disastrous fire which nearly destroyed the Intendant's palace a few months after his arrival, he seems to have yielded to the temptation of retrieving his fortunes by recourse to trade, a practice which was contrary to the King's orders. He was severely rebuked by the minister on that account.[2] Nevertheless, he was an able public officer. He fostered as well as he could the progress of agriculture, the fisheries, and the lumbering and mining industries, and it was under his administration, as recorded above, that the postal service was inaugurated in Canada.

Bégon's successor, Dupuy, remained only two years in office. They were troublesome years. He was a gifted man, learned in law, a fluent writer and a powerful legal reasoner. But, on the other hand, he was obstinate, haughty, pugnacious, and had no sense of economy. From the beginning, he quarrelled with the Governor, first on questions of minor importance, and then on more serious matters. But the great fight between Governor and Intendant took place at the death of Mgr de Saint-Vallier, Bishop of Quebec. A difficulty arose about the funeral celebration, between one of the clerical dignitaries, Archdeacon de Lotbinière, and his fellow members of the Chapter of Quebec. Dupuy, who had been named testamentary executor, interfered violently and ordered the funeral to take place clandestinely at night and without any of those usual ceremonies so fitting on such an occasion. A long controversy ensued, in which Dupuy took the most prominent part. He summoned the members of the Chapter before the Superior Council. They declined the jurisdiction of that body on such a question. The Intendant published an ordinance strongly asserting the supremacy of the State over the Church, and he ordered that an "information" be opened before "the lieutenant civil and criminal" against a certain canon for having read some document in the pulpit. The fight went on for weeks. At last, the Governor, as head of the Government, deemed that it should be stopped. But his interference added new fuel to the flames of public discord. He gave an order forbidding the Superior Council to receive and hear the *appels comme d'abus*, and such other proceedings, and he decreed the suspension of all ordinances published in connec-

---

[1] *Can. Archives*, C. 11, vols. cv, cviii.   [2] *Ibid.* B, Pontchartrain à Bégon, 13 juillet 1715

tion with the conflict. Dupuy roared and strove to meet the Governor's strictures against his conduct. He ordered the incarceration of Rageot, the bailiff of the Superior Council, guilty of having obeyed the Governor's injunctions. Then, Beauharnais sent soldiers to rescue the prisoner forcibly. In the meantime, he issued two *lettres de cachet*, putting under arrest Gaillard and d'Artigny, members of the Council. The feud was protracted for months, till the reception of letters from the minister, whereby Dupuy was recalled.[1] But Beauharnais himself was blamed for having adopted arbitrary measures, such as the putting of two councillors under arrest and the sending of soldiers to break into the gaol. This incident gives an insight into the Old Regime at one of its weakest points, that is to say, the ill-balanced powers of the Governors and Intendants.

Dupuy was succeeded by a man of a very different temper. Gilles Hocquart was conciliatory, though not lacking in steadiness. Clearsighted, painstaking, devoted to the public weal, he was one of the best Intendants that the mother country ever sent to her Laurentian colony. For once, the two civil heads of New France lived in perfect harmony. Beauharnais and Hocquart worked hand in hand. They never ceased to praise each other in their respective letters to the Home Government. It was under Hocquart's administration that some of the Canadian industries showed their greatest development, especially shipbuilding and the iron works. The opening of highways, already mentioned, was equally one of his main cares. He also tried to benefit the Canadian population by fostering the manufacture of salt, an article urgently needed in the colony, and imported at a somewhat high cost.[2] After Talon, Hocquart deserves the second place in the list of the Intendants of New France.

Very noteworthy is the power of expansion which the striving colony displayed from its earliest days. From Champlain to La Vérendrye, its explorers and discoverers pushed always forward and opened east and west, north and south, new avenues for trade, civilisation and Christianity. Champlain paved the way, and his traces were followed by a host of discoverers, interpreters, traders and missionaries, who explored successively Lake Champlain, the River Ottawa, the River Nipissing and the Georgian Bay, the Hurons' country, the Great Lakes Ontario, Erie, Huron, Superior, Michigan; penetrated west as far as Green Bay, Fox River and the Mascoutens country; and going north beyond Lake St John reached the Northern Sea (Hudson Bay).[3]

When Talon came back to Canada in 1670, one of his great aims seems to have been the discovery of new territories and the opening of new alliances and trading relations with the Indian tribes. It was

---

[1] See Registre du Conseil Supérieur, 1727–8, Archives provinciales, Quebec; also "La grande querelle de 1728", by "Ignotus", in *La Presse* of Montreal, Oct. and Nov. 1901.
[2] *Édits et Ords.* II, 390. [3] *Canada and its Provinces*, I, 45 and 108.

for that purpose that he sent de Saint-Lusson to take possession of the country around Lake Superior. On 14 June 1671 a great meeting of fourteen nations took place at Sault Ste Marie. Saint-Lusson and Father Allouez, a Jesuit, addressed the gaudy gathering. The former ordered a cross to be erected with the arms of the French King; and, at night, an immense bonfire, illuminating the dark forest and foaming rapids, closed that impressive ceremony.[1] At the same time, the Governor and the Intendant had sent the famous Cavelier de la Salle towards the south-western country, in order to try, if it was possible, to find a waterway leading to the Mexican Sea. La Salle had reached the Ohio in 1669–70. It seems that, in 1670–1, he pushed as far as the Illinois river and country. In the same year, Talon directed an expedition headed by Father Albanel and de Saint-Simon, to explore the country north of the River Saguenay and of Lake St John. They reached James Bay, at the bottom of Hudson Bay on 28 June 1672 and took possession of the country. The crowning feature of the great Intendant's efforts in exploration was the mission entrusted to Louis Jolliet and Father Marquette, which ended with the discovery of the "Meschacebe", the mighty Mississippi, in 1673.

Thus before 1700 French and Canadian explorers had realised great achievements. Hand in hand, priest and trader, missionary and *coureur des bois*, prompted, the one by his apostolic devotion, the other by his eagerness for wealth, and both by the noble ambition of extending and enhancing their nation's influence and prestige, had accomplished a work of wonderful magnitude. Through them, New France had stamped her name on three-fourths of the known North American continent. Her influence, moral, political and commercial, expanded beyond her borders to the west, south and north. She had planted the cross and the fleur-de-lys from the burning shores of Arkansas to the icy waters of Hudson Bay, and from the waves of the Atlantic to the remotest confines of the great inland seas. This expansion was to go on during the eighteenth century. After the discovery of the Mississippi, the expeditions of Cavelier de la Salle in the south, and the foundation of Louisiana by d'Iberville and his brothers, the objective of the Canadian explorers was the Western Sea. The very important explorations of Pierre de la Vérendrye and his sons in 1731–49 are described in a later chapter.[2]

The Treaty of Aix-la-Chapelle which brought to an end the War of the Austrian Succession (1744–8) gave back Louisbourg to France and came as a respite for the Laurentian colony. During the captivity of de la Jonquière, de la Galissonnière, another distinguished naval officer, had been named Governor *ad interim*. De Beauharnais

[1] *Rel. des Jés.* 1671, pp. 20–7 and 28.
[2] See *infra*, chap. xvi, also Burpee, L. J., *Pathfinders of the great West*, i, 146; Margry, P., *Découvertes et établissements des Français dans l'Amérique Septentrionale*, vol. ii; *Can. Archives*, C. 11, Postes des pays de l'Ouest (1679–1759).

left Canada in September 1747, after having been nearly twenty years at the head of the colony. He was one of the best Governors of New France under the Old Regime. De la Galissonnière's stay in Canada was short, but he remained long enough to prove himself a most brilliant and able administrator. His term of office was marked by an unceasing activity. His reports to the Home Government were brimming with clear-sighted views and proposals. He saw the urgency of keeping free the intercourse between Canada and Louisiana, and with that in view, he entrusted Céloron de Bienville with the mission of leading an expedition towards the Ohio River, called by the French "*La Belle Rivière*", for the purpose of taking possession of that country. He remained only two years at the head of the colony. Under his administration, a new Intendant had come to replace Hocquart. His name, fated to a shameful celebrity, was François Bigot—the evil genius of the dying days of New France. Around him, and very often associated with him, a gang of embezzlers and vile speculators gathered, plundered the State and private individuals, and organised a scandalous system of official theft. De la Galissonnière left Canada in the fall of 1749, when de la Jonquière came at last to take charge of the government to which he had been appointed three years before. This new Governor's term of office was also very short. He died at Quebec on 17 March 1752, having won a well-deserved fame in the French navy. But in Canada, he was accused of nepotism and greed, and of being unduly interested in the western trade.[1]

His successor was the Marquis Duquesne de Menneville, a captain in the King's navy, who remained in office a little less than three years. A new war between France and England was now imminent. The joint commission appointed to study and settle the complicated question of the respective boundaries of the English and French colonies seemed unable to reach a satisfactory solution, and, on the other hand, the condition of European politics pointed to renewed hostilities between the great powers. In view of those ominous prospects, the Marquis Duquesne made strenuous efforts to reorganise the Canadian militia and to strengthen the western frontier. He directed the construction of new forts to the south of Lake Erie and in the Ohio country, namely Forts Presqu'Île, le Bœuf and Duquesne, the last one on the site of the present city of Pittsburg. These moves startled the English colonies, which resolved to put a stop to the alleged French encroachments on a territory claimed by the English Crown. The ensuing events, the expedition led by a young Virginian colonel of militia named George Washington, the death of the French officer Jumonville, the fight at Fort Necessity, and all the subsequent happenings on the Ohio and the Monongahela,[2] marked virtually the beginning of a war which was to seal the fate

---

[1] *Mémoires sur le Canada* (1749–60), pp. 10, 24, 26.   [2] See vol. i, p. 470.

of New France. In 1755 Duquesne was replaced by the Marquis de Vaudreuil, a son of the first Governor of that name, who assumed the government of Canada on 23 June. The history of his administration is little else than the history of the Seven Years' War in America and will be found in another chapter. In 1760 the capitulation of Montreal put an end to the Old Régime.

To sum up, the old Canadian Regime appears to us as a political and social fabric whose component parts are well delineated and strongly linked, though some may seem deficient and unsound and prone sometimes to clash together. New France has three heads: the Governor, representing the King, the highest authority in the land; the Bishop, representing the Church and exercising his jurisdiction over the clergy, the religious communities and the laity; the Intendant, invested with great administrative power in judicial, police and financial matters. Then comes the Superior Council, a kind of small parliament—in some respects resembling the *parlements* of old France—partly court of law, partly legislative body. Under the Council, other courts co-operate in the administration of justice; first the lowest, the seigneurial court, for minor cases; then the *Prévôté* at Quebec and the *Juridiction Royale* at Three Rivers and Montreal, sitting in appeal for the small law-suits, and in first instance for the most important ones. The colony is divided into three districts, Quebec, Montreal and Three Rivers. The town of Quebec is the seat of government, where the Governor-General resides in the picturesque Château St Louis, on the summit of the cliff. Montreal and Three Rivers have each their local Governor, and the former has a delegate of the Intendant, named the *Commissaire-Ordonnateur*. The settled country on both sides of the St Lawrence and on such rivers as the Richelieu, is parcelled out in seigneuries and parishes, the one usually overlapping the other. The seigneury represents the land tenure, the settlement of the country, the colonising expansion and activity. The parish is the religious bond, uniting the groups of Canadian families under the same spiritual direction, and gathering them at the foot of the altar under the shelter of the Church in whose sacred precincts the small communities seek and find their purest joys and their noblest inspirations.

In the country the rural population is devoted to the clearing of the land, the tilling of the soil and the home industries. Often, too often, the farmer is called away for military service, and returns only after many weeks, or even months. He has then much to talk about, lively descriptions and reminiscences to unfold. But the farm has suffered by his absence. There is also the young man who, one day, has been tempted by the allurements of the far-away western trade. He has gone, and, sometimes after many years, he comes back, introducing into the peaceful and uneventful parish a breath of romance and a glamour of wonderful deeds. In the Canadian community, the clergy and the religious orders occupy a large place and exercise a great influence over the social life. In 1754 there are in Canada 150 priests or members of religious orders, that is to say, Jesuits and Recollets. Also there are 225 nuns, Ursulines, Hospitalières and sisters of the Congregation.[1] The last-named, here and there in the country, have convents where they give education to the young girls of the neighbourhood.

In the course of the year, there are for New France two seasons of capital importance and of lively interest, the spring and the fall. When, after the long months of the severe and tempestuous winter, the St Lawrence, under the milder winds and the warmer sun of April, is freed of its icy *carapace*, when the migratory birds begin to flock back to their summer haunts, when the vernal sap is striving in the swelling buds, and when the lawns begin to revive, a feeling of joyous expectation pervades the whole population of Canada. The long seclusion is over at last, and soon the white sails—migratory as the birds—will shine once more over the great river's waves, coming from far-away France and bringing in their folds news from friends and relatives, from the remote and beloved mother country. Sometimes sooner, sometimes later, sometimes in May, more often in June, the ardently desired ships arrive. Quebec is all alive. Letters, official and private, goods and necessaries of every description are spread over town and country, and the flow of ships, of merchandise, of messages, lasts for six months. But short are the Canadian summers. With October, the east wind blowing from frosty Belle Isle, begins to kill flowers and leaves, and to darken ominously the St Lawrence. It is time to prepare for another winter, to write the last letters, to close the last accounts, to send the last orders, to exchange card money and *ordonnances* for drafts on France. Soon, too soon, the ships begin to sail back. By the middle of November, the harbour of Quebec is deserted; and the barrier of space, of ice and ocean rises again for seven months between Old and New France.

A year comes when the white sails of France do not return. In the spring of 1760, on 9 May, the ship, which from Cape Diamond is seen rounding the Point of Orleans, hoists the colours of England. And not for almost a century does a French flag wave again in the Quebec breeze. The long struggle is over. United in a common purpose, the English colonies have seconded the great effort displayed by England to attain this object—the destruction of New France. The goal has been reached at last and the Canadian Old Regime is no more. But persistent traces of its life and institutions have subsisted. And, after 170 years, some of the latter still remain unshattered, living monuments of bygone days, safeguarded by the faithful adherence of a surviving nationality.

[1] *Can. Census*, 1871, IV, 61.

CHAPTER IV

THE STRUGGLE FOR SUPREMACY
IN AMERICA

(I) 1682–1748

As has already appeared, the British and French settlements in North America, following the lines taken by their respective explorers, placed the two peoples in situations where growth involved conflict. England asserted her right to the coasts of Newfoundland, Nova Scotia and Maine, on the ground of prior discovery and (with the exception of Nova Scotia) actual settlement. France, however, claimed the whole of that peninsula, also the western shore of the Bay of Fundy down to the Kennebeck River, and large parts of the coast of Newfoundland; and, in times when the fisheries formed the supreme issue, these pretensions bred constant strife.[1] But the supreme crux was the region of the St Lawrence and its tributary lakes. Both by discovery and prior settlement the French claimed that great basin, the southern feeders of which lay at the back of certain of the English colonies. On the other hand the English settlers by their original patents held their titles good to all the western lands as far as the Pacific. Yet the climatic urge and the westward push of the French fur-traders and *coureurs des bois* cut athwart these unsubstantiated claims, leaving the prize to the nation which best supported its pioneers. In 1664 when Louis XIV assigned all non-Spanish America to the French West India Company,[2] the struggle assumed a national aspect, which, in the infancy of those settlements, could be settled decisively only in Europe. In America the strife for the hinterland turned on the possession of the key-positions on the outfalls of the Great Lakes and on the portages between the chief river routes, especially those between the Mohawk River and Lake Oneida, between the Upper Hudson and Lake George, and between the Chaudière and Kennebeck. Access to ice-free ports (a still more vital question for Canada) centred chiefly in the possession of Acadia and the coast to the southward as far as the Kennebeck, the source of which was near to that of her river, the Chaudière.

After 1660 the first collision took place in time of nominal peace amidst the sub-Arctic wastes on Hudson Bay. Here the fundamental cause was the clash of English maritime discovery with the push of the French fur trade. In 1668 Prince Rupert, resuming the quest for the North-West Passage, which had baffled many Englishmen from Frobisher to Hudson, determined to carry the flag of St George

[1] *Cal. St. Pap., Am. and W.I.* 1574–1660, pp. 26, 102, 119, 152, 239.
[2] Parkman, F., *The Old Régime in Canada*, p. 234.

through Hudson Bay to the Pacific for the trade of Cipangu and Cathay. Chance then brought to London two French-Canadian explorers, Radisson and Groseilliers, who, having met with injustice at Quebec and neglect at Paris, now offered their services to the Prince. He commissioned them to search for the northern passage, and in 1668 they sailed for Hudson Bay in two ships. Groseillers in the *Nonsuch* (navigated by Gillam of Boston) alone reached the bay. The result was the foundation of Charles Fort near Rupert River, the return to England with a valuable cargo of furs, and the foundation in 1670 of the Hudson's Bay Company for the search for the "South Sea" and the establishment of a trade in furs and minerals in "Prince Rupert's Land". The two men sailed thither in 1671 and founded posts at Moose and York Factory near Port Nelson. In 1676 the furs exported thence were valued at £19,000;[1] and the French traders, even far south, feeling the competition, resolved to expel their rivals from Hudson Bay. Accordingly Quebec merchants formed *la Compagnie du Nord* to which Louis XIV granted the trade of Hudson Bay; and its strategic advantage over scattered English posts, rarely succoured from the Ocean, conduced to the outbreak of hostilities even in time of peace (1682). Radisson and Groseilliers, now acting for the French, captured two English ships and two of the Hudson's Bay Company's posts. Thus began a struggle which went generally in favour of the French, until war broke out between the two nations.[2]

"King William's War" (1689–97) pitted some 12,000 Canadians against about 100,000 English colonists in New England and New York. New England alone boasted a militia of 13,279 horse and foot and an annual revenue of about £12,000 sterling.[3] Possessing ice-free harbours, a more genial climate, and far greater wealth, the English should easily have disposed of the Canadians, whose leaders with soaring imagination grasped at immense spaces far beyond the peopling powers of a population checked by celibacy and cramped by autocratic coddling. Yet, the ardent loyalty of these sons of France to Church and King, their feudal upbringing, their life of hunting and trapping in a rigorous climate, made them fine soldiers, inured to hardship. Moreover their *bonhomie*, their chivalrous manners, even the vices of the *coureurs des bois*, early won over the Indians, whose natural bent was towards the Canadian Esaus and away from the New England Jacobs. The savage might chaffer with the Boston fur-dealers, but he foregathered gladly with the stout *voyageurs* who brought him fire-water. Not from them was there danger that the plough would encroach on the forest, whereas it was soon clear that New England energy and Puritan thrift would dispossess the red man more and more of his hunting grounds. Thus, the French soon had

[1] See chapter xvi; also Schooling, W., *The Hudson's Bay Co.* 1670–1920, chap. i; Willson, B., *The Great Company*, p. 173; Biggar, H. P., *Trading Companies of New France*.
[2] Parkman, F., *Lasalle and the Discovery of the Great West*, p. 76; Garneau, *Hist. du Canada*, i, 408–13. [3] *Cal. St. Pap. Col.* 1689–92, pp. 261, 270.

the help of the northern and eastern tribes—a matter of the first importance in border warfare. So far back as 1636 the young Harry Vane reported to his father the condition of Massachusetts as "very tumultuous", for the French on the north had armed the natives and were continually encroaching.[1] Reprisals of course followed; but in the main the French had Indian support, with one notable exception, that of the Five Nations or Iroquois. Champlain, as we have seen, had committed the mistake of attacking one of their tribes; and to affront one was to bring down vengeance from all. During more than a century they kept up the vendetta; and it is not too much to say that Champlain's error of judgment lost France a good chance of conquering North America; for the five tribes shielded the colony of New York on the north and New England on the west, and were always ready to raid Canada. Probably their fury was due less to English intrigues and bribes than to an undying hatred of the French and their allies among the tribes. But the outcome was a crescendo of frightfulness during every war, with the logical sequel that one or other of the white races using Indians as allies must suffer political extinction in North America.

In the twelve English colonies all the elements of military weakness abounded. Lacking any form of union except the gossamer threads connecting them with the English Crown, widely diverse in interests and outlook, they resembled each other chiefly in an ingrained habit of opposition to the royal Governors, which boded ill for obedience in the field. Further, the Revolution of 1688 in England gave rein to the spirit of faction in the colonies. At Boston the mob (desirous of "free trade") deposed and imprisoned Governor Andros and "debauched" the garrisons of eight frontier forts on or near the Kennebeck. These easily fell to the French, who, with their fierce Indian allies, now ravaged the borderland. Letters from Boston pictured a state of anarchy,—"they are not afraid to say that the Crown of England has nothing to do with them". Others saw hope only in strong government from England.[2] Meanwhile the Leisler faction, now dominant in New York, so demoralised the defenders of Schenectady, on the Mohawk River, that early in 1690 a party of French and Indians easily surprised it by night and massacred some sixty persons, in revenge (so they said) for the recent savage Iroquois raid on Lachine near Montreal. New York, then a poor colony, was in despair, and blamed wealthier New England for deserting it.— "If a Governor come not soon, the country will be lost".—"We are the ignorantest, weakest and poorest people in the world". Such is the burden of two letters from Albany early in 1690. Yet the danger common to all did not end the local schisms. These multiplied until in October New England dissolved into ten units—Pemaquid, Maine,

[1] Cal. St. Pap. Am. and W.I. 1574–1660, p. 239.
[2] Cal. St. Pap. Col. 1689–92, nos. 336, 912, 929, 949.

New Hampshire, Massachusetts, Plymouth, Rhode Island, King's Province, Connecticut, and East and West Jersey.[1]

Over against these squabbling communities stood Canada, strong in her monarchical institutions, wielded by the strongest of her early governors. For Louis XIV now sent back to her Count Frontenac —a name of terror to the Iroquois. In 1672–82 "Onontio" had for a time cowed them, and now in his seventieth year he came back to win them over, first by terrorism (as at Schenectady), then by war-like display, war dances, presents—and the hope of scalps. By contrast with the Leislerites and the wrangling New Englanders his heroic figure and theatrical ways seemed to presage victory. On the whole, then, the imponderables of war balanced numbers, wealth, and for a time even sea power, thus postponing to the year 1760 an issue seemingly attainable in 1690.

In this year, the New Englanders, stung to action by Frontenac's border raids, prepared a joint-stock expedition for the reduction of that centre of Acadian privateering, Port Royal, and thereafter of Quebec. As Old England, a prey to invasion fears, could send no help, New England would work out her own salvation. Such was the counsel of William Phipps, a self-made man whose masterful ways endeared him to the Bostonians and procured him the command of the expedition. The threat of it was helpful, compelling raiders and privateers to concentrate. Accordingly, Phipps found the Penobscot Fort deserted by the French, and then, sailing across the Bay of Fundy, easily reduced Port Royal (11 May), thereupon rifling the church, pulling down the high altar and breaking the images. Boston next sent forth a force of five armed vessels and twenty-nine transports, which without difficulty sailed up the St Lawrence. Delays below Île d'Orléans prevented the hoped-for surprise at Quebec, and enabled Frontenac to sail down betimes from Montreal, issuing orders everywhere for the militia to follow him. Strengthening the weak defences of Quebec, he on 16 October defied Phipps's summons to surrender. On the 18th some 1200 English under Major Walley landed below the Charles River and began to skirmish forward, but the Canadian militia by day and sharp frosts by night took heavy toll of them. Phipps, having little ammunition, should have postponed action by the ships till his soldiers could attack in force. Instead his armed ships blazed away at the defences before Walley could attack from the Charles River. The ships' guns, badly aimed, splintered much rock but left intact the defences, whose guns dismasted the flagship *Six Friends* (44) and beat off the others. On the 19th a final check to the land force led at nightfall to a rush for the boats and the abandonment of five guns and all the stores. Disease on the homeward voyage completed the discomfiture; and the comment of one of the "undertakers"—"we are almost run aground"—

[1] *Ibid.* nos. 783, 929, 1157; *N.Y. Col. Docs.* III, 693–6, 708.

reveals the despair at Boston. The debt of Massachusetts mounted to £50,000; and paper money was issued even for the value of two shillings. Frontenac now begged Louis XIV to spare a few squadrons to "crush the Bostonians in their den and the English of New York as well".[1] But *le grand monarque* could spare none.

In June 1691 Phipps besought the English Government to send two frigates, one to strengthen our very doubtful hold over Nova Scotia, the other to convoy to Quebec a New England force, along with 2000 muskets, 100 cannon to fortify Île d'Orléans, and four mortars to bombard Quebec from the south, he himself commanding the whole. England, however, was then in too great danger to throw away ships and stores on this fool's errand; and the local strifes swayed to and fro indecisively. A raid into Canada by our allied Maqua Indians ended with their total destruction (December 1691); and until Major Pieter Schuyler organised the defence of Albany, that town and indeed New York were in danger, which New England did nothing to avert.[2]

After the victories of Barfleur and La Hogue in the summer of 1692 England was safe from invasion and could at last spare a squadron for the colonies. Under Admiral Sir Francis Wheler it was first to capture Guadeloupe, and then, picking up reinforcements which were requested at Boston, sail on to capture Quebec. Far too much was attempted, and also, owing to dockyard delays, too late in the season. Arriving in the West Indies when the rains and heat were due, Wheler's men died like flies and effected nothing. He reached Boston early in July (six weeks late) with only 650 soldiers and one-third of the crews efficient. To his request for the promised reinforcements Phipps replied that the Quebec project needed 4000 men, whom he could not collect within four months. On the 24th Wheler begged for 400 men to help him attack Placentia, the French privateering base in Newfoundland; but Phipps declined, on the plea that he had dissolved the Massachusetts Assembly on the 15th and could not now send men out of the colony.[3] Wheler, deeming his fleet too weak to tackle the forts of Placentia, sailed home, having accomplished nothing.

The Phipps and Wheler fiascoes greatly encouraged the French, who in July 1694 with a band of Acadians and Indians massacred some sixty settlers on the Oyster River in New Hampshire, in a "strangely barbarous" manner, killing even infants in the cradle. Indeed, Frontenac's policy of fierce border raids achieved a temporary success by inducing the local militia to defend its own districts. New York was in urgent distress.[4] Despite Governor Schuyler's local successes our Iroquois allies could not be roused to effective action

---

[1] *Cal. St. Pap. Col.* 1689–92, nos. 1239, 1299; Parkman, *Frontenac and New France*, chaps. xii, xiii; Garneau, I, 383–6.
[2] *Cal. St. Pap. Col.* 1689–92, nos. 1660, 1968, 1969; New York Hist. Soc. (1891), p. 73.
[3] *Ibid.* 1693–6, nos. 136, 441, 475. See too *C.H.B.E.* vol. I, chap. xvii.
[4] *Ibid.* nos. 1153, 2040, 2054; Parkman, *Frontenac*, chaps. xvi, xvii; Le Sueur, W., *Frontenac*, chap. xi.

and lost half their number under Frontenac's persistent attacks. Fundamentally his successes were due to England's inability to spare a large force overseas, to the selfish and perhaps disloyal conduct of Phipps in 1692, above all to the obstinate dissidence of all the English colonies. A New Englander, John Nelson, who was captured by the French in Nova Scotia in 1691 and spent over four years in captivity in Canada or France, laid stress on these truths, adding that the Canadians won over the savages by conversion (which we neglected), by profuse presents, by making their best youths lieu-tenants, and by sending several (even a few Iroquois) to France to behold the glory of Louis XIV and of his armies in Flanders. Ac-cordingly in 1696 there were at Versailles six deputations of Indians from Canada, Nova Scotia, and Hudson Bay asking for help against us; while our friendly Indians went over to the French or "stand doubtful what to do".[1] In that year, the French also laid waste the border of New England, capturing its sea bulwark, Pemaquid Fort. Their leader, Pierre le Moine d'Iberville, having been trained in the French navy, united discipline with daring, and now sailed off to devastate the English settlements in Newfoundland, thereafter with one warship beating three of our armed merchantmen in Hudson Bay and capturing Fort Nelson (1697). In the sequel he raided our West Indies. A scheme was also on foot for the capture of New York by a French squadron, when peace came to end these strifes.

By this time it was clear that the fate of America would be decided on the high seas and in Europe.[2] There Louis XIV's overbearing policy had aroused against him forces so superior as to exhaust his treasury and compel him to sign the Treaty of Ryswick (September 1697). Its basis being the restitution of conquests, Acadia was restored to France; but the settlement of the Hudson Bay disputes was relegated to commissioners, and turned to the advantage of the French. They succeeded also on the south border of Canada. One of the last acts of Frontenac was to receive at Montreal signs of sub-mission from the humbled Iroquois; and his daring and haughty spirit lived on, impelling his successors to far-reaching plans which embraced the Mississippi and the lands around the Great Lakes. New France was to become a greater Old France. In the south that most daring of Canadian warriors, d'Iberville, completed the work of la Salle on the Mississippi, by exploring its delta and there building the fort of Biloxi fifty miles from the mouth (1699). Thereafter some 400 Huguenot refugees in the Carolinas applied for permission to settle in "Louisiana" but received the official reply that Louis XIV had not expelled them from France to found a republic in America. Thus d'Iberville's settlement remained a solitary military outpost, strengthened, however, in 1701 by Fort Louis in Mobile Bay, the

---

[1] *Cal. St. Pap. Col.* 1696–7, no. 250 (rec. 23 Sept. 1696).
[2] See vol. I, pp. 321–2, 511–15.

creation of his brothers Serigny and Bienville.[1] The grandiose designs of Louis XIV appeared in the despatch, in the summer of 1701 (before the outbreak of war), of a powerful fleet of twenty-eight sail under Admiral Chateaurenaud, for a surprise attack on the British West Indies. The plan miscarried.[2] D'Iberville's good fortune also failed him. Instead of harrying first Barbados and then New England, he was beset by illness after illness, the last carrying him off at Havana in 1706. His exploits, ranging from Hudson Bay to Louisiana, prepared the way for the great French scheme of encircling the English American colonies by conquests extending from the sub-arctic to the sub-tropical zone. Thanks to Louis XIV's insensate ambition and bigotry the scheme wilted for lack of men; for his wars condemned many thousands of Frenchmen to die fruitlessly beyond the Rhine, and his rigid Catholicism denied to Louisiana the hundreds needed to till her soil.

The overweening policy of Louis also ranged against him the half of Europe in the War of the Spanish Succession (1702–13). Consequently, England and her Dutch allies soon gained maritime supremacy, and their capture of Gibraltar in 1704 and of Minorca in 1708 not only sealed up the Toulon fleet but blighted French efforts in America. Even so, the issue there remained doubtful owing to the miserable divisions. The mayor and council of Albany in their poverty begged the Home Government to build a stone fort to protect the town, which had little help from New England. Colonel Quary reported on the inefficiency of the colonial militia, which was in general ill armed and worse disciplined. Nothing but a good garrison at Albany "can steady the Five Nations to the English interest". If they desert us, all may be lost. A quota system for general defence should be imposed on the colonies. This, however, proved to be difficult; for Governor Dudley of Massachusetts could scarcely induce his Assembly to raise men and money against threatened Indian raids from the north-east. Many young men even absconded to Rhode Island, which harboured them and would not help in defence measures. The Hudson's Bay Company bewailed the recent French encroachments which deterred Indians from coming to Fort Albany, the only British post on the bay, thus reducing the trade by four-fifths. They therefore begged for three warships and 250 troops to expel the French entirely from the bay. St John's in Newfoundland feared conquest by the French garrison of some 500 men at Placentia.[3] Lieutenant-Governor Usher, of New Hampshire, foretold the loss of that colony. Meanwhile the French sent to Placentia forces which ravaged St John's and our other settlements. Consequently piteous appeals came thence for help, especially for defence on land, which is "absolutely requisite to maintain that fishery". In general the

---

[1] Garneau, I, 436–43. [2] See vol. I, chap. xvii.
[3] *Cal. St. Pap. Col.* 1702, nos. 40, 260, 306, 348, 962, 999, 1135.

inability of the navy to defend our colonies and commerce from French raiders increased the resentment against Marlborough and the Whigs for concentrating too much on the war in Flanders.[1]

Accordingly, the Tories, seeking proleptically to bring in the New World to redress the balance in the Old, now pressed for the conquest of North America. This feat, which would rival the "barren" victories of Marlborough in Flanders, seemed easily attainable. As exhausted France could spare neither ships nor troops for Canada, that exigent nursling could not long survive the grip of England's sea power. Moreover, in 1709–10 New England had some 17,000 men under arms waiting for British help which never came; but the menacing attitude of their advanced guard at Wood Creek, north of Albany, at least "amused" the Canadians and checked the usual border forays. Clearly the best means of defending New York and Boston was to threaten Montreal and Quebec. Similarly, the only sure way of protecting Anglo-American commerce was to burn out those wasps' nests, Placentia and Port Royal, the latter of which was dubbed "the great pest and trouble of all the navigation and trade". Naval considerations also prompted the conquest of Nova Scotia and Canada. Already the seaboard of New England was being recklessly deforested; and the "mast-fleet" for England sometimes sailed with scanty cargoes—a matter of deep concern for the navy in war time, especially when access to the Baltic lands was doubtful. To increase the area of accessible British forests was therefore important; and Governor Dudley and the Council of Massachusetts urged those conquests because then "all the trade of naval stores, enough for all Europe, will be entirely in H.M.'s disposition".[2]

In 1710, however, the defence of Portugal diverted most of the forces destined for Quebec; and it was a small and belated contingent under Colonel Nicholson which in July reached Boston to pick up the five New England regiments. After the usual delays the whole force sailed thence in mid-September to attack Nova Scotia, "the key of all the eastern colonies".[3] Port Royal, being weak and weakly held, surrendered on 2 October. But Nicholson's task was only begun. The Acadians, refusing to accept British rule, began to attack the capital (now renamed Annapolis Royal) so that he recommended their deportation unless they would become Protestants. A frigate would be needed permanently to defend it from French privateers and from "the illegal trade of Your Majesty's neighbouring colonies". Colonel Vetch of Boston, left behind as governor, did nothing to conciliate them, and in June 1711 reported that he was blockaded by a French force landed recently in Baie Verte.[4]

Meanwhile the Tories, lately come to power, were preparing for

[1] *Cal. St. Pap. Col.* 1710–11, nos. 85, 91.
[2] *Ibid.* nos. 81, 380, 491, 504; see too Albion, R. G., *Forests and Sea Power*, pp. 160–76, and chap. vi. [3] *Corresp. of W. Shirley*, II, 149.
[4] *Cal. St. Pap. Col.* 1710–11, nos. 460, 613, 879, 887.

the conquest of Canada. Taking from Marlborough some 6000 fine troops, they entrusted them to General Hill, brother of the Queen's new favourite. Party reasons may also explain their appointment of an inexperienced admiral, Sir Hovenden Walker, to command the fleet, consisting of nine sail of the line, four frigates and many transports. These, along with a colonial contingent from Boston, were to sail up the uncharted St Lawrence and attack Quebec, while Nicholson led a colonial force through the Hudson-Richelieu rift to attack Montreal or Three Rivers. The plan, it will be seen, resembled in large outline those of Phipps and Wolfe. In execution it fell far below the amateurish effort of 1690 and serves but to add lustre to Wolfe's right-hand man, Admiral Saunders. In 1711 everything went awry. Walker, sailing from Plymouth on 4 May, reached Boston on 24 June. There nothing was ready; Vetch had not arrived from Annapolis or Nicholson from New York; and preparations were delayed quite a fortnight by "the ill nature and sowerness of these people", who overcharged for stores, harboured deserters (amounting to 250) and otherwise thwarted the plan, apparently from fear that it might lead to the union of all the colonies, along with Canada, under the direct government of the Crown.[1]

Such was the belief of General Hill and Colonel King. Hill, as "a four-bottle man", got on badly with the Puritans of New England. Still, he pushed on the preparations, which were complete by the end of July. Walker soon had friction with the sea-captains unwillingly impressed for service as pilots up the St Lawrence. Very foolishly, he had detached to Annapolis on special service the most skilled, Captain Southack, and soon the "averseness and unsufficiency" of the others were apparent. Walker, not knowing the estuary, requested Vetch, who had been up it with Phipps in 1690, to lead in a light frigate; but owing to misunderstanding or pique, this plan was not followed. The admiral therefore trusted a pilot brought from France, who probably betrayed him. In blowing, misty weather Walker took far too northerly a course; and on 23 August eight transports and two store ships were dashed on the rocks of Egg Island, with the loss of 742 lives. Even so enough survived to go on, as Vetch urged. But as the pilots unanimously refused, Walker flinched and made for home, a council of war deciding against an attack on Placentia because their provisions would scarce carry them to England.[2] Nicholson's force now having to retreat in haste, the land war ended with the usual raiding, despair and demoralisation. Massachusetts begged the Queen to send another expedition in 1712, but expected to be excused furnishing its quota. Albany traders made a secret pact with the enemy, and Vetch by his peculation and harshness at Annapolis alienated the Acadians.[3]

---

[1] *Cal. St. Pap. Col.* 1711–12, nos. 46, 61, 96.   [2] *Ibid.* nos. 92, 94.
[3] *Ibid.* nos. 401, 403, 433, 448, 452; Garneau, I, App. ccxii.

The petty whims of Queen Anne, leading to the dismissal of Marlborough, served to balance even the colossal blunders of Louis XIV. The result was seen in the Treaty of Utrecht (April 1713). England, weary of war, had long been bargaining with France. As to American affairs, the Hudson's Bay Company urged the complete expulsion of their aggressive rivals from the bay, and, on St John (Bolingbroke) consulting the Board of Trade and Plantations, it pressed for expulsion, and successfully. Our demands for Nova Scotia and Newfoundland were also granted in the main; but the French negotiators stood out firmly for the retention of Cape Breton Island, hitherto deemed an annexe of the adjacent peninsula. In April 1712 St John consulted the Board whether the proposed gains in Hudson Bay, Nova Scotia and Newfoundland might warrant our giving way over Cape Breton Island. The Board demurring to this view, the responsibility for that concession at Utrecht rests with him.[1] The Board also recommended a clear definition of the bounds of Nova Scotia, viz. the River St Croix on the west and "Canada River" on the north. His failure to get any clear definition inserted in the treaty invited a campaign of chicanery, evasion and friction.

Thus in May 1719 Governor Nicholson reported from Annapolis the non-arrival of the official French order for the surrender of Acadia; and in 1721 his successor, Colonel Philips, stated that 700 French were working on the fortifications of Louisbourg.[2] Indeed, for the Canadians Utrecht was not a settlement but a challenge. After Walker's fiasco and St John's weakness (or worse), what spirited people would not hope to overcome mere numbers without organisation and to baffle counsels devoid of foresight or firmness? Consequently the encircling policy now entered on a new and more formidable phase, Father Bobé in 1720 claiming for France the whole of the continent and the expulsion of the English as usurpers. The rebuilding of Fort Niagara and the construction of several forts in the west formed part of this design. The only retort was Fort Oswego, which Governor Burnet of New York built at his own expense (1727). In 1731 the French built a fort at Crown Point within the bounds claimed by the Mohawks and New York.[3]

Accordingly, in the war of 1744-8 the French began with many advantages; for their increasing inferiority in numbers was counterbalanced by military preparedness and unity. The Governor of Cape Breton Island easily seized the small redoubt at Canso, and then, raising the Acadians, nearly captured Annapolis. Clearly, Nova Scotia would never be safe while the French could easily threaten it from across the narrow strait. New England therefore determined to capture Louisbourg. In that now well-fortified harbour lay all

[1] *Cal. St. Pap. Col.* 1712-13, nos. 365, 374.
[2] *Ibid.* 1718-22: entries of 23 June 1719, 1 Oct. 1721.
[3] Garneau, I, bk VI, chap. iii; Parkman, *Half Century of Conflict*, chaps. ix, xiii, xvii.

the strategic potency of Port Royal and Placentia combined. Stronger than either for defence, it also more immediately dominated the one good passage to the St Lawrence; and the capture of twenty-five Boston vessels in May–September 1744 by its privateers marked it out as the Dunkirk of American waters. Further, the recent danger to Annapolis showed that, unless the island were reduced, "the French will soon be masters of Nova Scotia". William Shirley, Governor of Massachusetts, who in January 1745 sent home this warning, had already persuaded his Assembly to assist in raising a New England force, which, with help from British warships, would attack Louisbourg before French succours arrived. He added that its capture would facilitate that of Canada—a country which from its fur trade, fisheries and naval stores "may be reckoned a more valuable territory to Great Britain than what any kingdom or state in Europe has belonging to it".[1]

Two years earlier the same advice, clinched by a similar estimate of the value of Canada, had been urged on the Admiralty by Commodore Peter Warren, who now commanded a squadron in the West Indies.[2] The two men therefore worked together heartily in making the enterprise a conjoint effort of the British navy and New England levies. Great credit attaches to both—to Warren because he dared even to denude the Leeward Isles of naval defence in order to attack Louisbourg; to Shirley, for overcoming local difficulties and raising promptly a united force of thirteen small armed vessels, and ninety transports carrying some 4000 New Englanders. New York sent ten cannon, the rest of the middle and southern colonies nothing. Warren from Antigua met them at Canso, with a squadron which, when strengthened from home, numbered six warships.

Louisbourg occupied all but the tongue of a low triangular promontory on the south-west side of a spacious harbour, the mile-wide entrance to which was half closed by rocks and commanded by a fortified islet. Almost unassailable by ships' guns from the open, the town was difficult of access on the harbour side; for a detached work, the grand battery opposite the entrance, would rake the assailants while they struggled past the island fort. The landward approach was also difficult; for it lay across hillocks and swampy hollows. A sea beset by storms or even more baffling fogs crowned the difficulties opposed by nature which dwarfed all that the puny efforts of man could oppose. Accordingly, even the stout New England mariners doubted of the success of an enterprise, which, beginning with a landing on a surf-beaten shore, would struggle across a wide undulating waste against ramparts reared by the pupils of Vauban. Shirley, an ex-barrister, having chosen for the command on land a shrewd merchant of Kittery, William Pepperell, the scheme was characterised by a local

[1] *Corresp. of W. Shirley* (ed. Lincoln, C. H.), I, 161–77.
[2] Richmond, H. W., *The Navy in the War of* 1739–48, II, 202.

wit as having a lawyer for contriver, a merchant for general, and farmers, fishermen and mechanics as soldiers. The sarcasm flew wide of the mark; for numbers, backed by determination, energy and seamanship go far. Moreover, the garrison of Louisbourg consisted of only 560 regulars (mostly Swiss malcontents) and about 1400 raw militia; and the place lacked the needful reserves of ammunition and stores. The issue, therefore, depended on the arrival of succours from France; but already, before Warren's appearance, the New England flotilla under a Bostonian named Tyng had captured some relief vessels. When the whole British force appeared, demonstrations along the coast facilitated a bloodless landing in a cove two miles away on the south-west. The moral superiority thus won by the assailants was still more evident on 2 May when 400 of them marched behind the hills to the north-eastern horn of the harbour and fired some storehouses. The volumes of smoke spread alarm in the detachment holding the grand battery near by, which fled in panic, leaving thirty guns but half spiked and the ammunition almost intact. Thus came to pass the prophecy of Boston zealots that Providence would provide the Protestant Gideonites with arms.

Still, Pepperell's levies (though strengthened by 300 of Warren's gunners and marines), for all their firing, produced little impression on the fortress itself. Fortunately, Governor Duchambon made no determined sortie, and in general the defenders showed little enterprise, probably because they awaited succours by sea. In this they were disappointed. Warren's warships (finally numbering eleven and mounting 524 guns), with the help of Tyng's light craft, captured ten French store ships by 19 May, and on that day brought down the flag of *le Vigilant* (64). To clinch these successes Pepperell and his many amateur advisers planned a boat attack by night on the fortified islet, but rash and disorderly execution led to complete failure and the loss of 189 men (24 May). Nevertheless, the close blockade and constant bombardment by sea and land did its work, and the threat of a conjoint assault brought Duchambon to surrender (16 June). Fundamentally, this remarkable success was due to the active and harmonious co-operation of an English fleet with New England forces. Warren supplied munitions of war without which the bombardment must have ceased, and he sent on shore 300 men, not "three or four" as Parkman states. Above all, without his squadron French ships would easily have thrown in reinforcements and supplies to a fortress which, with them, could have held out indefinitely. Finally, Warren took away to France 1200 of the inhabitants, thereby long rendering innocuous that haunt of privateers. England also repaid to the contributing colonies their expenses in the expedition.[1]

[1] Richmond, ii, 209–16; Parkman, *Half Century of Conflict*, ii, 85–139; *Shirley Corresp.* i, 196–205, 222–41; Wood, W., *Louisbourg*, chap. ii.

As in the previous contests, the issue depended, not on the desultory border warfare but on the staying power of the mother countries. In Europe the last rounds were curiously equal, the French army under the Maréchal de Saxe having signally worsted the Allies in the Netherlands, while France herself was growing faint under the strangle-hold of the British navy. For on 3 May 1747 Anson, well seconded by Warren, had overpowered la Jonquière's fleet of thirteen warships and twenty-five transports bound for Canada with the aim of recapturing Louisbourg and Nova Scotia. In a running fight forty leagues north of Cape Ortegal Anson captured twelve warships and six transports, whereupon the survivors fled back to port. The blow was the more severe because in 1746 a similar expedition was shattered by a tempest. Nor was this all. On 14 October 1747 in the same waters Hawke won a victory nearly as crushing as Anson's.[1] Together they ruined the enemy's navy and mercantile marine. The scales of war being balanced, both protagonists were weary of the stalemate and sought any means of escape. London financiers prophesied bankruptcy unless peace came soon; and the French Controller of Finances declared that he saw hell open before him if the war continued.[2] Louis XV also being tired of campaigning, la Pompadour imperiously ordered the French plenipotentiary, St Severin, to bring back peace from the conference at Aix-la-Chapelle. London opinion wobbled between the pacifist propaganda of Lord Chesterfield, that Louisbourg was worthless, and the chameleonic views of Hardwicke, that everybody thought it must be given up.[3] Accordingly, at the conference the formula of the *status quo ante bellum* was discovered to be an easy and speedy means of huddling up all the disputes. The Duke of Newcastle sought to avert one of its corollaries, the restitution of Cape Breton Island to France; but St Severin insisted that in that case France must retain all her Flemish and Dutch conquests.[4] Regard for the safety of London and loyalty to our allies forbade any such solution. Consequently by the Treaty of Aix-la-Chapelle (April 1748) Austria and the Dutch Republic recovered their lost Netherland territories; and Madras and Cape Breton were restored to Great Britain and France respectively. These terms registered the dominant fact, that the issue of the war was determined, not by the desultory strifes in the colonies, but by the campaigns in Europe and the high seas.

The peace was no peace. It elicited from the justly incensed New Englanders the gibe that *their* conquest, Louisbourg, was bartered away for "a petty factory in India", whereas in reality it was bartered for Madras *plus* the Belgic and Dutch lands conquered by France. Her resentment at the loss of the Barrier fortresses, together

---

[1] Richmond, III, chap. iv.
[2] *Lord Chesterfield's Letters* (ed. of 1905), II, 866; Broglie, Duc de, *La Paix d'Aix-la-Chapelle*, 131-3, 143-6, 160.   [3] Yorke, P., *Life of Hardwicke*, I, 629, 631.
[4] Ld. Sandwich to D. of Newcastle, 12 Apr. 1748 (Sandwich Papers), quoted by Richmond, III, 240-2.

with Antwerp and Ostend, crystallised into the proverb *bête comme la paix*. Nevertheless, thanks to French solidarity and English discords, she held her own in North America; and the value which she attached to Louisbourg as the seaward bulwark of Canada appeared both in the negotiations and in the energy with which her Canadian officials pushed on the policy of encircling the English colonies. With reason, a year later, did the General Court of Massachusetts declare—"The danger on the westward is greater because of our exposed state to the eastward, upon the giving up Cape Breton to the French".[1]

(II) 1749–1760

The Peace of Aix-la-Chapelle was followed in Europe by an eight years' cessation from hostilities; in North America it achieved much less. There, it had left unchanged the causes of conflict—it had not settled the question, now rapidly becoming acute, of the ownership of the lands west of the Alleghanies and south of the Great Lakes, it had not delimited the frontier of Acadia, and though commissioners were appointed to adjust this boundary, their protracted deliberations proved completely abortive.

The Acadian question, though devoid of the vast potentialities involved in the rivalry for the Ohio valley, had in 1748 reached a more advanced stage and was the point of acutest conflict in North America. Not only was the boundary in dispute—the French claiming that the Peace of Utrecht had not ceded to Great Britain the northern portion of the modern Nova Scotia, the British seeking for "Acadia" a less restricted connotation—but the situation of the French inhabitants of the portion acknowledged as British also caused serious friction. The Canadian authorities had never ceased to teach these Acadians that their obligation to Great Britain was very limited and that they still owed obedience to France. Contention had centred upon the oath of allegiance to King George, which certain priests at the bidding of Quebec had urged the Acadians to refuse or to take only with reservations calculated to make it meaningless. To end this anomalous situation the British authorities now demanded from the Acadians an unequivocal and binding oath, though they granted recusants the right of withdrawal into French territory. At the same time it was resolved to secure the position by building a fort on the Chignecto isthmus, which connects the Nova Scotian peninsula with the mainland, and to establish a substantial British colony on Chebucto Bay, now Halifax. Opposition was actually, though ineffectually, offered to the building of Fort Lawrence on the isthmus (September 1750), and the Canadian authorities promptly established two new posts, Fort Beauséjour, immediately opposite Fort Lawrence, Fort Gaspareau on Baie Verte, incited the local Micmac Indians to

[1] *Shirley Corresp.* i, 481.

attack the British and redoubled their efforts to spread discontent among the Acadians of Nova Scotia.

The responsibility for this policy must be shared between those actually on the spot, notably the energetic but fanatical Abbé le Loutre, the authorities at Quebec, where de la Jonquière had just become governor, and the ministers at Versailles. If the latter wished to avoid an immediate renewal of the war their actions hardly suggest it: de la Jonquière's instructions from the Minister of Marine, dated 4 May 1749, emphasised the necessity of expelling the British from Oswego on Lake Ontario, and of anticipating their westward progress by securing the Ohio valley. For the moment a moderate line was enjoined as regards Acadia,[1] but before long that trouble had become acute again, and in April 1754 the General Court of Massachusetts declared that the French were fortifying themselves, breaking the peace everywhere and clearly planning the conquest of all North America.[2]

Over the Ohio meanwhile the French had no intention of giving way; indeed, Duquesne, who succeeded de la Jonquière in 1752, had definite instructions to expel from that region the British traders, 300 of whom were estimated to be frequenting it. As yet the Alleghanies marked the limit of effective British settlement, but all along the Pennsylvanian and Virginian borders backwoodsmen were steadily encroaching on the forests. Indeed the local Indians usually preferred French traders to British, mainly because the former confined themselves strictly to trade, whereas the latter tended to cultivate the country round their trading posts. As early as June 1749 de Céloron had attempted to establish French influence in this region, but the British traders had flouted his orders to them to quit the district, and not till after Duquesne's arrival did an expedition led by Marin establish two new posts, one on Lake Erie, named Fort Presqu'Île, the other on the Rivière aux Bœufs, and definitely challenge the British by capturing or driving out such traders as it encountered (summer 1753). These traders mostly belonged to the Ohio Company, formed in 1748, which had influential backing in Virginia and Maryland, and its complaints were taken up by the Governors of those provinces and of Pennsylvania. In November Governor Dinwiddie of Virginia despatched Major Washington of his militia to Fort le Bœuf with a formal protest to the commandant requiring him to evacuate "the King of Britain's territories". The British declared that the original patents for the colonies granted them all the lands westward to the ocean[3] and contended that the territory in dispute belonged to the Iroquois, whom the Treaty of Utrecht had recognised as under British protection; the French replied that France through her explorers had already established claims over the

---

[1] Minister of Marine to de la Jonquière, 12 Sept. 1750.   [2] *Shirley Corresp.* II, 47–9.
[3] Osgood, *The American Colonies in the XVIIIth Century*, IV, 287–90.

Ohio valley before the Iroquois had moved into it. Such arguments, however, were mere futilities. British and French had come into open collision in territory of which neither was in effective occupation, and force alone could decide their quarrel unless pacific tendencies at home were strong enough to restrain the local tendencies to conflict. But neither from England nor from France was any definite or deliberate policy forthcoming. Too far from the scene to exercise effective control, both Governments, while professing pacific intentions, prepared to back their claims by arms.[1] Yet Newcastle, while determined to support the colonies,[2] imagined that peace could nevertheless be maintained, and refused to proceed beyond half measures while any chance of peace remained.[3]

With neither Power prepared to give way, war was inevitable, and could not be restricted to the disputed area. The national character of the struggle could not be disguised, as in India, by representing the combatants as mere auxiliaries. It was possible, however, that the new contest might be kept free from European complications. In that case the problem before France would be how to bring her great military strength to bear against a weaker military power whose territories were not directly accessible to her troops, being everywhere separated from them by seas whose mastery was an indispensable preliminary to effective action. In war against Great Britain France could only profit by her military superiority if she could dispute the control of the seas which the British navy, as soon as it could be sufficiently expanded again from its reduced peace establishment, would probably re-assert. Should the British navy dominate the ocean waterways, the British army might well achieve more than the much larger French army, were the latter debarred by naval weakness from reaching the scene of a conflict confined to overseas possessions. It might take time, however, to secure control of the seas, and if, while control was still unsecured, France could substantially reinforce her garrisons in Canada the local situation gave her some prospects of a successful defence.

Superficially the Canadian chances hardly appeared promising. On the map the area claimed for Louis XV exceeded that which owed allegiance to George II: but effective French settlement was limited to the St Lawrence valley, hardly extending even to the shores of Lake Ontario; and while the white population of Canada was in 1755 only 55,000,[4] the British colonies contained over a million whites besides fully 250,000 negroes. But the French obeyed one ruler instead of being divided into thirteen independent communities, more inclined to quarrel than to co-operate, with particularist traditions and

[1] Waddington, R., *Louis XV et le Renversement des Alliances*, chap. i.
[2] Newcastle to Albemarle, 5 Sept. 1754, Brit. Mus. Add. MS. 32850, f. 218.
[3] Charteris, B. M., *Cumberland and the Seven Years' War*, p. 122.
[4] Parkman, F., *Montcalm and Wolfe*, I, 23.

divergent interests, devoid alike of effective military organisation and of an adequate executive. In Canada the Governor, if occasionally hampered by friction with the Intendant or the commanding officer of the troops from France, enjoyed unquestioned authority;[1] in the British colonies the Governors had little power, depending even for their salaries on local Assemblies whose exercise of the "power of the purse" was usually more rigorous than reasonable. Further, as has already appeared, the almost feudal authority of the Canadian seigneurs gave the country a semi-military tone, while the population, if poorer and more backward than that of the longest settled British colonies, was more warlike and could put into the field a larger proportion of its man power. The British colonies were more absorbed in peaceful pursuits, and though on the borders men had to live and work under arms, the French and the Indians menaced some colonies only, and the others were disposed to leave the backwoods settlers to provide their own protection. For defence, the British colonies were indifferently equipped; for offensive warfare there was no preparation. Except for some "Independent Companies" of King's troops at New York and in the Carolinas, regulars in name rather than in training, and three weak battalions garrisoning Nova Scotia and Newfoundland, the British colonies were without troops, whereas in the "Colony Regulars", mostly recruited from France and administered by the Ministry of Marine, Canada possessed some 2000 effective soldiers, while her 15,000 militiamen were better organised and more effective than their British counterparts.

Besides her better military organisation, Canada possessed certain advantages in her geography, though seriously handicapped by having no ice-free ports: she was cut off from France for at least five months in the year while the St Lawrence was frozen. Between the St Lawrence valley and the British colonies a trackless wilderness of forest-clad mountains, sparsely inhabited by Indians, interposed a formidable barrier, only to be penetrated with difficulty even where lakes and rivers provided natural arteries of communication. From New York the Hudson was navigable for schooners as far as Albany, but the route thence by Lakes George and Champlain and the Richelieu River involved much labour in portages and in road-making before it could be made practicable for an attack in force, as experience was to show. An alternative line, which branched off westward up the Mohawk River and reached Lake Ontario by Lake Oneida and the Oswego River, would establish successful attackers between the main French settlements and their western outposts, but it was a roundabout approach to Montreal and no easier. Indeed a rapid advance in force against Canada was possible only by ascending the St Lawrence, and its dangers, which the French perhaps deliberately exaggerated, had been emphasised by the ill-fated

---

[1] Parkman, *Montcalm and Wolfe*, I, 479–81.

expedition of 1711, even before Louisbourg had provided the naval forces of the defence with a good base flanking this approach.

Washington's perilous mission to the Ohio proved fruitless, and, with the Home Government's sanction, Dinwiddie decided to assert the British claims by forcible means. With considerable difficulty he extracted from the Virginian Assembly funds to equip a few hundred militia and despatched a detachment to establish a fort where the Alleghany and the Monongahela unite (April 1754). This party had barely arrived before the French appeared in force and compelled it to retire, themselves completing the unfinished works and naming them Fort Duquesne. Shortly afterwards a French reconnoitring party encountered Dinwiddie's advanced guard under Washington, and in the skirmish which followed the French were overpowered, and their leader, de Jumonville, killed. Washington, who had 300 Virginian militiamen and the South Carolina Independent Company,[1] thereupon started to fortify a post, appropriately named Fort Necessity, at Great Meadows, midway between Fort Duquesne and Wills Creek, his advanced base on the Potomac, but was attacked (3 July) by double his force. After a brief defence he had to capitulate, being allowed to retire to Wills Creek.

These skirmishes on the Monongahela had far-reaching effects. Though the fiction of peace was not discarded till May 1756, neither England nor France proposed to recede, and in November 1754 two British battalions received orders to proceed to Virginia. These orders were not kept secret and the French promptly protested again, proposing that both sides should refrain from further hostile acts. As the French were simultaneously preparing extensive counter measures, including the despatch to Canada of six battalions, or over 3000 men, and had sent orders to Quebec for the destruction of Shirley's recently established post on the Kennebeck River, it looks as if their main purpose was to gain time, especially as their expedition did not leave Brest till four months after the British reinforcements had sailed. Meanwhile Washington's defeat had enormously improved the local situation of the French, securing for them the wavering Indians of the disputed region and shaking the adhesion of the Six Nations to the British, whose traders were either murdered or forced to take refuge east of the Alleghanies.

The British plan of operations was drawn up by Cumberland,[2] though a very similar scheme was also propounded by Shirley.[3] While the troops from home were to advance on Fort Duquesne, expeditions recruited in New England and the Middle Colonies were to attack Crown Point and Niagara, and the Nova Scotian garrisons assisted by New Englanders were to dispossess the French of their forts on the Chignecto isthmus. If too ambitious and complicated for the forces and means of transport available,[4] the plan did not

[1] *Amherst Papers*, I, 12.   [2] Charteris, pp. 127–9.
[3] To Sir T. Robinson, *Shirley Corresp.* II, 144.   [4] Osgood, IV, 342.

go beyond excluding the French from the territory in dispute, and the securing of defensive positions from which, should war follow, an eventual offensive might be developed.[1] However, the battalions ordered to Virginia, the 44th and 48th Foot, mustered under 400 apiece and, though raised to 500 by drafts from other regiments before they left Cork (January 1755), only reached their establishment of 700 by enlisting recruits in Virginia. They were thus hardly homogeneous or representative of the infantry who had fought so well at Dettingen and Fontenoy. The 48th indeed had served at Lauffeldt, that second Fontenoy near Maastricht, but the 44th's warlike experiences had been confined to Prestonpans, and in the main the two battalions were new to active service. Their commander, General Edward Braddock, has, like his battalions, usually been misrepresented. A stern disciplinarian he clearly was, and something of a martinet, and in that age men of his vigorous and courageous type were usually prone to violence and brutality in speech and action; but his reputed incapacity seems to rest largely on Horace Walpole's gossip and is hardly borne out by Wolfe's description of him as "a man of sense and courage",[2] while his selection by Cumberland for a difficult and important task, the tone of his letters,[3] and the record of his ill-fated expedition, if carefully considered, justify a different judgment.

On reaching Virginia (February 1755) Braddock found the local authorities so remiss in providing transport and supplies[4] that the troops could not be collected at Wills Creek, now renamed Fort Cumberland, till well into May. There was, he wrote, "a great lack of spirit in the people to forward the expedition". Indeed, but for Benjamin Franklin[5] the horses and wagons would not even then have been forthcoming, while the provisions supplied were both deficient and bad. At Fort Cumberland Braddock was 120 miles from Fort Duquesne, he had to make his road as he advanced, to carry with him all his supplies, and this over two densely-wooded mountain ranges "of excessive height and steepness with many strong rivers and creeks to cross".[6] Starting on 10 June, he spent eight days over the first thirty miles, and though he then pushed ahead with 1400 men and ten light guns, leaving the remaining troops to bring along the bulk of the artillery and wagons, he took another three weeks to reach the Monongahela. On 9 July his advanced guard, when within six miles of Fort Duquesne, was suddenly attacked by 900 men, two-thirds being Indians. Braddock had not neglected precautions against surprise, scouts were leading the way, flankers protected the column, and the first exchange of shots was in his favour. The British

[1] Corbett, *England in the Seven Years' War*, i, 25.
[2] Willson, H. Beckles, *Life and Letters of Wolfe*, p. 274.
[3] *Amherst Papers*, vol. LXXIII, *passim*.
[4] Braddock to Robinson, 18 March and 14 April, *ibid*.
[5] *Shirley Corresp.* ii, 173, and Braddock to Robinson, 5 June (*Amherst Papers*, vol. LXXIII).
[6] Braddock to Robinson, 5 June, *Amherst Papers*, vol. LXXIII.

volleys and the fire of the vanguard's guns struck down the French commander, de Beaujeu, and sent the Canadian militia flying. Most of the Indians were following their example when the next in command, Dumas, rallied them and brought them back to support the handful of Colony Regulars who were standing their ground unflinchingly. Then before Braddock's main body could form line to meet the attack, the vanguard threw it into confusion by recoiling upon it, whereupon the two battalions, full as they were of recruits, soon lost all order. Conditions were entirely against Braddock. Firing from the cover of the trees and brushwood at the red coats which provided admirable targets, the Indians themselves offered the poorest of marks, and the gallant efforts of officers and men to close with their unseen foes only meant that the best men were the sooner shot down. Gradually the men huddled together on the road, firing ineffectively and at random into the forest. For the two hours that their ammunition lasted the ineffectual resistance continued; finally the survivors gave way and fled in disorder. Braddock, who had exposed himself recklessly and had five horses killed under him, fell mortally wounded, of ninety officers over two-thirds went down, and barely 500 survivors rejoined the rear column. It, to make matters worse, abandoned guns, ammunition and supplies, and, to Dinwiddie's consternation,[1] recoiled hastily to Fort Cumberland, sixty miles away. This retreat left the frontiers of Virginia, Pennsylvania and Maryland exposed to the Indians, who swooped triumphantly down on the backwoods settlements, doing tremendous destruction and committing terrible outrages.[2] Washington, to whom the defence of the frontier was entrusted, had only 1000 untrained and undisciplined militia, and could offer no effective resistance to these savages.[3]

Braddock's defeat naturally caused widespread dismay in the British colonies and corresponding elation in Canada, nor did success elsewhere compensate for it. Shirley's advance against Niagara was so much delayed by troubles over transport and supplies that he reached his advanced base at Oswego late in August, long after the French, who had learnt his designs from Braddock's captured papers, had strongly reinforced their western posts. He could merely strengthen the defences of Oswego, and, leaving 700 men in garrison, returned to Albany. His expedition was to have been covered by an advance against Crown Point of 6000 New England militia under Sir William Johnson, the sole superintendent of the Six Nations, over whom he enjoyed a remarkable influence. Johnson managed to convey his raw and ill-organised levies to the bend of the Hudson forty miles above Albany, where less than twenty miles of land separate its waterway from Lake George. But to carry guns and stores over this short distance was infinitely harder, and it was 27 August before about 2500 men reached Lake George

[1] Osgood, IV, 351.   [2] *Dinwiddie Correspondence*, II, 118 ff.   [3] *Ibid.* II, and Osgood, IV, 356.

and, encamping there, began collecting boats and stores for an advance down the lake. They were soon rudely interrupted by Baron Dieskau, a Saxon officer in the French service, who had just arrived from France with reinforcements and had hastened to Ticonderoga, where the outfall from Lake George flows into Lake Champlain, with two of his battalions from France and all the available Colony Regulars and militia. From Ticonderoga he pushed on with 1500 men, mainly Canadians and Indians, hoping to effect a surprise. Johnson, however, having received warning, despatched 1000 men to meet him. But the New Englanders, less careful than Braddock of protection on the march, blundered into an ambush and were quickly sent flying back. Dieskau pressed on against Johnson's camp, but his Indians and Canadians would not attempt to storm its rough defences, and Johnson managed to rally his men. Then, having gained superiority in a prolonged fire-fight, thanks largely to his artillery, he sallied out and routed his enemies, Dieskau himself being taken (8 September). On hearing the news Shirley optimistically urged a dash at Ticonderoga, but Johnson, who had never had more than two weeks' provisions in hand,[1] realised that his men were quite unfit for the offensive, even if he could have transported them to Ticonderoga or maintained them there. Accordingly, after erecting and garrisoning a fort, named William Henry, on the shore of Lake George, he had to let the rest of his men disperse to their homes. Dieskau's defeat had redeemed Johnson's operations from total failure, but the French hold on Lake Champlain was unshaken.

Only in Acadia had the British been successful. There Monckton with 2000 New Englanders and the regulars of the Nova Scotian garrisons had easily reduced the feebly defended Forts Beauséjour (16 June) and Gaspareau. This success had been followed by the famous expulsion of the Acadians, for which the local authorities had long been anxious. The step may be justified as a political and military necessity and certainly the Acadians' demand to be allowed to remain neutral was quite inadmissible.[2] For the hardships suffered by the Acadians the main responsibility must rest with those French officials and priests who had systematically endeavoured by underhand measures to nullify the cession of Acadia to Great Britain, thereby placing the unfortunate Acadians in an ambiguous position leading inevitably to their expulsion.

Hostilities meanwhile had not been confined to the North American continent. When the French preparations to reinforce Canada had become known in England, Newcastle's ministry, while flinching from Cumberland's policy of open war,[3] took the extraordinary step of despatching a squadron under Boscawen (27 April) to the American

[1] Osgood, iv, 366.
[2] Doughty, *The Acadian Exiles*; Parkman, *Montcalm and Wolfe*, vol. i, chap. viii.
[3] Charteris, chap. xv.

coast to intercept the French ships and prevent them from landing their troops in Nova Scotia or proceeding to Quebec. However, in the fogs and rainstorms of the Newfoundland waters nearly the whole French squadron evaded interception and safely reached either Louisbourg or Quebec. Two ships only, the *Alcide* and the *Lys*, carrying about a tenth of the reinforcements, were taken (10 June). Boscawen, as Hardwicke wrote to Newcastle, had done "too much or too little". Only complete success, the capture of all the six battalions which were to be the mainstay of the defence of Canada for the next five years, could have redeemed Newcastle's attempt to act as if the maxim "No peace beyond the Line" still applied to North America. One result of this encounter was the recall (23 July) of the French ambassador, Mirepoix, though negotiations still continued and war was not declared till May 1756; another, the refusal of the Dutch to fulfil their treaty obligations when war did break out, on the plea that the British were the aggressors.

For 1756 the British proposed to renew the attacks by Lakes Ontario and Champlain, while if Pennsylvania and Virginia could provide the necessary forces, Fort Duquesne might again be assailed. But Newcastle, alarmed by French threats of invasion, had despatched only two battalions as reinforcements. Lord Loudoun, the new Commander-in-Chief, did not arrive till late in July, and Abercromby, his second in command, who preceded him, was not equal to organising an effective force out of the untrained and undisciplined mob which was collected between Albany and Fort William Henry without transport, proper administrative services or sanitary arrangements.[1] No advance on Ticonderoga could be attempted, and in the sporadic encounters between reconnoitring parties to which both sides confined themselves the French fared best. Still, they merely strengthened their position on Lake Champlain and made no effort to profit by their chances in an offensive. Elsewhere they were active enough. In May a squadron under de Beaussier, which the British had failed to intercept, had reached Quebec, bringing a new Commander-in-Chief, capable and of high character, the Marquis de Montcalm, and two fresh battalions. Montcalm was soon at variance with the Governor-General, de Vaudreuil, who, if not actually concerned in the rampant corruption which disgraced the Canadian administration, made no effort to suppress it, but this friction did not prevent Montcalm from descending in August with three battalions of regulars, 1000 Canadians and many Indians upon Oswego, to the capture of which post Vaudreuil attached special importance as it was "the direct cause of all the troubles that have overtaken the Colony".[2]

Strategically a menace to the French communications with the west, Oswego had been successfully reinforced and supplied earlier in the year by an expedition under Bradstreet, an energetic colonial

[1] *Shirley Correspondence*, II, and Osgood, IV, 388 ff. [2] Doughty, *Siege of Quebec*, I, 160.

officer whom Wolfe described as "an extraordinary man for expeditions".[1] Even so, the post was not strong and its garrison consisted mainly of invalids or half-trained troops; its wooden stockades could offer only a feeble resistance to the siege-train which Montcalm's flotilla had enabled him to transport to the spot, and on 14 August it surrendered after a four days' siege. It was a serious blow to British prestige,[2] though Montcalm did nothing to follow up his success. However, as Colonel Webb, who was on his way to reinforce Oswego, promptly retired to Albany on hearing the news, destroying two forts and obstructing the navigation of the Mohawk River, the Mohawk-Oswego line of attack on Canada was virtually put out of action. In the west Fort Duquesne had been left unmolested, for Pennsylvania and Virginia were not even able to defend their frontiers effectively against the Indians and Canadian rangers, though a line of forts and blockhouses nearly 500 miles long was constructed along the borders from Virginia to New York.[3] Altogether, then, 1756 had gone badly for the British.

However, before another campaign opened Pitt's advent to office (November 1756) improved the prospects substantially. If his strategy was not always impeccable and if he has often been credited with other men's work, like Anson's administrative reforms, he certainly infused into the conduct of the war a vigour hitherto lacking. Seven battalions, escorted by fifteen sail of the line under Admiral Holbourne, were promptly (February) ordered to America,[4] there to unite with Loudoun who could collect 5000 men more for an attack on Louisbourg. This attack, the necessary prelude to a blow at Quebec, was the main feature of Pitt's plan, which coincided in all essentials with that already prepared by Loudoun.[5] Meanwhile, three regular battalions and a large body of provincials under Webb were left to guard the northern frontier, where there had been constant skirmishes all through the spring and early summer, notably an attempted surprise of Fort William Henry, which the garrison, mainly the survivors of the 44th Foot, had successfully repulsed.

Unfortunately for Loudoun adverse winds[6] detained the reinforcements at Cork till 8 May, and it was 9 July before they reached Halifax: moreover the British watch on the French naval bases was not yet sufficiently well established to prevent three separate French squadrons from escaping and uniting at Louisbourg[7] a force stronger than Holbourne's.[8] In face of this French superiority at sea Loudoun's transports could not proceed beyond Halifax and the

[1] Willson, H. Beckles, *Life and Letters of Wolfe*, p. 369.
[2] Kimball, G., *Corresp. of Pitt with colonial Governors*, I, 162.
[3] Shirley to Robinson, 8 March 1756, *Amherst Papers*, vol. LXXIII.
[4] Knox, *Journal of the Campaigns in N. America*, I, 16.
[5] Kimball, I, 53.   [6] Knox, I, 17.
[7] Kimball, I, 71.   [8] Knox, I, 63.

British strategy was completely foiled.[1] Holbourne did, however, establish a watch which kept the French fleet fixed at Louisbourg, and maintained the watch till in September a violent gale crippled half his ships[2] and allowed the French to slip out and regain Brest, though too late to interfere with the first of Pitt's offensive measures against France, the abortive Rochefort expedition. But in the meantime two new battalions with 1100 drafts for the original six had evaded the British efforts to intercept them and had reached Canada in safety.[3]

In Loudoun's absence from the frontier Montcalm had taken the offensive with success. Concentrating at Ticonderoga his six regular battalions, the Colony Regulars, 3000 militia and nearly 2000 Indians, he advanced up Lake George at the end of July. Though held by over 2000 men, two-thirds provincial militia, Fort William Henry proved an easy prey.[4] Its defences were not calculated to resist the heavy artillery Montcalm's flotilla had brought up, and on 9 August it surrendered, the garrison being promised a safe-conduct to Fort Edward, though they might not serve again until exchanged. Unluckily for Montcalm's reputation and for the unfortunate garrison, its departure was followed by an Indian attack upon the defenceless column and a horrible massacre followed in which several hundreds were killed or carried off. Once the attack started Montcalm and many other French officers did their best to stop it, but he had foreseen its likelihood[5] and should have taken more adequate precautions. He had been in Canada long enough to know what to expect of the Indians, not long enough to tolerate and even condone their conduct, as did some of the Canadian authorities.[6]

Could Montcalm have followed up his success by advancing against Fort Edward, as Vaudreuil wished,[7] he would have found it weakly held. But the water-carriage which had brought his heavy artillery to Fort William Henry would no longer serve him, as Burgoyne was to discover twenty years later; the Canadians melted away to gather their harvest, the Indians retired home with their spoils, provisions and transport were lacking,[8] and Loudoun, after reinforcing Nova Scotia so as to secure that province against attack from Louisbourg,[9] hastened back to the Hudson with half his force.[10] Montcalm, therefore, could only demolish Fort William Henry and retire to Ticonderoga. He had had the best of the campaign but had not altered the strategical situation appreciably. Indeed had the naval situation, for which Loudoun could not be held responsible, only allowed that luckless commander to carry out his orders, he might have more than balanced Montcalm's success.

[1] Knox, I, 43.   [2] Ibid. I, 101; Kimball, I, 114–16.
[3] Doughty, I, 213.   [4] Knox, I, 67 ff.
[5] Paris Documents, x, 614, quoted in Doughty, I, 189.
[6] Parkman, I, 525–9.   [7] Paris Documents, x, 660.
[8] Ibid. x, 631.   [9] Knox, II, 594.   [10] Ibid. I, 44.

To master the salt-water route to Canada was the soundest strategy, and Pitt's plan for 1758, drafted on 30 December 1757,[1] virtually repeated the scheme for the previous year. But instead of adopting the defensive on the Hudson, Ticonderoga was to be attacked by Abercromby, who now succeeded Loudoun, with 15,000 men, 9000 of them provincials, while Amherst tackled Louisbourg with 12,000, nearly all regulars, one of his three infantry brigadiers being James Wolfe of the 67th Foot. Subsidiary expeditions under Bradstreet and Forbes, consisting mainly of provincials, were to renew the attempts against Lake Ontario and Fort Duquesne. Moreover, while Pitt had provided substantial reinforcements, the new energy and order which Anson had infused into British naval strategy and administration were being felt, and the French efforts to reinforce Canada were successfully frustrated. De la Clue, with the Toulon fleet, trying to slip through the Straits, was driven into Cartagena, Duquesne's attempt to relieve him was defeated by Osborne (February 1758), and Hawke swooped down upon a large convoy lying in Aix Roads with 3000 troops on board and destined for Canada, and put it and its escort out of action (5 April). A few vessels slipped through, singly or in small parties, bringing two more battalions for Louisbourg and some supplies; but effectually Canada was isolated.[2] This was the more serious because the colony was not as yet self-supporting as regards supplies, and both garrison and civil population had to endure considerable hardships.

Amherst and his naval colleague, Boscawen, were considerably delayed in crossing the Atlantic with the reinforcements from England. The admiral reached Halifax only on 9 May and it was 2 June before the fleet and convoy were off Louisbourg and bad weather and a heavy surf then caused further delays.[3] The main difficulty of the attack on Louisbourg was to get the troops landed. Wolfe wanted to land at Miré and Laurembec, some way north-east of the town, under cover of demonstrations off the harbour mouth and in Gabarus Bay, just west of it,[4] and was not pleased at Amherst's decision to try to land the whole force in face of opposition in Gabarus Bay where the French were strongly posted. The attempt, "rash and ill-advised" though Wolfe pronounced it,[5] proved successful (8 June), despite the surf and the French. Two boats of Wolfe's division reached the shore at a point where projecting rocks provided some cover, whereupon Wolfe, promptly directing the rest to the spot, landed and stormed a couple of batteries. The defenders, taken by surprise, offered only a feeble resistance, and streamed back to Louisbourg in disorder.[6] For some days afterwards the high winds and "the great swell upon this coast"[7] interrupted communication with the fleet and

---

[1] Kimball, I, 133–53.   [2] Corbett, vol. I, chaps. xi–xiii.   [3] Knox, I, 215.
[4] Stopford Sackville MSS. II, 259.   [5] Willson, H. Beckles, p. 384.
[6] Knox, I, 243, III, 99; Doughty, I, 105–7.   [7] Knox, I, 184.

delayed the landing of the besiegers' artillery, but the first difficulty
had been overcome at the cost of only about one hundred casualties.
Closely blockaded by Boscawen, and with Amherst's siege operations
progressing steadily, Louisbourg was soon hard pressed. Drucour,
the Governor, had over 3000 French and Canadian regulars in
garrison, besides the crews of six ships of the line and seven frigates.
This squadron had failed to get away before the blockade was
established, and though a few vessels succeeded in escaping, the
majority, at Drucour's request,[1] remained to assist in the defence,
four of them being sunk on 29 June, and two more soon after, to block
the entrance to the harbour.

The preparations for the attack were steadily pushed on, but they
involved "an incredible deal of labour".[2] Not only had batteries to
be thrown up, fascines and other materials constructed and the camp
fortified for protection against attack by Canadian rangers and Indians,
but roads had to be made to connect up the lines with the landing-
places before the artillery could get forward.[3] This was perhaps "the
most painful of our labours",[4] and was largely responsible for the
apparent slowness of the operations, which Wolfe criticised severely,[5]
condemning the engineers as "ignorant and inexperienced" and
the conduct of affairs as slow and cautious.[6] His active and impatient
spirit hardly made sufficient allowances for the necessary delays in
landing stores and constructing roads, and Amherst, who was "indefatigable in visiting our outposts and batteries" and "in concerting
plans by which he can accelerate the siege",[7] did not do badly to
get his siege works begun by 23 June and his bombardment started
by 19 July.[8] Boscawen co-operated wholeheartedly, putting his
marines at Amherst's disposal and landing seamen to assist in forwarding the siege works. Wolfe wrote, "He is no bad *fantassin* himself
and an excellent back-hand at a siege".[9]

Wolfe himself was extremely active. On 12 June he had pushed
round to the east of the harbour with a strong detachment of picked
troops and had established a battery on Lighthouse Point. This opened
fire a week later against Goat Island in the middle of the entrance,
and effectually silenced its defences (25 June).[10] He carried out
several other successful minor enterprises and took his full share in
the work of the trenches, being prominent in repulsing several sorties
on which Drucour ventured[11] without, however, achieving much
success or appreciably retarding the progress of the siege. The
besiegers' guns, once the bombardment was opened, soon made an
impression on the defences which, although reputed the strongest
in America, were in several respects defective. Drucour held out,
however, till a practicable breach had been effected and an assault

[1] Knox, I, 219, III, 102.   [2] *Ibid*. I, 245.   [3] *Ibid*. III, 12.
[4] *Ibid*. I, 247.   [5] Stopford Sackville MSS. II, 265.
[6] Wright, *Life of Wolfe*, p. 448.   [7] Knox, I, 247.   [8] *Ibid*. III, 15.
[9] Stopford Sackville MSS. II, 264.   [10] Knox, I, 245.   [11] *Ibid*. I, 246.

was on the point of being delivered. Meanwhile (25 July) boats from Boscawen's fleet entered the harbour and captured or destroyed the remaining ships of the line, which had escaped destruction when four days earlier the besiegers' guns had set the others on fire. On 26 July Drucour surrendered unconditionally[1] with over 5500 men.[2]

"The Gibraltar of North America" had cost Amherst and Boscawen 600 casualties, but the price was not reckoned high. Wolfe urged that the successful besiegers should push on at once against Quebec, which indeed had been the original plan.[3] Amherst favoured the idea, for Quebec was but lightly held, most of the French troops being with Montcalm on Lake Champlain, but the time taken on the passage out and Drucour's protracted defence had made it rather late for so considerable an undertaking, and naval opinion was against the venture.[4] The decisive reason, however, was that Amherst with half his force was called off to the Hudson where the great advance had failed lamentably.

The colonies had responded far better than before, not only to the call for troops but to the demands for transport and supplies, though Abercromby found his preparations retarded by the want of arms and of tents.[5] However, when he advanced from Albany at the end of June he had the largest force ever collected in America, and an ample supply of boats awaited him on Lake George, the energetic Bradstreet having constructed them near the site of Fort William Henry. Montcalm meanwhile had concentrated his battalions from France at Ticonderoga with some hundreds of Colony Regulars and militia—a counter-stroke from Oswego against Abercromby's communications, which Vaudreuil had planned, having been abandoned just in time to let Lévis reach Ticonderoga before the British appeared.

With 15,000 men against under 5000 Abercromby's success should have been certain, but on the day (6 July) that his troops landed above the rapids which connect the two lakes, Lord Howe, whom Wolfe reckoned "the best officer in the British Army" and in whom the whole force had unbounded confidence, was killed in an advance-guard skirmish. Without him Abercromby was helpless. He fell back to his landing-place, forgoing all chance of a *coup de main* and giving Montcalm time to complete the construction of a formidable abattis of felled trees in front of his position. But though impregnable to infantry this barrier could not have resisted the heavy artillery Abercromby had left with his boats. Howe might have induced him to postpone the assault while guns were being fetched, but on 8 July Abercromby, alarmed by reports, exaggerated as it proved, that large French reinforcements were at hand,[6] hurled his men at the abattis and persisted in renewed attacks, unenlightened by the bloody

---

[1] Doughty, I, 122.   [2] Kimball, I, 291–3, 302–7.
[3] Willson, H. Beckles, p. 393.   [4] *Ibid.* pp. 390, 393.
[5] Abercromby to Pitt, 22 May 1758, *Amherst Papers*, vol. LXXIII.
[6] *Ibid.* LXXIII, 171 ff.

repulse of the first assault. For six hours the unavailing efforts continued till nearly a third of his 6000 regulars had fallen and the survivors were completely exhausted.[1] That, when Abercromby at last stopped the fruitless slaughter, the shattered battalions retired in disorder is hardly surprising. Even so, he had nearly treble Montcalm's force, and his superior artillery might have reversed the verdict had he undertaken systematic siege operations, as Montcalm expected, but he retired as precipitately as he had attacked and spent the rest of the summer inactive at the southern end of Lake George, not even resuming the offensive after Amherst had reinforced him early in October.[2] Montcalm, however, despite lectures from Vaudreuil on the desirability of taking the offensive,[3] was too weak to counter-attack even when reinforced by 3000 Canadians and Indians; indeed, in face of the possibility of a renewal of the attack, he could make no detachments to interfere with Bradstreet and Forbes.

Bradstreet, despatched, not without misgivings, by Abercromby late in July with 3000 men, only 200 of them regulars, reached Oswego by the Mohawk route on 22 August. Though sickness and desertion[4] reduced his force seriously, he was strong enough to cross the lake to Frontenac, the French post on the site of the modern Kingston. Frontenac had been denuded of troops to reinforce Ticonderoga and had to surrender (27 August) before help could arrive from Montreal. Bradstreet, however, made no attempt to retain the position, or to attack Niagara, which the fall of Frontenac had isolated. He did not even re-establish a post at Oswego, though he carried off an immense booty and destroyed not only the fortifications but the flotilla of armed vessels with which the French had controlled the lake. As a raid, for it was no more, his expedition fully merited Wolfe's verdict, "Frontenac is a great stroke. An offensive, daring kind of war will awe the Indians and ruin the French".[5]

An additional set-off to Abercromby's defeat was contributed by the success of Forbes. That officer, a Scottish soldier of real capacity, had under him a newly-raised battalion of Highlanders, another of the "Royal Americans", four battalions of whom had been recently levied among the German settlers in Pennsylvania, and 4000 provincials, whom he described as "an extream bad collection of broken innkeepers, horse jockeys and Indian traders".[6] Though delayed by the remissness of the provincial authorities in providing transport and stores, and further retarded by having to make a new, though shorter, road north of Braddock's, he proceeded methodically, making each stage good with fortified posts and establishing magazines. Despite "incredible difficulties",[7] his own ill-health, a disastrous

---

[1] Knox, I, 189–95.   [2] *Amherst Papers*, LXXIII, 195.   [3] Doughty, I, 240.
[4] *Amherst Papers*, LXXIII, 184.   [5] Willson, H. Beckles, p. 397.
[6] Kimball, I, 312.   [7] Knox, I, 270.

check to his advance-guard under Major Grant, who displayed more enterprise than discretion (14 September), and the rains of an abnormally wet autumn, he persevered in his "painful campaign"[1] and on 23 November had the satisfaction of finding Fort Duquesne evacuated. His diligence in road-making allowed of the retention of the post, and though he returned to Philadelphia only to die (March 1759) he had achieved a success more solid than Bradstreet's. The fall of Fort Duquesne was an object lesson to the local Indians, three tribes of whom had already deserted the French cause, and the long-vexed Pennsylvanian and Virginian frontiers soon ceased to be troubled.

Though Abercromby's failure had largely neutralised Amherst's success, 1758 had seen the tide turn. The St Lawrence route was uncovered, Acadia was definitely secured for the British,[2] the hold of the French on the Ohio valley was virtually gone and their communications with the west endangered. If the citadel still held out, important outworks had fallen, and in face of the stricter blockade now established over the French ports substantial assistance from France was unlikely to reach the besieged colony. Indeed the French authorities, recognising the difficulty of evading the British squadrons, contented themselves with risking at sea only very few transports and store ships. They concentrated their efforts rather on Choiseul's scheme for invading England, which was to be foiled by the vigilance of Boscawen and Hawke and the culminating triumphs of Lagos and Quiberon. That the troops allotted to the invasion might have turned the scale in the Minden campaign and thereby presented Choiseul with Hanover as a tangible set-off against colonial losses may be admitted; it does not detract however from the general soundness of Choiseul's conception of a direct blow at his enemy's heart, even if this aim was over ambitious for the naval force available.

For the next campaign the plan of 1758 was to be renewed.[3] Amherst with 6000 regulars and over 5000 provincials[4] was to take the Lake Champlain route. Prideaux with three regular battalions and 2500 New Yorkers was to follow the Mohawk line, re-establish Oswego, capture Niagara and threaten Montreal from upstream. Wolfe with 12,000 men, almost entirely regulars, was to be escorted up the St Lawrence to Quebec by a powerful fleet under Saunders, which, besides transporting the expedition and its stores to its goal, would co-operate with its guns in the army's operations.

Wolfe's selection for this command—he was but a colonel and received local rank as major-general for the expedition only—was greatly to Pitt's credit, even if he was not alone in recognising Wolfe's merits. Good services in Scotland and on the continent as a junior officer had long before this earned Wolfe the approval of Cumberland, and his appointment to the command had been requested by

[1] Knox, I, 270. [2] *Ibid.* II, 594. [3] Kimball, I, 414-24. [4] Knox, I, 474.

three of the ablest colonels then serving in America, Monckton, Murray and Burton.[1] In Saunders he had a capable colleague, one of Anson's "Centurions", whose cordial co-operation he was to find invaluable. Neither Vaudreuil nor Montcalm had anticipated a serious attack on Quebec by the St Lawrence, believing that its difficult navigation with its strong current and tortuous channels put that out of the question; one reach in particular, known as "the Traverse", was reckoned impracticable for ships of any size. Unluckily, before Saunders could reach American waters, all chance of effecting a surprise had been lost. Whereas Durell, the naval commander on the station, had orders to be off the St Lawrence directly navigation opened, he had waited at Halifax on account of the ice, which was unusually thick and late,[2] and, to Wolfe's disappointment,[3] Saunders found him still there on 30 April. In the meantime a convoy from France, in all three frigates and seventeen store ships,[4] had done what Durell believed impossible,[5] and slipping past had ascended the St Lawrence unhindered, bringing not only supplies and 350 reinforcements but timely warning of the intended attack. Had Durell only intercepted this convoy Quebec might have been but ill-prepared when, on 26 June, Saunders, three weeks after leaving Louisbourg, anchored below the town. He had left his larger ships of the line below the Traverse, but the other warships and all the transports had surmounted the famous difficulties of the approach.[6]

To have reached Quebec without losing a single vessel was an astonishing triumph for Saunders and his navigating officers, among them James Cook, the future explorer; and the French were surprised and disheartened by their success.[7] But it was one thing for the navy to bring Wolfe within striking distance of Quebec and to give him mobility and a choice of points to attack, another thing to take Quebec. For miles upstream steep cliffs seemed to preclude a landing, even if the ships could run the gauntlet of the batteries which swept the narrows opposite the town. For six miles downstream, on the bank where Wolfe had intended to land,[8] Montcalm had constructed entrenchments, known as the Beauport lines,[9] which defied the attackers to land above the Montmorency River, while if they landed below it and succeeded in forcing its extremely difficult passage, an advance on Quebec through the forests in face of Montcalm's troops would be a most hazardous undertaking.

Montcalm's force, if not all equal to Wolfe's in quality, outnumbered it considerably. He had five battalions of French regulars, 1200 Colony Regulars, 1200 men from the ships, 1000 Indians and several thousands of militia, probably 14,000 all told.[10] Pitt had not

---

[1] Cal. St. Pap. Col. vol. LXXVI.   [2] Townshend's Journal in Doughty, v, 229.
[3] Ibid. VI, 52.   [4] Kimball, II, 162.   [5] Amherst Papers, vol. XLII.
[6] Knox, I, 360 ff. Also Wood, W., Logs of the Conquest of Canada.
[7] Doughty, II, 61.   [8] Ibid. II, 65.
[9] Knox, I, 378.   [10] Doughty, II, 52.

provided the full force Wolfe had asked for, and as some units originally allotted to the expedition could not be spared from the West Indies, while others were much under establishment, the winter's wastage not having been made good from home,[1] Wolfe was 3400 short of the 12,000 men on whom Pitt had reckoned.[2] He could count on some assistance from the marines and sailors of the fleet and from Saunders' guns, but even so, his force was hardly adequate to its difficult problem, especially as the advantages of position were against him. True, with the naval forces "masters of the river",[3] Wolfe could reckon on a superior mobility which would allow him to vary his point of attack freely. Montcalm, however, enjoyed the defender's trump card, that it would be enough for him to maintain the *status quo*, which in the circumstances was much easier than to alter it. As Wolfe wrote, "The enemy puts nothing to risk and... has shut himself up in inaccessible entrenchments so that I can't get at him without spilling a torrent of blood".[4]

After occupying the Île d'Orléans just below Quebec (27 June) while Saunders successfully beat off a midnight attack (28/29 June) by fireships, Wolfe proceeded, largely at Saunders's instance,[5] to seize Point Lévis also. This point, which faced Quebec and was only 1200 yards from its walls, was secured by Monckton's brigade, after some resistance from a large body of Canadians and Indians.[6] The fleet was thus provided with a more satisfactory anchorage,[7] and from Point Lévis Quebec could be bombarded, but though the bombardment, which was opened on 12 July,[8] inflicted considerable damage on the lower city, it could not solve Wolfe's main difficulty or bring the attackers nearer to the walls.

The problem indeed was formidable. Wolfe in his Journal (3 July) speaks of consultations with the admiral after a reconnaissance above Point Lévis and of resolving to land above the town if possible. No such attempt, however, was made, and on 9 July a brigade of Townshend, who had come out with Saunders, was landed below the Montmorency, where a camp was entrenched and batteries erected to enfilade the left of the Beauport lines.[9] But the Montmorency was in a deep gorge and for some miles inland there was no practicable passage, and it soon became evident that the road to Quebec did not lie that way. On the night of 18/19 July, however, a fifty-gun ship and five smaller vessels successfully passed the "Narrows", despite heavy fire from the town batteries.[10] This offered a prospect of effecting a landing above Quebec, but reconnaissance showed the enemy to be on the alert and well prepared, while Wolfe feared that it might be difficult to reinforce the troops first landed before the

[1] Wolfe to Whitmore in Doughty, VI, 38. [2] Knox, I, 358–60.
[3] Doughty, II, 54. [4] Willson, H. Beckles, p. 469. [5] Knox, I, 386, II, 61.
[6] *Ibid.* I, 393. [7] Wolfe's despatch of 2 Sept. in Doughty, II, 252.
[8] Knox, I, 415. [9] Townshend Papers in Doughty, V, 241 ff. [10] Knox, I, 429.

enemy's whole force could be upon them.[1] However, the presence of these ships above Quebec threatened Montcalm's communications and compelled him to detach troops up-river to guard possible landing-places.

Wolfe meanwhile, abandoning the idea of a landing above Quebec, had resolved upon attacking the left of the Beauport lines, formidable as that position was. He hoped to entice the French from their en-trenchments by capturing a detached redoubt near the water's edge which appeared to be out of supporting distance of the lines. Half Monckton's brigade from Point Lévis was to land from boats on the beach in front directly the tide was low enough for Townshend's men from the Montmorency camp to ford that river near its mouth. Wolfe apparently hoped that Montcalm would leave his entrench-ments to defend the detached redoubt,[2] and calculated on sub-stantial assistance from the fire of Townshend's guns from across the river,[3] but it is clear that the attack was a hazardous venture (31 July).[4] Actually, after some delays and difficulties,[5] the first boat-loads landed successfully, whereupon the French evacuated the redoubt, but while Townshend's brigade was wading the Montmorency, and before all Monckton's men had landed, the picked battalion of massed Grenadier companies suddenly and unaccountably dashed forward up the steep slope against the lines. One other battalion followed, but the headlong folly of this partial and premature attack met with the inevitable result. Swept down by the "repeated heavy fire of the enemy"[6] the Grenadiers were thrust back with over 400 casualties. Montcalm did not venture the counter-attack which the situation seemed to invite, possibly because a violent thunderstorm had wetted the ammunition of both sides, and his inactivity allowed Wolfe to withdraw, much disheartened, not merely at the failure and the heavy losses but at the undisciplined rashness of his best troops.[7]

Wolfe's repulse was specially welcome to Montcalm, who was receiving bad news from other quarters. Prideaux had reached Oswego by the middle of June and, after rebuilding the fort, had started for Niagara on 1 July. Arriving on 6 July he opened siege operations, and though he himself was killed, Johnson, his successor, cleverly ambushed and routed (24 July) a relieving force of 1200 men under de Ligneris, collected from posts further west.[8] On the following day Niagara capitulated, the survivors of the relieving force retiring impotently to Detroit, after burning several other forts. The reduction of Niagara, which the French regarded as "the key to all these inland seas",[9] coupled with Haldimand's defeat of a French attack on Oswego,[10] left the British masters of the chief lakes,

[1] Wolfe's despatch of 2 Sept., cf. Knox, II, 64.   [2] Ibid. II, 65.   [3] Doughty, II, 150.
[4] Wolfe to Saunders, ibid. II, 151.   [5] Knox, II, 66.   [6] Ibid. I, 452.
[7] Ibid. I, 449–57; Doughty, II, 148–51, IV, 189–90, 286–7, V, 254–5; Hist. MSS. Comm. Rep. XI, App. 4.   [8] Amherst's letter to Wolfe in Doughty, VI, 40; Knox, II, 183.
[9] Knox, II, 191.   [10] Ibid. I, 495.

and contributed substantially to the success of Stanwix's efforts to secure the country between Lake Erie and the Ohio.[1]

Amherst meanwhile had moved from Fort Edward to Lake George on 21 June, but had had to spend another month in bringing forward supplies, preparing bateaux, and training his provincial troops,[2] and it was 21 July before he could embark for Ticonderoga. Bourlamaque, who was commanding on Lake Champlain, had three French regular battalions, brought up by Canadians to 3000,[3] and his orders were to delay Amherst as long as possible without committing himself to a definite stand. He slipped away therefore from Ticonderoga directly Amherst started siege operations (26 July)[4] and evacuating Crown Point (4 August) also retired down the lake to the Île aux Noix. Could Amherst have followed at once he might well have reached Montreal before August was out, but "to the unspeakable mortification of the General and the Army",[5] some French sloops controlled Lake Champlain:[6] two months were spent in constructing vessels to oppose them, and when at last they had been disposed of,[7] it was too late to operate against Île aux Noix. All Amherst had done to help Wolfe was to keep Bourlamaque's regulars away from Quebec. It is easy to condemn his slowness, but without a road or the free use of the waterway of the lake he could not advance.[8] He is more open to criticism for not having provided himself with gunboats originally; he may well have calculated on being detained some weeks before Ticonderoga and Crown Point, whose evacuation was unexpected. But the delay in his advance fully justified Gage, now in command on Lake Ontario, in not risking an advance on Montreal, which seemed to lie open to him. To do so with the other converging forces held up would have invited a concentration against him.

Thus neither from the Great Lakes nor from Lake Champlain was a solution of the deadlock at Quebec likely to be forthcoming; if Pitt's plan was to be redeemed from failure, Wolfe must do something, and that without delay, for time was beginning to run short. Saunders could not remain indefinitely in the St Lawrence: his ships must be clear away before winter set in. Yet, as Wolfe wrote on 2 September, "we have almost the whole force of Canada to oppose",[9] and failure stared him in the face. Anxiety and strain were telling on his enfeebled constitution and for days he was prostrated through illness. All through August there had been sporadic fighting, with constant skirmishes;[10] Quebec was intermittently bombarded and suffered still more damage.[11] The right bank was raided and ruthlessly swept bare of supplies, while Murray with 1200 men was conveyed some distance up-river by the ships already above Quebec

---

[1] Knox, II, 198 ff.
[2] *Ibid.* I, 477–81. [3] *Ibid.* II, 69. [4] *Ibid.* I, 508.
[5] *Ibid.* II, 194. [6] *Ibid.* I, 509–11. [7] *Ibid.* II, 196.
[8] Amherst's Journals in Knox, III, 20–68. [9] Doughty, II, 253.
[10] Knox, II, 70. [11] Doughty, II, 174.

and made several descents on the left bank, notably at Deschambeau.[1] Thereon Montcalm, now increasingly dependent for supplies on his communications with the interior, despatched 1500 men under Bougainville to Cap Rouge, seven miles upstream, and the most likely spot for the descent in force which he anticipated. He had already, on hearing about Niagara, sent Lévis to Montreal with 1000 men, and as many of the militia departed, with or without leave, to gather in the harvest, the force at Quebec was reduced by fully a third. Casualties and disease had also thinned Wolfe's ranks and by 1 September his effectives numbered only 6000.[2]

Just after Murray's return from up-river (27 August) Wolfe requested his brigadiers' advice on the course to be pursued. He himself propounded three alternative plans, all involving an attack on the Beauport lines.[3] The brigadiers' reply[4] suggested a descent above Quebec, somewhere near Pointe aux Trembles, where the roads leading westward from Quebec unite, in order to intervene between Montcalm and his supplies. Such a move might well have drawn Montcalm away from his vantage ground at Quebec and committed him to a frontal attack in which his militiamen would be of little use, while the lie of the land would allow the ships' guns, useless just above Quebec, to bear effectively. Defeat at Pointe aux Trembles followed by a vigorous pursuit might have meant the surrender, not only of Quebec, but of Montcalm's whole force.

Wolfe, in his own words, "acquiesced" in the brigadiers' proposal,[5] and, abandoning the project of again attacking the Beauport lines,[6] proceeded to evacuate the Montmorency camp. This was successfully accomplished without interruption,[7] the troops being transferred to Point Lévis. Here they were embarked on vessels already above Quebec and proceeded upstream towards Pointe aux Trembles.[8] Montcalm, who had at first expected an attempt on Beauport,[9] now became apprehensive of an attack higher up and promptly reinforced Bougainville,[10] whose strenuous endeavours to keep level with the shifting ships and be ready to oppose the threatened descent soon left his men exhausted. These movements may have been all along intended to "amuse the enemy"[11] and to divert Montcalm's attention from the real objective,[12] but it may equally be that Wolfe quite intended to carry out the brigadiers' scheme and only decided to attack nearer Quebec after reconsideration. He has left no record of his reasons, but in any case it must be remembered that, had he adopted his subordinates' suggestion, the responsibility in case of

[1] Mahon, *Life of Murray*, pp. 100–20; Knox, II, 9–14, 45, 68.
[2] Knox, II, 105.   [3] Doughty, VI, 90.
[4] *Ibid.* VI, 92; Mahon, pp. 124–7.
[5] His despatch of 2 Sept. in Doughty, II, 252.   [6] *Ibid.*
[7] Knox, II, 71; Townshend's account in Doughty, V, 263 ff.
[8] Knox, II, 72 ff.   [9] Doughty, II, 261.
[10] *Ibid.* IV, 93–5.
[11] Townshend's despatch, *ibid.* V, 216.   [12] Knox, II, 79.

failure would have been his, and his alone, as commander of the expedition. What is certain, however, is that Wolfe was solely responsible for the final plan which, although it also involved attacking above Quebec, differed essentially from theirs and did not emanate from them.[1] Indeed they wrote to him on 12 September[2] asking for more information as to his proposed attack, "the several parts which fall to our share in the execution of it", and "the place or places to be attacked".

Wolfe's selection of the Anse du Foulon, a little cove less than two miles above Quebec, for his point of attack involves some obscurities. A French post guarded the top of the steep track which gave access to the Heights of Abraham, but its commander, de Vergor, had a bad reputation, and Wolfe may have learnt from a deserter, many of whom had come over recently, that his watch was far from vigilant and may have concluded that surprise here was reasonably likely. The theory has been advanced that traitors in the French camp, probably Bigot, the Intendant, and Cadet, the chief storekeeper, deliberately arranged to facilitate Wolfe's success by giving the negligent, or even treacherous, de Vergor this post and by helping Wolfe's boats to pass themselves off as French provision boats which, as supplies were running low,[3] were anxiously expected from up-river.[4] Bigot and Cadet were notoriously deeply involved in the abuses rampant in the administration and might have hoped to find security through services to the English, but their return to France after the fall of Canada largely discounts this theory. There is no need to conjecture that Bougainville had been deliberately lured away by Cadet to explain his failure to reach the battlefield before the day was decided. Holmes's boats, returning upstream with the flood tide for additional stores, may well have distracted his attention,[5] and drawn him off westward in accordance with his explicit orders.[6] Even if he had heard the firing when Vergor's post was rushed he would not necessarily have thought it important or known what it meant, and when definite information did reach him he had still to collect his scattered forces. Similarly Vaudreuil's failure to bring up all the troops from Beauport may be ascribed to nothing more recondite than his fears of a landing from the ships demonstrating off the lines.

Whatever his motives, Wolfe achieved his object. His first "debarkation" landed unopposed[7] an hour before sunrise, scrambled up the gully, surprised Vergor's post and captured the battery near Samos.[8] Without loss of time he established himself on the heights

---

[1] Holmes's letter in Doughty, IV, 296; Townshend's Journal, *ibid.* V, 267; *ibid.* VI, 60-1.
[2] Knox, II, 48; Doughty, VI, 59.
[3] Doughty, III, 99.   [4] Mahon, chap. viii; Doughty, IV, 112.
[5] Doughty, III, 17, III, 96, V, 216.
[6] Montcalm to Bougainville in Doughty, IV, 117.
[7] Holmes's letter in Doughty, IV, 295 ff.   [8] *Ibid.* III, 92.

and within an hour Townshend's division had reinforced him.[1] In Quebec and in the Beauport lines all was turmoil and confusion, Montcalm and Vaudreuil issuing conflicting orders, while the British fleet increased the confusion by opening a heavy bombardment of the lines and by lowering boats filled with marines, as though for a landing.[2] The French had been taken completely by surprise and Wolfe's whole force landed unopposed; indeed he had got a couple of field guns up[3] and had advanced within a mile of the city before Montcalm's main body arrived, soon after 8 a.m.[4] One battalion was guarding his rear, two were thrown back on his left under Townshend to deal with the Canadians and Indians in the thickets which fringed the plateau, from whom had come the only opposition as yet encountered.[5] This left him about 3000 bayonets for the main fight, and though Montcalm's force exceeded that number, the ranks of his regulars had been swelled by incorporating militiamen whose quite different training and tactics made the increase of numbers a doubtful blessing.

Montcalm has been criticised for attacking at once instead of waiting for Bougainville to arrive to take Wolfe between two fires. According to some accounts Montcalm could not understand why Bougainville had not appeared already and feared that further delay would let Wolfe entrench and establish himself solidly on the heights. More probably he knew that if he stood on the defensive he could not prevent Wolfe from attacking, while he wanted the moral advantage of taking the offensive, specially important in view of the surprise which Wolfe had effected. Moreover, he had collected all his regulars, the only troops to be relied on in a pitched battle in the open. Anyhow, about 9 a.m. his men advanced to the attack, deployed into line when 400 yards from the British and though galled by Wolfe's guns and sharpshooters[6] pushed forward, opening a rather ineffective fire when still 150 yards away, while on the flank the Canadians and Indians maintained a brisk fight with the British flanking parties.[7] Wolfe, owing to the long frontage to be taken up, had had to draw up his men two-deep, instead of the usual three-deep formation,[8] and his line, despite some casualties as the French drew nearer, withheld its fire in perfect silence[9] with unflinching discipline[10] till the enemy were within 40 yards. The French were already somewhat disordered, for the militiamen incorporated in their ranks had, as their custom was, thrown themselves down to reload.[11] Then the British fired with decisive effect, sweeping the French down wholesale. Promptly reloading they poured in another destructive volley

---

[1] Townshend's Journal, *ibid.* v, 268.
[3] *Ibid.* II, 99 and 101; Doughty, v, 222.
[4] Doughty, III, 127.
[6] Doughty, III, 132.
[8] Doughty, v, 107; Knox, I, 350, 487.
[10] *Ibid.* II, 101 and Doughty, v, 104.

[2] Knox, II, 93.
[5] Knox, II, 99 ff.
[7] Knox, II, 175.
[9] Knox, II, 79.
[11] Malartic's Journal, p. 88.

and as they charged forward the French line collapsed:[1] the militia, unused to close quarters, would not stand, and the British charge scattered the survivors of the French regulars, who streamed back towards Quebec, so vigorously pursued that no stand could be made,[2] especially as Montcalm had been mortally wounded in trying to rally the fugitives. Luckily for them, in the moment of victory Wolfe, already twice wounded, had received a fatal shot, and his orders to the reserve to hasten down to the St Charles and intercept the French retreat were not carried out. There was some delay too while the Light Infantry and Highlanders drove off the Canadians in the woods on the flanks, not without sharp fighting and considerable losses;[3] moreover, an advanced party of Bougainville's men had just appeared about 11 a.m. near the Anse du Foulon. This was quickly beaten off, and Bougainville, discovering what had happened, recoiled upstream, but the diversion helped to check the pursuit, and Townshend, now in command, as Monckton also was disabled, called his men off and started entrenching in front of the walls, and preparing to get up heavy guns to batter them.[4]

Some of the French had taken refuge in Quebec, most had fled across the St Charles to the Beauport lines, where at a hastily collected council Vaudreuil decided on immediate retreat by the St Charles valley, leaving Ramezay with 2000 men, mainly sailors and militia, to make what terms he could for Quebec. Had Vaudreuil been a man of spirit, the position was not hopeless. If the French casualties were fully twice the 655 British,[5] there were at Beauport and with Bougainville as many fresh troops as had been in action. But Vaudreuil's men were mainly undisciplined militia, the loss having fallen heaviest on the battalions from France, while the British, despite Wolfe's fall, were flushed with confidence after their eleventh-hour victory. Still Vaudreuil might have passed into Quebec the supplies which he abandoned, for want of which Ramezay had to capitulate on 18 September. At that moment the French troops were at Pointe aux Trembles, Lévis, who had arrived and taken command on the previous day, having arrested their retreat in the hope of succouring Quebec.

Townshend had given the garrison good terms[6] because it was essential to secure Quebec before the beaten army could rally. To make the battered city defensible, and to prepare for the winter's rigours, absorbed all his energies in the short period which elapsed before the fleet had to quit the river.[7] Had the margin of time been larger, a prompt move up-river to bring the French to action again would have been sound strategy. The victory of 13 September, which

---

[1] Doughty, v, 272.   [2] *Ibid.* v, 105, 217; Knox, ii, 102.
[3] Doughty, iii, 172, v, 53.
[4] Townshend's Journal in Doughty, v, 54, 218, 289; Knox, ii, 103, 113, 119, 121.
[5] Knox, ii, 118.
[6] Doughty, v, 219; Kingsford, iv, 305.   [7] Knox, ii, 179.

Wolfe might have made more fruitful had he lived, had left the French still a force "in being", and till Lévis was disposed of the conquest of Canada was incomplete. As it was, Lévis withdrew unmolested to Montreal and, during the winter, so successfully restored the efficiency of his force that in the spring he could advance against Quebec with 7000 men, while his four frigates, which, much to Wolfe's annoyance,[1] had avoided destruction in the previous year, completely overmatched the small British naval force and assured him the mastery of the St Lawrence.

The garrison left under Murray to hold Quebec, originally 7000 strong, had been sadly reduced during an unusually inclement winter.[2] The troops had had a hard time in 1759, and what with incessant toil, inadequate clothing and fuel, indifferent accommodation in the half-ruined city, and a monotonous diet consisting largely of salt provisions, they went sick by scores, mainly with dysentery and scurvy. Over 700 died, and by April the effectives, many of them only nominally fit, mustered barely 3500. Murray had been as active as possible and gained several minor successes over bands of Canadians and Indians, but the hard frosts had prevented him from making his intended improvements in the wretched defences of Quebec before Lévis arrived at Lorette (26 April).[3] Skirmishing between outposts covered Murray's withdrawal of his outposts from Cap Rouge and Ste Foy to Quebec (27 April); and next day, as Lévis advanced, Murray moved out to counter-attack him.[4] The action, fought rather farther to the west than Wolfe's battle, began by Murray's dislodging Lévis' advance-guard from a large house it had seized on the Ste Foy road, and driving it right back. Pursuing too far, Murray's men were in their turn attacked and thrust back, but he re-established the fight with part of his reserve, and for two hours maintained the unequal struggle till two French battalions worked round through the woods and, attacking in flank, dislodged the British left from two small redoubts. The French left also succeeded in outflanking its opponents and the whole British line recoiled in disorder, leaving eighteen of its twenty field guns behind, though two battalions from reserve interposed successfully to cover the retreat.[5] The casualties, 110 officers and 994 men,[6] amounted to a third of the force engaged,[7] but Lévis' success had been dearly bought, his French battalions having 600 casualties and the Colony Regulars and militia another 350.

For a brief period disorder prevailed in Quebec,[8] but Murray soon had the situation in hand, and, with discipline re-established, the garrison made a good defence, working hard, making frequent sorties and keeping the besiegers' works under an effective fire. Lévis

[1] Willson, H. Beckles, p. 470.   [2] Knox, II, 201–380.
[3] *Ibid.* II, 449.   [4] *Ibid.* II, 380–9.
[5] *Ibid.* II, 390–6.   [6] *Ibid.* II, 397.
[7] Murray to Pitt in Kimball, II, 295; Knox, II, 396.   [8] Knox, II, 405.

had little artillery and the rocky ground seriously impeded siege operations; he had made only slight progress when, on 9 May, the arrival of H.M.S. *Lowestoft* proved that the St Lawrence was again open for the expected reinforcements. This prospect encouraged the garrison enormously,[1] and five days later substantial assistance[2] arrived in the shape of more warships under Commodore Swanton, who promptly engaged and destroyed Lévis' frigates, and with them his transports and store ships.[3] Lévis had therefore to raise the siege and retire on Montreal (18 May), but, though in desperate case, he resolutely rejected Murray's overtures for negotiations. But there was no hope of help; the French Government had practically left Canada to its fate, and though a tiny squadron from Bordeaux did evade the British in the Bay of Biscay (April), it reached Anticosti to find Swanton ahead of it, and, taking refuge in a river in Chaleur Bay, was soon discovered and destroyed by Commodore Byron.[4]

The final British converging movement on Montreal was now in progress. Murray actually was the first to sight Montreal. He started from Quebec on 14 July with 2500 picked troops,[5] the garrison having been augmented to over 4000 men by the recovery of sick and wounded. With three frigates escorting his flotilla he pushed on steadily,[6] disarming the inhabitants of the riverside parishes and making Lévis' militiamen desert in numbers by threatening to burn their farms unless they returned home. Encountering only negligible opposition, for Lévis was greatly handicapped by lack of munitions, Murray reached Sorel at the mouth of the Richelieu River by 13 August, and four days later two battalions from Louisbourg reinforced him, whereupon he advanced again, arriving near Montreal (27 August) ten days before Amherst appeared. His operations had greatly facilitated the advance of the central column, now under Havilland, by taking its opponents in flank.[7] The chief obstacle in Havilland's way was the Île aux Noix; once it had been taken (27 August), St John's and Chambly quickly followed, and he pushed on to Montreal unopposed. Amherst meanwhile, with 5500 regulars and over 4000 provincials, "reserving the most difficult department for himself",[8] had reached Oswego early in July,[9] embarked there on 10 August, a large flotilla having been collected, and proceeded to descend the St Lawrence. Fort Lévis, above the head of the first rapids, gave little trouble, surrendering on 25 August,[10] but the shooting of the Cedars Rapids cost nearly 100 lives.[11] By 6 September, Amherst was at Lachine just above Montreal and two days later Vaudreuil surrendered, though even then the indomitable Lévis would have held out.

[1] Knox, II, 415.   [2] Ibid. II, 425.   [3] Wood, *Logs*, pp. 330–5; Kimball, II, 290.
[4] Knox, II, 440; Kimball, II, 334.   [5] Knox, II, 463.
[6] Ibid. II, 466 ff.   [7] Ibid. II, 529.
[8] Ibid. II, 526.   [9] Ibid. III, 78–95.
[10] Ibid. II, 544.   [11] Ibid. II, 557.

By Lévis' own admission[1] Murray's movement had attracted his attention and prevented his doing more to impede Havilland and Amherst. The latter, however, had played the decisive part in the campaign, as his advance had effectually barred any chance of the French escaping to the westward to prolong their resistance. If the operation was marked by no dramatic battle, it was a substantial testimony to Amherst's capacities as an organiser and administrator.[2] The distances to be covered and the difficult country to be traversed enhance its merits considerably. Amherst's determination to ensure success may have tended to make that success slow in coming, but in the special circumstances of North America, where the chief difficulties were geographical and administrative rather than tactical, "slow but sure" was no bad motto.[3]

In the reduction of Canada, army and navy played complementary parts. Without Hawke and his colleagues to keep the seas open for our troopships and to bar them to those of France, thereby preventing the French from reinforcing Canada, the army's task would have been indefinitely increased. Without Saunders's ships Wolfe could not have reached Quebec, or "misled, mystified and deceived" Montcalm after getting there.[4] But the mere isolation of Canada was not enough, however effective, nor was it enough for Boscawen to escort Amherst to Louisbourg or for Saunders to give Wolfe the chance to scale the Heights of Abraham. The troops once landed, the navy could do little more. The army's first venture in North America had been inauspicious, but before Montreal fell the British regular had learnt enough of backwoods fighting to compete with Canadians and Indians in skirmishing.[5] Without the British regular Canada would never have been conquered. At Louisbourg and at Quebec under 10 per cent. of the troops had been provincials, and useful as the local troops were, they cannot claim any of the outstanding successes of the war. The reasons for this ineffectiveness have already been indicated. Not even Pitt could obtain from the colonies all he wanted. Provincial jealousies and the lack of effective machinery for raising troops or taxes were too much even for Pitt's inspiring exhortations, and performances lagged behind promises. The thirteen colonies had to be united before they could be effective in war. Pitt's personal share in the successful attainment of the British aims was, however, substantial; though, if he selected Wolfe and Amherst and Saunders for their commands, he had not trained them, and the army owed almost as much to Cumberland's reforms as the navy to Anson's. The conception of the strategy which ultimately proved successful does not differ radically from the original scheme, whether that emanated from Shirley or from Cumberland,[6]

[1] Knox, II, 472.
[2] Ibid. II, 591.
[3] Ibid. II, 200.
[4] Ibid. II, 132.
[5] Ibid. I, 207, 504, II, 339.
[6] Charteris, p. 205.

while "conquering America in Germany", in its way almost as essential as the reduction of Louisbourg and Quebec, was imposed on Pitt by the French, whose failure to achieve their purpose does not make the conception less theirs. Pitt's chief contributions to the victory lay in his vigour in providing reinforcements and supplies, in his insisting that Wolfe should have the subordinates he wanted even if they were out of favour at court, and in his success in substituting enterprise and the will to win for the discouragement and apathy previously prevailing. When Forbes renamed Fort Duquesne he was happily inspired.

CHAPTER V

NEWFOUNDLAND TO 1783

THE colony of Newfoundland and its adjacent territory of Labrador were the first lands in the western hemisphere to be visited by Europeans, and their discovery ante-dates the voyages of Columbus by nearly 500 years. Before the end of the ninth century Norwegian vikings passed across the sea to Iceland and thence a hundred years later to Greenland and the shores beyond. The Icelandic sagas record that in the year A.D. 977 Gunnbjorn, a sea-rover, driven by a tempest to the westward, saw the snowy mountains of a land beyond the ocean, and thither Erik the Red sailed from Iceland in 983 in search of fresh homes for himself and his men. He called the new land "Greenland" and planted settlements there that were continuously occupied until the fifteenth century. In 999 Leif the Lucky, Erik's son, sailed from Norway with missionary priests to convert the Greenlanders to Christianity, but on his way he was driven far to the south-west and came to the coast of a pleasant land where self-sown wheat and wild grapes grew. He called it "Vinland the Good" and continuing his voyage he carried the news of his discovery to Greenland. In 1001, according to the tale, Thorfinn Karlsefne, an Iceland merchant, determined to sail thither in search of trade. He came first to a cold, stony land that he called *Helluland* (i.e. land of slate, probably Labrador), and thence to a less mountainous coast covered with bushes called *Markland* (i.e. land of wood) which is clearly the eastern coast of Newfoundland.

The saga narrative, with its wealth of pointed and picturesque detail, has generally been accepted in its entirety. But Dr Nansen has cast doubts upon the historic authenticity of the discovery of "Vinland the Good" and has shown that the parts of the story that can be confirmed from independent sources are less striking but more directly in accordance with probabilities. He contends that the Vinland story is founded on vague memories of the Greek myths of the "Fortunate Isles" and is purely legendary.[1] The discovery of Helluland and Markland, however, is a historic fact that can be confirmed independently. There is no doubt that the Greenlanders at various times during the centuries of their occupation made voyages westward and southward in search of wood and furs. Traces of their landing have been found as far west as Baffin Land, and from the Icelandic annals we have confirmation of their visits to Markland in search of timber as late as 1347. But no permanent settlement on those coasts was attempted, and the adventures of the Norse voyagers

[1] Nansen, F., *In Northern Mists*, 1, 352–3, etc.; but see Williamson, J. A., *Voyages of the Cabots*, pp. 128–9.

were unknown to the rest of Europe until long after the western continent had been revealed by other discoverers.

John Cabot's discovery of lands beyond the Atlantic in 1497 and the disappointment of his second voyage in 1498, having been already mentioned in this History,[1] need not be discussed in this connection. The site of Cabot's landfall and the land he formally annexed for Henry VII have been identified by some writers with Newfoundland, but they are now generally placed in Cape Breton Island. The earliest map showing the northern discoveries was that of Juan La Cosa of 1500, which marks the coast of what appears to be part of Newfoundland as "discovered by the English" and sets an English flag on its extreme westerly point "Cavo de Inglaterra".[2] The coast is not separated from the adjacent mainland, and for the next thirty years at least cartographers marked *Terra Nova* as continuous with Labrador and sometimes even with Greenland, the whole coastline being made to run as a rule from west to east. The English discovery of the "new lands" was, however, soon forgotten, and they were usually[3] marked as lands of the King of Portugal in consequence of the explorations of two brothers from the Azores, Gaspar and Miguel Corte-Real. Between 1500 and 1503 they explored and mapped much of the coast of Newfoundland, and certain of the most prominent features still bear their names. Some, like Cape Race, Cape Bonavista and Conception Bay, are little changed, but others have been corrupted like Cape Freels, originally called after Frey Luis, the chaplain of the voyages. Though its existence was probably known earlier, it was not until 1534 that Jacques Cartier explored the Straits of Belle Isle and clearly separated the island from the continent. But cartographers still continued in great doubt about its outline, some marking it as a group of islets and others as one insular mass with a serrated coast. These doubtful problems were cleared up, in the years 1762–7, by the celebrated explorer, Captain James Cook.[4]

The lasting results of the Cabot and Corte-Real voyages sprang, not from their discoveries on land, but from their revelation of the riches of the sea. In Cabot's account of his first voyage nothing was of greater interest to his backers among the Bristol merchants than his description of the fisheries off the "new land". As the Milanese agent at the court of Henry VII wrote to his master (18 December 1497): "They affirm that the sea is covered with fish which are caught not merely with nets but with baskets, a stone being attached to make the basket sink in the water, and this I heard the said Master John [Cabot] relate. And the Englishmen, his companions, say they will fetch so many fish that this kingdom will have no more need of Iceland, from which country there comes a very great store of fish which are called stock-fish".[5] These tales were hardly exaggerated. The

---

[1] See vols. I, 25 and VI, 17, 18.   [2] Harrisse, H., *Terre Neuve*, Plate II.
[3] But the globes of Gemma Frisius (c. 1530) seem to have preserved a memory of English claims.
[4] *Ibid.* pp. 351–3.   [5] Biggar, H. P., *Precursors of Cartier*, p. 20.

shallow waters on the Banks lying to the south and east of Newfoundland are probably the most prolific fishing grounds in the world, for
favourable breeding conditions with a gravelly bottom and cool
water from the Arctic current combine with an abundant food supply
of the smaller forms of marine life to yield stores of codfish that seem
inexhaustible. The struggles of the men of various nations who fish
those waters for cod have been inseparably associated with the
development of Newfoundland for 400 years. The exploitation of
the sea has demanded the use of its shores, and a unique and essentially amphibious society has grown up. From the beginning the
fishermen have caught the cod with lines and hooks baited with
herrings, capelan or other small fish that must be sought in coastal
waters.[1] The catch is prepared for market on stages or "rooms"
erected on the narrow beaches of the coast fjords, and thus there was
every summer a constant coming and going between the fishing
grounds and the shore that filled those seas with activity. From the
sixteenth century until the nineteenth the fishing fleets of the nations
of western Europe sailed out on annual voyages across the Atlantic
from February to December, so that endless opportunities occurred
for international rivalry both at sea and on shore. The fortunes of
the fishery were governed by the politics of Europe, and there is no
colony whose prosperity has been so much the sport of diplomacy
as that of Newfoundland. The development of the land colony could
never proceed independently of controversies relating to the sea
fisheries, and until our own day[2] it has always been hampered by
restrictions imposed for the benefit of rival fishing industries.

The first fishermen to exploit the new grounds that Cabot had
discovered were the Portuguese, who began to sail thither in 1500 or
soon after. By 1506 the industry had become so important that a
special tithe was levied by King Emmanuel on the catch,[3] and the
new lands became known to western Europe for a century or more
by their Portuguese name of *Tierra dos Baccalaos*[4] (i.e. the lands of
the codfish). Bretons and Normans were also active competitors
soon after the beginning of the century, but Englishmen did not come
until later. Henry VII granted patents in 1501 and 1502 to certain
merchants of Bristol and the Azores for discovery and colonisation
in the new lands, but their efforts were probably directed to the
coast of Labrador and its fur trade. The fate of the enterprise is
unknown save that it soon failed and was remembered only by
Hakluyt's mention of its connection with Robert Thorne the elder
and so with later schemes.[5]

When Henry VIII's shipmaster, John Rut, in the *Mary of Guilford*
visited the harbour of St John's on 3 August 1527, he found eleven

[1] Peret, R., *Géographie de la Terre-Neuve*, p. 179.
[2] Anglo-French Agreement, 1904; Hague Arbitration with U.S. 1910.
[3] Emmanuel I to Diogo Brandã, 14 Oct. 1506. Printed in Biggar, *Precursors*, pp. 96–7.
[4] Or, more correctly, *Bacalhaos*.
[5] Hakluyt (ed. of 1907), I, 27–8.

Norman, one Breton and two Portuguese barks but no Englishmen fishing there.[1] The French usually fished from the harbours on the south coast to the west of Cape Race, and the Portuguese from the east coast between Cape Race and Cape Bonavista,[2] but Rut's testimony shows that there can have been no recognised delimitation. In fact, the harbours of the island until the seventeenth century were always "no man's land", and their beaches lay open to the first comer. In the account of Henry Hore's disastrous voyage to the south coast of Newfoundland in 1536 there is no mention of English fishermen on the Banks, but his crews were saved from starvation by plundering a well-found French fishing vessel that came unsuspectingly into the harbour where they were stranded.[3] An Act of Parliament of 1541[4] forbidding the purchase of fish at sea excepts the produce of the "new land", but there is no indication that Englishmen were fishing there. Probably we may date the regular opening of our west-country industry from about the year 1555, the time of the interruption of French enterprise by their bitter privateering war with Spain.

Spanish fishermen began to make annual voyages to Newfoundland waters about the same date, those from the southern ports coming first for cod, and the Basques from Biscay to seek for whales off the Labrador coast.[5] The wars of Henri II led to fierce battles between the French and the Spaniards in the Newfoundland harbours,[6] and enabled our fishermen to increase their industry at the expense of both combatants. The number of English barks annually crossing the Atlantic rapidly increased under Elizabeth and soon equalled the number of the Portuguese, whose man-power was drained by their wars in the Indies. They were considerably outnumbered, however, by the French and Spanish, and in 1578 Anthony Park-hurst informed the elder Hakluyt that in one year there were on the average above one hundred sail of Spaniards that come to Newfoundland to take cod, twenty or thirty Biscayans hunting whales for train, one hundred and fifty sail of French and Bretons, fifty Portuguese and fifty English barks.[7]

A system was already growing up whereby the men of each nation usually frequented different harbours, the English congregating most in the harbours round St John's, the French round Placentia opposite Cape Breton, the Spaniards at Spanish Harbour and so on. Before Parkhurst no one had paid any attention to the possibilities of the interior of the island, and he was the first to explore them. But his search was resented by the fishermen, and he told Hakluyt that "the

[1] Purchas, XIV, 305; Williamson, J. A., *Maritime Enterprise*, p. 254, and *Voyages of the Cabots*, pp. 256–61.
[2] Ramusio, *Viaggi*, III, 423.
[3] Hakluyt, v, 338–41.   [4] 32 Hen. VIII, c. 2, § v, *Stats. of Realm*, III, 828.
[5] Brown, V. L., in *Report of Can. Hist. Assoc.* 1925, p. 67; Harrisse, *Terre Neuve*, pp. lviii, lix.
[6] See Inquisition held at San Sebastian, 15 Oct. 1555, *cit.* Harrisse, p. lx.
[7] Writing from Bristol, 13 Nov. 1578; Hakluyt, v, 344.

Western men suppose that I find some secret commodity by reason that I do search the harbours, creeks and havens, and also the land much more than ever any Englishman hath done". He gave an excellent account of the fertility and goodness of the country and tested it for himself by sowing wheat, barley, peas, etc., the first seeds that were set in Newfoundland. Parkhurst was the first to urge upon Queen Elizabeth the advisability of annexing and fortifying the island, so that Englishmen might become the "lords of the whole fishing";[1] and his letter foreshadows the long struggle to found a colony to monopolise for England the wealth of the fisheries. It was still tacitly accepted that the King of Portugal held whatever shadowy claims to the *Tierra dos Baccalaos* were conferred by right of prior discovery, but the fertile ingenuity of Dr John Dee recalled to the memory of Englishmen that John Cabot under the standard of Henry VII had anticipated the Portuguese by three years, and he did his best to persuade the Queen and Burghley that this gave England a valid right to Newfoundland against other nations. They listened to him sceptically and refused any official help, for they knew how little such arguments weighed in practical politics. However, he had set the ball rolling, and his friends among the advocates of colonisation took up his idea with enthusiasm, and by their writings soon firmly established the statement of England's prior claim in the public mind. This supplied good material for propaganda against the Iberian claims to a monopoly of oceanic power, but the struggle for the fisheries could not be decided by appeals to antiquarian learning. It demanded practical and effective occupation of the disputed territory, and Sir William Monson fairly expressed the legal position when he wrote some thirty years after Dee—"We can challenge no right of inheritance [to Newfoundland], wanting proof of possession which is the law acknowledged by the right of discovery".[2]

The first attempt at formal annexation came from Dee's friend, Sir Humphrey Gilbert, in 1583, which was considered in our first volume.[3] His proceedings were not especially directed by a desire to dominate the fishing as Parkhurst had proposed. His aim was to found a great lordship in America, and what he did in Newfoundland was to have been only an incident on his way southward to *Terra Florida*.[4] He crossed by the "trade way" because the fishing merchants informed him that he could obtain supplies cheaply in the Newfoundland harbours. St John's was an *entrepôt* for the fishermen of all nations, and when Gilbert arrived (3 August 1583) he found it "populous and frequented" and an abundance of provisions of all kinds that was "unexpected in that desolate corner of the world".[5] He had to force his way in against the objections of the fishermen, who knew what to expect from a "gentleman adventurer". Their fears were

---

[1] Hakluyt, v, 348.   [2] Churchill, *Voyages*, III, 203.
[3] See *C.H.B.E.* vol. I, pp. 67, 105–6.   [4] Hakluyt, VI, 8.   [5] *Ibid.* VI, 17–19.

justified, for he proceeded at once to levy contributions of provisions from the masters of the barks at St John's and in all the neighbouring harbours, whether English or strangers. Under his guns they could not refuse, and when he went on to proclaim with imposing formalities the annexation of all the territories for 200 leagues around, the fishermen had to submit. But only seventeen days after his arrival Gilbert's pageant came to an end. After much spoil and destruction by his unruly crews he sailed away to continue his voyage (20 August 1583), and Newfoundland settled down again to its accustomed business with entire disregard of his annexation, his laws and his leases.[1] The episode had no direct effect on subsequent history, and England's claims to the island were neither more nor less valid than before.

The next expedition, undertaken by the orders of the Government, had permanent effects upon the fishery. Between 1555 and 1585 the Spaniards furnished the largest contingents to the annual fishing fleets, and their trade attained a prosperity that was never afterwards approached. The growing demands of the Indies flotas for sailors and Philip II's drafts upon the fishing ports for his Armada for the invasion of England crippled the Spanish industry, and in 1585 it received its death-blow at the hands of an expedition sent out under Sir Bernard Drake as one of the first strokes in the naval war. More than 600 Spaniards and Portuguese were taken prisoners and 60,000 quintals of fish were seized. The Spanish fishing fleet never recovered, and whereas before 1585 some 150 barks sailed annually to the Banks from the Biscayan ports, even in the best of later years their numbers were reduced to ten or under, manned by Basques who pretended to be subjects of the King of France. Only the English and the French were left as serious competitors, and Spain and the Mediterranean countries had to purchase their supplies of stock-fish from them even in time of war and pay for them mostly in money. This was one of the reasons that made the Newfoundland trade so valuable in the eyes both of English and French statesmen. In exchange for nothing but the export of labour and some food supplies the nation was enriched by the influx of treasure and the encouragement of mariners. In time of war the fisheries supplied a reserve of skilled and experienced men for the fighting fleets and their barks an indispensable addition of auxiliary craft. Arguments such as these carried great weight, and they account for the favour with which even the most exacting demands of the fishermen were listened to for a couple of centuries.

During the Wars of Religion the French fleets declined, but by the end of the sixteenth century more fishermen sailed annually from French than from English ports, though the English would not admit

---

[1] Hakluyt, VI, 25.

it.[1] Competition in the markets of southern Europe became more and more acute, and the fishing merchants on both sides of the Channel resisted everything that might add to the prime cost of their merchandise. In France edicts were procured to keep down the wages of the fishermen and to lighten dues, while in England the leaders of the west-country industry were loud in their complaints to Parliament and began their long and bitter fight against every attempt to found permanent colonies in Newfoundland. It was in the vicissitudes of this fight that the English colony was born, and they have left an indelible impress on its history.

Both parties in the struggle aimed at accomplishing the same purpose—to become "lords of the whole fishing". The colonisers maintained that this could best be done by planting settlers in the island and fortifying it so as to deny the use of its harbours to men of other nations. They would raise supplies and sell them to the fishing fleets, and would also aid in catching fish for sale to merchants who would carry it to market. The men of the smaller ports feared that if settlers remained in the island during the winter, they would monopolise the best places for drying stages and would gradually exclude the annual voyagers from the harbours. If this happened, the profits of the trade would pass on the one hand to the colonists who would supply the labour, and on the other to London and Bristol merchants who had sufficient capital to send out large store ships[2] and to give credit to buyers in the southern markets. The small employers of Poole, Barnstaple, Fowey and the other western ports were at one with the fishermen who manned the voyages on a profit-sharing basis. They were determined to withstand the threat to their prosperity and rarely has any part of England ever spoken with so united a voice on any economic matter. This united appeal to the predominant mercantilist theory of national prosperity was both powerful and persistent, and only a complete change of imperial outlook was responsible for its ultimate defeat.

Though isolated Englishmen may occasionally have been left behind by the fishing fleets to winter in Newfoundland, no organised group settled there until the season of 1610–11, when John Guy and William Colston of Bristol went out with a party of colonists and established themselves at Cupid's Cove in Conception Bay. They were sent by a Company to which advocates of colonisation like Hakluyt and Chief Justice Popham and certain Bristol capitalists had subscribed. With the support of Sir Francis Bacon they obtained an elaborate charter from the Crown as "the Treasurer and Company of Adventurers and Planters of the City of London and Bristol for the Colony or Plantation in Newfoundland",[3] but the difference

---

[1] Musset, G., *Les Rochellais à Terre-Neuve, passim.*
[2] Known as "Sack ships".
[3] For patent see *Select Charters of Trading Cos.* (Selden Soc. XXVIII), pp. 51–62.

between the enterprise and other colonising schemes is to be found in the Instructions[1] with which Guy was furnished. The purpose of the colonists was to introduce new methods into the fishing industry. Instead of sending out fishermen and supplies annually to Newfoundland waters, permanent settlers were to be established securely in the island to sell the cargoes of large supply ships and to freight them for London and Bristol with stock-fish and train oil prepared by themselves or purchased from others. The instructions for the planting of food crops and the rearing of sheep were incidental to this main purpose and the aim was clearly to change radically the traditional system of organisation. Though freedom of fishing for all was expressly safeguarded, it was clear that permanent settlers with property in the soil would have more favourable opportunities to secure the best fish-curing stations than those who depended upon their early arrival each spring for the first choice in every harbour, as had been the custom for a century.

The fishing merchants of the western ports were at once up in arms, and when in August 1611 Guy under the provisions of his charter issued ordinances[2] for the management of the harbours and the prevention of disorderly fishing, the issue was fairly joined. The ordinances were drafted in the common interest and along traditional lines, but they were contrary to the ancient practice as being enforceable by a resident governor in place of the skipper of the first ship arriving in any harbour, who, as "fishing admiral", had customarily held authority for the season. Great pressure was brought to bear upon the Government in England to secure the cancellation of the company's charter, and in Newfoundland the fishermen refused to recognise Guy's authority or to obey his ordinances. With only a small company of forty men behind him Guy could do little against thousands of English fishermen and their allies among the men of other nations. In 1612 sixty men and women were sent out by the Company, but this did not help. Pirates of all nations now made their bases in some of the Newfoundland harbours where they found a ready market for their plunder among the men of the fishing fleets, and Guy had to stand idly by while they stole his stock and commandeered his stores and the barks of the fishermen.[3] If he had had sufficient force to make headway against the marauders, he might have secured some respect for his pretensions, but the resources of the Company were quite insufficient to undertake forcible measures, and no help was forthcoming from the English Government. In 1615, however, a commission of vice-admiralty was issued to Sir Richard Whitbourne to go out at his own charges to keep order in the harbours and to defend the fishermen from pirates, recouping his expenses by collecting fees. Whitbourne had had a long experi-

---

[1] Instructions to Guy in Brit. Mus. Cott. MSS. Otho, E. VIII, 5. Printed in part in Prowse, D. A., *Hist. of Newfoundland*, pp. 94–6.   [2] Text in Prowse, p. 99.
[3] Whitbourne, R., *Discourse*, reprinted in Purchas, XIX, 424–40. See p. 426.

ence in the trade, for he had begun to make summer voyages to Newfoundland as early as 1583.[1] He was a skilful sailor, both in peace and war, having commanded his own ship against the Armada of 1588, but with insufficient means he could secure no more respect for the King's commission than could Guy for his patent, and he came home to press upon the Privy Council and the public the need for support of the colony on a considerable scale in order to vindicate England's rights to the island and the command of the fishery. It was all without avail, for James I had no funds to spare, and the proceeds of the collections in parish churches that were authorised for the support of Whitbourne's schemes were negligible.

Guy's scheme was not one of the attempts to form a land colony on theoretical lines which failed so often under James I and Charles I. It was a practically conceived effort to organise the fishery on new lines, very similar to those that were successful 200 years later. If the plan could have been carried into effect, it is probable that Englishmen would have won the foremost place in the fishery much earlier, for they would have monopolised the beaches, but the conservative opposition of the western fishing merchants was too strong for the Newfoundland Company, and its resources were soon exhausted. Like most other unsuccessful holders of Crown grants at the time its last attempt to make a profit was by disposing of its nominal rights to any who would take them over. This led to five or six ill-supported and abortive schemes for land colonisation in Newfoundland that need not long detain us, for they had no influence on the subsequent history of the island. Sir William Vaughan tried with Whitbourne's assistance to make a settlement of Welshmen at Trepassey on land purchased from Guy's Company (1616–30), but he soon disposed of part of his rights to Henry Cary, Viscount Falkland, who as Lord Deputy of Ireland was interested in a scheme for settling Irishmen in Newfoundland (1623). He called the land near Placentia Bay "South Falkland", and bought another tract on Trinity Bay from Guy direct and named it "North Falkland". But he did little or nothing in either place and soon abandoned the idea. The schemes led to the publication of certain colonising tracts[2] and the insertion of various high-sounding names in the maps adorning them, like "Britannioll", "Cambrioll Colchor", "Golden Grove", and so on, that had as ephemeral an existence as the colonies themselves.[3] The most serious attempt was made by Sir George Calvert, then Secretary of State, who in 1621 sent out a Welshman, Captain Wynne, with a few colonists to settle in the south-eastern peninsula of the island and in 1622 and 1623 obtained grants from the Crown of the region which he called the Province of Avalon, a name that

---

[1] Whitbourne, R., *Discourse*, in Purchas, XIX, 425.
[2] E.g. Vaughan, W., *The Golden Fleece* (1625).
[3] See Mason's map of 1625 reproduced in Prowse, p. 106, and Rogers, J. D., *Hist. Geog. of Newfoundland*, p. 65.

has persisted. Wynne established his headquarters at Ferryland Head, a name corrupted from the name Farelhaõ (= rocky) originally given to it by the Portuguese. There a strong stone house was built and Calvert sent out various small parties of settlers in 1624, 1625 and 1627 at his own expense. In 1628 he brought out his wife and family, but, finding the climate not to his liking, transferred himself and the remnant of his colonists to Maryland.[1] Meanwhile the first fight had occurred in the long struggle between England and France for the fisheries. War between the two powers had begun in 1626 and soon degenerated into an affair of privateering raids on both sides. In 1628 three French privateers attacked the English barks fishing near Cape Broyle and made several captures. Calvert (now Lord Baltimore) came to the rescue from Ferryland near by and having retaken the prizes he launched a counter-raid against the Frenchmen fishing farther south off Trepassey. Seven French vessels were taken and considerable destruction was done.[2]

The capture of the colony of Canada by the Kirkes[3] had an important influence on the affairs of Newfoundland, for it led to the appearance in the island of Sir David Kirke, the founder of the first permanent colony and one of the most striking figures in its early history. As was stated in an earlier volume,[4] the fishing merchants strongly opposed the policy pursued by the Government when new and valuable fisheries were opened up off the New England coast about 1620. They wished to prevent the colonisation of New England for the same reasons as moved them in Newfoundland. At that period and for long afterwards the exploitation of North American waters was regarded as one problem, and in the long debates on free fishing in the House of Commons between 1620 and 1629 there was no differentiation between the two regions. The Council of New England was established on the inspiration of Sir Ferdinando Gorges as much to control the fisheries as to promote colonisation, and its schemes were brought to naught mainly by the opposition of the fishing merchants. It was not until the successful establishment of the land colony in Massachusetts Bay that the two lines of development diverged. By the middle of the 'thirties the fisheries to the south were passing completely into the hands of the New England colonists and the English fishing merchants were restricted as before to the waters off Newfoundland.

The Government first took up the question of regulating the fisheries after the debates of 1620–1, and Gorges, Sir William Alexander and others were commissioned to draw up rules "for establishing order among the fishermen of Newfoundland", a term that here certainly includes the waters of Nova Scotia and New England in which the principal commissioners were specially interested. This

[1] See vol. i, p. 168.   [2] *Cal. St. Pap. Col.* 1574–1660, p. 93.
[3] See chapter ii.   [4] See vol. i, p. 147.

fanned the resentment of the fishermen, and the efforts at control that were made by Gorges' vice-admirals were wholly disregarded. It was not until after the French war that the Government was again moved to take action, and this time on the petition of the fishing merchants themselves. The war and the attacks of French privateers had badly crippled the industry. The English had now undisputed use of the harbours on the eastern coast of the Avalon Peninsula, but their annual fleet, which had numbered 250 in 1618, had shrunk to forty barks in 1629.[1] The French, on the other hand, were increasing rapidly and beginning to capture the markets for Newfoundland fish in the Mediterranean, while the Dutch, who needed large quantities of dried cod to provision their East Indian fleets, began to purchase it direct in the Newfoundland harbours instead of through English middlemen. The loss of the New England fishery to the new Puritan colonists brought matters to a head, and in 1633 an influential petition from the western ports was presented to the Crown praying for the regulation of the fishery and its support in view of its great importance to the nation and the navy. The newly-established Commission for the Plantations supported the petition after careful enquiry, and on 24 January 1633/4 the Privy Council issued an order[2] of great importance which as the "Western Charter" of the "Fishing Charter" lay at the base of all regulations concerning Newfoundland for more than a century and a half.

The eleven regulations, being in the main a codification of the traditional customs of the fishery, need not be detailed here. But certain new regulations of a unique kind were made that consolidated the western fishing interest and made it a powerful antagonist in the struggles over the development of the colony in subsequent years. The mayors of Southampton, Weymouth and Melcombe Regis, Lyme, Plymouth, Dartmouth, East Looe, Fowey and Barnstaple were authorised to take cognisance of all complaints, examine witnesses on oath concerning offences committed in the Newfoundland fishery and move the vice-admirals of Hants, Dorset, Devon and Cornwall to arrest the ships and persons of the offenders. The "fishing admiral", who, as has been stated, was traditionally the first shipmaster arriving in each harbour at the beginning of the season, was authorised to keep order and despatch delinquents to England, and in recompense for his duties he was allowed to hold an additional fishing "room" on the beach besides that which he had first chosen. If murder or felony were committed at the fishery, the murderer was to be tried by the Earl Marshal of England, i.e. according to martial law. The code was an attempt to provide a means of

---

[1] *Cal. St. Pap. Col.* 1574–1660, p. 96; *Cal. St. Pap. Dom.* 1628–9, p. 103; Prowse, p. 146.

[2] Called erroneously by Prowse and others "Star Chamber Rules". The Privy Council chanced to be sitting in the Star Chamber when the order was made, but it had nothing to do with the Court of Star Chamber. P.C. Register, *A.P.C. Col.* I, 192–7. For amendments of 1671 see *ibid.* I, 558–63.

orderly government in an amphibious society without permanent settlement, where the most usual offences were those akin to piracy, and it must be remembered that the order was drawn up at that period of Charles I's arbitrary government when he was endeavouring to use the summary processes of martial law wherever possible in place of the tedious procedure of the Common Law. It takes its place, therefore, alongside the other experiments in the evolution of extra-territorial jurisdiction which were being made at the period and to which reference is made elsewhere.[1] The order was reissued with some amendments on subsequent occasions after the Restoration[2] and it therefore plays a very important part in the history of Newfoundland. To have secured the "Western Charter" was a great victory of the fishing merchants over their rivals, but it was not long before there was a fresh attempt at colonisation which this time succeeded.

When the Kirkes were compelled to restore Quebec and their booty to the French in 1632,[3] they were left with certain claims against the Crown, and in 1637 some compensation was given for these by the grant of two patents for the colonisation of the whole of Newfoundland. The first of these was issued to a company including Sir David Kirke together with the Marquis of Hamilton and other peers, but the second and effective grant was to Kirke alone. It contained, probably in deference to the representations of the fishing interest, a provision that no settlements were to be established within six miles of the coast—a regulation which was frequently repeated in later years and gave trouble for nearly a century. Kirke took no notice of it, however, and when he proceeded to the island with a hundred colonists in 1638, he made his headquarters at Ferryland in the "Mansion House" built by Lord Baltimore ten years before.[4] He found some few persons remaining from the earlier unsuccessful colonies, and at once began to govern with vigour. He was determined to make a self-sufficing colony and not a mere fishing station, but from the first he found his greatest source of profit in the fishermen. He charged all aliens visiting the eastern harbours 5 per cent. on their catches, and when in 1639 the French ambassador complained against this, the Privy Council replied that Kirke was within the rights conferred by his patent, and that the imposition was justified by the similar tax levied by the French upon English fishermen.[5] When the French tried to evade the imposition, Kirke used force to make them pay, and in the same way he made Englishmen pay rent for their "fishing rooms" in the harbours near Ferryland. The "rooms" were granted on yearly leases, and thus, in spite of the

---

[1] See vol. I, chap. v. [2] E.g. 26 Jan. 1661, 23 Dec. 1670, etc.
[3] See chap. iii.
[4] See Field, A. M., "The Government of Newfoundland". An unpublished thesis in the Library of the University of London.
[5] Dom. Corr., Car. I, 10 May 1639.

fishermen's protests to the Government at home, a breach was made in the traditional customs. Kirke's merchant backers in London sent over large ships with miscellaneous cargoes for sale, and for the return voyage they loaded fish caught and cured by the settlers. Thus Kirke established a rival system of trade to that of the western fishing merchants, and was able to send cargoes of dried cod to southern Europe while the enterprise of others was hampered by the Civil War.[1] The Governor did a great trade not only with the fishermen and his settlers but also with the New England colonies,[2] and Newfoundland for a time became a regular *entrepôt* for the English colonies on the American coast.

After 1642 considerable numbers of settlers fled from England to the colony, and Kirke ruled them efficiently and with a strong hand. Under him the attacks of the French and of sea-rovers upon the fishermen ceased, and Newfoundland knew a period of unaccustomed peace. By 1648 the exodus of trained seamen and fishermen to take service under Kirke began to cause serious alarm to the Long Parliament,[3] and the fact that many Royalists had fled to Newfoundland made the party in power fear that Prince Rupert might make the island a base for his fleet. The complaints of the western ports were taken into serious consideration and Cromwell determined to send out commissioners backed by force to bring Kirke to subjection. In 1651 he was compelled to return to England and justify himself before the Committee on Plantations, and the commanders of the three men-of-war sent out to protect the annual fishing fleet against the French and royalist privateers were ordered to take charge of the affairs of the fishery.[4] These were the first of the convoy captains who afterwards played so important a part in the history of Newfoundland, and with their commission a new period opens. Kirke left the island in the autumn of 1651, the interests of the colonists were ignored, and the fishing interest again came into the ascendant.

The case against the Governor dragged on for three years while his work in Newfoundland went to pieces, and Cecilius Calvert, the second Lord Baltimore, brought an action for trespass. He died in 1654 soon after it had been decided to return to him a remnant of his property but to abolish the organisation he had built up. He deserves to be remembered with honour among the pioneers of the Empire not only because of his skill and determination to develop a prosperous colony on sound lines that afterwards were justified, but also because he saw how Newfoundland might serve other purposes of benefit to the Empire than those of an intermittently used fishing stage, "a great English ship moored near the Banks during the fishing season for the convenience of fishermen".[5] In a memorandum

---

[1] See Interregnum, Entry Book, xci, p. 545. Quoted by Field, p. 61.
[2] Brit. Mus., Egerton 2395, no. 259.   [3] Interr. Entry Book, cxv, 7.
[4] Interr. Entry Book, xciii, 244, 8 April 1651.
[5] William Knox in *Second Report to H. of C. Committee on Newfoundland Trade*, 1793.

presented to the Council of State to justify his actions, he pointed clearly to the inevitable struggle with France for the possession of the island. "The French, if once the island be fortified", he wrote, "will be destroyed of their nursery of mariners, this being the only place, with Canada and Acadia and the Banks, where they come for supply of fish for that nation. Without fish from that place that nation cannot be supplied nor the King of France's navy furnished with fish.... Newfoundland is a key to the Gulf of Canada which if the English were in possession... they might give the law to all foreign kings".[1] Thus, he foreshadowed the strategic ideas that were to guide our policy in the struggle until victory was won at Utrecht in 1713.

By 1653 the English were in sole possession of the coast from Cape Bonavista southward to Trepassey, and there were about 500 permanent residents including some 350 women and children in thirty or forty separate settlements, of which St John's, Bonavista and Conception were much the largest. Besides, there were about 1000 boatmen and servants who came over to find employment in the fishery and stayed for a summer or two and then usually drifted away to New England in search of the higher wages that were paid there. There was no husbandry, and the settlers had very little live-stock. They made their living entirely by fishing with hired boatmen near the shore, and they did much better than the deep-sea fishermen from England, for they took nearly one-third of the catch, though they and their employees were outnumbered every summer by three to one. To contemporary observers it seemed contrary to sound policy to consider the interests of a handful of scattered settlers in preference to those of the much larger number of nomadic fishermen. In their view the settlers added nothing to the national strength either in men or money, while the fishermen made a splendid reserve of experienced and hardy sailors for the navy, and their 200 or more ocean-going vessels could furnish valuable auxiliaries in time of war. The Council of State of the Commonwealth therefore in 1656 took into serious consideration the demands of the west-country ports that the "prosecuting of the Plantation should be discontinued".[2] Fresh instructions for the management of the fishery were issued on the basis of the "Fishing Charter" of 1634, but without the anomalous provisions giving jurisdiction to the western mayors and the Earl Marshal.

After the Restoration the "Fishing Charter" was renewed in 1661 and in 1670, when fresh rules were added forbidding the fishermen to carry out passengers and directing that they should include one apprentice or "green man" to every four sailors. This was a direct attempt to increase the national reserve of trained mariners, and the fishermen were compensated for the requirement imposed upon them by a re-enactment of the rule forbidding settlers to hold

[1] Brit. Mus., Eg. 2395, no. 259.   [2] St. Pap. Dom., Interr. LXXVII, f. 532.

property within six miles of the shore. Since every settlement in Newfoundland lay at the water's edge, the rule was bound to be a dead-letter unless the colony were destroyed. The question as to the possibility of effecting this was repeatedly debated between 1656 and 1675, and both in 1671 and 1675 the Government, influenced by the powerful advocacy of Sir Josiah Child,[1] definitely decided to remove the settlers to Jamaica and St Christopher. The decision[2] was not lightly taken, but was a carefully considered though misguided attempt to restore prosperity to an industry of national importance that had suffered a series of unexampled disasters.

These disasters befell the industry partly from natural causes and partly at the hands of our national enemies, although the fishing merchants attributed their main misfortunes to the fishing of boatmen employed by the resident population, called in the papers of the time "bye-boatmen". In May 1665 Admiral de Ruyter raided the English fishermen and captured their first ships leaving with full cargoes for the Mediterranean. He sailed into the undefended harbour of St John's, destroyed the shipping and burned the planters' houses and the fishing stages. The voyages of 1666 and 1667 were ruined by Dutch privateers in the English Channel and the threat of more raids, while Algerine pirates repeatedly attacked the fleets and carried off their sailors as slaves. In 1673 Evertsen, one of de Boes' captains, returning from his recapture of New York, raided and burned Ferryland,[3] while the French menace, as we shall see later, was ever becoming more threatening. The New Englanders, too, were making serious inroads upon English profits. They not only employed local boatmen and carried off the catch to sell in the West Indies for the profit of the Boston shipowners, but they did a roaring trade in smuggled goods from Europe in flagrant defiance of the Navigation Acts. To mercantile theorists it seemed that the interests of the nation both public and private were being sacrificed for a mere handful of settlers, a large proportion of whom were recently arrived Irish Papists whose loyalty was more than doubtful.

The cod like other fish is uncertain, and between 1663 and 1675, owing to severe weather and a change in the direction of the usual migration, the fishing was uniformly bad on the Newfoundland coast,[4] although the French on the Banks and in the Gulf of St Lawrence were making large catches. The voyages from 1670 to 1673 were particularly disastrous for the western ports, for their boats returned almost empty, and great distress prevailed from Southampton round to Barnstaple. This fact more than anything else brought matters to the crisis of 1675, and in the minds of those in power amply justified their decision after full and painstaking

---

[1] Child, Sir Jos., *A New Discourse of Trade*, pp. 195–204.
[2] *A.P.C. Col.* 1, 565, 621–5.   [3] *Cal. St. Pap. Col.* 1669–74, p. 525.
[4] See Field, pp. 113–14, etc.

enquiry[1] to undertake drastic measures, the most striking being the removal of the colonists. The assertion made by one of the best-known historians of Newfoundland and accepted by other writers that the Committee on Trade and Plantations was debauched by the lavish bribery of Sir Josiah Child[2] is demonstrably unjustified. From 1675 onwards the system of naval convoy to the fishing fleets which had been irregularly used was better organised and made annual, and thus began that strong naval influence which was to save the island from the anarchy that had prevailed since the departure of Sir David Kirke. Amid the warring factions, the convoy captains were the only source of acknowledged and unbiassed authority, and the Privy Council knew that it was only from them that impartial and accurate evidence could be obtained. Their original purpose in 1675 was to organise the removal of the colonists, but they were also instructed to answer a number of well-chosen questions about the trade. Accordingly, in 1676 and 1677, the Government began to receive the first of a series of reports that continued for more than a hundred years. They provide a source of direct information that is almost unique. Their immediate result was to convince the Council that the most serious danger was to be found, not in the conflict of rival interests, but in the likelihood that, unless England bestirred herself, Newfoundland might fall wholly into the hands of the French.

Indeed this danger had become acute. In the first half of the seventeenth century the French alone fished along the southern shore of Newfoundland from Trepassey westward to Cape Ray, but they made no permanent settlements. At the close of the Spanish war Louis XIV determined to establish a fortified base at the entrance to the Gulf in order to protect Canada from attack, and in 1660 Placentia, the best harbour and fishing beach on the coast, was chosen as its site. It had long been frequented by French fishermen and in 1662 it was formally annexed and garrisoned by Du Mont. Sieur Gargot took out families of settlers from La Rochelle in 1663, and by 1668 Placentia was firmly occupied, with a resident governor,[3] and alien intruders were warned off along the whole southern shore which was proclaimed to be French territory. The French fishery was at the height of its prosperity from 1678 to 1689. Whereas about 1640 the English had 270 ships employing 20,000 men, by 1678 the average number of ships in each annual voyage had sunk to less than eighty, if the figures given are reliable. The merchants of La Rochelle, Morlaix, St Malo, and other French ports, on the other hand, at that period sent out annually nearly 300 vessels every year with some 20,000 men,[4] and their produce almost monopolised the Mediter-

---

[1] See *Cal. St. Pap. Col.* and *Cal. St. Pap. Dom.* 1674–5, *passim*.
[2] Prowse, p. 195.   [3] *Cal. St. Pap. Col.* 1661–8, p. 537.
[4] Peret, *Terre-Neuve*, p. 236; Musset, G., *Les Rochelais à Terre-Neuve*, pp. 93 ff.; Bellet, A., *La Grande Pêche de la morue à Terre-Neuve*, p. 55.

ranean markets. The industry was highly favoured by the King and Colbert, and the haphazard traditional customs of the fishing admirals were codified by an *Ordonnance* of 1681[1] into an organised system.

Sir William Poole, who was sent out as Commissioner in 1678 to report upon Newfoundland, gave the English Government a detailed account of the French activities and recommended that the orders for the removal of our colonists should be withdrawn, that instead the colony should be fortified and receive a governor, and that the French should be expelled from the southern shore.[2] Accordingly, the Privy Council (14 April 1678) decided to retain and fortify the colony;[3] and the issue with the French was fairly joined upon the outbreak of war in 1689, when Newfoundland became one of the lesser prizes to be fought for in the international struggle. That it had a connection with other causes of war in the minds of the powerful mercantile interests in the House of Commons who supported William III's policy is certain. If a French King ruled over Spain and Naples, the Mediterranean trade in stock-fish was likely to be closed to Englishmen and the profits of the industry would disappear, whatever happened in Newfoundland. It was as a subordinate part of the greater whole that our policy in the island was changed, and the settlers were freed from the threat that hung over them. The colony was reprieved, and the newer methods of the larger ports were preferred to the conservatism of the small western merchants because the Government saw the double part played by Newfoundland in supporting our power at sea. The fishery provided a nursery of seamen, it was true, but it was also true that unless the English navy could find a victualling base in Newfoundland waters, there could be little hope of success against enemies who were firmly planted in Canada.

The interval between 1681 and 1689 saw a lull of hostile activity on both sides. The treaty of neutrality as to America signed in November 1686[4] provided that neither power should molest or intrude upon the possessions of the other. If it were true, as was stated soon after the Restoration, that Charles II had made a secret agreement with Louis XIV to recognise French monopoly of the fishing from Cape Race to the westward and from Cape Bonavista northward,[5] apparently receiving in return recognition of our exclusive rights in the south-east, then the neutrality treaty was based on the principle of *uti possidetis* in Newfoundland as elsewhere. At this period the trade in contravention of the Navigation Acts of the New Englanders and New Yorkers was increasing, and the collectors of customs in the American colonies found the island one of the most dangerous loopholes in the trade system. Charlevoix states that the

---

[1] See de la Roncière, Ch., *La Question de Terre-Neuve*, p. 24.   [2] See Field, App. IV.
[3] *A.P.C. Col.* I, 887.   [4] Dumont, *Corps Diplomatique*, VII, pp. ii, 141.
[5] See the evidence of Lady Hopkins, sister of Sir David Kirke, writing in 1660, Brit. Mus., Eg. 2395, no. 266.

annual commerce of the merchants of St John's amounted to 17,000,000 *livres*,[1] but the secrets of this illicit trade were so carefully guarded that his statement cannot be verified.

With the outbreak of the war with France the life of the island was shadowed by raids and the fear of raids on both sides. The fishery was only one of the prizes to be fought for, and neither party could spare any considerable force from the main theatres of war. The forces engaged never amounted to more than a few hundreds, and generally the English were worsted. The ultimate possession of the island, however, was decided not by what happened there but by the results of the war in Europe. The first move against the French came in February 1690 when Captain Herman Williamson, an English privateer, took and plundered Placentia just before the fishing fleet was due to arrive. French privateers retaliated in the following year by raiding Ferryland and Bay Bulls, but in neither case was any lasting injury done. In 1692 and 1693 English fleets returning from the West Indies bombarded Placentia but did nothing more, and it was not until 1696 that serious action was attempted on either side. In the summer five English men-of-war attacked the French forts, but were unable to take them since de Brouillon, the new Governor, had put them in a good state of defence. The French in the autumn took Ferryland, shipped the inhabitants to England and burned the English buildings all along the coast save at St John's. Further, in November, the famous adventurer, d'Iberville, led a mixed force of French and Indians through the woods and surprised the settlement, and the inhabitants, being without any military defence, were compelled to capitulate. They were shipped off to Europe, and d'Iberville raided northwards until he was foiled by the stubborn defence of a handful of settlers at Carbonear. The blow was serious, for almost all the English settlements were sacked and burned and hardly an Englishman was left in the island. For once all interests were united in agreeing that the island must be garrisoned, and in June 1697 Colonel Gibson, an engineer, was sent over with four companies to fortify St John's. Twelve men-of-war were also sent out to dislodge the French on the southern shore, but the result was a disgraceful failure. With the Treaty of Ryswick (1697) came a short breathing space, nothing much having been gained by either side.

When war broke out again in 1702, little had been done to fortify St John's and the English were almost as defenceless as before, for the small military garrison was ill-paid and ill-furnished, and there were constant desertions to New England. In contrast the French during the interval of peace refortified Placentia and made it stronger than before, while the Malouins and Basques, exploiting fresh fisheries in the north and on the west coast, completely outsold

---

[1] Charlevoix, P. de, *Hist. de la Nouvelle France*, II, 185.

the Englishmen in Spain because their catches were better cured and arrived two months earlier. Captain Graydon,[1] who reported on the state of the island in 1701, showed that three-quarters of the New-foundland coast was in French possession,[2] and we seemed hopelessly beaten. The French made two or three successful raids with their Indian allies against isolated settlements, while the British Govern-ment was unwilling to spare any attention to the island other than to order certain of the West Indian expeditions to bombard Placentia on their way home. Admiral Graydon went so far in pursuance of these half-hearted orders as to reconnoitre the fortress in the autumn of 1703. Further French raids followed, but there were no reprisals, for the degenerate officers of the petty garrison at St John's spent their time in quarrelling and lining their pockets by illicit trade. Subercasse, the new Governor of Placentia, knew his enemies' weakness, and in January 1705 he led his forces through the woods and surprised the town of St John's. Many of the Irish settlers assisted him, but a remnant of Englishmen under Colonel Moody shut themselves up in the fort and refused to surrender. After five weeks of ineffectual siege Subercasse was compelled to retire with the booty he had wrung from the defenceless inhabitants and turned his attention to the other settlements. These he cruelly sacked and destroyed practically all English property outside St John's.

The disasters of 1705 decided the Government to make the military commandant supreme in the island in place of the annual convoy captains. But the disorders were worse than ever, and the soldiers found it impossible to manage the unruly fishermen or to keep the disaffected Irish from traitorous correspondence with the French. The smugglers from New England openly scoffed at the Acts of Trade and did as much business with the enemy as with the English fisher-men whom they debauched with illicit supplies of rum. The Board of Trade made repeated appeals to the ministry to give a settled government and a proper armament to the colony, but without effect. Neglect and disorder left the way open to a new French attack, and on 21 December 1708 St John's was surprised and taken for the third time. As there were no Indians with the French troops of de St Ovide, there was no barbarity, but he exacted a heavy ransom and practically forced all the English inhabitants along the eastern shore who would not abandon the island to accept French sovereignty. The loss of St John's was viewed in England almost with indifference, for with the change of government the old fishing interest regained its influence, and, as usual, could observe with complete equanimity the depopulation of the colony. The war, too, seemed nearly over, and the Newfoundland question passed into the hands of the diplomatists with whom it was to remain for exactly

[1] Later Admiral Graydon.   [2] *Cal. St. Pap. Col.* 1701, pp. 529–31.

200 years.[1] In the official instructions of 1709 to Marlborough and Townshend, one of the essential conditions was that France should "restore" Newfoundland and Hudson Bay,[2] and thenceforward this condition was regularly insisted on. The merchants kept their demands before the Government by repeated memorials, and finally France was compelled to yield. In the Thirteenth Article of the Treaty of Utrecht (11 April 1713) she acknowledged British sovereignty over the whole island of Newfoundland with the adjacent settlements on the islands of St Pierre and Miquelon, but the extraordinary and far-reaching concession was made that her subjects should be permitted "to take and dry fish" on the coast from Bonavista round the north and west coast to Point Riche,[3] a clause that entailed endless difficulties. The concession was only made to facilitate diplomatic bargaining about other things by plenipotentiaries who cared little and knew less about actual conditions in the fishery, but their ignorance was their own fault, for ever since Henry St John in April 1712 had asked the opinion of the Board of Trade as to the feasibility of allowing the French "a general right to fish and dry their fish in the sea of Newfoundland and on that coast as they have hitherto done",[4] the Government had been in possession of several reasoned memorials from experts strongly opposing any such concession.[5] However, the mischief was done, and so matters had to remain for the next fifty years. Another but lesser difficulty was introduced into the treaties without a full balancing of the circumstances. Spanish fishermen came to Newfoundland in the latter half of the seventeenth century in only negligible numbers, though Basque harpooners from Guipuscoa still found employment in the whaling industry. Spain, however, had a long memory for her past glories, and the Spanish plenipotentiaries at Utrecht were instructed to press for the inclusion of a clause safeguarding her ancient rights in the fishery. The English envoys agreed, and an ambiguous form of words was inserted in the treaty signed on 2 July 1713 stating that "Her Britannic Majesty consents...that all such privileges as the Guipuscoans and other people of Spain are able to make claim to by right, shall be allowed and preserved to them".[6]

Of our many changes of policy in the government of Newfoundland during the years of war, little need be said. In 1698 an "Act to encourage the Trade of Newfoundland" was passed.[7] It established most of the traditional rules upon the authority of Parliament in place of the earlier charters which came from the Crown. The existence of a colony of settlers was recognised by implication, and

---

[1] Until the decision of the Hague Court on American claims, 1910.
[2] *Hist. MSS. Comm. VIIIth Rep.* p. 36.
[3] Dumont, VIII, 341, Art. xiii.   [4] C.O. 194, V, 10.
[5] *Cal. St. Pap. Col.* 1711–12, nos. 234, 373, 374, 388.
[6] Dumont, VIII, 396, Art. xv.
[7] 10 Will. III, c. 14.

for the first time they were permitted to acquire legal titles to land. But the authority of the fishing admirals was also confirmed, and the inhabitants were forbidden to take "rooms" before the visiting fishermen were provided. Only those "rooms" held before 1685 might be retained, but even this gave to the inhabitants their first legal title. No regular form of government was provided for the colony, but the convoy captains were made supreme over all other authorities including the commandant of the garrison during their stay in the island every summer. They were the chief mainstay of order during the succeeding period, and came to be looked to as the only impartial dispensers of justice. When in 1728 a further step was taken and by Order-in-Council[1] the convoy captain was formally appointed governor, holding office usually for three years, the Government came to the form that it retained until the early years of the nineteenth century. In 1729 the first resident justices of the peace were appointed, and one of them served as deputy-Governor during the winter absence of the naval Governor, thus preserving some of the continuity of administration whose lack had been one of the most serious misfortunes of the colony in earlier years.

The Act of 1698 was almost the last victory of the western adventurers over their competitors, for their industry was declining fast, but there was a final attempt to revive the old restrictive policy in 1718. In that year the Board of Trade and Plantations, acting on the representations of the western ports and also moved by the great increase of New England's illicit trade, advised the Government that the fisheries had been obstructed not only by the late war but by "the irregularities of the inhabitants, traders and fishermen who reside in and resort to Newfoundland". They added that "the fishery has flourished as the inhabitants have been discouraged"[2] and urged once more that all the colonists should be removed. But such an idea was forty years out of date, and the Government wisely neglected it. It might have been practicable in 1676, but in 1718 it was ludicrous.

The mechanism of the trade at this period indicates by what means the small western ports had been beaten. The conflict was not merely one between nomadic fishermen and settled colonists, as has so often been stated. Prowse attributes most of the troubles to the venality or tyranny of the Home Government, but his own evidence shows that such an explanation is too simple. It was a struggle, like so many economic struggles, between an inefficient and outworn system and new and more profitable methods.[3] The smaller ports kept to the old ways and used barks which ran up to about seventy-four tons with a crew of some twenty-two men. On their arrival in the island in the spring they used the small boats they had brought

---

[1] *A.P.C. Col.* III, 218.
[2] *Journal of Commissioners for Trade and Plantations*, 1718, p. 15; Prowse, p. 191.
[3] See Field, *passim*.

with them, and after drying and salting their catch, barrelling it and lading it into their holds as early as they could, started off separately for Spain or Portugal to secure the first market and the best price. The cargoes they could carry were necessarily small, and the men who worked on shares with the owners were at the mercy of every accident and had no chance of making up for bad fishing in one place by good in another. Poole and Dartmouth abandoned the earlier methods before the end of the seventeenth century and followed the practice of London and Bristol in sending out large "sack-ships" filled with men who paid their passage or were employed on wages. On arrival the passengers took service as "bye-boatmen", while the hired employees used their masters' boats that had been left in the island during the winter and were got ready just before the fleets arrived. The sack-ships obtained their cargoes partly from their own men and partly by bartering the miscellaneous goods they had brought. They also tried to fill up their lading as early in the season as possible and sailed for the Italian markets as well as those outside the Straits of Gibraltar which the lesser men avoided. They were able to overcome difficulties that were fatal to the smaller men, and they were much better provided against dangers from the Algerines and other pirates. Most of their men were not skilled sailors like those of the lesser ports, but they made much better profits for the merchants, and before 1729 almost all the western adventurers had gone out of the business. Barnstaple and Bideford were the last to adhere to the old system (1735).[1]

Towards the middle of the eighteenth century the sack-ship men in their turn were driven out of the shore fishery and found their cargoes on the Banks 200 miles from the coast which until that period had never been frequented by Englishmen. The fishery of the southern and eastern shores passed entirely into the hands of the Newfoundlanders under the lead of a few principal merchants of St John's. In fact, as in most other industries, a division of labour took place. The catching, curing and sale of the cod were no longer concentrated in one set of hands, but three or more classes of employer specialised, each in one part of the industry. Even the fishing admirals suffered a change, and whereas they had once been rough and uneducated fishermen, by the middle of the eighteenth century the same names recurred again and again in their lists, many of them belonging to well-known and respected families like the Holdsworths of Dartmouth. With these changes St John's became a busy and prosperous town, deriving its profits not only from the cod but also from sealing, whaling and, even at so early a date, salmon fishing. Unfortunately for the British Exchequer a good deal of its prosperity was drawn from less reputable sources than the fisheries. The authorities found it impossible to put a stop to contraventions of the Acts of

[1] See Rogers, p. 118, quoting reports of convoy captains.

Trade and trafficking with the enemy in time of war. Much of the building materials for the French forts at Louisbourg and the provisions for its victualling were obtained through St John's, and Newfoundland fish was one of the chief articles carried by the New Englanders to pay for the contraband sugar of the French West Indies. It was often argued seriously by interested persons that since Newfoundland had never been formally recognised as a "Plantation", it was not provided for in the Navigation Acts and it was no offence to carry foreign goods there. Conversely it was a British "possession", so that it was no offence to import goods from thence into America. As in so many other niceties of the Acts of Trade the question could be and was argued both ways by the same quibbling merchants. For some inexplicable reason no custom-house was established in Newfoundland until the general tightening-up of the system in 1762; official laxity allowed the island to remain an anomaly in the fiscal arrangements of the Empire and a perpetual leak in the regulations that on paper seemed so water-tight.

Though certain merchants in St John's were prosperous, the rest of the colonists were miserably poor and at the mercy of the owners and storekeepers. The only standard of exchange was fish, and there was a truck system that loaded the fishermen with debt. Since there was little or no husbandry or other industry, they were utterly dependent upon the year's fishery, whether good or bad. The population increased four-fold between 1713 and the opening of the Seven Years' War, and a large proportion of the newcomers were Irishmen with very low standards of life. During the winter there was little employment, and since the commonest commodity in the island after the all-pervading codfish was rum, disorder was rampant. The alternation of intense summer labour and winter idleness made the people reckless and shiftless,[1] and not until the Society for the Propagation of the Gospel began to support a resident clergyman in 1703 were any of the elevating influences of religion provided.[2] Education there was none, and the conflict between the jurisdiction of the fishing admirals and the local justices of the peace left the preservation of order largely dependent upon the strong but rough and ready ideas of justice of the convoy captains. The picture is a painful one, but that things were not worse is a testimony to the sound common sense and high ideals of duty of a long succession of officers of the Royal Navy. Many well-known men who rose to high distinction served as naval governors in the eighteenth century, and names like those of Sir John Leake (1702), Lord Vere Beauclerk (1728), Rodney (1749), Graves (1762) and Sir Hugh Palliser (1764) are merely outstanding examples of a line of capable and diligent officers who saw service on a somewhat thankless station.

[1] Pedley, C., *Hist. of Newfoundland*, p. 205.
[2] The first church was built at St John's in 1699 and ministered to by a naval chaplain.

After the turmoil of the seventeenth century the history of New-foundland in the eighteenth seems featureless, and its main interest lies in the part played by the fishery question in European diplomacy. As the population increased the thin line of English settlements along the eastern shore stretched northwards, and the colonists began to resent bitterly their exclusion from the northern shore where were some of the best fishing grounds. The fatal provision of the Treaty of Utrecht began the long course of bickering with France about Newfoundland that stretched into the twentieth century; but before considering it brief reference must be made to the Spanish claims. In the spring of 1715 the Basque ports, relying on the new treaty, fitted out a fleet for the fishery, but when the vessels arrived in Newfoundland waters they were warned off by the English naval commanders and compelled to return empty. The Spanish am-bassador in London lodged a strong protest and claimed that as the original discovery of the fishery had been made by the Basques and they had frequented it ever since without molestation in time of peace, to refuse them access was in clear defiance of the treaty. This appeal to history was repeated in many subsequent memorials, but it had as little sound foundation as the British rejoinders which gave an entirely different version. On both sides demands were made for documentary evidence, and when there was practically none forth-coming, the deficiency was supplied by rash assertions that gave a travesty of the island's history. Diplomatic documents referring to Newfoundland after 1713 are characterised by an amount of hard swearing that makes them utterly untrustworthy as historical sources. In the Treaty of Madrid (1721) Great Britain promised to maintain the articles of the Treaty of Utrecht, but the access of Spanish fishermen was still prohibited by the officers in Newfound-land and the protests continued.[1] In the Treaty of Aix-la-Chapelle (1748), despite Spanish representations at the conference, no reference was made to the claims, but in that of Paris (1763) Spain was com-pelled to agree to their relinquishment, and by Art. XVIII all doubt about the exclusion of the Biscayans was removed.[2] French attempts were made to raise the question in the peace negotiations of 1780, but the claims to a share in the fisheries were ultimately withdrawn in return for the retrocession of East Florida[3] and the dispute was finally closed.

After the ratification of the Treaty of Utrecht France withdrew her garrison from Placentia to Louisbourg, but many of her fishermen remained in the island of St Pierre and in isolated harbours along the southern shore, notably at Port-aux-Basques. They did not refuse obedience to the English officers who came into contact with them,

[1] See Brown, V. L., in *Reports Can. Hist. Assn.* (1923), pp. 64–82.
[2] Martens, *Recueil des Traités*, I, 43.
[3] P.R.O. Treaty Papers, 68. Florida Blanca to Hussey, 2 May 1780, *cit.* Brown.

but official visits were very few. Placentia was occupied by a small English garrison in 1714 and placed under the Governor of Nova Scotia, but it was little used by our fishermen until after 1745, when it came under the administration of Newfoundland. French activities in the south were concentrated in Cape Breton Island and the idea of recovering their old possessions seems to have been abandoned. They made very full use of their privileges in Petit Nord, however, and warned off any British subjects who came there. The limits of the French shore as laid down in the treaty were debatable, for, though the position of Cape Bonavista was clear enough, there were permanent English settlements to the north of it that could not be removed. The position of Point Riche, the boundary point on the western coast, was quite uncertain, for while the French maintained that it coincided with Cape Ray, the south-western point of the island, the English put it more than 200 miles further north. But, save for occasional hunting parties from the French posts on the other side of the Straits of Belle Isle, the western shore of Newfoundland was almost unvisited before the middle of the century, and the matter did not become important until Labrador passed into British possession by the Treaty of Paris (1763).

During the Seven Years' War the garrison of the colony was neglected, and in June 1762 a French expedition under the Comte d'Haussonville landed a strong force of regulars at Bay Bulls without resistance. They marched overland to St John's and the tiny British garrison, outnumbered more than twelve to one, surrendered. The blow was serious, the whole year's fishery being destroyed. Captain Graves[1] was then on his way out in charge of a large convoy, and learning of the capture when off the Grand Banks he took prompt action. Troops were summoned from New York and Louisbourg, and Placentia was reinforced. Early in September 1762 a force a little weaker than the French appeared off St John's and troops were landed in the face of some resistance. The French squadron slipped out of the harbour under cover of a fog leaving their land forces to their fate, and seven days later d'Haussonville with some 800 men surrendered to Colonel William Amherst and was granted passage back to France.[2] The part played by the Newfoundland question in the peace negotiations has been discussed elsewhere,[3] and here we need refer only to the result. By the Treaty of Paris France was confirmed in possession of the fishing rights guaranteed at Utrecht, and the small islands of St Pierre and Miquelon off the southern shore were granted to her as an unfortified shelter for her fishermen since the Cape Breton harbours were denied to them. This concession was greeted with a storm of protest from the merchants engaged in the

[1] Afterwards Admiral Lord Graves.
[2] Despatches from *London Gazette*, 12 Oct. 1762, in Prowse, pp. 412–16.
[3] See vol. I, chap. xvii.

American trade, but it was without avail, and France has ever since retained these tiny remnants of her once vast possessions in North America. The cession of Canada involved that of Nova Francia or Labrador, which raised new questions for solution.

The War of the American Revolution gave rise to no serious threat to Newfoundland. The island was strongly garrisoned and was used as a base for the British squadrons on the North American station. American privateers raided the fishermen on several occasions before and during the war, and more than once small parties landed and burned some of the lesser settlements, but no lasting injury was done. In September 1783 the Treaty of Versailles with France confirmed the rights conceded by former treaties, but with two modifications. St Pierre and Miquelon were recognised as French territory in full right and without restrictions, and the French interpretation of the south-western limits of their fishery was recognised by substituting Cape Ray for the debatable Point Riche. On the eastern shore the actual state of affairs was recognised by substituting for Cape Bonavista Cape John, north of which no English settlements were to be found. The most serious concessions were made in the Declaration handed to the Comte de Vergennes immediately after the treaty had been signed. In this the promise was made that on the French shore "His Britannic Majesty will take the most effective measures for preventing his subjects from interfering in any manner by their competition with the fishery of the French during the temporary exercise of it...and he will for this purpose cause the fixed settlements which shall be formed there to be removed". Thus, as will appear later,[1] the colony was placed in shackles and sacrificed to the exigencies of the general diplomatic situation.

In the reorganisation undertaken in Newfoundland and Labrador after 1763 the first necessity was an exact survey of the island coasts, the lack of any accurate map having greatly hampered our negotiators. The task was entrusted to Captain James Cook who had been a "master" in one of the frigates in Wolfe's expedition against Quebec in 1759. The celebrated navigator was engaged upon this task for the greater part of the years 1762–7, and the publication of his admirable map[2] in 1768 gave for the first time a true delineation of the island coasts and the Straits of Belle Isle. As naval Governor in 1764–8 Sir Hugh Palliser took a strong and definite line. He defined the rights of the French under the treaty and showed clearly that they were there on sufferance. All trading with the inhabitants was suppressed and the regulation of the cod fishery was kept in English hands. Frenchmen who remained in the island after the season was over were deported, and any who attempted whaling had their vessels confiscated. On the other hand, any interference with the acknowledged French rights was drastically suppressed, and much stricter

[1] See chapter xvii.   [2] Reproduced in Prowse, p. 317.

order was enforced in the colony than ever before. Palliser devoted great attention to the suppression of illicit trading by the New Englanders, and he had a large measure of success in bringing it to an end.

The newly-annexed territory of Labrador having been placed under the Governor of Newfoundland, Palliser took prompt measures to establish British control[1] and develop new fisheries. Fort Pitt was built on Château Bay and garrisoned with marines; friendly relations were established with the Montagnais Indians, and endeavours were made to protect the Eskimos who then came as far south as the Straits of Belle Isle. The fishermen who were driven off the French shore passed to Labrador, and Palliser had very great difficulty in controlling the New Englanders who came with them. They attacked and plundered the Eskimos and refused to obey any regulations.[2] His successors found even more difficulty as relations between the Home Government and the American colonies became more and more strained. By the Quebec Act (1774)[3] Labrador was removed from the government of Newfoundland and placed under the control of the Governor of Canada, and many of Palliser's measures were abandoned. But his advice was much relied on by the Government in passing a new Act for the encouragement of the fisheries[4] by which bounties were paid for British vessels employed in the Newfoundland trade. The wheel had come full circle. Whereas in 1676 the visiting fishermen outnumbered the inhabitants twenty to one and all that seemed necessary to encourage the trade was to deport the colonists, now, a hundred years later, the inhabitants were more than 15,000 and the fishermen only 9000,[5] so that the Government had to attempt to increase their numbers by bounties and other artificial means. Despite neglect, and sometimes in the face of positive hostility, a true colony had grown up, and henceforward its development became more normal, its peculiar amphibious character gradually passing away.

[1] See Labrador case before the Judicial Committee of Privy Council (1927). *Evidence*, vol. III, pp. 930 seqq.
[2] Palliser to Governor Bernard of Massachusetts, 7 Aug. 1766, *cit.* Prowse, p. 327.
[3] 14 Geo. III, c. 83.   [4] Palliser's Act, 15 Geo. III, c. 31.
[5] Palliser's Report of 1765, *cit.* Prowse, p. 325.

CHAPTER VI

THE PROBLEM OF GOVERNMENT, 1760–1774

THE conquest of Canada presented Britain with a gigantic problem. Hitherto the Empire had grown chiefly by peaceful expansion and settlement rather than by conquest. Now, at one stroke, a huge territory was taken over, a territory already settled by another European people with a civilisation very different from that of Britain and as old and fixed. What was she to do with it and its inhabitants? The acquisition of Acadia, fifty years earlier, had given a foretaste of this problem. If Britain could have worked out a solution there, the experience would have been invaluable. But the policy of religious toleration and non-interference had, as we have seen, been ineffectual and had ended in the tragic deportation of 1755. The difficulty of incorporating this French and Roman Catholic colony into an English and Protestant Empire was aggravated by special circumstances. Britain and France, then chronic foes, might soon again be at war. Would not the Canadians look with longing eyes towards the mother country from whom they had been torn? The French, moreover, were not to remain the sole inhabitants of Canada, for a small but important English mercantile community immediately appeared, adding a disparate element which made the problem more complex. Difficulties also arose from the proximity of the old colonies whose dependence upon the mother country was now lessened by the expulsion of France from America. A government adapted to Canadian conditions might easily rouse their suspicions. Another embarrassment in the American background was Britain's new responsibility for the management of the large Indian population formerly bound by close ties to the French. Already disquieted by the pressure of English settlement, and now dismayed by the surrender of the French, they might rise at any time. Indeed, the attempt to forestall the fierce native rising known as Pontiac's revolt was to precipitate an unfortunate settlement in Canada.

The problem of the government of Canada called for higher statesmanship than was forthcoming after the accession of George III and the subsequent dislocation of British political life. Then in succession came the American revolt and the French Revolution, upheavals that were to postpone any real solution until a century after the country was conquered. Fortunately, such statesmen as George III could trust did not at once shoulder the responsibility for the administration of the new colony. They left it to the chiefs of the victorious army who formed the first British Government of the country. Though Quebec fell in 1759 and the whole colony was surrendered a year later, Canada was but an occupied territory until ceded by the Treaty of Paris, 10 February 1763. As the treaty allowed all who wished to retain their French nationality a further period of eighteen months to withdraw themselves and their possessions, the people of Canada could not be regarded as wholly British until 10 August 1764. Thus the "military regime" or "*règne militaire*" lasted in all nearly five years in Quebec and four years in Montreal and Three Rivers.

The Canadian people whom these army leaders governed numbered between 60,000 and 65,000. The towns of Quebec and Montreal together contained about a fifth of the population. Three Rivers was only a straggling village of 600. The rest, except for a few small colonies at Detroit and further west, were settled along the St Lawrence valley from just above Montreal. The tradition of a general exodus of the better classes when the country fell to the British is no longer accepted. Almost all the old seigneurial families, and apparently most of the bourgeoisie and the professional classes remained, while the clergy stood solidly by their flocks. The departure of the French army drew a number of Canadian officers to France, but many of these came back after a few months, disappointed with their reception in the land of their forefathers. But if there was no social decapitation, there was an administrative decapitation, for the whole body of responsible civil officials, natives of France and appointed by the Home Government, departed with the French forces and left the commanders of the British army to improvise a Government.

The completeness of the British victory inclined the Canadians to submit to British rule, but there were hidden reservations. New France, staunchly Catholic, had fallen to a Protestant conqueror and in this supreme crisis its Church was without a head. Bishop Pontbriand had died just before the surrender of the colony and though the chapter elected three vicars-general to govern the diocese, Briand of Quebec, Perrault of Three Rivers and Montgolfier of Montreal, these lacked the vital power to ordain priests. A bishop was essential to the life of the Church, but there was no prospect of a bishop. Amherst had flatly refused Vaudreuil's demand for a continuance of the old arrangement of appointment by the French Crown, and appointment by the Protestant King of Great Britain was equally impossible. Hence there was a certain hollowness in the capitulation's promise of toleration. The hope that France, refusing to desert her child, would insist on a restoration at the close of the war operated to allay the natural uneasiness, but it also retarded the reconciliation of the people. When the treaty dashed this hope, the religious apprehensions of the Canadians were livelier than ever, for now the promise of toleration was qualified by the clause, "as far as the laws of Great Britain permit". This delicate religious situation, while calling for no immediate action, portended trouble for the future.

During the military regime, Canada had three Governments, those of Quebec, Three Rivers and Montreal. They were directly under the Commander-in-Chief who resided in New York, and were quite independent of each other. The first was formed immediately after the capture of Canada's citadel with Brigadier-General James Murray, fifth son of the Scottish Lord Elibank, as Governor. The other two were formed a year later upon the surrender of the country. Canada had been divided by the French into three districts. These Amherst continued without alteration, placing Colonel Ralph Burton over Three Rivers and Brigadier-General Thomas Gage over Montreal. Murray remained in Quebec until the end of the military regime, when he became Canada's first British Governor, but the others were shifted. In October 1763 Gage took over the command-in-chief from Amherst and was succeeded in Montreal by Burton, and Colonel Frederick Haldimand, who had temporarily replaced Burton during his absence on an expedition to Havana from May 1762 to March 1763, now succeeded him in Three Rivers. All the military Governors spoke French. Murray was particularly noted for his proficiency in that tongue, and Haldimand, a Swiss by birth, was so little master of the English language that Gage often wrote to him in French. Their secretaries, through whose hands all the detailed business of government passed, were French by blood. One was from French Switzerland, the others were of Huguenot families settled in the British Isles.

The new Government, thus largely French at the head, was purely French below. Under the Old Regime, the two most important local functionaries were the *curé* and the captain of the militia. The latter, who was much more than a militia officer, was commonly the leading "habitant" of the parish. Very naturally, Murray immediately made use of them, particularly the layman, and when Amherst became master of the country, he followed in Murray's steps, directing the Governors of Montreal and Three Rivers to recommission and employ the captains of militia. They proved an invaluable link between the people and the new Government. They disarmed the population at the beginning, and with the *curés* took the census. As before the conquest, they published all Government documents by reading them on Sunday at the church door after service, and almost every order of the Government was carried out by them or under their direction. They supervised the maintenance of roads, the repair of bridges, and the provision of fuel and straw for the garrisons. They were responsible for policing their districts and the people were commanded to obey them. In addition to their old duties, they assumed the important function of justices of the peace.[1] Appeals lay to courts of British army officers who also possessed an original jurisdiction. These

[1] Burt, A. L., "Who was the 'Com(man)d(ant) de la Troupe dans Chaque Coste'?" *Can. Hist. Rev.* Sept. 1926, VII, 226.

tribunals seem an exception to the French character of the Government, but they had Canadian assistants, they followed the old laws as closely as possible, and, except for a very few entries, their records were all in French. One poor English merchant being sued in Quebec asked for a copy of the case against him that he might have it translated into English. The judges, his fellow-countrymen, granted his request but ordered him to reply in French, the language of the country.[1]

The law of Canada was accepted as it was found. The preamble in one of Gage's decrees implies that the unsettled fate of the country was the cause, but the treaty brought no attempt at change. The further reason was the principle, which the military Governors consciously applied, that the laws of a conquered country remain until expressly altered by the new sovereign.[2] The legislation of the period,[3] issued rather indiscriminately as proclamations, ordinances, decrees and orders, effected only necessary innovations. Courts of justice had to be established and reformed; the circulation of the heavily depreciated paper currency had to be stopped, and the value of the many different coins which now appeared, out of hiding or imported by the army, had to be fixed; prices had also to be regulated, for the influence of worthless paper lingered. Apart from these alterations, which were no more English than French in character, the legislation of the conqueror dealt chiefly with markets, butchers and bakers, fire prevention, roads and traffic, the protection of game during the mating season, the rights of seigneurs and the countless other details of daily life. It was inspired by one idea, the preservation of Canadian society as it existed. Even the spirit of the Old Regime breathes through these new ordinances, which were often appeals rather than commands. Hearing that his "proclamation" against hucksters was not obeyed, Burton called upon the militia captains "if you please, to refresh the memories of the inhabitants"; and Gage, after ordering "the mourning which must be worn for His late Majesty King George II", added that "an exact observance of the regulations before mentioned will not be insisted upon".

But signs of change soon appeared. Freed from the distractions of war, the "habitants" struck deeper roots than ever into the soil. When the Commander-in-Chief called for Canadians to aid in crushing Pontiac's rising, they were very slow to volunteer. They objected, not to fighting the Indian, but to fighting at all, for they had tasted the sweets of peace. The conquest also brought new ideas of liberty, even against the Church. In 1762 Murray reported daily resistance to the collection of the tithes. But more important was the freedom of the

[1] Pub. Arch. Can. *Registre d'audiance du conseil militaire de Québec*, 1760-2 (transcripts from originals in Quebec), II, 129.
[2] Pub. Arch. Can. *Series C.O.* 5 (transcripts from originals in Public Record Office), LXV, 89.
[3] Pub. Arch. Can. *Report* 1918, App. B.

individual in secular affairs. Instead of being ordered to fight or labour for nothing, or to surrender his produce for worthless paper, he was now paid for almost everything which he did or supplied at a good market price and in real money. There was also an end to all cramping monopolies. All that was necessary for trade was a licence which could be had for nothing. Amherst's famous "placard",[1] promising that the old laws would be retained, that the army was to pay its own way, and that trade would be free, was a veritable charter of liberties to the conquered. Equally significant was the attitude of the conqueror. At once the English "private" was on cordial terms with the "habitant", helping him in the field and his daughter in the kitchen. During the second winter in Quebec, when the English merchants and officers collected over £500 to relieve the distressed Canadians in that city, the soldiers insisted on giving up one day's provisions a month to the same cause.[2] This spontaneous feeling of the rank and file was shared by those in authority. In November 1759 Murray wrote to Amherst: "*En bonne politique* it [Canada] should be perhaps destroyed, but there may be reasons why it should remain, as it is a guarantee for the good behaviour of its neighbouring colonies. . . . Until I have the Honour to receive your orders, I shall follow the natural dispositions of my heart, which dictates Clemency; This Conduct can do no hurt, because the Effects of it may be undone in one week; It may have a permanent advantage".[3] Immediately after Canada was surrendered, Amherst instructed the military Governors that "the inhabitants of this country are now as much His Majesty's subjects as any of us", and ordered them to see that the troops lived "in good harmony and brotherhood with them",[4] and a year later the Secretary of State was more explicit.[5] But such orders were quite unnecessary, for they were executed before ever they were issued. The Secretary of State, however, was inspired by design rather than by sentiment. As Monckton and Murray had earlier urged,[6] he now insisted that the Canadians must be persuaded to remain in Canada to preserve the value of the conquest. In the interests of the Empire and of Canada, the Canadians were to be won. Not until the following century, when an unfortunate experience gave rise to a different tradition, were the happy memories of this courting time of French and English forgotten.

Thus the military conquest was followed by a moral conquest which makes this regime unique in the history of military occupations. It was well that the wounds of battle should be cleansed by those who had inflicted them, and not by civilians who might have troublesome

---

[1] Pub. Arch. Can. *Report* 1918, p. 21.
[2] Pub. Arch. Can. *Murray Papers* (transcripts from originals in Bath), III, 49.
[3] *Ibid.* I, 6.   [4] Pub. Arch. Can. *Series C.O.* 5, LIX, 250 seqq.
[5] Pub. Arch. Can. *Haldimand Papers, Series B* (Brit. Mus.), XXXVII, 10.
[6] Pub. Arch. Can. *Series C.O.* 5, LXIV, 61.

notions about English laws supplanting French laws. These years deserve more attention than they have usually received. They were of untold importance in the history of Canada, for then were laid the foundations of French-Canadian trust in the justice of British rule, a trust which is vital to Canada with her dual nationality. These years were also important in the history of the Empire, for the French of Canada were the first great body of another race to enjoy that liberty which is the secret of the British Empire.

There is another side to the history of the military regime that had important consequences. On the morrow of the conquest a small English-speaking mercantile community appeared. Its members were called "old subjects" in contradistinction to the Canadians who were known as "new subjects". The first merchants came with the army as sutlers, but they were few compared with the numbers that poured in after the fall of Montreal. Five days after that event, Amherst issued a general invitation to the "traders and adventurers" in the neighbouring colonies to come to Montreal and Quebec with supplies necessary for the comfort of the troops and of the population. Promising them a good market and every encouragement, he specified a number of articles for which they would find a particular demand, and undertook to facilitate their transport by the Lake Champlain route, for he thought the season too late for them to sail up the Gulf.[1] Within a fortnight the invitation was published in New England, and the "rush" began both by sea and by land. Goods to the value of £60,000 were shipped to Canada by the beginning of December.[2] How many merchants came at this time is not definitely known, but with the sutlers they appear to have formed the backbone of the English "colonies" of Quebec and Montreal. In 1761 their numbers were increased by new arrivals, many of them from England. After that, they only trickled in, though there may have been a considerable immigration at the time of the treaty. At the close of the military regime, they were only about four hundred, and their dependents were few, for many of them were young bachelors. Except a handful of Jews all were Protestants. The great majority were born in the British Isles, but so many of them had lived in the old colonies that their society had a distinct American tone, particularly in Montreal, which was in constant communication with neighbours to the south. They settled in the towns of Quebec and Montreal, and few of them acquired any more property than was necessary for the conduct of their business. They were the chief importers and exporters of Canada, the bulk of their trade being with the mother country. Many who established themselves in Quebec became interested in the fisheries of the Gulf, which they developed, while their brethren of Montreal tended to be drawn into the fur trade of the upper country, for which enterprises they employed

---

[1] *Ibid.* LIX, 174 seqq. [2] *Ibid.* LIX, 361; LX, 3.

native Canadians. Their character has been much discussed. Murray and, later, Carleton condemned them as the scum of the earth, masquerading as its salt, only to evoke the reply that solid London business houses would never grant such extensive credits to a lot of worthless nobodies.[1] Of course there were some rascals among these adventurers on the frontier of the Empire, but the majority appear to have been of respectable character and of no mean education.

Not ill conduct, but an utter incompatibility of character embroiled them with the army that had called them in. Socially they were separated by an impassable gulf from the officers of that day. The merchant was apt to regard the soldier's as a barbarous profession, while the officer looked down on the trader's as a mean calling. Politically they were civilians to the core, worshipping British liberty as much as their military rulers believed in British order. They insisted that they carried English laws "on their backs", and that neither French laws nor military authority could touch them.[2] They eschewed the established courts, settling their own differences by arbitration. But sometimes they were haled before the courts of army officers for misdemeanours or violations of military Governors' decrees, or disputes with Canadians or members of the army, and then their defiant attitude and the officers' scorn led to at least one flagrant miscarriage of justice.[3] The friction, noticeable in 1762, was a serious factor in the life of the colony by the end of the next year. One amusing incident in the strife was a ball given by the Quebec officers in the fall of 1763; they invited the merchants' wives without their husbands, and the latter never forgave the insult.[4] The peace treaty and the royal proclamation of 7 October 1763 intensified the feud by stiffening the merchants' attitude. Now that Canada was finally British and had the promise of English laws, why should this military and French regime be continued? To many merchants it was plain tyranny. An explosion might have occurred had they known what was passing in correspondence across the Atlantic. Home officials challenged the jurisdiction of military courts over civilians, and Gage replied, half in dismay and half in anger, that the Home Government was responsible for this flaw in the Canadian administration because the King had given it his general approval.[5] Murray alone had suspected this defect and from the beginning had tried to evade the awkward responsibility by punishing civilians with words rather than with fines and imprisonment;[6] but his sharp tongue made things no easier in Quebec than in Montreal. It is hard to blame either

---

[1] Pub. Arch. Can. *B.M. Add. MSS.* 35915, *Hardwicke Papers*, p. 19.
[2] Pub. Arch. Can. *Series C.O.* 5, LXV, 89.
[3] Transcripts from Pub. Arch. Can. *Series Q*, X, 95 seqq.
[4] *Ibid.* V, 626.
[5] Pub. Arch. Can. *Series C.O.* 5, LXV, 88 seq.
[6] Pub. Arch. Can. *Murray Papers*, II, 29, 53; III, 52.

merchants or military Governors, for both were largely justified. Nevertheless, the whole episode stored up trouble for the future.[1]

Meanwhile the alternative of retaining or of restoring Canada had been a burning question at home. A flood of pamphlets discussed the problem from every angle, the security of the old colonies, their dependence upon the mother country, the development of shipping, and the material value of the conquered territories. The argument settled down to a choice between Canada and Guadeloupe.[2] This little island exported half a million pounds' worth of sugar and cotton while Canada produced only a few thousand pounds' worth of furs. But Canada won. It was believed that Guadeloupe would soon fall an easy prey to British sea power now that North America was solidly British, and the tide of policy was turning away from tropical islands, which supplied only raw produce, towards populous continental colonies, which promised an expanding market for growing British manufactures.[3] By the Treaty of Paris, 10 February 1763, France renounced all claim to Canada and its dependencies, and in return Britain promised to grant the Canadians toleration, "as far as the laws of Great Britain permit". The French objected to this qualification, but had to yield. They had accepted it fifty years before when ceding Acadia, and now they were told that the King of Great Britain had no power to grant toleration in any other manner.

Having secured Canada, Britain faced the problem of giving it a Government. The solution was comprised in the Royal Proclamation of 7 October 1763, in Murray's commission as Governor, 21 November 1763, and in his instructions, 7 December 1763. All were the work of the Board of Trade and Plantations, then responsible for the detailed administration of the colonies. The Proclamation established Governments in the new territories of North America and the West Indies and created a vast Indian reserve in the heart of the continent. In addition to defining the new Governments of East and West Florida and Grenada, it changed Canada's name to Quebec and greatly reduced its size. The southern boundary was drawn so as to cut off lands not yet settled by the French that they might be added to Nova Scotia, which then included the three maritime provinces of to-day, in the expectation that it would develop as a solid English colony. Labrador was cut off on the east and added to Newfoundland to prevent smuggling and possible French encroachments in that quarter. All the western territory from close to the Ottawa River was severed as a necessary part of the new policy of placating the restive Indians by preserving their hunting grounds from the invasion of settlers. While forbidding any settlement and any private purchase of lands in this great reserve, the Proclama-

---

[1] See Kennedy, W. P. M., *Constitution of Canada*, chs. iv, v; Mahon, R. H., *Life of General Murray*.

[2] See vol. i, pp. 503, 591 and Grant, W. L., "Canada versus Guadeloupe", *Am. H.R.* July 1912, xvii, 735.   [3] Beer, G. L., *British Colonial Policy*, 1754–65, chap. viii.

tion promised free trade. Any Governor would supply a licence gratis to each trader who gave security that he would observe the regulations imposed. To draw settlers to the new colonies, the Proclamation promised Assemblies as soon as possible, "the Enjoyment of the Benefit of the Laws of our Realm of England" immediately, and, except in Grenada, special inducements to officers and soldiers to take up lands. Murray's commission empowered him to create courts of justice and to legislate with the advice of a Council and Assembly. His instructions prescribed a Council of four officials and eight nominees from among the residents, with which he was to make necessary regulations until he could summon the Assembly. Both Council and Assembly were to be Protestant. The instructions also contained elaborate provisions for the attraction of an agricultural population from the congested colonies to the south and for the gradual conversion of the Canadians. In short, this old French colony was to be remodelled on the English type.

To some modern eyes, this solution of the problem has seemed so impossible that an ingenious argument has been advanced to palliate the blunder.[1] But English eyes of those days saw differently. Though the Government had designs upon the religion of the Canadians, it had no idea of violating the treaty guarantee, which was limited to "worship" according to the "rites" of the Roman Catholic Church. "The laws of Great Britain" distinctly forbade the exercise of any foreign ecclesiastical jurisdiction. The Canadians were not to be coerced; they were to be persuaded to see the light. The Board of Trade was soon to elaborate a plan of Church government for Quebec which was permeated with this idea, and already Governor Murray, about the best friend the Canadians ever had, was toying with various schemes to convert them. The Proclamation "gives every body great Content and Satisfaction", he reported in January 1764.[2] If the influx of land-seekers from the south had come then instead of a generation later, the new system of government would not have remained without a foundation. How could the Home Government foresee that the appeal of the royal promise would be vain, and that Murray's Proclamation[3] advertising Canadian lands would also fail, though it was published at considerable expense in the old colonies[4] and had all the allurements of a modern immigration poster? Moreover, the normal government of all British colonies was by Governor, Council and Assembly. Only experience could teach the necessity for a different policy in the new colony.

On 10 August 1764 Murray became civil Governor of the whole province and began to erect the new system. He was all ready with his Council, which deserves special notice for it assumed an

---

[1] Alvord, C. W., "The Genesis of the Proclamation of 1763", in *Proc. of Michigan Hist. Soc.* 1908.

[2] Pub. Arch. Can. *Murray Papers*, II, 63.   [3] Pub. Arch. Can. *Report* 1918, App. C, p. 3.

[4] Pub. Arch. Can. *Minutes of Legislative Council*, B, p. 155.

unexpected importance. Of the four official members two never appeared, for Gage and Burton refused appointments as Lieutenant-Governors of Montreal and Three Rivers, whereupon these two offices disappeared. The third, the Surveyor-General of the American Customs, rarely appeared. Only the Chief Justice attended regularly, and as the first holder of that office carried no weight, Murray's nominees were practically the whole Council. Sharing his sympathy for the Canadians, they were to be the nucleus of the "French party" which practically governed Canada until 1787. Colonel Irving, a solid Englishman, and Adam Mabane, a warm-hearted Scot, were its first leaders. Irving returned home in the spring of 1768, but Mabane spent the rest of his life in Quebec. He was surgeon of the garrison and senior judge of the Common Pleas, and, after a pre-liminary quarrel, became the intimate of Carleton and the almost sole confidant of Haldimand. This Council took its responsibility seriously, passing a resolution for weekly sessions but often meeting more frequently, for it regulated practically everything of importance affecting the civil government of the province.

The administration of justice was provided for by an ordinance of 17 September 1764. This was drafted by Chief Justice William Gregory and Attorney-General George Suckling, who had been ap-pointed by the Home Government and had already arrived in the colony. The ordinance created a superior Court, or Court of King's Bench, and an inferior Court, or Court of Common Pleas. The Chief Justice presided over the former, which possessed both criminal and civil jurisdiction based on the laws of England and the ordinances of the province. French and English were to be admitted without dis-tinction to juries in this court. The Court of Common Pleas, intended for the Canadians, had only a civil jurisdiction. In cases arising before 1 October 1764 it could apply French law, but in all other suits it was to apply equity, keeping as close as possible to English law, which was ultimately to prevail. Canadian advocates might plead in this court, but there was no mention of Canadians on juries, which were optional. The ordinance also gave an extensive juris-diction to justices of the peace and provided for the appointment of bailiffs from among the "habitants". For all offices except the last, which was a burden, Roman Catholics were legally disqualified. Their admission as jurors in the King's Bench and as advocates in the Common Pleas was a conscious waiving of the law, for which Murray excused himself to the Home Government.

The keystone of the arch of government was never laid. Grenada got an Assembly at this time, but Grenada's Governor went out fresh to his job[1] while Murray had lived in Canada since 1759 and knew its people. He refused to call an Assembly because that would place

[1] Higham, C. S. S., "The General Assembly of the Leeward Islands", *E.H.R.* July 1926, XLI, 366.

65,000 Canadians at the mercy of a handful of English-speaking merchants. The new constitution was an utter misfit. It was not English because its arrested development left the mercantile minority under what they regarded as an arbitrary Government. Nor was it Canadian; for the natives of the country were shut out of every office but that of bailiff, their laws were proscribed, and their religion was in jeopardy. The system pleased no one, least of all Murray. He sympathised deeply with the Canadians but his hands were forced against them. Therefore he sent his secretary, Cramahé, home to press for an adjustment in their favour. This mission, the petitions of the Canadians, and Murray's pleading despatches drew attention to the injustice committed in Quebec, and started a reaction which was ultimately to lead to the Quebec Act. It began with the report of the Attorney- and Solicitor-General, 10 June 1765, affirming that the penal laws of England did not apply to Canada. Then the Board of Trade denounced the ordinance of 17 September 1764. One criticism was that it refused Canadians full equality with other British subjects in the courts, and Murray was therefore instructed to remove the discrimination. Meanwhile, to quiet the fears of the Canadians for their property, he himself had issued an ordinance continuing French laws of tenure and inheritance until 10 August 1765, and the judges of the Common Pleas, though they lacked specific authority for so doing, had made French law the rule for judgments affecting the property of Canadians, and admitted Canadians to sit on juries.

Still more delicate was the question of the headship of the Church. As neither the old nor the new sovereign could nominate a bishop, the dean and chapter of Quebec seized the opportunity to revive the ancient custom of election. But Murray distrusted Montgolfier, their choice, and believed that Canada might do without a bishop. Could not the vicars-general continue to administer the diocese and priests educated in the Quebec Seminary be sent abroad for consecration? But when the Canadians planned to send a deputation to Great Britain to plead with the Government for a bishop, he acquiesced in their going and intimated his preference, if a bishop were to be allowed, for Briand, whom he commended in the highest terms.[1] Montgolfier was obliged to forego his hopes, and the chapter now elected Briand who crossed the Atlantic to further the Church's cause. During the months of negotiation which followed, he made a good impression. But the intervention of the French ambassador, the machinations of a renegade Jesuit from Canada, and difficulties at Rome, all conspired to delay a settlement. Offended by the double election in Quebec, Rome preferred to govern the Canadian Church through a vicar apostolic, which the British Government could not tolerate. Finally Rome agreed, and Briand was unofficially told that he might return as superintendent of the Church in the colony if he

[1] Pub. Arch. Can. *Series Q*, 1, 251 seqq.

were consecrated quietly, as he was in the spring of 1766. When he returned to Quebec in June of that year there was great rejoicing, for the crisis in the history of the Canadian Church had passed. To the Canadians, Briand was bishop; to the Government, he was only superintendent of the Roman Church in Quebec. He played his difficult rôle admirably. Sharing the simple life of the seminary priests and avoiding all outward pomp, he gave no offence to any Protestant except the Huguenot Masères.

In contrast with the quiet attitude of the Canadians, the English-speaking merchants made a great noise. Exasperated by Murray's sympathy for the "new subjects" and his breach of the royal promise contained in the Proclamation of 7 October 1763, they determined to force an Assembly upon him or to drive him home in disgrace. Feelings pent up during the military regime broke loose, and the province was soon in an uproar. The first grand jury of Quebec, selected so as to include some of the worst malcontents,[1] arraigned the Government of the colony and demanded that every ordinance and all public accounts be passed by a grand jury. The fourteen Protestants on the jury brought in an additional presentment denouncing the admission of Roman Catholics to juries, and the seven Canadians, discovering what had been done, declared that they had been hoodwinked. More serious was the trouble in Montreal where there were no barracks for the troops, and the merchants who had been chosen justices of the peace insisted that they alone had power to billet soldiers. Some of them exercised their new authority to pay off old scores against the army. The ringleader was Thomas Walker, a Londoner who had lived in Boston. He so roused the ire of the army that a party of soldiers broke into his home, beat him thoroughly and carried off part of his ear as a trophy. Murray and his Council rushed up to investigate and some of the culprits were laid by the heels. Every effort to bring them to justice, however, was baffled by the blind rage of Walker and his friends.[2] The upshot was a confused three-cornered quarrel. The civilian faction blamed the army for shielding the criminals and the Governor for assisting them to escape; Murray accused Walker and the other civilians of blocking the course of justice and the army of protecting the guilty; while the army believed that the Governor had combined with the merchants to persecute innocent officers and men.

In their efforts to wreck the Governor, the mercantile minority tried to bring pressure upon the Government at home. They made political capital out of their finding a vent for British manufactures, they used their debts to London business houses to enlist their powerful interest, and they engaged Fowler Walker, a barrister of Lincoln's Inn, to conduct the campaign. From Canada and from

[1] Burt, A. L., "The Mystery of Walker's Ear", *Can. H.R.* Sept. 1922, III, 233.
[2] *Ibid.*

London, a storm of petitions blackened Murray's character, demanded his recall and the appointment of a "civil" governor. Regarded as the *protégé* of Bute and of Lord George Sackville, Murray was easily prejudiced in the eyes of the Home Government. The Walker episode capped the climax and the Governor was summoned home to give an account of his administration.

Some have blamed Murray's temper for his troubles, but he was placed in an impossible situation, forced to impose an English yoke upon the Canadians whom he admired, and to withhold the Assembly which should never have been promised. He was also ill supported by the Home Government. Robbed of all military authority the moment he became civil Governor, he was set over against Burton who commanded the army. Hotheads on both sides embittered relations until the Governor was actually refused admission to his own capital.[1] This division of authority was excused on the ground that it was insisted upon in the other colonies. But nothing can excuse the appointment of poor tools instead of able instruments to help the Governor. The Chief Justice had a shady past, knew little law and less French, and his closest companion was the worst rogue in Canada, while the Attorney-General was a legal pedant, utterly ignorant of human nature and of the language of the country. They repeatedly betrayed Murray into legislation that incurred the censure of the Home Government. It was a much wronged Governor who sailed from Quebec, 28 June 1766; but already the tide of opinion was setting in his favour. The King warmly welcomed him, showing approval of his policy by promising him Canadian judges, and the Government were now convinced by his replies to the malicious charges against him. His accusers shrank from the official investigation which they had demanded, and an Order-in-Council publicly vindicated him.[2] Though retaining his title of Governor, Murray had no desire to return to the turbulent politics of the colony, and this first British Governor to win the hearts of the Canadian people, as they themselves said,[3] passed out of Canadian history.

Colonel Guy Carleton landed in Quebec three months after Murray's departure. Although he did not succeed him as Governor until 1768 and meanwhile was only Lieutenant-Governor, Carleton had full control of the Government from his arrival. Like his Scottish predecessor, this Irish soldier was a brilliant officer who had served under Wolfe at the siege of Quebec. He resembled him also in his sympathy for the Canadians and was soon to share his disdain for the English-speaking merchants. But he had a very different temper. It did not explode; it smouldered. There was also a cold formalism about him which was lacking in Murray. The ferment in the colony subsided upon his arrival, but for this Carleton was only partly

[1] Pub. Arch. Can. *Murray Papers*, II, 229.
[2] Burt, A. L., "Governor Murray and the Brit. Govt.", in *Trans. R. Soc. Can.* 1928.
[3] Pub. Arch. Can. *Report* 1888, p. 18.

responsible. He did not labour under all Murray's handicaps. He had not to face the difficult task of inaugurating civil government, and he enjoyed the full support of the Home Government. He had able legal advisers in Chief Justice William Hey and Attorney-General Francis Masères, who replaced the incompetent Gregory and Suckling, and he was commissioned as Brigadier-General in order to close the breach between military and civil authority. The mere fact of a change was wholesome. The mercantile factions of Quebec and Montreal were ready to welcome any successor to Murray. Carleton reciprocated by befriending them, particularly their leaders, George Allsopp and Thomas Walker, and in a few weeks he purged the Council of Murray's chief friends, Irving and Mabane. This high-handed action, the injustice of which he concealed from the Home Government, pleased the merchants who had been causing most of the trouble and had a general disciplinary effect.[1]

Whatever his mistakes, Carleton had the interests of the Empire and of Canada at heart. He brought large views to bear upon the problem of government and contributed more than anyone else to the working out of a new solution. He tore aside the illusion that the colony might be assimilated to the common English type. Immigrants from Europe, he pointed out, would prefer the "more chearful Climates and more fruitful Soil" of the southern colonies, and therefore "this Country must, to the end of Time, be peopled by the Canadian Race, who already have taken such firm Root, and got to so great a Height, that any new Stock transplanted will be totally hid, and imperceptible amongst them, except in the Towns of Quebec and Montreal".[2] Having formed this conclusion, he insisted upon a new policy. The Canadians must be attracted into the service of the Crown, their old laws and customs assured to them, and every just grievance removed. What he wanted was a Government, Canadian in character, such as would permanently incorporate the new possession in the Empire. Other considerations drove him in the same direction. In 1759 Murray had seen that Canada might be used to keep the old colonies in order, and now that the storm-wrack of the coming tempest was clearly apparent Carleton had the same vision. Some have impugned his motives, charging him with the attempt to make Canada a British weapon to overawe the restless colonies to the south. But he was only doing his duty as a British commander when he urged the erection of strong forts along the Lake Champlain route to link Quebec and New York securely. With the eye of a strategist, he saw that this would give British military power the key to America.[3] Nor were the old colonies his only concern. He feared a

[1] Burt, A. L., "Sir Guy Carleton and his First Council", *Can. H.R.* Dec. 1923, IV, 321.
[2] Pub. Arch. Can. *Documents relating to the Constitutional History of Canada*, 1759–91, ed. Shortt, A. and Doughty, A. G., 2nd ed. 1918, p. 284.
[3] *Ibid.* p. 280.

war with France, which might cause a rising in Canada and perhaps the loss of the country. Whether his fears of the old colonies and of the old enemy France dictated or only reinforced his policy of justice for the Canadians, for which he is deservedly honoured, or whether all three motives were so fused in his mind that no one was dominant, cannot be decided now and may never be settled, for all his private papers were destroyed after his death.

With the limited authority of a governor, Carleton was not free to apply his sweeping programme, but he pressed it upon the British Government and enacted such reforms as lay within his power. One abuse caught his eyes immediately—the heavy fees collected by every functionary from the Governor down. Murray had complained but had done nothing; Carleton acted at once, remitting all his own fees except those for licensing public houses and these he turned over as part of the provincial revenue. Others' fees he could not stop, for they were mostly in lieu of salary and were based on law, but he did check the vicious tendency to enlarge them quietly, and to the end of his regime he continually urged the Home Government to abolish the whole business. He also criticised the judicial administration and blamed Murray's ordinance of 17 September 1764 for sweeping away the only laws that the people of the country knew and for "introducing all the chicanery of Westminster Hall into this impoverished Province". The attempt to substitute English for French law had broken down. French law had forced its way into the courts, jostling with English law and producing intolerable confusion. Litigants appealed to one or the other law according as their immediate interest lay and not according to the tongue which they spoke, and the same judges applied both laws. From this miserable tangle Carleton turned to the French regime for guidance. To assist his studies, he commissioned F. J. Cugnet to prepare his famous abridgment of the old laws. Within a year the Governor had a solution—the repeal of the objectionable ordinance, the restoration of Canadian laws "almost entire", and the appointment of local judges. As a step in this direction he ordered Masères to draw up two ordinances.[1] One provided for monthly sessions of the Court of King's Bench, "to gratify the Canadians in their desire of having the proceedings of the courts of justice carried on with more expedition than had yet been used, and in a manner that might bear some resemblance to the diligence they had been accustomed to see in the time of the French Government, when all their courts of justice sat once a week". The other provided for French law to govern the tenure and inheritance of land. Neither was submitted to the Council and therefore neither was enacted. To see whether the first would be acceptable, Chief Justice Hey presented it to a grand jury of the province, but his recommendation was in vain. "Some of the English mer-

[1] Masères, F., A Collection of Several Commissions, 1772, pp. 58 seqq.

chants of that jury, desirous to delay causes of actions for debt in the then low state of commercial credit in the province, did not approve so much expedition of judgment; and therefore the English part of the jury never acquainted the Canadian part".[1] The other, because of its "great extent and importance", Carleton hesitated to pass without the approval of the Home Government, which demurred because an investigation into the whole legal and judicial system was already being made.

This investigation was rather belated. In the spring of 1766, Attorney-General Charles Yorke so roundly condemned the work of 1764 that the Government ordered the Board of Trade to prepare new instructions for a complete recasting of the judicial administration of the colony. Among other reforms, Canadians were to be admitted to all offices except that of judge in the supreme and circuit courts, now to be established, and they were to be allowed their old laws governing real property and inheritance.[2] Carleton would have acted upon such instructions, but they were never sent. Immediately after their completion in June 1766 the Rockingham Ministry fell, and they were forgotten until the Duke of Richmond attacked the Government in the House of Lords nearly a year later. Then the Government hesitated to effect such drastic changes without more information and ordered the Governor and Council, with the assistance of their legal advisers, to report upon the judicial administration of the province. Maurice Morgann was sent out in 1768 to assist the work and to carry home the results, which he did in 1770. Masères drew up the first report, but Carleton rejected it impatiently. Masères, though he had a fine mind and a sterling character, was a Protestant bigot and his consequent "antipathy to the Canadians" irritated Carleton. Disliking the coldness of the climate and of the Governor, Masères had asked leave to retire from the country, and as soon as the investigation was completed he departed. Meanwhile Morgann prepared a report that pleased the Governor, but Hey objected to this and drew up a third.[3] Finally Carleton combined these two so as to present a full statement of the conclusions which he had already reached. He was for restoring the laws as they stood on the eve of the conquest. The only changes which he would allow were the substitution of English criminal law, the introduction of the Habeas Corpus Act, and trial by jury for torts as well as criminal cases. These he urged as good in themselves and as giving every satisfaction that the "old subjects" could expect. Hey and Masères formally disagreed. They favoured the old laws of real property and inheritance but would stop there, for they were reluctant to abandon

---

[1] Shortt and Doughty, *op. cit.* p. 466.
[2] Pub. Arch. Can. *B.M. Add. MSS.* 35914, *Hardwicke Papers*, pp. 72 seqq.
[3] Pub. Arch. Can. *Shelburne Papers* (transcripts from originals in Ann Arbor, Michigan), LXVI, 25 seqq.

the policy of assimilating the province to the common type of an English colony.[1]

Meanwhile Carleton was justly impatient with the Commission of the Peace and resolved to reform it immediately. The justices of the peace had more power than those at home and were less qualified to use it, for they were selected from the merchants and the few retired officers in the colony. The more successful merchants preferred to devote themselves wholly to business and only a few accepted a commission from a sense of duty; the less successful sought it for the fees attached to the office. Abuses crept in to make a bad system worse. Powers already too large were illegally stretched, and agents, some of them with blank citations ready to be filled in, appeared in various parishes inciting the inhabitants to litigation. Costs were often many times the amount of the original debt, and for trifling sums "habitants" were sometimes sold up and even lodged in prison.[2] Carleton's remedy was the ordinance of 1 February 1770. Instead of one Court of Common Pleas which sometimes sat in Montreal, there were now two Courts, one for each district, which were to sit continuously, except for short vacations, for they took over all the civil jurisdiction of the justices of the peace. Costs were reduced and debtors received reasonable protection. The Montreal merchants raised a great cry, but the Governor was firm. If he needed any proof of the wholesome effect of the reform, the Montreal jailor supplied it. He petitioned for a salary because his fees dropped with the number of his prisoners.[3]

The judicial system was not the only thing wrong in Canada. The whole edifice of government erected in 1764 was cracking because of the missing keystone. The failure to call an Assembly had unforeseen consequences much greater than the unrest of the mercantile minority. It robbed the Government of the colony of the two vital powers of legislation and taxation. The instructions forbade the Governor and Council to pass regulations "that shall any ways tend to affect the life, limb or liberty of the Subject, or to the imposing any duties or taxes". In his efforts to begin and to establish civil government, Murray had repeatedly overstepped these narrow bounds. Some of his transgressing ordinances the Home Government disallowed, others they permitted to stand. Carleton avoided offence only by cutting down legislation to a minimum, but this irked him and he demanded a freer hand. More serious than this limitation was the want of authority for the thirty odd ordinances that were passed and not disallowed. They rested only on the instructions, and these could confer no power not granted by the Governor's commission under the great seal, which empowered the Governor to legislate only with an

[1] British Museum, King's MSS. ccvii, 5 seqq.
[2] Pub. Arch. Can. *Report* 1890, pp. 1 seqq.
[3] Pub. Arch. Can. *Minutes of the Legislative Council*, C, p. 97 v.

Assembly. On this ground alone, all the ordinances were *ultra vires* except that establishing courts of justice, which was based on the commission. Moreover, there were grave doubts, later substantiated by Mansfield's famous judgment in Campbell *v.* Hall, whether even the commission could have given legislative competence to Governor and Council alone after the Royal Proclamation had promised an Assembly. The first to find this fatal flaw were the merchants in the colony or their agent in London, Fowler Walker. Masères was presented with it directly he reached Canada in September 1766,[1] and there is reason for believing that Lord Shelburne, then Secretary of State, saw it not long afterwards.[2] The absence of an Assembly, which was necessary for the imposition of new taxes, also left the province without a revenue when the old revenue, or rather the only important part of it, collapsed in a surprising manner. The most important revenue inherited from the King of France was derived from the customs duties. In 1760 Murray hit upon them to help defray the expenses of his Government. He remitted those which would restrict trade with Britain and slightly modified the others. Though they paid these duties during the military regime, the merchants complained that they were illegal. Finally, in the summer of 1765, several of them prosecuted the collectors of the customs in the superior court, apparently in vain.[3] Meanwhile the Attorney- and Solicitor-General at home reported that the King could collect all the duties in force at the time of the conquest, and the Government appointed a receiver general for the colony and instructed him to exact payment according to a scale differing little from that applied by Murray. The demand of these duties in 1766 met with a flat refusal. Some of the resisters were prosecuted at once, but a jury of their fellows returned a verdict of "not guilty" in defiance of the Chief Justice's charge. This stopped the duties in Quebec and inspired several merchants to pursue Murray at home to recover what they had paid while he was military Governor. He was defended by the Government because he had accounted to the Treasury and because the revenue of the province was at stake. Chief Justice Sir Eardly Wilmot, who presided over the Court of Common Pleas where the suit was commenced in January 1768, had no doubt of the legality of the old duties, but had no opportunity to pronounce upon it, for the suit was compromised. It transpired that Murray had demanded a little more than the old rate on rum, but the plaintiffs were surprised by the strong evidence of the defence on the main point. Therefore they accepted an offer to refund the excess. With renewed confidence, the Treasury repeated their orders to collect in Quebec, where another trial was held in 1769. Again the Chief Justice instructed the jury to bring in a special verdict, and again they returned a general verdict of not

---

[1] Pub. Arch. Can. *Shelburne Papers*, LXIV, 109. [2] *Ibid.* LXIV, 125.
[3] Pub. Arch. Can. *Murray Papers*, II, 224 seq.

guilty. Further attempts to collect were abandoned; the opposition was too strong. The plea that these were not the old duties because the goods were not imported from France or the French colonies was only a quibble, but it was backed by the general American spirit of resistance to taxation by Britain and by the conviction that the King had no power to tax without the consent of the promised Assembly.[1]

From 1767 the Home Government was wrestling with the general problem of the administration of the colony, and Lord Hillsborough, who returned to the Board of Trade after he assumed the new office of Secretary of State for the Colonies in January 1768, kept writing to Carleton promising an early settlement. At the very time that the latter was busy with his report in Quebec, the former was ready with his plan. On behalf of their correspondents in the colony, the London merchants had been petitioning for an Assembly, and Hillsborough made this the principal feature of his new scheme. But it was not to be a purely Protestant Assembly such as had been contemplated for Canada in 1763 and had since brought trouble in Grenada. Following the suggestion of the merchants, the test was to be waived, as it soon was in Grenada, to allow a Roman Catholic minority to sit in the Assembly and in the Council. Hillsborough was also ready to turn his back upon the investigation proceeding in Canada and to adopt the abortive instructions of 1766 as the basis of a new judicial system. His programme for the Church was a modification of the plan which his Board had drawn up four years before in conjunction with the Archbishop of York.[2] The Jesuits and the chapter of Quebec were to be dissolved immediately; other religious houses were to be closed to new members; the seminaries of Quebec and Montreal were to be consolidated at Quebec; the property of all these bodies was to be vested in the Crown, with allowances for those already dependent upon it, to be used for the support of the seminary and a Protestant clergy; and the "superintendent" was to be closely restricted in his functions by the Governor, who would preserve the ecclesiastical supremacy of the Crown. Proceeding to questions of finance, he set forth details of a civil establishment and of the revenue necessary to support it, and suggested that the Governor should persuade the Assembly to. make this revenue perpetual.[3] Carleton had requested leave that he might advise the Government in person, but Hillsborough urged immediate action without waiting for his return and at the same time wrote to Carleton that he must remain until the Government had reached some decision upon the proposed new constitution. Hillsborough, however, could not persuade his colleagues to adopt his measures until Morgann's return, for they regarded the settlement of the laws as the foundation upon which

[1] Masères, F., pp. 288 seqq.
[2] Pub. Arch. Can. *Shelburne Papers*, LIX, 11 seqq.; *Series C.O.* 42, VII, 6 seqq.
[3] This section is omitted from Shortt and Doughty, but may be found in Pub. Arch. Can. *Series Q*, XVIII, A, 64 seqq.

everything else must be built. Thereupon he sent Carleton permission to return and also a copy of the plan, remarking that "it will very nearly coincide with your own Opinions".[1] It did not. Hillsborough, though no friend of the American colonies and their political ideas, was for going on; Carleton was for going back.

In the summer of 1770 Carleton handed over the Government to Cramahé, who was made Lieutenant-Governor in the following year, and sailed for England. But just before he left, Carleton made a memorable decision to solve one of the most delicate problems of the colony. Briand's consecration was only a temporary solution of the crisis in the Church and Carleton was worried by the prospect of confusion after his death. Rome had empowered the bishop to nominate a coadjutor who would succeed automatically, but Carleton had withheld his consent during nearly four years. Now, fearing what might happen should another Governor take his place, he was all impatience. He picked out a member of a distinguished Canadian family then serving as parish priest in the Island of Orleans and pressed Briand to consecrate him immediately. The bishop agreed with the Governor's choice, but not with the hasty method which he urged, for that in his eyes would have been illegal. The necessity of procuring bulls from Rome delayed the consecration until the summer of 1772. Apparently Carleton did not consult the Home Government, for when Cramahé reported what had been done he received a warm scolding from the Secretary of State, Lord Dartmouth. The latter, who had just succeeded Hillsborough, could find no trace of any sanction given by the Government and was alarmed at the whole proceeding.[2] However, the principle of episcopal succession was settled, and incidentally the Governor's choice marked an epoch in the history of the Canadian Church, for Desgly was the first Canadian-born bishop of Quebec.

Four years elapsed between Carleton's departure from Quebec and his return with the Quebec Act in his pocket. The Home Government was distracted by the growing American troubles and by a mass of contradictory evidence and advice, both official and unofficial. Except upon the question of the Assembly, which all condemned, and the revival of French laws governing real property, which all upheld, the Governor, the Chief Justice and the Attorney-General of the colony disagreed, and when the legal advisers of the Home Government were consulted they also gave conflicting opinions. The Canadians pleaded for their old laws and the opening of all offices upon equal terms. The English in the colony clamoured for an Assembly and they found plenty of backing in London. The merchants of the capital insisted on an English constitution as essential for the life of trade, and Masères, who had retired to his chambers in the Inner Temple, was a staunch friend of the mercantile minority whose agent he became. Though he only forwarded and never

[1] *Ibid.* VI, 129.   [2] *Ibid.* VIII, 166 seqq.

supported their petitions for an Assembly, he poured forth reams of arguments against a return to the Old Regime. Not until the latter part of 1773 was the drafting of the bill begun. Dartmouth introduced it into the House of Lords, 2 May 1774, and the Commons, who made slight amendments, passed the third reading six weeks later. Apparently to avoid a protracted debate, the Government withheld the preliminary official reports, though they allowed the House to examine Carleton, Hey, Masères, Advocate-General Marriott, and Lotbinière, a Canadian seigneur. Attorney-General Thurlow and Solicitor-General Wedderburn were of course present in the House as members and supported the measure. But Marriott, with a brilliant wit that refreshed the weary House, parried every effort to extract any information or opinion. Lotbinière objected to a nominated Council and wanted an Assembly half of which should be composed of seigneurs. Hey and Masères repeated their previous criticisms, while Carleton gave his approval to the bill as it stood. Indeed the Government, embarrassed by a wealth of difficult material, seem to have fallen back upon the advice of the Governor whom they trusted. Although they rushed it through in the fag-end of the session, to hasten a settlement in one important part of the troubled American Empire, the Quebec Act was no hasty ill-considered measure.

The first clause enlarged the boundaries so as to include the territories which the Proclamation had cut off on the east and on the west. Both French and English in Canada were unanimous in urging this change. The seal fishery, the chief activity on the Labrador coast, was conducted from Canada in the dead of winter and depended upon permanent establishments on the spot. The regulations of the Newfoundland Government threatened its extinction and the destruction of the capital invested in it, for they were designed for the cod and whale fisheries pursued in the summer by craft from home or from the old colonies.[1] As there was no essential conflict between these two enterprises, the restoration of this territory was only just. Much more important was the extension of the boundaries to the Ohio and the Mississippi. When separating this great Indian Reserve in 1763, the Government had intended to set up a special administration for it, which raised the question as to who should meet the expense involved. The British tax-payer could hardly be expected to shoulder an additional burden for something that would chiefly benefit the colonists, and the latter refused to be tax-payers at all. The whole design was abandoned in 1768, and the regulation of the Indian trade was handed over to the individual colonies. This necessitated a co-operation which was impossible. New York invited Pennsylvania and Quebec to join in a conference and proposed a system of regulation by means of imposts upon the trade, but the Quebec Council had no power to levy duties and, moreover,

---

[1] Pub. Arch. Can. *Minutes of Legislative Council*, B, pp. 85 seqq.

believed that the policy suggested would ruin the trade. The encroachments of French traders who came up the Mississippi and the growing confusion in this western country, thus left derelict, constituted a serious problem. The simplest solution was to give the territory a government by annexing it to one of the colonies. There was only one choice. Historically it belonged to Canada. Geographically it was linked with it as with no other colony, by great waterways which were then the only means of communication into the heart of the continent. Economically it was dependent upon it, for the fur trade was focussed at Montreal. Moreover, its only inhabitants were a few Canadians and the Indians. The latter could be more effectively managed through the Governor of Quebec than through any other, for he alone was unhampered by an Assembly. These reasons are sufficient to explain the re-annexation of this territory, but if they had not existed the mother country might have done the same thing, for she could hardly have been expected to give the keeping of this great land to any of the colonies on the brink of revolution. In one most important respect, this policy of 1763 was unchanged—the preservation of this country as an Indian Reserve. Hillsborough, now out of office but consulted by the Government, wanted to have this stipulated in the Act, but it was left implicit. The polity established in Canada and extended to these lands was deemed a sufficient discouragement to prospective settlers.

It has often been said that the Quebec Act was a blow aimed at the American Colonies and that it contributed to their revolt, for they were offended by the establishment of Roman Catholicism, the revival of French civil law and the denial of an Assembly, and they were greatly alarmed by the reinforcement of the policy of eleven years before. Britain seemed to have stepped into France's shoes in America, threatening the old colonies from Canada and trying to coop them up on the Atlantic seaboard. This fear was real and it had some justification, but it is doubtful whether the Revolution would have been slower in coming without the Quebec Act or the Quebec Act very different without the coming of the Revolution. In the penal legislation against Massachusetts, the Government had just dealt an open blow, and having done this, could have no motive for concealing the designs hinted at by opponents across the floor of the House. Indeed, sections two and three of the Act protected the old colonies in any legal claims they might have to the hinterland.

The Quebec Act also added legislative force to the treaty guarantee of toleration and took two steps to give it practical value. In place of the old oaths designed to exclude Roman Catholics from office, the Act substituted a new oath framed to admit them. Although it was inserted only in the committee stage in the Commons, the principle had been earlier accepted. Carleton had pressed for this very thing in order to open the doors of the Council to Canadians, and five years before the Act Hillsborough had intimated that it might be granted.[1] Much more momentous was the legal recognition of the tithe. Roman Catholics were to pay it to their own Church and Protestants were made equally liable for the maintenance of a Protestant clergy. Of all the officials who advised the Government, Masères alone opposed this provision, but Huguenot blood was still hot in his veins. According to Knox, the Colonial Under-Secretary, the Government was convinced that the conquest had not impaired the legality of the tithe, and therefore the Act was only declaratory, except in exempting Protestants from the obligation to support the Roman Catholic Church. Whatever were the grounds of this opinion, the purpose of the Government was to preserve the religion of the Canadians as they found it. Though there had been talk of regulations for the Church, the Act contained none. Carleton opposed the proposal to suppress all the religious communities in the colony. He would condemn only the Jesuits, whose order was already dissolved by the Pope. To deal with "this very delicate business" of the Church, he demanded a free hand[2] and he got it.

As the establishment of Roman Catholicism has sometimes been criticised from a Protestant standpoint, it should be remarked that the Act did not make it *the* established religion, for the royal supremacy was preserved and the Church of England was legally *the* established Church. To estimate the effect of this part of the Act is in fact difficult. The tithes had been collected since the conquest and they continued to be collected by spiritual authority. The practical value of the change depends upon whether there was any real or potential resistance to the tithe. That there was resistance is supported by Murray's statement of 1762 and Masères' later assertions, but by no other direct evidence that has yet come to light. The only indirect evidence on the point is the gratitude of the clergy for an Act which placed the tithes beyond any danger. But the danger which they feared may have been from the British Government rather than from the "habitant". The Act may have rivetted Roman Catholicism upon French Canada and, by imposing the tithe upon reluctant "habitants", have contributed to Canadian sympathy for the American cause. But even if this supposition could be established there would still be room for difference of opinion over the policy.

To settle the form of government, the Act expressly revoked the troublesome promise of an Assembly and reimposed the existing system in a modified form. Government by Governor and Council, hitherto a temporary arrangement, was made permanent and carefully regulated. The Governor and Council became the recognised Legislature. Their power was wider than that intended by Murray's

---

[1] Pub. Arch. Can. *Series Q*, VI, 37 seqq., 67 seq.
[2] Pub. Arch. Can. *Dartmouth Papers* (transcripts from originals in Patshull House), II, 239.

instructions but not so extensive as that conferred by his commission upon Governor, Council and Assembly. Because it was not a popular body, the new Legislature could levy no taxes except for local improvements, and, without the royal consent, could enforce no ordinance touching religion or imposing any punishment greater than fine or three months' imprisonment. All ordinances were to be sent home within six months for approval or disallowance, and to give the widest practical scope to the latter possibility, legislation was confined to the first four months of the year, just before navigation opened. The new Council was practically double the size of the old body, for it was to have not less than seventeen nor more than twenty-three members. The Governor's instructions, which were passed in the following January, named the new Councillors—twenty-two in all. Apparently the Home Government accepted Carleton's list. It included all the old Councillors who were in attendance, except one who had been temporarily added to make a quorum. George Allsopp, who had been deputy secretary, became a member of the Council, and Adam Mabane was restored to his old seat, for he was now reconciled to the Governor, probably through their common feeling for the Canadians. Eight of the twenty-two were Canadians. One was a Protestant and an old member; the other seven were Roman Catholics admitted by the new oath. Numerically they were a minority, but practically they were not, for most of the other members were strongly Canadian in sympathy. Except the Council the Act set up no machinery of government. It simply reserved to His Majesty the right to constitute courts of justice. The revenue was established by a separate measure known as the Quebec Revenue Act which imposed customs duties and a fee for public-house licences and preserved "the territorial or casual revenues" that had belonged to the Crown before the conquest. The proceeds were to be deposited with the receiver general of the colony for the support of the civil administration.

The Act was criticised for refusing an Assembly; but an Assembly was out of the question, the Canadians as a whole neither understood nor wanted it. Another and more reasonable criticism was that the Act should have established the system of Governor and Council for only a definite period. But the Government replied that this would cause uncertainty and unrest in the colony, the very thing which the Act was designed to stop, and that there was no need for it because Parliament could change the system whenever it saw fit. There was, however, one grave defect in the new Legislature, and that was its personnel. George Allsopp stood almost alone as the champion of the mercantile minority which was therefore little likely to get justice from such a Council.

The Act also attempted to unravel the tangled skein of the laws by prescribing English criminal law and French civil law with certain qualifications. French civil law was not to apply to lands already granted or to be granted in common soccage, nor was it to prevent the execution of wills according to English law. An earlier draft of the bill had also provided for the possible transformation of existing feudal tenures into freehold, but Carleton objected and the provision was dropped. This omission was in harmony with the new land policy just adopted and already showing signs of promise. Carleton, seeing that there was no demand for Canadian lands, had persuaded the Government in 1771 to revive at once the old system of granting *en fief et seigneurie*, but without any right of feudal jurisdiction. The result was a swarm of petitions for seigneuries in 1772.[1] Though the American Revolution was to forestall any action upon these petitions, this could not be foreseen when the Act was being prepared. Moreover, Carleton believed in the feudal system because it gave the Government "great power over the Seigneur, which power will be done away by changing the Tenure into free & common Soccage".[2] There was also the general qualification that English criminal law and French civil law were to hold "until they shall be varied" by provincial legislation.

There was no criticism of the establishment of English criminal law. It was more humane than French criminal law, and its regular application since the conquest had given general satisfaction. Though the discussions leading up to the Act brought out a number of objectionable features which have since disappeared from English criminal law, it was assumed that the Governor and Council would prevent their evil effects in the colony. But the establishment of French civil law has aroused strong criticism. There was a definite separation of interest, the English minority controlling the bulk of the trade and the Canadians being chiefly concerned about their lands. It is said that both interests should have been reflected in the legal settlement by the establishment of English civil law except for real property. This criticism ignores several important considerations. When the Quebec Act was passed, the English population in the colony was very small and had been growing smaller since 1770. It seemed unjust to introduce the general body of English civil law when the French outnumbered the English thirty to one and would probably outnumber them still more as years passed. Also, in addition to the uncertain effect of tearing one part of the law away from the other parts that were knit to it, there were strong objections to particular features of the English civil law of that day. Arrest for debt had alarmed the Canadians, while the English law of bankruptcy had raised such opposition among some English merchants in Canada that Carleton had stopped its application.[3] Finally, there has been an

---

[1] Pub. Arch. Can. *Minutes of Legislative Council*, C, pp. 113 seqq.
[2] Shortt and Doughty, p. 553.
[3] Pub. Arch. Can. *Series Q*, v, 248 seqq., 367 seqq.; *Series C.O.* 42, vi, 236 seq.

illusion about English mercantile law. Developed from the law merchant of Europe, it was only at this time taking shape in the Court of King's Bench under the presiding genius of Lord Mansfield.[1] During the discussions prior to the Act, it was commonly taken for granted that the law merchant was the only possible rule for the settlement of commercial disputes because it was common to all trading nations. Thus the Act cannot be blamed for robbing the merchants of what they had not possessed—a definite body of English mercantile law. But it did prevent them from enjoying this law as it developed and it robbed them of two rights which they had enjoyed—those of Habeas Corpus and of jury trials in civil suits.

These were grave defects, but the Act itself provided for their elimination and the instructions directed it. While establishing French civil law as the general rule, the Act empowered the Governor and Council to modify it, and the instructions urged provincial legislation to introduce the right of habeas corpus and to allow English law for "personal Actions grounded upon Debts, Promises, Contracts, and Agreements, whether of a Mercantile or other Nature; and also of Wrongs proper to be compensated in damages", particularly when "old subjects" were concerned. It has been argued that these instructions, which were drawn up later, betray a change of mind on the part of the Government after the Act was passed.[2] This is improbable because Carleton, who sailed immediately afterwards, must have carried with him the knowledge of the Government's intention to allow the merchants no just grievance. Dartmouth's letter of surprise at Carleton's failure to report the satisfaction of the "old subjects" with the new constitution appears conclusive upon this point.[3]

But why did the Government leave these holes in the Act if they were to be patched up in the colony? Of the three just grievances of the minority, the omission of English mercantile law is explained by its inchoate condition. The introduction of the Habeas Corpus Act, though supported by Carleton's report, was condemned by the legal advisers of the Home Government on the ground that it would be dangerous. The great bulk of the population of Canada still had fond memories for France, Britain's chronic foe, and had been quite unaccustomed to such a privilege. At the same time the Government did not wish to deprive the English minority of their birthright. The only escape from the dilemma was to trust the Governor and Council, who were on the spot, to find some safe way of introducing the law. For the elimination from the Act of jury trials in civil suits, the English in Canada were themselves to blame. Nearly a fortnight after he had introduced the bill into the Lords, Dartmouth secured

---

[1] Holdsworth, W. S., *History of English Law*, 3rd ed. I, 572.
[2] Coupland, R., *The Quebec Act*, pp. 126 ff.
[3] Shortt and Doughty, p. 585.

Lord Chancellor Apsley's consent to a clause allowing disputes between merchants to be tried by jury. But the Chancellor immediately recalled the fate of the old French duties and withdrew his consent. He thought it better "to stand the harangue of the day than to yield to the request which certainly squints at the revenue".[1] Here also there was no thought of robbing the merchants of their just right, and the Government sought to escape from the dilemma of granting too much or too little by relying on the provincial Legislature. Thus the English mercantile minority would have had no real grievance if the instructions had been carried out. Here lies the great tragedy of the Act. By secreting his instructions and concealing his disobedience from the Home Government, Carleton warped the new constitution.[2]

There is still another criticism often flung at the Quebec Act. It has been charged with hardening French-Canadian nationalism by giving it a charter of liberties, and some have linked 1837 with 1774. The Act reinforced this nationalism by preserving the old laws and may have had the same effect by strengthening Roman Catholicism. But it is idle to imagine that the French of Canada could have been assimilated. One race has been merged in another only when the assimilated did not possess an old and fixed civilisation or when they were a minority. Neither of these fundamental conditions existed in Canada. If the policy of 1763, instead of being abandoned, had been enforced and developed, it would have driven Canada into the American Revolution, or it would have created a new Ireland on the banks of the St Lawrence.

[1] Pub. Arch. Can. *Dartmouth Papers*, II, 280.
[2] Smith, W., "The Struggle over the Laws of Canada", *Can. H.R.* June 1920, I, 166–86.

CHAPTER VII

BRITISH NORTH AMERICA AND THE
AMERICAN REVOLUTION, 1774–1791

OF the old-world communities in America none seemed to differ more widely than New France and New England. In the eyes of the law, Protestantism did not exist in New France; the counsels of the colony were believed to reflect the opinion of the Society of Jesus, that militant branch of the Church whose special duty it was to defend the citadel of Roman Catholicism against the invasion of Protestant heresy. In New England, Roman Catholicism was heresy; there, as Burke declared, was "the Protestantism of the Protestant religion", so thorough that the moderate ceremonial of Anglicanism was considered a dangerous compromise with the devil. The valley of the St Lawrence had not provided a favourable soil for the growth of political liberties; the injunction of Colbert, to refrain from giving a corporate form to the inhabitants of Canada, had been obeyed with a rare fidelity. New England regarded itself as the offspring of religious freedom and civil liberty; the principles of liberty had flourished and grown sturdy in its clear, rare atmosphere. Not alone in religion and in politics was the fundamental difference in the spirit of the two peoples made manifest. In industry and commerce, New England displayed an intensity and aggressiveness which were wholly foreign to New France. And yet, in large measure because of these differences, the political development of each of these communities was influenced greatly by the other.

Difference of religion not only prevented the close association of New France and New England but inspired a mutual suspicion and distrust. New England feared the power of Roman Catholic France in North America because the Church of Rome was believed to have designs on the Protestant communities of the northern seaboard. Fear of France and a realisation of her own weakness begat in New England feelings of dependence on the parent State, towards which there had been but slight manifestation of filial devotion. Petr Kalm, the Swedish naturalist, who had travelled extensively throughout the North American settlements before the conquest, regarded the dominion of France over the St Lawrence valley as "the best means of keeping the colonies in their due submission".[1] When Britain was debating the relative advantages of Canada and Guadeloupe, she had been warned that the retention of Canada might

[1] Kalm, P., *Travels in America*, I, 207.

involve the loss of her older American empire. Such warnings were ineffective; France was driven from the northern mainland and the danger of Roman Catholic aggression ceased to be a factor in the relations of the southern colonies to the motherland.

As the government of Canada presented very real difficulties, British statesmanship was inclined to proceed with caution. In the determination of a Canadian policy due consideration was given to the attitude of the Atlantic colonies. There were those who saw in the growing spirit of independence in the south the fulfilment of the dire predictions of 1763 and who agreed that the provisions of the Treaty of Paris should be neutralised by limiting the conquest of Canada to a change of sovereignty and by preserving the fundamental characteristics of French-Canadian civilisation. Sir Guy Carleton, the Governor of Quebec, was inclined, for various reasons, to accept the consequences of this view. As early as 1768, he had warned the British Government that "should France begin a war in hopes the British colonies will push matters to extremities, and she adopts the project of supporting them in their independent notions, Canada, probably, will then become the principal scene, where the fate of America may be determined".[1] Whatever may have been the inmost thoughts of Carleton and of British ministers regarding the Quebec Act, the influence of that measure on the conduct of Americans, both French and English, was determined by what were popularly believed to have been the motives which inspired it. Its reception in Quebec and in New England influenced very greatly the subsequent relations of the two communities.

In Quebec there were four distinct groups—the English officers of the army and of the civil administration, the English merchants, the Roman Catholic clergy and the *gentilshommes*, among whom were included the seigneurs, and the officers, civil and military, of the Old Regime, and finally, the "habitants", comprising the vast majority of the people of the colony. It was in the interest of the English official class to support the policy of the Government. The official recognition of the Church and the restoration of the French civil law won the loyal support of the clergy and of the *gentilshommes*. The majority of the "habitants" were probably indifferent to the Act, although there were those who, since the conquest, had abandoned the habit of paying tithes and seigneurial dues and did not regard their restoration with favour. Here, at least, was material upon which the ardent critics and defenders of the change could let loose their powers of persuasion. There was no doubt regarding the position of the majority of the English merchants. The most influential of those at Montreal were of American origin and in the regular course of business maintained a constant communication with Boston. The

[1] Carleton to Hillsborough, 20 Nov. 1768, in *Documents relating to the Constitutional History of Canada*, 1759-91, ed. Shortt, A. and Doughty, A. G., 2nd ed. 1918, p. 326.

British element predominated at Quebec and corresponded with the London merchants engaged in the trans-Atlantic trade. The merchants had demanded that the promise of a popular Assembly and of English law contained in the Proclamation of 7 October 1763 should be redeemed. Not only were they refused an Assembly but the English commercial law which they had been accustomed to follow in their own transactions was swept away and the entire French civil law restored. They felt that their request for bread had been answered by the gift of a stone.

The attitude of the English merchants contained the seed of real trouble. Particulars of the Quebec Act had already reached Canada when Carleton returned in September 1774. It is significant that during this same month citizens of Quebec sent a thousand bushels of wheat to the Boston Committee of Donations as evidence of their sympathy with the leaders of the popular party in the distress caused by the closing of that seaport, and that Montreal gave expression to kindred feelings by the contribution of a substantial sum of money. In both cities there were doubtless many who were moved by a vague, general sympathy with the aspirations of Adams, Warren and their associates. The keen and bitter disappointment caused by the Quebec Act created a consciousness of grievances and clarified and reinforced the kindly feelings of the English merchants toward their American friends. A committee was chosen at Montreal to consider grievances; delegates were sent to Quebec and the "town-meeting", different, however, from the Boston type, became a factor in public discussion among the English inhabitants.[1] Soon, petitions to the King, Lords and Commons were prepared requesting the repeal of the Quebec Act.[2]

The English colonies were directly interested in two of its provisions—the extension of the boundaries of Quebec and the official recognition of the Roman Catholic religion. The company which the measure kept in its march through Parliament—the Port Bill, the Quartering Bill, the Charter Bill, the whole series of "intolerable Acts"—raised a strong presumption that it concealed some sinister design. And such was not difficult to find. Many of the colonists thought that the Seven Years' War had been fought to drive France from the interior of the continent and to ensure room for the expansion westward of the seaboard colonies. The necessity of maintaining order in the back country and the interests of the fur trade may have amply justified the extension of the boundaries of Quebec to the Ohio and the Mississippi, but, to the leaders of colonial discontent, the real reason for the change was to be found in the hostility of the Home Government to the colonies. The error of the conquest of Canada had been discovered, it was argued, and it now became the

[1] Shortt and Doughty, p. 586, Carleton to Dartmouth, 11 Nov. 1774.
[2] *Ibid.* p. 589.

deliberate policy of the British Government to restore, as far as possible, the conditions along the northern and western frontier which existed prior to 1760. It had even been suggested—so said Dame Rumour—that the Province of Quebec, as lately defined, should be ceded or given up to France.[1] But the policy of the Quebec Act was quite as effective in the achievement of such a purpose and much more subtle. The establishment of the Roman Catholic religion and the introduction of French civil law in the vast hinterland created a barrier to English migration quite as effective as if the country had been restored to France. If, then, the French in Canada and the Roman Catholic Church were to be used again as instruments for the repression of the English colonists, it behoved the leaders of the popular party to adopt measures of self-defence.

The manifestations of discontent in Canada because of the Quebec Act suggested a course of procedure. The first Continental Congress, on 24 October 1774, prepared a letter to the "Inhabitants of the Province of Quebec" which dilated on the iniquity of the Quebec Act in withholding a popular Assembly and invited the Canadians "to accede to our Confederation" and to send delegates to the Congress to be held in the following May.[2] Copies of the address were sent to Thomas Walker in Montreal for circulation; a French translation was prepared and distributed broadcast in the Montreal district. The Provincial Congress of Massachusetts decided to send John Brown of Pittsfield as delegate to Canada to explain the projects of the Congress and to endeavour to obtain the co-operation of the Canadians. Brown arrived in Montreal in March and at several meetings at the Coffee House discussed plans with the disaffected there and with delegates from Quebec. The English merchants did not propose, however, to permit their sympathies to betray them into foolish action. The time was not yet ripe for open association with the Continental Congress, whose policy of non-importation, if adopted in Canada, would have involved the English merchants in ruin. But the mission was not in vain; friendly communications were established with Montreal and Quebec, and plans were perfected for keeping the southern colonists advised about hostile movements in Canada. There the matter stood when unexpected developments in another quarter completely altered the posture of affairs. A sudden attack by less than a hundred "Green Mountain Boys" of the New Hampshire Grants district, under the joint command of Ethan Allen and Benedict Arnold, forced the surrender of the small British garrison at Fort Ticonderoga (10 May 1775). Two days later they captured the British post at Crown Point and then Arnold surprised the fort at St John's with its garrison of a dozen regulars, seized a sloop, destroyed the other boats and retired without firing a shot.

[1] See Smith, J. S., *Our Struggle for the Fourteenth Colony*, I, p. 85.
[2] *Journals of the Continental Congress*, ed. Ford, W. C., I, 105.

These stirring incidents on the Canadian frontier found Carleton wholly unprepared for an effective defence. In 1767 he had urged that the fortifications at Crown Point, Ticonderoga, Fort George and the walls at Quebec should be repaired, and had advocated enlisting the French Canadians in local militia units; but none of his recommendations had been adopted. Early in 1774 the 7th, 8th, 10th, 26th and 52nd regiments were stationed in Canada; in September, as clouds began to overhang the horizon at Boston, General Gage, commanding the British forces there, requested Carleton to send him the 10th and 52nd regiments. Carleton readily agreed to the transfer of these troops because it would give the Canadians the opportunity, which he had represented they eagerly awaited, of demonstrating their attachment to the Crown. "A Canadian Regiment would compleat their Happiness, which in Time of need might be augmented to two, three or more Battalions".[1] Carleton sent to St John's all his available troops which included a small corps of Canadian volunteers. He himself went up to Montreal and on 9 June proclaimed martial law and called out the Canadian militia supposed to be enrolled under the old French law. By this time Carleton was beginning to realise the real temper of the Canadians. The *noblesse* were anxious to demonstrate their gratitude for the protection afforded them by the Quebec Act. The vast majority of the clergy loyally supported the Government. But the habitants were thoroughly alarmed by the declaration of martial law. With few exceptions, despite the urgings of the clergy, they refused to enlist under the seigneurs; some declared their willingness to follow British half-pay officers or their own captains of militia.

Vital factors in the life of the Canadian habitants which had been obscured from Carleton's view were now becoming manifest. The feudal social structure transplanted from the Old World had not flourished in the soil of the St Lawrence valley; the harsh conditions of pioneer life tended to reduce the elevations and fill in the depressions of social gradations. During the French regime this process of erosion had proceeded steadily; after the conquest, the remaining peaks of feudal authority almost crumbled to dust. The foundations of the ancient authority both feudal and ecclesiastical had been shaken and the influence of seigneur and priest, upon which Carleton had relied, was found largely to have vanished. In such conditions, the Quebec Act, which proposed to restore the ancient power of seigneur and of priest, would scarcely arouse the enthusiasm or the gratitude of the habitants. "An Act passed for the express purpose of gratifying the Canadians", declared Chief Justice Hey, "is become the first object of their discontent and dislike".[2] Unconsciously Carleton had prepared the soil for the seed of disaffection scattered

---

[1] Shortt and Doughty, p. 584, Carleton to Gage, 20 Sept. 1774.
[2] *Ibid.* p. 668, Hey to Lord Chancellor, 28 Aug. 1775.

broadcast by the friends and emissaries of the revolting colonists, and he was now reaping the harvest. The dismal promise of one feature of the unhappy situation had not been fulfilled. The majority of the English merchants at Montreal, although not friendly to the Administration, had hesitated to give active aid to their American friends; they had sent James Price as unofficial delegate to the second Continental Congress, but the value of the British connection to their commerce caused them to pause on the threshold of revolt. A few of the more zealous partisans such as James Livingston and Thomas Walker—whose zeal the loss of an ear had redoubled—were prepared to cast in their lot with the revolting colonists. At best, however, Carleton's resources in the southern part of the province were utterly inadequate to the resistance of invasion.

After the engagement at Bunker's Hill the dogs of war were let loose. Congress was persuaded that it was the intention of Carleton to employ the Canadians and the Indians in an attack on the colonies. To anticipate such a stroke, Congress decided, late in June, on the invasion of Canada. The execution of the project was entrusted to General Schuyler who was directed, should he find it not "disagreeable to the Canadians", to "immediately take possession of St John's, Montreal, and any other parts of the Country".[1] A second expedition under the direction of Benedict Arnold, who had been replaced in the Lake Champlain command, was ordered to proceed to Canada, through the wilderness of Maine and by way of the Chaudière, to join the southern army before Quebec. Ill-health compelled the retirement of General Schuyler, and the command of the Lake Champlain project devolved on Richard Montgomery, who, in 1760, during his service with General Amherst, had gained an intimate knowledge of the district. Early in September, Montgomery's army moved northward. Ethan Allen, ever in search of glory, appeared upon the scene and was employed in scouting expeditions among the Canadians. In conjunction with a Major Brown he evolved a plan for the surprise and capture of Montreal. With a party of about 150 men, of whom nearly half were Canadians, Allen attempted to carry out the foolhardy project. His plans miscarried; he himself was captured with about forty of his men and was confined in the hold of the *Gaspé* pending his transportation to England for trial. Walker, who was implicated in the raid, was arrested and confined to gaol. The folly of Allen accomplished more, however, for the enlistment of the Canadian habitants under the British standard than all the threats and exhortations of Carleton and his priests and seigneurs. In a short time, 900 had enrolled and were encamped at Chambly.

The fort at St John's was defended by Major Preston of the 26th with less than 700 men, of whom 120 were Canadian volunteers.

[1] Secret Journals of Congress, 27 June 1775.

Chambly, further down the Richelieu, was held by Major Stopford and 80 regulars. Carleton, learning of Montgomery's advance, had requested Gage for the aid of two regiments. Howe, who succeeded to the command on the recall of Gage, was prepared to send the troops, but Admiral Graves, who commanded the transports, refused to undertake the passage to Quebec. Carleton, therefore, was left to his own puny resources. Montgomery's operations against St John's were impeded by the lack of artillery and by internal dissensions and his only hope seemed to be in starving the garrison into submission. Events took an unexpected turn when, on 18 October, the fort at Chambly with an ample supply of provisions, guns and ammunition surrendered to Major Brown and James Livingston with a force of 350 untrained men, of whom 300 were Canadians. The fate of St John's had now been decided, and on 2 November Major Preston and his garrison surrendered. The way was open to Montreal. The banners of victory seemed to have an uncanny attraction for the French Canadians, on whose support no reliance could be placed. Montreal could not be defended. On 11 November Carleton set out for Quebec, and two days later Montgomery and his men entered the city.

Carleton's plight was desperate indeed. The Americans erected batteries at Sorel which seemed to command the St Lawrence. Carleton and a few trusted officers, disguised as habitants, embarked in a whale-boat and, successfully eluding the American batteries, reached Quebec on the 19th. His fleet was less fortunate, however, and was forced to surrender with all its cargo. One passenger, Thomas Walker by name, rejoiced in the capture, for it brought freedom and escape from judicial process which he had not contemplated with pleasure. Montgomery, who sorely needed ships to transport his troops to Quebec, was able to use his prize to good advantage. On his return to Quebec, Carleton had barely avoided Arnold's force which, but a few days previous, had come down the Chaudière to the St Lawrence and was now resting at Pointe aux Trembles in preparation for the attack on Quebec. Arnold had begun the ascent of the Kennebeck in late September with a force of 1100 men. The march across the height of land to Lake Megantic had been most trying; provisions failed and, had it not been for the timely aid of friendly French Canadians, the greater part of the army would have perished of starvation. On 8 November he reached the St Lawrence with two-thirds of his original force but was unable to cross to the north shore until the 14th. In the hope that the effort to arrest Montgomery's advance had emptied Quebec of its effective defensive forces, Arnold summoned the city to surrender, only to receive from Cramahé, the Lieutenant-Governor of the province who was in charge during Carleton's absence, a decisive answer in the form of an 18-pound shot. Arnold's men were utterly exhausted; their clothing, tattered and torn, was unequal to the rigours of the advancing winter; they lacked ammunition and provisions and were incapable of conducting a siege of the renowned fortress. A report that Colonel Allan Maclean, who had recruited a corps of Royal Highland Emigrants, was about to attack sent Arnold up the river to Pointe aux Trembles to await the arrival of Montgomery.

That officer's early military experience taught him that his hold on Canada was most insecure so long as the British standard floated above the citadel of Quebec. His lack of adequate siege equipment, the need of proper clothing for a winter campaign, the limited service for which his men enlisted seemed to dictate delay until the spring. But consideration of the aid which Arnold's men could give and of the prospect of Carleton receiving reinforcements in the spring left no alternative. By early December the two forces had united and commenced the siege of Quebec. The combined armies numbered about 2000 men, an undisciplined force, with little military experience, and inadequately supplied with artillery. Within the fortress Carleton had about 1800 men, of whom about 400 were regulars, including Maclean's Highlanders, another 400 marines and seamen from the British ships in the harbour, between 300 and 400 militia of British birth and the remainder Canadian militia. The opposing forces were thus nearly equal in number. Carleton possessed a real advantage in the quality of his troops and a distinct superiority in military equipment and provisions. Montgomery decided on an attack on the Lower Town which contained most of the wealth of Quebec; he would attack from below Cape Diamond while Arnold's force would approach from the St Charles. Major Brown's Provincials and Colonel Livingston's Canadians were expected to divert attention from the main assault by attacks on the Cape Diamond bastion and the St John's Gate respectively. The main attack began in a blinding snowstorm early in the morning of 31 December; Montgomery's force encountered unexpected resistance as it approached the Lower Town; the general and a dozen of his men were killed, whereupon the remainder of the 900, who had not hitherto faced artillery fire, turned and fled. Arnold, meanwhile, had worked his way through the Lower Town to the point fixed for the junction with Montgomery. But neither Montgomery nor his forces arrived. Arnold's men, their commander disabled by a wound, soon found themselves surrounded and were compelled to surrender.

Carleton's losses were 7 killed and 11 wounded; of the Americans 30 were killed and nearly 450 surrendered. The siege continued during the winter but in a wholly ineffective manner. The rising tide of adversity completely quenched the enthusiasm of the habitants for the cause of "Liberty". Desertions among the Provincials undermined the attachment of the Canadians. In the earlier days the Americans had paid for supplies with cash, but with the appearance of paper money, which recalled very bitter memories of the worthless French *ordonnances*, Jean Baptiste's interest in the principles of democracy suffered a serious relapse. Instances of abuse of Canadians by undisciplined Provincials did not improve the situation. Moses Hazen, a retired half-pay officer, farmer and miller at St John's, was entrusted with the task of raising a second Canadian regiment, but could enlist only 250 men. Several hundred men were sent to reinforce the army before Quebec. Disease and dissension, however, seriously interfered with its operations, and the arrival of reinforcements from England early in May 1776 was the signal for the retreat of the Provincials. About the middle of May a minor engagement occurred at the Cedars a short distance above Montreal where Captain Foster, who commanded the British post at Ogdensburg, with a small force of regulars, Canadians and Indians, attacked an American force and secured nearly 500 prisoners. The Quebec army fell back to the Richelieu while British reinforcements under Burgoyne were sent up the St Lawrence. Three Rivers was recovered by the British early in June, and Arnold, now in command at Montreal, fearing that his retreat would be cut off, retired hastily to the Richelieu. Chambly and St John's were abandoned, and on 18 June Arnold, the last of the American invaders, bade a sad farewell to Canada.

The Provincials, however, still retained control of Lake Champlain and the "back-door" of Canada. By the autumn, Carleton's army was substantially reinforced by troops from England and numbered 10,000 men, stationed mainly in the vicinity of Montreal and on the Richelieu. During the summer, boats were constructed to replace those captured by the Americans. By October, Carleton was prepared to follow Arnold to his retreat on Lake Champlain, and on the 11th he encountered the American vessels off Valcour Island, some fifty miles north of Crown Point. Fighting continued intermittently until the 13th, when twelve of the fifteen American vessels surrendered. Crown Point was destroyed by the Americans and the remnant of the naval force retired southward below Ticonderoga which was strongly held by General Gates. Carleton decided that the season was too far advanced to justify the siege of Ticonderoga and, well satisfied with having secured control of Lake Champlain, retired to St John's for the winter. He was severely censured by Lord George Germain, the Secretary of State for the Colonies, for this decision, but the judgment of an experienced commander "on the spot" was entitled to more favourable consideration, as Carleton tartly remarked, than that of "a great general at 3000 miles distance".

While, during the subsequent course of the war, Gates, Lafayette, and Washington at different times proposed the invasion of Canada, such a project was not again undertaken. Carleton's successful defence demonstrated alike the sources of weakness in Canada and the difficulties of invasion. The position of the mass of the Canadians was clearly demonstrated. "I think there is nothing to fear from them, while we are in a state of prosperity, and nothing to hope for when in distress".[1] The necessity of providing an adequate garrison was clearly recognised, and Carleton's successors were not left in his former precarious position. The American campaign had assumed two distinct phases—political and military. The revolutionary leaders, too, had learned the uncertainty of Canadian support; the modes of thought and the manner of life of Catholic French Canada differed fundamentally from those of Puritan New England. Religion rendered political union between French Canada and the revolting colonies impossible. From the military point of view, the importance of Quebec in the defence of Canada had been demonstrated and, without such naval superiority as would ensure the command of the St Lawrence, Quebec could not be held. Yet, the American campaign had not been wholly a failure. Invaluable experience had been gained; the necessity of a co-ordinated command, of sterner discipline and of a national, as distinct from a provincial, outlook had been made manifest in a campaign in which reverses had not been fatal to the main purposes of the Provincials. It is significant that the Declaration of Independence, the symbol, at least, of national unity, followed close on the heels of the failure of the invasion of Canada.

The Revolution was America's first civil war. Long before the relations of the colonies to the motherland became an issue, the natural forces of Conservatism and Radicalism had created parties in the several colonies which, while not primarily political, profoundly influenced political action. In New York, for instance, distinctions of wealth, of social position and of religious affiliation created factions as early as the beginning of the eighteenth century.[2] The sapling of English political theory and practice, transplanted to America, sent its roots deep down into the native virgin soil and produced a fruit the like of which had not been gathered from the parent tree. Ideas of popular representation, as distinct from class representation, were the peculiar product of American conditions and were current in all except ultra-Conservative circles. The American view of the principles underlying colonial obligations to the mother country was accepted by the vast majority of the leaders of thought in the colonies, but there was a real and honest difference of opinion regarding the best method of making such principles effective. The Conservative, because of his innate aversion to revolution, desired to maintain the British connection as the foundation of economic and political stability. More anxious was he, therefore, than the Radical to correct by constitutional means the abuses which were generally admitted to exist in the colonial system. "On its political side loyalism stood for

[1] Shortt and Doughty, p. 675, Carleton to Germain, 28 Sept. 1776.
[2] Flick, A. C., *Loyalism in New York*, p. 16.

the recognition of law as against rebellion in any form, for the unity of the empire as against a separate, independent existence of the colonies, and for monarchy instead of republicanism".[1] As an economic force, loyalism stood for stability and for the protection of the rights of property against the Radicals, the disturbers and the adventurers on new and uncharted seas of commercial and financial practice.

Loyalism did not follow any of the recognised lines of social or economic distinction. While it included "the aristocracy of culture, of dignified professions and callings, of official rank and hereditary wealth", it numbered among its adherents the tradesman and the artisan, the village blacksmith and the coloured labourer, men of all vocations and from well-nigh every corner of the colonies as well as the recent immigrant who had found neither vocation nor permanent place of abode. Public officials, from governors to township magistrates, found a special reason for loyalty; clergy and devoted adherents of the Church of England gave honour to George III as a duty of even more pressing urgency than godly fear; merchants, bankers, shippers feared the dislocation of business which the revolutionary upheaval might cause. And in the country villages and along the western frontier were those of whom the world heard little who still took pride in the motherland and were determined to remain subjects of its King. Nor was this new political earthquake a respecter of family ties. The arch-Whig, Benjamin Franklin, found his son, Sir William, arrayed against him. John Randolph, the King's Attorney-General of Virginia, was opposed by his son, Edmund, later the first Attorney-General of the United States. Colonel John Butler was obliged to lead his rangers against the forces of his Whig cousins, Colonel Zeb Butler and Colonel William Butler. Nor was there any assurance that individuals would be found in the same camp on successive days. As great a personage as Alexander Hamilton moved from the party of the Crown to that of revolt, and Arnold, leader of the provincial forces in Canada, with much less justification, deserted to the Tories.

Loyalism had little chance to thrive in Puritan New England. The Puritan colonies had never been distinguished for attachment to the throne; for the seed of revolt had been carried to America in the *Mayflower* and the growing plant had been faithfully nurtured by New England nonconformity. Loyalism, when it attempted to assert itself in Massachusetts, was subjected to a fierce verbal onslaught by the Adamses and their disciples. And yet, the Loyalists of New England were numbered by thousands. Virginia, of all the colonies, should have remained firm in its attachment to the Crown. In its social structure and habits, in its religious associations and intellectual interests it more closely resembled rural England than did any other part of America, but the policy of the Home Government, which pre-

[1] Flick, p. 11.

vented the occupation of the lands west of the mountains, alienated many of the wealthier and more influential Virginians. Many of the planters were hopelessly submerged in debt to English merchants and, in sheer despair, were driven to seek escape by repudiation.[1] The causes of revolt in Virginia were very different from those operating in Massachusetts and, when the movement had become well established, its leadership passed from the northern to the southern colony. The influence of Washington, Patrick Henry and Lee provided a very real obstacle to the growth of loyalism in Virginia. In New York, where social and denominational affiliations had already created parties, the De Lanceys, large landed proprietors and leaders of loyalism, were Anglicans, while the Livingstones, Presbyterian and leaders of the opposing faction, espoused the cause of independence. In New York and Pennsylvania the forces of loyalism and revolt were very evenly divided, and, in the opinion of John Adams, had it not been for the influence of Massachusetts and Virginia, these two colonies might have joined the British and seriously imperilled the movement of revolt.[2] In the Carolinas the loyalist party outnumbered the Whigs, as the Radicals were called. In Georgia it was so strong that, but for the surrender of Cornwallis at Yorktown, the colony would probably have completely dissociated itself from the revolutionary movement.[3] Throughout the colonies as a whole, in the opinion of John Adams again, the Whigs and Loyalists were each entitled to claim a third while the remainder were indifferent,[4] prepared, like many of the Canadians, to cast in their lot with the winning side. The forces of loyalty, sadly deficient in leadership, were strangely dissipated; yet it has been stated that during the war more colonials fought under the royal standard than with the Provincials.[5]

Following the example of Massachusetts, committees of correspondence, committees of safety, local and provincial, temporary and standing, were appointed in the several colonies even in districts where the Sons of Liberty composed but a small fraction of the inhabitants. These local committees then began a vigorous persecution of those suspected of loyalist sympathies. By various forms of intimidation, by social ostracism, by commercial boycott and by methods much less gentle, pressure was exerted to undermine the loyalty of the Tories. "If I must be devoured", cried the "Westchester Farmer", "let me be devoured by the jaws of a lion and not be gnawed to death by rats and vermin".[6] The non-importation association of the first Continental Congress gave way, in the fol-

[1] For details see Bemis, S. F., *Jay's Treaty*, p. 103; also Harrell, I. S., *Loyalism in Virginia*, chap. i.
[2] Adams, J., *Works*, x, 63.
[3] Tyler, M. C., "Loyalists in the American Revolution", *Am. H.R.* I, 28.
[4] Adams, J., *Works*, x, 87, 110.
[5] Channing, E., *History of the United States*, III, 215.
[6] The "Westchester Farmer", *Free Thoughts*, p. 13.

lowing June, to a defensive association which held "those persons inimical to the liberties of the colonies who shall refuse to subscribe this association". By the spring of 1776 an organisation for the suppression of loyalism had been completed from the Continental Congress to the village committee.

After the Declaration of Independence in July 1776, the persecution of loyalism was undertaken with redoubled severity. A new State claiming sovereign rights had been created, and all citizens were required to declare their allegiance. Loyalism now became treason, and a fresh element of animosity marked the persecution of its votaries. In many districts they had formed associations which, necessarily, operated in secret, but now, without the active support of British troops, were of little avail. The plan of paying for the war by the seizure of loyalist property gradually took form and in November 1777 the Continental Congress recommended that the States confiscate loyalist property and invest the proceeds in Continental loan certificates. The Loyalists were disfranchised; they were disqualified from practising their professions; they were denied the protection of the courts for their persons and property; they were forbidden freedom of speech and of the press; their merchants and traders were not allowed to sell their goods; many were exiled, others were imprisoned and some were tried and executed for treason. After the Declaration of Independence, no real effort was made towards conciliation. It seemed perfectly obvious that, unless he speedily renounced his British allegiance, the Loyalist was not wanted in those regions to which the authority of Congress extended.

Already the royalist forces had been largely recruited from the colonies. Colonel Maclean's Royal Highland Emigrants included many Scottish refugees from the estates of Sir William Johnson which, on his death in 1774, descended to his son, Sir John. During the summer of 1775 a large number of Loyalists were enrolled in the "Royal Fencible Americans", and in May 1776 Sir John Johnson escaped to Canada and received authority to raise two battalions of 500 men each of the King's Royal Regiment of New York, popularly known as the "Royal Greens". Several battalions were recruited among the Loyalists of eastern New York and were used most effectively in the operations along the seaboard. In the valley of the Mohawk and of the Wyoming and along the western frontier, such units were raised as Rogers's Rangers, Simcoe's Queen's Rangers, and Jessup's Corps which grew out of the first battalion of "Royal Greens". A large number of Loyalists were with Burgoyne at Saratoga and, after that disastrous affair, were employed chiefly in the southern colonies and in border raids along the Canadian frontier. It has been estimated that in New York alone 23,500 Loyalists were under arms.[1] At least an equal number were enlisted in other colonies, bringing the total to ap-

[1] Flick, pp. 112, 113, n. 1.

proximately 50,000 men. Not only in the actual enrolment of soldiers but in raising money, providing clothing and supplies for the armies and organising relief for the destitute did the Loyalists render valuable aid to the cause of the Crown. Indeed, had it not been for the contempt of the British regular officer for the colonial, the issue of the war might have been far different.

The instinct of self-preservation dictated to the Whigs a policy of segregating the Loyalists. Connecticut, which seemed to have few Tories of its own, received a supply, under guard, from New York and New Jersey, others being sent to Pennsylvania, while many of the Quaker colony's suspects were sent to Virginia. The more active and dangerous Loyalists were confined to gaol. The disposition of these prisoners and exiles constituted a very real problem at the conclusion of the war. Other Loyalists, again, to escape imprisonment or persecution, made their way, often with the greatest difficulty, to regions which were held by British forces. Thus, before the withdrawal of Howe, Boston became a city of refuge for Massachusetts Loyalists. Later, Newport, Charleston, Savannah, Philadelphia, and New York became concentration centres for loyalist refugees. Before the close of the war, all of these towns had been abandoned by the British except New York, which therefore became the chief place of refuge for the loyalist exiles.

While hostilities ceased in 1781, the fate of the Loyalists was not determined until the Treaty of Paris of 1782. The treaty provisions relating to boundaries and to the Loyalists were of peculiar importance to Canada. The British public had not extracted much comfort from the military operations in America and was heartily sick of the entire affair. This attitude was reflected in the policy of the Government and its agents in the negotiations with the colonies. The nation wanted the American business ended and was prepared to pay a reasonable price for peace. A comparison of the relative abilities of an Oswald and a Franklin is not necessary to an understanding of the Treaty of Paris.[1] The subject-matter of the negotiations was essentially American and the colonial delegates were naturally on more familiar ground than their British associates. The definition of the limits of the United States represented an effort to secure a satisfactory natural boundary. Britain surrendered the territory between the Ohio and the Great Lakes which had been included in Quebec by the Act of 1774. The fur-traders represented British interests in this area but, in 1783, the British merchants engaged in the fur trade did not enjoy the favour of Government. Many of them were suspected of sympathising with the revolting colonists and of having aided them during the war. In any event, the interests of the western fur trade were disregarded and a boundary was accepted which alienated a most valuable fur-producing area.

[1] See vol. 1, chap. xxv.

The Loyalists regarded the provisions of the treaty as utterly inadequate for their protection. It was agreed that creditors on either side should meet with no lawful impediment to the recovery of debts, that there should be no further confiscation, and that Congress should recommend to the Legislatures of the States to provide for the restitution of the property of Loyalists who had not borne arms. The State Governments were responsible for the execution of these provisions and, because of local influence and the deep-rooted hatred of the Loyalists, the attitude of the State officials was very different from that of the Federal Government. In these early years of experiment, before a central authority had been firmly established, the Federal Government was obliged to proceed with caution in exerting pressure on State Governments for the protection of the rights of those who were regarded as enemies of the Republic. Hence the aid of the Federal Government was not the most effective means of protecting the Loyalists.

The definite acknowledgment of the independence of the States by Britain in the treaty of peace made an end to the fond hopes of many Loyalists who, to the last, had relied on provision for some form of British supremacy. The acceptance of the Republic or exile were the only alternatives now offered. In the early stages of the war many of the Loyalists sought refuge in regions where the authority of the Crown was not brought in question. A great many merchants, landowners, royal officials and Episcopal clergymen retired to England. Others, in the south, crossed to the West Indies. From the Atlantic seaboard there was a steady migration to Nova Scotia. When Howe withdrew from Boston in March 1776, nearly 1000 Loyalists accompanied the army to Halifax. From western New York another stream wended its way northward to Canada. In July 1778 nearly 1000 loyalist refugees were receiving provisions from the Government of Quebec.

It seemed natural that the Loyalists of the Atlantic coast should look to Nova Scotia for a permanent home. It was within easy access from Boston and New York; there was an abundance of unoccupied lands and British authority seemed to be firmly established. The city of Halifax, which became known as an important naval base during the Seven Years' War, had been established in 1749 around the excellent harbour of Chebucto Bay. In the following year it became the capital of the province and a stream of settlement from Britain and the continent began to flow in its direction. A large migration of German Protestants was directed mainly to the Lunenburg district in the years immediately preceding the Seven Years' War, and after the war the lands left vacant by the expulsion of the Acadians, the most fertile in the province, were rapidly occupied by immigrants from the New England colonies. After the restoration of peace, Nova Scotia became the frontier of New England. The Philadelphia

Company, in which Benjamin Franklin was interested, sent many settlers northward to the district which later became Pictou County. In 1767 the total population of Nova Scotia was 13,374, of whom more than half had come from the older American colonies. This migration northward continued steadily until the outbreak of the Revolution. The western portion of the peninsula—the Annapolis valley and the fertile lands at the head of the Bay of Fundy—became the centre of New England influence. Migration from the mother country meanwhile had not been suspended; the *Hector*, in 1773, brought 200 Highland settlers to Pictou Harbour, the advance guard of a substantial Scottish immigration which was destined to leave its impress on the Pictou and Cape Breton districts.

The government of Nova Scotia had been entrusted in the early years after the founding of Halifax to a Governor and nominated Council, although instructions were given to the Governor to summon a popular Assembly to aid in legislation. The first Governor, Cornwallis, and his successor, Lawrence, preferred to dispense with the elected Assembly, until, finally, the protests of Halifax merchants and of English settlers compelled Lawrence to convene one. The first election was held in the summer of 1758 and five of the fifteen members chosen were of New England origin. Although many of the New England emigrants to Nova Scotia were sympathetic to the cause of the Whigs, the preponderance of loyalist sentiment throughout the colony gave them little encouragement to proclaim their faith. The advances and threats of the Continental Congress were alike ignored. The New England Loyalists, therefore, might rely on finding in Nova Scotia the authority of the Crown firmly established and representative institutions similar to those with which they were familiar.

In the autumn of 1782 a party of about 500 Loyalists was sent from New York to Annapolis Royal on the Bay of Fundy. Scouts sent to explore the Annapolis valley and the mouth of the St John River across the Bay brought back glowing accounts of the country. In the spring of 1783 the task of finding homes for the thousands of Loyalists huddled together in New York was undertaken in earnest. In April a fleet of twenty vessels carried 7000 refugees to Port Roseway on the south-east coast of Nova Scotia and to the mouth of the St John. During the summer and autumn the fleet of transports was kept busy. Governor Parr of Nova Scotia estimated that by the end of September 18,000 refugees had arrived and by the end of the year the number had increased to 30,000. New York was not evacuated by Sir Guy Carleton, who now commanded the British forces, until 25 November 1783, because he prolonged his stay to make certain that provision was made for every Loyalist who applied for the protection of the Crown. By the end of November, therefore, the stream of migration northward had largely subsided, although a few who found it difficult to re-establish themselves in their former homes sought more congenial surroundings in Nova Scotia. By the summer of 1786 the movement northward had spent itself.

The total number of loyalist immigrants to Nova Scotia may be placed, on the most reliable estimates, at 35,000 or approximately double the population of the colony before the migration began. Thirty thousand of these came by way of New York City and 20,000 had formerly resided in the colony of New York.[1] These new settlers were distributed in various parts of Nova Scotia. Lands were granted on the St John River northward, a distance of 150 miles, while another settlement was formed at Passamaquoddy Bay. Many of the immigrants, however, attracted by the advantages of the capital, remained in the vicinity of Halifax; while the Annapolis valley had been popular from the beginning of the movement northward. Digby and Fort Cumberland became the centres of flourishing loyalist colonies, although the most interesting of all the settlements was located at Port Roseway. The first loyalist settlers went there in 1782 and within two years the population had increased to 10,000. Stores and churches were built, streets were laid out and plans made for the construction of a metropolis which should rival Halifax and ultimately become the capital of the colony. But these ambitious plans were doomed to cruel disappointment; the site had not been wisely chosen; the surrounding country was unable to support a large population and, in a few years, Shelburne, as the settlement was known, was but a haunted monument of its erstwhile greatness.

Prince Edward Island, likewise, received its quota of Loyalists. On the faith of the promise of lands similar in extent to those granted in Nova Scotia and Quebec, many Loyalists went to the island colony. Others, again, some 600 in number, who were dissatisfied with conditions in Nova Scotia, crossed over to the island. Difficulties were encountered in securing title to their lands, which, unfortunately, were not settled for many years. About 3000 Loyalists settled in Cape Breton Island, which consequently received a separate administration, with a Lieutenant-Governor (1784).[2]

The resources of the Government of Nova Scotia proved quite inadequate to the reception of a large number of immigrants. Satisfactory provision was made for the relatively small migration prior to 1783, but the flood of settlers which swept over the province in the summer and autumn of that year completely swamped the administrative system then under the control of a pretentious but inefficient Governor, John Parr. The Government was unable to supply the refugees with provisions or with lumber for the construction of even temporary shelter. Serious delays occurred in the allotment and survey of lands. Dissatisfaction alike with the size and location of grants of land became widespread. Many of the immi-

[1] Flick, p. 175.
[2] Wallace, W. S., *The United Empire Loyalists*, p. 63.

grants were very keenly disappointed and declared that they had been the victims of misrepresentation. There was a very real difference between the loyalist and the pre-loyalist migrations from New England to Nova Scotia. The earlier immigrants had been frontiersmen, accustomed to the hardships and privations of pioneer life, while many of the Loyalists were town-dwellers, officials, clerks, tradesmen, unable to pursue their accustomed vocations in their new homes and unfitted for the rigorous demands of frontier life. The plight of these people was truly pitiable and many of them preferred the ignominy and humiliation of returning to their former homes to enduring the privations of life in "Nova Scarcity" as the Maritime colony came to be known among the disaffected. Others, again, were prepared to gamble on the superiority of distant pastures and migrated to the northern shores of the upper St Lawrence and of Lake Ontario.

The Loyalists who settled north of the Bay of Fundy suffered more keenly from the breakdown of the administrative system than did those in other parts of the province. They were far removed from other settled communities from which aid might have been received and were too far distant from the seat of government effectively to present their grievances or to secure prompt redress for inequalities and delays in the allotment of grants of land. A very large number were discharged officers and men representing no less than thirteen loyalist units which had served with distinction during the war. They seemed, therefore, to possess an *esprit de corps* which distinguished them from those who settled in the peninsula. To certain of their leaders the prospect of a large population occupying the country north of the Bay of Fundy seemed to justify the creation of a separate government, a suggestion made by Edward Winslow as early as July 1783. Dissatisfaction with the existing Administration gave impetus to the movement for separation. The opportunity of securing office may not have been absent from the minds of certain of the more ardent advocates of separation. The imperial authorities were convinced of the wisdom of dividing the province, and in May 1784 their decision was communicated to Governor Parr of Nova Scotia. A line drawn across the isthmus from the Missiquash River to its source and thence to the Baie Verte became the boundary between the two colonies, and Colonel Thomas Carleton, a younger brother of Sir Guy, was appointed the first Governor of the new province of New Brunswick.

The administration of the new province was entrusted to the Governor assisted by an appointed Council and an elected Assembly. The chief administrative and judicial offices were allotted to Loyalists. The Rev. Jonathan Odell, who had acted as private secretary to Sir Guy Carleton in New York, became the secretary of the province; George Duncan Ludlow, prior to the revolution a judge of the Supreme

Court of New York, became the first Chief Justice and a member of the Council; James Putnam, formerly Attorney-General of Massachusetts, became a puisne judge and a Councillor; Jonathan Bliss, a graduate of Harvard and former member of the General Court of Massachusetts, was appointed Attorney-General; Daniel Bliss, likewise a Harvard graduate, was appointed to the Council, while Ward Chipman, also a graduate of Harvard, became Solicitor-General. In few British colonies has it been possible to draw on such extensive reserves of talent and experience for the initiation of civil government as were found among the Loyalists of New Brunswick in 1784. The colony was divided into eight counties for electoral purposes and in November 1785 the first provincial election was held.

The other main stream of loyalist migration wended its way westward and northward to Canada. Many of the refugees crossed to the colony of Quebec at Niagara, at Oswego, Sackett's Harbour and Ogdensburg, others went by way of Lake Champlain and the Richelieu while many arrived by way of the Atlantic and the St Lawrence. As early as June 1774 Loyalists from the western frontier began to make their appearance at the British posts on the Richelieu. The measures of repression taken against those who manifested Tory leanings during 1775 and 1776 sent many to Canada, and from these refugees the militia units which participated in border warfare were largely recruited. The reverse to the British cause at Saratoga in 1777 started fresh movements northward. By the autumn of 1778, at least 3000 Loyalists had gone to Canada. More systematic arrangements for the relief of the refugees were made by Sir Frederick Haldimand, who in 1778 succeeded Carleton as Governor, than by Governor Parr in Nova Scotia. A temporary settlement was established at Machiche, near Three Rivers, where the Loyalists received shelter and provisions at the expense of the Government. The northward migration continued until the conclusion of peace when the floodgates were let loose. A second camp was established at Sorel, and stations were formed at St John's and Chambly, at Quebec and Montreal for the supply of provisions. Many of the disbanded troops, still retaining their military organisation, chose to go to Canada. Carleton reported that in July 1783 eight companies of Loyalists, organised as militia, had embarked from New York for Canada[1] while other companies left in August and September. These immigrants wintered at Sorel and received lands in the following spring. In all, approximately 20,000 came to Canada, of whom, it was estimated, 15,000 came from the colony of New York.[2]

In the spring and summer of 1784, the task of the allocation of lands was undertaken in earnest. Naturally, the newcomers preferred to be segregated for the purpose of preserving their own language and

[1] See Carleton to Haldimand, 6 July 1783, Pub. Arch. Can. *Series B*, CXLVI, 65.
[2] Flick, p. 179.

customs. In July 1783 special instructions were issued to Haldimand authorising him to grant to every non-commissioned officer 200 acres and to privates and to civilian heads of families 100 acres with 50 acres additional for each member of the family. The seigneury of Sorel, which had been acquired by the Government in 1780 and in which the camp was located, was divided among them, each receiving, however, only 60 acres and a town lot while the remainder of his lands was allotted in the districts which had not hitherto been opened for settlement. Another smaller settlement was formed in the Gaspé peninsula. The district later known as the Eastern Townships, bordering on the States of New York, and Vermont seemed to offer another suitable location; but Haldimand feared that friction might occur with the Americans and that, possibly, some of the new settlers might be won from their attachment to the Crown.

Settlement in the occupied areas of Quebec did not accord with loyalist ideals and, for that reason, the vast majority sought lands beyond the settlements of the French along the upper St Lawrence, Lake Ontario and Lake Erie. In the autumn of 1783, on the receipt of his instructions regarding the granting of lands, Haldimand sent surveyors to the shores of the Bay of Quinté and five townships were laid out in lots. In the following spring, eight more townships were surveyed between the Bay of Quinté and the Ottawa; and in the spring of 1785 transportation from the camps at Machiche, Sorel and St John's was commenced under the direction of the new superintendent, Sir John Johnson. The five townships immediately west of the seigneury of Longueuil were allotted to the men of Sir John's regiment, the first battalion of the King's Royal Regiment of New York. Many of these men were Scottish Highlanders of the Roman Catholic faith who had come from the Johnson estates in the Mohawk valley and whose impress on the county of Glengarry remains to this day. To the men of Jessup's Corps were allotted the remaining three townships. The five townships extending from Cataraqui westward were given to civilian immigrants and to disbanded men of the second battalion of the Royal Regiment of Jessup's Corps and of Rogers's Rangers. The Niagara peninsula provided a refuge for another group which included many refugees from southern New York and Pennsylvania. Many of the frontiersmen enlisted in Butler's Rangers received lands in the Niagara district at the close of the war. Provision was likewise made for the Indians of the tribes of the Six Nations who remained steadfast to Britain. A reservation for the Indians was made in the township of Tyendenaga west of Cataraqui and near the settlement of the Rangers with whom the Indians had served during the war. Another and larger reservation was made on the Grand River, flowing into Lake Erie. This settlement, which was nearer to the old home and kinsfolk, was the more popular and ultimately attracted many of the Indians from the Quinté district.

The Loyalists who settled in Canada were of a somewhat different type from those who went to the Maritime Provinces. A larger number came from the western frontier, farmers, mechanics, labourers, strangers to a life of ease and luxury, but familiar with the limitations and vicissitudes of the pioneer. Few of them were drawn from professional life or had enjoyed the privileges of a university education, yet their training in the rough and unrefined school of backwoods experience fitted them admirably for the strenuous conflicts of frontier life. Because they were, as a rule, less familiar with the comforts and luxuries of the older communities of the east, the new settlers in Canada expected less and were less liable to disappointment than their fellows who went to Nova Scotia. Although occasionally expressing dissatisfaction with their lot, few of the Canadian Loyalists returned to their former homes. The Maritime Provinces reaped the benefits and paid the penalty of receiving the aristocracy of the Loyalists; Canada received the yeomanry and gave them a task worthy a yeoman's mettle. Until they could become self-supporting the refugees in Canada received aid from the Government in the form of material for clothing, tools to aid in the conquest of the forest and in the building of houses, and a gun which afforded protection from wild animals and aided in obtaining food. Their persistence, industry and frugality gradually released them from the privations and limitations of pioneer life and ushered in a new day of comfort and prosperity.

When it became apparent that several of the States had no intention of restoring property taken from Loyalists during the war, the British Government gave friendly consideration to claims for compensation. The Coalition Ministry in July 1783 appointed a royal commission to enquire into this question; and the commissioners found it necessary to go to America to enquire specifically into claims. Ultimately, compensation was limited to loss of property and of income derived from office or profession. The labours of the commission were not concluded until 1790 and bitter complaint was aroused by the delay. In the end, the Loyalists would seem to have been very generously treated. In addition to the aid which had already been granted in various forms and to the lands which they had received the British Government paid over three million pounds to those found by the commission entitled to compensation. Later, Lord Dorchester proposed that some mark of distinction should be accorded to those "who had adhered to the unity of the empire" and authority was given to Loyalists and their descendants to affix the letters "U.E." to their names "alluding to their great principle, the unity of the empire".[1]

The immigration of thousands of English-speaking settlers into British North America became a political factor of the first importance.

[1] See Minutes of Council, Quebec, 9 Nov. 1789; also Sabine, L., *The American Loyalists*, and Van Tyne, C. H., *The Loyalists in the American Revolution*.

The old continental empire was now but a memory. In so far as British policy relating to Canada had been influenced by consideration of the older colonies, there was now to be a change. British dominion on the North American continent was in future to be established on the foundation of interests but recently acquired or considered of substantial value. Canada and the Maritime Provinces thus came to occupy an entirely new place in Britain's oversea policy. This change in the position of Canada involved the abandonment of one hitherto dominant principle. Carleton had proceeded on the assumption that "barring Catastrophe shocking to think of, this Country must to the end of Time, be peopled by the Canadian Race".[1] British statesmanship had therefore only flirted with the plan of maintaining the ascendancy of French institutions in Canada. Not only had the conditions which seemed to justify such a policy been removed, but the assumption on which the feasibility of its operation had been based had now been disproved. The loyalist migrations concluded that experiment; the new position of Canada demanded a new departure.

These changes were reflected very soon in the attitude of the French Canadians. The attachment of the French Canadian to his Church and to his civil institutions had never been seriously undermined. When no danger threatened the supremacy of his Church or of his laws, he could afford to be critical. The new menace to French-Canadian ascendancy, however, completely changed the situation. The French Canadian has been essentially conservative and his conservatism has been manifested in a special manner in his determination to preserve a mode of life which is peculiarly the product of his own mental habits and of the conditions in which he has lived. The preservation of his language has been essential to the perpetuation of the ideals embodied in his mode of living. His Church has been the citadel around which all the forces of conservatism have rallied for the preservation of those factors in life which he values most highly. When he saw in the migration to his province of thousands of English Protestants a challenge to the supremacy of his Church and language he rallied loyally to their support. The Quebec Act, which, under very different conditions, many of the French Canadians were inclined to criticise, now became the chief bulwark of his defence. The supremacy of his Church and of his civil law was guaranteed by that measure which, thereafter, came to be regarded as the Magna Carta of French-Canadian liberties.

The position of the English-speaking minority was also affected by these new conditions. They had not ceased to advocate the introduction of English commercial law and the constitution of a popular Assembly. Carleton's instructions had, in fact, suggested that the English commercial law might be introduced by ordinance of the Council, but,

---

[1] Shortt and Doughty, p. 284, Carleton to Shelburne, 25 Nov. 1767.

during the period of danger, Carleton thought it wise to avoid the possibility of local dissension by refraining from disclosing his instructions—a topic discussed in the previous chapter.[1] Haldimand took the soldier's view of the Quebec situation and went even farther than Carleton, refusing, after the most explicit directions, to disclose his instructions. In April 1784 the English party in the Council endeavoured, without success, to secure the appointment of a committee to draft a petition to the King and Parliament requesting the constitution of a popular Assembly. Haldimand, who resolutely opposed the project of the English minority, retired as Governor in the following November and was succeeded by Henry Hamilton as Lieutenant-Governor, who was much more sympathetic to the demand for an Assembly. The radical difference between the policies of Hamilton and of his predecessors inevitably brought him into conflict with the Council and led to his recall in August 1785. He was succeeded by Colonel Henry Hope who, in turn, gave way to Guy Carleton in the following August, appointed Governor-in-Chief of all the British North American provinces except Newfoundland.

The appointment of Carleton, now elevated to the peerage as Baron Dorchester, to such a position was significant. It indicated a desire to maintain a more intimate union among the remaining British colonies through a strong central executive and, likewise, it gave the British Government, in a new and difficult situation, the benefit of the advice of an officer who surpassed all possible nominees in his knowledge of Canadian conditions. Dorchester reached Quebec in the autumn of 1786, accompanied by William Smith, Loyalist and former Chief Justice of New York, with whom he had returned to England from America in 1784 and whose appointment to a similar post in Quebec had been made at his urgent request.

Already the British Government was confronted with the problem of revising the system of government in Quebec. The English at Montreal and Quebec had derived much satisfaction from the influx of the Loyalists, regarding them as allies in the conflict with French-Canadian conservatism and reaction. In the autumn of 1784 the older English of the province addressed a petition[2] to the Crown in which they urged the creation of a representative Assembly with the powers of taxation necessary to enable it to meet the expenses of government. They advocated increasing the membership of the Council, making it more independent of the Governor and giving it more effective control over the administration; they asked that the commercial law of England should be introduced and that the right of Habeas Corpus, enjoyed by virtue of an ordinance of the Council, should be embodied in the constitution of the province. This petition, represented as expressing views both of the French and

---

[1] See Shortt and Doughty, p. 599, for Article 12 of Carleton's Instructions.
[2] *Ibid.* p. 742.

English subjects, prompted the leaders of the French Canadians to present an address to the King disapproving the request for a popular Assembly and indicating their fear that the colony could not bear the taxes which "must necessarily ensue".[1] The Loyalists, likewise, presented a petition in the spring of 1785 requesting that the settlements above Montreal should be constituted a separate district distinct from the province of Quebec and under the administration of a Lieutenant-Governor and Council, subordinate, however, to the Governor and Council of Quebec. These petitions indicated to the British ministers three different methods of approaching the settlement of Canadian affairs.

In the spring of 1786 Powys, a private member of the House of Commons specially interested in Canada, was refused leave to introduce a bill incorporating most of the requests in the petition of the older English of Quebec; for Pitt urged that no action should be taken until Dorchester's report on conditions in the colony had been received. Dorchester realised fully the difficulties of the situation and in June 1787 confessed to being "at a loss for any plan likely to give satisfaction to a people so circumstanced as we are at present". He urged, however, that the instructions relating to the granting of lands, which had been framed in 1771 in accordance with his own recommendations, should now be modified in such a manner as to permit the introduction of the freehold tenure. Ministers perceived the impossibility of obliging the Loyalists to accept lands under a tenure with which they were wholly unfamiliar; and in September 1787 Lord Sydney, the Secretary of State charged with the control of colonial affairs, pointed out that a change in the system of land holding was being recommended, that this suggested a division of the province, but that no alteration in the Quebec Act was contemplated because of the difficulty of evolving a satisfactory plan for an Assembly.[2]

The English of Quebec and Montreal, not satisfied with the progress being made by the British Government, sent one of their number, Adam Lymburner, to London as special agent for the prosecution of their cause. He was heard at the bar of the House in May 1788, when he urged the remedies they advocated. Powys again endeavoured to persuade the Commons to consider the Quebec situation, but again Pitt counselled delay on the ground that the Government was not yet sufficiently informed regarding conditions in the colony. This debate indicated that the Canada question must be considered during the next session. From the premise that a change in the system of land tenure was necessary the Government was moving towards a division of the province, with the creation of a popular Assembly as a possible expedient. In the autumn of 1788 a special packet boat was de-

---

[1] Shortt and Doughty, p. 762.
[2] See Shortt and Doughty, p. 863, Sydney to Dorchester, 14 and 20 Sept. 1787.

spatched to Quebec with a request that Dorchester should immediately advise regarding the basis of the objection of the French to an Assembly.

Lord Dorchester approached this problem with a more intimate knowledge of conditions in the American colonies than had been gained by any of the ministers and his suggestions were based on his American experience. He did not deem it necessary to form the Loyalist settlements above Montreal into a separate government. The four districts into which the upper country had been divided might be placed under the direction of a Lieutenant-Governor subordinate to the Governor-in-Chief at Quebec. The creation of a new province seemed to tend towards disintegration at a time when the more intimate union of the remaining British North American colonies appeared to him essential to the maintenance of the British connection. If, however, a new province were created he saw no objection to giving it a representative Assembly.

By the autumn of 1789 the ministers reached a decision regarding the government of Canada and embodied their ideas in a draft bill, which was sent to Lord Dorchester in October for his comment and criticism.[1] The purpose of the bill, as stated by William Grenville, the Secretary of State, was "to assimilate the Constitution of the Province to that of Great Britain as nearly as the difference arising from the manners of the people and from the present situation of the province will admit". The most significant features of the Government's policy were the division of the province and the creation of a popular Legislative Assembly in each part. It could not be denied that the settlement of the Loyalists in Canada created a new situation which could be met only by intervention of the British Parliament. The Loyalists insisted on having recourse to English law, particularly the law of real property; two systems of law could not be administered satisfactorily within a single province. That condition alone seemed to justify a separation of the Loyalists from the French Canadians. The Loyalists of the upper country were accustomed to representative institutions in the American colonies; their brothers who went to Nova Scotia and New Brunswick enjoyed the benefits of a popular Legislature. Less than this could not be expected to satisfy the Canadian Loyalists. Assuming, therefore, that the new settlers must have a popular Legislature, it could not without injustice be denied to the English of Quebec and Montreal. Should there, then, be one or two Legislatures? The Government decided that the union of all the English and French, particularly with the promise of a rapid increase in the English population through immigration, would tend to introduce racial and religious disputes into the Legislature and thus

---

[1] See Grenville's views as stated in the Duke of Richmond's letters to Earl Bathurst of 24 Nov. 1818, and 16 May 1819, in *Bathurst Papers*, Hist. MSS. Comm. 1923, pp. 460 and 471; also in *Dropmore Papers*, Hist. MSS. Comm. 1892, I, 496, 506.

interfere with the experiment in representative government. These conditions seemed to justify the division of the province and the creation of two Legislatures.

Within these broad limits, the details of the administrative system devised for the Canadas were determined largely by the views entertained by ministers regarding the causes of the loss of the American colonies. Parliament was "about to communicate the blessings of the English constitution to the subjects of Canada because they were fully convinced that it was the best in the world".[1] The supreme virtue of the English constitution was found in its well-balanced and happy combination of the aristocratic and democratic elements. The American colonies had been lost because unbridled democracy had been allowed to run wild and the proper balance of the constitution had been disturbed. In Britain the House of Lords checked the excesses of democracy while a hereditary aristocracy and an established Church supported the authority of the Crown. The absence of these conservative institutions having been fatal in America, a similar error must not be made in the Canadas. The constitution of the Legislative Council, corresponding to the House of Lords, presented an opportunity for laying the foundations of a Canadian aristocracy. The final draft of the bill fixed the membership of the Legislative Council of Upper Canada at not fewer than seven and of Lower Canada at not fewer than fifteen and provided for conferring hereditary titles of honour which should carry the right of membership in the Council. Despite the warning of Lord Dorchester that "the fluctuating state of property in these Provinces would expose all hereditary honours to fall into disregard", much emphasis was laid on the benefits to be derived from this provision in creating an influential class in the colony whose interest would lie in supporting the authority of the Crown and of the Governor. In the debate in the Commons, Fox raised doubts regarding the feasibility of forming a colonial aristocracy capable of commanding respect and urged that the Council should be made elective with a higher property qualification both for members and electors than applied to the Assembly. He saw in the distance separating Canada from the mother country a practical difficulty in the exercise by Parliament of control over the Governor's advisers, and hoped, by making the Council elective, to render it independent of the Governor and capable of fixing on his counsellors a sense of responsibility for their recommendations.[2] Time justified the prediction of Lord Dorchester and this part of the Act remained a dead letter.

The Assembly of Upper Canada was to have a minimum membership of sixteen and that of Lower Canada of fifty. The bill presented to the House, in accordance with the suggestion of Lord Dorchester,

---

[1] Grenville (then Lord Grenville) in the debate on the Quebec Government Bill in the House of Lords; *Parl. Hist.* XXIX, pp. 655–8.
[2] *Speeches of C. J. Fox* (ed. 1815), IV, 202–36.

gave the Lower Canadian Assembly a minimum membership of thirty. In committee Fox objected to the membership of both Assemblies on the ground that it was incapable of giving them a truly representative character. When the bill was reported, Pitt agreed to increase the membership of the Lower Canadian Assembly to fifty. The Governor or Lieutenant-Governor of each province was authorised to form counties for the purpose of electing representatives. British subjects of the age of twenty-one and owning property in the country of the yearly value of 40s. and, in the towns, of £5 were entitled to vote. The Council and Assembly were required to meet at least once a year. The life of the Assembly was fixed at four years subject to the right of dissolution at any time by the Governor or Lieutenant-Governor. Bills passed by the Assembly and Council might be reserved for the royal assent and unless this assent was given within two years such bills would not become law.

An Executive Council for each province completed the machinery of government. The Council of Quebec had acted both as a Legislative and an Executive Council. The quorum of the Council acting as an executive body was lower than when it assembled for purposes of legislation; fewer members attended the executive sessions and, as we have seen, Carleton thought it proper to invite only specific members of the Council to advise him on questions of policy. Under the new Act there was a definite intention to maintain a distinction between the Executive and Legislative Councils, although members of one Council might belong to the other. The constitution of an Executive Council did not require statutory authority; directions for its creation are found in the new instructions issued to the Governor of the two provinces after the Act became operative. The Act itself assumed that a Council would be appointed in each province and entrusted it with the duties of a final court of appeal in civil cases arising within the province.

The attempt to extend the influence of the Church of England and to use it to strengthen the English interest in the colony may also be traced to the loss of the American colonies. Had the intimate association between Church and State which existed in England been maintained in the colonies, many argued, they would not have revolted; for by its teaching and organisation the Church of England tended to support authority. The transplanting of the British system of government involved not necessarily the creation of a State Church in the colonies, but the maintenance of an intimate connection between the Established Church in England and the colonial administration. "For the support and maintenance of a Protestant clergy" the ministers decided to create an endowment in the form of lands which would increase in value and become productive of a revenue as settlement advanced. The Crown was therefore authorised to reserve from the waste lands of each province a quantity equivalent to one-seventh of the lands granted and likewise to erect parsonages or rectories "according to the establishment of the Church of England" and to endow them from the lands reserved for the clergy. In employing lands as an endowment for the Church the Government followed a well-defined precedent which had been adopted in New France and, to a limited extent, in some of the older colonies, but, unintentionally, created a situation productive of much embarrassment in the Canadas.

Other provisions in the Canada Bill dealt with the problem of land tenure. The English tenure of free and common socage was introduced into Upper Canada and persons holding land there in any other manner were permitted to secure fresh grants in freehold. In Lower Canada a grantee was given the right to demand that lands should be conveyed according to the English tenure.

The division of the province contemplated by the Act was effected by an Order-in-Council of 25 August 1791[1] and at the same time the Secretary of State was authorised to direct the Governor of Quebec to fix a date for the commencement of the Act not later than 1791. Under this authority the Act became effective on 26 December 1791.

The Constitutional Act was an odd combination of Liberalism and reaction. The policy of the Government was formulated only after careful consideration of the Canadian situation and with a sincere desire to place the relations between the colonies and the homeland on a satisfactory basis. A failure to realise the political implications of new-world conditions was responsible for the attempt to introduce certain exotic institutions. Nature triumphed over the doubtful wisdom of statesmen and these efforts did not interfere seriously with the working of the new system. Most of the defects revealed by subsequent experience may be traced to conditions which could not have been anticipated in 1791. By introducing representative institutions, however, the Act did mark a distinct advance in the evolution of self-government in Canada. It provided a medium for the expression of popular opinion, which, although at first unable to make itself effective in directing public policy, ultimately could not be denied a hearing. It promoted discussion of public affairs and the education of the Canadian people in the rules of the political game. Without the introduction of representative government the Canadian people could neither have attained to political consciousness nor have acquired the training and discipline necessary for the conduct of their own affairs and the expression of their own national ideals.

---

[1] *Documents relating to the Constitutional History of Canada*, 1791–1898, ed. by Doughty, A. G. and McArthur, D., p. 3.

CHAPTER VIII

BRITISH NORTH AMERICA UNDER REPRESENTATIVE GOVERNMENT, 1791–1812

THE city of Quebec, the ancient capital of French Canada, became the seat of government of the Lower Province, while Newark, at the junction of the Niagara River with Lake Ontario, yet barely a village though the oldest English settlement in the province, became the seat of government of Upper Canada. Lord Dorchester was appointed Governor-in-Chief of each of the new provinces and Major-General Alured Clarke, the Lieutenant-Governor of Quebec, retained the same position in Lower Canada. There had been competition for the Lieutenant-Governorship of Upper Canada. Dorchester strongly recommended Sir John Johnson, whose appointment seemed justified by valuable services during the war and an intimate knowledge of the problems of the Loyalists. The choice of the Ministry, however, was Lieutenant-Colonel John Graves Simcoe, Member of Parliament and officer commanding the Queen's Rangers during the later part of the American campaign.

Simcoe had taken an active part in the discussions in Parliament on the Constitutional Bill of 1791 and before his departure for Canada discussed policies with Henry Dundas, the minister who now supervised colonial affairs. Dorchester, who regarded the appointment of a single Governor-in-Chief as one of the most important features of the new arrangement, returned to Britain in the autumn of 1791 and was absent from Canada for more than two years. During this period the Canadian administration had been allowed to start on lines widely divergent from those contemplated by him. The appointment of Simcoe in preference to Johnson had not improved the personal relations between the Governor and his lieutenant in Upper Canada. Dorchester, who in the trying days before the evacuation of New York probably saw the Loyalists in the worst possible light, was completely out of sympathy with Simcoe's exuberant enthusiasm for the Loyalist and other American immigrants. In the absence of Dorchester and because of his earlier personal association with Dundas, Simcoe initiated the practice of corresponding directly with the Colonial Secretary rather than through the medium of the Governor-in-Chief. This disintegration of the authority of the chief executive officer seemed to Dorchester a repetition of the errors of the old American administrative system and to threaten fatal consequences. Such conditions as these made the veteran Governor-in-Chief most unhappy in his new position.

Relations between Britain and the United States were now very critical and required delicate management. The fortified trading posts along the border—Oswegatchie, Oswego, Niagara, Fort Erie, Detroit, Michilimackinac, and Pointe au Fer and Dutchman's Point on Lake Champlain—all within territory belonging to the United States by the treaty of 1783, were still retained by Britain. The treatment of the Loyalists immediately following the war formed the pretext at first for refusal to surrender the posts, but, in all the States except one, the objectionable legislation was removed and a new federal court was created to which British creditors and others claiming rights under the treaty could resort. Nevertheless, the posts were retained. The reasons for this policy must be sought in conditions not openly disclosed at that time. The surrender of the posts involved the abandonment of the western Indians and serious loss to the fur-traders. James McGill reported the western fur trade to be worth in 1785 £180,000, of which £100,000 came from territory ceded to the United States.[1] The border posts could not be abandoned until the continued friendship of the western tribes had been assured and arrangements made for the diversion of the trade to Canada. There were many in Britain who, regarding the federal experiment of the former colonies as doomed to failure, confidently expected that certain of the colonies, at least, would return to the imperial fold. Should these predictions be fulfilled the border posts might be retained indefinitely.

Simcoe and the officers administering Indian affairs found themselves in a very difficult situation. The British Government was genuinely anxious to prevent the occurrence of any incident in the west country which would disturb friendly relations with the Republic. The fur-traders, on the other hand, were most insistent that such aid should be given to the natives as would enable them to resist the advance of the Americans. Simcoe and his associates hoped that the mediation of Britain might be acceptable to the United States and that thereby the sovereignty of the Indians might be preserved over territories constituting a "buffer state" of such a character and extent as to assure the continuation of the fur trade. They were, therefore, careful to maintain neutrality between the Indians and the Americans. Simcoe instructed Colonel McKee, Indian agent at Detroit, to remove from the minds of the natives all hope of intervention by Britain on their behalf other than by mediation.[2] That this was done appears from the assurance given by McKee to Simcoe that "whatever fears you may have entertained of a contrary tendency...the West Indians are so firmly convinced of our resolution not to commence a war with America, that now they neither individually or

---

[1] James McGill to Hon. Henry Hamilton, 1 Aug. 1785, quoted in Pub. Arch. Can. *Report* 1890, p. 56.
[2] Simcoe to McKee, 30 Aug. 1792, *Simcoe Papers*, 1, 207.

collectively entertain such an expectation".[1] Washington and his ministers, however, contended that the Indian lands had been ceded to the United States, that the Indians were subject to the Republic and that a purely domestic issue did not require the offices of a mediator. The Canadian officials did not deem it wise to discontinue the issue to the Indians of the customary provisions—on which they had learned to depend—or of guns and ammunition necessary to enable them to procure fresh meat. This undoubtedly aroused suspicion in the United States that the Canadians were not preserving strict neutrality.

Early in 1793 England was at war with France and could not afford to arouse the further enmity of the United States lest it be driven into alliance with the French Republic. Genêt, the agent of the French revolutionaries in the United States, was known to be directing propaganda in Lower Canada designed to detach the French Canadians from their British allegiance.[2] The situation seemed to Dorchester most threatening, though he earnestly desired to maintain peaceful relations with the United States. He undertook to warn the Indians of the villages of Lower Canada, assembled at Quebec in February 1794, of the impending dangers, declaring that the patience of Britain with the United States was "almost exhausted" and that he would not be surprised "if we are at war with them during the course of the present year".[3] The report of this speech spread rapidly to the western tribes and was used by traders and others to incite the Indians against the Americans. John Jay, appointed a special envoy to London to adjust outstanding differences with Britain, had but recently arrived when the report of Dorchester's speech reached the ministers. John Randolph, the Secretary of State of the United States, regarded the utterance of Dorchester as "hostility itself", and as particularly dangerous because his recent return from Britain might indicate that he expressed the views of the British Government. At the same time Dorchester directed Simcoe to occupy a post on the Miami River which had been abandoned after the war. These measures taken by Dorchester as reasonable defensive precautions caused serious embarrassment in London. Dundas felt obliged to advise the Governor that there was apprehension lest his conduct should provoke hostilities.[4] In the conditions then existing Dorchester was not anxious to remain in charge of the Government of Canada and requested leave to resign. He was not permitted to retire, however, until July 1796, when he was succeeded by Major-General Robert Prescott.

Meanwhile Jay's negotiations in London were highly successful. In November 1794, the treaty to which his name has been given was

[1] McKee to Simcoe, 13 Oct. 1792, Simcoe MSS.
[2] Turner, F. J., *Corresp. of the French Ministers to the U.S.* 1791–7, II, 204, 232.
[3] Pub. Arch. Can. *Series Q*, LXVII, 109.
[4] Dundas to Dorchester, Pub. Arch. Can. *Series Q*, LXVII, 177.

signed providing for the withdrawal of all troops from the posts within the territory of the United States by 1 June 1796. Already difficulties had arisen in the location of the boundary fixed by the treaty of 1783 and provision was made for the appointment of a commission to determine the identity of the St Croix River, part of the boundary, and likewise the course of the boundary west of the Lake of the Woods. Mutual trading concessions were likewise made which remained effective until 1807.[1]

In Upper Canada, Simcoe was confronted with problems of settlement and with the organisation of a pioneer community. The Loyalists, in his view, were ideal settlers and by the building of a strong Loyalist province in Upper Canada he hoped to salvage much that was lost in the American rebellion. Agents were sent to various parts of the United States to proclaim the advantages of settlement in Upper Canada and generous offers of free land were made to induce American farmers to migrate thither. Discontent in several of the American States coupled with the prospect of cheap land did, indeed, start a steady stream of migration northward. Simcoe exercised a certain discrimination in the admission of settlers and insisted that they take the oath of allegiance to the King before receiving grants of land. He likewise favoured the stationing of troops at strategic centres throughout the province with a view to their ultimate permanent settlement. This scheme failed to meet the approval of the Commander-in-Chief, Dorchester, who preferred to dispose of the troops on the basis of military considerations alone. A battalion of about four hundred and fifty men, named the Queen's Rangers, after Simcoe's old unit, was sent to Canada from England, and was employed in clearing land and building roads and bridges. Simcoe was keenly alive to the importance of transportation facilities to meet the requirements of the fur trade and of settlement. In the summer of 1793 he journeyed on foot north from York to Holland River and thence proceeded by canoe to Lac aux Claies, which he renamed Lake Simcoe in honour of his father. Across the lake he entered the Severn River whose windings finally led him to the Georgian Bay, an inlet of Lake Huron. He saw in this route an alternative to the Great Lakes and to the Ottawa-French river systems for the transport of merchandise to the Indian country, and hoped that the region about York might be able to win from Detroit some of the trade in food supplies with the western posts. The construction of the overland portion of this new route, extending from York to Lake Simcoe and named Yonge Street in honour of Sir George Yonge, Secretary at War, was commenced in 1793 and completed three years later. To meet the needs of the pioneer settlements Simcoe planned the construction of a highway extending from the east to the west of the province, and began the survey of that

---

[1] Bemis, S. F., *Jay's Treaty*, chaps. xii, xiii, App. vi.

part, leading westward from York, which became known as Dundas Street.

The attention of the Legislature of Upper Canada was very early directed to the problems of judicial organisation and of local government. During the first session, the law of England was made the rule of decision in all cases affecting property and civil rights, and trial by jury was introduced. In 1794, District Courts and a Court of King's Bench for the entire province were established. The Lieutenant-Governor or Chief Justice and any two members of the Executive Council were constituted a court of appeal. In the determination of the form of local government a very real conflict arose between old-world and new-world ideals. Simcoe's confession of political faith was very clearly expressed in a letter to the Duke of Portland in which he declared, "I have therefore endeavoured to establish the form as well as the spirit of the British constitution by modelling all the minutest branches of the Executive Government after a similar system and by aiming as far as possible to turn the views of His Majesty's subjects from any attention to the various modes and customs of the several provinces from which they emigrated, to the contemplation of Great Britain itself, as the sole and primary object of general and particular imitation".[1] New England had devised new forms of local government which reflected the democratic spirit of the new world and these forms had been assimilated, in part at least, by New York from which the majority of the Upper Canadian Loyalists migrated. In New England the town or township elected its own council, which passed by-laws and supervised municipal administration. The English system, which was transplanted to Virginia, placed the direction of local government in the hands of the justices of the peace appointed by the Crown, and left only very minor duties to elected parish officers. Simcoe naturally desired to introduce the English system, while most of the members of the Legislature preferred the form of popular control with which they were familiar in the older colonies. No agreement was possible in the first session, but in the following year a compromise was reached which preserved the essential features of the English system and conceded the principle of popular election in a few of the inferior offices. To give additional support to the aristocratic principle in government, Simcoe later introduced the English office of county lieutenant to which he usually appointed a legislative councillor. This scheme, however, failed to obtain the approval of the Colonial Secretary and the office was allowed to lapse.

Dorchester and Simcoe held such widely divergent views regarding most matters of public policy that it was impossible for them to work in harmonious co-operation. Simcoe came to Canada a young man of untiring energy and stirred by an ambition to render distinguished

[1] Pub. Arch. Can. *Series Q*, 281, Pt 1, p. 220; Doughty and McArthur, p. 200.

service to his sovereign and his nation. He soon discovered that neither he nor his cherished projects could find a place in Dorchester's scheme of administration. The disillusionment was tragic in its completeness. His resignation was submitted in December 1795, and in the following July, the month of Dorchester's retirement, he handed over the reins of office to Peter Russell as administrator until a successor should be appointed.

Simcoe's successors prior to 1812 found that their attention was largely absorbed in keeping the machinery of government running smoothly and in making satisfactory arrangements for the settlers who were pouring into the province in increasing numbers. Newark was not satisfactory as the seat of government because of its proximity to the United States. Simcoe at one time looked with favour on "the forks" of the Thames River where London now stands, but it was too remote from the commercial centre of the colony. Kingston was the chief point of transfer from the river to lake boats for the imports coming *via* the St Lawrence, and, largely for that reason, was of first importance commercially during the years immediately following the formation of the province. The greater part of the post-Loyalist immigration from the United States moved across the border and settled around the western end of Lake Ontario and in the south-western peninsula where the land was more suitable for agriculture than along the St Lawrence. Newark's position did not permit of its becoming a distribution point for these new settlements. The village of York, situated nearer the centre of the region more recently occupied, became the terminus of much of the lake transportation. Simcoe's highways—Dundas Street extending westward, and Yonge Street, northward, from York—not only directed the course of settlement but made that village an important trading centre by providing facilities for transport. Although of later origin than Kingston, York soon challenged the commercial supremacy of the eastern centre. Simcoe decided to move the capital to York because, while being more distant from the boundary than either Newark or Kingston, it also possessed an excellent natural harbour, seemed capable of adequate defence and its place in the commercial life of the colony appeared assured. Not until 1797, however, were the offices of government actually moved to York.

The problem of land grants presented real difficulties. In the earlier days large tracts—in some cases, entire townships—had been granted to a "leader" and his associates on the understanding that settlers would be brought out and placed on the land. But this system had been much abused. Large grants of land in the best positions were made to public officers and to friends of the Government. These lands, remaining unimproved, hindered seriously the settlement of the province, the construction of highways and the organisation of the life of the local community. The flow of migration from the United States continued unabated. The restrictions enforced by Simcoe to ensure loyalty to the Crown were abandoned by his successors and the gates were thrown wide open. It was estimated that in 1813 less than 20 per cent. of the population of Upper Canada were natives of the British Isles and their children, while 80 per cent. were of American birth and three-quarters of these were non-Loyalists attracted to Canada mainly by cheap land.

Gradually there developed at York a petty colonial aristocracy which included the members of the Executive and Legislative Councils and officers of government. This group, later known as the "Family Compact", may be traced to Simcoe's day and, with frequent changes in the office of chief executive, it acquired an effective control over the provincial administration.[1] It took good care of its own members and friends in appointments to office and in the distribution of the public lands. Naturally this group aroused the jealousy of those on the outside and the resentment of many of the settlers whose progress was impeded by unimproved lands. This opposition soon became manifest in the Legislative Assembly. William Weekes, an Irish-American immigrant who had secured admission to the bar of the province and subsequently was elected to the Legislature, assumed the leadership of the malcontents. He had as allies several of the members in whose constituencies the land problem was of serious consequence and, beyond the Legislature, such men as Justice Thorpe, Charles Wyatt, the surveyor-general of the province, and Joseph Willcocks, sheriff of the county of York. Party distinctions were beginning to emerge, determined largely by social and economic differences. The wealthy classes, most of the professional men, and merchants to whom the favour of government meant much, naturally associated themselves with the Administration, while those disappointed in the race for office, the socially "outcast" and the pioneer who found his efforts to improve the conditions of life impeded by special privileges, economic and political, enjoyed by the friends of Government, formed the incipient Opposition.

The leadership of this group, at this stage much more conscious of the existence of grievances than of a method of reform, was largely of American origin because of the preponderance of the American element in the population of the province. The experience which directed its procedure and such measures of improvement as it devised were American rather than British. Had this movement not been interrupted and its leadership changed, reform in Upper Canada would have followed a very different course. By the time of the outbreak of the war with the United States discontent was manifest and a division of the people and of their representatives in the Legislature into the friends and opponents of the Administration had become clearly outlined.

[1] See chapter x (B).

The development of Lower Canada was complicated by several factors which were not found in the Upper Province. Difference of race and religion, of temperament and ideals, and of economic interest involved the Administration of the Lower Province in unusual difficulties. The French-Canadian soon adjusted himself to the requirements of the new system of representative government. A very substantial majority of the members of the first Legislature were French Canadians drawn from the seigneurs, the notaries, the advocates, the merchants and the wealthier habitants. They soon demonstrated their solidarity by electing one of their number as Speaker and by providing for the equality of their language in the formation of the rules of procedure of the House. A new judicial system was introduced creating superior courts or Courts of King's Bench for the districts of Quebec and Montreal and inferior or circuit courts which met in the counties. Taxation was imposed to meet the cost of the administration of justice. During the life of the first Parliament relations between French and English, if not cordial, were at least sufficiently harmonious to prevent obstruction of public business.

After the second provincial election, held in 1796, a new spirit became manifest in the Assembly. The representative system, with its declamations and appeals on the hustings for popular support and with its speeches on the floor of the House, made demands on political leadership which the seigneur was both unwilling and unable to meet. Such leadership as he had hitherto exercised had been based on his position and not on the favour of those whom he regarded as his inferiors, and he shrank from the disagreeable incidents of the new system. The notary or the advocate, on the other hand, frequently descended from the habitant class, felt no such restraint in appealing for the franchise of his fellows. And likewise, his experience in dealing with the affairs of other people, and, in the case of the advocate, his training in the courts, gave him an advantage over the seigneur in the presentation of political issues on the public platform and before the Legislature. Gradually the leadership of the French Canadians became transferred to the advocate and the notary and, as a consequence, relations with the English were substantially modified. The new leaders represented a different social stratum and were not admitted to the homes of the prominent English merchants as were the members of the old Council and many of the seigneurs representing the French-Canadian *noblesse*. The social contacts which formerly reduced the asperity of political conflict began to disappear and a new element of bitterness and rancour complicated the relations of the two groups in the Legislature. In the appeal for the franchise of the habitants it became good politics to pose as the defender of the rights of the French-Canadian country dweller against the attacks of the wealthy English merchant. The introduction of the representative system provided a forum for the discussion of the principles of French-Canadian nationalism, a method by which it might be made more articulate and a motive for exalting its importance.

At Quebec, as at York, the friends of the Administration formed a small and exclusive clique. Most of the members of the Executive Council belonged likewise to the Legislative Council appointed by the Governor. There were French Canadians in both Councils, but they were no longer representative of the French-Canadian people and were regarded as having sacrificed their racial allegiance on the altar of royal favour. The fur-trading and commercial element was most influential in this group which, because of the preponderance of Scots among the traders, came to be known as the "Scotch party". It was essentially progressive, anxious to promote immigration, to improve transportation by building roads and bridges, to develop the resources of the province and increase its production and commerce, but, although in control of the two Councils, it found its programme blocked by the French-Canadian majority in the Assembly. The French Canadian was wholly out of sympathy with the projects of the English commercial group. He preferred to save the resources of the province for the benefit of future generations of French Canadians. He saw no advantage in the settlement of English-speaking Protestants on the waste lands of the province which otherwise would be reserved for his own children and grandchildren. He preferred the inconvenience of rough roads to the payment of taxes for the improvements advocated by the English.

It was inevitable that the French and English ideals of provincial development, so widely divergent in character, should soon come into conflict. The struggle was complicated by the fact that each group controlled one branch of the Legislature. As early as 1805 a definite conflict of interest arose. It became necessary to raise funds for the erection of gaols at Quebec and Montreal. The English group proposed a tax on land; the French Canadians advocated a tax on imports which they hoped would fall chiefly on the merchants. The Legislative Council thought it wise to pass such a measure despite the protests of the merchants. The controversy which the bill aroused bore fruit in the founding by leaders of the Canadian party in the Legislature of a paper, Le Canadien, which became the organ of French-Canadian nationalism.

By 1807, when Sir James Craig, a veteran of many campaigns and thoroughly imbued with the soldier's ideals of discipline and obedience, became Governor-in-Chief, the two groups had attained clearly defined positions and had commenced to consolidate their forces. In the election held in May 1808, largely through the influence of Le Canadien, the French-Canadian group in the Assembly was substantially increased. In the session which followed much attention was given to a measure which proposed to disqualify judges from

membership in the Assembly, and to the dispute as to the right of
Ezekiel Hart, a Jew who adhered to the English party, to sit in the
Assembly because of his alleged inability to subscribe to the oath of
office. Craig considered their efforts a waste of time and, on the
advice of his Executive Council, prorogued and then dissolved the
Legislature. The hostility of the Governor provided the leaders of
the popular party with excellent political ammunition and in the
new Legislature the English party was still further reduced.

The French-Canadian leaders recognised the weakness of their
position so long as they lacked control of the administrative officers.
They therefore proposed to raise by provincial taxation sufficient
revenue to defray the cost of civil government. The power of the purse,
which had been so effective an instrument in the hands of the popular
Legislatures in the old colonies, now threatened to become a factor
in the political game in Lower Canada. The administrative party
was not so easily entrapped, and the offer of the Legislature was not
accepted. The Legislature also proposed the appointment of a provincial agent in London who should be entirely independent of the
Governor and be a direct channel of communication between the
Assembly and the British Government. Attention was again directed
to the disqualification of judges, and while a bill dealing with the
problem was still before the Assembly, a resolution was passed
declaring Judge de Bonne, one of the members, incapable of sitting
or voting in the House. Craig regarded this as an invasion of the
constitutional rights of the Legislative Council and of the Governor
and again dissolved the Legislature. He seized the press of *Le
Canadien* and imprisoned the proprietors. The election took place in
April 1810, and resulted in very little change in the standing of the
parties. Pierre Bédard, a member of the Legislature and one of the
founders of *Le Canadien*, refusing to admit his guilt, was held in gaol
until March 1811. Whether they were growing weary of the struggle
or whether overhanging war clouds diverted their attention, the
members of the new Legislature were much less inclined to provoke
conflict. De Bonne did not offer himself for re-election and soon
afterwards retired from the Bench. Craig was prepared to recommend
drastic measures to improve the unhappy situation. The reunion of
the provinces was proposed, but Craig feared that by creating a more
equal division in the Assembly the difficulties might be still more
seriously complicated. He favoured, rather, a return to the earlier
form of control by Governor and Council and the diversion of the
revenue derived from part of the estates of the Jesuits and the
Sulpicians to the maintenance of civil government. The European
situation and the danger of war with the United States absorbed the
attention of the British Government and no change was made. The
prospect of being involved in active military operations induced
Craig to suggest the appointment of a younger man as his successor.

He was allowed to retire in June 1811, a year before the outbreak of war.

The operation of the representative system in Lower Canada, as in the Upper Province, had succeeded, by the time of the outbreak of the war with the United States, in bringing into clear relief certain fundamental differences in economic and political interests. The Loyalist migrations completed the foundation of French-Canadian nationalism; Craig's opposition helped to create the superstructure. The programme of nationalism was now clearly defined, and it had found in the elected Assembly a ready instrument for the promotion of its aims. While in Lower Canada the racial factor created a much sharper line of cleavage, in both provinces the party of opposition to the Government aimed to give the Assembly the control of provincial administration—a problem solved, only after the shedding of blood, by granting, in addition to the form of the British constitution, its vitalising spirit which had been withheld in 1791.

The course of development of Nova Scotia and the eastern colonies was necessarily greatly influenced by the Loyalists. The resources of government were strained to the utmost in providing shelter for these immigrants and in aiding them to adjust themselves to their new surroundings. As in the other provinces, many of the Loyalists were disappointed and shrank from the hardships and privations of pioneer life. Some returned to their former homes, while others, including several of the wealthier families, took passage for Upper Canada and became leaders of the Loyalist group in that province. Those who remained were incorporated gradually in the material and intellectual life of the province. This loss was made good, at least in part, by immigration from the United States and the United Kingdom, in particular, from Scotland. Between 1790 and 1805 several thousand Highlanders, chiefly from the Isles and the west coast, migrated to Nova Scotia, settling in Pictou county, where there was already a substantial Scottish settlement. Many of these were fishermen and readily found employment in the rapidly increasing fisheries of the colony.

Agriculture, however, continued to be the chief industry. In consequence of the destruction of Louisbourg, and especially after the loss of the older American colonies, Halifax became an important naval base and provided an excellent market for provisions. British policy contemplated reducing trade with the United States to a minimum, yet it proved necessary for many years to permit the importation of food-stuffs from the old colonies because the production of Nova Scotia could not satisfy the local demand. There was, therefore, but little surplus of agricultural produce for export to the West Indies during the early years. The European war, enhancing the price of provisions and greatly increasing the military and naval forces using Halifax as a base, stimulated agriculture and the supply of food-stuffs in Nova Scotia. Also during the years when materials were required for houses for the Loyalists, the lumber industry was encouraged by a provincial bounty for the erection of saw-mills. Governor Parr reported in 1785 that there were ninety saw-mills in the province, twenty-five erected since 1783, and that these would be nearly sufficient to supply the West Indies with lumber. Nova Scotia was more favourably situated than the other provinces for the marketing of lumber, fish and agricultural produce in the West Indies because of the unrivalled advantages in transportation possessed by Halifax. The fishing industry grew rapidly, and with it the shipbuilding industry, until the early years of the new century, when the risk of capture on the seas and the desertion of seamen to the United States placed it under a serious handicap. At Halifax, Shelburne and in the Pictou district shipbuilding flourished and each year many new ships were sent out, some to Britain laden with lumber, others with supplies to the West Indies, where boat and cargo alike were sold.

The European wars and the war with the United States brought unprecedented prosperity to Halifax and to Nova Scotia. Letters of marque were issued to Nova Scotian shipowners and many prizes were brought to Halifax and condemned. Money poured into Halifax and was freely spent. The restraints imposed by the United States on trade with Britain and the virtual neutrality of the New England States during the War of 1812 made Halifax the port of entry for commodities urgently needed by the United States. Her merchants took advantage of their opportunities and reaped an abundant harvest. Their prosperity, in turn, was reflected in a greater demand for most of the products of the rural settlers.

On more than one occasion during the years before the War of 1812 the political horizon of Nova Scotia became heavily clouded, but each time the good sense and sanity of its leaders prevented a serious storm and avoided damage to the vital interests of the province. The Anglo-Saxon habit of compromise was developed, and later conducted Nova Scotia in safety through the more serious political crisis which in the Canadas involved rebellion and bloodshed.

The Loyalist immigration changed the basis of political alignments. Previously the original settlers of the late 'forties and the 'fifties endeavoured to hold the political fort against the new American settlers, but now the pre-Revolution settlers were forced to combine to resist the democratic ideas introduced by the Loyalists. Governor Parr was much alarmed by the reforming tendencies of a group of younger Loyalists led by a Halifax attorney, Jonathan Sterns, who, said Parr, aimed at being the Wilkes of Nova Scotia. Their attack was aimed chiefly at abuses in the administration of justice. These clouds soon rolled away and, as an early historian of the province has stated, by 1792, "the heterogeneous elements of which its population was composed were now settling down into good neighbourhood and harmony".[1] But other lines of cleavage made their appearance. From 1782 to 1808 Nova Scotia had but two chief representatives of the Crown. On Parr's death in 1791, Sir John Wentworth, Loyalist and former Governor of New Hampshire, became the representative of the Crown and brought to his office an ingrained prejudice against democratic tendencies in government. Politically as well as commercially and socially Halifax bulked large in the life of the province, and it was inevitable that an Administration party should form around the chief executive, composed of the conservative and socially superior elements of the community, and determined to secure stability of government by solidifying its own control of the chief administrative offices. Such families as the Haliburtons, the Brentons and the Wentworths imparted solidarity to the group. Their interests were entirely different from those of the farmers and the fishermen. The farming community desired above all else the building of highways and bridges, and their representatives in the Legislature insisted on substantial appropriations for such purposes, frequently against the wish of the Administration party in the Assembly and Council. Economic and social differences created two distinct parties and by 1812 that line of cleavage had already been drawn which paved the way for Howe's magnificent constructive work in securing responsible government.

A desire to minister to the spiritual needs of the community and to maintain the authority of government prompted a generous support to the Church of England in Nova Scotia. In 1787 the Rev. Charles Inglis, Loyalist and former rector of Trinity Church, New York, was consecrated first bishop of Nova Scotia, with spiritual jurisdiction extending to the Canadas. For nearly thirty years he laboured and laid firmly the foundation of the Church of England in British North America. Keenly interested in education, he was largely instrumental in the founding at Windsor in 1788 of a "religious and literary institution" which became King's College. Halifax possessed a grammar school in 1789, but not until 1811 was provision made for similar schools in the more populous counties. At the same time the province undertook to grant more generous aid to the common schools. In many respects these years constituted the "Golden Age" of Nova Scotia. Sir John Wentworth maintained an elaborate establishment and entertained with lavish hospitality. The war brought many distinguished officers, both military and naval, to Halifax; the cup of social enjoyment was filled to overflowing by the residence within the province of two royal princes, Prince William Henry and Prince Edward, later Duke of Kent. A provincial regiment was recruited to replace a part of the garrison; provincial officers and

[1] Murdoch, B., *A History of Nova Scotia*, III, 99.

men achieved distinction in the capture of St Pierre and Miquelon. Life at the provincial capital possessed an exhilaration and a zest hitherto unknown, and this expansive energy made itself felt in the intellectual as well as the social life of the province. The *Nova Scotia Magazine and Comprehensive Review of Literature, Politics and News*, a monthly journal, was founded in 1789 and printed by John Howe. It was succeeded by the *Acadian Magazine*, a publication of the type of *Blackwood's*, which provided an outlet for the literary talent of the province. The debates in the Legislature manifested a dialectic skill and an eloquence unknown in later days, except in the fiery battles of Joseph Howe. In these early years were created the conditions which enabled Nova Scotia to contribute much beyond her share to the political and intellectual life of the Canadian people.

As we have seen, the organisation of New Brunswick as a separate province was effected late in 1784. The population of the province was then estimated at 16,000, of whom 12,000 were Loyalists, 2500 old English inhabitants and 1500 French. The Council, which first assembled in November 1784, was composed of nine members, of whom seven were Loyalists and two represented the older residents. The unusual training and experience of the councillors proved to be a source both of strength and of weakness. It assured capable administration; but the social and intellectual differences between the councillors and the mass of the settlers deprived the Council of a representative character and tended to divide the people of the province into two factions. From the outset, two distinct forces, both of American origin, may be observed in the development of New Brunswick. The Loyalists were American and brought with them American conceptions of local government and of the structure of colonial government. Such quarrel as they had with the old system of colonial administration did not concern its structure but rather the relation between its parts. Governor Thomas Carleton and the members of the new provincial oligarchy attributed the troubles with the old colonies to the undue influence of the popular Assembly and were determined that this mistake should not be repeated in New Brunswick. The American Revolution forced the administrative parties in the remaining colonies into a reactionary position and thus into conflict with the liberal or radical ideas which filtered in with the Loyalist settlers. Carleton, therefore, accepted an Assembly as a necessary evil but deferred its inauguration until all the measures for the creation of a provincial establishment which lay within the competence of the Crown had been taken. He hoped by strengthening the executive powers of government to weaken the new democratic tendencies. A site farther up the St John River was selected as the provincial capital with the name of Fredericton. To appease the inhabitants of Parrtown, the present Saint John, and at their earnest request, he gave the town a charter as a city corporation modelled after New York. The aldermen, assistants and constables were chosen by popular vote, while the Governor appointed the mayor, sheriff, recorder and clerk. Already American influence had made itself felt in the most populous centre in the province.

The material progress of the colony was disappointingly slow. At the end of twenty years its population had increased by less than ten thousand. After the wave of settlement from the old colonies subsided, there had been little immigration to New Brunswick. A substantial number of the Loyalists, finding the adjustment to frontier conditions difficult, became discouraged and left the province. Some were attracted by the milder climate and seemingly better opportunities of Upper Canada; others, as has been seen, returned to the United States. Of the twenty-six men elected to the first Legislative Assembly, six left the province during the life of the Legislature. Markets for the produce of the settlers were limited. Agriculture progressed slowly, and it was necessary, until the early days of the new century, to import provisions from the United States. The lumber industry became firmly established during the first years of settlement, when the demand for building materials was abnormally high, and later adjusted itself to the requirements of the West Indian market. Conditions were most favourable for shipbuilding and a flourishing industry developed on the St John and other streams flowing into the Bay of Fundy. Most of the ships found profitable employment in the West Indian trade. From the beginning the fishing industry enjoyed a healthy local market. Lumber, fish and such flour and grain as the province could export were sent to the West Indies in exchange for sugar, rum and molasses. From an early date the mining of gypsum for the United States market became of importance.

The spiritual and intellectual interests of the settlers were not neglected. The British Treasury contributed handsomely to the erection of churches of the Church of England, while the Society for the Propagation of the Gospel aided in the payment of the salaries of clergymen. Soon after the formation of the province lands were set aside as an endowment for higher education. A grammar school had been established at Fredericton where the children of the councillors and officers of government received education. From this a provincial Academy emerged which received aid from the province after 1792, and became, in turn, the University of New Brunswick. The Academy, however, served but a limited number of students. It was not until 1802 that the province granted aid to common schools in the various parishes where the children of the country dwellers might receive a rudimentary education. Three years later provision was made for establishing a grammar school at Saint John and state-aided public schools in the several counties.

At a relatively early period the distinction between privileged and non-privileged became the basis of political cleavage in New Brunswick, as it did later in Upper Canada. It was natural that the representative of the Crown should ally himself with the conservative elements in the community. Carleton's choice of Fredericton as the capital was not popular and caused keen disappointment in Saint John, the commercial centre of the province. At Fredericton the Lieutenant-Governor was surrounded by a group of public officials, such as the judges and the senior administrative officers from which the Council was recruited, who were anxious to extend their own control over the government of the province. They knew little of the problems of the commercial classes or of the rural inhabitants. It is not surprising, therefore, that the Assembly, representing the people of the province, frequently found itself in conflict with the Council and the Lieutenant-Governor. An Opposition party gradually emerged in the Legislature under the leadership of James Glenie, a Scottish Radical, and former officer of the Royal Engineers, who settled in the new province. The Assembly supported Saint John in its desire to have certain of the sessions of the Supreme Court held there; the Council steadily refused its request. The Assembly included in a general appropriation bill provision for the payment of members' salaries; the Council for several successive years rejected the bill and left the provincial service without an appropriation for salaries. Through the intervention of the Duke of Portland a compromise was reached by which the appropriation for members' salaries was made in a separate bill which was accepted by the Council. Carleton retired to England in 1803 and until his death in 1817 the Government was administered by the senior member of Council or the commander of the forces as President. During these years the political situation was undisturbed, and in material things the province began to reap the harvest of the toil and self-denial of its pioneers.

The history of new lands depends far more on pioneers than politicians. But unfortunately the latter tend to fill the stage and crowd out the men who make the material which Parliament merely manipulates. To some extent this is inevitable; for the work of the distant toilers cannot be focussed, whereas intrigues, debates and Acts possess both concentrated effect and personal appeal. Rarely does a searcher find documents, which will briefly illustrate the life of the people. A table of the exports of British North America is here appended; for the details throw much light on the economic conditions of the British North American colonies in these years and indicate the relative importance of fishermen, farmers, millers, hunters, trappers, lumberers, timber merchants, exporters and shipmen in the old colonial life. For lack of space only typical years of war and peace have been chosen.[1]

---

[1] The tables are in *Commons Journals* (1816), App. II. Those for 1813 are missing owing to fire.

Exports from Canada to Great Britain

	1800	1807	1812	1814
Ashes (pearl and pot) (in cwts.)	31,367	35,566	59,195	13,341
Codfish (in cwts.)	3,083	742	6	—
	(in 1801)			
Wheat (in qrs.)	19,420	25,267	22,378	—
Wheat flour (in cwts.)	6,421	6,970	4,015	9
Train oil (in tuns)	224	113	—	52
Seeds of flax and linseed (in bushels)	1,280	3,528	8,056	6,772
Skins (per head)				
Bear	48,290	13,186	3,706	9,694
Beaver	245,321	19,140	135,849	128,250
Deer	369,327	50,895	20,301	16,031
Fox	21,052	5,378	657	4,045
Marten	74,912	36,786	596	25,095
Mink	16,694	5,888	65	3,872
Musquash	20,341	3,357	22,011	354,197
Otter	34,952	6,589	3,139	14,559
Racoon	243,310	18,827	8,976	3,163
Seal	8,652	3,046	150	1,243
Wolf	8,232	1,030	1	5,384
Deals and pine boards (in cwts.)	305	556	2,574	760
Masts under 12 in. (in cwts.)	13	151	1,282	463
Masts 12 in. and upwards (in loads)	55	2,753	14,019	668
Timber, fir (in loads)	323	2,700	32,716	8,349
Timber, oak (in loads)	804	5,733	18,047	4,431

Other exports, e.g. annotto, castor, spruce essence, hides, rice, spirits, sugar, tar and pitch, turpentine, whalefins, wines, cotton wool, sheeps' wool, were very small.

The imports into Great Britain from Nova Scotia and New Brunswick in 1800–14 were similar; those of timber were as follows:

		1800	1807	1812	1814
Deals and pine boards	N.S.	1	117	226	161
(in cwts.)	N.B.	43	103	433	89
Masts under 12 in.	N.S.	93	215	797	360
(in nos.)	N.B.	67	727	3,304	627
Masts of 12 in. and upwards	N.S.	5	31	524	44
(in loads)	N.B.	792	1616	2,125	221
Timber, fir	N.S.	565	9475	25,203	10,742
(in loads)	N.B.	783	7062	75,870	20,932
Timber, oak	N.S.	39	—	56	13
(in loads)	N.B.	—	12	2	3

The imports into Great Britain from Prince Edward Island and Cape Breton Island in 1800–14 consisted almost entirely of timber, but did not begin until the year 1805; also there were shipments of skins from Prince Edward Island in 1803 and 1808.

The exports from Canada, Nova Scotia and New Brunswick to the British West Indies and Bermuda increased in 1800–14. Those of wheat began in 1803. The mass of exports from all the provinces consisted of salt fish, boards, shingles and staves, New Brunswick sending 2,131,000 boards in 1803 and 3,240,877 in 1814. All sent train oil, bread, flour and salt meat. Nova Scotia began to send apples in 1805.

Of the imports from the British West Indies into British North America from 1800–14 coffee rose from 13,050 lbs. to 63,929 lbs., rum rose from 73,970 gals. to 605,699 gals. Clearly, then, inter-colonial trade increased fast under the artificial stimulus of war.

CHAPTER IX

THE WAR OF 1812

THE War of 1812 between Great Britain and the United States was a product of two political upheavals, the revolt of the American colonies and the French Revolution. Few Britons, seemingly, realised the significance of the union of the old colonies in a separate and independent State. The structure of British oversea commerce had been reared on a foundation which included the American colonies and they, in turn, had profited from their enjoyment of special privileges as trading partners with the mother country and with the other colonies. The recognition of American independence raised the question of the dissolution of this partnership.

There were those who urged that Great Britain should disregard the fact of political separation and continue to extend to the former colonies the benefits of the Navigation Laws and other regulations as in pre-revolutionary days. This policy would ensure the West Indies a necessary food supply, would impede the development of industries in America and would help to preserve a market for British manufacturers. It might conceivably lead to an alliance based on kinship, common traditions and mutual commercial advantages, by which the former sympathetic interest of the old colonies might be revived. On the other hand, Britain might elect to treat the American Republic as a foreign State, beyond the pale of the British mercantile system, with whom commercial intercourse on the part of the remaining colonies should be discouraged. The advocates of this policy hoped to substitute the remaining American colonies for those which had seceded in the trade with the West Indies and the mother country. Many Britons regarded the dual experiment in federalism and republicanism as foredoomed to failure and complacently awaited the day when the prodigal colonies, tired of the husks of independence, would, singly or in groups, crave reinstatement within the Empire. Then the old commercial system might be restored on a more satisfactory basis because of the chastening experience of the period of separation.

The first course found many advocates, including Pitt and Shelburne; the commercial interests, however, saw greater advantage in the second and persuaded British statesmen to adopt an attitude of hostility to American trade. From this time the interests of Britain and the United States definitely diverged. British statesmanship unwittingly set in motion forces destined to establish the authority of the Republic at home and to make it respected abroad. The dependence of the former colonists on Britain for credit, merchandise and markets gave her a practical advantage in diplomatic relations with the new Republic and, in conjunction with the reputed impotence of the Federal Government, introduced an element of severity and rigidity in her relations with the Americans which was not productive of greater friendliness.

The mercantile influence in British politics manifested itself in restrictions on American trade with the continental colonies and with the West Indies, and in the attempt to retain the fur trade of the region south of the Great Lakes which by the Treaty of 1783 had become part of the United States.[1] The outbreak of war with France early in 1793 introduced fresh complications in Anglo-American relations. Britain's success in the war depended on her control of the trade of the Atlantic. The United States determined to observe neutrality but their definition of the rights of neutral commerce was not accepted by Britain. The United States maintained the principle of "free ships, free goods", while Britain claimed for a belligerent the right to seize enemy property on neutral ships. She also considered all goods to be contraband which enabled the enemy to carry on the war, thereby including necessary food supplies, whereas the United States regarded as contraband only such materials as could be used for military purposes. British maritime policy, enforced by Orders-in-Council of June and November 1793, aroused intense resentment in the United States and, in conjunction with the holding of the border trading posts, strengthened the already strong trend towards an alliance with France.[2] Such an issue was prevented by the partial repeal of the latter order and by the Jay Treaty of 1794 which granted the United States a minimum of concessions. While stipulating the surrender of the posts by June 1796, and the settlement of debts and of boundary differences by references to special commissions, it obliged the United States to accept the British definition of contraband. Although accepted by the Senate with modifications, the treaty was extremely unpopular in the United States and aggravated the popular feeling of resentment towards Britain.

In the meantime party alignments were being formed in the United States which determined the character of its government. On one side were Washington, Hamilton, Adams, and their followers, now designated the "Federalists"; on the other were Jefferson, Madison and the "Republicans". Washington and Hamilton were suspected of an unduly warm admiration for the social and political gradations which flourished in Britain. They derived political support from the

[1] *Vide supra*, chapter vii.
[2] See despatches of the French ambassadors to Washington, MM. Genêt and Létombe, as to the fitting-out of American corsairs against British commerce, and plans for the conquest of Canada, in *Report of the Amer. Hist. Assoc.* (1903), vol. II, pp. 212–18, 1025; also the *résumé* of the official British statement in *Annual Register* (1814).

seaboard and from the trading interests of the north-east which had intimate associations with the financial and commercial houses of Britain. They saw alike in the radical agrarianism of the American frontier and in the rampant democracy of France a menace to private rights in property and to stability in government. Jefferson, descended from good frontier planter stock, was a democrat, a Radical and an idealist. He knew the problems of the west-country farmers who supported him consistently and he had not been drawn into the meshes of banking and commercial alliances. He was not without sympathy for the Radicalism of France and looked askance at Britain partly because he disliked Hamiltonianism and partly because he saw no evidence in British policy of friendliness towards the United States. The election of Jefferson to the presidency in 1800, with the support of the newly-formed frontier States, was not without its significance in Anglo-American relations.

The struggle between Britain and France was renewed in 1803. The collapse of the continental resistance to Napoleon left Britain without effective military aid in her attempt to arrest the progress of Napoleonic despotism. If her sea-borne trade were crippled, her people faced bankruptcy and starvation. The sea remained her last bulwark of defence and also provided a means for breaking the French offensive. There ensued a series of exclusive measures by Napoleon against Britain's commerce to which she replied by Orders-in-Council excluding neutral trade from the coasts which he closed to her.[1] Further, the British practice of searching neutral vessels for deserting seamen provided cause for friction with the United States. The treatment accorded to sailors on British war-ships made the navy unpopular. American merchantmen offered higher pay, fewer risks and better conditions of service. Desertions from British to American ships became so numerous as to create an acute crisis. From sheer necessity Britain resorted to the practice of searching American vessels for deserters and removing them by force. International law permitted the search of neutral vessels with a view to determining whether by reason of the nature of its cargo or of the persons it carried neutrality was being violated; it permitted the detention of a vessel in a belligerent port where, by recognised legal process, the complaint might be investigated. But this procedure was much too complicated and involved too great delays to satisfy the exigencies of the British naval service. British sea-captains adopted a more speedy process and assumed the double rôle of prosecutor and judge. Britain did not admit the right of British-born seamen to alienate themselves and refused to recognise the certificates of nationality issued by American consular officers. Similarity of speech complicated the problem of determining the nationality of seamen while a knowledge of the fate which awaited the impressed effectively

[1] See Mahan, A. T., *Sea Power in its Relations to the War of* 1812, I, 104–13.

dissuaded the accused from making any compromising admissions. In practice doubtless many *bona fide* British seamen escaped and many subjects of the United States were impressed into the British naval service. By the process and in its results the sovereignty of the United States was violated.[1]

The restrictions imposed on American trade and the impressment of seamen were the subjects of negotiation when the *Chesapeake* affair inflamed the public of the United States. In June 1807, the American frigate, *Chesapeake*, suspected of having engaged seamen deserting from the British service, refused to allow the captain of H.M.S. *Leopard* the right of conducting a search. The *Leopard* then fired into her, killed three men and wounded eighteen others, and, after a search, took off four seamen. One of these proved to be an Englishman and was hanged; the others were Americans who had been impressed into the British service and had escaped. The British Government disavowed the action of the captain of the *Leopard* but refused to make any concession regarding the right of impressment. Had the United States possessed armed forces capable of defending their rights of sovereignty, the *Chesapeake* incident might have drawn them into war. Napoleon had been equally inconsiderate of American trade, but his comparative impotence on the high seas deprived his fulminations of terror. Britain's ability to enforce her aggressive naval policy made her the chief offender against American rights. Nevertheless Jefferson determined to exhaust the resources of peaceful retaliation before resort to hostilities. A Non-Importation Act prohibited the import of certain British goods and an Embargo Act restrained American vessels from leaving American ports for those of Europe. Despite these regulations American vessels slipped away without clearance papers and were welcomed in British ports. Although a flourishing export trade in flour and provisions developed by way of Lake Champlain and the St Lawrence and from Nova Scotian ports, the total trade of the United States declined seriously and in its fall threatened to involve the Republicans in ruin. New England Federalism flourished on the embargo, and, had war become necessary, might have forced the United States to join Britain against France. The Embargo Act gave way to a Non-Intercourse Act which likewise failed to modify British maritime policy.[2]

In 1808, Madison, for eight years Secretary of State, succeeded Jefferson as President. For a decade and a half the United States had submitted to the invasion of their sovereign rights rather than resort to war. Had impressment and the restriction of trade been the paramount issues, war should have been declared after the *Chesapeake* affair and after the obnoxious Orders-in-Council of November 1807. But for four years further the United States tolerated the limitations imposed by British policy and during that period came to the verge of war with

[1] *Ibid.* I, 114–28.   [2] *Ibid.* I, 155–215.

France. It would therefore seem necessary to seek elsewhere the forces which finally drove the American people to war. These will be found in conditions of life on the western frontier of the United States.

After the transfer of the border trading posts in 1796, Fort Malden, at the southern corner of Upper Canada, became the centre of the trade with the tribes which roamed the valleys of the Maumee, the Wabash, the lower Ohio and the Mississippi. The valley of the Wabash was the most thickly populated Indian region in Western America and by 1809 the United States had purchased lands which brought the zone of settlement up to the Wabash Indians. The westward advance was thus confronted with a serious obstacle. The civilisations of the white man and of the red man, based on entirely different social and economic conceptions, seemed incapable of harmonious adjustment. The white man's virtues and vices were alike subversive of Indian welfare; the greater the skill he devoted to the use of land, the less its value for the Indian. The laxity as well as the refinements of his mode of life carried destruction to the native. Indian statesmen such as Tecumseh and his brother, the Prophet, perceived the fatal consequences of contact between the two races and sought to keep them apart by arousing the tribesmen to peaceful resistance to the American advance. As settlement continued, quarrels became more frequent and Tecumseh found it impossible to restrain his warriors. The resulting Battle of Teppecanoe of November 1811 demonstrated the necessity of dislodging the native if settlement were to continue its westward march. The interests of the British traders in Canada were identical with those of the Indians. In the ordinary course of business they sold to them guns, ammunition and knives, necessary to their normal peaceful pursuits, but capable of becoming deadly weapons. The Indian menace was in reality a British menace because British agencies made the Indian dangerous and capable of resistance. By 1810 this frontier situation had introduced a new element both into Washington politics and Anglo-American relations. The representatives of the frontier saw in war with Britain a solution of the Indian problem and the prospect of capturing the valuable Indian trade.

This programme, at first purely defensive, soon became part of a project of Imperialism and national aggrandisement. The new transmontane states, which in 1810 and 1811 sent a vigorous group of Radical Republicans to the support of Madison, assumed the leadership of a new aggressive nationalism. Excellent soil, abundance of timber and water-power, proximity to a waterway to the Atlantic made Upper Canada attractive to the prospective settler. Canada came to be valued because of its potential contribution to the development of the American nation. Under the intoxicating influence of the new wine of expansion free rein was given to the imagination. The doctrine of "manifest destiny" was revealed to frontier members of the House who seemed to enjoy the Divine confidence to a unique degree. Johnson of Kentucky announced that "the Great Disposer of Human events" intended that the Mississippi and the St Lawrence should belong to the same people,[1] while Harper of New Hampshire believed that the "Author of Nature" had "marked our limits in the south by the Gulf of Mexico and on the north by the regions of eternal frost".[2]

The designs of the western war party thus went through a rapid but radical metamorphosis which was promoted by conditions in Canada. The stream of Loyalist migration to Upper Canada had long since dried up, and the European war restricted British emigration. Between 1795 and 1812 thousands of non-Loyalist Americans had poured into Upper Canada, attracted by cheap land rather than by a preference for British institutions. By 1812 they composed a majority of the people of the province. They were almost wholly Nonconformists, and the parent churches in the United States, regarding them as still within their jurisdiction, had sent missionaries to minister to their religious needs. Through the agency of the Church and by other means they maintained connection with the people "back home", thus retaining an intellectual and spiritual kinship with the Republic and preventing their complete identification with a British community. The American frontiersmen learned that Upper Canada was a goodly land, that most of its settlers were of the same stock as themselves, shared their political views and would welcome release from the yoke of Britain. The bitter conflict of French and English in Lower Canada was deemed to make that province an easy prey to the invader. "The acquisition of Canada this year (1812) as far as the neighbourhood of Quebec, will be a mere matter of marching", said Jefferson.[3] Thus the ambitious projects of the "expansionists" were encouraged.

The policy of expansion advocated by Clay, Calhoun and other western Republicans threatened to rend their own party in twain. The Federalists, opposed to war with Britain for commercial reasons, found further cause of opposition in the addition to western agrarian influence involved in the conquest of Canada. The cleavage between North and South, free and slave states, was even now a fundamental fact in American politics. Western Republicans found it difficult to enlist the support of their southern associates in the annexation of Canada by which northern political influence would be increased. Expansionism thus became double-barrelled; the acquisition of Florida, then a possession of Spain, Britain's ally in the war, was linked with the conquest of Canada; the interests of North and South were safeguarded and the unity of the party was preserved.

Two movements of antagonism to Britain, one arising out of resentment caused by her maritime policy, the other avowedly designed

[1] *Annals of Congress*, 12 Congress, I, 457. [2] *Ibid.* I, 657.
[3] *Jefferson's Writings*, ed. Ford, P. L., VI, 75.

to capture Canada, combined their forces in the spring of 1812 and carried the Administration rapidly in the direction of war. By May 1812 the Orders-in-Council seemed about to disappear, and on 16 June Lord Castlereagh announced the intention of the British Government to suspend them. Two days later, Madison's recommendation of a declaration of war was approved by Congress. In opposition to war the Federalists were joined by Republicans but not in sufficient numbers to defeat the Administration. The United States learned of the suspension of the Orders-in-Council in August. Impressment, the only major issue outstanding, seemed an inadequate justification for war, but the "expansionists" were now in the saddle and did not intend to forego the conquest of Canada and Florida. Negotiations for an armistice were foredoomed to failure.[1]

On the part of the United States the War of 1812 was a sectional war. New England and the Middle East, whose wealth was required to provide the sinews of war, were openly opposed to hostilities. West and South were pursuing different objectives and found agreement difficult. Madison and Monroe, his Secretary of State, representing the "Virginia dynasty" and the plantation interest, were accused of indifference regarding the Canadian campaign.[2] Monroe, in fact, instructed the American *chargé d'affaires* at London to urge on the British Government the desirability of agreeing to an early settlement before the invasion of Canada should arouse a popular demand for permanent occupation.[3] British interests could be injured most effectively by an attack on Canada; the western expansionists could not be satisfied without its conquest. Hence both military and political expediency demanded the invasion.

The conflict became one in which both naval and military forces would be engaged. Although the activities of Napoleon made it necessary to concentrate the strength of the British navy in European waters, the forces at Halifax and Bermuda were capable, by careful management, of preventing the American navy from seriously interrupting trans-Atlantic trade. Water-communication on the Upper St Lawrence and the Great Lakes was of supreme importance because of the economic dependence of the upper country on Montreal and the utter inadequacy of the roads. Britain enjoyed a slight superiority in naval forces on Lakes Ontario and Erie, an advantage however which an aggressive building programme could readily overcome. On the outbreak of war the United States had enlisted approximately 10,000 regulars distributed over several widely separated garrisons; a further 25,000 had been authorised, but the long term of service— five years—had discouraged enlistment. There remained the volunteer force and the State militia but the control of both organisations by the States impaired their value, particularly for the invasion of

---

[1] For details see Pratt, J. W., *Expansionists of 1812*, chap. ii.
[2] *Writings of James Monroe*, v, 291.
[3] *Ibid.* v, 212.

foreign territory. The higher command, composed of officers of advanced years and of little military experience, was notoriously weak. Despite ample warning, the outbreak of hostilities in June 1812 found the United States utterly unprepared for aggressive warfare. Yet their far greater wealth and vastly superior population—6,000,000 whites as against 600,000 in the British North American colonies—promised an easy conquest of Canada.

In many respects conditions in Canada did not promote the organisation of an effective defence. The American and republican sympathies of a great part of the inhabitants of Upper Canada occasioned much anxiety. Many of these would probably remain neutral until it should become clear which side the fortunes of war favoured. There was no doubt about the position of the Loyalists who, though a minority, were the most influential element in the province; they had old scores to settle and eagerly seized the opportunity which the outbreak of war provided. Lower Canadian conditions would have been much worse had not the tact and conciliatory attitude of the new Governor, Sir George Prevost, gone far to restore the confidence of the French Canadian, although at the cost of antagonising the English official and commercial minority. Yet in a contest with the United States the English element in Lower Canada could not afford to be disloyal. When war was declared there were in Canada slightly less than 4400 British regulars, about 4000 Canadian regulars and an equal number of incorporated provincial militia who had received military training and were subject to the same military discipline as the regulars. The urgent demands of the European situation made it impossible to expect reinforcements from the mother country. Britain, however, possessed a distinct advantage in the greater skill and experience of the officers commanding the forces in Canada and in the superior discipline and training of her military force.

Natural conditions made Upper Canada peculiarly vulnerable. Settlement had followed the St Lawrence and Great Lakes waterway which became the principal channel of communication with the world outside. At Montreal, Kingston, Niagara, Detroit, Michilimackinac the channel was relatively narrow; command of these ports would have interrupted communications with the country above. The St Lawrence front from Montreal to Kingston was the most vulnerable portion of the waterway; loss of control of any part of this section would have cut off the Upper Province from its economic base at Montreal. Nature provided the United States with two avenues of approach to this portion of the St Lawrence—one by way of Lake Champlain, the other by the Mohawk and Lake Oneida. Had the United States been prepared for war, a sudden thrust at this vulnerable area might have reduced the Upper Province to speedy submission.

Political considerations determined the American plan of campaign. The west country had pressed for the conquest of Canada and was expected to provide the force required for the invasion. Hence the western rather than the eastern end of the lake-and-river channel became the first object of attack. It was proposed to invade Canada from Detroit and from Niagara. In the south-western peninsula, between these two points, were to be found the majority of the new American settlers whose support was expected to contribute to the success of the campaign. By this means the Indian country would be cut off and the danger of attack from the natives removed. General Hull, Governor of the Territory of Michigan, was entrusted with the command of the invasion by way of Detroit. He assembled a force of 2000 regulars in western Ohio and reached Detroit early in July. He crossed the river to Sandwich on the night of 11 July, and on the 13th issued a flamboyant proclamation offering the Canadians emancipation "from tyranny, and oppression" and restoration "to the dignified station of freemen". So great was his confidence that he did not ask their assistance but merely that they remain peaceably at home.

The Upper Canadian forces were under the command of Major-General Sir Isaac Brock, the administrator of the province, a soldier since boyhood although possessed of little experience under fire. He had learned of the declaration of war on 28 June and, fully appreciating the importance of the Indians, had proposed to Captain Roberts, commanding at St Joseph's Island, an attack on Michilimackinac if his forces seemed adequate. Roberts, with a party of 400 Indians, 180 French Canadians and 45 regulars, departed on 16 July and by what he described as "the almost unparalleled exertions of the Canadians who manned the boats", covered the fifty miles before daybreak of the following morning. The garrison of 57 effectives had not yet learned of the declaration of war and were incapable of defending the post. The surrender of Michilimackinac on 17 July completely altered the situation at Detroit. The western Indians friendly to the British were confirmed in their attachment, while those inclined to neutrality were impressed by this demonstration and joined the British. Meanwhile Hull was wasting valuable time at Detroit. Fort Malden and Amherstburg were held by a force less than a quarter of the strength of his army and probably could not then have withstood attack. Brock was held at York endeavouring to obtain from an unwilling Legislature provisions for the adequate defence of the province. He sent Colonel Procter of the 41st to take command at Amherstburg and, after proroguing the Legislature on 5 August, hastened to the Detroit area with 300 men. The threatened interruption of his communications southward and the surrender of Michilimackinac obliged Hull to withdraw from Canada to Detroit. Brock reached Amherstburg on 13 August, and after consultation with Tecumseh decided on an immediate attack on Detroit. With a force of 1300 effectives, of whom half were whites, he immediately crossed the river and moved northward to the fort at Detroit sup-

ported by the *Queen Charlotte* on the river. The war-whoops of the
Indians intimidated the undisciplined Americans and on the 16th
Hull decided to surrender. The capture of Detroit gave Brock control
of the Territory of Michigan and of a vast quantity of supplies which
were sorely needed for the maintenance of the Indians. This action
cemented the Indian alliance and caused the Americans in Upper
Canada, who expected the army of the Republic to advance in a
triumphal procession, to reconsider their position. Psychologically
Brock's victory at Detroit saved Upper Canada.

Brock then hastened to the Niagara frontier where General Dearborn had been making preparations for the invasion of Canada.
Dearborn had encountered great difficulties in assembling an army;
the Governors of Massachusetts and Connecticut refused to honour
his requisitions while the New York troops had little enthusiasm for
the campaign. Brock would have struck at once at Niagara and
Sackett's Harbour but was prevented by an armistice arranged by
Prevost after it became known that the Orders-in-Council had been
suspended. The chief effect of the armistice, which expired on 8 September, was the interruption of Brock's offensive when the British
moral was at its best and the American force had not yet been properly organised. Profiting by this delay the Americans had been able
by 12 October to concentrate a force of nearly 7000 on the Niagara
front while Brock had no more than 1700 men. On 9 October
the Americans captured the British brig *Caledonia*, which had conveyed Roberts's force to Michilimackinac, and the *Adams*, taken
by the British at Detroit, both now anchored at Fort Erie. This
incident greatly improved the American *moral* and prepared the
way for the attack across the river. The American forces were divided
between Major-General Stephen Van Ransselaer of the New York
militia, stationed below the falls, and Brigadier-General Alexander
Smyth of the United States army who commanded the troops above
the falls. It seems to have been the intention of Van Ransselaer to
make a feint against Queenston and to direct his main attack against
Fort George. The British seeming prepared for this offensive, the
American plans were changed to make Queenston the chief objective.
On the morning of the 13th Van Ransselaer sent troops across the
river from Lewiston to Queenston and 350 men gained a position on
the heights above Queenston. Brock and Sheaffe, his second-in-
command, were both at Fort George and until the early morning did
not know in what direction the main attack would be launched.
Brock hurried to Queenston and discovering the Americans on the
heights led a small party against them. The Americans were forced
back but Brock was mortally wounded and the British retired to the
village. A second attack under Lt.-Colonel John Macdonnell, the
Attorney-General of Upper Canada, also failed and Macdonnell was
killed. Finally Sheaffe's force advancing from Fort George encircled

the Americans whose numbers had now increased to 1600 men. Smyth refused to aid in the attack, and many of the New York militia, maintaining that they had enlisted for service in the State only, watched the engagement from the American shore. As Sheaffe's force closed in, the spirit of the Americans was broken and they failed to offer effective resistance. Their losses included 950 captured and 300 killed or wounded. The British loss was 150, but this included Macdonnell and Brock, whose stout courage and unerring genius had been the chief defence of the province. Van Ransselaer resigned his command to Smyth who late in November launched an unsuccessful attack against Fort Erie. After his failure there he secured leave and was soon dismissed from the army. Meanwhile on the sea the Americans had been more successful, their heavy frigates having won two notable successes over the *Guerrière* and *Macedonian* besides diverting the British naval force with sufficient success to permit their merchantmen to return in safety to harbour.[1]

The failure of the Americans in 1812 was attributed, in part at least, to their inability to control communications on Lake Erie and Lake Ontario. During the autumn of 1812 and the following winter strenuous efforts were made to remedy this defect. Captain Chauncey, a vigorous and capable officer, was placed in charge of the Lakes force and selected Sackett's Harbour as his base. Here he rushed forward the construction of new warships for the spring. Across the lake at Kingston the British were engaged with feverish activity in a similar task. Commander Oliver Perry was given command on Lake Erie and supervised the construction of a flotilla at Presqu'Île. By the end of July 1813 he had a larger and more effective naval force than the British, who were handicapped by their inability to get men and materials. The American campaign of 1813 aimed at securing control of the Lakes, cutting off the upper part of the province from its base and then striking at Montreal.

Late in April, Dearborn and Chauncey set out from Sackett's Harbour for York and Fort George, sailing clear of Kingston which was of much greater strategic importance. York, though the capital of the province, was not adequately fortified and offered little resistance. Sheaffe retired in the direction of Kingston after losing over 100 regulars. One of the batteries exploded as the Americans were taking possession, killing or wounding more than 200 of their men. They thought a mine had been sprung by the British, and in revenge burned the Parliament Buildings and did extensive damage to private property. Dearborn and Chauncey then crossed the lake to Fort George. Here Colonel Vincent, who succeeded Sheaffe in the Niagara command, had only 2400 men as against Dearborn's 6000. Fearing his retreat would be cut off by the superior force he evacuated the fort and fell back to Burlington. During the progress of this

---

[1] Mahan, i, chaps. vi, viii.

engagement Sir George Prevost, who had come to Kingston earlier in the year, and Sir James Yeo, now in command of the British naval forces on Lake Ontario, attempted an attack on Sackett's Harbour. The expedition was well timed and seemed likely to succeed when an order to retire was given. Lack of co-operation between the land and naval forces and, seemingly, a fatal indecision and inertia on the part of Prevost were responsible for the failure.

Dearborn did not take full advantage of his victory at Fort George. By 5 June the main American force, 3000 strong, had reached Stoney Creek in pursuit of Vincent. On the night of the 6th, a Canadian raiding party of about 700 men under Colonel John Harvey completely surprised the Americans and obliged them to retreat, leaving behind their guns and stores. The British losses were larger than the American, but the American captives included two brigadiers. Yeo's vessels now began to harass the Americans who retired to the Fort George-Queenston line. Later in the month an American force of 600 men under Colonel Boerstler, marching inland from Queenston in an effort to dislodge an advanced British party under Lieut. Fitzgibbon, was threatened with extinction by the Indians on its flanks and preferred to secure safety by surrendering to the British.

The position in the western part of the province depended on the command of Lake Erie. Captain Barclay, the capable British naval commander on Lake Erie, had been unable to obtain either the men or materials with which to equip an adequate naval force. The provisioning of the western Indians had exhausted the British supplies and Procter's army was placed in grave danger. As long as Perry's fleet was at large there was no assurance of relief. Gathering together such guns and ammunition as he could obtain at Fort Malden, Barclay staked everything on an engagement with Perry. The Americans possessed an advantage in numbers, but in equipment and in the quality of the crews there was little difference. They met at Put-in Bay on 10 September and fought until the British, completely exhausted, were compelled to surrender. During the remainder of the war the Americans held undisputed possession of Lake Erie. Procter's position was now extremely precarious; his only hope of safety lay in establishing speedy connection with Niagara by land. He delayed his movement eastward until the 26th, giving General Harrison, who succeeded Hull, opportunity to close in on him. Harrison overtook the British and the Indians at Moraviantown on the Thames on 5 October and gained a decisive victory. Tecumseh died fighting after Procter had fled from the field, and with his loss and the interruption of the western communications British influence with the Indians rapidly declined.

Preparations for the two-fold attack on Montreal were not completed until the late autumn. General Hampton, proceeding by Lake Champlain, was expected to effect a junction with General Wilkinson advancing from Sackett's Harbour down the St Lawrence, whereupon the combined forces under Wilkinson's command would proceed to Montreal. Hampton's force of 7000 men had reached the Châteauguay River by late October and found its progress blocked by a force composed chiefly of French Canadians under Colonel George Macdonnell and Colonel Charles de Salaberry, a French Canadian trained in the British army. The defending force was composed of 1500 men, but de Salaberry and Macdonnell placed these so skilfully that less than 500 defeated an advanced party of 1500 Americans and gave Hampton the impression of such strength that he decided to retire. Wilkinson did not begin his advance down the river until 5 November and by the 11th had reached the foot of the rapids near Cornwall. Another American force of 2000 under Colonel Boyd had crossed the river and followed in the wake of the main army. On 11 November Colonel Morrison with 1000 Canadians attacked Boyd's army at Chrystler's Farm and inflicted heavy losses. Hampton in the meantime had commenced to move back to Lake Champlain and abandoned all thought of a junction with Wilkinson, who thereupon took his army into winter quarters. The closing incidents of the campaign of 1813 reflect little credit on either side. The American forces in the Niagara peninsula, after the reverses of the summer, retired to Fort George, and in December recrossed the river. On the eve of evacuating Fort George they set fire to the village of Newark and burned 150 houses without apparent justification on military grounds. Revenge followed swiftly. General Gordon Drummond, newly appointed Lieutenant-Governor of the province, directed a successful attack on Fort Niagara. Other British parties crossed farther up the river burning all the American villages along the river front.

The campaign of 1814 opened on the eastern front. Wilkinson resumed his advance on Montreal in March and by the 30th had reached the La Colle, a small tributary of the Richelieu. His advance was blocked by a small British force under Major Handcock which had the protection of an old stone mill. Wilkinson's force was much larger than Handcock's and should have had little difficulty in forcing its way. In the face of stubborn resistance offered by the Canadians, Wilkinson decided to retire. Thus ended the project for the capture of Montreal. Early in May a combined military and naval force under Drummond and Yeo captured the fort at Oswego, burned the barracks and carried off the stores. The La Colle fiasco led to the retirement of Wilkinson and the appointment of General Jacob Brown, one of the relatively new men who had come forward rapidly during the earlier campaigns. The Niagara front was selected for the main American offensive and Brown crossed the river with a force of 4000 men and took possession of Fort Erie. He then began to advance along the Niagara and on 5 July encountered a British force of slightly more than 2000 at Chippewa. His advance was stubbornly contested but the British were obliged to give way. He had expected co-operation from Chauncey in an attack on Fort George and Fort Niagara, but the naval commander was still at Sackett's Harbour. Brown then decided to strike across the peninsula for Burlington, but again his advance was checked at Lundy's Lane where the most bitterly contested battle of the entire war was fought. Drummond and Riall with 3000 men defended an advantageous position against Brown and Winfield Scott with a force of 4000. The battle raged from afternoon to late night of 25 July with varying success and heavy losses on each side. Finally, however, the Americans were compelled to retire to Fort Erie which they successfully defended against determined assaults. Early in November they destroyed the fort and retired to winter quarters.

By the spring of 1814 the European situation had so changed as to release some of Wellington's veterans for service in Canada. During the summer 16,000 of these seasoned troops had come up the St Lawrence, and Prevost had 10,000 of them available for an invasion of American territory with Plattsburg on the western side of Lake Champlain as the objective. The British naval force on the lake was expected to co-operate with the army in a decisive thrust. A new gun-vessel, the *Confiance*, was scarcely completed when on 11 September Captain Downie, the British naval commander, at Prevost's urging, engaged the American flotilla in Plattsburg Bay. Numerically the naval forces were nearly equal, but the Americans possessed an advantage in *personnel*. On land Prevost had twice the numbers of his opponents and the best trained army which had seen service during the war. Downie was killed early in the engagement and his ships were gradually overpowered. Meanwhile Prevost lost valuable time disposing his troops and when the naval engagement was terminated had not yet come to grips with the enemy.[1] With American control of the lake assured he decided that Plattsburg would be untenable, withdrew his men and retreated to Canada. There was bitter controversy over Prevost's action; he was summoned home to answer charges laid by Sir James Yeo, but died before the court-martial assembled.

Neither party had been able to secure undisputed supremacy on Lake Ontario until the autumn of 1814. Yeo undertook the completion of the *St Lawrence*, a large warship carrying 102 guns. Though delayed by the capture of her guns on the Atlantic, the ship was ready by mid-October, and as Yeo now possessed definite superiority, Chauncey sought refuge in Sackett's Harbour where his fleet remained until the end of the war. Meanwhile British naval superiority had asserted itself on the Atlantic. The British blockade

---

[1] For new letters on this fight see the *Bathurst Papers* (Hist. MSS. Comm. 1923), pp. 285-94, 302.

extended only to the southern part of the Atlantic coast; New England was permitted to trade subject to British supervision and reaped a handsome profit from this privilege. Hence, New England not only took no part in the invasion of British territory but gave Britain the practical benefits derived from commerce. This did not mean, however, that New England ports provided a safe harbourage for American warships. In the summer of 1813, Captain Broke, of the *Shannon*, sent a polite challenge to Captain Lawrence of the *Chesapeake*, then in Boston harbour, inviting a test of strength. In equipment the ships were practically equal, but the superior training and discipline of Broke's crew gave him a distinct advantage and he was able to bring the *Chesapeake* as a prize into Halifax harbour. Halifax was abustle with activity during the war years. When the New England attitude became known, the Governor of Nova Scotia issued a proclamation designed to prevent any molestation of the Americans along the frontier. Nova Scotia and New Brunswick were not invaded and were able to send troops to Canada. Privateering became extremely profitable, and Halifax, as the base of the Atlantic squadron and free from the dangers of invasion, reaped an abundant harvest of prosperity.

In the autumn of 1814 the British organised a joint naval and military expedition under Admiral Cochrane and General Ross to harass the Atlantic coast as a diversion in favour of Prevost's invasion and with the further incidental object of retaliating for the destruction of civilian property in Upper Canada. The expedition proceeded to Chesapeake Bay and, after encountering a feeble resistance at Bladensburg, reached Washington on the evening of 24 August, although an attack on the capital had not been originally contemplated. They burned the Capitol and the President's residence while the Americans themselves set fire to other public buildings. Their subsequent attempt on Baltimore failed. For the same general purpose and also with a view to the revision of the Maine-New Brunswick boundary, Sir John Sherbrooke organised another joint expedition in the autumn of 1814 which captured the port of Castine, at the mouth of the Penobscot, and Fort Machias. Castine was retained until after the close of the war, and in British possession became the centre of a flourishing trade with the surrounding country, bringing a substantial revenue to the coffers of Nova Scotia. The campaign of 1814 closed with a futile attempt on the part of the force which had operated in the Chesapeake to capture New Orleans.

The fall of Napoleon in the spring of 1814 completely altered the situation in America. It then became apparent that the United States could not conquer Canada. Enthusiasm for the war waned rapidly. Britain, too, wished to end the American complications. Consequently negotiations for peace opened at Ghent in August 1814, and were greatly influenced by those proceeding at Vienna at the same time. At first, Britain insisted on the creation of a neutral Indian "buffer" state to include the lands of the western tribes with whom the British had commerce. The Americans would not agree to this and the project was finally abandoned. The Treaty of Ghent, which was signed on 24 December 1814, provided for the restoration of all conquered territory and for the appointment of several commissions to settle the various outstanding boundary disputes. It contained no reference to the right of impressment or to rights of neutral trade.[1] These very issues which had been employed to arouse war sentiment remained undetermined when peace was restored, but a foundation had been laid for the settlement of questions which otherwise would have caused friction with Britain and with Canada.

The War of 1812 is of great significance in Canadian development. It arrested the flow of American emigration to Upper Canada—a migration, the continuance of which for a decade would have altered materially the character of the province. Also it purged Upper Canada of republicanism and obliged the Americans who remained to cut their former ties and to become British subjects in reality. Further, the Loyalists who were the heart of the British resistance in Upper Canada now deemed themselves the saviours of the country and, therefore, entitled to dominate its government. The war, coming at a time when grievances were being discussed and remedies sought, made the Upper Province definitely British in regard both to allegiance and to political consciousness. American methods and programmes being now discredited, the reforms of the future were destined to be guided by British leaders along British lines of development. The war also demonstrated the possibility of successful co-operation among all Canadians regardless of their origin, and thus brought the Canadian people into more intimate association. In its losses and sacrifices as well as in its victories was laid the foundation of a new Canadian tradition—one of the first which Canadians shared in common, and which has been woven into the background of a distinctive Canadian nationality.

[1] Koch and Schöll, *Traités*, III, 202; *Bathurst Papers*, pp. 286–9, 302, 316; *Camb. Hist. of Brit. Foreign Policy*, I, chap. v; Updyke, F. A., *The Diplomacy of the War of 1812*.

CHAPTER X

BRITISH NORTH AMERICA UNDER REPRESENTATIVE GOVERNMENT

(A) LOWER CANADA (1815–1837)

THE conclusion of the war with the United States, the retirement of Sir George Prevost in April 1815, and the election in the same year of Louis-Joseph Papineau as Speaker of the Assembly are three events that taken together mark an epoch. The war left the long international boundary lines unimpaired. Consequently the original transportation routes to the West continued to serve the principal Montreal and Quebec merchants, whose import and export trade extended their economic and political outlook to embrace the British connection with Canada as a whole. By strange fortune, as leaders of the English-speaking communities of the two cities whose prosperity they established, they became by juxtaposition the antagonists of their French-Canadian fellow-subjects, both giving[1] and receiving the provocation that embittered reciprocally the two races. Of Sir James Craig, and of his severity towards the French-Canadian press they could approve. But for Sir George Prevost's concessions to the French-Canadian side they had a hearty contempt.

Prevost, like Dorchester before him, was expected to administer a government whose constitution both promoted and accentuated race discord. Had it not been imposed upon a province divided very unevenly between two races it would have produced other discords such as exhibited themselves in Upper Canada. Prevost sought, not to procure an alteration of the constitution, but an amelioration of its working in the interests of the race of the majority, which, while electorally free, seemed to be shut out from the administration. For whilst the Act of 1791 established a representative parliamentary constitution, it did not establish a representative parliamentary government. On the contrary, the features that appeared to invite an approximation to English parliamentary procedure were nullified by Colonial Office control and the provincial patronage that went with this control. The elective body that represented the people of the province and a governing clique (the Château Clique) appointed through the Colonial Office could find no common ground to stand upon. From the Governor and Lieutenant-Governor down through the Bench, the Executive Council, the Legislative Council and the departmental services, positions of honour or emolument in the province were

---

[1] Cf. Chapais, T., *Cours d'Histoire du Canada*, III, 110.

within the gift of the Secretary of State for the Colonies. The result was an intrusion of office holders not Canadian by birth. Between them and the English-speaking minority there grew up an understanding by which the two arrogated to themselves pretentiously the duty of maintaining a British ascendancy in face of the French-Canadian majority of the population. In the days of Craig, their spokesman, Chief Justice Sewell, and Ryland, the civil secretary,[1] had offered the advice that led to that Governor's blunders. Prevost put these two out of countenance by procuring the elevation of two French Canadians to the Bench, by increasing the stipend of the French bishop, and by utilising conspicuously French-Canadian regiments in the war and French-Canadian *voyageurs* for the intelligence and the inland transport services. The wisdom of Prevost's concessions is not the point in question here, but their result was manifest in the altered relations of the two races. Previously the English-speaking minority had affected to tolerate, perhaps only temporarily, the nationalist survival of French Canada through the retention of its language, its Church and its civil law. Recognition rather than toleration seemed to be implied in Prevost's course; from recognition it would be a simple matter for the French to aim at the control of the patronage and thus inaugurate a French ascendancy.

The election of Papineau as Speaker of the Assembly in 1815— he was not its actual leader until later—suggests a sketch of the procedure this tribune of the French-Canadian people was expecting to follow. Within the parishes and towns of the province he received support as the champion of French Canada; and in every general election between 1815 and 1837 he and his followers carried the polls. Within the Assembly he and his party took a different position. They advocated, not the rights of French-Canadian nationalism, but the rights of the Assembly under a representative constitution. So that what appears on the surface as a constitutional struggle was quickened and invigorated by issues felt beneath the surface. For the French-Canadian people, regarded as a separate race, had no separate legal status. The law and the constitution regarded them as British subjects only. But, as the majority of the British subjects of the province, having the majority in the Assembly—an Assembly that came ultimately to represent them almost exclusively—they had a well-defined status which the custom and usage of English representative government recognised. Yet the theory and practice of Colonial Office government at this period could not tolerate a Legislature after the English model. It requires little perspicacity to see that this theory and practice would be challenged on constitutional grounds by the Assembly, and that the representative

[1] Kennedy, W. P. M., *Documents of the Canadian Constitution*, especially nos. LXVII, LXXV, LXXVII, LXXIX, LXXXIII. Ryland's copies of his letters are in McGill Univ. Library MSS.—*The Ryland Letter Book*.

branch of the Legislature would endeavour to control the Administration—especially when there was something more than a constitutional advantage to be gained. Within the Assembly, and for purposes of political reform only, Papineau was supported by a liberal reforming element among the English-speaking minority—men like John Neilson of Quebec, whose sane and sturdy Liberalism took the direction of an attack upon administrative privilege. Papineau and Neilson together represent under Canadian conditions and in the exceptional French atmosphere of Lower Canada the same effort to broaden and liberalise the basis of politics that marked contemporary political agitation in England. Papineau and his French followers were careful outwardly to represent themselves only as aggrieved members of the provincial Assembly. So that apparently the Colonial Office had on its hands only a dispute between an elected Assembly and the beneficiaries of its own patronage. Officially, also, neither the Governor nor the Colonial Office could recognise that the animus within Papineau's mind was of nationalist and not of parliamentary origin; and that his political acts needed translating into terms of his nationalist motives quite as much as many of the public documents of the time, appearing in English, need to be read in the light of their French originals.

A more vexatious attack could scarcely have been devised than the one Papineau was to launch to meet an equally vexatious relegation of the Assembly—and thus of the French-Canadian people—to a position of political subordination. In his angrier moments Papineau might declare that his people were slighted, aggrieved and insulted: in his judgment and in theirs that unfortunately was the case. Injured national esteem, and not any substantive grievance, was the malaise from which the body politic suffered.[1] It explains the sharpness and vehemence with which, from the French side, Papineau's agitation was carried on—likewise its concentration against the very persons in public office whose conduct gave offence in this direction. The Assembly began by a recourse to impeachments, and up to the very year of the suspension of the constitution it still hoped to perfect this means of bringing to legislative trial those who in a sense hostile to itself too openly advised or supported the Administration; it then sought to control supply in order to control patronage, provoking thus the most serious and determined of all its disputes with the Colonial Office; and following this it proposed an elective Legislative Council, or Upper House, in order to carry its bills of supply—all the while forwarding to the Home Government protests, petitions and remonstrances based upon the assumption that under a representative Government the wishes and opinions of a majority of the electorate, expressed through a majority of the representative house, are entitled to adoption.

[1] See Hansard, 3rd ser. xxxix, 1484, for Grote's opinion in 1837.

The outstanding case of impeachment was that which was directed against Chief Justice Sewell before Prevost retired.[1] With Sewell was associated Chief Justice Monk. The principal charge against them was the publication on their own authority of the Rules and Order of Practice for their courts, alleged to be an infringement of legislative authority. The prime mover in the impeachment was James Stuart, a former Solicitor-General, whose dismissal from office, and influence in the Assembly subsequently acquired, incited him to retaliation. The Assembly counted upon sending Stuart to London to plead the charges; but when a money bill to furnish Stuart's expenses was sent from the Assembly to the Legislative Council, that body refused its concurrence. In the Privy Council the case was called and considered without the Assembly being heard; and when the decision went in favour of the two judges the Assembly could not but feel that the judgment was due in part to their not being represented by counsel. When Sir George Drummond, who served as Governor between the Administrations of Prevost and Sherbrooke, received notice of this decision through Lord Bathurst, then Secretary of State for War and the Colonies, he was instructed that, should the Assembly not accept this decision as final but take steps to renew the impeachment, he was forthwith to proclaim the Assembly dissolved. It so came about that the Assembly had recourse to a petition to the throne. On the first intimation of this, Drummond, probably against his own better judgment, was obliged to order a dissolution. The punitive and disciplinary character of this dissolution could not be disguised. Intended most unwisely as a reprimand, it displayed to the province an unexpected contrariety between the independence of public opinion and Lord Bathurst's displeasure. On purely legal grounds the articles of impeachment may have seemed frivolous; Sewell's real offence sprang from his being the arch-enemy of the survival of French Canada (*la survivance française*).[2] Mortifying as it must have been to the Assembly not to procure his removal, even more mortifying was the cumulative effect of the three steps by which the designs of the Assembly had been frustrated: the loss of its bill for expenses in the Legislative Council; the charges not being argued by counsel; the arbitrary dissolution to forestall further action. The elections that followed endorsed the Assembly's action completely, returning members a shade more intransigent than before.

Sir John Coape Sherbrooke was Governor when the new Assembly held its first session. He came with instructions from Lord Bathurst, of more than passing interest, as they reveal Lord Bathurst's misconception of the force and vigour of colonial public opinion especially in conjunction with the privileges of a representative House.

---

[1] Pub. Arch. Can. *Documents relating to the Constitutional History of Canada*, 1791–1898, ed. Doughty, A. G. and McArthur, D., II, 443–77; also 504–36.

[2] Kennedy, no. LXXIV, esp. p. 268.

In Bathurst's way of thinking the Assembly had acted contrary to public opinion, which the Colonial Secretary strangely pictured to himself as controlled by Sewell and his fellow office holders (*les bureaucrates*) in collusion with the French Catholic clergy! Sherbrooke strove to undeceive him on this point, and his letter sounded a warning note as to what might be expected in the province if public opinion, decisively expressed, were too sharply crossed. Fortunately for Sherbrooke the new Assembly had set its mind upon securing a salary for its Speaker. It asked for the Governor's consent. Sherbrooke, in turn, suggested that the Speaker of the Legislative Council—at that time Chief Justice Sewell himself—should receive a like salary. To this the Assembly agreed, and Papineau, as a salaried officer, evinced a cordial support of the Governor. When Stuart attempted to revive the question of Sewell's impeachment he found the Assembly no longer disposed to follow him; the members turned to Papineau for leadership.

To Sherbrooke fell the task of taking the first definite steps to place upon a constitutional footing the provincial finances and the control of supply. The provincial treasury received funds from two sources: first, the proceeds from the Quebec Revenue Act and from the Crown revenues of the province; second, the taxes levied by the provincial parliament. By 1818 the receipts from the former met only half of the required annual expenditure, the Government paying off the balance by drawing upon the second—though at first without asking for parliamentary sanction. Technically, on the part of the Colonial Office, this meant incurring a debt towards the province. To regularise for the future the appropriation of this provincial money, Bathurst instructed Sherbrooke to ask the Legislature annually for the amount required, reserving to himself the control of its expenditure. In 1818 the Assembly voted the total sum requested of it as an unspecified appropriation, sufficient to balance the budget Sherbrooke laid before them after the Crown revenues and the proceeds from the Quebec Revenue Act had been expended. Before the next session Sherbrooke had retired, the Duke of Richmond succeeding him. The session of 1819 is memorable for the first overt challenge by the Assembly of the system of administrative control over supply. The Assembly saw the tactical advantage to themselves of an annual appropriation specified at their own discretion. When in 1819 the total amount of revenue required was laid before them, they proceeded, on the ground that the budget was essentially one, to specify the expenditure from both sources of revenue, even to the point of revising the stipends of those included within the administrative patronage, thus taking the control of supply out of the hands of the Administration. The Legislative Council rejected the bill of 1819 on the ground that, were it adopted as a precedent, it would make every office holder in the province responsible to the Assembly.

Clearly the Assembly had discovered a constitutional method of embarrassing the Government through the stipends of its irresponsible office holders; clearly, also, the Government would have to rely upon the subservient votes of those same office holders in the Legislative Council to stay the attack. For this reason Papineau was to agitate later for an elective Legislative Council. The rejection of the bill of 1819 left the Government without the necessary authority to use the funds required to meet its obligations for that year. The Duke of Richmond—who, it is known, esteemed Sewell's opinion—suggested to Bathurst imperial acts rather than provincial acts for the internal taxation of the province: a procedure no minister, mindful of the American Revolution, could contemplate. Richmond's untimely death in 1820 brought Lord Dalhousie to Quebec as Governor; and with the accession of George IV as King in the same year, the consequent dissolution brought into being a new Assembly.

In the session of 1821 the Legislative Council announced its determination in regard to the control of supply. Briefly it required either a general appropriation for the lifetime of the sovereign, or else an annual budget voted in the exact form, item by item, applied for by the Governor. In other words, the discretionary power of the Assembly over separate items was to be nullified, leaving as a prerogative of a group of office holders the irresponsible expenditure of provincial money. As between the Council and the Assembly the issue involved more than the constitutional control of supply; it involved the ascendancy of the French-speaking majority over the English-speaking minority. With the growing conviction that the entire control of supply belonged of right to the Assembly, its leaders began to take high constitutional ground and to merge the issue of supply into the broader question of abstract popular rights as against bureaucratic irresponsibility. In this way Papineau and his party widened their platform and attracted to their support a group from among the English-speaking community. From men like John Neilson of Quebec this group shaded down to types of recent immigrants, bringing with them the radical feeling for popular rights then prevalent among the English, Irish, and Scotch of their class. Papineau himself was well informed in the republican traditions of France, and in the views and principles of the French doctrinaires. He drifted into contact with English Liberals and Radicals, particularly with Roebuck, and, as his voluminous collection of letters reveals, he had many friends and correspondents in the United States. Under a government in which an elective Assembly was expected to furnish money without controlling its expenditure, Papineau could feel that his was much the same cause, within the small compass of a colonial population, that gave to the Liberals and Radicals of Europe their fighting spirit before 1830.

The declaration of the Legislative Council in 1821, and the refusal of the Assembly to consider a permanent supply, suggested a possible compromise. Before negotiations were begun an untoward move on the part of certain business interests in Montreal, bringing influence to bear privately upon the British Cabinet, provoked an indignant public protest from both Upper and Lower Canada. The move was occasioned by an application from Upper Canada to have its quota of revenue derived from the customs at Montreal and Quebec readjusted on the basis of its increased population. The Cabinet was prevailed upon to make the reapportionment of the common revenue of the two provinces an opportunity to reunite them under a single Legislature and Administration, without either province being consulted as to its wishes in this respect.[1]

Two provisions of the proposed legislative union call for especial comment.[2] First: constituencies were to be distributed, not uniformly over the population of the two provinces as a whole, but upon the basis of an equal quota in representation from each, the assumption being that a solid English-speaking vote from Upper Canada added to a handful of English-speaking members from Lower Canada would keep the French Canadians in a permanent minority. Arbitrary as this was—ordinary common sense would have seen that the vote of Upper Canada could not be manipulated indefinitely as a solid vote to redress the balance against the French Canadians from Lower Canada—it was as nothing to a further provision which threatened, as it was intended to do, the survival of French Canada. This was that after fifteen years French should cease to be a language of debate and record in the combined Legislature. In justification of the private interests behind this measure it must be said that they overlooked questions of language and race in view of the paramount need of securing Government assistance in promoting the economic prosperity of the country, particularly in assuring through subventions and through the credit of the public treasury increased facilities for national help in transportation: a matter, then as now, of prime importance in public policy.[3] To Upper Canada the proposed union with the French population of the Lower Province was distasteful; to the people of Lower Canada it seemed to threaten annihilation.[4] Signatures by the thousand were procured to a petition against the bill. Papineau from Montreal and Neilson from Quebec were deputed to proceed to London with the petition. Papineau went as an outraged nationalist;[5] Neilson as an outraged Liberal. By securing the friendly services of the Whig Opposition the two delegates managed to have the bill set aside on the ground that it had been framed without the wishes and opinions of the people of the provinces being first taken.

---

[1] Hansard, 2nd ser. VII, 1199.   [2] Kennedy, nos. LXXXVIII and LXXXIX.
[3] Ibid. nos. XCII, XCIII, XCIV and XCV for petitions in support of the union.
[4] Ibid. nos. XCVI, XCVII, XCVIII for petitions and resolutions in opposition to union.
[5] Ibid. no. XCI; Chapais, III, 263–82.

The impassioned oratory which in 1822 fired the province with the conviction that its public opinion was regarded as a negligible quantity was repeated with greater vehemence five years later, and on that occasion it involved Dalhousie more personally. Within the interval Dalhousie had proposed a compromise in the control of supply. The Civil List should be separated from the provincial expenditure proper; the latter only should be detailed annually at the discretion of the Assembly. If Dalhousie had been inclined to take high ground against the Assembly in the matter of the administrative control of supply, he was placed at this juncture in a most uncomfortable and embarrassing position through the Receiver-General at Quebec. This official, who held his office without bonds, and whose accounts were not subject to provincial audit, found that his private investments of public money had miscarried, and that he stood in debt to the province to the amount of £96,000. The Assembly made the most of the Receiver-General's delinquency, exploiting the incident as a grave reflection upon administrative irresponsibility.

With the temporary absence of Dalhousie from the province in 1825 Sir Francis Burton, Lieutenant-Governor, became Acting Governor. Though appointed to the post of Lieutenant-Governor in 1808, he had held the office as a sinecure, continuing to reside in England. Upon an address from the Assembly forwarded through Lord Dalhousie, he was required to proceed to Quebec and to continue to reside there during the tenure of his office. In the budget for 1825 Burton unwittingly framed his application for a supply in such a way as to name the total amount required, and to ask the Assembly to furnish the difference between the permanent revenue and the total named. The Assembly was careful to vote the supply exactly as the Governor had requested it, to that extent meeting the conditions laid down by the Legislative Council. But it most adroitly denominated its supply a bill to provide for the expenses of the provincial government and the administration of justice, thus including the Civil List within the scope of its grant, at the same time attaching to the bill a schedule of detailed appropriations which the supply was intended exactly to cover. In this form the Legislative Council accepted the supply, an action of which Lord Bathurst strongly disapproved.[1] When the "model" of 1825 was tried again next year Bathurst's disapproval required its rejection. In 1827 Dalhousie adopted the expedient of not submitting a Civil List at all, and only the items chargeable to provincial taxation were scheduled. Declining to vote a supply on these terms the Assembly, by way of reprimand, was dissolved.

This, the second punitive dissolution under Bathurst's regime, left upon the mind of the province a more abiding impression than the first. It exposed a complete breach between administrative authority

[1] Kennedy, nos. CII, CIII.

and the Assembly. To the mind of French Canada the inference was conclusive that the Assembly represented the province, while the Governor represented an external authority under external influence in sympathy only with the English-speaking minority. The more clearly the Governor was viewed in this light the more fully did French Canada come to dissociate administrative authority from the people at large. It began to regard the Assembly and the Speaker of the Assembly as the sole centre of its political existence, seeing in the Governor an antagonist to be resisted or at least tolerated on sufferance. Thus Papineau came to represent French Canada— Dalhousie to embody all that French Canada held in aversion. From Papineau's conduct in the elections following the dissolution it must be inferred that he took Dalhousie's action as a personal affront to himself and to his people; he was prepared with Gallic intensity to see that the affront was requited in full to Dalhousie's discomfiture and discredit. The subsequent effect was to aggravate a popular distemper, that, spreading over French Canada, rendered the relations between the province and its administrative officers increasingly difficult. The immediate effect was to sting Dalhousie into personal resentment against Papineau for the gratuitous public abuse and contempt the latter had heaped upon him from the hustings.[1] When Papineau, fresh from his victory and that of his party at the polls, was chosen Speaker again at the opening of the next session, and the Assembly formally asked the Governor to confirm their choice, Dalhousie declined. As the Assembly refused to elect another Speaker at the Governor's bidding, and as Dalhousie remained obdurate, the constitutional machinery of the province was brought to a sudden stop.

The time seemed propitious to send to London a delegation to lay before the Government the state of the province. Lord Bathurst's long tenure of the Colonial Office came to an end in 1827; his successors, especially William Huskisson, were less inclined than he to regard with an unfriendly eye popular opinion expressed constitutionally through a Colonial Assembly. A change of policy was partly indicated by a change of governors. Lord Dalhousie being transferred to India, Sir James Kempt succeeded him in Quebec in 1828, with the avowed intention of beginning an era of conciliation. Although Dalhousie's attempt loyally to carry out Bathurst's instructions contributed to bring on the disastrous crisis of 1837—apart from his administrative relations with the Assembly—no other governor of the period showed a finer public spirit towards the general welfare of the province or took leave of it more universally well regarded.

The representations of the delegates from Lower Canada inclined

[1] Election speech of L.-J. Papineau at Montreal, 1827. (Pamphlet, McGill Univ. Library.)

Huskisson to ask for a parliamentary committee to hear evidence upon the state of the province from every interest concerned. As the Canada Committee this committee made recommendations to the following effect: (1) that the revenue of the province be placed at the disposal of the Assembly in the hope that the Assembly will provide a permanent and not an annual Civil List; and (2) that placemen, particularly the judges, shall no longer be drawn upon for the membership of the Legislative Council. In both recommendations the spirit of compromise can be seen—a compromise that was welcomed by neither side in the province.

Sir James Kempt remained in Quebec but two years. His acceptance of Papineau as Speaker disposed of the personal dispute left over by his predecessor. But the Assembly set aside the Governor's request for a permanent Civil List and voted a budget after the model of 1825. For two successive sessions this model was followed, the Legislative Council acquiescing. One long-standing complaint of the English-speaking settlers in the Eastern Townships was ended by a reform in representation. The membership of the Assembly was increased from fifty to eighty-four, involving the creation of new counties and the rearrangement of others. The redistribution satisfied the claims of the Townships; although, among the English-speaking sections of the province, those who feared or affected to fear a French ascendancy noted with apprehension the employment of French county names in preference to English. Kempt must have been sensible of the fact that the antagonism towards the system of government he was expected to administer lay too deep to be touched by official conciliation and good will. His retirement after two years of effort in this direction brought to Canada Lord Aylmer.

The year 1830, which marked in France a successful revolution, in England the accession of William IV and the calling to office of Earl Grey and a Whig Cabinet, increased the political ferment in the province. French Canada had begun to take stock of its past and to look to its future. It wished jealously to remain a separate community, living within its own Church and its own language, and to respect and maintain traditions that it could not possibly share with an English-speaking Protestant community (*l'Anglicisme, voilà l'ennemi*). Calling itself *La Nation Canadienne*, thinking of the province as *La Patrie*, it was growing abnormally sensitive both as to its position within a mixed population and as an unrecognised nationality under British rule. It elevated the idea of its own race identity to a plane of devotion for which in English experience there is hardly a category. To remain under British protection but apart from all other British fellow-subjects became both a political objective, and, within the province, something like a race challenge. Anglicisation was to be faced with defiance, and the least attempt to promote it became persecution. A historical tradition—later to find expression

16-2

in the pages of Garneau—was already beginning to shape itself, and to furnish a basis for the criticism of current events. It goes without saying that Craig, Sewell and Dalhousie are adopted by this tradition as the enemies of French-Canadian nationalism. But it remained for Lord Aylmer to feel the full force and effect of nationalist recrimination.

French Canada had viewed at first with suspicion, but latterly with increasing alarm, the tide of British immigration flowing into the country. Against the settlers that passed on to Upper Canada nothing could be said, but the rapid peopling of the Eastern Townships with newly arrived farmers and farm labourers gave rise to the fear of some sinister design against the survival of French Canada. When the cholera scourge visited Britain in these years it was practically inevitable that the emigrant vessels from England, Ireland and Scotland should bring the dread disease amongst their passengers. The scourge touched Quebec and exacted its death roll.[1] Lord Aylmer maintained quarantine and isolation, but that was not sufficient to prevent the malicious rumour that the disease had been allowed to come to the province to decimate the French-Canadian population. A people capable of attaching credence to such a suggestion could naturally be carried off its feet by the street shooting that occurred in 1832 in connection with a by-election in Montreal.[2] On the last day of polling troops from the garrison were marched to the scene to preserve the peace. The troops, held in check by their officers, were treated at first to a fusillade of jeers and reproaches, later of stones and other missiles. Provoked beyond endurance the officers ordered the detachment to fire. Three of the crowd fell dead, others were seriously wounded. In the popular imagination this incident—which ought never to have been allowed to happen—was magnified into a deliberate massacre. Papineau with ostentatious officiousness watched the inquest and haughtily summoned Lord Aylmer from Quebec to attend to the affair personally. He contrived to allow the "massacre" to rankle quite unnecessarily in the popular mind; and whilst no open threats of retaliation were uttered, popular opprobrium was concentrated deftly against the Governor personally. A movement on the part of the English-speaking population of Montreal to enrol themselves into volunteer companies and to be drilled in readiness for eventualities, was stopped by Lord Aylmer, who, had he sanctioned it, could not have refused a similar move on the part of the French.

It is practically impossible, in portraying Papineau, to separate

---

[1] *The Quebec Mercury*, Oct. 1832, published figures of interments in Quebec, 7 June to 30 Sept., as follows: Protestant grounds, 1244; Catholic grounds, 1574; at St Roch, 474. Total for less than four months, 3292. Christie, R., *Hist. of Lower Canada*, III, 409.

[2] Christie, III, 396–407; Kingsford, IX, 480–8, with references to the *Minerve* (Montreal), *Spectateur* (Quebec), *Quebec Gazette*, *Herald* (Montreal) and *Gazette*. Tracey, the successful candidate, edited the *Vindicator*, "a newspaper of rather violent politics".

the Canadian and the French Canadian in him. His nationalism was not altogether bounded by his race; his views befitted a colonial statesman who felt his country restive under the unnecessary tutelage imposed upon it through officials foreign to its atmosphere, disconnected from its traditions, and too often estranged in sympathies from its people.[1] To what extent he contributed to the ending of this irresponsible system of government in Canada no critic has yet cared to estimate. His career is in many respects the outstanding tragedy of the incompatibility between colonial statesmanship and the smothering of self-government inherent in Colonial Office control. The eventual winning of responsible government meant the recognition of a distinctively Canadian statesmanship, hitherto, as in Papineau's case, repressed and frustrated. And amongst those who contributed to establish a statesmanship of this kind Papineau takes a high place. As the colleague and associate of Neilson he stood for political and constitutional interests broader than those of one race alone. But during Lord Aylmer's tenure of office Papineau and Neilson were to drift apart. The occasion for this was the adoption by the Assembly at Papineau's behest, but against Neilson's opposition, of the ninety-two resolutions —a combined Great Protestation and Grand Remonstrance drawn up principally by Papineau himself.

Already the two had differed in opinion upon a proposed settlement of the budget. By the Howick Act of 1831 the Imperial Government had allocated to the province the whole of the permanent revenue, with the provision that a fixed Civil List of £19,500 only should be reserved.[2] Consistently with the status of a colony as then understood it was a fair compromise upon the control of supply. Neilson voiced his approval, and was prepared to consider the unseemly wrangle over the budget, continuously distracting to the province since 1819, as definitely settled. Not so Papineau, whose Gallic disposition and relentless categorical mind could be satisfied only with a settlement upon his own terms. He required imperatively a complete surrender.

The introduction of the ninety-two resolutions in the session of 1834 marks the climax of Papineau's career.[3] The resolutions were impressive only by their number and their length. They reveal Papineau as a student of revolution and of revolutionary constitutions, particularly of the French constitution of 1790–1 with its all-powerful Legislative Assembly, and the federal constitution of the United States. Their contents were at the time and have been ever since a target for sarcasm; but their contents were as nothing

---

[1] Cf. Kingsford, IX, 479.

[2] Kennedy, no. CX, Canadian Revenue Control Act 1831; Hansard, 3rd ser. II, 690.

[3] The text in French and in English appears in the *Journal of the House of Assembly*, 1834, pp. 310–35, and in Kennedy, no. CXLV; also in abbreviated form in *History of Canada* by Kingsford, IX, 544–54.

beside the spirit and temper by which they were inspired.[1] They express the feelings of a revolutionary of a somewhat visionary and academic cast of mind. Neilson and those of a like disposition voted against the resolutions; and the list of these voters included a group of French Canadians whose conservative instincts recoiled from their compatriot's inflexible and irreconcilable manner. Neilson, as a Reformer and a Liberal under colonial conditions, resented equally with Papineau the subordinate rôle assigned to the representative branch of the Legislature by administrative practice under the Constitutional Act, but he would have been contented with a sensible working correlation between the representative body and the Administration. Papineau, it is clear, wanted to reverse the whole administrative practice under representative government by making the representative body the absolute and controlling authority in government. He wished to see the Legislative Council elective, thus bringing it into harmony with the majority of the Assembly; he wished the Assembly to have complete and unrestricted control over the public finances so as to attach all placemen by ties of responsibility to itself; also a High Court in the province to try cases of impeachment laid against judges and others in public office. The combined effect of these demands would have been to make the Assembly omnipotent, bringing everything else under its authority and control. Incidentally it would have made of Papineau himself, as Speaker of the Assembly, and as tribune of his people, the leading personage of the provincial Government.[2]

By stressing the place of the people and of popular control in his scheme for a new provincial Government, Papineau, it could be seen, was drawing away from long constituted traditional authority, and making himself spokesman of a populace upon whose passions he would have to play: the descent to the rôle of popular agitator would follow. It came definitely in his break with ecclesiastical authority. A bill before the Assembly, which Papineau furthered, sought to revolutionise the *fabrique* of the parishes by allowing parishioners to attend and to vote at its meetings; in other words, to supersede the authority of the curé and the churchwardens by something resembling a parish meeting. The Church interests felt obliged to overreach Papineau by appealing to the Legislative Council to have the bill set aside. Papineau had committed the grave error of echoing the anti-clericalism of the French revolutionaries.[3] In the judgment of many he had forfeited any further

---

[1] Cf. Roebuck's remark: "The provinces are at this moment in a state nearly approaching open revolt"; Hansard, 3rd ser. XXII, 767.

[2] For a supporting petition from Lower Canada see Hansard, 3rd ser. XXV, 920–3. For the countervailing petition, *ibid.* XXVI, 1013.

[3] Chapais, III, 245–61, especially Papineau's remark, p. 254. Papineau's library contained *Les Œuvres de Boullanger* (N. A. Boulanger), 4 vols. Amsterdam, 1794. Marginal notes in Papineau's hand show the anti-clerical passages that appealed to him. These four volumes are in McGill Univ. Library.

claim to be the political spokesman of French Canada as a community; others continued to recognise his leadership, but with misgivings. The extent of his influence was found to be contracting. Conservative Quebec grew lukewarm, and the *patriote* ranks narrowed down to a younger element, in individual cases tinged with anti-clericalism, to be found in Montreal and its vicinity. With this group were combined a small handful of the English-speaking community—men of defiant radicalism like Dr O'Callaghan, and men of a sentimental predilection for righting popular wrongs. In this very narrowing and intensification of the militant *patriote* and radical force lay its danger to the peace of the province. Of this the Home Government was well advised by petitions and memorials from the Loyal and Constitutional Associations of the English-speaking communities in Montreal, Quebec and the townships. These petitions reflect the traditional views and difficulties of the English-speaking minority in contact with the French.

With the ninety-two resolutions of the Assembly before them, and with petitions and memorials from the English-speaking community in a contrary sense, the Home Government reserved its decision. Neither with propriety nor with dignity could it either modify the Howick Act or repeal it entirely to satisfy Papineau; to make the Legislative Council elective and therefore French would be to take away one of the constitutional devices for an English ascendency and for imperial control; to keep the entire Administration under threats of impeachment before a High Provincial Court would be worse than useless. Even admitting the evils complained of, the remedies proposed seemed too ill-advised to be considered. In the dilemma the Government resorted to the Liberal expedient of a commission of enquiry. A commission was to be appointed to proceed to Quebec, the chairman of the commission serving as Governor of the province in place of Lord Aylmer, who was to be recalled.

After Lords Canterbury and Amherst had both declined the task, the duty was entrusted to Lord Gosford, a genial but undistinguished nobleman. With him were associated Sir Charles Grey and Sir George Gipps.[1] The commissioners reached Quebec in 1835, and Gosford as Governor, ignoring the imminence of a political crisis, began—injudiciously as it appeared later—a course of official entertaining and public amiability, to the consternation of the English-speaking community and to the bewilderment of the French. In the meantime his two colleagues traversed the province forming, or appearing to form, a judgment upon its political difficulties. In the course of the next year Sir Francis Bond Head, Governor of the Upper Province, read to the Provincial Assembly in Toronto the text of his official instructions, known to be identical with those of

---

[1] Cf. Reports in Christie, IV, 243–302 (especially p. 264). See also Kennedy, p. 366, n. 1, and nos. CXV, CXVI, CXXII, CXXVII. For instructions to Commission see *ibid.* no. CXVIII.

Gosford. From the instructions it appeared that both Governors were to practise social conciliation but not to temporise with the wish for reform. These disclosures placed Lord Gosford in anything but a favourable light before the *patriotes*; when, later, the report of the commissioners was made known and it was discovered that no constitutional changes had been recommended, the *patriotes* faced the complete frustration of their hopes.[1] Lord John Russell's ten resolutions followed.[2]

The excitement in Montreal foreboded a crisis, especially in view of the indignation manifested over Lord John Russell's resolutions.[3] One section of these resolutions, intended to deal with the affairs of Lower Canada, empowered the Governor to use the funds of the provincial treasury without the authorisation of the Legislature for all outstanding claims upon the Government. Virtually this was to declare the Cabinet's intention of suspending representative government in the province. A boycott of English imports, designed as a protest as well as a means of cutting off the receipts from the Imperial Revenue Act,[4] obliged the *patriotes* to garb themselves in native homespun. Representatives in motley array gathered in Quebec in August 1837 for what was to be the last Parliament under the Constitutional Act. A supply was refused on the ground that grievances had not been redressed,[5] and the Assembly was prorogued. The summer of 1837 passed with *patriote* meetings held in many parts of the province—meetings seditious and insurrectionary in language, but leading to no overt breach of the peace; for nothing like a general insurrection had been contemplated. A rising in Montreal was probably averted by the timely and resolute action of Mgr Lartigue, bishop of the diocese. In an episcopal charge issued to the clergy he enjoined them to admonish the faithful against the sin of rebellion and insurrection.[6] He urged his people not to be misled into thinking that the small number of militant *patriotes* could speak for French Canada as a whole. The injunctions were answered with the utmost disrespect by the anti-clerical writers of the *patriote* press—a fact not without its influence in displaying the militant *patriotes* as undesirables, beyond the pale of the Church.

In November, fearing that the presence of Papineau and O'Callaghan in Montreal might accidentally precipitate a crisis, friends of

[1] *British Parl. Papers*, 1837, XXIV.

[2] For the text see Hansard, 3rd ser. XXXVI, 1303; also Kennedy, no. CXXIV. For the debate, Hansard, 3rd ser. no. XXXVI, 1287–1362; no. XXXVII, 76–147; no. XXXVIII, 198–217; especially Russell's statement of 6 March 1837: "That part of the constitution which requires that the ministers of the Crown shall be responsible to Parliament, and shall be removable if they do not obtain the confidence of Parliament is a condition which can only exist in one place, namely, the seat of empire. Otherwise we should have separate independent powers existing not only in Great Britain but in every separate colony".

[3] Cf. Hume's prophecy, *ibid.* XXXVIII, 215.   [4] *Ibid.* XXXIX, 1456–63.

[5] Kennedy, no. CXXVI, especially p. 440.

[6] For text (Eng. transl.) see Christie, IV, 417–21.

the two urged them to withdraw from Montreal. They left the city and proceeded in the direction of St Hyacinthe. The move was interpreted as the prelude to an uprising, and warrants were issued for the arrest of several well-known *patriotes*, including Papineau and O'Callaghan. At St Denis and St Charles, two small villages on the Richelieu, the *patriote* villagers, with a small handful of English-speaking sympathisers, stood embattled to resist the arrests. Thus the so-called "rebellion" of 1837 was started. With considerable difficulty two small detachments of troops sent from Montreal dispersed these gatherings, but Papineau and O'Callaghan both escaped arrest by making their way across the border to the United States. Sir John Colborne who, from being Governor of the Upper Province, had passed to the command of the forces, repaired to Montreal in the course of the year. With the Richelieu valley pacified he was able in December to move to St Eustache and the neighbouring village of St Benoit, and there disperse, after much loss of life on the part of the insurgents, the one formidable gathering that arrayed itself against the Government during that year.[1] Reports magnifying the "rebellion" far beyond all proportions—for it was an uprising on a very small scale and within a very small compass—reached London within a few weeks.[2] The seriousness of the situation called for more than ordinary care in determining, for the guidance of the Cabinet, precisely what the character of the disturbance was. The Cabinet needed accurate information and reliable advice from some statesman who, with cultivated political discernment, could really explain the crisis and indicate its solution. The result was Lord Durham's mission.

The province about to come under the scrutiny of Lord Durham was still industrially backward. Not only did the countryside south of the border present a reproachful contrast, and point to a more successful way of mastering trans-Atlantic conditions, but the province itself was acutely conscious of its handicap. The industrial outlook of the habitant did not transcend a primitive rural economy, impounded within a separate Church, a separate tongue and a separate land tenure. If this element consecrated its politics to the maintenance of such an economy, and viewed the withholding of self-government as a challenge to its survival—what is to be said for the English-speaking minority: the mercantile class in Montreal and Quebec, and the farmer settlers in the Eastern Townships? These men eager for prosperity lived for projects and opportunities held beyond their grasp. Keenly aware of the need of transportation

---

[1] Decelles, A. D., "The *Patriotes* of '37" (*Chronicles of Canada*), chaps. viii, ix; Chapais, IV, 193–207.

[2] *Ann. Reg.* 1837, p. 415: "The news that a civil war had broken out in one of our colonies was received by the whole [Radical] party with undissembled delight and triumph". For the debate see Hansard, 3rd ser. xxxix, 1428–1507.

facilities, of a trade less restricted by imperial control, of capital, proverbially suspicious of a Canadian venture, of an improved postal service, of better municipal government and better education, and particularly of a British immigration to develop the land and exploit natural resources, they desired above all things a prosperous commercial colony, and the assistance of Government to that end, and found themselves balked by the indifference, if not by the open hostility, of French Canada.

Thus when Lower Canada was merged into the Union there was outstanding as against the provincial treasury no public debt that had been incurred for internal improvements, or for the furtherance of a general public policy, beyond the paltry obligations of £113,975 currency, contracted just before the union, for the improvement of the Montreal harbour and the completion of the canal at Chambly. A union with the English-speaking Upper Province promised relief in that direction. The fur trade, better organised after the amalgamation of the North-West Company and the Hudson's Bay Company in 1821, concentrated its export, import and banking interests in Montreal. Shipbuilding, encouraged by the War of 1812, and lumber helped to make Quebec an industrial city; though the application of steam to river navigation tended to enhance the maritime position of Montreal. At the same time the construction of the Lachine Canal, opened in 1824, made that city more directly accessible by the western water route. It grew as the metropolis of the Townships and through its control of the larger part of the traffic with the United States. The export of wheat and flour proved remunerative until the repeal of the Corn Laws dislocated entirely this Canadian industry. The construction of the Erie Canal through New York State (opened in 1825) diverted to New York City much of the western traffic of the United States that otherwise would have used the Great Lakes and St Lawrence waterway. The Old North-West Territory of the United States, between the Ohio and the Mississippi, included within the Province of Quebec by the Quebec Act of 1774, and sacrificed to the United States in 1783, attracted with its abundant professional and industrial opportunities a goodly portion of the English-speaking population of the Canadas. In that way many a British family that crossed the Atlantic to make its home in Canada passed on, along the western waterway, into Ohio, Illinois, Indiana and Wisconsin. Phenomenal as the increase of population through British immigration was, its constant depletion through emigration across the border bears testimony to the economic and political shortcomings of Canada that Lord Durham's *Report* was soon to expose. The devastating commercial panic spreading from England and from the United States into Canada in 1837 and 1838 served only to intensify the ills for which he was expected to find the cure.

(B) UPPER CANADA (1815–1837)

The history of a young rapidly expanding colony is concerned with social growth rather than political discussion. Its official archives tend to be misleading. Between the year of the general peace and the arrival of Lord Durham the record of Upper Canada was one of normal growth, accompanied by the usual signs of growth—confusion, imperfect organisation, social friction and clumsy attempts to adjust means to ends. The so-called "rebellion" with which the period closed—a local disorder—was not the logical conclusion to a quarter of a century's activities; it was an unnecessary and criminal episode, precipitated by folly and inexperience. A constantly increasing community of settlers, whose mere energy was greatly in excess of their political experience, had to be guided towards self-control by a benevolent but rather timid Home Government. The agents of that Government, being neither Burkes nor Chathams, were likely to make the miscalculations so easy to inexperience and imperfect sympathy. The true heroes of the story were not governors or agitators, but quiet dull men with ploughs and axes, whose main ambition was to ward off famine and to increase the meagre comforts of life. To such men professional politicians were at best a doubtful and costly luxury.

It is dangerous to generalise too much on the character of the population, for that was continually changing. Beginning with numbers somewhere about 80,000 in 1815, the community had increased by 1824 to 150,066, by 1830 to 213,156, and by 1841, the year of union, to 455,688.[1] At first the main strain was American—Loyalists and those who followed where they had blazed the trail, but in the East the Highland Scots were strong, in part direct from Scotland, in part refugees from the United States. North of the capital, York, and farther to the West, there were Germans and French Canadians. At the close of the wars it was hoped that many settlers from Scotland and Ireland would go out in the transports sent for the returning troops, and the Colonial Secretary, Bathurst, gave strict injunctions to the commander of the forces, Drummond, that he must not grant land to subjects of the United States, but use his best endeavours to prevent their settlement.[2]

The years after Waterloo saw no great rush from Britain. Indeed, until 1830, the numbers of British emigrants were not conspicuously greater than in the later eighteenth century, but British North America was the usual goal, and British policy favoured settlement in Upper Canada. A Scottish colony, in essence military, created the town of Perth in and after 1815, and by their success drew other Scottish emigrants out to join them; while, later, a larger party

---

[1] Estimates from Gourlay, R. F., *Statistical Account*, 1822, and Blue-books for Canada.
[2] Bathurst to Drummond, 10 January 1815.

supported by emigration society funds and private subscriptions, established themselves at Lanark on land granted by Government. A second Talbot conducted a party of Irish to Western Canada, near London, in 1818. English settlers peopled the region round Peterborough, and Peter Robinson in 1823 and 1825 conducted two Irish experimental expeditions under the auspices of Wilmot Horton and the Colonial Office.[1] Perhaps the happiest episode of the period, although not for its hero, was the founding of the Canada Land Company in 1824–6, and the efforts of John Galt, on the spot, to make the great Huron grant a model colony. Galt's reputation as a pioneer has suffered, partly through his greater fame as writer, partly through his inability to propitiate conventional officials and economical directors, but there were few qualities of the practical coloniser, save the gift of advertisement, and the power of attracting social influence, in which he was not easily Edward Gibbon Wakefield's superior. Guelph, Goderich and the towns of Western Ontario owed more to him than Adelaide and Wellington to the other.[2] After 1830 the number of immigrants increased, although it is doubtful whether the quality did not deteriorate.

The first practical problem for the new population was that of land settlement.[3] It is futile to dwell too much on abuses, for nowhere outside eighteenth-century Prussia has land distribution ever been conducted with wisdom; still, except in specially controlled districts like the Talbot settlement or Perth, Upper Canadian management exhibited all the mistakes that were possible. The normal procedure had been to grant 200 acres to each settler, at first free, later subject to fees which showed a tendency to rise; later still, quit-rents had to be paid and land bought in auction sales. Here as elsewhere regulations existed apparently in order that officials and politicians should break them. At first the districts settled were chequered with blocks not only of Clergy Reserves but also of Crown Reserves, in which lack of owners and cultivation held back the organisation of the rest. Rules made in Britain were steadily disobeyed by colonial authorities; surveys were altogether inaccurate; vast grants were made to interested parties, some of whom were as remote from the scene as the Bishop of Quebec, and these swamped the little holdings of the genuine settler; unnecessary and heartless delays in the completion of formal grants drove immigrants in despair to practise "squatting". Lord Durham's *Report* condenses into a few figures the natural result: "The area of the surveyed part of the province is stated to be 17,653,544 acres. Out of this there have been reserved for roads 450,000, for the clergy, 2,395,687; there have been granted and appropriated

---

[1] *Canada and its Provinces*, XVII, 75–84.
[2] Galt, *Autobiography*, 1833, epochs 6 and 7.
[3] Authoritative summary in Lord Durham's *Report*, App. B (Sir C. Lucas's edition, III, 29–130).

13,660,838, and there remain to be granted 1,147,019". "A very small proportion", his Land Commission reported, "perhaps less than a tenth, of the land thus granted has been even occupied by settlers, much less reclaimed and cultivated".[1] Travellers, wherever they strayed from the common tracks, gave depressing accounts of conditions in the pioneer settlements; and Sir Peregrine Maitland had some romantic notions dispelled when he paid a governor's visit to that home of heroes, Glengarry. "I was disappointed in the Glengarry settlement", he wrote shortly after his arrival in Canada. "There is but little cleared, and the people are not so comfortably housed as I had in my imagination fancied they would be. They are very poor.... The people are of a good sort, but they brought neither funds nor notions of comfort from the Highlands".[2]

Here then was the material foundation of the life of the province—a vast stretch of virgin country, cleared at intervals along the river and lake front, at Cornwall, Brockville, Kingston, the Bay of Quinté, York and to the West, with one or two invasions of the hinterland like Perth, Hull or Peterborough; a land of rough scattered villages, and settlements not yet villages; a population whose sober industry was in part counteracted by the selfish folly and indolence of officials in York, but who still fought indefatigably, perhaps unimaginatively, on, founding their new civilisation on the graves of the children and women and sick folk who succumbed in the struggle, and on the loss of all the luxuries and tastes which Europeans counted life. It is significant that when Gourlay drew up his summary of actual provincial complaints, all of them dealt with details of land settlement.[3]

It had been the ambition of the founders of the province to give it an ecclesiastical framework; and indeed in a pioneering settlement religion is the one interest which forces itself into the brute struggle for existence; for even the roughest pioneer accepted birth, marriage and death more resignedly when accompanied with religious rites. It was difficult for organised religion to keep pace with the expansion of the province, and undesirable that religious energy should be dissipated in sectarian strife. But, at worst, the State Church, controlled from York by the most aggressive human force and political monopolist in Upper Canada, John Strachan, Archdeacon of York and, later, bishop there, planted its churches and missionaries with reasonable pertinacity. Statistics of religion for the period suffer from a terminological inexactitude surpassing even that of politicians; still it seems likely that by 1827 there were thirty Anglican clergy and thirty-five churches with ten more churches building.[4] Colborne, an honest Christian and churchman, was disquieted, when he

[1] Durham, *Report* (ed. Lucas), III, 52; II, 223.
[2] C.O. 42/361, Maitland to Bathurst, 19 August 1818.
[3] Gourlay, I, 623-5.
[4] *Letter to R. J. Wilmot Horton, by the Rev. Dr Strachan*, dated 16 May 1827, p. 4.

arrived, rather at the quality than at the numbers of the Church. "There are not more than three clergymen in the province that are fit for the position in which they are placed. The supineness of our Church is lamentable".[1]

The Scottish Church, which ultimately secured State recognition on an equal footing with that of England, possessed certain features in common with its sister Church, but racial characteristics in it were also strongly marked. Apart from a rather more aggressive religiosity, the Scots in Canada, who settled in communities, demanded that in their new parishes there should be the same religious centre as at home, and, because more highly organised, they told in the province out of proportion to their actual numbers. By 1832 they had seventeen ministers and a provincial synod.[2] At Kingston, long the chief town in Upper Canada, the Scottish minister visited among a people at least 1500 in number, and counted 350 communicants. Through the same racial clannishness the Highland Roman Catholics, chiefly in Glengarry, received Government recognition, and found in Alexander Macdonnell, the first Roman Catholic Bishop of Kingston, a champion not less redoubtable than John Strachan himself.

But the form of religion most natural to the province was Methodism, and Methodism with a strongly American flavour. In 1828 the formal connection with the American Methodist Episcopal Church was severed, and in 1833 the Canadian Methodists joined hands with the British Wesleyan Methodists, but, down to 1830, the American element, whether Loyalist or of more recent origin, remained predominant in the province, and the Church of this racial section was neither Anglican nor Presbyterian but Methodist. After the peace the Government at York was plagued with fears of American propaganda through American Methodist preachers. Drummond in 1814 had foreseen inroads of "itinerant fanatics, enthusiastic in politics as well as in religious matters", who might pervert the faithful by their noxious principles.[3] These unjustifiable prejudices yielded very slowly before facts, and Strachan utilised them most unpardonably in that religious chart of 1827 which marks the zero point of Canadian ecclesiastical honesty, speaking of the preachers as "certain to render a large portion of the population, by their influence and instruction, hostile to our institutions, both civil and religious".[4] In actual fact Methodism was the most natural expression of the province in religion; it was active and unselfish, perhaps not the most disciplined and educated agency at work, but in the hands of a very notable Loyalist, Egerton Ryerson, a power both for political order and steady loyalty. In 1835 Ryerson claimed

[1] Colborne to Hay, 31 March 1829.
[2] Return of U.C. Clergy, etc., July 1834, p. 3.
[3] C.O. 42/355, Drummond to Bathurst, 20 March 1814.
[4] *Letter to R. J. Wilmot Horton, by the Rev. Dr Strachan*, dated 16 May 1827, p. 2.

that between 1825 and 1835 provincial Methodism had increased from 41 ministers and 6875 members to 93 ministers and 15,106 members; and the quadrupling of these figures would not exaggerate the total influence of Methodist efforts.[1]

If history were indeed a compilation of organised petitions against grievances, and official answers, it might seem true that religious life in Upper Canada was a whirlpool of ecclesiastical claims and jealousies, with the desolation of the Clergy Reserves as a melancholy background for Christian futility. As a matter of fact, for so young a settlement, religion had taken wonderfully firm root. The mere religiousness of men ignored the surface frets and disputes. In Kingston, Dr Machar of the Scottish Church found a kindred spirit in his Anglican colleague, Cartwright, and John Beverley Robinson, the representative Anglican layman in the West, paid warm tribute to the work of Methodist missionaries, and assisted in their church building schemes.[2] Against the conventional over-emphasis on religious differences may be set the dying words of an Anglican clergyman: "The nearer I approach to eternity, the more I see those veils rent asunder which separate Christians from one another".[3] Further, in the heats, past and present, of the Clergy Reserves dispute, it is also too easy to ignore the fact that of all the payments made from provincial funds to religious bodies in 1832, while the Anglicans received £4430, the share of the Church of Rome was £1500 and that of the Presbyterians £1121: and that, in addition, some £4000 were "placed at the disposal of the Presbyterian Synod, Methodist Conference, and Roman Catholic Bishop and Clergy, for the purpose of building churches and chapels".[4]

The development of education in the province followed along lines not dissimilar. The hard physical work in which most of the community shared left little time and less inclination for letters. Individuals inheriting some older tradition, like the Cartwright family of Kingston, possessed an excellent knowledge, at least of English literature. "There was hardly a passage of excellence", wrote C. E. Cartwright of his father, "in Shakespeare, Milton, Dryden, Pope, Thomson, and Goldsmith, that he could not repeat".[5] Unusual new arrivals like Mrs Jameson brought with them the intellectual interests of the set they had left in England; and lists still remain of little libraries chiefly stocked with dusty volumes of forgotten American sermons. But plain men had to study life at first-hand, not in books. The first impulses towards education came in most cases through religion. John Strachan's schools at Kingston,

---

[1] Ryerson, E., *Story of my Life*, p. 149.
[2] *Memorials of the Rev. J. Machar*, p. 63; Robinson, *Life of Sir J. B. Robinson*, p. 179.
[3] *Memorials of the Rev. J. Machar*, p. 64.
[4] *Statement showing what payments were made to Bishops, etc., in U.C.*; ordered to be printed 23 July 1834.
[5] Cartwright, C. E., *Life and Letters of Hon. R. Cartwright*, pp. 26, 27.

Cornwall, and York, set a fair standard for later secondary education. He too was the effective if pugnacious agent in forcing the idea of a University on the Government, however narrowly he interpreted that idea. A spirit of emulation drove Ryerson and the Methodists to create the Upper Canada Academy at Coburg to offset Anglican activity.[1] However much the fact may be deplored, the higher education of Upper Canada owed everything to the contending ambitions of the Churches. It would be unfair to deny to the legislative bodies their share in the work.[2] Eight district schools had been established in 1807 by a Government grant of £800 a year, and later acts amended the original project. It became a shibboleth with keen reformers to object to these because their cost and their distance from outlying regions made them useless except to a few wealthy inhabitants. So while the district schools found advocates in the more aristocratic Legislative Council, the Assembly, after 1816, became the patron of the more democratic common school system, to which an Act of that year granted £6000 a year— or, as it worked out in detail, a maximum of £25 to the individual school.[3] Under Maitland a general board of education, regarded by reformers as a doubtful gift, was appointed to direct all schools in receipt of state aid, and to control funds allocated to education. Thereafter, until union, the politicians fought over education, Council and Assembly each backing its favourite, forgetful of the interest of teachers and taught alike, who struggled, often unsuccessfully, with adversity. There were many schools where absence of fuel prevented the meeting of classes in winter, and schoolmasters were hard to find and keep—a teacher of twelve months' standing was counted a prodigy.[4] In refreshing contrast to the sterile argument of the politicians stands the effective zeal with which Sir John Colborne set up his Upper Canada College and made it at once the most respectable educational centre in the province. At the same time private enterprise had done something to fill in the gaps. If Barnabas Bidwell failed to enter politics, perhaps he served the province better by his academy in Ernestown, and in the Midland District a committee of good Kingston citizens, inspired by religious motives, founded the Midland District School Society, and provided education, in three schools, for 300 children, often of the poorest class.[5] Here, as in Church matters, one must postpone attention to the outcries of agitation, and recognise the real constructive work of men, not vocal but practical. Upper Canada could have dispensed more easily with self-named reformers in education than with the autocrats and sectarians who founded schools.

As population flowed in, and business expanded beyond the limits

---

[1] Ryerson, p. 113.   [2] *Canada and its Provinces*, XVIII, 277–300.
[3] Herrington, W. S., *History of Lennox and Addington*, p. 115.
[4] *Ibid.* chap. vi.   [5] *Memorials of the Rev. J. Machar*, p. 61.

of the townships, the question of intercommunication came to the front. Mr Gladstone used to dwell on the "liberation of intercourse" and its chief agent, the penny post, as one of the most admirable developments of useful civilisation; nowhere was this better illustrated than in Upper Canada. Bad roads long remained an obstacle to Canadian prosperity, for except over the frozen snow the network of ordinary roads, plank and corduroy roads, mud trails and forest paths, provided more obstructions than facilities to intercourse, and the Crown and Clergy Reserves enormously increased the difficulties. The history of the Post Office,[1] which was the chief agent in use of these routes, furnishes important evidence of the life of the community. At this time even the Governor-General at Quebec found his despatches lingering on the road from November to February, and emigrants to Upper Canada sometimes waited four months for letters from home. It was a serious disadvantage that the deputy postmaster had his headquarters at Quebec, and received his orders from London. But Stayner who took over the position in 1827 did probably as much as any locally appointed official could have done, increasing the offices in Upper Canada from 90 to 270, arranging five trips a week between Montreal and Niagara, and attempting to keep in touch with newly developed settlements. Provincial needs forced Canadians to improvise services to the United States, and through New York to England, thus making good the defects of the Government monopoly. Organisation naturally lagged behind life, without actually losing touch with it. Reformers served a useful purpose in goading the authorities into greater efficiency; yet it is significant that while the agitators dwelt largely on the misuse of the surplus which the Canadian offices were contributing to the English revenue, Stayner kept steadily at work, attempting to deliver more letters through offices spread over a constantly widening area to a vastly greater number of new settlers.

In this essential work of binding together the scattered population another factor began at this time to affect the social life of Canada—the building of canals. Until late in the 'forties, with the exception of a diminutive line in Lower Canada, the colony remained in the pre-railway age. But it witnessed the first real effort to develop water transport. Two great lines of operation were planned before 1837, and carried to rough completion. Warned by dangers to their lines of communication in the American War, the Home Government began to construct an inner line, running up the Ottawa River, and thence by canal to Kingston and Lake Ontario. The project involved not only the improvement of minor works along the course of the Ottawa, but the canalisation of 150 miles of stream and lake between Kingston and what is now Ottawa. A Select Committee reported in

[1] Smith, W., *History of the P.O. in British North America*, especially chaps. viii, ix, and xi.

1832 to the House of Commons that some £993,022 had been, or would immediately be, spent, and that by the expenditure of another £171,515 on locks at the Grenville Canal and the Island of Montreal, it would be possible to send steamboats 134 ft. long, 33 ft. broad, and 5 ft. in draught, from Montreal itself through to Kingston and Ontario.[1]

Interest in the other line, by the St Lawrence and the Great Lakes, centred in these years chiefly in the Welland project to connect Lakes Erie and Ontario. Older canals evading the Cascades, Cedars and Coteau Rapids had been improved, and by 1824 the Lachine Canal removed difficulties just above Montreal. But in the West the early struggles of the Welland pioneers furnished by far the most exciting story of provincial enterprise. At what is now St Catharine's, the first representative of the Canadian Middle West entered practical politics in the person of William Hamilton Merritt. Merritt was an American-born settler of Loyalist stock who served, and continued to serve, his apprenticeship at a multitude of trades, land-owner, storekeeper and bookseller, flour miller and lumber seller, with half a dozen minor activities to complicate his accounts. A dreamer of amusingly materialist dreams, he had a mind full of notions but incapable of exactitude. Among his visions was one of Montreal as a port in the hands of the Upper Province, passing its ships on to the westernmost of the Great Lakes, with a Welland Canal between Ontario and Erie as the chief link in the long chain. Merritt's reach invariably exceeded his grasp, and his projects furnished the happiest touches of unconscious humour in the period. But by hook or crook he, or some of his victims, accomplished his ends. His first rude survey was vitiated by a hundred per cent. error in calculating heights. The finance of his Welland Company suggests Wilkins Micawber rather than Lombard Street, and Francis Hincks found it difficult in 1836 to discriminate between truth and fiction as he audited the books. On 30 November 1829 Merritt recorded the first navigation of his new waterway, characteristically proving that the canal could now be traversed in twenty-four hours by confessing that he had taken sixty, and that he had grounded midway on a bar, "where, being Sunday, we remained all day".[2] But his confused and guileful optimism involved more cautious heads than his own, and he finally harnessed the provincial and Imperial Governments with the completion of his scheme.[3]

Such were the salient social features of the time—abundance of steady spade work, politics properly and usefully arising only as the pioneers compelled the organised government to relate itself to their gallant improvisations. Settling, logging, ploughing, building, the

---

[1] *Report of Select Committee on Canal Communications in Canada*, ordered to be printed 29 June 1832.
[2] Merritt, J. P., *Life of W. H. Merritt*, 1875, p. 123.
[3] *Ibid. passim*; *Canada and its Provinces*, x, 523–9.

provincials found that they must have better roads, honester land settlement, post offices which would bring and carry letters, a clergy who would preach, marry and baptise, and schools in which instruction might be possible. Unfortunately not only later historians but contemporary politicians conceived of government as a thing of fixed institutions and grandiose statements of rights and duties. Most of them, except Sir John Colborne, hampered their efforts by using a rhetoric of voice and pen appropriate perhaps in Johnson's London, but preposterous by Lake Ontario. Misfortunes came because of their failure to seek simple and honest roads to the material happiness of their unpolitical constituents.

The charter of the province was, of course, the Constitutional Act of 1791, but the legal details were of less importance than the human agents who converted its clauses into practice. At the centre was the Lieutenant-Governor, ruling, in spite of legal technicalities, at his little capital, York,[1] as a despot limited only by inexperience and the British Parliament. Such was the position, inevitable in 1815, when colonial posts were not attractive to Englishmen of the first rank, and when the additional pay which soldiers drew made it natural to appoint officers of Wellington's army. Events between 1815 and 1837 revealed no one in the colony who would have performed the duties of Lieutenant-Governor better than the average good British officer of the day. Of the three men who ruled between 1818 and 1837, Peregrine Maitland (1818–28) was a Tory guardsman, admirably fitted to play his part in a polite circle, or on a battlefield where some wiser head was in command; but with no flexibility of mind or power of resisting prejudice, and, in partnership with his wife—a daughter of the Duke of Richmond—inclined to head a social clique or court. Under strain he became querulous, and towards political opponents he betrayed little interest in seeing that justice was impartially administered.[2] His successor, Sir John Colborne (1828–36) was a very different man—an able soldier, who at Waterloo had displayed tactical powers of the first order, a solid administrator with a nice discrimination between the respective values of action and of speech; a Christian whose religion was not the less sincere for its zealous churchmanship. Colborne had the good soldier's gift of obeying orders faithfully even when his opinions were on the other side; he was too sound a gentleman not to spurn in his heart the ignoble turmoil and crude exaggerations of the men who thwarted him; and if he failed intuitively to recognise the solution to his political problems, he failed in company with almost every Englishman of the time before Durham.[3] Sir Francis Bond Head (1836–7), the last of the series, brought into high relief the good qualities of his

---

[1] After 1834 renamed Toronto.
[2] Despatches of Maitland to the C.O., 1818–28.
[3] Moore Smith, G. C., *Life of Colborne*, 1903, *passim*.

predecessor. For his inexperience the Cabinet which appointed him may be held responsible, but besides inexperience Head revealed an incapacity to learn how incompetent and ignorant he really was. He exhibited a spasmodic self-sufficiency which under strain broke down in panic and violence. He lacked sense, modesty and discipline, and contrived to combine insults to his subjects with disobedience to his superiors. With Dogberry he must be written down an ass.[1]

Arrayed over against the Lieutenant-Governor was the House of Assembly, twenty-six in number in 1826 but increased by 1836 to sixty-nine. By the Act of 1820 one member was allotted to counties and towns with a population of 1000, and two in the case of counties with more than 4000.[2] All forty shilling freeholders in the counties had the franchise, and in the towns, five pound freeholders and ten pound copyholders. Upper Canada, then, had a popular Assembly far more representative than was the British House of Commons even after 1832; and throughout the period one may watch popular moods play across its meetings as clouds and sunshine over the surface of the provincial forests on a blowy day. Doubtless it did not control the executive, nor, even after 1831, had it the full power of the purse; but to call it a mere debating society is ridiculous. It was completely representative, and therefore endowed with all the powers which adequate representation always confers. Varying in opinion from time to time, it incurred the discredit of extreme factiousness and violent tyranny, but it never failed to reflect the temper, however transient, of the constituents by whom it was elected.

Between Governor and Assembly lay the two Councils, Legislative and Executive, differing in function and to some extent in membership, but for practical purposes a unit. Here, if anywhere, resided that Family Compact of which so much has been written. There was no Family Compact.[3] A primitive community had to provide an upper house and a working government, and, since most communities receive the governments which they deserve, Upper Canada was provided with such wisdom, honesty and public spirit in its councils as a colony less than 100,000 strong can usually provide. Working together, these councillors developed common vested interests, with, now and then, internal splutters of petty animosity. They clung to power because they liked it, and felt themselves fit to govern. Between 1815 and 1837 this changing but growing "council crowd" found as their leaders the two ablest men in the province, John Strachan and John Beverley Robinson, the former a man of the type whence popes and cardinals come in the greater

[1] Head, Sir F. B., *Narrative and Emigrant*; despatches to and from Glenelg, 1836–7.
[2] C.O. 42/365, Maitland to Bathurst, 7 March 1820.
[3] Dent, J. C., *Story of Upper Canadian Rebellion*, vol. 1; Kingsford, W., *History of Canada*, vol. x; Wallace, W. S., *The Family Compact*.

world, the other an educated and opinionative gentleman in a land where education, a fixed creed, and a correct manner were all solid assets. Strachan, who fought not unequally with every governor from Colborne to Elgin, was unlikely to accept dictation from eccentric and ill-mannered agitators. It seems clear that *this first Canadian party* developed its perverted form under the influence of Sir Peregrine and Lady Sarah Maitland and that Dr Baldwin, if his be the credit,[1] coined the phrase "Family Compact" at the moment—1828—when the group had reached its maximum of strength, although not of influence. Regarded as a party, as Burke conceived of party, it claimed the right to office—to monopoly of office if that were possible. One may discriminate between its younger better days when Robinson guided it arrogantly but wisely, and the years of unwisdom after 1829 when Boulton and Hagerman, the Attorney-General and the Solicitor-General, misled it to their own undoing.

The British Parliament provided the last primary factor in government. It is easy to be unjust to an agent which suffered from the imperfect understanding which is the natural consequence of remoteness. Fair judgment will confess that no other single element displayed so much good temper, steadiness, and benevolence. While Liverpool was Prime Minister and Bathurst Colonial Secretary, direction of overseas affairs was unenlightened but in no sense tyrannical. From 1828 onwards the most admirable expressions of political wisdom, apart perhaps from the views of the younger Bidwell and Robert Baldwin, all came from Westminster. The *Report* of the Select Committee in 1828 was benevolent and fair-minded. Its desire that "all other changes should, if possible, be carried into effect by the local Legislatures themselves in amicable communication with the local Government", was the soil from which true autonomy was to spring.[2] Goderich and Colborne between them conferred a substantial benefit in 1830–1 when they handed over to the province the funds annually arising from the Quebec Revenue Act. Goderich's despatch to Colborne of 8 November 1832 is a masterpiece of quiet rebuke to grievance-mongering and a generous promise of co-operation. "His Majesty's ministers", it declared, "are and ever have been prepared to refer to the Provincial Legislature the consideration of every question directly or remotely affecting the interest of the province".[3] Even Glenelg with his feeble grip, and lack of penetration, gave Head instructions in 1835 which nothing but Head's folly could have rendered fruitless. Let it be granted that, before Durham, no English leader discerned the one thing needful for Canada; that English ways were leisurely;

[1] Wallace, pp. 3–4.
[2] *Report of Select Committee*, ordered to be printed 22 July 1828.
[3] *Papers respecting alleged grievances in Canada*, ordered to be printed 20 August 1833, pp. 3–14.

that Colonial Secretaries after 1828 changed with embarrassing frequency and that the last of them was a weakling. It is still true that the Imperial Government ruled with honesty and steadiness, and that no other system, then in existence, or which could have been created before 1838, would have done the work better. It is a historical fact rather than a political grievance that down to 1839 no merely English politician was able to think of colonial self-government as compatible with imperial unity.

The political situation developed through phases determined as much by political opinion in the province as by the character of the existing Lieutenant-Governor. In 1817 the Government of Upper Canada still retained its old war suspicions concerning Americans and other seditious characters, and therefore held itself aloof from thoughts of reform. On it broke the storm of Robert Gourlay's agitation. Gourlay was a Scotsman of good position and intelligence, but of enfeebled fortunes, who had conceived the idea of founding a new prosperity through land-owning in Canada. He had practical knowledge and ideas, but his judgment was poor, his mental balance unstable, and he over-estimated the scope and initiative permitted, even to an abler man than he, in an organised colony. Before he had been long resident in Upper Canada he launched a circular containing some thirty-one questions, mostly pertinent, and in answer received some most enlightening replies. A little later, thwarted in his personal ambitions, and souring in temper, he proposed to hold a convention of delegates by whose collective wisdom and criticism Canada might be saved. In a more highly developed state, such violent personal action would at once have proved self-destructive. In Canada Gourlay first attracted much attention and some sympathy; then, as his projects were one by one snuffed out, he developed a frantic mood, in which it was only too easy for the executive attacked by him to intervene. Smith, who was acting head in Gore's absence, directed his Attorney-General to watch Gourlay's progress,[1] and although the accused was twice acquitted in 1818 of a charge of sedition, the legal authorities of the province secured first his condemnation and finally his expulsion by the scandalous perversion of the statute passed in 1804 for the protection of the province against wandering Irish rebels. The chief importance of the episode is that it marked the beginning of organised grievance-hunting—in this case *bona fide* grievances; that it summarised existing faults in the control of emigration and land; but even more that it revealed the unwillingness of the Government to acknowledge their errors and set them right. Gourlay, who never was a rebel, and who behaved with conspicuous good feeling when in the United States he heard of the Canadian rebellion, passed out of Canadian history leaving behind him a strange medley called a Statistical Account, and a precedent

[1] C.O. 42/365, Smith to Bathurst, 28 April 1818.

for later reformers to quote against a retrograde and brutal Government.[1]

Until 1824 the atmosphere remained comparatively tranquil. After 1821 the conspicuous ability of the new Attorney-General, Robinson, controlled the Assembly and kept partisanship within the limits of decency. For the moment Upper Canada was deeply concerned in securing from Lower Canada its fair share of the duties levied on imports at Quebec. Proposals were made in England to combine an Act of Union with the necessary rectifications in trade regulations; but the measure, primarily of interest to the Lower Canadian British, met with little support in Upper Canada. The Canada Trade Act of 1822, which was saved from the wreckage of the Union Scheme, safeguarded the financial interests of Upper Canada, awarding the province one-fifth of the duties collected between 1819 and 1824, and providing arbitration for the settlement of outstanding and possible future difficulties.[2] At the same time, and on to its solution in 1828, the Alien question which affected the rights of American-born Canadians provided a legitimate political interest and a means of educating provincial politicians in the methods of constitutional criticism. Legislation under George III had at first sought to attract settlers from the South; but the War of 1812 introduced another spirit. Bathurst, it will be recalled, had forbidden Drummond to grant land in any case to subjects of the United States, but natural law had proved too strong for executive timidity. In 1817 Lieutenant-Governor Gore had found local feeling strong against exclusion.[3] But in and after 1821 the election of an able American, Barnabas Bidwell, to the Assembly, and later, on his defeat, the candidature of his son Marshall Spring Bidwell, raised the whole question. Some years of involved and confused action followed, the incontrovertible fact being that Americans had settled, would continue to settle, and must receive their full rights as citizens. Finally, common sense prevailed, and a bill introduced by the younger Bidwell in 1828 removed the last disability of genuine settlers from the United States and left their future unprejudiced.[4] The affair had served to introduce, in M. S. Bidwell, the ablest leader of moderate reform who appeared in Upper Canada before 1837. Between his election in 1824 and the rebellion, Bidwell never failed in discerning the true issues of the constitutional struggle; his moderation in language and action was a model alike to friend and foe. His only weakness lay in a certain lack of physical and intellectual robustness which in the end gave Head his chance of sending Bidwell from the province, and cost Upper Canada his leadership in quieter times.

[1] Gourlay, R., *Statistical Account* and *General Introduction*. The earlier part is attributed to Barnabas Bidwell.   [2] Dunham, A., *Political Unrest in Upper Canada*, chap. iv.
[3] C.O. 42/359, Gore to Bathurst, 7 April 1817.
[4] For the whole question see Dunham, chap. v.

Beneath the surface, the administration of the Clergy Reserves both as a church endowment and as a disastrous form of land settlement, provided an unfailing source of political friction. Nothing could be more explicit in criticism than the judgment of the House of Commons Report of 1828 on this nuisance: "These reserved lands, as they are at present distributed over the country, retard more than any other circumstance the improvement of the colony, lying as they do in detached portions of each township, and intervening between the occupations of actual settlers, who have no means of cutting roads through the woods and morasses which thus separate them from their neighbours". Yet, more and more, Strachan and Robinson assumed a die-hard attitude on the question; and Maitland revealed his incapacity for balanced judgment when he reported that the old-established practice of interspersing the Reserves among grantable lots—the very root of all mischief—was preferable to any other.[1]

Grievances, reforms, even normal legislative action all made for the grouping of provincial statesmen into Conservatives and Reformers, while the Lieutenant-Governor's social prejudices, and his refusal to act as honest broker between the parties accentuated the cleavage, making the Reformers seem less loyal and more democratic, and giving the Government party an autocratic and domineering air. The separation assumed disastrous form in Maitland's last years of office, 1824 to 1828. Then Maitland became the centre of a party of domination, especially in the Executive and Legislative Councils, and in society; and the group, in full possession of all places and social prestige, treated their critics with a contempt which cut deeper than mere injustice. "With the exception of his son", wrote Maitland in 1828 of Dr W. W. Baldwin, "he is the only person throughout the province *in the character of a gentleman*, who has associated himself with Mr Hume's projects"[2]—that is, who has voted against the Government.

On the other side chance had arrayed some very able leaders— Bidwell the younger, Dr John Rolph, a competent but evasive Englishman who would have played a greater part if his frankness and good faith had equalled his ability; Dr William Baldwin of York, and his son Robert, the solidest and most moderate of those who tried to discover the new formula which would bring peace to Canadian politics. At this time, too, a Scot who had passed through a multiplicity of minor employments, from draper and general store-keeper to journalist, transferred the office of his *Colonial Advocate*, a paper started in 1824, to the capital. Concerning the character of William Lyon Mackenzie there is far less room for difference than partisan writing suggests. He possessed some critical ability, and real disinterestedness in money matters. On the other hand, he over-estimated his capacity for political leadership, and had an

[1] C.O. 42/368, Maitland to Bathurst, 29 June 1822.
[2] C.O. 42/384, Maitland to Sir George Murray, 18 September 1828.

imperfect appreciation of political realities. He possessed that easiest of all gifts to those who care to own it—fatal fluency in melodramatic journalism and in personal abuse. He never really proposed a working substitute for the Government he denounced. Overstraining his very meagre powers, and yet unable to rest from self-expression, and to let others take the lead, his self-control vanished after 1836, and the kindest verdict on his efforts thereafter is that mind and nerves had completely lost their balance.[1] Meanwhile he brought a resounding reinforcement to the cause of reform.

Unfortunately for themselves Maitland and his friends had provided fuel in plenty for a blaze. Between 1825 and 1828 a series of law-suits discredited the Administration. Already Maitland had been a consenting party to the persecution of Gourlay; he had removed from office Thomas Merritt for affording that culprit too much liberty under arrest; and he had excluded Gourlay's partisans from their legitimate war claims to land grants. Young men of good society in York disgraced themselves by an attack on Mackenzie's printing office, and the destruction of his plant in 1826. A little later, on his own initiative and using Royal Engineers for the work, the Lieutenant-Governor destroyed the property of an hotel-keeper at Niagara, whose faults and trespasses it lay with the law to mark and punish.[2] Then, further discredited by unskilful handling of Judge Willis, a presumptuous and wrongheaded lawyer fresh from England, and the excessive punishment of a worthless Irish journalist, Francis Collins, Maitland, his ministers, and his set—what may by this time be termed the party of Government House—formed the target for incessant attacks which culminated in the election and rout of 1828. For two years the House of Assembly lay in the power of the party of reform—or rather of grievances; M. S. Bidwell made an admirable Speaker and official head to the majority; Mackenzie in print and speeches kept up a running fire on the discredited Administration; and when Sir Peregrine Maitland left his Government in November 1828 for Nova Scotia, he handed over a very delicate situation to his successor, Sir John Colborne.

Colborne has received too little credit for the extraordinary coolness and clearheadedness with which he met a dangerous situation in 1828. Whether a successful rebellion would ever have been possible in Upper Canada may be doubted; but had an injudicious governor like Head assumed office at this point he might have produced a crisis four-fold more serious than that of 1837. The prestige of the Government had badly deteriorated, and one might justifiably talk of misgovernment. The Government party, defeated at the polls, were yet in possession of office and power, and of everything but

[1] Lindsey, C., *Life...of W. L. Mackenzie*; Dent, *Upper Canadian Rebellion*; despatches from Maitland and Colborne, 1818–36.
[2] *Correspondence relative to Mr Forsyth's Petition to House of Assembly*, ordered to be printed 18 July 1833.

moderation and common sense. They were even more dangerous to stability than the agitators. Mackenzie was now in full pursuit of grievances and abuses, threatening, as unbalanced and incompetent propagandists always do, to create more public disorder and confusion than he professed to cure. Colborne, especially in England and with the Whig Reformers, seemed from the first to be Governor in a dependency which produced, lived on, and exported only grievances. But they were not his creation. After 1830, when one set of extremists made way for another, to the outside world it was Colborne, and not the Assembly, who persecuted Mackenzie and broke the law. Once more, when in 1835 agitation broke loose afresh and the Seventh Report on grievances proclaimed the sins of the Government of Upper Canada, Colborne had to accept discredit for abuses of which he was not the author, and feel the effects of ill-tempered and mendacious agitation. Through it all he kept his head and temper—the nearest approach to a first-rate man which these years produced. Loving deeds better than words, he bade his province cease talking and do something—make decent roads, and provide better schools. With amazing celerity he organised and started Upper Canada College. No case of injustice stands against his name. Accusations against him of surrendering to the Compact are ill-founded. He had no illusions about the "Venetian" executive and Upper House which tried to exploit his name and authority. He thought the favoured Church "supine" and ill-staffed, and Strachan in his eyes was killing his religious influence by his political activities.[1] He believed the Anglican charter of the new university to be a mistake. He announced to the Colonial Secretary his intention to weaken the Compact at its centre: "We have now in the Executive Council the archdeacon and three of his scholars, the Chief Justice, his brother, and Mr Markland. I really think that it is right, as this establishment cannot be broken up, to increase it gradually".[2] At the same time he cherished no illusions about his power to change the independent tone of the Assembly, but suggested a union of all the provinces in which "the little demagogues of a small community, and the jealousy and suspicion of the local government might disappear".[3] His most serious error was the foundation and endowment of forty-four rectories just before he left in 1836. The action suggests a concentrated effort on the part of Dr Strachan to utilise the last chance favourable to the Anglican Church. In any case the way had been prepared for the measure by correspondence between Bathurst and Maitland, and more definitely in private letters from Goderich. Still the measure was ill-advised, and reflects unfavourably on Colborne's usually cool judgment.[4]

---

[1] C.O. 42/388, Colborne to Hay, 31 March 1829.　　[2] C.O. 42/389, Colborne to Murray, 1 October 1829.　　[3] C.O. 42/391, Colborne to Murray, 20 January 1830.
[4] *Correspondence between Lieut. Governor of U.C. and the S. of S. for the colonies on the creation of the rectories,* 1839.

Strangely enough it was the victory of the Government party in 1830 which really ruined Colborne's chances of success. Reinstated in public confidence in 1830, largely through the prevailing trust in the new Governor, a violently Tory majority proceeded to outrage law and the very spirit of the constitution by their treatment of Mackenzie, whom they not only expelled five times[1] after legitimate elections, but declared incapable of sitting and voting. All this was in no sense the work of Colborne, but the violent misuse of power by the representatives of the people of Upper Canada. Colborne's only public share was his direction in 1833 that Mackenzie should be admitted to take the oath.

Beneath these apparent troubles the province was actually not discontented, nor unprosperous; but Mackenzie's voice was louder than the quiet sounds of industry and peace from all the province outside York. The stars in their courses were fighting against the Lieutenant-Governor. The story of Mackenzie's expulsion and incapacitation had startled the Whig Cabinet in England, and embittered provincial opinion. The election of 1834 saw the Reformers once more in the ascendant in the House, and Mackenzie prepared for a vast orgy of grievance-hunting[2] which ended in the famous Seventh Report. That report seems finally to have convinced the British Ministry that a change of Governor was desirable. Indeed it may be admitted that in the critical state of Canadian opinion a subtler, more flexible, perhaps less honest mind might cope more easily with the situation. But Sir John Colborne left amid the regrets of the community—as a Toronto paper expressed it with unusual felicity, "never before had there been witnessed so much feeling with so little show".[3]

With the arrival of Sir Francis Head came the last calamitous phase of Upper Canadian history. Glenelg sinned often, but Head's appointment was his worst offence. He did nothing rightly, although, in sudden spurts of activity, again and again he seemed about to win the game. His instructions, although they refused to permit responsible government, were generous. But the new Lieutenant-Governor, after a bold attempt to modify his Council towards the reforming party, flung aside the experiment and turned suddenly to a course of daring but foolish autocracy. His failure dated from the day—12 March 1836—when Robert Baldwin, John Rolph, and J. H. Dunn resigned their recent appointments. His reservation of money bills in answer to the refusal of supplies by the Assembly merited Glenelg's implied reproof[4]; and his election campaign in

<hr>

[1] On Kingsford's reckoning four times (Kingsford, x, 322 n.).
[2] *Seventh Report from the Select Committee of the House of Assembly*, Toronto, 1835, answered in Glenelg's Instructions to Sir F. B. Head, 5 December 1835; Kennedy, W. P. M., *Documents*, pp. 412 ff.
[3] Kingsford, x, 296. The paper was the *Toronto Courier*.
[4] C.O. 42/434, Glenelg to Head, 6 September 1836.

1836 was a disaster to the Government which no Loyalist majority could possibly retrieve. By a strange fatality the electoral victory, which really meant defeat for Head, proved the crisis also in Mackenzie's career. The great agitator lost his seat at York, and with his seat went the last remnants of his political sanity. While Head was involving himself in recall by refusing to obey Glenelg's instructions to reinstate Ridout, a man whom he had quite unjustly deprived of office, and to offer Bidwell the next vacant judgeship,[1] Mackenzie passed rapidly through sedition to open treason. His newspaper *The Constitution* outdid the old *Colonial Advocate* in violent abuse. Attracted by the stir in Lower Canada, and ultimately acting in concert with the rebels there, he and his fellow extremists drew up in the "Declaration of the Reformers of Toronto" the first draft of a new declaration of independence, and proposed the calling of a convention and the appointment of commissioners who should join hands with representatives from Lower Canada. The autumn of 1837 saw arms collected, pikes forged, and drilling commenced. Cheered by Head's rash despatch of all his troops to the east, Mackenzie made his last visitation of the country, and fixed the day for his rising, 7 December 1837.

The disorders which began on 4 December 1837 cannot in any way be compared with the more serious revolt in Lower Canada. They were the fruit of Mackenzie's insane and disingenuous propaganda reiterated in primitive communities who were thus taught that the only remedy for their undefined grievances lay in a resort to violence. The rebel plans were dislocated at the outset by the sudden alteration of the day fixed for the attack from 7 December to 4 December. By the evening of Monday, 4 December, parties of deluded farmers, hungry, ill-armed, undisciplined, and without any intelligent leadership, had begun to collect round Montgomery's tavern, a public-house a few miles north of Toronto. For an interval of perhaps twenty-four hours the inaction of Sir Francis Head made the capture of the town a possibility; but even had Toronto fallen into the hands of the insurgents that would merely have intensified their final ruin. The men of Upper Canada had no intention of deposing Head to make Mackenzie president of a new republic; and even if the main body of public opinion had been less steady than it was, there never was a period in which Colborne, if he had been present, could not immediately have re-established order with half a battalion of regulars. While, in Toronto, Head was thwarting the sound plans of soldiers like Fitzgibbon, Mackenzie at Montgomery's tavern was behaving like the furiously incompetent commander of an ill-trained territorial battalion who has lost his bearings on a field day.

On Monday night, 4 December, each side had killed a man in

[1] On Ridout, Glenelg to Head, 5 April 1837; on Bidwell, Glenelg to Head, 14 July 1837 and 24 November 1837, all in C.O. 43/46, 47.

casual encounters. There was an exchange of shots on Tuesday between a loyal picket and the main body of insurgents, in which, after the first two volleys, both sides took to their heels. On Thursday, the date originally fixed for the rising, the Loyalists who had been crowding in to offer their services advanced, more than a thousand strong, against less than half that number of rebels who still loitered round the tavern. In twenty minutes the whole affair was over. The casualties were one rebel killed in action, and about twenty Loyalists and rebels wounded. The vanquished scattered on all sides to find shelter and hiding places, many, including Mackenzie, escaping to the United States. A similar but even less important rising took place in the London district, in which the numbers involved never seem to have exceeded 300, and in which the same utter lack of organisation led to the same collapse before the concentration of Loyalist volunteers. The one real danger to Canadian peace came in the later scattered attacks along the whole provincial frontier from Windsor to Prescott, conducted by groups of escaped rebels supported by American border ruffians; in their train these criminal excesses brought the risk of complications with the United States. For Mackenzie in exile attempted to use the violent anti-British prejudices of the American border population in his private war against the Canadian Government. At least one of these efforts nearly succeeded; for after Mackenzie had established a rebel outpost at Navy Island on the Canadian side of the Niagara River, and had begun to use the American steamer *Caroline* to keep up his communications with American sympathisers, a daring "cutting out" expedition led by Captain Drew, an old naval officer, destroyed the little craft in American waters, and set opinion in the border states aflame. Indeed, for the next two years, border incidents, all in some way connected with this unhappy rising, embittered intercourse between the two countries, and more than once threatened actual war.[1]

But already quieter and shrewder minds had diagnosed Canadian ailments and proposed the only adequate remedy. In 1828, Dr Baldwin with other reformers had petitioned that "a legislative Act be made in the Provincial Parliament, to facilitate the mode in which the present constitutional responsibility of the advisers of the local Governments may be carried practically into effect; not only by the removal of these advisers from office when they lose the confidence of the Parliament, but also by impeachment for the heavier offences chargeable against them".[2] Impeachment was too clumsy and obsolete a weapon for modern use, and the hotter heads had preferred the Lower Canadian outcry for an elective Legislative Council and other less essential projects. But Robert Baldwin, who shared little in the heats, and who had only once, in 1830, entered the Assembly as member, defined the true position in a clear and careful statement

---

[1] Dent, vol. II, *ad fin.* [2] Dunham, p. 166.

to Glenelg. The remedy, he held, "consists in nothing more than having the provincial government, as far as regards the internal affairs of the province, conducted by the Lieutenant-Governor (as representative of the paramount authority of the mother country) with the advice and assistance of the Executive Council, acting as a provincial Cabinet, and composed of men possessed of the public confidence, whose opinions and policy would be in harmony with the opinions and policy of the representatives of the people". Baldwin also shrewdly saw that "there was nothing in the charter which forbade the application of such a principle".[1] Twelve years later he helped to administer the scheme he had so clearly defined.

If the rebellion was an illogical and unnecessary episode in Canadian history, it still served to administer just such a rude irrational shock to slow-footed British wisdom as so often seems necessary for the production of the greater efforts of British statesmanship. As Gladstone based his Irish programme in 1868 on the effects of Fenian outrages, Durham's mission and *Report* were prepared for by Mackenzie's fiasco. It was essential that means should be found through which to reconcile executive authority with popular opinion. It was even more essential that some man of unusual competence and authority should come, acceptable to the colonists, trusted by the Imperial Government, and furnished with credit and resources sufficient to meet the material as well as the theoretic needs of the Canadians. Lord Durham's happy combination of sound doctrine and personal authority made his arrival at Quebec in 1838 an epoch in Canadian history.

(C) THE MARITIME PROVINCES (1815–1840)

In 1767 the old province of Nova Scotia—as yet undivided—possessed the only Assembly that was to survive the American Revolution. Homogeneous, as Quebec could never be, in population and economic interests, it inherited the naval and maritime traditions of the first Empire. Its political traditions too were rooted in New England. Thus while the cataclysm of the Quebec Act divorced that province in effect from the first Empire and gave to Canadian history an exotic strain for half a century, "the American question" continued without intermission in Nova Scotia until it was finally solved by "responsible government". Colonial policy after the Revolution found here an ideal environment. Within ten years the old Whig traditions were fairly submerged beneath the Loyalist migrations. The province was broken into four fragments, three of which were never again to be reunited. Nova Scotia, New Brunswick, Prince

[1] C.O. 42/434, 43/46, Baldwin to Glenelg, 13 July 1836. Enclosed in a despatch, Glenelg to Head, 20 August 1836. See too in *Report on Can. Arch.* 1923, p. 329.

Edward Island and Cape Breton still struggled with the sea and the wilderness as a homogeneous people, but it was necessary to grope their way forward towards self-government as isolated communities, reproducing, with rancour often intensified by its very pettiness, the chronic problems of the first Empire.

To their solution, however, each made a very distinctive contribution. New Brunswick, *par excellence* "the Province of the Loyalists", though the most conservative of the British provinces was the first to force a change in the Executive Council and to obtain the control of the Crown lands and revenues in return for a fixed Civil List. Nova Scotia with the oldest of popular Assemblies was also the first to achieve responsible government in its final form. Prince Edward Island, inheriting from the first Empire the intolerable burdens of absentee proprietorship, was in many respects the least harmonious of the British provinces. If New Brunswick was the first to control its Crown lands Prince Edward Island was the last. The province had been granted away in a single day. The ravages of that blunder were not repaired for more than a century until Prince Edward Island—the last of the American provinces—joined the Canadian Confederation in 1873. In so brief a survey many a local celebrity and many issues which in effect were solved in triplicate must be sacrificed to the broader perspective, and where differentiation is necessary the more distinctive achievement must prevail.

From the first Nova Scotia was a "frontier" of New England, with much which that term implies in the popular theory. For Shirley, the greatest of the colonial governors, Nova Scotia was "the key to British interests and dominion in America"—"the key of all the Eastern Colonies upon the Northern Continent".[1] Shirley's "Great Plan" of New England expansion northward was only partially effected, chiefly at the hands of others, but by the eve of the Revolution more than half the population of the province was classified as American. The settlements at Cornwallis, at Horton, at Liverpool, at the mouth of the St John, at Sunbury and the head of the Bay of Fundy were drawn from this source. "Their mark", writes Mac-Mechan, "is on every settlement they made to this day".[2] Other elements were less homogeneous. The first settlers at Halifax in 1749 were British, many of them disbanded troops and but too many of them "the King's bad bargains". The stolid thrifty Germans of Lunenburg County, a handful of Acadian French surviving "the expulsion", a few settlers from the north of Ireland and a vanguard of Highland Scots completed the *personnel* of settlement at the American Revolution. Then it was that the basic political traditions of the Maritime Provinces were definitely laid.

Governor Legge, resolute and honest but almost incredibly arro-

---

[1] Osgood, H. L., *The American Colonies in the XVIIIth Century*, III, 576; *Corresp. of W. Shirley*, ed. Lincoln, I, 346, 499; II, 148, 592, etc.   [2] *Canada and its Provinces*, XIII, 110.

gant and vindictive, followed Carleton in Quebec in reversing the "Great Plan" of Shirley and of Halifax for New England expansion northward. It required the concerted efforts of the Council and finally the secret Addresses of the Assembly to Crown, Lords and Commons to procure the Governor's recall. Legge's recall and the manner of it, however, confirmed the faith of the Assembly in the Board of Trade and the British connection. The Address of June 1775, drafted in secret within a few weeks of Lexington, invoked "the Spirit of Concord" in the cause of "Constitutional Freedom, to the British Race, in every part of the Globe".[1] That tradition of "confidence and moderation" was never broken. It became the first principle of local policy, and was doubly confirmed by the Loyalist immigrants, who nearly trebled the population of the province and held even the old Assembly suspect of "republican ideas".

The dismemberment of the old province was too prompt and systematic to be the result of local preferences. In William Knox's memorandum upon *New Establishments for the American Loyalists*, drawn up for Lord North in 1783, is to be found the project of "a new province" designed to "cherish monarchical principles and to repress republican ideas".[2] It became the order of the day to concentrate the executive and to disintegrate representative institutions—to govern, as Durham afterwards observed, "by means of division, and to break them down as much as possible into petty isolated communities, incapable of combination, and possessing no sufficient strength for individual resistance to the Empire".[3] The Loyalists had "had enough of Assemblies". In the Nova Scotian Assembly the old traditions survived. In that of New Brunswick the "American spirit of innovation" was more easily submerged. Cape Breton was denied an Assembly altogether, and Prince Edward Island narrowly escaped the same fate.[4] Thus was the second Empire to correct what Knox deemed to be the "vices" of the first. The fact that it ran the same course and but for better counsels would have invited the same dissolution was the challenge to a wiser statesmanship.

Even the War of 1812—a time of abounding prosperity—failed to isolate the British provinces from New England. The West Indian and inter-colonial trade from which Knox had sought in vain to exclude the independent states after 1783[5] was now in British hands, but New England was bitterly opposed to the war, and in the end almost defied the Union in order to continue its intercourse with the British provinces. Castine, established by the British in the State of Maine in order to accommodate this lucrative traffic, yielded a

---

[1] Pub. Arch. Can. *Series A* (transcripts of originals in P.R.O., London), xciv, 11.
[2] *Extra Official State Papers*, ii, Appendix xiv.
[3] *Report*, ed. Lucas, Sir C., ii, 66–7.
[4] "Reducing the Civil Establishment of it to a parallel with Cape Breton", Sydney to Parr, 29 May 1784, *Report on Can. Arch.* 1894, p. 419.
[5] Knox, ii, Appendix xiii.

buoyant revenue which afterwards contributed to the founding of Dalhousie College. In truth many thousands of the Loyalists had returned and "remained Citizens of that Government". In 1817 Dalhousie found "the connection between the respectable inhabitants of this Province, and the States...yet very intimate; scarcely a family that has not Fathers, Brothers, and near relations settled there".[1] To Howe and to Haliburton alike the gravest economic and national peril of the province was this fatal gravitation to New England, though their remedies were characteristically different. Mere allegiance was not an issue. Dalhousie himself was unable to detect "the most distant doubt of the Loyalty of this Province".[2] In political temper all three provinces were irrevocably British. In economic outlook however they continued to move within the orbit of New England. In these two grim facts—both of them dominant, yet mutually antagonistic—is to be found for a century and a half the basic problem of the Maritime Provinces.

The most lucrative early industries were the fisheries, lumbering, shipbuilding and privateering. During the Napoleonic Wars the Vice-Admiralty Court at Halifax once put up at auction twenty-three prize-ships in a single day. The fortunes of Captain Barss of the *Packet*, of Captain Godfrey of the *Rover*, of Enos Collins and the Cunards are but incidents of a long tradition. At Windsor fifteen square-rigged vessels were to be seen upon the stocks at one time. In two decades Pictou exported timber to the value of £2,000,000. The best masts for the British navy came from the St John.[3] In less than three years 150 square-rigged ships, sloops and schooners were built in New Brunswick, many of them by co-operative enterprise, long traditional in the New England fisheries. The whole process from the felling of the timber to the sale of ship and cargo in a British port was frequently the work of the same resourceful crew. The foundations of the Cunard shipping interests were laid at Halifax and on the Miramichi. In 1830 more than 1320 ships were owned in Nova Scotia alone, and the sea-faring population was estimated at 4500.

These conditions were curiously reflected in the politics of the period. In Nova Scotia the banking and mercantile interests flourished at Halifax—the only free port in the province—where the Government, the garrison and the chief naval base on the North Atlantic were already concentrated. Distances however were short, and carriage roads east and west from Halifax for 250 miles were "better than in any other Colony".[4] Agriculture, ruthlessly criticised in 1818 by Young in his *Letters of Agricola* in the *Acadian Recorder*, responded quickly to Young's enterprise and to Dalhousie's unfailing

[1] Pub. Arch. Can. *Series A*, CLVII, 159; CLX, 59.   [2] *Ibid.* CLVII, 10.
[3] Albion, R. G., *Forests and Sea Power*, pp. 292, 356.
[4] Pub. Arch. Can. *Series A*, CLXVIII, 18.

interest, but the contrast between adventitious wealth and official opulence in Halifax and the hard-driven thrift of the farmer embittered many a political contest. Five members of the Council were at one time partners in the Halifax Banking Company. All but one lived in Halifax, and nine of the twelve belonged to the Anglican Church, which comprised but one-fifth of the population. Blanchard and Howe thus found their natural allies among "the stout yeomen of the counties".

In Prince Edward Island politics followed still more closely the lines of economic cleavage. Across the Bench and the press, the Council and the Crown itself, is to be traced the trail of absentee landlordism. A few of the original holdings had been bought up by colonisers like Lord Selkirk, whose enterprise left its mark upon the whole history of the island,[1] and whose holdings were afterwards carefully dissociated from the endless feud over "the land question".[2] An Address of the Assembly in 1797 revealed that twenty-three of the sixty-seven townships had not a single settler. In twelve others there were thirty-six families. In 1802 £59,162 of quit-rents remained unpaid. On the other hand, the Assembly's agitation for the escheat of proprietary holdings was not altogether disinterested. The contest between the "Escheaters" and the proprietors—the "Snatchers" and the "Sticklers"—dominated every Administration. Governor Fanning's early ardour for reform cooled rapidly when arrears of quit-rents and enforced land-sales sufficed to sate the salaried officials and "the land hunger of these local speculators".[3] Governor Smith (1813–24), brother of the hero of Acre, championed "the sanctity of property" and rode rough-shod over all opposition. He confessed himself at loggerheads with the Assembly and half of his Council, with his Attorney-General and his Chief Justice; but with the help of his two sons-in-law he was ready to take on the whole round of devils. His son in petty spite once broke the windows of the Assembly room. John Stewart, when about to leave for England with an Address for the Governor's recall, narrowly escaped arrest by the Governor as chancellor of his own court. Haszard of the *Register* was laid "by the heels" for libel for printing these proceedings. Tremlett the Chief Justice and Smith himself were in the end cashiered, but the bad feeling which riddled the island threatened to infect the other provinces. Archibald the suave and adroit Speaker of Nova Scotia was appointed Chief Justice in 1824. He found little "beyond a continued history of quarrels and contentions.... I am desirous the example should never gain ground

---

[1] Selkirk, Earl of, *Present State of the Highlands*, Pub. Arch. Can. *Selkirk Papers, passim*; Macphail, in *Canada and its Provinces*, XIII, 354 seqq.; Warburton, *History of Prince Edward Island*, pp. 268 seqq.; Martin, Chester, *Lord Selkirk's Work in Canada*, pp. 21 seqq., 177 seqq.

[2] *Selkirk Papers*, 19180, 20311, 19079, etc.

[3] Harvey, D. C., *The Centenary of Edward Whelan*, p. 10.

among us". Governor Kempt of Nova Scotia was satisfied that "Squabbles" over the supply bill, even under Governor Reedy's conciliating Administration (1824–31), "will have a bad effect both in this Province and in New Brunswick. The whole Revenue about which the Council and Assembly are at Open War does not amount to £2000 a Year!!!...It is really too bad".[1]

During the 'thirties the agitation for either escheat or the penal taxation of wild lands culminated in an exhaustive joint memorial by the Legislature in 1838. Out of revenues of £107,600 less than £7500 had been contributed by the proprietors. Durham commended the memorial in a scathing letter which remained unknown until 1875. His *Report* charged "a handful of distant proprietors" with stifling the colony "in the very cradle of its existence".[2] In 1839 Cooper, the Speaker, went as a delegate to England, but was denied an audience at Downing Street. Against escheat, at least, the Colonial Office definitely set its face.[3] For sixty years of the second Empire, Prince Edward Island is strangely reminiscent of Maryland during the first.

The good fortune of New Brunswick in this respect was exceptional among the British provinces. Saint John as an incorporated city—the first in Canada—was not the capital of the province and was thus never tempted to play the rôle of Halifax in Nova Scotia. After the removal of the Crown monopoly over pine timber for the navy, wealth and commercial enterprise were more evenly distributed than in any other province in America. Alexander Stewart of Nova Scotia once stressed in a confidential memorandum the difference between the Nova Scotia and New Brunswick Assemblies. Crane and Wilmot, Simonds and Johnston—"in fact nearly all the members" in New Brunswick—were "men of considerable and some of them of large property, while our House, are comparatively poor men".[4]

The commercial depression which followed the War of 1812 drew many political issues in the three provinces into the same channels. The convention of 1818 with the United States, as *Agricola* notes bitterly, left "the American flag...triumphant in the port of Halifax". For eight years addresses and petitions innumerable sought "the same freedom of trade with all the world which the people of the United States have acquired". Here, as during the Revolution, the temper was intended to be exemplary. A joint Address of Council and Assembly in Nova Scotia "as the senior British Government in the North American Colonies" was circulated among the other provinces. It appealed, not to "factious and seditious murmurings",

[1] Pub. Arch. Can. *Series G*, cccix, 154; cccx, 89, 152, 198, 251, etc.; Archibald to Kempt, 12 May 1828; Kempt to Hay, 14 May 1828, N.S. *Series A*, clxix, 64, 63. Huskisson had decided the issue in favour of the Assembly (*ibid.*).
[2] *Report*, ed. Lucas, ii, 198; Campbell, D., *History of Prince Edward Island*, p. 89.
[3] C.O. 226/60, Russell to FitzRoy, 17 Sept. 1839.
[4] Pub. Arch. Can. *C.O.* 217 (photostatic copies of originals in P.R.O.), clxv, 693.

but to the "confidence and assistance of the Mother Country".[1] In truth the reforms of the trade laws in 1826 were a landmark in colonial history. In his *Proposal for Confederation* in that year the aged Uniacke—once a "Cumberland rebel" but for more than forty years Assemblyman, Speaker, Attorney-General and Executive Councillor of Nova Scotia—asserted that the loss of the thirteen colonies "would not have taken place" had British policy "met the wishes of the North American Colonies fifty years ago with the same liberality".[2]

A contest with the British Treasury after 1826 for the control of customs revenues ran true to the same traditions.[3] Again the Nova Scotia Assembly—"a Pattern to other Colonies for Moderation and Harmony"—was disposed to be "liberal and moderate in all their Proceedings and thereby set a good example to the other Colonies" by appropriating the revenues but voting the salaries of customs officials in their own supply bill. "No other Colony", noted Governor Kempt, "has made such an offer". Before the issue was set at rest, however, the House under the able leadership of Alexander Stewart and C. R. Fairbanks had taken up ground which they refused "under any circumstances, to compromise or relinquish". The following year (1830) came the famous "brandy dispute"; and Fairbanks left at Downing Street a memorandum of prophetic insight for the reform of the Executive Council. "The remedy is to be found in applying to the colonies the same principles on which the Government is conducted at home". Advisers of the Governor ought to be sought in the Assembly which "ought to possess powers similar to those exercised by the House of Commons. They have repeatedly claimed these as their right and *will* exercise them".[4]

To this traditional temper and moderation the Maritime Reformers attributed the distinctive achievements which we have now to examine. Thus while the stormy experiences with Mackenzie and the Canadian "ultras" and Tories deterred Glenelg from granting an interview even to Robert Baldwin who had crossed the Atlantic upon that mission in 1836, the access to the Colonial Office from New Brunswick and Nova Scotia remained assured and uninterrupted.[5] In the pigeon-holes of Downing Street were to be found memoranda from Simonds, Chandler, Crane and Wilmot, Fairbanks, Archibald, Huntington and Young among the Reformers and from the aged Uniacke, from Baillie, from Wilkins and Stewart and Samuel Cunard

---

[1] Pub. Arch. Can. *Series A*, CLX, 59 seqq.

[2] Uniacke to Bathurst, 11 Apr. 1826, *ibid.* CLXVII, 332 seqq.

[3] In abolishing fees the British Treasury had directed the payment of salaries of customs officials directly from customs revenues.

[4] Kempt to Horton, 17 Apr. 1826; 10 Feb., 8 Apr. 1827, Pub. Arch. Can. *Series A*, CLXVII, 61; CLXVIII, 10, 42; CLXXII, 86 seqq.; *Journals*, 23 Mar. 1829.

[5] This does not apply to Prince Edward Island. Cooper, Speaker of the Assembly, went to London in 1839 to urge escheat but could not get access to the Colonial Office. Campbell, p. 93.

and officials unnumbered from the circles of the provincial "Compacts". In 1838 Howe himself appeared at the Colonial Office without introduction and was taken in for half an hour with Glenelg. "What passed", notes Howe in his diary, "not fit to put into Note Book which might fall into other hands".

The only instance, Howe notes in 1839 in the first of his *Letters to Lord John Russell*, where a dominant Assembly had displaced an Executive Council was in New Brunswick, but "the struggle lasted as long as the Trojan War", and it failed to establish a practice for the future. For two generations official life there had moved in an atmosphere of affluence and staid respectability. The first Governor had held office for thirty-three years, fourteen of them as an absentee in England. Jonathan Odell and his son William held the office of Provincial Secretary for nearly sixty years; the first mayor of Saint John held office for ten and his successor for twenty years. For thirty years every member of the Executive and Legislative Council was an Anglican, and every judge of the Supreme Court until 1851. The first three Attorneys-General held office for sixty-three years, the first Surveyor-General for thirty-two years and the first Solicitor-General for twenty-five. "The members of the Council", says Raymond, "grew old together".[1]

Under Sir Archibald Campbell (1831–7) many issues common to all the provinces arose at last in New Brunswick. The Dissenters' Marriage Bill—an issue sagaciously adjusted by the Supreme Court in Nova Scotia—was frustrated by the Council for ten years and carried only in 1834. On the other hand, Goderich's instructions of 1832 for the separation of the Executive and Legislative Councils were thwarted, as we shall see, in Nova Scotia, and carried out almost perfunctorily in New Brunswick.[2] The Crown lands issue, however, was indigenous and its solution was unique. The commercial panic of 1825 had concentrated attention upon the abuses in the Crown lands department. The Commissioner, Baillie, was one of Bathurst's nominees, and his position as a "stranger, i.e. not the descendant of a loyalist" was "sufficient *of itself* (wrote Campbell) to create ill-will".[3] But there was more than this in the criticism. A revenue of £14,913 from the Crown lands cost £5929 to collect, and Baillie himself admitted a salary and fees (1827) of £2600 per year. No doubt private interests were involved, but the Governor refused the returns demanded by the House, and by 1833 both the Governor and Baillie were employing all the stock phrases of the Tory vocabulary against "Mischievous Agitators", "self interested and mischievous demagogues", bent upon "Paralysing the Arm of the Executive". "I think I see republican principles fast

---

[1] *Canada and its Provinces*, XIII, 167.
[2] *British Parl. Papers*, 27 Aug. 1839, (579) pp. 6, 55.
[3] Campbell to Goderich, 5 Mar. 1833, Pub. Arch. Can. *C.O.* 188 (transcripts from the P.R.O.), XLV, 117.

rising in this Province". There was a "love of innovation which... would speedily lay the respectability and prosperity of the Province prostrate at its feet".[1]

As early as 1832 the House had proposed "to take upon itself the civil List", in return for the Crown lands and revenues. Petitions poured in to the Assembly, and a Committee of Grievances sat with closed doors. "Two brothers of the name of Simonds", wrote the Governor, "are the demagogues of the day". In 1833 Charles Simonds and E. B. Chandler were appointed by the Assembly to carry their protest to the Colonial Office. The Governor refused letters of introduction, but referred them to Goderich's "well known accessibility".[2] When Simonds and Chandler reached London they found E. G. Stanley in office and Baillie himself in attendance there with "the unreserved confidence of Sir Archibald Campbell".[3] In truth both the Governor and his *protégé* appear to poor advantage beside the studied moderation of the "Mischievous Agitators". By 4 August Stanley was prepared to agree to a Civil List of £14,000. A Treasury Memorandum adds that in controlling "the whole of the local resources" the Assembly "must necessarily exercise a complete control over all persons employed for that purpose".[4] Baillie declined a lucrative position which Stanley offered him in Jamaica, but in November 1833 Sir Archibald, almost articulate with vexation, applied for the government of Nova Scotia. "Take the wicked from before the King", quoted the Fredericton *Courier*, "and his throne shall be established in righteousness".

But the contest was not so easily won. The Assembly had scarcely passed their resolution of acceptance when an express despatch sent through New York reserved the proceeds from the Nova Scotia and New Brunswick Land Company—a colonising venture of great promise—from the revenues to be surrendered to the Assembly. "The bargain was up.... Mr. Stanley had not kept faith with the Assembly", reads the scathing indictment of Crane and Wilmot in 1836. "He would not have acted in such a manner towards an independent State".[5] It was not until 1836 that a second delegation, William Crane and L. A. Wilmot, renewed negotiations with Glenelg. The details were easily settled, and a draft Civil List Bill was prepared by the Lords of the Treasury. But the administration of the Crown lands, as distinct from the revenues, was no longer included in the agreement. For a time Crane and Wilmot urged a "peremptory rule" that the Executive Council must include representatives of the

---

[1] Pub. Arch. Can. *C.O.* 188 (transcripts from the P.R.O.), XLV, 75, 117, 139; XLIII, 167.

[2] *Ibid.* The Simonds family of Saint John were pre-revolutionary New Englanders of great wealth and influence. *Journals*, 15 and 18 Mar. 1833, pp. 123, 133.

[3] "...Who has commissioned me". Pub. Arch. Can. *C.O.* 188, XLVIII, 8.

[4] *Ibid.* XLVI, 70, 212.

[5] *Journals*, 1836–7, Appendix, p. iv.

Assembly, but Glenelg held resolutely that "the prerogative is unfettered", and commended the "just delicacy" of the delegates in waiving the point.[1] The Assembly passed the draft bill without the alteration of a syllable, "with hearts full of the warmest duty and gratitude". But Sir Archibald had not yet shot his last bolt. He reserved the bill; and the House in exasperation sent Crane and Wilmot again to Downing Street with a brief that was not to be gainsaid. The Governor and his Council had "lost the entire confidence of the country". The only two votes recorded in opposition were cast appropriately by Messrs End and Street.

Upon their second arrival in London, however, Crane and Wilmot found that Sir Archibald had already sent in his resignation. Glenelg bore witness that the Assembly "had acted in the most liberal and handsome manner".[2] Sir Archibald Campbell had solemnly avowed that "implicit reliance cannot be placed on the scrupulous observance of any engagements the House of Assembly may be willing to Contract". To Sir John Harvey, Campbell's successor, Glenelg wrote in a different strain. The Assembly offered to add £500 voluntarily to the Civil List to cover unforeseen charges for exchange. Such was their "cordiality", their "strict and honorable...adherence to the spirit rather than the letter of the pledges given on their behalf by Messrs Crane and Wilmot". Sir John Harvey's assent to the Civil List Bill was given on 17 July 1837. Upon his own responsibility he added to the Executive Council those who in the words of Charles Simonds himself—now Speaker of the Assembly—commanded the "entire confidence" of the House. Wilmot moved for a "full length portrait" of Glenelg to be hung in the Assembly Room. Sir John Harvey closed the chapter appropriately by a tribute to Glenelg's "noble support", and for Queen Victoria "the homage of...heartfelt gratitude".[3] The accrued revenues from Crown lands (£150,000) which now fell to the disposal of the Assembly must have accounted for much of their complacency. When Sydenham visited New Brunswick in 1840, he reported that it was "impossible not to be struck with the difference between the political state of New Brunswick and that of the other Provinces of British North America. While elsewhere Society is distracted...there reigns in New Brunswick the most perfect tranquillity and an entire harmony between the Executive and the Legislature....No doubt much is due to the good sense of the Inhabitants".[4] But the problem of "colonial government" was not yet solved, for the Assembly had expressly decided to

---

[1] *Journals*, 20 Dec. 1836—1 Mar. 1837, Appendix, p. xvi.
[2] Glenelg discussed with Crane and Wilmot the feasibility of a union of the British provinces shortly afterwards projected by Roebuck and Durham. *Ibid.* 6–22 July 1837, Appendix, no. 1.
[3] 10 Mar. 1832, Pub. Arch. Can. *C.O.* 188, XLIII, 167; *Journals*, 6–22 July 1837, pp. 423, 461; *British Parl. Papers*, 27 Aug. 1839, (579) p. 76.
[4] Thomson, P., to Russell, 27 July 1840, Pub. Arch. Can. *Series G*, CLXXXIV, pt 2.

"repudiate the claims set up by another Colony" for an Executive Council "at all times" subject to the Assembly.[1]

Before tracing the grim contest of that other colony for responsible government in its final form, a word must be said of another issue which deeply affected the temper and interests of the Maritime Provinces. An attempt to arbitrate on the Maine boundary dispute had failed in 1831. The "Madawaska Settlers"—chiefly French Acadians —had established themselves upon the upper reaches of the St John River as early as 1786, but by 1835 the coveted pine timber of the Restook, the Madawaska and the Fish Rivers, western tributaries of the St John, had attracted the most aggressive timber crews of both nationalities in the "disputed territory". The fact that it could reach the mills only through British territory by way of the St John was an advantage which the New Brunswick lumbermen were not slow to seize. By 1839 both Governments professed a policy of respecting the "disputed territory". In February the New Brunswick warden found nine crews at work there and confiscated their timber. Meanwhile the Maine Legislature met with closed doors, and the Governor of the State sent Rufus McIntire, senator and land agent, to the Restook River. The Woodstock lumbermen—"hardy, brave, loyal, and I will add submissive Subjects", as Sir John Harvey wrote to Glenelg—retaliated by "borrowing" 250 muskets from the militia. At the Governor's proclamation "every Stand of Arms and Round of ammunition" was dutifully returned; but not, adds Harvey, before the American senator and two of his officers had been captured and carried off to Fredericton, whence the Attorney-General hastened to liberate them on parole.[2]

Counter-arrests followed. Harvey had 1000 militia and nearly 500 regulars on the St John, when the fortunate appearance of General Scott, Harvey's "gallant and talented friend" and enemy in the War of 1812, gave an opening for conciliation. In March a truce was made between Harvey and Governor Fairfield, but the "declamation, bluster and excitement" in the Maine Legislature which Harvey contrasted with the grim resolution of his own made a more permanent settlement imperative. In the following year an American party took a post on the Fish River, and Harvey wrote in November that "not a moment should be lost" in sending troops into the district.[3] The Governor-General responded with cool resolution, only to discover that Harvey had reopened negotiations with Fairfield, compromising both the Governor-General and himself, and virtually promising the withdrawal of the troops. Sydenham's scathing resentment and Harvey's recall after a "career of Public Service of 47 years" (as he wrote bitterly to Lord John Russell)

[1] *Journals*, 6–22 July 1837, p. 475.
[2] Harvey to Glenelg, 18 Feb. 1839, Pub. Arch. Can. N.B. Despatches Sent, vol. VII.
[3] Harvey to Sydenham, 14 Nov. 1840, Pub. Arch. Can. *Series G*, CCLII, 271.

cannot be examined here; but the appearance of regular troops on both sides freed the issue at least from the "blustering Warriors" of the hustings in the State of Maine.[1]

For the treaty which finally closed the dispute no wiser British plenipotentiary could have been chosen than Lord Ashburton. As head of the Baring financial interests his knowledge of American conditions was unsurpassed. He was a director of the St Andrews and Quebec Railroad Company then projected through the disputed territory. His opponent, Daniel Webster, as the *Baring Papers* show, was under the deepest personal obligations to him. The "war of maps" which was scarcely less fantastic than "the Restook War"— the "war of pork and beans" as it was jocularly known at that time— is traced elsewhere;[2] but though the results for the United States were "under all the circumstances, to say the least, favourable for them", as Lord Ashburton wrote to Bagot,[3] the terms have been defended with authority from the British point of view.[4] New Brunswick obtained nearly 900 square miles formerly awarded to Maine by the abortive arbitration of 1831.

During "the Restook War" the Reform Assembly of Nova Scotia, as we shall see, voted £100,000 and called out the militia. But the Reformers there were more radical than those of New Brunswick in their temper and more discerning in their tactics. Within four years they moved with precision to the neatest and perhaps the most temperate of all demonstrations of responsible government.

The biography of Joseph Howe has long done service for the history of that contest in Nova Scotia. No figure of that day so dominates the background of local history. Son of John Howe, King's Printer, Postmaster-General and founder of the *Weekly Chronicle*, he had begun as a "printer's boy" with Tory traditions, but with an instinctive distrust for "the caprice of men in office". As editor of *The Novascotian* he won a unique place in the confidence of his native province and in British American journalism. In the throes of conflict he sometimes descended to extravagances which impaired his cause and led him at his worst into indiscretions which passed at the Colonial Office for cardinal sins. At his greatest Howe was the Burke of the second Empire. In magnanimity, in breadth of view, in grasp of first principles and of British traditions at their best, both were pre-eminently right. In the realm of political litera-ture, too, both have the prodigality of genius, and such genius at its height transcends criticism. Consistency frequently rewards the narrower intensiveness of mere talent. But in Howe's temper, as in Burke's, there was much that was "meant for mankind", and to

---

[1] Captain Webster (U.S.A.) in Maclauchlan to Reade, 2 Feb. 1841, Pub. Arch. Can. *Ganong Papers*, M. 744.   [2] Vol. II.
[3] 26 July 1842, Pub. Arch. Can. *Bagot Papers*, II, 482.
[4] White, J., in *Canada and its Provinces*, VIII, 815 seqq.

this day tradition records his abounding energy, his long rambles to the remotest villages of his native province, his love for the solitudes of its forests and for the sea, his abiding faith in his countrymen. At one of the darkest hours of his life—a certain "Black Saturday" in London—he records the reflection that they "have never failed me". In truth their "steadiness" for which he thanked God in the hour of his triumph was the reward of his own, for never were followers more responsive to confidence than Howe's in Nova Scotia.

The first forecasts of responsible government, as we have seen, were not his. But between his day and the earlier influence of Fairbanks and Alexander Stewart and S. W. G. Archibald, there is a great gulf fixed. Murdock, Sydenham's secretary, once revealed ingenuously the traditional tactics of the Colonial Office in dealing with troublesome reformers. Fairbanks at the height of his influence was translated out of the Assembly into the Vice-Admiralty Court; Stewart to the Legislative and Executive Council. Archibald, the venerable Speaker, who poured oil upon the troubled waters for twenty years, once remarked that "Assemblies require to be moulded by men of understanding". He too passed to his reward as Attorney-General and Master of the Rolls. No fewer than three Executive Councillors had served their time in the Speaker's chair, and one of them was known to deplore the "Supply of Patriots" in the Assembly: they would "thwart and embarrass the Executive Government because it cannot employ and reward them".[1] For Howe too the net was spread. A couplet in his commonplace book is characteristic:

> As Bees on Flowers alighting, cease their hum,
> So, settling upon Places, Whigs grow dumb.[2]

But there were less sardonic traditions of "honourable ambition" in Nova Scotia. Nowhere did official life reach a higher level of honour and of private integrity. In truth the quixotic resentment of the Council against the new order is the measure of their prestige and of their sensitiveness. In the famous "brandy dispute" of 1830 they threw out a supply bill and a revenue of £25,000 because the Assembly had "outraged the rules which regulate the intercourse of Gentlemen". Seven years later by the same tactics they forced Howe to rescind the Twelve Resolutions because a phrase in one of them imputing self-interest "at the expense of the public" violated "that decorum which regulates the intercourse of society".[3] But the cultured and exclusive circles of Halifax were not, as James Stephen of the Colonial Office notes, a school for "Public Spirit". The voice of Nova Scotia, attuned to a more robust and native patriotism, was

---

[1] Scrope, G. P., *Life of Lord Sydenham*, 1843, p. 117; Archibald to Kempt, 12 May 1828, Pub. Arch. Can. *Series A*, CLXIX, 64; CLXXIII, 14.

[2] For "Places" offered to Howe see Pub. Arch. Can. *Series A*, CLXV, 589; *Howe Papers*, I, 21, etc.

[3] Pub. Arch. Can. *Series A*, CLXXI, 125; Chisholm, J. A., *Speeches...of Joseph Howe*, I, 142.

to be found in the *Acadian Recorder* of the Holland family, in the *Colonial Patriot* of Jotham Blanchard, and in the *Novascotian* of Joseph Howe. The libel action against Howe in 1835 was a direct challenge to this new order, and after his dramatic defence Howe appealed fittingly to his followers to "teach their children the names of the twelve men who had established the freedom of the press".

It is impossible here to linger upon Howe's spectacular rise to the leadership of the Reform Assembly of 1836-40—his breach with Stewart, his "flashes" (as he used to call them) of political insight, his incomparable courage. Howe's *Legislative Reviews* in the *Novascotian* since 1830 account for much of this mastery; and it was confirmed by his tactics—one of his "flashes"—in rescinding the Twelve Resolutions and substituting an Address to the Crown. In that Address the early preference for an elective council is tempered by a broader expediency. Thenceforth the Nova Scotian Reformers concentrated with growing incisiveness upon the separation of the Executive from the Legislative Council, and the employment there of ministers "who *enjoy the confidence of the people* and can *command a majority in the popular branch*". Three years later the inflexible resolution of Herbert Huntington—the Baldwin of Nova Scotia—and the incomparable tactics of Howe had brought the Colonial Office to a pass of perplexity and consternation that it taxed the mercurial genius of Sydenham himself to ward off that "objectionable principle".

Glenelg's response to the Address confirmed that much maligned statesman in the esteem of the Maritime Provinces. Nothing could exceed his "candour, and frankness, and liberality". The separation of the two Councils—directed by Goderich in 1832 and deliberately thwarted at Halifax[1]—was now made peremptory. In desperation Glenelg directed the publication of the despatches—a retribution, as James Stephen notes, "which Sir Colin Campbell has brought upon himself".[2] For the first time four Executive Councillors were to be chosen from the Assembly and could answer there for government policy.

But with the Canadian imbroglio it was clear that responsible government was in no "state for decision nor even discussion" in Downing Street. A solemn protest by Howe as early as 1835 against Papineau's "uncompromising and offensive spirit" was now published in an attempt to salvage the cause in Nova Scotia from "the two maddest rebellions on record". Papineau's insensate tactics were opposed by "at least seven-eighths of the population", and his addresses were "left on the Table" by the Assembly.[3] Even the Durham mission served only to confound the reorganisation of the Council.[4] A delegation from Nova Scotia, with the old Compact still

---

[1] *British Parl. Papers*, 27 Aug. 1839, (579) p. 5; Pub. Arch. Can. *Series A*, CLV, 145.
[2] Pub. Arch. Can. *Series A*, CLXIII, 845. [3] *Ibid.* CLXI, 605.
[4] Through an error in Durham's Commission.

in the ascendant, met Durham only after the fatal breach with Melbourne, and contributed little but an impression of "striking ability...and polish of manners which are even less commonly met with in colonial society". Howe too added a paper of great power and moderation, but the "Durham fiasco", as it appeared at the time, cast a shadow of gloom and despair.[1] Even the New Brunswick Assembly, as we have seen, went out of its way to "repudiate the claim set up by another Colony" for responsible government. In Nova Scotia alone, it seemed, the Reformers held grimly an unbroken front. In desperation such as they had never known they determined to send Huntington and George Young to face the issue with the Colonial Office.

Their only credentials—the exemplary traditions of the Assembly— were spectacularly enhanced upon the eve of their departure. Amidst cheers that were caught up in the lobbies and spread to the streets of Halifax, the House unanimously voted £100,000, and called out the militia, as we have seen, for the defence of the New Brunswick boundary in the threatened "Aroostook War". "Never", wrote Howe in the *Novascotian*, "have we witnessed such a heart-stirring scene". But the Council threw out the vote for the expenses of the delegates, and they finally sailed from Halifax at their own expense, as forlorn a hope, Huntington wrote bitterly, as ever championed a desperate cause.

The delegation of 1839 achieved more than appeared upon the surface; though its immediate mission was foredoomed to failure, for in June Lord John Russell announced his pontifical doctrine of "colonial government". But the invaluable counsels of Charles Buller established contacts that were never broken. Huntington and Young returned to find that Durham's *Report* had run like wildfire through the columns of the *Novascotian*, while Howe himself in another of his old "flashes" was forging his four open *Letters* against the "cleft stick" of Lord John Russell's Olympian logic.

By common consent the *Letters to Lord John Russell*[2] have been enshrined with Durham's *Report* and Buller's *Responsible Government for the Colonies* in the political literature of the language. Two only of Howe's theses can be noted here. Lord John Russell had predicated an Executive Council under a "Governor receiving instructions from the Crown on the responsibility of a Secretary of State". Howe and Buller between them—perhaps the nearest akin of British and colonial Reformers—crowned this bicephalous hobgoblin of "colonial government" with satirical laughter. The "responsibility" of "Mr Mother Country" Buller traced to the clerks in the attics of Downing Street, while Howe overwhelmed with merciless badinage the solemn

---

[1] Buller, C., *Sketch of Lord Durham's Mission*, Pub. Arch. *Report* 1923, p. 358; Pub. Arch. Can. *Durham Papers*, III, 126.

[2] Kennedy, W. P. M., *Documents of the Canadian Constitution*, pp. 480 seqq.

fiction of a transient governor in the hands of virtual life-councillors, presuming to govern by "instructions from the Crown". "He may flutter and struggle in the net...but he must at last resign himself to his fate". There could be no end to colonial grievances until the Governor could "shake off this thraldom" by an "appeal to the people".

But Howe's *Letters* closed upon a more poignant note which made them an epitome of Nova Scotian traditions. "Have we done anything to justify the alienation of our birthright?...This is not the race that can be hoodwinked with sophistry....All suspicion of disloyalty we cast aside as the product of ignorance or cupidity; we seek for nothing more than British subjects are entitled to; but we will be contented with nothing less." In truth, though the *Letters* were addressed to a Secretary of State, the sure touch of a master moulded them to the deepest political instincts of the race.

Less than a month after Howe's four *Letters* Lord John Russell's despatch of 16 October 1839 at last broke the Governor's "thraldom" to his life-councillors by authorising him to change his Executive Council at will upon "motives of public policy". Few documents of so momentous an import have been so curiously misconstrued. Sir John Harvey in New Brunswick referred to it as "a new, and... improved Constitution",[1] and Howe claimed truly that "it bestowed all that was required" for responsible government. But its immediate purpose was vastly different—in Russell's own phrase, "freedom of action" for the Executive. Sir Colin Campbell interpreted it bluntly as "intended...merely to strengthen the hands of the Governor by enabling him more effectually to control refractory Public functionaries"; and Vernon Smith of the Colonial Office adds the conclusive comment that Sir Colin was "right in his interpretation of Lord John's letter".[2] This, too, was Sir John Harvey's conception, as a careful examination of his *Circular* makes manifest. Russell himself barred Howe from the Executive Council because "it might appear a sanction to the opinions of his recent publication".[3] In truth Lord John Russell's conception of "colonial government" at this time, with all his benevolent "motives of public policy", was governance and not self-government, and it was to be as thoroughgoing as his imperial logic.

But the despatch, as Howe saw at a glance, could be made to serve a very different purpose. In Canada the Governor-General had just avowed the Queen's instructions to govern "according to the well understood wishes and interests of the people". For the first time the House could test, to a certainty, whether the Governor was disposed to employ those who had the confidence of "*a majority*

[1] Pub. Arch. Can. N.B. Despatches Sent, *C.O.* 188, III, 24 Dec. 1839.
[2] Governor's *Letter Book*, Halifax, 1 Mar. 1840; Pub. Arch. Can. *Series A*, CLXXIV, marginal note on Campbell's despatch of 4 Apr. 1840.
[3] *British Parl. Papers*, 1840, (181) p. 6; Pub. Arch. Can. *Series A*, CLXXI, 433.

in the popular branch". On 3 February 1840 Howe moved four resolutions with the now classic formula that "the Executive Council, as at present constituted, does not enjoy the confidence of the Commons". In a speech of great power and magnanimity he appealed to both parties "to unite to give a constitution to our country" with seemly pride that the foundations of "these great changes should be laid here".[1]

For the Governor there was now no escape. He was not at liberty to change his Executive Council "collectively", and Lord John Russell, with the spectre of responsible government now clearly before his eyes, hastened to reaffirm that refusal. Sydenham, too, issued the warning that "the demand...involves the establishment of this objectionable principle" which "could only be met when thus urged by a refusal".[2] Howe's flawless tactics had demonstrated beyond a doubt either that the Governor had violated his instructions or that he had been instructed to withstand responsible government. Inspired by the austere resolution of Herbert Huntington, "five-and-twenty stern men" voted the next step—an Address for the Governor's recall. Howe who drafted "every line of it" once called it "the severest trial of my life....If ever I performed a task with a heavy heart it was that". In truth gallant old Sir Colin, chained by his instructions, and Howe like a soldier "called out on a firing party", were but symbols of an issue which lay with Lord John Russell himself. He it was who claimed "the responsibility", and his, as we shall see, was the sorry stratagem by which both Sir Colin's blunt *insouciance* and the most magnanimous of appeals for responsible government were for the time circumvented.[3]

With the Assembly's vote of want of confidence—thirty to twelve— J. B. Uniacke, son of the old "Cumberland rebel" and afterwards the "first premier overseas under responsible government", resigned from the Executive Council amidst the execrations of the Family Compact and joined the ranks of the Reformers. "From that hour", exclaimed Howe, too confidently, "they might date...a constitution of which no power on earth could now deprive them".[4]

---

[1] Chisholm, I, 292.
[2] Pub. Arch. Can. *Series A*, CLXXIV, 275; *Series G*, CCCLXXXVII, 209; vol. CLXXXIV.
[3] See below, chapter xiv, and Martin, Chester, *Empire and Commonwealth*, chapter iv.
[4] Chisholm, I, 295.

CHAPTER XI

THE MISSION OF THE EARL OF DURHAM

IN 1838 England, on the threshold of a great period of colonial expansion, was struggling in perplexity towards a policy for her new Empire, and in Canada men were still seeking for some practical expedient which would bring into unison the discordant elements which persisted in thwarting and cancelling each other's chances of development. It was the lot of the Earl of Durham, by his impetuous indiscretions as well as by his wisdom, to discover for his country the answer to its perplexities, and to begin the reconciliation of the warring forces in Canada to each other and to the mother country. This he did in a brief mission of five months and by the precipitate compilation of a report. Eighty years earlier Chatham had imposed on a distracted England the idea of empire; now it fell to Durham to play the part of a second Chatham, less experienced, masterful and self-sufficing, to proclaim the essential unity between England and her colonies, to quicken the political imagination and shatter the hampering conventions of the governing classes, and to commit them to a greatness which they had not sufficient audacity to understand.

Between 1830 and 1838 the Earl of Durham had been the ugly duckling of English politics. Seldom had the organised government of England been less in touch with the living powers of the country than in the year when Earl Grey became Prime Minister; and the reforming Whigs, with all their good intentions and bold practice, soon felt the numbing power of an unsympathetic monarchy, a hostile House of Lords, and the tyrannical spirit of social and political conventionality. Radical reform, chafing at the incompleteness of the surrender to its demands, grew boisterous, ill-mannered and extravagant. It was Durham's misfortune that he had a place in neither camp. Important as his influence had been while the scheme of Parliamentary reform was in the making, it declined within Grey's ministry as experience revealed how incompatible his views of national reform were with those of the orthodox Whigs. Earl Grey himself, whose daughter Durham had married, watched his son-in-law's progress with constantly decreasing patience; Sir James Graham declared him an impossible colleague;[1] and he was too completely Lord Melbourne's opposite in temper, manners, and understanding, to be pleasing to Grey's successor in the headship of the party. On the other hand Durham found it increasingly difficult to accommodate himself to Joseph Hume's addlepated Radicalism, or the

[1] Parker, C. S., *Life and Letters of Sir J. Graham*, I, 180.

more advanced ideas and methods of the extreme left. The Radical group was a vague and changing shadow, and in any case Durham had no inclination to be the Mirabeau of an English Revolution. After his resignation from office in 1833, he remained a conspicuous, influential, puzzling figure in politics—one whose future it was impossible to predict, but whose present standing was as uncomfortable to his former colleagues as to himself. His embassy at St Petersburg, between 1835 and 1837, relieved the Government of their most dangerous friend and critic, while it gave Durham himself temporary occupation for powers probably more considerable than those of any of the ministers whom he served. It was not unnatural, as Canadian affairs grew darker throughout 1837, that his should be the name which occurred to Melbourne for an experiment in imperial knight-errantry in North America.

The character of the Earl of Durham will reveal itself in the story of his misadventures and victory, but at the outset it is important, among impressions of irascibility, moodiness, love of display, and impatience with fools or sluggards, to remember the real singleness of mind which led him always to identify himself with the work he had in hand;[1] and, even more, an unexpected and secret humility, which intimates alone suspected, and which, robbing him, as it did, of the appearance of success, gave him at the end self-control sufficient to subordinate his private discontents to the welfare of the colony which he had governed. "He had an abundance of political courage, sometimes, perhaps, a little approaching to rashness", Hobhouse noticed, "but in his intercourse with his friends he was by no means overbearing, nor, excepting in public controversy, arrogant or overbearing. In fact he did not attach so much value to his character or opinions as to give himself a sufficient amount of self-confidence in matters of importance".[2] The swelling port and regal display which caught the eye of gossips in England and Canada were only Durham's peculiar way of impressing on those with whom he worked the grandeur of the imperial idea which possessed him.

The history of the mission began with a letter from Melbourne in July 1837, in which the Prime Minister invited Lord Durham to render a great and important service to Her Majesty, her ministers, and the country, by undertaking the settlement of the affairs of British North America.[3] In retrospect it is now clear that whoever entered on the task did so with two fatal handicaps. One was that, from 1834 until Peel's victory in 1841 stabilised politics, the service of the Empire was at the mercy of party rivalries and caprices. With the partial exceptions of Wellington, Peel, Russell, and perhaps Howick, the members of the Imperial Parliament consisted then of

---

[1] Trevelyan, G. O., *Life and Letters of Lord Macaulay* (popular edition), pp. 355–6.
[2] Broughton, Lord, *Recollections of a Long Life*, v, 291.
[3] Reid, S. J., *Life of Lord Durham*, II, 137–9.

two bodies of high-spirited and irresponsible gentlemen, thinking much less of the immense interests which depended on their votes than on the fascinating and depraving game of party "ins and outs". The other was equally serious—the character of the Prime Minister. About the time when Durham decided to take office, Howick, the strictest critic of the day, wrote of Canadian affairs with manly plainness to Melbourne:

From what I have observed I cannot be mistaken in concluding that you have not taken the pains necessary for acquiring [an accurate knowledge of the real state of things]. Let me entreat you to rouse yourself from your past inaction, to make yourself really master of the facts by which your opinion must be guided, and having done so, to set yourself resolutely to consider what can be done to repair the fatal errors of the last three years.[1]

Melbourne was that characteristic product of an old political civilisation—the finished gentleman and *amateur*; competent to manage the delicate work of educating a young queen in politics; a fascinating host; an imperturbable figure in the whirl of politics; but indolent, indecisive, and uninformed in the gross details of responsible statesmanship. Success in political compromise blinded that generation (perhaps our own also) to the difference between compromise as a practical accommodation between conflicting men and views, and compromise as mere reluctance to face ugly facts and the exclusion of awkward primary issues from political programmes. The mission about to be arranged had as its object nothing less than the perpetuation of the British colonial fabric by the concession to Her Majesty's subjects overseas of their just rights. Yet Melbourne with weak pessimism confessed, as he sent Durham to his work, that "the final separation of those colonies might possibly not be of material detriment to the interests of the mother country".[2] He flinched from contemplating realities coolly and boldly; he also seems to have refrained from checking his instinctive dislike of Durham's character and methods.[3] At the end of 1837 he had chosen his man, because he thought that Durham might act with boldness as well as prudence. Within eight months he was talking of the same man as one "on whom no dependence could be placed", because he had ventured to act with that boldness.[4] There is a limbo in history reserved for fashionable statesmen whose courage and fidelity are unequal to their social gifts.

Durham's conduct throughout his mission was so completely conditioned by the terms on which he had accepted it that no doubt must be left concerning these terms. In 1837 he had not encouraged Melbourne's advances, and when, on 7 January 1838, the Prime Minister renewed his offer, admitting that "it was not a tempting one, nor unattended with risk", Durham consented, "depending on

[1] *Lord Melbourne's Papers*, ed. Sanders, pp. 423–4.   [2] Reid, II, 137.
[3] Broughton, v, 162, diary for 16 August 1838.   [4] *Ibid.*

the cordial and energetic support of Her Majesty's Government, and on their putting the most favourable construction on his actions". The reply could not have been more explicit. "As far as I am concerned", wrote Melbourne, "and I think I can answer for all my colleagues, you will receive the firmest and most unflinching support".[1] This pledge received additional impressiveness from the royal message which expressed the Queen's anxious wish that the Earl of Durham should undertake "this important and difficult duty". It was in the spirit of these letters that Durham made his moving statement in January, bespeaking "the cordial, energetic support of my noble friends, the members of Her Majesty's Cabinet, the co-operation of the Imperial Parliament, and the generous forbearance of the noble lords opposite".[2] From the first, however, the signs were adverse. When Brougham opened his campaign against the man whom in his perverted soul he hated—his first speech was on 18 January—Hobhouse significantly recorded in his diary a boast of Roebuck: "As we are deserted by Durham, we must trot out the old horse"[3]—as if Brougham required prompting. About the same time, in addition to initial errors in the Government project which Peel set right, and the futility of some of Glenelg's instructions, the Opposition, through Sir William Follett, began its attempts to limit the new High Commissioner's powers. Russell accepted these limitations with special reference to land tenure and religion, but the terms of limitation were left terribly indefinite, a fact which involved disaster later.[4] It was also ominous that, at this time, Greville, who represented steady old Whig opinion, spoke of Durham as "generally an object of personal aversion to the Whigs".[5] The situation was so delicate, and Durham's undertaking so hazardous, that only by the strictest honour and most faithful courage on the part of the Cabinet could success be ensured.

Durham was now Governor-in-Chief of all the British North American provinces except Newfoundland, High Commissioner for special purposes in Upper and Lower Canada, and Governor-General of all British North America.[6] From first to last he interpreted his position in a viceregal sense, regarding it as an ambitious Indian Viceroy might do. He had no intention of remaining, like earlier Governors, a mere servant of the Colonial Office, for in his own eyes he was, equally with members of the Cabinet, a minister responsible for acts which technically were those of the Crown. He acted with all the dignity which ought to belong to such a position, and men about town like Hobhouse smiled as they noted bills of fare at a great dinner headed "*Dîner de son Excellence*",[7] and jested

---

[1] Reid, II, 149–50.   [2] Hansard (here and henceforth 3rd ser.), XI, 242.
[3] Broughton, V, 116.
[4] Hansard, XI, 590–2, 595.   [5] *Greville Memoirs*, IV, 56.
[6] Lord Durham's *Report* (ed. Lucas), vol. I, chap. iv.   [7] Broughton, V, 127.

at the band which accompanied him on his voyage. It was unfortunate that he did not equally realise the need for a speedy departure. Charles Buller had already urged in Parliament that his Lordship should "repair soon to a place where he is much wanted", and afterwards he held that, by failing to act while the sense of urgency compelled the acquiescence of doubtful politicians, Durham had greatly weakened his position in England.[1] His selection of Staff was also open to criticism. No one could doubt the ability and technical fitness of the men he chose. Of his right-hand man, Charles Buller, it might be said that, even including W. E. Gladstone, he was almost the foremost young politician of his time. But Edward Gibbon Wakefield, to whom Durham intended to delegate all matters affecting land and emigration, had never established himself in society as a respectable character, in spite of his peculiar genius. About Thomas Turton who had, seventeen years previously, offended against the moral law, but whose claims as an able lawyer and a fitting subject for compassion E. J. Stanley and Hobhouse had pressed on Durham, it is sufficient to quote Buller's comment that his appointment in Canada, and, one might add, the willingness to take him on the mission, were matters to be regretted.[2]

In the adventure which began on 24 April 1838 and ended on the publication of the great Report, the most impressive feature must always remain the industry and rapidity with which the Governor-General and his Staff worked—industry and rapidity the more remarkable because Durham went out a sick man, and returned a dying man. On the voyage, which lasted over a month, the members of the mission had leisure in which to read the many documents of their case, and to outline some kind of preliminary basis for action. From the day, 29 May, on which they landed, they were entirely engrossed in their great experiment. Durham had hardly published his initial proclamation, with its appeal for co-operation and cessation of factiousness, and its promise of free, liberal, British institutions, when he found himself forced to act in a serious diplomatic affair. Complications with the United States, which for the last year had hung like a thundercloud on the southern horizon, began to threaten in serious form through the seizure of a Canadian steamer, the *Sir Robert Peel*, in Canadian waters. Durham's answer to the danger revealed him at his best. Offering a thousand pounds reward for information about the assailants, and mobilising his military and naval resources as a frontier police, he refused to allow leisurely correspondence to give time for fresh complications. At once he despatched Colonel Grey to Washington where, within a fortnight, the Government had not merely promised, but had begun to afford, military assistance, in co-operation with the Canadian Government, to keep the frontier quiet.[3]

[1] Buller, C., *Sketch of Lord Durham's Mission*, in Lucas, III, 338.   [2] *Ibid.* III, 338–9.
[3] C.O. 42/282, Durham to Glenelg, 2 June 1838; Report of Col. C. Grey, 22 June 1838.

Meanwhile the High Commissioner was finding abnormal difficulty in making any kind of connection with the French Canadians, a fact easy of explanation since Great Britain through its new representative did not disguise the intention to deprive French nationality of its existing powers of obstruction. By August he was compelled to admit the "disaffected temper of the French Canadians *as a people*". On the other hand, both in Quebec and, later, at Montreal, while steadfastly maintaining the legitimate rights of the French, he slowly but surely won over the British population of Lower Canada by the soundness of his views.[1] Sir John Colborne strongly advised an early visit to Upper Canada, but before his departure thither the High Commissioner took two important steps. He created a special Council for Lower Canada, consisting of his three secretaries, the commissary general, and the provincial secretary, purposely excluding local politicians of either side or race, that the Council might appear completely unpartisan and unprejudiced.[2] Whatever the judgment of the British Parliament might be, a French Canadian revealed one advantage peculiarly grateful to his compatriots: "Il a fait déjà une bonne chose", said he, "il a tué les deux conseils".[3] His second important decision was made through the Council. In the settlement of outstanding questions concerning political prisoners, he and his Council issued an ordinance proclaiming an amnesty subject to the exception of two classes—on the one hand those who after rebelling had, like Papineau, left the country; on the other some eight men of acknowledged treasonable views whom he decided, on their confession of guilt, to send to Bermuda, there to be restrained from re-entering the colony by a threat of capital punishment. Of this ordinance much more remains to be said below. These measures were followed by a most necessary reform of police which Durham pushed through without delay. He had found that there was no system of rural police—a mere pretence in Quebec, and nothing better in Montreal. Before June had passed he had ordered into existence a body of thirty-two men for Quebec, increased by October to seventy-five; and before the Report was published Montreal could boast a force of one hundred, organised on the model of London.[4] About the same time Wakefield, with Hanson to mask his active but forbidden influence, was set at the head of a commission on waste lands, whose report remained one of the chief successes of the mission.[5]

Between 5 July, when Durham arrived at Montreal from Quebec, and 1 November, when he sailed for Plymouth, he concentrated into a few weeks as much decisive work as all his predecessors had accomplished since 1815. Reconciling the important British population in Montreal to his point of view, and choosing from them, as

[1] Durham to Glenelg, 9 August 1838, in Kennedy, *Documents*, pp. 455 ff.
[2] C.O. 42/282, Durham to Glenelg, 29 June 1838.   [3] Lucas, III, 343.
[4] *Ibid*. II, 132-3.   [5] C.O. 42/282, Durham to Glenelg, 29 June 1838.

assistant in the investigation of municipal institutions, perhaps the ablest of them, Adam Thom,[1] he passed on to Upper Canada. There, within less than a fortnight, he visited the chief centres of population, including the capital, Toronto, invited opinions from either side on the great vexed question of the Executive Council, and made a demonstration of British military strength at Niagara, which impressed American opinion only less than his previous clemency towards rebels and the courtesy which he now extended to the officer commanding the American frontier troops and to numerous less distinguished American citizens. He saw enough of the Welland Canal to make its further extension a vital part of his programme for Canada, and on his way back he descended the Long Sault Rapids on the St Lawrence, in order to have actual experience of the need for more efficient canalisation of the river.[2] At Montreal, on his return, he found time to deal with the relations between the Seminary of Saint-Sulpice and the town of Montreal, administering a cold *douche* of rebuke to the bigotry of the less open-minded Protestants of the place. Throughout all this period it must be remembered that, to use Lady Colborne's expression, he was "constantly laid up for days together, and Mr Buller as bad".[3] In view of the persistent nagging with which the Opposition in Britain continued throughout these months to comment on his doings, the definite approval by Sir John Colborne of the things actually accomplished by the mission was of extreme importance. As was natural, Colborne, his wife, and presumably many of the military set, cherished shrewd suspicions that Durham's final summing up would prove offensive to their Tory sensibilities. But Lady Colborne has left an exact description of her husband's judgment, passed after Durham had accomplished more than half his work: "He by no means desires it should in future be thought that he placed full confidence in the future under Lord Durham's administration. He only, *as far as it went*, and *up to the period* of his approving his measures, gave him his hearty concurrence and assistance".[4] The precisely defined approval of the old soldier was worth all the half-hearted support which Melbourne's Government afforded him.

August saw Durham making a first draft of his Report in the memorable despatch in which he gave his maturing opinions on French *nationalité* and on Canada's relations with the American people. In September he met representatives from Nova Scotia, Prince Edward Island, and New Brunswick, and in council with them began to re-shape his views on union, federal or legislative, for all British North America.[5] At the same time he received and began to give

[1] Buller, *Sketch*, in Lucas, II, 360.
[2] C.O. 42/282, Durham to Glenelg; despatches between 12 July and 24 July 1838.
[3] Moore Smith, G. C., *Life of John Colborne*, p. 299.
[4] *Ibid*. pp. 298–9; letter of 14 September.
[5] Buller, *Sketch*, in Lucas, III, 362–4.

effect to the definitive report on land and emigration which Hanson and Wakefield had handed in.

But now the work of the Governor-General was suddenly arrested by news of the complete disapproval of his Bermuda Ordinance by the Imperial Parliament. Already there had been trouble at Westminster over Turton and Wakefield, while in July Ellenborough and Wellington had done their best to cut down by interpretation the powers presumably in possession of the head of the mission. But the new attack affected the very essentials of Durham's policy and position, and it was unexpected. On 31 July Glenelg, while confessing that there might be legal inaccuracies in the Bermuda Ordinance, assured Durham that "all reasonable people here approve your conduct" and that he and his colleagues were in entire agreement. It was also reassuring when Earl Grey wrote at the same time to say that his conduct had seemed "the most lenient and humane which could be justified": still more so when Melbourne sent assurance of royal approval.[1] On 19 September the whole situation was changed. For some time prior to that date Durham had been contemplating resignation; for the incessant, if petty, attacks at home had fretted his proud spirit; and Buller had found it necessary to place before him with a plainness creditable to both men the probable consequences of retirement.[2] Besides this, Durham had always cherished misgivings as to the reception of the ordinance, and, while awaiting news, was in so deep dejection that, as Buller says, "he would for some time do nothing himself, nor let me do anything".[3] But he seems to have been unprepared for the completeness with which the Imperial Parliament and Cabinet had undone his work, news which affected him all the more keenly because he first heard of the full extent of his defeat, not from a despatch, but from an American newspaper.[4] At a meeting of the delegates from the provinces, he told them in painful phrases how he had suddenly been arrested in his mission by the interference of a branch of the English Legislature, in which the responsible advisers of the Crown had deemed it their duty to acquiesce; and he announced his intention to resign.[5] Under the strain of the situation he broke down, and it was of this period that Buller wrote so movingly: "I saw that Lord Durham's health was fearfully affected by all that had passed. Such a degree of nervous agitation did his disease produce, and such a reaction of that agitation on his bodily health was constantly going on, that it was evidently impossible for him to bear up against the anxieties and labour of his government".[6]

---

[1] C.O. 42/282, Glenelg to Durham, 31 July, Grey to Durham, 31 July; C.O. 42/307, Melbourne to Durham, 28 July 1838.

[2] Buller and Wakefield to Durham, 7 September 1838.

[3] *Report of Canadian Archives*, 1929, Charles Buller to J. S. Mill, 13 October 1838.

[4] Lucas, III, 364.   [5] Reid, II, 236–40.

[6] Lucas, III, 365–6.

The Proclamation of 9 October, in which Durham expressed most unrestrainedly his views concerning Canada, his protest against the conduct of the Imperial Parliament and ministry, and his reasons for resignation, is so important that it demands treatment in detail below. The chief interest of the last four weeks of the mission lies in the amazing mass of work performed, the weight and wisdom of the decisions arrived at by a defeated and tormented man. He kept in view the necessity for friendlier relations with the United States, and planned to pass through that country on his way home—a plan frustrated by new threats of trouble in Lower Canada. He received and answered addresses from all the important towns as they besought him not to abandon them. He reviewed the evils which had hitherto prevented the development of Prince Edward Island and promised to recommend a measure in England which would remove them.[1] In Stuart he appointed the man best fitted to act as Chief Justice in Lower Canada; and met the problem of "squatting", which mal-administration of land grants had created, by giving all *bonâ fide* squatters up to 10 September the right of pre-emption of their holdings. He discussed many things with Glenelg: the dangers threatening from the Maine frontier, the injustices inflicted on rank and file by the existing system of military pay, problems of crime and gaols, and the affairs of the British North American Land Company. He held grave consultation with Colborne concerning the new unrest, and it must have given him satisfaction to know that so competent and honest a counsellor not merely advised his immediate return to England, but thought that his presence in London was of the utmost importance.[2] On the very morning on which he sailed, he had to interview Sheriff Macdonell, who reported the reluctance of the volunteers from Upper Canada to serve a Government indifferent to their fate, and he attempted to disabuse them of their error.[3]

Then, on 1 November, he sailed in the *Inconstant*, parting with his Canadian friends amid a silent sympathy which left an undying impression on all who witnessed the departure. "The streets were crowded; the spectators filled every window, and every house-top; and though every hat was raised as he passed, a deep silence marked the general grief for Lord Durham's departure". The melancholy voyage was also persistently stormy up to the very day of arrival in Plymouth Sound, 26 November.[4]

No faithful narrative of the mission dare avoid careful consideration of three grave decisions made by Lord Durham in Canada—the passing of the ordinance by which prisoners were sent to Bermuda, the resignation with which he met the attacks on his policy, and the

[1] C.O. 42/284, Durham to Glenelg, 30 October 1838.
[2] *Ibid*. Colborne to Cowper, Quebec, 19 October 1838.
[3] *Ibid*. Durham to Glenelg, 1 November 1838.　　　　[4] Lucas, III, 370.

Proclamation of 9 October, in which he stated his case in the hearing of all Canada.

Sir John Colborne had, quite properly, left the problem of the political prisoners to be settled by the High Commissioner; and Durham could not avoid making their treatment a significant act of policy. It was certain that there would be little chance of conviction before French-Canadian juries. It was desirable that some act of generosity should display the benevolent intention of Great Britain towards the great majority of the accused. Durham, advised especially by Buller, and with the approval of Colborne, decided on an amnesty, but an amnesty which excepted those who had fled from justice and which prescribed special treatment for the ringleaders in prison. The Proclamation and ordinance which secured these results were promulgated on 28 June—the coronation day of the Queen—as an act of grace and favour in the Queen's name.[1] In a despatch of 29 June Durham explained that he had chosen Bermuda as a place of detention for the eight chief prisoners since residence there, as compared with the great penal colonies, would not "affix a character of moral infamy" on the exiles, or make them, as possibly they might become in Australia, centres of trouble as political martyrs.[2] As for Papineau and the *émigrés*, he chose rather to scare them away from Canada by definite threats of capital punishment, than lure them to destruction by permitting their return through an ambiguous silence. His critics took full advantage of the fact that this was the first important act of that special Council which they had already attacked so fiercely.

The reception of these acts in England formed the crisis, and provided the tragedy, of the mission. They contained two obvious irregularities, one the infliction of a suspended sentence of death on Papineau and the *émigrés* of 1837; the other the transportation of men to Bermuda, a region over which the Council had no jurisdiction. In both cases Durham was using his extraordinary powers as High Commissioner, and he naturally looked to the ministry at home to make good any irregularities by special legislation. Whatever the law might say, no one in Canada doubted the wisdom of the policy. But in England, even without Brougham's insane hatred to act as stimulus, the Opposition recognised the excellence of the ground for a joint attack on Durham whom they hated, and the ministry which they wished to wreck. Brougham's "petty and personal feelings"[3] forced him to the front, the Opposition peers followed willingly, and the Imperial Parliament was persuaded into a course of action disastrous not merely to the colony but to British prestige and credit. The Declaration and Indemnity Bill which was

[1] Reid, II, 205.
[2] C.O. 42/282, Durham to Glenelg, 29 June 1838.
[3] Words of Russell, Hansard, XLIX, 1228.

discussed and passed between 7 August and 15 August not merely condemned and then gave indemnity for the explicit error about Bermuda; it cancelled the whole ordinance. The discussion did more. The Opposition and, with a few exceptions like Lord John Russell and the law officers, the Whigs either condemned, or permitted to be condemned, the special Council through which Durham proposed to do his work; still worse, they made it doubtful whether Durham possessed more than very ordinary powers, and left it uncertain whether he could even suspend the Habeas Corpus Act. Melbourne had indeed introduced and then feebly withdrawn an amendment, declaratory of the powers of the Governor-General and special Council of Lower Canada, "to pass such acts as may be necessary for the safety of the province, providing for the punishment of, and detaining in custody persons who have been engaged in conspiracies against Her Majesty's Crown and Dignity".[1] By the withdrawal of this amendment Durham's position was really left much weaker than before, and although Russell in a speech not merely generous but extraordinarily able tried to undo the evil by interpreting the original grant of powers in the widest sense, and by taking upon himself all consequences which might flow from Lord Durham's accepting this enlarged interpretation of his powers, it is no exaggeration to say that nothing but immediate resignation could be expected from the High Commissioner. His critics, then and since, have not faced the natural consequences of this discussion on the character of the High Commissioner's authority. His Council had been condemned and its first act of high policy had been cancelled. But infinitely more disquieting was the disclosure that, in face of the abnormal conditions prevailing in Lower Canada, the very authority of the High Commissioner had been challenged and that, in spite of Russell's manly acceptance of responsibility, any use made by Durham of his special powers would most probably not be sustained by the Imperial Parliament. Here was something more than a vote of censure; it was the rescinding of an authority without which Durham never could have been induced to go to Canada. His resentment and resignation were therefore not temperamental excesses; they were the proper and constitutional reply to an act of folly persisted in, despite remonstrance, by the Imperial Parliament.[2]

The Proclamation of 9 October 1838 was the natural sequel to the Act of Indemnity. Durham had already felt bitterly the attitude towards him of the House of Lords, and Melbourne's "expressive silence" there, but the proceedings of 7, 9, and 10 August especially forced a decision on him. "I have resolved", he wrote on 25 September, "on resigning an authority which has now indeed become

[1] See Hansard, vol. XLIV, for both debates on the ordinance.
[2] C.O. 42/283, Durham to Glenelg, 28 September 1838; Proclamation of 9 October.

thoroughly inadequate to the ends for which it was created".[1] Three days later he declared with unanswerable directness:

I shall not err in representing the policy of the Imperial Government as one for the production of insecurity at present, and of doubt, uncertainty and want of confidence, as to the future. A delegated authority when not sustained by the power which has bestowed it loses all moral force. By retaining an authority which has become merely nominal as regards the greater purposes for which it was created I should wilfully delude the public with false hopes, and deliberately provide for a more bitter disappointment.[2]

It is disquieting to those who believe in the imperial responsibilities of senates to witness a house of peers break faith with their most distinguished proconsular servant at the bidding of an insane rhetorician like Brougham.

Durham had now not only to publish the disallowance of his ordinance, but to settle, with doubtful powers, the fate of the eight deported men. He had another duty. The whole fabric of policy on which he had lavished so much enthusiastic labour threatened to tumble about his ears, even before he left Canada. Unless something decisive were done, one more fatal blunder would be added to the long list of failures attributed by the colonists to England. There therefore appeared on 9 October a Proclamation which still represents perhaps more completely than any other document the temper and methods of Durham's genius. It announced the indemnification of all parties to the carrying out of the ordinance. It met the case of the transported men very boldly, by stating that "no impediment exists to the return of the persons who had made the most distinct admission of guilt, or who have been excluded by me from the province on account of the danger to which its tranquillity would be exposed by their presence". It made formal announcement of his resignation. Then, by a very notable break with ordinary convention, it took the Canadian public into the confidence of the Governor-General, stated his case against his opponents, and promised to defend Canadian interests against the influence of "some persons too apt to legislate in ignorance and indifference".

So general and sweeping was the condemnation in England of this document, so deeply does its character affect the reputation of Lord Durham, that comment on it cannot be refused. On the decision that no action now lay against the Bermuda exiles the opinion of Charles Buller, on whose advice the decision was made, seems conclusive. The former settlement had been annulled; the exiles might return; returning they would be arrested, and between the odium incurred by a fresh prosecution and the discredit following on the certain acquittal by any jury likely to be called, the very evils which the ordinance had originally sought to avert would arise in four-fold strength. The old legal maxim *non bis in idem* had its

[1] C.O. 42/283, Durham to Glenelg, 25 September 1838.
[2] *Ibid.* Durham to Glenelg, 28 September 1838.

bearing on the case, and, apart from that, the diminished authority of Durham left him crippled for future action. Actually no other course than that which Buller advised seemed to have equal advantages.[1]

Durham's outspoken defence of his conduct and policy now appears a piece of bold wisdom. He had been hampered throughout by malicious and cruel persecutions at home, where the High Commissioner and his mission were regarded as legitimate objects for irresponsible attack. There is unfortunately a kind of convention in England by which men may employ whatever calculated and destructive cruelty they please towards unusual forms of original genius, so long as social decorum is maintained, and victims who are rash enough to strike back usually do so to their own destruction. But Durham proved himself a dangerous subject for treatment of this description, and shattered the convention by his counter-strokes. Goaded to madness by the continued attacks on Turton, he silenced his critics on his return by threatening "an inquiry into the case of every man who may have received official employment after having committed adultery";[2] and in his Proclamation he replied to a series of parliamentary insults far less pardonable than his answer to them. He knew that genteel surrender would leave the colonies unenlightened as to the real intentions of the best minds in England towards Canada, and permit Government after Government to continue blundering on, always missing the goal in imperial policy through indolence, timidity, or unintelligent conservatism. His Proclamation made decisive action on the part of England inevitable. It proved an effective introduction to the Report, and a guarantee of the reforms which now must be attempted. In Canada it enlisted the support of all classes. As Buller put it in his dashing style, "I do not think it would have been impossible for Lord Durham to have made himself King of Canada, if he had been fool enough to wish it".

The return of the mission still left its most important task incomplete, the presentation of a definitive Report on the affairs of the North American colonies; and the months of December 1838 and January 1839 were among the most strenuous and exciting of Durham's life. Current gossip, gaining respectability by Mill's assertion that Lord Durham's Report was "written by Charles Buller partly under the inspiration of Wakefield",[3] denied him the credit of authorship. But his correspondence indicates quite clearly what happened. Glenelg lost no time in calling for a statement, but Durham told him that Buller's presence was necessary for the completion of the Report. Buller arrived on 21 December, and on 31 January 1839 Glenelg received the proof sheets of the document.[4] After the arrival of the mission in Canada Durham had wisely done his work

---

[1] Buller, note A, in *Sketch*; Lucas, III, 377-80.   [2] Hansard, XLV, 600.
[3] Mill, J. S., *Autobiography*, p. 124.
[4] C.O. 42/284, letters from Durham, 8, 20, 31 December; from Glenelg, 10, 26 December 1838, 5 February 1839.

through departments, Buller acting as chief of staff, Wakefield and Hanson attending to land and emigration, Turton to legal questions, and, after July 1838, Adam Thom to municipal institutions. He himself had paid particular attention to French-Canadian nationalist problems and relations with the United States, and he had interviewed and corresponded with the opposing leaders in Upper Canada, the Baldwins and Beverley Robinson, on the vexed question of responsible government.[1] It is also plain that he was the moving spirit in the discussion with provincial delegates in September on Union.

The Report naturally followed on the lines adopted in the mission. The technical sections investigated by commissioners were bound to owe everything to the experts, even the phrases in which their essential points were expressed; just as the speeches of British Chancellors of the Exchequer owe their details to the officials of the Treasury. Further, Buller's strong views and personal force were bound to tell, for Durham had always expected competent assistance from his chief staff officer. All this meant that Lord Durham, in what were obviously for him weeks of strenuous labour, used just so much, and no more, assistance from his colleagues as great statesmen are accustomed to ask from competent assistants. His own words—his was a singularly clear and honest mode of speech— are unambiguous about his labours: "I was urged repeatedly", he said in the House of Lords on 11 February, "by Her Majesty's Government to produce this report at as early a date as possible, in order that it might be ready before the meeting of Parliament. I did so; but it was at the expense of considerable labour, and great anxiety of mind".[2] No one who has studied the more characteristic qualities of Durham's temper and mode of expression, whether in speech, letter, or despatch, can mistake his touch in all the great moments of the Report.

The history of its appearance shares in the abnormality which marked everything else in the mission. It was sent in proof sheets to the ministry, completed just before Parliament met in 1839, so that no opportunity was given for judicious eliminations by the Cabinet; a few of Durham's friends had a private view of it immediately after Glenelg had acknowledged its arrival, and Gibbon Wakefield, who had been encompassing the work with his manifold attentions and acting as a self-elected press-agent, and who feared lest at the last moment ministers might cut out some fundamental section before publication, enabled *The Times* of 8 February to reveal some of the secrets to the public. This he did without Durham's knowledge.[3] So Melbourne, caught by the impetuous haste of Durham's methods

---

[1] *Durham Correspondence:* W. W. Baldwin to Buchanan, 26 July; R. Baldwin to Durham, 23 August; J. B. Robinson to Durham, 6 September 1838,—in *Report of the Canadian Archives,* Ottawa, 1923, pp. 186, 188, 326–8.

[2] Hansard, XLV, 208–10.

[3] *Ibid.* XLV, 206–15; Greville, IV, 168–9, with doubtfully correct notes by Reeve.

and Wakefield's doubtful intrigues, found himself pledged to an unabridged Report and an immediate discussion, which took place on Monday, 11 February 1839. The Report appeared without its weighty appendices, but these were hurried on, A, mainly on the Clergy Reserves, being presented on 6 February; B, on waste lands, 28 February; and by 31 May the last accounts had been printed.

What was it in the document which so arrested men's attention throughout the Empire in 1839, and has kept its pages fresh and influential to the present day? The Report, said Buller in 1839, would be the text-book of the colonial reformer, until it became the manual of the colonial government of Great Britain.[1] But like all the fundamental documents of our constitutional progress, it possesses none of the regular logical and abstract features of a treatise on political science. Its form, affected by the several purposes which it had to serve, is clumsy and dislocated. It is easy to mark those points at which separate statements have been dovetailed into each other. It varies greatly in interest, power, and even style. Its earlier portion may be regarded as a study in the pathology of French-Canadian national sentiment based on adequate information, but not, perhaps, on adequate sympathy. Then follow more or less perfunctory descriptions of the other provinces. There is an extremely able and arresting section on land settlement and emigration, reinforced, in Appendix B, by a masterly enquiry into the whole subject, which betrays Wakefield's hand on every page.[2] But the essence of the Report lies in its conclusion, in which Durham (for it is hardly conceivable that he allowed others to state his definitive policy for him) laid down the lines along which British colonisation was to develop.

No one formula or line of argument will do justice to the Report as a whole. It may be regarded as a programme of definite practical reforms calling for immediate legislation. Durham's recommendation to organise in Lower Canada, and develop in Upper Canada, an adequate system of municipal institutions was eagerly adopted by Sydenham and passed into law in 1841. Improvements in the means of transport and development of public works like the Welland Canal it also fell to Sydenham to carry out, to be paid for by the guaranteed loan which also Durham suggested.[3] The idea of a Supreme Court of Appeal for all the provinces had to await the day of confederation—it was created in 1875. Nothing had seemed to Durham so disastrous as the irregularity of Canadian money votes, and he demanded that "the rule of the Imperial Parliament, that no money vote should be proposed without the previous consent of the Crown"[4] be at once established, a recommendation which naturally met with the approval of a trained parliamentarian like Sydenham. The land and

---

[1] Hansard, XLIX, 186.   [2] Lucas, III, 34–130.
[3] Appendix B, Lucas, III, 126–8.   [4] Lucas, II, 286–7.

emigration policy Durham had adopted from Wakefield as it stood, for like Wakefield he thought the waste lands of the colonies a great strategic reserve to be retained in English hands for the support of a new British Empire. Wakefield always placed the need for British control of waste lands before the claims of colonists for complete internal self-government; but from phrases in the Report it seems likely that Durham would have surrendered that control into the hands of a united Dominion Legislature.[1] However that may be, the Wakefield policy suffered early shipwreck when it was decided to hand over the control of land in Canada to the provincial authorities, and a series of special statutes between 1840 and 1852 made the necessary surrenders.[2] All that remained were some effectual criticisms of old mismanagement, and the creation by Lord John Russell of a Colonial Land and Emigration Board. Of the Report as a programme of reforms, then, it may be said that it was Durham who supplied Sydenham and Russell with materials for the legislation between 1839 and 1841 on which modern Canadian progress is founded.

More interesting because more speculative were Durham's diagnosis of, and remedy for, the evils of French-Canadian nationalism. He had already proved the sincerity of his sympathy with positive and useful national sentiment, in his early defence of the rights of Norway, and of the revolt of the Belgians in 1830. It is now perhaps fashionable to forget that all nationalist claims are not just claims, that racial solidarity is only one of many guiding principles in the shaping of nations and empires, and that the evils of the future will probably in part arise from the concession of national status to communities unfit to administer the gift. No one could accuse Charles Fox of imperfect sympathies either with freedom or with France; yet, on this very French-Canadian question, Fox in 1791 had opposed the separation between British and French in Canada, saying that "the most desirable circumstance was that the French and English inhabitants of Canada should unite and coalesce into one body and *that the different distinctions of the people might be extinguished for ever*".[3] It was Durham's honest view, founded on deep thought, that the future of the French-Canadian race must be a partnership with all the other North American colonies, not existence as "a petty and visionary nationality",[4] ruining itself by inbreeding and isolation, and interfering in a kind of racial petulance with the prosperity of its neighbours. Doubtless he lacked that intimate knowledge and fine sympathy with the French which Dorchester had always shown; nor had he the easy tolerant temper which led Melbourne to tell Russell that "swamping the French population would not do in these days".[5] His phrases ring with a note of ruthlessness: "I entertain no doubts

---

[1] Lucas, II, 314 and note.   [2] Keith, A. B., *Responsible Government in the Colonies*, II, 1047.
[3] See Gourlay, *Statistical Account*, II, 10.
[4] Lucas, II, 265.   [5] *Melbourne Papers*, p. 444.

as to the national character which must be given to Lower Canada; it must be that of the British Empire"; and, again, "The French Canadians are but the remains of an ancient colonisation, and are, and ever must be, isolated in the midst of an Anglo-Saxon world".[1] He proposed to break down all artificial barriers, and leave the French to find their proper place in the midst of the numerical majority of a loyal and English population. That majority must permanently predominate.

This he planned to effect by a project of union. He had gone out to Canada with visions of federal union for British North America. These he set aside mainly because "he could not doubt that any independent powers within the federation which French Canada might possess would be used against the policy and the very existence of any form of British Government".[2] There still remained the project of a great and inspiring legislative union, with its postal system, land policy, judicial organisation and commercial and banking institutions, planned on an ambitious scale and its citizens stimulated by the greater opportunities which the new dominion would give them. In idea he never abandoned such a union. He merely recognised that, with all the separate provincial interests demanding accommodation, the scheme required time, and that his special *Canadian* questions called for instant settlement. He compromised therefore on a legislative union between Upper and Lower Canada, and saw his project successful just before he died.

Nevertheless, he under-estimated the resisting powers of French nationality combined with French Catholicism and the astonishing fertility of the French-Canadian race. He has been called an arrogant Englishman who wished to destroy the specifically French qualities in the Canadian French. His union scheme, hateful to the French, galled them from first to last, and his doctrine of representation in proportion to population,[3] in the hands of George Brown, brought on a later crisis, and helped to produce the final confederation. But in spite of Durham's fixed resolution to anglicise Lower Canada, another of his fixed ideas seemed likely to make his union less drastic than he planned. He was extremely anxious to protect against the central authority "powers of local management and of distributing funds for local purposes"; and he definitely said that he would prefer that the Provincial Assemblies should be retained with merely municipal powers,[4] rather than that the Legislature of the Union should possess the right to local interference. It was really a question of degree, and had Durham remained in Canada he might have come to admit that the extent of these inalienable provincial rights practically involved a federal constitution. It must also never be forgotten that the resolute conception by him, and administration by Sydenham, of a strict union between Upper and Lower Canada rid the French

---

[1] Lucas, II, 291.   [2] *Ibid.* II, 307.   [3] *Ibid.* II, 324.   [4] *Ibid.* II, 322.

of some of their impracticable ideas, and that Elgin was able to do them fuller justice, because in the interval they had learned that, whether they would or not, French Canadians must accept their place in a world in which the Anglo-Saxon element must play the dominant part.

When all has been said, however, Lord Durham's Report still stands and lives because it prescribed for Canada, and through Canada for the rest of the English-speaking Empire, the one form of government by which imperial unity could be preserved. The remedy, colonial self-government, was so heroically simple, so free from the need for legislation and lawyers, that this final achievement of the mission appears now almost commonplace. But in the light of events between 1815 and 1840 it seems the most original practical experiment of the time. No one doubted that for England Cabinet government was the only possible constitution. But for the colonies it was quite another matter. It is needless to dwell on the authoritarian doctrines of Wellington and his followers.[1] The strange thing is that the Whigs were, in point of theory, little better. Glenelg in his elaborate instructions to Sir Francis Head was not only confused and negative in what he said about responsible government; he actually thought the constitution of the Legislative Council "a subject of far more importance".[2] Again and again Lord John Russell proclaimed that "there was one place in which the power of the Executive could be entirely controlled—the seat of the Imperial Government"; and he sent Poulett Thomson out to execute Durham's projects fatally embarrassed by Whig sophisms as to the ultimate seat of responsibility for the colonies.[3] When pressed, English statesmen preferred that the responsibility for colonial government should be brought home to Governors through petitions to the Crown from their subjects; and Durham never scored more heavily than when he pointed out the fatal weakness for the Executive involved in such a course and in leaving the Governor a mere subordinate officer, receiving his orders from the Secretary of State for the Colonies,[4] and liable to be appealed against and disgraced by judiciously timed petitions, or even, as in Colborne's case, recalled because of a mere general turmoil in the Assembly. In Canada only two or three politicians knew, and could describe intelligently, what they wanted. Nothing illustrates better the extreme confusion of Canadian thought than the attitude of the Upper Canadian Tories in 1839.[5] They deplored the constitutional ideas of the

---

[1] See *Quarterly Review*, LXIV, 462–85.
[2] C.O. 43/45, Glenelg to Sir F. Head, 5 December 1835.
[3] Hansard, XL, 26; Russell to Poulett Thomson, 14 October 1839, in Kennedy, *Documents*, p. 522.
[4] Lucas, II, 101.
[5] Report from the Select Committee of the Legislative Council of Upper Canada on the *Report of the Earl of Durham*, 1839, in Kennedy, pp. 470 ff.

Report as likely to lead "to the overthrow of the great colonial empire of Great Britain"; yet, in actual fact, they were themselves the majority in a popular Assembly conspiring with an Executive Council of their own party to challenge the policy of an Imperial Cabinet. The reformers were still quite vague in their definitions, and many of them with Mackenzie had surrendered to the superior attractiveness of an attack on the Legislative Council. Outside the circle of the two Baldwins, no one cared to say in plain language that the exact remedy required was the introduction into Canada of the British Cabinet system, with all that the Cabinet system involved; and only the Baldwin group seemed to recognise that the change could take place without any fresh legislation.[1]

Durham had been bred in the Fox tradition—his father had been Charles Fox's friend—he must therefore have known that wisest of all Fox's judgments, delivered in the hot debate of 1791, that "it was our interest as well as our duty to give them [the colonies] as much liberty as we could to render them happy, flourishing, and as little dependent as possible".[2] It has been suggested that Wakefield was Durham's master here, but Wakefield was a confused thinker in constitutional matters; his favourite land policy led Durham to think of limiting the scope of his political doctrines, and in the Metcalfe crisis Wakefield, when tested by practical politics, took the wrong side. Durham was really maintaining the liberal ideas of the advanced Whigs, enlightened by advice from Robert Baldwin. A single sentence will express his opinion: "Every purpose of popular control might be combined with every advantage of vesting the immediate choice of advisers in the Crown, were the colonial Governor to be instructed to secure the co-operation of the Assembly in his policy by entrusting its administration to such men as could command a majority; and if he were given to understand that he need count on no aid from home in any difference with the Assembly, that did not directly involve the relations between the mother country and the colony".[3] He made it quite plain that his system "would in fact place the internal government of the colony in the hands of the colonists themselves".[4] At the same time, believing with all sound statesmen in a strong Executive, he was convinced that the rights of the Legislature and the strength of the Executive were necessarily connected; and that while, on the existing system, the dignity of the Crown was lowered, the power of the Governor reduced to nullity, and the rights of the Assembly denied, his project would satisfy every desire of the Assembly without impairing a single prerogative of the Crown.[5]

[1] R. Baldwin to Glenelg, 13 July 1836; R. Baldwin to Durham, 23 August 1838, in *Report of the Can. Archives*, 1923, pp. 326 ff.
[2] See Gourlay, II, 98. All Fox's speeches on 11 May 1791 are important.
[3] Lucas, II, 279–80   [4] *Ibid.* II, 281.   [5] *Ibid.* II, 278.

Lord Metcalfe, whose political ideas came to him from England by way of India, thought that Durham meant only to appoint isolated heads of departments, each in his separate sphere well-pleasing to the Assembly; but the text of the Report reveals Metcalfe's error. Durham talked of the rude machinery of the Executive Council in which there was no specialisation of office but all ministers attended to every kind of business. In place of that he proposed "a system of administration by means of competent heads of departments". He was contrasting such heads, not with the joint responsibility of an English Cabinet, but with the promiscuity of a Canadian Councillor's business.[1]

The one important reservation in Durham's plan was rather that he proposed to retain for the Imperial Parliament "the constitution of the form of government, the regulation of foreign relations, and of trade with the mother country, the other British colonies, and foreign nations, and the disposal of the public lands". The most authoritative of Durham's modern critics has remarked how very limited the powers were which Durham left to the colonial Government.[2] That, however, was not Durham's opinion. The exceptions, he said, were few. He might also have said that these exceptions were in exact accordance with the wishes of the wisest Canadian Reformers. Robert Baldwin, who understood the business if any man did, limited his constitutional petition with the words "as far as regards the internal affairs of the province", and he told Durham himself that "the Imperial Parliament is the tribunal in whose hands should be retained all the powers of general legislation essential to the welfare of the Empire as a whole".[3] After all, Durham and Baldwin, being practical statesmen, suited their plan to the actual needs of Canada. It was not their business to make a constitutional Utopia, but to provide a good working Government. Besides this the reservations lose their formidable appearance the more closely they are examined. Wakefield's idea had been that the control of waste lands must be in British hands; yet, in the Report, Durham himself showed, as has been already said, an inclination to vest that control in a Dominion Legislature when it should come into existence. What he feared was local jobbery.[4] As for foreign policy and commercial regulation, these were, in 1839, either not strictly concerns of Canada, or, as in the boundary disputes and the desire for commercial reciprocity with the United States, difficulties much more simply handled by the Imperial than by the Provincial Government. Men's rights are

[1] Kaye, Sir J. W., *Life and Correspondence of Lord Metcalfe*, pp. 414–15. The view here taken differs from that expressed by the writer in *British Supremacy and Canadian Self-Government*, p. 244.

[2] Lucas, II, 282 and note.

[3] R. Baldwin to Durham, 23 August 1838, enclosing letter to Glenelg of 13 July 1836, in *Report of Can. Archives*, 1923, pp. 326 ff.

[4] Lucas, II, 314 and note.

their advantages; and Peel and Elgin proved that the most profitable right possessed by Canada was its claim on British support in negotiations with the United States. By control of "the constitution of the form of government" he most probably meant to show that an inclination towards American republican institutions would involve a definite break with England.

Whatever he meant, Durham was giving everything; for the gift of self-government can be limited only by the desires of those who receive it. As trade regulation became an important feature in the Canadian budget, as Canadian diplomacy turned more and more to business arrangements with related powers, the exceptions to the gift of autonomy melted away. It was then actual and expansive self-government which the Report described, and which Durham urged with all his power on the Whig Government.

There is little space for a description of the influence exerted by the Report in the years which followed. The resistance offered to his ideas in Canada and Britain has now only the interest attaching to obsolete prejudices and bad political logic. The real test of their value was the speed with which those who could profit by them, or who could elevate their statesmanship by employing the maxims of the Report, accepted and used them. Already, by the end of 1839, Wakefield, who kept a shrewd eye on the colonial press, wrote of the Report: "It has now gone the round from Canada through the West Indies and South Africa to the Australias, and has everywhere been received with acclamations".[1] Henceforth it became the standard by which colonial constitutionalists regulated their claims. Its history in Canada is well known. Sydenham took it over, with Russell's niggling limitations, and before his death he discovered that in practice Durham's plan alone was workable.[2] The third Earl Grey adopted his brother-in-law's theories and, on his acceptance of the Colonial Office in 1846, he gave them effect in a famous despatch to Sir John Harvey.[3] Lord Elgin, who married Durham's daughter, wrote in his first letters home from Montreal that "he had adopted frankly and unequivocally Lord Durham's view of government", and that the real and effectual vindication of Lord Durham's memory and proceedings would be "the success of a Governor-General of Canada who works out his views of government fairly".[4] To-day he needs no vindication; for the later history of the British Empire has been the fulfilment of his dreams through obedience to his precepts.

[1] Wakefield to Durham, 26 December 1839.
[2] Dent, J. C., *The Last Forty Years*, pp. 149–51.
[3] Grey, Earl, *Colonial Policy*, I, 209.
[4] C.O. 43/35, Earl of Elgin to Lady Elgin, 31 January and 4 March 1847.

CHAPTER XII

CANADA UNDER RESPONSIBLE GOVERNMENT,
1840–1854

I. LORD SYDENHAM (1839–41). The fourteen years from the proclamation of union between Upper and Lower Canada to the close
of Lord Elgin's governorship are the most important in Canadian
political history, for they witnessed the decisive stages in the constitutional experiment which determined the future, not only of
Canada, but of all the self-governing colonies of Great Britain. Yet
although these were years of excursions and alarms, fruitful in crises
and full of anxieties for timid souls, the troubles and dangers were
far less fundamental than political and constitutional critics incline
to assume. In politics the strength of the chain is that of its strongest,
not of its weakest links, and the danger to the British connection, so
persistently dwelt on by journalists and orators in those years, was
negligible, partly because the main body of the British community
in Canada had not the slightest inclination to abandon the British
flag, partly also because none of the alternatives to the imperial
connection was practicable or advantageous to the colonists. Similarly, in social and economic affairs, in spite of cycles of depression
and actual misfortunes, the Canadian community was, in its Spartan
way, really far better off than the majority of the inhabitants of
Britain, and continually upset the gloomy calculations of its publicists
and politicians by manifesting to shrewd observers all the symptoms
of disgustingly robust health.

This chapter will deal with the more startling phenomena, some
of them pathological, of political growth. It will prove misleading
if, at the outset, some affirmation is not made of the quiet happy
spaces of domestic life untroubled by politics, and the hard constructive pioneering work which did more for the province than all
the political discussion—of Canada, in a rhetorical phrase from Lord
Elgin, "with the bloom of youth yet upon her cheek, and with
youth's elasticity in her tread".[1]

For political purposes the period of so-called responsible government began with the imperial statute which united the provinces of
Upper and Lower Canada, and with Lord John Russell's despatch
of 16 October 1839, in which he declared that "the tenure of
colonial offices, held during Her Majesty's pleasure, will not be
regarded as equivalent to a tenure during good behaviour, but that
not only such officers will be called on to retire from the public
service as often as any sufficient motives of public policy may suggest

[1] Walrond, T., *Life and Letters of Lord Elgin*, p. 49.

the expediency of that measure, but that a change in the person of the governor will be considered as a sufficient reason for any alterations which his successor may deem it expedient to make, in the list of public functionaries".[1] By the Act of Union a sphere of political action was created, sufficiently large to allow British and French Canadians to learn the parliamentary game, and to correct each others' eccentricities; by the despatch, in which Russell never meant to confer what Canadian reformers called responsible government, the relation between the executive and all other factors in Canadian politics was freed from pre-existing limitations, and left open to the incalculable influence of future events.

Between 1840 and 1854 there are three clearly marked periods in the growth of the Canadian system of Cabinet government—the Governor-Generalship of Poulett Thomson (he became Lord Sydenham in August 1840) with Lord John Russell as Colonial Secretary, in which the general position was defined for further amendment; the critical years, 1842 to 1845, in which, under Lord Stanley's supervision, Sir Charles Bagot and Sir Charles Metcalfe subjected the ideas of Downing Street to the test of colonial practice and criticism; and eight years, all of them under Lord Elgin's control, and six of them with Earl Grey co-operating from the Colonial Office, at the end of which the province of Canada had, for working purposes, attained to Cabinet government, as nearly as possible on the British model.

Between 1839 and 1841 Russell and Poulett Thomson remade the province. Their joint programme included the legislative union of Upper and Lower Canada, the creation of a reasonable Civil List, the establishment of a system of local government, the settlement of troublesome problems like that of the Clergy Reserves, and the quickening of Canadian financial and economic life through the encouragement of public works and the guarantee by England of a new Canadian loan. Russell contributed an earnest desire to see the colony reformed and pacified, and the most perfect loyalty towards his Governor-General. He was, unfortunately, hampered by a doctrinaire and logical conception of the nature of the Governor-General's responsibility. Poulett Thomson brought to the task a mind trained in finance and parliamentary procedure and tactics, a civilised sense of public honour, an energy which few of his former British colleagues had ever suspected, and a gift for managing individuals, which in the eyes of his unsophisticated provincials latterly seemed a kind of unholy political mesmerism. The practical details of the programme presented no difficulties which could not be overcome by audacity, common sense, and hard work; no opening having been given to the French Canadians for a campaign against the hated Union in which their nationalism was to vanish.

---

[1] Lord J. Russell to the Rt Hon. C.E. Poulett Thomson, 16 Oct. 1839, in Kennedy, p. 324

But the constitutional theory which Russell imposed on Poulett Thomson promised immediate friction. The party of Reform in Upper Canada now knew perfectly what they wanted, "that the Crown should, as at home, entrust the administration of affairs to men possessing the confidence of the Assembly".[1] They assumed that the heads of departments must combine in a corporate unity as Cabinet or ministry, and that as a Cabinet they must work in union with the party or group of sections which possessed the majority in the House of Assembly.[2] From that position they never flinched, and to that position in 1848 they won the consent of the Governor-General and the Home Government. They were not anxious to define the actual extent of the responsibility which they demanded. Durham and Buller might enumerate the departments reserved for imperial control, but as yet Canadians had not interested themselves in delimiting the frontier between things domestic and things imperial. With Anglo-Saxon opportunism they simply asked that, in matters which interested them, they should control their own affairs; and already, in Crown land administration, they were inconspicuously annexing something allocated by Durham to imperial management.

Russell's instructions to Thomson were equally plain, although not equally practicable, and they held the field against the Canadian view between October 1839 and November 1846, when Grey altered the position of the Home Government in a notable despatch to Sir John Harvey.

"The power for which a minister is responsible in England", Russell had written to Poulett Thomson, "is not his own power, but the power of the Crown, of which he is for the time the organ. It is obvious that the executive councillor of a colony is in a situation totally different.... Can the Colonial Council be the advisers of the Crown of England? Evidently not, for the Crown has other advisers for the same functions, and with superior authority. It may happen therefore that the Governor receives, at one and the same time, instructions from the Queen and advice from his Executive Council, totally at variance with each other. If he is to obey his instructions from England, the parallel of constitutional responsibility entirely fails; if on the other hand, he is to follow the advice of his Council, he is no longer a subordinate officer, but an independent sovereign".[3]

The best comment on this policy which Stanley accepted, after 1841, as completely as Russell, and which both Colonial Secretaries reiterated to their Governors-General, lies in the adventures of Sydenham, Bagot and Metcalfe, who attempted to administer the system.

But apart from nice points of constitutional theory, the first Governor-General of united Canada had to carry out a most ambitious scheme of administrative reform. Poulett Thomson assumed authority on 19 October 1839. He came from Britain with

[1] Lord Durham's *Report* (ed. Lucas), II, 151.
[2] C.O. 42/470, Sir George Arthur to Lord John Russell, 1 March 1840.
[3] Russell to Poulett Thomson, 14 October 1839, in Kennedy, p. 522.

a reputation for shrewdness in political and economic matters, great personal vanity, and some moral levity. But, like two other great contemporary administrators, Gladstone and Dalhousie, he had served his apprenticeship in the best school for statesmen in Britain, the Board of Trade; and two years in Canada proved that vanity and levity were but surface flaws. In October he began a career of incessant useful administration, unbroken by intervals for rest, and qualified by singularly few errors. Within a month he had secured from the Special Council of Quebec their sanction, not only for a legislative union with Upper Canada, but also for the amalgamation of the provincial debts. Between November 1839 and February 1840 he had met the legislative bodies of Upper Canada, and, faced with extreme Reformers on the one hand, and the Family Compact men on the other, he had secured their consent to union by satisfactory majorities, and had actually contrived and carried a compromise on the Clergy Reserves. It is true that a legal ruling in Britain forced him to frame his compromise in an imperial statute, passed in a modified form, but the check in London was trivial compared with the victory in Toronto. A rapid dash into Nova Scotia enabled him to make at least a temporary settlement of political troubles there; he glanced, in passing, at New Brunswick, where the wisdom of Sir John Harvey had kept things quiet; and later in the summer of 1840 he made a progress through Upper Canada.

Meanwhile the fortunes of the Union Bill at Westminster were involving him in new labours. Moved by some criticisms from Edward Ellice in the debate, Lord John Russell had omitted the clauses dealing with local government.[1] Now the creation of a system of local government, to Sydenham as to Durham, seemed almost as vital for Canada as the Union itself. In the absence of local bodies, as Durham had pointed out, the great business of the Assemblies became literally parish work; and the new instrument of government for Canada would be fatally crippled by the omission of the municipal clauses.[2] Sydenham, as we must now call the Governor-General, gave free expression to his temper as well as to his opinions in a vehement despatch to his chief; and then, to save the situation, he passed an ordinance to serve his purpose in Lower Canada, judging with shrewd accuracy that if he could set up municipal machinery in the East, the West must acquiesce in a similar measure from Parliament when the new Parliament met. Sydenham had now to consider the measures which must accompany and implement the Act of Union. These by themselves would have occupied all the energies of a routine politician for all his time. He chose Kingston as capital of United Canada, not because it was ideally suitable, but because Quebec and Toronto were each disqualified by geo-

---

[1] Hansard, 3rd ser. LIV, 1263-4.   [2] Lucas, II, 92.

graphical position, and because Montreal, later a possible choice, could not be selected in 1841, when the French were in high revolt against the Union, and the British Loyalists still sore about concessions to the disaffected.

Next, Parliament had to be summoned and a suitable Executive Council chosen. The date for assembling Parliament had been fixed for the middle of May 1841, but, owing to the lateness of the season, and the difficulties incident on preparing the new capital for its responsibilities, it was ultimately postponed to 14 June. Before that date the Governor-General must have his programme ready, and his plans laid for the guidance of eighty-four popularly elected members of Assembly, most of whom had never acted together before, and whose knowledge of parliamentary procedure was slight. The charge has been laid against him that Government intervened decisively in the elections; but there has been some exaggeration on the point. An Administration in being cannot but tell on a Legislature coming into being. In any case, in Upper Canada the quiet industrious moderate men held opinions very similar to those of Sydenham himself. As one of them put the case to a kindred spirit: "Both Tories and Republicans would glory getting us into difficulties...but I think our earthly salvation depends on our agreeing with His Excellency".[1] In both Upper and Lower Canada there was much violence in which all parties and sections were involved; as an electioneering community Canada lay still in the eighteenth century.[2] The most definite accusation is that the Governor-General, by modifying the limits of city and county constituencies at Montreal and Quebec, helped himself to supporters, and disfranchised some French anti-unionists. The truth is that Russell adopted a most grave and sensible suggestion from Peel, recommending fuller representation for commercial interests, and Sydenham's modifications of the electoral districts in question were simply in accordance with a measure agreed to by both party leaders at home.[3] In the early months of 1841 Sydenham could not but be the chief functioning part of the Government of Canada, so that he appeared as a useful combination of Governor and Prime Minister. In view of the pre-existing chaos and the perfect novelty of the experiment, not only the Governor-General but even more the voters had reason to be thankful for the results. Sydenham had set his heart on creating a middle group, which would save the country from domination by representatives of either extreme; and indeed the salvation of the colony depended on obtaining a Government in which there would be a minimum of abstract discussion, and a maximum of practical legislation. That middle party the election more or less secured for him. The old "Compact" party might now be neglected—it had

[1] Merritt, J. P., *Life of W. H. Merritt*, p. 234.
[2] Dent, J. C., *The Last Forty Years*, chaps. iii, iv and v.
[3] Hansard, 3rd ser. LIV, 1125.

seven representatives. But there were twenty French members, all hostile to the Union Act by which alone they possessed what power they had; five reforming members were marked as *ultras*, and there were others of uncertain degrees of progressiveness, and of still more uncertain degrees of disinterestedness. The fate of the Legislature depended on the action of twenty-four so-called Government members, and twenty moderate Reformers.[1] Canada was about to make its first trial of Liberal-Conservatism. The success of the experiment would be determined by Sydenham's power to wean men from their old party associations.

His new Executive Council corresponded more or less to this idea of government by the centre. It was an eclectic group, astonishingly well chosen, apart from one lamentable but inevitable omission. But it contained no French Canadians. The Governor-General had found them either resigned to a sullen and reluctant submission, or bent on perverse, if passive, resistance. Since they differed from him on a fundamental issue, the Union, they could only be left in self-imposed isolation. In constructing his Council he had once more approached them, and more particularly Louis Hypolite Lafontaine, the most eminent of them. But, as his successor told the story, "members of that party who accepted office from him were invariably rejected from their seats when they sought to be re-elected, and an overture, made to the party through Mr Lafontaine, was abruptly broken off".[2] Among the others (who were either like W. H. Draper, the Attorney-General for Upper Canada, moderate Conservatives, or like S. B. Harrison, the Provincial Secretary for Upper Canada, moderate Reformers) Robert Baldwin, the Solicitor-General for Upper Canada, stood in a class apart. He had been long and intimately associated with the more extreme Reformers, although his character for loyalty and honour remained unstained, and it had been with reluctance that he had yielded to Sydenham's pressure, and become Solicitor-General in the new Executive, as iormerly he had reluctantly agreed to fill a similar place in the Executive of Upper Canada. Extreme conscientiousness had led him to refuse to take an oath, on assuming office, which seemed unjust to his Roman Catholic fellow-representatives; and, to safeguard his working theory of responsible government, he had written to four of his new colleagues, warning them of his lack of political confidence in them. It was his intention, imperfectly understood by the Governor-General, to acquiesce in his position until the meeting of Parliament enabled him to act in accordance with what he held to be the correct constitutional procedure. Meanwhile, for Sydenham, he counted as a reforming member of a Council which represented all shades of reasonable opinion.

[1] Scrope, G. P., *Memoir of...Lord Sydenham*, p. 217.
[2] C.O. 42/495, Sir Charles Bagot to Lord Stanley, 26 September 1842.

The first parliamentary session of United Canada remains notable for many things, but especially for its achievements, which were Sydenham's achievements, in practical legislation. After two and a half months of unceasing labour he summed up what had been accomplished with a natural self-satisfaction: "The five great works I aimed at have been got through—the establishment of a Board of Works with ample powers; the admission of aliens; a new system of county courts; the regulation of the public lands ceded by the Crown under the Union Act; and lastly this District Council Bill".[1] He might have added the improvement of education through the province, and preparations for the negotiation of a loan of £1,500,000 for public works.

During the same months a fierce constitutional battle was being waged over the definition of ministerial responsibility. It had originated on the eve of Parliament in Baldwin's proposal of 12 June. As there now existed an organised Reform party, which, if the French were counted in, possessed a majority in the country, it was his opinion that the Executive Council should be relieved of all those members whose views were unacceptable to that party. Sydenham took up the gage of battle, accepted Baldwin's proposal as an explicit resignation, and concentrated his group of moderates.[2] The struggle continued intermittently down to the end of the session; when, on 3 September, the Governor-General, through Harrison, gained a tactical but not a substantial victory. In place of resolutions proposed by Baldwin, Harrison carried counter-resolutions which were subsequently to be much quoted, and which certainly seem to mark a decided weakening from the firm attitude of Russell's despatch:

1. That the head of the executive government of the province, being within the limits of his government the representative of the Sovereign, is responsible to the imperial authority alone; but that nevertheless the management of our local affairs can only be conducted by him by and with the assistance, counsel, and information of subordinate officers in the province.

2. That in order to preserve between the different branches of the provincial parliament that harmony which is essential to the peace, welfare, and good government of the province, the chief advisers of the representative of the Sovereign, constituting a provincial administration under him, ought to be men possessed of the confidence of the representatives of the people; thus affording a guarantee that the well understood wishes and interests of the people, which our gracious Sovereign has declared shall be the rule of the provincial parliament, will on all occasions be faithfully represented and advocated.

3. That the people of this province have moreover a right to expect from such provincial administration the exertion of their best endeavours that the imperial authority, within its constitutional limits, will be exercised in the manner most consistent with their well-understood wishes and interests.[3]

It is always useful to prevent extreme statements of constitutional dogmas; and it is counted a tactical victory when resolutions are

---

[1] Scrope, pp. 242–3.
[2] C.O. 42/479, Sydenham to Baldwin, 13 June and 23 June 1841.
[3] Scrope, pp. 258–61; Dent, I, 149–56. For the fourth resolution see Kennedy, p. 564.

carried which on the surface seem to deny the case of the Opposition. But it is mere blindness not to see that, for working purposes, these resolutions conceded almost everything of the Reformers' case which was worth struggling for.

A fortnight later the first session of the Union Parliament closed; and with its close Sydenham's life also ended. He received fatal injuries, falling from horseback on 4 September, and he died on 19 September, the day after that on which his Parliament stood prorogued. He has had many critics, and their criticism has cut deep; but none of them has ever shown how sullen French nationalism could have been forced, by means other than those used by him, to accept the Union, through which alone lay the path to their fortune as a race; and the crude tactics and bald logic of the ultra-Reformers are the best evidence that before responsible government could be perfectly achieved in Canada, its advocates must learn those very lessons which Sydenham's restrictions taught them. French and British alike, they were all of them still at school in politics, and Sydenham was their perfect teacher. But schoolmasters are seldom popular.

II. BAGOT AND METCALFE (1842–5). Lord Sydenham's system of government for Canada had been explicit, if not simple. The unrest in the province could be removed only by sound practical legislation and resolute administration; and these benefits only the Governor-General's initiative was competent and disinterested enough to secure. They must however be secured in co-operation with the people of Canada, as represented by the provincial Parliament; and that Parliament must be organised, not into parties which, in Canada, for Sydenham were merely factious groups, but into a solid central body of moderate men, bent on business. His executive councillors must be selected, partly because they were competent, partly because they were acceptable to this central body. When individuals ceased to be so, they should be replaced. Connected thus with public opinion in Parliament, the Governor-General, as Sydenham interpreted his vocation in practice, was neither autocrat nor irresponsible as of old, but really the permanent Prime Minister of Canada. The position was stable because power to remove him lay with the British Cabinet; it was non-partisan because support came, not from sectional groups, but from average moderate opinion. There were two sides to his government—energetic administration, and intelligent co-operation between Executive and Legislature. Co-operation being a means to the true end, administration, it was futile to squander time on discussing the exact constitutional theory which should regulate the methods of co-operation.

The instructions of his successor, Sir Charles Bagot, from Lord Stanley were in exact accordance with this system. Bagot was to recognise no distinction of national origin or religious creed; he was to consult the wishes of the mass of the population; but he must refuse to reopen the discussion of constitutional doctrine, "a chapter which has already led to such serious consequences, and in the prosecution of which I contemplate seriously the prospect of the dismemberment of the Empire".[1] Unfortunately, when Bagot arrived in Kingston on 10 January 1842, he found his instructions less simple to put into practice than they had been to formulate. Public opinion continued, in spite of all the late Governor's efforts, to organise itself into party groups, one of them racial in character. The French were still in revolt against the Union, and bitter over the reasons which had made their inclusion in the Government, or their acceptance of office, impossible. The Upper Canada Reformers refused to consent to any form of government less popular than that which would render the Executive completely responsible to the majority in the popular Assembly. The executive councillors recognised how powerless they must be in the face of a hostile House of Assembly, and with Sydenham's restraining hand gone, the majority were certain to hold that no useful legislation could avail that was not prefaced by a complete acceptance of their theory of responsibility. The next five years were occupied with statements and restatements of this political problem.

Sir Charles Bagot had been chosen, not as an adept in parliamentary management, but because relations with the United States were so strained that, in Sir Robert Peel's judgment, capacity to live at peace with the Republic was the first requisite in the new Governor-General.[2] Bagot had served at Washington, and was a *persona grata* among the governing classes there. He had admirable social qualities which his family circle reinforced; a direct and humorous eye for facts; a spirit of friendliness, and a remarkable ignorance of business methods and parliamentary procedure. Whatever Peel may have thought, the Colonial Office and its head, Lord Stanley, had little confidence in him.[3] Administrative progress, so far as that depended on the Governor-General, suffered a check, although Bagot took some interest in the evolution of the university project for Upper Canada, and reported favourably of the development in Upper Canada of Sydenham's new local government machinery. Finance, and more particularly some of the details of the guaranteed imperial loan, were terribly mismanaged. But even had Bagot been a master of domestic administration, the political situation would have halted him at once. Happily there were some months of leisure before the next session of Parliament fell due, and Bagot's kindliness and diplomatic skill proved useful. In a series of appointments he

[1] C.O. 43/36, Stanley to Bagot, 8 October 1841.
[2] For Peel's most authoritative statement see *Can. Hist. Rev.* VIII, p. 46.
[3] *Bagot Correspondence*, especially after the events of September 1842.

revealed his impartiality, for while he chose Francis Hincks, the ablest financier in the province and a Reformer, as Inspector-General, his new Solicitor-General for Upper Canada was a Tory, Sherwood. Stanley had cautioned him about the French,[1] but Bagot found himself, quite early in his regime, attracted by French manners, and distressed by the exclusion of French-Canadian leaders from office. Among other appointments, that of M. Vallières de St Réal, a very distinguished member of the community, as Chief Justice of the King's Bench in the district of Montreal, proved most acceptable. At the same time Hincks's influence made for conciliation, and his ministers must soon have realised that on vexed questions like the control of the Civil List, and the granting of an amnesty to those still suffering for their conduct during the rebellions, the policy of the Governor-General might easily take a popular and generous trend.[2]

But none of these promising circumstances could alter the hard fact that when Parliament met on 8 September there would be a hostile majority in the Assembly, and a challenging motion declaratory of provincial rights, in terms violently contradictory to the ideas of the Home Government. The crisis was further complicated because the old Tories, recommended by Stanley as men on whom he should rely in a crisis,[3] had themselves made factious advances to the French Canadians and to the extreme Reformers. They were prepared to combine with these groups in order to overthrow the existing Executive Council, heedless of the inconsistency of such a course, and of the difficulties in which its success would place the Governor-General.[4]

Either of the two more obvious alternative solutions was impossible. Bagot might have met the Assembly, as Stanley later told him he ought to have done, countered their attack through his ministers and supporters, allowed the enemy to show their hand, and then have appealed to the country through a dissolution.[5] But in view of the undeniable exclusion of the French from influence, and since Sydenham's resolutions of 3 September 1841 really favoured the ideas of the Reformers, the ministerial case was very weak, and in the absence of an autocrat like Sydenham to dominate the elections, a dissolution would have ensured defeat. On the other hand, he might surrender outright to Baldwin, Lafontaine, and the party of unmitigated responsible government; but that could only mean instant and ignominious recall at Stanley's hands. Advised especially by W. H. Draper, the ablest, after Hincks, of all his ministers, and strongly urged by him to adopt a policy of

[1] C.O. 43/144, Stanley to Bagot, 1 April 1842.
[2] C.O. 42/503, Bagot to Stanley, 26 January 1843.
[3] *Bagot Correspondence*, Stanley to Bagot, 17 May 1842.
[4] C.O. 42/495, Bagot to Stanley, 26 September 1842.
[5] *Bagot Correspondence*, Stanley to Bagot, 3 November and 3 December 1842.

justice towards the French,[1] Bagot followed his diplomatic inclinations and chose a middle course. Between the opening of Parliament on 8 September and the debate on the Governor-General's address, he approached Lafontaine and ascertained his terms. These required four seats in the Council and the admission of Robert Baldwin to office. Consenting to this as the only possible course, Bagot was startled to find his offer refused by the group whose terms he had accepted; but flinging ordinary usage aside, he let the Assembly, which had already begun its attack on the Government, know the extent of the offer which the Opposition leaders had refused. Draper read the Governor-General's letter of surrender to the House. The unusualness of Bagot's action, the extent of his concession, and his obvious *bona fides* sufficed to end the onslaught. Baldwin, Lafontaine, and two other Reformers accepted office, with the certainty of a fifth place for another French Canadian. Room had been made for two of the new ministers by the highly irregular process of accepting ministerial resignations before these had been either invited or offered. Indeed from first to last Bagot's methods made havoc of the delicacies and proprieties of ordinary procedure, but they won the day, and the House of Assembly expressed its unmingled satisfaction at the course adopted.[2]

The Council thus reorganised, and given a strong Reform and French colour, has been called the first Baldwin-Lafontaine ministry, but mistakenly so. It was not a perfectly homogeneous Cabinet; it did not represent the supremacy of a single victorious party in Parliament; and in it no one was officially recognised as chief minister. But the event stands out as one of the most important in Canadian parliamentary history, for it involved the ultimate defeat of the policy proposed by both Russell and Stanley, and administered by Sydenham. It is true that the reluctance, not only of Stanley, but even of Peel's Cabinet, and the obvious displeasure of the Colonial Office, destroyed the value of their acquiescence in what had been done[3]; and that Bagot's successor was selected with a view to at least a partial recovery of imperial control. It is equally true that Bagot regarded himself as having acted "without the least sacrifice of British interests, or the least danger to British institutions in the province".[4] Nevertheless, although the Governor-General had not, in set terms, surrendered to the party and doctrine of responsible government, actually he had done so; and the illness, which very shortly removed him from all active participation in politics, completed the transfer of real power into the hands of the new ministers. In short, if the British imperial position as defined by Russell be accepted as sound, Bagot's conduct was indefensible. If,

[1] Wrong, E. M., *Charles Buller*, p. 295.
[2] C.O. 42/495, Bagot to Stanley, 26 September 1842.
[3] C.O. 43/144, Stanley to Bagot, 2 November 1842.
[4] C.O. 42/495, Bagot to Stanley, 26 September 1842.

on the other hand, as Lord Elgin discovered a few years later, the one remedy, whether for Canadian unrest or for British dread of separation, really lay in acceptance of Baldwin's view of colonial government, and Lafontaine's claims for French nationality, then Bagot was wiser than his British masters, and his action in undermining the Russell compromise was a piece of unusually sound common sense.

It would be inaccurate to say that in Canada tranquillity was restored, for when Robert Baldwin stood for re-election after his appointment, the election was contested by means of "bludgeons, swords, and fire-arms", as well as votes, and the new minister lost his seat. But at the centre government had become possible once more; the province had gained a more genuine unity from the amelioration of French opinion, and in French Canada the population displayed their friendliness towards their afflicted Governor "in a mode which never before greeted a governor of these provinces, in masses and public prayers".[1] In the opinion of Bagot's chief secretary, no one was likely, after he was gone, to obtain the same complete confidence from a population which he had rescued from political isolation, and treated with affectionate justice.

The assumption of office by Sir Charles Metcalfe, on 30 March 1843, marked a new complication in the political situation. Between 1842 and 1847 the dominant factor in politics was not the Governor-General, but the mood of the Canadian people, varying in temper from point to point, but always in the ascendant. Throughout 1843 the prevalent attitude was one of watchful support of the more progressive ministers, while Baldwin and Lafontaine were equally *en vedette* to maintain the political advantages gained under Bagot.

In Metcalfe[2] Canadians had a personality to cope with very different from that of his suave and malleable predecessor. A preposterous legend arose later in Canada that Lord Stanley had sent Metcalfe out to destroy responsible government. The characters of both Metcalfe and Stanley offer sufficient refutation to that melodramatic myth; but a private minute, jotted by James Stephen on a later despatch, gives the surest indication of Stanley's attitude at this time: "So far as I have means of knowledge, Lord Stanley has been acting during the last four years on the conviction that he could not, and, I believe, on the principle that he ought not to, fetter the governor's discretion about anything".[3] Stanley had deeply regretted Bagot's concession, and Metcalfe was, of all men in Britain, the statesman best fitted to retrieve the situation in Canada; but there was no secret conspiracy to overthrow either Canadian liberties, or even what extreme Reformers thought their liberties.

Metcalfe's thirty-seven years in India had given him a position

---

[1] Rawson to Blackwood (of the Colonial Office), 27 December 1842.
[2] Kaye, J. W., *Life and Correspondence of Lord Metcalfe*; Dent, *Forty Years*; Hincks, F., *Reminiscences*, chaps. vii, viii.
[3] James Stephen, in a note concerning instructions for Lord Cathcart, 12 January 1846.

there somewhat similar to that later attained by John Lawrence. Wisdom, courage, liberality of outlook, and generosity of temper had marked all his doings down to the days when he became Acting Governor-General. In Jamaica he had apparently solved a problem not dissimilar to that which called him to Canada. His administrative experience was unequalled, and his political opinions were those of a progressive British Whig.[1] But his were the ways of a man accustomed to acknowledge authority, whether as principal or subordinate, and he knew what Stanley's wishes were. He believed in discipline and strict honour, and he expected his subordinates to play the game according to the accepted rules. He laboured under the disadvantage of having to learn his subject as he went along, but he made a most careful study of what Durham and Sydenham had written about his province. His reading convinced him that whether Sydenham had intended it or not, his rule "had rendered it inevitable that the council should obtain, and ascribe to themselves, in at least some degree, the character of a cabinet of ministers".[2] The concession of such a point seemed to him to involve breach of the connection; and he evolved from a study of Durham's *Report* an alternative idea of the Governor carrying on his Government by heads of departments in whom the united Legislature reposed confidence. "The general responsibility of heads of departments, acting under orders of the governor, each distinctly in his own department, might exist without the destruction of the former authority of Her Majesty's Government".[3]

Once more administrative efficiency and progressive legislation had to take a place subordinate to constitutional discussion. It soon became apparent that Governor-General and ministers had little in common, whether in politics or in political manners. From the first the natural unwillingness of an honest and conscientious administrator to allow his ministers such liberties in jobbing patronage as those to which American practice had accustomed them furnished occasion for disagreement. It seems also probable that, determined as he was to hold the balance level between factions, and finding among the better-class Conservatives men who spoke his own language more nearly than did his ministers, Sir Charles Metcalfe associated, as his ministers thought, too freely with the Opposition. In his little capital, Kingston, where political scandal was a natural stock-in-trade, and men proclaimed from the housetops rather more than was spoken in private councils, the personal equation was bound to enter to an unpleasant degree into all political disputes. In any case troubles sprang up at once. In the third session of the Union Parliament which met on 28 September 1843, the Government attempted to put down the disorders which in those days accom-

---

[1] Kaye, II, 455.   [2] Metcalfe to Stanley, 5 August 1843, in Kennedy, pp. 565 ff.
[3] Metcalfe to Stanley, 5 August 1843, in Kennedy, *ibid.*

panied political elections, and incidentally tried to spike the Tory guns, by passing three Acts, two of them quite admirable, the third an unfortunate imitation of the earlier British effort to check the energies of Orange Lodges, in Canada as elsewhere centres of Tory feeling. There is little profit in recording the complicated series of conversations, misunderstandings, charges, and counter-charges, which ended in the resignation of all the Executive Council, with one negligible exception, on Sunday, 30 November. The general charges made by the ministers were that Metcalfe had not given them his confidence; that he had made appointments without consulting them; that he had reserved a bill on which their hearts were set; and that he was aiming at a policy of mediation between parties, instead of accepting his ministers from the party dominant in Parliament. So they left him to carry on the government of Canada, assisted only by Dominic Daly, nicknamed for his adherence to office the "Perpetual Secretary".[1] If Bagot's affair may count as the first pitched battle in the seven years' war for responsible government, this was the second; and those who remembered Bagot's surrender might have expected another victory for the Reformers. But Metcalfe had not been trained in a school of surrender. "You desire to perpetuate your union with the British Empire", he wrote in answer to one of the myriad addresses which friends and foes showered down on him at this time. "Do not imagine that this purpose can be promoted by obstructing Her Majesty's Government, in order to reduce its authority to a nullity. You have every privilege freely granted that is compatible with the maintenance of that union. Her Majesty's Government has no inclination to exercise any unnecessary interference in your local affairs; but can never consent to the prostration of the honour and dignity of the Crown; and I cannot be the traitor that would sign the death-warrant of British Connexion".[2]

With painful efforts the Governor-General built up a new Council, refusing, with a wisdom never fairly acknowledged by his critics, to fling himself for relief straight into the hands of Sir Allan McNab and the old "Compact" party. He added Viger to conciliate the French, Draper to steady the centre; and Smith, D. B. Papineau, and Morris, all men of reasonably good reputations, came in during the testing months after the crisis. None of them, however, not even Draper, possessed the proper kind of influence and authority in the country.[3] Even if his Council had made a braver public appearance than it did, it never could have faced a new session of the existing Parliament, and a dissolution followed in September 1844. The election of 1844 long remained a subject of anecdote and myth among Canadian

---

[1] Kaye, II, 492–527; Dent, I, chaps. xiv, xv; Wrong, pp. 296–333; *Letter on the Ministerial Crisis*; Hincks, chaps. vii, viii.
[2] Kaye, II, 536.   [3] C.O. 42/525, Metcalfe to Stanley, 13 May 1845.

politicians. It was a fight without gloves, neither side sparing any trick or violence which might gain the victory. Metcalfe's character places him above the murky fog of bribery, brutality and chicanery which hung over the province during the struggle; but there are indications that he regarded himself as free to interpret legitimate means of persuasion somewhat generously. In these days, A. T. Galt, the son of the Scottish novelist, was spending his best energies in the Eastern Townships in the service of the British American Land Company. Friends at court are always useful, and Galt, in an interview with the Governor-General, indicated that his company was not unwilling to support the Government, desiring in return not concessions but simple justice. "You may rest assured", said Metcalfe, "those who support me, I will support". In answer the Townships sent a solid block of six representatives to support Metcalfe and the flag.[1] But the dominant fact on the Governor-General's side was not violence or corruption; it was his conviction, publicly declared, that the struggle was one to maintain the connection with Britain. It is always dangerous to turn the Union Jack into a party colour; but Metcalfe claimed to be fighting against party, and his obvious sincerity and patriotism, and the reports of his unstinted generosity towards those who required help, told on the mass of British Canadians, who might have sympathy with the Reformers, but who placed union with the mother country first in their political creed. It was a bitterly fought campaign, and a hard-won victory for Sir Charles Metcalfe. His own estimate of the results was far too optimistic—forty-six for the Government, twenty-eight for the Opposition, and some nine undeclared and uncertain.[2] At best he could count on a working majority of somewhere between three and six. With most of the debating and fighting strength on the other side, there was bound to be a progressive decline in that of the Government.

There is something almost tragic in the last struggles of a man who in 1845 was literally dying on his feet. A cancerous growth on his cheek, which had long afflicted him, was now rendering existence a torture. The sight of one eye was gone, that of the other weakened; eating and drinking became more and more painful exercises. Yet Metcalfe never flinched from what he counted an imperial duty. As pitiful as his sufferings were the tactics by which he and his ministers attempted to retain their political control. Warned of an Opposition motion for the removal of all the remaining restrictions in the use of the French language, they anticipated it by a Government proposal. Again, when the dormant question of compensation for those in Upper Canada who had suffered losses in the rebellion

[1] Skelton, O. D., *Life of Sir A. T. Galt*, pp. 134–6—an extract from a letter of A. T. Galt, 7 December 1844.
[2] Kaye, Sir J. W., *Selections from the papers of Lord Metcalfe*, p. 437.

was reawakened, and it seemed possible to conciliate French opinion by the extension of the idea to Lower Canada, the Government party assisted in carrying an address that "His Excellency would be pleased to cause proper measures to be adopted in order to ensure to the inhabitants of that part of the province formerly Lower Canada indemnity for just losses sustained during the rebellion of 1837 and 1838". Although commissioners were appointed, and claims collected and corrected, the move effected nothing in the world of French political opinion, and the incident ended, to re-emerge in startling fashion under Lord Elgin.[1]

A peerage, with its assurance of royal favour, and the warmest of support from Stanley and Peel, brought some little comfort, but Metcalfe's race was run, and he left Canada at the end of 1845, a dying but not a defeated man. The Canadian verdict on Lord Metcalfe's career, formulated in the days after admiration for his generous and loyal pugnacity had faded into disillusionment, stands clear—an unfortunate episode presided over by a misguided but noble-hearted autocrat. The opinion of Peel's Cabinet, even in its more progressive section, was as definite on the other side. "The favour of his Sovereign and the acknowledgment of his country", wrote W. E. Gladstone, in his short-lived Colonial Secretaryship of 1846, "have marked his administration as one which, under the peculiar circumstances of the task he had to perform, may justly be regarded as a model for his successor".[2] But the most searching comment was made, in the privacy of the Colonial Office, by that much misunderstood official, James Stephen.

"I will venture to say in general", he wrote in 1846, for Mr Gladstone's guidance, "that Canada appears to me to have shaken off, or laid aside, the colonial relation to this country, and to have become, in everything but name, a distinct state....It is my own opinion that a governor of Canada is best instructed by resorting to the commonplaces which present themselves on such an occasion, but whose best recommendation is that they convey little or no meaning. A man fit to govern Canada must and will act, as Lord Metcalfe has always done, on his own judgment and responsibility. A man not fit to govern Canada will, I believe, but have that unfitness increased and rendered the more dangerous, if he is hampered by any rules of conduct from this country, to which he may think it his duty to adhere, even when adherence to them becomes impossible. There are at this moment, in Canada, almost as many Europeans as there were in the United States when they declared their independence—a very pregnant fact in many ways".[3]

As will be seen, the greatest of Sydenham's successors held opinions not so very different from this, but drew an entirely different conclusion. Bureaucrats faced with novelty are naturally pessimistic.

Nothing was added to the tale of responsibility in 1846, the year of Lord Cathcart's rule. Cathcart let constitutional questions severely alone. It was his unfortunate lot to rule Canada in the

---

[1] Hincks, letter to Lord Elgin, 9 February 1849, which was later printed in Canada.
[2] C.O. 380/5, instructions to Lord Cathcart, from a draft dated 3 February 1846.
[3] A minute on Lord Cathcart's instructions, 12 January 1846.

decisive year of British economic reform; and he was the channel through which colonial merchants, damaged by the rectifications of Peel's third Free Trade budget, and deprived of the advantages of colonial preference, warned the free-traders of Britain of the incalculable ruin they were preparing for the colonies. Through him also Mr Gladstone communicated to the province the chief truths of the Cobdenite gospel in despatches which would have done honour to a professor of economics.[1] The Governor-General had also to face the possibility of war with the United States. Through the entire period, indeed, relations between Britain and the American Republic with special reference to Canada remained obscure. Out of the rebellion had arisen incidents such as the burning of the *Caroline* by Canadian Loyalists, and the unjust imprisonment and trial of Macleod in the state of New York, which threatened frontier warfare.[2] In both East and West there were boundary difficulties which American orators proposed to solve by violence. Each new presidential election saw American parties prepared to catch votes by conniving at some fresh variety of insult to Great Britain, the Oregon boundary furnishing in 1844 the most famous of their war-cries, "Fifty-four forty or fight". Durham had steadied the situation for the moment, and although border provocations in Maine had proved almost too much for Sydenham's patience, Bagot's known friendliness towards Washington counted for something, and Metcalfe was most courteously received as he passed through the state of New York to Canada in 1843. Peel, too, had in these years steadfastly set his face against war, and the so-called surrenders of the Ashburton and Oregon treaties in 1842[3] and 1846[4] were the price he paid in order that Britain and the United States might escape the crime of mutual strife, and Canada the wastage of war. But no one who had intimate knowledge of the irrational animosities on either side of the Canadian frontier could afford, in 1846, to feel optimistic; and it was well that at the critical moment the Governor-General of Canada was also a soldier.

III. LORD ELGIN (1847–54). Under Lord Elgin the troubles of the Canadian community ended. The British Whigs through their Colonial Secretary, Earl Grey, had removed the chief obstruction in a despatch to Sir John Harvey, now Lieutenant-Governor of Nova Scotia. Harvey was recommended to allow the formation of party ministries, so long as he himself remained unassociated with any one party, and acted as a mediator and moderator between the influential of all parties.[5] For Canada these instructions meant that the Governor-General was expected to accept the contentions of the Reformers, and to exercise his authority indirectly and in the form

---

[1] Gladstone to Cathcart, 3 March and 18 May 1846.   [2] See chapter x (B).
[3] See chapter xiv.   [4] See *C.H.B.E.* vol. ii.
[5] Grey, Earl, *The Colonial Administration of Lord John Russell*, i, 209–13.

of influence. For such a rôle no one could have been better fitted than the eighth Earl of Elgin. He was one of the distinguished group of young Liberal administrators whom Peel had gathered round him. His Scottish origin and name were likely to propitiate a perfervid section of the colonial Reformers: and his marriage with Lady Mary Lambton made him seem a natural continuator of his father-in-law's policy. His chief qualities were those of easy accessibility, fair-mindedness, acute political judgment, and common sense raised to the pitch where it passes into statesmanship. Unlike his predecessors, he came to Canada not an invalid but in the prime of life, and his eight years in Canada were the most stirring and fruitful in a career compact of strenuous imperial service. Like Sydenham he possessed the absolute confidence of the Colonial Office, and even more than with Sydenham his and not theirs was the guiding and constructive mind.[1] It was a singular advantage, too, that so far from regarding concessions to Canada as disastrous to imperial unity, he thought the new Liberal policy the only possible basis for that unity. In an age when British ministers of all shades of opinion were indulging in jeremiads over the fate of an Empire whose fundamental strength they seemed incapable of perceiving, Lord Elgin never flinched, and his official chiefs had to endure some very plain speaking on the duty, for Cabinet ministers, of optimism and courage.

His first achievement was the concession to the colony of complete self-government in domestic administration. On his arrival he found that the emergency ministry which Metcalfe had created in 1844, and which Cathcart had continued, was powerless and discredited. Its ablest members were already taking thought for a doubtful morrow by seeking appointments on the Bench. Attempts made to conciliate French opinion met with no response in Lower Canada. Indeed, the so-called Sherwood-Daly ministry, through which Elgin governed the province in 1847, marks the lowest point of strength and capacity reached by a Canadian Administration in the last century. At times it actually possessed a bare majority in the Assembly, but defeat was its natural atmosphere. The election at the end of the year, in which this fiasco inevitably ended, was decisive. A great majority in both Upper and Lower Canada returned to support Baldwin and Lafontaine; their candidate for the Speakership was carried by fifty-four to nineteen, and an amendment to the address by fifty-four to twenty. The new ministry, under the two great Reform leaders, entered office on 11 March 1848. It is a striking evidence of the changed attitude of the British Government that, after the arch-rebel, L. J. Papineau, had returned from exile, and had found a seat in the new Parliament, Grey, who did not realise for how little Papineau now counted among the French

[1] Based on the *Elgin-Grey Correspondence*, 1847-52.

Canadians, told Elgin that he would not oppose his inclusion in the Government, "if his being included in the arrangement should be insisted upon by the leaders of a party which can command a majority".[1] It was in accordance with British traditions that the revolutionary change, by which it was determined that the British Empire should develop into a loose federation of self-governing Dominions, was expressed in nothing more sensational than a few wise despatches, and a slight modification in the method of selecting executive councillors in Canada and Nova Scotia.

The years from 1848 to 1854 fall into two divisions—the first to 1851, in which the new instrument of government was proved under Baldwin and Lafontaine; the second from 1851 to 1854, in which Elgin, mainly with Hincks as his lieutenant, but, at the end, in co-operation with the Tories, established, as the best means of operating the new system, government by a central, or moderate, or Liberal-Conservative party, with efficient administration, not abstract political doctrine, as its inspiration.

The great Baldwin-Lafontaine ministry disappointed all the fears and prophecies of its critics, perhaps also the bright hopes of its more enthusiastic partisans, by three years of sober, constructive, and conservative legislation. Elgin soon found that his chief ministers, so far from being firebrands, were perhaps the most truly conservative statesmen in the province. As for disloyalty he assured Grey that Robert Baldwin was worth three regiments to the British connection, and that the last hand to wave the British flag on American ground might well be that of a French Canadian.[2] In 1848 and 1849, years of revolution and stress in Europe, the only threats which British rule in Canada had to face were futile movements of Irish-American discontent, and the unprincipled use of anti-British propaganda by candidates for the American presidency, designed to catch the Irish vote.[3] The legislation of these years was steady and useful rather than brilliant—an Amnesty Act long overdue; educational reform, including the establishment of the University at Toronto on an unsectarian basis; improved municipal organisation; a Chancery Act to remedy the abuses of the existing court, and the first beginnings of railway legislation. There were, however, two incidents of a more sensational character. The first was that of the Rebellion Losses Bill. Lafontaine, determined, as he had a right to be, that the provision, initiated under Metcalfe, for compensation to claimants in Lower Canada who had sustained damage in the rebellion, should be made effective, carried a bill for that purpose. Elgin, who privately disliked the measure,[4] stood loyally by his ministers, refused to shift the responsibility from his

[1] *Elgin-Grey Correspondence*, Grey to Elgin, 22 February 1848.
[2] *Ibid.* Elgin to Grey, 4 May 1848.
[3] C.O. 42/589, Elgin to Newcastle, 28 January 1853.
[4] *Elgin-Grey Correspondence*, Elgin to Grey, 4 January 1849.

shoulders to those of the Home Government, and was on two separate occasions subjected in Montreal to fierce hostile demonstrations, accompanied by crude violence. At the same time the mob, which consisted in part of well-dressed and respectable individuals, destroyed the Parliament House with its records and library; and later in the summer another Montreal mob committed an assault on the house of the French-Canadian leader, Lafontaine, in protest against the trial of the leaders of the April riots. It was the last flare-up of diseased animosity towards the French, and the frank confession of the old "Compact" party that their day was over. The words in which Sir Allan McNab, the leader of the group, refused to intervene as a moderator in the disturbances mark the shame and discredit in which his party was disappearing: "If we don't make a disturbance about this", he told a moderate who was remonstrating with him, "we shall never get in".[1] Elgin, who acted with amazing self-restraint and wisdom throughout, gained thereafter the unfailing support of the French; and, as his tour in Western Canada in the autumn of 1849 proved, the equally sure respect of all that was decent and responsible among the British settlers.

The second episode, the annexationist movement of 1849, was a consequence of Peel's Free Trade movement and is discussed in a subsequent chapter. The remedy for a movement primarily economic was, as Elgin saw, the arrangement of some kind of reciprocity of trade with the United States. The incessant emphasis in his letters to Grey, not only on the difficulties in which Canadian business men were involved, but on the need for immediate diplomatic action in Washington, proves how clearly he understood this side of Canadian life, and in a sense his Reciprocity Treaty of 1854 was the perfect answer to the agitation of 1849. As it was, Baldwin made it clear that he would countenance no trafficking with disloyalty, and subscribers to the manifesto in favour of annexation who held offices under the Crown suffered deprivation of them. The movement barely touched the West, and the prosperity of 1851 gave the lie to some of the exaggerations of 1849.

Meanwhile the political situation was developing in two opposite directions. On the one hand extreme opinion, disappointed by the moderation of the ministry, was organising itself into radical groups, Rouges among the French, and Clear Grits in Upper Canada. On the other hand, these extremists tended to drive the ministers into a central position. Now that the great theoretic dispute over responsibility had been settled, many men, chief among them Francis Hincks, the Inspector-General, felt inclined to banish abstract discussion from politics, and to concentrate on the promotion of Canadian material prosperity. As chapter xv relates, the early 'fifties were the period of railroad exploitation and the average Canadian had

---

[1] Elgin to Cumming Bruce, 14 January 1850.

come to think in economic and financial terms rather than in political. In 1851 the two leaders of the old Reform party disappeared from political life, Baldwin, because the new Radicals had challenged his chancery legislation, and were prevented from abolishing the Court of Chancery only by the loyal support of Baldwin's French friends; Lafontaine, partly because of ill-health, but also because he was at heart conservative, and had little sympathy with the Reformers of the extreme left.

The new Hincks-Morin ministry,[1] which was supported by both French and British in the election of 1851, provided, far more than the late Administration had done, a programme and leaders fitted to guide the province into its era of expansion. Its moderate temper and utilitarian objects expressed more appropriately than the zeal of 1847–8 the ideals for which first Sydenham and then Elgin had striven. The new call was for the self-government of Canada, established through utilitarian administration by practical men.

The work of the ministry revealed itself between 1852 and 1854 in a mass of domestic legislation and in the prolonged negotiations with the United States which Lord Elgin brought to a successful termination in 1854. Its period of greatest strength was covered by the long session, broken by one adjournment, which lasted from 19 August 1852 to 14 June 1853. Acts dealing with every aspect of provincial life were passed; for railways and a trans-Atlantic service of steamships; for increased representation in the House of Assembly; for the adoption of a decimal coinage; for the organisation of a ministry of agriculture. A score of other measures met the popular demand for material development, and the final success of the reciprocity negotiations, in which Hincks played a considerable part, opened up fresh markets for an increasingly productive Canada. But this absorption in practical measures was preparing trouble for Hincks and his supporters. In Upper Canada Hincks, although easily the ablest provincial statesman of his time, was losing weight. He was too intimately connected with the French to please his western supporters; and, like other politicians who have blended business with politics, some of his transactions, while judged in the courts to be legitimate, were not regarded as judicious in a Cabinet minister.[2] The ministry had also inherited two awkward questions from its predecessors, the demands for secularisation of the Clergy Reserves, and for the abolition in Lower Canada of seigneurial tenures. The latter was in response to real grievances inflicted on the Lower Canadian community by relics of the old French colonial system. It affected vested interests there, and Lafontaine with his conservative mind had approached the subject with caution, if not with reluctance. Hincks, Morin, and indeed the Governor-General, were inclined to

---

[1] Hincks, chaps. xii–xv; Dent, II, 245–304.
[2] *Report of a Select Committee of the Legislative Council.*

move slowly. So also with the Clergy Reserves. Sydenham had done his best to reconcile Upper Canada to a compromise; but times had changed. The demand for complete secularisation had increased with the increased importance of the non-Anglican element in the population. The Presbyterian Scots had been affected by the Free Kirk movement in Scotland, and were being evangelised in the interests of a voluntary system by George Brown, editor of *The Globe*, and, through its columns, the most influential propagandist in Canada. John Strachan, Bishop of Toronto, who never learned to leave well alone, but whose devotion to the Church of England in Canada almost atoned for the lack of scruple with which he prosecuted Anglican interests, was rousing old rancours through his agitation for an Anglican University.

Unfortunately for Hincks and Morin, events in Britain made it difficult for them to meet the demands of their more radical supporters. In 1851 the Russell Government was too weak to pass the necessary preliminary imperial legislation through the House of Lords. Then the short-lived Derby Government of 1852 did its best to cancel Elgin's work by its ignorant and prejudiced colonial and ecclesiastical outlook;[1] and Hincks who visited Britain in 1852 suffered a double rebuff at its hands—in railway projects and over the Clergy Reserves. When the Aberdeen Coalition gave the necessary sanction for provincial legislation on the Clergy Reserves, it had become important in Canada to delay the bill for secularisation until parliamentary representation had been reformed and the House of Assembly given its enlarged numbers. These delays, together with a growing impression that the reforming party was no longer eager to reform, shook the stability and reputation of the ministry.

The last year of Lord Elgin's regime, 1854, was in many ways a decisive one. It witnessed the overthrow of an Administration to which he had looked for the realisation of his policy for Canada; an election and party crisis; then, the accomplishment of practically every object which the Governor-General and his most trusted advisers had hoped to obtain.[2] Elgin himself had spent the later months of 1853, and the earlier part of 1854, on furlough at home; the early summer saw him launched on the special mission to Washington in which he secured the Reciprocity Treaty. Hincks, too, had been an absentee. In the interval the political situation had not improved. It was a fresh count in the impeachment that, when the ministers met Parliament on 13 June 1854, the earliest possible date after Elgin and Hincks had returned from the United States, they had evaded by a single day an infraction of the law

[1] Elgin to Cumming Bruce, 2 October 1852.
[2] The final authority for the closing months is found in two unpublished and unofficial letters to Sir George Grey, 9 September and 15 September 1854 (C.O. 42/595).

which required not more than a twelvemonth to intervene between two sessions of Parliament. The attack broke on the Government from every quarter, and defeat in the debate on the address seemed certain. The ministers advised an instant dissolution, and the Governor-General accepted their advice. But this created a new offence, for according to Canadian usage no session of Parliament counted as such unless at least one measure had passed into law during its existence. As the Speaker, not without personal *animus*, drove home his technical point, in the presence of the Governor-General, observers noticed that Elgin's face revealed, for the only time on record, his deep chagrin at Canadian political factiousness.[1] "My Parliament has been trying to diminish my sentimentality for this country by behaving very badly", he wrote to his wife, "but I have sent them about their business".[2] It was a justifiable chagrin, for half a dozen major issues were calling for parliamentary settlement, chief among them the provincial ratification of the Reciprocity Treaty.

Whatever the event might be for Hincks, it proved for Elgin merely the last and completest of his victories. The summer election came and went, and it was soon apparent that while the ministerial group would outnumber any other single section, the other groups by combining might snatch a victory; and although the political opinions of these groups varied from the obsolescent Tory views of McNab to the aggressive Radicalism of the Clear Grits, enmity to the ministry seemed adequate excuse for the abandonment of party creeds and honour. On 8 September the Hincks-Morin Cabinet resigned; on 11 September the McNab-Morin Cabinet entered office.

The victors in this arrangement were not the Tories, but the Governor-General and the province. Much lay implicit in the change. It enabled Elgin to give spectacular evidence of his adherence to the principle of responsible government, for he was not only accepting a new ministry at the dictation of a parliamentary majority, but he was replacing old friends with men, some of whom, in both word and action, had insulted and injured him in a fashion for which no apology could atone. But, further, it was a victory, not for the old Tories, not even for John A. Macdonald and the new Conservatives, but for that central moderate party through which Sydenham had done his really effective work, and to reconstitute which had been the main aim of Elgin, and, with him, of Hincks. The new ministry was not merely blessed by Hincks and Baldwin; it included the solid mass of Hincks's French colleagues, together with two representatives of Upper Canadian moderatism. This marked the official beginning of that Liberal-Conservative party and programme which came to be associated so closely with the future of Canada. Its true founders were Sydenham, Elgin, and Hincks.

But Elgin believed in measures as well as men, and the change

---

[1] Dent, II, 294.   [2] *Letters of the Earl of Elgin* (privately printed, 1864), p. 6.

effected his purposes because the first steps taken by the new ministry were to complete and pass bills for the secularisation of the Clergy Reserves, and the abolition of seigneurial tenures, which the Governor-General and his late councillors had delayed only that they might secure the greatest measure of unanimity possible in the province.[1] Now, the party formerly pledged to the maintenance of old establishments, and headed by McNab, the most unrepentant "die-hard" in Canada, accepted the reforming programme which their predecessors had drafted.[2] In addition they ratified the great trade agreement with the United States, on which Elgin, Hincks, and the moderates had spent so much labour. Between 1841 and 1854 it had been far too frequent a practice for parties either to suggest in opposition projects which they knew to be impracticable, or, more frequently, to oppose with violence measures which the welfare of the province demanded. Elgin did something to end this party factiousness by forcing the bitterest partisans in Parliament to accept the very address which their opponents had drawn up, and to complete the legislative programme sketched out in 1848 by the moderate Reformers.

By 1854 Baldwin and Lafontaine, the Radicals of 1841, had mellowed into reasonable Whigs, and then fallen silent. The "Compact" group was either extinct, or served in Cabinets devoted to causes which they had once reviled. In Britain, Secretaries of State for the Colonies no longer composed abstract essays proving that the inevitable was absurd, or expected a high-spirited and intelligent people to receive guidance in domestic details from Downing Street. An immense victory for common sense and progress had been won. But while the chief beneficiaries had been the Canadian people, whose moderation and loyalty had entitled them to all they secured, the credit must remain with Sydenham and Elgin, the two most notable figures among the Governors of Canada. Of the two, the first place must be given to Elgin; for while, with Sydenham, he saw the folly of Canadian factions, and the clamant need for a central group bent on a constructive programme, he also saw that the future of the province must depend on a real partnership between French and English. In pursuit of Canadian prosperity he cherished no animosities, and remembered no insults, but conceived of himself, his Reformers, and his Conservatives, as forming parts of an indivisible whole. As he returned in melting mood from his last progress through his province, he wrote home with pardonable complacency, "It is impossible for me to go through the country without feeling that I have a strong hold on the people of the country; that I occupy a place here which no one ever filled before".[3]

---

[1] Elgin to Lady Elgin, 25 August 1854.
[2] The same to Sir George Grey, 15 September 1854.
[3] The same to Lady Elgin, 7 October 1854.

CHAPTER XIII

CANADA UNDER RESPONSIBLE GOVERNMENT,
1854–1867

THE year 1854 divides the quarter century of the Union experiment in the Canadas into two distinct periods. It was a year of marked significance. It saw the departure of Lord Elgin, last of the proconsuls. It brought the definite liquidation of the old political parties and the assumption of office by a Liberal-Conservative coalition. It produced the settlement of the Clergy Reserves and seigneurial tenures questions, the last of the great issues which had given the parties of reform their mission and their unity. It was the year, finally, of the signature of the Reciprocity Treaty, indicating a new economic orientation and a beginning in the shaping of foreign policy.

The years from 1841 to 1854 had witnessed the struggle for responsible government and its achievement; the years from 1854 to 1867 were to witness the attempt to make responsible government work and to develop its three-fold implications in party government, Cabinet government, and colonial self-government. The first period was dominated by the governors, a period remembered as the day of Sydenham and Bagot, of Metcalfe and Elgin; the second was the day of the prime ministers and party leaders, of McNab and Morin, of John A. Macdonald and Cartier, of Brown and Dorion, Galt and McGee, of Taché and Sicotte and John Sandfield Macdonald. The first period was one of testing the working of the union of Upper and Lower Canada in a single province; the second, of seeking a remedy or a substitute for that union. In the first period the constitutional issue concerned the relations between Governor and Assembly; in the second, the relations between section and section. The endeavour of the French-Canadian element of Canada East to escape from the subordination and the denationalisation marked out for it by the framers of union was followed by an agitation in English-speaking Canada West to escape from "French-Canadian domination". The first period saw the break-down of the old preferential system which united the colonies with the mother country in political and economic bonds; the second, the trial of reciprocity, linking British North America in trade with the other great branch of the English-speaking peoples. The first period saw the beginnings of large-scale financial and corporation enterprise, of canal and railway building, of wider commercial contact with the outside world; the second, the outcome in prosperity, speculation, economic crisis and sober recovery.

The general election of August and September 1854, though warmly contested, was indecisive. Hincks and Morin had hoped that an appeal to the country would solve the difficulties created by the growing cleavage between the moderate and radical wings of the dominant Liberal party and by the clash of rising personal ambitions. In the event their difficulties were multiplied. The party situation in the new Assembly, which met on 5 September, was confused, but two results were clear: that there was a decisive majority for the secularisation of the Clergy Reserves and for the abolition of seigneurial tenures, and that there was not a majority for the Hincks-Morin Administration. The groups in the Assembly were many, and the lines of demarcation far from definite. The union of the Canadas had brought party alliance rather than party fusion, and each section of the province retained and multiplied its separate groups. In each there was a Centre party, with a Left and a Right.

In Canada West, the Ministerialist or Centre party, led by Hincks and comprising the majority of the moderate Reformers who had followed Baldwin, had lost in numbers on both flanks, but remained the largest group. On the right stood the Conservatives, themselves divided into the die-hard Tories who had opposed responsible government and fought for the union of Church and State, with Sir Allan McNab, Cayley and Murney and John Hillyard Cameron as their chiefs, and a mellower and more opportunist wing, prepared to accept the people's verdict on these issues, and finding a leader in the youthful member for Kingston, John A. Macdonald. On the left there was a motley group of Independents and Clear Grits, with George Brown, fiery Covenanter, William Lyon Mackenzie, unsparing critic of all autocracies, and John Sandfield Macdonald, a more supple opportunist, most notable among them.

In Canada East, the Ministerialists, with Morin, Drummond, Chauveau, Taché and Cartier on the front benches, had also lost in strength but retained the lead. On their left, the Rouges, followers of Papineau and exponents of a radicalism of French and United States inspiration, had reached nineteen in number; their chieftain had retired to seigneurial seclusion at Montebello, but Antoine Aimé Dorion, radical in view and moderate in temper, his brother Eric, *l'enfant terrible* of the *curés*, Papin and D'Aoust and Laberge, all with the fire and certainty of youth, had taken up his torch. Loosely allied with the French-speaking Rouges were a number of English-speaking Liberals, Luther Holton, John Young, and, for a time, A. T. Galt. There was not so definite a right wing, but Joseph Cauchon, hating what he termed the "socialism" of Clear Grit and Rouge, and clerical in sympathy, had a following or "tail" which tended to draw away from the Centre group.

The Assembly now consisted of one hundred and thirty members, sixty-five from each section. The two Centre or Ministerialist parties, controlling from fifty-five to sixty votes, fell short of a majority; the Conservatives, and the Clear Grits and Rouges combined, each numbered between thirty-five and forty. How could a stable majority be secured, a majority which would carry out the evident will of the electorate as to the Clergy Reserves and seigneuries? It was not possible to reunite the Liberal party of Baldwin and Lafontaine: there was a greater cleavage of temperament and personal antagonism between the Liberal Ministerialists and their Clear Grit and Rouge wings than between Liberals who had been six years in office and Conservatives who had been six years out. Three other combinations were contemplated. Brown had supported Macdonald and other Conservatives against Ministerialists in the election, emphasising "the small differences which now divide Conservatives and Reformers in Upper Canada, and the exceeding probability that ere long they will be found together in the same harness working against the common enemy".[1] He was sanguine enough to believe in the possibility of a union of moderate Conservatives, Clear Grits and Rouges, but the event showed that it was easier to work against a common enemy than for a common purpose. Hincks looked to winning over some of the Conservatives who had accepted secularisation; any wider coalition seemed to him improbable, for he had "no idea whatever that Sir Allan McNab...would be willing to form a government on the basis of carrying the secularisation of the Clergy Reserves".[2] But it was precisely the possibility of this third plan of a wider coalition, between the Conservatives of Canada West and the Ministerialists of Canada East, and perhaps of Canada West as well, based on acceptance of the electoral verdict on Clergy Reserves and seigneurial tenure, that Sir Allan, lured by the chance of power and spurred on by Macdonald, was now exploring.

The decision was not long deferred. Hincks summoned a party caucus to ensure united backing for George Etienne Cartier as Speaker, but the left wing refused support. The anti-Ministerialist groups planned to give a complimentary nomination to Louis Sicotte, of the Rouge group, and then to unite on John Sandfield Macdonald, who had clashed sharply with Hincks in the closing hours of the preceding session. Their plans carried to the extent of defeating Cartier by sixty-two to fifty-nine. But when Sicotte was named, and appeared in an unquestioned minority, Hincks, preferring the lesser evil, suddenly called out, "Put me among the yeas", and so blocked the path of his nearer rival. Even so, the end was only postponed. Two days later the Government was defeated on a minor question of privilege, and at once resigned. Sir Allan McNab, as the leader of the recognised Opposition, was sent for by the Governor-General. Without hesitation, McNab accepted the task of forming an Administration. Through Macdonald he entered into negotiations with Morin, who readily agreed upon a coalition, stipulating, however,

[1] *Toronto Globe*, 7 Aug. 1854.
[2] Letter to John Wilson, 14 Sept. 1854, in *Reminiscences*, p. 336.

that the Ministerialists from Canada West should be offered representation. Hincks, the most expert parliamentarian and most practical administrator of his day, but under fire for adventures in the shady borderland of politics and finance, found it advisable to withdraw to a West Indies governorship. Two members of his group, Robert Spence and John Ross, joined the new Administration.[1]

The formation of the Liberal-Conservative coalition ministry and party was not an accidental result of sudden shifts in parliamentary tactics. It was the natural outcome of the passing of old issues, the cleavage between radical and moderate Reformers and the merging of mellowed Tories and disillusioned Whigs. The Coalition was recognised and blessed in retirement by Baldwin, Whig champion of the old causes, and so recognised and opposed in the Assembly by Dorion, pressing on to yet new aims.

The McNab-Morin Government set vigorously to work to carry out the policies it had inherited. Legislative effect was given to the Reciprocity Treaty. The Clergy Reserves were secularised. Future proceeds from the sale of reserves were to be distributed among the municipalities in proportion to population. No further payments were to be made to any Church, though provision was made for continuing all stipends charged upon the reserves during the lifetime of existing incumbents and for commutation of these payments if desired, a provision which involved the establishment of a small permanent fund and therefore roused the wrath of the root-and-branch men who could not tolerate even the shadow of a continuing endowment. The two-century-old endeavour to implant a frontier version of the feudal system in the New World did not survive the two-generation endeavour to establish a frontier form of State Church. The Seigneurial Tenure Act abolished all feudal rights and duties, but not at the expense of the seigneur. Provision was made for judicial determination of the rights of the seigneurs as distinct from their unauthorised claims, and for indemnifying them at the expense of the province for the *lods et ventes* or transfer dues, the *droit de banalité* or milling obligation, and all other lawful charges except the *cens et rentes*. The *cens et rentes*, an annual rental usually amounting to a sou an arpent, the habitant continued to pay, but this charge, equivalent to the interest on a very light mortgage, was redeemable at any time by payment of a corresponding capital sum. As the province assumed the burden of freeing the habitant of Canada East from his obligations, it became politically

---

[1] McNab-Morin Administration, 11 Sept. 1854:
Canada West. Sir Allan McNab, President of Council and Minister of Agriculture; John A. Macdonald, Attorney-General West; William Cayley, Inspector-General; Robert Spence, Postmaster-General; John Ross, Speaker of the Legislative Council.
Canada East. A. N. Morin, Commissioner of Crown Lands; L. T. Drummond, Attorney-General East; P. J. O. Chauveau, Provincial Secretary; E. P. Taché, Receiver-General; J. Chabot, Commissioner of Public Works.

necessary to make an equal grant to the municipalities of Canada West, and a proportionate grant to the Townships of Canada East, where the seigneurial tenure was not in force.

The day after the adjournment for the Christmas recess, on 19 December 1854, Lord Elgin, who in his seven years of office had watched over the experimentings of Tory, Reform, and now Liberal-Conservative Administrations, made way for his successor. Sir Edmund Head, Oxford don, Poor Law Commissioner, and latterly Lieutenant-Governor of New Brunswick, was a man of ability and of stiffness on occasion, as George Brown was to discover, but he did not hold the centre of the stage. Early in his term he ceased to attend the meetings of Council, and learned of the policies of the Cabinet only when formulated, instead of sharing in the discussion while they were still in the shaping. Even in relations with the Imperial Government, the growing practice of ministerial visits to London came to afford an alternative channel of consultation.

During the recess the postponed reorganisation of the Canada East wing of the Government was effected. Morin retired to the Bench, Taché succeeded as leader, and Cartier and Cauchon entered the Cabinet in place of Chauveau and Chabot. The strength of the Administration in the East was consolidated by the changes, and John A. Macdonald and Cartier entered upon the close political and personal partnership which for the greater part of the next twenty years was to form the basis of government in Canada.

When Parliament reassembled in February, it continued a programme of constructive legislative activity comparable to the early years of the Baldwin-Lafontaine regime. The municipal and road system of Canada East was revised. The franchise was extended. The withdrawal of some British regular forces to strengthen the armies in the Crimea stimulated a reorganisation of the militia system. The sedentary militia, consisting of all male inhabitants between eighteen and sixty, was continued, with no training beyond the convivial farce of the single annual muster day, but increased provision was made for its arming and for its mobilisation in emergency. Side by side, a new volunteer force was set up, with from ten to twenty days' training. Both bodies as yet merely supplemented the British regular force, which provided the Staff and organisation. The Grand Trunk Railway, in financial difficulties because of rising construction and capital costs and management by absentees and contractors, received a "loan" of $900,000 to complete construction. A measure for making the Legislative Council elective was rejected by the Council in 1855, but it passed a year later, the main achievement of the session. The new Council consisted of forty-eight members, twelve chosen every second year for an eight-year term, by the same voters as elected the members of the Assembly but grouped in fewer and larger constituencies; the existing members were to retain their seats for life. An elective

Upper House was based on United States rather than British precedent and fitted dubiously into a system of Cabinet responsibility, to say nothing of Cabinet patronage, but during the brief decade the experiment lasted the new Council did little harm, if little good, and did not come into serious conflict with Cabinet or Assembly: at worst, candidates found the large constituencies inconvenient and costly to canvass. But the reform had been a demand of the old Liberal party and the passing of the Act completed its traditional mission.

The new Government was favoured during its early years by the extraordinary prosperity which pervaded the colony. Railway building was at its height. The mileage of the province grew from two hundred in 1853 to over eighteen hundred in 1859. Some £15,000,000 currency was expended on railway construction in four years. British capital, provincial credit, municipal ambitions and rivalries pooled in the Municipal Loan Fund, all offered tempting opportunities for promoters, at home and overseas. Charters and lobbyists multiplied. New towns were planned, land values in town and country soared (the Great Western paying $700,000 for land costs estimated to require $60,000), wages rose, supplies found readier market, and prices between 1852 and 1854 doubled or in some cases trebled. Thus the Canada Company recorded the rise of price of cows from an average of £4 to £9 or £10 per head; flour, from £1 to 38s. or £2 per barrel; while pork doubled, and oats trebled in price.[1] The Crimean War raised interest rates disturbingly; but in compensation, with Russian wheat out of the British market, grain prices rose to golden heights; the price of fall wheat at Toronto, which had varied little from 4s. a bushel between 1840 and 1853, rose to 10s. 11d. in May 1855.[2] Reciprocity opened wider markets to the south, and if the trade between the provinces and the Republic was largely one of neighbourhood convenience and exchange of similar products, it was none the less profitable. New banks secured charters with an ease which fell into laxity, and the old ones increased their capital and still more their note-issue. New gold supplies in California, Australia and British Columbia were enhancing prices and giving a fillip to industry everywhere. Immigrants poured into the province, particularly into the West; in 1854 over 50,000 landed at Quebec, and 7000 more came from the United States, and though the majority passed on to the Western States, enough remained to turn the wheels of business still more rapidly. Toronto's population rose from 13,000 in 1842 to 30,000 in 1852 and 42,000 in 1856, and its property values more than doubled between 1851 and 1856; London, in Canada West, grew from 5000 to 15,000 between 1850 and 1856. Wholesale and retail business

---

[1] Widder, F., *Information for Intending Emigrants of All Classes to Upper Canada.* 1855.
[2] *Ibid.* p. 14.

multiplied and specialised. As in the railway eras thirty and sixty years later, optimism was unbounded and speculation discounted the progress of years to come.

The day of reckoning came in the bleak year 1857. It was a year of financial crisis in Britain and the United States, but the troubles in Canada were only secondarily influenced by developments elsewhere: the restriction of British investment had begun earlier and the United States crisis was more definitely a banking panic. The tide of prosperity had turned in Canada itself. Railway building and railway promotion were approaching an end, and with their ending came a collapse of land speculation. The Crimean War was over and wheat had fallen. The harvest of 1857 was poor in quantity and quality; the harvest of 1858 was a complete failure. Inflated land values tumbled. Railways which had been meeting interest out of capital called on the province to make good its guarantees or grant doles. Municipalities which had recently discovered how easy it was to borrow discovered now how hard it was to repay, though they discovered later how politically feasible it was to shift their burdens to the province. The province itself found its revenues falling as its burdens grew. Bankruptcies spread in widening circles, and though the Canadian banks withstood the immediate test much better than the banks of the United States, and payments were not suspended during the crisis, weaknesses had been incurred which brought collapse later. Immigration through Quebec fell in 1858 to one-sixth the height of 1854. It was only a temporary check in the onward sweep of development, but it was a serious and a salutary one.

The economic crisis inevitably brought harder going in politics. The secure mastery of the early years of the Coalition was challenged. Old programmes had been carried out; the new had not yet taken shape. In the interval personal bitterness and political corruption flourished. John A. Macdonald emerged more and more as the dominant figure, but constantly under fire. A violent quarrel with Brown on the floor of the house, a threatened duel with one of his own followers, Colonel Rankin, and growing friction with his titular leader, marked his stormy progress. Defeated on a motion for enquiry into charges of failure on the part of a Roman Catholic judge and jury to render justice in the murder of a Protestant at a fair in Canada East, and also, so far as the Canada West members were concerned, on a proposal to make Quebec the permanent capital instead of alternating between Quebec and Toronto, McNab was forced to resign, and was left smouldering in gouty rage while his junior supplanted him, in May 1856, as western leader in a Taché-Macdonald ministry. Later in the year Cartier took the place of Taché.

The two incidents just noted were symptoms of the rising sectional and religious antagonism which was to create new issues and reshape parties. The root difficulty was that two communities, differing in language, in race, in creed, in social customs, found themselves yoked together under a single government. Durham's hope that union would force assimilation of the French minority to English ways had proved illusory. French nationalism was more conscious, more assured, more firmly rooted than in Papineau's day. The two sections of the province had been brought closer in trade and transportation, but in education, in legal systems, in social atmosphere, the cleavage continued and the task of finding solutions acceptable to both grew harder. Nor was that all. It was not the minority but the majority that complained. The minority was more homogeneous, more conscious, as is the way with minorities, and less evenly divided into parties: in nearly every year there was a party in Canada East strong enough to unite with either majority or minority in Canada West and still control the Assembly. It was Canada East which was accused of domination, Canada East which was to be charged with forcing separate schools on Canada West, Canada East which was attacked as extracting a greater share of local expenditures out of a treasury to which it made a smaller contribution. The fact that the immigration-fed population of Canada West was growing more rapidly, leaving Canada East further behind each year after 1850, did not make the nominal equality in seats and the actual inferiority in influence easier to bear, and gave ground for demands for a radical revision of the Union experiment

But it was not merely the failure of Union and responsible government, it was also their success that counted in creating new issues and new solutions. Out of Union came deadlock and out of deadlock Confederation; but out of Union also came the growing national consciousness and confidence and the expanding economic organisation which were to make it possible to overcome deadlock by the wider union. Responsible government was giving to the statesmen of the provinces, to Macdonald and Cartier, Brown and Galt, as well as to Tupper and Howe and Tilley, a training in facing problems, a skill in managing men, an ambition for wider fields, which were new and essential factors in the situation. Responsible government was bringing to the people a consciousness of a distinct entity, of present weakness and potential strength, out of which were to grow the urge to expansion, the will to nationhood. Responsible government inspired the will, Union provided the means, for the vigorous policy of canal and railroad building which, with all its extravagance and misdirection, was giving the Canada of the 'fifties a rapidly growing population, an economic diversity, and an ease of intercourse which profoundly altered its outlook. With closer settlement and improved transportation there were coming a growing diversity and specialisation of occupation, an increased trade within the province and without, in which potash, timber and wheat served as the most easily marketed staples, and a rapid expansion of the towns and cities in which the trade and industry involved in this increasing interdependence were centred.

It was not merely within the province but on every border that new issues were emerging. The imminent struggle in the Republic to the south was already making the more far-sighted weigh the strength and weakness of a federal system and was soon to provide a hammer of Thor to forge a wider union. The eastern provinces were slowly rising above the political and economic horizon as the project for an intercolonial railway took spasmodic shape. But it was chiefly the West that gave a new trend to provincial ambitions.

While Canada had prospered exceedingly, it was coming to be feared that limits were set to its expansion. It was the epoch of the opening of the prairie West. The open plains of Illinois and Iowa, of Nebraska and Minnesota, were filling up at tremendous speed with American frontiersmen and European immigrants. The province of Canada had little cheap land to offer in rivalry. A lavish land policy in early days had left little at the disposal of the Crown except in the granite wilderness half-way between Lake Ontario and the Ottawa; here colonisation roads were built and free land offered, but fortunately with little avail. It was in vain that it was demonstrated that an ordinary axeman could underbrush and chop an acre of hardwood forest in eight days, that women and children could fire the brush-heaps, and five men with a yoke of oxen pile the logs for burning, and the ashes yield half a barrel of potash, worth some six or eight pounds currency a barrel:[1] to most homeseekers the treeless prairie carried greater appeal than the forest clearing. The need came home of a Canadian West to balance the new United States West.

That West appeared to be had for the seeking. The Hudson's Bay Company was losing its grip on its vast domains. Settlers and "free" or independent fur-traders in the Red River were challenging its control, and its exclusive trading licence over the North West Territories, not included in its charter grant of Rupert's Land, was to end in 1859. The Company had done high service in staking out a great empire and in maintaining good relations with the Indian tribes, but its desire to hold that empire as a monopolist fur preserve blocked settlement, and without settlement, as Oregon had already demonstrated, the advancing tide of United States absorption could not be stayed. A vigorous agitation for taking over this heritage arose in Canada, particularly after 1856. Sullivan and Morris in pamphlet and lecture, McDougall and Brown in the press, urged Canadians to rise to their great opportunity. While it was on the explorations of the men from the Lower St Lawrence that the province's claims to a rightful share in western sovereignty were based, it was in Canada West that the demand was loudest: a new Canadian territory in the West would bring settlers and markets, traffic for railways, votes to

[1] *Canada, the Land of Hope*, by the Editor of the *Canadian News* (1857), p. 13.

offset Canada East, and a barrier to United States expansion. Investigation by a committee of the Assembly in 1857, the appointment of Chief Justice Draper in the same year to urge Canada's claims before a British select committee, the despatch of the Dawson-Hind expedition to explore the possibilities of water and land routes from Lake Superior to Red River, the incorporation in 1858 of the North-West Transportation, Navigation and Railway Company, and the arrival at Fort Garry of aggressive Canadian settlers armed with a printing-press, indicated the growing interest. And beyond the prairies beckoned the Pacific. California drew all men's eyes in 1849; in 1858 the rush to the gold diggings on the Fraser emphasised the fact that British North America could match California as it could match the prairie West. And beyond the Pacific the wars in China and the Mutiny in India compelled still further vision, as men began to look westward to the Far East.

Both in domestic and in external issues it was naturally the Opposition that pressed hardest for change. It was no accident that gave George Brown and his journal, the *Globe* (Toronto), the foremost place alike in the denunciation of the domination of Canada East and in the demand for westward expansion.

The fifth Parliament was now drawing to its end. Hammered by Brown because of "subservience to priest and politician" in Canada East, deserted by Cauchon because of failure to grant the North Shore Railway in Quebec its due allotment of land subsidy, and harassed by the economic crisis, yet strong in the art of managing men, Macdonald and Cartier won success in the general election of December 1857. It was a success ominous of deepening sectional conflict. The opponents of the Government had secured a majority of seats in Canada West, but their cry of French and Catholic domination had proved fatal to their allies, the Rouges, who came back much weakened in numbers and in spirit.

It was in the following year, 1858, that the conviction of the necessity of some constitutional change definitely crystallised. Continued business depression, the impotence in the Assembly of the party with the majority in Canada West, the controversy over the seat of government, and the passions roused by the short shrift of the Brown-Dorion ministry and the chicanery of the "Double Shuffle", gave new bitterness to party controversy and new force to demands for a change. The session of 1858 was notable for exhaustive debates in which all the weaknesses of the existing system were emphasised and every solution canvassed.

There have been few Parliaments in Canada better fitted to discuss a great issue. John A. Macdonald, George Etienne Cartier, Louis Sicotte, Thomas Loranger, Philip Vankoughnet, John Rose, on the Treasury benches; W. H. Merritt, Joseph Cauchon, J. C. Chapais, Hector Langevin, and Christopher Dunkin on the seats behind them;

George Brown, John Sandfield Macdonald, W. L. Mackenzie, Malcolm Cameron, Oliver Mowat, William Howland, M. H. Foley, A. A. Dorion, C. J. Laberge, L. J. Drummond, and D'Arcy McGee opposite, and A. T. Galt figuratively on a cross-bench, illustrated the high proportion of a country's ability drawn to Parliament in days when politics still provided the chief field and outlet of ambition.

The proposals for change naturally came mainly from the Opposition. The Government could find little seriously wrong in a system which gave it power: the troubles of the province were clearly due to unscrupulous agitators, with George Brown as prince of evil. Macdonald and Cartier were temperamentally averse from what they considered premature and academic discussion of constitutional changes. Macdonald lacked the vision of Galt, the quickening eloquence of McGee, the intensity of Brown, the constructive courage of Tupper, the fighting force of Cartier, but he possessed powers of patience and skill in handling men which were to prove equally indispensable in the outcome. For the present Macdonald and Cartier adhered to the policy of the coalition of 1854; they were content to rely on party manœuvres and personal influence; time after time prominent members of the loosely-knit Opposition, Galt, Smith, McGee, were detached and brought into the governmental camp.

The most simple solution advocated was to cut the Gordian knot, repeal the Union and allow each separate province to follow its destiny unfettered. Characteristically, it was the surviving leaders of the pre-Union period who urged this simple and drastic reversion to the days of their youth—Papineau, returning from exile to find Lafontaine reigning in his stead, and Mackenzie, robbed of some illusions by close contact with his republican neighbours in exile, but still watchful of usurpers, and reaching a wide public with his *Repealer's Almanac*. But the solution was not to be found by turning back. Union had brought joint assets and joint responsibilities: "A man and his wife may agree to separate, but what were they to do with the children?" Malcolm Cameron asked at the Reform Convention a year later. There were tasks of material development, railway building, canal maintenance, which only the larger unit could carry out effectively. Repeal would revive the old disputes as to the division of customs duties. It would reduce Canada, nucleus of a nation, already stirring with desire for continent-wide expansion, to petty colonial disunity. Not with that solution could a growing people be content.

Assuming that Union was to continue, two policies were urged as safeguards against the oppression of one section by the other—the double majority and representation by population. The double majority solution was a parliamentary device which made special appeal to opportunists and parliamentary tacticians. Hincks and John A. Macdonald found it useful at times, but it was peculiarly the hobby of

Cauchon and John Sandfield Macdonald. Let the Administration be based on the majority group in each section, or at least insist that no legislation affecting one section be passed unless with a majority from that part, and there would be no danger of undue interference or oppression. This policy, it was urged, was the logical extension of the recognition of the separateness of the two sections involved in the double Cabinet leadership, the two sections of the Administration, the retention of distinct legal, municipal and school systems and the constant enactment of laws applying to one section alone. It had precedent in its favour, urged Cauchon and John Sandfield Macdonald in a debate in May of this session on a double majority motion: Hincks had resigned in 1854 because he had not the confidence of his own section, and McNab had been ousted in 1856 on the same plea. But the objections were felt to be overwhelming. The double majority principle might prevent interference but it would enthrone deadlock. It would mean union in form but repeal in fact and perpetuate sterility and strife, declared Sicotte in the same debate. It would yoke together majority groups of antagonistic principles, Galt contended, give a minority of the whole House a veto power, and fail to provide a positive remedy for the evils charged. The finishing stroke was given in a pronouncement by a Committee of the Canada East Opposition, Dorion, Drummond, Dessaules, and McGee, in a manifesto on the various constitutional solutions, issued in 1859: "The impossibility of clearly defining the cases to which the double majority should apply...is felt by all, but were it even possible, it would only lead to new phases of difficulty by compelling majorities professing opinions and principles diametrically opposed to each other to unite, and thereby effectually to extinguish the influence of the one or other minority or both". In practice, a principle which served the purpose of leaders in opposition, but was discarded by its own advocates whenever they came to power, was hopelessly inadequate.

Representation by Population, as its abbreviation into "rep. by pop." indicated, was not a parliamentary device but a popular war-cry. Although at the date of union Lower Canada had four people to Upper Canada's three, each section had been given the same number of seats in the Assembly. By 1850 the western section, thanks to the stream of immigrants, had forged ahead, and continued to gain, until in 1861 it held fourteen people to every eleven in the eastern section. Inevitably this growing disparity brought demands for a change in representation. In vain was it insisted that the Act of Union was a treaty which no one party could change, for it had been changed.[1] In vain was it recalled that Canada

---

[1] The Union Act Amendment Act, passed in 1854 by the Imperial Parliament after an address from the Assembly, repealed the provision that the number of members in the Assembly could be altered only by a two-thirds vote of both Council and Assembly.

East had been under-represented at first: Canada West had now suffered an equal number of years of under-representation, and could be patient no longer. It was worse than vain for Cartier to declaim that wealth as well as heads must be computed, "the codfish of Gaspé Bay" weighed against "the Grits of Upper Canada". To be held inferior in voting power touched individual pride and racial prestige in Canada West: inevitably the demand for "rep. by pop.", taken up first by Tories, later by Clear Grits, as the exigencies of opposition prompted, more and more became gospel in the west—and equally inevitably anathema in the east. The demand was difficult to answer, but its own wiser advocates came to realise that it was inadequate. Given larger representation, the west might still be evenly divided; if it did vote solidly, it would be the turn of the east to fear oppression. In the 1858 debate Cauchon's motion for a six months' "hoist" was carried by sixty-four to forty-two, with only ten votes from Canada West among the majority.

By a process of exclusion it was coming to be realised that the only positive solution lay in the adoption of a federal system. But for what area? The simpler and more practicable plan appeared to be to transform the existing province of Canada into a federation. "There would be no difficulty", Dorion declared in 1856, "in getting the people of Upper and Lower Canada to set up a general Legislature with control of commercial interests, railway interests, public works and navigation, while at the same time education and matters of local character might be left to local Legislatures". But why not widen the scope of the experiment, bring in the unknown empire west of the Great Lakes and the colonies by the Atlantic, already half linked by rail, and make a federation comparable to the great Republic to the south which thrust its example on all men's vision? During this session, Galt, its most persistent and effective parliamentary advocate, urged the wider federation as an alternative policy during the "rep. by pop." debate, and later formally moved a resolution in support of a federal system for Canada, with provision for incorporating east and west. A federal system, he contended, would solve the conflicts which now raged in Canada by assigning the most controversial subjects to local Legislatures; it alone could make possible the occupation of the West and union with the East; it would bring economic unity and military strength: "half a continent is ours if we do not keep on quarrelling about petty matters and lose sight of what interests us most". But the obstacles yet appeared too great: no other leader of the Assembly supported Galt's motion.

The difficulty of ensuring stability was strikingly illustrated by the party fortunes of the session of 1858. The issue of the seat of government compelled attention. The compromise adopted in 1849 of spending four sessions alternately in Toronto and in Quebec had yielded some incidental advantage in giving the members first-hand knowledge of both sections of the province, but it had been irksome and inconvenient for administration. As a permanent capital, Montreal, Quebec, Kingston, Toronto, all had claims and persistent supporters. The Government had sought a year earlier to avoid a perilous choice by referring the selection to the Queen; on Head's advice, the lumber village of Bytown or Ottawa had been selected. It was a reasonable geographical compromise, but it satisfied none of the more ambitious aspirants. On 28 July the sum of the disappointed rivalries resulted in a vote of sixty-four to fifty in condemnation of the choice. Brown moved the adjournment as a test of confidence; his motion was lost by fifty to sixty-one, but the ministry decided to resign. Sir Edmund Head accepted the resignation and called upon Brown to form a government. To the surprise of his opponents and of some of his friends Brown succeeded in enlisting the co-operation of Dorion, in bringing together a strong group of ministers, and in securing tentative agreement upon a common policy.

The new ministry was sworn in on 2 August.[1] To find support in Parliament was a harder task. In a House with a normal majority for the late Government, with the new ministers absent on account of accepting office, and with some uneasiness in each wing of their supporters as to whether the speedy union of Canada West and Canada East groups had not been achieved through a sacrifice of the principles of one or both groups, the Brown-Dorion Administration met overwhelming defeat. There was some ground for believing that the verdict of the electorate would be different, and Brown at once advised a dissolution. The Governor had taken pains to notify Brown, after inviting him to form a ministry but before it had been formed, that he would make no pledge as to dissolution, to which Brown had replied by refusing to discuss the question until constitutionally entitled to act as the Governor's adviser. Sir Edmund now refused to accept the advice. On the practical ground of avoidance of an unnecessary election and on colonial precedent the Governor made an effective reply to Brown's demand, but his answers savoured somewhat of debating points (worthy, the *Globe* remarked, of the author of *Shall and Will, or Two Chapters on Future Auxiliary Verbs*). The incident left an acidulous impression of personal hostility: Sir Edmund was above intrigue but he was not exempt from prejudice. After a summons to Galt, as a man of middle ways, which was declined, the Governor called upon the former leaders, with Cartier

---

[1] Brown-Dorion Administration, 2 Aug. 1858:

Canada West. George Brown, Inspector-General; John S. Macdonald, Attorney-General West; James Morris, Speaker of the Legislative Council; M. H. Foley, Postmaster-General; Oliver Mowat, Provincial Secretary.

Canada East. A. A. Dorion, Commissioner of Crown Lands; L. T. Drummond, Attorney-General East; L. H. Holton, Commissioner of Public Works; F. Lemieux, Receiver-General; J. E. Thibaudeau, President of the Council.

now titular Premier and with Galt as Inspector-General, or as it was now first termed, Minister of Finance. With a prudent desire to avoid by-elections, the returning ministers took advantage of a statute which provided that a minister who resigned his office and within a month accepted another should not thereby vacate his seat; each minister was now sworn in to a different post from that he had held the week before, and then immediately shifted to his normal post. This "Double Shuffle" was within the letter of the law, but it lent colour to Brown's claim of popular support and fire to his denunciation: with Macdonald attacked for shabby intrigue and petty chicanery, and Brown portrayed as over-reaching himself by greed of power, politics took on an added bitterness.

The search for a solution continued. More important than the debates in Parliament were the party conventions and committees, a new form of democratic control borrowed, like the party caucus, from the south. The Reform Convention of Canada West, called in 1859 "to consider the relations between Upper and Lower Canada", definitely recognised that Union had failed, that representation by population, though just and necessary, was not enough, that the double majority expedient was unworkable, and that a federal union of the Canadas was the true remedy. In Canada East in the same year a committee of the Rouge party reached the same conclusion as to the true solution, in a memorandum more penetrating in its analysis but less effective in popular support. Meanwhile the reorganised Government was also active. Galt had made an enquiry into the possibility of the wider federation a condition of entering the ministry; the proposal held promise of offsetting the "rep. by pop." cry and postponing a decision as to the seat of government, and was accepted. Accordingly, in the autumn of 1858, Galt, Cartier, and John Ross proceeded to England to discuss with the British Government two special questions, both of significance in the project of eventual expansion, the completion of the Intercolonial Railway to the East and the absorption of the Hudson's Bay Territory in the West, and at the same time to urge the British Government to take the initiative in summoning an intercolonial conference to discuss the union of all the provinces. They found the Colonial Office indifferent if not hostile, and the other provinces lukewarm, and the project lapsed.

All parties in Canada were now on record as to the necessity of a change. Galt, Cartier, and Ross, in the memorial to the Colonial Secretary presented on 23 October 1858, declared:

It is our duty to state that very grave difficulties now present themselves in conducting the Government of Canada in such a manner as to show due regard to the wishes of its numerous population.... The result is shown by an agitation fraught with great danger to the peaceful and harmonious working of our constitutional system and consequently detrimental to the progress of the province. The necessity of providing a remedy for a state of things that is yearly becoming worse, and of allaying feelings that are daily being aggravated by the contention of political parties, has impressed the advisers of Her Majesty's representatives in Canada with the importance of seeking for such a mode of dealing with these difficulties as may for ever remove them.

In the session following the Reform Convention, Brown summed up its conclusions in two resolutions, defeated by more than two to one, but still of significance as a declaration of faith. The first declared that

the existing legislative union between Upper and Lower Canada has failed to realise the anticipations of its promoters; has resulted in a heavy debt, burdensome taxation, great political abuses, and universal dissatisfaction; and it is the matured conviction of this Assembly, from the antagonisms developed through differences of origin, local interests and other causes, that the union in its present form can be no longer continued with advantage to the people;

and the second, that the remedy lay in the establishment of two or more local governments with one joint authority in control of common affairs.

The political motives for change were now reinforced by economic and military factors. The development of transportation, always a dominant interest, was taking new forms. The bush trail had been followed by the corduroy road, and the corduroy road by the gravel or macadam or plank road, with its constant toll-gates; canal building had made possible fuller use of the magnificent waterway system and a proud and lively steamship traffic thronged the St Lawrence and Great Lakes. The first outburst of railway building was now spent; between the crisis of 1857 and Confederation no new local lines were constructed. The provinces and municipalities were staggering under a burden of debt, and shareholders faring leanly, but with two thousand miles of road completed by 1860 the local and export needs of the British North American community were excellently served and its whole industrial outlook transformed. The completion, for the moment, of the local programmes turned attention to the gaps in the intercolonial plan. A through line ran from Sarnia to Rivière du Loup, two hundred miles beyond Quebec; two north-ward tentacles were thrust up in New Brunswick, and a line from Halifax had reached Truro. Between Rivière du Loup and Truro there stretched a wilderness gap of five hundred miles. Clearly no single province could bridge it; even joint action was considered inadequate, and with reviving hope the three provinces turned to seek imperial aid. Macdonald and Rose from Canada, and Johnston and Archibald from Nova Scotia, journeyed to London in 1857, and Cartier, Ross and Galt, with Tupper, Henry and Dickey from Nova Scotia and Fisher and Smith from New Brunswick, made the same pilgrimage in 1858. They asked the British Government, in view of the imperial and defence interests involved, to contribute half a guarantee of £120,000 a year, or merely to grant steamship subsidies similar to those paid the Cunard line by which Boston was being built up at the expense of British American ports. The interviews were vain; Disraeli as Chancellor of the Exchequer had more pressing demands to meet nearer home. The project perforce lapsed until the military factor gave it fresh urgency.

Industrial change was bringing political consequences. With growing population and railroad communication, rising standards of living and thronging inventions, the province, especially Canada West, was rapidly passing through the pioneer stages of manufacturing. Home production was giving way to village service and village service to urban factories. The saw-mill and the cabinet-maker were followed by the furniture factory; the blacksmith shop at the corner or the village foundry developed into a waggon and carriage works or implement factory; flour-mills added new machinery; woollen mills took the place of the cottage spinning-wheel and loom, and tanneries made ready the way for boot and shoe factories. With this growth came concern for markets, and in the first instance for the protection of the home market. It was significant that Galt, the chief parliamentary exponent of federation, took a foremost part in railroad planning and construction and as Minister of Finance gave expression in his tariff of 1859 to the rising spirit of economic nationalism.

A gaping Treasury called for higher taxes, and in the primitive industrial condition of the colony higher tariff duties were the only adequate solution. But the industrial centres, feeling the pinch of hard times and falling consumption, were demanding higher duties for protection as well. The rising tide of protection in the Northern States was proving more compelling than the example and precepts of free-trade Britain: Isaac Buchanan of Hamilton assumed the rôle of prophet of protection played by Horace Greeley in the United States. Cayley's budget in 1858 had shown the effect of this double pressure in schedules of 15 and 20 per cent., or an average increase of 5 per cent., on the most important manufactured imports, and Galt's budget added another 5 per cent. to the textile and iron and steel schedules. Ten years before, Hincks had declared that to set up a protective tariff in Canada was tantamount to a declaration of independence. Galt made that declaration now. To a protest from Sheffield manufacturers and a warning from the Colonial Secretary, Galt replied:

Self-government would be utterly annihilated if the views of the Imperial Government were to be preferred to those of the people of Canada. It is, therefore, the duty of the present government distinctly to affirm the right of the Canadian Legislature to adjust the taxation of the people in the way they deem best—even if it should unfortunately happen to meet the disapproval of the Imperial Ministry.

The immediate effect of the Cayley-Galt duties was to relieve the needs of the Treasury, but they had other and more varied effects. So far as the province itself was concerned, it became necessary to retrace these steps if the low-tariff colonies by the sea were to be reconciled to federation, and Galt's budget of 1866 lowered duties practically to their former level, with the avowed double purpose of meeting Maritime views half-way and of making Canada a "separate and distinct nationality" by adopting a tariff policy different from that of its neighbour. But in the meantime the higher duties had had repercussions abroad. In Great Britain many men echoed Roebuck's exclamation, "Of what use are our colonies to us if they are allowed to tax our products?" and the view that separation of the colonies from the mother country was alike desirable and inevitable grew apace. In the United States, the increased duties on manufactured goods were held to violate an implicit understanding that free trade in natural products, considered of chief advantage to Canada, would be balanced by continuing low duties on the other products of the United States. Galt had no difficulty in demonstrating the fallacies in this contention, but the belief persisted and had much to do with the eventual decision of the United States to end the reciprocity experiment. The shadow of sectional conflict in the Republic was deepening. The abandonment of the Missouri Compromise, the Dred Scott decision, John Brown's raid on Harper's Ferry, the cleavage of parties and churches on the slavery issue marked the growing tension. Canadian interest was keen, but the possible significance of the coming conflict in the movement for the union of the provinces was foreseen by few.

For the moment, as the 'sixties dawned, that movement was in eclipse. Returning prosperity removed the spur of economic discontent. Party readjustments postponed the breakdown of the political machine. In the Opposition ranks opportunism triumphed, and it seemed possible that both parties would be content to endeavour to carry on without recourse to the drastic solutions of "the extremist and the doctrinaire". John Sandfield Macdonald had ousted Brown in leadership, or rather primacy, in the loosely organised Reform Opposition of Canada West, while the equally supple Sicotte, who had resigned from the Cartier-Macdonald Cabinet late in 1858, had supplanted Dorion. No longer hampered by Brown's forthrightness, the Opposition gained strength in Canada East, though it could not do more than hold its own in Canada West. The general election of July 1861 shook the Government, revelations of maladministration and of ministerial inattention to duty weakened it during the first session of the new Parliament, and in May 1862 an adverse vote on a Militia Bill forced its resignation, and brought to power the Sandfield Macdonald-Sicotte ministry.

A former supporter, John Rose, wrote as follows to Thomas Baring on 23 May 1862:

Their defeat was ostensibly on the Militia Bill, but many other causes have brought it about. There was a very general feeling that they had existed long enough; that they could, from the force of circumstances, do nothing in the way of financial reform; the later reconstruction was another source of break-up; the maladministration in certain departments was very damaging, and finally Galt's budget sent many of their staunchest supporters to the cross-benches. They were adroit enough to fall on the second reading of the Militia Bill, on the very day when a vote of non-confidence was to have been moved which would have left them in a minority of 35 to 40.[1]

The Militia Bill was an incidental outcome of the great conflict which had now broken out in the Republic. When the Civil War began, Canadian sentiment had been overwhelmingly in sympathy with the anti-slavery cause. Later, the influence of pro-Southern sympathy in the English governing classes and resentment against the clumsy efforts of a section of the Northern press, which sought to heal the Union by uniting North and South against British foes and for Canadian conquest, brought a reversal of opinion. The *Trent* crisis in December 1861 had shown that if the conflict came Canada would not flinch from its full share. The vote on the Militia Bill in May demonstrated that Canada would decide for herself what that share should be. The ministry, with the assistance of imperial officers, had planned a sweeping reorganisation of the defence forces, with the backbone in an active force, composed of volunteer militia in the towns, and of regular militia recruited by volunteering backed by balloting in the country, and subject to training four weeks a year for a period of three to five years: the project involved a five-fold jump in the outlay on defence. It was too drastic a proposal for the public view either of Canada's danger or of Canada's responsibility, and proved the last straw on the ministry's back.

The more enduring effect of the Civil War was to stimulate the movement for federation. In Canada, and in the colonies by the sea, the danger of invasion, however discounted, powerfully reinforced the political and economic forces making for union. The fable of the bundle of sticks took on a new appositeness. In Great Britain, opinion passed from the careless indifference of the 'fifties, through the wounded anger of the controversy following the rejection of the Militia Bill, into a settled conviction that a connection which yielded no trade profit and involved military weakness possessed little value, and that the prudent and the decent thing to do was to aid the colonies to find strength in union and perchance safety in independence. In this mood, the project of an intercolonial railway, which many considered a necessary forerunner of intercolonial union, found fresh support on both sides of the Atlantic, though repeated negotiations in 1861 and 1862 failed to reach common ground and in the end

[1] *Baring Papers*, Canadian Archives.
Sandfield Macdonald-Sicotte ministry, 1862:
Canada West. J. S. Macdonald, Attorney-General West; M. H. Foley, Postmaster-General; W. P. Howland, Minister of Finance; W. McDougall, Commissioner of Crown Lands; James Morris, Receiver-General; Adam Wilson, Solicitor-General West.
Canada East. L. V. Sicotte, Attorney-General East; A. A. Dorion, Provincial Secretary; T. D. McGee, President of the Council; U. J. Tessier, Commissioner of Public Works; F. Evanturel, Minister of Agriculture; J. J. C. Abbott, Solicitor-General East.

intercolonial union was necessary to secure an intercolonial railway. In yet another way the Civil War advanced the cause of federation. Undoubtedly the resentment felt by the North against the pro-Southern sentiment of the governing classes in Britain and a considerable section in Canada counted strongly in the decision to terminate the reciprocity agreement. Thus, about to be shut out of the United States market, the colonies naturally explored with new seriousness the possibilities of finding recompense in the wider home markets which would be opened and sheltered by federation.

The Macdonald-Sicotte Government pursued a cautious course, cutting down expenditure, passing a more modest Militia Bill which found general acceptance, and advocating intercolonial railway extension, though not at all costs. In the session of 1863 it was compelled to deny the main principle of its chiefs, the double majority, in order to save a Separate School Bill, consolidating the position of denominational schools in Canada West. George Brown, back in Parliament after a brief absence, led the Clear Grit wing against the bill, and it was passed only by Canada East votes. In May 1863 the Government found itself in a minority of five on a straight want of confidence motion. Macdonald advised the Governor-General, Lord Monck, an Irish peer who had succeeded Head in 1861, to grant a dissolution, and this time the advice was accepted. Before the election, Macdonald sought to placate his left wing critics by a Cabinet reorganisation which put Dorion in Sicotte's place and strengthened the Clear Grit membership. The election of June 1863 brought the inevitable seesaw of gain in Canada West and loss in Canada East. The opposition of the galled ministers who had been dropped in the reconstruction, Sicotte, McGee and Foley, made Macdonald's position precarious. The approach of sectional as well as party deadlock was significantly marked in the annual vote on "rep. by pop." in the ensuing session. In 1856, the vote had stood twenty-two for to sixty-one against, with Canada West divided seventeen to twenty-five, and Canada East five to thirty-six; in 1863, the figures were forty-three to sixty-four, with Canada West voting forty-two to thirteen and Canada East one to fifty-one. After surviving this session with majorities dwindling from eight to three, and beginning a second with still more dubious outlook, the Government anticipated its fate by resigning in March 1864.

The policy of patchwork was nearing its end. On the existing basis no enduring combination could be formed that would escape deadlock. Fergusson Blair and Dorion, Cartier and Macdonald, Taché and Campbell, were combinations mooted in vain. When at last a Taché-John A. Macdonald ministry was formed, with "rep. by pop." significantly left an open question, by-elections went against the Government, a majority of two passed into a minority of two, and by 14 June this last effort of the old regime had failed.

Three, or in fact four, ministries, and two general elections, in three years, hostility and deadlock between Canada East and Canada West, a paralysis of constructive legislation, bitter and personal controversy and the dubious influence of the odd man—these evidences of the failure of the Union experiment combined with the rising hopes and fears which made for a national vision to compel the search for a broader foundation. Fortunately the remedy was at hand. By a dramatic conjuncture, a select committee of nineteen members appointed on Brown's motion to consider the constitutional problem had reported the very day of the Government's defeat, indicating confederation, applied to the Canadas alone or to the whole of British North America, as the solution. Brown, McDougall, Galt, Cartier, Cauchon, Chapais, Dorion, were among the majority; a minority stood out, John Sandfield Macdonald, Scobie, Dunkin and John A. Macdonald, who was not yet persuaded that if a wider union came it should take the form of a federal rather than a legislative union.

The further fortunes of confederation are discussed in a later chapter.[1] All other developments of the remaining three years of the Union were subsidiary to this overshadowing change. The termination of the Reciprocity Treaty by the United States in 1866 was in the main an echo of the political misunderstandings of the war period. Raids and rumours of raids upon Canada by motley armed bands of Fenians from the United States in 1866 reflected the same smouldering irritation, strengthened and directed by the physical force wing of sympathisers with Irish freedom who saw in Canada only a colony and hostage of England. Economic and military reprisals alike strengthened the popular will to union in British North America, and led the British Government and its representatives on the spot to throw all their influence into the federation scale. In the party field the period ended as it had begun, in coalition, but at the end as in the beginning coalition became a name; Brown found himself a hostage in Macdonald's Cabinet; though the Liberal party, save the Rouge wing which had not been included in the coalition, continued to support confederation, the Liberal representation in the Cabinet gradually faded. The last Parliament of the Province of Canada held its session of 1865 in the new capital on the Ottawa, making ready to hand on the torch of responsible government to the first Parliament of the Dominion of Canada.

[1] See chapter xviii.

CHAPTER XIV

THE MARITIME PROVINCES, 1840–1867

HOWE'S resolution of want of confidence[1] was the first clear challenge to Russell's scheme of "colonial government". The consternation of Downing Street is to be traced in a variety of minutes and marginal notes. Lord John himself dropped the magic word "Cabinet" and conceded that there was "something untold" when "a few factious demagogues", as Campbell had described them, could command resolute majorities of two-thirds of the Assembly.[2] In the "present circumstances of the Canadas" it was decided that Sir Colin must go. The alternative, as the Governor-General pointed out from Montreal, was the "objectionable principle" of responsible government itself. Even Sir Colin's recall must not "afford a triumph to a little knot of persons who certainly ought not to receive one".[3] To Sydenham himself with his magic wand was entrusted the task of arranging the details, and thus was Lord John Russell "relieved [as he wrote to Sir Colin] from the necessity of entering into many explanations".[4]

In truth the Russell-Sydenham doctrine never had a narrower escape than in Nova Scotia, nor Sydenham's amazing adroitness and versatility a more spectacular triumph. His fortnight at Halifax bore two vastly different interpretations. In his official despatches Sydenham's policy still conformed to the pontifical doctrine of Lord John Russell. The Executive Council if properly managed could be a "very useful and powerful engine in the hands of the Governor". With a new Governor, a new Assembly, and "so much good sense amongst the People" a forthright policy of "practical measures" could "divert men's minds from the agitation of abstract points of government". It was clear that Howe could no longer be proscribed from office, but Sydenham enclosed an article from the *Novascotian* to offset "any difficulty on the score of his pamphlet".[5]

But Sydenham's famous interview with Howe and their subsequent correspondence will bear another interpretation. One lingers upon the picture of Howe reading aloud his proscribed *Letters to Lord John Russell* for Sydenham's ingratiating criticism, and both falling insensibly into each other's confidence. "Before Mr Thomson left Nova Scotia", notes Howe, "it was apparent that the old system was doomed". They were to "bring out the new policy discreetly". To

---

[1] See above, p. 286.　　　　　　　　　[2] *C.O.* 217, CLXXIV, 323.
[3] Thomson to Russell, 27 May 1840, *Series G*, CCCLXXXVII, 209.
[4] *C.O.* 217, CLXXIV, 275.
[5] Thomson to Russell, 27 July 1840, *Series G*, CLXXXIV; *The Novascotian*, 23 July 1840.

the appeal "to lessen, if possible, the difficulties with which...the Governor-General was beset" in his desperate problem of the Canadas, Howe responded with characteristic magnanimity. He gave his "pledge to serve for two years...without fee or reward" in one of those "hermaphrodite" coalitions of the Sydenham regime. Herbert Huntington roundly rejected every overture as a delusion and a snare. Howe too had his misgivings. It was not long before he was writing to Sydenham of the attempt of his Tory colleagues "to make the whole affair bear the same appearance of trick and humbug as did the former Council".[1]

Howe relied, as he always maintained, upon the introduction of responsible government "by degrees"—"as early as circumstances would permit"—and "upon the distinct understanding with Lord Sydenham, that thereafter the House of Assembly was to possess and freely exercise its right, by a vote of want of confidence...to change the policy or dismiss the advisers of the Governor".[2] Had Grey instead of Stanley succeeded Russell in 1841 it is possible that "the great experiment" might have succeeded without those violent reactions which distorted the struggle in Canada, and "without displacing or injuring a single person drawing his living from the public funds".

Huntington, as it happened, was the shrewder prophet. Falkland, the new Governor, had been Whig whip in the House of Lords. He began with every promise of carrying out Sydenham's *concordat* with Howe. The retiring councillors "died hard, but were in firm hands".[3] The return of Peel to power in Great Britain, however, brought a revival of Toryism in Nova Scotia. Responsible government was soon on the defensive. The coalition councillors were "openly and shamelessly intriguing with each other". One of them approached Uniacke with a proposal to "embark in the same boat" and "throw Howe overboard". Uniacke indignantly rejected the overtures, but Howe, now convinced that the coalition "cannot go on", yielded at last to Huntington's resolute demand for a homogeneous party government.

The feud which rent the coalition of 1840 left scars that never healed. No courtlier spirit ever graced Nova Scotian politics than James W. Johnston—moderate to the point of Liberalism in his outlook, an aristocrat in education and temper, austere and incorruptible alike in private and in public life, and gifted above all with that "polish of manners" that had so impressed Durham and Buller in Quebec. In the portrait of him in the old province building, the finely-chiselled features in meditative repose contrast strangely with Howe's stormy countenance on the other side of the Speaker's chair. The instinctive

---

[1] Chisholm, *Speeches...of Joseph Howe*, I, 328; Howe to Falkland, 3 Apr. 1843; to Falkland, n.d.; to Thomson, 12 Aug. 1840; *Howe Papers*, VI, X, 12.
[2] Howe to Falkland, 3 Apr. 1843, *Howe Papers*, vol. VI.
[3] Howe to Huntington, n.d., *Letter Book*, 1839–1845, *Howe Papers*.

feud between them was embittered by religious and educational conflict.[1] Falkland, almost boycotted at first by the society of Halifax,[2]
now turned instinctively to Johnston's courtly counsel in accord with
Stanley's Tory regime at Downing Street. A sudden dissolution in
order "to escape the necessity of immediately forming a Party
Government" further weakened the reform wing of the coalition,[3]
and when Falkland appointed Almon, Johnston's brother-in-law, to
the Executive Council in defiance of every protest, it was clear that
responsible government "by degrees" was reverting "by degrees" to
the old order. Within a few days of the Metcalfe crisis in Canada,
Howe, Uniacke and McNab resigned. If a Liberal "party government" was impossible they could at least force a Tory party government.[4] Such were the first-fruits of coalition. It was necessary, as
Huntington observed bitterly, to begin the long contest over again
for the unquestioned ascendancy from which Sydenham had lured
them in 1840.

In Nova Scotia, as in Canada, the struggle that followed was
perhaps the bitterest in the history of the province. In Canada the
ex-councillors deluged Metcalfe with vituperation as "Charles
the Simple", "old Square Toes", "the old squaw" and worse;
and Metcalfe retaliated against "rebels" and "republicans" whose
professions of loyalty were "utterly worthless". In Nova Scotia Falkland's tactical blunders, culminating in the *gaucherie* of defending himself in the press, brought from Howe's pen a deluge of badinage and
pasquinade, which covered him with ridicule. But the loss of dignity
was scarcely less costly to Howe than to his adversary. For two years
he retired to his farm "like Cincinnatus to his plough". "We are a
body of honest and well-meaning people", he wrote bitterly, "going
to capture the Sepulchre, with good intentions—and we have to deal
with pagans, who, while they trust in the Prophet, know the value of
close ranks, discipline and chain mail". With Charles Fisher in New
Brunswick, with Adam Fergusson in Canada, with John Kent in
Newfoundland, and above all with Charles Buller in England and the
resolute spirit of Huntington in Nova Scotia, Howe took counsel and
tried to bide his time. The dawn broke first in England. In 1846 the
Whigs came back to power, and the third Earl Grey, with Charles
Buller and Hawes in the background, authorised in Nova Scotia
the first fully responsible government in the British dominions overseas.

The direct contribution of Buller and of Howe to that event cannot

[1] Johnston championed the Baptist Tory interests against Howe's plan for a non-
sectarian provincial university.
[2] Falkland to Stanley, 22 Dec. 1841, Leg. Libr., Halifax, *Governor's Letter Book*, no. 116,
p. 128.
[3] Falkland to Stanley, 28 Nov. 1843, *Letter Book*, no. 117, p. 122.
[4] The Reformers though once more reunited stood in a minority ranging from one to
four in the new Assembly.

be traced here.[1] "If this Whig Government disappoints us", Howe wrote desperately, "you will have the questions I have touched discussed in a different spirit, ten years hence, by the Enemies of England, not by her friends". The elections of August 1847 were followed with intense interest in the other provinces. "If Nova Scotia strikes the first blow", wrote Fisher from New Brunswick, "I do believe that the next election in Canada will follow suit and it must have some effect here".[2] The Reformers carried twelve counties with a resolute majority of seven. Sir John Harvey, Falkland's successor, made every effort to short-circuit responsible government by another specious coalition. But Howe had learnt his lesson. He was no longer afraid of "party government". Sir John's overtures for a "mixed government"—addressed to his "excellent and talented friend"—Howe had met with invincible resolution. In truth the issue was now broader than Nova Scotia. "Political principles and the rights of vast bodies of people" were at stake. None but "an apostate and a deserter" could "abandon or sacrifice these after a ten years' contest". Six weeks later Grey's despatch of 3 November 1846, followed by another equally famous on 31 March 1847, reconciled Harvey to the inevitable.[3]

No more momentous despatches ever left the Colonial Office, for in Grey's own words they established for the first time "principles of general application to all colonies having a similar form of government" and were those given to Elgin for his guidance when he went to Canada.[4] But there was credit for this due elsewhere. Upon the first of Sir John Harvey's overtures in 1846 there is a marginal note in Howe's meticulous handwriting: "This was my first communication...from Gov't House, after my 'proscription' and banishment therefrom for several years. During all that period I was a disaffected and dangerous man. Now I am my Sovereign's Representative's most excellent and talented friend. I thank God, and the steadiness and intelligence of my countrymen for the change". Secure now in the inevitableness of responsible government Howe "went into the woods and called moose with the old hunters...forgetting the bitterness of conflict". When the House met in January 1848 the resolution of want of confidence of 1840 was repeated with vastly different results. For the first time it terminated one Administration and installed the Opposition in power. The new Cabinet, with Uniacke as Prime Minister, took office on 2 February 1848. Without the shedding of a drop of blood—as Howe was wont to boast—without a blow, without the breaking of a pane of glass, responsible government was won.[5]

[1] Martin, Chester, "Corres. of [J.] Howe and [C.] Buller, 1845–1848", *Can. Hist. Rev.* Dec. 1925, pp. 315, 317 ff.; Livingston, "First Responsible Party Government", *ibid.* June 1926.   [2] 12 June 1847, *Howe Papers*, I, 238.

[3] *Howe Papers*, I, 158; *Brit. Parl. Papers*, 10 Aug. 1848 (621), pp. 7, 29.

[4] Earl Grey, *The Colonial Policy of Lord John Russell's Administration*, I, 209, 213.

[5] A permanent Civil List was not arranged until 1849. Nova Scotia was thus the only province to force responsible government without that prerequisite.

The parallel contests in the other two provinces lacked the dignity of an imperial issue which the Nova Scotian Reformers instinctively felt in their own. In New Brunswick the victory of 1837—perhaps the most distinctive reform in the British provinces up to that time— was followed by seventeen years of kaleidoscopic coalitions. The Assembly not only "repudiated" Howe's doctrine of responsible government but found in Lord John Russell's famous despatch of 16 October 1839 "nothing...to call forth any expression from the House, on the Subject of Colonial Government".[1] In the elections of 1842 the Reformers were in a hopeless minority, yet in the following April Wilmot, their avowed champion, took office single-handed in coalition with seven Tories. A few months later ebullient addresses from New Brunswick appeared in Canada in support of Metcalfe's "noble stand" in resisting the "extravagant demands" of his ministers upon the patronage of the Crown.[2]

This gratuitous chivalry soon brought its own freakish retribution. A week after the death of Odell, the Provincial Secretary, in 1845, Lieutenant-Governor Colebrooke appointed to the office his own son-in-law, Alfred Reade, an utter stranger to the province. Wilmot and four of the Tory councillors indignantly resigned. The Assembly condemned the appointment by a vote of 26 to 4 and Stanley himself hastened to cancel it. It was clear that constitutional principles in New Brunswick were not unrelated to loaves and fishes. The first formal approval of responsible government marked an equally violent reversal. A resolution by Fisher to secure "the accountability of the Executive Council to the Assembly" was lost by 23 to 12. A few months later Fisher carried a resolution through the same House, 24 to 11, approving the principles of Grey's famous despatch to Sir John Harvey which had appeared in the interval. There was more of Martha than of Mary in the phlegmatic political temper of New Brunswick.

Coalitions continued until 1854. Charles Fisher describes the "mongrel Government" of 1847 to Howe, then in the midst of "the great election" in Nova Scotia. A victory there would "give new courage to the few among us who adhere to principle". The result stirred even those who had been "given over to their idols £ s. d." but the province was still "too loyal and too ignorant".[3] A few weeks later Fisher himself entered a Tory coalition. Wilmot described the New Brunswick elections of 1850 in much the same terms. "You say you do not understand our political parties. I am not surprised at this when I cannot understand them myself—Our People are running wild".[4] Wilmot as Attorney-General was still able to play "some

[1] *Journals of Assembly*, 29 Feb. 1840, p. 126.
[2] *Journals of Assembly*, 1844, p. 87; *Series G*, CDLIX, 343.
[3] 12 June, 25 Aug. 1847, *Howe Papers*, I, 238, 253.
[4] Wilmot to Howe, 25 June 1850, *ibid.* I, 354.

strange pranks", as Elgin wrote, with Grey's apostolic doctrine of *laissez faire* but next year he left politics altogether for the Bench. In 1852 Sir Edmund Head disclaimed "all idea of the system in this Province being different from that pursued in Nova Scotia or Canada", but it was not until 1854 that Fisher and the Reformers swept the province and formed the first homogeneous party government.[1]

Prince Edward Island on the other hand narrowly missed being the first of the British provinces to win responsible government—a distinction due less perhaps to sustained effort than to the traditional asperities of that province.

From 1845 all official intercourse was permeated by a violent feud between Lieutenant-Governor Huntley and Joseph Pope, Executive Councillor and Speaker of the Assembly. Until Pope was suspended from the Council, Huntley roundly maintained that "nothing was heard about confidence" in that body; Pope had thrown in his lot with the "party of the 'Escheators' to secure unlimited control". An Address of the Assembly in April 1846 urged for the first time "the principles of Responsible Government".[2]

Huntley's own views of this "abstruse subject" at this time were enlivened by a ready wit and a vein of complacent sarcasm, but it soon became clear that he was prepared to outbid his "vindictive, passionate and overbearing" antagonist for the support of the Assembly. Pope had carried a resolution (8 April 1846) that the House had "no confidence in Sir Henry Vere Huntley". It was not long before Huntley could claim the "attachment of the Members... induced by Mr Pope... to prefer complaints against me".[3] It is hard to say how much Huntley's sudden conversion owed to the personal feud with Pope, how much to the return of the Whigs to power in Great Britain and how much to the sincere conviction—a corollary of the local feud—that hostility to government policy ought to make "the resignation of the Councillor imperative". The House resolved (18 March 1847) that an Executive Council ceasing to "retain the confidence of the majority... ought to resign", and Huntley pledged his "best support".[4] Thenceforth, despite much special pleading, Huntley's despatches to Grey are among the ablest papers for responsible government from a colonial governor of that time.[5]

Behind Huntley now appeared the men who eventually won the day. George Coles, first Premier of the province in 1851, was an "honest, intelligent, fearless debater" with unpretentious natural ability and a "degree of moral courage [added Huntley] that I have

---

[1] *Grey-Elgin Correspondence*, 10 May 1850. The "pranks" were bounties to the fisheries. See Grey's *Colonial Policy*, I, 279 ff.; Pub. Arch. Can. New Brunswick Despatches Sent, *C.O.* 188, vol. CCVI, 28 Feb. 1852.
[2] Huntley to Grey, 17 Apr. 1846, *Series G*, CCCXV, 284; *Journals*, 1846, p. 137.
[3] *Journals*, 1846, p. 99; Huntley to Grey, 13 July 1847, *Series G*, CCCXV, 428.
[4] *Journals*, 1847, pp. 63, 145.
[5] See Huntley to Grey, 9 May 1847, *Series G*, CCCXV, 408 ff.

not before seen in the island".[1] James Warburton, afterwards Provincial Secretary, was chairman of the drafting committee in 1847. Edward Whelan, who had served his apprenticeship with Howe in Nova Scotia, brought to the Assembly a Celtic eloquence and a knowledge of the broader field. In 1847 he threw his "fearless principles" behind Huntley in the columns of the new *Examiner*. The Address to which Huntley pledged his support passed the House by a vote of 18 to 3. Responsible government seemed assured. Governor Bannerman afterwards deplored to Grey himself (1851) the subsequent delay as a "futile source of agitation".[2]

Earl Grey, however, had other views. In numbers, wealth and talent, the island was not ready for "any fundamental change"—an opinion which Grey retained as late as 1854.[3] He applied to Elgin to prescribe an Executive Council including all parties upon the model of Jamaica, and Huntley went to Canada to discuss the situation. Elgin conceded that the old oligarchy of the "Compacts" was "of all forms of Colonial Government...the worst", and that reform lay "in the direction of Responsible Government". But Huntley's zeal betrayed itself. Was it "deliberate conviction" or the feud with Pope and Haviland?[4] A petition had already gone forward for an extension of his term of office, in the interests of responsible government. Grey, however, had already decided against the petition. Behind his resolution lay "deeper considerations of a special kind"—the demand for a fixed Civil List and the ugly "subject of the Land Tenures". What protection would there be for the "rights of proprietors, especially absentees"?[5] Campbell's Administration (1847–50) was filled with an angry contest resulting in "want of confidence" and the stopping of supplies. Grey also summarily stopped the parliamentary grant and disallowed a Civil List Bill because it embodied the proviso that "a system of Responsible Government...shall be granted to and established in this island". Responsible government must be based not upon statutory conditions but "on the faith of the Crown".[6] In 1851 Bannerman brought an ultimatum from Grey upon the Civil List and the Assembly with wry faces swallowed the leek. "The faith of the Crown" was nobly redeemed. On 24 April 1851, with Coles as first Premier, Bannerman formed the first responsible Government in Prince Edward Island in the "belief...that the agitation and excitement...so prejudicial to this Colony are drawing to a close".[7]

Awaiting the achievement of responsible government were many of

---

[1] Huntley to Grey, 13 July 1847, *Series G*, CCCXV, 428.   [2] *Ibid.* CCCXVI, 1, 320.
[3] Grey to Campbell, 1 Jan., 2 Oct., 27 Dec. 1847; 18 Feb., Confidential, 1850; *Journals*, 1849, Appendix D; *Series G*, CCLXXXIV, 205, 284, 345; *Colonial Policy*, I, 274.
[4] Elgin to Grey, 14 Sept. 1847, *Grey-Elgin Correspondence*; 25 Sept. 1847, *Series G*, CDLXI, 160.
[5] Grey to Campbell, Confidential, 18 Feb. 1850, *Series G*, CCLXXXIV, 345; to Bannerman, 12 Feb. 1851, *Journals*, 1851, Appendix Y.
[6] Grey to Bannerman, 31 Jan. 1851, *Journals*, 1851, Appendix D.
[7] *Series G*, CCCXVII, 3.

the gravest economic problems of the century, accompanied, too, by the prosaic work of local self-government—schools and roads, fisheries and Crown lands, "rum and politics". Population in the three provinces increased from 400,000 to nearly 700,000 in twenty-one years. The ship-yards were still busy, though the days of "masting" and square timber were over, while the annual export of spruce deals from New Brunswick alone increased from less than 80 to nearly 250 million feet in two decades. But above all, it was the age of railways; and for a brief moment the spirit of railway projection lifted the Maritime Provinces upon the crest of the most spectacular economic revolution of the century, only to pass them by at last in the trough of the wave. "Editors as well as Legislators", says Fenety, took "glimpses of the moon" and could "see nothing but railroads".[1] Scarcely two years after the first passenger railway in Great Britain a double project was launched in New Brunswick for an intercolonial railway to Quebec "to convey the whole trade of the St Lawrence, in a single day, to the Atlantic waters", and an international line to the United States for "passengers, mails and light articles". The St Andrews and Quebec Railroad Company was incorporated in 1836 and Lord Ashburton became one of the directors. The New York press emulously attacked the scheme as "one of the most magnificent that has yet been projected upon this continent".[2] This first phase of projection closed only with the Papineau rising and the dispute about the Maine boundary.

Interest was revived in 1845 by Sir Richard Broun's project in London for a Halifax and Quebec Railway to be accompanied by an elaborate scheme of colonisation. Two years later Sir John Harvey rated the project "second in importance to none which has ever engaged the notice of any Colonial Legislature in any portion of the British Dominions...destined at no remote period to connect the Atlantic with the Pacific Ocean".[3] Surveys by the British Government culminated in the Robinson report of 1848, which recommended virtually the route of the Intercolonial of 1876. But a fatal divergence had already appeared between the two historic motives of railway construction—commerce, on the one hand, and political or military considerations on the other. For Nova Scotia a line from Halifax to the isthmus would subserve both purposes. For New Brunswick the issue was not so clear. The British Government might support the Intercolonial for political reasons, and capitalists might support the International for commercial reasons, but in the end neither could support both, while the province, torn by the conflicting interests of east and south, could support neither without the other. Nothing but heroic methods could reconcile these divergences. With his friend

---

[1] *Political Notes and Observations*, I, 318, 321.
[2] Fleming, S., *The Intercolonial*, pp. 6, 14 n.; Skelton, O. D., *Railway Builders*, p. 57.
[3] *Journals*, Leg. Counc. 1847, p. 9.

Major Carmichael-Smyth, Joseph Howe became the apostle of public ownership in what he once called "the noblest scheme of colonial policy ever devised"—a system of railways to be built at half the normal cost by the expedient of securing for provincial debentures the guarantee of the Imperial Government.[1] In 1850 Howe and Smyth together wrestled with Grey's opposition to the guarantee. Perhaps no greater exploit in advocacy is to be found in Howe's whole career than his success in expunging from the records of the Colonial Office Grey's initial refusal on that "Black Saturday" of 28 December 1850. With the promise of an imperial guarantee of £7,000,000 Howe's mission to Canada and New Brunswick was a triumphal procession. In his report he pictured a "great scheme of intercolonial policy…in our own time reaching the Pacific".[2]

The imbroglio with Grey and Hincks, which quenched these hopes and postponed the Intercolonial for twenty-five years, remains one of the enigmas of Canadian history. In 1852 Grey unaccountably excluded from the guarantee the line to the American boundary in which New Brunswick was chiefly interested, while Hincks precipitated from the Colonial Office a stark refusal which delivered the whole project of publicly owned railways "into the arms of the great contractors".[3] By 1858, Nova Scotia had struggled forward under provincial credit with railways from Halifax to Windsor and Truro at a cost of £800,000. At an equal cost New Brunswick rescued the Saint John and Shediac from the contractors and completed the line in 1860. Meanwhile the Grand Trunk had begun its meteoric career and a last concerted attempt to obtain imperial aid for the Intercolonial failed in 1858.[4] Thus it came to pass that instead of the railways subserving "a great scheme of intercolonial policy", it was confederation alone which eventually brought the Intercolonial Railway.

For the Maritime Provinces, as for Howe himself, the failure of the railways was climacteric. In 1852 Howe and Jackson, who personified the devious influence of the British contractors in the wake of the Grey-Hincks imbroglio, were fellow-passengers for England. "God help poor Nova Scotia", notes Howe in his diary, "if she submits, or quarrels with such a man and such a combination". Canada, after two rebellions costing over £4,000,000, had received a gratuitous loan of £1,500,000. "I know of no terms in which I can describe what my countrymen will feel", Howe had urged, "if they are refused the guarantee of half that amount".[5] In the hour of trial the long tradition of "moderation and harmony" had proved a broken reed. With

[1] Chisholm, II, 318. Major Smyth was Thackeray's step-father and the original of Colonel Newcome. His *National Railway between the Atlantic and Pacific* was published in 1849.
[2] 20 July 1851, *Journals*, 1852, Appendix no. 6, p. 18.
[3] Chisholm, II, 316. Hincks's "tart letter" to Pakington is in Fenety, I, 444.
[4] Fleming, p. 56; *Brit. Parl. Papers*, 1859 (112).
[5] Chisholm, II, 110.

baffled faith there came for provincial politics, as for Howe himself, a lowering of the *moral*, a coarsening of the fibre. The Reciprocity Treaty of 1854 too added an element of unprecedented bitterness. For the Maritime Provinces as a whole no measure since the trade reforms of 1826 promised so much, but for two of them at least the manner of it served only to hasten the descent into Avernus.

Prince Edward Island had advocated reciprocity for many years. In 1849 a tentative Act was passed for "Free Trade with the United States". In 1849 and again in 1852 joint Addresses of Council and Assembly had urged even the "abrogation or relaxation of the Treaty of 1818" excluding United States fishermen from the in-shore fisheries. This generosity was variously attributed to the suicidal policy of Crown fishery reserves—the whole coastline to the depth of 500 feet—which obstructed local enterprise, and to the local practice of selling fish to the Marblehead and Cape Cod fishermen who thus took it to the United States markets duty free. A minute of Council notes that Prince Edward Island was "the first North American Colony that has shewn any disposition to reciprocity with the United States".[1]

Other views, however, prevailed in New Brunswick where local enterprise had developed the fisheries, and in Nova Scotia where they formed the staple industry of the province. Under the commercial restrictions before 1854 the exports of Nova Scotia to the West Indies and other markets more than trebled those to Great Britain and the United States combined, while New Brunswick exports to Great Britain alone were more than seven times those to the United States.[2] Under reciprocity, trade with the United States more than doubled in ten years,[3] and one of Howe's most famous speeches—to nearly 600 delegates of 30 Boards of Trade at Detroit in 1865—advocated the extension of the treaty.

The "gratuitous surrender" of the in-shore fisheries in 1854, however, had brought the bitterest protest ever recorded in the *Journals* of Nova Scotia. Upon this issue both the larger provinces were in agreement. In 1852 the Council in New Brunswick wanted the treaty of 1818 "rigidly enforced" with "no deviation...from that policy".[4] In 1852-3 for the first time provincial rights were enforced by the British Government supported eagerly by provincial resources. The results were "acknowledged to be of momentous concern" to the United States, with very material results in expediting negotiations for reciprocity. An Address of the Nova Scotia Assembly in 1853, however, stipulated that "no treaty be negotiated...which would surrender to foreigners the reserved fisheries on our sea coasts". It

---

[1] *Journals*, 1855, Appendix G.
[2] Andrews, *Trade and Commerce of the British North American Colonies*, p. 19.
[3] From 7½ millions in 1853 to over 16 millions in 1863. Secretary to the Treasury, quoted in *The Reciprocity Treaty*, Harvey, A., p. 14.
[4] *Journals*, 1853, p. 19.

would have a "most disastrous effect" and could be "purchased by no equivalent".[1]

A chapter of accidents led to the signing of the treaty without consultation with Nova Scotia, and the Cabinet there learnt the terms "literally from rumour and public journals". Webster's pledge to protect the United States fishermen "hook and line, bob and sinker" was interpreted in the light of the voluminous report of Andrews, the American Consul, as a sign that the Maritime fisheries were the price paid for American concessions. What barbed the injury was the fact that the in-shore fisheries were immediately thrown open for the best "run" of the mackerel season, while the American Government pleaded constitutional difficulties for deferring the opening of their own markets until the formal ratification by the provinces. Johnston and Howe vied with each other in denying "the right of Lord Elgin to concoct, or of the Imperial Government to ratify" stipulations thus "arbitrarily removed from their control". The sacrifice of provincial rights had stultified "a century of loyal attachment and devotion".[2] The treaty was finally ratified in all three provinces—in Prince Edward Island on 7 October, in New Brunswick on 3 November and in Nova Scotia on 13 December—but two of them resented a "humiliating position, too painful to contemplate". Passing from the magnanimous contest for responsible government to the railway fiasco and the "fisheries grievance" one is conscious of an anti-climax which was to culminate finally in the bitterness which attended the entrance of Nova Scotia into Confederation. How far, with the fisheries as bait, a renewal of the Reciprocity Treaty was still a feasible alternative for the Maritime Provinces it would be hard to determine. As late as 1868 two advocates of it from the United States Congress came to Prince Edward Island and Nova Scotia, but the movement was bluntly discountenanced by the Colonial Office in favour of confederation.[3]

Elsewhere in this volume will be found the story of "Maritime union" which, with the support of the Colonial Office, began to over-shadow provincial politics during the 'fifties and culminated under Tilley and Tupper in the larger Confederation during the 'sixties. The smallest of the provinces, however, was the last of that day to enter the Dominion, and it remains to trace its emancipation from the most repressive, perhaps, of all the anachronisms of the first Empire.

There are few more depressing themes than the "land question" of Prince Edward Island. There was scarcely a political issue in the island for a hundred years which was not either dominated or vitiated by it. The rule of the "Compacts" was riddled by it. In its extreme form—the agitation for escheat—it convulsed the province during the

---

[1] *Journals*, 17 Feb. 1853.
[2] *Ibid.* 1854–5, p. 578.
[3] *Series G*, cccxxi, 65.

'thirties and survived the "unalterable opposition" of the Colonial
Office of that day to appear before the Imperial Commissioners as
late as 1861 "from the day the court opened until it closed". It
appeared in Protean forms without number. When the door was closed
upon escheat, Bannerman noted the prevalent belief that responsible
government, by acquiring the Crown rights in the province, "would
lead...to the confiscation of property".[1] Grey's final objection to
responsible government, as we have seen, was "the subject of the
Landed Tenures". He was prepared to use "military force" if
necessary in defence of "rights of property", and when responsible
government became inevitable in 1851 troops were sent for three
years to accompany the concession. Ten years later troops again appeared in the island, as the Tenant League proclaimed, to support
the "rent-leeches" in that "rent-ridden and slave-holding Colony".[2]
The solution of the land question became one of the chief inducements to confederation, and it was finally effected by what Campbell
calls "the most unconstitutional act" that ever received the sanction
of the Crown.[3] For a hundred years it had been the original sin of
the body politic. From 1852 to the Land Purchase Act of 1875 it
dragged its serpentine length over 360 days of discussion in the
Legislature, "to the exclusion of all sound politics". It was "Ireland
on a small scale". "The amount of money and time wasted in public
controversy", wrote the commissioners of 1861, "no man can
estimate".

The stages from Cooper's futile mission for escheat in 1839 to the
Land Purchase Act of 1875 would be tedious to recount. Both Grey and
Lytton (1850 and 1858) had invited the appointment of commissions;
and Labouchere and Stanley (1855 and 1858) for a time favoured an
imperial guarantee for a project of land purchase. The second was soon
emphatically disavowed, but the purchase of the Worrell and Selkirk
estates—some 140,000 acres—in 1854 and 1860 under a local Purchase
Act pointed the way to the easiest solution of the land question.

The classic attempt to explore the whole basic problem was made
by the Imperial Commission of 1860. The Assembly's support was
almost solid—the only dissentient being the "notorious escheator,
Mr Cooper".[4] Joseph Howe was chosen by unanimous vote of the
Assembly to represent the tenants, while J. H. Gray of New
Brunswick represented the British Government and J. W. Ritchie of
Halifax, the proprietors. Beginning in September 1860, the Com-
mission toiled for ten months through a "controversy unexampled,
perhaps, for length and virulence, in the history of colonisation".[5]
The *Report* was unanimous in opposing escheat but in recommending

[1] *Series G*, cccxvi, 320.
[2] *Journals*, 1851, Appendix Y; *Series G*, cccxx, 143, 154, etc.
[3] *History of Prince Edward Island*, p. 168.
[4] Daly to Lytton, 13 May 1859, *Brit. Parl. Papers*, 26 July 1864 (528), p. 1.
[5] *Ibid.* pp. 7, 17.

an imperial guarantee of £100,000 for a project of land purchase, arbitration in case of disagreement and "*compulsory power of purchase at some price*" in the last resort.[1] The Assembly immediately embodied these provisions in legislation.

But the sequel was characteristic of the land question. Scarcely a phase of the *Report* escaped the devastating criticism of the Colonial Office. Newcastle dismissed at the outset the "notion of any imperial guarantee or advance of money"; he disallowed both provincial Acts for implementing the *Report*, found "insuperable objections" to a "multiplicity of separate local arbitrations", and sustained as "conclusive" the objections of the proprietors to compulsory proceedings of any sort. The principles of the *Report* of 1861 were eventually vindicated, as we shall see, by the Dominion, though Howe did not live to see that day; but for ten years deputations, proposals and counter-proposals appeared from every quarter. The Howe award "being now out of the way", Newcastle himself, in what must be conceded to be one of the ablest despatches ever drafted on the land question, finally advocated Sir Samuel Cunard's "machinery of redemption" on the basis of "eight years' purchase of the reserved rent, plus eight years' purchase of the average actual receipts", two-thirds of this to be supplied by the Government through the issue of debentures.[2] In 1866 the Cunard estate of 212,000 acres —more than one-seventh of the whole island—was purchased for £53,000. Two years later the Governor reported that out of 1,400,000 acres in the province some 450,000 remained in the hands of the proprietors, nearly 400,000 had been purchased by the Government, some 450,000 acres were already held in fee simple by former tenants, and more than 200,000 were still under lease. Among the coercive measures towards confederation not the least was the blunt intimation that "the Imperial Government would probably cease to concern itself" with the land question.[3]

The terms offered by the Dominion in March 1873 were so far augmented in the following May as to remove at last "the eternal land question" from the limbo of undetermined causes. In lieu of land revenues the province was granted $45,000 per year (5 per cent. on a capitalised value of $900,000) and the Dominion undertook to advance funds as required to the amount of $800,000 for the purchase of 381,720 acres of proprietary holdings. A compulsory Land Purchase Bill was disallowed by instructions from Downing Street in 1874, but to the astonishment of the proprietors the "act of spoliation" passed the Governor-General with "unprecedented haste" in 1875.[4] Under the Land Purchase Act and a long series of amendments the miasma of

---

[1] For the *Report* in detail see *Journals*, 1862, Appendix O.
[2] *Brit. Parl. Papers*, 26 July 1864 (528), pp. 67 ff.
[3] *Series G*, CCCXX, 234, 441; CCCIII, 70.
[4] See Martin, Chester, Report on *The Natural Resources Question*, pp. 63 ff.; Montgomery, *An Experiment in Communism and its Results*.

the land question began slowly to lift from the horizon of provincial politics.

The dominant theme of the 'sixties in the Maritime Provinces—the carrying of Confederation—is traced in another chapter.[1] In truth Confederation marked, though it did not necessarily effect, the passing of an economic as well as a political era. In one respect at least it was decisive. The buoyant trade with the United States under the Reciprocity Treaty came to an end, and the representatives of Congress, seeking renewal with the Maritime Provinces, found the situation dominated, as we have seen, by Canadian and Imperial policy. Meanwhile the Canadian delegates to the Charlottetown conference had painted more roseate prospects of "a market of four millions of people", with "the great resources of the West" streaming to the Maritime ports "over the immense railways of Canada".[2] But elsewhere the slow process of economic change was less dependent upon policy. The principle, now so obvious, that trans-Atlantic trade depends upon shortening railway transport to the sea rather than ocean transport to the land, proved fatal to the early hopes of the Maritime Provinces. New Brunswick continued to rely upon her matchless inland waterways; the other two provinces upon coasting facilities and the closest network of roads to be found in the British provinces. All three were soon to find themselves passed by in the building of the great trunk lines which dominated westward expansion. The vast hinterlands of the west opened a field not for the Maritime trade but for the steady emigration of thousands of their population. The census returns of the Maritime Provinces have never reached the ratio of increase shown by the decade after 1861.[3]

The revolution in the staple industries of the Maritime Provinces however belongs to a later period, though the tendencies were already discernible. In the 'sixties trade was still buoyant, the fisheries still prolific, and shipbuilding to outward appearances more prosperous than ever. In 1864 nearly 500 ships were built in the three provinces, with a gross tonnage of nearly 170,000. In New Brunswick the barque, the clipper ship and the brigantine of heavy tonnage predominated. Over 1000 ships, including 23 steamships, were registered in that province in 1865.[4] In Nova Scotia and Prince Edward Island too the ruinous practice of building ships for sale—resulting in "jerry-building" and the neglect of legitimate commerce —was slowly rectified by the enterprise of the Cunards, of Captain George McKenzie of Pictou and other shipowners.[5] But iron and steam had already struck the knell of the wooden sailing ship. When

---

[1] See below, chap. xviii.
[2] Speeches on *The Union of the British Provinces*, ed. Hon. Edward Whelan, pp. 46, 52.
[3] The population in that year was as follows: Nova Scotia, 330,857; New Brunswick, 252,047; Prince Edward Island, 80,857.
[4] *Journals*, Appendix no. 16, p. xiii.
[5] Patterson, *History of the County of Pictou*, pp. 430 ff.

Samuel Cunard with the *Britannia* secured the contracts for the British mails in 1840 he began an enterprise which, like the railways, outran the local interests of his native province. The *Persia*, the first of the iron mail-ships (1855), and the *China*, the first of the propeller ships (1862), were the heralds of a new commercial age. It remained for a chronicler of the next generation in contemplating the deserted ship-yards of Windsor, of the St John and the Miramichi, to reflect with poignant recollections upon "the golden age of the Maritimes".

CHAPTER XV

THE FINANCIAL DEVELOPMENT OF BRITISH
NORTH AMERICA, 1840–1867

FROM the reaction after the highly artificial prosperity during the War of 1812 Canada recovered in the following decade. The new economic expansion took place chiefly in the decade 1823–33, especially in the years from 1825 to 1831. Trade was good, and numerous enterprises such as the Welland and Rideau Canals were undertaken, the Lachine Canal being already in working order. New roads were opened up and older ones improved. The operations of the Canada Company and other private land enterprises were bringing to Canada many of its best settlers.

Numerous local industries were begun or expanded in various parts of the Maritime Provinces, and in Upper Canada in particular. This development was largely due, in the latter province, to difficulties of transportation, even by roads. Facilities for establishing water-powers were numerous; millwrights and persons skilled in building timber structures of some size were in demand. At first the equipment for the mills came chiefly from the United States, but, later, foundries were established in Canada, as at Montreal, Kingston, York (afterwards Toronto), Dundas, and even at Marmora near Belleville, where was established an iron works producing malleable iron from local ores. In the immediate neighbourhood of each grain mill there was also often established a saw-mill, a cooperage to provide barrels for the export of flour, a small woollen mill providing yarn and coarse cloth. A special woollen factory was erected on the Humber near York.[1] A blacksmith shop was connected with each mill site, where often a great variety of fairly skilled work was produced, such as simple agricultural implements and even wagons. At many of these centres there were also stills, producing alcoholic beverages, whisky, not beer, being chiefly favoured. Among the more important iron products brought from a considerable distance, especially from the old French iron works re-established at Three Rivers in Lower Canada, were domestic stoves, large potash and sugar kettles, the latter of which, on occasion, were found most useful for many purposes, domestic and other.[2] Special industries were located at particular places, as, for instance, a nail factory at Port Hope in 1826.[3] A noted paper factory was established in Upper Canada by James Crooks.[4]

---

[1] *Colonial Advocate*, 13 Dec. 1827.
[2] See the newspapers of Quebec, Montreal, Kingston, Toronto and Niagara, etc.
[3] *Kingston Chronicle*, 13 Sept. 1826.　　　　　　　[4] *Ibid.* 7 July 1826.

On the paper there produced, most of the leading newspapers of the province were printed.

Naturally many of these groups of local industries centring around a water-power were owned by single persons or partnerships. A general store was usually a commercial and social centre of exchange for all the essential imports of the neighbourhood, as groceries, dry goods and hardware; also the place of receipt for all the natural products exported from the same extensive neighbourhood. This concentration of the ordinary business of a considerable community, within a few hands, reduced much of the processes of exchange to a form of comparatively simple book-keeping, with the minimum use of money or credit instruments. On the other hand, most of these scattered centres, through their leading moneyed citizens, held somewhat similar relations to the few larger centres in each province, such as York and Kingston in Upper Canada, Quebec, Three Rivers, and Sherbrooke in Lower Canada, while Montreal was the ultimate centre of the larger houses of import and export, which dealt also with commercial exchange. Although geographical conditions were somewhat different in the Maritime Provinces, where the leading centres communicated with each other by sea, yet even there a considerable and similar local economic development and enterprise took place.

To facilitate the commercial dealings of the various outlying districts with the provincial sub-centres, and through them with Montreal, several stable banking institutions had been created before or during this period. Such were: the Bank of Montreal, established chiefly by American capital, the Bank of Quebec, the Bank of Upper Canada at York, the *Banque du Peuple*, and the Commercial Bank at Kingston. Others, somewhat less stable, were brought into being by the prosperity of the time, but few survived the critical period which followed. Most of these institutions depended chiefly upon the privilege of issuing bank notes or paper money, which, when properly secured, furnished a very desirable and efficient medium of exchange.

During this period of comparative prosperity and expansion, there was a considerable development in immigration and settlement, alike in the Canadas and Maritime Provinces. In the Canadas this took place chiefly in the Eastern Townships of Lower Canada, and throughout the more northerly and westerly sections of Upper Canada. The rapid expansion of the English element naturally gave rise to considerable apprehension on the part of the French population. Encouraged by the Quebec Act, the French section had come to regard Canada as essentially a French-Canadian country, although the British Government had gradually come to ignore its original pledges in that respect. Moreover, the increasing numbers of persons of British origin were more and more inclined to regard existing facts and future prospects rather than ancient pledges and constitutional rights, and there was thus a growing tendency to assume that Canada must in the end be a British colony, at least in its economic development and its public law and institutions, the French however retaining their religious freedom and domestic usages. It is true the commercial French element of Quebec and Montreal had been already more or less incorporated by the English element, thereby losing most of their influence with the general body of the French village and urban population.

The rebellion of 1837 largely paralysed the prosperity of the two provinces. This did not mean much for the general body of the French Canadians, whose economic standing remained practically the same; but it meant everything for the majority of the English element whose economic progress was arrested for a time. It caused also an almost complete cessation of immigration from Britain, and the departure for the United States of many of the more recent arrivals, especially those possessed of means. Finally, after the suppression of the rebellion and the more extreme French-Canadian nationalist hopes, a number of French Canadians sought refuge in several of the neighbouring States, where they tended to gather in small communities of their own.[1]

In conformity with Lord Durham's Report and various other communications the British Government, as we have seen, decided to unite the two provinces, with the hope and expectation that the English element, with or without a French wing, would control the majority of votes in the Assembly. Otherwise the situation which had brought the Legislature of Lower Canada to a deadlock would be repeated, the direct power of the Crown would have to be exerted, while nothing like responsible government would be possible. This, of course, would mean that economic enterprise in Canada would be brought almost to a standstill. The rural contentment of the French-Canadian settlers might, indeed, be considered to be preferable to the restless type of Anglo-Saxon colonial life, which would naturally pass almost entirely to a more kindred atmosphere in the United States. The Act providing for the union of the two provinces duly passed the British Parliament, 23 July 1840.[2] To bring this measure into operation in Canada was the task allotted to the new Governor, Charles Poulett Thomson, better known to history as Lord Sydenham, who arrived in Canada in November 1839.

The vindication of the Union meant much for the political future of the Canadas, but it implied much more for the economic future of the country, and it was on this new basis that the subsequent economic development of Canada was to proceed. In the interval of racial struggle between 1834 and 1839, the economic reaction on both public and private enterprise in the Canadas had been very severe.

[1] Emigration Report of Select Committee of the Legislative Assembly, Montreal, 1849.
[2] British Statutes, 3 and 4 Vict. cap. 35.

Canadian resources and credit had receded to a low ebb. In 1834, public works in the way of roads, canals, preparations for construction of railroads, etc., were relatively as advanced as in the neighbouring States. A severe economic crisis had occurred both in England and the United States in 1837, yet down to 1840 the Canadas, outside of the French rural districts, were very greatly depressed. Even before the arrival of Lord Sydenham, it was known that one of the chief inducements which the British Government had to offer for the successful introduction of the policy of union was a substantial financial assistance towards the resumption and promotion of the central public works of the country. The mere prospect of a liberal assistance towards the relief of the financial burdens of the country tended to be discounted immediately by the commercial element, including, as usual, the French merchants of Montreal. Thus, in 1839, there occurred a premature revival of trade. In Montreal and the chief commercial centres connected with it there were extensive importations from Britain, which were sent chiefly to the former centres of active trade in Upper Canada and the Eastern Townships of Lower Canada. Conditions were not so bad this year, but in 1840 they became rather stringent. While many of the new supplies were welcome enough to the people, yet payment for them was very difficult.[1] In the chief Canadian trading centres, especially Montreal, British imports were being sold on the wholesale markets by auction, as in London. As a natural result prices were demoralised.[2] On the other hand, the somewhat slow recovery from the crisis of 1837 in England and the United States limited the demand for Canadian produce.[3] To a certain extent similar conditions prevailed in the Maritime Provinces up to 1843.[4]

It was soon found that Lord Sydenham, in economic and political matters alike, was his own Prime Minister. There certainly was at that time no one else in the country who properly understood the special functions of leadership pertaining to that position in the British system of responsible government. Thus, Sydenham proceeded to select a body of men as his Council or Cabinet from the representatives returned to the Legislature, such as might be expected to command the majority in the Legislature and otherwise contribute valuable elements to the Government. Then, while consulting them on the various points upon which each could furnish the best information and judgment, he nevertheless framed his own measures, in outline at least, and convinced his Council of their soundness and practicability. His exceptional capacity in this respect both captured the intelligence and enlisted the enthusiasm of the members of his Council in proportion to their own ability. On this basis he framed

---

[1] *Examiner*, Toronto, 10 Jan. 1840.
[2] *Chronicle and Gazette*, Kingston, 14 July 1840; also *Examiner*, 15 July 1840.
[3] *Examiner*, 15 July 1840.
[4] *Novascotian*, Halifax, 30 Sept. and 14 Oct. 1841; also 12 June 1843.

a programme for the united Legislature, both extensive in range and important in its details. In nearly all cases he secured the necessary majorities in a new and untried Legislature, with a nationalist French representation entirely bent from the first on wrecking the Government if possible. The significance of this achievement is effectively pointed out by Lord Seaton, formerly Sir John Colborne, who as a Governor in Canada had endured much while the French were endeavouring to render British government impossible there. In a letter to Sir George Murray, to be passed on to Sir Charles Bagot, the successor of Sydenham, Lord Seaton indicates that Sydenham, by his personal ability and political diplomacy, had to combine the ultra-conservative mercantile and financial element of Lower Canada with the more radical elements of Upper Canada, in order to secure the Union and carry on the Government for the first session. He intimates, however, that from the very success of these measures it was inevitable that he should retire at the close of that session, to permit a new successor to build upon the foundations which he had laid. On this ground Lord Seaton considers that Sir Charles Bagot, the new Governor, may hope to recover the French element; which was just what Sydenham expected, and what Bagot successfully accomplished.[1]

Only on one important point did Sydenham fail to carry his Cabinet with him, viz. in his proposal to introduce a Government Bank of issue on the British model. On the basis of sound banking and as a legitimate source of public revenue in a commercial atmosphere such as that of Britain at the time, or of Canada after confederation, his policy was perfectly sound. He failed to realise, however, the peculiar relations of the Canadian banks to the miscellaneous and highly seasonal character of Canadian domestic exchange at the time, and the vital relation to all this of the note issues of the country. On this subject he found himself definitely confronted with the practical experience of some of the ablest men of the country, both within and beyond the Cabinet. His political wisdom, rather than his financial judgment, caused him to drop his central bank scheme.

One of the chief elements in Sydenham's success as leader of the Government was his capacity, first to select and then to command the respect and support of able men for the most important public positions to be filled. Special mention may here be made of Francis Hincks, in view of his future career, more particularly in connection with the economic development of Canada. At that time he was an almost unknown person, generally regarded as a Baldwin Reformer, yet, as events proved, with a far clearer insight into the real meaning of things than his patron. Hincks had managed for a time, quite successfully, a rather obscure institution known as the People's Bank, afterwards taken over by the Bank of Montreal. He had recently

[1] Can. Arch. MSS. *Series M*, CLVIII, 148.

appeared as the editor of the *Examiner*, which Bagot declared to be "by far the best written paper in this country", an estimate which was echoed as far away as Halifax by Joseph Howe in the *Novascotian*. The important and difficult task for which Sydenham selected him was that of investigating and putting in order the public finances, which Sydenham, with his practical knowledge of such matters, had suspected to be in a very unsatisfactory condition. Hincks having successfully accomplished this task, Sydenham bequeathed him to his successor, Sir Charles Bagot, as Inspector-General, or Minister of Finance in his Cabinet. Bagot, in proposing him to Lord Stanley as the first incumbent of this new and important office, acknowledged that he was a Radical but was confident as he had supported Sydenham that he would support him also. In any case he was quite sure there was no other man in the country so fitted for the position.[1] Thereafter, in his various intervals of office, chiefly as Minister of Finance, Hincks played far the most important part of any single individual in the development of the Canadian banking system from 1841 to 1871.

We may here note an incident which, though more or less accidental in its origin, nevertheless had very important consequences for the financial future of all the British North American colonies. For some time previously to 1837, the official Canadian financial interests in Britain and the United States had been conducted through a well-known but limited Anglo-American house known as Thomas Wilson and Company, with headquarters in London. In 1837, the Hon. John Henry Dunn, Provincial Treasurer of Upper Canada, had gone over to England on official business. Immediately on his arrival in London he naturally went to the office of Thomas Wilson and Company, only to find that the firm had failed the day before. Other houses were suggested to him by his friends, but he was told that, if it were possible to make connections with the great house of Baring Brothers, already extensively connected with American finance, he might consider himself and his Government especially fortunate. Accordingly, he applied to the Barings, was graciously received, his pressing wants supplied and future possibilities left for later consideration. He at once communicated with the Canadian Government, recounting both his evil and good fortune, and urging that the Government make, if possible, immediate and permanent arrangements with the Barings as the financial agents for Canada for the future. In the meantime the fast packet service by way of New York brought word to the Canadian Government of the failure of Wilson and Company. Taking immediate advice through the best media in Montreal, the Government decided to link with another firm, Messrs Glyn, Halifax, Mills and Company. This they at once proceeded to do through messages to Dunn and the Glyns.

[1] Can. Arch. *Series M*, CLX, 59.

These papers from and to London crossed on the Atlantic. Glyn, Halifax, Mills and Company duly accepted the proffered Canadian account, but the Canadian Government immediately instructed Dunn to close with the Barings also, and for a time, at least, divide the Canadian account between them. Dunn managed to effect this arrangement, both houses being on very intimate terms with each other. Henceforward these two firms continued to divide the Canadian account between them down to confederation and thereafter until 1891, when, by the mutual agreement of all parties, the Canadian account in London was transferred to the Bank of Montreal. The period from 1841 to 1871 was by far the most difficult for Canadian finance, and the support of these powerful financial houses proved to be of inestimable advantage to Canada on many critical occasions, especially in connection with her great public works such as canals, railways, municipal borrowings, etc.[1]

Sydenham, himself a maternal cousin of the Barings, from his knowledge of financial conditions recognised that the debts already contracted for public works, as yet only partially completed, threatened the credit of Upper Canada with ultimate ruin.[2] He concluded, therefore, that the assistance of the credit of the Imperial Government was practically indispensable for the rehabilitation of Canadian credit, the completion of the public works already begun, and the undertaking of others equally essential.[3] The direction in which Sydenham considered that such assistance would prove most effective for the benefit of United Canada was that of further improving by means of canals, etc., the navigation of the St Lawrence, including the connecting links between the lower lakes which together constituted the central highway of the two provinces.[4] The Home Government adopted these suggestions, and Sydenham was authorised to promise that it would guarantee the interest on a loan of £1,500,000, equivalent to $7,500,000, for these purposes.[5] It appears from a letter of Lord John Russell to the British Treasury, of 24 July 1840, that the British Government had in contemplation to guarantee the existing debt of Upper Canada, which was then about £1,226,000.[6] Lord Sydenham did not make public this communication in Canada, but in another Act, "to appropriate certain sums of money for public improvements in this province", etc., provision was made for specific public works amounting to £1,659,689. This was assented to 18 September 1841, the day before Sydenham died. While the works specified were to be completed with as little delay as possible, the

---

[1] Through the generosity of the houses of Barings and Glyn Mills the present writer has been instrumental in securing for the Canadian Archives the extensive MS. collections dealing with these and similar matters in the years 1821–71.
[2] Sydenham to Russell, 22 and 25 Feb. 1841, *Series M*, CLXV, 1.
[3] Sydenham to Russell, 27 June 1840, *Series M*, CLXV, 1.
[4] Sydenham to Russell, Feb. 1841, *Series M*, CLXV, 2.
[5] Russell to Sydenham, 3 May 1841, *Series M*, CLXV, 3.
[6] *Ibid.* p. 11.

expenditure was expected to be "spread over a period of five years necessary for their completion".[1] Lord Sydenham, it appears, had expected that the interest on most of this additional appropriation of £1,659,689 would be derived from an increase in the provincial revenue, which he expected to provide chiefly from the contemplated Government Bank of issue and a revision of the customs duties.[2] The expected revenue from the Government note issue, however, disappeared with the abandonment of that measure. Lord Sydenham's death undoubtedly prevented any readjustment of his fiscal measures, and left the provincial finances in considerable confusion. The consequences were fully set forth by C. E. Trevelyan, Chief Secretary of the British Treasury, in a confidential communication to the Cabinet on the subject of Canadian finances[3], in which he showed that public works were not necessarily profitable and criticised severely the improvidence with which nearly the whole of the Canadian debt had been incurred and the proposals for a lavish development of the miscellaneous public works of Canada at the expense of the British Government.[4] Most of his strictures on passing conditions were entirely justified, while his predictions for the future were as amply fulfilled. Among the most important consequences from the expenditure of relatively large sums on public works in a country like Canada were the successive waves of exceptional prosperity produced in the country while the great expenditures of capital were taking place, to be followed by equally marked periods of reaction and stagnation when such expenditures ceased, or were greatly diminished. These waves of artificial prosperity, followed by times of stagnation and economic distress, were never more marked in Canada than between 1841 and 1867.

There was naturally much impatience in the province for the effective realisation of the loan of £1,500,000, and the undertaking of the various public works provided for in the Act of 1841, cap. 28. But important considerations connected with the embarrassment of the programme of public works left by Lord Sydenham, coupled with inadequate sources of revenue for meeting them, had to be considered. The upshot was that the British Government, by an Act of Parliament of 1841–2, guaranteed merely the interest on the loan of £1,500,000, at a rate not to exceed 4 per cent., from which alone the repayment of such part of the existing debt as might be called for was to be provided first, while only the remainder might be applied to public works.[5] This latter was understood to be the limit of the amount available from the provincial Act of 1841, cap. 28, above referred to, authorising specific public works to the extent of £1,659,689. As Bagot reported to Stanley, the Canadians

[1] Russell to Sydenham, 3 May 1841, *Series M*, CLXV, 6.   [2] *Ibid.* p. 8.
[3] *Ibid.* pp. 9–10.   [4] *Ibid.* pp. 10–11.
[5] Brit. Statutes, 5 and 6 Vict. cap. 118.

were displeased with this curtailment of the extensive prospects which they had been led to entertain.[1] However, to give effect to the Imperial Act, the Canadian Act was passed again authorising the raising, by way of loan in England, of £1,500,000 for the construction and completion of public works in Canada.[2]

In the meantime surveys, begun in 1839, had been undertaken by the British engineer, Colonel Philpotts, whose final estimates were presented to Sir Charles Bagot. Only then was it possible to begin the actual work on the canals. His plans were certainly calculated to suit the most ambitious. His estimate amounted to about £6,000,000, but Bagot anticipated that more than double that amount would be required.[3] Alarmed by the miscellaneous programme of the works contemplated by the Legislature, Stanley wrote to Bagot, in June 1842, praying him to warn the Legislature not to get out of its depths financially by undertaking too many public works, but to keep closely to the chief projects on the St Lawrence route.[4] Bagot admitted that the public in Canada were most anxious for the beginning of the public works from the promised loan,[5] but stated that the more he looked into the question of financial assistance from England, the more he was convinced that the matter should be very cautiously dealt with. The funds supplied by Great Britain should not be placed in the hands of the Canadian Legislature simply to be scrambled for.[6]

For years to come, in confirmation of Trevelyan's forecast, the prospective revenues to be derived from the tolls on the public works in aid of transportation were constantly paraded as the ultimate justification for extravagant expenditures. A typical statement of this character, setting forth the great commercial advantages accruing both to Canada and Great Britain from the canals and other public works connected with the opening of the St Lawrence water-route to the head of the lower Great Lakes, was made by Sir Randolph Routh, the Canadian Commissary-General: "Let the resources of this country begin at least to develop themselves before the present [military] force has materially diminished. Once open the St Lawrence to the Lakes, and you have the States of Michigan, Indiana, Illinois and Ohio, ready to send all their shipments through that channel, and also the western portion of the State of New York". He adds that, as the revenues from this water-way increase, the duties on English manufactured goods may be reduced, with the result that an immense import trade to these same States will ensue. "Montreal will become the greatest commercial city on this continent, and that in the course of ten years".[7]

Something may here be said of the development of the St Lawrence water-way before 1841, the control of which was entirely in the hands

---

[1] *Series M*, CLXV, 71.   [2] Can. Statutes, II, 1842, cap. 8.
[3] *Series M*, CLX, 151.   [4] *Ibid.* CLXV, 100.
[5] *Ibid.* CLX, 17–18.   [6] *Ibid.* CLX, 198.
[7] *Ibid.* CLXV, 13.

of the Legislature of Lower Canada until 1822, and practically until 1841. The Lachine Canal alone received any consideration, and between 1822 and 1829 about £100,000 had been expended on it, yet, owing to the very limited size of the locks, it was virtually a mere boat canal.[1] The Legislature of Upper Canada had made some surveys of the water routes in that province, but the only practical attention paid to them was due to the imperial interests in providing safe military routes to the interior of the province. The Rideau Canal was therefore undertaken and carried through between the years 1826 and 1830 at the sole expense of the Imperial Government.[2]

The Commissioners of Upper Canada, in their Report of 1825, frankly attributed the neglect of the St Lawrence route to the efforts of Lower Canada to discourage any improvements on the river above their province.[3] In the meantime, private enterprise undertook the construction of the Welland Canal between Lakes Erie and Ontario. Down to the year 1840 £491,771 had been expended upon it, £117,800 representing privately-owned stock, which was afterwards taken over by the Government in 1841. To replace the wooden locks with stone structures and put the canal in good serviceable shape, it was estimated, in 1841, that £450,000 would be required.[4] Meanwhile Upper Canada endeavoured to promote the construction of the Cornwall Canal on which, down to 1839, upwards of £354,000 had been expended; and Keefer, the engineer, considered that another £57,671 would complete it for traffic.[5]

Just before the political crisis of 1837 in Upper Canada, £245,000 of additional stock was authorised for the Welland Canal in order to replace the original wooden locks then rapidly decaying. Finally, with characteristic lavishness and improvidence, the Legislature of Upper Canada voted credits for £930,000 for internal improvements.[6] Of course, nothing of any practical consequence was actually undertaken, and everything was ending in financial and political chaos when the union of the provinces was decided upon.

Of other works to be completed after the Union the most important was a canal to overcome the heavy rapids between Lakes St Francis and St Louis, completing the link between Cornwall and Lachine. In 1841, Keefer estimated the construction of such a canal at £255,900.[7] This was afterwards provided for by the Beauharnais Canal. Then the Lachine Canal would require to be enlarged at an estimated cost of £225,300.[8] Other minor improvements on the river, above and below Montreal, completed the total estimate given.

---

[1] Keefer, T. C., *Canals of Canada, their Prospects and Influence*, p. 13.
[2] Mactaggart, J., *Three Years in Canada*.
[3] Keefer, p. 14.
[4] Memorandum on various public works by H. H. Killaly, 1841, Can. Arch. Series M, CLXV, 15.
[5] *Ibid.* CLXV, 16.
[6] Keefer, pp. 17–18.
[7] Can. Arch. *Series M*, CLXV, 16.
[8] Keefer, p. 16.

In 1845, the Beauharnais and the enlarged Welland Canals were opened. As this event coincided with other favourable, albeit highly artificial economic conditions, there was a notable increase in the business of the St Lawrence route,[1] which proved, however, to be merely temporary, so that by 1848–9 Canadian prospects began to assume a very gloomy aspect, aggravated by the blunders of the Lafontaine-Baldwin Government. At this time there vanished, temporarily at least, the dream of so many, that Canadian public works would not only amply repay the capital expended upon them, but return a handsome contribution towards the relief of provincial taxation. Some, however, and among them so shrewd and well-informed an observer as Keefer, still argued that, at least in minor forms, the subsequent influence of the Canadian canals would be not only, as everyone admitted, beneficial to Canadian trade, but even remunerative on the capital outlay. Keefer argued that eventually the St Lawrence canals would be the means of transferring the trade of the Maritime Provinces from the United States to Canada, and would prove a powerful factor in securing reciprocity with the United States.[2]

After the practical completion of the St Lawrence water-route from the Great Lakes to the sea, and the opening of this system for the free passage of American shipping, in virtue of the Reciprocity Treaty of 1854, the results were found to be anything but encouraging. In the Report of the Select Committee of the Canadian Legislative Council, in 1861, one of the causes of this was said to be the facilities afforded by railroads from Chicago to the Hudson. There was also an immense preponderance of American over Canadian shipping on the upper Lakes. It was found that only 2 per cent. of the produce which passed the Welland Canal went down the St Lawrence, the greater part being taken to New York *via* the Erie Canal and the Hudson. The facilities afforded by the customs at Quebec and New York were practically the same. Yet goods to the value of only $21,505 passed through Canada for the Western States, while goods to the amount of $7,692,531 passed through the United States for consumption in Canada. It would seem that the costs of shipping below Montreal constituted an important factor in neutralising the advantages above that port. Among these costs were the towing charges and the high rates of insurance in the latter part of the year. From 1845 to 1859 the tolls on the Canadian canals averaged at first about five cents per bushel, but in the end only about three-fifths of a cent per bushel. And even that the commissioners thought might be practically abolished.[3] Among the remedies advocated was the deepening of the St Lawrence canals to a minimum of $10\frac{1}{2}$ ft., so as to permit vessels to pass directly from the Great Lakes to Great Britain. The Hon. John

[1] Keefer, pp. 26–7.
[2] Keefer, p. 47.
[3] *Report of the Select Committee....* Printed by order of the Legislative Council, Quebec, 1861.

Young of Montreal, who had devoted much attention to this subject,[1] stated that the rivalry between the Canadian and American routes to the West had developed with the completion of the St Lawrence canals in 1849. Down to 1847, the trade of Western Canada was confined to the St Lawrence by reason of the preferences on grain and flour sent to Britain by that route. Then, in 1849, the American Government introduced the bonding system, by which Canadian produce could pass through American ports to Europe free of duty, while goods from Britain reached Canada in the same way. But the British Corn Laws and Navigation Acts were completely abolished by 1849. There was thus perfect equality between the Canadian and American routes, and this was further promoted by the Reciprocity Treaty of 1854. The export of Canadian grain to the United States, above the St Lawrence canals, increased from 124,000 bushels in 1849, 2,334,000 bushels in 1852, and 3,812,000 bushels in 1854, to 8,337,000 bushels in 1860. In the last period the total receipts at Montreal from both Canada and the Western States amounted to only 6,558,000 bushels. Young showed how little of the Canadian and American export trade of the West reached the ocean through the lower St Lawrence. He specially advocated the opening of the Lake Champlain Canal, in connection with the Richelieu River route to the Eastern States from Montreal, in order to permit Canadian produce to reach the growing markets of the Eastern States. He also urged the further improvement of the St Lawrence both above and below Montreal, and expressed his conviction that the St Lawrence route could still be made the cheapest and best.[2]

The most persistent impediment to the employment of the St Lawrence route by vessels having the option of going to either Canadian or American ports, or to both, arose from the fact that it was practically impossible to obtain return cargoes to Canada at all equivalent to the bulky freights of grain or timber from Canada outward. The general result was that vessels which came to Canada had to charge the outward cargo with the whole cost of the round trip. As practically no steamers could undertake such a trade, those coming to Canada had to be heavily subsidised by both Britain and Canada, through mail and other contracts.[3] The restriction of the St Lawrence traffic to the summer months was also a continued handicap. Consequently the British Navigation Acts added very materially to the disadvantages of the St Lawrence route, and could only be offset by special countervailing privileges, such as were afforded by the free import of Canadian flour and grain to Britain from 1843. But with the complete abolition of the Corn Laws, between 1846 and

---

[1] Young, J., *Rival Routes to the Ocean from the West*, etc., Montreal, 1858.
[2] See the above *Report*, Appendix VI, p. 12.
[3] See the contracts with the Cunard Co. 4 July 1839. Can. Arch., MS. Correspondence with the Colonial Office, XII, 97, 449.

1849, the Canadian and Maritime Governments, Boards of Trade, etc., naturally agitated for the abolition of the Navigation Acts which confined the trade between all ports of the British Empire to British or colonial vessels navigated by British masters and by three-fourths, at least, of British crews. The Home Government, realising the necessary logic of their trade policy, duly abolished the Navigation Acts in 1849, thus permitting the vessels of all nations to resort to the St Lawrence.[1]

At the outset of the Canadian Union in 1841, there emerged a question which had long been the subject of much desultory discussion between Canada and the Mother Country; to wit that of the admission of Canadian flour and grain to the markets of Great Britain under special privileges. To a certain, though much more limited, extent this question had also engaged the attention of agricultural interests in the Maritime Provinces, especially Prince Edward Island. In this as in many other matters, however, the interests of Upper and Lower Canada differed considerably. The farmers of Western Canada desired an effective duty against American grain imported for home consumption, although not for transmission through the province. On the other hand, the French Canadians, who did not quite feed themselves, favoured the admission of cheap flour from the United States.[2] The millers of Montreal and neighbourhood especially desired the free import of wheat. In the meantime, on behalf of the Home Government, the Hon. Henry Labouchere proposed, as one of the stepping stones to the ultimate repeal of the Corn Laws, to reduce the duty on grain from the colonies to a uniform rate of five shillings per quarter. This proposal was supported in Canada by Hincks,[3] who also took up the whole question of the Free Trade movement in England, and its prospective effects upon Canada. He predicted the ultimate adoption of complete Free Trade in England, and in the meantime anticipated the free admission there of Canadian grain and flour.[4] The free admission of Canadian produce to Britain had been strongly advocated by Lord Sydenham.[5] Naturally, in the course of the general break-up of the protective system in the Empire, many varieties of interests became urgently vocal. Petitions poured in upon the Canadian Governors to be forwarded to the Home Government, while others were sent directly. In a petition, through Lord Sydenham, from George Moffatt, an exporting merchant of Montreal, it was explicitly stated that, should it be decided to admit Canadian produce to Britain free of duty, the duties on American produce coming to Canada should be fixed at suitable rates, and once these were paid all such produce (including all food-stuffs) should be accepted as Canadian in the British markets.

[1] Speech of H. Labouchere, 15 May 1848. Hansard, vol. XCVIII, 992–1021.
[2] *Examiner*, Toronto, 23 Dec. 1841.   [3] *Ibid.* 12 May 1841.
[4] *Ibid.* 19 May 1841.   [5] Sydenham to Russell, 21 Jan. 1841.

Similar arrangements were advocated in the Maritime Provinces as suited to their special needs.[1]

As to the admission on the same basis of both Canadian and American grain and flour, the new British Conservative Government, under Peel, was not at first prepared to make so radical a change, although willing to make a move in that direction. Stanley, writing to Bagot, intimated that the Canadian Legislature might place a moderate duty on wheat coming from the United States, which would be contingent on a reduction of duty on Canadian wheat and flour to one shilling per quarter. He did not wish the proposal to come from the Executive Government in Canada, but from the Provincial Legislature.[2] This was promptly acted upon in Canada, the duty on American wheat being fixed at three shillings per quarter.[3] The bill was, of course, reserved by Bagot to ascertain whether it might be supplemented in Britain by the admission of Canadian wheat and flour. After further discussion and enquiry as to practical details, including the amounts of grain and flour obtained from Canada, the United States, etc., the Home Government implemented its side of the arrangement by confirming the Canadian Act, and by passing an Imperial Act permitting American wheat ground in Canada to be sent to Britain as colonial produce, at a duty of one shilling per quarter for wheat, and a proportional duty on wheat flour.[4] This arrangement gave an immense stimulus to the Canadian milling industry, especially in the neighbourhood of Montreal, and greatly promoted Canadian shipments *via* the St Lawrence, but proved only a stage in the irresistible movement in Britain, ending in the abolition of the Corn Laws in 1846. For the benefit of Canada the reduction in the protective duties was extended over the period from 1846 to 1849.

The loss of the Canadian preference in British food supplies coincided with other political and economic troubles precipitated by the Lafontaine-Baldwin Government in Canada, and produced, in 1849, a severe and complex crisis centring in Montreal. As is described in an earlier chapter,[5] riots occurred there, culminating in the burning of the Parliament buildings, and the mobbing of the Governor, Lord Elgin. The commercial and financial interests, in despair of both the economic and political future of Canada as a separate country, organised and advocated, albeit in very moderate and reasonable terms, with expressions of the friendliest sentiments towards Great Britain, a proposal for the annexation of Canada to the United States. They argued quite calmly that, inasmuch as Great Britain had found it to her interest completely to break through the existing bonds of mutual economic interdependence between Great Britain and Canada, it was incumbent on the latter to seek for and adopt such

[1] Can. Arch. P.F. LXXVII, 506.
[2] Stanley to Bagot, 3 Mar. 1842, Can. Arch. *Series M*, CLXV, 38.
[3] Can. Statutes, 1842, cap. 31.
[4] Brit. Statutes, 6 and 7 Vict. 1843, cap. 29.   [5] See chapter xii.

other connections as might provide some reasonable substitute for those which had been lost. The only course which seemed to promise a reasonably stable future was that of annexation to the United States.[1] The persons who took the lead in this movement were among the most prominent men in commerce, finance and politics in Montreal. Later, several of them held very prominent positions as ministers of the Crown in Canadian Cabinets, two of them being afterwards Prime Ministers. At the time the Government of Lafontaine and Baldwin, although having a fairly good theoretic conception of responsible government, and at first enjoying a majority in the House of two to one, proved to be singularly incapable of devising or adopting any effective measures to offset these unfortunate developments, in spite of repeated appeals and remonstrances from such persons as Hincks, Minister of Finance.[2]

In the face of the declining financial credit of Canada, greatly aggravated by the development of the domestic crisis, Hincks had naturally a difficult task to accomplish in attempting to reassure the Canadian financial agents in London. The Barings, in a letter to him,[3] stated frankly that, whatever the causes of the agitations against the Canadian Government, they were at all events very real in their effects upon Canadian credit. Riots in Canada on the ground that the Government was undertaking to pay rebels, and an influential movement for separation from the Empire, seriously affected the security for much of the money already borrowed by Canada and her future credit. Consequently people would not buy the colonial bonds of British North America. As to the suggestion that if they find it difficult to sell 6 per cent. Canadian bonds, they might increase the rate to 7 per cent., that would be absolutely fatal, since a Government offering 7 per cent. bonds on the British market would simply mean that such a Government had no credit at all. Hincks, in his replies, naturally exhibited considerable embarrassment. In his letter of 29 February 1849, virtually confessing that the measures of the Canadian Government had led to the exceptional disorders in the country, he endeavoured to minimise the evil effects on Canadian credit in Britain, and concluded with the futile aspiration, "I do trust that local and party quarrels here will not be allowed to produce any effect on the minds of British capitalists injurious to our interests", as though the British investor could ignore what the Government of Canada had not the capacity to prevent. In the circumstances, however, the Barings and Glyn Mills saved Canadian credit from a ruinous collapse by placing their own extensive credit at the service of Canada, and tactfully withholding Canadian securities from the market, until their value was gradually restored. This restoration

[1] *Circular of Committee of Annexation Association of Montreal* (1849); also Report of Annexation meeting on 8 Dec. 1849.
[2] Hincks to Baldwin, 26 Oct. 1849 (Toronto Public Library), vol. A 51, p. 142.
[3] Of date 12 Jan. 1849.

occurred only when Hincks himself, in association with Morin, took control of the Government and entered upon a new and constructive line of policy.

Among the more injurious practices to which the Canadian Government in its extremity had previously resorted was that of handing out to various local creditors, such as banks and construction companies for public works, various forms of bonds or securities which either directly or indirectly were brought upon the London market, where they appeared in direct competition with the regular Canadian securities, to the obvious detriment of Canadian credit. Another practice, though less injurious to Canadian credit abroad, was the issue of paper securities in Canada in form and amounts suited to the purposes of a circulating medium.[1] In reply to the vigorous remonstrances of the Barings as to the irregular securities from Canada which came on the London market, Hincks assures them that under his administration of Canadian finances, "you may rely on it that no bonds will be placed on the London market through any other channels than through your own house and Messrs Glyn, in concert with each other. The Canadian Government will be guided entirely by your advice in its financial operations".[2] At that time Canada was arranging for a loan of £500,000, and in connection with this it was declared to the Barings that it was the intention of the Canadian Government not further to increase the provincial debt, whether for railways or anything else. On the contrary, it was their purpose to take measures to reduce the debt.[3] At the same time the Canadian Executive Council had to admit that it was committed to afford assistance to certain railroads, but with small probability of their ever requiring it, the guarantee being merely intended to assure the success of their own corporate financing. Yet the Council blandly asserted that in all such matters it would act under the advice and with the co-operation of the Barings and Glyns.[4] Hincks himself explained that in an Act of the last session, affording the guarantee of the province to the bonds of railway companies on certain conditions,[5] every precaution had been taken to make the guarantee a merely nominal one. In case, however, it should become necessary to call upon the guarantee, the Government had taken authority to add anything up to 10 per cent. to the customs duties. He then explained how amply protected were the holders of the provincial securities by the private and corporate interests pledged to the support of the corporations whose bonds have been guaranteed.[6]

While these confident expectations were at least partially realised

[1] *Globe*, 22, 26 and 29 July 1848; 13 and 20 Sept. 1848.
[2] Hincks to Barings, 16 July 1849.
[3] This was also stated in a letter to the Barings of L. M. Viger (Receiver-General of the Canadian Department of Finance), 6 Aug. 1849.
[4] L. M. Viger to Barings, 30 July 1849.
[5] Can. Statutes, 1849, cap. 29.
[6] Hincks to Barings, 31 Oct. 1850.

during the ensuing boom in railroad building and provincial prosperity in general, the ultimate result of these assurances was anything but happy, becoming the basis of vigorous attacks on the good faith of the Canadian Government by the *Times* and other British journals. It is noticeable also that such confident declarations of financial faith as regards the merely nominal use of the public credit in support of railroads and similar corporations were common to the whole North American continent, and preceded the ultimate financial collapse of public credit in many States of the American Union.

In the meantime, however, the new Hincks-Morin Government, 1851–4, soon restored tranquillity in Canada, and directed the energies of the province into new channels. By promoting the movement for a Reciprocity Treaty with the United States, they killed the annexation effort, and by directing the corporate interests towards the construction of railroads, at first as subsidiary to the St Lawrence canal system, but ultimately as largely independent of it, they opened new avenues for the influx of foreign capital, resulting in increased population and a marked extension of several towns.[1] In the rural districts of Western Canada in particular, exceptional prosperity came in three ways, first, in a greatly enlarged domestic market for their secondary produce, such as dairy products, vegetables, fruits and the coarser grains, while the Reciprocity Treaty afforded them a valuable outlet for nearly all their agricultural products, especially hay and grain. Then the Crimean War at least doubled and occasionally trebled the ordinary prices for wheat, while nature vouchsafed exceptionally bountiful harvests. The financial commitments national and corporate which accompanied, as both cause and effect, this exceptional period of prosperity were naturally very heavy, and the boom deceived even the Barings and the Glyns. The inevitable collapse, however, took place from 1857 to 1860. Then conditions were ameliorated in some respects, though aggravated in others, by the outbreak of the American Civil War, at the close of which political and economic conditions in Canada brought the conception of a general union of the British North American provinces from the more or less speculative sphere into that of urgent practical politics.

Probably the most important event in this period was the negotiation and final adoption of the Reciprocity Treaty with the United States. From the time of American independence the question of reciprocal trade between the British Colonies and the United States was often to the front. Undoubtedly the Hon. Richard Cartwright at Kingston, supported by his partner the Hon. Robert Hamilton at Niagara, was the first to advocate the possibilities of this trade, setting forth, even before 1791, its prospective advantages to Canada, as affording at once an outlet for the surplus agricultural products of

[1] See chapters xiii and xxxiii (B).

Upper Canada and an inlet for the manufactured British goods indispensable to these early settlements. He, therefore, urged that the
St Lawrence route should not be obstructed by tariff burdens and
customs regulations; but as the chief objects of Dorchester and
Simcoe were military and not economic this advice was ignored. The
British Government then undertook, by a series of inconsistent regulations, to direct the commercial relations of the British North American
provinces, including those with the United States, which regulations
sometimes favoured, for a time at least, special colonial interests.
The intervening periods of disadvantage to colonial interests were
commonly mitigated, locally at least, by a very extensive system of
smuggling, which under such conditions carried with it little moral
or social stigma. In their larger aspects the international trade relations were matters of periodic discussion in the press of both the
United States and the colonies. Thus, in 1844 the New York *Journal
of Commerce* pointed out that, while most of the products of the
Eastern States were admitted freely into New Brunswick and Nova
Scotia, yet they could be paid for only in products from these provinces, and the American duties on these were so high that little
exchange could take place, to the obvious detriment of many
important interests in the United States.[1]

Next, in 1846, the repeal of the Corn Laws left Canada without any
advantage over the adjoining State of New York in sending American
flour to the British market. Before their actual repeal the Canadian
Legislature petitioned the Home Government that, should it be in
contemplation to admit from the United States free of duty grain and
food-stuffs, the condition should be imposed that a like privilege
should be granted to similar articles passing from Canada to the
United States.[2] No such arrangement, however, was made; but in
that year Congress passed an Act permitting Canadian imports and
exports to pass through the United States in bond without duties, a
blow at the costly St Lawrence transportation system then nearing
completion. Among those who took an active interest in promoting
reciprocity was W. H. Merritt, previously the chief promoter of the
Welland Canal. On 1 July 1847, he introduced to the Provincial
Legislature a resolution embodying the chief features of a reciprocal
trade arrangement between the United States and Canada.[3] Merritt
managed to persuade the Government to follow this up by sending
him in charge of a delegation to Washington in 1848.[4] In that year the
Canadian Government appeared to be very confident that they could
obtain free entry to the United States of Canadian natural products
in exchange for granting to the Americans the right of navigating the
St Lawrence, and in this Hincks was evidently the prime mover.[5]

[1] *Examiner*, 6 Mar. 1844.   [2] Petition of 12 May 1846.
[3] Keefer, T., *Sketch of the Rise and Progress of the Reciprocity Treaty*, Toronto, 1863.
[4] *Ibid.* p. 4.
[5] Can. Arch. P.F. vol. LXXVIII, no. 43, p. 1; also p. 5, Memorandum by Hincks.

Prominent American papers doubted whether these appeals to Washington would meet with anything but courtesy, on account of there being so much to ask and so little to grant in return.[1] Yet Grinnell introduced a bill which passed the House of Representatives accepting the Canadian offer, although it afterwards met with strong opposition from the New England and Southern States, the measure being regarded as simply of special interest to Canada and New York State. Early in 1849, the Canadian Legislature passed an Act[2] to admit free from the United States certain goods, on condition that they should admit free the same articles from Canada. The list included practically all kinds of food-stuffs, vegetable and animal, all kinds of wood, hides, wool, mineral ores and potash. In an open letter from Hincks to a friend, he represents reciprocity as the one effective cure for the unrest and pessimism underlying the agitation for annexation, which he declares to be almost entirely due to the lack of free access for Canadian produce to American markets. He declares also that there was a false idea abroad that Great Britain was indifferent to the fate of Canada. On the contrary, the Home Government was entirely willing to assist Canadians to obtain reciprocity with the United States.[3] Here Hincks was undoubtedly speaking with considerable inside knowledge. In a despatch of Lord Grey to Lord Elgin there was enclosed a copy of the instructions of the Foreign Minister, Lord Palmerston, to Sir Henry L. Bulwer (the new British minister to the United States), relating entirely to the question of a possible reciprocity treaty with the United States. It is found, however, that the British Government took a much wider view of reciprocity than the Canadian Government had done. Crampton, the retiring British minister, had reported, on 30 July 1849, that in conjunction with Hincks as a member of the Canadian Government, he had at first brought the matter, on the basis of the Canadian proposals alone, to the attention of Clayton, United States Secretary of State, who had intimated that the United States Government wished to await the action of the British Parliament as to the repeal of the Navigation Laws. He also stated privately to Crampton that, unless all the British North American provinces and the subject of the Atlantic fisheries were included in the arrangement, the President could not undertake to recommend the proposal to Congress. Now, the British Government, says Palmerston, wishes especially to secure the free entry to the United States of the articles specified by the Canadian Legislature. Manufactured articles cannot be included without interfering with customs tariffs. Incidentally, it is suggested that the United States might make some concession to Canada on account of the free admission of her products into Great Britain. The British Government is quite willing to have reciprocity extended to

[1] *British Colonist*, Toronto, 27 July 1849.   [2] Can. Statutes, Act of April 1849, cap. 3.
[3] *British Colonist*, 26 Oct. 1849.

the other British North American colonies except Newfoundland, and to throw open to the Americans all the Atlantic fisheries, except the inshore fisheries of the rivers and inlets, with permission to land to dry their nets and cure their fish, so long as they do not interfere with private property or the operations of British fishermen. In return all fish, fresh or cured, from the British colonies must be admitted free to the United States. It is willing also to allow to the United States' vessels and citizens the free navigation of the St Lawrence and its canals, and is anxious that coal should be included in the articles of free exchange, as this would be of importance to Nova Scotia. But, should opposing private interests in the United States on this point threaten the success of the treaty, the matter need not be insisted upon.[1]

At this time the United States consul at Saint John, New Brunswick, was I. D. Andrews, from Eastport, Maine, a typically shrewd and well-informed New Englander, possessed of a unique personality. Long engaged in the boundary trade, and familiar with most phases of frontier smuggling, he became a strong advocate of reciprocal free trade between the United States and the British North American colonies.[2] After the passage of Grinnell's Reciprocity Bill, Andrews was summoned to Washington to discuss the subject. Possibly following the lead of the Executive Government, he criticised the measure as too narrow, and advocated the inclusion of the Maritime fisheries and the navigation of the St Lawrence and the St John. In 1849, after passing the reciprocity measure referred to, the Canadian Government again sent Merritt to Washington, where Grinnell's bill was again introduced to Congress only to be again lost in the Senate. In July 1849, Andrews was appointed by the American Executive Government as a special agent to visit the provinces of British North America to collect statistical and other information on their past, present, and prospective conditions. Keefer, on the recommendation of Merritt, was selected by Andrews as assistant in his work.[3] In January 1850, another American bill was before Congress when the President died; then the slavery agitation paralysed all action for a time. The Andrews' first report was published in 1851, but he was again commissioned by Corwin, Secretary of the Treasury, to visit the British North American provinces to collect "full and complete statements of their trade and commerce with the United States, and with other parts of the world, inland and by sea, for 1850–1, with such information as can be procured on the trade of the Great Lakes".[4] Keefer was employed on this also, and the joint result was the preparation of the large and important report of 1853 by Andrews on the lake trade.

---

[1] Pub. Arch. Can. *Series G*, vol. cxxxv, Grey to Elgin, 17 Nov. 1849, with Palmerston's instructions enclosed, pp. 150–73.
[2] Keefer, p. 5.   [3] *Ibid.* p. 6.   [4] *Ibid.* p. 8.

The New York Chamber of Commerce petitioned Congress to obtain reciprocity, but little was done in 1851–2. In 1851, Hincks again went to Washington, hoping to get through his original measure for Canada alone, but failed. He then joined forces with the railway delegates from the Maritime Provinces and adopted an aggressive attitude towards the United States, closing to them the canals, putting prohibitory duties on their imports and taking active measures to protect the fisheries; from which incident the Canadian navy dates. Webster intimated to the British minister, Bulwer, that these petty annoyances must cease before he would resume negotiations. The British Ministry, with its own political life at stake, did nothing before it fell in 1852. The new British Government took action by sending a small fleet, under Admiral Seymour, to protect the British fisheries, and the Americans sent another under Admiral Perry. These officers took the matter good-naturedly, exchanging courtesies instead of shot until the politicians should reach, before fighting, what would still have to be accomplished after fighting, a basis for adjustment. Under the powerful influence of the Barings in England, and their intimate financial connections in the United States, a reasonable basis was soon reached, and negotiations were resumed. In December 1852, and February 1853, President Fillmore sent messages to Congress favouring a convention, the details of which were worked out by Everett, who succeeded, on the death of Webster, as Secretary of State. He agreed to admit provincial fish free of duty, on condition that the American fishermen were admitted to the shore fisheries.[1] In March 1853, Pierce became President, with Marcy as Secretary of State, and Buchanan as Minister to England, both intimately connected with the chief British economic interests. The President availed himself of the special knowledge of Andrews, who strongly recommended "that no attempt should be made to drive a bargain with the colonies, but that they should be treated in the most liberal and considerate manner".[2] The President approved of his views, and commissioned him to visit the British North American colonies to explain to them the attitude of the American Government, and to endeavour to induce them to agree to the basis of a common treaty. He was largely instrumental in achieving this result.[3] At first the Maritime Provinces were either indifferent or opposed to the treaty; but it turned out in the end that they had most to gain from it and that it was western and not eastern conditions which led to its abrogation. The treaty was agreed upon by the negotiators in August 1853, yet it had to be ratified by Congress and by the various British North American Legislatures. Hence it did not actually pass until 5 June, and only went into effect by executive action in Canada, 18 October 1854, and by proclamation in the United States, 16 March 1855.[4]

[1] Keefer, p. 11.   [2] Ibid. p. 12.   [3] Ibid. pp. 12, 13.
[4] Harvey, A., The Reciprocity Treaty.

Those who benefited most from the treaty were, as a rule, the general body of producers on the one hand, and of individual consumers on the other, supplemented by groups of middlemen who handled the various products. The objectors were, chiefly, those who suffered from the competition of free goods in their previously protected markets, and these classes are commonly more distinctly vocal than the others. It is impossible here to present adequate tables of statistics covering the chief features of the operation of the treaty, or the careful interpretation required to give such statistics their proper meaning and application. The argument *post hoc ergo propter hoc* is especially inadmissible here without, at least, very important qualifications. In the first place, it soon appeared that local conditions and cost of distribution had more to do with the result of the Reciprocity Treaty than the mere nature of the articles produced and exchanged. In a general survey of international trade along the extensive boundary between Canada and the United States, it was commonly found that the very articles which bulked largest in the American imports from Canada were just those which bulked largest in the Canadian imports from the United States.[1]

As a rule the Canadians were highly satisfied with the result of the treaty, especially as its earlier operations coincided with the development of prosperity in the provinces, although this was largely due to the increasing expenditure of foreign capital in the building of railroads, etc., and the exceptional demand at high prices for Canadian wheat, caused by the outbreak of the Crimean War. Yet much the larger share of these beneficial results was attributed to the Reciprocity Treaty. This popular conviction in retrospect accounts for the permanent impression in British America as to the exceptionally beneficial effects which may be expected from a re-establishment of reciprocity with the United States in restoring prosperity in Canada when periodic depressions are being experienced. The chief American objections to the treaty were expressed by the Hon. Israel T. Hatch in 1860. He was charged with the special duty of examining not so much the operation of the treaty as the practice and policy of the Canadian Government in relation to the general trade with the United States. He admitted that the principle of reciprocity with British North America was accepted by all political parties in the United States; but he claimed that in practice Canada constantly endeavoured to cause it to operate entirely to her own benefit.[2]

Within the first year of the operation of the treaty, many Americans perceived that their chief interest in the trade with Canada would lie not so much in the direction of the exchange of natural products as in finding a rapidly expanding market there for manufactured goods.

[1] Trade with the British Provinces. Letter from the Secretary of the Treasury, 31 Mar. 1868, p. 15.
[2] Hatch, I. T., *The Reciprocity Treaty, A Report to Congress*, Washington, 1860.

Thus the New York Board of Trade urged the extension of the terms of the treaty to include all forms of goods and all shipping routes, including the coasting trade, the general effects of reciprocity being clearly beneficial to both countries. One special American advantage was that Canadian trade *via* the St Lawrence had been reduced, while that *via* New York had been increased, and Canadian purchases of American manufactured goods had also increased. Congress was therefore urged to pass an Act for an unlimited reciprocity, to take effect when the Canadians passed a similar measure.[1] It may be noted that at the annual meeting of the Board of Trade of Toronto this idea of an unlimited reciprocity in trade and shipping was strongly supported. This was natural enough, however, considering the interests represented in such a Board, as the members were almost entirely engaged in trade between the two countries. Further, the Board strongly urged the establishment, at Washington, of an independent Canadian representative, in addition to the regular British minister.[2]

On the other hand, the enormous expansion of the provincial expenditure on public works, such as the subsidising of railroads, etc., entailed an increasing demand for public revenue, and this was sought almost entirely through the medium of customs duties, which fell largely on the imports of manufactured goods coming chiefly from the United States and from England. According to Hatch's report he evidently assumed, like so many other Americans in discussing this subject, that the chief advantage to Canada was that of having access to the extensive markets of the United States for her natural products, while the corresponding advantage to the United States was to be found in an increasing Canadian market for their manufactured goods. It would appear, however, from the newer features of the Canadian tariff and transportation developments, that Canada had adopted a policy of erecting barriers against American manufacturers, and of confining her trade to her own transportation routes, including her export and import trade with Europe. Indeed, it is claimed that one of the great objects of the Grand Trunk Railway system was to capture the American carrying trade of the West. But British exporters to Canada presented equally vigorous protests, as in the case of Sheffield, against the increase of Canadian tariff rates. They argued that, inasmuch as the Mother Country had adopted Free Trade, the colonies should have done likewise, at least as regarded British goods.[3]

On the surface at least these criticisms seemed valid. The Hon. A. T. Galt, Canadian Minister of Finance, had given repeated

---

[1] Report of the New York Board of Trade, 3 Jan. 1856, in the *Globe*, Toronto, 24 Jan. 1856.
[2] Report of the Annual Meeting of the Toronto Board of Trade, the *Globe*, 29 Feb. 1856.
[3] *Report of the Minister of Finance on the Reciprocity Treaty with the U.S.*, etc., Quebec, 1862, p. 21.

expression to the policy of the Canadian Government in promoting a system of transportation through Canada by water and rail which would serve not only Canada but, as far as possible, attract the American western trade.[1] Moreover, one of the chief objects of the Reciprocity Treaty was to afford to Americans and their vessels the free use of the St Lawrence route, and international discourtesy could scarcely be imputed to the Canadians for seeking to improve this route and desiring to see their American friends make use of it. As a matter of fact, however, complaints were made that too much of the western trade was passing through American channels only.[2] Further, the tariff could not be said to have any connection with the framing of the Reciprocity Treaty. Galt, however, did not hesitate to state that although the central object of the Canadian tariff was the indispensable one of raising revenue, and that in consequence the Government had been forced from time to time to increase duties moderately, yet so far as that policy might encourage the production of certain goods in Canada, instead of their importation, such a result was to be welcomed. Galt had taken occasion also, in his replies to similar remonstrances of Great Britain as regards the tariff, to point out that relatively the British enjoyed a considerable advantage over the Americans.[3]

While the American contentions could be shown to have no necessary connection with the Reciprocity Treaty, yet at the same time in the course of the development of the two countries, with the manufacturing cities of the United States, more or less in proximity to Canada and the Maritime Provinces, the markets for the products for British North America tended to become steadily better, while there was a lessening inducement to send such articles from the United States to Canada. On the other hand, the manufactured goods of the United States were those which chiefly sought a market in Canada, and naturally suffered most from increasing Canadian tariffs. With the outbreak of the American Civil War, all ordinary lines of international trade were more or less demoralised, but under the terms of the Reciprocity Treaty some advantages were derived by a number of special Canadian interests. At the close of the war, with changed but equally abnormal conditions, it became evident that, when its period was run, the treaty would be abrogated. Needless to say there were endless discussions on the subject, especially from the Canadian side, and scores of proposals were made for the renewal of the treaty on a somewhat modified basis. Nevertheless, final notice of abrogation was served in the spring of 1865, and the treaty ended automatically a year later.[4]

[1] Galt, A., *Canada 1849–59*; also his Report, *op. cit.* pp. 5, 6.
[2] *Report of the Select Committee*, Quebec, 1861.
[3] Galt, *Canada 1849–59*, pp. 30, 34.
[4] Larned, J. N., *Report on the state of Trade between the U.S. and Brit. N. America*, Washington, 1871, pp. 1–25.

The prospective and actual abrogation of the treaty had naturally much to do with the movement for confederation. But it was discovered, incidentally, that one of the chief effects of the treaty on the British North American provinces was that their trade had been directed into north and south channels to the detriment of their east and west economic connections. There was, therefore, an immediate revival of the already well canvassed but temporarily discarded project for a line of railway connecting the Maritime Provinces with Canada. Accordingly, the building of an intercolonial railway became a central feature in the terms of confederation.

We have already seen that Hincks, in his attempts to retrieve the unfortunate effects of mistaken policy and apathy on the part of the leaders of the Lafontaine-Baldwin Government, had ardently promoted the Reciprocity Treaty. Joined with this was his other and for a time even more successful diversion of public interest to the promotion of a system of railways, at first subsidiary to the St Lawrence route but afterwards largely independent of it. Thus, in that politically disastrous year, 1849, Hincks introduced and secured the adoption of an Act "to provide for affording the guarantee of the province to bonds of railway companies on certain conditions, and for rendering assistance in the construction of the Halifax and Quebec Railway". Owing to difficulties between the representatives of the provinces affected and the Imperial Government, the latter part of the scheme came to naught for a time. The Government assistance promised to railway enterprises in general was a guarantee of 6 per cent. interest on the bonds of any railway company whose line should extend to seventy-five miles or upwards, and to the extent of one-half the cost of construction of such railway. The terms on which such a guarantee could be claimed virtually implied that the guarantee would be merely nominal, private enterprise and capital amply taking care of each adventure. Although in the early 'thirties the periodical press of English-speaking Canada had been filled with railroad propositions, yet previous to 1847 there was in operation but one line of fifteen miles between Laprairie, opposite Montreal, and the Richelieu River at St John's, and a short coal road at Pictou in Nova Scotia. At the time of passing the Act of 1849, there were less than fifty miles of completed railroad in Canada. Hincks's appeal, therefore, came at the psychological moment. The first corporations to make good their claims to the Government guarantee were the Great Western Railway, already under construction from Niagara to Detroit, and the North Railway from Toronto to Georgian Bay. So many others, however, were preparing to claim the prospective Government assistance, that, apparently under the warning advice of the financial agents in London, the purely general character of the Government offer was modified by an Act of 1851, being confined to the two roads already mentioned, and a third and more important, the Grand Trunk

Railway from Quebec to Toronto, afterwards extending the line below Quebec to Rivière du Loup and beyond Toronto to the western boundary of Canada at the St Clair River. Although many projects had been long in contemplation for parts at least of this through line, yet it was only reduced to practical realisation through the chartering of the Grand Trunk Railway in the session of 1852–3.

In connection with the formation of the Company in England, Hincks had arranged with the firm of Peto, Brassey, Betts and Jackson to construct this trunk line. Immediately after it was chartered, the Company entered into a contract to take over the Atlantic and St Lawrence Railroad from the Canadian frontier to Portland, Maine, thus affording a winter outlet to the Canadian system. It was also arranged to connect this Portland line with Quebec. In the meantime, Hincks had come to terms with the Barings and Glyn Mills, who joined in this project. In the voluminous correspondence and reports on this undertaking among others, as preserved in the Baring Papers, we have a complete inside history for the first twenty years of this great Canadian enterprise and all its vicissitudes. The prospectus of the Company presents the scheme as a great national undertaking with the Canadian Provincial Treasury as virtually the chief partner. The Hon. John Ross, member of the Government, was president, and five of his colleagues, including Hincks, were on the Canadian board of directors. Baring and Glyn were members of the London board.[1] American experience was ignored and English standards of construction and equipment introduced regardless of cost, while the expected profits on the undertaking were rated at $11\frac{1}{2}$ per cent. on the capital invested. Under such distinguished auspices the stock was for a time readily disposed of in Great Britain, and Canada was assured of the expenditure in it of previously undreamt-of millions. Then the Government authorised municipalities, urban and rural, to take stock in any such railways as might be chartered to open up the country. In order to aid the municipalities in raising capital on the British market at reduced rates, the Consolidated Municipal Loan Fund was established in 1852.[2] Through these channels many additional millions of British capital were brought to the country. The Grand Trunk Company estimated its expenditure at upwards of $75,000,000 in building and equipping the railway, including the Victoria Bridge at Montreal. About $30,000,000 were borrowed by the Government in Britain in addition to its contributions to the Grand Trunk Railway. The Municipal Loan Fund brought in about $12,000,000, while several municipalities raised large additional loans on their own account; and between 1852 and 1860, the Government spent an additional $11,500,000 on the canals. Accordingly, an exceptionally prosperous period was enjoyed by Canada between

[1] *Prospectus of the Grand Trunk Railway Co.* April 1853.
[2] Can. Statutes, 1852–3, cap. 22.

1852 and 1857, and yet the effects of this prosperity, for the great mass of the people, including the new settlers, were exceptionally ephemeral. Many farmers, instead of paying off their debts, enlarged their land holdings at high prices, and also enlarged their mortgages. Villages grew into towns and towns into cities. The latter in particular found themselves loaded with municipal debts for civic improvements, and at the end of the boom many of them were unable to meet their obligations. In such cases both principal and interest went ultimately to increase the national funded debt. Further, the wages of labour, clerical services, etc., were greatly enhanced, correspondingly raising the cost of construction for railways and all other public works. Yet the rapidly increasing cost of living rendered the advantages of higher incomes much more apparent than real. Under exceptional prosperity extravagance in living became the order of the day. Thus, when the collapse of 1857 closed the pockets of British investors, there was astonishingly little reserve wealth to be found among the Canadian people from the millions spent in the country in the previous five years. There were numerous exceptions, but this was true of the great mass of the people.

Recovery began with the outbreak of the American Civil War, supplemented at its close by the ephemeral activity connected with the special operations of the last year of the Reciprocity Treaty, which in turn was supplemented by the expectations from Confederation and the beginning of the construction of the Intercolonial Railway. Thus Confederation was inaugurated on its economic side with a more or less speculative commercial activity, and high expectations for the future.

CHAPTER XVI

THE OPENING OF THE WEST

THE history of what is to-day known as Western Canada, or that part of the Dominion extending from Lake Superior to the Pacific and from the international boundary to the Arctic, may be said to begin in 1610, when Henry Hudson sailed through the Straits into the Bay that bears his name, and in so doing opened up one of the two great water routes into the heart of the continent. Between that year and 1631 both the east and west coasts of Hudson Bay were explored, and the way was paved for discoveries inland from the Bay. Three-quarters of a century before Hudson's discovery of the Bay, the other great water route had been found in the Gulf of St Lawrence, and in the next century and a quarter the St Lawrence waterway was explored from the Gulf to the head of Lake Superior, the discovery of the western shores of the latter being associated with the names of Pierre Esprit Radisson and Daniel Greysolon Du Lhut. Here again the way was clear to the interior. The western shores of Lake Superior and Hudson Bay were to become the starting-places for the discovery of the great western plains and all that lay beyond.

Before attempting to tell the story of the exploration of the prairie region of Canada, it will be convenient to describe very briefly how the two water gateways became linked with the name of that singular adventurer, Radisson; how the Frenchman who had explored Lake Superior and learned there of the wealth of furs that were to be obtained in the country about Hudson Bay became instrumental in creating the Hudson's Bay Company; and how his enterprise was to affect profoundly the history of what is now Western Canada. In 1665 Radisson, having failed to interest the French authorities in an expedition he had planned to Hudson Bay, sailed for England, where he succeeded in enlisting the support of Prince Rupert and several influential merchants. Three years later the *Nonsuch* sailed for the Bay, and in 1669 returned with a rich cargo of furs. The following year King Charles granted a charter to the Hudson's Bay Company, "for the discovery of a new passage into the South Sea, and for the finding of some trade for furs, minerals, and other considerable commodities". By the terms of this momentous charter the Hudson's Bay Company was granted "the sole trade and commerce of all these seas, straits, bays, rivers, lakes, creeks and sounds, in whatsoever latitude they shall be, that lie within the entrance of the straits, commonly called Hudson's Straits, together with all the lands and territories upon the countries, coasts and confines of the seas, bays, lakes, rivers, creeks and sounds aforesaid...and that the said land be from henceforth reckoned and reputed as one of our Plantations or colonies in America, called 'Rupert's Land'". The boundaries of this land were extremely vague, and for many years the Hudson's Bay Company was content to leave them so; nor did the directors concern themselves overmuch with the obligation to discover a new passage into the South Sea. It was not in fact until they began to feel the competition among the inland tribes, first of the French traders and later of the British merchants from Montreal, that they aroused themselves from the dream of a comfortable monopoly on the shores of Hudson Bay and sent expeditions inland for discovery and the development of trade. Before dealing with these expeditions it will be convenient to follow the course of exploration west of Lake Superior up to the close of the French period.

Pierre Gaultier de Varennes, Sieur de La Vérendrye, born in Three Rivers on the St Lawrence, was the last of the great explorers of New France. With rare singleness of purpose, determination and public spirit he devoted himself and his sons to the search for an overland route to the Western Sea. Although he failed in his main design, his actual achievement was much more significant. He was in a very real sense the discoverer of the Canadian West, of that vast prairie region that in a few short years has become one of the principal grain-producing areas of the world. Of all the path-finders of Canada, French or British, of the first rank, La Vérendrye alone was native-born. Between 1731 and 1742 he built posts on Rainy Lake, the Lake of the Woods, Red River, Assiniboine River, Lake Winnipegosis and the Saskatchewan River. The country between Lake Superior and Lake Winnipeg was in La Vérendrye's day very difficult, a wilderness of rocks, swamps and small waterways to Rainy Lake, and a succession of dangerous rapids on Winnipeg River. West of Lake Winnipeg travel either by land or water was less arduous. The French Government having refused to give him financial support, but offering instead a monopoly of the western fur trade, these posts were built partly for trade and partly as stepping-stones toward western discovery. The monopoly was in reality an incubus. There was too much unselfishness and idealism in La Vérendrye's character to make a successful fur-trader; and yet, as he had been compelled to go into partnership with several Montreal merchants to obtain the means of equipping and paying his men, he must waste a great deal of his time and energy in bartering with the Indians for furs. Because of the penuriousness of the French Court he was persistently hampered in his explorations. None the less his life was embittered by baseless insinuations and open charges at Quebec and Paris that he was neglecting the cause of discovery in order to make a fortune out of the fur trade.

From his post on the Assiniboine, Fort La Reine, he travelled in 1738 over the plains to the villages of the Mandan Indians on the Missouri. Of this remarkable tribe, which was afterwards visited and described by Lewis and Clark, Catlin and Prince Maximilian of Wied, he had heard such fabulous accounts from other tribes that he expected to find a settlement of white men, from whom he could obtain particulars of the country to the westward and the most practicable route to the sea. He was correspondingly disappointed to learn that they were merely Indians, though they lived in walled villages and cultivated the soil. Four years later he sent two of his sons to the Mandans, having in the meantime obtained from them through an interpreter information as to other tribes that were said to occupy a region toward the west not far from the ocean. The sons procured guides from the Mandans and set out over the plains toward what they hoped would prove to be the *Mer de l'Ouest*, but were mortified to find that their route was turning toward the south-west rather than the west. They came into contact with many tribes, some of whom had never met white men before, while others had apparently been in touch with the Spaniards from Mexico. Finally they reached a range of mountains—evidently an outlying spur of the Rockies— beyond which, they were told, lay the sea. To their bitter disappointment they were turned back at the foot of these mountains by the hostility of one of the tribes. After an absence of over twelve months they returned to Fort La Reine without having achieved their purpose, but with a wealth of information as to the country they had visited and its native inhabitants.

Having failed to reach the sea by way of the Missouri, La Vérendrye turned to the Saskatchewan, but his enemies at Quebec had by this time finally triumphed over him. Before he could accomplish anything to the purpose by this new route he was recalled by the Governor. Impaired in health and heavily in debt, he died in 1749, heartbroken and disillusioned. His sons begged to be allowed to complete their father's work, but hostile influences made even this impossible. They were without honour in their own country, although they and their father had added by discovery to New France an immensely rich region west of Lake Superior, between the Missouri and the Saskatchewan.

Meanwhile the Hudson's Bay Company was showing an interest in the exploration of the interior. In 1691 it had sent Henry Kelsey inland to visit some of the tribes. From his journal, which is obscure, it would appear that he travelled by the Nelson or Hayes routes to the Saskatchewan, then turned south to the west of Lake Winnipegosis, until he reached an encampment of Indians, who would seem to have been Mandans, somewhere about the Assiniboine River.

A more definite and important expedition was made by Anthony

Hendry, of the same Company, in 1754–5. Starting out from York Factory, on Hudson Bay, he followed the Hayes River to Oxford Lake, and by a series of small lakes and rivers reached the Saskatchewan. From here he struck overland, crossed the South Saskatchewan, and travelled over the plains to the country of the Blackfeet, in what is now the province of Alberta. He wintered among this tribe, the first white man who had visited them, and his narrative contains a very interesting account of their manners and customs, which is supplemented by the journal of another employee of the Hudson's Bay Company, Matthew Cocking, who reached the Blackfeet in 1772. Hendry's statements as to the Blackfeet riding on horses, and the immense herds of buffalo that in his day blackened the western plains, served to discredit his narrative among the officers of the Hudson's Bay Company, who knew nothing about the buffalo and had never heard of mounted Indians. On his return journey Hendry visited a French fort on the Saskatchewan, where he met La Corne, an officer who had been sent out to continue La Vérendrye's explorations, but had accomplished nothing. This visit has some significance as the only occasion during the French regime when British and French explorers met in the country beyond Lake Superior.

The expeditions of Kelsey, Hendry and Cocking had for their principal object to draw some of the more remote tribes to the trading posts of the Company. That of Samuel Hearne (1770–2) made a more direct contribution to the cause of exploration. One of its two purposes was probably to discover "a new passage into the South Seas". The other was to search for rich copper mines, word of which had been brought down to the Bay by northern Indians. The journey had the negative result of proving that no passage existed through the continent, at least as far west as the Coppermine River. It had the positive result of throwing a good deal of light upon the immense area, hitherto quite unexplored (much of which remains so), lying between Hudson Bay and the Coppermine River, and between the Arctic coast and a line drawn from Prince of Wales Fort, at the mouth of the Churchill River, to Great Slave Lake. The search for copper mines was rewarded with a few insignificant specimens of ore. Hearne left Prince of Wales Fort in December 1770, with no white companions, but with a party of Chipewyan Indians led by a shrewd and masterful chief named Matonabbee. Their course was roughly north-west to the Coppermine River, some distance above its mouth, thence down to the Arctic. The return journey was almost due south to Great Slave Lake, and east from the mouth of Slave River to Prince of Wales Fort, the whole forming an immense triangle.

Hearne tells a characteristic story of Matonabbee. When they were discussing the arrangements for the journey, the question arose as to whether or not women should be included in the party. The Governor of Prince of Wales Fort demurred, but Matonabbee was insistent. Women, he said, were indispensable. They were obviously made for labour; they could carry, or haul, as much as two men; they could pitch the tents; make and mend clothing; in fact, said he, there was no such thing as travelling any considerable distance or for any length of time in this country without their assistance. Moreover, he added, "though they do everything, they are maintained at a trifling expense, for as they always stand cook, the very licking of their fingers in scarce times is sufficient for their subsistence". Hearne was a young man, active, intelligent, curious; he kept his eyes open, saw much that was interesting, and afterwards put it into a narrative that makes exceptionally good reading. He lacked the strength of character of such an explorer as Alexander Mackenzie, and found himself powerless to prevent the wanton massacre by the Indians of his party of a number of inoffensive Eskimo, men, women and children, at what was afterwards appropriately called Bloody Falls, on the Coppermine. Nevertheless it must not be forgotten that he was a solitary white man among savage Indians, far from the nearest trading post, and that under these difficult conditions he carried out important explorations.

These several expeditions sent out by or on behalf of the Hudson's Bay Company, whatever their other purposes, added very materially to the sum of geographical knowledge. The interior had been penetrated from Hudson Bay to the upper waters of the Saskatchewan, to the mouth of the Coppermine, and to Great Slave Lake. A distinction must, however, here be drawn. Hearne's discoveries became public knowledge on the publication of his *Journey* in 1795. Kelsey's narrative, such as it is, was printed in the *Hudson's Bay Report*, 1749. Nothing, however, outside the carefully guarded circle of the Hudson's Bay Company, was known of the discoveries of Hendry and Cocking until comparatively recent times.[1]

Throughout this early period of discovery in the interior of Western Canada, the men who led the expeditions were in every case both fur-traders and explorers. Ostensibly, fur-trading was their vocation and path-finding their avocation; but in reality their hearts were in discovery, and fur-trading was but a means to that noble end. This applies with equal force to the next group of explorers, some of whom were associated with the Hudson's Bay Company and others with its great rival, the North West Company. One of these, David Thompson, forms a link between the two corporations, as he served for some years under the former and then for a longer period under

---

[1] See "Hendry's Journal" (ed. Burpee, L. J.) in *Trans. Royal Society of Canada*, 1907; "Cocking's Journal" (ed. Burpee, L. J.), *ibid.* 1908; also *The Kelsey Papers* (ed. Doughty, A. G. and Martin, C.), Public Archives of Canada and Public Record Office of Northern Ireland, 1929.

the latter. But before describing his work it will be well to consider briefly the geographical achievements of several earlier and minor explorers in this field, some of whom were attached to the Hudson's Bay Company and others were fur-traders from Montreal.

Peter Pond, a native of Connecticut, who had fought at Ticonderoga and Fort Niagara and had been an officer in the army led by Amherst down the St Lawrence to Montreal in 1760, entered the western fur trade about five years later. He made his headquarters for a time at Michilimackinac, on the strait between Lakes Huron and Michigan, and in 1775 travelled into the country west of Lake Superior, with Alexander Henry, Thomas and Joseph Frobisher and other Canadian traders. Pond's journal of his western travels is one of the most curious documents in the literature of the Canadian West. It throws an interesting light on the manners and customs of some of the Indian tribes in his day, but is chiefly remarkable as an amazing example of phonetic spelling, so grotesque in fact that the journal was at one time, though quite unjustly, supposed to be a silly fabrication. It was discovered in the home of one of his descendants, where it was being used to light the kitchen fire. Unfortunately the part relating to his discoveries in what is now Western Canada had been destroyed before the manuscript was rescued; and it is now only possible to reconstruct his work in a fragmentary fashion by means of his manuscript maps and the occasional notes of his contemporaries.

Between 1775 and 1788 Pond travelled over a large part of what are now the provinces of Manitoba and Saskatchewan. From Lake Superior to Lake Winnipeg and the Saskatchewan River he had been anticipated by La Vérendrye; nor was he the discoverer of the canoe route from the Saskatchewan to the Churchill by way of Frog portage; but Pond must be credited with the original exploration from Île à la Crosse Lake through La Loche Lake and over Methye portage to the Clearwater River, a branch of the Athabaska. He had thus taken an important step, for he had crossed over from waters that emptied into Hudson Bay to those that flowed into the Arctic. He descended the Clearwater to the Athabaska, and the latter to Lake Athabaska. There is reason to believe that he also explored part of the Peace River, and that either he or his men followed Slave River down to Great Slave Lake, where they built a trading post. Pond therefore linked his own discoveries with those of Hearne. It is interesting to remember that before 1788 at least one continental water route had been explored from the Gulf of St Lawrence to the Arctic, by way of the Great Lakes, Lake of the Woods, Lake Winnipeg, the Saskatchewan, the Churchill, the Athabaska, Lake Athabaska, Slave River, Great Slave Lake, the Yellowknife and the Coppermine—a distance of about five thousand miles. Pond seems to have been morose and ill-tempered, got into trouble with some of the other traders in the West, was tried for having killed one of them in a duel, and finally returned in disgust to the land of his birth. One of his maps is said to have been of service to the United States Commissioners in settling the boundary line between their country and Canada. What is more to our present purpose, his maps, the work of an unscientific traveller, are extremely inaccurate.[1] He over-estimated his distances, put Great Slave Lake much farther west than its true position, and consequently assumed that the Pacific coast was but a comparatively short distance from that lake. He also learned of the existence of the great waterway afterwards to be known as Mackenzie River, but supposed that it emptied into the Pacific. Both these misconceptions were to influence the course of future discovery. His contemporaries, Alexander Henry and the Frobishers, although important figures in the history of the fur trade, added little to geographical knowledge beyond the discovery of the portage route from Cumberland House on the Saskatchewan to Frog portage on the Churchill and to Île à la Crosse Lake.

In the last ten or twelve years of the eighteenth century two officers of the Hudson's Bay Company, Philip Turner and Peter Fidler, carried out explorations in the Athabaska country. Turner had been brought out by the Company from England, at the suggestion of the department charged with colonial affairs, to clear up the uncertainty as to the position of Great Slave Lake and its distance from the Pacific. A competent and painstaking surveyor, he laid down on his manuscript map[2] the Saskatchewan up to the Forks, the portage route to the Churchill, that river up to La Loche Lake, the Clearwater and Athabaska to Lake Athabaska, that lake and Slave River and a small part of the south shore of Great Slave Lake. He also showed, with tolerable accuracy, the North Saskatchewan and the Peace, although in this case he had to depend upon Indian report.

Fidler succeeded Turner as surveyor and astronomer of the Hudson's Bay Company, and also left a manuscript map, or rather a map prepared from his surveys by George Taylor, of the country from Hudson Bay to the Peace River,[3] as well as voluminous journals. The map has been preserved, but unfortunately the journals have disappeared. From this map it appears that Fidler, in 1790–1800 and later, explored and surveyed both branches of the Saskatchewan, parts of the Athabaska and the Peace, together with Lesser Slave Lake and the route between the two rivers by way of that lake, and Churchill River from Frog portage down to Hudson Bay. He also

[1] See Burpee, L. J., *The Search for the Western Sea*, pp. 322–49. Cf. Innis, H. A., *Peter Pond*.
[2] In the Archives of the Hudson's Bay Company.
[3] In the office of the Geographer at Ottawa. Parts of the Journals were found by J. B. Tyrrell at York Factory. For extracts see *Trans. Royal Society of Canada*, 1913.

appears to have explored the route from the Churchill by way of Reindeer River and Reindeer Lake to Lake Athabaska—a notable achievement. A comparison of this map with the Arrowsmith map of 1811 makes it tolerably clear that the latter got much of the additional information incorporated in that map from the surveys of Fidler.

This brings us to David Thompson, who entered the service of the Hudson's Bay Company in 1784, studied practical astronomy under Philip Turner, and left behind him a series of manuscript journals filling forty-five volumes and covering the amazing period of sixty-six years, as well as a very remarkable manuscript map.[1] He spent thirteen years in the employment of the Hudson's Bay Company and then left it for that of the North West Company. Like Turner and Fidler he had served the older Company as surveyor and astronomer, but became convinced in 1797 that his services in that capacity were no longer required. He had no objection to fur-trading as a side issue, but as a sole occupation it did not appeal to him. During these thirteen years Thompson made careful surveys of the known water routes between Hudson Bay and the Rocky Mountains, including both branches of the Saskatchewan, and explored and surveyed new routes between the Nelson and Churchill, the Nelson and Saskatchewan, the Saskatchewan and Athabaska. He also surveyed the route by way of Reindeer Lake from the Churchill to Lake Athabaska, connecting his surveys on the south shore of the latter lake with those of Turner. Much of this was very difficult country, rock and muskeg and long and difficult portages around waterfalls and rapids. It is impossible to say at this time whether Thompson or Fidler first discovered Reindeer Lake.

This bald statement gives but a very inadequate idea of the magnitude and value of Thompson's achievement. He seized every opportunity of travelling over a waterway that was new to him, took infinite pains to make his surveys accurate and to fix his positions by astronomical observations, and was constantly accumulating information for his map of the West He also kept a systematic record of meteorological and other data. All this was done without neglecting his duties as a fur-trader. As an example of the extraordinary accuracy of his work, it has been said by J. B. Tyrrell, himself an eminent surveyor, that the ascertained position of Cumberland House, on the Saskatchewan, after fluctuating from time to time, has now been definitely established, and that the Dominion Government surveyors have found that their observations agree almost exactly with those of Thompson taken more than a century and a quarter ago, with the cumbersome instruments of his day. Thompson was warmly welcomed by the partners of the North West Company, who

[1] In Provincial Archives at Toronto. See too Thompson's *Narrative* (Champlain Soc. 1916).

accorded him every facility to carry on his scientific work. As a matter of fact they were very glad to have his assistance at this time, for the terms of the Treaty of Peace, 1783, and of Jay's Treaty, 1794, made it necessary that they should ascertain as soon as possible whether certain of their western posts were on the British or the United States side of the boundary. Thompson carried out this task and also in the next few years made important explorations and surveys in the country between Lake Superior and the Red River, between the Assiniboine and the Missouri, and on the upper waters of the Saskatchewan. In 1807 he had nearly completed his surveys of the country between Hudson Bay and Lake Superior, on the east, and the Rocky Mountains, on the west. He still had before him five years of strenuous work west of the mountains, to be carried out with the same painstaking care, but this will be dealt with later.

While Thompson was with the Hudson's Bay Company, a fur-trader from Montreal, Alexander Mackenzie, had boldly penetrated into the extreme North-West. Leaving Fort Chipewyan, on Lake Athabaska, in June 1789, he descended Slave River to Great Slave Lake, where he was detained for some time by the ice. Finally he made his way to the west end of the lake and found himself floating down one of the great rivers of the world. At this time nothing was known about the Mackenzie, and the explorer confidently believed that it would carry him to the Pacific. He was correspondingly disappointed when he finally found himself in the Arctic. Nothing daunted, however, he at once began to lay his plans for another expedition, and in order that he might be well equipped he travelled from Fort Chipewyan to London to secure the best instruments and improve his knowledge of their use. In the summer of 1792 he sent men to build a post on Peace River, east of the mountains, and he himself wintered there so that he might start west as soon as the ice broke up in the spring.

In May of the following year he set forth on his second expedition, accompanied by Alexander McKay and a party of French-Canadian voyageurs or boatmen. Not without difficulty they followed the Peace up through the mountains, and then ascended its tributary the Parsnip. From the headwaters of the latter they crossed over to the Tacouche Tesse (afterwards known as the Fraser), and descended that stream to a point later named Alexandria in honour of the explorer. Convinced that he was getting too far south, and anxious to find a shorter route to the sea because of the rapidly diminishing stock of provisions, Mackenzie turned back to the mouth of the Blackwater. His men were disheartened and mutinous, and only his iron will kept them to the task. He ascended the Blackwater toward the west. From its upper waters he crossed a ridge of mountains and arrived on the banks of the Bella Coola. He and his men had had little or nothing to eat for days and were very thankful to reach a village of friendly Indians where they feasted on salmon, the staple food of all the coast tribes. Obtaining a canoe from these Indians, Mackenzie and his men paddled rapidly down the Bella Coola and found themselves on salt water, Bentinck Arm. Having reached the Pacific, the explorer was anxious to start on his return journey at the earliest possible moment, partly because he was dependent for a supply of provisions on the continued friendliness of the Bella Coola Indians, and partly because he now found himself followed and threatened by hostile Coast Indians. It appears that they had had a misunderstanding with some of Vancouver's men, who had reached Bentinck Arm by sea some time before, and seemed inclined to wreak vengeance on these other white men.

Mackenzie, however, was determined not to turn back until he had ascertained his position. "My people", he says in his *Journal*, "were panic-struck, and some of them asked if it was my determination to remain there to be sacrificed". He replied that he would not stir until he had accomplished his object. Having finally obtained the latitude, and painted on the face of a rock this inscription: "Alexander Mackenzie, from Canada, by land, the twenty-second of July, one thousand seven hundred and ninety-three", he embarked with his men and turned his face toward the east. This rock, it is believed, has been identified, and the Canadian Government has placed there a monument to commemorate Mackenzie's notable achievement—the final realisation of the dream of an overland route to the Pacific, that dream that directly or indirectly had inspired the explorations of most of the great discoverers of the Canadian West. In fact it may be said that Mackenzie successfully completed the search for the Western Sea whose history goes back to the voyages of Jacques Cartier and Henry Hudson.

About a decade after this memorable expedition through what was to be known as New Caledonia, now northern British Columbia, Simon Fraser and John Stuart were sent by the North West Company to establish trading posts west of the mountains. Fraser, like Mackenzie and Thompson, while a loyal and competent trader, was keenly interested in discovery, and welcomed the instructions of the Company to explore the Tacouche Tesse (Fraser) from Mackenzie's farthest point, Alexandria, to the sea. Having made his preparations, he started from Fort George, at the mouth of the Nechaco, in May 1808, with John Stuart, Jules Maurice Quesnel and nineteen *voyageurs*, on one of the most difficult journeys in the history of exploration. As one watches to-day, from a car window on one or other of Canada's transcontinental railways, the tumultuous flood of the Fraser rushing down to the sea through its forbidding gorges, one gets a faint idea of the tremendous difficulties which the explorer and his companions had to surmount. Again and again they escaped death by a miracle.

The Indians assured Fraser that it was madness to attempt to run a canoe down that tempestuous river, and told him of a safe route by another stream (which he later named after his fellow-explorer Thompson) that would bring him to the comparatively navigable waters of the Tacouche Tesse many miles below. "But", says Fraser, "going to the sea by an indirect way was not the object of the undertaking. I therefore would not deviate". There speaks the obstinate Scotsman; but one finds a blood-stirring quality in the spirit of the man. His orders were to explore this particular stream, and he would do it though death lurked behind every foot of the way. His indomitable pluck carried him through to the mouth of the river, which has since most properly borne his name.

Fraser took observations, at a point not far from where the city of New Westminster stands to-day, and was disappointed to find that the river he had been following was not, as he had supposed, the Columbia, the lower part of which had been explored by Lewis and Clark three years before. Curiously enough, while in 1808 Thompson was actually upon the upper waters of the Columbia, Fraser supposed that he was on the upper waters of the river he had named the Thompson. Facts like these make one realise how often explorers are forced to grope blindly for landmarks, and are sometimes led astray by plausible evidence.

The discoveries and surveys of David Thompson have already been traced west to the Rocky Mountains. In 1807 he determined to cross those mountains, by what is known as Howse Pass, which leads from the upper waters of the North Saskatchewan to those of the Columbia. This would bring him into that extraordinary region of mountain ranges and long valleys that is now southern British Columbia. He had been stationed for some time at Rocky Mountain House, a trading post of the North West Company, on the North Saskatchewan, where he had been brought into close and friendly relations with the Blackfeet, and particularly with a tribe of that confederacy known as the Piegan Indians. They knew of Thompson's plans to cross the mountains and, realising that he would then be brought into touch with their ancient enemies the Kootenay Indians, and by supplying them with firearms would make them formidable, they determined to block his passage. Accordingly, they stationed a party of warriors at the eastern approach to Howse Pass, and warned Thompson that they would not permit him to cross the mountains.

Thompson, thoroughly familiar with the Indian character, was neither dismayed nor discouraged. He made his preparations and bided his time, knowing that sooner or later the Piegan would be thrown off their guard by some more exciting object. His faith was amply justified. Some time before a number of Piegan had attacked the Lewis and Clark expedition and suffered loss, and when a war party was organised among the tribe to avenge the dead, the warriors on guard at Howse Pass promptly abandoned their post to join the party. Thompson lost no time, made his way over the pass, and built Kootenay House near the headwaters of the Columbia. In the years that followed he thoroughly explored the Columbia from source to mouth, as well as its great tributary the Kootenay. Down to the point where Lewis and Clark had struck the Columbia in 1805 Thompson was the original discoverer, and his is the sole comprehensive survey of the entire river not only in his day but even down to the present time.

Thompson left the West in 1812, and the remainder of his life was spent in Eastern Canada, where among other important undertakings he was engaged in the work of the International Boundary Commission. In 1813 and 1814 he prepared his great map of Western Canada for the North West Company, on a scale of about fifteen miles to an inch. A comparison of this map with other maps of the period reveals the extraordinary contribution he made to our knowledge of Western Canada. Not only did Arrowsmith borrow from him, without acknowledgment, much of the information incorporated in his maps, but, as J. B. Tyrrell has pointed out, "when in 1857, forty-five years after the termination of Thompson's work, the Government of Canada began to look westward and wanted a map of Western Canada, the very best that it could do was to republish[1] Thompson's map of 1813 without, however, giving him credit for it except by a small note in one corner; and to this day some parts of the maps of Canada published by the Canadian Government, the railway companies, and others, are taken from Thompson's map".[2]

The exploration of the Pacific coast from the sea had been practically completed before the dates of any of these overland expeditions. The story can be told only in the barest outline. It goes back to Drake's voyage of 1577–80 in the *Golden Hind* and the Spanish expeditions from Mexico in the same century. It was not, however, until James Cook's voyage of 1776–8 that an Englishman discovered any portion of what is now the coast of British Columbia. Cook sailed up the coast, landed on the outer side of what was afterwards called Vancouver Island, discovered and named Prince William Sound and Cook's Inlet, and penetrated through Bering Strait into the Arctic. On his return voyage he was murdered by the natives of Hawaii in the Sandwich Islands. Cook discovered the Pacific coast of Canada, but it remained for George Vancouver, who had been with him, to explore and survey it in his voyage of 1791–5, which he did with such thoroughness that little remained but to fill in minor gaps in that intricate coastline with its outer fringe of islands.

The extent, though not the reality, of the Russian and Spanish

---

[1] This is perhaps a little misleading, as Thompson's map had never been published. The original hung for many years in the dining hall at Fort William.
[2] Introduction to Thompson's *Narrative*.

discoveries is somewhat problematical. Semen Dezhnev is said to have seen the islands in Bering Strait in 1648, Fedorov and Gvozdev to have landed on the mainland of America near Prince of Wales Cape in 1732, and Bering and Chirikov to have discovered the coast between lat. 55° 30' and 60° in 1741. Juan Perez is reported to have sailed north from Mexico as far as the Queen Charlotte Islands in 1774, and Quadra to have reached Chichagov Island the following year, making a rapid survey of the coast on his return south. Upon the explorations of Bering and Chirikov, and the subsequent establishment of Russian trading posts, was based the claim of Russia and afterwards of the United States to the coastal strip known as the Panhandle of Alaska, which shuts out much of British Columbia from the sea.

The exploration of Western Canada from Hudson Bay and from Lake Superior to the Pacific has now been outlined in its larger aspects. It remains to complete the story of discovery in the far north. The expeditions of Hearne and Mackenzie have already been described. They represented two long lines of penetration through the north country, with two ascertained points on the northern coast of the continent, the mouth of the Coppermine and the mouth of the Mackenzie. In the century that followed, the Arctic coast was explored from Point Barrow in the west to Melville Peninsula in the east; the broad outlines at least were ascertained of the immense region lying between the northern half of Hudson Bay and Alaska; and a series of Arctic voyages, in which men of various nationalities revealed the heights to which human pluck and endurance may be carried, resulted in the discovery and partial exploration of the vast Arctic archipelago that now constitutes the District of Franklin.

Incidental results were the discovery by (Sir) James Clarke Ross in 1831 of the North Magnetic Pole on the west coast of Boothia Peninsula, the actual discovery of the North-West Passage by (Sir) Robert McClure in 1850, and the first and only voyage through it by Roald Amundsen in 1903-6. The Passage that for hundreds of years had inspired the hearts of some of the world's most intrepid discoverers, and in the search for which many of them had given their lives, which had been the subject of more extravagant hopes than perhaps any other object in the history of exploration, and upon whose quest millions of pounds had been expended, was finally proved to be a reality, but like the North-East Passage, utterly worthless for all practical purposes.

Half a century after Hearne's journey, and about thirty years after that of Mackenzie, (Sir) John Franklin started inland in 1820 from York Factory on his first overland expedition to the Arctic. He had been sent out by the British Government, and reached Fort Chipewyan by way of Hudson Bay and the usual route of the fur-traders. With him were (Sir) John Richardson, (Sir) George Back and Robert Hood. Richardson and Back were to lead subsequent expeditions to the Arctic; Hood was to come to a tragic end on this journey, murdered by the *voyageur* Michel crazed with hunger.

From Great Slave Lake Franklin travelled up the Yellowknife River and wintered near Winter Lake. In the spring he descended the Coppermine to the sea and explored the coast eastward around Coronation Gulf, Bathurst Inlet and Melville Sound, to a point on Kent Peninsula which he named Turnagain. Returning to Hood River he ascended it and attempted to make his way back overland to Winter Lake. The conditions of travel were exceedingly difficult, provisions were soon exhausted, and although he and his companions finally won through, they were reduced to eating lichen scraped from the rocks and such things as even the wolves had left behind.

Three years after his return Franklin commanded a second expedition again accompanied by Richardson and Back. They wintered, 1825-6, on Great Bear Lake, where they built Fort Franklin, and in June descended the Mackenzie to the delta. Dividing his men into two parties, Franklin succeeded in exploring the coast in one season from Gwydyr Bay, near Point Beechey, to the mouth of the Coppermine. In 1833-4 Back added Great Fish River, now Back River, to the map. From the eastern end of Great Slave Lake he made his way by a series of rivers and lakes to the source of Great Fish River, and the following year descended that river to the sea, and explored the Arctic coast to Point Ogle, the north-easternmost point of Adelaide Peninsula.

Four years later Thomas Simpson, of the Hudson's Bay Company, carried Franklin's farthest exploration on to Point Barrow, filled in the big gap between Turnagain and Point Ogle, and followed the coast north-eastward from the mouth of the Coppermine to Castor and Pollux River. In 1846-7 Dr John Rae crossed the isthmus from Repulse Bay to Committee Bay and explored the coast of the Gulf of Boothia from Melville Peninsula round to Ross Peninsula. Seven years later he extended Simpson's discoveries from Castor and Pollux River to Cape Porter. Richardson's expedition of 1848 and that of James Anderson in 1855 did not add materially to what was already known of the Arctic coast. As a result of these various land expeditions, the Arctic coast of North America was traced, with one or two exceptions, from Point Barrow to Melville Peninsula. Melville Peninsula was explored by (Sir) William Parry in 1822, and Boothia Peninsula by the same Arctic discoverer in 1829-32. Incidentally lines of exploration were carried through that immense region which, according to Vilhjalmur Stefansson, has been misnamed the Barren Grounds. The bare recital of these discoveries will be misleading if one does not remember that they were carried out under conditions that were often extremely hazardous, through difficult country, where human life might depend upon the uncertain movements of the caribou herds, and where the summer was very brief and winter long and dark and deadly cold.

Only in the briefest possible way can the results of Arctic maritime exploration be noted, in so far as they relate to the discovery of the Arctic islands of Canada and of the various sounds, channels and straits that separate them. That story of heroic achievement covers a period of three and a half centuries. It goes back to the voyages of Frobisher in 1576 and Davis in 1585, and includes the famous names of Ross, Franklin, McClure, McClintock, Parry, Sverdrup and Amundsen. It put upon the map in fairly correct outline the great islands of Baffin, Ellesmere and Victoria, and such lesser islands as Somerset, Devon, Bathurst, Melville, Banks and Prince of Wales.

Similarly the exploration of the extreme North-West, the District of Yukon and the adjoining corner of British Columbia, must be dismissed in a very few words. Finlay River, the northern branch of the Peace, was explored by Samuel Black, of the Hudson's Bay Company, up to its source in Thutade Lake, in 1824. Ten years later John McLeod, of the same Company, ascended the Liard River from the Mackenzie, then the Dease to Dease Lake, and crossing over to the Stikine explored its upper waters. In 1840 Robert Campbell, also of the Hudson's Bay Company, followed the Liard to its source; three years later he traced the Pelly down to where it becomes the Yukon; in 1848 he built Fort Selkirk at the junction of the Lewes and Pelly; and two years later descended the Yukon to the mouth of the Porcupine. In 1842 John Bell, of the Hudson's Bay Company, discovered the Porcupine, and in 1844 explored it down to the Yukon.

The exploration of Western and Northern Canada having now been briefly outlined, it will be convenient to describe, with the same brevity, the history of the Hudson's Bay Company, the North West Company and the X Y Company, as well as their relations to each other and to the natives with whom they bartered blankets, cotton, knives and kettles, flints, beads, vermilion, twine, tobacco, firearms and ammunition, and a variety of other articles, including liquor, brought mostly from the British Isles, for beaver, fox, otter, marten, mink and many other more or less valuable skins.

Something has already been said about the origin of the Hudson's Bay Company. Its first trading post was built in 1667 at the mouth of the Rupert River, James Bay, and was named Fort Rupert. Between 1682 and 1688 York Factory was established near the mouth of the Nelson, Fort Albany at the mouth of the Albany, Moose Factory at the mouth of the Moose, Fort Severn at the mouth of the Severn, and Fort Churchill at the mouth of the Churchill, all on James or Hudson Bays. Fort Churchill was replaced between 1733 and 1747 by Prince of Wales Fort, built of massive masonry. To these trade centres the Indians of the inland tribes brought down their furs annually and returned laden with various commodities obtained in exchange. As the weight of French trade opposition from Canada began to be felt, smaller posts were built on the upper waters of some of the rivers flowing into James Bay; but it was not until 1774 that the Company moved boldly into the interior of the continent, building Cumberland House on Sturgeon Lake, a point of strategic importance commanding that great natural thoroughfare, the Saskatchewan, as well as the canoe route between the Saskatchewan and the Churchill. From about this time dates the long-continued rivalry between the Hudson's Bay Company and the British traders from Montreal presently to be organised as the North West Company.

The North West Company was not, like its competitor, a chartered company, nor is there evidence that it was even incorporated. Dating from 1783–4, it was a partnership of merchants, functioning under an agreement that was renewed from time to time. What it lacked in dignity, however, it made up in energy and aggressiveness. The men who controlled its destinies were for the most part shrewd and resourceful Scotsmen, while the rank and file were largely made up of French Canadians equally familiar with the conditions of life and travel in the Indian country and with the character of the Indians themselves. The traders of the North West Company, following the route already opened by their French predecessors, built trading posts at Grand Portage and at convenient points on the inland waterways. Trade here followed, not the flag, but the explorer. As new water routes were discovered, new rivers and lakes, new districts, forts were quickly built and trading relations established with the surrounding tribes. In this way a network of posts was created, spreading out like an immense fan from Lake Superior to the Rocky Mountains, and ultimately to the Pacific.

As the Hudson's Bay Company brought its trading goods and articles of food and equipment by sailing ship from England, so the North West Company supplied its interior posts from Montreal, its brigades of canoes following the long-established thoroughfare up the Ottawa River to Lake Nipissing and Georgian Bay, through the lakes to Grand Portage, thence to Lake Winnipeg and the various posts. As a matter of fact London to a large extent furnished the trading goods of both Companies, and to London also went ultimately the furs which had become the bone of bitter contention between them.

There was fierce competition between the North West Company and the Hudson's Bay Company, and the North West Company had also for some years to meet the opposition of a Canadian rival, the X Y Company, founded in 1800. There were times when the three organisations maintained trading posts within a stone's throw of one another, their respective traders resorting to every expedient that cunning could suggest to outwit each other. But for the most part the opposition of the X Y Company was to the North West Company, and it finally became of so ruinous a nature that the leaders on both sides were compelled in 1804 to seek relief in union.

It might have been supposed that an experience that had brought both Companies to the verge of bankruptcy would have cured them of the folly of cut-throat competition. So far was this from being the case that they had no sooner buried their own hatchets than they dug them up again to make a united attack on the Hudson's Bay Company. It is of course only fair to say that the responsibility for this conflict rested equally upon both the North West Company and the Hudson's Bay Company. Both clung tenaciously to what they conceived to be their rights and would yield not an inch to the other. The Hudson's Bay Company, entrenched within the extremely generous terms of its charter, regarded the North West Company as interlopers, and branded its traders as "pedlars". The latter scornfully denied the right of the Hudson's Bay Company to monopolise the trade of half a continent, throughout much of which its own men had been first in the field.

So the fight went merrily on, sometimes good-natured and aboveboard where the rival traders were of the better sort and had learned to respect each other, but often bitter, uncompromising and unscrupulous. One very unfortunate result was that, in their desperate efforts to win the trade of the Indians, each made free use of that irresistible bribe, liquor, a dangerous expedient as more than one trader found to his cost. Finally, in 1821, the same solution was found as in the conflict between the North West Company and the X Y Company—the Hudson's Bay Company absorbed its Canadian competitor. Thereafter the strength and experience of the three furtrading corporations that at one time had struggled for the mastery were consolidated, and the Hudson's Bay Company reigned supreme over that land of immense distances and illimitable resources that is known to-day as Western Canada. Indeed the time came when the flag of their ancient and romantic partnership flew over trading posts as far removed as Labrador and Vancouver Island, the Yukon and California.

From time to time the fur-trading corporations of Canada came into contact, friendly or otherwise, with those of the United States and Russia. Early in the nineteenth century John Jacob Astor of New York conceived the idea of developing the fur trade of the Pacific coast. He tried to interest the North West Company, but the negotiations fell through. He then organised the Pacific Fur Company, drew into it several Canadians who had had experience with the North West Company, and sent out two expeditions, one by sea and the other by land. In 1811 Astoria was built near the mouth of the Columbia. The following year a party of North West

Company men descended the Columbia with news that war had been declared between the United States and Great Britain, and that a British war vessel was on its way to seize Astoria. Making a virtue of necessity the Pacific Fur Company turned over Astoria to the North West Company, by whom it was renamed Fort George. After the war it was restored to the United States Company. This incident was not without influence upon the long-continued controversy over the Oregon boundary. Similarly the relations entered into between the Hudson's Bay Company and the Russians, the rivalry between the British and Russian fur-traders, and the leasing of the coast strip to the Hudson's Bay Company for a term of years in consideration of an annual rental of two thousand land-otter skins, were to become important factors in another controversy with the United States over the Alaska boundary.

No account of the western fur trade would be complete without some reference to the sea-otter trade of the Pacific coast. Here if anywhere the stories of fabulous profits in the fur trade had some basis in reality. Bering's last voyage of 1741 revealed the fact that the skins of the sea-otter, at that time abundant everywhere on the north-west coast of America, would bring enormous prices in the Chinese market. For a quarter of a century Russian adventurers rushed to Alaska, and suffered incredible hardships, but reaped a rich harvest. About 1785 British fur-traders entered the field, and they too found a very profitable market in China for skins purchased from the Coast Indians for trinkets and bits of iron. A few years later they were joined by ships sailing from New England ports. The frantic greed of these independent traders of various nations led in a few years to the practical extermination of the sea-otter.

It is perhaps unsafe to generalise as to the influence of the fur trade in Western Canada upon its native inhabitants. Much depended upon the character of the individual trader. The Hudson's Bay Company or the North West Company might lay down a certain policy, but the headquarters of those corporations were remote and the officer in charge of a particular district or a particular post had all the powers of an autocrat within his own realm. That there was a very seamy side to the fur trade we have ample evidence in such narratives as the Journal of Alexander Henry the younger. On the other hand, we know that men like David Thompson were not only respected by the Indians but exerted upon their lives an influence that was altogether good. On the whole one may perhaps safely say that the Indians of Western Canada gained more than they lost by reason of their contact with white traders. It is not without significance that Canada has had very little trouble with her aborigines, and it is not unreasonable to assume that that fortunate circumstance is due at least in some measure to the fact that the Indians had learned from generations of contact with traders that the attitude of the white man was friendly and that his word could be relied upon.

Much has been written about the exorbitant profits of the fur trade and the unfair advantage that was taken by white traders of the unsophisticated Indian. That charge was no doubt true in the early days of the fur trade, or when traders first came into contact with a particular tribe, valuable furs being willingly exchanged for a needle, a few beads, or other trifles, but it was not always true. While tribes and individuals varied in mental capacity, the average Indian was by no means deficient in shrewdness, and it did not take him long to gain a pretty fair idea of the market value of his wares. Ross Cox, who wrote from personal knowledge, bears witness to this. Describing the methods of trading among the Indians, he says, "They are shrewd, hard dealers, and not a whit inferior to any native of Yorkshire, Scotland, or Connaught, in driving a bargain".[1]

Further, if the traders exchanged for valuable furs goods that originally cost them a comparatively small sum, they had to transport them very long distances, their overhead expenses were considerable, and they had to wait a long time for the return on their investment. In such an extreme case as Fort Yukon, no less than seven years elapsed before the returns reached the market. The first year the trading goods reached York Factory by sea from England; the second year they were transported inland to Norway House, at the northern end of Lake Winnipeg; the third year they were carried through the long water-communication to Peel River, near the mouth of the Mackenzie; the fourth year they were hauled over the mountains and taken down the Porcupine to Fort Yukon; the fifth year the furs obtained in exchange were made into packs and carried to the Mackenzie; the sixth year they arrived at the depôt at Fort Simpson; and the seventh year they reached the London market.

It is a debatable question how far the fur trade paved the way for the settlement of Western Canada. As was to be expected, the attitude of the fur-trading companies was not favourable to settlement; for settlement and the fur trade can hardly co-exist for any length of time. As the former increases the latter must inevitably be crowded out, and the traders must seek their peltries somewhere beyond the frontiers of civilisation. Nevertheless, without their pioneer work it is doubtful whether the settlement of the west could have been accomplished in anything like the same period of time. So much may be said of the unconscious and unintentional influence of the fur trade. Where, on the other hand, it was brought into direct contact with settlement, and recognised it as its enemy, as in the case of the North West Company and the Selkirk Colony, the fur trade made its enmity unmistakably felt. That conscious influence was, however, only temporary and sporadic, however formidable it

[1] Cox, R., *Adventures on the Columbia River*, II, 78.

may have seemed at the time, and it does not affect the general conclusion that, however unwittingly, the fur trade blazed the trail for
colonisation. Moreover, in many cases the centres of the fur trade
became in course of time the centres of settlement. To-day the
provincial capitals of Manitoba, Alberta and British Columbia cover
the sites of Forts Garry, Edmonton and Victoria. Fort William, once
the headquarters of the North West Company, of which Washington
Irving has given a romantic account in his *Astoria*, is now the busy
transhipping point for Canadian grain from rail to lake steamer. The
rival American port of Duluth covers the site of the old fur-trade
post of Fond du Lac. Also during the period of the fur trade many
of the time-expired servants of the North West Company and the
Hudson's Bay Company, rather than return to a civilised East with
which they had little in common, made homes for themselves and
their half-breed families around the trading posts. These also became
the nuclei of settlement.

As the history of the fur trade overlaps that of exploration in
Western Canada, so, but to a much more limited extent, the period
of early settlement overlaps that of the fur trade. The outstanding
event in that period was the establishment of what is sometimes known
as the Selkirk Colony and sometimes as the Red River settlement;
and the outstanding man in the history of the Red River settlement
was Thomas Douglas, Earl of Selkirk. A man of high ideals but
indifferent judgment, he had made two attempts at colonisation
before directing his energies towards Rupert's Land. His attempt at
settlement in Prince Edward Island met with some degree of success;
his venture in Upper Canada was, for various reasons, a dismal
failure. The Red River country seemed to offer a more promising
field and, with the idea of promoting colonisation through the
Hudson's Bay Company, he made considerable purchases of stock.
The directors of the Company, however, looked coldly upon his
project, and in the end he undertook it alone, the Company granting
him an area of 116,000 square miles of what proved to be exceedingly
fertile land in the valley of the Red River.

From the outset Selkirk's plans were opposed by the North West
Company which, in addition to the general objections of fur-traders
to settlement, saw in this particular scheme a deliberate attempt to
shut it out of the rich fur country of the west. From its point of
view Selkirk was merely an ally of the Hudson's Bay Company, and
therefore an enemy to be fought with every available weapon. The
opposition began in England, but quickly moved to the actual
scene of operations in the West, with serious consequences as will be
seen later. Selkirk lost no time in developing his plan of colonisation.
He secured the services of Captain Miles Macdonell, from the
Glengarry settlement on the upper St Lawrence, and set to work to
secure recruits for his colony. Petty obstacles of every kind seemed

to clog the wheels of the expedition, but finally a party of High-landers with a few Irish sailed with Macdonell from Stornoway in July 1811. They had a stormy voyage, and arrived at York Factory too late to go inland that season. Petty jealousies between the officers of the Hudson's Bay Company and Selkirk's men added to the other discomforts of a winter on the shores of Hudson Bay.

In the spring Macdonell with twenty-three men made his way by the Hayes route to Lake Winnipeg and the Red River, where the land granted to Selkirk was formally transferred by the Hudson's Bay Company to his representative. Selecting a site for the per-manent settlement, within the boundaries of the present city of Winnipeg, and leaving a few men to begin work on the buildings and break up land for wheat, he led the main party up the river to the junction of the Pembina with the Red River, on the international boundary. Buffalo were numerous and fish could be procured in abundance, so that the settlers spent a comparatively comfortable winter. A second party of settlers came out in 1812, recruited mainly from the Hebrides and the west of Ireland. They reached York Factory without misadventure, under the leadership of Owen Keveny, and left early in September for the interior. A third party, about a hundred in all, sailed from Stromness in June 1813. Typhoid fever broke out on the voyage, and to add to their misery the un-fortunate settlers had to winter at Fort Churchill. But these sturdy Highlanders, women as well as men, nevertheless managed to tramp all the way on snow-shoes from Churchill to York Factory in April of the next year; and in the following month made their way to the Red River. In 1815 a much larger party of settlers, chiefly from Sutherlandshire, came out under the leadership of Robert Semple.

Of the long conflict between Selkirk and his settlers and the Hudson's Bay Company on one side, and the North West Company on the other, only a very brief sketch can be attempted. Early in 1814 the smouldering hostility of the Nor'Westers was brought to a blaze by the action of Macdonell in prohibiting the export of pem-mican from the hunting grounds of Assiniboia, which lay within the area granted to Selkirk. This was a direct challenge to the Cana-dian traders, who had been accustomed for years to secure here large quantities of pemmican to supply their various posts and brigades. For a time Macdonell seemed to have the upper hand, and seized several shipments of pemmican from men of the North West Company. The latter bided their time, gradually drew the settlers from their allegiance, arrested Macdonell on a warrant, and burnt the colony buildings. Most of the settlers went to Upper Canada, while a loyal remnant waited for reinforcements from Hudson Bay.

In 1815 Semple arrived with his settlers at Red River and pro-ceeded to re-establish the colony. Here he was joined by Colin Robertson with a considerable party of Canadian traders and *voyageurs* recruited in Montreal for Selkirk. In spite of the heavy blow struck by the North West Company, the Red River settlement seemed stronger than ever, and the Hudson's Bay Company was at last actively engaged as an ally of Selkirk. The lull that followed was, however, but the lull before the storm. The North West Company was as determined as ever to stamp out the infant colony. They had already made use of the half-breeds, who were attached to their interest, to sow dissension among the settlers, and were now enlisted, under the leadership of Cuthbert Grant, in a more active rôle. A Hudson's Bay Company brigade was seized, in retaliation for one of the North West Company captured by Colin Robertson some time before; and in June 1816 a determined attempt was made to capture Fort Douglas, the headquarters of the colony. Semple, instead of remaining within the walls of his fort, rashly marched out with a number of his men, and in the skirmish that ensued he was killed as well as a score of his followers.

This tragic incident of "Seven Oaks" became the turning point in the relations between the Hudson's Bay Company and the North West Company, and ultimately led to their union in 1821. In the meantime, however, the long-suffering colony was not yet at the end of its misfortunes. Selkirk had arrived in Canada in the winter of 1815, and the following June left Montreal for the West, taking with him a number of officers and men of two disbanded regiments. Learning on the way of the "Seven Oaks" disaster, he seized Fort William, arrested the partners of the North West Company assembled there, and took possession of their papers and furs. The first gave him valuable information, and the seizure of the latter at least temporarily crippled the resources of the enemy.

Miles Macdonell was sent on to Red River with some of the disbanded soldiers and a couple of field pieces, and found little difficulty in recovering Fort Douglas. Meanwhile Lady Douglas had persuaded the Governor at Quebec, Sir John Sherbrooke, to send two Commissioners, Coltman and Fletcher, to the Red River settlement to investigate the "Seven Oaks" affair and the relations between the fur-traders and the colonists. On the other hand, the North West Company won a diplomatic victory. They had sent one of their men with a warrant to Fort William, but Selkirk had refused to recognise its authority. Representations were made to the Colonial Office, and a peremptory despatch was sent to Sherbrooke ordering Selkirk's arrest.

Of the report of the Commissioners, and the interminable litigation that followed in Upper and Lower Canada, it is impossible to say anything here. Charges of robbery, grand larceny, stealing, riot, false imprisonment, assault and battery, were brought by the North West Company against the Hudson's Bay Company and the Red River settlers; and charges of murder, arson, burglary, robbery, grand larceny and malicious shooting by the latter against the North West Company. The final result on both sides was inconclusive. Selkirk died in 1820, and in the following year the two fur-trading Companies were united. Thirteen years later the settlement was transferred by the Selkirk family back to the Hudson's Bay Company. The bitter hostility of the North West Company was a thing of the past, but it was too much to expect that the older corporation would do more than tolerate a colony whose very existence seemed to them inconsistent with the best interests of the fur trade.

After 1816 the development of the settlement was not, however, hampered so much by human opposition as by natural calamities and misguided paternalism. For three successive years crops were destroyed by a plague of locusts, and several years later a disastrous flood in the Red River shattered the hopes of the long-suffering colonists. The various experiments tried by the Selkirk estate, experimental farms, a scheme for producing cloth from buffalo wool, ventures in flax, tallow and other commodities, proved lamentable failures. Had it not been for the stubborn optimism of the Scottish settlers the colony could not possibly have survived. After the flood of 1826 their faith was justified. Abundant harvests proved the extraordinary richness of this Red River land, and probably had something to do with the reconveyance of the settlement to the Hudson's Bay Company.

The period from 1834 to the sale of Rupert's Land to Canada in 1869 and the entry of the Red River settlement into the Confederation the following year as the Province of Manitoba, calls for no particular comment. No very unusual incidents marked these years of slow but quite definite growth and prosperity. They have been not inaptly described as a "period of obscure and prosaic development".[1] In a few short years the progress of what had once been the Red River settlement was to become neither obscure nor prosaic, but on the contrary more than realised the most extravagant dreams of its founder.

No enthusiastic Selkirk laid the foundations of what were some day to become the Provinces of Saskatchewan and Alberta, except in so far as the creation of the Red River settlement may be said to have influenced settlement farther west. Generally speaking those provinces developed from very small and obscure beginnings, such as the half-breed settlements that, as already mentioned, grew up about the trading posts of the North West and Hudson's Bay Companies. At the time of Confederation the white population was still negligible, and it was not until many years later that, as the result of influences and conditions that lie outside the scope of this chapter, it grew to sufficient proportions to justify the organisation of the region between Manitoba and the Rocky Mountains as the North

---

[1] Martin, Chester, *Selkirk's Work in Canada*, p. 175.

West Territories; then as the Districts of Assiniboia, Saskatchewan, Alberta and Athabaska; and finally as the Provinces of Saskatchewan and Alberta.

The settlement of British Columbia dates back to the middle of the nineteenth century, and for some years was confined to Vancouver Island. It was the result nominally of the grant of the island in 1849 to the Hudson's Bay Company, one of the obligations of the grant being that the Company should bring out settlers. As a matter of fact the Company was not keenly interested in colonisation, and if it had been left to its unaided efforts, little if any progress would have been made. More potent factors were the extraordinary success that had attended the efforts of the United States to establish settlements in Oregon; and the widespread interest in the entire Pacific coast created by the discovery of gold in California. Fort Victoria had been built by the Company on Vancouver Island in 1843, and six years later the western headquarters of the Company had been removed there from Fort Vancouver. This became the nucleus of the infant colony. The opening of a coal mine at Nanaimo in 1851 also had a minor influence upon the course of settlement. If the colonisation of Vancouver Island was influenced by the flourishing settlement in the valley of the Columbia, that settlement in turn owed a great deal to Dr John McLoughlin of Fort Vancouver, who for many years directed the affairs of the Hudson's Bay Company on the Pacific coast. McLoughlin's attitude towards the American colonists was indeed so friendly, so paternal in fact, that he brought upon himself the severe displeasure of the Company and resigned. Like many another benefactor he experienced nothing but ingratitude from the people he had befriended.

Settlement on the mainland was the direct result of the discovery of gold on the Fraser in 1858. The gold rush of that year was amazing. Thousands of gold-seekers hastened by sea and land to the new Eldorado from every quarter of the world. As mining licences had to be taken out at Victoria, that place was transformed with disconcerting speed from a village to a city. Its harbour was filled with ocean steamers, and every species of craft that could be kept afloat; food became scarce and fetched fabulous prices; for a time most of the population of San Francisco seemed to have moved north to Victoria.

On the Fraser mining towns sprang up with the same mad speed at Langley, Hope, Yale and other points, and New Westminster became the seat of government of the new colony on the mainland. In 1859 gold was discovered farther up the Fraser, and a few months later the famous Cariboo rush was in full swing. Settlements were formed at Quesnel, Barkerville and at many other points on the upper Fraser and the Thompson, as well as in the intervening country. The Cariboo gold-fields not only yielded in seven years gold to the value of 25,000,000 dollars, but also led to the permanent settlement of the interior of British Columbia.

An incident of the discovery of gold in Cariboo was the emigration of gold-seekers from Ontario and parts of the eastern States to British Columbia. The most important of these overland expeditions was that of 1862. Its members gathered at Fort Garry, and travelled overland by way of Forts Ellice, Carlton and Edmonton to the Yellowhead Pass, and thence to Quesnel and the North Thompson. Their story is one of rare pluck and endurance. They were of the pioneer breed that made possible the settlement of the West. The settlement of that most remote district of Western Canada, the Yukon, hardly comes within the scope of the present chapter. But here, as on the mainland of British Columbia, settlement was the direct result of the discovery of gold.

Civil government, as generally understood in British communities, that is, government by representatives of King or people of some recognised political division of the British Empire, can hardly be said to have existed in the Red River settlement. That settlement was not in the strict sense of the term a public community. From 1812 to 1834 it was to all intents and purposes a private estate, controlled first by Lord Selkirk and after his death by his executors and his son; between 1834 and 1869 it was part of Rupert's Land and controlled by the Hudson's Bay Company. It was not in fact until the transfer of Rupert's Land to Canada in 1869, the creation of Manitoba and its entry into the Confederation in 1870, that civil government may be said to have had its beginning.

It is nevertheless true that under both the Selkirk regime and that of the Hudson's Bay Company, the affairs of the Red River settlement were administered by a Governor and Council acting under the authority vested in the Hudson's Bay Company by its charter, and to that extent civil government began with the founding of the settlement in 1812. After the colony was transferred to the Hudson's Bay Company it was divided into four districts, each presided over by a Justice of the Peace; and in 1839 a Recorder was appointed. Order was preserved by a volunteer corps commanded by a Sheriff.

The situation in Vancouver Island between 1849 and 1858 was somewhat similar to that in the Red River settlement. The island was the property of the Hudson's Bay Company. But, so far as civil government was concerned, there was this marked distinction that the Governor was appointed, not by the Company, but by the Crown. A Council was appointed by the Governor in 1851; and in 1856, under instructions from the Colonial Office, the Governor took the momentous step of summoning a representative Assembly. The colony was divided into four electoral districts, and the Assembly consisted at first of seven members. Its representative character was perhaps somewhat dubious, the members being either employees

or retired employees of the Hudson's Bay Company. The Assembly
was in fact a species of Family Compact. In 1858 an Act was passed
for the government of the mainland, and James Douglas became
the Governor of both British Columbia, that name being applied
at first only to the mainland, and Vancouver Island. At the same
time the Crown repurchased the island from the Company. Douglas
governed the island with the assistance of an Assembly, and the
mainland with the advice of a Council. In practice, however,
Douglas ruled alone in British Columbia.

One important result of the gold rush was that it both demanded
and made possible the construction of the Cariboo Road, from
Ashcroft on the Thompson River to Barkerville east of Quesnel on
the Fraser; several hundred miles through an exceedingly difficult
country. This very remarkable piece of road-making was the work
of the Royal Engineers, and was carried out between 1862 and 1865.
A practicable road had already been built from Ashcroft down to
navigable waters on the Fraser. The island also was provided with
roads quite adequate to the needs of a very young colony. Partially
representative institutions were granted to the mainland in 1864;
two years later island and mainland were brought under one
government; and in 1871 British Columbia entered the Confederation.

Names, in alphabetical order, of the chief explorers and traders of Western Canada:

Amundsen, Roald (1872–1928), Astor, John J. (1763–1848), Back, Sir George (1796–
1878), Campbell, Robert (1808–94), Cook, James (1728–79), Douglas, Sir James (1803–77),
Drake, Sir Francis (1540?–96) DuLhut, Daniel G. (1636–1710), Fidler, Peter (1769–1822),
Franklin, Sir John (1786–1847), Fraser, Simon (1776–1862), Hearne, Samuel (1745–
92), Hendry, Anthony (–   ), Henry, Alexander, the elder (1739–1824), Henry,
Alexander, the younger (–1814), Hood, Robert (–1821), Hudson, Henry
(–1611), Kelsey, Henry (–   ), La Vérendrye, Pierre (1685–1749), McClintock,
Sir Francis Leopold (1819–1907), McClure, Sir Robert (1807–73), Macdonell, Miles
(1767–1828), Mackenzie, Sir Alexander (1755–1820), McLeod, John (1788–1849),
McLoughlin, John (1784–1857), Parry, Sir William (1790–1855), Pond, Peter (1740–1807),
Radisson, Pierre E. (1635–1710), Rae, John (1813–93), Richardson, Sir John (1787–
1865), Ross, Sir James Clarke (1800–61), Selkirk, Earl of (Douglas, Thomas) (1771–1820),
Semple, Robert (1766–1816), Simpson, Thomas (1808–40), Sverdrup, Otto (1855–   ),
Thompson, David (1770–1857), Vancouver, George (1757–98).

CHAPTER XVII

NEWFOUNDLAND 1783 TO 1867

THE story of early settlement of Newfoundland and its relation to the British Isles was in chapter v brought down to 1783. The selfish effort of the West of England merchants to make the island a close preserve, the transition from the irregularities of the fishing admirals to the embryonic forms of a constitutional administration, the rivalry with the French for the actual possession of the country— these form the environment by which the character of the New-foundlander was first influenced. In the subsequent development of the community the primary factors of nationality, occupation, and religion as affected by the climate and physical features of the island all play their part.

Newfoundland was settled by a hardy type of mariner from the south-western counties of England. Coming originally to catch cod-fish, they made a practice of calling at Waterford and Cork on their way out, not only to buy Irish woollens, but also to engage young Irish servants. These "youngsters" (or green men) were apparently engaged for two summers and the intervening winter, and gradually settled down, intermarrying with the "planter" or settler families.[1] They were of a fine type but comparatively few in number. Un-fortunately, towards the end of the eighteenth century they were fol-lowed by discontented and lawless individuals, whose objection to orderly government left a permanent mark on Newfoundland.

The almost universal occupation of the settlers was the cod fishery, conducted chiefly along shore or in small vessels "supplied" by owners who kept the fishermen in their debt. This calling involved hardship, its returns were irregular, and its methods bred a distrust between man and man which extended to the Administration and hampered honest attempts at impartial government. The seal fishery developed somewhat later. The religious partisanship of the age was aggravated in a thinly settled country where the more excitable element adhered to the Roman Catholic faith. The isolated communities proved highly receptive of religious influences: their enthusiasm led them into col-lisions in which religion and political ambition reacted sharply on one another. The topography and climate of Newfoundland also had a full share in moulding the character of the settlers. Within the few miles of the sea-coast then known the island appealed intensely to all the elements of the population; here recalling parts of Scotland or Ireland, here reproducing the local atmosphere of Dorset or Devon-shire, it gave at once a sense of home to the immigrant from the old

[1] Prowse, D. W., *History of Newfoundland*, p. 201.

country. At the same time the violent extremes of climate, the rapid transitions from brilliant sunshine to piercing chill, with the prolonged severity of the winter, tended to produce a specially hardy and self-reliant type.

In the history of these people the year 1783 marked a fresh starting point. By the Treaty of Versailles the French finally relinquished their claim to sovereignty over any part of Newfoundland, and yet by a diplomatic declaration concurrent with the treaty received certain rights of fishery which were destined to breed trouble on the coasts of the island for more than a century to come.[1] The rights conceded to the French placed upon the settlers irritating and sometimes intolerable obligations. These affected even the fisheries of the North Atlantic with which the island by its position and the quality of its local industry was inseparably bound up.

The French negotiators had claimed the exclusive right to the Newfoundland fishery from Cape St John on the north-west corner of Notre Dame Bay to the northernmost point of the island, and then down the whole of the west side to Cape Ray. Such a claim practically wiped out the English ownership of half the island: the English declined to admit anything of the sort in the draft treaty and negotiations came to a deadlock. As a way out Alleyne Fitzherbert (afterwards Lord St Helens) proposed that the difficulty should be met by an undertaking on the part of the English Ministry to secure by executive instructions the rights demanded for the French fishermen. This actually happened. While Article IV of the treaty confirmed to England the sovereignty over Newfoundland and Article V renounced the fishing rights conferred on France by the Treaty of Utrecht, a secret declaration of 3 September 1783 undertook to prevent British subjects from interfering in any way with French rights. This amazing interference with the rights of the settlers, even to the extent of removing British settlements, may be explained by the long-standing conception of Newfoundland as solely a fishing centre; it seemed to ministers absolutely within their competence: but it bound on a British colony a burden which for more than a century hampered its whole political life.

In 1783 there was still no settled government in the colony.[2] An Admiral was granted a commission as governor for three or four years, coming out each summer to reside for some four months. In 1783 the Governor was Vice-Admiral John Campbell. He found a growing indignation at the serious and increasing scandal surrounding the Courts of Oyer and Terminer, originally established in 1763 as an alternative to carrying all disputes to the court of an English county. Incompetence and corruption marked their pro-

[1] Prowse, pp. 352–5. For the text of the declaration see Appendix to the *British Case in the North Atlantic Coast Fisheries Arbitration* (1909–11), Pt I, p. 11.
[2] "The present Government...such as it is, is in the Admiralty". Dr Gardner of Boston in 1784. Brit. Mus. MS. 15,493.

ceedings. Yet it was not till 1789 at the instance of Aaron Graham under Governor Admiral Mark Milbanke that definite steps were taken for establishing courts upon a sounder footing. The first attempt, curiously enough, proved irregular. The Governor under his commission established a Court of Common Pleas: this did not suit the merchants, who at once impugned the legality of the act: their view was admitted by the law officers of the Crown, but attention was thus called to the pressing need of a duly constituted court, and in 1791 an Act of the British Parliament[1] created "the Court of Civil Jurisdiction of our Lord the King at St John's in the Island of Newfoundland", under which John Reeves, a legal adviser to the Board of Trade, was appointed Chief Justice on the modest stipend of £500 a year. In 1792[2] the Court became the Supreme Court of Judicature in the Island of Newfoundland, and was continued from year to year for nearly twenty years before it was made permanent. Chief Justice Reeves, though he presided over the Court for only two years, laid the foundations of a sound and impartial administration of justice. His successors were not always lawyers, yet the value of the Court was maintained, until it was made a permanent part of the administration. Soon afterwards definite legal qualifications were also required for the Chief Justice.

Admiral Campbell's name is also connected with the declaration of religious liberty by a proclamation of 1784, apparently coincident with Dr James L. O'Donel's arrival in the colony as Prefect Apostolic. Gathering up the threads of previous efforts, the newcomer lost no time in acquiring a site for a suitable chapel and laid the foundations of that vigorous Roman Catholic sentiment which has played so important a part in the story of the colony. He became bishop in 1796. In his diocesan statutes of 1801 he embodied the basis of his political teaching and example—"that the priests should use every means to turn aside their flocks from the vortex of modern anarchy, that they should inculcate a willing obedience to the salutary laws of England, and to the commands of the governor and magistrates of this Island".[3] But he had meanwhile to encounter much jealous opposition, not only from Protestant partisans, but also from certain of the official hierarchy. His activities doubtless stimulated adherents of the Church of England, which had had a foothold in the colony since early days, and as far back as 1703 received a grant from the Society for the Propagation of the Gospel. In 1786 the Anglican church at Placentia was built largely under the patronage of Prince William Henry, afterwards William IV, and in 1787 Bishop Charles Inglis was appointed Anglican Bishop of Canada, New Brunswick, Nova Scotia, and Newfoundland.[4] One indirect but interesting result of the recognition of the Roman Catholic Church was improved cultivation near

[1] 31 Geo. III, cap. 29.   [2] 32 Geo. III, cap. 46.
[3] Prowse, p. 364; Howley, *Eccl. Hist.* p. 204. [4] Prowse, p. 653.

St John's: the young Irishmen, who came to the colony full of the desire to acquire land and settle down, naturally wished to be as near their church as possible: the farms and homesteads of Avalon are, next after the Devonshire settlers, due to these Irishmen.

The war which broke out between England and France in February 1793 had an immediate effect on Newfoundland, the Admiral Governor of which, on 14 May 1793, seized Île St Pierre. In the following year a regiment of infantry, the Royal Newfoundland Fencibles, was raised: preparations were made for defending Signal Hill and the Narrows of St John's Harbour: the sustained efforts were so successful that when on 1 September 1796 the French fleet appeared off the capital, the sight of large encampments and their activity sufficed to secure St John's from attack. The French turned down shore and attacked Bay Bulls, setting the little town on fire: they also damaged the town at St Pierre, but effected practically nothing.

The mutiny in H.M.S. *Latona* in the harbour of St John's (1797)—an echo of the mutinies in the home fleets,—and a conspiracy known as that of the United Irishmen (1799), clearly traceable to the Irish rebellion[1], brought Newfoundland into the wash of European troubles: otherwise the colony in 1800 was peaceful. The fisheries were successful, the competition of the foreigner being largely removed; the only special trouble seems to have been the constant attempt of American traders to smuggle in provisions and smuggle out Newfoundland fishermen. In December 1803, Vice-Admiral James (afterwards Lord) Gambier recommended the grant of a local government in Newfoundland. This has been cited as a plea for "responsible government",[2] but all that Gambier proposed was that there should be "a power in the island for framing laws for its internal regulation, and for raising the sums necessary to promote any measure of public utility by which expense must be incurred"; for as yet there was no sort of local Legislature. To Gambier also credit is due for attempts to promote education—by the St John's Charity Schools, one for Roman Catholics, another for Protestants—to uphold the influence of the clergy and to rescue the remnant of the original Indian inhabitants.

In 1804 the colony had 20,000 inhabitants, who caught and cured 600,000 quintals of fish, besides 107,000 seals.[3] The chief markets for the cod were Spain, Portugal and the West Indies. The prosperity of war-time still persisted; yet the old tyranny of merchants towards the fishermen and dealers kept the majority of the colonists in poverty. The system of supplying material for the fishery at a fixed price and setting off the debt against the prices realised for the catch left the dealers and fishermen in the traders' hands.[4] Sir Erasmus Gower's

---

[1] Document reproduced by Prowse, p. 418. [2] An error of Prowse, p. 376.
[3] Prowse, p. 378. Quintal = 1 cwt. [4] *Ibid.* p. 379 (a Fogo petition).

regulation of 12 September 1805, requiring declaration of prices and so checking the truck system, is evidence of a gradual improvement, also shown in other directions. The capital with some 8000 citizens was steadily increasing in size and importance: Gower Street, one of its main thoroughfares, was opened in 1804 and named after the Governor, as was Duckworth Street a little later. "A primitive post office"[1] was established in 1805; the first newspaper, the *Royal Gazette*, was instituted in 1806. The Benevolent Irish Society, established in 1806, was a sign of improving ideals: founded by James McBraire, who was not himself a Roman Catholic, it was simply Irish in its conception, but not unnaturally it became, and still is, the leading Roman Catholic organisation in the island: it is the centre of all Roman Catholic charities and education, though its constitution still nominally opens the door to all denominations. In 1809 (as has been seen) a permanent Court of Justice was established. The new Governor, Vice-Admiral Sir John Duckworth, set himself to reduce the buildings of St John's to something like order, and had a large share in procuring the Act whereby much of the foreshore of the harbour of St John's was at last made available for private occupation.[2] He also made a more determined effort than Gambier to save the Beothucks, whose story, however, is for the ethnologist or antiquary.[3]

The principal imports into Great Britain were sealskins, furs and seal-oil: codfish came irregularly and chiefly on its way to Spain and Portugal. A remarkable war feature was the great rise in direct importations of codfish into Spain during the Peninsular War—611,960 cwts. in 1811 and following years, as against a previous average of some 300,000. A growing trade with the United States was sharply checked by the non-intercourse policy (1808) and killed by the War of 1812. But the growth of trade with the West Indies seems to have been regular and natural: an average of 91,503 cwts. sent to them prior to 1805 became an average of 123,975 for 1811–15, and the quantities of molasses and rum shipped back by the schooners point the same way.[4] There is some evidence that the policy of the United States in and after 1808 gave an impetus to the trade between Newfoundland and the West Indies.[5] The first decade of the century had seen distinct progress.

In 1812–14 Great Britain and the United States were at war and Newfoundland prospered greatly. Besides abnormal prices for fish and oil, there was the profit from numerous prizes which were continually brought into St John's. The Governor's unceasing

[1] Prowse, p. 380.

[2] 51 Geo. III, cap. 45: "for taking away the public use of certain Ships' Rooms in the town of Saint John" (*sic*).

[3] Cf. *B.T.* 1, 63. See Howley, J. P., *The Beothucks or Red Indians, the aboriginal inhabitants of Newfoundland*, 1915.

[4] *Report of Select Committee of H. of C. on Newfoundland Trade*, 26 June 1817. Cf. *C.J.* of 1816, App. 11.

[5] Cf. *B.T.* 1, 64 with *C.O.* 137, 114–16.

vigilance kept the colony free from all danger of attack, though some damage was done on the Labrador coast, and a few sealing schooners were captured. Naturally every increase of prosperity meant some step forward in the consolidation of the colony. In 1813 a fund was raised to secure legal recognition of the right to erect private buildings on the lands in and around St John's. This action, urged by more than one Governor, had been frustrated by the selfish policy of the west country merchants. A certain Dr William Carson, who had in 1808 come from Birmingham to St John's, took a lead in the agitation, demanding the establishment of a civil government and a Legislature under a resident Governor; with which he closely linked "the appropriation and cultivation of the lands". The Home Government seized on the second limb of the recommendation and issued instructions for the lease and grant of lands, particularly near St John's. Some 110 grants were issued in the year 1813.[1] The Governor's report[2] in that connection is instructive:

St John's, with a population of nearly 10,000, seems to have grown out of its original situation, and to be changing its character from a fishery to a large commercial town, and for a considerable time past has offered such advantages to the farmer and gardener as to overcome all the restraints which nature and the policy of government had laid on the cultivation of a soil certainly less sterile than it has generally been considered.

Doubtless from that time dates the systematic importation of the lilacs and laburnums, the black currants and apple trees, so regular a feature even in distant outports of the colony.

The prosperity of war time was followed by the inevitable reaction. In 1814 an enormous fishery, a large catch of seals, and high prices marked the crest of the wave: the next year was also good, but then came the crash. Just as happened over a century later, with the first threatening of stringency the traders went to pieces. Though the fishery of 1816 was good, the low prices demanded cool and calm management, and this was absent. In such a crisis troubles not seldom come together. During the years 1815–18 there was scarcity amounting to famine, both in St John's and the outports, credit was contracted, and food-stuffs were short. A series of fires added their horrors. In 1816 the town, built chiefly of wooden houses, was almost destroyed by a fire. In 1817–18 "a frost that sealed up the whole coast commenced early in November, and continued almost without intermission through the entire season, and on the nights of the 7th and 21st November 1817 three hundred houses were burnt, rendering two thousand individuals, in depth of that cruel winter, homeless".[3] Outbreaks of lawlessness everywhere threatened property and life. The courage and resource of Captain Buchan, the senior naval officer on the station, alleviated suffering, and kept up the heart of the community to an extent which gives his name a definite place in the island

---

[1] Prowse, p. 655.   [2] *Ibid.* p. 399.   [3] *Ibid.* p. 405.

story. And other help was forthcoming: the Home Government sent
£10,000: Halifax contributed liberally: and Boston despatched a brig
with food supplies. A good seal fishery in 1818 brought fresh hope to
the colony, but recovery was slow. In September 1818 and again in
1819 bad fires ravaged the capital: yet ultimately they bore good
fruit in the attempt to improve the laying-out of the town.[1]

One result of all this trouble was the decision to appoint a Governor
as direct representative of the Crown. Admiral Francis Pickmore had
been ordered to remain in the colony, but he died during the severe
winter: his successor, Sir C. Hamilton, was the first resident Governor
definitely so appointed. He arrived in July 1818: for the first time, also,
a Governor's lady was in residence at Fort Townsend,[2] the barracks
on the north-west of the town, where the police headquarters now
stand. The new departure was in other ways opportune, for the life of
Newfoundland was bound up with the North Atlantic fisheries; and
two recent treaties had given the colony an unenviable position in
the wrangles of diplomacy which it retained for a century. In
1815 the final peace confirmed to the French fishermen their previous
rights to the fishing on the Newfoundland shores, despite the urgent
petition of the Newfoundlanders that all foreigners might be excluded:
in 1818 a convention was concluded with the United States which
gave them the liberty to take fish of every kind on part of the
southern coast of Newfoundland and up the western side into and
beyond the Straits of Belle Isle, with liberty for ever to dry and cure
fish in unsettled harbours.

The close of George III's reign coincides with a new era in the
political history of Newfoundland, which now definitely passed out of
the status of a mere fisheries centre. The old naval governors had out-
lived any justification: the obligation of residence led naturally to the
civil governor. In 1819 the flogging of two men at Harbour Grace
(the second town in the island) for alleged contempt of court brought
up the whole question of local administration, and eventually Parliament[3] empowered the Crown to establish a Supreme Court with
jurisdiction as complete as the High Court of Judicature of Great
Britain. The charter under this Act was issued in 1825, and in the
same year Sir Thomas Cochrane became the first civil governor: the
new Supreme Court was inaugurated with much *éclat* in January
1826. Cochrane threw himself with wise energy into the life of the
colony: he pressed on the public roads leading from the capital;
encouraged agriculture and projected better public buildings;
aroused interest in education; and generally showed a grasp of affairs
and capacity, which, aided by the feeling of public satisfaction at the
new departure, gave him a special reputation amongst the governors
of the colony. Nevertheless the agitation for a local Legislature con-

---

[1] By Act 1 Geo. IV, cap. 51.   [2] Prowse, p. 409 n.
[3] By Act 5 Geo. IV, cap. 67.

tinued. An Irishman, Patrick Morris,[1] became an active ally of Dr Carson; the movement spread to the best known merchants in St John's. The West of England still strenuously opposed any idea of granting a Legislature:[2] there was also opposition of a genuinely thoughtful character, as from the Roman Catholic bishop: but the reform could not reasonably be denied to a British colony. In 1832 Parliament passed an Act to grant a representative Assembly to Newfoundland: and instructions were issued to the Governor to summon a Council of six members which was to have legislative powers concurrent with those of the Assembly when constituted.[3] In the autumn the general election took place and a House of Assembly met early in 1833. The Council promptly distinguished itself by contending that the Assembly had no power to pass a Revenue Bill and, even after reference to the Home Government, persisted in a course of bickering and obstruction which, not too wisely handled by the officials of the Assembly, soon reduced the Legislature to a mere bear garden: two quarrelsome protagonists on each side, one of whom was the Chief Justice, involved both branches: the press and public meetings added fuel to the fire: the Council tried to cut down the Assembly's expenditure and threw out the Revenue and Supply Bills: the Governor by issuing warrants on the Colonial Treasury for civil expenses unduly strained his constitutional rights. All this discord and irregularity introduced a chronic state of irritation and ill-will into public life. The noisy extremists dominated the situation, and men of moderate views were hounded out of the colony. Sectarian dissension gave a new bitterness to the quarrels. Much of what is unseemly in the local politics of after years can be traced to this inauspicious beginning.

A change of Governors in 1834 failed to calm things down. The spirit of political disorder was rife, and when in 1836 the first Assembly expired at its statutory period, the new election presented a scene of disgraceful riot and outrageous personal assaults. The local law officers maintained that a second general election was necessary. Yet even when at last an Assembly was duly constituted, the quarrels between the two branches of the Legislature broke out anew in an aggravated form. An appeal to the Home Government seemed the only hope of salvation. A deputation (Carson, Morris and Nugent) was sent to England by the House of Assembly in 1837. The Chief Justice, the leader of the Council, was dismissed; in the opinion of some being made a scapegoat.[4] This did not bring peace. In the following year Kielly, a practitioner in St John's, came to high words with Kent, a member of the Assembly, who appealed to the House to vindicate his honour. Kielly was called to the bar of the House

---

[1] His pamphlets began in 1823; see bibliography.
[2] See Prowse, p. 428.
[3] Instructions to Governor, 1832: see App. to *Newfoundland Consolidated Statutes of* 1916.
[4] Prowse, p. 444.

and ordered to apologise and throw himself on its mercy. This he declined to do in the form dictated by the House, and was sent to gaol. On application to the Court he was released on the ground that the House had acted *ultra vires*. The Assembly then issued a warrant for the arrest not only of the alleged offender, but also of the Sheriff and the Judge concerned. The Governor by proroguing the Legislature put a stop to the farce. The question of the power of the Assembly came before the Supreme Court and eventually was carried to the Judicial Committee of the Privy Council which decided that, though the House of Assembly had every power reasonably necessary for the proper exercise of their function and duties, they had not the "exclusive privileges which the ancient law of England has annexed to the House of Parliament".[1] That decision was afterwards re-affirmed in all cases of similar claims by colonial Legislatures: without a local or imperial statute they are invalid.

Meanwhile the second Assembly had come to an end, and a serious election riot at Carbonear in 1840 led to the appointment of a Committee of Enquiry by the House of Commons. Governor Prescott was directed to dissolve the Legislature and return home to give evidence before the Committee. For nearly two years the constitution was suspended: there was no Legislature. Then as a temporary measure the Crown took power[2] to constitute by instructions to the Governor an Executive Council of advisers and to abolish the Legislative Council as a separate unit, its members being merged with those of the Assembly: the result was a single legislative chamber partly nominated—an arrangement which has been not infrequent in the colonies. Under James Crowdy, the Colonial Secretary, as Speaker, with a conciliatory and courteous Governor in Sir John Harvey, this Legislature worked tolerably well for the six years that it lasted. There was less personal squabbling and public business was more readily transacted.

Undue stress has been laid by some writers on these political outbursts. Despite them the colony was making solid progress. From about 1830 for reasons not easily determined the spring seal fishery was developed on new lines and steadily became a more profitable and enthralling enterprise; hard work and forethought were required for the preparations, and the winter instead of a period of drunken orgy became a season of activity and labour. A stout race of seamen and small owners was bred on the industry; the general standard of comfort was raised: the outports round Conception Bay and north to Fogo and Twillingate became flourishing centres.[3] Between 350 and 400 vessels annually sailed for the ice fields: their sailing and return became an occasion of excited demonstrations on the part of the entire

---

[1] *Kielly v. Carson* (the Speaker), 4 Moore, P.C. p. 63. The case is reprinted in App. to *Newf. Law Reports.* See also Prowse, p. 447.

[2] Acts 5 and 6 Vic. cap. 120.

[3] Prowse, pp. 450–1.

population, to whom the hazard of this chase peculiarly appealed. These vessels were afterwards used for the summer cod fishery on the coasts and off Labrador. The success of these fisheries is reflected in other developments. In 1834 the Government Savings Bank was established: in 1836 the newly chartered Bank of British North America opened a branch in St John's; and the first lighthouse was erected at Cape Spear. With the growing importance of the towns on Conception Bay came better roads. Round the Bay and across to Placentia and southward along the coast to Bay Bulls and Trepassey tolerable carriage-ways began to open up the country. A geological survey (by J. B. Jukes) was undertaken between 1838 and 1840, but, confined to the coast region, it resulted in a cursory report that there were no traces of coal-measures or minerals. The fisheries were still without a rival, and special legislation to aid the whale fishery was discussed in 1840. In 1842 steam communication with Halifax was established. Yet it was steam which was to alter the whole character of the development of the fisheries: when some twenty years later steamers became the chief agents in the seal fishery, the richer St John's merchants absorbed the trade at the expense of the outports: these gradually declined, and not till the Great War of 1914–18, when steam carriage was difficult to obtain, did they recover for a time a semblance of the prosperity which they enjoyed in those palmy days in the middle of the new century.

The contemporary records show that already the nucleus of administration was organised on exactly the lines subsisting to-day: stipendiary magistrates at the head of each district, customs officers protecting revenue, local constables, schools under religious control.[1] The religious life of the people had also in that decade received fresh stimulus. In 1839 Newfoundland was constituted a separate see, with Bishop Aubrey Spencer as first Anglican Bishop. St Thomas's Church was consecrated in 1840 and became the garrison church. A year later the foundation stone of the Roman Catholic Cathedral was laid by the Bishop, Dr Michael A. Fleming. In 1844 the appointment of Dr Edward Feild as Anglican Bishop began an era of indefatigable missionary effort embracing the whole island.

In the wood-built towns of North America fire was a special danger. In 1845 there had been disastrous fires at Quebec and Saint John, New Brunswick, to both of which Newfoundland had sent relief. On 9 June 1846, St John's was almost destroyed by fire within twelve hours. The two principal streets for a mile were blotted out. The premises destroyed carried all the names best known in Newfoundland enterprise. The disaster brought practical sympathy and aid from all quarters; and the citizens of St John's, thus encouraged, strove to replace the old town by something much better. With equal pluck they faced the damage done by a disastrous gale only three months later.

---

[1] See, for instance, *Journals of Assembly*, 1844.

In 1847 Sir John Harvey left Newfoundland and the old constitution was revived: but neither his diplomacy nor the disasters just mentioned had quenched the agitation for a more popular system of government. It received a special impulse from the dissatisfaction of the Roman Catholics at their treatment under the existing regime. In 1848 a new Roman Catholic bishop, Dr John T. Mullock, arrived, and, joining forces with P. F. Little, an able lawyer from Prince Edward Island, organised a "Catholic Liberal" party. Their first appeal to the Home Government, just after a new Assembly had been elected, elicited the reply that "the introduction of what is termed Responsible Government will by no means prove to [the colony's] advantage".[1] The bigger merchants preferred the Government of the Crown; and the Protestants were inclined to resist change simply because it was advocated by Roman Catholics of marked ability.[2] In 1852 the Home Government still held back,[3] but a change was near; three delegates visited England during 1853 and pressed matters on. In the Cape of Good Hope the grant of self-government was being accorded, and the more complete autonomy which had been given to the North American colonies was being conceded in Australia: it became invidious to withhold it from Newfoundland. In 1854 the British Ministry[4] were ready to grant responsible government as soon as certain preliminary conditions were satisfied, including proper provision for officers who would be displaced; but friction between the Governor and Legislature hampered progress,[5] and when eventually arrangements were made for enlarging the House of Assembly and forming new electoral districts,[6] no real pains were taken to provide on a sound basis for the representation of all classes of the colonists.[7] As a result the Roman Catholics were in a position to monopolise the Administration under the new constitution.

Early in 1855 Mr (afterwards Sir) Charles Darling was sent out as Governor, and lost little time in bringing the new regime into operation: he had not received his final instructions or all the instruments which he thought essential, but without waiting for these he formed what he called an *ad interim*[8] Administration on the basis of full ministerial responsibility, appointing under the instructions issued to him[9] an Executive Council (of Ministers) of not more than seven, and, on the nomination of Ministers, a Legislative Council of not

[1] P.R.O. Earl Grey, Sec. of State, 14 May 1849.
[2] P.R.O., despatches of Governor Le Marchant, e.g. 19 Nov. 1851; 13 Feb. 1852.
[3] *Ibid*. Sir John Pakington, Sec. of State, 3 Apr. 1852. Cf. Gov. Baillie Hamilton's despatches of 21 Feb. 1853 and 4 May 1853.
[4] *Ibid*. Duke of Newcastle, S. of S., 21 Feb. 1854.
[5] P.R.O., Gov. Baillie Hamilton's despatch no. 86, 23 Feb. 1854.
[6] Act 18 Vic. cap. 3, 30 Nov. 1854.
[7] Prowse, p. 467.
[8] P.R.O., Governor's Speech to Legislature, 4 Aug. 1855.
[9] *Newfd. Gazette*, 19 June 1855.

more than fifteen. The elected House of Assembly consisted of thirty members from ten electoral districts. In the first Assembly there was a marked religious cleavage. The Ministry, composed of able and enlightened politicians, with Little as Premier and Attorney-General, was dominated by the Roman Catholic element. The new ministers happened on good times: 1855 and the ensuing years were years of excellent fisheries and general prosperity, aided by the establishment in 1856 of telegraphic cable communication with the neighbouring continent.

There is a certain irony in the fact that during the very first year of the new constitution the principle of local autonomy which lies at the root of responsible government was violated in an extraordinary manner by the Home Government. To appreciate what actually happened it is necessary to review briefly the claims of the French. Owing to unsettled conditions and twenty years of war following the declaration of Versailles, it was not till after 1816 that questions could well arise. In 1824 the British Parliament passed an Act to enforce the treaty rights of France; it was continued from time to time up to 1834, when it was left in abeyance. The French by degrees became more aggressive in the assertion of their claims, and by 1844 they were pressing for clearer definition of their rights. Local negotiations led to discussions in Paris in 1846. These came to nothing, but were resumed in 1851 at the request of the French, anxious particularly to obtain the right of taking bait on the south coast. The outcome was a proposal for a compromise whereby the French should give up their rights along most of the west coast, but should acquire an exclusive right of fishery and the use of the strand for fishery purposes from Cape St John in Notre Dame Bay northward to the Quirpon Islands and so to Cape Norman, as well as to five named harbours on the west coast. British subjects were to be prevented from erecting any buildings on strands reserved to the French. There were further stipulations as to concurrent rights.

It is difficult now to imagine how a British plenipotentiary could propose, and a British Ministry contemplate, the permanent concession to a foreign State of an exclusive territorial right in a British colony. The incident illustrates the contemporary attitude of Englishmen towards the colonies: these were assumed to be ready to accept such obligations towards foreigners as the Central Government determined to be right. There was no clear thinking as to the claims of Newfoundland apart from certain fishing rights in its waters: nor did ministers realise that the right to discuss questions affecting the colony's territory was a corollary of the grant of responsible government. There was an immediate outburst in the colony. In the Legislature all parties and creeds joined in determined opposition to "any attempt to alienate any portion of our fisheries or our soil to any foreign power without the consent of the local Legislature".[1] They declined to assent to the terms of the convention. Delegations were sent to Canada to seek moral support and to England to protest against the convention. Promptly the Secretary of State announced that "the proposals contained in the Convention having been now unequivocally refused by the colony, they will of course fall to the ground...the consent of the community of Newfoundland is regarded by Her Majesty's Government as the essential preliminary to any modification of their territorial or maritime rights".[2] This formal statement did not end the squabbles and collisions between French and English fishermen, or the determination of the French to press extravagant claims to exclusive rights. For another half-century the peaceful development of the colony was hampered by restrictions on Newfoundland schooners in Newfoundland waters, by the French opposition to settlements on British soil, by attempts to enforce claims which were never contemplated by treaty. Much of the story of Newfoundland is written in terms of the ship and shore fisheries. Still, with the successful assertion of its rights in 1857, Newfoundland may be considered to have thrown off the leading strings. The ten years commencing with 1855 were a vigorous period which laid down the lines for the future.

The interior was very little known, but along the coasts the outports were steadily acquiring greater wealth and comfort, followed by the spread of religious establishments and education. Harbour Grace, one of the oldest British settlements, and Placentia, the old French capital, were fairly important towns and the centre of considerable trade. Trinity, Bonavista, Fogo, and Twillingate to the north, Ferryland, St Mary's, St Lawrence, and Harbour Breton to the south, were substantial settlements. Along the southern coast the Jersey "Rooms"[3] shared the fishery with the agents of big firms at the capital. St John's, an epitome of the colony, was the commercial centre and clearing house, the seat of the Legislature and Courts of Justice: it was also at that time a garrison town: daily between Fort William and Fort Townsend along Military Road marched detachments of troops. In the eastern quarter of St John's and near Government House were official residences of the principal military officers. Military society gave a stimulus and tone to social life which were lost a few years later when the Royal Newfoundland Companies—the "old red coats" as they were affectionately called—were finally disbanded and the garrison removed. Prior to that a short-lived volunteer force was raised early in 1860 and was prominent at the reception of the Prince of Wales (afterwards King Edward VII) later in that year.

From this too brief reference to the real life of the colony it is neces-

---

[1] Prowse, p. 474. The exact passage has not been traced in the Record Office, but the substance in much the same terms is repeated in the House of Assembly or in petitions from public meetings.

[2] C.O. 194/150, Labouchere's despatch no. 10, 26 Mar. 1857.

[3] Prowse, p. 450 n.

sary to turn to the squabbles of political parties, which, indeed, arise from causes deep down in the life of the people: they have had serious results in the public life and mentality of the Newfoundlander, and they have usually a direct bearing upon relations with the outer world.

The extent to which the Roman Catholics monopolised the first Administration naturally brought a reaction: the growing strength of the Protestant outports demanded a share of political power. In the elections of 1859 the Opposition had their first chance of bidding for it. The Roman Catholics called themselves the Liberals, the Church of England and other Protestants being dubbed Conservatives, but the names did not mean much. The Roman Catholics for the moment carried the day. The new Premier was John Kent, but the leading spirit of the Government was Mr (afterwards Sir) Ambrose Shea, the Speaker: both were able men, but lacking in stability. The Roman Catholic bishop threw the weight of his influence against them because they would not accept a contract for a steam service to which he had committed himself; so the "Liberals" were divided against themselves. The bad fishery of 1860 and ill-judged expenditure on poor relief led to further mischief. When the House met in the spring of 1861, dissension as to the application of relief moneys soon spread to other matters: but the break-up came in another way. The Prime Minister in the Assembly[1] openly accused the Governor of siding with the judges, the lawyers, and a minority of the House in opposing proposals of the Government as to the payment of salaries. The Governor called upon the Prime Minister for an explanation: the latter declined: the Governor dismissed the Ministry and requested the Opposition leader, Mr (afterwards Sir) Hugh Hoyles, to form one. This he did, and immediately asked for a dissolution. A general election gave him a good working majority, but left very sore feeling behind it. When on 13 May 1861 the Governor opened the new House of Assembly, he was hooted by the Roman Catholic section of the mob: the unelected candidates for Harbour Main forced their way into the House, and were ordered to withdraw: when one of them, Hogsett, was removed by the police, their supporters tried to break into the Chamber. Riots ensued—first in front of the House of Assembly, where the police had to clear the steps— then in the city generally, ending in an order to the troops to fire on the rioters. The unfortunate wounding of Father Jeremiah O'Donnell infuriated the mob: but the soldiers had shown great restraint, and the Roman Catholic prelate, Dr Mullock, successfully appealed to his excited congregation. Next day the city was comparatively quiet.[2]

This riot, following election riots at three principal centres, brought the struggle for religious ascendency in politics to a head. People

---

[1] Prowse, p. 488.
[2] Prowse (p. 490 n.) quotes a newspaper account which is not altogether supported by papers in C.O. 194/165.

were frightened: it was recognised that some compromise was essential.[1] From that date began the effort to make a fair adjustment of political patronage which has now resulted in an arrangement to divide everything from the Government downwards into equally balanced thirds, representing the three leading religious denominations, the Church of England, the Roman Catholics, and the Methodists. As regards the action of the Governor which in fact started all the trouble, there can be no question that it was amply justified. In such a case, the criterion by which to judge a Governor's action (i.e. the action of the Crown) is the extent to which a general election affects his new Ministry. On this occasion the response of the electorate was unequivocal.

This incident gives a particular place to the name of Sir Alexander Bannerman, whose term of office in other ways coincided with a very interesting period in the development of the colony—the completion of telegraphic communication with the outside world, the introduction of steam into the seal fishery and mail services, and the first conscious efforts to administer Labrador. Further, the opening of the Tilt Cove copper mine in 1864 raised the promise of a great industry. A year later Murray's geological survey was commenced, although such results as it produced belong to a later period, since it was spread over some twelve years and was at first naturally tentative.[2] In 1865 also an effort was made to lay an Atlantic cable to Newfoundland: the cable broke, and the work was thrown back a year: but when in 1866 the *Great Eastern* successfully landed a new cable, the 1865 cable was also picked up and landed at Heart's Content, which is still the chief cable station of the colony.

The educational development of the whole community was closely linked with the efforts of the religious denominations, and had now reached a point at which more regular progress was possible. Bishop Feild's energy—backed by the Colonial and Continental Church Society incorporated in 1862—had made the little missionary schooner *Hawk* an institution in all the waters of the colony: with the outports in mind he established a Church of England Academy (now Bishop Feild College) on the lines of an English public school and reorganised the Theological College. A Bishop coadjutor was consecrated in 1867— the more necessary because of the responsibility for Bermuda, linked to Newfoundland by diocesan administration as well as by close business associations. The Roman Catholics had enjoyed a line of remarkable prelates in O'Donel, Fleming, and Mullock, and their school, St Bonaventure's College, lately instituted, aimed at the highest Roman Catholic ideals. The Wesleyan Methodists were rapidly becoming a powerful body, and the Scots Church met the needs of some of the most successful settlers.

---

[1] Cf. Prowse, p. 491.
[2] Murray, A. (and Howley, J.), *Geol. Survey of Newfoundland.*

Thus Newfoundland was on the threshold of a new era, when the question of federating the North American Provinces came up for serious discussion. The story of federation is told in the following chapter. The Home Government was anxious that all North American colonies should accept the new regime—and it has been suggested that the new Governor of Newfoundland, Mr (later Sir) Anthony Musgrave, quite expected to bring his ministers to that view. However, they showed great caution: when in September 1864 they were invited to the Conference at Quebec, they accepted as a matter of courtesy only, and sent Mr (afterwards Sir) Frederick Carter, the Speaker, and Ambrose Shea, the leader of the Opposition, as a delegation to observe and report without agreeing to anything. At the beginning of 1865 the question was brought before the Assembly, which deferred discussion until after the next election in the autumn. Carter had become Prime Minister in the course of the year, and his Government was sustained at the general election by a large majority. It was his duty to bring the question of joining the proposed Union before the new House, and he did so promptly and fairly. It was worthy of discussion in a temperate and thoughtful manner, but a remarkably vigorous opposition gradually developed, and finally the anti-federation party preferred to rely on exciting an ignorant electorate. Extraordinary tales were circulated about grinding taxation, and the terrors of the "desert sands of Canada". The outport fishermen were thoroughly frightened.[1] Charles F. Bennett, who led the opposition, was capable of discussing the question from the higher point of view,[2] but lent himself to the electioneering method, and appealed even to the Irish hatred of the Union with Great Britain. For four years the question stood in the forefront of political thought, and at the election of 1869 became the test question. The overwhelming victory of its opponents was a decisive negative. Yet there was a confident expectation in Canada that Newfoundland must enter the Dominion: and for some years in various official publications it appears as a province of Canada with information on the same lines as for other provinces.

How far it is the interest of Newfoundland to join the Canadian Dominion is not exactly a matter for the historian. A small community thoroughly well governed may be a happier and more competent member of political society than if its interests are merged in those of a larger area: individuality in the State as with persons has great advantages. On the other hand it is difficult in a small community to obtain that constant succession of high-minded and unselfish statesmen who really make for good government. It is common to hear enlightened men in Newfoundland sigh for the return of the sound and stable administration which Crown government usually secures.

---

[1] Prowse, p. 495.
[2] See his pamphlet on the financial aspect, pub. in 1870 (C.O. Library).

CHAPTER XVIII

THE COMING OF CONFEDERATION

SOON after Britain recognised the independence of the United States, dreams of uniting those northern remnants of America which remained in British hands began to take form. Early proposals, however, were evidence of optimism in the advocate, rather than the result of political exigency or economic necessity. The proposals were generally imitative of the federal union in the neighbouring Republic, and usually the chief argument advanced in their support was the assertion that the colonies united would be less liable to absorption by the United States than the colonies separate. This argument drew its strength from memories of the revolutionary struggle, reinforced by the bitterness engendered by the War of 1812; it was sustained by the spectacle of a clamorous "manifest destiny" finding piecemeal fulfilment as the years went by, and it finally proved tellingly effective in the time of stress during and after the American Civil War. But until the middle of the nineteenth century the provinces were engrossed in the task of laying local foundations, social, economic, and political, without which no union of the whole, at any rate no free union, could be effected. The isolation of the several provincial communities, and their lack of unifying interests, the result of mingled factors of race, geography, and pioneering conditions, rendered the earliest proposals essentially futile. Durham, it is true, envisaged a united British North America as the ultimate goal of British and colonial statesmanship, but he was compelled to realise that for the time being the obstacles were insurmountable. Nevertheless, in his Report, he sounded strongly the note of British-American nationality as an aim for the future, necessary, he thought, in order to give the people of the provinces a worthy political existence, off-set the preponderance of the United States on the continent, and ensure the permanence of British institutions in North America. He appreciated the close relation there must be between railway building and political consolidation and emphasised the need for an intercolonial railway to draw the provinces together.

The annexation agitation of 1849 in Canada was countered by the formation of a British American League, which proposed as the best antidote to annexation the union of all the provinces. But as the league was dominantly Conservative, its advocacy of federation was weakened by the partisan source of the proposal. Hence its overtures to leaders in the Maritime Provinces on behalf of union were ineffective, even had the time been ripe.[1] Nevertheless in Nova Scotia James W. Johnstone, Opposition leader, introduced a resolution in the Assembly in 1854, approving of "the union or confederation of the British Provinces on just principles" and authorising the Government to confer with the Governments of the other provinces and with the Imperial Government respecting the proposal. Joseph Howe, however, believed political union impossible until the provinces were more closely connected physically by the building of railways; it might then follow naturally. He did not oppose the ideal, but seized the occasion to make a brilliant but non-committal speech on the larger question of closer organisation of the Empire. No division was asked for upon the motion. Nova Scotian interest in the subject continued to live. In 1857 James W. Johnston, now Premier, and A. G. Archibald, sent to England on provincial business, were instructed to bring the subject of union before the Secretary of State for the Colonies. Labouchere was indifferent. In the absence of a united request from the colonies the Government would not feel warranted in dealing with the question.

The apparent indifference of the Colonial Office to the proposal on this as on former occasions is hardly surprising, for the physical barriers in the way of political union were too great, the resulting administrative and economic advantages too slight, the political problems and dangers to be overcome too trivial and immaterial, to warrant the expenditure of much energy upon the question. But the time was now rapidly approaching when it would become a live political issue, the focus, indeed, of British North America's most pressing problems. In the later 'fifties and early 'sixties there developed a complex array of factors much more diverse and impelling than before, which stimulated the growth of interest in the idea. In the Province of Canada, as has been seen, the party game was becoming increasingly difficult to play under existing rules and conditions, the clash of sections, the racial rivalry, the jealousies of religious groups threatening eventually to render responsible government unworkable. The essential and permanent duality of the province was becoming ever more apparent, and therefore the need of constitutional readjustment more obviously urgent. Upper Canada, passing Lower in growth of population and wealth, was increasingly jealous of the latter's retention of that equal share of legislative power which it enjoyed under the Union, while Lower Canada was unwilling to part with the safeguard of its interests which that equal share ensured; and the economic distress of the late 'fifties accentuated the political dissatisfaction. As early as 1856 the Reformers of Lower Canada advocated in the Legislature the transformation of the existing union into a truly federal relationship between the two sections. Three years later the same expedient was supported in a resolution adopted at a

[1] Howe to Moffatt, 8 May 1849, *Speeches...of Joseph Howe* (ed. Chisholm, J. A.), II, 25.

Reform Convention in Toronto, at which time Lower Canadian Liberal members of the House, unable to attend the Toronto meeting, issued a manifesto supporting the proposal. While some of the supporters of this proposal were, as will be seen, urging the acquisition of the North West by the Province of Canada, the inclusion of the eastern provinces in a general federation was not yet advocated by the Liberal party; indeed, A. A. Dorion, on the floor of the House in 1856, and the resolutions of the Toronto Convention in 1859, expressly set aside the latter idea as impracticable.

Meanwhile, however, the idea of a union that should include the Maritime Provinces was winning ground. Outstanding among its advocates at this stage was Alexander Morris, a brilliant young lawyer, who lectured in Montreal early in 1858 on "Nova Britannia"; his glowing account of the growth and possibilities of British North America, from the Atlantic to Vancouver Island, along with his ardent prophecy of its political unification, was widely distributed afterwards as a pamphlet, and constituted a most effective bit of educative propaganda. In the same year the federation ideal first found a leading place in the programme of a provincial government. For this A. T. Galt, with the approval of Governor Head,[1] was responsible. He presented to the Assembly resolutions in favour of a federal system which should take in not only the Canadas but also the eastern provinces and the western territories. Although the ensuing debate elicited little support for the resolutions, within a few weeks he found his opportunity. Taken into the Cartier-Macdonald Government at the time of the "Double Shuffle" to help secure its stability, he made it a condition of his entrance that the question of federating all the provinces should be taken up officially. Overtures were shortly made to the British and Provincial Governments, and when Cartier, Galt, and Ross were sent to England to confer with the British Government on various matters, they were charged with the duty of following up this question. Arguing from both the constitutional difficulties of Canada and the desirability of removing danger of absorption by the United States, they presented confidentially a scheme of federation, similar in outline to that finally adopted, and they urged that the Home Government should instruct the provinces each to appoint delegates to discuss the subject. Bulwer Lytton, the Colonial Secretary, showed so much coolness towards the proposal that Galt felt it advisable to warn him against placing difficulties in the way of federation by pointing out that the only alternative for the provinces lay in "ultimate absorption in the United States".[2] While no formal indication of sympathy could be elicited from the Colonial Secretary, his final word to the Canadian Government avoided

---

[1] Martin, C., in *Can. Hist. Assoc. Report* for 1929.
[2] Galt to Lytton, confidential, 22 Nov. 1858, in Skelton, O. D., *The Life and Times of Sir A. T. Galt*, pp. 251 f.

equally any hostile expression and based the refusal to sanction a conference upon the reluctance of Her Majesty's Government to commit the Maritime Provinces "to a preliminary step towards the settlement of a momentous question, of which they...[had] not yet signified their assent to the principle".[1] The Canadian Government did not at once drop the question. For a little while they hoped, though vainly, to get favourable action by the other provinces. Galt, in England in the following winter, was instructed again to seek British sanction for a conference. But Newcastle, Colonial Secretary in the new Palmerston Ministry which had replaced Derby's in the summer, apparently gave him no encouragement.[2] Meanwhile, also, the Cartier Government had weathered the difficulties which had helped to give to Galt's proposal its temporary prominence. Yet henceforth union was a subject of more frequent discussion by both politicians and public than ever before.

Champions of the cause found in 1860 a uniquely favourable opportunity, when the youthful Prince of Wales made his celebrated visit to North America, under the wing of the Colonial Secretary. If the tour was educative to the prince, it was no less so to his mentor. Friends of union made the most of the occasion. For example, upon the party's landing at Halifax, P. S. Hamilton followed up notable earlier pamphleteering on the subject by addressing to the Duke of Newcastle an open letter urging him to enquire into the state of feeling among the colonists concerning the question of provincial union. During the succeeding weeks the duke used his eyes and ears to good effect. Soon this topic became the subject of legislative consideration, although this time the scene was not Canada but the Maritime Provinces. Dr Charles Tupper, upon whom was falling the mantle of James W. Johnston, felt that advocacy of the proposal was again in order. In November 1860 he lectured at Saint John, New Brunswick, on "The Political Condition of British North America", and extolled the advantages attainable by union of the provinces. It would, he claimed, establish a British North American nationality which could later include the great West, and, besides elevating the tone of public life and strengthening defence, would bring freedom of interprovincial trade and economy in administration, and render concerted action possible in the "vitally important question of intercommunication". The address, warmly supported on this occasion by Premier Tilley of New Brunswick and J. H. Gray, leader of the Opposition there, soon gained wide publicity, as it was reported fully in the press and repeated at Halifax and other centres in Nova Scotia. Tupper believed, however, that union of the Maritime Provinces, Nova Scotia, New Brunswick and Prince Edward Island, was more immediately

---

[1] Lytton to Head, 26 Nov. 1858, Pub. Arch. Can. *Series G*, vol. CLVIII. Printed in Skelton, pp. 252 f.
[2] Galt to Newcastle, 18 Jan. 1860, Pub. Arch. Can. *State Book U*, pp. 650 ff. See also Head to Newcastle, 13 Feb. 1860, *Series G*, vol. CDLXIII.

feasible, that it promised advantages in trade and economies in administration, and would be a step towards the larger union. On this more practicable if less rosy theme he delivered a lecture the next evening at the town of Portland, near Saint John.[1]

The Government of Nova Scotia did not wish to leave to the Opposition a monopoly of the expression of these high hopes for the future. In the next session of the Legislature Joseph Howe, the leader of the Government, introduced, on 15 April 1861, a resolution referring to the discussion in all the colonies of the question of a union, either of all the provinces or only of the Maritime Provinces, and to the necessity of consultation among the leading men of the colonies, and with the Imperial Government, if the obstacles were to be overcome. He therefore moved that the Colonial Secretary and the other provincial Governments be communicated with "in order to ascertain the policy of Her Majesty's Government, and the opinions of the other colonies, with a view to an enlightened consideration of a question involving the highest interests, and upon which the public mind in all the provinces ought to be set at rest".[2] The resolution was passed unanimously, but the Government was steering doubtfully through manifold political difficulties, and having taken the wind from the Opposition's sails in this matter was content to let the subject drop for the time. Thirteen months, indeed, passed before any such action as was foreshadowed in the resolution was taken. It so happened that the intervening period was crowded with developments which tended to create, both in the provinces and in Britain, a more favourable atmosphere for consideration of the union idea.

It will be recalled that the decade just closed had been a period of rapid and extensive railway building in British North America. There had been great accomplishment, but more was needed. While Canada had now an extensive railway system in the Grand Trunk, and Nova Scotia and New Brunswick both had short lines of their own, all efforts to arrange for the financing of a connecting intercolonial railway across the intervening sparsely populated and unproductive Appalachian upland had hitherto failed. The other outstanding fact in the railway situation in 1861 was the failure of the Grand Trunk to realise the sanguine hopes of its promoters. Numerous favours from the provincial treasury had not sufficed to place it on its feet financially. The generosity of the Canadian public was now exhausted and the growth of traffic under existing conditions was not sufficient to promise adequate relief.

For the salvation of the Grand Trunk several things must be done. Whether further governmental aid could be obtained or not, there must be reorganisation of the management to secure the maximum economy of operation, and steps must be taken to increase traffic.

---

[1] Tupper, Sir C., *Recollections* (1914), pp. 14 ff.; Saunders, E. M., *Life...of Sir Charles Tupper*, I, 80; Saunders, E. M., *Three Premiers of Nova Scotia*, pp. 343 ff.
[2] *Journals of Assembly, Nova Scotia* (1861), p. 125.

Would not the latter be accomplished if an intercolonial railway could be built to link Canada with the Maritime Provinces and the Grand Trunk with their ports? So thought Messrs Baring Brothers, who were not only financial agents for Canada, along with Messrs Glyn Mills and Co., but were also the most important London financiers behind the Grand Trunk. Edward W. Watkin, whom the share-holders now elected to represent them as superintending commissioner to clear their troubles, held such views, and already had the hope of further revivifying the Grand Trunk by securing such an extension of communications westward to the Pacific as would not only bring about the settlement of the West and produce a growing traffic with that region, but would also, as forming the shortest route between western Europe and the Far East, reap golden profits from the growth of a heavy and lucrative oriental trade. Before accepting the com-mission Watkin had several long interviews with Newcastle, who was now enthusiastic about the possibilities of the future development of the provinces through which he had recently travelled,[1] and eager that the British Government should lend assistance to the proposed intercolonial railway, although he felt that the undertaking must first secure satisfactory backing by the provinces.[2]

When Watkin, joint lieutenant of the Barings and their associated interests and of Newcastle, arrived in the provinces in the summer of 1861, his first task was to investigate the administration of the Grand Trunk. Its affairs he described as an "organised mess",[3] but under a new manager, C. J. Brydges, it was not long before they were in much more orderly shape. As further financial assistance from the provincial Government could not be looked for and the western project would as yet be premature, Watkin set himself to re-vive the plan of an intercolonial railway. In this he was so far successful that negotiations were resumed among the provincial Governments. In September under Grand Trunk auspices a joint delegation from the Governments of New Brunswick and Nova Scotia toured Canada (going *via* Portland, and from Detroit on to Chicago) so as to become acquainted with Canada and Canadians.[4] At Quebec, on 30 September, the delegates met in council with members of the Canadian Administration and it was resolved to renew to the Imperial Government the offer of October 1858 to aid in the construction of an intercolonial railway, and to send delegates to England to press the project upon the attention of the Home Government.[5]

Having accomplished this much, Watkin hastened back to England to pave the way for the coming of the delegates. He records that in

[1] Watkin, Sir E. W., *Canada and the States: Recollections*, 1851–86, chap. i; Trotter, R. G., *Canadian Federation: Its Origins and Achievement*, ch. xiii.
[2] Crawford to Lords of the Treasury, 25 Feb. 1862, *Brit. Parl. Papers*, H. of C. (1862), ccix, 5.
[3] Watkin, p. 519.   [4] Trotter, pp. 187 f.
[5] Minute of Council, 30 Sept. 1861, *State Book W*, p. 407, in *Brit. Parl. Papers*, H. of C. (1862), ccx, 16.

numerous interviews with Newcastle concurrence was reached in a programme for building a railway under an imperial guarantee, and it was further agreed to make a start as soon as possible at "Pacific transit" across the West, also that some solution should be sought for the difficulties involved in the position of the Hudson's Bay Company, and that the federation project should be pushed.[1] When the delegates arrived they were presented by Watkin to the duke. After some discussion a memorial was prepared by the delegates for Newcastle to lay before the Cabinet. This was presented to him on 2 December, but prompt consideration of it was prevented by the Cabinet's absorption in the crisis over the *Trent* affair. Only after the delegates had returned home to attend the meetings of their respective Legislatures did their proposals receive full consideration, and then they were rejected.[2] Although the delegation of 1861–2 failed in its official mission, its presence in London was marked by steps towards the formation of a permanent organisation there to promote British North American interests and constitute a regular means of communicating with the Government. Howe drew up its prospectus before his departure and shortly afterwards the organisation was effected. This British North American Association comprised a large number of the financial leaders in the City and received as well subscriptions from Nova Scotia, New Brunswick and Canada. Although organised primarily for business convenience it later proved a valuable means of focussing interest upon the federation project and securing support for it.[3]

The economic desirability of the Intercolonial Railway, viewed from whatever angle, was as great as ever. And by events of the winter the old argument that it would be useful for defensive purposes had gained new and effective point. The spectacle of some thousands of troops, sent from Britain after the *Trent* affair, driving several hundred miles in sleighs in the depth of winter in order to reach the posts of need in Canada, was a dramatic revelation of the delays and perils involved in the then backward interprovincial communications. Thus, although the negotiations of the winter of 1861–2 had fallen through, hope of their renewal survived. Watkin was in Canada in the winter and again for a short time in the early summer, but the Cartier-Macdonald defeat in May precluded any immediate renewal of formal interprovincial negotiations. In September, however, a notable conference was held at Quebec, when delegations from the Governments of Nova Scotia and New Brunswick met with representatives of the Canadian Government. Encouraged by a further statement from the Colonial Secretary as to what the British Government was willing to do, and by the informed optimism of Watkin, who returned to Canada for the meeting, the conference agreed upon a new proposal for sharing

[1] Watkin, pp. 80 f.
[2] Newcastle to Monck, 12 Apr. 1862, *Brit. Parl. Papers*, H. of C. (1862), ccx, 22.
[3] Howe to Thomas Baring, 31 Dec. 1861, Pub. Arch. Can. *Baring Papers*.

the burden of building the railway and decided to send delegates again to England.[1] This conference of September 1862 considered several other problems of common concern, all of them closely related to this subject. One of these was the question of forming a commercial union of the provinces, which had been discussed sporadically for several years. To the members of the conference the benefits to be derived from the lowering or removal of tariff barriers among the provinces were obvious, and they felt them to be an "indispensable consequence" of the building of the Intercolonial Railway, but the question was postponed because the Nova Scotia and New Brunswick delegates felt that the Maritime Provinces could not then afford the loss of revenue which would be involved.[2]

The conference also took up the question of political union. Significantly, this was now done with the approval of Downing Street. Although immediate action in the direction of carrying out Howe's resolution of April 1861 had seemed inexpedient to the Nova Scotia Government, the developments of succeeding months had given the question renewed importance, and the resolution had at length been transmitted to the Colonial Secretary in May 1862 with the opinion that in view of the growing feeling in favour of some sort of union there should take place a meeting of "leading men of the different provinces...in the hope that...some practical scheme...[might] be devised to which the public attention...[might] be directed in the future consideration of the subject".[3] Newcastle's reception of the overture was cordial, in contrast with his marked coolness towards Galt's advances little more than two years previously. His reply voiced appreciation of the importance of the two measures alluded to in the resolution, Maritime union and union of all the provinces, and expressed the view that a proposal for the adoption of either "should emanate in the first instance from the Provinces". He gave assurance that "if a Union...should hereafter be proposed with the concurrence of all the Provinces to be united...the matter would be weighed by the [British] public...Parliament, and...Government, with no other feelings than an anxiety to discern and to promote any course which might be the most conducive to the prosperity, the strength, and the harmony of all the British Communities in North America".[4] Upon the authorisation thus obtained Howe acted promptly, suggesting to the several Provincial Governments that it would be well if the question could be taken up at Quebec and "be set at rest by such a formal discussion as would promote such a

---

[1] 12 Sept. 1862, *State Book X*, p. 536. Printed in *Brit. Parl. Papers*, H. of C. (1864), DXXX, 3.
[2] Howe to Newcastle, draft, 13 Sept. 1862, Pub. Arch. Can. *Howe Papers*, VIII, 316 ff. See also *Brit. Parl. Papers*, H. of C. (1864), DXXX, 13.
[3] Mulgrave to Newcastle, no. 47, miscellaneous, 21 May 1862, *Journals of Assembly*, *N.S.* (1863), App. no. 17.
[4] Newcastle to Mulgrave, *N.S.* no. 182, 6 July 1862, *ibid.* Also in Pope, Sir J., *Confederation Documents*, pp. 303 f.

union, if there be any general desire to effect it, and save much time, if there was not".[1] At Quebec it was concluded that the question should be postponed, as it could be more conveniently taken up after the Intercolonial Railway should have prepared public opinion for union by increasing intercourse among the provinces.[2]

Defence has already been mentioned in its bearings upon the transportation problem. In other respects also it was linked in this year to the affairs of the provinces as a group. In May the Canadian Legislature, by defeating the Militia Bill of the Cartier-Macdonald Government, seemed, in the eyes of much British opinion, to repudiate Canada's due responsibilities. Better, it was said, let so indifferent a colony go its own way. It was a burden, not an asset. But Newcastle, unwilling to assent to the theory that the colonies should be set adrift, proceeded to cope with the militia problem in a constructive spirit. In a despatch to Monck he made several suggestions, among them stressing the desirability of a uniform system of militia training and organisation for the provinces, which Her Majesty's Government would institute if assured that it would be acceptable to their people. "The political union of the North American Colonies", he added, "has often been discussed. The merits of that measure and the difficulties in the way of its accomplishment have been well considered, but none of the objections which oppose it seem to impede a union for defence. This matter is one in which all the Colonies have interests common with each other and identical with the policy of England". He wished to know the attitude of the Canadian Government and suggested that Monck consult with the Lieutenant-Governors of Nova Scotia and New Brunswick, who were to be at Quebec for the approaching conference of delegates.[3] The conclusion reached, both by the Canadian ministers and by Monck and the Lieutenant-Governors, was that means of communication were not yet "sufficiently easy to enable the three provinces beneficially to avail themselves of the services of a common head to their militia forces". Monck did not himself "believe that the move would be acceptable either to the Canadians or to the inhabitants of the Lower Provinces".[4]

In accordance with the railway agreement reached by the provincial representatives at Quebec, delegates soon went to London to negotiate further. While Howe and Tilley were interested mainly in securing an intercolonial railway, the Canadian delegates, Sicotte and Howland, had been instructed to insist upon associating with it negotiations for the extension of communications westward to the

---

[1] Howe to Dorion, Tilley, Pope, respectively, 14 Aug. 1862, and replies from Parent and Tilley, *Journals of Assembly, N.S., loc. cit.*

[2] Howe to Newcastle, draft, 13 Sept. 1862, *Howe Papers*, VIII, 316 ff.

[3] Newcastle to Monck, no. 163, 21 Aug. 1862, *Series G*, vol. CLXVIII, in *Brit. Parl. Papers* (1862), [3061], pp. 40 ff.

[4] Monck to Newcastle, no. 147, 30 Oct. 1862, *Series G*, vol. CDLXIV, pp. 315 ff., in *Brit. Parl. Papers, loc. cit.*

Pacific, a project more popular than the intercolonial with most Canadians, who had already a satisfactory winter outlet by way of Portland (Maine). Watkin, in close touch with the delegates, was working for both schemes. The western phase of the story will be dealt with in the next chapter. Here it should be noted that the Canadian delegates were disappointed in their hope that the British Government would consider any Canadian expenditure upon an intercolonial railway as a contribution towards imperial defence; and they declined at the last minute to agree to the sinking fund stipulated by the British Government as a prerequisite to its guaranteeing a provincial railway loan. Nova Scotia and New Brunswick were ready to proceed, and there was much acrimonious controversy with the Canadian Government over its insistence that negotiations must now begin again *de novo*. The project, however, was by no means dead. Before many months plans were made to determine the feasibility and cost of the road by an exploratory survey, which, after some unsuccessful bickerings, the Canadian Government on its own responsibility at length entrusted to Sandford Fleming, an engineer of experience and a believer in a future united British North America.[1]

Meanwhile circumstances provided the propagandists for political union with arguments by which a most effective appeal might be made to the general public. As the American Civil War went on, the people of the Northern States became increasingly hostile. The provincial authorities and the Administration at Washington co-operated in amicable efforts to avoid trouble, but public feeling was largely beyond their control, especially when, despite their efforts, Canada was made the base for attacks upon the North.[2] Expressions of American hostility awoke in the provinces dread of violent consequences. Fear also grew lest, even if the mailed fist were withheld, there be a fulfilment of threats to abrogate the Reciprocity Treaty of 1854 and withdraw the bonding privilege under which colonial goods crossed American soil by rail without paying duty. As time went on it became obvious that the former of these threats was liable to be carried out, in part from economic motives but largely with the hope of making the position of the provinces untenable and inducing them to seek economic salvation in annexation to the United States. The assumption that the provinces were perforce dependent upon American favour for economic prosperity, and could be coerced by withdrawing that favour, proved erroneous. It was used as an argument for establishing interprovincial free trade, which would be a natural accompaniment of federation, and as an added reason for an intercolonial railway, which would give relief from the necessity of using the American roads.[3] The fear of military aggression, however, both

[1] Trotter, pp. 198 ff.
[2] MacDonald, Helen G., *Canadian Public Opinion on the American Civil War*, pp. 112 f., 187 ff.
[3] *Ibid.* pp. 199 f.; Trotter, R. G., "Some American Influences upon the Canadian Federation Movement", *Can. Hist. Rev.* Sept. 1924, p. 223.

came earlier than the economic fear, and also carried more weight with the mass of the people.

The man for the occasion was D'Arcy McGee, orator and poet, once a malcontent in Ireland, now a patriot in British America. In the press and on the platform, in the Maritime Provinces as well as in Canada, he bore the standard of a "new nationality", and everywhere he effectively rang changes on the idea that a federal union of the provinces under the Crown was "the only means to perpetuate a future connection between Great Britain and the trans-oceanic Provinces of the Empire".[1] He emphasised the danger of American aggression, more, indeed, than the Reform press thought justified by facts, but the Conservative Opposition, into whose ranks he had been driven by Sandfield Macdonald's enmity and drawn by John A. Macdonald's skilful overtures, took in general a gloomy view of the helplessness of the province in its existing state of defence. For the most part, however, they made this view the basis of attacks upon the policy of the government of the day rather than used it as an argument for hastening the consummation of a union of British North America. As late as 1861 John A. Macdonald had expressed views favourable to future union, when attacking in the Assembly a proposal for representation by population.[2] But in the elections since that time the project had formed no part of the programme of the Conservatives as a party, or indeed of any party, as such, in the Province of Canada.

Yet the only hope of real cure for the now chronic political deadlock in that province seemed to many to be constitutional change of some sort. With sentiment in Upper Canada becoming overwhelming in its demand for "rep. by pop.", and with sentiment in French Canada still adamant in its resistance to a surrender of its rights by such a change under the existing union, there was a growing possibility that the idea of a general union might be taken up seriously by politicians of opposing parties as a way through the threatening impasse. When, in March 1864, Sandfield Macdonald felt compelled to abandon his attempt to carry on the government, both Lord Monck, the Governor-General, and he hoped that a coalition might now be formed to grapple with the constitutional question. But the hope proved impossible of present fulfilment, and the Conservatives, who took office under Taché and John A. Macdonald, were carefully non-committal upon the fundamental issue, both in its provincial and its wider implications, although they were ready to seek "a more intimate commercial union" with the other provinces and to favour the development of communications both eastward and

---

[1] McGee, T. D., "A Plea for British American Nationality" and "A Further Plea for British American Nationality", *British American Magazine*, Aug. and Oct. 1863; his *Speeches and Addresses, Chiefly on the Subject of British American Union*; and Skelton, Isabel, *Life of T. D. McGee*, pp. 419 f.

[2] Pope, Sir J., *Memoirs of Sir John A. Macdonald*, 1, 228 f.

westward,[1] measures which were widely held to be more fitly the prelude than the outcome of political union.

Meanwhile, in the Maritime Provinces, efforts had begun, which, though local in their first intention, nevertheless tended to promote the confederation of British North America. The leaders, in despair of getting constructive co-operation regarding a railway from the succession of precarious governments in Canada, and convinced that a general political union, even if desirable, was at best a remote possibility, had now revived the project for a legislative union of their three small provinces. By it they hoped to secure considerable economies and improvements in government and to create a more respectable sphere for the exercise of political talents, as well as provide an enlarged market for the budding industries of their artificially separated communities. Early in 1864 resolutions were accepted by the respective Legislatures authorising the appointment of delegates to consider union of those provinces "under one Government and Legislature".[2]

News of what was being planned down by the sea reached the legislators at Quebec before the shift of government there in March. Some, at least, of the advocates of federation were admiringly envious of the forward step of the Maritime leaders and were eager to emulate it. But gloomy as they might feel about their own situation, constitutional change was nevertheless in the air. The first move had already been made by George Brown, who had come to see that "rep. by pop.", for which he had led so loud a clamour, could be obtained for Upper Canada only as a part of some larger scheme which would offer at the same time safeguards to Lower Canada. Hoping to gain the support of the Conservative leaders who half a decade earlier had advocated a general federation, he had moved for a select committee on the constitutional question in such phraseology as to link it skilfully with their former proposal. His resolution came up again for discussion in May, and although, because of its sponsor, some of the oldest friends of federation found convenient excuses to withhold their support, it was nevertheless carried, by the first vote favouring constitutional change since the present difficulties had arisen. The committee, drawn from all parties, and including several men who for one reason or another had opposed Brown's motion, reached almost unanimous agreement that the most promising remedy for Canada's constitutional ills lay "in the direction of a federative system, applied either to Canada alone, or to the whole British North American provinces". And when they reported to the Assembly on 14 June they felt that they had made sufficient progress to warrant

---

[1] Monck to Newcastle, no. 43, 31 Mar. 1864, and enclosure from *Quebec Chronicle* of 31 March, *Series G*, CDLXV, 61 ff.
[2] Gray, J. H., *Confederation*, p. 17; Whelan, E., *Union of the British Provinces*, p. 4; Tupper, *Recollections*, p. 39; Hannay, J., *Sir Leonard Tilley (Makers of Canada)*, pp. 69 ff.

their recommending that the subject be again referred to a committee at the next session.[1]

Postponement of the issue, even for so brief a time, proved unnecessary, for on the very day on which Brown's committee reported the Taché-Macdonald Government fell. The coalition which had proved impracticable in March now, after a week of negotiation, became a reality. Within less than twenty-four hours of the defeat and chiefly through Alexander Morris, of "Nova Britannia" fame, who was now a Conservative member and an eager unionist, word had been passed from Brown to the Conservative leaders that he was willing to co-operate with any government that would set itself to a final settlement of the constitutional difficulties. A Conservative caucus decided in favour of attempting a coalition,[2] and the House was treated to the astounding spectacle of the ancient enemies, Brown and John A. Macdonald, conversing amicably in the middle of the floor. Formal negotiations followed, in which Galt, Cartier and Taché joined, and continued until Wednesday, 22 June, when the result was announced. The meticulous detail of the "Ministerial Explanations"[3] then read to the House, in English by Macdonald, and in French by Cartier, strikingly evinces the need felt by these old foes of guarding most explicitly their reputations for political integrity throughout the negotiations. During these epoch-making deliberations the Government's representatives kept in close touch with their colleagues, and Brown with his political friends. The question at issue being more than that of Brown's personal adherence, he had to carry with him his group of Reformers. Sandfield Macdonald and some other Upper Canadian Reformers would not go with him, nor would those of Lower Canada, French or English, but the votes of the Upper Canadian group whose allegiance he could count upon promised to ensure stability to the Administration.

Two questions had to be thrashed out: upon what programme could the Conservatives and Brown's Reformers unite, and what should be the relation of the latter to the Government? As to the programme, Brown was at first reluctant to support the federation of all the provinces, since, though he believed "it ought to come, and would come about ere long", he held that "its adoption was uncertain and remote". He would have liked to insist upon his old remedy of representation by population in the existing Province of Canada, but the others were sure that no government could carry such a measure, and that the only likely basis of settlement lay in the federal principle suggested by the report of his committee. While they preferred first to attempt its application to all the provinces, Brown and his friends wished the effort to be concentrated on the narrower

[1] Mackenzie, A., *Life...of Hon. G. Brown*, pp. 85 f., 221 f.
[2] *Globe*, Toronto, 16 June 1864.
[3] In full in Pope, *Macdonald*, 1, 344 ff. Following quotations are from this document unless otherwise noted.

project of federating the two Canadas. Eventually a satisfactory compromise was reached, by which the Government pledged itself

to bring in a measure next session for the purpose of removing existing difficulties by introducing the federal principle into Canada, coupled with such provisions as will permit the Maritime Provinces and the Northwest Territory to be incorporated into the same system of Government; and...[to] seek, by sending representatives to the Lower Provinces and to England, to secure the assent of those interests... beyond the control of our own legislation to such a measure as may enable all British North America to be united under a General Legislature based upon the federal principle.

Concerning the relation which Brown and his followers should bear to the Government there was also much discussion, due, on the one hand, to Brown's personal repugnance to becoming a colleague of men whom he had so bitterly opposed, and to the Reformers' feeling that they should have half of the places in the Cabinet, while, on the other hand, the Government negotiators and the Conservative caucus insisted upon Brown's entrance into the Cabinet as the best guarantee of the support of his friends, and argued that half the Upper Canadian seats in the Cabinet were all that could be granted. The caucus of Upper Canadian Reformers decided almost unanimously to accept the proposed programme and three Cabinet posts, urging, however, that Brown should accept one of these. Brown's reluctance was at last overcome, partly by the tactful persuasions of the Governor-General, Lord Monck, who, indeed, had been active throughout the crisis as a genial apostle of conciliation.[1] When the successful outcome of the negotiations had been announced, the necessary business of the session was speedily concluded and on 30 June the Legislature was prorogued, the *Gazette* forthwith announcing the names of the new ministers—George Brown, Oliver Mowat, and William McDougall. As soon as the ministerial by-elections had been held, the Government "diligently applied themselves to the great object of the coalition".[2]

The problem to be attacked was ready at hand. Decision whether to promote first a federation of all the provinces or to start with a federation of the Canadas was made easy by the situation in the Maritime Provinces. Correspondence with their Governments shortly made it clear that at the approaching conference, which was arranged to meet on 1 September, Canadian delegates would be welcomed to present their proposals, but also that the Maritime delegates had not been authorised to deal there officially with any wider proposal than that of local union.[3] Such informal opportunity as the conference would afford offered sufficient opening if the Canadians could be ready with their case. They set themselves in earnest to its preparation. In addition to such study as was given to the problem by

---

[1] Trotter, R. G., "Lord Monck and the Great Coalition of 1864", *Can. Hist. Rev.* June 1922.

[2] Pope, I, 265 ff.

[3] The correspondence is in *Journals of Assembly, N.S.* (1865), App. 3. For Monck's report on it see Monck to Cardwell, no. 124, 26 Aug. 1864, *Series G*, vol. CDLXV.

Ministers individually, the Cabinet as a whole devoted a series of council meetings in August to discussing, under Brown's presidency, the issues involved.[1]

Meanwhile the education of the public to a British North American outlook was proceeding apace. In August a large number of Canadians enjoyed a unique excursion to the Lower Provinces. Its originators were McGee, who knew the Maritime Provinces from his lecturing tour of 1863, and Sandford Fleming, who was now in charge of the exploratory survey for an intercolonial railway. Alike painfully aware of the mutual ignorance or aloofness of the peoples concerned, they conceived the happy idea, in conversation at Quebec shortly before the coalition was formed, that an excursion of Canadian legislators to the seaboard would bring mutual knowledge, promote good will and co-operation, and facilitate union. Fleming secured invitations to the Canadian Legislature from the boards of trade of Saint John and Halifax. Even then the plan would have fallen through had not McGee and his friend Ferrier of the Legislative Council, a director of the Grand Trunk, moved to bring that railway to the rescue. Ever alert to seize opportunities in the cause of wider vision and common feeling among the provinces, C. J. Brydges, the Grand Trunk's general manager, invited the members not only of both Houses but of the Canadian press as well to go down as guests of the railway. The route was by train to Portland, Maine, and thence by boat. More than a hundred members of the Legislature and representatives of the press availed themselves of the invitation. McGee was the only Cabinet Minister to do so, as the rest of the Coalition remained at Quebec to work on the federation problem. The excursionists reached New Brunswick early in August and spent two weeks there and in Nova Scotia, being welcomed everywhere with marked cordiality. At the festivities in honour of the guests there was much enthusiastic talk of the proposed union of the provinces. Both in visitors and in hosts the intercourse bred a new sense of the largeness of their common interests, and the reports borne back to Canada did much to educate the public there. It would have been hard to conceive a more desirable preliminary to the official negotiations soon to follow.[2]

The Governments of the three Maritime Provinces, in selecting delegations to represent them at the Charlottetown Conference, all approached the problem without partisan spirit and appointed men of both parties. In Nova Scotia, however, Joseph Howe, still the most important Liberal in the province though no longer a member of the Legislature, felt compelled regretfully to decline Tupper's invitation to act as a delegate, on the ground of his pressing duties as a fishery

---

[1] Mackenzie, p. 227; Skelton, Isabel, p. 518.
[2] Burpee, L. J., *Sandford Fleming, Empire Builder*, pp. 90 ff.; Skelton, Isabel, pp. 516 ff.; Saunders, *Tupper*, 1, 99 f.

commissioner under the Reciprocity Treaty of 1854.[1] The Maritime delegates assembled at Charlottetown on 1 September, and decided to postpone consideration of Maritime union until the Canadians should have an opportunity to present their ideas. The latter arrived from Quebec aboard the Canadian Government steamer *Queen Victoria*. The party comprised eight members of the coalition ministry, including Macdonald and Cartier, Brown, Galt, and McGee. The newcomers were given the floor on 2 September and proceeded for two full days to outline the proposed union and argue its advantages. Then followed several days of "free and frank discussion".[2] There was unanimous conclusion that a "Confederation of all the British North American colonies would be highly advantageous to all the provinces, provided equitable terms...could be agreed upon", and it was felt that no insurmountable obstacles to an agreement had been encountered. Tentative agreement was reached that the union should be federal, that population should form the basis of representation in the Lower House of the Federal Parliament, and that the Upper House should comprise equal representation from each of the three regions: Upper Canada, Lower Canada, and the Maritimes. Some progress was made in defining the respective shares of central and provincial governments and also in regard to other matters, but all features were left open for full and free discussion *de novo* at Quebec.[3]

At Charlottetown, and later at Halifax and Saint John, the delegates attended banquets where toasts were drunk to the success of the union cause and speeches of varying degrees of exuberance were made. Men were caught up by the rapid sweep of recent events. The goal loomed near and sure of attainment. John A. Macdonald seemed to voice the general opinion among the leading men of the several provinces when he said at Halifax: "I have been dragging myself through the dreary waste of colonial politics. I thought there was no end, nothing worthy of ambition, but now I see something which is well worthy of all I have suffered in the cause of my little country.... There may be obstructions, local prejudices may arise, disputes may occur, local jealousies may intervene, but it matters not—the wheel is now revolving and we are only the fly on the wheel; we cannot delay it—the union of the colonies of British America under the Sovereign is a fixed fact".[4] By the time the Canadian delegates rejoined the *Queen Victoria* for the return trip to Quebec, which they reached 18 September, they had gained a new respect not only for the natural resources and possibilities of development of those provinces, but also for the intelligent and thrifty quality of their people and their public life. Men like George Brown, who had

[1] Chisholm, II, 434 f.
[2] Tupper, p. 40.
[3] See "Confederation of British North America", in Montreal *Gazette* of 23 Sept.; also Mackenzie, p. 228, and Gray, pp. 29 ff.
[4] Whelan, p. 43.

doubted whether it was yet really worth while to make an effort to attract the distant and insignificant "Maritimes" into a union with Canada, doubted no longer.[1] Apart altogether from any mere question of the convenience which their accession might be in helping to solve the constitutional tangle in the Province of Canada, it was obvious that those little provinces could bring no mean contribution to the national life of a united British North America.

When the date set for the Quebec Conference approached, the *Queen Victoria* was sent to convey the Maritime delegates and their wives and daughters to Quebec as guests of Canada. In due course there gathered at the historic old capital delegations from Nova Scotia, New Brunswick and Prince Edward Island, all bi-partisan, as they had been at Charlottetown, and also two representatives of Newfoundland, and on 10 October 1864 the epoch-making conference, comprising these representatives and the full Coalition Cabinet of Canada, began its deliberations.

The records[2] of the proceedings of this body are scanty, but it would be a mis-reading of the evidence to assume from that fact that the assembled statesmen were blind to the importance of the work to which they had set their hand. The seeming haste with which agreement was reached is more apparent than real, for, although the Quebec Conference spent only three weeks at its task and on some days sat but a short time, as a matter of fact most of the spade work was accomplished elsewhere. The subject, it must be remembered, was no new one. It had received more or less careful study for years at the hands of a chosen few. Galt, especially, had for a long time devoted his comprehensive and subtle mind to mastering the inherent problems and shaping practicable solutions. In lesser degree McGee and other Canadians and such Maritime leaders as Tupper and Tilley had already made themselves more than superficially acquainted with the question before the events of 1864 brought it into the foreground of political activity. In the past few months there had been the deliberations in Brown's committee, then the work of the Coalition in preparation for the Charlottetown Conference, and the informal discussions at that gathering. Upon returning to Quebec the Canadian Ministers had continued their consideration of the subject, as they had agreed to present to the approaching conference a scheme of federation in all its details.[3] Their special labours did not end even with the convening of the full conference, for they continued to meet by themselves as occasion permitted in order further to thrash out details for presentation to the larger body.[4] Not only has

---

[1] Canada, *Parl. Debates . . . on Confederation* (Quebec, 1865), p. 97.
[2] See Pub. Arch. Can. *Macdonald Papers*, especially those in Pope, *Confederation Documents*: also A. A. Macdonald's "Notes on the Quebec Conference", ed. by A. G. Doughty in *Can. Hist. Rev.* March 1920; Gray; Whelan, and *Debates on Confederation*.
[3] Whelan, p. 17.
[4] Mackenzie, p. 228; Pope, *Confed. Docs.* p. 8.

regret often been expressed at the paucity of the records left by the "Fathers of Confederation" as to the course of their work in Cabinet and in conference, but there has been astonishment at the apparently casual attitude with which they approached their task. It may be borne in mind, however, that they were following their accustomed tradition of informal Cabinet procedure so far as their foundation work was concerned, and even in the Conference they were thinking, as the very slightness of the record shows, rather of the practical results they were arriving at than of leaving to posterity a detailed view of the process by which the results were attained. Since what they did would receive its technical validity through an ordinary Act of Parliament, they were in a sense merely doing virtually what all of them had done many times before on a lesser scale, when drafting the basis of a bill for legislative consideration.

Yet, scanty though the record may be, it is still sufficient to enable one to reconstruct the main course of discussion in the Conference and to appreciate the chief problems which were there encountered. The press was denied admittance, as at Charlottetown. The chairman was the veteran Canadian Premier, Sir Étienne Taché. Voting was by provinces, each province having one vote, Canada being considered for purposes of voting as two provinces. Most of the resolutions proposed by the Canadian Ministers were brought in printed in groups as "Draft Resolutions" for the better convenience of the members of the Conference.[1] Although a great many of these were accepted without modification it would be a mistake to suppose that the Conference provided merely a rubber stamp for the proposals of the Canadians. A number of the more important points not only aroused vigorous discussion but were settled with grave difficulty and only by compromise.

The first formal decision was to endorse the formation of a federal union. It was already clear that only by the preservation of provincial governments could union be made at all acceptable either to the French Canadians or to the Maritime Provinces. A unitary, or, as it was then generally styled, a legislative, government for the proposed union would be worse in the eyes of Cartier and his followers than the "rep. by pop." which they dreaded for the existing Canada, while federation, by contrast, had the advantage that it would leave French Canada free to maintain and develop her individuality. In the eyes of the Lower Canadian ministerialists the addition of the Maritime Provinces was attractive as an off-set to Upper Canada. Maritime feeling was so strong that, as will be seen, it almost wrecked the federation project. It would certainly have blocked a legislative union. But there were some, of whom Macdonald was the most prominent, who did not conceal their preference for the latter type. Since it was not feasible, however, they stressed the necessity of giving the paramount

[1] Examples of these are in *Macdonald Papers*, "Confederation 1", pp. 286 ff.

power to the Central Government, arguing that the calamitous civil war then being waged in the United States and still threatening the possible disruption of the Republic was chiefly the result of the wide extent and sovereign nature of the power of the individual States. With this view there was, indeed, general agreement. In the division of powers, therefore, between central and local authorities, the "residual powers", those not specifically allotted to either, fell to the Central Government, in contrast to the course followed in the constitution of the United States. By entrusting to the Federal Government the power to disallow provincial acts, hitherto exercised by the British Government, it was expected also to reinforce the central authority. It was assumed that, should disputes arise over jurisdiction, they would be settled by the existing imperial tribunal.

Accustomed to legislative supremacy, and realising that federation would be technically brought about by an ordinary Act of Parliament, the "Fathers" took for granted that any alterations in the scheme that the future might demand would be secured by regular legislative procedure. Great as might be the step which they were planning they did not think of it as revolutionary but as evolutionary. Thus their task was also simplified by continuing in the provinces the type of responsible government to which they were already accustomed and adopting the same type for the new Federal Government. In a sense the application of parliamentary government to a large federation was a bold venture of faith, but to most of the "Fathers" it seemed the natural way.

Although British and colonial institutions largely formed the basis of the new scheme, these offered no suggestion for solving the strictly federal aspects of the problem. Here the experience of the United States proved helpful. The problem of representation was solved, as it had been in the Republic, by basing representation in the Lower House upon population and in the Upper upon equality of sections. While these sections in the United States were the individual States, in the new federation they were to be Upper Canada, Lower Canada, and the three Maritime Provinces considered as one section, Newfoundland to receive additional members should it come in. This question of the distribution of members in the Upper Chamber occupied three days and nearly broke up the proceedings. Its successful solution was the outstanding compromise of the Conference. Discussion waxed warm, too, over the mode of choosing the members of the Upper House. Should they be appointed or popularly elected, and if the former, by provincial or federal authority? Election was rejected because it was felt that two elective Houses were incompatible with the responsible Cabinet system. It might, moreover, lead to a demand for representation by population in the Upper as well as the Lower House. Nor was there serious support for the principle of provincial appointment except by Prince Edward Island.

Appointment by the federal Government therefore won the day, to be based in the first instance upon provincial nominations but thereafter made with a free hand. The Upper House was not intended to be a rival of the Lower in power or importance; it was relied upon, however, to safeguard sectional interests, to serve as a useful legislative check, and to ensure due representation of property and of conservatism in the federal Parliament.[1]

The financial problem proved peculiarly difficult, and upon that rock also the Conference almost went to pieces. If the Central Government was to receive practically all sources of revenue, except direct taxation for local purposes, a grave difficulty would be created for the Maritime Provinces, which had no municipal system and no direct taxation, and so were accustomed to meet local needs from the provincial treasury. The Canadians, already used to local taxation, and in the habit of letting turnpike companies build many of their roads, found it hard to appreciate the situation in which those provinces would be placed. But after protracted discussions by a special committee a compromise was reached. The Central Government was to take over the provincial debts, up to certain fixed limits, and out of the federal revenues grant annually to the provinces, in consideration of the transfer of their powers of taxation, a sum equal to eighty cents per head of the population according to the census of 1861. It was further agreed that the Central Government should assume responsibility for the prompt construction of an intercolonial railway: this was a *sine quâ non* to the entrance of the Maritime Provinces into a union. Canada, however, being more interested in the westward development of communications that would tap the trade of the new American West and hasten the opening of the British North West, would shoulder the Intercolonial Railway only if the "Maritimes" would sanction this westward development as well. The latter was therefore declared to be a subject of the highest importance to the proposed federation, and accordingly to be undertaken as soon as finances would permit.

Upon leaving Quebec the delegates visited the chief cities of Upper as well as Lower Canada, finding everywhere an enthusiastic welcome and making the most of the opportunity to educate public opinion. The project won prompt approval from the British press, and, with minor exceptions to certain details, from the Colonial Secretary, Edward Cardwell,[2] who had recently succeeded Newcastle upon the latter's retirement on account of ill-health. More than two years were to pass, however, before it proved possible to carry out Cardwell's suggestion that delegates should proceed from the provinces to London to co-operate in the drafting of a bill upon the basis of the Quebec Resolutions.

[1] MacKay, R. A., *The Unreformed Senate of Canada*, ch. iii.
[2] Cardwell to Monck, no. 93, 3 Dec. 1864, *Brit. Parl. Papers* (1865), [3426], pp. 11 f.

The least difficulty was encountered in the Province of Canada, where, in February and March 1865, after a debate of some weeks, the Legislature agreed to the "Resolutions" and adopted an address requesting the Imperial Government to pass legislation embodying their provisions. The debate is justly famous. Explained and defended in masterly fashion by the best minds of the Coalition, the federation proposals were also subjected to searching analysis and vigorous attack by those who believed them impracticable or undesirable. Upper Canadians were naturally almost unanimous in support of a scheme that would gain for their section the long desired "rep. by pop.", although some of the "Grits" adhered to their earlier programme of a federation limited to the two Canadas. Among Lower Canadians there was naturally more difficulty, because the French would be in a minority in the new federal Government and the English in that of the French province. The most vigorous opposition came from Lower Canadian Liberals, both French and English. A. A. Dorion voiced the hostility of those who thought the Intercolonial Railway was sheer waste, and all the worse because its construction might be of some assistance to the Grand Trunk Railway and was favoured by that Company and its friends. Christopher Dunkin, in a remarkable effort which occupied many hours, subjected the whole scheme to a most meticulous and critical examination. The chorus of opposition from Lower Canadian Reformers was augmented by a group of French-Canadian Conservatives who were afraid of placing Lower Canadian interests, even in general matters, in the hands of an English majority. But Cartier's strong hold upon his followers, reinforced by the influence of the Church, was sufficient to quiet the fears of most of the French, while Galt's assurances to his English-speaking Protestant compatriots in Lower Canada that their interests would be safeguarded carried great weight with them. The bulk of Conservatives there, of both races, thus supported the federation project. In both Houses of the Legislature the address was adopted by large majorities.

The Maritime delegates had been so confident of the success of the Quebec scheme that at an adjourned meeting of the Maritime Conference held at Toronto on 3 November they had decided to postpone the question of the smaller union.[1] But when they reached their homes, their rejoicing was changed to foreboding. Already opposition was active. Its causes were not difficult to see. The natural instinct of the smaller community against coalescing with the larger that might exploit it, and dissatisfaction with the proposed financial terms, found common voice in the popular slogan that the people were being sold to Canada at eighty cents a head. The Lieutenant-Governors of Nova Scotia and New Brunswick were hostile and lent their encouragement to opposition. It was sufficiently disappointing to those

---

[1] *Journals of Assembly*, N.S. (1865), App. 3, p. 30.

who had set their hopes on the scheme's success that Prince Edward Island and Newfoundland should fail to accept it, but the cause was lost unless the tide could be turned in the mainland provinces. And lost it soon seemed to be when, in New Brunswick, the key province geographically, an election in March resulted in the overwhelming defeat of the Tilley Administration and with it of the cause of federation. In the circumstances, to bring on the issue at once in Nova Scotia, where Howe had become a leader of opposition, would be to ensure defeat; Tupper therefore dodged it by securing the passage of a motion to renew negotiations for Maritime union.[1]

In little more than a year New Brunswick changed its mind, and in a second election (May–June 1866), reinstated the federationists. Diverse influences co-operated to produce this second turnover.[2] On sober second thought many New Brunswickers decided that, after all, the terms of union were not altogether unfavourable. The promised Intercolonial Railway would mean more to this province than to any other. The British Government was convinced that the Quebec scheme ought to be passed, partly by arguments in its behalf by a Canadian delegation which visited London in 1865, partly by the influence of London financiers with a heavy stake in provincial economic development, and partly by its own desire to simplify the North American problems of the Colonial Office, the War Office and the Foreign Office. It did not conceal its attitude, but urged federation repeatedly in official despatches. It withheld approval from renewed proposals for Maritime union except as a part of the larger scheme. Lieutenant-Governor MacDonnell was replaced at Halifax by Sir William Fenwick Williams, popular as a Nova Scotian and as the hero of Kars, and a staunch believer in federation. Lieutenant-Governor Gordon of New Brunswick, on a visit to England, became a convert to the cause.

The situation in the United States was a powerful aid. Abrogation of the Reciprocity Treaty was at last definitely decided upon in January 1865, to take effect at the earliest date possible under the terms of the treaty, which would be 17 March 1866. Attempts to avert it by securing a renewal of reciprocity arrangements before that date failed. Even at an international commercial convention held at Detroit, in July 1865, to consider the possibility of a new treaty, and when resolutions were adopted in favour of it, political antagonism to the provinces found a voice. At British suggestion a Confederate Council of Trade was formed representing the provincial governments, to provide a means of provincial participation in the diplomatic efforts of the British Government. The Council failed to effect its main purpose, but took the initiative in sending a joint trade commission in the fall of 1865 to study possibilities of trade developments in the West Indies and Brazil which might afford some

[1] Saunders, *Tupper*, I, 114 ff.   [2] Trotter, *Canadian Federation*, pp. 126 ff.

compensation for the threatened loss of the United States market. It was obvious that such missions would be more effective if they represented a single government, rather than a group of separate provinces.[1] A further effect of the Republic's policy was to strengthen the feeling that there must be free trade among the provinces, which federation would bring. And, in so far as abrogation was associated with the desire of certain Americans to induce the inhabitants of the provinces to welcome annexation, it not merely failed of its purpose, but strengthened the determination to find some other way to economic salvation. These developments could not have been better timed to exert a maximum effect upon New Brunswick opinion. And to cap the climax came the Fenian scare. Following the close of the Civil War the Fenians in the United States conceived the unhappy notion that the way to free Ireland was to attack Britain in her American provinces. Their threats of invasion were voiced openly for months, and in the spring of 1866 they gathered in menacing numbers, armed and well officered, on the Canadian and New Brunswick borders. While the invasion on the Niagara border, when it came in June, proved a fiasco, and on the New Brunswick border the United States authorities finally prevented hostilities, great excitement if not panic prevailed in the provinces, and proved to be a godsend to the federationists in New Brunswick. Again when the Fenian crisis became acute, the provincial Government resigned, practically forced out of office by Gordon. In the election thus precipitated the Fenian scare was effectively used to convince the people of the necessity of union.

The victory of the federation cause in New Brunswick made it possible to move ahead. Nova Scotia as well as New Brunswick appointed delegates to go to England to discuss the matter further with delegates from the Province of Canada and with the British Government and to draw up a basis of union. After some delay the London Conference opened at the Westminster Palace Hotel on 4 December 1866. It took the Quebec Resolutions as the basis of its work, and the London Resolutions, which it adopted before Christmas, were in general on similar lines although modified to meet objections which had been raised in the provinces.[2] The term "federation" was replaced by the less appropriate word "confederation", apparently because of the looser connotation of the latter. In view of the Maritime demand the pledge in regard to the building of the Intercolonial Railway was made more explicit and a distinct provision included for an imperial guarantee in aid of it. Federal subsidies to the provinces, also, were somewhat increased. And on Galt's motion a clause was inserted guaranteeing to Protestant or Roman Catholic minorities in both sections of old Canada the rights regarding separate schools enjoyed previously to federation. When the London Resolutions had

[1] Rogers, N. McL., "The Confederate Council of Trade", *Can. Hist. Rev.* Dec. 1926.
[2] Pope, *Confed. Docs.* pp. 94 ff., 305 ff.; Gray, pp. 385 ff.

been agreed to by the provincial delegates under Macdonald's chairmanship, there followed shortly further sessions under the chairmanship of Carnarvon, the Colonial Secretary in the new Derby Government. Other British officials, as well as Lord Monck, who had gone over for the purpose, assisted at this stage in preparing the measure for Parliament. To meet British objections the pardoning power was transferred from the provincial Lieutenant-Governors to the Governor-General as the direct representative of the Crown, and the number of members in the Upper House was made slightly flexible as a possible advantage in avoiding deadlock. Provision concerning governments which would have to be set up in the new Provinces of Quebec and Ontario had been made in the last session of the Canadian Legislature and was embodied in the bill.[1] The choice of a name for the new Confederation was made at this stage. The title "Kingdom of Canada" would probably have received the preference but for Lord Stanley's suggestion that the monarchical term might offend the republican susceptibilities of the United States.[2] There is a well-authenticated tradition that Tilley pointed out the special appropriateness with which the old term "Dominion" might be applied to the continental federation of the future in view of the word's use in Psalm lxxii—"He shall have dominion also from sea to sea, and from the river unto the ends of the earth".[3]

The course of the bill through the Imperial Parliament was altogether unexciting. Sponsoring it in the Lords, Carnarvon made a speech marked by enthusiasm, understanding, and vision. In the Commons it received the intelligent support of men of both parties who were familiar with British North American affairs either because of official associations with colonial matters or through their financial connections with the provinces. But the rank and file seemed to know little and care less about the whole subject. A delegation from the Opposition group in the Maritime Provinces had come to England under Howe's leadership and had campaigned vigorously and virulently against union. By asserting that the will of a people had been over-ridden Howe had won some sympathy, notably from John Bright, who lifted his voice against the bill in Parliament. But the campaign had no chance of success against a measure which promised so much more convenience for Downing Street and so much greater security and opportunity for British investors. The British North America Act became law on 28 March 1867. A supplementary measure, the Canada Railway Loan Act, authorised an imperial guarantee of interest on a Canadian loan of £3,000,000 for the construction of the Intercolonial Railway. On 22 May a Royal Proclamation declared that the three provinces, Nova Scotia, New

[1] Pope, *Confed. Docs.* pp. 89 ff.
[2] Pope, *Macdonald*, 1, 313.
[3] L. P. D. Tilley (son of Sir Leonard Tilley) to George S. Holmested, 28 June 1917, Pub. Arch. Can.

CHAPTER XIX

EXPANSION OF THE DOMINION, TO 1880

THE vision of those who, in choosing the name Dominion, saw their land in prospect stretching "from sea to sea" was in 1867 still very far from realised. The new Confederation would be an achievement of relatively slight consequence if it remained restricted within the bounds of the original four provinces, while on the other hand its expansion to the continental limits would ensure it a great and significant future. Prophets of the "new nationality" like Alexander Morris and D'Arcy McGee had pictured the wider vision in glowing terms. Brown and McDougall had long and ardently preached westward expansion, and numerous political and business leaders in the country appreciated its desirability and believed in its practicability. It may well be that many of those who joined in the celebrations on 1 July 1867 hardly expected the Dominion to grow territorially in the immediate future, but to-day, when one surveys all the attendant circumstances, one finds little cause for surprise at the rapid movement of events which soon added to the new Canada the great North West, the Pacific coast, and Prince Edward Island.

Active Canadian interest in the West was of comparatively recent origin. While it is true that in the French period and in the earlier years of British rule Canadian activity in the western fur trade had been strikingly large, it had ceased after the absorption of the North West Company by the Hudson's Bay Company in the 'twenties and the latter's virtual abandonment of the old Canadian trade-route that the Nor'westers had used. Then for some decades Canadian energies were concentrated upon the task of absorbing a heavy immigration, transforming a straggling frontier into a compactly settled community, and securing a large measure of political autonomy. By the middle of the century enough of this task had been done for Canadians to lift their eyes to spy out new areas of activity farther afield. At this juncture the growing dissatisfaction among the settlers at Red River made itself heard, and there came, from various causes, an awakening in Canada to the wealth of natural resources in the West. From 1847 onwards Brown's Toronto *Globe*, and before long McDougall's *North American*, merged in a few years with the *Globe*, published articles and editorials the general purport of which was to point out that this western country was of great value and that Canada should challenge the validity of the Hudson's Bay Company's regime there and win a chance to share in the advantages of its development. Through the 'fifties the need of action, unless the opportunity was to be lost, became increasingly urgent, for that decade saw the population of Minnesota increase from less than 5000, at its organisation as a Territory in 1849, to more than 172,000 in 1860, two years after its admission as a State of the American Union. St Paul, the Minnesota metropolis, became also the metropolis for the Red River country, with which communications were so relatively easy that from 1858 the Hudson's Bay Company itself employed that route for much of its traffic. The inauguration of steamer navigation on the Red River in 1859 measurably improved connections between St Paul and the British North West.[1]

Informed of these developments as they progressed, the Toronto business community, as well as journals of the city, were stirred to larger ambitions to compete with American enterprise by the establishment of Canadian connections, and rejoiced when the whole subject of the past, present, and future of the North West came into the limelight through the British parliamentary enquiry of 1857 into the affairs and the governing powers of the Hudson's Bay Company.[2] Interrogation from the Company in regard to the renewal of its licence in the North-Western Territory, as distinct from Rupert's Land where its rights were by charter, precipitated the enquiry, as, in view of the dissatisfaction among the settlers at Red River and the Canadian desire for an opportunity to take part in the exploitation of the West, the British Government decided that the licence should not be renewed until the whole question had been studied thoroughly. The Canadian Government was invited to present its views to the select committee, and in doing so it argued the need for the rapid opening of the West by Canadian enterprise and over a Canadian route, if the expanding United States settlements were not to imperil the British hold upon the western country. It further contended that because of early French-Canadian activities in the West, the rightful boundary of the Province of Canada lay at least as far west as the Rockies and possibly at the Pacific. Moreover, Canada challenged the validity of the charter under which the Company operated. After hearing a great mass of evidence from many quarters the committee refused to commit itself on the points of law involved concerning the boundary and the charter. It held that in such country as was best fitted for the fur trade the Company should continue to exercise a monopoly beneficent in its effects upon the Indian population, but it expressed the hope that arrangements might be made under which, as rapidly as it became practicable for the settlement of any given region to proceed, a way might be found for its equitable cession to Canada. The region west of the Rockies should ultimately be joined with the colony of Vancouver Island.

Changes of government in Britain and the insistence of the Canadian

[1] Hartsough, Mildred L., *The Twin Cities as a Metropolitan Market: A Regional Study of ...Minneapolis and St Paul*, pp. 24 f.
[2] Trotter, R. G., *Canadian Federation: Its Origins and Achievement*, especially pp. 234 ff., 249, 253.

authorities upon their technical contentions prevented any agreement being reached under which the British Government might have been willing to renew the Company's licence, and it therefore lapsed in 1859, the Company continuing, however, to exercise a *de facto* jurisdiction beyond the bounds of Rupert's Land except in the colony of Vancouver Island, which, in accordance with a recommendation of the committee, was withdrawn from under the Company's aegis.

While public opinion in Canada was being educated by such proceedings to a greater appreciation of the western problem, some of the business leaders and the Government were proceeding to action in the interest of the province. The task of gathering data for the Canadian case before the British select committee aroused the provincial Government to the desirability of exploring forthwith the possibilities of establishing regular communications with the Red River. A party was sent out that very year, and in the next season, 1858, its work was followed up by further exploration both of the route from Lake Superior to the settlement and also beyond in the region of the Assiniboine and Saskatchewan Rivers. The explorations would probably have been carried still farther west had there not already been an official British party exploring the passes through the western mountains. In 1858 and 1860 the Government also procured reports on the feasibility of a canal from the St Lawrence to Georgian Bay *via* the Ottawa-Lake Nipissing route, which it was expected would assist in drawing the expanding trade of the new American North West into Canadian channels as well as shorten the distance from Montreal to Red River.

A transcontinental railway on British soil had found its occasional advocates almost since the earliest days of steam railways, and for a Government ̶e̶n̶ persons had attempted to demonstrate its practica- hey proceed ̶ ̶the settled parts of Canada itself were supplied, or t and Tele ̶th the new means of transport, a westward extension of the provincial system attracted the promoters' interest, though the deplorable financial condition of the railways in the old-established settlements was hardly calculated to encourage the private investor or the provincial or British Government to wholesale speculation in a new line through the wilderness. While in 1858 a Toronto group headed by Allan Macdonnell secured a company charter to construct lines of railway between navigable waters and thus provide facilities from the Great Lakes to the Pacific, it proved impossible to obtain the necessary backing to carry through the project. As a more modest venture another Toronto group, led by W. McD. Dawson and Lewis Moffatt, placed a steamer on the upper Great Lakes and proposed a wagon and steamboat route to Red River. They received provincial grants towards opening the communication and for carrying mails. A mail service was inaugurated by steamer and canoe and in winter by courier and dog-sled, but was very irregular, and operations were abandoned in 1861. And their further plan for a North West Transit Company to carry mails and passengers by wagon and steamboat across the continent, while its political advantages were appreciated by both Canadian and British Governments, failed to draw from either sufficient promises of financial aid, even by way of postal subsidies, to make the project practicable.

The advocates of North West transit gained new strength and courage as a result of Watkin's visit to Canada in 1861 in the interests of the Grand Trunk Railway. Mention has already been made of a transcontinental railway as part of the plans for placing the Grand Trunk upon its feet. Accordingly, while Watkin was working to secure an intercolonial railway in the East he was making equally strenuous efforts for the establishment of communications across the West, although his first idea, in favour of a railway there, gave way to the more immediately feasible scheme of a wagon road and telegraph. The British capitalists with whom he was associated took up the question, and negotiations were pressed with the Canadian and British Governments and with the Hudson's Bay Company. The Company was reluctant to make any outlay, though expressing a willingness to surrender the whole or any part of its territorial rights for fair compensation. The Canadian Government, at least its Upper Canadian element, was eager for the project, more so than for the Intercolonial Railway; the British Government was sympathetic, but insistent upon coupling the intercolonial with the western project. When Canadian delegates were in London late in 1862 the scheme formed a chief object of their attention. The Company was now willing to grant a right of way, but as a grant so limited would be in itself no source of income the promoters felt it would be necessary to ask aid in the form of guarantees from the Imperial Government and the provinces of Canada and British Columbia. T███████led to form in London the Atlantic and Pacific Transi██████graph Company, and their project so far won Newcastle's support that he recommended it for the acceptance of the colonial Governments.[1]

Meanwhile, from 1 December 1862 negotiations had been proceeding for a reorganisation of the Hudson's Bay Company. Though a right of way was all it would give to the Transit Company, it was not averse from selling out altogether.[2] Watkin and his associates made a brave effort to induce Newcastle to have the British Government itself become the purchaser, but to no avail. Why not buy out the old Company themselves? Thomas Baring and the elder Glyn concluded that without the direct participation of the Imperial Government the Pacific scheme involved too much risk for private persons to take, but the rest of the group went on, found the ready cash by forming the International Financial Society, Limited, and forthwith became

---

[1] Trotter, R. G., *Canadian Federation: Its Origins and Achievement*, pp. 267 ff.
[2] Watkin, Sir E. W., *Canada and the States: Recollections*, 1851–86, pp. 115–20.

themselves the owners of the old fur-trading Company. The new proprietors were to carry on the existing trade under the charter, but planned to administer the Company's affairs "on such principles as to allow the gradual settlement of such portions of the territory as admit[ted] of it, and facilitate the communication across British North America by telegraph or otherwise".[1]

Watkin spent much of the summer of 1863 in Canada working in the interests of the new Hudson's Bay Company. The political problem involved in the western settlement he discussed with the Governor of Rupert's Land and with leaders of both political parties in Canada as well as with high dignitaries of the Roman Catholic Church. He reported that he found Sandfield Macdonald, John A. Macdonald, Cartier, and Cazeau, the Vicar-General, all in favour of setting up a separate Crown colony, but Brown and the "Grits" eager to annex the territory to Canada in the hope of giving a permanent preponderance to Upper Canada. Watkin did not think Lower Canada would brook that possibility and suggested that a Crown colony, federated with the Canadas in such a way as not to alter the balance between them, and with free trade with Canada, would obviate present difficulties and promote the future union of all the British North American provinces which he assumed would some day be consummated.[2] At this time he also grappled with the communications problem and proceeded to make tentative arrangements for the construction of various sections of telegraph line. But the Company declined to endorse these tentative agreements. The Canadian Government, also, proved unwilling to guarantee a mere line of telegraph, and insisted that a road must be part of the undertaking from the beginning, since without it a telegraph line would do little to promote settlement. Canada, moreover, had become no less hostile to the charter because the Company was now in new hands, and the provincial authorities determined to push for a settlement of the legal question. Why, it was urged, pay anything for the West if it might become Canadian without compensation?[3] But Newcastle was no readier than in the past to dismiss the Company's claims in summary fashion. He therefore pursued negotiations with Sir Edmund Head, the new Governor of the Company, looking to the purchase of the latter's territorial rights by the Crown. Cardwell succeeded him as Secretary of State while these negotiations were in progress, and would not accept the Company's latest proposals without modification. Before proceeding farther in regard to them he waited to learn whether Canada would be willing to take over the government of any portion of the territory.[4] His enquiry reached Canada shortly after the formation of the great coalition of 1864.

[1] Head to Newcastle, 3 July 1863, *Brit. Parl. Papers*, H. of C. (1863), ccccxxxviii, 17.
[2] Watkin, pp. 171 ff.
[3] Minute of Council, 18 Feb. 1864, *Brit. Parl. Papers*, H. of C. (1864), cccccii, 15 f.
[4] Cardwell to Monck, 1 July 1864, *ibid.* DL, 1 f.

The inclusion in the coalition of Brown and McDougall, with their long record as advocates of Canadian acquisition and development of the North West, was enough to ensure recognition of the problem in the succeeding interprovincial negotiations, even had there not been the general Canadian interest in the question which now existed. Maritime demands made the Intercolonial Railway a *sine qua non* of federation. The Canadians would accept it only on condition that the Lower Provinces agree as well to the improvement of western communications by the new Federal Government. This was provided for in the Quebec Resolutions. Provision was also included for the later admission of the western lands into the union. Cardwell's query of the spring could now be answered in the affirmative, and Brown was sent to England to negotiate terms on which Canada might give all the aid possible towards opening up the country. In accordance with his instructions he "urged that the Imperial Government should without delay secure the extinction of the Company's claims, and that the Government of Canada would be prepared to assume the duty and cost of opening up communication into the country and establishing local government in the settled portions".[1]

As Brown lacked time to push matters to a close, he arranged for them to be resumed later when Canadian delegates would again be in England, and returned for the meeting of the provincial Legislature. In the ensuing debate therein upon the Quebec Resolutions much was made of the argument that federation would hasten the solution of the North West problem, though critics of the whole scheme saw in its western aspect another device for aiding the Grand Trunk and its friends of the new Hudson's Bay Company.[2] The Canadian delegation which went to England soon after the Legislature rose comprised Macdonald, Cartier, Brown, and Galt. They soon became convinced of the impossibility of enforcing Canada's technical contentions in regard to the Company's rights without, at best, lengthy and expensive litigation, and concluded "that the quickest solution of the question would be the best for Canada". Accordingly they "proposed to the Imperial Ministers that the whole British Territory east of the Rocky Mountains and north of the American and Canadian lines should be made over to Canada, subject to such rights as the Hudson's Bay Company might be able to establish; and that the compensation to that Company (if any were found to be due) should be met by a loan guaranteed by Great Britain". The Imperial Government gave its consent, and the delegates anticipated little trouble in arriving at a valuation of the Company's territorial rights that would satisfy the Company itself.[3] The course thus agreed upon was the one finally

---

[1] For Brown's Report of 26 Jan. 1865 see Pub. Arch. Can. *State Book AB*, pp. 209 ff., in *Brit. Parl. Papers*, H. of C. (1864), ccccII, 16 ff.

[2] See Dorion's speech, Canada, *Parl. Debates on ... Confederation*, p. 263.

[3] Report of the delegates, 12 July 1865, Canada, Parliament, *Papers Relating to the Conferences between Her Majesty's Government and a Deputation from Canada*, etc. (1865), pp. 3 ff.

followed, but when the Company would willingly have proceeded with negotiations, the Canadian Government favoured postponement in view of the probability of the province being soon absorbed in the proposed Union.[1]

In the interval that elapsed before the Dominion came into being, events furnished renewed incentives to early action. A group of Anglo-American capitalists made proposals to buy out the Company's rights with a view to colonising the country.[2] Against such a move being even thought of, the Canadian Government protested, arguing again from the danger of Americanisation of the territory and its consequent loss. In Minnesota there was a group actively interested in trying to secure by peaceful arrangement the annexation of the neighbouring British North West to the United States. Whether or not the eastern provinces might be driven into the arms of the Republic by the abrogation of reciprocity, at least it was hoped that Britain might consent to cede the North West in compensation for the "Alabama Claims". The discussion evoked in Congress by the introduction of a bill, 2 July 1866, to facilitate peaceful annexation of any part of British North America had a decidedly stimulating effect upon the provincial desire to secure the country for the Confederation at an early date.[3] A resolution that was passed without opposition in the House of Representatives on 27 March 1867, expressing solicitude at the proposed Confederation as a step likely to increase the embarrassment already existing between Great Britain and the United States, was hardly calculated to ease the minds of provincial friends of Confederation. A few days later a treaty was signed between the United States and Russia for the purchase of Alaska, and, while the purchase had quite other origins, it was popularly acclaimed, and the heavy expense involved was defended, on the ground that it was a brilliant stroke towards shutting off from the Pacific the Dominion that was about to be formed.[4]

Meanwhile there was a diversity of hopes among the settlers at Red River. Some desired a Crown colony, some wished annexation to the new Confederation, while a few sympathised with the hopes of their Minnesota neighbours. A petition to the British Government from some of the settlers, for the establishment of a Crown colony, was forwarded by Sir John Michel, in command of the forces in British North America and temporarily administrator of the Government of Canada. With the caution of the professional soldier he opposed either a Crown colony or union with Canada "until a safe communication for military purposes" should have been completed to Fort

[1] Minute of Council, 22 June 1866, *State Book AC*, pp. 560 ff.
[2] Correspondence enclosed in Godley to Pres. of Exec. Council, 14 March 1866, *Series G*, vol. CLXXV.
[3] Blegen, T. C., "A Plan for the Union of B.N.A. and the U.S., 1866", *Mississippi Valley Hist. Rev.* March 1918; Watkin, pp. 227 ff.
[4] 30 March 1867. See Callahan, J. M., *The Alaska Purchase and Americo-Canadian Relations*, pp. 22 ff., 30, and *passim*.

Garry.[1] The colonial delegates in London, however, thought far otherwise, and on 3 April 1867, a few days after the passage of the British North America Act, they considered the question in conference at the Westminster Palace Hotel and adopted resolutions, for transmission to the Colonial Secretary, in which they expressed their opinion that, provision having been made in the Act just passed for the admission of the North West into the Union "on such terms and conditions as the Parliament of Canada may propose and Her Majesty approve, it would not be expedient to anticipate the action of that body, or to create institutions or systems of government in any part of British America, which would not be of long continuance, and which would probably retard the policy of union".[2] The delegates realised that without prompt action by the Dominion the North West would inevitably become, in an economic sense at least, an appanage of the United States.

The first Parliament of the Dominion met early in November, and within less than a month McDougall introduced a series of resolutions in the House of Commons for an address to the Crown asking for the union of Rupert's Land and the North-Western Territory with Canada A dilatory amendment offered by Holton was defeated and an address adopted. In July 1868 the British Parliament passed an Act to enable the Crown to accept a surrender of the lands and rights of the Hudson's Bay Company and to transfer Rupert's Land to Canada by Order-in-Council. In the autumn Cartier and McDougall were sent to London as the Dominion's representatives to complete negotiations. Some delay resulted from the fall of the Disraeli Government, but in April 1869 an agreement was reached under which the Company consented to surrender to the Crown its trading monopoly and its territorial rights in Rupert's Land, retaining, however, its trading posts and extensive lands as well as the liberty to trade without hindrance. Canada was to provide the sum of £300,000 as compensation for the Company's claim, also buying at cost price the materials on hand for the construction of the telegraph line.[3] The Canadian Parliament promptly adopted an address accepting the terms agreed upon, and it was soon arranged that before the end of the year the Crown should transfer to Canada both Rupert's Land and the North-Western Territory. In anticipation of that event an Act was passed at Ottawa to provide for the government of the whole region. The administration of these North West Territories, as the whole was to be called, would be in the hands of a Lieutenant-Governor appointed by the Dominion Government and responsible thereto, and assisted by an appointed council. McDougall was shortly appointed Lieutenant-Governor under this Act and left in September, going by way of St

[1] Mem. encl. in Michel to Carnarvon, no. 30, 22 Feb. 1867, *Series G*, vol. ccccLXVI, in *Brit. Parl. Papers*, H. of C. (1870), cccCXLIII, pp. 6 ff.

[2] Pub. Arch. Can. *Macdonald Papers*, "Confederation 5", pp. 179 ff.

[3] For full terms and other documents see *Brit. Parl. Papers*, H. of C. (1868-9), ccccXL.

Paul, in order to be on hand to take up his official duties when the transfer should take place on 1 December.

Trouble, however, was brewing.[1] The eagerness of the Canadian Government to acquire the territory had unfortunately not been matched by an equal care to ensure the good will of the people of the settlement. Negotiations had taken place entirely without consulting the interests or desires of the latter. Many of the Company's men, still harbouring a grudge because they had been ignored in the transfer of the Company in 1863, disliked these new arrangements made by distant outsiders, although they were prepared to acquiesce in them without violent resistance. The *Métis*, the largest element in the settlement and under their clergy the most cohesive, became alarmed, perhaps needlessly, for the security of their rather uncertain land tenures, when there appeared an unannounced survey party, sent by the Canadian Government with the Company's permission, to begin a survey of the settlement. Though in earlier years eager for union with Canada, they had been more recently antagonised by settlers from that province, especially since the establishment of the *Nor'wester* in 1859 with its clamorous voicings of British-Canadian ambitions in and for the settlement and its continual depreciation of the abilities and prospects of the French settlers. Neither the latter nor their religious leaders were eager to be swamped by an alien tide from the east or governed autocratically by a regime that would be strange to their traditions and careless of their rights. Americans in the settlement, among whom there was an open movement for annexation to the United States, were naturally disappointed at the rapid evanescence of their hopes. Support of the Dominion's policy, indeed, was virtually limited to the Canadian element, although the older British element was acquiescent. McDougall, therefore, faced a difficult situation. The *Métis* being already prepared for resistance, he was unable to enter the settlement, and had to remain at the border. When he reported the critical state of things to the Dominion authorities they sent word cautioning him to move very slowly and carefully, and asked the Imperial Government to postpone transfer of the territory. This was done, but McDougall, without waiting for instructions, assumed that the transfer was made, and invited ignominious failure by attempting to assert his authority.[2] His policy merely strengthened the position of the "National Committee". Louis Riel, its leading spirit, was now virtual dictator, Governor McTavish's untimely illness rendering it impossible for him to maintain his legal authority as the Company's official.

Ill feeling had by this time reached such a pitch that a Canadian mission which arrived shortly could accomplish little, and Bishop

---

[1] Martin, C., "The First 'New Province' of the Dominion", *Can. Hist. Rev.* Dec. 1920; Morice, Father A. G., *History of the Catholic Church in Western Canada*, ii, ch. xxii.
[2] Pope, Sir J., *Memoirs of Macdonald*, ii, 52 ff.

Taché, unfortunately absent in Rome, was called home to aid in bringing reconciliation. Macdonald interviewed him at Ottawa on his way and authorised him to assure the malcontents that if the Company's authority were restored there would be full amnesty, and that the colony would promptly receive representative institutions.[1] Before the bishop reached his destination Riel planted the seeds of future bitterness by the impolitic execution of Thomas Scott, who had ventured to question the authority of his *de facto* rulers. This event strengthened the already-formed determination of the Canadian Government that, to avoid uncertainties both as to Riel's good faith and possible moves by American sympathisers, Fenians and others, a military expedition must be sent to take control.[2] Under the command of Colonel Garnet Wolseley a combined force of British regulars and Canadian militia made its way by Lake Superior and overland to Fort Garry, reaching its destination in August 1870, to find that Riel and his followers had decamped upon its approach. During the winter there had again been talk in the American Senate, by men from the North-Western States, looking to negotiations with a view to the annexation of the British North West, but this had been based largely on the assumption that Canada would find it impossible successfully to assume jurisdiction. Whatever possibility of international difficulty this talk may have suggested vanished, therefore, upon the successful reassertion of legally constituted authority at Red River.[3]

The policy of the Dominion Government towards the settlement had been definitely altered by the insurrection, as seen in the assurances given to Taché. Emissaries from the settlement were received at Ottawa, and not only was their demand for immediate provincial status agreed to, but a separate school system like that of Quebec was granted. The Canadian Government, however, decided to retain control of public lands, with the avowed object of obtaining from them repayment for the £300,000 paid in compensation for the Company's claims, and also in order to ensure the means to build a Pacific railway and to obviate the possibility of local obstruction of rapid settlement; but it consented to recognise existing titles and provide for special grants to the families of half-breeds. The measure in which provision was made for establishing the new province and regulating these other matters was not considered subject to any confirmation by Riel and his associates since that would have involved giving them official recognition.[4] As the Manitoba Act it was passed by the Canadian Parliament in May 1870, and was confirmed by an Imperial Act of the following year. The old district of Assiniboia formed the new province, the remainder of the territory which was

[1] Macdonald to Taché, 16 Feb. 1870, *Macdonald*, II, 312 f.
[2] Macdonald to Rose, 11 March 1870, *ibid.* II, 62 f.
[3] Trotter, p. 300, n. 22.
[4] Martin, pp. 369 ff.

to be ceded by the Crown now constituting the North West Territories, which were to be administered for the time being in accordance with the Canadian Act of 1869. An Imperial Order-in-Council, issued on 23 June 1870, and effective on 15 July, formally transferred Rupert's Land and the old North-Western Territory to Canada.

The progress of the federation movement in the older provinces and in the North West did not go unnoticed on the Pacific slope. Hardly had Vancouver Island and British Columbia been united by Act of Parliament in 1866 when a movement for entrance into the Confederation that was being planned by the older provinces assumed considerable proportions among the ten thousand white inhabitants in the western colony. The popular demand and the influence of the elected minority in the single-chamber Legislature were sufficient to cause tentative overtures concerning admission to the Dominion at its inception, but the Colonial Secretary took the ground that consideration of the question must wait until the intervening territory should have been incorporated with the Confederation. Governor Seymour and the official circle were reluctant to see union in any event, for it would inevitably mean the introduction of responsible government and an end to their privileged position, a fact which added to its desirability in the eyes of the popular party. Strengthened by the Colonial Secretary's stand, the opponents of union in the Legislative Council, in April 1868, refused to adopt resolutions intended to define terms of union and pray for admission. Seymour reported the action to London, enlarging upon the difficulties of union in existing circumstances and declaring that its advantages were remote.[1]

Unofficially, however, the movement was already gaining headway. At a public meeting in Victoria in January union was enthusiastically urged, and a memorial embodying the terms proposed was sent to the Canadian Government. The essential terms were responsible government for the province, representation in the Dominion Parliament, a subsidy from the federal treasury and federal assumption of the provincial debt, and the construction of a wagon road from Lake Superior to the Fraser River. A strong Confederation League was formed soon after, and its open meetings developed into popular demonstrations. The culmination of its gatherings was a convention of leading federationists, held at Yale, B.C., in mid-September, which still further consolidated the sentiment for union and endorsed a set of definite proposals regarding it, framed under Amor de Cosmos' leadership. The Canadian Government had welcomed the memorial received early in the year and had sent it on to England. In August they had been interviewed at length on the questions involved by D. W. Higgins, a leading unionist who had made the trip from the coast to

---

[1] Howay, F. W., "Attitude of Governor Seymour toward Confederation", *Trans. Roy. Soc. Can.* 3rd ser. xiv, sect. 2, pp. 34 ff. For the correspondence on the entry of B.C. see *Brit. Parl. Papers*, H. of C. (1868–9), cccxc.

Ottawa at his own expense.[1] The resolutions of the Yale Convention were forwarded to the Colonial Secretary, but in doing so Seymour discredited their importance as much as possible, and in February 1869 the Legislative Council passed a resolution urging the British Government "not to take any decisive steps towards the present consummation of such union".

Sir John Macdonald suggested the replacement of Seymour by Anthony Musgrave, who as Governor of Newfoundland had proved himself a friend of confederation.[2] Seymour's death, on 10 June 1869, accentuated the need of action, and Musgrave was appointed to succeed him. Lord Granville's instructions to the new Governor were clear and mandatory. Now that agreement had been reached concerning the fate of the land lying between Ontario and British Columbia, and the prevailing opinion in the coast province seemed favourable to union, he had no hesitation in stating that union was the wish of Her Majesty's Government. The instructions were to be published and Musgrave was to do what he could to promote "favourable consideration of the question".[3] He used his influence to good purpose among the official group, and the subject, on his initiative, was brought up for debate in March 1870, soon after the Legislative Council met. Resolutions were adopted embodying acceptable terms, and a delegation was sent to Ottawa via San Francisco. The Canadian Government was eager to seize the favourable opportunity to round off the western boundary of the Dominion and scotch the hopes of the annexationists, and within a few weeks of the delegation's arrival terms were agreed upon. The idea of a wagon road as a preliminary to the railway was dropped as an unnecessary expense in view of the pledge now given to begin the railway within two years and complete it within ten. The British Parliament passed an Act giving the province a Legislative Council more than half elective, and in January 1871, after an election had been held, that body unanimously ratified the terms. The Canadian Parliament took up the question in March and carried favourable resolutions. By an Imperial Order-in-Council of 16 May 1871 British Columbia became a province of the Dominion on 20 July following, gaining at the same time a fully-elective Assembly and responsible government.

Prince Edward Island[4] was still outside the fold. Separatist forces had proved even stronger there than in Nova Scotia and New Brunswick. Before the end of 1864 public feeling against the Quebec scheme was strong and when the Legislature met an address was carried overwhelmingly, asking the Crown to refuse assent to any

[1] Gosnell, R. E., *The Story of Confederation*, pp. 85 ff., gives items from Higgins' diary.
[2] Pope, *Macdonald*, ii, 144.
[3] Granville to Musgrave, no. 84, 14 Aug. 1869, *Brit. Parl. Papers*. See also Howay, F. W., "Governor Musgrave and Confederation", *Trans. Roy. Soc. Can.* 3rd ser. xv, sect. 2, pp. 15 ff.
[4] The Prince Edward Island negotiations are in *Series G*, vols. ccic, ccc, cccxx, cccxxi.

measure that would bring the province into a federal union with Canada or any other provinces. It was argued that the island must remain dependent upon agriculture and fisheries and therefore must seek to retain its markets in Britain, the United States and the West Indies. To be compelled by a tariff union to seek manufactures in Canada rather than abroad would curtail exports as well as imports and injure the community's basic industries. The Quebec scheme was criticised as unjust; Prince Edward Island, where natural conditions must always keep the population small, was offered an inadequate and eventually decreasing representation; the exceptional position of the island in regard to its land system and its communications should, it was said, have brought an offer of a financial arrangement very different from that embodied in the Quebec Resolutions. In short, recognition of a duty to aid in defence was not felt to require the province to take a step which, it believed, "would prove politically, commercially, and financially disastrous to the rights and best interests of its people". Nova Scotia's suggestion to resume negotiations for a Maritime union was rejected. The Colonial Secretary's despatch on behalf of further and favourable consideration of the larger project merely drew from the island Legislature, in May 1866, renewed and almost unanimous resolutions of dissent and protest against entering any scheme of union whatever, and the request that this decision be deemed conclusive. Therefore the province sent no delegates to the conference at the Westminster Palace Hotel in the winter of 1866–7, despite inducement held out in the way of probable financial assistance in settling the local land question.[1] J. C. Pope, leader of the island Government, happened to be in London during the conference, and although he had voted in the Assembly against any union he was favourably impressed by an offer of the conference that the Dominion would allow the sum of $800,000 to extinguish proprietary rights. Before he could submit the question to the Legislature, however, his Government was defeated on other issues at a general election,[2] and the new Government was opposed to federation.

When the Dominion had been established, the island still found itself courted by its neighbours. In the summer of 1868 a United States congressional committee appeared to investigate possibilities of securing free trade with the province and inshore fishing privileges for American fishermen. In the autumn representatives of Nova Scotia's anti-confederation Government arrived with vague proposals for "political relations" with the Maritime Provinces. Nothing came of these missions, and hardly more came of another in the following year, when a Canadian delegation conducted an informal and private discussion, upon the basis of which the Dominion Govern-

---

[1] See also Gray, J. H., *Confederation*, p. 384.
[2] Pope, *Macdonald*, II, 146 f.; Pope, *Confed. Docs.* p. 308.

ment in December made a definite offer of so-called "better terms", for the terms were promptly rejected by the provincial Administration.

After a time, however, efforts to finance an island railway produced difficulties from which the only escape seemed to lie in union with Canada and the latter's assumption of the railway burden. Overtures to the Canadian Government elicited the information that the way was open, and a delegation proceeded to Ottawa. The negotiations were successful, and on 1 July 1873 Prince Edward Island entered the Confederation.[1] The manner in which settlement of the land question was thereby facilitated has already been recounted in a previous chapter.[2] The entry of the province was particularly welcomed by the Dominion Government because the latter feared that otherwise the island's nearness to the shores of Nova Scotia and New Brunswick and its extensive fisheries would make it a rendez-vous for smugglers and complicate control of the Gulf fisheries.[3]

Union with Newfoundland was a matter of less consequence, a fact fortunate for Canada, since it was impossible to arrive at terms satisfactory to both the Dominion and the colony. Early in 1866 the Legislature of the latter, while recognising the abstract advantages of union, postponed consideration of the Quebec scheme in view of the uncertain state of public sentiment on the subject and the lack of information as to what course the other provinces would pursue. Newfoundland did not participate in the London Conference of 1866–7, but shortly after the establishment of the Dominion the friends of union in the colony deemed the time more auspicious, and the Governor, Musgrave, entered into private communication with the Canadian Premier.[4] Official negotiations were resumed in 1868 and in the following spring a delegation visited Ottawa, where a tentative agreement was reached.[5] In the provincial election of that autumn, however, the Government was overwhelmingly defeated and federation repudiated. The financial terms were thought to be not sufficiently generous, the provision for a mail steamship service was too vague to win much support for union, and the ancient enmity of the ignorant "out-harbour people" towards Canada played its part in strengthening opposition. There was fear, also, that Canada might neglect the interests of the island as a fish-producer, particularly in reciprocity dealings with the United States. Restored prosperity after a period of hard times accounted in part for the people's readiness to face the future alone.[6]

In the 'eighties divided counsels in regard to negotiations with the United States impressed the Canadian Government once more with the desirability of securing Newfoundland's adhesion to the Confederation.

[1] *Sessional Papers*, Canada (1873), 68.   [2] See chapter xiv.
[3] Pope, *Macdonald, loc. cit.*
[4] Pope, *Correspondence of Sir John Macdonald*, pp. 44 f., 50, 61 ff.
[5] *Sessional Papers*, Canada (1869), 51.
[6] *Vide supra*, chap. xvii; also Prowse, D. W., *Hist. of Newfoundland*, pp. 494 ff.

Accordingly, Sir Charles Tupper called at St John's in 1887 and discussed the question with leaders of both parties, but the terms which he suggested did not prove acceptable to the Government.[1] The hard times of the middle 'nineties brought virtual insolvency to the "ancient colony", and thus led to the broaching of the subject once more, when Newfoundland sent delegates to Canada. The Canadian Government declined to burden itself with the whole debt of the colony, believing that the latter's financial straits would compel it to accept more moderate terms, and so negotiations were fruitless.[2] With the gradual return of prosperity, opinion in Newfoundland again set in strongly against entrusting the colony's highly specialised interests to Canada with its different and more varied interests. "We think", said a prominent citizen of Newfoundland to the Canadian Club in Ottawa in 1921, "that Ottawa would not be able to appreciate our viewpoint".[3]

The transfer of the North West to Canada in 1870 had left undefined the northern limits of the Dominion's territory and jurisdiction. Any uncertainty in the matter was set at rest by an Imperial Order-in-Council of 31 July 1880, annexing to Canada, from 1 September of the same year, all British possessions in North America with the exception of Newfoundland and its dependencies. The validity of this order was ensured in 1895 by the passage of the Colonial Boundaries Act.[4] Thus the Dominion, which expanded "from sea to sea" in the years 1867 to 1873, may be said to have fulfilled also another phrase of the national psalm now that it extended "from the river unto the ends of the earth".

---

[1] Tupper to Macdonald, 17 Aug. and 31 Oct. 1888, Pub. Arch. Can. *Tupper Papers*; Tupper to Macdonald, 18 Sept. 1888, Pope, *Corres. of Macdonald*, p. 422. See also Tupper, *Recollections*, p. 312, and Saunders, *Tupper*, II, 92.

[2] Prowse, pp. 541 ff., 552 ff.; *Sessional Papers, Canada* (1895), 48.

[3] McGrath, Sir Patrick, *Ottawa Citizen*, 7 Nov. 1921.

[4] 40 and 41 Vict. cap. 47.

CHAPTER XX

POLITICAL PARTIES AND RAILWAY POLICY,
1867–1885

THE British North America Act came into force, so far as the original colonies entering the Canadian Confederation were concerned, on 1 July 1867. Of the new Dominion Lord Monck, who had been Governor-in-Chief of United Canada, was appointed Governor-General; and he confided the task of forming its first Government to John Alexander (or, as he now became, Sir John) Macdonald. For this choice there were good reasons. Lord Monck and Macdonald had worked hand in hand to bring about federation; and though Macdonald had not been one of the first crusaders in the cause of national unity, he had, when the project came within the realm of practical politics, become its chief architect and protagonist. Especially after George Brown, the Liberal leader, had withdrawn from the Great Coalition in Canada at the end of 1865, Macdonald stood without a rival. "Men who had been in almost open revolt against him in 1865", a witness none too friendly to him has confessed, "now admitted that he was supreme in his own way".

It was Macdonald's conviction that the Government which presided over the infancy of the Dominion should be, like that which had presided over its birth in Canada, a coalition. He even denounced on the hustings the evils of party. "Party", he quoted, "is merely a struggle for office, the madness of many for the gain of a few". In making appointments to the Senate, or nominated Upper House of the Dominion, he had little difficulty in applying this idea. The British North America Act laid down the number of senators to be appointed from each province; and all Macdonald had to do was to select from the members of the pre-Confederation Legislative Councils an equal number of Liberals and Conservatives, having due regard to the part which his nominees had played in the movement toward federation. But in the formation of his Cabinet, Macdonald found the difficulty of applying the coalition principle all but insuperable. In the government of Canada under the Union, the convention had grown up that the Cabinet should reflect the various political, religious, and regional elements in the party or parties supporting it. This convention Macdonald felt bound to respect. "I do not want it to be felt", he said, "by any section of the country that they have no representative in the Cabinet and no influence in the Government". But, with the limited number of portfolios at his disposal, this was more easily said than done. The various provinces had to receive in the Cabinet representation roughly proportionate to their population; recognition had to be given to the various Protestant denominations, as well as to both Irish Roman Catholics and French Roman Catholics; and when to these considerations there was added the necessity of apportioning portfolios among both the Conservatives and the Liberals who had supported federation, it will be seen that the problem became a veritable Chinese puzzle.

For a week Macdonald wrestled with the problem, but without success. He was on the point of giving it up, and advising the Governor-General to send for George Brown, when Charles Tupper, the leading exponent of federation in Nova Scotia, came forward with a solution, namely, that he, the representative of the Conservatives of Nova Scotia, and D'Arcy McGee, the representative of the Irish Roman Catholics, should stand aside in favour of Edward (afterwards Sir Edward) Kenny, an Irish Roman Catholic from Nova Scotia, who had the additional advantage of having Liberal antecedents. There were perhaps no two men who had greater claims to a portfolio in the first Government of the Dominion of Canada than Tupper and McGee; for the entrance of Nova Scotia into the Confederation had been mainly the result of Tupper's efforts, and McGee had been the Mazzini of the movement toward national unity in British North America. Their self-abnegation in offering to stand aside in favour of a politician whose name is now forgotten is one of the brightest spots in Canadian political history, and proves that even in politics it is not always safe to assume the lowest motives. Their action solved the last of Macdonald's difficulties, and he was able to present to the Governor-General a Cabinet which satisfied the demands of all conflicting interests.

Even without Tupper and McGee, the first Government of the Dominion was one which commanded respect. From Ontario there were five ministers, two of whom were Conservatives, and three Liberals. The Conservatives were Macdonald himself and his friend Alexander Campbell; the Liberals were William McDougall, W. P. Howland, and A. J. Fergusson Blair. From Quebec there were four ministers, George E. Cartier, Hector Langevin, J. C. Chapais, and (as the representative of the English minority) Alexander T. Galt. Nova Scotia and New Brunswick each had two representatives— Nova Scotia, A. G. Archibald and Edward Kenny; New Brunswick, S. L. Tilley and Peter Mitchell. The Cabinet thus formed went to the country, in the first parliamentary elections of the Dominion, in August and September of 1867. On the whole, the result was distinctly favourable to the Government. In Ontario, where George Brown had already raised the standard of opposition, the "Brownites" carried only fifteen seats out of eighty-two, and Brown himself was defeated; in Quebec, where many of the *parti rouge* continued their opposition to confederation, the Government carried all but twelve seats out of sixty-five; and in New Brunswick only three Opposition candidates were returned. Only in Nova Scotia did the Government fail to obtain a majority. Here Joseph Howe, who had already launched his campaign for the repeal of confederation, carried everything before him; and out of nineteen members returned, only one, Charles Tupper, was a government supporter. But as the Opposition members from Nova Scotia, when Parliament met, refused to coalesce with those from Ontario and Quebec, Macdonald found himself not only supported by a large parliamentary majority, but faced with a divided Opposition.

The first task confronting the new Government was the completion and consolidation of the work of federation. In the first place, the administrative machinery of the new federal Government had to be created; and in the second place, there were a thousand problems to be solved in regard to the relations of the Dominion with the provinces—problems that still sometimes vex Canadian politics. "Confederation", as Macdonald put it, "is only yet in the gristle", and he prophesied that it would be several years "before it hardens into bone". Especially difficult was the problem of the reconciliation of Nova Scotia to confederation. Howe's agitation for "repeal" had swept the province; and for the first year or two after 1867 Macdonald watched the situation there with anxious care. When Howe went to England in 1868 to launch there an agitation for the repeal of confederation, Macdonald promptly sent Tupper to London to counteract his campaign. Howe succeeded in enlisting the support of no less powerful an advocate than John Bright; but the British Government resolved to adhere to the terms of the British North America Act, and Tupper, in a memorable interview, persuaded Howe himself that the agitation for "repeal" was doomed to failure. This interview paved the way for one of the most amazing illustrations of Macdonald's skill in the art of managing men. When Howe returned to Nova Scotia, Macdonald with some of his colleagues went down to Halifax to meet him; and there the great "tribune of the people" was speedily won over by "John A.'s" arguments. Not only did he agree to desist from his opposition to confederation, but he was actually persuaded to enter the Dominion Cabinet as President of the Council and later as Secretary of State for the Provinces. He exacted, as the price of his adherence to confederation, "better terms" for Nova Scotia; and his attitude was well expressed in his reported remark, "You have got us, and now you must keep us". But his conversion marked the end of the campaign for "repeal" as a pressing danger to confederation, and it illustrated very strikingly the preeminence of Macdonald among Canadian statesmen.

The danger of the secession of Nova Scotia from the Dominion having been averted, Macdonald now turned his attention toward the extension of the Confederation from the Atlantic to the Pacific— "from sea to sea, and from the river unto the uttermost ends of the earth". As recounted in the previous chapter, this feat of expanding, within five short years, the unstable union of Ontario, Quebec, New Brunswick and Nova Scotia into a well-knit Confederation covering practically the whole of the northern half of North America, unquestionably confers the highest credit on Macdonald and his colleagues. It was at this time that Bismarck and Cavour were completing the work of German and Italian national unity; their Canadian contemporary Macdonald in his task of uniting British North America displayed qualities that may even be compared with theirs.

The five years immediately following confederation were perhaps the most creditable of Macdonald's whole career. He had by this time reformed his private life, which had been somewhat irregular; and he had risen to the height of his great responsibilities in a truly statesmanlike manner. The task of directing the affairs of the new Confederation, however, taxed even his superb gifts in the art of government; and fortune was not always with him. At the very outset, two of his leading colleagues, Galt and Cartier, took serious umbrage because Macdonald was knighted for his services in connection with confederation, while they received only the C.B.[1] Macdonald himself was in no way responsible for this discrimination, and he sought to remedy the slight by obtaining a baronetcy for Cartier and a knighthood for Galt.[2] Cartier was completely mollified, and continued to act in concert with Macdonald until his death in 1873. But with Galt the salve was not so effective. In 1867 he had a second disagreement with Macdonald, in connection with the winding-up of the Commercial Bank, in which Galt had been interested; and he made this disagreement the excuse for resigning from the Cabinet.[3] This "double C.B." incident (as it was known) did Macdonald no good, for Galt was a statesman held in high estimation by men of all parties, and his resignation was a distinct loss to the Administration.

During these years, in truth, there occurred in the personnel of the Government an abnormal number of changes, which did not always tend to strengthen it. In 1867 Fergusson Blair, one of the Liberal ministers from Ontario, died, and Howland and McDougall were repudiated by a Liberal convention held in Toronto. Macdonald soon replaced them by more serviceable colleagues. Howland became in 1868 Lieutenant-Governor of Ontario; and McDougall was appointed in 1869 Lieutenant-Governor of Rupert's Land and the North West Territories. The result was that the Government lost the aspect of a coalition, and became predominantly a Conservative Administration. It is true that, as we have seen, the veteran Howe was induced early in 1869 to enter the Cabinet; and in that year Macdonald succeeded in pressing into service as Minister of Finance Sir Francis

[1] See also Wallace, W. S., *Sir John Macdonald*, chap. 7.
[2] Skelton, O. D., *Life and Times of Sir A. T. Galt*, p. 421.   [3] *Ibid.* pp. 422–8.

Hincks, who had been Liberal Prime Minister of United Canada from 1851 to 1854, and who had since that time been absent from the country. But both these accessions disappointed expectations. Howe failed to achieve at Ottawa the dominating position he had enjoyed at Halifax. Hincks also was found to have lost touch with Canadian conditions, and in February 1873, discovering that his "resurrection" had not realised expectations, he resigned from the Cabinet; while, in May 1873, only a few weeks before his death, Howe accepted the lieutenant-governorship of Nova Scotia.

Meanwhile, the opposition to the Government was strengthening itself in the country. Though George Brown had been defeated in 1867, and was out of Parliament, he had gathered about him the remnants of the Liberal party, and had raised aloft once more the Reform banner. As Macdonald lost, one after the other, his Liberal colleagues, those Liberals who had supported him drifted back, in many cases, into the "Brownite" fold. It must be confessed that there was in 1867 little immediate justification for the revival of party spirit in Canada, and, as there were no great principles at stake, George Brown was not unfairly accused of carrying into the new era the political quarrels of a bygone age. But an Opposition has always, under the British parliamentary system, a useful function to perform; and under Alexander Mackenzie and Edward Blake, the Liberals, though few in number, made their influence felt. Their first success was won in 1871 when, in the provincial elections in Ontario, they wiped out the majority of Sandfield Macdonald's "patent combination"—the Coalition Cabinet to which Sir John Macdonald had entrusted the government of Ontario—and then, in a series of brilliant attacks, forced its resignation under fire. Sir John Macdonald complained bitterly that Sandfield Macdonald had thrown away his chances, and this was no doubt the case; but the Liberal victory in Ontario was a distinct blow to the prestige of the Government of Ottawa, and seemed to presage ill for the future.

Hardly less serious than the revived strength of the Liberal party was an embarrassing rift which occurred at the same time among Macdonald's supporters. The basis of Sir John Macdonald's power was at all stages an amazing alliance of the Orangemen of Ontario and the Roman Catholics of Quebec. On several occasions, however, the task of driving in tandem the orange and the *bleu* required all his skill and adroitness. The first of these occasions occurred in 1869 when there broke out in the Red River valley an *émeute* of the *Métis* or French half-breeds. As has already appeared,[1] the negligence of the Government was partly responsible for this rising, which opened the flood-gates of racial and religious feeling. Naturally, the French-speaking population of the province of Quebec sympathised with the French half-breeds of the Red River valley in their fight for what they regarded as their rights.

---

[1] See chapter xix.

On the other hand, the English-speaking element in the Dominion regarded the rioting of the *Métis* as nothing more or less than rebellion, and the execution of Thomas Scott as plain murder. The Liberal Government of Ontario, under Edward Blake, with a just appreciation of the political situation, actually offered a reward for the apprehension of Scott's murderers. This placed Sir John Macdonald in an awkward predicament. He had crushed the so-called "rebellion" of the *Métis* with military force; and it is only right to say that, where law and order were at stake, Macdonald never faltered. But if he dealt severely with the "rebels", he was bound to offend the French of Quebec, and to alienate perhaps some of his French-Canadian colleagues. If he did not deal severely with them, he would offend equally his supporters in Ontario and the Maritime Provinces. In the end he succeeded, with marvellous dexterity, in preventing a split both in the party and in the Cabinet; but it was only by conniving at the escape of Louis Riel. Had Riel been captured in 1870, the Conservative party would have been hopelessly divided on an issue of prime importance.

In 1872 the life of the first Parliament of the Dominion of Canada came to an end; and Macdonald had to submit his record to the judgment of the electors. The result was the vindication of his policies, though by a reduced majority; and it seemed likely that his Government was assured a new lease of life for five years, which was the term of Parliament's existence. But Nemesis lurked round the corner. During the first session of the new Parliament, there occurred a spectacular episode which swept Macdonald from power, and for a time indeed threatened to end his political career.

British Columbia had entered the Confederation in 1871 on the definite condition that a railway should be built within ten years, which would link British Columbia with Canada, just as the Intercolonial Railway was linking Canada with the Maritime Provinces. Macdonald lost no time in addressing himself to the problem of building this railway; and there were those who were unkind enough to suggest that, in bringing British Columbia into the union, and in undertaking to build the Pacific Railway, he was playing for the votes which the members from British Columbia would have in the Dominion Parliament. Be that as it may, there is no doubt that Macdonald and his colleagues devoted to the question of the building of the railway the most careful consideration; and in the end they gave a charter for the building of the railway to a group of Canadian financiers headed by Sir Hugh Allan, of Montreal, the founder of the Allan Line of steamships.

With this action no fault could be found. But in the general election of 1872 Macdonald and Cartier were so indiscreet as to go to Sir Hugh Allan for contributions to their party funds. In those days there was no party organisation to look after such matters, and it was customary for the ministers themselves to manage the campaign funds. From Sir Hugh Allan contributions were obtained which amounted to the surprisingly large total of nearly $300,000. In some way the Liberals heard of these contributions; and they succeeded in obtaining from the office of J. J. C. Abbott (afterwards Sir John Abbott), who was Allan's lawyer, copies of the correspondence which had passed between Allan and Abbott on the one hand and Macdonald and Cartier on the other. When Parliament opened, Lucius Seth Huntington, one of the Liberal leaders, charged Macdonald with having sold the charter for the Pacific Railway to Sir Hugh Allan and his friends in return for very large contributions to the funds of the Conservative party.

Macdonald at first most indignantly denied all these charges; and the resolution proposed by the Liberals was rejected by the Conservative majority in the Commons. But it was felt that the charges were too serious to be thus dismissed; and Macdonald himself brought forward a motion for the appointment of a select committee of the House to investigate them. This committee, of course, would have been predominantly Conservative; and the Liberals consequently refused to have anything to do with it. Macdonald then proposed the appointment of a royal commission of three judges to take evidence under oath, and to report to Parliament. But this proposal, like the former, failed to meet with the approval of the Liberals. They objected that it was a commission appointed by Macdonald to enquire into charges made against himself; and their objection was well illustrated by a clever cartoon of the period, in which a court-room was depicted, with a judge sitting on the Bench, a counsel pleading at the Bar, and a prisoner standing in the dock— all three figures possessing the unmistakable features of Sir John Macdonald. The Liberal leaders declined to appear before the commission; but they did not hesitate to publish in the newspapers the documentary evidence which had come into their possession. Some of this was very compromising, notably a telegram which Macdonald had sent to Abbott, which ran as follows: "Immediate, private. I must have another ten thousand—will be the last time of calling. Do not fail me; answer to-day". This evidence, together with that taken before the royal commission, created a painful impression both in the country and in Parliament.

In the debate over what came to be known as "the Pacific Scandal", the attack was opened by Alexander Mackenzie, who, in consideration of the facts disclosed, moved that the Government had merited the "severest censure" of the House. Macdonald's reply was one of the great efforts of his life. He did not deny the receipt of campaign funds from Sir Hugh Allan; but he insisted that there had been no connection between these contributions and the granting of the charter for the railway. In other words, the charter had been granted on the merits of the case; and had no reference to any contributions which Sir Hugh Allan might later have made. The accusation of corrupt motives Macdonald rejected with emphasis. "These hands", he vowed, with a dramatic gesture, "are clean". But his effort was in vain. The disclosures made by the Opposition shocked the none too tender conscience of the country, and a number of Macdonald's supporters wavered in their allegiance. When Donald Smith (afterwards Lord Strathcona) announced in the House that he could no longer "conscientiously" support the Government, it was clear that the fate of the Government was sealed; and Macdonald, without waiting for a vote, submitted his resignation to Lord Dufferin, who had succeeded Lord Monck as Governor-General. Donald Smith's defection stirred Macdonald to an outburst of anger; and he is said to have asseverated that he "could lick that man Smith quicker than hell could frizzle a feather". But in a cooler mood he realised that he had been beaten, and he lost no time in accepting, and indeed in anticipating, the verdict of Parliament.

Over half a century has elapsed since the "Pacific Scandal"—or, as Sir Charles Tupper described it, the "Pacific Slander"—and we are now able to view the incident in a dispassionate light. It was, without doubt, most regrettable that the Prime Minister of Canada should have accepted money, even for purely party purposes, from a railway contractor. Yet it cannot be denied that, in doing so, Macdonald did what many other politicians have done both before and since that time. Parties need campaign funds; and if they cannot obtain them from their friends, where are they to obtain them? Macdonald was unfortunate in having the acceptance of these funds made public through the theft of private papers, and in having an interpretation placed upon the incident which it did not properly bear. But we may fairly conclude that, in accepting campaign funds personally from Sir Hugh Allan, he was guilty of a grave indiscretion, rather than of a serious moral offence. At any rate, as we shall see, this was the verdict of the Canadian people five years later.

When Sir John Macdonald resigned, the Governor-General sent for Alexander Mackenzie, the leader of the Liberal party in Parliament, and invited him to form an Administration. Mackenzie, like Macdonald, was a Scotsman by birth. He had come to Canada in 1842, when twenty years of age, and had become first a stonemason, and then a builder and contractor. "Mr. Mackenzie", Goldwin Smith is reported to have said at a later date, "was a stonemason; he is a stonemason still". This was without doubt an unfair verdict; but it contained an element of truth. Mackenzie was a politician of scrupulous integrity, of great industry, and of remarkable debating power. But he was lacking in many of the attributes of a political leader. He had little personal magnetism, and he was deficient in boldness and imagination. That the leadership of the Liberal party in the Dominion should have been confided to him, rather than to Edward Blake, the new Prime Minister of Ontario, was a serious error in judgment on the part of the managers of the Liberal party. There is evidence that Blake was indeed offered the leadership, and that Mackenzie was willing to stand aside in his favour; but apparently sufficient pressure was not brought to bear upon Blake, and Mackenzie was thereupon induced to accept the duties of leader in the federal sphere.

As a Cabinet-maker Mackenzie proved distinctly inferior to Macdonald. At the outset he failed to secure in his Cabinet the presence of several leading Liberals, notably that of Luther H. Holton, who had been a member of the Brown and Sandfield Macdonald Cabinets before confederation; and it was with difficulty that he persuaded Edward Blake to become even a minister without portfolio. He did prevail upon A. A. (later Sir Antoine) Dorion, the leader of the *parti rouge*, to become Minister of Justice, though Dorion retired to the Bench after a few months; and he pressed into service also Albert J. (later Sir Albert) Smith, a former Prime Minister of New Brunswick. But the rest of his Government were almost wholly without Cabinet experience, or indeed without striking ability or distinction. Richard J. (afterwards Sir Richard) Cartwright, his Minister of Finance, became later, it is true, a stalwart of the Liberal party; but in 1873 he was a recent convert from Conservatism, and had never before held office under the Crown. William Ross, Isaac Burpee, D. A. Macdonald, Télesphore Fournier, David Laird, Thomas Coffin, David Christie and R. W. Scott, were all estimable politicians whose names are nearly forgotten to-day.

After some hesitation, Mackenzie decided to ask the Governor-General to dissolve Parliament, and to appeal to the country in a general election. This took place in the beginning of 1874. The Conservative party went to the polls, of course, with defeat sitting at their helm; but even they perhaps hardly anticipated the extent of the disaster which overtook them. The country had been so shocked by the "Pacific Scandal" that only 45 Conservatives were returned, out of a total of over 200 members; and many of these held their seats by narrow majorities. Sir John Macdonald himself was all but defeated in his own constituency of Kingston, which he had represented without serious opposition for thirty years; he was unseated on an election petition, and then re-elected by a still narrower majority. The rout of the Conservative party appeared decisive. To most people, and even to Macdonald himself, it seemed as though his star had set. He called together the remnants of his following, and placed in their hands his resignation as leader of the party. He was, he said, "an old man who had done his share of the fighting"; he urged the desirability of appointing, as leader of the party, a younger man who had not been the target, as he had been, for so many shafts of calumny and abuse; and he begged to be allowed to doff his armour. But his followers refused to accept his resignation; and, confident of the loyalty of the "Old Guard" (as he called those of his supporters who had survived the election of 1874), he was prevailed upon to face the duties of leader of the Opposition.

During the first year or two of his administration, Mackenzie had fairly clear sailing. In the sessions of 1874 and 1875 Macdonald, not anxious to advertise his weakness, refrained even from dividing the House. "Give the 'Grits' rope enough", he said, "and they will hang themselves". Consequently, Mackenzie and his colleagues had a free hand in devising their policies; and the amazing thing is that they did, as Macdonald prophesied, proceed to "hang themselves". In some respects, it is true, they achieved notable results. In 1875 Mackenzie set up the Supreme Court of Canada, which acted at Ottawa as a buffer for the Judicial Committee of the Privy Council; and in 1876 Edward Blake, who had been prevailed upon in 1875 to accept the portfolio of Justice, succeeded in bringing about changes in the royal Instructions to the Governor-General which formed another landmark in the history of responsible government. Not only in regard to the exercise of the power of pardon, but also in regard to the reservation of bills for the signification of the Queen's pleasure, Blake whittled down the prerogatives of the Governor-General to a minimum. On the constitutional side, Mackenzie and Blake thus made a decided contribution to the development of Canadian nationality. But on the economic side, they took an attitude totally different. Toward the building of the Canadian Pacific Railway they were almost hostile. They terminated the contract with Sir Hugh Allan and his syndicate; and they substituted for the original plan an amended arrangement whereby only parts of the original railway were to be built, and use was to be made of marine transportation where water routes were available. Similarly, they proved hostile to the growing demand for increased protection of Canadian industries. Mackenzie was a fervid free-trader; and he would not . entertain the idea of a high protectionist tariff—which is, after all, only a manifestation of nationalism in the economic sphere.

Just after confederation there had sprung up in Canada an organised nationalist movement. It originated with a group of young men, nearly all under thirty years of age, who had met together in Ottawa in 1868, and had pledged themselves to do all in their power to stimulate the growth of "a national sentiment". The group adopted the motto of "Canada First", and the movement they inaugurated came to be known as the "Canada First Movement". At first it was non-political, and it devoted itself to such enterprises as the North-West Emigration Aid Society. But gradually the temptation to invade the political field became too great to be resisted; and in 1874 the Canadian National Association was formed, with a definite programme, which is one of the most significant documents in the political history of the Dominion. Among its items were the following: (1) British connection, consolidation of the Empire, and in the meantime a voice in treaties affecting Canada.... (6) Encouragement of immigration and free homesteads in the public domain. (7) The imposition of duties for revenue so adjusted as to afford every possible encouragement for native industry. (8) An improved militia system, under the command of trained Dominion officers.

The way in which this programme anticipated the lines along which Canada was destined to develop during the next half-century can only be described as uncanny. The first and eighth clauses forecasted important phases of the growth of Canadian autonomy; the sixth outlined the policy of "building up Canada"; and the seventh contained in germ the doctrine of the National Policy. In fact, the political history of Canada since 1874 has been essentially the story of how the two traditional parties of the Dominion have raided the platform of "Canada First" for most of their ideas.

At first, the entrance of "Canada First" into the political arena promised well. The National Club in Toronto was formed, with Goldwin Smith as its first president; a weekly journal, significantly named the *Nation*, was founded in Toronto as the organ of the party; and in a by-election in West Toronto the nominee of the group, Thomas Moss (afterwards Chief Justice of Ontario), was triumphantly elected to the Dominion Parliament. Lastly, in the autumn of 1874, "Canada First" obtained for the moment a leader of the first rank in Edward Blake, who had retired from the Mackenzie Government, and seemed not unwilling to place himself at the head of a nationalist party. On 3 October 1874, Blake delivered at Aurora, Ontario, a speech—still famous as the "Aurora speech"—which was little more than an amplification of the programme of the Canadian National Association, and definitely aligned him with "Canada First". "The future of Canada, I believe", he said, "depends very largely on the cultivation of a national spirit".

It seemed as though "Canada First" were on the eve of a great future. W. A. Foster, the spokesman and guiding spirit of the group, expressed the hope that the old-line parties would break up. But the hope was hollow. In the spring of 1875, Edward Blake was prevailed upon to return to the Liberal camp, and to accept office in the Mackenzie Government as Minister of Justice. It was as though the captain of the host had deserted in the face of the foe.

> Just for a handful of silver he left us,
> Just for a ribbon to stick in his coat.

The members of the group lost heart, and the party itself gradually broke up. The *Nation* ceased publication; the National Club became a purely social institution; and the Canadian National Association disappeared from view. The movement died probably a pre-ordained death. It was before its time. But it exerted nevertheless a potent and profound influence on the future course of Canadian politics. Once the ideas of its exponents ceased to be confined to a party programme, they spread among all classes and parties, and came to be the common heritage of Canadians. As Charles Mair wrote in his lines in memory of W. A. Foster in 1888,

> The seed they sowed has sprung at last,
> And grows and blossoms through the land.

The "Canada First" movement caused at first no small concern to the Mackenzie Government—a concern fully evidenced by the broadsides which the *Globe*, the chief Liberal newspaper, poured into the "Canada First" ranks. But after the movement received its quietus as a political adventure, the Liberals gave it little further thought. In this they made a fatal mistake. Had they adopted the "Canada First" programme, not only on its constitutional, but also on its economic side, they would no doubt have placed themselves in line with the aspirations of the Canadian people, and thus have ensured to themselves a long lease of political power. But they left it to Sir John Macdonald to develop the idea of the National Policy of fiscal protection; and the result was the decisive defeat of the Mackenzie Administration when the Parliament of 1874 reached its legal termination.

There were in 1878, of course, other causes that contributed to the defeat of Mackenzie. Repeatedly, he showed himself to be lacking in political common sense. His initial mistake was in taking himself the portfolio of Public Works. This brought him into direct contact with all those persons in Canada typified by the gentleman who, when asked what his politics were, said succinctly, "Contracting". Under previous Administrations, government contractors had been allowed some latitude, if they contributed handsomely to party funds; but Mackenzie, with his rigid honesty, held all contractors to the letter of their contracts, and so alienated the good will of those who should have been friendly to him. The scrupulous attention which he devoted to the business of his department, moreover, left him little time for his duties as Prime Minister. It was a case of the captain of the ship spending most of his time in the engine-room. Sir John Macdonald, when Prime Minister, always allowed his particular department to run itself, and gave all his thought to the leadership of the Government. But not so Mackenzie. He allowed the Government to run itself, and gave his chief efforts to the administration of his department.

The result was apparent in several ways. Mackenzie never became master of the Government; and Blake, for instance, entered and left the Administration at his pleasure. Persuaded to accept office in 1873 without portfolio, he resigned after three months, and re-entered the Cabinet, as we have seen, in 1875 as Minister of Justice. This office he resigned in 1877; and though he became President of the Council, he took no part in the elections of 1878, and indeed virtually withdrew from the Government. In the same way, Mackenzie allowed Dorion, the leader of the French-Canadian Liberals, to retire to the Bench in 1874; and in 1875 he brought into the Cabinet, as the leading French Canadian, J. E. Cauchon, a politician with so malodorous a reputation that the young Wilfrid Laurier declined to sit at the same council board with him. It was only after Cauchon's retirement in 1877 that Laurier could be persuaded to enter the Cabinet. Had Laurier been brought into the Cabinet in 1875, he might have had a chance to strengthen the hold of the Government in Quebec; but by 1877 the elections were so near at hand that Laurier had not a fair opportunity to show his powers. Had Mackenzie devoted to the composition of his Cabinet half the thought which he devoted to the details of the administration of his department, the result of 1878 might have been very different.

In many ways Mackenzie was too conscientious. He disliked the spoils system; and when he took office, he declined to dismiss the civil servants appointed under the previous regime. The result was that his Government had only the half-hearted allegiance of those entrusted with the execution of its policies. There is reason for believing, indeed, that the Conservative Opposition was indebted to civil servants, during the Mackenzie regime, for information and co-operation. "We lived", complained Sir Richard Cartwright later, "in a glass hive". Furthermore, Mackenzie was too generous toward his political opponents in Parliament. In 1874 he had it in his power, apparently, to drive Sir John Macdonald from the House of Commons; but he hesitated to hit an opponent who was down, and he reaped the reward of his magnanimity in his defeat in 1878.

As will appear in later chapters, the most powerful factor in his defeat was economic. During his period of office, there occurred three of the worst harvests in Canadian history; and these coincided with a severe financial depression in the United States. That Canada came through the crisis as well as she did reflected no discredit on the Mackenzie Administration. But there were naturally many who laid the blame for the prevailing "bad times" at the door of the Government. This was especially true after Mackenzie, an ardent free-trader, had declined to entertain the proposal that a high protective tariff should be imposed, as a remedy for Canada's economic ills.

Probably Sir John Macdonald was also at heart a free-trader. It is significant that he declined to commit himself on the question of a high protective tariff until after Mackenzie had nailed the free-trade flag to his masthead. As late as 1877, when Goldwin Smith rallied

Macdonald on his rumoured conversion to protection, Macdonald replied that he had not got himself into that hole yet. But when Mackenzie had committed himself, Macdonald—like the true opportunist he was—promptly proceeded to get himself into that hole; and when Goldwin Smith upbraided him with this change of front, he airily retorted that protection had done so much for him, he felt he must do something for protection. To his protectionist programme he applied, by a stroke of genius, the name of the "National Policy"; and on this policy the apparently discredited politician of "Pacific Scandal" fame was in 1878 returned to power, with a majority no less emphatic than that by which he had been defeated in 1875.

Up to the moment of polling, Alexander Mackenzie refused to believe that the people of Canada would fail to re-elect a Government so conscientious and economical as his had been. But like many another reformer, he had too great a faith in human nature, and he failed also to appreciate the strength of the growing nationalist feeling of the Canadian people. A "national policy" —a policy of "building up Canada"—was what the Canadian people demanded at that time; and it was this policy which Sir John Macdonald, more by accident than by design, offered them.

Sir John Macdonald once described himself in a visitors' book as "John A. Macdonald, cabinet-maker"; and certainly few politicians have understood the delicate art of making a Canadian Cabinet better than he. The Administration which he formed at the end of 1878 was not perhaps spectacular in its personnel. It could not be described as "a ministry of all the talents". But it was a masterpiece of political sagacity. In the first place, Macdonald drew the members of his Cabinet mainly from the "Old Guard" which had stood by him so gallantly, both in the Upper and in the Lower House, from 1874 to 1878. From the "Old Guard" in the Commons he took Charles Tupper as Minister of Public Works, John Henry Pope as Minister of Agriculture, James Colledge Pope as Minister of Marine and Fisheries, Hector Langevin as Postmaster-General, L. F. R. Masson as Minister of Militia, Mackenzie Bowell as Minister of Customs, and L. F. G. Baby as Minister of Inland Revenue; and from the Senate he chose J. C. Aikins as Secretary of State, Alexander Campbell as Receiver-General, and R. D. Wilmot as Speaker of the Senate. John O'Connor, who became President of the Privy Council, and James McDonald, who became Minister of Justice, had both been out of Parliament during the Mackenzie regime; but they had supported Macdonald during the crisis of the "Pacific Scandal", and had gone down to defeat in 1874. The only member of the Cabinet of whom the "Old Guard" might have felt jealous was S. L. Tilley, who had spent the years 1873–8 in safe retirement as Lieutenant-Governor of New Brunswick. No one could accuse Macdonald of lack of loyalty to his followers.

At the same time, he solved with marked success, in the formation of his Cabinet, the jig-saw puzzle of province, race, and religion. The Maritime Provinces had adequate representation in Tupper, Tilley, James McDonald, J. C. Pope, and Wilmot; Quebec had Langevin, Masson, Baby, and J. H. Pope; Ontario had Macdonald himself, Boswell, and Campbell; and the West was represented by Aikins. But Macdonald's chief triumph was the inclusion in the Cabinet of both Mackenzie Bowell, the Grand Master of the Orange Association, and Hector Langevin, the political leader of the French-Canadian clericals. The presence in his Cabinet of such discordant and anti-pathetic elements proved later to be, on occasion, a cause of weakness and embarrassment; but it was based on a tacit understanding to let sleeping dogs lie, and for the moment it ensured to Macdonald a majority both in Ontario and in Quebec. For once, moreover, politics harmonised with statesmanship. Macdonald's success in driving in harness the orange and the *bleu* showed the people of Canada that it was possible for the most diverse elements in the body politic to work together for good.

During the years that followed there were, perhaps, more than the usual number of changes in this Cabinet. In 1880 Baby was appointed to the Bench, Wilmot was appointed Lieutenant-Governor of New Brunswick, and Masson resigned from ill-health. Their places were taken by J. A. Mousseau, D. L. Macpherson, and Adolphe Caron. In 1881 James McDonald resigned to go on the Bench; and A. W. McLelan, who resigned from the Senate to re-enter the Commons, was taken into the Cabinet. The year 1882 saw further changes. Aikins resigned to become Lieutenant-Governor of Manitoba; Mousseau, in order to become Prime Minister of Quebec; O'Connor, to become later a judge; and J. C. Pope, from ill-health. The vacancies thus created were filled by John Carling, who had been a member of the first Government of Ontario, by J. A. Chapleau, who had been Prime Minister of Quebec since 1879, by John Costigan, an Irish Roman Catholic from New Brunswick, and by Frank Smith, a Roman Catholic from Ontario—the last without portfolio. Finally, in 1884 Tupper left the Cabinet to become Canadian High Commissioner in London; and in 1885 Tilley was compelled by ill-health to retire from politics, and to assume once more the Lieutenant-Governorship of New Brunswick. These frequent changes, entailing the appearance of new faces at the council board, greatly altered the complexion of the Cabinet, and emphasised the pre-eminence of Macdonald. Especially after the retirement of Tupper and Tilley, Macdonald was left without a rival near the throne, absolute master of the Administration.

Nor were all these changes fortuitous. In many of them was seen the hand of the master strategist. There was, for instance, in the frequent changes among the Quebec ministers more policy than accident. Macdonald seems to have followed, among his French-Canadian colleagues, the precept *Divide et impera*. He played off Langevin against Caron, Caron against Chapleau, and Chapleau against Langevin. It is not necessary here to enter into the intricacies of Quebec politics in the 'eighties; but nothing is more certain than that Macdonald used them for his own ends. Langevin he apparently regarded as his ultimate successor—"because", he said, "he has always been true to me"—but he did not wish Langevin to be able to bring to bear upon him the full pressure of a united Quebec. For this reason he brought upon the stage, first Mousseau and Caron, and then Chapleau. In the same way, it appears that the translation of Tupper to the Canadian High Commissionership in London was not wholly without design. Sir Richard Cartwright (no mean authority) asserts that Macdonald had offered to retire from the premiership in favour of Tupper, but that he found it difficult to carry out his intention, since (as he reported) some of his supporters declined to follow Tupper, and that consequently the appointment of Tupper to the High Commissionership was the only way out of the dilemma. However this may be, it is clear that Macdonald used even Tupper as a pawn in the game of politics.

To the end of his days, Macdonald was a politician first, and a statesman afterwards. Perhaps this was, in Canada at that time, a condition of successful statesmanship; nor was it an unnatural condition. The trouble was that Macdonald devoted so much attention to the details of politics that he was sometimes unable to give to the problems of statesmanship the time they deserved. "I have no doubt", said Sir Richard Cartwright, "that Sir John often thought long and hard how best he could strengthen his hold on power and keep his party well in hand, but I very strongly suspect that he never bestowed half-a-dozen hours of serious study on the problem of how best to promote the settlement of the North West, or how to stop the exodus, which was steadily increasing, of our people to the United States".

The first problem which Macdonald attacked, after his return to power in 1878, was the carrying out of the National Policy. He had promised to give Canada a protectionist tariff, and he was as good as his word. Hitherto Canada had had a tariff "for revenue alone"; now it got a tariff designed to protect to the full its nascent industries. Even Alexander Mackenzie admitted that Macdonald "had gone the whole hog". Whether the National Policy was a sound policy, and whether it achieved the results expected of it, are questions on which political parties in Canada are still divided. But it was an intelligible policy; and once Macdonald had adopted it, he had no hesitation in carrying it to its logical conclusion. "I will say this for that old scoundrel, John A. Macdonald", observed Sir Richard Cartwright, "that if he once gave you his word, you could rely upon it".

A natural concomitant of the National Policy was the building of a national transcontinental railway, which would facilitate inter-provincial trade. Indeed, if trade was to flow east and west, rather than north and south, a transcontinental railway was not only a desideratum, but a necessity. The arrangements originally made by Macdonald in 1872 for the building of the Canadian Pacific Railway had been rendered abortive by the "Pacific Scandal" and Macdonald's subsequent fall from power; and the Mackenzie Government, as we have seen, had proceeded with the building of the railway in a very half-hearted and piecemeal manner. Now that the National Policy, however, was a *fait accompli*, Macdonald was able to turn his attention once more to completing the Canadian Pacific Railway, and to carrying out thus the pledge he had given to British Columbia when it had entered the Confederation in 1871. With the lapse of the charter for building this railway which Macdonald had given the Allan syndicate in 1872, the Mackenzie Government had reverted to the idea of constructing the railway as a public work under government control; and what work was done on the railway between 1874 and 1878 was done by government contractors. During 1879–80 Tupper, first as Minister of Public Works, and then as Minister of Railways and Canals, had continued this policy, but with decidedly unsatisfactory results. In 1880, therefore, Macdonald and Tupper decided to go back to the project of building the railway through the agency of a private company, which would push through the completion of the railway with the greatest possible speed.

In the summer of 1880 Macdonald, with three of his colleagues—Tupper, J. H. Pope, and D. L. Macpherson—went to England for the purpose of finding capitalists who would undertake to finance the construction and working of the railway. After much negotiation, they were successful. A syndicate was formed, which came to be known later as the Canadian Pacific Railway Company, which undertook both to build and to work the proposed railway. The leading members of the syndicate were George Stephen (afterwards Lord Mount Stephen), Sir John Rose (who had been the second Minister of Finance of the Dominion), J. J. Hill (a Canadian who became a great railway-builder in the United States), and Donald A. Smith (afterwards Lord Strathcona). Owing to Donald A. Smith's estrangement from Macdonald in 1873, his name did not appear, his interest being held by other parties; but he proved a chief mainstay of the venture, and subsequently, on his reconciliation with Macdonald, his connection with the Company was made public. Stephen, Smith, and Hill had all been members of the syndicate which had in 1879 taken over the St Paul, Minneapolis, and Manitoba Railway, which had first given access by rail to the Canadian North West, and they were personally conversant with the possibilities of a Canadian transcontinental railway route.

The terms on which the railway was to be built were, in the nature of the case, not unattractive. The Company, on its part, undertook to complete the line by 1891, and to deposit with the Government of Canada the sum of one million dollars as an evidence of good faith. But it was to receive on the other hand, as a subvention, twenty-five million dollars and twenty-five million acres of land along the route of the railway between Winnipeg and the Rockies. These conditions were undoubtedly generous; and when the contract came before Parliament for ratification at the beginning of 1881, they were bitterly attacked by the Liberal Opposition. Edward Blake, who had in 1879 succeeded Alexander Mackenzie as leader of the Liberal party, prophesied that the Canadian Pacific Railway would not "pay for its axle-grease", and appealed to Parliament not to throw the hard-earned money of the Canadian tax-payers "down the gorges of British Columbia". Under Liberal inspiration, a rival syndicate was formed which offered to build the Canadian Pacific Railway on much less onerous terms; but the *bona fides* of this Company was open to doubt, and in any case its offer came too late. The Government, with its parliamentary majority, was able to ensure the approval of the contract into which it had entered for better or worse.

British Columbia had been promised in 1871 that the Canadian Pacific Railway would be completed within ten years. These ten years had now elapsed, and thanks to the inaction of the Mackenzie Government, less than three hundred miles of track along the main line of the railway had been laid. In fairness to British Columbia, it was desirable that the rest of the railway should be completed with all possible despatch. The new Company rose to the situation magnificently. The final surveys were pushed forward with energy; contracts were let for the construction of the various sections of the railway; and on 7 November 1885, Donald Smith drove home the last spike at Craigellachie, a lonely spot in British Columbia—less than five years after the building of the railway had been resumed.

This great feat was not accomplished without the conquest of many difficulties, both in engineering and in finance. The difficult country to the north and west of Lake Superior, and still more the vast barrier of the Rockies, interposed problems which taxed the skill and ingenuity of the Company's engineers to the utmost. But the chief difficulties were financial. The attacks which had been made on the project by the Liberal Opposition undermined the Company's credit, and made it difficult for it to borrow money, or even to realise on its lands. By the end of 1883, the Company was in financial straits; and Macdonald was compelled to cable to Tupper, who had gone to London to take up his duties as High Commissioner, "Pacific in trouble, you should be here". Tupper returned immediately, and in the session of 1884 he fought through Parliament a bill whereby a loan of $22,500,000 was advanced to the Company from the public funds. This measure of relief solved the financial difficulty for a time;

but only for a time. Early in 1885 the Company found itself once more without resources. The general manager telegraphed to the president, "Have no means of paying wages, pay-car can't be sent out, and unless we get immediate relief we must stop". Stephen, the president, appealed to the Government for a further loan of $5,000,000. But his appeal was not cordially received. The majority of the Cabinet felt that to grant any further loans would be merely a justification of the prophecies of the Opposition. Even Macdonald seems to have made up his mind that further assistance was out of the question. It was a critical moment, not only for the Canadian Pacific Railway, but for Canada itself. Fortunately, at the last moment, Pope persuaded Macdonald to call an emergency meeting of the Cabinet to reconsider the matter. At this meeting Macdonald placed the issue squarely before his colleagues, and braver and wiser counsels prevailed. By the sheer exercise of his personal authority, Macdonald brought his recalcitrant followers into line; and Parliament was prevailed upon to vote the necessary loan. From that day all went well. The railway was completed without further misadventure; and ultimately both loans were fully repaid. But seldom has the fate of a great enterprise trembled so precariously in the balance as that of the Canadian Pacific Railway in those early days of 1885.

Meanwhile, the Government had appealed to the electors, and had been returned by a large majority. In this election, which took place in 1882, the chief issue was the building of the Canadian Pacific Railway; but a decisive factor, in the opinion of the Liberal Opposition, was a redistribution bill which Macdonald had put through Parliament prior to the election. The census of 1881 had shown that Ontario was entitled to a larger representation in the House of Commons; and Macdonald seized on this as an excuse for altering the boundaries of a large number of constituencies in Ontario in such a way as to favour the Conservatives. The process, to which the name of "gerrymander" is commonly applied, was described by Macdonald himself as "hiving the 'Grits'". Liberal districts were added to constituencies already decidedly Liberal in complexion; and Conservative districts were added to constituencies where the issue was doubtful. Sir Richard Cartwright estimated that the redistribution robbed the Liberals of no less than twenty seats. This was no doubt an over-estimate, since the "gerrymander" aroused such opposition that it may have lost the Conservatives as many votes as it gained them. But it had, no doubt, an influence on the result; and, in any case, it was not a specimen of Macdonald's state-craft at its best.

Scarcely less reprehensible was the Franchise Bill which Macdonald introduced into Parliament in 1885. In principle, this bill had much to commend it. Hitherto the provincial voters' lists had been used in the federal elections; and not all the provinces had uniform franchise laws. It was proper and natural that the Dominion Parliament should seek to control the voters' lists for its own elections. But Macdonald inserted in the bill provisions whereby the voters' lists were to be prepared and revised by paid agents of the Government; and it was feared by the Liberals that this would result in the "stuffing" of these lists against them. There were those, indeed, who insisted that the disfranchisement of Liberals was the chief object with which the bill was introduced. Against the bill every form of parliamentary obstruction was brought into play. For weeks the debates lasted until dawn. Eventually, Macdonald, unwilling to appeal to the country on such an issue, was compelled to compromise; and the more objectionable features of the bill were amended. But both the "gerrymander" of 1882 and the Franchise Bill of 1885 illustrated the lengths to which Macdonald was prepared to go, in tampering with the representative system, in order to retain power.

There is no doubt that, in some respects, the political morality of Sir John Macdonald was not of a high order. He studied human nature, as Goldwin Smith said, "too much on the weak side". Though incorruptible himself, he was not above the indirect bribery of others, and he never hesitated to dispense with rules in playing the game of politics. At the same time, it must be confessed that he merely took things as he found them. Both pathos and common sense appear in his reply to an elector who had objected to his political methods: "Send me better men, and I will be a better man myself". Possibly a statesman imbued with higher ideals of morality would have failed where he succeeded. Certainly, judged by the standard of achievement, Macdonald stands head and shoulders above his contemporaries. He it was who founded and organised the great Liberal-Conservative party; if not the initiator, he was the master-builder of Confederation; he was the sponsor of the Canadian Pacific Railway; and he was the author of the National Policy of protection of native industries —a policy which has never been really reversed from that day to this. In the critical years of its youth the Dominion of Canada was to a large extent the work of his hand.

CHAPTER XXI

THE CONSERVATIVE AND LIBERAL
ADMINISTRATIONS, 1885–1911

HAD he consulted his own wishes, there is no doubt that Macdonald would have retired from politics in 1885. "With the Canadian Pacific Railway finished, and with my Franchise Bill become law", he wrote, "I feel that I have done my work, and can now sing my *nunc dimittis*". He was over the age of three score years and ten; and he had no ambitions unfulfilled. He was not to be permitted, however, to put off his armour. His followers were far from united on the choice of a successor; and there had occurred, moreover, during 1885 an event which damaged greatly the prestige of the Government, which even threatened to disrupt the Liberal-Conservative party, and which made essential his continuance in office.

This was the second North West rebellion. The building of the Canadian Pacific Railway and the incoming of settlers had alarmed the half-breeds on the Saskatchewan, as the half-breeds on the Red River had been alarmed fifteen years before. They were unable to get from the Canadian Government satisfactory titles to the lands they held, and they were afraid they would be dispossessed. A little diplomacy would have allayed these fears; but Sir David Macpherson, the Minister of the Interior, though an able and honest administrator, was not alive to the situation. Despairing of justice, the half-breeds appealed to Louis Riel, the leader of the Red River rebellion of 1869–70, who had taken refuge in Montana; and Riel returned to Canada, and organised a revolt of the half-breeds and of some of the Indians. At Frog Lake there was a massacre of white settlers by a band of Indians under a chief named Big Bear; and a wholesale Indian uprising, with all its attendant horrors, seemed imminent. A force of Canadian militia, under General Middleton, was hurried to the North West by the newly-built railway; and succeeded with little difficulty in crushing the rebellion. At Batoche Riel's half-breeds were defeated, and he himself was captured. But out of the rebellion developed a situation which threatened to dissolve the Confederation.

Twice had Riel been guilty of rebellion against the Crown. His first offence had been allowed to pass into oblivion; there is even reason for believing that he had been encouraged to keep out of the way. But his second offence convinced Macdonald that the time for leniency was past. There were certain principles with which he never trifled. One of these was the preservation of law and order. Riel was brought to trial on a charge of treason, was found guilty, and was hanged at Regina. His conviction was the signal for an outburst of racial and religious feeling. In Quebec, French Canadians, both Liberal and Conservative, had, on account of Riel's French blood, vehemently opposed his execution. In English-speaking Canada, on the other hand, his death had been demanded with equal vehemence. The Cabinet itself was divided on the matter. But Macdonald had made up his mind. "He shall die", he exclaimed, "though every dog in Quebec bark in his favour". An attempt to save him from the gallows on the plea of insanity was unsuccessful, and when he paid the price of his criminal folly, a wave of bitter passion swept over Quebec.

Of this sentiment Edward Blake, the Liberal leader, strove to take full advantage. Though he disclaimed any desire to make political use of the "Regina scaffold", he opposed and condemned the course of the Government throughout; and his championship of Riel's cause proved a source of the strength which the Liberal party has had in the province of Quebec since that time. Whether Blake's attitude toward the execution of Riel strengthened the Liberal party as a whole may, perhaps, be questioned. Losing in Ontario what he gained in Quebec, he failed to carry with him many of the leading English-speaking Liberals in Parliament.

Had the Liberal party during this period enjoyed the leadership of a more practical politician than Blake, there might have been a different story to tell. All he needed to do was to hold his own followers together, and to divide the Government forces. But he succeeded in doing neither of these things effectively. The truth is that, as leader of the Opposition, Blake was a comparative failure. Despite his great abilities, he was singularly lacking in political sagacity. Shy and reserved in temperament, he held himself aloof from his supporters, and his "repulsive nod" did not win for him their affection. He seldom consulted his colleagues, and his actions repeatedly caused consternation among them. In 1883 he went out of his way to offend the powerful Orange Association by deliberately opposing the bill for its incorporation. Later he aggravated the results of this blunder by gratuitously advocating in the Canadian House of Commons the cause of Home Rule for Ireland; and when he espoused the cause of Riel in 1885 he finally ruined his chances of ever polling a majority of votes in Ontario. His speech on the execution of Riel, which took seven hours to deliver, and which is said to have taken him three months to prepare, was a masterpiece of legal disquisition; but its only effect was to put his supporters to sleep, and to relieve greatly the minds of his opponents. On occasion, he was known, on the floor of the House, to carry his researches to five places of decimals; and he once upbraided one of his lieutenants for failing to see more than two sides of a question. With his profound and exhaustive mind he was without a peer in the court-room; but he never completely adjusted himself to the political arena.

Meanwhile, Sir John Macdonald had been busy strengthening his entrenchments. In 1887 he persuaded Sir Charles Tupper to resign temporarily the Canadian High Commissionership in London, and to return to Canada as Finance Minister; and he also reinforced his Cabinet by the inclusion of several notable new men. One of these, John S. D. Thompson, who took the portfolio of Justice and was regarded by Macdonald as the "greatest find" of his political career, ultimately became Prime Minister of Canada; another, George E. Foster, who became Minister of Marine and Fisheries, was subsequently Minister of Finance and Minister of Trade and Commerce in successive Conservative Administrations; and a third, Thomas White, who became Minister of the Interior in 1885, displayed signal abilities until his career was cut short by death in 1888.

With this Cabinet Macdonald submitted his record to the judgment of the electors in the general elections of 1887. He appears to have been genuinely apprehensive of the result, and with reason. When the returns were in, it was found that the Government's majority had been cut in half; and there was doubt as to the party loyalty of twelve or more of the Quebec members who were officially labelled Conservative. Could these be detached from the Government side, the Conservative majority was hardly likely to number a baker's dozen. Another election within a year or two was, in these circumstances, not improbable; and in this election the Liberals, with the tide setting in their favour, might easily win. But Blake, by one of his characteristically abrupt actions, threw the game away. During the session of 1887 he suddenly addressed a circular letter to his supporters resigning the leadership of the Liberal party. His motives in taking this extraordinarily inconsiderate action are difficult to discern. Chagrin at his failure to carry the country and a desire to anticipate any demand for his retirement were, no doubt, present in his mind. But his failure to confer with his supporters, while typical of the man, took the Liberal party unawares, and disorganised its *moral*. It seemed as though Achilles, with victory at last in sight, had gone off to sulk in his tent.

With heavy hearts, the Liberals turned to face the problem of choosing a new leader. The most obvious choice was Richard Cartwright, who, as Minister of Finance in the Mackenzie Administration, had earned the *soubriquet* of "the Rupert of debate". With his Tory antecedents and his vigorous fighting instincts, Cartwright would have been an admirable leader of the Opposition; but, as the Liberals could not hope to gain much ground in Ontario, it was deemed wise to offer the leadership to a French Canadian. The choice of the party therefore fell on Wilfrid Laurier; and no happier choice of a political leader was ever made. Laurier, still a young man, was without family ties; he had an unrivalled command of both the English and the French languages, a mind of singular clarity and moderation and urbane and courtly manners which endeared him to all with whom he came into contact. He had begun his political career in the ranks of the *parti rouge*; but his sympathies, unlike those of many of that party, were with English Liberalism—the Liberalism of Burke and Fox—rather than with French republicanism. There was, of course, at first difficulty in reconciling the Scots Presbyterian Liberals of Ontario—the quondam followers of George Brown—to the leadership of a French Roman Catholic; but eventually Laurier completely won even their allegiance. The time came, indeed, when he was more concerned over his supremacy in Quebec than over his hold on the votes of English-speaking Liberals.

For the moment, however, Laurier's position was far from happy. He had hardly assumed the leadership of the party when there emerged on the political horizon a question which caused him no small amount of embarrassment. This was the question of the Jesuits' estates. When the Society of Jesus had been suppressed by the Pope in 1773, its estates in Canada had reverted to the Crown; and in 1867 they had come under the control of the Legislature of the province of Quebec. In 1887 there came into power in Quebec the Liberal Government of Honoré Mercier, a bold and clever politician who had placed himself *en rapport* with the ultramontane wing of the Roman Catholic Church in the province. In that year Mercier placed on the statute books of Quebec an Act reconstituting the Society of Jesus as an incorporated body; and in 1888 he followed this up with an Act authorising the payment to the Jesuits of $400,000 as compensation for the estates they had lost. This Act had some objectionable features, notably a provision whereby the settlement was subject to the ratification of the Papacy; but it was accompanied by an increased grant to the Protestant schools in Quebec, and among the Protestants of Quebec there was little opposition to it. In Ontario, however, it roused a furore. Led by Dalton McCarthy, a prominent Conservative, the extreme Protestants of Ontario, both Liberals and Conservatives, united to form what was known as the Equal Rights Association, and demanded the disallowance of the Jesuits' Estates Bill by the Federal Government. Sir John Macdonald was too shrewd a politician to invoke the power of disallowance in the case of a financial measure which was so obviously a matter within the competency of the Quebec Legislature; but McCarthy pressed the matter on the attention of the Federal Parliament, and though he could muster only thirteen votes—"the noble thirteen", they were called in Ontario—he created a serious split in the Conservative party, and gained widespread support in the English provinces.

Laurier was placed in a difficult position. He did not wholly approve of the Jesuits' Estates Act; but he did not believe in the exercise of the federal power of disallowance of provincial legislation, and he was satisfied that the Quebec Legislature was entitled to throw its own money into the sea, if it so desired. At the same time, he hesitated to appear to support Mercier, since he knew that his support would be attributed to the fact that he was a French-Canadian Roman Catholic. His apprenticeship in the *parti rouge* had not, moreover, inclined him toward Mercier's ultramontanism. Accordingly he hesitated; but he finally took his stand on the ground of provincial rights; and he courageously carried the war into the enemy's territory by going to Toronto and defending his views in a magnificent speech before a vast audience in that citadel of Orange Toryism—an audience which, though at first hostile, became first respectful, and then half-persuaded.

With the leaders of both parties opposed to the disallowance of the Jesuits' Estates Act, the agitation of the Equal Rights Association gradually died down; though not before the fires of religious animosity had been rekindled in both Ontario and Quebec, and lines of cleavage had been driven into both the Liberal and the Conservative parties. Which party suffered most is a matter for speculation. The chief support of the Equal Rights Association came from the Conservatives, and there is no doubt that Macdonald had to face a serious insurrection among his supporters in Ontario; but there were many Liberals who sympathised with the movement, and identified themselves with it. On the other hand, Macdonald, by his attitude, recovered in Quebec some of the ground he had lost during the agitation over the execution of Riel; whereas the day was postponed when Laurier was able to win the complete confidence of the Liberals of Ontario. Perhaps, on the whole, Laurier suffered more from the Equal Rights movement than did Macdonald.

Meanwhile, fortunately for Canadian unity, a question of another character forced itself into the political arena. This was the question of commercial union or "unrestricted reciprocity". The National Policy had not produced all the results prophesied of it. It had not, by itself, brought about any pronounced revival of industry in Canada; and it had failed to stem the tide of Canadian emigration to the United States. Had Sir John Macdonald accompanied his fiscal policy with an attempt to develop the great natural resources of Canada, there might have been a different tale to tell; but Macdonald's interest lay in politics rather than in economics. During the 'eighties, consequently, a movement had sprung up toward closer commercial relations with the United States. The father of this movement was Erastus Wiman, a Canadian who later made his mark in New York; and Goldwin Smith lent to it the support of his powerful and incisive pen. Among the professional politicians the chief advocate of the idea was Cartwright, who, like his old chief Mackenzie, was a convinced free-trader. Cartwright was not able to commit the Liberal party to the undiluted policy of commercial union; but he did succeed in committing it to the more practical policy of "unrestricted reciprocity" with the United States, and this was the chief plank in the platform on which the Liberals appealed to the country in 1891.

Here again Laurier's position was difficult. He was not a doctrinaire free-trader, and he was opposed to the idea of commercial union, both on political and economic grounds. He accepted the idea of "unrestricted reciprocity", though apparently with some misgiving; and he must have been unhappy in the knowledge that Blake, who was still in Parliament, was out of sympathy with the new policy of the party. It was with difficulty, on the eve of the elections of 1891, that Blake was restrained from attacking publicly the idea of "unrestricted reciprocity"; and his attack was only deferred until the day after the elections, when he published his celebrated *Address to the electors of West Durham*. Whatever may be thought of the ethics of Blake's post-election repudiation of the policy of the party which he had ceased to lead, there is no doubt that his studied silence before the elections was damaging to the Liberal cause, and was a source of worry and embarrassment to the new leader of the party.

Macdonald's course, on the other hand, was clear. He was no stranger to the idea of reciprocity with the United States, and had frequently advocated it. As late as 1890, he would have been quite willing to "dish the Whigs by stealing their clothes". But once the Liberal party was irrevocably committed to the idea of reciprocity, Macdonald fell back on the National Policy. Unrestricted reciprocity he denounced as the inevitable precursor of political union with the United States; and with that gift for telling phraseology which he revealed at critical moments, he coined the famous sentence, "A British subject I was born, a British subject I will die. With my utmost effort, with my latest breath, will I oppose the 'veiled treason' which attempts by sordid means and mercenary proffers to lure our people from their allegiance".[1] His party went into the campaign with the battle-cry of "the old man, the old flag and the old policy"; and they were able to give point to this cry by making use of an unpublished pamphlet by Edward Farrer, the chief editorial writer on the Toronto *Globe*, in which the annexation of Canada to the United States was prophesied.

The result was the defeat of the Liberals in the elections of 1891, for the fourth time in succession. The Conservative majority was not large, but it was adequate. To a great extent, it was a personal triumph for Macdonald himself, who had been represented as appealing to his friends for their suffrages for the last time. The appeal was prophetic. On the day of the elections, worn out by his electioneering efforts, Macdonald took to his bed; two months later

[1] Pope, Sir J., *Mems. of Macdonald*, II, 336.

he suffered a slight stroke, and then a more severe one; and on 6 June 1891 his great and gallant spirit took flight. It is not too much to say that his death marked the close of an epoch in Canadian history. He had been in Canadian politics for nearly fifty years, and during this time had exerted a continuous influence upon the fortunes of the country. He was not without grave faults; nor has any attempt been made in these pages to minimise them. But he was at heart a patriot. It is easy to say that he was unprincipled; but there were some principles on which he knew no compromise—the integrity of the British Empire, the preservation of law and order, the keeping of promises, and his own personal incorruptibility. After enjoying public office for thirty years, during the greater part of which he was first minister of the Crown, he died in 1891 a poor man. To Canada his death was a calamity; to the Conservative party it was a disaster. But his memory is still a fragrant and potent influence in Canadian politics. As *Punch* put it, on his death, with a touching allusion to his nickname of "Old To-morrow":

> Canada's "Old To-morrow" lives to-day
> In unforgetting hearts, and nothing fears
> The long to-morrow of the coming years.

Once the hand of the master strategist had been removed, the Conservative Government and the Conservative party gradually went to pieces. The process of disintegration was spread over five years, and at times it seemed as though it had been arrested. But the stars in their courses were fighting against Sisera, and in 1896 came the débâcle. Difficulty occurred, in the first place, over the choice of Macdonald's successor as Prime Minister. The two chief candidates for the office were Thompson and Bowell. Thompson (now Sir John Thompson) was, however, a Roman Catholic convert from Methodism, and as such proved unacceptable to the Orangemen of Ontario; whereas Bowell, the grand master of the Orange Association, was regarded as unacceptable to the French-Canadian Roman Catholics of Quebec. In the end the party selected a compromise candidate—J. J. C. (later Sir John) Abbott. He, the Government leader in the Senate, was on good terms with both the Orangemen and the Roman Catholics in the party, besides being a lawyer of ability and astuteness. No longer a young man, however, he was regarded by the party managers as little more than a stop-gap until the dissensions in the party might be healed. He held office as Prime Minister for about eighteen months; but at the end of 1892 ill-health compelled him to retire from political life, and he died in 1893.

During his brief regime Abbott revealed an unexpected degree of political sagacity. He took over the Cabinet of Sir John Macdonald intact; and he had the wisdom to confide the leadership of the House of Commons to Thompson. On more than one occasion he completely outgeneralled the Opposition. But he did not find his lot a bed of roses. During the session of 1891 Israel Tarte, an able and audacious French-Canadian journalist who had hitherto been Conservative in his leanings, brought forward against Sir Hector Langevin, the Minister of Public Works, concrete charges of departmental corruption. The charges were referred to the committee on privileges and elections; and the evidence produced before this committee made it clear that Thomas McGreevy, one of the Conservative members of the House of Commons, had been mainly instrumental in obtaining from the Department of Public Works corrupt favours for contractors who had contributed to party funds. The political washtub was for the moment black with the linen cast into it. McGreevy himself was expelled from the House; but the committee differed as to the culpability of Langevin. The majority held that Langevin was innocent of any connection with the irregularities in his department; and the House sustained their verdict. But it appeared that McGreevy and Langevin had lodged together in Ottawa; and in any case Langevin could not be acquitted of the charge of negligence. He was compelled to resign office; and the Conservative party lost its chief leader in the province of Quebec.

The McGreevy scandals told heavily against the Government. They revealed a degree of laxity and corruption in the Administration which shocked even some of the Conservative members. But, fortunately for the Conservative cause, charges of corruption no less reprehensible were almost immediately levelled against the Liberal Government of Honoré Mercier in the province of Quebec. Evidence was forthcoming to show that the Mercier Government had trafficked in public contracts for the benefit of the campaign funds of the provincial Liberal party. The connection of Mercier with these frauds was not proved any more than that of Langevin with the McGreevy frauds, but the revelations provided the Conservatives with an unanswerable *tu quoque*, and made it impossible for the Liberals in the Federal Parliament to reap the benefit of the McGreevy-Langevin charges. Mercier was dismissed from office by the Lieutenant-Governor of Quebec, and in the ensuing elections the Liberal party in that province suffered defeat. From the standpoint of party politics, the downfall of Mercier was a veritable godsend to the Conservative party in the federal arena.

When Sir John Abbott retired from office the Conservative party seemed, no doubt, as strong as, if not stronger than, it had been at the time of Sir John Macdonald's death. Under Abbott, indeed, its parliamentary majority was considerably augmented. But the appearance of strength was superficial. The retirement of Langevin left the Conservatives without any leader of the first rank in the province of Quebec, with the exception of Sir Adolphe Caron; and Caron himself had been under attack. On the other hand, the defeat of Mercier left Laurier the unrivalled leader of the

Quebec Liberals, and in fact the only political leader of the first rank in the province. The disappearance of Langevin and Mercier had thus the result of enhancing Laurier's prestige, and of hastening the day when he was able to appeal to his own people as their "favourite son".

Sir John Abbott was succeeded in 1892 by Sir John Thompson. Abbott's shrewd and patient leadership had composed the party differences which had been acute in 1891; and Mackenzie Bowell himself, though no longer grand master of the Orange Association, exerted his efforts to ensure the support of Thompson by the Orange lodges. Thompson was a very able man. As a lawyer, he was hardly inferior to Edward Blake; and he had a trustworthy solidity which Blake lacked. His chief defect was a cutting Irish wit which occasionally got the better of him. "Thompson", Sir John Macdonald had once said, "has just two faults. He is a little too fond of satire, and a little too much of a Nova Scotian". By 1892 he had got over the latter fault, but he never got over his love of satire. On one occasion he even let it play about the wife of the Governor-General. When dining at Government House, he was much troubled by the mosquitoes, and when his vice-regal hostess suggested closing the windows, he replied with sarcasm, "Oh, pray, do not bother. I think they are all in now". His mordant wit did not endear him to everyone; and he would never have achieved the popularity of Sir John Macdonald. But his ability and his integrity won universal recognition, and had he lived longer he might have rehabilitated the fortunes of the Conservative party.

Thompson's Cabinet contained few surprises. He himself retained the portfolio of Justice, and Foster that of Finance. Caron, Ouimet, Bowell, Charles H. Tupper, Haggart, Costigan and others of the Old Guard remained at the council board. Chapleau retired, and was succeeded by A. R. Angers, whose term as Lieutenant-Governor of Quebec had expired. W. B. Ives, a politician from the Eastern Townships, became President of the Council, and Sir Frank Smith and Sir John Carling were ministers without portfolio. The most notable change was the appointment of a comptroller of Customs, a comptroller of Inland Revenue, and a Solicitor-General, who were to be members of the ministry, but not of the Cabinet; and it was significant that the post of comptroller of Customs was filled by the appointment of N. Clarke Wallace, who had succeeded Bowell as grand master of the Orange Association. The comptroller of Inland Revenue was John F. Wood, and the Solicitor-General, John J. Curran.

With this Cabinet Thompson governed Canada successfully for two years. He had his difficulties with internal politics, especially with the question of the tariff and with that of the suppression of Roman Catholic separate schools in Manitoba which is discussed below. Even among his own supporters there was complaint with regard to the high protective tariff, and he was compelled to promise to "lop the mouldering branches away". He was embarrassed also by the action of the Manitoba Government in abolishing separate schools in Manitoba; but he was able successfully to shelve this issue—when the intervention of the Dominion Government was demanded—by the device of referring the question to the courts. He took, in fact, no strong line in regard to domestic problems, and his chief energies were devoted to foreign and imperial affairs. Most of his time was occupied in negotiations as the representative of Great Britain at the Behring Sea arbitration at Paris, and as the representative of Canada at the Intercolonial Conference in Ottawa in 1893, and in London in 1894, in regard to copyright and merchant shipping. In the later negotiations he showed himself no mean successor of Edward Blake as a champion of Canadian autonomy. His chief interest lay, in fact, in the legal aspects of Canada's foreign and imperial relations; and herein lay also his chief contribution to Canadian development.

It was while he was in England at the end of 1894, in connection with negotiations over these matters, that he died suddenly at Windsor Castle. His death was unexpected, and took the Conservative party unawares. Within four years they had lost by death three Prime Ministers. Such a succession of disasters was enough to demoralise any political party, and especially a party which had held office for over fifteen years, and was fighting with its back to the wall. With every government, dry rot sets in after a prolonged period of office, and life and vigour depart. Such was the fate of the Conservative Government after the death of Sir John Macdonald, and especially after the death of Sir John Thompson. The chief problem of the party became that of clinging to power, and a party which is preoccupied with such a problem is heading for disaster.

The task of forming a new Government was confided to Mackenzie (later Sir Mackenzie) Bowell. Bowell was entitled to the Premiership both on the grounds of seniority and as a concession to the Orange Association, which had loyally accepted the leadership of Thompson in 1892. He was an honest, straightforward, bluff, and somewhat mediocre politician, who might in other circumstances have risen to unexpected heights. But he succeeded to the leadership of the party at a time when the Archangel Gabriel might have fallen short of what was expected of him. He had to take over, almost without change, the Cabinet of his predecessor; and this Cabinet was one neither of outstanding distinction nor of conspicuous loyalty to himself. Sir John Thompson's place as Minister of Justice was taken by the young Charles Hibbert Tupper; Bowell's place as Minister of Trade and Commerce was taken by W. B. Ives; and two ministers without portfolio were added to the Government—Donald Ferguson, from Prince Edward Island, and Dr W. H. Montague, from Western Ontario. But in the main the Cabinet was the same as under Thompson.

At this juncture, moreover, a question became acute which, after causing successive Conservative Governments no small amount of concern, was destined to be the cause of the downfall of that party. This was the question of separate Roman Catholic schools in Manitoba. The province of Manitoba had contained from the first a considerable French-Canadian Roman Catholic population, the descendants of the *engagés* of the fur trade; and the Manitoba Act of 1870 had contained provisions intended to safeguard separate denominational schools. In its first session the Legislature of Manitoba had established a school system modelled upon that of Quebec; and the provincial grant for education was apportioned between the Protestant and the Roman Catholic schools. At an early date, however, it became apparent that Manitoba was to be predominantly an English-speaking Protestant province; and a movement sprang up for the abolition of separate Roman Catholic schools. This movement, stimulated by the Equal Rights agitation in Ontario, resulted in 1890 in the abolition of all denominational control of Manitoban schools, and in the establishment of a system of non-sectarian public schools. The Roman Catholic minority, robbed of what they regarded as their dearest rights, fought this legislation with bitter determination. They appealed to the Lieutenant-Governor to withhold his assent, but in vain; they appealed to the courts to declare the legislation unconstitutional, but without success; and finally they appealed to the Dominion Government to introduce remedial legislation.

To a Conservative Government such an appeal was embarrassing in the highest degree. The French-Canadian supporters of the Government, backed by the Roman Catholic hierarchy, insisted that a grievance existed, and that a remedy should be found. The Orangemen, on the other hand, were opposed to separate schools, and consequently to any remedial legislation. It was in vain that the Government sought to evade the difficulty by again referring the matter to the courts. Had the Roman Catholic minority in Manitoba the right to appeal to the Governor-General in Council? The Supreme Court of Canada ruled that it had not that right; but the question was carried to the Judicial Committee of the Privy Council at Westminster, and in the beginning of 1895 the Privy Council ruled that such an appeal was in order. This meant that the new Bowell Government was at last forced to face the question squarely, and make up its mind whether it would introduce remedial legislation or not, and if it did, what form that legislation would take.

The dissensions in the Cabinet were pitiful to behold. In the summer of 1895 Angers resigned because the Cabinet would not immediately introduce a remedial bill; and later in the year Wallace resigned because he could not exact a pledge that such a bill would not be introduced. Bowell succeeded in holding together, for the moment, the rest of his Cabinet; and he even got them to agree to

introduce, in a modified form, a bill restoring separate schools in
Manitoba. But discontent with his leadership had been gathering
head even in the Cabinet itself; and in the beginning of 1896 there
occurred one of the most amazing episodes in Canadian political
history. No less than seven of the ministers—C. H. Tupper, Foster,
Ives, Dickey, Wood, Haggart and Montague—resigned suddenly
while Parliament was sitting, and left Bowell stranded almost alone.
Bowell complained bitterly that he had been living for months in "a
nest of traitors"; but the truth seems to be that the "bolters"—all
Protestants—were alarmed at the prospect of trying to carry through
the coercion of Manitoba under a leader of such indifferent abilities
as Bowell, and had determined to force him to make way for a
stronger man. Bowell strove hard to form a new Government, but
his efforts were frustrated by pickets which watched every train
coming into Ottawa; and eventually a truce was patched up, whereby
most of the deserters were to return to their posts on condition that
Bowell should eventually make way for Sir Charles Tupper. Tupper,
answering the call of the party, resigned the High Commissionership
in London, returned to Canada, and at the end of April 1896
assumed the office of Prime Minister, with the understanding that he
would attempt to force the Remedial Bill through Parliament.

Sir Charles Tupper was no longer a young man; but his eye was
not dimmed, or his natural force abated. The "old war-horse", as
he was sometimes called, scented the battle from afar. His first task
was the reorganisation of the Government. He had not much Cabinet
timber to work with. He persuaded Angers to return to the Government; but he made the mistake of allowing Caron and Ouimet to
retire. Among the English-speaking ministers, there was only one
significant change: Hugh John Macdonald, the son of Sir John
Macdonald, was pressed into service as Minister of the Interior, and
it was hoped that his name would be a talisman of success. Sir
Charles Tupper's son, Charles Hibbert Tupper, on the other hand,
though appointed Solicitor-General, was not a member of the
Cabinet. Backed by this Cabinet, Tupper faced the situation with all
his old-time courage and determination. If these qualities had had
time to make their influence felt, the course of events might have been
different. But the seventh Parliament of the Dominion was rapidly
approaching its legal termination; and, moreover, Tupper found
himself faced by an antagonist who by this time had acquired an
adroitness in the art of politics in some respects hardly inferior,
and in others superior, to that of Sir John Macdonald. Wilfrid
Laurier had at first assumed toward the Manitoba schools question a
neutral and non-committal attitude. He sympathised with the desire
of the minority in Manitoba for separate schools; but refused to declare himself on the question of remedial legislation until the legislation was introduced. "I stand", he said in a famous speech, "within

the lines of Torres Vedras, and I will not come out before I choose my time". When the Remedial Bill was introduced, and then only, he came out and chose his ground of battle. Under the astute guidance of Israel Tarte, who had deserted the Conservatives, and who knew the politics of Quebec as no one else did, he opposed the Remedial Bill, on the plea that it contravened the Liberal doctrine of provincial rights. It combined, in his view, the maximum of coercion with the minimum of relief for the minority. Provincial rights had been since confederation a cardinal feature of the Liberal creed. Sir John Macdonald had always sought to assert the paramount authority of the Dominion Government and Parliament over provincial legislation; but Oliver Mowat, the Liberal Prime Minister of Ontario, had espoused the cause of provincial rights, and had won the day in repeated cases carried before the Judicial Committee of the Privy Council. The Privy Council, in a famous case, had even ruled that the provincial Legislature had, within its sphere, "authority as plenary and as ample . . . as the Imperial Parliament in the plenitude of its power possessed and could bestow". In taking his stand on the ground of provincial rights, Laurier was in full accord with sound Liberal doctrine.

At the same time, his attitude required courage. The bishops of the Roman Catholic Church, satisfied that the Remedial Bill was the best they could hope for, gave it their blessing; and the whole weight of the hierarchy was thrown into the scale to persuade Laurier to accept the bill. Laurier was a faithful son of Mother Church, and the pressure brought to bear on him must have caused him no small concern. But it was not for nothing that he had received his baptism of fire in the ranks of the *parti rouge*. In politics he declined to accept his orders from the Church. He had, moreover, a shrewd idea that the political principles of the *parti rouge* might triumph even in Quebec. The French-Canadian habitant, faced with the alternative of voting, at the behest of the clergy, for an English-speaking Prime Minister, or of voting, against the behest of the clergy, to place in power a French-Canadian Prime Minister, might easily choose the latter alternative. On the other hand, it was certain that Laurier's opposition to the Remedial Bill would greatly strengthen his hand in Ontario and the other English-speaking provinces.

These calculations proved correct. Tupper attempted, in the dying days of Parliament, to force the Remedial Bill through; but without success. The Liberals employed every means of obstruction known to parliamentary law, even to the extent of keeping the House of Commons in continuous session for ten days and nights, barring Sunday; and eventually Tupper was compelled to give up the struggle and to go to the country.

The result of the elections was a signal vindication of the wisdom of Laurier and Tarte. Manitoba, it is true, by a freak of politics, voted for its own coercion; but in nearly every other province the Liberals achieved a majority. In Ontario they carried, with their allies, fifty-one seats, as against forty-one for the straight Conservatives; in the Maritime Provinces they ended almost even; in British Columbia and the North West Territories they won six out of nine seats; but in Quebec they broke all records by capturing forty-nine out of sixty-five constituencies. "Jean-Baptiste" had voted for Wilfrid Laurier against the bishops. In all, the country had returned a Liberal majority of over thirty. Sir Charles Tupper, accepting the inevitable, promptly resigned; and the Governor-General sent for Laurier.

The Government which Laurier formed in 1896 was not inaptly described as "a ministry of all the talents". Never perhaps in Canadian history has so able and distinguished a group of men gathered about the council board. This was the more remarkable since of the Mackenzie Administration most of the members had passed from the scene. Only Laurier himself, Richard (shortly afterwards Sir Richard) Cartwright, and R. W. (later Sir Richard) Scott survived from the earlier to become ministers in the later Cabinet. Laurier, avoiding Mackenzie's mistake, did not take a department, but became merely President of the Council; Cartwright became Minister of Trade and Commerce, and Scott, Secretary of State. The other ministers were without administrative experience in the federal arena, but not all of them were without experience in provincial government. No less than three of the Liberal Prime Ministers in the provinces were persuaded to join the Administration: Sir Oliver Mowat, the veteran Prime Minister of Ontario, became Minister of Justice; W. S. Fielding, the Prime Minister of Nova Scotia, became Minister of Finance; and A. G. Blair, the Prime Minister of New Brunswick, became Minister of Railways and Canals. A few months later Clifford Sifton, Attorney-General in the Government of Manitoba, was appointed Minister of the Interior. The other ministers were Louis H. (later Sir Louis) Davies of Prince Edward Island, Frederick W. (later Sir Frederick) Borden of Nova Scotia, Israel Tarte, Sir Henri Joly de Lotbinière, C. A. Geoffrion, Sydney Fisher, R. R. Dobell, and Charles (later Sir Charles) Fitzpatrick of Quebec, and William (later Sir William) Mulock and William Paterson of Ontario.

With a Cabinet of such calibre Laurier proceeded to give the country a Government which contrasted strongly with that of the weak and moribund Administrations which had preceded it. He first addressed himself to a peaceful solution of the Manitoba schools question. With Liberal Governments in power both in Ottawa and in Winnipeg, it became possible to get the Manitoba Legislature to make amendments to the school law of the province which redressed some of the more serious grievances of the Roman Catholic minority.[1] These amendments did not go so far as Laurier would have liked; but he recognised that, in existing circumstances, they embodied the best

[1] For details *v. infra*, chap. xxii.

terms the minority could hope for, and on this ground he defended them. "The smallest measure of conciliation", he held, "was far preferable to any measure of coercion". The compromise effected did not, it is true, satisfy the *intransigeant* element in the Roman Catholic Church; and the hierarchy continued their crusade against the Liberal party. But a number of Roman Catholic Liberals appealed, in their private capacity, to the Vatican; and, in order to deal with the situation, the Pope sent out to Canada an envoy, Monsignor Merry del Val, who wisely put a damper on the extremists in the Church; and the agitation died down. The question of separate schools in Manitoba ceased to trouble the waters of federal politics; and thus the moderation and sanity of Laurier's policy were vindicated.

In a similar spirit of moderation Laurier dealt with the question of the tariff. Since the days of Mackenzie a powerful wing of the Liberal party had been in favour of lower tariffs and indeed of free trade, especially with the United States. On the other hand, the tariff had not been a dominant issue in the elections of 1896; and the Liberal party had obtained the support of many voters who were frankly protectionist. In these circumstances, it would have been folly for the Cabinet to surrender to the free trade wing of the party. Nor was Laurier convinced that free trade was either practicable or desirable in Canada. What he did was to appoint a tariff commission which heard evidence in various centres, and gathered detailed information on which a revision of the tariff might be based. When in 1897 Fielding introduced his first budget, it was seen that, while certain much-needed readjustments of the tariff had been made, no revolutionary changes had been introduced, and in the main the National Policy had not been disturbed. But one important innovation was adopted—namely, the principle of a minimum and maximum tariff. A flat reduction of $12\frac{1}{2}$ per cent., increased later to 25 per cent., on all goods except wines and liquors, was granted to countries which admitted Canadian products on terms as favourable as Canada offered. This amounted in practice to a preference on British imports over virtually all others, and came to be known (rather inaccurately) as "the Imperial Preference". Whatever its effects from the economic point of view (and these were generally recognised as beneficial), the Imperial Preference was a shrewd move politically. It created a most favourable impression in the Mother Country, and effectually gave the lie to the hoary cry that the Liberal party was disloyal and anti-imperial. That it should have been introduced by a Government of which a French-Canadian was first minister, was regarded as a remarkable circumstance, and greatly enhanced Laurier's reputation both in Great Britain and in the English-speaking provinces of the Dominion.

In like degree he gained in prestige from his visit to England and France at the time of the Diamond Jubilee of Queen Victoria in 1897.

As the French-Canadian Prime Minister of the greatest of Britain's overseas Dominions—a living and vivid illustration of the British genius for empire—he was, with his courtly manners, his eloquent command of the English tongue, his subtle air of distinction, the lion of the hour. Nothing could have exceeded in happiness the phrases in which he avowed the loyalty of Canada to the British throne, except possibly the phrases in which he described, in France, the attitude to Great Britain and to France of himself and his own people. "We are faithful", he said, "to the great nation which gave us life, and we are faithful to the great nation which has given us liberty". Never did any man rise to meet the demands of a difficult and exacting situation more superbly than Wilfrid Laurier during those close-pressed months of the summer of 1897. The knighthood conferred on him by Queen Victoria was regarded by Canadians as a none too signal acknowledgment of his services to Canada and the Empire.

There had been those in 1896 who had doubted Laurier's capacity for the leadership of a Government. A student and a scholar, with gentle and old-world manners, and little experience of practical affairs, he seemed ill-fitted to be first minister in a country where politics and practical affairs were, and are, closely inter-related. Seldom, however, were expectations more signally falsified. In a very short time Laurier was recognised as the unquestioned master of the Administration; and indeed nothing about him was more striking than the ruthless way in which, as time went on, he discarded the lieutenants who opposed his will. Beneath his velvet glove there was an iron hand. The fact that he retained power for fifteen years—a longer consecutive period of office than had been enjoyed even by Sir John Macdonald—proved that he was not deficient in the art of politics. As one of his own supporters has said, if he had affinities with Sir Galahad, he had also affinities with Machiavelli.

The first dissension in the party occurred in 1899, at the time of the outbreak of the South African War. This event fanned into flame in English-speaking Canada the national and imperialist feeling which had been kindled by the Imperial Preference and the Diamond Jubilee. This was the period, moreover, of the activities of the Imperial Federation League. Laurier had never subscribed to the ideas of the imperial federationists; but he had been to some extent influenced by the vigour of their propaganda. He hesitated over offering the services of a Canadian contingent in the South African War, partly because he thought such an offer unnecessary, and partly because he realised that Quebec was lukewarm. But he was impressed by the demand in the English-speaking provinces that Canada should give some sign of imperial solidarity; and three days after the declaration of war the Canadian Cabinet passed an Order-in-Council authorising the despatch to South Africa of a contingent of one thousand men. A week later the despatch of a second contingent was authorised; and before the war was over Canada had sent to the theatre of war over seven thousand soldiers. The action of the Government in authorising these contingents roused the opposition of one of Laurier's ablest followers, Henri Bourassa, a grandson of the famous Louis-Joseph Papineau, who now definitely broke with his leader. Bourassa stood at first almost alone, even among the French-Canadian Liberals; but gradually he gathered about him increasing support, and the time came when he was able to head in the province of Quebec a revolt against Laurier's leadership which caused the Premier no small degree of concern and distress.

For the moment, however, Laurier had little difficulty in holding his supporters together; and the exploits of the troops of Canada on South African battlefields not only increased her prestige abroad, but also the prestige of the Government at home. Consequently, in the general election of 1900, the Conservatives were reduced to the straits of playing for the votes of the extremists in both Ontario and Quebec. In Ontario Laurier was attacked as half-hearted in coming to the relief of the Mother Country, and in Quebec as too eager to drag the sons of the habitant into the vortex of imperialist militarism. "Sir Wilfrid Laurier", exclaimed Sir Charles Tupper in Quebec, "is too English for me". This double-faced campaign failed, however, to produce results; and in the elections the Laurier Government was returned with an increased majority.

The turn of the century was a time fraught with great events. Not only was the South African war in progress, but in 1901 Queen Victoria passed, after her long reign, to her rest. It seemed as if one era had ended, and another begun. Laurier was not slow to take advantage of the psychology of the moment. "The nineteenth century", he exclaimed, in one of his characteristically simple and eloquent declarations, "was the century of the United States; the twentieth century will be the century of Canada". And Laurier identified himself with the aspirations of which this statement was an expression. He became, as it were, in his own person—until disillusionment came—the embodiment of the idea of Canadian progress.

In the first place, he identified himself with the idea of the growth of Canadian autonomy within the Empire. As early as 1897, in the midst of the celebrations attendant on the Queen's Jubilee, he had described Canada as "a colony, yet a nation—words never before in the history of the world associated together". At a later date he eloquently described the British Empire as "a galaxy of free nations". In his view there was one Crown, but the Canadian Government was as much the adviser of the Crown for Canadian affairs as the British Cabinet was for British affairs. This conception he championed against all comers at the Colonial Conference of 1902, and at the subsequent Imperial Conferences, as well as continuously on Parliament Hill at Ottawa. Laurier was, in fact, among Canadian states-

men, the first great and unqualified nationalist. His contributions to
the growth of Canadian autonomy were many. It was under his
regime, in 1900, that the last British troops were withdrawn from
Canada, and the fortifications at Halifax and Esquimalt were
handed over to the Canadian militia; it was under him later that the
Canadian militia ceased to be commanded by an imperial officer, and
that the policy of a Canadian navy was launched—that, in short,
Canada assumed the full responsibility for her own defence, both
military and naval, internal and external. In 1908 he finally safeguarded the interests of Canada in regard to the signing of imperial
treaties by the arrangement whereby no imperial treaty should be
binding on Canada without Canada's explicit consent; and in 1910
he successfully asserted the right of Canada to control and regulate
British immigration into the Dominion. He it was who dotted the
"i's" and crossed the "t's" of Rudyard Kipling's famous lines about
Our Lady of the Snows:

> Daughter am I in my mother's house,
> But mistress in mine own.

In the domestic sphere, Laurier's nationalism was also not without
significance. Like D'Arcy McGee he rejected the idea of British-
Canadian, or French-Canadian, or Irish-Canadian nationalism—
"patriotism", as McGee had said, "rejects the prefix"[1] but strove
to foster an all-Canadian nationalism in which all the racial elements
in Canada could find common ground. "Our respective forefathers",
he had said in his maiden speech in the Quebec Legislature in 1871,
"were enemies and waged bloody war against each other for centuries.
But we, their descendants, united under the same flag, fight no other
fights than those of a generous emulation to excel each other in trade
and industry, in the arts and sciences of peace".[2] As a result, there
were during his premiership none of those conflicts between "the
two races" in Canada which have marred other periods of Canadian
history. To bring about harmony between the French and the English
in Canada was perhaps his dearest ambition; and while he was Prime
Minister he lost no opportunity to achieve this ambition. It was the
tragedy of his life that, after he had lost power, circumstances arose
which threatened to destroy his life's work; and if, when faced with
an unavoidable dilemma, he clave, like Ruth, unto his own people,
who shall blame him?

But the most notable contribution of the Laurier Government to
Canadian progress in the domestic sphere was probably its aggressive
immigration policy. In 1892, as we have seen, Laurier entrusted the
portfolio of the Interior to Clifford (later Sir Clifford) Sifton, a
westerner; and Sifton was fully impressed with the fact that the
paramount need of the Canadian West was settlers. He lost no time
in establishing immigration offices all over the United States, the

[1] Brady, A., *T. d'A. McGee*, p. 53.   [2] Laurier, Sir W., *Speeches...*, ed. Barthe, U., pp. 2, 6.

British Isles, and even continental Europe. At first, the results were disappointing. Some of the agents sent to the United States resigned in despair. "The people", said one of them, "did not even know where Canada was". Gradually, however, the stream of immigration began to flow. In 1897 the total number of immigrants from the United States was less than 2500; by 1907 the number had increased to over 60,000; and by 1911 it reached the total of 125,000. In 1897 the total immigration into Canada from all countries was barely 20,000; by 1911 it had grown to a third of a million annually. These figures did not take into account the contemporaneous exodus to the United States (now partially stemmed), in regard to which satisfactory statistics were not available. But, with all necessary deductions, the figures were nevertheless impressive, and constituted a notable tribute to the energy and foresight of the Laurier Administration.

The opening up of the country consequent upon the success of this immigration policy entailed on it a policy of railway expansion. The Canadian Pacific Railway had provided Canada with a transcontinental railway linking Halifax and Saint John with Vancouver; but it became clear that this single line would soon be inadequate to meet the needs of the rapidly growing West. The Canadian Pacific between Port Arthur and Winnipeg was a bottle-neck in which freight traffic was already becoming hopelessly congested. In these circumstances, the Grand Trunk Railway, the oldest railway corporation in Eastern Canada, which had long felt the need of through connections, applied to the Government for aid in building a second transcontinental railway, to be known as the Grand Trunk Pacific. At the same time, two daring and ingenious Canadian railway-builders, William Mackenzie and Donald Mann, had, by buying up the charters of a network of small railways, created the beginnings of a third transcontinental system, the Canadian Northern; and they, too, applied to the Government for aid. Laurier made an attempt to bring the Grand Trunk and the Canadian Northern together; but the two railways were determined to pursue each its own course, and Laurier was not able to bring about a pooling of their interests, or indeed any measure of co-operation. The Government finally granted a charter to the Grand Trunk Pacific, which was to run from Winnipeg to the Pacific; and it undertook itself to build an extension of the Grand Trunk Pacific, to run through northern Ontario and Quebec from Winnipeg to Nova Scotia, and to be known as the National Transcontinental. This line the Grand Trunk was to lease from the Government for fifty years at a small rental. Meanwhile the Canadian Northern continued to seek and to obtain aid, by means of the guarantee of bonds and even by means of cash subsidies, both from the Dominion Government and from some of the provincial Governments.

This ambitious programme of railway-building was the storm-centre of much controversy; and it was the occasion in 1903 of the resignation of Laurier's Minister of Railways, A. G. Blair, whose policies Laurier had rejected. There is no doubt that, after his failure to bring the Grand Trunk and the Canadian Northern together, Laurier became convinced that Canada could support three trans-continental railway systems. In nothing, perhaps, during his period of office was his lack of business capacity more signally, more tragically, displayed. The disastrous results of his railway policy have sometimes been attributed to the World War, and to the conditions created by it, conditions which bore hard on railways in all countries; but it is highly probable that his policy would have ended in disaster, even if the World War had never taken place. The National Trans-continental, built under political auspices, cost in the end three times the original estimate; and eventually it proved to be a white elephant. Both the Grand Trunk Pacific and the National Transcontinental, moreover, required, before they were completed, additional aid from the public exchequer; and when the war broke out, the solvency of both railways was open to grave question. The war, without doubt, greatly aggravated the situation. But only blind partisanship can now deny that Laurier's weak handling of the railway problem was the chief blot on his regime.

There is in the case of governments a law of diminishing returns. The first fine frenzy of reforming zeal is in time replaced by the "administrative mind" and the mere desire to cling to office. This was the fate of the Laurier Cabinet. In the general elections of 1904 and 1908 the Liberals carried the country with little difficulty. The leader of the Conservative Opposition, R. L. (later Sir Robert) Borden, who had succeeded Sir Charles Tupper in 1901, was a man of high character and sound judgment, but he possessed no great personal magnetism; and he had to face on more than one occasion a cabal against his leadership in the party itself. Further, the very weakness of the Opposition contributed in no small measure to the undoing of the Government. For one thing, it perhaps encouraged Laurier to jettison ruthlessly some of his ablest lieutenants. First Israel Tarte, his right-hand man in the province of Quebec, was dis-carded in 1902, because of the heterodox views he expressed publicly in regard to the tariff; then Blair, as we have seen, was forced to resign in 1903 over the railway issue; and in 1905, Clifford Sifton, the author of the Government's immigration policy, parted company with Laurier over the question of separate schools in the West. These ministers Laurier replaced by men who were mainly notable for their party loyalty. When Laurier was reproached by an old friend on the score of one of these appointments, his defence was that "So-and-so has never made any trouble for me". By its third parliamentary term, the Government had become mainly an office-holding Adminis-tration, and was obviously on the down grade.

Gradually, moreover, rifts began to appear in the party lute; and incidents occurred which injured the prestige of the Government. The first of these was what was known as the "Dundonald incident". In 1902 the Earl of Dundonald, an able and enthusiastic soldier, assumed command of the Canadian militia. From the first Lord Dundonald was out of sympathy with the ideas of the ministry regarding the militia. He had come to Canada bent on its reorganisation and efficiency; and he was much disturbed when, in his first interview with Laurier, the Prime Minister suavely remarked, "You must not take the militia seriously, for though it is useful for suppressing internal disturbances, it will not be required for the defence of the country, as the Monroe Doctrine protects us against enemy aggression". "Here was I", wrote Lord Dundonald later, "sent out to reorganise the militia, and the Prime Minister saying quite frankly that he advised me not to take the force seriously". When, however, the acting Minister of Militia, Sydney Fisher, went in 1904 so far as to interfere in purely military appointments to a cavalry regiment in the Eastern Townships, Lord Dundonald's patience came to an end, and he made a public attack on the minister. As a result, he was summarily dismissed from office by Order-in-Council; and with him the practice of appointing Imperial officers to the command of the Canadian militia terminated. There is no doubt that, in attacking publicly his political superior, Lord Dundonald was technically wrong; but there were many people who felt that he was morally right. There was more than a suspicion that the Government was not really anxious to have an efficient militia, since this would be in-compatible with the exercise of political patronage. After his dismissal, Lord Dundonald was the object of wild ovations in Toronto and Montreal, and it was noted that there were many Liberals among those who acclaimed him. On the whole, the episode probably did the Government much more harm than good.

The next serious dissension occurred in 1905 over the schools question in Saskatchewan and Alberta. When these provinces were carved in 1905 out of the North West Territories, it became necessary to legislate with regard to the establishment in them of separate Roman Catholic schools. It might have been expected that Laurier, who had resisted the coercion of Manitoba in 1896, would have been careful to avoid coercion in 1905. But by this time political conditions had changed, and Laurier was perhaps loth to defy the French-Canadian bishops again. He therefore embodied in the Act constituting the new provinces provisions safeguarding the rights of the minority in regard to separate schools. These provisions roused among the Liberals of Ontario and the West such opposition that they were somewhat amended; but the episode cost Laurier one of the ablest of his colleagues, Sir Clifford Sifton, and it seriously undermined his position in the English-speaking provinces.

A more important matter, in Laurier's own view, however, was a revolt from his leadership in the province of Quebec. In 1899, as we have seen, Henri Bourassa had broken with him over the despatch of Canadian troops to South Africa. Bourassa, a man of courage and ability, launched in Quebec a nationalist movement. He was bitterly anti-imperialist, and some of his followers, if not he himself, seemed to contemplate the establishment of a French-Canadian republic on the banks of the St Lawrence. Unlike his grandfather Papineau, he was strongly clerical and ultramontane; and thus he gained the support of many of the French-Canadian clergy. He played frankly on the religious and racial prejudices of the people of Quebec; and it appeared as though he would supplant Laurier as the "favourite son" of the habitant. When, in 1910, Laurier's old constituency of Drummond-Arthabaska returned to Parliament in a by-election a Nationalist candidate, it looked like the handwriting on the wall. Quebec was, and is, the pivot of the Confederation; and if Laurier lost Quebec, he lost his citadel.

As the Parliament elected in 1908 began to approach its legal termination, it became clear that some decisive stroke was necessary to rehabilitate the Government in the eyes of the country. At this juncture, by what seemed singularly good fortune, it was discovered that the Republican Administration in the United States was favourable to a measure of reciprocity in trade arrangements with Canada. Reciprocity with the United States had long been a lode-star with Canadian politicians. The Reciprocity Treaty of 1854–66 had been an undoubted blessing to British North America; and since 1867 repeated attempts had been made to renew closer trade relations with the United States, though these attempts had been met with repeated rebuffs. If the Laurier Government could now succeed in negotiating an agreement whereby the vast market of the United States would be thrown open to Canada, it was thought that such an achievement would ensure for it a new lease of life.

Fielding, the Canadian Finance Minister, went to Washington and succeeded in negotiating an agreement for reciprocity between Canada and the United States in natural products. This has commonly been described as the "Reciprocity Treaty", though it was not properly a treaty, but merely an agreement to bring in concurrent legislation. On the strength of this agreement, the Laurier Government appealed to the country. At first, the Conservatives were nonplussed. Sir John Macdonald had so often looked with favour on reciprocity in trade with the United States that Borden was loth to oppose it. But stouter counsels prevailed. The Conservatives remembered that they were the traditional exponents of the "National Policy" of high protection; and they decided to fight. The election which followed was one of exceptional bitterness. The Conservatives argued that reciprocity was merely the precursor of commercial, and possibly political, union. They pointed out that, since 1867, Canada had followed a policy of inter-provincial and intra-imperial trade, with railways spanning the country from east to west; and they contended that to open up even partial free trade from north to south would be to reverse that policy, with perhaps disastrous results. Finally, they raised against the Liberals the old cry, so deadly in a country settled originally by the Loyalists of the American Revolution, of disloyalty to the Empire; and it was unfortunate that some leading Republicans in the United States used language which seemed to give colour to the cry. President Taft, for instance, described Canada as being "at the parting of the ways". In the United States Congress passed the necessary legislation but in Canada the result of the elections was the decisive defeat of the Government. In British Columbia not one Liberal was returned; and in Ontario only thirteen Liberals were elected as against seventy-two Conservatives. In the Maritime Provinces, in Quebec, and in the Prairie Provinces, the Liberals had a slight advantage; but even here their losses had been great. In Quebec, Laurier carried only thirty-eight out of the sixty-five constituencies, as against twenty-seven captured by the Conservatives and Nationalists. This was the result of an "unholy alliance" between the Conservatives and the Nationalists in Quebec, whereby, while Laurier was attacked in Ontario as too French to be British, he was attacked in Quebec as too British to be French. Such are the devices to which political parties sometimes resort.

Laurier's defeat cut him to the quick. He lost no time in submitting his resignation to the Governor-General, and some bitter phrases escaped his lips. "It was not reciprocity that was turned down", he wrote, "but a Catholic Premier". He found it also hard to forgive those compatriots of his in Quebec who had deserted him. But he soon recovered his usual serene and philosophic calm; and when the new Parliament met, he turned with his old-time dignity and courtesy to take up again the duties of leader of the Opposition. He had, in truth, nothing of which to be ashamed. During his fifteen years of office he had brought Canada out of the commercial doldrums of the end of the nineteenth century, and had ushered in an era of unprecedented prosperity. The great need of Canada had been men and money, and these were now flowing toward her in copious measure. Best of all, the exodus of Canada's youth to the United States—that running sore of the Canadian body politic—had been staunched. In the same way, Laurier had appreciably increased the political stature of Canada. He found her a colony; he left her a "sister nation" to the Mother Country. Largely through his efforts the British Empire had been transformed into the British Commonwealth of Nations, in which Canada enjoyed, not a subordinate, but an equal status. What George Washington achieved in 1776–83 by the bloody disruption of the British Empire, Laurier achieved in 1896–1911 without a hint of bloodshed, and without breaking the silken thread that binds the Empire Commonwealth together.

CHAPTER XXII

THE SETTLEMENT OF THE PRAIRIES, 1867–1914

In the year 1867 the population of the country that became Manitoba totalled about 10,000 souls. A census begun in October 1870 gave a population of 11,963, of whom 9840 were *Métis*, French and English, 1565 white, and 558 Indian settlers on the land.[1] As for the Territories, when they were formed in 1870, the Indians were not yet settled on reserves, nor grouped in settlements. There were few whites in Saskatchewan, apart from mission settlements and fur-trading posts. Of the latter there were: Fort Pelly, Cumberland House, Fort à la Corne, Fort Carlton, Fort Pitt, Fort Touchwood and Fort Qu'Appelle. In Alberta the Red Deer River divided spheres of influence between the Hudson's Bay Company and free-traders on the north and Americans on the south, who had established trading posts to carry on their brisk trade in whisky.[2] Indian tribal war was rife. Missionary enterprise was confined to the north. There was an important trading post at Fort Edmonton and mission centres at Victoria and St Albert.

In 1870, then, the prairies possessed one considerable community near the present Winnipeg, and incipient settlements at Portage la Prairie, Prince Albert and Edmonton. Apart from these and out-lying mission centres and fur-trading posts they were still a Great Lone Land, over which passed wandering tribes of Indians, great herds of buffalo, and traders bringing supplies along the rivers to the Company's forts and returning with convoys of canoes laden with pelts. Such were still the prairies—their great solitudes broken only occasionally by the creaking of a Red River cart or the bustle and stir of a buffalo hunt.

In 1870 the prairies were transferred to the Dominion. The hopes of those who favoured political union with the East were amply fulfilled. In the decade 1871–81 the population of Manitoba increased from 18,995 to 65,954. Settlers came by way of the United States, for as yet there was no railway from the East. For some the trek did not end at the Red River. Already the more adventurous or dissatisfied spirits were pushing further westward. The community at Prince Albert was augmented by arrivals from Kildonan. After the troubles of 1870 (which have been described in a previous chapter[3]) discontented half-breeds squatted near St Laurent on the South Saskatchewan and at Willow Bunch in the Wood Mountain. Homestead

---

[1] *Canada and its Provinces*, xix, 99.
[2] McDougall, J., *On Western Trails in the Early Seventies*, p. 10.
[3] *Vide supra*, ch. xix.

grants were first made in 1873, and soon farm settlements stretched to Westbourne and Rapid City, to Turtle Mountains and Fort Ellice. "At the close of 1879", says Begg, "farm houses and cultivated fields were in sight all along the main road for 250 miles west of Winnipeg".[1]

In 1874 surveyors for the telegraph line used for headquarters a spot on the Battle River, called "Telegraph Flat". Its name was later changed to Battleford. This site was chosen for the Government Buildings of the North West Council erected in 1877, and soon became the centre of a settlement. The following suggestions to intending settlers were issued in March 1882:

Intending settlers having horses, cattle and implements, will do right by bringing them along with them; but those not having livestock can purchase outfits at Winnipeg; or, if not caring to encumber themselves with farming implements, can purchase them at Battleford. The prices at Winnipeg are: Double waggons, $65 to $75; Red River carts, $10 to $15; iron bound carts, $30 to $35; Buckboards, $50 to $75; Waggon harness, $30 to $40; Cart harness, $6 to $10; single harness, $20 to $30; Canadian teams, $250 to $400; Native ponies, $50 to $80; Yoke of oxen, $150 to $175.

Camping Outfit: A good tent, tin stove, frying pan, tin cups, axes, spades, hammer, brace and bits, or auger, drawing knife, saw, nails, assortment of waggon bolts, logging chain, hobbles and ropes for horses, a shot gun, powder and shot as game is plentiful. Provisions: Flour, bacon, beans, dried apples, sugar, tea, baking powder, etc. Route: Take train from Winnipeg to Brandon, or to the end of the C.P.R. Waggons drawn by Canadian horses—the load should not exceed 1,500 lbs. Good oxen in carts—from 500 to 800 lbs. The best time to travel is in early spring. A fair average rate per day is for oxen 15 miles, for horses 15 to 25 miles.[2]

Settlements in the southern part of Saskatchewan made but slow progress before the coming of the railway. Indians gathered around the communities at Willow Bunch, Qu'Appelle and Touchwood Hills, but the white population was only gradually augmented. In the north a small community grew up around Carlton. On or near the south branch of the Saskatchewan five French settlements came into existence: St Laurent, St Louis de Langevin (McDougall's crossing), Duck Lake (or Stobart), St Antoine (Batoche), and Fish Creek. A flourishing community developed at the Carrot River. The most progressive settlement in the Territories was Prince Albert.[3] A letter dated 13 September 1880 comments on its progress:

The old trading-shops of bygone days of the fur trade have given place to handsome, well-stocked, modern-fronted stores, which have been hoisted into life by the rapidity of settlement and growth of the farming interest. There is a marked solidity about improvements which suggests permanence, and the tasty residences do not in the least savour of the "mushroom-ness" of the Far West. The "Old Settler" now meets a great many strangers—well-dressed, watch-wearing, cigar-smoking men of the East. They have come here to remain and pursue their trades and professions. The large farms will compare with those of any country. Those belonging to Captain McKay, Charles Mair, the Hudson's Bay Company, Captain Young, William Miller, and a score of others are nearly 200 acres under cultivation and the grain is the finest in the world.

[1] Begg, A., History of the North West, II, 388.
[2] Saskatchewan Herald, March 1882.
[3] Oliver, E. H., "The Beginnings of White Settlement in Northern Saskatchewan", Trans. Roy. Soc. Can. 3rd ser., 1925, XIX, 87–91.

Within Alberta the Indian population still outnumbered the white. The census of 1881 gives a population of 1203 including the *Métis*—at Edmonton, 230 English, 480 French; at the Bow River, 180 English, 100 French; at the Peace River, 18 English, 195 French. Before the building of the railway the chief means of transportation were canoe, Red River cart and sledge. The major trails ran westward from the Red River, the chief being the Portage trail. Minor trails connected the growing settlements. The trails followed old fur-trading routes. In the western prairies one connected the boundary line, Fort Macleod, Calgary, Edmonton and Athabaska Landing; another ran from Edmonton *via* old Fort Assiniboine to the confluence of the Smoky and Peace Rivers. In Saskatchewan trails led from Fort Ellice to Touchwood Hills, to Humboldt, to Carlton both *via* Gabriel's Crossing and *via* Batoche's Crossing, to Battleford both *via* the "River" trail and the "Plain" or "Outer" trail; also from Humboldt to Battleford *via* Gabriel's Crossing and the "River" trail; from Battleford to Fort Pitt; from Fort à la Corne to Prince Albert and Carlton; from Touchwood Hills to Qu'Appelle.[1]

During the 'seventies the buffalo hunts abruptly ceased. This was a revolution for the Indians, who were forced to give over their old nomadic habits and to adopt a more sedentary existence. But a still greater economic change was at hand. Through the coming of the railway, trader and hunter gave way to rancher and farmer, for the building of the railway opened up the prairies. The half-breed Uprising attracted attention to the West. Settlers from Eastern Canada and the British Isles brought with them their household effects and ideas of social organisation. The Ontario settlers were the gift of the Canadian Pacific Railway, and have always tended to predominate along this railway, particularly along its main line and older branches. The coming of the railway in the early 'eighties produced a "boom" in Manitoba that promised to make a city of every hamlet fortunate enough to find itself on the railway. Morris or Minnedosa might become a metropolis. Nothing, it was felt, could prevent the growth of important towns wherever the railway intersected streams. Prophets were divided in their predictions of impending greatness as between Selkirk and Winnipeg, and their disagreement as to the most suitable place for the railway to cross the river yielded a double boom as advocates advertised the attractions of the town in which they had invested. The completion of the Pembina line stimulated the boom in the boundary country and brought in speculators by rail. When the Canadian Pacific Railway arrived, unrestrained advertising, unscrupulous mishandling of public confidence, subdivision exploitation, sudden opulence, later so familiar to the West, disturbed the little prairie communities as train-load after train-load of speculators was dumped down.

[1] Oliver, pp. 96–8.

Public improvements were undertaken out of proportion to the population of the towns. In Winnipeg "the civic assessment was more than trebled; a new city hall, street lighting by gas, street railways, the telephone and nearly five million dollars in buildings remained to commemorate the boom".[1] Though immigration was for a time stimulated, depression followed when the boom broke. Only slowly and by painful efforts were general credit and industry re-established.

An attempt was made to bring in settlers through Colonisation Companies,[2] which contracted with the Dominion Government to people reserved areas at the rate of $120 for each settler. Some Companies brought in not a single settler. In Saskatchewan, where they were particularly active, only seven Companies placed more than fifty settlers each. The Temperance Colonisation Company founded Saskatoon. The site was picked by John N. Lake: "We thought of Minnetonka for a name, but we found some Saskatoon berries and that settled it".

Hard upon this movement of population from Ontario followed English settlers and Scottish crofters, who were settled in groups, or who, when possessed of capital, sought to establish large farms. But large farms, of which an outstanding example was the Bell farm of 64,000 acres at Troy, in the main proved disastrous. Of the Crofter settlements may be mentioned the Benbecula or Gordon-Cathcart colony south of Wapella. A different type of settlement was made south of Moosomin in 1884 of colonists from the east end of London. To each family Baroness Burdett Coutts advanced $500 on security of the farm. A Jewish settlement was located between Pipestone Creek and Moose Mountain by the London Mansion House Committee. This included the families of ten Polish and Hungarian, ten Austrian and nine German and Russian Jews. It was organised by Mr Wurtheim of Winnipeg. "They have found", wrote Professor Tanner in 1884, "a new and happy home in Canada and a freedom from all persecution and injustice". In 1886, German, Swiss and Hungarian colonies were established in Eastern Assiniboia at Alsace, Bismarck, Hohen-Holme and Esterhazy. To counteract a report that the country between Moose Jaw and Calgary was unsuited to cultivation the railway established experimental farms along the track at ten different stations, six in Saskatchewan and four in Alberta.

The comparatively slow growth of population on the prairies was due to many causes. Alternate sections of land were reserved for the railway, and this scattered settlement and retarded the establishment of schools and churches. In Manitoba provincial railway charters

---

[1] *Canada and its Provinces*, XIX, 115.
[2] For statutes dealing with these see 1874, ch. XIX, secs. 14, 15; 1881, ch. XVI, sec. 10; 1883, ch. XVII, sec. 38; 1886, ch. XXVII, sec. 9; 1886, *Rev. Stat. of Can.* ch. LIV, sec. 44; 1887, ch. XXXI, sec. 6; 1889, ch. XXVII, secs. 4, 5, 8; 1891, ch. XXIV, secs. 8–11; 1897, ch. XXIX, sec. 16; 1900, ch. XX, sec. 3; 1901, ch. XX, sec. 4; 1906, *R.S.C.* ch. LV, secs. 145–57. See also *Annual Reports* of Dept. of the Interior.

were disallowed, and throughout the prairies the building of branch lines was not prosecuted. A resolution of a farmers' convention in Winnipeg got into Eastern papers and discouraged immigration:[1] "That this convention cannot advise immigrants to settle in the province till full redress of the grievances complained of by this convention shall have been attained". The Norquay Administration in Manitoba, politically embarrassed, accomplished little to attract settlers. In the Territories the Council possessed neither initiative nor power; but the Assembly inaugurated in 1888 an aggressive policy of advertising the resources of the country, and the "uprising" drew the attention of the East to the possibilities of the prairies. The result was that during 1888–97 the annual rate of immigration to the Territories increased five-fold over that of the previous decade.

In 1896 Clifford Sifton became Minister of the Interior. Henceforth in the Dominion Cabinet there was a western representative who knew the needs of, and had an unlimited faith in, Western Canada. A vigorous policy of advertising was inaugurated in the United States, the British Isles and Europe, and a network of agencies established to impart information and to assist immigrants. Exhibitions of the produce of the country were arranged. Illustrated publications describing opportunities in the West were scattered broadcast in many countries. The peasants of Europe began to read, each in his own language, of the "Last and Best West", which offered free land.

In the early 'nineties Eastern Canada was losing many of her sons to the United States. At the opening of the Laurier regime this exodus, however, turned more and more to the prairies. Those from Ontario were the most widely distributed; those from Quebec tended to gather into communities, e.g. in the French settlements of Manitoba, at Gravelbourg, Vonda and Montmartre in Saskatchewan, and in northern Alberta; those from the Maritime Provinces attached themselves generally to urban communities. Harvesters' excursions encouraged settlers from Eastern Canada by giving a very desirable type of worker a first-hand knowledge of western conditions. Even within the prairies themselves a distinct movement of population took place. Farmers in Manitoba, originally come from Ontario, moved further westward to enable their sons to homestead, or themselves to purchase larger holdings, where land was cheaper.

The American invasion, which developed slowly from the time of the World's Fair in Chicago (1893), gathered strength under the Sifton scheme of advertising. The flow of population became a steady stream from 1900 and, under the allurement of free and cheap land, increased in volume till homesteads were exhausted. The building of J. J. Hill's railways, the opening of the Soo Line, the booming of real estate, the coming of Mormons to Alberta and of other religious and

[1] *Canada and its Provinces*, XIX, 117.

racial groups to other districts all combined to swell this tide of immigration. The Great War, however, and the growth of economic difficulties associated with credit conditions, sale of machinery and grain marketing served to check the movement. In general the Americans have kept to lines that run north and south, and, having followed them up, have turned off to western branches. Of the American immigration about one-third is North-European of the second generation. The fathers came from North Europe to the northern Central States, and the children in the next generation pushed northward to the prairies. By this way came many Norwegians and Swedes, but not Icelanders, who, for the most part, came directly to Canada. A second third of the American immigration is of Yankee stock. They belong to the westward movement that came from New England and other eastern sections of the United States, by way of Ohio and the Mississippi, to the American North-West, and thence to Canada. This journey probably required about three generations to complete. The remaining third consisted of British and Eastern Canadian folk who were repatriating themselves, sometimes in the first, sometimes in the second, generation.

Particularly after the Boer War, attention was directed to the overseas Dominions by unsatisfactory labour conditions in the British Isles. In no other part of the world was the Dominion propaganda so effective. The British population of the prairies increased rapidly during the 'nineties, but the growth was phenomenal in the pre-war period of the new century—in Saskatchewan, for example, from 40,094 in 1901 to 251,012 in 1911. Settlements grew up in all three provinces almost entirely of British stock. But the Barr Colony, settled at Lloydminster, attracted the greatest attention of all. It made a most valuable contribution to the development of the country from Bresaylor to Vermilion. The notoriety which it gained did more, perhaps, than the whole output of immigration literature distributed prior to 1903 to attract British attention to the Territories. To its association with the Barr colonists Saskatoon owes the impulse that launched it on its career as the leading distributing centre of central Saskatchewan.

English-speaking newcomers did not exhibit so great a tendency to live together as others more directly influenced by religious motives or a common language. But throughout the prairies were planted little communities, rural municipalities, school houses, churches, railway stations, bearing such names as Huron, Ottawa, Boston, Stornoway, Kindersley, Cupar, Colonsay, Saltcoats, Tuffnell. In these places was usually a small group or individual family with a memory of "back home". And "back home" was almost invariably Ontario, the United States and Great Britain.

In the 'eighties the Primitive Methodists organised a Colonisation Company to introduce settlers to the prairies. Other religious groups undertook to establish settlements. The first Jewish community was founded in 1885 at the Moose Mountain by Baron Hirsch. Although this proved unsuccessful, flourishing colonies grew up at many centres, e.g. Hirsch, Oxbow, Wapella, Lipton, Edenbridge, Sonnenfeldt and Alsask. A colony of German-American Roman Catholics settled at Muenster, and ultimately became a separate ecclesiastical jurisdiction. All the French settlements, of which there were many in all three provinces, tended to become religious groups. An advance guard of German-speaking Mennonites—the first Europeans to settle in the prairies after confederation—came from Russia to Manitoba as early as 1874 with a promise of their own schools on the part of the Dominion Government. By 1875 they had established an extensive community of 6000 in Manitoba. They demonstrated the possibilities of open prairie farming and the feasibility of growing flax. Later many settled in Saskatchewan in the neighbourhood of Warman, from Herbert to Swift Current, and in smaller communities at Guernsey and elsewhere.[1] The Mennonites have made more than one journey for their faith, and some have left Canada on a further pilgrimage for Mexico and Paraguay. Their schools have been a source of trouble to the authorities. Their curriculum contained a little arithmetic, a little Bible history and a good deal of catechism. Their teachers have received wages in kind—oats, barley, wheat. Scarcely any have been able to speak English. An attempt to force their children to attend public schools miserably failed. Their one desire was to be left alone.

Another religious group was the Doukhobors. They took up land in Saskatchewan between Kylemore and Verigin, and between Langham and Prince Albert. They were "Spirit Wrestlers", dissenters from the Orthodox Russian Church. The Community Doukhobors were under the leadership of Peter Verigin as a Christian Community of Universal Brotherhood. Many, however, broke away from his sway and became independent. Owing to difficulties over lands all but one-tenth of the Community Doukhobors moved to British Columbia.

The largest racial group from central Europe on the prairies is constituted of Ukrainians or Ruthenians. They are Little Russians, but not all from Little Russia or the Ukraine. Some of them are Ruthenians of Galicia, Bukowina and districts north-east of old Hungary. They belong, for the most part, to the Uniat Church, acknowledging the authority of the Pope but keeping the Greek ritual. The Ruthenians, despoiled and exploited in their own country, cherished in their hearts the seeds of economic and social discontent. When the story reached their ears of new lands across the sea they were ready to respond. The first Ruthenians to reach the prairies came in 1894, nine families in all, and settled at Star, near Ed-

[1] Oliver, E. H., *The Country School in non-English-speaking Communities in Saskatchewan.*

monton. It was three years before the general migration gathered momentum. Unlike the Doukhobors the Ruthenians made no striking appeal to the imagination. They were neither martyrs for their faith, vegetarians, communists, nor passive resisters. They were dirty, poor, ignorant Slavs. They arrived in such numbers that their very picturesqueness became common. They were willing to work and eager to become Canadians. Strong and industrious, they knew how to accommodate themselves to western conditions. They showed a disposition to select bushy and slightly hilly homesteads near water-courses, a type of country which recalled their native land. They built little one-storey houses with walls of poplar trunks filled and faced with smooth whitewashed mud. Here the wife and children re-mained to cultivate with neither horse, ox, nor plough, while the husband went as navvy on the railway. Out of infinite frugality and untiring industry they saved enough to purchase an ox and plough for a second year's operations. By slow, but sure, degrees they won a livelihood and success. As soon as Ruthenian settlements were established their fellow-countrymen joined them. Many hardships of the earliest immigrants were in this way obviated for their successors. The steady stream of emigration, however, began by 1904 to de-preciate the value of farms in Galicia and Bukowina. From that year a larger percentage of people left their families behind till they could earn enough to bring them out. The Ruthenians have, on the whole, kept to the country, and to northern sections of the prairies.

Magyar communities developed at Woodridge, Manitoba, and near Lethbridge, Alberta, but larger and more numerous settlements within Saskatchewan. The first Magyar group took up homesteads near Esterhazy in 1886. In 1892 a small colony of 125 settled at Otthon. Then another Hungarian settlement was made at Crooked Lakes (Wakaw). In 1902 Zoltan von Rajces of Rosthern founded still another at Matthewsfield (Matyas Fold). Soon there were settle-ments at Otthon, Beaver Hill, Saxon Hill, Plunkett, Melville, Lestock, Wakaw, Regina, Bekevar, Stockholm, Bukowina, Touchwood, Middle Lake, Esterhazy, Kaposvar. A survey of 55 typical Hungarian families some 20 years after their coming showed that on their arrival all adults and children of school age were able to read Magyar, but none had been able to speak English. At the time of the survey practically all children of school age were able to speak and read English and, thanks to home instruction and church services and such journals as reached them, nearly as many were able to read Magyar. It was rare for a woman to speak or read English with either ease or proficiency, although nearly all under-stood common words of salutation, the language of counting, of ad-dressing horses, and a few common phrases. The men, brought into greater contact with life outside the settlements, exhibited a larger mastery of the English language. Of 55 families 30 took one Magyar periodical and 3 more than one, 12 took English papers and 5 two or more. All but 5 owned land; 23 one quarter-section; 17 two quarters; 6 three quarters; 2 one section; 2 less than two sections. Of the land-holding families practically all had a fuller complement of stock than was the average for the prairies; 14 owned automobiles, and 12 telephones. All families but one had gardens and much finer gardens than those of English-speaking Canadians; and 17 families owned some kind of musical instrument. Three had sent their children beyond the public schools.

Scattered through the central prairies are a dozen Bohemian settlements, of which the earliest dates from 1904. The largest, between Esterhazy and Langenburg, contains 150 families mostly from South Russia. At Marriot and Valley Centre were settled 60 families who came by way of the United States. The writer investigated a settlement of 37 families near Glenside, formed in 1904. He found a Moravian group chiefly from 4 villages south of Brno (Brünn) in Moravia. A second group came to Canada from South Russia. Settlers from Bohemia had established themselves in the province of Cherson Kaja north of the Black Sea. But land hunger, opposition to conscription, social unrest in Russia and letters from the United States and Canada rendered them dissatisfied, and they grasped the opportunity to migrate to Canada.

Of the Germans comparatively few came from Germany itself, the majority coming from Russia or the north Central States of America. We have already noted St Peter's Colony near Humboldt. Other groups settled near Rosthern, Holdfast, Dundurn, Perdue, Haultain, Odessa, Kipling, Melville, Lanigan, Middle Lake, St Walburg, St Brieuc. These have proved thrifty settlers and deserve the prosperity which they have reaped. Their social life has been enriched by church activities, and their consciousness of racial distinctiveness deepened by publications in their own language.

No group exhibited greater capacity to adapt themselves to Canadian life than the Icelanders. About 1876 some 250 came to the shores of Lake Winnipeg. The Icelanders have been particularly successful in Manitoba, and, more recently, in Saskatchewan. Many have attained to positions of eminence in the political, academic and economic life of the prairies.

Scandinavians have come mostly through the Middle States, although some, as a result of assiduous propaganda, came directly from their homelands. They settled in large numbers near Macoun along the Soo Line, near Outlook and Conquest. In Saskatchewan the census of 1901 showed but 1452 Scandinavians, that of 1911 no less than 33,991.

About 1906 a settlement of Finns was established west of Dunblane. They have proved radical in their economic views. Scattered throughout the prairies are other racial groups. Poles are interspersed among the Ukrainians. Roumanians are found in various centres, though not in large numbers. There are even a few Persians north of North Battleford. In the cities Greeks came to compete for the better-class restaurant business. The Chinese almost monopolise the laundry trade, apart from steam laundries, and there are few towns where they have not established an "eating-house".

The following surveys of the origins of settlers[1] reveal the composition of two rural municipalities in the Central Prairies in 1914: Insinger Municipality: Bukowina, 1841; Galicia, 562; Poland, 187; Scandinavian countries, 270; Iceland, 28; Germany, 19; Bohemia, 8; Russia, 5; Roumania, 6; Jews, 27; United States, 56; Great Britain, 163; Canada, 124. Total, 3296. Theodore Municipality: Scandinavians, 223; Bukowinians, 123; Galicians, 12; Germans, 19; Jews, 14; Poles, 6; Icelanders, 3; Bohemian, 1; Americans (mostly Scandinavians), 27; British, 85; Canadian, 70. Total, 583.

The prairies are wide. The mutual intercourse of these peoples has been hampered and their interaction retarded owing to the vast area over which settlement has spread. But there has been the unifying influence of common economic environment, common political institutions and like educational systems for children. Intermarriages have taken place on a considerable scale. The writer investigated 19,025 marriages of the period 1906–12. In 73.4 per cent. both contracting parties were English-speaking; in 8.1 per cent. the union represented a process of speedy assimilation where the next generation would be thoroughly Canadian; 3.2 per cent. produced only tardy assimilation to Canadian customs and manners, although children born of such marriages would be more Canadian than either parent. No less than 15.2 per cent. of the marriages tended to perpetuate racial and national characteristics that are non-Canadian.

In the making of the West the big things have been done by Eastern Canadians and Britons. Thus, apart from outstanding exceptions like Van Horne, railroads were built by Canadians and British. Order was established by the Mounted Police, largely British. The old Hudson's Bay Company was chiefly the work of Scotsmen. The development of government, of political, social, religious and educational institutions has been the achievement of Canadians. The feeling for "land" as the fit place to make homes is the gift of the Europeans. But to Americans the people of the prairies owe much in alertness of mind, in practical initiative, in courage, in shrewdness, in determination to exploit and to make the most of the country.

The growth in the population of Manitoba for the period 1871 to 1911 was as follows:[2] 1871, 25,228; 1881, 62,260; 1891, 152,506; 1901, 255,211; 1911, 455,614.[3]

---

[1] Conducted by Rev. J. A. Doyle of the Methodist Church.
[2] *Census of Canada*, 1911, p. 522.
[3] Given as 461,394 in *Census of Canada*, 1921, I, 354–5.

In Alberta the increase of rural population for the decade 1901–11 was 180,327, of urban 121,314; in Manitoba the rural increase was 70,511, the urban 129,892; in Saskatchewan the rural increase was 287,338, the urban 113,815.[1] In the same period Alberta made an increase in total population of 413·08 per cent., Manitoba 78·52 per cent., and Saskatchewan 439·48 per cent.[2] The following table gives the population of Manitoba, Saskatchewan and Alberta for 1901 and 1911:

	Manitoba		Saskatchewan		Alberta	
	1901	1911	1901	1911	1901	1911
Total population	255,211	461,394[3]	91,279	492,432	73,022	374,295
British	164,239	266,562	40,094	251,010	34,903	192,629
European	73,092	160,574	33,031	199,781	24,110	132,921
Asiatic	210	970	42	1,224	248	2,097

In the political development of the Prairies[4] there have been two distinct trends—that of the Red River and that of the Territories. The whole region was originally under the sway of the Hudson's Bay Company. For the Red River settlement responsible self-rule came with the transfer to Canada: the Territories possessed no form of government prior to incorporation in the Dominion.

The landmarks in the growth of Manitoba are the coming of the Selkirk colonists, the development of the Council of Assiniboia, the passing of the Hudson's Bay Company as a governmental body and its transformation into a commercial enterprise, the enactment of the Manitoba Act, and the abolition of the Legislative Council. In 1867 the Red River settlement was governed by the Council of Assiniboia, a representative, but not responsible, Council. This Council had organised a board of works, committee of economy, volunteer corps, legal and judicial machinery, tariff system and postal facilities. It appointed public officials and erected necessary buildings. It supervised the whole social life of the settlement, imposing duties and restrictions on the sale and importation of liquors, superintending the building of roads, the issue of marriage licences and the encouragement of native industries.

The series of Dominion Acts relating to the Prairies begins with "An Act for the temporary government of Rupert's Land and the Northwestern Territory when united with Canada", 22 June 1869. This Act sought to prepare for the transfer of the Territories to the Government of Canada. A year later the Manitoba Act (33 Vict. c. 3) launched upon its independent constitutional career the old District of Assiniboia, henceforth in possession of self-government. The Lieutenant-Governor in the first days of the province occupied an important position in the Administration. For a short time there was a temporary Government with two ministers and the Legislative

[1] *Census of Canada*, 1911, p. 5.   [2] *Ibid.* p. 522.
[3] See text and note at foot of p. 530.
[4] Henceforth this term, when used in a political sense, will be printed "Prairies".

Assembly. After this, government was carried on with the Legislative Assembly and a Legislative Council, but without a Premier. At the end of six years the Council was abolished. Without a Council but with a Premier and an Assembly, the province assumed the constitutional form which has endured to the present.

The transfer of the settlement to the Dominion, however, was not accomplished without a disturbance, of which an account has been given in a previous chapter. When the regulars under Colonel Wolseley came on 24 August, Riel and his associates had fled. Donald A. Smith (the future Lord Strathcona) continued the administration for the Company till Adams G. Archibald arrived by canoe on 2 September. The province of Manitoba, already since 15 July within the Confederation, had now a Lieutenant-Governor appointed by the Dominion Government. The Red River expedition made a contribution to the settlement no less than to the good order of the country out of all proportion to its cost. The total expense was under $500,000, although Wolseley had had to transport 1400 men through a wilderness. But the expedition of 1870 showed that the western plains could be reached and colonised. In fact both in 1870 and in 1885 Louis Riel unwittingly drew the attention of Eastern Canada to the undeveloped possibilities of prairie settlement.

The first Legislature in March 1871 set about the task of laying foundations. In the autumn Gilbert McMicken arrived as Dominion lands agent, and allotment of lands began. A group of half-breeds sullenly withdrew to the Saskatchewan. Meantime the spectre of Riel hovered over the new province. His flight in August 1870 had postponed for the Dominion Government the awkward question of the amnesty promised by Bishop Taché. But the threat of the Fenian Raid of October 1871 revived interest in this matter. Riel and Lépine rallied the half-breeds to resist the raid. Before they could render practical assistance, it was broken up. But when Governor Archibald publicly thanked them in a review at St Boniface, and shook their hands, an outcry was raised in Winnipeg and throughout the East. The action of the Lieutenant-Governor, it was declared, compromised the Canadian Government over the amnesty to Scott's murderers. Riel, elected by acclamation as member of the House of Commons for Provencher, had the audacity to sign the roll. He was expelled from the House. Lépine was brought to trial and found guilty. On his own responsibility the Governor-General commuted his sentence to imprisonment for two years and forfeiture of political rights. Riel himself was declared an outlaw. After confinement under an assumed name in an asylum he retired to the United States.

In December 1872 the Hon. Alexander Morris, Chief Justice of Manitoba, became Lieutenant-Governor. Attorney-General Clarke guided the Administration till replaced in 1874 by Marc A. Girard who, however, after only a few months gave way to Davis as Premier.

For four years Davis carried out his programme of "economy and retrenchment" till he, in turn, was succeeded in 1878 by John Norquay. For ten years the Government was controlled by Norquay, the "native Premier". Then, in 1888, after the briefest interim, during which Dr Harrison was Premier, Thomas Greenway assumed control. "The control of public affairs", writes Chester Martin, "passed to a generation that knew not the Red River Settlement".[1]

The period 1870–88, then, was the time of foundation-laying. Creditable beginnings were made in the legislative, economic and educational phases of provincial life. The provincial treasury was so restricted in resources that the severest economy had to be practised. In 1876 the Legislative Council by a self-denying Act voted its own demise. Of these years not the least important incident—in view of coming events—was the agitation for a "purely non-sectarian system of Public Schools".[2] It became clear in the expanding life of the province that French influence was passing. Men were more concerned with real estate speculation and its attendant boom, with the railway agitation, with the material development of the Prairies than with preserving the balance of power between Red River races, nationalities and tongues.

But railways were vital to the growth of the Prairies. Uneasiness developed when Alexander Mackenzie held out little hope of realising the promises made to the West at confederation. After delay due to financial crises in the United States, railways began to push up to Manitoba from the south. The St Paul and Pacific was extended to the boundary. In 1879 Stephen, Smith and Hill formed the St Paul, Minneapolis and Manitoba Railway Company. Then came strife with the Dominion Government over the granting of charters to lines exclusively within the province, and the disallowance of the charter of the Manitoba South Eastern Railway in 1882. Railways became a party issue, with Thomas Greenway stoutly contesting "monopoly clauses" and championing "provincial rights". The Norquay Government fell, oppressed by difficulties associated with the disallowance of railway charters, with its failure to secure "better terms" at Ottawa, and with a contest, in which the protagonists were primarily Ontario and the Dominion Government, concerning the eastern boundary.

What the Dominion Government was unwilling to do for friends in the Norquay Government it felt itself forced to concede to opponents in the Greenway Administration. Disallowance was abolished by the surrender of the offensive "monopoly clause" by the Canadian Pacific Railway Company.[3] Greenway immediately threw his energies into the task of providing greater railway facilities. After an unseemly contest at "Fort Whyte", which, fortunately, proved bloodless, the Dominion ceased to interfere with local railway development.

---

[1] *Canada and its Provinces*, XIX, 121.   [2] *Ibid.* p. 108.   [3] *Ibid.* p. 122.

Scarcely had the railway strife subsided when the schools question came to the fore. Immigration had greatly increased the strength of the Protestants, who resented the larger grant per pupil paid to the Roman Catholic schools. The issue was forced by Joseph Martin, Attorney-General in the Greenway Government. He took a decisive stand against the use of French in courts and Legislature and against separate schools. The conflict, involving religion, race and language, became a matter of bitterest debate in public discussion, in the press and among the lodges, and finally spread to the older provinces. School bills were brought down in 1890. A Department of Education with an Advisory Board was established. The so-called "treaty rights" of the Roman Catholic minority, evidently kept "in secret reserve" for a score of years, were invoked in vain. The Public Schools Bill passed the Legislature, and French was abolished as the official language of courts and Legislature. The question of taxing Roman Catholics to support public schools was carried to the Privy Council, but the contention of the Manitoba Courts was upheld.[1] Then by invoking the Manitoba Act redress was sought from the Governor-General in Council. At length the Dominion Government, forced into action, interfered in a remedial order. This order the Greenway Government declined to obey, and, on appeal to the electors, was returned to power by a decisive majority. Laurier, leader of the Dominion Opposition, promised a "better way than coercion". Over this issue the Dominion elections of 1896 were fought. The Conservatives were defeated. By negotiation Laurier, largely through the co-operation of Clifford Sifton, effected a settlement[2] which, if not entirely satisfactory, has never been seriously disturbed. The Schools Act was amended to permit religious teaching, when authorised by the trustees or on petition of ratepayers, between 3.30 and 4 o'clock in the afternoons or on certain days of the week. Further, at least one Roman Catholic teacher was to be employed where the attendance of Roman Catholic children averaged at least 25 in any school in rural districts and villages, or 40 in towns and cities, provided the parents of the children made formal petition for this privilege. These children might be segregated for religious, but not for ordinary school, instruction, and provision was made for bilingual teaching of non-English-speaking students in cases where ten or more such were in attendance.

After the removal of the schools question from practical politics, the extension of provincial boundaries, the state of the province's finances and the handling of liquor became live matters of debate. Hugh John Macdonald succeeded to the Premiership. He passed a stringent measure to prohibit the sale of intoxicating liquor except under licences granted to druggists. This Act the Privy Council de-

[1] Lefroy, A. H. F., *Canada's Federal System*, pp. 652–66; Report of Decision of Privy Council in the Manitoba School case.   [2] *Vide supra*, chapter xxi.

clared to be constitutional. Nevertheless Roblin, who had succeeded to the Premiership on Macdonald's return to Dominion politics, referred the liquor question to a referendum. He caught the Temperance forces disorganised. As a consequence a majority of nearly 7000 was piled up against the Macdonald Act. With this reverse, the liquor question dropped out of practical politics until after 1914.

The issues that confronted the province during the remainder of this period were less political than economic. The Government continued to encourage railway expansion and nearly 4000 miles of line were completed by 1910.[1] The ownership and control by Government of utilities that were natural monopolies became the policy of the Roblin Administration. The Government purchased the equipment and interest of the Bell Telephone Company and installed a government system. The venture into the elevator business proved less successful, and the Government rented the system to the Grain Growers' Grain Company. Other features of the period were the extension of the provincial boundaries to Hudson Bay and the agitation for "better terms". The Borden Government signalised its accession to power and its friendliness to the Roblin Administration by increasing the area of the province, placing Manitoba on a financial equality with the sister provinces of the Prairies and increasing the subsidy from $840,000 in 1911 to $1,350,000 in 1912.

When the province of Manitoba was created on 15 July 1870 it was granted responsible government, but there was no thought of bestowing responsible, or even representative, government on the remainder of the Prairies. Apart from the few whites at the Forts and Missions there were only Indians and half-breeds resident in the Territories. Consequently the administration of that vast stretch of country was vested in the Lieutenant-Governor of Manitoba. He governed with the assistance of a Council, whose members also were resident in Manitoba.

The growth of population, due in the first instance to the removal from the Red River to the Saskatchewan of discontented *Métis*, and an outbreak of serious disorders among the tribes of the south-west as a result of bootlegging and whisky-trading in the Whoop-up country induced the Dominion Government to take three steps. It organised the North West Mounted Police. It entrusted the supervision of Territorial matters to a new Department—the Department of the Interior. And it appointed a separate Lieutenant-Governor for the Territories. He was to govern under the terms of the North West Territories Act, 1875. The first step towards responsible government was now taken. Henceforth government was to be by men resident within the Territories, not by men who governed from an adjoining

[1] See below, chapter xxv.

province. In keeping with this step the Territories received a capital of their own. Battleford was selected for that honour. For one year, till buildings were erected at Battleford, the seat of government was at Livingstone, Swan River, and here in the spring of 1877 the first session of the new North West Council was held. Then in 1878, 1879 and 1881 the Council met in Battleford.

The Swan River Council consisted of one appointed and three *ex-officio* members—the Lieutenant-Governor, two magistrates and the Commissioner of the Police. But the opening session of the Council at Battleford saw the first recognition of the citizens of the Territories themselves. Pascal Breland, a merchant of the Cypress Hills, was appointed a member of the Council. A still more important step in advance was made in 1881. Under the North West Territories Act, 1875, provision had been made for the erection of an electoral district when an area of 1000 square miles contained a population of 1000 inhabitants of adult age. The first election under this arrangement was held in the district of Lorne in the Prince Albert settlement. Here Chief Factor Lawrence Clarke was elected over Captain Moore by a vote of 250 to 143. This constituted another step towards the goal. The people themselves had chosen their first elected representative to occupy a seat in the Council. The development of the country and the attendant increase of population still further altered the composition of the Council. This became evident on the transfer of the capital to Regina. The erection of each new electoral district meant an increase in the elected members of the Council—1 in 1881; 6 in 1883; 8 in 1884; 13 in 1885; 14 in 1886 and 1887. After 1883 they exceeded the appointed members. Provision had been made by the North West Territories Act that when the elected representatives reached 21 the Council should terminate and a Legislative Assembly be constituted. Though that number was not reached, the session of 1887 proved to be the last meeting of the Council. In 1888 a Legislative Assembly came into being with 22 members. This was in accord with the demands made by the elected members of the Council.

The change due to the addition of elected members had aroused within the Council itself an aspiration for a greater measure of self-rule. The elected members exhibited a growing interest in all matters that concerned the people—schools, agriculture, finance, and municipal organisation. The Council could dispose of only such funds as came from the administration of Territorial ordinances, e.g. fines and licence fees, and from direct taxation which was restricted to electoral districts. But in 1886, as a result of representations made, the powers of the Council were enlarged. Henceforth it could levy direct taxation within the whole Territories for Territorial, including municipal, purposes.

From 1884 the elected members of the Council were in the majority. Each year they became more articulate in the expression of the needs of settlers. The most aggressive members of this group came to be Frederick W. G. Haultain, a lawyer of Fort Macleod; Frank Oliver, a journalist of Edmonton; and James H. Ross, a rancher of Moose Jaw. As early as 1884 Oliver and Ross, with Turriff of Moose Mountain and Geddes of Calgary, were asking for the transfer of revenues arising out of natural resources from the control of the Dominion to the Council. From the same year dates the struggle to secure for the elected representatives the control of all money devoted to the purposes of government. At this time Lieutenant-Governor Dewdney made some feeble efforts to satisfy this demand for responsible government. Small sums of money—$1000 in 1884 and $500 in 1886—were placed at the disposal of the elected representatives to spend on their various districts. In 1885 a committee was appointed to devise a method for enabling the elected members during recess to keep the Lieutenant-Governor advised in regard to their districts. In the following session all the elected members were constituted a committee to report upon a scheme of responsible government for the Territories. A report was brought down in 1887. This criticised the administration of the previous decade on the ground that it excluded the people from controlling the public money. It asked for an elected Council presided over by one of their own number. A further feature was the request that the Lieutenant-Governor carry on his executive functions with the advice of an Executive Council of Three who should hold seats in the Council. In the Legislative Assembly that met on 31 October 1888 were embodied some, though not all, of the suggestions made by the report. In this Assembly, for the first time, all parts of the Territories were represented by elected members. Another step had been made towards responsible government. Every qualified resident might now vote for a member of the Assembly and make his influence felt in the Government. The Government was for the first time completely representative. The more acute phase of the struggle lay ahead— to make the Government responsible to the people through their representatives.

Where was enthusiasm for responsible government to be found when Lieutenant-Governor Royal assumed office in 1888? Not in Ottawa, either on the part of the Government itself or on the part of the majority of Territorial members of the House. Not in the Territories, on the part of all districts, for Saskatchewan was opposed and even in Regina and its vicinity there was strong opposition. Some Territorial newspapers were lukewarm, others, in fact, actively opposed, while still others, such as the *Macleod Gazette* and the *Edmonton Bulletin*, were staunch advocates. Whatever support the cause found was from members of the old Council, or the new Assembly. These were anxious to extend the control of the representatives of the people from purely Territorial funds to all expenses of administration and all matters of government. Much depended upon the attitude of the new Lieutenant-Governor, upon the determination of the members of the recently created Assembly and upon the pressure put on the Dominion Government. Perhaps most of all depended on the general Territorial situation. The coming of the railway had opened the way for an influx of population. A substantial beginning had been made in the establishment of schools. An incipient municipal organisation was in operation. The uprising of 1870 had drawn the attention of the East to the Prairies, and, through the coming of troops, dispelled the thought that the plains were fit only for Red Men and buffaloes. The needs of the Prairies increased with the growth of population. No one was better acquainted with these needs than the members of the Assembly. It was felt in the Territories, particularly in the Assembly itself, that if the money available for government were spent by men acquainted with local conditions settlers might be attracted to the Prairies.

The active struggle for responsible government in the Territories falls in the regime of Lieutenant-Governor Royal, 1888–93.[1] In that struggle the initiative was borne by members of the Assembly. In their fight for control of the purse they were placed in the position of waging a contest with the Lieutenant-Governor who represented the Dominion Government.

Differences of opinion between the Lieutenant-Governor and the Assembly arose with regard to the extent of the powers and responsibility of the Advisory Council. The Lieutenant-Governor held that the Assembly was not entitled to have a statement of public accounts laid before it on the ground that the moneys unaccounted for were part of the Dominion vote to the Territories. The Assembly considered that these moneys had been voted by an Ordinance of the Assembly, and should be duly accounted for to the Assembly. The Lieutenant-Governor held that the Advisory Council was responsible to the Assembly with respect to Territorial revenue only. The majority of the Assembly held that the Act of 1888 meant *all* matters of finance, including the Dominion grant. When the Lieutenant-Governor refused to modify his views the majority in the Assembly protested by refusing to vote the Territorial estimates and by withdrawing powers previously granted the Advisory Council under the Ordinances.

The issue passed from the Assembly's right of control over the Dominion grant to the Assembly's right of control over the Advisory Council, or, as it came to be, the Executive Committee. So acute became the contest that within a period of five years there were nine different Advisory Councils and Executive Committees. Lieutenant-Governor Royal's tenure of office terminated in the early autumn of

---

[1] Oliver, E. H., "The Contest between Lieutenant-Governor Royal and the Legislative Assembly of N.W. Territories, 1888–1893", *Trans. Roy. Soc. Canada*, 1923.

1893. During his term power passed almost completely into the hands of the representatives of the people. It is agreeable to find that the Lieutenant-Governor before laying down his office expressed his satisfaction at the gains that had been made:

When, on 4 July 1888, I was sworn in as Lieutenant-Governor of the Territories, the functions of that office were as totally different from those of the Lieutenant-Governors of the Provinces as they will be from those to be performed by my successor. I was responsible to the Privy Council of Canada alone for the executive acts done in the Territories. The Assembly had hardly a voice in the Government of the Country and the Lieutenant-Governor was practically a Political Commissioner under whose direct supervision and authority the affairs of the Territories were conducted and administered. Now all this has been changed materially, and hence my satisfaction. The Legislature to-day practically enjoys the rights and privileges of self-government.

After long agitation in the Territories, led by the Premier, Hon. Frederick W. G. Haultain, the Parliament of Canada in 1897 passed legislation giving the Territories such a form of responsible government as was possible while they still continued to be Territories and lacked provincial status. The Executive Committee was replaced by the Executive Council. By that time the foundations were laid for the educational, municipal, political and judicial systems of the Territories. Responsible self-rule had been achieved. But a Territorial Administration had not the powers of a Provincial Government. And the difficulties of government were tremendously increased by the remarkable growth of population due to the success of the Sifton policy of immigration. The Dominion Government doubled the annual grant to the Territories. This increase was not sufficient to meet the needs, for the expenditure on government in 1905 was four times that in 1897. Financial necessities developed constitutional aspirations. The agitation for provincial autonomy produced a constitutional discussion over "provincial rights" and precipitated a sectarian controversy of much bitterness over separate schools. A debate developed whether there should be one or two provinces. Provincial autonomy became a matter of Dominion-wide discussion. It was charged in the public press that the Dominion Government hesitated to take action on account of the problem of separate schools; that the hierarchy of Quebec would not permit the Manitoba situation to be duplicated in the newer provinces. When Laurier introduced the autonomy measures he declared that they continued the educational system already existing. It was urged by many, however, that the Dominion was imposing separate schools upon the Territories, and Sifton resigned from the Cabinet. The educational clause that was ultimately carried safeguarded all rights or privileges which any class enjoyed at the passing of the Acts.

On 1 September 1905 two provinces were erected, Saskatchewan and Alberta. The financial arrangements were satisfactory, but the Dominion retained control of the natural resources. Mr Haultain, who had guided the Territorial Assembly for nearly twenty years and had opposed features of the Autonomy Bills, was passed over in the selection of new Premiers. He became leader of the Opposition in Saskatchewan.

The period 1905–14 witnessed the laying of foundations of the most important provincial institutions and the erection of public works. To Walter Scott fell the honour of the Premiership of Saskatchewan, and to A. C. Rutherford that of Alberta. Scott continued in office to the end of our period. In Alberta Rutherford was succeeded in 1910 by the Hon. A. L. Sifton. Upon the basis of Territorial legislation a complete system of government was established in each province, the educational system expanded, a judicial system set up, long-distance telephones constructed and operated, municipal institutions organised for urban and rural communities, public roads, bridges and buildings constructed, support granted to railway extension, and aid given to every phase of agriculture. Laws were enacted relating to public health, the public service, the professions, the organisation and extension of advanced educational institutions, universities, cities, towns, villages and rural municipalities. During this period new lines of railway were constructed, and immigration developed to such an extent that free homesteads practically came to an end. When the Great War broke out, the provinces were fully organised and equipped with provincial institutions.

The stages in the growth of municipal institutions in the Province of Manitoba are marked by the years 1871, 1873, 1883 and 1900.[1] In 1871 the County Assessment Act and the Parish Assessment Act made provision for dealing with local finance. The former concerned the tax roll of the province; the latter, purely local improvements and assessments for the parishes within each of the five counties. An Act of 1873 provided for the erection of a local municipality in districts containing not less than thirty freeholders. In 1883 the province was divided into twenty-six counties and three judicial districts. This Act copied closely the Ontario Act of 1849. In the working out of the Act it was found in many particulars to be unsuited to Western conditions. By the General Municipal Act of 1900 every city, town, village and rural municipality became a body corporate. Over all, excepting cities having separate charters of incorporation—Winnipeg, St Boniface and Portage-la-Prairie—was placed the general supervision of a Department of Municipal Affairs.

In the North West Territories (Saskatchewan and Alberta) we find among the ordinances one "respecting Municipalities" (1884). This contained provisions for the establishment of certain rural municipalities and the towns of Regina, Moose Jaw, etc. Only a limited number of rural municipalities came into being under

[1] See articles by present writer in *Canada Year Books*, 1915, 1921.

this ordinance. In 1896 legislation was passed de-organising certain municipalities where the system proved unpopular. In 1897 the Legislature passed a Statute Labour Ordinance. The year following produced the Local Improvement Ordinance which, with its amendments, was observed until 1904. The average area of each district was one township. In 1903 a new Local Improvement Bill de-organised all one-township districts and abolished the provision for statute labour. The new bill provided for local improvement districts with an area of four townships, each electing a councillor annually. The four thus secured formed a Council Board. In 1904 the Legislature made financial provision for enquiry into municipal organisations in order to provide a safe, economical system of rural municipalities and to improve the ordinance under which cities, towns and villages were administered. The breaking up of the Territories in 1905 into the present Provinces of Saskatchewan and Alberta caused delays; but municipal commissions with urban and rural sections were appointed. As a result of the experience gathered during Territorial days and later, and of the findings of these commissions, Local Improvements Acts were amended, Rural Municipality, Town and Village Acts were passed in both provinces, and a City Act was passed in the Province of Saskatchewan.

The pioneers of education in the West were the missionaries. The Council of Assiniboia gave support that was only occasional and entirely inadequate. In March 1853 a despatch from the Company was received by the Council disapproving of grants for education totalling £130 as being a misapplication of public funds. The attitude of the Council is exhibited in a minute of 22 February 1866:[1]

> The President laid before the Council a petition from the Settlers at Point Coupee to the number of 27, representing that, with a view to the instruction of their children, numbering about 60, they had lately built a school house, but had not the means of paying a school master. The Council by a majority of votes granted 10 Pounds to be payable to the Schoolmaster himself. But in granting that sum, the Council wished it to be distinctly understood by all concerned, that it would not be continued, being given for the present year only, and that it was not to be drawn into a precedent.

In 1870 the churches were almost entirely responsible for education, and they continued their interest. In 1871 Manitoba, and in 1884 the Territories, established systems of schools. In both cases the Boards of Education were divided into two sections, Protestant and Roman Catholic. In Manitoba the churches continued for many years to be responsible for higher education, for the church colleges were vigorous institutions long before the provincial University became a force. And the inspectors of schools were clergymen till 1888.

In 1871, Manitoba had 24 school districts, 12 being Protestant and

---

[1] Oliver, E. H., *The Canadian North-West; its Early Development and Legislative Records*, I, 100.

12 Roman Catholic. Within a dozen years Protestant schools had outstripped the Roman Catholic. There were 40 Roman Catholic schools with an attendance of 1941; the Protestant numbered 271 with an enrolment of 10,831. In 1882 the Protestant School Board of Winnipeg established a high school. In the same year the Roman Catholic section of the Board established a normal school at St Boniface; two years later the Protestant section established one in Winnipeg. In 1888 the Protestant section ceased to employ clergymen and appointed five full-time inspectors. In 1890 the denominational aspect of education was abolished, and all schools brought under the Public Schools Act. This action, as shown already, ultimately precipitated the Manitoba schools controversy. Under the final adjustment of this question a Department of Education was created and all public schools became non-sectarian. Religious exercises, at the option of trustees, might be observed prior to the closing of school in the afternoon. A conscience clause permitted parents to withdraw their children during the religious instruction.

Further problems arose from the incoming of settlers from Europe. The Mennonites were particularly difficult to deal with. They sought to maintain private schools with low educational standards, almost entirely devoted to religious training. Owing to language difficulties an experiment was made in establishing special training-schools for teachers for Ruthenians and Poles. Other problems have been the low average attendance, the existence of small and inefficient schools and sparsely settled communities. The establishment of consolidated schools was designed to remedy these evils. At the end of our period there were nearly 50 consolidated school districts in the province. In 1882 a collegiate department was established in Winnipeg. Similar departments followed in Brandon, and Portage-la-Prairie. From 1888 a system of secondary schools has existed. In 1911 two technical schools were erected in Winnipeg.

Not the least difficult problem was afforded by the University. It was begun in 1877 on the model of the University of London as a federation of Colleges: St Boniface, St John's, Manitoba. Wesley College was not added till 1888. In 1907 a commission was appointed to consider the University situation. As a result of its report, by no means unanimous, the present policy of University education was inaugurated, emphasising the University as against the Colleges. Dr J. A. McLean was appointed President. In Manitoba the Agricultural College was established independently of the University. The University of Alberta was opened in 1908 with Dr H. M. Tory as President, and the University of Saskatchewan in 1909 with Dr W. C. Murray as President.

In the Territories the school system was inaugurated in 1884. The Board of Education had two sections—Protestant and Roman Catholic —which remained till the Board was abolished in 1892. At this date a Council of Public Instruction was established with two Protestants and two Roman Catholics as assessors, and the actual administration placed under a superintendent. In 1901 the Executive Council itself undertook the administration of the school system. The guarantee of the privileges of minorities, as existing in 1901, was perpetuated by the Saskatchewan and Alberta Acts.

In 1888 a high school system was inaugurated. Both provinces have developed secondary schools, normal schools and provincial Universities. Alberta, however, did not employ a Secondary Education Act. The main development of education in the Territories has coincided with that of Manitoba, except that the new provincial Universities received larger support and powers at a relatively earlier stage in their history, and, also, larger privileges were extended to separate schools by reason of the autonomy measures.

Some indication of educational progress in the Prairies can be gathered from the following tables:

Receipts and Expenditures for Public Education[1]

Year	Manitoba		Saskatchewan		Alberta	
	Receipts	Expenditures	Receipts	Expenditures	Receipts	Expenditures
1906	$2,358,888	$2,249,558	$1,465,361	$1,448,915	$1,289,921	$1,259,107
1914	$5,674,349	$6,079,720	$9,020,411	$9,072,296	$7,304,188	$7,834,891

Elementary and secondary publicly controlled schools[2]

Year	Manitoba			Saskatchewan			Alberta		
	Schools	Teachers	Pupils enrolled	Schools	Teachers	Pupils enrolled	Schools	Teachers	Pupils enrolled
1906	1847	2365	64,123	873	1296	31,275	570	924	28,784
1914	2688	2864	93,954	2966	5140	118,927	2027	3978	89,910

There was no church life on the prairies before the coming of the Selkirk colonists. The great fur companies had at times encouraged exploration, but never missionary enterprise. But when the Red River settlers came a new era was inaugurated. By 1867 the leading churches had established themselves. The next half-century was for all alike an era of great Home Mission effort and of unparalleled development.

The majority of the original Selkirk settlers were Presbyterians. But they waited for a minister of their own for four decades, till John Black came to Kildonan in 1851. In 1875 there were only two self-sustaining congregations west of the Great Lakes—Kildonan and Knox Church, Winnipeg. On 31 December 1914 the strength of the Presbyterian Church on the Prairies was:[3]

[1] *Canada Year Book*, 1914, pp. 126–7.   [2] *Ibid.* p. 119.
[3] *Minutes and Reports of General Assembly, Presbyterian Church in Canada*, 1915, p. 521.

Synods	Manses	Elders	Preaching stations	Families	Com-municants	Total amount raised in 1914
Manitoba	142	916	484	6108	28,599	$597,491
Saskatchewan	154	589	936	7214	18,581	$499,696
Alberta	80	439	535	5048	13,283	$316,614

The outstanding figures in this development were John Black, James Nisbet, Lucy Baker, Dr John Carmichael, Principal King of Manitoba College and, above all, the "Great Superintendent", Dr James Robertson.

The Wesleyans applied themselves to mission enterprise in the West as early as 1840. James Evans established a mission at Rainy Lake, and Robert T. Rundle at Fort Edmonton. The Wesleyans did not, however, become securely established till the 'sixties. The outstanding Methodist leaders during our period were Dr George Young, Dr James Woodsworth and Principal Sparling of Wesley College. In 1914 Manitoba Conference had 23,816 members, and raised for all purposes $482,617; Saskatchewan, 18,748 members, and raised $430,313; Alberta, 16,049 members, and raised $297,950.

The most striking feature in the religious life of the two churches mentioned has been the agitation for Church Union. To prevent over-lapping and to promote co-operation a movement to unite the Con-gregational, Methodist and Presbyterian Churches was launched in 1902. The union was not actually consummated till 1925, but already before 1914 votes were taken and policies shaped with a view to that event.

The first Church of England minister to arrive in the West came in 1820—John West. Robert Machray became Bishop of Rupert's Land in 1864 and continued in that office till 1904.

At his consecration [writes Canon Tucker[1]] there were eighteen clergymen in this vast diocese: one in the Yukon, two in the Mackenzie River district, three on Hudson Bay, four in what is now Saskatchewan and eight in Manitoba. There was not a baker, a butcher, a tailor or shoemaker in the whole land. No collection was taken up in any of the churches....During his term Bishop Machray saw eighteen clergy grow into two hundred, and scores of thousands of dollars contributed where offertories had been non-existent.

A synod was organised in 1867. In 1872 the diocese of Rupert's Land was divided by the formation of the see of Moosonee; in 1874, Saskatchewan and Athabaska; in 1884, Qu'Appelle and Mackenzie River; in 1887, Calgary; in 1891, Selkirk, now Yukon; and in 1899, Keewatin.

At the time of the transfer there were between Lake Superior and the Rocky Mountains four Roman Catholic bishops, Taché, Grandin, Faraud, Clut, all Oblates, as many secular priests, Ritchot, Dugas, Kavanagh and Giroux, 30 Oblate missionaries, about 30 lay brothers and seven establishments of Grey Sisters. In 1914 there were 247,000 Roman Catholics on the Prairies as follows: Manitoba, 80,000; Saskatchewan, 98,000; Alberta, 69,000. The Territory was divided

---

[1] *Canada and its Provinces*, XI, 228.

into six dioceses: the archdioceses of St Boniface, Winnipeg, Regina and Edmonton, and the dioceses of Prince Albert and Calgary.

From 1803 the jurisdiction of the Courts of Upper and Lower Canada extended in criminal matters to the Prairies.[1] In 1839 a General Court of Assiniboia was established. In 1871 the Legislature established the Supreme Court of Manitoba, later known as the Court of King's Bench.[2] The Court was not put into operation until the Hon. Alexander Morris became Chief Justice on 14 August 1872. In 1906 a Court of Appeal was created. In 1914 the Court of King's Bench of Manitoba consisted of a Chief Justice and five puisne judges. In addition there were county courts, surrogate courts, and minor courts presided over by magistrates and justices of the peace.

The North West Territories Act, 1875, made provision for establishing a regular judiciary in the Territories. In 1878 three judicial districts were created with district courts. In 1886 the Supreme Court of the North West Territories was established with five judges. In 1907 Saskatchewan established a Supreme Court and also a surrogate court as court of record. In the same year Alberta took similar action. Both provinces also have systems of district and inferior courts.

That from the outset the Territories enjoyed security in spite of a native population, which in the early 'seventies, especially in the south-west, was none too tractable, was due to the North West Mounted Police. On 11 September 1874 the new police force, after a ride of nearly 800 miles, arrived at what is now Lethbridge. Assistant-Commissioner Macleod proceeded to Belly River near Fort Whoop Up. In the heart of the Blackfoot country he established headquarters. His aim was to protect the Indians, restrain all lawlessness, and repress the illicit liquor traffic of Americans. He built Fort Macleod on Old Man River. In a year's time he stamped out the whisky trade and put an end for ever to the riots, murders, robberies and lawlessness that had disgraced the country. Largely because of the efficiency of the Police there was no "Wild West" on the Canadian prairies.

The only other serious interruption to good order in the Territories was the Uprising of 1885. Half-breeds had emigrated from Manitoba in the early 'seventies, and settled along the South Saskatchewan. There they had cherished their grievances till they assumed the dignity and dimensions of a Bill of Rights. They repeatedly laid their claims before the Dominion Government. But, although the North West Council had supported them, they received scant attention at Ottawa. Their demands related to patents, the payment of dues on timber, rails and firewood, breaking and "cropping" on pre-emptions, contracts for public works, the Hudson Bay route, elections and natural resources. They wanted the Territories divided

[1] 43 Geo. III, cap. 138. [2] 34 Vict. cap. 2.

into provinces, the sale of 500,000 acres to build schools and hospitals and to purchase seed-grain and implements, money grants to religious institutions, better terms for Indians and 240 acres for each half-breed. Exasperated at the failure of the Dominion to listen to them, they brought back their old leader, Louis Riel, from the United States to the Saskatchewan, to fight their cause. The old buffalo-hunter, Gabriel Dumont, became military leader. In March 1885 hostilities broke out at Duck Lake. The rising was an act of sheer madness with no chance of success, but there was danger that the Indians might rise throughout the West. Canadian troops were brought to the Prairies by the new Canadian Pacific Railway. They marched northward in three columns—from Qu'Appelle, Swift Current and Calgary. The insurrection was soon suppressed. The chief engagements were at Cut Knife Hill, Fish Creek and Batoche. By 12 May all resistance was over. Riel was tried in Regina and hanged on 16 November 1885.[1]

In the sphere of economic development this period of less than fifty years witnessed the change from the most primitive industries, and, indeed, from the stage of hunting to the most advanced grain-growing. It witnessed the passing of trader and freighter to a life of settled occupation, the coming of workers from the ends of the earth, the weaving of a vast network of railways, and the growth of populous cities, towns and villages where, in 1867, only buffalo and Indians roamed.

In that year the only advanced settlement was at the Red River, where farming was of a primitive character, there being no other market than the settlement itself. A considerable portion of the community eked out an existence by hunting and freighting. Supplies from outside were shipped from St Paul. Railway connection was through the United States, and had to be supplemented by a trek overland of 400 miles.

When the West was transferred to Canada, rapid development began. "In ten years", writes Dafoe,[2] "the country had been taken over, the title to the land secured, law and order enforced over the whole territory, a definite railway policy adopted, and an initial demonstration on sufficiently generous lines of the fertility of the soil had been made". It will be of interest to record some beginnings. In 1871 came a stage line from Abercrombie, Minn., and a telegraph line from Pembina. In 1872 the steamer *Selkirk* arrived at Winnipeg carrying supplies and put an end to freighting from the south. In 1871 surveying was begun on the block system, and the country made ready for homesteading in 1873. In the latter year was concluded the first of eight treaties with the Indians for extinguishing their title in the land. In 1876 wheat was first exported from the settlement; the shipment consisted of 878 bushels.[3] The first train reached

---

[1] *Vide supra*, chapter xxi.   [2] *Canada and its Provinces*, xx, 298.   [3] *Ibid*. 294.

St Boniface on the Pembina branch on 9 December 1878. In the late 'seventies the buffalo herds came near to extinction and the hunts came to an end. In 1881 the first sale of Canadian Pacific Railway land was made near Brandon to Charles Whitehead.[1] In 1883 the main line of that railway was completed to Winnipeg.

In 1886 the government inspection of wheat began. The production of hardy varieties such as Red Fife and Marquis added greatly to the area in which wheat could profitably be grown.[2] A marked increase has taken place in mixed farming. In Alberta dairy and live-stock enterprises developed in the central section; in the southern portion ranching long predominated, but irrigation has made possible a great variety of crops.

In the period 1901–14 the capacity of country elevators in Manitoba more than doubled while those of the area of the North West Territories increased almost twenty-four-fold.[3] The total acreage and yield of grain for the Prairie Provinces became: wheat, 9,335,400 acres, 140,958,000 bushels; oats, 5,353,000 acres, 150,843,000 bushels; barley, 936,000 acres, 19,545,000 bushels.[4] And this development in grain growing was paralleled by a similar increase in the farm live-stock of the Prairie Provinces.

Nor was the development of the Prairies confined to the products of the farm. In the first fifteen years of the century the value of manufactures for the Prairie Provinces increased seven-fold, and the number of manufacturing establishments advanced from 429 to 1019.[5] In the period 1907–14, the increase in the number of motor vehicles registered was from 99 to 20,107. By 1914 the mileage of telephones had become 364,117, and of railways 11,710. In 1902 Manitoba had 52 branches of banks; in 1905, 95; in 1915 the number had become 204. In 1902 Saskatchewan and Alberta together had 30 branches of banks; in 1905, 87; in 1915 there were 401 for Saskatchewan and 258 for Alberta.

The ordinary revenues and expenditures of the Prairie Provinces grew in the period 1908–13 as follows:

| Year | Manitoba | | Saskatchewan | | Alberta | |
	Receipts	Expenditures	Receipts	Expenditures	Receipts	Expenditures
1908	$2,891,582	$2,534,799	$1,844,371	$2,091,613	$2,849,650	$2,823,831
1913	$5,788,070	$5,314,849	$4,668,754	$4,656,800	$5,399,905	$5,225,584

Down to the outbreak of the Great War the general trend of development had been westwards. But the opening of the Hudson Bay Railway, the finding of vast mineral deposits, the realisation of the untapped wealth in fisheries and timber, the discovery of varieties of wheat more hardy and ripening earlier, were later to inaugurate another movement in a northerly direction, likely to be of equal significance in attracting settlers to Western Canada.

---

[1] *Canada and its Provinces*, xx, 302. [2] *Vide infra*, chapter xxv (ii).
[3] *Canada Year Book*, 1914, pp. 457–8. [4] *Ibid.* p. 164. [5] *Ibid.* 1921, p. 363.

CHAPTER XXIII

THE SETTLEMENT AND PROGRESS OF BRITISH COLUMBIA, 1871–1914

CONFEDERATION effected a complete change in the status of British Columbia and in the political power of its people. With the step from colony to province came responsible government. There were many who believed that the country was not ripe enough in settled population to justify the measure; but influential supporters of confederation had resolved that union and responsible government should synchronise.[1]

With confederation, too, came renewed faith. The burden of debt had been lifted. And yet the province was very much as Governor Frederick Seymour had described it—a wagon road, with a gold mine at one end and a seaport at the other. As Cariboo continued to wane, other sources of wealth—other forms of employment—were sought. Agriculture, spreading from the vicinity of the Cariboo Road to the valleys of the Thompson and the Fraser, drew to itself many of the miners, tired of following fickle fortune. The coal mines of Nanaimo were producing 30,000 or 40,000 tons annually and employing two or three hundred men. Salmon packing had commenced, and lumber was being exported to Australia, China, and South America.

The Lieutenant-Governor selected as Premier John Foster McCreight, a prominent lawyer. He was in no sense a politician and, moreover, had opposed the introduction of responsible government, so that the choice was a disappointment to its ardent supporters, who had hoped that the test of the system might have been inaugurated under one of its advocates. The Legislative Assembly, as constituted by the Act of 1871, consisted of twenty-five members: thirteen from the mainland and twelve from Vancouver Island.[2] This balancing of the two divisions, without regard to relative population, prevailed down to 1894. In 1871 the census of the province was 37,247: being, mainland 5627, island 5959, with 25,661 Indians, undistributed.[3] In the new order of things it was difficult to find a dividing line between Government and Opposition. However, as the island with twelve members had two salaried ministers, while the mainland with thirteen members had only one, a cleavage along the line of mainland against island resulted. It was, indeed, an old and easy line of fracture. To this nucleus other local and personal differences attached themselves.

---

[1] Tupper, Sir C., *Recollections of Sixty Years in Canada*, p. 127.
[2] *Acts passed by the Leg. Counc. of British Columbia*, 1871, no. 3, sec. 7.
[3] *Can. Census*, 1891, 1, Table 6, p. 366.

The McCreight Government lived through only one session; yet that afforded the opportunity to enact many laws necessitated by the new conditions. The legislation which touched the vital spot was the cancellation of the tolls on the Cariboo Road.[1] These had been imposed to repay the cost of construction; but, as with confederation the debt had vanished, the reason for their existence was gone. The greatest forward step McCreight made was to abolish tuition fees and local levies and to substitute free education, placing the whole cost of the public schools upon the public revenue, where it remained until 1891.[2] McCreight also planned to substitute vote by ballot for the old-fashioned open voting; but before he could carry his intention into effect, he was defeated, and his Government resigned.

About this time came the end of the San Juan boundary trouble with the United States which had dragged on since 1853. The Treaty of Washington, 1846, fixed the boundary between British and American possessions along the 49th parallel "to the middle of the channel which separates the continent from Vancouver's Island and thence southerly through the middle of the said channel and of Fuca Straits to the Pacific Ocean".[3] The interpretation of these words was difficult, for between the continent and Vancouver Island lay the Haro Archipelago, comprising San Juan and other islands with a total area of about one hundred and seventy square miles. On the northern side was Haro Strait, which the Americans asserted was the channel; on the southern side, Rosario Strait, claimed by the British as the channel. The question was which, if either, of these waterways was "the channel" of the treaty. To prevent trouble the two claimants ordered their representatives to refrain from any acts in the disputed area that might provoke conflict.[4] The Hudson's Bay Company had large herds of cattle on San Juan Island, where, also, many Americans had squatted. A dispute between the Company and one of the squatters regarding the value of a pig furnished, in July 1859, an excuse for a fire-eating officer, General Harney, to order the occupation of San Juan by American troops.[5] British men-of-war were immediately despatched to the scene; but they landed no men, being content with the display of immensely superior force.[6] General Winfield Scott, the head of the United States army, soon arrived. He reprimanded Harney for his precipitate action, withdrew all the troops except one company, and arranged for a joint occupation by them and a company of British marines.[7] Numerous attempts were made to settle the

[1] *Statutes of B.C.* 1872, no. 2.
[2] *Ibid.* no. 16; 1891, chap. 40.
[3] Milton, Viscount, *A History of the San Juan Water Boundary Question,* p. 42.
[4] *Affairs in Oregon. House of Repres.* 36th Congress, 1st Session. Ex. Doc. no. 65, pp. 6 f.
[5] *San Juan Water Boundary,* p. 258.
[6] *Affairs in Oregon.* Ex. Doc. no. 65, pp. 28 ff.; Egerton, Mrs Fred, *Sir Geoffrey P. Hornby,* pp. 64 ff.
[7] *Island of San Juan. House of Repres.* 39th Congress, 2nd Session. Ex. Doc. no. 24; *Message from the President of the U.S.* December 21, 1866, pp. 192 ff., 229 ff.

question, but it was not until 1871 that the two nations requested the German Emperor to decide, which of the two—Haro Strait or Rosario Strait—was "most in accordance with the true interpretation of the treaty". The question in this narrow form the Emperor, on 21 October 1872, decided in favour of the Haro Strait and the contention of the United States.[1]

Amor De Cosmos, a brilliant but eccentric man, who succeeded McCreight as Premier, was also a member of the Dominion Parliament. He endeavoured to avoid the mainland against island cry by appointing two salaried ministers from each section. This not only failed to stifle that cry but raised another—that of inconsistency, inasmuch as, while preaching retrenchment and economy, he had added the expense of a new minister. To the credit of the short-lived De Cosmos Government are: the introduction of vote by ballot and the abolition of dual representation.[2] The latter compelled De Cosmos to choose between the two fields. He chose the larger, and on 9 February 1874 resigned his seat in the Provincial Legislature.

George A. Walkem, who had been Chief Commissioner of Lands and Works in the McCreight Government and Attorney-General under De Cosmos, now became Premier. Much of his administration touches the railway difficulties with the Dominion Government. The franchise under which Confederation had been accepted had been limited to British subjects having certain property qualifications; but in 1874 the Walkem Government introduced manhood suffrage. At the same time Chinese were excluded from voting, a privilege which they had exercised, if otherwise eligible, from the earliest days of elections on the mainland.[3] The province was passing through a period of depression, accentuated by the failure to commence railway construction and by the steady decrease of gold mining. Cariboo continued to dwindle; and search where they might in Omineca or in Cassiar the miners could find no diggings with promise of large and long-continued production. The population of the towns was at a standstill. The vast areas of vacant land still remained vacant. Even for the produce of lands already occupied no sufficient market existed. To tide over the situation, to prevent a recurrence of the conditions of 1866–8, the Government in 1875 entered upon a programme of public works much in advance of the requirements.

The debt-free condition resulting from union lasted for six months. Then began an era of deficits. By the end of 1874 these amounted to more than $300,000; and in consequence the Walkem Government floated the first provincial loan.[4] The great expenditure of 1875 created a further deficit of $260,000. The Opposition declared that

[1] Cushing, C., *Treaty of Washington*, etc., pp. 204 f., 221 ff.; *Correspondence respecting the award of the German Emperor*, 1873, pp. 2 f.
[2] *Stats. of B.C.* 1873, no. 16, p. 81; *Can. Stats.* 1873, no. 2, p. 4.
[3] *Stats. of B.C.* 1871, no. 12; 1874, no. 12; 1875, no. 2.
[4] *Ibid.* 1874, no. 21.

this expenditure had been incurred with an eye to the approaching election. Perhaps the charge was justified, for the Walkem Government now repealed manhood suffrage and substituted a statute under which the qualifications varied in different sections of the province.

The elections occurred in 1875. The Government appeared to have been placed securely in power, but early in the session of 1876 it met defeat. One of the first measures of the new—the Elliott—Government was to re-enact manhood suffrage. This Government had a short and stormy life, for the acute form of railway trouble, known as "Carnarvon Terms or Separation", caused intense friction, as appears from the fact that, when Lord Dufferin, Governor-General of the Dominion, visited Victoria, he was expected to drive under an arch bearing the motto "Separation". Hearing of this, he tactfully requested the mayor to change "S" into "R", but, as this was not done, he drove round the arch.[1] But, further, the Government suffered from the looseness, or rather the absence, of ties between it and its supporters. Andrew C. Elliott had been so unwise as to admit into his Cabinet a minister with whom he soon found it impossible to work, and who, on being dismissed, not only joined the Opposition, but took his personal friends with him. Crippled by this defection, the Elliott Government hobbled along with a majority of two.[2] In this precarious situation Elliott was injudicious enough to introduce a bill enlarging the Legislature to thirty-three. A bitter fight began. For more than a month he tried, but failure met him at every turn. His incapacity as a leader was plain in this struggle. In the end he was forced to abandon his bill, and accept a compromise whereby, supply having been voted, a new election should be held.[3]

In that election Elliott was defeated and his opponent formed the second Walkem Government, which held office from 1878 till 1882. Much of this period was occupied with railway troubles: first, the failure to commence the construction of the Canadian Pacific Railway; and, secondly, the refusal to build what was called the "Island section" from Esquimalt to Nanaimo. Until 1882 Walkem had usually a majority of seven or eight in a House of twenty-five. The rock on which he came to grief was the Esquimalt graving dock. This had been estimated to cost £100,000, and grants equalling that amount had been promised by the Imperial and Dominion Governments. It soon became plain that the cost would exceed the estimate. More than $180,000 was spent by the local government for site and plant. The people of the mainland complained of this expenditure at a time when roads and trails were a crying necessity. It was another phase of "mainland v. island". Walkem, thinking that the promised

---

[1] Lyall, Sir A., *Life of Lord Dufferin*, chap. 7; Hamilton, Lord Frederic, *The Days before Yesterday*, 1920, p. 249.

[2] *Journals of Leg. Ass. of B.C.* 12 Mar. 1877; 12 Feb. 1878.

[3] Kerr, J. B., *Dict. of well-known British Columbians*, p. 89; *Journals*, 9 Apr. 1878.

grants would complete the undertaking, stated in reply to a direct question that the dock "would not cost the people one cent more". At that time the Government had agreed to supply the cement, which was supposed to be merely a matter of $3500. When it was known that this item would probably reach $150,000 the excitement became intense. A Parliamentary Committee reported against the Government.[1] The House divided twelve to twelve; the Government was saved only by the vote of the Speaker.

The census of 1881 showed: on the island a population of 17,292, on the mainland, 32,167, making a total of 49,459—an increase of about 13,000;[2] but the House still contained only twenty-five members. Though it had been agreed that the readjustment of seats should be considered in 1882, Walkem, perhaps remembering the experience of his predecessor, evinced no intention of so doing. There was need for adjustment: Kootenay, which in the election of 1878 had polled only 15 votes, had two members; Esquimalt with 160 voters had two members; New Westminster District with 800 voters had two members. A resolution condemning the inaction of the Government was rejected by the casting vote of the Speaker.[3] Elliott with a majority of two had been unable to control the House; Walkem did so on the Speaker's vote. He was bold and resourceful; he succeeded in winning over one of his opponents, and, after voting supply, steered the ship of state safely into prorogation. Soon after the close of the session he was appointed to the Supreme Court of the Province.

Robert Beaven, the Minister of Finance, then formed a government, and in June 1882 went to the country. When the polls had closed the Beaven Ministry was seen to be in full rout: only eight of its supporters were to be found amongst the twenty-five. Nevertheless Beaven and his one colleague retained office. The Opposition members presented to the Lieutenant-Governor a "round robin" to show that the Government had been defeated. He refused to act, for he regarded the party ties—if such they could be called that were but personal—as too loose to justify any serious action. The Opposition clamoured for the resignation of Beaven, or for his dismissal, or for the summoning of the House. Beaven would not resign; and the Lieutenant-Governor would not act. So affairs drifted along for months with Beaven and his one minister as a sort of skeleton government. Finally, in response to a memorial signed by three-fifths of the members-elect, the Lieutenant-Governor directed that the House be summoned for 25 January 1883.[4] Beaven, with a majority of eight against him on the floor, went through the solemn farce of laying down the policy of his so-called Government in the Speech from the Throne. But the House was in no humour to endure the mockery and

---

[1] *Sessional Papers of B.C.* 1882, p. 485; *Journals B.C.* pp. 65 ff. and pp. i ff.
[2] *Census of Canada*, 1891, I, Table 6, 366.
[3] *Journals B.C.* 1882, pp. 25 f.
[4] *The British Columbian*, New Westminster, 9 and 29 Dec. 1882.

at once condemned the ministers for violating the spirit of responsible government in failing to advise its prompt meeting.[1] So died the Beaven Ministry. As regards the finances of the province up to 1883, each year, except 1879 and 1881, saw a deficit, ranging from about $50,000 in 1880 to about $340,000 in 1876. The gross debt in 1882 was $800,566.[2]

The Government that came into power in 1883 existed under changing names—William Smythe, A. E. B. Davie, John Robson, Theodore Davie, and John H. Turner—and varying personnel until 1898. Smythe, the new Premier, determined to clear away the discord that had arisen over the Island Railway, and to relieve the province from the incubus of the graving dock. Negotiations with the Dominion Government secured the accomplishment of both these objects. The Island Railway, now called the Esquimalt and Nanaimo Railway, was to be built: the province granting in aid 1,900,000 acres and the Dominion contributing a bonus of $750,000. The graving dock was to be taken over by the Dominion, which gave to the province $250,000 and repaid the money already expended, $182,000. A large area, 3,500,000 acres, in the Peace River country was also granted to the Dominion in lieu of lands alienated within the railway belt. In 1883 and 1884 these arrangements were crystallised into Acts and declared to be a complete settlement of all claims between the two Governments.[3]

The province now entered upon a period of material development. On the mainland railway construction proceeded apace; on the island, too, the long-looked-for Island Railway approached completion. These works offered the market so fervently desired. The fertile valley of the Fraser and the rich farming and grazing lands of the interior were being occupied and cultivated; Saanich, Cowichan and other farming districts on Vancouver Island were receiving population. The country was at last filling up. Between 1881 and 1891 the number of inhabitants in Victoria, New Westminster and Nanaimo increased three-fold.[4] New lumber and grist mills, salmon canneries and manufactories were being established; railway construction brought a great increase of population, families coming where only individuals had come before. Settlement spread out from the railways as a base. The lengthening lines of rails gave to farmer, grazier, and manufacturer the means of access to new markets.

In this development the Indians shared. They entered slowly into the new economic life, taking their parts as farmers, fishermen, or unskilled labourers. Unfortunately they, too frequently, yielded to the vices of civilisation. Miners and settlers, especially on the Nass

[1] *Journals B.C.* 26 Jan. 1883.
[2] Cowan, G. H., *B.C.'s Claim for Better Terms*, pp. 16 f.
[3] *Sess. Pap. B.C.* pp. 453 ff.; *Stats. of B.C.* 1883, chap. 14; 1884, chap. 14.
[4] *Canada Year Book*, 1914, p. 50.

and Skeena Rivers, came into conflict with their tribal rights and ancient hunting and fishing privileges. These difficulties, however, were always adjusted by firm, yet sympathetic, treatment.[1]

At this time came the downfall of the Metlakatla mission. This station, established in 1857 by William Duncan, a layman, for the Church Missionary Society, had proved that the Tsimshian Indians, one of the fiercest of the coast tribes, could be trained in the arts of civilisation and brought under the influence of Christianity. The village of contented, civilised, and Christianised Indians, with its neat homes and well-built streets, its imposing church, its community organisation, cannery, saw-mill, and store, attracted the attention and won the admiration of everyone interested in the improvement of native races. For nearly twenty-five years it flourished, then a disagreement concerning church services and ritual led to turmoil, riot, and factional dissension which became so intense that a war-vessel was sent to the scene. In the end the community was rent in twain, and Duncan and his followers left the village to establish a new Metlakatla in Alaska.[2]

The membership of the Legislature had stood steadily at the original twenty-five; but in 1885 the Smythe Government added two members. In doing so the balance between island and mainland was preserved: each section received an additional representative.[3] In this period of expansion, the Government, with constantly recurring deficits, entered upon a policy of giving bonuses to transportation and development schemes.[4] Fortunately many of them fell by the wayside. Those that were carried through, e.g. the Eagle Pass Wagon Road and the Kootenay and Columbia Canal, benefited their promoters, but brought nothing of permanent value to the province. Under the terms of union the Canadian Pacific Railway ended at tide water on Burrard Inlet, but the Smythe Government granted 6000 acres for its extension to Coal Harbour. There in 1885 began the City of Vancouver, a city of marvellous growth, which in thirty years had reached a population of over 100,000. The completion of the railway in November 1886 was followed by the inauguration of the trans-Pacific trade, first to China and Japan, and later to Australia and New Zealand. The effect of rail connection with Eastern Canada is shown by the census of 1891. From 1871 to 1881 the increase was about 30 per cent., but in the next ten years, being the period of building and early operation of the railway, the population increased 100 per cent., and in each subsequent decennial census a similar growth has appeared.[5] The coal mines of Nanaimo reflected this

[1] Sess. Pap. B.C. 1887, pp. 251 ff.; 1884, pp. 277 ff.
[2] Metlakathlah Inquiry, 1884: Report of Commissioners, in Sess. Pap. B.C. 1885, pp. 131 ff., 277 ff.; Depositions, in Sess. Pap. B.C. 1885, pp. 317 ff.
[3] Stats. of B.C. 1885, chap. 3.
[4] Ibid. 1883, chaps. 25, 35; Sess. Pap. B.C. 1887, pp. 315 ff.
[5] Canada Year Book, 1913, p. 51.

growth: in 1874 they produced 81,000 tons; in 1879, 241,000; and in 1887, 413,360.

In 1890 the Robson Government increased the membership of the Legislature from twenty-seven to thirty-three; still retaining the vicious, but seemingly imperative, balance of power: seventeen on the mainland and sixteen on the island.[1] This action was the main point of attack in the elections of 1890; but in the changed conditions caused by the influx of population the cry was not: mainland against island. The newcomers had no interest in, or knowledge of, the facts that had fostered and fomented the sectional feeling. Criticism was directed to the varying unit of representation: for example, 7111 voters on the island elected sixteen members; while 6566 on the mainland elected only six members. The demand was for "Fair Representation"; but Robson, able, astute, and far-seeing, disarmed his opponents by admitting that the bill was only a temporary measure, intended to give a modicum of relief pending the decennial census of 1891. Robson had usually a majority of eight or ten, but after the elections of 1890 this was increased to about seventeen in a House of thirty-three.

Meanwhile the sealing industry had developed apace. In 1866 the Indians informed a trader of the facility with which fur-seals could be obtained thirty or forty miles off the coast of Vancouver Island. This was the germ of pelagic sealing. Year by year the number of schooners engaged in it increased. Year by year the Victoria schooners followed the seals northward farther and farther, until about 1883 they entered Bering Sea.[2] The herd was making for the rookeries on the Pribylov Islands, which were under lease to the Alaska Commercial Company. In 1886, without warning, United States revenue cutters seized British sealing schooners in Bering Sea, though seventy miles from the nearest land. The Americans claimed that sea as territorial water of Alaska. Until 1899 these seizures continued, though occasionally they were varied by an order to leave. In all fifteen British vessels were seized and confiscated and five others were ordered out of Bering Sea.[3] This high-handed conduct became the subject of many protests and much correspondence between Great Britain and the United States. Ultimately a tribunal of arbitration was established and sat in Paris in 1893 to decide what exclusive rights Russia had had in Bering Sea; how far they had been recognised by Great Britain; to what extent they had been transmitted to the United States; and what, if any, rights of protection or property the United States had in the seal herd beyond the three mile limit. If their findings were adverse to the United States the arbitrators were authorised to frame regulations for the government of pelagic sealing.[4] The arbitrators decided that Russia, and consequently the United

---

[1] *Stats. of B.C.* 1890, chap. 7.
[2] *Fur Seal Arbitration: Proceedings of the Tribunal of Arbitration at Paris*, 1893, II, 187 f.
[3] *Ibid.* I (Award and Declarations), 83; IV (Schedule of Claims), 133 ff.
[4] *Ibid.* I, 9 ff. (note).

States as her successor in title, had no jurisdiction beyond the three mile limit; that Bering Sea was a part of the Pacific Ocean; that the United States had no rights of protection or property in the seal herd after it had passed out of territorial waters—that is, beyond the three mile limit. Under the authority to enact regulations the Board prohibited sealing within a zone of sixty miles around the Pribylov Islands and also forbade, between 1 May and 31 July in each year, any sealing east of 180° longitude and north of 35° latitude. The remainder of the regulations dealt with the weapons and vessels to be used and the records to be kept.[1] The persons interested in the twenty schooners, that had been seized or interfered with, pressed their claims for damages which in 1896 were judicially investigated and fixed at $463,454.[2] The regulations did not affect the Asiatic side of Bering Sea and the Pacific Ocean, and sealers resorted thereto under an agreement made in 1893 between Great Britain and Russia, whereby British vessels were permitted to take seals in those waters except within a zone of thirty miles around the Russian seal islands.[3] This was the state of affairs down to June 1911 when, by agreement between Great Britain, the United States, Russia and Japan, all pelagic sealing ceased north of the 35th parallel. The United States, Russia, and Japan, all of whom had territory on which were seal rookeries, granted to Great Britain a certain percentage of the returns therefrom. Then the sealing fleet, which for forty years had been the pride of Victoria and had brought wealth to many of her citizens, was dispersed in every direction and into all classes of service. The owners, however, still share under the agreement which expired in 1926.[4]

In 1893 magnificent Parliament Buildings were constructed at Victoria. In 1894 the old idea of the balance of power between island and mainland tottered to its fall. The redistribution of the seats in that year left the number at thirty-three, but the traditional policy of allowing one member more to the mainland than to the island disappeared. Instead there were nineteen members on the mainland to fourteen on the island.[5] In 1895 Davie, the Premier, became Chief Justice, and again the Government was reorganised as the Turner Government. From 1883 when its predecessor, the Smythe Government, came into power, down through the A. E. B. Davie, Robson, Theodore Davie, and Turner Governments there was in each year a deficit varying from $28,912 in 1891 to $561,408 in 1898, and to the enormous sum of $1,010,899 in 1894. In those fifteen years the accumulated annual deficits reached $4,734,782. To provide for

---

[1] Fur Seal Arbitration: Proceedings of the Tribunal of Arbitration at Paris, 1893, 1 (Award and Declarations), 78 ff.
[2] Howay and Scholefield, History of B.C. II, 465.
[3] Foster, J. W., Diplomatic Memoirs, II, 47.
[4] Howay and Scholefield, II, 465 f.
[5] Stats. of B.C. 1894, chap. 26.

capital expenditures and these deficits the Governments were forced into continual borrowings. In 1884 the gross debt of the province was $770,812; by 1898 it had grown to $7,425,262.[1]

The demand now became insistent that the country must live within its income and that these repeated borrowings must cease. This feeling of dissatisfaction was evident when in preparation for an appeal to the people the Turner Government introduced a redistribution measure whereby the number of legislators was increased to thirty-eight.[2] In the votes on this bill its majority fell to seven; and then to five. It was plain that despite every effort the Turner Government was losing ground. In July 1898 the elections were held. The result was doubtful, but it appeared that the Government had been defeated, having only fifteen supporters in a House of thirty-eight. Twenty-nine election petitions were launched increasing the uncertainty. In August 1898, before any of these had been heard, and before a deferred election had been held, the Lieutenant-Governor (Thomas R. McInnes) dismissed Turner and, after some vacillation, called upon Charles A. Semlin.[3]

Internal difficulties in the Semlin Government led, in 1899, to the resignation of the Attorney-General, Joseph Martin, the "stormy petrel" of Canadian politics, who, following the custom of those days, joined the Opposition. During the session of 1900 the Semlin Government, though weakened by his defection, battered by his attacks, and crippled by the capricious support of one of its adherents, staggered along, sometimes with a majority of one and sometimes on the casting vote of the Speaker, until on 14 February 1900 it was defeated by a vote of 19 to 18. The Lieutenant-Governor then informed Semlin that he must within a fortnight either resign or ask for a new election. Semlin did neither; he arranged for support, and reported that he could control the House. The Lieutenant-Governor, notwithstanding, dismissed him and called upon Martin to form a ministry.[4] The Legislature at once resolved that it had no confidence in Martin.[5] Shortly afterwards, when His Honour arrived to prorogue the House, every member, with one exception, rose and left the chamber, and the brief Speech from the Throne was read to empty benches. The scene was unparalleled in a British Legislature, but it was deemed necessary to mark the intense disapprobation of the course taken by the Lieutenant-Governor. As he left the hall the members filed in again, singing "God save the Queen!" and an uproarious scene followed: resolutions condemnatory of his conduct were mingled with patriotic songs and general disorder.[6]

All this boded ill for Martin. However he went bravely to work and

---

[1] B.C.'s Claim for Better Terms, pp. 16 f.   [2] Stats. of B.C. 1898, chap. 38.
[3] Gosnell, R. E., Sixty Years of Progress: British Columbia, Part 2, p. 144.
[4] Ibid. p. 146; Journals B.C. 14, 22, 23, 27 Feb. 1900.
[5] Ibid. 1900, p. 79.
[6] Gosnell, R. E., History of British Columbia, p. 144.

formed a ministry, if such it can be called, composed of men quite unknown in the public life of the province. More than three months elapsed between the dissolution and the election. That interval Martin used in an aggressive campaign. Loud were the complaints that a body of men, five-sixths of whom had never been members of the Legislature, should for three months govern the country without the authority of the people. Such a condition, it was said, had no parallel in the history of responsible government.[1] The elections were decisive; out of thirty-eight members only thirteen were supporters of Martin. His opponents pressed for the dismissal of the Lieutenant-Governor, who, it was urged, had acted unconstitutionally in dismissing a minister with a working majority and calling upon a man who had no following—who led no party. Upon his refusal to resign Lieutenant-Governor McInnes was dismissed.[2]

James Dunsmuir, a wealthy coal mine operator, without political training, experience, or aptitude, formed a ministry, that in reality was a coalition, in which the only bond of union was opposition to Martin. For a year all went well; in some of its legislation the Government even had Martin's support. Dunsmuir, in September 1901, took into the Cabinet one of the Martin party. This move, so subversive of the *raison d'être* of his ministry, led to disruption; and he was only saved from defeat by the support of four members of the Martin wing.[3] In that year the Dunsmuir Government, in fulfilment of its promise to introduce a fair measure of representation, increased the membership of the Legislature to forty-two, of whom twelve were from island constituencies.[4] And so it remained until 1915 when the number became forty-seven.[5]

Dunsmuir resigned the leadership in November 1902. His successor, Colonel E. G. Prior, faced a difficult task; the original majority of seven had dwindled to two or three; there was little coherence amongst his supporters. By-elections reduced this small margin of safety. Clouds darkened deeply in 1903 upon the Prior Government. A committee was ordered to investigate the circumstances connected with the grants of coal and oil lands to a railway company and their subsequent cancellations.[6] While the enquiry was proceeding, Prior requested and obtained the resignations of two ministers who had been closely connected with these strange transactions. As usual they joined the Opposition. The Government no longer controlled the House and existed only by the indulgence of its opponents. Then came the final blow. The Premier had a controlling interest in a certain company. The charge was made that he had awarded to it a contract

---

[1] Letter of Hon. R. W. Scott, to Lieut.-Gov. McInnes, 2 June 1900, in *The Daily World*, Vancouver, 5 July 1900, and in *The Daily British Columbian*, New Westminster, 6 July 1900.
[2] Gosnell, *Sixty Years* (Part 2), pp. 147 f.
[3] *Ibid.* (Part 2), p. 150; *Journals B.C.* 1902, pp. 56, 57, 64, 67.
[4] *Stats. of B.C.* 1902, chaps. 42 and 58.
[5] *Ibid.* 1915, chap. 14.   [6] *Journals B.C.* p. 61 and Appendix.

under circumstances arousing a suspicion that the figures of other tenderers had been known to the company before the submission of its tender. A parliamentary enquiry was ordered; the evidence obtained was placed before the Lieutenant-Governor; and on 1 June 1903 he dismissed Prior.[1]

Richard McBride, an energetic young man of thirty-three, the leader of the Conservatives, now formed a ministry. He resolved to introduce Dominion party lines into local politics.[2] In the thirty-two years since confederation, the non-party system had been fully tried. There being no bond of affiliation the support was personal, and, in consequence, on a breach of relations the dismissed minister or disgruntled supporter went over to the enemy, taking with him his personal following. The strongest argument was the practical failure of the non-party system during the past five years: in that time there had been five governments—Turner, Semlin, Martin, Dunsmuir and Prior. The history of the decline and fall of the Semlin, Dunsmuir and Prior Governments had been markedly similar.

Those five years had been black financially. Like the preceding fifteen they had been marked by constant deficits, varying from $287,077 in 1900 to $1,348,552 in 1903. The gross debt in 1898 had been $7,425,262; in 1903 it was $12,542,086: an increase of over five million dollars in five years.[3] In the decade from 1891 to 1901 the population had increased from 98,173 to 178,657.[4] From 1872 down to 1903, with the exception of 1879 and 1881, the financial story had been one of continual deficits, regardless of population, social conditions, or the government in power. In that interval the province had piled up a gross debt of twelve and a half million dollars. Even the surpluses for the two excepted years vanish when examined: the figures for 1879 only cover six months, and the deficit of the ensuing year swallowed up the supposed surplus; as to 1881, while that was a real surplus, it was obtained by the simple expedient of starving the public works.[5] This continual failure to keep expenditure within income, regardless of the pilot, gave rise to a feeling, which soon crystallised into a conviction, that the revenue had been and always would be insufficient to meet the expenditure; that the effort to govern with such limited income had, while causing extremely high direct taxation, exhausted the credit of the province, and yet had failed to balance the budget; and, in short, that it was impossible for British Columbia to carry on her ordinary expenditure under the existing terms of union.[6] Hence the demand for "Better Terms". Dunsmuir and Prior had both brought the situation before the

[1] Journals B.C. 1903, pp. 62 ff.   [2] Ibid. 1903, p. 66, 2 June 1903.
[3] Howay and Scholefield, II, 526 f.
[4] Canadian Year Book, 1913, p. 51.
[5] Howay and Scholefield, II, 538 f.
[6] Procter, F. J., The Financial Crisis in British Columbia, pp. 8 f.; B.C.'s Claim for Better Terms, p. 18; Report of the Delegates to Ottawa, 1903, in Sess. Pap. B.C. 1903, pp. K 3 ff.

Dominion Government and had argued that the failure of twelve finance ministers steadily through thirty years of varying conditions to produce a real surplus must be due to permanent causes. These, they suggested, were: (1) The cost of administration, owing to the physical character of the country. (2) The distance from the commercial, industrial, and administrative centres of Eastern Canada. (3) The non-industrial character of the province, as compared with Eastern Canada, whereby a larger percentage of goods was imported and consumed, increasing the contributions to the Federal treasury in the way of taxes in a ratio of three to one. (4) The disadvantage of the province in relation to markets for its special products.

The contention was that the financial arrangements in the terms of union were in reality a leap in the dark on both sides; that there was no unalterable quality in the terms; and that a state of affairs, not anticipated by either the Dominion or the province, had arisen as a result, which established a moral right to, and a sound constitutional claim for, an increased grant.[1] The subject of "Better Terms" was discussed year after year in the Legislature, and again and again with the Dominion Government, but no result was obtained. In 1906 a conference of Dominion and provincial representatives was held at Ottawa. McBride, armed with a unanimous resolution of the Legislature in favour of "Better Terms", attended and pressed the claim for special treatment. He asked for an impartial judicial tribunal to examine the question and report its findings. The other provinces refused to recommend that course and, after protest, McBride retired from the meeting. The remaining representatives then resolved that, owing to its large area, geographical position, and very exceptional physical features, British Columbia was entitled to special treatment, which they fixed at $100,000 a year for ten years.[2] The conference also recommended certain increases in the subsidies applicable to all the provinces. The Dominion Government embodied the findings in an amendment to the British North America Act, which, as drafted, provided that these payments should be, as the conference requested, "a final and unalterable settlement" of the claims of the various provinces. British Columbia protested against the insertion of those words and sent McBride as a special delegate to London to support the protest. As a result the obnoxious words, which in any event had no binding force, were omitted from the statute.[3] No further steps have been taken to press the claim for "Better Terms".

We turn to the burning question of the coastline. In 1824 there still remained three out of the original four claimants to the northwest coast of America. The portion belonging to Russia was de-

---

[1] Report of Delegates in *Sess. Pap. B.C.* 1903, p. K 6; *ibid.* 1907, pp. 28 ff.
[2] *Ibid.* 1907, p. D 12.
[3] 6 Ed. VII, cap. 11.

limited by the treaty of 1825. The line of boundary was to commence at the southernmost point of Prince of Wales Island and

ascend to the north along the channel called Portland Channel as far as the point of the continent where it strikes the 56th degree of north latitude; from this last mentioned point the line of demarcation shall follow the summit of the mountains situated parallel to the coast, as far as the point of intersection of the 141st degree of west longitude;

and thence along that meridian to the Frozen Ocean. The treaty, after providing that Prince of Wales Island should belong entirely to Russia, went on to state:

That whenever the summit of the mountains which extend in a direction parallel to the coast, from the 56th degree of north latitude to the 141st degree of west longitude, shall prove to be at a distance of more than ten marine leagues from the ocean, the limit between the British possessions and the line of coast which is to belong to Russia as above mentioned shall be formed by a line parallel to the windings of the coast and which shall never exceed the distance of ten marine leagues therefrom.[1]

In 1867 the United States purchased Alaska from Russia. The discoveries of gold in Omineca and Cassiar caused British Columbia to urge repeatedly the necessity of ascertaining the meaning of the language of the agreements and the exact position of the boundary line on the land.[2] But nothing was done. For twenty-five years the question drifted on, with occasional discussions; then it sprang into great and practical importance with the discovery of the Yukon gold-fields. Something had to be done, for there were thousands of adventurers "mucking" over the Chilcat and Chilcoot passes towards the latest river of gold. In 1898-9 a Joint High Commission considered a number of matters in dispute between Canada and the United States. No agreement was reached, though the contentions on each side were clarified, but a conventional boundary was fixed on the Dyea and Skagway trails at the summits of Chilcoot and White passes.

At last, after more than thirty years, a tribunal was created in 1903 to interpret the treaty and fix the course of the line. It was to consist of "six impartial jurists of repute who shall consider judicially the questions submitted to them".[3] Those questions were somewhat complex; but the important point in the controversy was whether the boundary should be drawn ten marine leagues from the heads of the inlets, so as to shut British territory off completely from the ocean, or parallel to and ten marine leagues from the general trend of the coast. Next in interest was the question whether the water boundary ran north or south of four uninhabited islands near the mouth of Portland Canal. The tribunal met in London in

---

[1] *Proceedings of the Alaskan Boundary Tribunal*, II, 12 ff.
[2] *Journals B.C.* 12 Mar. 1872, p. 36; 7 Jan. 1874.
[3] *Corresp. respecting the Alaska Boundary*, 1904, pp. 41 ff., 45 ff.; cf. article in *Can. Hist. Rev.* VI, 332 ff.

September 1903 and in the following month made a majority award deciding that the boundary line should be drawn so as to give two out of the four islands to each claimant, and that the line extended around the heads of the inlets, shutting out British possessions from the ocean.[1] In England the award was calmly received as a settlement of a disturbing question; but in Canada the belief that the American "impartial jurists" had been selected because of their fixed views created a feeling of intense dissatisfaction. The boundary, so obtained, greatly limits the possible development of the extreme northern portion of British Columbia.

Returning to internal politics we note that, when McBride took office in July 1903, the gross debt was more than $12,500,000 and there were besides floating liabilities of about $1,500,000. A loan of one million dollars to meet the pressing claims could only be had at 5 per cent. and upon the agreement to repay it in ten annual instalments. The condition was so bad that the banks refused further credit. The new Government faced the problem firmly. The people, too, saw that sacrifices must be made to regain financial safety. There was a feeling that stable government had come at last.

Yet, despite the financial position of the Government, the province was advancing in wealth and population and was developing her natural resources. The lode mines of the Kootenays had been steadily increasing in importance and widening in extent, embracing the gold mines of Red Mountain (Rossland), the silver of Toad Mountain (Nelson), the silver-lead of Slocan and East Kootenay, and the copper of the boundary country. With the advent of railways the trade and transportation which had flowed to and through the neighbouring states were, in great part, secured to the province. The vast coal measures of the Crow's Nest were opened; and, a supply of coke therefrom being assured, smelters were erected at numerous places in the Kootenays. Towns, dependent upon the mines and the smelters, sprang up in every direction, throve with those industries, and languished as they waned. Agriculture and fruit-growing spread to the Kootenays and thence into the Okanagan, which had theretofore been, principally, a grazing country. The building of the Grand Trunk Pacific opened up the great northern part of the province and, besides giving rise to numerous small towns, brought into being the City of Prince Rupert at its western terminus. The fisheries of the coast expanded to include the herring and the halibut; whaling stations were established. Lumbering spread along the lines of the railways. The vast supplies of paper-making woods led to the establishment of pulp and paper plants at a number of places along the coast; and around them sprang up neat towns supported entirely by

---

[1] *Proc. Alaskan Boundary Tribunal,* 1 (Award), 29 ff.; Foster, J. W., *Diplomatic Memoirs,* II, 197 ff.

that industry. The population of the agricultural districts increased steadily. Coal mining on Vancouver Island continued to extend the area of its operations. All of these forces reacted upon trade and trade centres, stimulating new manufactories and forms of industry.[1] The population in 1901 was 178,657; and in 1911, 392,480.[2]

The McBride Government, in an effort to balance the budget, practically doubled taxation and at the same time reduced expenditure. In 1903 the deficit had been $1,348,552; in 1904 it was $224,534. Then came an era unprecedented in the history of the province: an era of surpluses, commencing in 1905 with one of $618,044 and reaching in 1910 the enormous sum of $2,417,748. In seven years, 1905 to 1911, a surplus of $10,925,346 was accumulated. In 1910 the net debt stood at $8,969,778. Thus in seven years a surplus exceeding the net debt had been secured.[3] Then unfortunately the old era of deficits returned. Beginning in 1912 with about $400,000, it grew in 1913 to $2,976,295; but in 1914 the deficit was $5,283,653; and so it went on through 1915, 1916 and 1917. In the result the surplus accumulated between 1905 and 1911 was engulfed by the deficits from 1912 to 1918 and the days of borrowing returned.[4]

With the first influx of miners came the Chinese. During the prosperous days of Cariboo their numbers increased unnoticed. Content with a small but sure return they usually worked ground that was thought too poor to attract the white miner. In 1864 they numbered about 2000.[5] With the decrease of mining they plodded along, gleaning, or became traders, packers, farmers, gardeners, or domestic servants. In 1875 it was estimated that there were 949 Chinese in Cariboo as against 1800 whites. Their simple needs and low cost of living gave them a great advantage in competition. The agitation against them began in 1864[6] and continued unsuccessfully for more than twenty years, rising with dull times and falling with prosperous ones. Between 1872 and 1885 anti-Chinese legislation was frequently debated. The resolutions or bills usually authorised a special tax on Chinese or prohibited their employment on public works. They invariably failed to become law, or were disallowed, or declared unconstitutional.[7] Between 1876 and 1880 the increase in the Chinese population was 2326;[8] in 1879 the Legislature stated that there were 6000 Chinese in the province; the contractors for the Canadian Pacific Railway brought in about 6500.[9] The Chinese were

[1] Gosnell, Sixty Years, p. 161.　　　　[2] Canada Year Book, 1913, p. 51.
[3] Year Book of B.C. 1911, 1914, pp. 278 ff., 391 f.
[4] Canada Year Book, 1925, p. 792.
[5] Macfie, M., Vancouver Island and B.C.: their History, Resources, and Prospects, p. 386.
[6] Report of Royal Comm. on Chinese Immigration, 1885, p. 109.
[7] Journals B.C. 1872, pp. 15 f.; 1874, p. 18; 1876, p. 48; 1878, p. 82; Stats. of B.C. 1878, chap. 35; Journals B.C. pp. 20, 47, 55 and p. xxiv; Chinese Immigration Report, Appendix G.
[8] Chinese Immigration Report, p. 5.
[9] The British Columbian, 22 Apr. 1882; 10 May 1882.

alleged to be subject to loathsome diseases and demoralising habits; were charged with evasion of civic responsibility and of tax contributions; in short, were said to be an unassimilable people whose presence retarded the settlement and prosperity of the land.[1] In 1884 the Legislature passed three Acts against the Chinese: to prevent their immigration; to impose an annual poll tax of $10; and to forbid their acquisition of Crown lands.[2] The first was disallowed as an interference with Dominion rights of legislation over immigration; and the second was declared unconstitutional by the courts.[3] As a result the Dominion Government appointed a Commission to enquire into Chinese immigration. The report exonerated them from the charges of bad morals, public burdens, and criminal tendencies. It opposed exclusion and recommended moderate restriction.[4] In pursuance of the recommendation the Dominion Parliament in 1885 imposed a tax of $50 on every Chinaman entering Canada.[5] The province then legislated against their employment on public works and in coal mines. Much of this legislation was declared unconstitutional as being aimed at a particular race. They continued to arrive in large numbers. In 1891, 1893, 1894, 1895, 1897, and 1899 the province urged the increase of the tax.[6] The constant demand bore fruit; in 1900 the tax was raised to $100. This was only a temporary measure. A Commission investigated the whole subject, and upon its recommendation the Dominion Parliament increased the tax to $500.[7] At that amount it stood until 1923 when the immigration of Chinese (unless merchants, students, government representatives or persons born in Canada) was forbidden.[8]

The Japanese, though perhaps more dangerous competitors than the Chinese, passed unnoticed until about 1900 when the Legislature enacted that all immigrants must be able to read in some European language. Aimed at the Japanese, this plain trespass upon the field of Dominion legislation was promptly disallowed. It was re-enacted in 1902, 1904, 1905, 1907 and 1908, but in every case either failed to secure the assent of the Crown or was disallowed.[9] The Dominion Government had an understanding with the Emperor of Japan that he would forbid the emigration of his subjects to Canada; but the Japanese evaded the prohibition by obtaining passports to Hawaii and continuing their journey to British Columbia. Anger at this subterfuge underlay the Asiatic riots that occurred in September 1907 in Vancouver. In 1908 the Japanese Government agreed to limit the

---

[1] *Journals B.C.* 1879, pp. 20, 47, 55 and p. xxiv.
[2] *Stats. of B.C.* 1884, chap. 3, chap. 4 and chap. 2.
[3] *Dominion and Provincial Legislation*, 1867–1895, 1896, pp. 1092 ff.
[4] *Chinese Immigration Report*, pp. lxxxii, lxxxvii, cxxx ff.
[5] *Stats. of Can.* 1885, chap. 71.
[6] *Journals B.C.* 1891, pp. 50 f., 53, 56; 1893, pp. 77, 91; 1894, p. 10; 1895, p. 55; 1897, pp. 12, 14; 1899, pp. 10, 99.
[7] *Stats. of Can.* 1900, chap. 32; 1903, chap. 8.   [8] *Ibid.* 1923, chap. 38.
[9] *Journals B.C.* 1902, p. 79; *Sess. Pap. B.C.* 1902, p. 1314; 1903, p. J 1; 1909, p. G 36.

number of passports to Canada and the Canadian Government undertook to admit the holders of such documents, while refusing entry to
all others. As a result Japanese immigration fell from 7601 in 1908 to
495 in 1909; and with one or two exceptions the annual entries remain
about that figure.[1] Of all the problems of the province there is none
whose solution calls for more courage, sacrifice, saneness, and breadth
of view than this question of oriental immigration. Despite tax
barriers and agreements there were in 1926 probably 40,000 Chinese
and 18,000 Japanese in the province.[2] Their invasion of provincial
industries continues. The remedy lies in the Dominion's power over
immigration. The province is alive to the danger, but powerless; the
Dominion powerful, but unable to appreciate fully the inroads that
Chinese, Japanese and East Indians are making upon the industrial
life of British Columbia.

The aboriginal population at confederation was supposed to be
25,661; forty years later the census gave 24,581.[3] The Indians are the
wards of the Dominion Government who by the terms of union undertook to follow as liberal a policy towards them as had been pursued
by the colony of British Columbia.[4] The province agreed to set apart
the necessary lands for their reserves; in 1876 a Commission fixed the
areas. Chiefs and councillors are elected by the bands and have
power to enact bye-laws in trivial matters. Metlakatla showed that
the Indian could be civilised and Christianised. Industrial, boarding,
and ordinary day schools have, following that example, been established amongst them, sometimes by the Dominion Government
and sometimes by religious denominations. And thus slowly the
Indian is advancing along the path toward civilisation. In 1914
there were more than 8000 who could speak English or French. The
income from their agriculture, fishing, hunting, and other industries
reached in that year the sum of almost $2,000,000.[5] In recent years
the Indian Title Question has appeared. The claim is that their pos-
sessory rights have never been extinguished, except as regards the
southern part of Vancouver Island. The fact is not denied. Yet the
provincial Government has consistently refused to recognise such
title, claiming that the setting apart of ample reserves and their
occupation by the Indians is a virtual equivalent or extinction of any
title they may have possessed.[6] The question is one of the unsettled
problems of the province.

---

[1] *Canada Year Book*, 1925, pp. 181 ff.
[2] Nelson, J., *The Canadian Provinces: their Problems and Policies*, p. 188.
[3] *Canada Year Book*, 1913, p. 604.
[4] Clause 13, Terms of Union, in Howay and Scholefield, *History of B.C.* II, 697.
[5] *Canada Year Book*, 1914, pp. 640 f.   [6] *Year Book of B.C.* 1911, pp. 164 f.

CHAPTER XXIV

THE PIONEERING SPIRIT

THE age of the pioneer in Canada is almost gone. Much land still remains to be possessed: men will push into solitudes in the North and among the mountains; the French habitant will make inroads into the forest, the prospector will thread the wilderness; but the country East and West has now been occupied so strategically that adventure into the unknown is no longer the usual lot of the settler. Retreating figures from that era are still to be met in the West; men and women, for example, who remember how Sir George Simpson used to come up the Red River in state; or Sheriff Inkster, still on active duty in Winnipeg, who tells how in 1865 it took him a fortnight to drive Dr Machray, the new bishop, from St Cloud in Minnesota to his "palace" at St John's on the Red River. But the change from the "Great Lone Land" of 1870 to the Prairie Provinces of 1929 is one of the most rapid transitions in recent history.

Every part of Canada has exacted a heavy toll of suffering from the pioneer, and only stout and enduring hearts could have come through. On the banks of the St Lawrence in the early seventeenth century, and in English-speaking Canada from the coming of the Loyalists in 1784 until the middle of the nineteenth century, there was many a tragic tale, though few equalled in disappointment that of the 10,000 Loyalists from New York who eked out an existence for a few years on the barrens of Shelburne harbour in Nova Scotia.[1] The story of the immigrant is familiar; the long drawn out passage in old wooden ships over the stormy and cold Atlantic, the slow ascent of the river to Lake Ontario, the hardships of winter, the ravages of disease. Some of the trials Mrs Susanna Moodie has told in her *Roughing it in the Bush*, and Mrs Anna Jameson gives a glimpse of a better side in Toronto and the Talbot Settlement in her *Winter Studies and Summer Rambles*. About the same time the Rev. Featherston Osler and his gifted wife began their missionary career north of Toronto in a settlement of poor, ignorant and indifferent people, and, labouring among them at first in almost incredible hardships, did much to civilise that region. No vestiges of the frontier, however, were visible in their brilliant family.

Recently the letters of John Langton, a graduate of Cambridge and later Auditor-General of Canada, who in the 'thirties made a home for himself near Peterborough (U.C.), have been published. He had the pluck and the endurance of the pioneer. He speaks of the failure of "the lazy gentry" who enter the country about June and buy a

[1] *Dalhousie Review*, II, 179 ff., 313 ff.

cleared farm with a shanty, and soon nothing more is heard of them: "Canada is decidedly not the country we any of us thought it was... but I still think and hope that a livelihood may be made here". He writes again, "You all seem to run upon the subject of danger, as if we were exposed to any here: the fact is, with ordinary precaution, there is nothing in the life of a backwoodsman which is worthy of the name. Fatigue and inconvenience there is in abundance, but danger none, and as far as I have seen of the former, there is nothing which novelty at present does not make rather pleasant than otherwise, and to which custom hereafter will (not) reconcile us".[1] Here was the *joie de vivre* of the true young pioneer. Later he writes, "I know of no money-making business in Canada except the Law, Store Keeping, Tavern Keeping and perhaps I may add horse dealing"; but he himself found some profit in lumbering.

There were not a few families in Nova Scotia and in Old Canada who had traditions of refinement. Simcoe even hoped to establish an aristocracy, and the educated circles clung tenaciously to the privilege of governing. In fact the first educational effort in these provinces aimed at establishing the old order in them. Bishop Charles Inglis and Dr John Strachan both sought to provide schools and colleges first for the select classes. This was natural. The Loyalists left the revolted colonies because they hated republicanism and wished to preserve British institutions. Therefore their leaders took steps as soon as possible to have their sons educated in the ways that prevailed in England. The perpetuation of their society was a *raison d'être* of their being where they were. But this social order could not in the circumstances of the case be perpetuated in the wilderness. Change was irresistible and it found spokesmen political, educational and denominational. These were the pioneers in things of the spirit, but, though there were many, only two may be mentioned here, Dr Thomas McCulloch (1777–1843), the leader of the Scottish Presbyterians in Nova Scotia, who founded the famous Pictou Academy, and Dr Egerton Ryerson (1803–82), the Superintendent of Education of Upper Canada for nearly thirty years, during which he gave its form to the popular educational system.

The future lay with the average pioneer, whether Loyalist or later arrival. Even the "honest and industrious peasant...having to act and think for himself, and being better acquainted with the world... soon becomes a theoretical as well as a practical man, and consequently a cleverer and more enlightened person".[2] As a matter of course he had to concern himself primarily with making a living, but soon leaders appeared who gave him education. Contemporaneously a multitude of churches sprang up which divided an otherwise homogeneous society into cliques. The bitter controversies of older lands

---

Langton, J., *Early Days in Canada*, pp. 75 f.
[2] Strickland, S., *Twenty-seven Years in Canada West*, I, 266.

were quite as bitter when transferred to the frontiers. Englishmen were Anglicans, Wesleyans or Baptists; Scotsmen were Presbyterians of three slightly differing types; Americans might be anything but Anglicans, or nothing. And politics often followed church lines. It was the common school that saved the situation and laid the foundation of a new people; and from these schools in the clearings came those who took the place in the towns of the families who at first had directed the affairs of the provinces.

Most of the settlements have had a happy history, in many indeed the quality of the people and their comfort were high, and in them was to be found the stock which has given a good character to Canada. Recently an accurate and discriminating account of two such townships, Darlington and Clarke, in Ontario was written by Professor John Squair, and his descriptions are typical of many portions of the province. He writes:

It was a heterogeneous, but British, population, with some bilingual Scottish Gaels. But it was homogeneous in one important sense; it had behind it a past of humble origins. Men and women, who had worked hard for generations and for small pay, were our ancestors. Our traditions were in favour of industry and thrift. Idling was not a good basis for reputation. Men and women were all industrious, but it was unusual to see women working in the fields. However, their indoor industry was prodigious. They were never idle. Their cooking, baking, cleaning, washing, mending, knitting and making of clothing were unending. They did the tailoring, the dressmaking and, in the earliest times, the spinning and weaving for their families. Models of piety and correct conduct, their presence in rough places like bar-rooms was unheard of.[1]

The backwoodsman or the farmer on the clearing found his relaxation in coming into the village settlement, any one of which was like any other. For example, in W. H. Smith's *Canada Past, Present and Future* (1851):

Newcastle, which contains about 500 inhabitants, is situated in the west end of the township, about a mile and a half from the lake. It contains a grist mill, with four run of stones, a planing machine, worked by a steam engine, a carding and fulling mill, three tanneries, an axe factory, a foundry and a nursery. There are also six churches, Episcopal, United Presbyterian, Wesleyan Methodist, Primitive Methodist, Episcopal Methodist, and Congregational.

There was no grammar school until 1859. In this village Daniel Massey had built a little machine shop and foundry in 1847, and in 1851 his son Hart A. Massey (from the proceeds of whose benevolent foundation Hart House in the University of Toronto was erected) joined his father, and together they prospered, the Massey Manufacturing Company having been incorporated in 1870 and moved in 1879 to Toronto, where to-day it is the Massey-Harris Implement Company doing business in several continents. These pioneering conditions had all but gone from old Ontario by the time that the federa-

---

[1] Squair, J., *The Townships of Darlington and Clarke* (1927), pp. 440 f.

tion of the provinces took place in 1867. Hereafter the higher task of the East was to enrich and widen the area of civilisation.

Many of the greatest pioneers displayed their vision and energy in the field of transportation. The necessities of their situation made them devise and accomplish large undertakings. At first rivers were the paths of communication, and where these ran into the sea and along the coasts brave men soon built ships and sailed them, and it is hard to say how much of the character of the maritime folk is due to the courage of the sailor and the fisherman. In war time privateers were fitted out in Nova Scotian ports, and their masters often made fortunes, as did the richest of all, Enos, the son of Joseph Collins, who came over from Boston. This Enos, born in 1774, "a determined, hard-faced man", was reputed, on his death in 1871 in England, to be one of the wealthiest of those who had come from America. Many a prize he had brought into Halifax during the French wars; he had carried flour and provisions through the blockade for Wellington's army in Spain, and had made the Americans yield him tribute in 1812–14.

A sea captain just home from a cruise leading a small procession of sailors carrying bags of treasure, flanked by a guard armed by stout cudgels or cutlasses was no uncommon sight on Water Street [Halifax] in those days, and as often as not these little bands turned into the stone warehouse at the head of Collins's Wharf.[1]

For nearly a century Canada was a great maritime state, and sent forth yearly between three and four thousand ships of more than five hundred tons burden. The vessels of Quebec, designed by English and French craftsmen on English lines, were built chiefly for timber cargoes and were usually sold in England, not a few for the Australian trade. For over half a century in the city of Quebec the same firms carried on extensive business in wooden ships. Even more enterprising were the builders and mariners of the provinces by the sea. In Saint John, Yarmouth, Pictou, Windsor and coastal hamlets large and comely ships were launched, were commanded by local captains and were manned by local crews. These vessels approximated to American models; indeed the greatest clipper fleet of the world was designed in the United States by a Nova Scotian, Donald MacKay. Everywhere their master-mariners had the reputation of being men of daring, resourcefulness and driving power who, often with wife and small children aboard, did not quail in shipwreck or mutiny; they were also thrifty traders. When the big ships came back to their home port or their inland base, the boys of the village learned from the crews something of the world outside, and in their turn became pioneers on the main. About 1885, with the arrival of the iron ship, the day of the wooden ship passed quickly, and after this there might be seen in almost any village along the coast an old sea captain who had traded in many a harbour, sitting in his garden in front of his white cottage,

[1] *History of the Canadian Bank of Commerce*, I, 42.

and now and then watching great ships sail by, but fewer and smaller year after year till only the schooner was left.

Most famous of Nova Scotian shipbuilders was Samuel Cunard, born in Halifax in 1787 of Loyalist parentage. He started his fortune by purchasing a prize vessel, and he established there the wharf which still goes by his name. Lumbering, whaling, banking were all profitable, but his greatest asset came to be his fleet of forty ships. In 1814 he made a contract with His Majesty's Government to carry the mails between Halifax, Boston, Newfoundland and Bermuda, and about fifteen years later he took shares in the *Royal William*, which the men of the provinces launched at Quebec in 1831 and fitted with engines at Montreal. This vessel in 1833 crossed the Atlantic Ocean from Nova Scotia to England by steam for the first time, disproving the fears of shrewd men of science and business. Cunard, "a bright, tight, little man with keen eyes, firm and happy manners", persuaded Robert Napier of Glasgow that the future was with steam, and their chance came in 1838. They had the powerful support of the Hon. Joseph Howe. On 26 April he and the Hon. Judge Haliburton sailed for England in Her Majesty's ten-gun brig *Tyrian* (one of the "coffins", so called because of their misfortunes). They were overtaken by the *Sirius*, a steamer which was recrossing the Atlantic on her first voyage, the mails were transferred to her and the passengers on the *Tyrian* with its flapping sails watched the *Sirius* steam over the horizon line. On 24 August Howe wrote a strong letter to Lord Glenelg urging that a condition of the new mail tenders about to be called for should be their conveyance on steam vessels.[1] The letter made an impression, and Cunard, having received through Robert Napier the support of George Burns of Glasgow and David McIver of Liverpool, established the "British and North American Royal Mail Steamship Company". They tendered for the delivery of the mails by steamships and were successful. Cunard sailed back on his own ship, the *Britannia*, and received ovations both in Halifax and Boston. Halifax was abandoned as a port of call in 1859; Sir Samuel Cunard died in England in 1865. Into his place in Canadian steamship transportation had stepped Hugh Allan, founder of the Allan Line, which from 1852 until its absorption by the Canadian Pacific Company did more than any other to promote sea-borne commerce to and from Canada.

The Great West has been the field of the pioneer for centuries. Names of forts, lakes and rivers that carry to the Easterner suggestions of the frontier are among the oldest in Canada. Even until the present the spirit of the fur companies lives on in some modern forms of Canadian enterprise. The Hudson's Bay Company, and especially the North West Company, were embodiments of as mighty a pioneering spirit as modern civilisation has seen. Only men of great experience, vision, and power could control such vast areas as they had to hold,

[1] *Speeches of Joseph Howe*, i, 187-91.

areas which until wheat and the railway came were traversed by the half-breed, and the Indian, in canoe and dog-sleigh harvesting furs; and to be successful they had to treat the natives fairly.

When the sovereignty of the Hudson's Bay Company waned, its spirit passed into the promoters of the Canadian Pacific Railway. One great figure, Donald A. Smith, bridges this period of transition. He spent most of his life in the routine service of the Hudson's Bay Company, learned at every stage its inner nature, and died as its Governor; but also he was one of the small group who initiated the Canadian Pacific Railway, and though neither its greatest financier nor its constructive genius, he was a steadfast believer in it and held on with fast grip in the darkest days. Simpson sent him first to Tadoussac, historic but far away on the St Lawrence and a poor centre for furs, and here he remained six years; from there he was appointed to the even more desolate Labrador; in 1853 he rose to be chief trader and in 1862 chief factor of the whole region, and in 1869 was transferred to Montreal as resident head. These thirty years in the wilderness made him a Labrador man and not a man of the plains. Consequently, during the difficult transition period when the Dominion was taking over the North West Territories, he proved to be a valuable mediator. Though he knew every detail of the fur trade, and won the confidence of the factors, he did not sympathise with their prejudices against immigrants and railways, but believed that the future lay with agriculture rather than skins. He realised that the old order, both at the Red River and on the Western plains, was rapidly passing. Simpson would not see this, and never allowed the Scottish farmers or Hudson's Bay settlers any freedom for markets, but Smith threw himself with his whole soul into the new Canadian regime and was the natural Commissioner from Canada to the Red River in 1869–70 at the time of the first uprising of the *Métis* under Riel. Also he was a useful interpreter of the West to Ottawa in the same crisis. The East knew nothing of and was indifferent to the West. Donald Smith's "unique significance in our history", says Professor John Macnaughton with much truth, "lies precisely in the achievement of that difficult synthesis" between East and West. He saw clearly that the primary demand of the new West was better communication with the outside world. He first found his own cousin George Stephen and converted him to a belief in the prairies: then he introduced him to J. J. Hill, an expatriated Canadian, and together they acquired the interests of the Dutch bondholders of the St Paul and Pacific Railway which they reorganised and called later the Great Northern. This Canadian-owned line became the first link by rail between the Red River and the outer world and proved to be the nucleus from which the mighty Canadian Pacific was shortly developed. That accomplished, the pioneering work of Smith was at an end. Younger and more venturesome men made the new Transcontinental, although there is the well-known photograph of him driving the last spike when the rails met at Craigellachie. In his old age in Montreal and in London as Lord Strathcona he was a larger figure in the public eye, but was of less real consequence to Canada than when in his prime he did not falter in his reasoned hope for the prairies. And for this he deserved well of his country.

Another great representative of the Hudson's Bay Company, who may be said also to bridge the gap between old and new, was Sir James Douglas (1803–77). He came to Canada in 1820 in the employ of the North West Company and, on the amalgamation in the next year, when John McLoughlin took charge of the Columbia Department, he went with that able man and shared with him many of the difficulties of that remote region. Shrewdly foreseeing what might happen in Oregon, Douglas abandoned Fort Vancouver as a port of the Company, and in 1843 established a new fort on Vancouver Island where the city of Victoria now stands. At this centre of government he reigned first as the Company's Governor of the island from 1851 to 1858, and from 1858 to 1864 as Imperial Governor of the new colony of British Columbia. From the beginning he was faced with troubles on account of new settlers whom the Company discouraged; but these were small in comparison with those that accompanied the inrush of miners to the Fraser River on the discovery of gold in 1855. By 1856 20,000 had moved in and Victoria had become a city. To cope with the situation the British Government created the colony of British Columbia in 1858 with Douglas as Governor. He was the man for the place. His firm and autocratic rule gave just government. The old pioneer knew his ground and his conditions. So completely had he won the confidence of the Indian that in his disputes with the miner entire reliance was felt in Douglas's impartial justice. Supported by Chief Justice Matthew B. Begbie, he kept British Columbia free from carnage such as had been so common south of the line. But when the demand for responsible government began to be heard Douglas realised that the autocratic period, to which he belonged, was passing, as had the rule of the Hudson's Bay Company, and he retired from the governorship in 1864, having fulfilled well his function as long as good administrative experience was required.

The English-speaking inhabitants of the Red River do not deserve the name of pioneer so much as do the early settlers in Ontario, for they were hardly forerunners. The Selkirk settlers had lived by the river since 1812, and the rest were officers and servants of the Hudson's Bay Company and French *Métis*. The first active pioneers of the West were the men from the East who came in to possess the country after 1870. But attention must be given to the life on the Red River, picturesque and even romantic. Brigades of York boats came up with their supplies in spring and fall, the *voyageurs* in brightly-coloured shirts and singing their *chansons* so that they could be heard round the bend of the stream; the carts creaked in from the buffalo hunt on the plains. Not infrequently the community was afflicted by cyclonic storms, floods, drought, fire and the failure of the buffalo. But Fort Garry and Kildonan did not suffer greatly from isolation. Among the families of the officers of the Company at the Fort there were women who had been educated abroad; dinners of ceremony were given at which ladies wore imported gowns, even if afterwards they danced in moccasins, and on occasion this outpost of civilisation was gay. The life of the Kildonan highlander, though comfortable, was more sober, as he was very tenacious of his religion and his standards of life. For both groups there was a background of hard, honest work, and their strength of character and integrity made a wholesome nucleus which has perpetuated itself in the Winnipeg of to-day.

The vast region between the Red River and the Rocky Mountains lay in solitude for two hundred years except when broken by nomadic Indian tribes within definite areas, and by the small groups clustered in Hudson's Bay forts or posts. But the way was being prepared for the coming of the white man not only by the treatment accorded to the Indian by the officers of the great Company but also by missionaries of religion. Joseph N. Provencher arrived at the Red River in 1818; Taché followed him; the pioneer of the Anglicans, the Rev. John West, came in 1820; James Evans, the Methodist, inventor of a syllabic system for the Crees, arrived in 1840, and John Black, the first Presbyterian, in 1851. Four others, however, may be singled out as representatives—Albert Lacombe, John McDougall, Robert Machray and James Robertson.

In the crypt of the church of the St Alban Mission overlooking the fertile Sturgeon Valley near Edmonton is the tomb of Père Lacombe (1827–1916), one of the greatest forerunners who made plain the path of civilisation in the West. The infusion of Indian blood in his veins helped this man from Quebec, which he left in 1852, to understand the "children of the prairies". He knew the Cree language better than the Crees did. To them he was "the man of the beautiful soul", and to the Blackfeet, as they saw him bearing his white flag with a red cross, he was "the man of good heart". Roaming from the Peace River to the Bow, he was a peacemaker among savage warriors, and again and again he took his life in his hands to allay their feuds. In encampments loathsome with dirt and disease and distressed with famine he chid, sympathised, pitied, and shared his own food with the starving. When the new settler entered and broke the soil and railway lines were laid, the buffalo disappeared, to the dismay of the fur trader and the Indian, and just such a man as Lacombe was needed at the crisis. Both then and later, when treaties had to be made, he was one in whom the Indian trusted. In the construction camps of the Canadian Pacific Railway he made himself at home with the men. Having won no less influence over the French *Métis*, both at Red River and on the plains, than over the Indians, he became in 1885 a great pacifier, and as he moved hither and thither through the lodges he stamped out discontent, which if it had got under way might have set the whole West aflame and swept the whites from the prairies. But this pioneer, most at home when roving the plains, could charm the magnates of Montreal and Paris and win the friendship of Van Horne, whose eulogy is proof of his wide human appeal: "His life, devoted and self-sacrificing, has been like peaceful moonlight—commonplace to some, but to others full of quiet splendour, serenity, mystery and of much more for which there are no words".[1]

Among the Protestants those who most resemble Lacombe were the Methodists George and John McDougall, father and son, but especially the latter. George's father had been in the British navy and fought on the Great Lakes in the War of 1812, and George himself was born in a frontier settlement of Ontario, where, as a young man, he traded with the Indians, learned their ways and the Ojibway language. John was his father's interpreter and companion in the wilds, and in 1860, the father having been sent to Norway House, he became a schoolmaster among the Crees. Many a journey father and son made by canoe in summer and by carriole or snow-shoes in winter, until in the bitter January of 1876 the father perished alone in a blizzard about thirty miles from Calgary and his horse came into camp without a saddle. John McDougall and Père Lacombe were almost contemporaries; they spent their later years within ten miles of each other and were only two months apart in death. In McDougall's life recurs the familiar story of the buffalo hunt, starving Indians, the bringing in of provisions in summer by the brigade of boats on the Saskatchewan and in winter overland; of pestilence stalking through camps; of prowling Crees and Blackfeet on the warpath; of debauchery through drink and the low-class white. By instinct understanding what the trouble at the Red River in 1870 might mean, father and son used all their tact to stay the Indians, tormented as they were by smallpox, from revenging themselves upon the whites in the posts and the mission stations. After the purchase of the Hudson's Bay territory John McDougall helped to negotiate treaties sometimes in company with the North West Mounted Police on the Saskatchewan, and later, when the advance of the Canadian Pacific Railway was alarming the Indians, he allayed their fears and accompanied surveyors in some of their most difficult journeys through the mountains. In the rebellion of 1885 he became chaplain to the Alberta field-force and as a scout under General Thomas B. Strange did much to keep the Indians of Northern Alberta loyal. These early missionaries placed the future in their debt, for they made ready for the coming white man at great sacrifice to themselves. In loneliness and much hardship they were more away from home than among their

[1] Hughes, K., *Father Lacombe* (Preface).

own families, but they protected the country against the greed and lust of the vicious white man and taught the Indian something as to what citizenship means.

A very different man from either Lacombe or McDougall, and working with a different object, was Robert Machray, later Archbishop of Rupert's Land, Primate of All Canada and Prelate of the Order of St Michael and St George. He was an Aberdonian Scot, a Fellow of Sidney Sussex College, Cambridge, had been rector of a good parish in England and as bishop set foot on the banks of the Red River in 1865. Tall, commanding, and with an intellect of exceptional vigour and cultivation, he became the pioneer of higher education on the prairies and the first Chancellor of the University of Manitoba in 1877. The twelve thousand people who were living at Red River when he arrived were disunited by great rivalries of race. Only a few hundreds of them were white, mostly Scots and English who looked with dislike upon the "alien and often insolent Canadians", and with anxiety upon Americans freighting from Minnesota into Fort Garry. The French far outnumbered all the others, and Indians prowled in the neighbourhood. The people of this isolated settlement lived by themselves, their future was uncertain and the impending change from Hudson's Bay to Dominion ownership was pregnant with trouble. The bishop was a strong advocate of confederation and a wise interpreter to the Secretary of State in London, and to the authorities at Ottawa, of the actual situation during the rebellion of 1870. In the terrible months of that winter, when one hasty act might have led to a massacre of the whites, he, along with Donald A. Smith, kept the white settlers in hand and restrained the rebels. Even then he had strong faith in the future and knew that plans must be laid to receive an incoming host. He kept oversight of his vast diocese and had it subdivided to meet emerging needs. But his greatest work was in education. He revived St John's College and himself taught in the school and the higher departments, living in the simplest manner among his scholars and masters. As Chairman of the Protestant Board of Education from the year 1871, he did much for many years to give tone to the schools of the province.

The fourth pioneer to be chosen for his work in upbuilding the social and religious life of the West is James Robertson (1839–1902), a Scot who came with his father in 1855 to seek a more favourable future in Ontario. There he took the regular Arts course in the University of Toronto, and was one of those who repelled the Fenian Raid at Ridgeway in 1866 when three of his fellow-students were killed and five were wounded. In due course he entered the ministry of the Presbyterian Church, and after serving some years in Ontario he went to Winnipeg in 1874. The times were hard, there were no markets, prices were high, but settlers kept passing along the black trails on prairie "schooners" and freighters heading out into the West and North, and Robertson had them on his mind and gave them a word of cheer on the way. It was said that his house was "an immigration office, an information bureau, and an employment agency". But he found Winnipeg too narrow a parish, and his Church appointed him to the superintendency of all its missions in the West. Back and forth he went on the railway line and from it followed by buggy and buckboard, cutter and "jumper" every trail in search of the groups of newcomers. "Once, and once only, in nineteen years did he eat Christmas dinner with his family". By his life of hardship he did much to prevent that lone land from becoming a "Wild West". "Intrepidity" was one of his favourite words, and when in 1897 gold was discovered in the Yukon he turned his eyes to the Klondike and sent young men in with the first rush of miners. Not the least of his services was his interpretation of the West to the East; he used his great powers of persuasion to induce promising men and women to take up homesteads on the prairies, and it was a familiar saying of his that it was necessary to pour Canadians into the mainland of British Columbia in order to prevent it being Americanised. His constant demand upon the East that it should support the West was a strong unifying factor; people got to know a country to the help of which they were induced to give.

A police force might be thought of as being only a negative factor in the life of a new country, but the North West Mounted Police were unique and have been a constructive agency of the first order for good. In no body of men could be found a finer quality of the pioneering spirit than informed the ranks of this celebrated force from the beginning, recruited as they were from all ranks of society, all subject to the same discipline, all supremely loyal and ready for any act of heroism. The observance of law such as was not known south of the border in the adjoining States was introduced when Major Macleod in 1874 marched his small company across the plains to occupy a permanent post. Almost their first work was to suppress the American whisky trader who demoralised the Indian; then by tact, fairness and force they won supremacy over and imposed order on belligerent Crees, Blackfeet and wandering tribes, often hunting out among them, at great personal danger even to life, the murderer, horse-thief or cattle-lifter. Many a story is told of individual prowess and self-control on long journeys in the severest weather. By meting out even-handed justice to Indian and white they won the respect of the red man which steadied him during the months of restlessness in the *Métis* rising of 1885. At no period was "this restrained but forceful oversight" more effective than in the days of the gold rush to the Klondike. Awful as was the toll of human life and suffering in that episode, it would have been immensely more awful, had not the trails been guarded by fearless and strong protectors in posts on which the British flag flew. They succoured the frail and the broken and drove the desperado relentlessly out of the territory.

But in quieter times a more original type of work was done by the Police in discovering what the new settlers were doing and in reporting upon the quality of the settlements. The patrol helped the newcomer to check the prairie or forest fire, and brought timely aid to families in dire straits even from starvation. Nowhere has a more original and beneficent method been devised for mapping out in such a short time, and keeping watch upon, such a vast country exposed to disaster from winter blizzards, summer cyclones, or the raids of the savage. What the cheery call of the patrol has meant to the solitary man in winter brooding over his disappointments, or to the lonely woman on the plains terrified by storm or Indian, none can tell. These few men stood for order, prepared the ways for the immigrant and strengthened the feeble knees of the disheartened. The advance of the railways imposed new tasks upon them, especially at the time when strikes disorganised the construction camps; and their worth is attested in the words of Van Horne to Colonel Irvine in 1883: "Without the assistance of the officers and of the splendid men under your command, it would have been impossible to have accomplished so much as we did. On no great work within my knowledge, where so many men have been employed, has such perfect order prevailed".

To-day the pioneering stage is all but over throughout vast areas and the force has undergone transformation; but that the first occupation of the Canadian West is so clean a page of history, so little stained by bloodshed, so free from crime, is due in large measure to these unique pioneers.

George Monro Grant, himself a man with the prophetic vision of a great pioneer, pays a generous tribute in his *Ocean to Ocean* (1874) to the ordinary surveyors and engineers as pioneers of civilisation, many of them men of good birth, some looking for adventure or supposed freedom, all of them "soldiers of peace":

In journeying often by hateful roaring streams, in perils of rapids, in perils of fires—working, eating, sleeping, sometimes short of food....We could see that continuous labour for one or two years in solitary wilderness or mountain gorges as surveyor, transitman, leveller, rodman, commissary or even packer is a totally different thing from taking a trip across the continent for the first time, when the perpetual novelty, the spice of romance, the risks and pleasures atone for all discomforts.[1]

The primacy of these engineers was held by Sir Sandford Fleming (1827–1915). In his old age at Ottawa in winter or at Halifax in summer he would talk gently and pensively of the early days, how he came near to being shipwrecked on his first passage from Scotland, and of his later manifold experiences on his surveys of the Dominion from the Atlantic to the Pacific. After railway work in Ontario from

---

[1] Grant, G. M., *Ocean to Ocean*, p. 359.

1852 to 1863 he laid out the line of the Intercolonial Railway from Halifax to Levis: then in 1872 he began to survey a route from Fort William to the coast. Dr Grant has told the story of his rapid crossing of prairies and mountains, and the passage of the Yellowhead Pass which Fleming strongly recommended. It was a great disappointment to him when the Government in 1880 decided to hand over the construction of the railway to the Canadian Pacific Railway Syndicate, but as Van Horne refused to accept his judgment in regard to the Yellowhead Pass, in 1883 he again crossed the continent and discovered, after much adventure, a possible route which is now the main line of the Canadian Pacific Railway through the Kicking Horse Pass, his party being the first white men to penetrate the almost impassable Rockies of this region.

As in the days of the North West Company, Montreal again produced men equal to the unprecedented occasion created by the Government when they discovered that it was too great a task for them to carry through a transcontinental railway. Behind the scenes the financial genius of the group was George Stephen, but more than that he was a leader of resourcefulness and indomitable courage, and of unbounded faith in the future of the West. When Stephen was looking for a superintendent to build the railway he turned to his friend J. J. Hill of St Paul, who strongly recommended him to take William Van Horne because "a pioneer was needed, and the more of a pioneer the better". Thus these two "pioneers of faith and vision", Stephen and Van Horne, were thrown together, one of the most remarkable conjunctions in the history of Canada—financial courage and impulsive constructive genius, in temperaments perfectly complementary to each other.

Though Van Horne was born in 1843 in a frontier village of Illinois, and had no advantages in early education, he inherited from his Dutch, German and French stocks many of the best qualities of American life, extraordinary energy, sustained power of work, accuracy in detail, determined judgment, quick resolution and withal a highly artistic temperament. On the one side he was a pioneer all his life through; on the other a designer of things of beauty even for his railways, the owner and lover of paintings, himself no mean artist, and a most affectionate family man. He rose with great rapidity from the position of a telegraph operator on a small local line in Illinois to be a general superintendent at twenty-eight, and soon such illimitable horizons were opening before him in his own country that his friends were greatly surprised that he was tempted by an enterprise of doubtful success in an alien country. But the idea of one continental line over which he would have control caught his imagination, and, though the difficulties seemed overwhelming, "the very immensity of the work challenged his fighting instincts". At once his marvellous energy and driving power put life into the enterprise. He went here, there, everywhere inspecting every detail and making everyone work, having previously brought in his supplies in enormous quantities. "He could divine the lie of a country, see how the roads should go from one end to the other and how they must get over or round obstacles which seemed to vanish when steeped awhile in his thought, like the rocks in the Alps under Hannibal's vinegar",[1] and, as Father Lacombe said, "He was a Napoleon in the planning of his work, in his control of it, and in the attachment of the men who worked for him. ...He gave that road from end to end of the continent one spirit". He did what seemed to be impossible: he built at the rate of between two and three miles a day for nearly 500 miles across the prairies in a season, and in forty-six months from his arrival in Canada, five years earlier than was promised, he completed the line, breaking all records in railway construction, and throughout at a higher standard than was required by the contract with the Government. He drove at this prodigious rate not merely to secure returns as soon as possible, but because he knew that the Americans were hoping to get their share of the North West. J. J. Hill expected that it would become a feeder to his lines, and he vehemently opposed Stephen and Van Horne when they determined to build round the head of Lake Superior, in itself the most difficult part of the whole line, but Van Horne knew instinctively that the rails must run from coast to coast and as near the border as possible; so against advice he sent it over the Kicking Horse Pass. The era of the wilderness ended in 1870. When the Hudson's Bay Company went out, who was to come in? The tenure of the Dominion was precarious until the line was completed from the East, and older Canadian immigration could without détour enter and occupy the vast plains before the American trekked north. So Van Horne built against time. In a real sense these two men, Stephen and Van Horne, changed the face of the West and did much to determine its national destiny.

After this feat Van Horne was offered almost any railway position in his native land that he might choose, but he preferred to complete, as far as in him lay, the work of this transcontinental road; so, to create trade, he erected grain elevators and flour mills and entered upon ocean transportation. To develop passenger traffic for the railway he gave his architects a lead in designing beautiful hotels on commanding sites. He "capitalised the scenery" but he also sought to promote the best permanent immigration into the West.

Canada is entering upon fuller economic life. Pioneers may still be met in Northern Quebec and Northern Ontario, in the Peace River area and in many parts of British Columbia, but pioneering in one phase has changed. We shall see no more builders like Mackenzie and Mann of the Canadian Northern Railway, or lumber kings like J. R. Booth. Great enterprise must show its courage and vision in

---

[1] Macnaughton, J., *Strathcona*, p. 293.

new ways. What is most distinctive of the constructive genius of Canada to-day is the great smelter or consolidated mines of British Columbia, development of the gold, nickel and silver of the pre-Cambrian shield, and the creation of pulp and paper mills by the harnessing of water-power in Ontario and Quebec. The attention of the country is fastened on what are really lesser tasks directed by huge combinations of men whose names are known only to a few. But these are made possible by the inflow of foreign capital which is itself due to the faith in Canada created mainly by the work of the railway pioneers.

Canadian society of the present is removed only one generation, or at most two, from the days of the pioneer. In so far as it depends upon wealth in Montreal, Toronto, Winnipeg or Vancouver it has behind it the fur-trader, the railway contractor, the lumberman, the miner, the manufacturer, the owner of the departmental store—these last having often developed out of the mechanic or the small shopkeeper. It is the result of the magnificent energy of those who without any initial privilege have with vision and will-power taken opportunity by the forelock.

The struggle with physical nature and the success attained in controlling it bred initiative, persistence and straightforwardness in the earlier generations. With something of the spirit of the Jack-of-all-trades, men were ready for every emergency and they were impatient of conventions. Society therefore has been and is fluid, and the man of to-day becomes the master of to-morrow; which means, of course, that contemplative virtues and the assurance bred by such tradition as is at once the grace and the strength of the old families of England are as yet rare in Canada. But spiritual forces have wrought in the heart of the pioneer, and it has been said with truth that "every major issue in the religious life of Canada has arisen on the frontier"—toleration in Quebec, equality of privilege in Nova Scotia and Ontario, unification in the West. It is to be hoped that this forthright vitality will continue to display itself in the coming generation in moral and intellectual integrity.

CHAPTER XXV

THE ECONOMIC DEVELOPMENT OF CANADA, 1867–1921

(I) COMMUNICATIONS

IN earlier chapters the history of the development of transportation was sketched in outline down to 1867, and it remains here to trace the changes which have taken place since that time, considering in turn highways, inland waterways, and railways.

About the middle and later parts of the nineteenth century the improvement of the highways involved the extension of the turnpike system and the macadamising, planking and gravelling of roads. But the maintenance of highways from the tolls which were collected was wholly unsatisfactory and legislation was passed at different times to facilitate the purchase of toll roads by the province or the municipalities.[1] Much difficulty was encountered in dealing with the problem of these roads, which were recognised as a failure, and it took many years to work out a solution. Some of the turnpike roads continued in existence, even in the neighbourhood of Montreal, until very recently, and the last vestiges of the system in Ontario remained until 1926, when the toll road between Sarnia and Petrolia was taken over.[2]

In the later years of the nineteenth century a new interest began to be taken in the roads, of which the organisation of Good Roads Associations is clear evidence. It was recognised that the means employed for the improvement of the roads had been "wasteful in the extreme",[3] and that the lack of good roads, so essential to the development of the province, had created "an almost revolutionary movement in favour of better roads".[4] Settlement had taken place over a large and relatively thinly-populated area. The methods by which municipalities had attended to the repair of their own roads had not produced the desired results, for the system of statute labour, by which each man had to do a certain number of days' work on the roads adjoining his land under the direction of local "pathmasters", who were appointed annually and had not the necessary knowledge, yielded at best only short stretches of passable road. Even the toll roads were but little better than the common highways. The time was ripe for a change, and in 1901 the Highway Improvement Act was passed. This Act set aside $1,000,000 (about £200,000) a year to provide for a government subsidy of $33\frac{1}{3}$ per cent. on all authorised

[1] *Statutes of Canada*, 1849, cap. 120; 1859, cap. 43; 1860, cap. 54; also *Statutes of Ontario*, 1901, cap. 33 (Toll Roads Expropriation Act).
[2] *Mail and Empire* (Toronto), 1 Mar. 1926.
[3] *Report* of A. W. Campbell, Provincial Road Instructor in Ontario, 1897, p. 10.
[4] *Ibid.* 1896, p. 7. The conditions in Ontario are taken as typical of those in the other eastern provinces.

county road systems, constructed according to government standards, after the county had ratified the system. By 1919 all the counties of Ontario had accepted this arrangement. As the work advanced, the grant was increased under the Acts of 1907 and 1912 to $2,000,000 a year.[1] By 1913 there were 3688 miles of county road.

In 1913 the Ontario Government appointed a commission to consider the highway problem and make recommendations concerning it. The report of this commission in 1914[2] and the consequent legislation of 1915[3] mark a new era in the provincial highway development, and since that time over $170,000,000 has been spent on the roads along the lines suggested by the report.[4] Emphasis was laid upon the fact that the work of construction and improvement should follow a thoroughly elaborated plan, which would benefit not only the main roads but also the chief market roads and local feeders. In the Act of 1915 provision was made, in the first place, for establishing a provincial Highway Department, with a minister, a deputy minister and a chief engineer as responsible heads of the system. Secondly, a provincial subsidy was to be given, amounting to 20 per cent. of the cost of maintaining county roads, provided these complied with departmental regulations regarding maintenance and repair. Thirdly, cities of 10,000 and over, in counties operating under the Highway Improvement Act, were required to contribute to the cost and maintenance of the leading suburban roads adjacent to those cities, by co-operation with the county council. Fourthly, in the case of main roads in which municipalities in one or more counties might be interested, a provincial grant of 40 per cent. of the cost of construction was to be given and the remainder of the cost was to be apportioned as the municipal councils concerned should decide. Finally, township councils were encouraged to appoint efficient road superintendents. It was hoped by this means to produce better work with many resulting economies.

The progress of the work requiring more and more money, this was provided by increases of the government grant, under amendments of the Highway Improvement Act. In 1917 provision was made under the Act for establishing a system of provincial county roads, towards which the province would contribute 60 per cent. of the cost of construction and maintenance. These were to provide extensions of the provincial highway system. In 1919 the government grant of 20 per cent. of the cost of maintaining county roads was increased to 40 per cent. In 1920, instead of the previous sources of revenue, a Highway Improvement Fund was instituted, composed of the unexpended balances of previous appropriations, $3,000,000

[1] Statutes of Ontario 1907, cap. 16 and 1912, cap. 11.
[2] Report of the Public Roads and Highways Commission, 1914.
[3] Ontario Highways Act, 1915, 5 Geo. V, cap. 17.
Statement, in advance of publication, by courtesy of the Highways Department.

yearly for five years, the annual receipts derived from motor vehicle licences, the sum of $1,580,000 as the revenue from motor vehicle licences in 1919, a sum equal to all repayments of loans under the Provincial Highway Act, and a further sum equal to the Dominion Government subsidy under the Canada Highways Act.[1] This Highway Improvement Fund was increased from year to year by additional provincial government grants, and later by a gasolene (petrol) tax.

The enlarged scale of expenditures on county roads under the Highway Improvement Act from 1903 to 1924 may be noted from the following table:

Years	Total expenditures	Government grants
1903–1910 incl.	$2,690,529.59	$896,843.16
1911–1917 incl.	$6,399,238.89	$2,163,161.57
1918–1924 incl.	$50,404,442.37	$23,076,643.99

In 1917 the Provincial Highway Act was passed,[2] with a view to the construction and maintenance, under the Department of Highways, of leading arteries throughout the province. This was desirable on account of the increased use of the motor vehicle for carrying passengers and freight and as a further inducement to the tourist traffic from the United States. This Act authorised the provincial Highways Department, with the approval of the Lieutenant-Governor in Council, to take over, on behalf of the Crown, any public highway and to assume thereafter all responsibility for the proper construction and maintenance of such highways. Work proceeded rapidly under this system, and a network of hard-surfaced roads, much of them of concrete construction, connects all the important communities. On them omnibuses run on regular schedules and both private and commercial motor trucks are in continuous operation.

In the newer and unorganised or unsurveyed sections of the province, or in organised townships where roads are necessary to give access to markets through unoccupied or sparsely settled districts, a system of colonisation roads has been established. This work has been carried out by the Northern Development Branch of the Highways Department, and the cost, while largely borne by the Government, is in part contributed by the municipalities. These roads are of great importance in opening up the northern and north-western sections of the province, and as these areas are being developed, larger and larger amounts are being expended on roads.

Finally, on the passing of the Canada Highways Act[3] in 1919, the Dominion Government set aside $20,000,000 to aid the provinces in their work of highway construction and improvement during the subsequent five years. Grants of $80,000 were to be made to every province during each of the five years and the remainder was to be

[1] *Statutes of Canada*, Act 9–10 Geo. V, cap. 54.
[2] *Statutes of Ontario*, Act 7 Geo. V, cap. 16; *Ontario Sessional Papers*, 1918, no. 15, p. 27.
[3] *Statutes of Canada*, Act 9–10 Geo. V, cap. 54.

allotted in proportion to their respective populations.[1] The grant was for construction only up to 40 per cent. of the cost, the province being required to furnish the other 60 per cent. and to guarantee the proper maintenance of the roads for which the subsidy was received. In Ontario, the grant was limited to expenditure on provincial highways only. At the end of the five years not all the original subsidy had been earned and spent, and an extension of time was granted for this purpose.

For transport purposes the only important waterways within Canada are those forming the Great Lakes-St Lawrence chain, which constitute the greatest system of inland waterways in the world. In the improvement of this system the most significant changes have been the construction of canals to connect the lakes, namely, the St Mary Canal between Lakes Superior and Huron, the St Clair Flats Canal to overcome the shallowness of Lake St Clair, the Welland Canal between Lakes Erie and Ontario, and the St Lawrence Canals to overcome the rapids in that river. As was noted previously, the Welland Canal was finally completed between Port Colborne, on Lake Erie, and Port Dalhousie, on Lake Ontario, in 1833; and in the years before 1850 the St Lawrence Canals were constructed, with the object of establishing the Great Lakes-St Lawrence route as the "natural" and strategic channel of trade between the central and western States and the trans-Atlantic markets.[2] In other words, the desire was to attract the traffic, especially the Atlantic grain traffic, of those States to the Canadian route and thus counteract the influence of the Erie Canal, which was built from Buffalo across New York State in order to absorb a large share of Canadian trade, and to retain the trade of the north central and western States in domestic channels. The growth of this traffic led to successive enlargements of the Welland Canal in 1841, 1853 and 1871, and, finally, in 1887 it was deepened to 14 ft. In the last two decades of the century the St Lawrence Canals were also deepened to 14 ft., so that vessels of that draught might carry traffic from the upper lakes to Montreal without trans-shipment.

In all the changes of canal dimensions and depth, the conditions prevailing along the Erie Canal, as well as the increasing size of vessels on the lakes, were kept constantly in mind. Almost invariably the dimensions of the Welland Canal locks lagged behind the dimensions of vessels on the upper lakes. From early times there was active competition between the St Lawrence and the Erie Canal route for the western grain trade. In the years 1860-70, which were the second decade of rapid railway-building in the United States, vessels of greater draught than the Welland Canal could accommodate

[1] *Ontario Sessional Papers*, 1920, no. 15, p. 25.
[2] Hincks, F., *Canada, its Financial Position and Resources*, p. 5; Coffin, W. F., *The Canal and the Rail*, p. 3.

carried the traffic to Buffalo, whence the railroads took the greater part of it to New York.[1] In 1870 the Erie Canal, in order to compete with the railroads, lowered its tolls by 50 per cent., thus creating a crisis for the Welland Canal, which was failing in its efforts to gain control of the western traffic and divert it down the St Lawrence. Consequently, in that year a commission was appointed to investigate the matter of canal transportation. Its report, issued in 1871,[2] reveals the inadequacy of the Welland Canal; for much lumber was going from the Georgian Bay region to Toronto by rail, and the increasing grain traffic was being diverted to the Erie Canal and the railroads across New York State. The size of the lake vessels had increased greatly and the larger vessels could carry cargo to Buffalo at rates with which the vessels of Welland Canal size could not compete. While the low rates on the Erie Canal and the improvements of railroad transport gave these agencies practical control of the western traffic, shippers in the western States complained of the inability of these transport agencies to handle all the traffic and urged that the Welland Canal should be enlarged to meet the requirements of the growing trade. The commission considered that, since the canal had in early years attracted much traffic from the Erie Canal, if it were now enlarged it would be put upon a much better competitive basis and part of New York's traffic would be attracted to Montreal. When once the "natural" channel was cleared of obstructions, traffic would go by that route rather than by the artificial Erie Canal. Hence the majority recommended that the Welland Canal should be enlarged for vessels with a minimum draught of 12 ft., although some wanted a depth of 14 or even 16 ft.

The minority of the commission, on the other hand, showed that the existing rates from Chicago to Montreal were about 8 per cent. less than those to New York; but they considered that New York had the advantage over Montreal because of its greater competition, its more abundant shipping, its open harbour all the year round, and its excellent banking and distributing facilities. Hence, even if rates by the St Lawrence route were reduced, they might not overcome these advantages possessed by New York. According to the commission's recommendation, the work of deepening the Welland Canal to 12 ft. was begun in 1871; but in 1875, at the request of many people interested in shipping, the Government decided to provide for vessels of 14 ft. draught, this depth being deemed necessary to divert trade from Buffalo. Chicago and other harbours on the United States side had been recently deepened to 14 ft., which promised to be the standard depth throughout the lakes. The question of deepening the St Lawrence Canals to 14 ft., to enable lake vessels to pass down to Montreal without breaking bulk, came up in the House in 1875, but

[1] *Ontario Sessional Papers*, 1909, no. 20 a, p. 36.   [2] *Ibid.* 1871, no. 54, pp. 17–35.

the motion did not pass;[1] and it was not till 1885–1901 that these were enlarged to accord with the Welland Canal.[2]

The high hopes centring in these canal improvements[3] were disappointed; for the Welland route rapidly fell behind in its proportion of western traffic owing to the constant increase in the size of vessels on the upper lakes.[4] Counteracting efforts in the early 'eighties to attract traffic to the Welland Canal by reducing the grain tolls, formerly 20 cents per ton, to 2 cents failed because the vessels on the upper lakes were too large for the canal.[5] Besides, these larger vessels were more economical and could carry freight at lower and lower rates, the average freight rate on grain from Chicago to Buffalo being reduced from 2.5 cents per bushel in 1899 to 1.5 cents per bushel in 1902.[6] These advantages by the United States route prevented the western grain from going down the St Lawrence route. Moreover, the United States vessels were able to get return cargoes of coal from Buffalo and other Lake Erie ports, while the Canadian vessels could seldom get return loads. Thus, the United States route through Buffalo retained its ascendency. Large vessels bringing grain down the lakes to Port Colborne, at the entrance of the Welland Canal, had to unload their grain into smaller vessels, which could pass through the Welland and St Lawrence Canals to Montreal. Later, to avoid the delay of such trans-shipment, a government elevator was constructed at Port Colborne to act as the intermediary in unloading and loading the vessels at this point.

With the great development of grain growing in Western Canada, and the increasingly large amount of the export trade in grain through the eastern ports of Canada and the United States, together with the large quantities of United States grain which came across the Great Lakes and went out through the Canadian channel, there was a demand that everything possible should be done to cheapen the cost of transport. The report of a Royal Commission, appointed to enquire into this matter, showed[7] that, on account of the larger and more economical vessels carrying to Buffalo and the excellent railroad facilities thence to the seaboard, the larger portion of the grain exported from Canada went through the United States. This United States route, it was stated, was aided also by the Canadian coasting laws, which compelled United States vessels taking on cargo at a Canadian port to unload the same at a United States port. When the rush movement of grain across the lakes in the fall drew great numbers of United States vessels into the trade, the movement of grain through the Buffalo gateway was greatly increased.

---

[1] *Debates of the House of Commons*, 1875, pp. 430, 590.   [2] *Canada Year Book*, 1925, p. 628.
[3] *Report of Chief Engineer of Canals*, 1880, p. 10; *Ontario Sessional Papers*, 1901, no. 20, p. xlii.
[4] *Ontario Sessional Papers*, 1909, no. 20 a, p. 16.   [5] *Ibid.* p. 16.
[6] *Ibid.* 1903, no. 20, Canal Statistics, p. 13.
[7] *Dominion Sessional Papers*, 1906, no. 19 a, Report of Royal Commission on Transportation, pp. 7–53.

The commission, therefore, recommended that, because of the increasing grain trade, the ports at the head of Lake Superior and those on the eastern side of the lakes, together with the elevator and transport facilities in the east, should be enlarged and improved in every possible way. It also urged that a through waterway from Lake Superior to ocean navigation be completed, so that the largest vessels on the upper lakes could continue their voyage to Montreal, or as near thereto as possible. If no better route could be found, the Welland Canal should be deepened so that the largest upper-lake boats could go down to the eastern end of Lake Ontario, 180 miles from Montreal, before breaking bulk.

Meanwhile some members of the House favoured the Georgian Bay Canal project for a waterway from that bay, *via* French and Ottawa Rivers, to Montreal. They were opposed to the improvement of the Welland Canal because, since the Canadian canals were free of tolls, the proposed improvement, carried out at Canada's expense, would benefit the United States as much as Canada; for the traffic which passed through the Welland Canal could then be diverted to Oswego or Ogdensburg for shipment through the United States.[1] But, in 1909, the engineers in charge of a survey of the Georgian Bay Canal reported that a 22-foot waterway along this route would cost $100,000,000, that its annual upkeep would cost $900,000 and that the time of passage would be 70 hours.[2] On the other hand, the estimated cost of the 25-foot channel by the Welland route was $50,000,000 and the time of passage six hours. The Minister of Railways showed that by the Welland route grain could be carried to Montreal at a rate with which even an improved Erie Canal could not compete.[3] The factors, therefore, which turned the decision in favour of the construction of the Welland Ship Canal were the greater accommodation provided by it, the much lower cost of construction and upkeep, the saving in the time of passage, and its remaining open longer in the fall when its facilities would be most wanted.[4] It was not until 1911 that the Government definitely made provision for the building of the canal.[5]

Between Lakes Erie and Ontario there is a difference of 325 ft. in the water levels. The existing canal overcomes this elevation by 25 locks, each 270 ft. long, 45 ft. wide and 14 ft. deep. The new ship canal will have 7 lift locks, each 800 ft. long and 80 ft. wide, with a depth of 25 ft. of water over the sills, and with a lift of $46\frac{1}{2}$ ft. Provision has been made that, if necessary to accommodate larger vessels on the upper lakes, the locks may be deepened to 30 ft. As a result of the rise of wages and prices during and after the War, the original esti-

---

[1] *Commons' Debates*, 1907–8, pp. 12,212–12,216.
[2] *Dominion Sessional Papers*, 1909, no. 19 a, Report of Engineers on Georgian Bay Ship Canal Survey, p. xix. [3] *Commons' Debates*, 1907–8, p. 4422.
[4] *Dominion Sessional Papers*, 1909, no. 19 a; and *ibid.* 1909, no. 20, Report of Deputy Minister of Railways and Canals, pp. 54–7.
[5] *Commons' Debates*, 1910–11, pp. 5058–60 (with reasons for this decision).

mated cost, $50,000,000, will not represent the final cost, which will probably reach $115,000,000 or more. When this work is completed, it is expected that a large amount of the Canadian grain which now goes out by way of Buffalo and the United States ports will reach the seaboard through the domestic channels.

The only other canal along the Great Lakes which need be mentioned is that constructed at Sault Ste Marie to overcome the difference of 19 ft. in the water levels of Lakes Superior and Huron. The original canal was inadequate to the increasing traffic, and in 1888-9 the Dominion Government arranged for the construction of a single-lock canal, the dimensions of which were finally fixed at 900 ft. long, 60 ft. wide, with a minimum depth of water on the sills of 18 ft. 3 ins.[1] Adjacent to this there are four United States canals of larger dimensions which were rendered necessary on account of the enormous development of the grain and ore trade from the ports at the head of Lake Superior and the increasing size of the vessels engaged in carrying these commodities. Latterly, another project has received particular consideration. The St Lawrence is navigable for ocean vessels up to Montreal, and with the deepening of the Welland route to 25 ft. there has come a proposal to deepen the St Lawrence Canals to the same depth so that ocean vessels may come up into the interior of the continent. There are many phases of this problem, particularly the economic and political, which call for careful and ample consideration before a final decision is reached.

The difficulties attending the construction and working of the early railways, such as the lack of capital and traffic, have been indicated previously, notably in the case of the Grand Trunk Railway. This road played a great part in the progress of Canada.[2] It was opened as a through line of 800 miles from Portland, Maine, to Sarnia, Ontario, in 1859.[3] The succeeding years brought the Company to the verge of ruin on several occasions, owing to the speculative conditions of the time, the Company's inadequate traffic and the active competition of other railways and waterways. Only the intervention of the Government saved it from disaster and the country from discredit.[4] When, in 1862, the Company defaulted on the interest payments on its bonds, the Government again came to its rescue, and in the accompanying capital reorganisation its bonds were converted into preferred stock.[5] Later, the Company extended its lines by construction, purchase and lease of other lines until it had obtained wide and important connections. In Ontario it touched nearly every

---

[1] *Canada Year Book*, 1925, p. 629. The canal was opened in 1895.
[2] Lovett, H. A., *Canada and the Grand Trunk*, 1829-1924, and Skelton, O. D., *The Railway Builders*.   [3] *Canada Year Book*, 1925, p. 588.
[4] Dominion Acts 18 Vict. cap. 174; 19-20 Vict. cap. 111; 20 Vict. cap. 11; 22 Vict. cap. 52; 29 Vict. cap. 56, etc. *Vide supra*, chapter xv.
[5] Act 25 Vict. cap. 56.

traffic-producing community and extended as far north as North Bay. In Quebec it reached the chief traffic centres. By 1873 it had obtained access to Chicago, so that its main through line extended from Portland to Chicago. Later, a series of other lines in Michigan came under its control.

Another milestone in railway development was attained in 1867, when, as a condition of their entering the Confederation, the Maritime Provinces insisted that there should be constructed a line of railway to connect them with the interior provinces.[1] Accordingly in 1867 the Dominion Government took over 196 miles of railway in Nova Scotia and New Brunswick as parts of the Intercolonial. The funds for this railway were provided by the Federal Government and in 1876 the line was opened from Halifax to a place near Levis, Quebec. Such a terminus, at a place out in the country, could not conduce to the development of traffic; but by subsequent purchase, lease and the acquisition of running rights over other lines, the Intercolonial obtained access to Montreal where it came in contact with a valuable traffic centre. On the whole, this railway system has not paid interest on its capital cost; but, as has been said, commercial considerations were not prominent when the road was planned.[2]

The era of the transcontinental railways began with the construction of the Canadian Pacific. Such a line had been advocated as early as 1849 but a parliamentary committee in 1851 reported against it. However, when British Columbia was admitted as a province of the Dominion in 1871, the Government gave its pledge to complete a railway to connect it with the East within ten years. Political complications ensued and efforts were made to have the road built by private capital; but these were unsuccessful and in 1874 the work was undertaken by the Government. As has appeared in earlier chapters, the line was finished by 1885 and was opened for through traffic in 1886 —an achievement which constitutes a great chapter in the history of Canada.[3] Much has been said in certain quarters as to the great amount of assistance which the Company received from the Government, but it is the judicious conclusion of an expert enquiry commission that the country has secured good value for the aid granted.[4] In refusing to allow any other company to build lines in the West between the main line of the Canadian Pacific and the international boundary, the Government desired to prevent United States roads from tapping this Canadian territory and to keep the flow of traffic east and west.

[1] *Vide supra*, chapter xviii.
[2] See an unpublished thesis (1916) by D. R. Cowan in the Library of the Univ. of Toronto.
[3] See Skelton, *The Railway Builders*; Innis, H. A., *History of the Canadian Pacific Railway*; MacGibbon, *Railway Rates and the Canadian Railway Commission*, ch. iii; Willson, H. Beckles, *The Life of Lord Strathcona and Mount Royal*; Vaughan, W., *The Life and Work of Sir William Van Horne*; MacBeth, R. G., *The Romance of the Canadian Pacific Railway*.
[4] *Report of Railway Inquiry Commission*, 1917, pp. xx, xxi.

At the time the Canadian Pacific was nearing completion, the small amount of traffic which it had induced many to think, and publicly to assert, that it could never pay. In 1884 and 1885 there were persons who sniffed at the railway as a philanthropic enterprise without any commercially successful future. Among these detractors were some of the Grand Trunk officials, whose criticisms were belied by the sequel. In truth the construction of the Canadian Pacific was an act of faith in Canadian development, as may be said also of the Canadian Northern, the Grand Trunk Pacific and the National Transcontinental Railways.

Unlike the British railways, which were built through well-developed country with abundant traffic, the Canadian railways were constructed through territory with very limited and frequently almost no population, and, in addition to using their utmost endeavours to develop settlement and traffic immediately tributary to the line, reached out to tap wider markets and sources of business. The influence of the Canadian Pacific in this way may be considered as typical of the activities of other railway companies in changing the life and prosperity of their respective districts. The vast range of its efforts and those of the Government soon induced settlement and immigration, and the richness of the soil attracted the ambitious of all classes and ages, from the older parts of the country as well as from trans-oceanic countries and the neighbouring Republic. The population of the three Prairie Provinces, which in 1881 was 25,228, in 1901 reached the total of 419,512;[1] and the number of bushels of grain carried by the railway increased from 7,842,343 bushels in 1885 to 42,763,253 bushels in 1899.[2] The total tonnage of freight carried by the railways in the fifteen years 1885-99 increased by an average of 20 per cent. annually. Farming districts were opened up rapidly and land values multiplied. Men of wealth and station became interested in the country's welfare. The railways brought about a unity of interests between the West and the East which made for the development of a national sentiment and aroused business optimism. The growth of the West stimulated the economic development of the East, whose mercantile and industrial interests found an enlarged market for their products.

During the time the Canadian Pacific was building its main line from Callander, near Lake Nipissing, to the Pacific Coast at Vancouver, the Company was taking active steps to get a network of feeders and distributors for this line. By acquiring the Central Canada Railway it gained access to Ottawa in 1883, and by stock control of the St Lawrence and Ottawa Railway in 1884 it secured connections with the St Lawrence River at Brockville and Prescott. In 1883 and 1885 it bought two divisions of the North Shore Rail-

---

[1] *Canada Year Book*, 1927-8, p. 101, and see above, chap. xxii.
[2] Annual reports of the Company.

way, built by the province of Quebec, and thus gained access to Montreal and Quebec. In 1881 a line was built by friendly interests between Ottawa and Toronto *via* Smith's Falls and was subsequently acquired by the Canadian Pacific. In western Ontario the Company acquired by long-term leases control of two lines which gave it access to the Georgian Bay (at Owen Sound) and Lake Erie (at St Thomas), and from the latter place it built an extension to Windsor. By means of construction and control, its policy of enlargement, absorption and amalgamation give it a network of lines in Eastern and Western Canada. Its western terminus is Vancouver and its eastern termini are Montreal and Quebec, on the St Lawrence navigation, and Halifax and Saint John, on the Atlantic Ocean. From Vancouver its trans-Pacific steamships connect with Japan, China and Australia, while from Montreal and Quebec in summer, and from Halifax and Saint John in winter, its vessels run to Great Britain and Europe. In this way, service is rendered by one company for two-thirds of the distance around the globe, and, along with its oceanic steamers, it claims with justice to be the greatest transportation agency in the world.

The second transcontinental was the Canadian Northern. It was begun in 1896 with the construction by Messrs Mackenzie and Mann of the 125-mile line from Portage-la-Prairie northward in Manitoba. The province of Manitoba guaranteed the railway's bonds and gave exemption from taxation, for it was eager to see competition established with the Canadian Pacific. From this time onward, largely by construction but also by lease, the Company developed a great system of lines in the Prairie Provinces and in 1902 extended its road to Port Arthur, at the head of Lake Superior. Not content to be a successful system of wheat-gathering roads in the interior of the West, the Company sought an outlet to the Pacific Ocean, which it obtained by a line chartered by the province of British Columbia. Its next objective was to build eastward from Port Arthur to the port of Montreal, with the purpose of completing its transcontinental line and linking it up with the few eastern sections of railway which it controlled. Probably no other such extensive work of railway-building has ever been undertaken by two men; and the business enterprise and political sagacity and strategy which they displayed were phenomenal. But before they had their transcontinental line completed they were overtaken by misfortune, the nature of which will soon appear.[1]

The third transcontinental railway was projected by the Grand Trunk. About the end of last century this railway began to look to the rapidly growing West with its increasing trade, especially in grain, as a fruitful territory to enter. It desired a share of the through trade, from which the Canadian Pacific was securing large revenues, and planned to open up new traffic areas in the northern part of the

---

[1] See further details in Jackman, W. T., *Economics of Transportation*, pp. 24–7; also *Canada Year Book*, 1925, pp. 589–90.

Prairie Provinces. Accordingly, its president, the late Charles M. Hays, sought a charter from Parliament for the construction of a line from North Bay, Ontario, *via* Winnipeg, to the north Pacific Coast, together with government aid to the extent of $6400 and 5000 acres of land per mile of line. The Government endeavoured to get the Canadian Northern, which had a good network of lines in the West, and the Grand Trunk, which had complete connections in the East, to join in forming one transcontinental railway; but the parties concerned could not agree and each set out to build its own transcontinental line. Instead of giving the Grand Trunk what it desired, the Government had a more ambitious project and made an agreement with this company that there should be a through line constructed from Moncton, New Brunswick, to the Pacific Coast; that the Grand Trunk, through its subsidiary, the Grand Trunk Pacific, should build with government assistance the western part of this line from Winnipeg to the Pacific at Prince Rupert, and that the eastern portion from Winnipeg through northern Ontario and Quebec, *via* Quebec city to Moncton, called the National Transcontinental, should be built by the Government.[1] Then, when the latter was finished, it was to be taken over for operation on a 50-year lease by the Grand Trunk Pacific, free for the first seven years, and thereafter at an annual rental equal to 3 per cent. of the cost of construction. To aid the Grand Trunk Pacific, the Government agreed to guarantee the interest on the Company's bonds to 75 per cent. of the cost of construction, but not to exceed $13,000 per mile for the prairie section, and $30,000 per mile for the mountain section. In 1904 this limitation was removed in the case of the mountain section, so that the Government became liable for a bond guarantee up to 75 per cent. of the cost of constructing that section.

The cost of building the Grand Trunk Pacific was much greater than had been anticipated owing to several causes: first, the road was built very substantially, as if it were passing through a well-developed territory with abundant traffic; second, owing to the advance in prices of commodities generally, the cost of the materials for the railway had greatly increased; third, owing to the great demand for labour in building the Grand Trunk Pacific at the same time as the Canadian Northern, the wages bill was swollen far beyond expectation; and, fourth, the road had been so long under construction that there was a large amount of accumulated interest due and unpaid.[2] Similarly, the cost of construction of the National Transcontinental was greatly inflated. The original estimate of its cost was $61,415,000; but when the cost reached $159,881,197, the Grand Trunk Pacific objected to carrying out its agreement. The Government, by accept-

---

[1] Dominion Act 3 Edw. VII, cap. 122.
[2] Down to 1 Jan. 1916, when the road was officially opened, this accumulated interest amounted to $26,938,139. *Report of Railway Inquiry Commission*, 1917, p. xxv.

ing the Company's refusal and commencing to work the line itself, in effect released the Company unconditionally.[1]

In 1914 all of the great railway systems except the Canadian Pacific were in financial embarrassment. The Canadian Northern had built too rapidly, so that the paying parts of the system were not able to carry the financial burden of the non-revenue-producing parts, and its heavy commitments for construction made it necessary to find large amounts of capital, upon which it was not likely to be able to pay interest, without assistance, for some years. The Grand Trunk Pacific had been receiving annual aid for several years from the Government to pay its fixed charges and a portion of its operating expenses, for the earnings of the parent Grand Trunk Railway were not sufficient to meet the financial requirements of its subsidiary.[2] If the Grand Trunk Railway could have been freed of the Grand Trunk Pacific, it would have been solvent; but since it was unable to meet or to repudiate this obligation, it had to share the bankrupt condition of the subsidiary line. Moreover, Grand Trunk earnings, amounting on the average to $3,600,000 annually, which should have gone to the upkeep of its property and the payment of its indebtedness on account of the Grand Trunk Pacific, were drained off illegally by authority of the London directorate to pay dividends to the stockholders in England.[3] With the outbreak of the war and the cessation of the preceding good times, the condition of these railways became critical. The money markets of the world were closed to private railway financing and the Canadian Northern came again to the Dominion Government for assistance. This was given, in 1914, in the form of a bond guarantee of the Company's securities amounting to $45,000,000, on the distinct understanding that the Company would be able to get the rest of the capital to complete its undertaking; but the Company was unable to realise its expectations, and in 1916 it came once more to the Government for aid. This was refused. Instead, the Government appointed a commission of three competent men to report upon the whole railway situation. The members of the commission were agreed that, since the Canadian Pacific was a strong road, it should be allowed to continue as it was; but concerning the disposition of the other roads opinion was divided. One suggested a plan for continuing the principle of private ownership, while the other two did not see any satisfactory way in which this could be accomplished. Instead, the latter, in their majority report, stated that the stockholders of the Canadian Northern had no equity in their property and since the people of Canada had found or assumed responsibility for the bulk of the capital, and would have to meet operating deficits and provide what further capital was needed, the

[1] *Ibid.* p. xxiii. The fuller history of this and the other roads is given in Jackman, *Economics of Transportation*, chs. i and xviii.   [2] See Jackman, ch. xviii.
[3] *Report of Railway Inquiry Commission*, 1917, pp. lxiv–lxv.

people should assume control of the property. The financial condition of the Grand Trunk and Grand Trunk Pacific was such that these two lines also should be surrendered into the hands of the people, who really owned them because of the financial assistance given to them. On account of these facts, the majority report suggested that the Government should take charge of these roads and hand them over for working to a board of trustees constituted as the Dominion Railway Company. The latter was to be a private company and its member trustees, to be appointed by the Government, were to be a "permanent, self-perpetuating body" and should not assume, or even be suspected of assuming, a political complexion.[1] To these railways the majority recommended that there should be added the National Transcontinental and the Intercolonial, so that all the government-owned roads should be worked under one administration. It is the carrying out of this plan, with all its modifications and deviations, which constitutes the railway history since 1917. At first in that year the Canadian Northern was taken over and worked by the former officers but under a new Board of Management. In March 1919 the Grand Trunk Pacific was taken over under receivership, and in October of the same year the Grand Trunk became the property of the Government. All these lines are now worked by the Canadian National Railways, organised as a private company under the Act of 1919.[2] The financial results from the consolidation of these lines have shown a progressive improvement, but along with this there has been a vast increase of the railway debt, incurred for capital expenditures, for the payment of interest on the debt and for the adjustment of interest payments upon interest accrued, due and unpaid. The indications are that it will be a long time before the people cease to make up in taxation the deficits of these lines which they now own.[3]

The present financial problems of the country through its ownership of these roads are directly attributable to the fact that there are more competitive east-and-west lines than are justified on economic grounds. Had purely business reasons controlled policy, the inevitable result would have been the construction of north-and-south lines to bring the railways into relation with the products of other climates and the large industrial centres of the adjoining country. But successive Canadian Governments have sought to promote national unity within the British Empire and, with this object in view, have encouraged transport, communication and trade by all-Canadian routes. As a consequence of this allegiance and the advancement of sovereignty, the railways were founded upon other than strictly economic principles, and their rates and operation show examples of the same forces at work to-day.

[1] *Report of Railway Inquiry Commission,* 1917, pp. lii, liii.
[2] Dominion Act 9–10 Geo. V, cap. 13.
[3] For a more complete study see Jackman, *Economics of Transportation,* ch. xviii.

(II) AGRICULTURE

The development of Canadian agriculture since confederation presents an interesting study. The increase in rural population has been small, but Canada has gradually acquired prominence among the contributors to the world's food supply. The general character and extent of its agricultural progress are illustrated in the following figures. In 1871[1] the area of improved land was 17,335,818 acres, in 1921[2] it had increased to 70,769,548 acres. Similarly, the area of occupied land increased from 36,016,401 to 140,887,903 acres during the same period, and the value of field crops, which in 1870 was placed at $111,116,606 (£22,223,000), by 1920 had risen to $963,045,936 (£192,609,000).

Canadian wheat production has grown with remarkable rapidity. In 1871 the wheat crop was 16,723,873 bushels. Most of this was produced in the Province of Ontario, but with the development of the great Prairie Provinces the total production had by 1915 reached 393,542,600 bushels. Wheat, however, is not the only grain crop of importance; the oat crop is also of large proportions, for though in 1871 oat production was 42,489,463 bushels, the crop of 1921 was 364,989,218 bushels. Barley, rye, mixed grains, hay, sugar beet and potatoes are other field crops produced in considerable quantity on a wide range of Canadian farms.

Of dairy products, Canadian butter, cheese, condensed and powdered milk are now of considerable importance. In 1870 the value of such products was only $15,023,968. In 1920 the value of the output of dairy factories alone amounted to $146,336,491.[3] For many years cheese was the great export product from dairy factories, but with the expansion of the fluid milk trade, the development of the ice-cream industry and the establishment of condensed and powdered milk factories, the quantity of cheese produced and exported has declined. With respect to the live-stock industry, the number of cattle sold or slaughtered in 1871 was given as 507,725. This number had increased approximately four-fold in 1921, when 2,097,390 cattle were marketed. The number of hogs sold or slaughtered has more than doubled in the same period, while the number of sheep sold or slaughtered has increased about twelve-fold. In regard to fruit, the production of apples has increased from 6,365,315 bushels in 1870 to 17,485,895 bushels in 1921, and other fruits and vegetables show greater increase than the apple crop. In the commercial canning of fruits and vegetables, in which 210 plants were engaged in 1921, an entirely new industry has developed since 1867.

Canadian agriculture thus shows a large increase in production,

---

[1] *Census of Canada*, 1870–1.   [2] *Ibid.* 1921.
[3] *Dairy Factories Report*, 1920 (Dominion Bureau of Statistics).

yet without remarkable increase in population. The rural population in 1871 was 3,003,238 and only 4,436,361 in 1921. There were approximately 367,862 farms in 1871 and 711,090 in 1921, and the occupied area increased more than five-fold during the same time. Only four provinces contributed to agricultural production in 1871, but in 1921 nine provinces had been opened up, including the vast wheat lands of the prairies. It is also interesting to observe that the average size of farm in 1871 was 97·9 acres, while in 1921 it was 197·97 acres, and further, while the value of field crops per farm was $302 in 1871, it was $1312 in 1921. Improvements in agricultural technique have undoubtedly aided in this increase in farm revenues. Finally, the importance of agriculture in Canadian economic life is seen in the fact that in 1920 agriculture contributed 41·3 per cent. of the estimated net value of production in the various provinces of the Dominion, while manufacturing contributed 32·7 per cent.[1]

In 1867 Canadian agriculture had reached the end of a period of prosperity which had begun in the early 'fifties, but with the cessation of the Civil War in the United States and the termination of the reciprocal trade agreement, Canadian farm products found fewer profitable outlets. Moreover, in many areas the second stage of pioneer life had been reached, the soil having lost some of its fertility; while live-stock enterprises, though of growing importance, had not attained large proportions. This was a transition stage in which the search for new markets took a prominent place. The decade 1871–81 was not encouraging. In this time of waning prosperity and financial crisis,[2] there arrived many immigrants filled with high hopes of rapid returns, but possessing little experience in the ways of a new country. Dissatisfaction showed itself in the organisation of the Grange.[3] This society had been established in the United States in 1868 by Oliver H. Kelly and his associates in the Federal Department of Agriculture, who sought to found among farmers a fraternal organisation for the solution of their economic and social problems. After varying fortunes it achieved a certain measure of economic success, especially in the Middle West. In Canada conditions were ripe for the establishment of such an organisation. The first Grange was constituted at Stanstead, Quebec, in 1872.[4] It spread to Ontario and there attained the greatest strength and importance. Briefly the Grangers proposed meeting together, talking together, working together and selling together. Of their economic programme, it is possible to give only the merest glimpse. At the outset the secretary of the local Grange assembled orders for goods which were transmitted direct to manufacturers who offered special prices to Grange members; when this system was

[1] *Canada Year Book*, 1922–3.
[2] *Vide* the section following.
[3] Wood, L. A., *A History of Farmers' Movements in Canada.*   [4] *Ibid.*

applied for the purchase of goods it was extended to implements; but the secretary soon tired of giving his services voluntarily. The Grange Wholesale Supply Company was organised with its headquarters at Napanee. Later, because of enlarged business, it moved to Toronto. The Ontario Salt and Soda Company was organised in 1882, an Insurance Company was formed in 1877, a Trust and Loan Company in 1879. None of these ventures was especially successful. Though the economic programme of the Grange failed because of internal strife, poor business management and ill-conceived ideas of business procedure, yet its social effects were permanent. Members met in school houses, or built halls in which to hold their meetings. In either case improvement in the community facilities resulted. Whereas farms had been isolated and social contacts all too few, the Grange gave the farmers and their wives something for which to come together. Community bonds were thus established. Moreover, the master of a Grange and his subordinate officers were persons of local importance. The Grange reached its greatest strength in 1879, when the membership was estimated to be 31,000. Though the Grange still lives, it is now largely supplanted by the "United Farmer" organisations. Its significance lies in the fact that it was an early attempt to improve the farmer's economic position by organisation.

In 1867 the farmer's calling was largely self-sufficient. His farm had been secured either direct from the Crown or through a land company, a few of which had been organised to develop the land, as, for example, the Canada Company, which developed a large part of Western Ontario. The farms might be said to have been of family size, the determining factor being how much land the settler could clear in a reasonable period. Soon farmers in Eastern Canada began to feel the effects of competition in grain-growing, through the development of the western United States, where land ready for the plough could be secured at nominal rates; in fact, as the Canadian West was still inaccessible, many farmers moved across the border.

Early in this period, hand methods of farming were still the rule, though the introduction of improved machinery was rapid during the 'seventies, for it is known that in Ontario in 1881 improved farm machinery was being used on 71 per cent. of the farms.[1] An examination of the records of a large implement manufacturing company shows the development of agricultural machinery in Canada.[2] In 1852 the Ketchum mower, the first to be made in Canada, was placed on the market. It was closely followed by the Burrell reaper. Again, in 1855, the "Manny" combined hand-rake reaper and mower was brought into use, and in 1863 the first self-rake reaper ever made in Canada was produced. According to the records of this company ploughs were made as early as 1846 by

[1] *Ontario Agricultural Commission Report*, 1881.
[2] Harris, M., *An Historical Sketch*, 1846–1926.

Elder John Harris, who settled on a farm near Brantford in that year. Even in 1867 the cutting of grain by other means than the cradle was new, but in 1869 a superior reaper was produced. This was a self-rake reaper, and in the same year the first steel rake was invented. Seven years later Sharp's horse dump-rake was placed on the market and in 1876 the first Canadian patent for a self-binder was granted, and the self-binder was complete by 1880. Before this date machines such as root pulpers and clover threshers were employed, and since this date the improvement in machinery has been rapid. Hay-loaders came into general use about the beginning of the present century. Tractors were not common in Eastern Canada until just prior to 1914. During the war they were largely used and to-day have established themselves as adaptable equipment on many farms. The Canadian farmer has acquired an automobile only in the last decade, but now-a-days the farmer who does not own an inexpensive car is behind the times. The distribution of electrical energy to farmers is making considerable progress in Ontario, but as yet only a minority are thus equipped.

The Canadian farmer, generally speaking, maintains a high standard of living, which has steadily risen. His food is probably of the same quality as in the early part of this period, but when we consider the advance in communication, his present opportunities may readily be appreciated. Rural mail delivery and telephones are almost universal, and both tend to offset the isolated position of the farm home. Road improvement, along with the replacement of the wagon, the democrat, and the buggy by the automobile, has brought the farmer much closer to the larger centres of trade, so that the goods and services which affect his standard of living are of higher quality.

Farming methods in Eastern Canada contrast with those in the Prairie Provinces. The farms in Western Canada are much larger than in Eastern Canada on account of the type of farming and the ease with which mechanical power can be applied to the more level lands in the wheat-growing regions. The use of tractors is more extensive on the prairies than in the East, and the number of horses per team is larger as well, for the implements are of greater capacity. Where the Ontario farmer might use a 6½ ft. cut binder, the Western farmer uses nothing less than an 8 ft. binder, and in the case of the combine it may be one of 15 ft.[1] When land is first broken on the prairie, the sod must be allowed to rot before a crop can be sown, and most farmers endeavour to get this work done before the middle of July. Many farmers in Western Canada do not plough their stubble land before seeding, but use heavy discs or cultivators to prepare the seed bed. Another practice is that of burning the stubble in the spring. This can of course only be followed in a new country where the land

[1] Hopkins, E. S. and Newman, L. H., *The Organisation...of the Experimental Farms*, p. 34.

is very fertile, and it is not adopted in Eastern Canada. In those parts of the West that have been settled for the longest period, mixed farming has become a necessity for the maintenance of fertility and the control of weeds.

In Western Canada the rainfall is not so great as in the East, therefore one of the western farmers' problems is to conserve moisture. This is more true in certain sections than in others. In fact in south-western Alberta irrigated lands have been offered for sale, and in both Saskatchewan and Alberta dry-farming conferences are held regularly. In Western Canada the summer fallow is still an effective means of controlling weeds, retaining moisture and improving the tilth of the soil. It has been largely discarded in Eastern Canada because farmers have discovered that by using hoe crops the land can be cleaned and at the same time losses due to the idleness of the land for the whole season can be overcome. In the West cereals are the most important crops. The system of farming is still that of the cash crop. In the East live-stock products, particularly dairy pro-ducts, are the important sources of income. The average farmer succeeds better when he develops some side-lines.

The development of rotations in Western Canada is still in the embryonic stage. In Eastern Canada—Ontario, for example—the better dairy farms are worked on a four-year rotation: (1) corn or mangolds, (2) oats and barley seeded with clover and timothy, (3) hay or pasture two years, with alfalfa not included in this regular rotation, but grown on a large scale. In the mixed farming areas longer rotations are the rule. Corn for ensilage, potatoes, turnips or mangolds, may constitute the first year's crop. The second year's crop may be either barley or mixed grain (oats and barley); with it would be sown clover and timothy. The third may be a crop of hay, and the following year the field would be pastured. The pro-cedure varies somewhat; for corn and potato some farmers prefer to plough up a green clover sod.

In harvesting grain the western farm methods are more spectacular than those in the East. The western farmer has to face a shorter season and since there is less space allotted to buildings the general practice is to stook the grain and then thresh it as soon as possible. The hazards in the West are greater than in the East, where the grain is cut, stooked and allowed to stand for several days until the moisture content is lowered beyond the danger point, when the sheaves are hauled into the barns. At a convenient time the threshing is done with the help of neighbours, a threshing machine being hired. In the West, stook-threshing is the rule. Usually the thresher provides the labour and most of the equipment, the operations being carried out on a large scale. The use of commercial fertilisers is, generally speaking, on the increase in the East, particularly in those areas where fruits and vegetables are produced, but even on dairy and the so-called "mixed" farms, the use of special fertilisers is coming to be recognised as essential, though the fertility of the land is still largely maintained through the application of farm manure and the ploughing down of leguminous crops.

Crop improvement in Canada is very closely associated with the names of two great experimentalists—Dr Charles E. Saunders, formerly of Ottawa,[1] and Dr C. A. Zavitz, formerly of the Ontario Agricultural College. Dr Charles Saunders, who was appointed Dominion Cerealist in 1903, was responsible for the development of new varieties of wheat. Early in the development of the West, the Red Fife variety was largely grown, but it required a relatively long season in which to mature, which was an objection particularly in the northern sections of the Western Provinces. If the wheat regions were to expand, early maturing varieties had to be found. The cereal breeding work at Ottawa was then under the direction of Dr William Saunders and he undertook to develop new varieties. First, a variety named Ladoga was secured from Russia. Unfortunately, though earlier maturing, the baking qualities were not very high. Failure to secure a better variety through importations resulted in attempts at cross breeding. From various crosses were secured Huron, Percy Stanley and Preston wheats, which, though their baking qualities were not high, enabled farmers who otherwise could not have grown wheat to do so and thus increase their returns. Dr Charles Saunders in 1903 crossed Red Fife and Hard Red Calcutta; the result was "Marquis". This new wheat has become the standard wheat in Western Canada and large acreages have been sown in the United States. It is not only early maturing, but also produces a flour of high baking quality. This is not the only improvement in cereal production, but the total resulting profit has amounted to millions of dollars.

In 1886[2] Dr Charles A. Zavitz began to develop new and improved varieties of crops. Among his more noted strains have been O.A.C. No. 21 Barley, O.A.C. No. 104 Wheat, and O.A.C. Nos. 72 and 144 Oats. Besides the development of these new varieties important work in breeding and selection in other crops has been carried on. The O.A.C. No. 21 barley is a selection from Mandscheuri barley which was made in 1903. In 1906 it was distributed to farmers co-operating with Dr Zavitz in the experimental work, and since then has become the most widely grown variety of barley. In the same year that O.A.C. No. 21 barley was selected from among its competitors, a large number of seeds of a variety of oats which had been imported from Siberia were sown. From among the plants was selected one which became the parent of the O.A.C. No. 72 variety, which is now

[1] Hopkins, E. S. and Newman, L. H., *The Organisation...of the Experimental Farms*, pp. 88 ff.

[2] Zavitz, C. A., *Forty Years Experiments with Grain Crops* (Ontario Dept. of Agriculture—Bulletin no. 332).

largely sown, particularly in western Ontario. While this variety does not mature earlier than the banner, another good variety of oats, it has a lower percentage of hull and a higher yield per acre. The 144 oat is an earlier maturing oat, particularly useful for crop mixtures. In much of this work of breeding and selection Dr Zavitz was ably assisted by the late Cecil R. Klinck.

Though Western Canada produces most of Canada's wheat, yet fall-sown wheat is still an important cash crop in Ontario. For many years the White Dawson variety was the most popular. In 1882 Robert Dawson selected a plant from his field and the seed grown from this plant resulted in the development of Dawson Golden Chaff. Later on this wheat was crossed with Bulgarian and the O.A.C. 104 was the result.

In the improvement of crops no more important step has ever been made than in the importation of alfalfa seed from Lorraine and Baden, Germany.[1] The first of these importations was indirect, two pounds of alfalfa seed being secured from New York State by Nathaniel Bethel of Welland County in 1871. The seed thus obtained had originally been brought from Lorraine. Bethel and his neighbours have been growing alfalfa of this variety ever since. Again, in 1875, Dr Colver who had a farm in Lincoln County imported seed from Baden, and not only sowed seed himself but distributed some among his neighbours. The blossoms on the plants in both cases are variegated in colour; consequently the variety has become known as the "Ontario variegated". It has proved to be most successful in Ontario and the acreage of alfalfa has very largely increased.

Dairy farming has been and still is one of the most important types of farming in Canada. The factory system of making cheese was introduced into Oxford County in Ontario in 1864 and the system rapidly spread to eastern Ontario, particularly Hastings County. The condensed and powdered milk business was first undertaken in Canada at Truro, Nova Scotia, in 1883.[2] There were in 1920 twenty-eight such plants in Canada. The first creamery was established at Athelstane in Quebec in 1873, and the first cream separator used in the country was imported from Denmark in 1882 and used in Quebec. These improvements in handling milk gave a great impetus to dairy farming, so that in every province dairying is an important source of income. In Nova Scotia, the chief areas of dairy production are in the vicinity of Halifax and Truro. The bulk of the dairy production in this province is in the form of butter, though the whole milk and condensed milk are also important.

In the Province of Quebec dairying is probably the most important system of farming. Some of the finest dairy farms in the Dominion are to be found around Howick, Ormstown, Huntingdon, Lachute

---

[1] Zavitz, C. A., *Alfalfa* (Ont. Dept. of Agric., Bulletin no. 280).
[2] *Dairy Factories Report*, 1920 (Dominion Bureau of Statistics).

and St Hyacinthe. While the greatest amount of milk is converted into cheese and butter, the cities of Montreal, Quebec, Three Rivers and Sherbrooke require large quantities of whole milk, and within recent years farmers well situated have found an outlet for cream in markets of the New England States. The development of dairying in Quebec may be indicated by the fact that in 1881[1] there were 162 butter and cheese factories; in 1911, 3041; in 1920, 1809.[2] The falling off in numbers does not indicate a decrease in volume of production, but rather an increase in output per factory.

In Ontario all the territory east of Trenton may be said to be devoted to dairying. In this region, cheese production reigns supreme. The soils in the central part of the region are rather shallow and the country somewhat rolling, so that the production of milk during the summer months has been the chief occupation of the people. The growing season though somewhat short is characterised by very rapid growth, providing abundance of pasture and roughage so essential to the success of a dairy farm. The central counties find a ready market for their milk in the city of Toronto.

In western Ontario, dairying centres largely in Oxford County and in the surrounding counties. For many years Oxford County has been considered to be the leading dairy county in the west of the province, and farmers in this county are regarded as the pioneers in dairying in that section. Whole milk is supplied to the city of Toronto and a large volume of cheese is produced, as well as pure bred cattle.

In the three Prairie Provinces dairying has been overshadowed by the production of cereals, as may be seen in the factory development. In Manitoba in 1900 there were only twenty-six creameries and forty cheese factories.[3] In 1920, while the creameries had increased to forty-four, the cheese factories had been reduced to four.[4] These figures and similar figures for the other provinces indicate that, while the dairy industry is increasing in importance, it will clearly be in the direction of butter production, because at the moment the distances are too great to permit the economical transportation of whole milk to cheese factories. In British Columbia some high-producing herds have been developed, and the dairy industry is well established, particularly in the Fraser Valley. This province is also the home of the most successful co-operative dairy in the Dominion.

Beef cattle form an important source of revenue for many farmers. Such cattle are not fed in large numbers in the Maritime Provinces, or in Quebec, though some excellent herds are to be found in both districts. In Ontario, Alberta, Saskatchewan and Manitoba, how-

[1] Chapais, J. E., in *Canada and its Provinces*, xvi, 505-70.
[2] *Dairy Factories Report*, 1920 (Dominion Bureau of Statistics).
[3] Ruddick, J. A., in *Canada and its Provinces*, vii, 651-74.
[4] *Dairy Factories Report*, 1920 (Dominion Bureau of Statistics).

ever, special areas are to be found where they are the sole source of income.

Ontario claims to be the home of good live-stock and has in fact been the breeding ground of this industry. The foundations of the live-stock business were laid in the period 1830–60, when English and Scotch settlers from good farming counties in the old land came to the wilderness to seek their fortune. Many of the migrants of the 'thirties had some capital and they were not long in this country before they saw the necessity of better live-stock. Noteworthy among these pioneers were the Millers of York County, F. W. Stone in Wellington County, Hon. John Brown in Brant County. In 1876 the Ontario Agricultural College introduced Aberdeen Angus cattle into Canada. These counties are still noted as centres of breeding and feeding live-stock, while Waterloo County, the north-western section of Middlesex, the County of Lambton and part of Kent, as well as Ontario and Durham Counties, east of the city of Toronto, now also play an important part in the industry.

In Western Canada the range conditions of the olden days are almost gone. Even in the Peace River country this is true. The ranching industry in Alberta was first established about 1879, when the Dominion Government brought 1000 head of breeding stock from the Montana ranges[1] to the foot hills of the Rockies about Fort MacLeod. The effort to demonstrate the possibilities of ranching in the West was successful enough to attract numerous ranchers with capital to establish holdings, but the industry had a hard struggle for some years. Those pioneer ranchers were a long distance from market, for there was at that date no railway, but after 1883, when transport became available, the industry rapidly expanded. The cattle were usually four years old when marketed, and with reasonably capable handling returned their owners satisfactory profits, even when exported to Great Britain. These were strictly range cattle; the losses due to the severity of the weather were at times large, particularly where the owners were careless or failed to provide supplies sufficient to support the cattle on a maintenance ration. It was, however, a spectacular development in Canadian agriculture. Even in 1908 there were 939 grazing leases in effect, covering 3,259,271 acres of land, of which 2,132,718 acres were in the Province of Alberta. In north-eastern and northern Saskatchewan the semi-ranching system prevails. The cattle in these areas are allowed to run in herds on fenced lands during the summer, and provided with cheap housing for the winter, where they are fed on hay and straw. In central Alberta and a large part of Manitoba, cattle in small herds are fed largely on the same systems as obtain in the mixed farming areas of Ontario, with the exception that corn silage is not used to any extent.

[1] Rutherford, J. G., *The Cattle Trade of Western Canada*. Special Report to the Dominion Department of Agriculture.

The "Western" cattle market was opened at Toronto in 1875.[1] It was, however, fifteen years before many shipments from the Western Provinces were received at these yards. The Harris Company in 1896 established the first beef-packing plant adjacent to this market. In the Western Provinces, the P. Burns Company, Gordon, Ironsides and Fares have been the pioneers. In 1871 there were 193 establishments slaughtering and packing meat, employing 841 people; in 1921 only 84, but these employed 7225 persons.[2] Consolidation and integration of business had taken place. Improvements in transportation and refrigeration have also meant much in the development of the cattle industry.

The swine industry in Canada has experienced many ups and downs within the last thirty years. The principal object has been to produce the Wiltshire side, which is so favoured on the English market. With this in view the majority of hog raisers have kept the bacon type, and probably the Yorkshire is the most popular breed. This type of hog was first introduced into Canada between 1878 and 1880.[3] The Brethours of Burford, Green and William Davies, were among the earliest importers of the Yorkshire breed. The Berkshire was imported to the Island of Montreal at a much earlier date, while Tamworths were first imported at the same time as the Yorkshires. Investigations carried on by the Dominion and Provincial Governments have shown the desirability of concentrating on this type of hog. The exports of Canadian hams and sides in 1921 were valued at $31,492,402.

The sheep industry is well distributed throughout the various provinces. The great sheep ranches are found in south-western Saskatchewan, southern Alberta and the interior of British Columbia. Despite this the provinces of Ontario and Quebec have most sheep. The total number in Canada in 1920 was estimated to be 3,720,783.[4] Of this number more than two million were in the provinces of Ontario and Quebec, where the flocks are small, the average farmer having possibly a dozen sheep, though some flocks of fifty or more are to be found. While the long wool breeds and most of the short wool breeds are found in Canada, the Shropshire, Leicester and Oxford are the most popular, the tendency being to favour the short wool breeds. The consumption of mutton in Canada is relatively not large, and a great many farmers raise sheep as a purely supplementary enterprise. In Quebec a large percentage of the wool produced is still used by the farmer's family in the manufacture of clothing. In the other provinces, however, except in isolated cases, wool is produced for sale. The climate of Canada is such that the merino type of sheep is not produced in large numbers, and as a

[1] Todd, S. E., "Making our Live-Stock Industry", *Farmers' Advocate*, 30 June 1927.
[2] *Slaughtering*, etc. 1921 (Dominion Bureau of Statistics).
[3] Todd, S. E., *loc. cit.*
[4] *Canada Year Book*, 1921.

result most Canadian wools are exported either to the United States or to England, our woollen mills importing wools of the type desired. There would seem, however, to be room for expansion of this industry in Canada, particularly in view of the fact that sheep growers now have facilities for selling their wool according to standardised grades, which compare favourably with those in other countries.[1]

Passing over the raising of poultry, which is generally a side-line on farms, we note that the production of fruits and vegetables has assumed importance in many provinces. Nova Scotia, Ontario and British Columbia have gained fame for their fruits, while Prince Edward Island, New Brunswick and Ontario have made rapid strides in developing potato production.[2] Fruit production is not of large proportion in Quebec, but certain sections adjacent to the St Lawrence and Ottawa Rivers produce apples of fine quality, the Fameuse and MacIntosh Red being the most popular varieties. Moreover, on the Island of Montreal, vegetables of very fine quality are grown. Though the snowfall is heavy, the growing season is long, and thus this area has become famous for its melons and vegetables. Owing to the expansion of Montreal city, there has recently been a tendency for farmers to move south and east of Montreal, though a few have gone to the north shore of the St Lawrence. In Ontario fruits and vegetables are produced in various sections. The Ontario Fruit Growers' Association was organised in 1859 and has been a vital force in improving methods of production. The chief areas of apple production are: (1) the counties of Prince Edward, Northumberland and Durham, (2) those counties lying between Toronto and Hamilton, and Norfolk County in the south-west, (3) those sections of Simcoe and Grey Counties lying between Collingwood and Owen Sound. Vegetable production is carried on extensively in the vicinity of Wellington in Prince Edward County and all along the shore of Lake Ontario to Niagara Falls, very intensive methods being employed about Leamington in Essex County and Blenheim in Kent. Other areas such as Elgin and Norfolk Counties produce quantities of vegetables, and celery growing is a well established business near Thedford.

As regards fruit and vegetables, the Prairie Provinces are consuming areas. Nothing can compare with wheat or cattle. The rancher and the grain farmer would scorn to trouble about crops requiring the care and attention that fruit and vegetables need. They want to do things on a large scale. British Columbia, on the other hand, is a large producer of fruit and vegetables, particularly in the Okanagan Valley. Much of the production in this area is on irrigated lands. The long distance which the fruit must travel to market affects the net return to the grower.

[1] Dryden, W. A. and Ritch, W. T., *The Sheep Industry in Canada, United States and Great Britain.* [2] See chapter xxvii for the Maritime Provinces.

Even after confederation—1867—the surplus production on many farms was small, and those farms tended to supply their own requirements for food and clothing. The small surplus of butter and eggs was usually taken to the country store and sold for cash or trade—mostly trade, for the storekeeper apparently was anxious to handle the produce. The prices of these farm products were always from 2 to 3 cents higher in terms of merchandise than in money. Very frequently merchants tendered due bills for produce; for example, if a farmer's wife brought in produce valued in goods at five dollars, but at the time she only needed goods to the value of two dollars, the merchant would give her due bills equivalent to three dollars. These could be tendered to this merchant at another time for goods. The due bills were not accepted generally, being a medium of exchange only between the merchant and his customer. This method of exchange was in vogue even at the beginning of the twentieth century in certain parts of Ontario. The country storekeeper thus assembled farm products which he shipped to a wholesaler or a broker in a large centre, such as Toronto. Many farmers also marketed their produce direct. Thus, in the fall of the year farmers might haul loads of potatoes twenty or twenty-five miles to a town where they would sell direct to storekeepers or to householders. Wheat, barley and peas were hauled long distances to small mills which processed these products or in turn sold them to larger operators.

In the early days much live-stock was sold dressed, because it could be transported more easily, and almost every farmer was able to do his own butchering. The cattle which were sold alive often had to be driven many miles, which reduced profits. In some parts of Ontario it was the custom to hold fairs. Until quite recently "horse fairs" were held in many small towns. They were usually held monthly, the horses being shown for sale on the square or on the main street. With the rise of motor transport, the horse fair has declined in importance.

The surplus which the farmer had to sell gradually increased: in 1881 a farmer in Hastings County from a farm of 180 acres sold barley to the value of $4500. A net income of $5000 was common on this farm even in those days. The increase in the surplus demanded more outlets and led to specialisation in handling farm products; hence the middleman system was extended. The tendency has been to use the services of the wholesaler, broker and commission merchant to a large extent. The auction system has never been very popular in Canada, although auctions take place at Montreal and Winnipeg. Public markets have been and still are important distributing agencies.

At the beginning of this century, farmers in Western Canada made a determined stand in favour of better marketing facilities.[1] The

---

[1] Booth, J. F., *Co-operative Marketing of Grain in Western Canada* (U.S. Dept. of Agriculture,

railway companies and the elevator companies failed to provide adequate facilities for the handling of grain. The western farmer, therefore, formed an organisation known as the Grain Growers' Association which undertook to secure revision of the legislation regulating the Canadian grain trade. As these efforts, though successful in large measure, did not secure all the advantages desired, the Grain Growers' Grain Company was organised in 1905. This company was successful from the beginning and extended its selling and elevator business over the three Prairie Provinces, though it had relatively little business in Saskatchewan, because in 1911 the Saskatchewan Co-operative Elevator Company was established, as a result of the report of a special local committee of enquiry. The latter company originally set out to provide elevator service for Saskatchewan farmers. Its selling activities developed later. The success of these companies created a demand in Alberta for a similar organisation to aid the Alberta wheat growers, which was finally provided by the Alberta Co-operative Elevator Company in 1913. This company was, however, not so successful as the older companies and it merged with the Grain Growers' Grain Company in 1917 as the United Grain Growers, Limited, which has been an outstanding success. In this connection it is worthy of mention that the grain market at Winnipeg is one of the largest in the world. The grain exchange handled a business of 1,446,892,500 bushels in 1921.[1]

Farmers have not confined their efforts to co-operative marketing of grain. In British Columbia practically all the fluid milk handled in New Westminster and Vancouver is sold through a co-operative company, which also manufactures butter and cheese, as well as condensed milk and casein. The Okanagan United Growers of Vernon, B.C., handle most of the apples shipped from British Columbia. In Ontario the United Dairymen's Co-operative, Limited, organised in 1920, has introduced the principle of selling cheese on grade and by auction. The Saskatchewan Co-operative Creamery Company was established in 1917. Its turn-over in 1921 was $3,500,000.

The United Farmers of Ontario conduct an extensive business, in which live-stock, poultry and eggs, as well as grain in large quantities are handled, and they possess the largest creamery in the province, having taken over the Toronto Creamery Company.

One of the most successful co-operative companies in Canada is the Canadian Co-operative Wool Growers, Limited, which handles wool from about 12,000 flocks in the Dominion. This company was organised in 1918 to provide a wool growers' selling agency, and in 1920

Technical Bulletin no. 63); Clark, W. C., *The Country Elevator in the Canadian West* (Bulletin of the Departments of History, etc., Queen's University, Kingston); Fay, C. R., *Co-operation in the Canadian West*; MacKintosh, W. A., *Agricultural Co-operation in Western Canada*; Moorehouse, Hopkins, *Deep Furrows*.
[1] *The Royal Grain Commission Report*, 1925.

handled 3,943,923 pounds.[1] In the Province of Quebec several successful companies have been formed, though Quebec's great contribution to co-operation has been in providing credit facilities. In 1900 Alphonse Des Jardins of Levis organised La Caisse Populaire, which has helped many farmers, as well as townspeople, in times of financial stress. In the Maritime Provinces, the most outstanding co-operative company is the United Fruit Company of Nova Scotia, with headquarters at Kentsville. This company, which was founded in 1912, is a federation of co-operative companies and manages the sales and finance of more than forty local companies.

Other companies, such as the Prince Edward Island Poultry and Egg Association, have done excellent work. Besides these companies, there are a large number of live-stock shipping clubs and local co-operatives whose total volume of business is large.

The economic significance of co-operative marketing, particularly in Western Canada, is so great that any account of the growth of Canadian agriculture would be incomplete without reference to it.

Tenancy is characteristic of English agriculture, and is important in certain of the United States of America, but Canada is a land of farm-owners. In 1921 tenants held only 7·9 per cent. of the total number of farms, while part owners and part tenants held 5·9 per cent.[2] This may be due in some measure to the low cost of land, but it is also due to an attitude of mind. Farm ownership is the goal. Should ownership not be possible, other occupations will be chosen.

Thus during the years 1867–1921 (little more than half a century) solid foundations have been laid for the development of agriculture, and, what is more important, a rural population possessing high standards of living has grown up.

(III) INDUSTRIAL DEVELOPMENT

In two respects confederation had an immediate influence upon the industrial growth of the colonies. (1) By removing the barriers of intercolonial tariffs, it provided an easy access to the markets of neighbouring provinces for the products of existing industries, thus enabling a national to supplant a narrow colonial economy. (2) The establishment of a strong central Government, relatively free from parochial importunities, gave greater scope to the State in the fashioning of a larger industrial life, and the history of Canada in the past sixty years vividly illustrates the deep influence of government on industry. Tariffs, bounties, public protection and development of

---

[1] Annual Report of the Canadian Co-operative Wool Growers, Ltd. 1921.
[2] Census of Canada, 1921.

natural resources, promotion of railway construction and subsidies in various forms bear witness to the modern mercantilism of Canadian policy.

At confederation industry was largely in the primary or extractive stage. It consisted in enterprises that utilised directly the natural resources of a country richly endowed, or in such infant manufacturing activities as could readily supply a local market. Foremost among the extractive industries and in general importance following closely upon the heels of agriculture was lumbering. In 1868 lumber in value represented almost one-third of Canada's total exports, some odd $18,000,000 (£3,600,000) out of $57,000,000 (£11,400,000).[1] The timber booms of the Ottawa, the St Lawrence and the St John helped to pay for the steel goods of Birmingham and the cottons and woollens of Lancashire and Yorkshire. But lumbering was not merely significant in that it strengthened Canada's foreign trade; it was a key industry. Dependent upon its products were secondary industries, which partly met the demand of local markets, and in a few cases helped to swell the volume of exports. Among these, the most prominent were shipbuilding, manufacture of agricultural implements, furniture and match making. Shipbuilding was particularly robust in the provinces of Nova Scotia, New Brunswick and Quebec. In Nova Scotia ships were built principally for use by the many shipowners in Halifax and Yarmouth who throve on seafaring ventures. In the period from 1860 to 1869 the little town of Yarmouth alone added to her fleet some 37 full-rigged ships, 104 barques, and a host of brigs, brigantines and schooners.[2] But in the other two provinces a goodly number of the wooden vessels were constructed for British owners. The greatest year of shipbuilding in the period was 1874, when 490 vessels aggregating 183,010 tons were built and registered in the Dominion.[3] From that date the industry steadily declined, and the year 1885 might be taken as marking the beginning of the end in the construction of the famous Canadian square-rigged wooden ships. The iron vessel with its greater economy had begun the conquest of ocean transport, and the forests of Canada were no longer of advantage in the support of a shipbuilding industry.

Two other industries that drew wealth from natural resources were fishing and mining. At confederation the value of their products was relatively small, the exports of fish from the whole of the Dominion being less than $3,500,000. But the succeeding decade witnessed a rapid growth, particularly in fishing, thanks in no slight degree to the federal Department of Marine and Fisheries, which provided a necessary central direction in the artificial hatching and distribution of fry. By 1879 the country's exports of fish had more than doubled, and

---

[1] *Canada Year Book*, 1870, p. 127.
[2] Wallace, F. W., *Wooden Ships and Iron Men*, p. 116.
[3] *Ibid.* p. 192.

Nova Scotia continued to be the premier province in the industry, with Quebec a close second.

Mining was in its infancy. Coal was the most valuable product, and, until British Columbia entered the Dominion, was mined exclusively in Nova Scotia, principally in the counties of Cumberland, Colchester, Pictou and the Island of Cape Breton. During the course of the Reciprocity Treaty (1855–66), and especially during the American Civil War, the industry expanded through exports chiefly to the United States, but the expiration of the treaty reduced the export trade. The Fathers of Confederation won the support of the Nova Scotian coal operators by their plea that they would find a market in the Canadas, and these inducements had much to do with the entrance of the maritime province to the Dominion. This prospective market unfortunately never came up to expectations. Quebec took coal from Pictou and Cape Breton, but the consumers of Ontario remained obdurate. Much to the discouragement of Nova Scotia all the advantages were and have remained in favour of Pennsylvania anthracite with its shorter haul. Another disappointment for the Atlantic province was the slow growth of a market for coal in industry. Although the provincial deposits of iron ore were plentiful, the early attempts to build up an iron and steel industry attained little success. The most ambitious iron plant was at Londonderry in the county of Colchester. It confronted many difficulties—the lack of adequate transport facilities and the unsatisfactory character of the native ore being the most pronounced—and throughout the 'seventies it dragged on an anaemic existence. Not till the 'eighties did any substantial development take place in iron and steel production. Copper came next in economic value to the mining of coal. The richest deposits of the metal were on the northern shores of Lakes Huron and Superior, whence it was shipped *via* the water route to the United States or Britain. The smelting took place abroad, and in the case of Britain principally at Swansea. Gold was also of some slight commercial importance. Previous to their federation the various provinces had their gold rushes, and, if smaller and less epic than those later to the Yukon and northern Ontario, they were large enough to raise vivid hopes among those who surveyed the resources of the country. As early as 1860 gold had been discovered in Nova Scotia, and in subsequent years had been mined in generous quantities. Later, Ontario shared in the excitement of gold discoveries. In the township of Madoc, Hastings county, gold was found in 1866, and for a few years after confederation gave rise to feverish, if not productive, operations. Silver mining could hardly be said to have existed, although in 1869 the rich Silver Islet mine was discovered, the first important silver property in Ontario. The mine was on a tiny island near Fort William, and was swept by the storms of Lake Superior, which time after time forced the miners to withdraw. The original holders, Montreal men, were unable or unwilling to put sufficient capital into its operation, with the consequence that it came largely under the control of New York financiers, who had by 1884 taken out of it some $3,500,000 worth of silver.[1] In such humble and hazardous circumstances silver mining in Ontario had its beginnings. In the decade 1867–77 the mining of other minerals was slight. Little capital, lack of transportation to the areas of mineral deposits, absence of adequate geological investigation, and uncertainty in regard to markets hampered the industry. Not until these circumstances were altered did the development of mineral wealth begin.

In addition to the extractive industries, the early Dominion had many manufactures but all of slender strength. The majority were, like those already mentioned, closely related to lumbering and agriculture, although others arose to supply the local Canadian market. Some of the miscellaneous objects manufactured were hardware, leather goods, boots and shoes, felt hats, machinery, farm tools, woollens and cottons, sugar, packed pork and alcoholic liquors. Notably of interest were cotton goods and refined sugar. Although dependent on imported raw products, these industries developed very rapidly and were strong enough to win special consideration when the National Policy was framed. Indeed, in the first decade of confederation, domestic cottons competed strongly with their Lancashire rivals. Almost all of the cotton factories were situated in Ontario, in the counties of Lincoln, Wentworth and Wellington. The hardware and leather manufactures matured from simple enterprises of frontier life: the smithy and the little crossroads tannery, erected to supply the requirements of neighbouring farmers. Canadian agricultural implements had already a cosmopolitan market. In the early 'seventies Chaplin, an enterprising manufacturer of St Catharine's, shipped forks, hoes and rakes to England, and an Oshawa firm sent similar implements to Great Britain, Germany, France, Australia and Brazil.[2] The woollen industry also had its triumphs. A contemporary wrote that "so completely have Canadian blankets, flannels, tweeds, friezes, knitted shirts and drawers taken possession of the market, that the imported article has become almost unsaleable".[3] Like other early manufactures, it was a domestic as well as a factory industry. It was estimated that 7,641,917 yards of woollen cloth and 1,771,140 yards of linen fabrics were made in the homes of the farmers, a quantity almost equal to that produced in all the textile factories.[4] With a population largely agricultural and a long and monotonous winter, textile manufacture naturally became established in the life of the people.

[1] *Papers of the Thunder Bay Historical Society*, 1911–12.
[2] *Report of Select Committee on Manufacturing Interests*, App. to Journals, Can. H. of C. 1874, no. 3.
[3] Small, B., *Products and Manufactures of the New Dominion*, pp. 142–3.
[4] *Census of Manufactures*, 1870–1, vol. 5, p. x.

During the first thirteen years of confederation, industry underwent no spectacular development. On the whole it was a period of humble beginnings, an era of stock-taking and preparation. Industries had not grown out of the pioneer stage, and the readjustment of production to home and foreign markets was only slowly effected. Up to 1873 some expansion took place. Credit was then relatively easy to obtain, thanks to the more than two dozen banks zealous to make loans on whatever seemed a tolerable security. Enthusiasm was fresh, and the political union of the colonies beckoned investors to be bold. But in 1873 a depression set in which continued until the end of the decade. Manufacturers now bemoaned their distress, specially those who exported abroad. The lumber trade suffered grievously from the falling off in the demand in the American and British markets. In 1876 it was claimed that the quantity of lumber manufactured would not exceed 50 per cent. of that produced in 1872 or 1873, and on account of low prices afforded a still lower percentage of profit.[1] Canadian producers were prone to look at home for the causes of the depression. But the fact is that Canada suffered from a general drop in the trade cycle, which affected other countries quite as much. Her sin was one of commission, the excessive trading of her merchants on long credit, but even in this fault she was not alone, as the commercial history of the United States in the same period showed. The depression after 1873 is adequate explanation for the relatively tardy growth throughout the decade, and provided the occasion for the National Policy of the next period. Nevertheless, while development in the 'seventies was not remarkable, it was very far from discouraging, as will appear from the Canadian census returns for production in manufacturing establishments in 1870–1 and 1880–1:

	Capital invested	Hands employed	Total gross value of the product
1870–1	$77,964,020	187,924	$221,617,773[2]
1880–1	$165,302,623	254,935	$309,676,068[3]

In the later census the extent of the Dominion was much larger, including in addition to the original provinces Manitoba, British Columbia, Prince Edward Island and the North West Territories. But the manufacturing production in the newer provinces was inconsiderable. The chief source of their wealth was the purely extractive industries, which are not included in the above statistics.

The period from 1880 to 1900 may be viewed as a second chapter in the industrial growth of the Dominion. It was an era of bolder experiments, and witnessed the rise of the National Policy, which first found expression in tariff schedules by the establishment in 1879 of protective duties. The demand for fiscal protection antedated confederation. As early as November 1847 it had been advocated by

[1] *Report of Select Committee on the Present Depression of the Manufacturing...Interests*, App. to Journals, Can. H. of C. 1876, no. 3.
[2] *Census*, 1870–1, III, 463.   [3] *Census*, 1880–1, III, 519.

Judge Sullivan at Hamilton and in the 'fifties and early 'sixties Isaac
Buchanan, often described as the father of the National Policy, ex-
pounded its merits from many platforms.[1] It received the blessings
of active politicians, the most distinguished being John A. Macdonald
and the eloquent prophet of confederation, Thomas D'Arcy McGee.
Conditions in the 'seventies gave the idea added force and extended
acceptance. Struggling manufacturers, harrowed by a trade depression, hopefully looked to protection as a panacea for their ills.
Farmers, who felt the pinch of American competition in the marketing
of their products, were scarcely less enthusiastic, and to many who
represented no special interests a protective tariff seemed an effective
mode of inducing the American Government to accept commercial
reciprocity, which they considered the surest step to the development
of Canadian resources. Thus many influences led to the tariff of 1879,
described by Tilley as modestly designed "to select for a higher rate
of duty those articles which are manufactured or can be manufactured
in the country, and to have those that are neither made nor are likely
to be made in the country at a lower rate".[2] The average level of
duties was not high. On American goods it was 25 per cent., and on
all dutiable commodities only 23·35 per cent.[3] In subsequent years,
alterations were made, mainly in an upward direction, and to the
present day the protective tariff has remained, although within the
twentieth century the average rate has been steadily reduced.

The precise influence of the tariff on industrial growth is difficult
to determine, because it synchronised with other factors that help to
fashion industrial organisation and to promote expansion. One of its
more immediate results was that of encouraging the establishment of
a few new industries and additional plants in those already existing.
The promise of protection to enterprises that could at all sustain themselves was a decisive factor with wavering capitalists, and induced
some American firms to open branch factories in Canada. The
principal industries whose development was encouraged were
jewellery, silver and plated ware, clock manufacture, cottons,
woollens, sugar-refining and iron and steel. Although most of these
would ultimately have grown without the National Policy, the increased tariff promoted activity earlier than would otherwise have
been the case. The stimulus unfortunately was not always lasting.
In the ensuing years manufacturers frequently complained that the
duties were inadequate to shelter them from American competition.
Those manufacturers who considered the duties inadequate could
scarcely find them a stimulus, but often, without the tariff, they could
not produce at all. The cotton industry particularly benefited. Between 1879 and 1885 nineteen new mills were established, principally

---

[1] Buchanan, I., *The Relations of the Industry of Canada with the Mother Country and the U.S.*
(*passim*).   [2] *Debates* (Canada), 1879, p. 418.
[3] McLean, S. J., *Tariff History of Canada*, 27. For schedule of duties see 42 Vict. cap. 15.

in Ontario and Quebec, and won a considerable share of the home market. In the twenty-three years subsequent to 1879, the increase in value of output nearly averaged $500,000 a year.[1] This expansion led to an injurious competition from which in the 'nineties escape was sought by consolidation. Combinations in this and other industries became the nightmare of the Canadian public, fearful lest they should be forced to pay a penalty in higher prices. Protection ensured some security to producers, but threatened evils to the body of consumers.[2]

The iron and steel industry, important from its intimate relationship to other enterprises, showed to what limited extent the National Policy might benefit. On account of its essential rôle in the promotion of industrial power, the iron industry became the cherished child of Canadian policy. In the tariff of 1879 the average duty on iron articles was only 16·17 per cent., a slight increase on the former rate. Pig iron was allowed to enter at two dollars per ton. In the succeeding years the rates on odd articles climbed upward until the schedule of 1887 provided substantial protection. The duties of that year were 8 per cent. higher than the average of 1879, and of particular note was the increase of the import duty on pig iron from $2 to $4. Three years previous to the imposition of the higher duties the federal Government had adopted another expedient for the promotion of the industry, a bounty of $1.50 a ton on the production of pig iron from Canadian ore. Thus by 1887 the iron and steel industry was favoured by a combined system of duties and bounties, which it retained with little modification to 1897. Not merely the federal authority, but the provinces also gave largesse to this basic industry. Ontario granted a bonus of $2 per ton on iron made from Ontario ore, and Quebec reserved 30,000 acres of colonisation land for the Canada Iron Furnace Co., in order that it might have a supply of fuel. Throughout the period there was a consistent, although not spectacular, growth in the secondary stage of the industry, partly due to protection, but attributable also to many other factors. The increase of railway mileage from 6858 miles in 1879 to 16,550 miles in 1897, gave a ready market for iron products.[3] Moreover, the secondary stages readily accommodated themselves to the tiny factories and limited capital of Canadian enterprise. The manufacturer of nails or horseshoes required only a small building, and wherever established could find an adequate local market. What has been true in the industrial development of all modern countries was no less evident in Canada. An industry grew only on the condition that it readily dovetailed into the economic life of the country. Its expansion then accompanied and was promoted by the general expansion. Notwithstanding the in-

---

[1] *Industrial Canada* (Toronto), March 1902.
[2] *Report of Select Committee on Combinations*, App. to Journals, Can. H. of C. 1888, no. 3.
[3] Donald, W. J. A., *The Canadian Iron and Steel Industry*, p. 123

creasing scale of bounties from 1883, the primary portion of the iron industry failed to mature as rapidly as the secondary, and the explanation is not far to seek. In the 'eighties and early 'nineties the industry was cramped by inadequate supplies of fuel and suitable ores, combined with a lack of sufficient capital. Protection and bounties could not supply these deficiencies. In the first thirteen years of the twentieth century the situation had altered. For the fiscal years 1909, 1910 and 1911, the combined production of pig iron amounted to 1,937,144 tons, over nineteen times that of the years 1896, 1897 and 1898, and the proportion of home produce to total consumption advanced from 36·2 per cent. in 1884 to 66·9 per cent. in 1911.[1] Rapid expansion took place in the twentieth century, although the industry received less protection, and the explanation is to be found in the change of general conditions. Suitable ores were readily imported from Newfoundland, technical improvements took place in the treatment of native ores, capital was more available from within the country and from abroad, and plants were thus enlarged to render possible production on a more extensive scale. Fuel resources were better utilised as a greater amount of capital moved into coal mining, and the shipping of ore and coal from the United States was facilitated by adequate railway transport. In addition the rapid economic development of the country, stimulated by elaborate railway construction, resulted in a larger home market for iron products. In these factors, perhaps much more than in the protective tariff, is to be found the explanation for the pronounced growth.

In other ways than by bounties and protective duties government encouragement was rendered to domestic industry. In the 'eighties the municipalities began to assist manufactures by exempting them from taxation or by granting loans and bonuses. As early as 1897 cotton factories in the Nova Scotian cities, Halifax and Windsor, received such aid.[2] But it was in Ontario that the practice became most prevalent. A provincial statute of 1884 authorised municipal councils to encourage manufactures by exempting them from taxation for ten years.[3] In 1887 they were given permission to grant a bonus on the approval by vote of two-fifths of the rate-payers.[4] Cities and towns now entered on a frenzied and unseemly competition for industrial plants. The statute could not itself promote general industrial growth, and probably did more harm than good in checking a wholesome localisation of industry. Although repealed in 1892, its essential provisions were re-enacted eight years later, and continued to exercise an influence on municipal action. The policy of granting loans to needy industries was an encouragement of a more defensible character, for it played a part in the establishment of many enterprises.

[1] Donald, W. J. A., *The Canadian Iron and Steel Industry*, p. 192.
[2] Statutes of Nova Scotia, 42 Vict. c. 27.
[3] Statutes of Ontario, 47 Vict. c. 32, s. 8.
[4] Revised Statutes, Ontario, 1887, c. 184, s. 479.

A form of political aid open to great abuse was that provided by government contracts, of which the famous "Clergue contract" of 1900 was an example. With the ostensible purpose of encouraging the steel industry in northern Ontario, the federal Administration contracted with the Algoma Steel Company, of which Clergue was the promoter, for 125,000 tons of "nickel steel" rails, 25,000 tons to be taken annually for five years for use on the Intercolonial Railway. While ministers pleaded that the contract was intended to encourage during its operation the production of steel rails in Canada, the Opposition did not fail to point out that it was made one month before a general election and that the price was seven or eight dollars a ton in excess of prices prevailing in England and the United States. It is difficult to avoid the suspicion that political motives have had as much to do with such contracts as economic policies, and the industrial benefits have been slight. But all measures that fitted into the National Policy of increasing production were the hopeful expression of a young country seeking quickly to become industrially strong and forced to press into service every expedient which promised to attain that result.

While in the 'eighties and 'nineties the National Policy promoted the rise of manufactures, the extractive industries passed through a period of leisurely development. The output of the fisheries grew with steady, monotonous consistency; that of the forests at a rate more rapid, particularly in the 'eighties. The National Policy was applied to fishing. In the thirteen years after confederation, the industry centred largely in the inland waters. To encourage sea fisheries, an Act was passed in 1882 to distribute $150,000 annually in bounties among the owners of fishing vessels and fishermen engaged in fishing from boats in the seas of Canada.[1] In 1891 this amount was increased by $10,000.[2] The Government sought to encourage the marketing of fresh fish in the interior by paying one-third of the ordinary express charges on shipments to points as far west as the eastern boundary of Manitoba and from the Pacific coast as far east as that boundary. These measures undoubtedly helped to develop fishing, but, as in all government bonuses, it is difficult to isolate their influence from that of other factors, such as the larger market that followed upon the growth of population.

By far the most interesting and fitful child of industrial growth was mining. At times it spurted strongly, and then at intervals lagged wearily, bringing disaster to its hitherto enthusiastic investors. It was different from the other extractive industries. They were old. From the establishment of the colonies, they had been important, and from the beginning of the nineteenth century their products had been prominent items in colonial exports. While the field, the forest and the lake readily revealed their wealth, the rocks hid their chief

[1] 45 Vict. c. 18.   [2] 54–55 Vict. c. 42.

treasures, until the pick of the prospector assisted by prolonged geological investigation exposed them. Moreover, the lack of railway transportation retarded mining. The rivers helped lumbering, fishing and agriculture, but in most cases only the railway could reach the back-country areas of mineral wealth, and mining awaited this means of communication. In addition capital was slow in entering mining enterprises of the pioneer character. Returns were so uncertain that the timidity of investors, although unfortunate for the industry, was justified. The 'eighties and particularly the 'nineties witnessed a change in these conditions. Foremost among the influences effecting this change was the development of more thorough geological knowledge, furthered by the activities of the federal and provincial Departments of Mines. As early as 1843 the Canadian Geological Survey was organised with a distinguished geologist, William Logan, as its chief. The work of carefully exploring, mapping and surveying eastern Canada was begun, and, after confederation, was extended to other portions of the Dominion. Annual reports upon the areas surveyed were issued, and prospectors had thus an intelligence service to guide their labours. The increase of geological knowledge combined with the extension of railways promoted growth in mineral production. The census figures[1] of the principal metals tell the tale succinctly:

	1871	1881	1901
Gold (oz.)	22,941	70,015	862,000
Silver (oz.)	69,197	87,024	1,157,807
Copper ore (tons)	13,310	8,177	259,561
Iron ore (tons)	129,363	2,223,057	301,143
Coal (tons)	671,008	1,307,824	5,321,715

Until the Yukon took the lead in the late 'nineties, the output of gold was greatest in British Columbia, where placer mining still prevailed in the valleys of the Fraser and Columbia Rivers, particularly in the Cariboo district. In production of silver that province was no less prominent, and from 1892 to 1906 led the other provinces. Copper also was produced in the western mountains, and exported, either in ore or in matte, for refining in the eastern United States. But Ontario and Quebec were not without their mining developments. The advance of the Canadian Pacific Railway through the northern section of Ontario led almost by chance to the discovery in the neighbourhood of Sudbury of rich copper and nickel fields. In 1899 the Canadian Copper Company was formed with a capital of $2,000,000, its intention being to work several claims as copper properties. Not till the autumn of the year was nickel discovered in the first shipment of ore, and henceforth attention was concentrated upon working the world's largest nickel bed. The opening up of the Sudbury mining area by the construction of the Canadian Pacific Railway had its close parallel twenty years later when the building

<hr />

[1] *Canada Year Book*, 1908, p. 114.

of the Timiskaming and Northern Ontario railway revealed the famous silver deposits of Cobalt, and led to the discovery of gold in Porcupine in 1909 and in Kirkland Lake in 1911. In Ontario mining of the precious metals has proved to be largely a rich by-product of railway construction. Throughout the period most of the provinces attempted the mining of iron ore, but no great triumphs were won, and the iron and steel industry grew largely by aid of imported ores from Newfoundland and the United States. As the statistics illustrate, coal production showed a noteworthy increase from 1881 to 1901, and in the latter part of this period the domestic market readily kept pace with production, nearly 75 per cent. of the coal being consumed in the homes of the community.[1] Other products entered into the wealth of the mining industry: petroleum, corundum, felspar, asbestos, gypsum and talc. Their discovery and use strengthened the basis for manufactures, and promoted industrial expansion in the twentieth century. Petroleum, which figures prominently in modern industry, was early found in south-western Ontario, in the counties of Kent, Essex, Brant and Lambton, where its production went on from the 'sixties of the last century. In the years 1900-15 production in Ontario fell off by one-half, but the decline was offset after the Great War by discoveries in the Turner Valley and other areas of Alberta.

The period 1900-21 stands out in bold relief, for it witnessed the most vigorous industrial growth in the country's history. The ventures of the previous thirty odd years were little more than experiments and beginnings, not rich achievements. The era of maturity and relative strength came with 1900. A few industries lagged behind and failed to fulfil their promise. The majority entered on a career of continued and quickened expansion. A steady enlarging home market —thanks to the thousands of immigrants who moved into the farm lands of the West—combined with a flow of capital from the investors of Europe and the United States maintained expansion on a stable basis, although the evils of a "boom" were too often evident. Mining continued the hopeful development begun in the 'eighties and 'nineties. The discoveries of gold in the Yukon, 1894-7, overshadowed temporarily the less glittering enterprises in the older provinces of the Dominion, but the opening up of Cobalt in 1903 recovered a goodly portion of mining investment for the East. Soon afterwards the gold area of Porcupine revealed its treasures, and Ontario became a great mining country. The masses of pre-Cambrian rock that extend from Labrador on the east and enclose the Hudson Bay basin began to open their storehouses of mineral wealth.

Fishing and lumbering grew with no less vigour than mining. The increase in the monetary value of the fisheries, 1900-12, was some 60 per cent.[2] and with due allowance for the depreciation of the

[1] *Labour Gazette*, I, 121.　　　[2] *Canada Year Book*, 1916, p. 261.

money unit the increase in output remained great. The distinctive growth in the twentieth century was in the fisheries of British Columbia. In 1900 the value of the catch in the Atlantic provinces of Nova Scotia, New Brunswick and Prince Edward Island was nearly three times as great as that in the Pacific province. But in the succeeding twenty years the situation changed. In 1921 the catch in British Columbia almost equalled in value the total catch in the Maritime Provinces. Both the deep-sea and inshore fisheries of the Pacific coast grew with rapid strides, and the major product of the industry, canned salmon, obtained world celebrity. Much of this development in British Columbia may be attributed to the greater scope in the newer province for applying machine methods and large-scale organisation. Especially in the canning of salmon, machinery was extended to almost every phase of the process, and the large companies with much capital reaped a decided advantage.

The forests as sources of industrial power became not less but more important in the twentieth century. There was not merely expansion of production, but the development of a more thorough state policy for the conservation of the forests and their greater economic use. In the case of no other industry was there such urgent need of government direction. The federal authority administered the forest lands in Manitoba, Saskatchewan, Alberta and a belt of territory in British Columbia, while in the Maritime Provinces, Quebec, Ontario and the greater part of British Columbia, administration was under provincial control. For long after confederation neither federal nor provincial authorities adopted an adequate policy. Attention was directed principally to facilitating the cutting of timber and perfecting the revenue collection. Maintenance of effective protection from fire, regulative control of logging operations, and conservation of existing forests were largely neglected, with a well-nigh irreparable loss to one source of industrial power. In the years 1900–12 much was done to rectify this unhappy situation. Particularly noteworthy was the legislation of the Dominion to set aside forest reserves for the provision of a permanent supply of timber.[1]

Along with the enactment of this conserving legislation, a young manufacturing industry, dependent upon forest wealth for its growth, moved in rapid strides to a position of great importance, and illustrated more forcibly than ever the economic value of Canada's timber. Woodpulp and paper production can claim the record among Canadian manufactures for phenomenal growth. In the census of 1871 pulp mills were not mentioned. In 1881 five mills were reported, employing sixty-eight men. The manufacture then began to grow, but the increase was leisurely until the twentieth century. Then it passed quickly its older competitors, until by the close of the Great War it ranked among the first two or three dominant manufactures in the country, com-

---

[1] 6 Ed. VII, c. 14; 1–2 Geo. V, c. 10.

panion to the old enterprise of flour milling. Its development was due to three factors; the country's great timber resources, water power and its utilisation, and an ever-widening world market for newsprint. The industry from the outset included three forms of activity, the operations in the woods with pulpwood as a product, the manufacture of pulp, and the manufacture of paper. The operations in the woods can scarcely be separated from ordinary lumbering activities, for large pulp and paper companies also worked sawmills to utilise such timber as might be more suitable for other purposes than pulpwood. All branches of the lumber industry were closely interlaced for the utilisation to the fullest extent of timber wealth. When the United States began to experience a shortage in its supplies of pulpwood, it became the ready market for the Canadian product, and to satisfy this market production increased. President Roosevelt's declaration of 1907, "We are out of pulpwood", was hardly the truth, but roughly from that date onwards the Canadian producer found in the Republic a zealous customer. It was estimated that two-thirds of the newsprint paper consumed in the United States was either of Canadian manufacture or made from wood or woodpulp imported from Canada.[1] The extending circulation of newspapers on the American continent was the ultimate explanation for the rapid growth of the industry.

While economic conditions largely determined pulp production, Canadian national policy played an influential part. Dominion and provincial legislation practically prohibited the exportation of unmanufactured pulpwood cut on Crown lands in every province except Nova Scotia, and thus decreed that the bulk of the raw product must be manufactured into pulp and paper in Canadian mills, instead of being exported as timber to be manufactured in the United States. Ontario, as early as 1900, was the first province to impose this restriction for the encouragement of the domestic industry.[2] In 1910 Quebec embodied it in an Order-in-Council, and in 1911 New Brunswick enacted a similar restriction, while in 1917 the Dominion applied it to the Crown lands in the Prairie Provinces.[3] Its effect in increasing production of pulp and paper in Canada was immediate. In 1908, when exportation from most provinces was free, the exports amounted to 63·6 per cent. of the apparent total production, but after 1912 declined steadily till 1922, when they were only about 25 per cent. of the total quantity of pulpwood cut in Canada.[4] Within the period 1912–22 the quantity of raw pulpwood consumed in Canadian mills increased by over 236 per cent. The manufacturing or secondary part of the industry hastened to keep pace with the primary operations in the woods, and in few cases was the definite influence of the

[1] *Canada Year Book*, 1922–3, p. 336.   [2] Statutes of Ontario, 63 Vict. c. 11.
[3] Statutes of Quebec, 1910, Ord. in Council, no. 291; N.B. Acts, 1 Geo. V, c. 10; Statutes of Canada, 1917, p. clvii.
[4] *Census, The Pulp and Paper Industry*, 1924, p. 6.

National Policy in encouraging domestic manufacture more clearly discerned. The legislative measures affected only the wood on Crown lands, not that cut from private land, but some 83 per cent. of the available spruce, balsam and hemlock was on Crown territories, and consequently the legislation covered the largest portion of the raw material.[1] Nevertheless demands were frequently made for an embargo upon the export of all pulpwood, and the issue was vigorously debated as a wider extension of the National Policy.[2] Within the period covered by this chapter, no action was taken.

While no other manufacture showed such impressive development as the pulp and paper, many grew with notable rapidity. The growth was particularly evident in those enterprises, not far removed from the extractive stage, with ample natural resources to give them an advantage over foreign competitors. In these industries the Canadian producer won a dominance at home, and became a prominent exporter to world markets. Old and virile industries that had developed as a direct consequence of expansion in agriculture were flour milling and meat slaughtering. Milling kept pace with the extension of wheat acreage. The advance of the plough throughout the valley of the Saskatchewan added to the wealth of millers in Montreal and at such points along the connecting railway line as Kenora, Fort William and Port Colborne. In addition modern milling, like pulp and paper, grew upon the cheap power provided by the hydro-electric developments. Slaughtering and meat packing accompanied the expansion in stock raising, and led to developments in the leather and boot and shoe industries. The canning of fruits, vegetables, lobsters and salmon shared in the general industrial growth, and obtained for its products a secure foothold in oversea markets.

Textiles showed progress, although they fell short of controlling the home market. The woollen industry prospered least, if it could be said to prosper at all. English and Scotch woollens easily held their own, and few in Canada were more keenly interested in high duties and more critical of the imperial preference than the manufacturers of woollen goods. Their discontent was the product of genuine tribulations. The 'eighties and 'nineties of the last century were their golden age. The industry had matured rapidly, and tolerable satisfaction was expressed with the fiscal protection which it enjoyed, viz. an average duty of 18·57 per cent. that rose on some manufactured goods, such as ready-made clothing and blankets, to 35 per cent. But after 1899 and synchronising with the establishment of imperial preference, which reduced duties roughly by one-third, the industry began to decline. During the next eight years, 88 mills were forced to close their doors. In 1910 only 78 woollen and worsted mills were working, producing approximately 7,616,000 yards of cloth, against

[1] *Report of the Royal Commission on Pulpwood*, 1924, p. 92.
[2] *Debates, Can. H. of C.* 1907–8, pp. 4774 ff.

an aggregate production in 1899 of 13,992,000 yards.[1] The only branch of the industry that retained vitality was the knitting mills. The competition of Yorkshire woollens was blamed for the general decline, and the blame was not ill placed. An old and accomplished technique, capacity for specialisation on particular goods, less expenditure on fuels and buildings, a strongly entrenched sentiment for British manufactures, a superior quality of raw wool, and a lower labour cost combined with the most modern machinery were all in favour of Yorkshire. In addition Canadian manufacturers complained that they had to contend not merely with Britain, but with Germany and Belgium, because goods of these countries were shipped to England in large bales, cut into short lengths, rolled on an English board, and then brought into Canada as British goods, getting the advantage of the preference.[2] Other factors undoubtedly exercised an influence. The decline in sheep raising since confederation made the Canadian manufacturers more dependent on imports of raw wool, which added to their embarrassments.[3] The tale of their grievances became somewhat less in the period immediately previous to the Great War, thanks to favourable tariff adjustments, and died away amid the expanding war market for woven and knitted goods.

The cotton industry had a more tranquil and prosperous history, largely because it was not so much exposed to British competition, and obtained readily the standard grade of raw product. In addition, the tariff genuinely assisted it in meeting its potential competitors, the New England producers. The value of the product more than doubled between 1900–10, and to the close of the period under consideration it remained the strongest of the textile group. Other industries then prominent were farm implements, rubber, the chemical industries utilising native mineral products, the automobile industry, and last, but by far the most distinctive, hydro-electric generation, which in the economic growth of Canada eventually bids fair to play the part that coal played in the earlier industrial triumphs of Britain.

The vital importance of hydro-electric generation became evident immediately before and during the Great War. In this period it became a basic industry, profoundly influencing the progress of milling, pulp and paper, mining and electro-chemical enterprises. In addition it revealed in the industrial field a collectivism, new to the American continent, where hitherto private enterprise had been dominant in the control of natural resources. In the early years of the century, the movement for public management of water power, instead of its exclusive utilisation by private corporations, developed in Ontario, largely because that province was in "the acute fuel zone", being dependent on her southern neighbour for the

---

[1] *Canada Year Book*, 1922–3, p. 450.   [2] *Industrial Canada*, Dec. 1902.
[3] *Canada's Wool and Woollens* (pamphlet, Toronto, 1908).

much-valued coal. Periodic shortages of coal made it evident that provincial industries must remain in a precarious condition, unless the most effective and economical use was made of water power. In 1906 the pressure of opinion resulted in the passage of a statute constituting an independent commission to provide for the transmission of electrical power to municipalities.[1] At the outset the commission was little more than a merchant, procuring and selling Niagara power to municipalities on economical terms, but in time it became a large manufacturer of power. In 1910 it supplied 750 h.p. to 10 municipalities; in 1921, 242,349 h.p. to 205.[2] General consumers, manufacturers, and farmers benefited from having power supplied at cost, and the stimulus to industry was pronounced. Other provinces followed in the steps of Ontario. Manitoba, Nova Scotia and New Brunswick created commissions in essentials similar to the Ontario system, and the idea of public control became firmly established. In the meantime private enterprises also were active in exploiting water resources, and a silent revolution in the use of water power was under way. By 1922 the developed water power amounted to 2,762,880 h.p., of which 476,503 h.p. were utilised by pulp and paper mills. It is difficult to translate the economic significance of this development into money values. But the actual cost to consumers was estimated not to exceed $30 per h.p. per annum, whereas power could not be developed in any other way than by water for less than $60 per h.p. per annum at the post-war cost of fuel and labour. Such economy, however, inadequately indicates all the advantages that Canada obtained from hydro-electric generation, whereby her many lakes and rivers began to play a new and vital rôle in industry.

The period 1900–21 witnessed not merely industrial expansion, but a pronounced change in the size of the business unit. The process of consolidation was at work, and reached its climax in the four years 1909–12, when 58 consolidations embracing 275 firms took place. The principal industries affected were pulp and paper, lumber, machinery, iron and steel, milling, canning, breweries, boot and shoe, bread, jewellery and meat packing. Between 1912 and 1920 twelve additional consolidations were effected, two of which were the largest in Canadian industrial history, the Riordon Pulp Co., Ltd., and the British Empire Steel Corporation. The consolidations were chiefly amalgamations in which the individual firms lost their identity, and formed new industrial units. The principal object set forth in the prospectuses was economy in production, with elimination of competition among salesmen and brokers, but motives to which publicity was not given exercised a weighty influence. Many firms were in a critical financial condition, and consolidation alone saved them from collapse. Others found that under existing competition profits were insecure, and

[1] Ontario Statutes, 6 Ed. VII, c. 15.
[2] *Canada Year Book*, 1922–3, p. 408.

sought through amalgamation the advantages of monopoly. The allure of promoters' profits was a powerful factor. Promoter sought to outdo promoter in the scope of activities and the amount of returns, and to struggling manufacturers they painted seductive pictures of the benefits that would accrue from their financing. Seldom did the benefits come up to expectations, and the history of the consolidations was a dreary tale of failures or partial failures. Reorganisations were imperative, and in the process the rights of investors and the obligations of companies were modified or obliterated, much to the injury of Canada's credit abroad. There was some justification for the bitter criticism of a London paper: "Canadians are fond of telling us that they are no longer children to be led in leading strings, but are a great nation. If they really desire to be regarded in this light, they must act a great deal more circumspectly in commercial matters, and not allow their desires to do business to out-run their financial discretion".[1]

The foreign investors, whom Canadian financiers often treated cavalierly, played a vital part in supplying the expanding industries with capital. It was estimated that during the years 1900–14, Great Britain loaned to Canada for industrial and mining enterprises some $300,000,000. In the same period six or seven hundred million dollars were raised in the United States, and went largely into Canadian industry.[2] There was a distinct difference between the influences exercised by Great Britain and the United States on Canadian economic growth. Great Britain invested much in industrial securities and little in branch factories. The United States invested liberally in branch factories, and relatively little in industrial securities. The British investor at a distance was content with a small return, provided that he had security, while the American sought the larger return that came with personal control over the business. Both in their respective ways assisted greatly in making Canadian industrial expansion possible.[3] The influence of the Republic was naturally the greater. In mining it was very pronounced, and in manufacturing scarcely less evident. Some Canadian industries, such as the manufacture of automobiles, were little more than an expansion of American enterprise to get round the tariff and benefit from the readier trade relations of Canada with the other portions of the Empire.

---

[1] *Financial Times* (London), Sept. 1913.
[2] *Report of the Board of Inquiry into Cost of Living in Canada* (1915), II, 1047.
[3] Field, F. W., *Capital Investments in Canada* (1914), chap. ii.

CHAPTER XXVI

THE ECONOMIC DEVELOPMENT OF CANADA,
1867-1921 (*continued*)

(1) FINANCE AND BANKING

EXPERIENCE has shown that there are certain characteristics always associated with the development of a stable and adequate financial order from the sporadic beginnings of credit, connected with small and scattered settlements, to a fully organised system of credit which supersedes the infertile stocking by methods which reward and utilise all savings. Indeed the essence of finance is the use of savings in the form of money. Thus, inevitably, what may be called the financial history of Canada, up to 1871, was mainly concerned with the establishment of a currency at once flexible and safe. This cannot be said to have been completely accomplished by the Bank Act of 1871, as will be explained later on, but at least it served its purpose, and the principles conducive to a permanent settlement were determined. But to make money savings fruitful and effective two further conditions had to be satisfied; first, that there should be a place both safe and accessible to lodge the money; second, that there should be some definite reward for so disposing of it.

The fulfilment of these two latter requirements could not be very rapid. The banks soon obtained the confidence of the larger communities in which their head offices were established, and where they had the support of various influential people associated with their foundation. But for some years the spread of branch offices was slow, and, in view of the limited resources at their disposal, must have seemed hazardous. Still, in these scattered country districts they could not hope to gain confidence without the accessibility that made them concrete realities in the minds of the country people. In truth the Canadian banks had great initial difficulties to overcome. Conceived and modelled in terms of English banking experience, they were for many years almost entirely without the English background of a thickly settled and stable country population long accustomed to the use of banks and the expanding industrial and commercial activities that created a steady demand for just the kind of short-term, fluid loans for which banking resources are most suitable.

Facts of geography and population made London a great financial centre and early tended to do the same for New York. The conditions in Canada made her financially dependent upon both. The problem of a scattered population is common, in varying degrees, to all colonial settlements, and the two factors of geography and population shape almost the whole of their economic structure.

40

There are, however, characteristics in the geography of Canada that differ fundamentally from those found elsewhere in the British Dominions, and create complications in external financial and economic relations that do not exist either in Australia or South Africa. North America tends to be a single economic area with New York becoming more and more the dominant centre of North American finance. Thus for Canada there have always been two competing financial centres, and not just a single one as in Australia and South Africa. This competing financial influence—alien and yet increasingly intimate—has expressed itself in different ways at all succeeding stages of Canadian development. No such disturbing contact has qualified the establishment in Australia and South Africa of self-contained financial systems with practically a single line of exterior communications concentrated upon London, and now crowned with central banks of their own.

For the formation of the new Canada the city of Quebec was the one available port of entry. The whole of the area now known as the province of Quebec was in effective occupation by the thrifty and prolific French Canadians. So there could be no extensive settlement of British people east of Montreal, and the heavily forested regions along the northern shores of Lake Ontario and Lake Erie had to be reached by a long and laborious journey before the real business of home-making could be commenced. Here was fought out the battle with nature, and here was established the core of progressive British Canada. Further westward, movement on a large scale had been for generations made impossible by 1000 miles of impenetrable wilderness that lay to the north of Lake Superior and guarded the gateway to the western prairies. A far more formidable obstacle to progress than were the Alleghanies in the United States, it served in Canada the same purpose of creating in the East a useful density of population as a base for the later migration to the West, which in the case of Canada was made possible by the Canadian Pacific Railway.

The great migrations of the nineteenth century passed Canada by, and her population increased comparatively slowly. In 1871 it numbered under four million people. Of these somewhat over a million and a half were settled in Ontario—a predominantly British community, mainly farmers owning their land, and hardened by the trials of pioneer settlement into the texture necessary for carrying the burdens of the present, and for leading the further adventure of settling and organising the western prairies. In the year 1867 the first Parliament of the new Dominion of Canada met, and took up its great task of creating a united country stretching from the Atlantic to the Pacific. In 1870 the new province of Manitoba was included in the Dominion, and in 1871, when British Columbia accepted confederation, the Pacific, the final goal of western extension, was reached. Among the powers specifically conferred on the Dominion

Government by the British North America Act were those of banking and currency control. Financial controversies that had occupied the Provincial Assemblies for fifty years were transferred to the Parliament of the Dominion, and the Bank Act of 1871[1] registered its decision and gave unity to the banking and monetary system of the whole country. The monetary unit adopted was a dollar identical in gold value with the American dollar, a decimal system that met with general approval.

Yet this identity in nomenclature of the monetary unit was almost the only point at which the Canadian banking and currency system followed the example set by the United States. In both countries there was a period of experiment and controversy. The United States arrived at a permanent settlement of principles during the Civil War, Canada in 1871, and the two settlements differed widely. The United States fixed upon a plan of currency fully secured by government bonds, inflexible and legalistic. They developed great numbers of small local banks and prohibited branches. They established fixed reserves and an elaborate system of state inspection. For many years previous to 1871 there were in Canada many strong advocates of the American ideas, and in 1869 these were embodied in a proposal put before the House of Commons by John Rose, the Finance Minister of the day. It was rejected *in toto*, and in 1870 the fundamentals of the existing system were moulded into a coherent plan, out of which emerged the Bank Act of 1871. The provisions of this Act contradicted almost every item of the American banking programme. It insisted on a large minimum capital, encouraged the establishment of branches, authorised the issue, without specific security, of notes up to an amount equal to the paid-up capital of each bank, demanded no fixed reserves, and made no provision for government or shareholders' inspection. From the beginning of their history as an independent nation the Americans have developed a legalistic way of thinking, and especially since 1830 have tended to rely more upon legal rules and inhibitions than upon the character and experience of men. In Canada there was but little of this confidence in the exclusive validity of restrictive regulation, and, as the decision of 1871 showed, Canadian opinion preferred the risks of entrusting financial responsibilities to persons unencumbered by too complicated a legal system, to the possible embarrassments of inelasticity implicit in the American plan.

But there was also an immediately practical reason for granting to banks the right of issuing their notes without the security of government bonds. In the absence of deposits adequate to meet their loan requirements the banks were compelled to rely upon their notes for a large proportion of their loanable funds, and a demand that they should furnish securities for the amount of the note circulation would, by just so much, have reduced their loaning power.

[1] 34 Vict. cap. v.

In regard to the permission to establish branches, and the development that occurred, it is probable that the narrowness of the line of settlement was an important cause. Where population must be extended upon a single, or at most a thin line, the selection of localities for branches offers no difficulties, and the impulse towards the growth of branch banking once created would be maintained. Large capitals were an obvious corollary of this form of growth, and as the banks were responsible to the Government in respect of their note issue, a small number of large institutions was clearly preferable. Thus after fifty years of debate the principles were settled on which, for the future, the development of Canadian banking would be based. It is interesting to note that this controversy was not concerned with minor differences but with one radical difference of principle. It was a fine thing that the small body of British folk who undertook the difficult task of creating Canada should, in spite of these immense exterior influences, have selected the broader principle of action and faith in personal honour upon which British enterprise and institutions are based.

Before proceeding to consider the details of the Bank Act of 1871, it is convenient at this stage to supplement the description of physical conditions and geographical situation, with which Canadian settlement was confronted, by some suggestions as to the nature of the business that had come into being by 1871 and with which the banks had to deal. A banking system situated in the midst of a vigorous industrial population is at once supplied with every advantage in the way of opportunity for fluid loans, and at the same time can obtain the requisite deposits as a basis for business. In Canada it was by no means so. Industry had at that time still the limits belonging to a scattered community in an undeveloped country. Nearly all the enterprise was associated either with agriculture or the primary industries, and many years elapsed before there was sufficient concentration of population or adequate market facilities to make a real industrial centre a possibility. In the meantime the banks were under the difficulties inevitable to a situation in which an adequate demand for fluid loans was impossible and much of their funds had necessarily to be tied up in advances not easy to liquidate. It must have required both skill and courage on the part of the bankers to be able to steer their way successfully—as, after all, the majority of them did—through the difficulties presented by that situation.

In those early days of the 'seventies a certain quality of grandeur was given to the proceedings of both politicians and financiers by the fact that all their activities were associated with a high purpose. This purpose in the main can be expressed under three headings—first, to establish a real physical connection between the eastern extremities of the Dominion and the Pacific Ocean; second, and concurrently with this, to preserve as far as possible the economic autonomy of the country; third, to preserve the tie with the parent stock in Great Britain. Political and social purposes determine the direction not only of political action but of financial responsibility, and the large expenditures of those days were all devoted to the completion of connecting railways.

It was natural, of course, that the consummation of Canadian confederation should enable the new Canadian Government to borrow more freely from London than could the scattered provinces in earlier days. At confederation the debts of the provinces were taken over by the Dominion Government as also their issue of government notes. Thus Canada started with a debt of about $80,000,000 (£16,000,000) and a note issue of $3,000,000 (£600,000).

Amongst the various details of controversy there had been one of a very important nature in regard to the proper relation of governments to the issue of notes. Many influential people held that it was proper for governments to regard a note issue as a possible source of profit. The right of issue of notes by banks had been conceded to them to some extent on account of their requirements for commercial loans; and it is probable that, if there had not been that urgent necessity, the claim on the part of some theorists that an unsecured issue of notes by the Government was the proper solution of the currency problem might have been accepted. As it was, it was adopted only to a very limited extent, and in course of time, as will be seen by later figures, this impulse entirely disappeared and the principle was ultimately established that government notes should be secured practically dollar for dollar by gold. Underlying this there is a very important principle involved. It is quite true that the banks were not subjected to the necessity of maintaining a reserve of any fixed amount, but then they were in possession, by the nature of their business, of a large body of fluid assets more than adequate to secure the payment of the limited amount of notes that they were allowed to issue. In the nature of things a government cannot possess any considerable amount of fluid assets; and the principle was therefore quite properly established that government issues should be fully secured by gold, as being the only fluid asset that they could secure and hold. In effect the Dominion notes came in time to be really of the nature of gold certificates—a fact all the more proper and important as it was insisted that the banks should hold not less than 40 per cent. of their reserves in legal tender notes, in which is implied of course that those legal tender notes were equivalent to gold. The final settlement of the bank note problem was not achieved in 1871. But the Bank Act of 1871 did include at least the beginnings of most of the principles that have ever since governed Canadian banking law.

The Act contained seventy-seven sections of which a considerable proportion was devoted to the care and transfer of stockholders' interest. It set out that the minimum subscribed capital for a bank must be not less than $500,000, and of this not less than $200,000 was to be paid up within two years. The note issue of each bank was not to exceed the amount of paid-up capital. No minimum reserve was established, but 50 per cent. if possible of such reserve as was kept was to be in Dominion notes, and never less than 33⅓ per cent. The voting power was to be one vote per share. Proxies were permitted but must be exercised by a shareholder not an officer of the bank. The directors had to be British subjects. Important restrictions were established in regard to the holding by a bank of real estate, which was only permitted as a permanent investment for purposes of bank premises. But mortgages might be taken as additional security.

In 1871 there were twenty-three banks in existence and about 150 branches. The total capital paid up at that time was $40,132,029, the note issue $24,480,627, the public deposits about $50,000,000, and the discounts about $92,000,000. It will be seen from this that the banks had not yet arrived at the point at which deposits were sufficient to provide for the loans. In fact these figures would show that to lend $93,000,000 it was necessary for them to use their entire deposits, all their notes and some of their capital.

The growth in industrial figures during the years between 1870 and 1890 is significant. The capital invested in 1870 was estimated at about $78,000,000, and the wages paid increased in the same period from about $41,000,000 to something over $100,000,000, and the value of products from $221,000,000 to $470,000,000. An important change had occurred also between 1871 and 1891 in respect of the ratio between deposits and loans. In 1891 the total deposits were about $152,000,000 and the loans $186,000,000, and in that year the numbers of the bank branches had increased to more than 400. This growth strikingly illustrates the progress of confidence both in the banks and in the custom of granting interest on deposits sufficient to create an inducement to withdraw savings from the stocking, and, as will be seen, in course of time this process continued until it is difficult to suppose there could be any money in the country apart from what was deposited in the banks.

The branch system of banking had an important effect in a country extending over great distances and as yet but thinly populated. It undoubtedly helped to modify the forces of provincialism and to give a certain coherence and unity to the thoughts and habits of otherwise remote and isolated communities, and as the Canadian banks later came to establish agencies not only in London and New York, but in places more remote such as South America and the West Indies, they inevitably acquired an international outlook that could not fail to create a certain nexus of interest and understanding between the small towns of Central Canada and the great world. It is also clear that the instinct which from the first insisted upon establishing large banks rather than small ones has been amply justified.

In the years between 1867 and 1886 the railway mileage increased from 2258 to 11,620 miles. This growth included the addition of the Canadian Pacific Railway extension to the Pacific and the Inter-colonial, both of which had been promised by the Dominion Government as conditions of federation. In the year 1886 the first passenger train passed over the tracks of the Canadian Pacific Railway to Vancouver, and the current of life began to pass freely from one end of the country to the other. At this point there became increasingly evident in Canadian economics what might be called a rhythm of progress. Owing to the shape of the country and the immense distances involved in movement from one part to the other it was essential that railway progress must go ahead of immigration. Consequently, while a new impulse of railway-building was being satisfied, a certain stimulus to economic and financial progress was provided. It was also inevitable that when railway-building and the construction work associated with it were for the moment checked, there came a time when it seemed as if the country was over-machined, prosperity lagged, and faith was needed to carry on until the framework established was justified by increased population.

The charters to banks involved in the Bank Act of 1871 provided for their continuance for ten years, and every tenth year the Bank Act has come before Parliament for reconsideration. In 1881 there was comparatively slight change, but it was established that bank notes were to be an unqualified first lien on the assets of a bank. The far more important revision of 1891 was preceded by another effort[1] to modify the Canadian banking system in the direction taken by the American. Again the controversy turned on the status of the bank note issue, and an important change was made. Later on will be given a table showing such losses to the public as had occurred through the notes. As a matter of fact, the main difficulty had been not the non-existence of assets sufficient to pay ultimately for the notes, but the need for some provision by which the notes of a bankrupt bank were immediately and automatically taken care of, and in 1891 a provision was introduced by which each bank must deposit with the Dominion Government 5 per cent. of the average circulation of the contributing banks as shown by the monthly return of notes. In this manner a fund was provided which ensured immediate payment of the notes of the defaulting bank on precisely the same basis as the notes of any other bank, and there could therefore be no feeling of uneasiness in respect of any notes held by the public.

In 1886 there were forty-one banks in Canada, the largest number it has ever had. Also at that time it must be noticed that the credit fund emerging from bank deposits had not yet reached the point of providing for all loan requirements. There is no doubt that the rather exaggerated capitalisation of banking in Canada

[1] An Act respecting Banks and Banking, 1890, cap. 31, s. 1.

was associated with the difficulties of acquiring funds for loaning purposes and the habit of using capital funds for that purpose.

The decade from 1890 to 1900 was one of quiet struggle.[1] Railway-building continued but mainly for extension of branch lines and the like, and no large enterprise stimulated Canada. The population of the country in that decade showed an increase of less than that of any similar period since confederation, being only about 11 per cent. The banking situation showed a moderate development in the fact that deposits increased from a little over $150,000,000 to about $300,000,000, and in that period also they passed the point at which they constituted an adequate supply of loanable funds for the country's needs. In 1890 there were thirty-eight banks; in 1901 there were only thirty-four. But it was felt that some organisation was necessary to give a certain unity to the policies represented. For that purpose there was created in 1900, by a separate Act,[2] the Bankers' Association. It was endowed with important powers and responsibilities, the chief of which were the appointment of a curator to deal with the affairs of a bankrupt bank and "the inspection of the disposition made by the bank of notes". The section dealing with this is as follows:

96 G. The Association may, at any meeting thereof, with the approval of two-thirds in number of the banks represented at such meeting (the banks so approving having at least two-thirds in par value of the paid-up capital of the banks so represented) make by-laws, rules and regulations respecting: (a) all matters relating to the appointment or removal of the curator, and his powers and duties; (b) the supervision of the making of the notes of the banks which are intended for circulation, and the delivery thereof to the banks; (c) the inspection of the disposition made by the banks of such notes; (d) the destruction of notes of the banks; and (e) the imposition of penalties for the breach or non-observance of any by-law, rule or regulation made by virtue of this section.

The slowly falling prices of this period, the low price of agricultural products, and the slackening of immigration reduced the rate of western extension and led to a tone of pessimism that was only resisted by the courage and faith of individuals and great corporations, of which a leading example was the Canadian Pacific Railway, whose directors retained their belief in the possibilities of the country. As in every period of depression in Canada, emigration to the United States was still active, and the change that came with the turn of the century was like a rebirth of the nation.

About this time the problem of rural credits began to come under discussion, and the subject has assumed a steadily increasing importance ever since. In the main the long-term loans have been provided by loan companies, trust companies and insurance companies, and the short-term loans by the banks; and this business in the Provinces of Ontario and Quebec as well as in the Maritime Provinces has been conducted smoothly, and on the whole to the satisfaction of both lenders and borrowers. These regions are the

[1] See also pp. 612–14.   [2] 63 and 64 Vict. cap. 93.

home of mixed farming carried on by a relatively stable population. But in the Western Provinces where agriculture is still chiefly devoted to a single crop—wheat—the full difficulty of seasonal production is experienced. The situation is further complicated by various legal exemptions that come ahead of mortgage or loan, the relative instability of the population, and a suspicion that the West is victimised by the East. Interest rates are higher in the West than in Ontario, but losses are greater, and expenses larger. The banks have made sincere efforts to meet the needs of the farmers, and in doing so have met heavy losses.

The twentieth century opened with a new spirit of optimism prevailing in Canada. The causes of this change of mood were not so much obscure as diverse. For one thing this fresh impulse in national growth is always associated with the appearance on the scene of groups of men of unusual vigour; so it was in Canada. Furthermore, the Liberal party, hitherto the exponent of a somewhat critical and cautious spirit, developed under the inspiring leadership of Sir Wilfrid Laurier an abundant faith in the economic possibilities of the country, and courage in giving enterprising endeavour the *imprimatur* of government support.

Coincident with these internal stimulants to activity two exterior phenomena lent power to expansion. The rise in the price of wheat, the chief product of the western prairies, and the exhaustion of free lands in the United States, brought on a movement of population both from the United States and Europe to the ample spaces of the Canadian West, and constituted the first experience of mass immigration to Canada. Finally the search-light of the London money market was turned on to the prospects of investment in Canada; and money for railway construction and municipal development became abundantly available. Expansion must be paid for, and the immense activities of the period between 1900 and the outbreak of the Great War involved financial operations on the grand scale. Canadian banking funds had become adequate for the satisfaction of the industrial and commercial demands of the country, but could supply but little of the vast sums required for so extensive a programme of railway construction. Almost the whole of the money needed for these purposes was supplied by London, and the London market was for the time a willing lender. The justification for such large expenditures must lie in the existence of an intelligible purpose, and, judged by that standard, the general conception of the railway construction carried out was supported by a perfectly valid idea. This was, that having established a line of settlement across the continent, the next step was to provide the means of broadening the area of habitation, for which purpose the great expanse of fertile lands to the northward of the Canadian Pacific Railway offered opportunity and reward.

As has been explained, circumstances favoured the belief that adequate immigration would follow the provision of transportation facilities. The leaders of enterprise were available. The money was to be had for the asking. Thus, as has already been described,[1] the work proceeded, the length of railways of Canada increasing in the period 1897–1915 from 16,550 to 35,582 miles. Practically all the money necessary for the carrying out of these great transcontinental projects had to be obtained from exterior sources, and of the money necessary the London market provided by far the largest proportion. From the same source, too, came nearly all the large sums expended in municipal equipment. In 1914 it was estimated by Sir George Paish that the indebtedness of Canada to Great Britain amounted to about £600,000,000. It was also estimated by another authority that borrowings from the United States during the same period amounted to between $600,000,000 and $700,000,000.

Estimates of the interest paid by Canada to exterior creditors during the period from 1900 to 1914 vary greatly, the lowest being $1,000,000,000 and the highest $1,500,000,000; but the amount was large, and in 1914 the annual charge for interest on external debt was probably not less than $200,000,000. During the years preceding the War Canada's borrowings in the London market exceeded those of any other country. Sir George Paish published in 1914 figures in regard to the seven years from 1907 to 1913 inclusive. According to these Canada heads the list with loans amounting to £250,000,000; the United States £164,000,000; Argentina, £118,000,000; Brazil, £88,000,000. The total of flotations in London was given as £1,127,000,000, so that Canada's share out of a list of forty-nine countries was not far short of a quarter of the whole amount. In these circumstances it is not surprising that prices in Canada rose rapidly. They did so in a ratio higher than that of any other country on record, and just twice as fast as in Great Britain.

Associated with this vast borrowing, indeed caused by it, was an era of extravagance on the part of the general public. The surplus of imports reached large figures. In 1913, the culminating year of the period, the surplus of imports from the United States was about $300,000,000. Much of this consisted of materials for the immense mileage of railway in process of construction, and the whole country throbbed with optimism and profitable activity. In the meantime, as will be seen from the following table,[2] immigration proceeded on a large scale, even although contemporary estimates were certainly too high.

In any case the increase in population was substantial and the incoming tide of settlers a fertilising one. All brought with them some useful additions to the country's wealth, and many of them, especially those from the United States, brought cash for investment in western farms. It was inevitable in these circumstances that industry should flourish, and from 1900 to 1915 the capitalisation of industry grew

[1] See chapter xxv (i). [2] See p. 641.

from \$447,000,000 to \$1,400,000,000. This form of investment proved attractive to United States capital, and some of the means for this expansion came from there. But large additions to capital were at this time made from accumulated profits. Banking figures for this period showed an expansion in accordance with the general growth of business. From 1900 to 1913 total deposits grew from \$305,000,000 to \$1,126,000,000 and total loans from \$280,000,000 to \$1,100,000,000. The immense inflow of capital from outside, and the profitable activities produced in Canada by this great stimulus, were sure to swell bank figures. The period was not without its troubles in the banking world. Two important failures occurred, the Ontario Bank in 1906 and the Sovereign Bank in 1910. In neither case did the public lose any money. The notes of these banks, as of the four small banks that subsequently failed, were all automatically paid in full.

The important monetary crisis of 1907 in the United States, while it caused inconvenience at the time in Canada, left no traces there of serious disturbance, and the Canadian banking system as a whole was in 1914 in a strong and fluid position. Branches of the banks had multiplied from 747 in 1902 to about 3000 in 1914. But the end of this time of easy borrowing and rapid development was visible in the autumn of 1912, and the banks adopted a policy of quiet liquidation, a policy which was continued and accentuated in 1913. To this they owed their sound position in August 1914 when a new test came.

One of the features of expansion in the Western Provinces was an excessive growth of urban centres. Their atmosphere was full of real estate excitements, and their judgment clouded. Assessments were increased to unwise figures, and both expenditure and borrowings were disproportionately large. In the autumn of 1912 some symptoms of disorder appeared. The population of the provinces began to diminish, and throughout 1913 their situation became increasingly difficult. But they stood bravely behind their liabilities, and the percentage of default in interest was trifling.

In the meantime the buying power of the western farmer was diminished. His chief product was wheat, and the price dropped seriously in the winter of 1912. General prices having at the same time risen since 1900 by 31 per cent., the reasonable equation between the price of his chief products and the cost of the things he had to buy was disastrously disturbed. The situation was further complicated by the fact that many settlers had become the owners of far too much land. The year 1913 was characterised by liquidation and tight money, and in the second half of the year by serious and growing unemployment. Once more it was apparent that, as in the 'nineties, only on a larger scale, railway construction and the development of industrial machinery had far outrun the requirements of the country. Time, courage and a fresh acquisition of population were the only remedies. But it was ordained otherwise, and while presently unemployment disappeared before the grim call of war, five years were to elapse before undivided attention could be given to the solution of fundamental problems of economics and finance.

In Canada, as in other countries, the shadow of coming war unsettled the financial equilibrium some days before physical conflict began. On 28 July the stock markets of Montreal and Toronto found it necessary to close, and in the next few days "runs" on banks and other symptoms of panic appeared. Prompt action was necessary, and the situation was successfully dealt with by a meeting of leading bankers called at Ottawa on Monday, 3 August, by the Minister of Finance, Thomas (now Sir Thomas) White. Before midnight the measures agreed upon were in print and communicated to the press.

There were no legal provisions in the Bank Act for times of panic, and the measures introduced by Order-in-Council were adopted in faith that Parliament would give its sanction. In brief, as passed by Parliament, and assented to on 14 August under the name of the Finance Act,[1] it was provided that:

1. Advances by Government to the banks in the form of Dominion notes could be made against approved securities deposited with the Minister. 2. The banks were authorised to make payments in their own notes in place of gold and Dominion notes. 3. The notes of the banks could be increased by an amount equal to 15 per cent. of their paid-up capital and rest, for the whole year, instead of from 1 September to the last day of February. 4. Redemption of Dominion notes in gold was suspended. 5. A moratorium was authorised [but was never declared].

These measures were accepted by the public with entire approval and all symptoms of panic disappeared. Thus an atmosphere of reasonable quiet was secured in which to deal with the problems pressing for solution. It is difficult to overstate the importance of the Finance Act, or the debt owed by the country to the Finance Minister, for his skill and foresight in its preparation and speedy enactment. It was still in 1921 in force as a whole, and the power of granting advances to banks against securities, including commercial bills, was a permanent contribution of great importance to the financial system of the country. Unemployment however persisted and, as a result of disordered trade, increased, so that it was necessary to continue public works, although money was immediately required for military organisation and revenue showed a disquieting reduction.

The preliminary war grant by Parliament, passed in August 1914, was for $50,000,000. The amount required in these first months of the War seemed large then, but in the perspective of the past now looks very small. Immediate requirements were provided by: £8,000,000 borrowed from the Imperial Government, $10,000,000 of Dominion notes issued by authority, $5,000,000 from the Bank of Montreal, and £3,000,000 negotiated in the London market in the form of six months' notes. This provided something under $70,000,000.

In the session of Parliament at the beginning of 1915 immediate

[1] Act of 22 Aug. 1914.

measures were adopted to increase revenue, by raising the tariff, by stamp taxes, and the like. The actual war expenditure down to February 1915 was $38,000,000. In August 1915 a loan of $45,000,000 was floated in New York, and in November 1915 subscriptions were asked for a $50,000,000 internal loan. This amount was named by the Minister with some trepidation as it seemed an incredible amount for the Canadian market, but the amount subscribed was over $100,000,000, and $100,000,000 was allotted. This was the first Dominion government loan ever floated in Canada and the result was a great surprise. A second and a third loan were floated in 1916 and in March 1917. In both cases the amount asked for was much over-subscribed. It was not until the end of 1917 that the amounts demanded from the public ran into larger figures, and the three succeeding loans in November 1917, November 1918, and November 1919, produced allotments amounting in all to nearly $1,850,000,000, bringing the grand total of war loans floated in Canada to about $2,200,000,000. In addition $150,000,000 was borrowed in New York.

Two significant points should be noticed in all these loans. In 1919 the Finance Minister in his budget speech stated that of the loans then outstanding $1,510,000,000 was held in Canada. Secondly, the banks in Canada were singularly free from any burdensome participation in war loans, and were thus able to use their resources for the industrial purposes created by the demands for munitions and war supplies generally.

The first war contract awarded in Canada was in September 1914. It took some months before machinery could be provided for the production of munitions on a large scale, and naturally there was a certain timidity on the part of capital to engage in a production felt to be full of unknown risks. But during 1915 and 1916 a steadily increasing volume of munitions was produced and vast quantities of other goods were sold to the Allies at high prices. Owing to the success of the last three loans, the Dominion Government was in a position to extend large credits for the supply of war requirements to Great Britain. These amounted during the War to $753,000,000. The banks subscribed another $100,000,000 and the British Government paid in cash through New York some $395,000,000.

High prices for all goods, high wages and an unlimited demand for everything that could be produced, created the money necessary for the immense war loans. A striking illustration of the way in which money had found its way into the hands of large numbers of people is exemplified in the number of subscribers to the three last loans—November 1917, 609,000 subscribers; November 1918, 1,140,000 subscribers; and November 1919, 795,000 subscribers. What had occurred, of course, was that a large part of the enormous addition to the Canadian debt had simply been transferred from the Government to individuals. Bank deposits rose from about $1,000,000,000 in June 1914 to $1,745,000,000 in 1919 and to $1,903,000,000 in 1920.

The total capital cost of the War to the Dominion was about $2,000,000,000, and out of this, as the Minister of Finance stated in 1919, some $276,000,000 had been paid for out of revenue. Such inflation as occurred was mainly in the form of bank credits. The increase of note issue was not alarming. Dominion notes in circulation reached a maximum of about $300,000,000 in 1919, with a gold reserve of $118,000,000. The bank note circulation increased from $105,000,000 in 1913 to a maximum of $228,000,000 in 1920.

The rise in prices, which was so closely related to such inflation as existed, was from the basic figure of 100 in 1913 to a maximum of 256 in 1920, and was followed by the drastic break in prices (beginning that autumn) to 150 in 1921. The management of the finances of Canada during the War was most skilful; the distribution of the war loans all that could be desired—more than three-quarters of their total being owned in Canada. The "maturities", too, were well arranged. But the addition to the public debt was unavoidably large.

In 1914 the net debt of the Dominion was $336,000,000 and the interest charges under $13,000,000. In 1921 these figures had risen to $2,340,000,000 and $140,000,000 respectively, and war pensions absorbed another $37,000,000. The two years from November 1918 to the autumn of 1920 belong in reality to the war period, and the high point of banking figures as of prices was reached in 1920. No bank failures occurred between 1914 and 1921, and in those years the number of branches in Canada grew from 3000 to 4659, besides which the number of their establishments in Great Britain, the United States, South America, the West Indies and other places outside Canada increased to 200.

From the first the Canadian banks have played an important part in the conservation and development of the business of the country, and their conduct of liquidation in 1912, their helpfulness and courage in the War, and their handling of the difficult readjustments of 1920-1, entitle them to high consideration.

The outbreak of the War brought with it important changes in Canadian finance. Up to that time London had been the obvious, and indeed almost the sole source of external credit. But the immense demands of the British Government for its own war expenses rapidly absorbed all the money that the London money market could supply. After the War was concluded, the situation still remained unfavourable for the flotation of Canadian loans in London; not only on account of scarcity of money, but also because of the disorder of the exchanges. With the pound sterling at a heavy and fluctuating discount, the borrowing of money in London by Canada became out of the question. In the meantime the Canadian public had become an extensive investor in its own securities, and had passed on from being a purchaser, mainly of government bonds, to becoming a buyer of municipal and industrial securities. More important still was the

rapidly growing American interest in all classes of Canadian investment. The financial relations of Canada with New York have, for
many years, been intimate, and it has long been the practice of the
Canadian banks to carry a part of their reserves in the shape of call
loans in that market. Five of the Canadian banks have their own
establishments there. But the foundation in 1914 of the Federal Reserve Bank in the United States was a momentous event. Immensely
strong, and ably and cautiously managed, it gave the initial proof of
efficiency in war finance, and the control of a gold situation that
must otherwise have been embarrassing. It has permanently stabilised
the New York money market, and made panics such as that of 1907
practically impossible. The creation since the War of an efficient bill
market has completed in New York the machinery necessary for an
adequate reserve centre.

Thus the North American continent has come to be, for financial
purposes, a more or less self-contained unit, with New York as its
great central market. This does not mean that London can be excluded from consideration in Canadian financial affairs. Far from it.
But it does mean that the enormous wealth of the United States and
its efficient concentration of power in New York have altered the
balance of Canadian interests. Proximity and continuously growing
intimacy have united with the accidents of war to change the orientation of Canadian finance.

The period dealt with in this chapter ends in 1921 and we must
conclude in a minor key, but not in pessimism. Like each succeeding
fall in the curves of Canadian development, it marks an interval of
hesitation, discomfort, and readjustment. It is true that the year
1921 was one of depression and that the national debt had reached
portentous figures. But it is clear that individual wealth had grown
in larger measure than the increase in public debt. In the period from
1914 to 1921 inclusive savings deposits in the banks showed an
increase of $577,000,000; Dominion war bonds held in Canada in
1921 not less than $1,600,000,000; municipal debentures bought by
Canadian investors, from 1914 to 1921, $277,000,000; purchases of
motors in same period, $400,000,000; making a total of $2,854,000,000.
To this large amount must be added other items of importance that
cannot be closely estimated. First; a large amount of Canadian
securities was repurchased from Great Britain. Second; much of the
increase in the capitalisation of industrial companies consisted of
accumulated profits. Thus it is clear that the vast transfer of wealth
to individuals, effected by government financing brought about by
the requirements of war, was associated with large additional profits
from the supply of war materials to the Allies, and a new distribution
and accretion of wealth ensued that needed only a fresh impulse of
enterprise to effect a return of general prosperity.

Canadian Bank Insolvencies since 1867

Name	Date of suspension	Paid-up capital ($)	Reserve fund ($)	Liabilities ($)	Assets ($)	Paid to note-holders (%)	Paid to depositors (%)
Commercial Bank of N.B.*	—	600,000		671,420	1,222,454	100	100
Bank of Acadia	April 1873	100,000		106,914	213,346	100	100
Metropolitan Bank	Oct. 1876	800,170		293,379	779,225	100	100
Mechanics' Bank	May 1879	194,794		547,238	721,155	57½	57½
Bank of Liverpool	Oct. 1879	370,548		136,480	207,877	100	96 6/17
Consolidated Bank of Canada	Aug. 1879	2,080,920		1,794,249	3,077,202	100	100
Stadacona Bank	July 1879	991,890		341,500	1,355,675	100	100
Bank of P.E.I.	Nov. 28 1881	121,000	45,000	1,108,000	953,244	59½	59½
Exchange Bank of Canada	Sept. 1883	500,000	300,000	2,863,884	3,779,493	100	66⅔
Maritime Bank of Dom. of Canada	Mar. 1887	321,900	60,000	1,409,482	1,825,993	100	103⅔
Pictou Bank	Sept. 1887	200,000		74,364	277,017	100	100
Bank of London in Canada	Aug. 1887	241,101	50,000	1,031,280	1,310,675	100	100
Central Bank of Canada	Nov. 1887	500,000	45,000	2,631,378	3,231,518	100	99½
Federal Bank	Jan. 1888	1,250,000	150,000	3,449,499	4,869,113	100	100
Commercial Bank of Manitoba	June 30 1893	553,650	50,000	1,341,251	1,951,151	100	75¼
Banque du Peuple	July 15 1895	1,200,000	600,000	7,761,209	9,533,537	100	17½
Banque Ville Marie	July 25 1899	479,620	10,000	1,766,841	2,267,516	100	75¼
Bank of Yarmouth	Mar. 6 1905	300,000	35,000	388,660	723,660	100	100
Ontario Bank	Oct. 13 1906	1,500,000	700,000	15,272,271	15,920,307	100	100
Sovereign Bank of Canada	Jan. 18 1908	3,000,000		16,174,408	19,218,746	100	100
Banque de St Jean	Apr. 28 1908	316,386	10,000	560,781	326,118	100	30½
Banque de St Hyacinthe	Jan. 24 1908	331,235	75,000	1,172,630	1,576,443	100	100
St Stephen's Bank	Mar. 10 1910	200,000	55,000	549,830	818,271	100	100
Farmers' Bank	Dec. 19 1910	567,579		1,997,041	2,616,683	100	†
Bank of Vancouver	Dec. 14 1914	445,188		912,137	1,532,786	100	†

* This bank was only in existence for three months and twenty-six days. Only some of its notes were redeemed on its reopening for a few days. The Dominion Government received 25 cents on the dollar on several thousand dollars' worth of the notes which it held.

† Liquidation incomplete.

Movement of Population, including estimated Natural Increase, recorded Immigration, and estimated Emigration, for the intercensal periods 1901–11 *and* 1911–21

Decades and Items		No.
Decade 1901–11:		
Population, census of 1 April 1901		5,371,315
Natural increase (1901–11), estimated		853,566
Immigration (1 April 1901 to 31 May 1911)... ...		1,847,651
	Total	8,072,532
Population, census of 1 June 1911		7,206,643
Emigration (1 April 1901 to 31 May 1911), estimated		865,889
Decade 1911–21:		
Population, census of 1 June 1911		7,206,643
Natural increase (1911–21), estimated...		1,150,659
Immigration (1 June 1911 to 31 May 1921)		1,728,921
	Total	10,086,223
Population, census of 1 June 1921		8,788,483
Emigration (1 June 1911 to 31 May 1921), estimated		1,297,740*
Net gain in population, 1901–11		1,835,328
Net gain in population, 1911–21		1,581,840

Sales of Canadian Bonds (in dollars)—Summary

	1910	1911	1912	1913
Government	55,000,000	5,675,000	35,639,700	53,066,550
Municipal	35,748,690	47,159,288	48,414,962	115,761,925
Railway	69,950,000	100,472,700	69,972,320	108,528,044
Public Service Corporation...	7,945,400	32,105,500	21,565,000	26,574,479
Miscellaneous...	62,356,500	81,400,500	97,346,000	69,864,297
Total	231,000,590	266,812,988	272,937,982	373,795,295
Percentage placed in Canada	17·00	16·86	13·82	12·20
Percentage placed in U.S. ...	1·50	6·58	11·35	13·56
Percentage placed in Gr. Brit.	81·50	76·56	74·83	74·24

	1914	1915	1916	1917
Government	85,415,330	214,814,133	208,621,933	675,182,500
Municipal	84,388,431	66,508,073	49,893,763	26,104,067
Railway	59,405,666	37,915,665	15,920,000	22,566,666
Public Service Corporation...	9,777,954	10,225,000	22,950,000	15,425,000
Miscellaneous...	33,947,686	12,430,000	19,531,666	17,067,800
Total	272,935,067	341,892,871	316,917,362	756,346,033
Percentage placed in Canada	12·09	43·71	33·56	74·63
Percentage placed in U.S. ...	19·77	42·11	54·89	24·71
Percentage placed in Gr. Brit.	68·14	14·18	1·55	0·66

	1918	1919	1920	1921
Government	704,632,729	781,812,000	113,455,500	133,488,500
Municipal	45,805,720	27,166,393	58,994,728	88,805,973
Railway	5,000,000	35,355,133	96,500,000	101,150,000
Public Service Corporation...	2,375,000	20,950,000	11,500,000	15,450,000
Miscellaneous...	6,155,000	44,100,202	33,381,853	61,290,345
Total	763,968,449	909,383,728	318,832,081	400,184,818
Percentage placed in Canada	94·87	76·89	32·82	50·36
Percentage placed in U.S. ...	4·70	22·54	67·18	45·49
Percentage placed in Gr. Brit.	0·43	0·57	—	4·15

* This figure includes also the 60,000 Canadian lives lost at the front and the soldiers (about 20,000) enlisting in the Canadian forces and receiving their discharge in the United Kingdom.

(II) COMMERCIAL POLICY AND THE DEVELOPMENT OF COMMERCE

The commercial history of Canada since the year 1867 falls naturally into several distinct periods—a period of comparatively rapid growth just after confederation, followed by a quarter of a century of steady but comparatively slow development until the middle 'nineties, then some sixteen years of rapid and accelerating progress, culminating about 1912 and succeeded by a brief reaction just prior to the commencement of the Great War, and finally seven years of war and its aftermath—the springs of immigration dried up together with the flow of capital, inflation and extraordinary enhancement of prices to about two and a half times the pre-war level (in the spring of 1920), succeeded by the acute deflation of 1920 and 1921—a deflation, however, from which the country has at the time of writing quite recovered.

As these alternate periods of quicker and slower growth in Canada have generally accompanied similar epochs in the history of other countries, especially new countries, they suggest a common cause. It is to be found, immediately at least, in the trend of world prices. From 1867 to 1873 world prices were generally rising, from 1874 to 1896 falling, from 1897 to 1914 once more steadily on the rise, and from 1914 to 1920 soaring higher still under the influence of war-time scarcity and inflation. Finally, the world price-level fell abruptly and disastrously in the latter half of 1920 and the whole of 1921, except indeed in countries where the currency was being still further inflated.[1]

Periods of rising prices tend to coincide with periods of rapid development and periods of declining prices with depression. Steadily rising prices such as prevailed between 1897 and 1914 necessarily operate as a bonus to productive enterprise—a bonus which at such times goes far toward meeting the interest charges of producers, who in new countries usually work with borrowed money. Steadily falling prices, on the other hand, impose a handicap upon producers, who, particularly in new countries, have little ready money to lose. Trade also, as based upon production, is necessarily influenced by the stimulus given to production in the one case and by the handicap placed upon production in the other. Thus there are two reasons for the comparative stagnation in the value of the external trade of the Dominion between the 'seventies and the 'nineties—first, the same dollar values in the latter years represented a considerably larger physical volume of trade than in the former; secondly, the great fall in prices during the twenty years, with the consequent handicap on production, tended to eliminate all but the soundest and best-managed of the industries of Canada. Conversely, the rising prices

[1] Layton, W. T., *An Introduction to the Study of Prices*, esp. chaps. vi–viii.

after 1897 involved, first, larger dollar values for the same quantity of commodities, and, secondly, a bonus on production which enabled even the less competent producers to earn satisfactory profits, thus stimulating production and consequently trade. This latter phenomenon, in an intensified form, was observable during the Great War.

Confederation, on its economic side, was the natural consequence of the denunciation by the United States of the Reciprocity Treaty of 1854—a treaty which had provided for the free interchange of the natural products of British North America and the United States, and had thus been advantageous to producers of food products and raw materials in the less advanced of the two countries—British North America—more especially during the American Civil War. The enduring memory of these advantages and the desire for their return were for at least a generation factors of the first importance in determining the commercial policy of Canada. During more than forty years all Canadian Governments were ready to send delegates to Washington to negotiate for the renewal of that treaty or for some similar arrangement. In the first session of the Dominion Parliament and at many later times overtures were made and representatives sent to Washington, but no success was achieved until the ill-fated Taft agreement of 1911 was carried in the United States but defeated by the people of Canada. Whatever may be said of the economic wisdom of their decision, it certainly marked the rise of a new spirit of national self-sufficiency; *Canada farà da sé*.

All modern experience, perhaps on account of the growth of national self-consciousness in the political sphere and of large-scale production in the economic, is in favour of making the economic and commercial unit at least as large as the political unit, or even larger, in the hope that the political unit may grow up to it, as in the case of the German Zollverein or the Mitteleuropa of the Great War period. It was therefore not surprising that the British North America Act, the fundamental law of the new Dominion, enacted in section 121 that "all articles of the growth, produce or manufacture of any one of the provinces shall, from and after the union, be admitted free into each of the other provinces".

In the British North American provinces, as in other new countries with little realised wealth, it had been found easier to raise a revenue by indirect than by direct taxation, and the chief source of revenue was the customs tariff, which in pre-Confederation Canada had had since 1858 a distinct flavour of protection to domestic industries. In the Maritime Provinces, however, the local tariffs were practically for revenue only, though in Nova Scotia some slight advantage was given to the manufacturers of the province by placing raw materials suitable for manufacture on the free list—a provision not found in the New Brunswick tariff. This divergence of policy as between the provinces is indicated by the fact that in Nova Scotia the general tariff rate was 10 per cent., in New Brunswick the general rate on goods not elsewhere specified was 12½ per cent., while in Canada, under the tariff of 1859, it was 20 per cent. However, in view of the advent of confederation and the consequent desirability of making concessions to the low tariff views of the Maritime Provinces, where the people were traders rather than manufacturers, the Canadian tariff on goods not elsewhere specified was reduced to the compromise rate of 15 per cent. in the tariff of 1866, which a year later became the first tariff of the Dominion.[1] Under this tariff certain luxuries were taxed 25 per cent.

The tariff policy of the new Dominion was naturally and necessarily determined largely by the direction and character of the existing trade and partly by the recognised potentialities of its enlargement. The fathers of Confederation were, however, realists, and the hard facts of the trade of Canada in 1868 were these: the total of the merchandise imported for consumption and the exports was approximately $120,000,000 (i.e. £24,000,000), viz. $67,000,000 of imports for consumption and nearly $53,000,000 of exports ($48,500,000 of domestic exports).[2] Thus Canada, a country with considerable interest payments to make and an "unfavourable" trade balance of $14,000,000, was obviously importing new capital on what was for those times a fairly considerable scale. And that capital was evidently coming from the United Kingdom, since the United States were still impoverished and on a paper basis as a result of the Civil War. Further, trade in those less complex days approximately reflected the facts of the financial situation. Imports from the United Kingdom were $37,600,000 or 56 per cent. of total imports for consumption, while exports to the United Kingdom were $17,900,000 or 37 per cent. of the total. Imports from the United States were $22,660,000 or 34 per cent. of the total, and exports to the United States $25,350,000 or 52 per cent. of the total, so that the United States remained Canada's largest customer in spite of the denunciation of the Reciprocity Treaty, trade still running in its accustomed channels. Thus the two great English-speaking countries in the first year of Confederation together supplied 90 per cent. of Canadian imports and took 89 per cent. of Canadian exports, and rarely in the subsequent years has their percentage of Canada's total trade fallen below 80 per cent. The natural result of this predominance of the United Kingdom and the United States in Canadian markets has been that Canada's commercial policy, apart from the question of the general rates of the tariff, has been mainly concerned with three great issues inextricably intertwined—the general question of a protective as compared with a revenue tariff, Canada's trade relations with the United States and those with the United Kingdom—in other words,

---

[1] McLean, S. J., *Tariff History of Canada*, p. 10.
[2] *Canada Year Book*, 1925, p. 456.

reciprocity with the United States and the British preference. This last issue includes, in the more recent years since Canada has become an important manufacturing country, her position as an exporter of manufactured goods to the other Dominions and the dependencies of the Empire. In addition to these questions of policy, we shall be concerned with the twenty-fold increase of trade during the period. From the small beginnings just described, the external trade of Canada in the fiscal year ended in 1921 reached the enormous total of $2,450,000,000. This figure, it is true, was recorded during a period of high prices and post-war inflation.

As already stated, the new Confederation was fortunate in commencing business on a rising tide of prosperity which culminated about 1873. Consequently the Canadians did not then greatly miss the American market, though they negotiated for the renewal of the Reciprocity Treaty, using as attractions the offer of the free admission of the Americans to the Canadian fisheries and the free navigation of the St Lawrence, together with admission on equal terms to the Canadian canals. In the first session of the Dominion Parliament, it was enacted that grain, flour and breadstuffs, animals and meats, poultry, fish, fruit, butter, cheese, timber and lumber from the United States might be admitted free of duty on condition of reciprocity.[1] Again, in 1869, Sir John Rose, then Minister of Finance in the Macdonald Government, was sent to Washington to co-operate with the British Minister in negotiating a reciprocity treaty, but without success. The hopes of the Canadians were still high, but they were dashed by the Washington Treaty of 1871, when the British delegates were held to have sacrificed Canadian interests to the general interests of the Empire, in order to conciliate the United States, in spite of the protests of Sir John Macdonald, who represented Canada in the negotiations. At any rate, under the treaty, Canada granted the free navigation of the St Lawrence for ever, and the use of her canals on equal terms throughout the duration of the treaty in return for the navigation of Lake Michigan and the St Clair Flats canal for the term of the treaty and of the Alaskan rivers for ever. She also conceded the free admission of Americans to her fisheries in return for admission to the American fisheries north of 39 degrees north latitude, the United States to pay money compensation for the superior value, if any, of access to the Canadian fisheries. This treaty deprived Canada of the special privileges by which she hoped to bargain for the admission of her natural products and was bitterly resented in Canada, though accepted at the entreaty of Sir John Macdonald as being in the general interest of the Empire. The anger of the Canadians might have been more lasting if the country had been less prosperous.[2]

[1] 31 Vict. c. 7, s. 4.
[2] *Canada and its Provinces*, IX, 126; Pope, Sir J., *Memoirs of Sir John A. Macdonald*, II, pp. 85 ff.

Considering the comparatively small scale of business in those times, there was certainly rapid progress between 1868 and 1873. Imports of merchandise increased in these five years from $67,000,000 to $124,500,000 or 85 per cent., exports from $52,700,000 to $86,000,000 or 63 per cent, total trade from under $120,000,000 to over $210,000,000 or 75 per cent. The adverse balance of trade rose from $14,300,000 in 1868 to $38,500,000 in 1873—indicating a great increase in the importations of new capital for the development of the country. This new capital was partly invested in new lines of railway, and the operating mileage of the railways rose from 2270 in 1868 to 3832 in 1873 and to 4804 in 1875. Again, the increase in imports involved a corresponding increase in customs revenue, which rose from $8,578,000 in 1868 to $12,954,000 in 1873, while total revenue receipts grew from $13,687,000 in the former year to $20,813,000 in the latter.[1]

The importation of new capital above described was not in this period unduly hindered by the height of the tariff. The compromise tariff of the time, besides introducing specific duties from the tariffs of the Maritime Provinces, had its *ad valorem* duties at three chief rates: 25 per cent., which may be described as a tax on luxuries, 15 per cent., the general rate and the rate on articles not elsewhere provided, and the 10 per cent. rate, most of the revenue being raised by the 15 per cent. rate. While the tariff may be described generally as a revenue tariff, there are certain indications in it of a protectionist trend, notably the free admission of raw materials and partially manufactured goods for further manufacture. Iron and colours imported for the use of wall-paper manufacturers are cases in point. Further, the ministers admitted on the floor of Parliament that protection was one of the ends of the tariff. In 1871, in the course of the discussion of a protest by the Montreal Corn Exchange against the grain and flour duties, Sir Francis Hincks took the ground that the Government, in imposing these duties, was acting in accordance with the National Policy.[2] There is thus evident a gradual trend in the direction of protection—a trend which appears natural enough when it is considered that the old province of Canada, which had already adopted a protective tariff, was the predominant partner in the new Confederation, having at the first Dominion census of 1871 over 76 per cent. of the total population.

As has been already recorded,[3] the first Liberal Administration of the Dominion took office in 1873 as a result of the defeat of Sir John A. Macdonald's Administration over the "Pacific scandal"—an issue entirely unconnected with tariff policy. It thus came into power at a very inauspicious time when the great period of prosperity and

---

[1] Breckenridge, R. M., *The History of Banking in Canada*, pp. 110-14.
[2] McLean, S. J., pp. 11 ff.
[3] See chapter xx.

rising prices which had culminated in 1873 had closed, and prices and general business were declining. Twenty-three years later, when the second Liberal Administration took office, the fates redressed the balance by bringing it into power at the very commencement of a period of expansion and prosperity when prices began to rise, business to "boom", and importation of capital from the older countries proceeded upon an unprecedented scale. Canadian Liberals have always had a leaning towards a tariff for revenue as distinguished from a tariff for the protection of domestic industries, but the increasing obligations of the Government for provincial subsidies, interest on debt and capital expenditure on railway construction, made an increased revenue necessary at the very time when the customs revenue was declining with the decline in trade. Consequently, in the new tariff of 1874, the general rate of duty on goods not elsewhere specified was raised from 15 to 17½ per cent. *ad valorem*, and the duties on spirits and tobacco were increased. A significant innovation was the imposition of a duty of 10 per cent. on "machinery for mills and factories, the like of which is not manufactured in Canada", an item previously on the free list; the change, however, was mitigated by a provision that such machinery might, by order of the Governor in Council, be admitted free of duty until 1875.

The great defect of a revenue arising in the main out of customs duties is its fluctuation—the likelihood of too large a surplus in times of prosperity and of a deficit in times of depression. Now trade continued to fall off and the revenue fell off with it, and an attempt in 1877 to increase the customs revenue by a readjustment and increase of duties, failed to fill up the gap between revenue and expenditure.

Meanwhile the Administration sent to Washington in 1874 the Hon. Geo. Brown, who had been appointed by the British Government joint plenipotentiary with the British ambassador, and who actually succeeded in making a draft treaty on the basis of the agreement of Canada to enlarge the Welland and St Lawrence Canals for the equal benefit of both countries and to admit free of duty specified manufacturing as well as all natural products. Canada was also to have the right to grant the same terms to the United Kingdom. However, like many another excellent arrangement, the treaty failed to pass the United States Senate.[1] Later on the fisheries arbitration arising out of the Washington Treaty of 1871 was resumed, and, largely owing to the ability of the Canadian negotiator, Sir A. T. Galt, Canada received in 1877 what is known as the "Halifax award" of $4,420,882 from the United States, as compensation for the superior value of her inshore fisheries, opened to the free use of the fishermen

[1] See J. Charlton's article on "Canadian Trade Relations with the United States", in *Canada: an Encyclopaedia of the Country*, I, 373.

of both countries.[1] A sum of $160,000, representing the interest on this amount, is still distributed annually by the Canadian Government in bounties to fishermen on the Atlantic coast.

The manufacturers as well as the traders of Canada were now feeling the full effects of the great depression, and, as was natural, blamed their own Government therefor, complaining bitterly of the dumping of the surplus products of British and American factories. Indignation was chiefly directed against the United States, both because it was a foreign country and because its markets were alleged to be barred against Canadian products while its products were received into Canada. Canadian manufacturers in 1874 professed themselves as willing to meet their American competitors on equal terms, but submitted that the existing terms were unequal. The slogans of the Conservatives in 1877 and 1878 were "The National Policy" and "Reciprocity of trade or reciprocity of tariffs", the former of these alternatives being generally recognised as preferable, if attainable. It was not attained, and the Canadian people in 1878 decided for "reciprocity of tariffs", though still hoping that retaliation might bring about a change of heart in the United States.

From the autumn of 1878 to the summer of 1896 the Conservative and protectionist party held power in Canada throughout eighteen years of rather chequered economic conditions, but with a general downward trend in world prices.[2] They were thus, on the whole, rowing against the economic tide. Their new tariff, the concrete expression of the "National Policy", was introduced in 1879, the Minister of Finance declaring that the Government's policy was to "select for a higher rate of duty those articles which were manufactured in the country, and to admit at a lower rate those which could not be made within the country". The general rate on goods not otherwise provided was raised to 20 per cent., but some duties were considerably higher. Protective duties were imposed on breadstuffs and a 25 per cent. duty on agricultural implements. The textile manufacturers received special consideration, the duties on woollens being practically doubled. Coal, whether anthracite or bituminous, was subjected to a duty of 50 cents per ton so as to enable Nova Scotian coal to compete with American coal as far west as Toronto. On the other hand, the duties on iron and steel were only slightly raised at this time, pig iron, previously free, paying $2 a ton (the attempt to create a Canadian iron and steel industry dated only from 1887). Finally, the rates of duty on furniture and clocks, carriages, glass-ware, wall-paper, silks, boots and shoes, buttons, rubber goods

---

[1] The fisheries articles of this treaty were terminated by the United States in 1885. On the Halifax award see Skelton, O. D., *Life and Times of Sir Alex. T. Galt*, chap. xvi. The total of the Halifax award was $5,500,000, but the balance went to Newfoundland (see *infra* chapter xxviii).

[2] The Canadian official index-number of wholesale prices dates only from 1890. It fell by 16 per cent. between 1890 and 1896.

and wooden-ware, were all substantially increased, and that on sugar was raised from 5 to 10 per cent. To a considerable extent specific duties were substituted for *ad valorem*, as providing a rather more stable yield in a period of depression and declining prices. Exclusive of the specific duties, the average *ad valorem* rate on 245 dutiable articles was 22·26 per cent., and the average total rate of duty collected on all dutiable goods in 1880, the first year of the operation of the new tariff, was 26·1 per cent. as compared with 21·4 per cent. in 1878. Meanwhile raw materials were in many cases allowed to come in free, with the evident object of promoting Canadian manufactures.

The tariff of 1879, as outlined above, underwent various changes in the 'eighties, mainly in an upward direction. The duties on coal were raised from 50 to 60 cents per ton in 1880, with the idea of enabling Nova Scotian coal to be brought as far as Hamilton. While the duties on finished manufactured products were from time to time increased, there was also evident a distinct tendency to take off the duties on raw materials and on any articles which were used in manufacturing processes. In 1887 there were a good many increases on such articles as printed and dyed cottons, cigars and cigarettes, also on iron and its products,[1] where the rates fixed by the Government were now about two-thirds of the corresponding rates levied in the United States. As a result of these and many other similar increases, the average rate of duty collected upon all dutiable articles reached its maximum in 1889, at 31·9 per cent. *ad valorem*. The highest average *ad valorem* rate of duty on all imports, dutiable and free, was 22·0 per cent. in 1888, so that these two years of 1888 and 1889 may be considered the climax of protection in Canada.[2]

In the early 'nineties the general discontent at declining prices and bad business led the Government to attempt to conciliate the people by removing the duties on articles of wide popular consumption. The most notable reform of this kind was the removal of the taxes on raw sugar in 1891, when the Government gave up taxation to the estimated amount of $3,500,000 per annum, while the duties on spirits and tobacco were increased. Again, in 1893 the duty of 25 per cent. *ad valorem*, which had been imposed on binder twine in 1890, was reduced to 12½ per cent. Also in 1894 there were many changes which, generally speaking, were in the direction of lower tariffs. The reductions were largely on agricultural products and on agricultural implements, cottons and woollens and iron and steel and their products, as well as on chemicals and leather. Apparently the Government was apprehensive lest the people might be carried off their feet by the anti-protectionist agitation of the Liberal Opposition.

[1] The rate on pig iron, for example, was raised to $4 per ton. In addition to the tariff, protection bounties were paid from 1883 to 1910 on pig iron produced from Canadian ore.
[2] *Canada Year Book*, 1925, p. 462.

In a young country which is importing capital for purposes of development, imports are probably a better test of prosperity than exports. The imports of Canada, which had been \$90,000,000 in 1878, fell to \$70,000,000 in 1880, and rose again to \$122,000,000 with the revival of prosperity in 1883. Thereafter they fell off in the renewed depression of 1884–8, averaging just about \$100,000,000 annually in these years, though even at this figure they exceeded the exports. A natural consequence of this stagnation was doubts and criticisms of the National Policy, and the Liberals, so badly defeated in 1878, raised their heads once more to complain of the short-sighted fiscal policy of the Government, and more particularly to press for better trade relations with the United States, whose tariff policy had not, as was hoped, been modified in favour of reciprocity with Canada by the retaliatory legislation of the Dominion. The Government, frightened by the rising tide of discontent and its declining majority at the general election of February 1887, sent Sir Charles Tupper to Washington in May of that year to negotiate a treaty, and to make what he afterwards described as "not an offer of unrestricted reciprocity, but an unrestricted offer of reciprocity"; but the Americans, irritated by alleged harsh treatment of United States fishermen by the Canadian authorities, were in no mood to listen to him, especially as, representing a protectionist Government, he was in no position to grant to American manufacturers freedom of access to the Canadian market.

Since the Conservative attempt to head off the growing discontent at the unsatisfactory commercial relations between Canada and the United States had been a failure, we find other means proposed to secure for both countries the advantages of freer trade. The programme of the Commercial Unionists included the freedom of the fisheries and of the waters of the St Lawrence system to the citizens of both countries, but more particularly a complete free trade between the United States and Canada; the assimilation of their tariffs against other nations; the abolition of customs-houses on the border; division of customs revenue; discrimination against the United Kingdom. This programme, the last item in which was particularly distasteful to most Canadians, was enunciated in 1887 by Erastus Wiman, a Canadian-born resident of the United States, who found allies in S. J. Ritchie, an American capitalist with large interests in Canada, and in Congressman Butterworth of Ohio, and, on the Canadian side of the border, in Goldwin Smith.[1] The scheme was in the beginning endorsed by the *Toronto Mail* and *Globe* and by the *Montreal Witness*, as well as by many farmers' organisations anxious to obtain admission for their produce to the American market. The Liberal Opposition, though they hesitated to incorporate Commercial Union into their

---

[1] *Handbook of Commercial Union: a Collection of Papers read before the Commercial Union Club, Toronto*, with introduction by Goldwin Smith.

platform, in the following year accepted in caucus a compromise policy known as "Unrestricted Reciprocity", including complete free trade between the two countries; no assimilation of tariffs; maintenance of customs-houses; no division of customs revenue; probably (though this was not made explicit) discrimination against the United Kingdom. Unrestricted reciprocity was the Liberal policy in the election campaign of 1891, and was perhaps defeated only by Sir John A. Macdonald's appeal to the patriotism of the Canadian people.[1]

The Conservatives won, but only by a narrow majority. Immediately after the election, however, a bomb was flung into the Liberal ranks by the publication of a letter from the Hon. Edward Blake, former Liberal leader, to the electors of West Durham, stating that in his opinion, unrestricted reciprocity would lead to discrimination against the United Kingdom and ultimately to political union with the United States.[2] The result of this attack was to kill the agitation for unrestricted reciprocity, and the Liberals, grown wiser, at the Ottawa convention in June 1893 made it a count against the existing tariff that "it has discriminated against Great Britain". Their declaration on reciprocity with the United States, except that they would include "a well-considered list of manufactured articles", was of a very gentle and innocuous character, such as might, but for the exigencies of party politics, have received the approval of the Conservatives themselves.[3] This abandonment of unrestricted reciprocity made it impossible for the Conservatives to avail themselves in 1896 of the patriotic ammunition which had served them so well in 1891, while the hard times made the electors feel that a change was desirable. In the summer of 1896 the change came.

The second Liberal ministry took office in July 1896, and a turn in the economic tide took place in the following year. Thereafter, throughout the fifteen years of the Laurier Administration, the Canadian ship of state was travelling with the tide and making excellent progress. One of the first steps of the Government was to send ministers to Washington to discuss reciprocity with the United States, but their reception was discouraging, more especially as the Republicans had been victorious in the presidential election of 1896 and were just introducing the Dingley Tariff, with rates of duty on Canadian products even higher than those of the McKinley Tariff of 1890. The question of trade relations came up once more in 1898, during the discussions of the Joint High Commission whose chief purpose was to settle the Alaska boundary dispute, but still the Americans were obdurate, and on his return to Ottawa the Prime

---

[1] Macdonald's election manifesto, in *Canada: an Encyclopaedia*, i, 398–401; also Laurier's election address, pp. 402–4.
[2] *Ibid.* i, 389 f.
[3] *Ibid.* i, 310, 311.

Minister declared, "There will be no more pilgrimages to Washington. We are turning our hopes to the old motherland".[1]

The Liberal party, after attaining office with its attendant responsibilities, realised more vividly than when in Opposition that changes must proceed gradually, with reasonable consideration of vested interests. Accordingly their 1897 tariff proposals did not go so far as was generally expected, and the chief changes which were made were in the direction of framing a new and specially low tariff for countries giving Canada favourable treatment rather than in a reduction of general rates.[2] A horizontal reduction of $12\frac{1}{2}$ per cent. in all customs duties except those on alcoholic liquors and tobacco was granted to the products of all countries giving Canadian products equally favourable treatment; the percentage of reduction was to be increased a year later to 25 per cent. This reduced tariff, originally known as the "reciprocal tariff", was understood to apply only to the products of Great Britain and certain low-tariff colonies, but Belgium and Germany were able to establish their claim (under treaties of 1861 and 1865 respectively) to have their products admitted on the same terms as those of Great Britain; and Argentina, Austria-Hungary, Bolivia, Colombia, Denmark, Persia, Russia, Sweden, Switzerland, Tunis and Venezuela obtained the same privileges under their most-favoured-nation treaties, while France secured the same treatment under the Franco-Canadian treaty of 1893. It looked as if half the world would get the advantages of the Canadian reciprocal tariff of 1897, but Great Britain saved the situation by denouncing the treaties with Belgium and Germany, thus enabling Canada to convert the reciprocal tariff, as she desired, into a British preferential tariff.

The British preferential tariff, with duties 25 per cent. lower than the general rate, came into force on 1 August 1898, and the percentage was raised to $33\frac{1}{3}$ on 1 July 1900, but four years later, in response to appeals from Canadian manufacturers, particularly in the textile industries, the minimum preferential tariff on woollens was raised from $23\frac{1}{3}$ to 30 per cent. and that on twine and cordage from $16\frac{2}{3}$ to 20 per cent. In 1906–7 there was a wider application of this principle of having special treatment for each article, and in the customs tariff of 1907 there were incorporated three rates for each dutiable item— the lowest, the British preferential rate; an intermediate rate, for use in granting favours on a reciprocal basis to foreign countries; a general tariff rate applicable to all other foreign countries. The customs tariff of 1907, with amendments, is still the tariff of Canada.

The grant of the British preferential tariff, heralded with a flourish of trumpets at the Diamond Jubilee, and supplemented by the denunciation of treaties with Belgium and the German Zollverein, which

---

[1] Fielding's budget speech of 22 April 1897. Also *Colonial Tariff Policies*, p. 666.
[2] Porritt, E., *Sixty Years of Protection in Canada*, 2nd ed. pp. 219 ff.

had been in force for over thirty years, had profound reactions upon world politics. In Germany, more especially, it was looked upon as a first step in the attempt to create a British Imperial *Zollverein*, and shut out German products from that equal treatment with British products which they had hitherto enjoyed throughout the length and breadth of the British Empire. Hence there arose in Germany, now a great exporter of manufactured goods, a cry for retaliation against Great Britain and Canada and a demand for an extension of German over-sea possessions which would provide markets for German manu-factured products and supply their own congested mother country with food products and raw materials. In 1899 Germany withdrew from Canada the benefits of her minimum tariff, in spite of the Canadian claims that German products were receiving as favourable treatment in the tariff as those of any other foreign country. In 1903 Canada retaliated by imposing a surtax of one-third the existing duties on the products of any foreign country which treated imports from Canada less favourably than imports from other States. This expedient was finally effective in inducing Germany to propose better relations, and in 1910 Canada agreed to withdraw the surtax, on Germany's grant of her minimum rates on a long list of Canada's exports.[1]

In the meantime the British preferential tariff, which had origin-ally extended to the goods of the United Kingdom, Bermuda, the British West Indies and British Guiana, was in 1898 extended to the products of India, Ceylon, the Straits Settlements and New South Wales. New Zealand granted a preference on a limited list of articles in 1903, and in the same year the South African Customs Union established a British preference, to which Canada was admitted in 1904. Negotiations with Australia for a mutual preference proved abortive; but in April 1912 representatives of the West Indies came to Ottawa and negotiated a special agreement giving them a 20 per cent. preference for ten years on their chief products, and imposing new duties upon foreign cocoa beans, limes and lime juice. In return Canada was to receive the same rate of preference on her chief ex-ports to the islands. She also extended the same preferences for three years to Newfoundland, Bermuda, British Honduras, Grenada and Jamaica, to give them an opportunity of joining in the arrangement. In 1920 this treaty was renewed and its preferences increased at a second conference in Ottawa, when Canada also agreed to provide steamship services to and from all the British West Indies.

The low-tariff Liberal victory in Canada in June 1896 was soon followed by a high-tariff Republican victory in the United States in November of the same year. Thenceforth for sixteen years the Re-publicans were in power in Washington, and the first-fruits of their

---

[1] Fleck, A. A., *Kanada: Volkswirtschaftliche Grundlagen und weltwirtschaftliche Beziehungen*, pp. 308–13.

administration was the Dingley Tariff of 1897, which struck even harder at Canadian products than the McKinley Tariff of 1890. Mr Fielding could only say, in his budget speech of 1897, that the time for approaching the United States on the question of reciprocity had not yet arrived. It did not arrive for some fourteen years thereafter, and when it came the United States made the approaches and the resulting agreement brought about the downfall of the long-lived Government of Sir Wilfrid Laurier. Their increasing prosperity rendered Canadians comparatively indifferent to the hostile tariff policy of the United States. In 1902 and 1907 the colonies, now committed to imperial preference, endeavoured to secure a preference in the markets of the mother country through the Colonial Conferences; but in 1902 the Conservative Government was not ready, and in 1907 the Liberal Government had been returned on a policy of free trade, so there was no response to their efforts. Thus Canadian statesmen, hopeless of getting any further with the United Kingdom, proceeded to negotiate commercial treaties with foreign countries on the basis of their intermediate tariff. Notable among these was a treaty with France, negotiated in 1907 but not ratified until May 1910, giving Canada the minimum rates of the French tariff on live cattle, fresh canned meats, dairy products, fish, lumber and pulp, agricultural implements, typewriters, various manufactures of iron and steel, furniture, boots and shoes, asbestos products and cement. Canada, on her side, admitted many important French products at favourable rates and later in the year extended the intermediate rates to the same products coming from Belgium and the Netherlands. In an agreement with Italy in the same year each of the countries extended favourable treatment to particular products of the other.

Meanwhile the United States threatened to retaliate against Canada under the Payne-Aldrich tariff of 1909, which contained provisions for a maximum and minimum tariff, the maximum to be imposed upon the goods of all countries discriminating against them. The United States claimed that the concessions made to France and other countries should also be granted to them, though there was no question of a *quid pro quo*. Finally Canada agreed to give the United States the benefit of the intermediate tariff on a few articles, whereupon they dropped their claim for treatment equal to France. In the course of the negotiations, President Taft had expressed his desire for better trade relations, and negotiations resulted in the United States offering complete free trade, which Canada declined. The agreement finally reached placed natural products on the free list together with some manufactured articles and reduced the tariff on others. All reductions which Canada gave the United States were by treaty to be extended to the British Empire and to the "most-favoured-nations". After a long debate, much obstruction and the calling of a special session of Congress, the United States accepted the arrangement. In

Canada, however, the fates were adverse. Long obstruction by the Conservatives led the Prime Minister to appeal to the country, and the electorate pronounced against him on 21 September 1911. From the purely economic point of view, the decision was probably a mistake, but unquestionably it was the expression of resentment at the attitude of the United States toward Canada in the past, and of determination to build up a country which would be independent of the vicissitudes of American politics. In support of this determination the opponents of the agreement could refer to the remarkable growth of Canadian trade in spite of the hostile attitude of their great neighbour.

As a result of the stimulus to greater production and trade, the aggregate external trade of Canada (merchandise only) increased from $221,000,000 in 1896 ($105,000,000 imports, $116,000,000 exports) to $356,000,000 in 1900 ($173,000,000 imports, $183,000,000 exports). Thereafter imports increased more rapidly than exports, indicating new importations of capital. By 1905 the total trade was $453,000,000 ($252,000,000 imports, $201,000,000 exports) and in 1910 it was $670,000,000 ($371,000,000 imports, $299,000,000 exports). In the fiscal year ended March 1914, it was $1,074,000,000 ($619,000,000 imports, $455,000,000 exports).

The outbreak of the Great War reduced Canadian trade, especially the overseas trade. The tonnage of sea-going vessels entered and cleared fell from 29,568,000 in the last fiscal year of peace to 25,402,000 in the first whole fiscal year of war. Again, imports fell from $619,000,000 to $456,000,000 in the same periods, as they could no longer be procured by borrowing in Great Britain. Exports, on the other hand, increased from $455,000,000 to $461,000,000, probably owing to higher prices of food products. Thereafter, with higher prices of food products and raw materials and manufacture of war munitions, Canada began to pile up a "favourable" trade balance contrasting vividly with her pre-war "unfavourable" balance. Canada's excess of exports during the war, however, went to support the 418,000 soldiers whom she despatched to Europe.

The trade of Canada, which, through customs duties on imports, had always borne the chief burden of the national taxation, was now affected both by the increase of that taxation and by war risks. Early in the war the customs duties on spirituous liquors and tobacco, sugar and coffee, were increased, and in the following year duties or additional duties of 5 per cent. *ad valorem* under the British preferential tariff and 7½ per cent. *ad valorem* under intermediate and general tariffs, were imposed on almost all goods in Schedule A of the Customs Tariff, whether previously dutiable or free. This naturally restricted imports, though the inflation which was already commencing disguised the truth of the situation. In addition, other taxes were added for the benefit of the revenue: an extra cent on letters, postcards, telegrams and cablegrams, a tax of 2 cents on every cheque, an extra

1 per cent. on railway and steamboat tickets, and an extra charge on every sleeping-car berth and parlour-car seat. Next, a business profits war tax of 25 per cent. was imposed in 1916 and a war income tax in 1917. In 1918 the taxes on parlour-car seats and sleeping-car berths were increased; and a luxury tax of 10 per cent. of the selling price of passenger automobiles, gramophones and records, piano players and records, and jewellery, was imposed.[1]

In 1919 the extra 5 per cent. *ad valorem* customs duty imposed under the British preferential tariff was wholly, and the extra 7½ per cent. *ad valorem* duty under the other tariffs was partially removed; also the duties on coffee and tea were reduced, together with the duties on the agricultural implements necessary to enable Canada to raise an increasing part of the quantity of food required throughout the world. In 1920, however, it became evident that the country had by no means balanced its budget, and a new tax, the sales tax of 1 per cent., was imposed upon wholesale and manufacturers' sales, a tax the rates of which were raised in 1921 and again in 1922.

So far as values go, the outstanding fiscal years in Canadian trade have been 1918, when exports of domestic produce aggregated $1,540,000,000 and imports $963,500,000, and 1921, when the domestic exports were $1,189,000,000 and imports $1,240,000,000. These, however, were years when prices were double or more than double pre-war prices, measured in paper dollars which were at a discount. Careful analysis of the trade statistics shows that Canada is now exporting a greater value of manufactured goods (including "partly manufactured goods") than she is importing. It is clear that the older conceptions of Canada as merely a "lumber lot" or a "granary" are utterly out of date, and that another important manufacturing nation has arisen. Indeed, Canada has been recognised by the League of Nations as one of the eight most important industrial countries of the world.

[1] *Canada Year Book*, 1925, pp. 760 ff.

CHAPTER XXVII

THE ECONOMIC DEVELOPMENT OF CANADA,
1867–1921 *(continued)*

THE MARITIME PROVINCES

THE economic history of the Maritime Provinces since confederation is largely a history of the effects produced on them by economic
movements in the countries of the western world and in particular
those of the Atlantic Basin. These provinces have reflected faithfully
the important economic changes in Canada, the United States, the
West Indies and Europe. The Civil War and subsequent industrial
development of the United States, the revolution in transport by land
and sea, the rapid growth of Canada since 1900 and the recent
European War all left a deep impression upon them.

The accuracy with which the Maritime Provinces have served as an
economic seismograph is the result of geography and the remarkable
adaptability of their people. Their geography has been influenced
fundamentally by a geology which has been well described as one of
pronounced "unconformity". The Acadian area is a subsidiary of the
Appalachian region. The profound geological disturbances in this
area, especially in Nova Scotia, have resulted in the shifting and
folding of sedimentary rocks and in the intrusion of igneous rocks;
and are responsible for scattered mineral deposits and ore bodies,
diversity of topography and soil, a serrated coastline, small lakes and
numerous rivers, and outlying submerged banks with their abundance
of fish. New Brunswick, since it belongs more closely to the Continent,
has longer rivers and greater possibilities for lumbering. As to climate,
the three provinces are a part of the easterly projection of the North
American Continent, and off their coast the cold waters of the
Labrador current meet the warm waters of the Gulf Stream from the
south. The summer flow of the St Lawrence River into the warm bays
and inlets of its land-locked gulf and the relative lack of disturbance
from tides make this area the fish hatchery of the north-western
Atlantic; the mingling of currents on the banks to the north-east of
Nova Scotia furnishes a rich supply of fish food; and the disturbed
waters of the Bay of Fundy produce an abundance of fish, with a
variety not found elsewhere. On land the cold north-westerly off-
shore winds of winter and the south-easterly onshore winds of summer,
in conjunction with the Labrador current, are responsible for the
prevailing cool and temperate climate. But again "unconformity"
is introduced by the Gulf Stream, as witnessed by the contrast between the orchard area of Nova Scotia and the limited possibilities of

agriculture in northern New Brunswick. Such in brief is the geographic background which has been responsible for the development of lumbering chiefly in New Brunswick, of fishing and mining chiefly in Nova Scotia, and of a specialised agriculture in all three provinces, but most particularly in the fertile seclusion of Prince Edward Island.

Furthermore, this background has been responsible in part for the sensitiveness of their economic activities. Situated in that part of North America which is nearest to Great Britain, and possessing numerous ocean ports open the whole year, they were subject, tariff or no tariff, to the industrial competition of the two most highly developed areas of western civilisation. Their industries, like their coastline, have been beaten upon by pitiless waves. The diversified character of their raw materials has limited the development of mass production, and cheap ocean navigation has exposed them to the competition of countries in which mass production has increasingly prevailed. The result has been to compel a readjustment of economic life and a concentration upon bedrock activities. They have exploited raw materials in which they had natural advantages, and developed by specialisation the distinctive resources of their soil. At confederation the population was chiefly English, Scotch and Irish; and apart from some increase of French in New Brunswick the racial constituents have remained, on the whole, unchanged. The population is homogeneous, highly individualistic and remarkably adaptable. Individual enterprise, acting on a variety of natural resources, is the keynote of their economic life.

The discovery and initial development of the Maritime Provinces proceeded from Europe, and their industries were developed from the sea in relation to European demands. Successively the basic industries have moved inland and since confederation each industry has felt the increasing pull of the land. First fishing, then lumbering and mining were developed; but over the course of their history, and especially in Nova Scotia, fishing has been of primary importance in respect of age, permanence and closeness of contact with the sea and with Europe. As late as 1891 more Nova Scotians were engaged in fishing than in any industry but agriculture; and the numbers rose until 1911. At confederation the dry fishing in cod was still the main branch of the industry. In the eastern counties of Nova Scotia and in Cape Breton the inshore fishery, conducted from small whale boats with two to four men at distances up to five miles from shore, was of first importance. In the western agricultural counties, in addition to the inshore fishery, large vessels of 25 to 100 tons manned by at least eight men fished on the banks off the coast from 1 April to mid-June and for the balance of the season in the Gulf of St Lawrence and further north. In 1873 the Lunenburg fleet extended its activities to the Grand Banks off Newfoundland. The fish when dried were marketed, as they had been for centuries, in tropical and sub-tropical countries with a numerous Catholic population. The old triangular trade persisted, fish to the West Indies and Mediterranean, sugar and fruits to England and France, outfits and general supplies to the Maritime Provinces. Cod was at once a food for local consumption and a basic export by which necessary imports were obtained.

On the technique and capital of the cod fishery other fisheries were built up, as the market was widened by improved transportation and new methods of preserving fish. Among these was the herring fishery, which found an expanding outlet in the United States. Its product was sold in a variety of forms the whole year round. The heavy tides of the Bay of Fundy permitted intensive operations by means of brush weirs, and new uses were found for the increasing catch. Fishing from the land by the aid of brush weirs facilitated rapid exploitation. The spawning habits of the herring saved it from depletion. But another group of fish, those known as "anadromous", which spawn up the rivers, were seriously depleted. Such were the salmon, shad and gaspereau. The ease with which these river fish could be caught, the high prices realised for the fresh product, the drying up of streams by the removal of forest, the blocking of the rivers by mill dams and refuse, led to the disappearance of some species and the rapid decline of others. Finally the herring, mackerel and cod, which had formerly been caught inshore, when they were pursuing the fry of the river fish, moved further out. The disturbance of the equilibrium of the fisheries was among the first fruits of industrialism.

Similar tendencies have been in evidence in the lobster and oyster fisheries. In 1867 lobsters were used as fertiliser along the Gulf shore, and the industry was limited to canning establishments at Sambro and Port Mouton for export to Great Britain, but in the 'seventies, with the exhaustion of the American fishery, districts adjoining the United States began to export live lobsters to Maine and Massachusetts. Canneries were established over a wide area; and by 1894 the lobsters provided a third of the total fish production of Prince Edward Island. With its cash return and steadiness of production and markets the lobster fishing was attractive to fishermen. As transport by steamship and rail became more regular and rapid, the wasteful process of canning was displaced, where possible, by the more profitable trade in live lobsters. By 1894 in districts adjacent to the United States canneries had been forced to close down. The oyster beds along the south of the Gulf and around Prince Edward Island have also been intensively exploited; and there has been a very serious decline in production from the high point of 1882. Overfishing, disruption of the beds by dredging for fertiliser, the introduction of disease by the importation of new oysters, poaching and difficulties of jurisdiction between the Dominion and the province are considered to be the causes of this decline.

In recent years the status of the inshore fisheries has been profoundly affected by the introduction of motor boats and extensive plants for the handling of the product. Capital has become important in an industry which used to rest primarily upon labour. In the Bank fisheries the steam trawler has been to the fore since 1908 and threatens the operation of the inshore and Bank fisheries on the old basis. Continued winter fishing is now possible and the persistent demands of the internal market for a steady supply have been met.

The effects of industrialism are manifest in the development of new fisheries on a large scale and in the marketing of new species in large numbers. In some years the lobster has surpassed the cod in value of catch. In 1920 over and above the live lobster trade it furnished material for 512 canneries employing 2000 workers and a capital of $2,000,000. Clams, scallops and tuna have increased in importance. By-product industries have been extended. Improved technique has shortened the time required for the catching, landing and marketing of fish. Artificial drying plants, bait-freezing plants and new freezing methods have made production more regular, and distribution has kept pace with production in the shape of improved express service to interior markets and improved steamship services to the West Indies. As a result, the fishing industry has been confronted with problems of depletion. The sea, the weather and the vagaries of fish migration have resisted the encroachments of industrialism, and even the lobster has been protected by the rugged exposed coast from Port Maitland to Cape Sable. But this was not a sufficient protection, and it has been necessary to enforce a policy of conservation under the Fisheries Act of 1868 and its amendments. Differences between the Dominion and these provinces have been largely settled. The opposition of the lumber interests on the rivers has been overcome. Regulations are in force to prevent overfishing. Size limits and seasons have been established for lobsters and other fish. Hatcheries have been opened at central points and reduction plants installed to keep down the dog fish, the enemy of all fishermen. Extensive research programmes have been carried out under the Biological Board of Canada at its stations in Halifax and St Andrews. Thus the technical response to industrialism has been thorough and on the whole adequate, but in the adjustment of labour less progress has been made. Excess labour has been forced into other industries; and in seasons of depression a pool of unemployment accumulates in the fisheries with results demoralising to the fishing population. The Fishermen's Union of Nova Scotia, which was incorporated in 1905, made no progress after 1909 and disappeared in 1913. The individualism of the fishermen has stood in the way of co-operative action.

The early economic development of Nova Scotia was characteristic of a peninsula with a coastline accessible to fishing grounds. New Brunswick, on the other hand, being part of the mainland, had large rivers, down which could be floated the softwood lumber of its forests. Therefore while in Nova Scotia the lines of exploitation were primarily external, in New Brunswick they were primarily internal.

Just as the fishing industry was erected on dry cod as a basic export, so the lumber industry of New Brunswick was reared on square timber of white pine. This tree was accessible, durable and large; easy to work, free from knots, and valuable in commerce. The logs were hewn, floated down the St John or Miramichi and exported chiefly to Great Britain. While the fishing industry was scattered along the coastline, the lumber industry was concentrated at the river mouths. The shortage by 1850 of large white pine led to the utilisation of smaller species and the production of smaller grades. Increased quantities of small logs called for a rapid expansion of machine industry and the extension and improvement of saw-mills. The Crimean War raised the demand for sawn timber and especially for spruce deals, the export of which doubled between 1850 and 1860; and the trade grew with fluctuations to a high point at the end of the century. Then once again the increasing proportion of small logs necessitated a change of product, this time to small size boards, planks and scantlings. As the more accessible forests of the United States approached exhaustion the Americans relied more on the Maritime Provinces; and the export of deals to Great Britain was replaced by that of smaller dimension lumber to America. Thus under the persistent pressure of industrialism the virgin forest was exhausted and the cutting interval was reduced to ten or twelve years. Still further encroachments on smaller trees followed the establishment of lath mills and the production of pulpwood and pulp, the raw and semi-raw material of the paper industry. The competition of Pacific Coast lumber, when this could reach eastern markets by the Panama Canal, stimulated the consolidation of the New Brunswick lumber industry and the development of pulp and paper. The lumber firms added various branches of the new industry to their existing activities, concentrating chiefly on the production of high grade sulphite pulp. The limited supply of water power was supplemented by steam power obtained from burning saw-mill refuse. But even as thus extended, the power was inadequate to meet the voracious requirements of the newsprint mills. Consequently pulpwood was exported to Three Rivers, Quebec. At Edmundston the export of sulphite pulp takes the ingenious form of pumping across the river to the paper mill at Madawaska, Maine.

The pulp and paper industry of Nova Scotia has been more seriously limited both as to power and raw material and cannot compare with that of New Brunswick. Most of the timber areas have been alienated to private hands and smaller operations have been the rule. Alienation made it impracticable to impose an embargo on the export of wood in an unmanufactured condition, as has been done in

New Brunswick on the Crown lands, where most of the forest lies. And this, together with accessibility by water to New England mills, smaller streams and the absence of large-scale organisation in the parent industry of lumbering, explains why large quantities of Nova Scotia's pulpwood are exported to the United States, and why the province has confined itself to the manufacture of groundwood pulp, a product with a low and fluctuating value.

As in fishing, so also in lumbering, industrial exploitation has been conditional upon improvements in transport. The heavy bulky character of softwoods and their capacity to float made water transportation of vital importance to the industry's early growth, although in recent years there has been a trend towards land transport and the American market. When transportation was by water, the lumber furnished not only cargo, but also the square-rigged wide-beamed softwood ship on which it was conveyed. Wooden ships were built at Saint John or on the Miramichi, filled with lumber, sent to Liverpool, England, and there sold. Such for example was the business of Pollok, Gilmour and Co., merchants of Glasgow, who played a prominent part in the early development of New Brunswick and became later the steamship line of Rankin, Gilmour and Co. of Liverpool. The skill of the lumbermen, an ample supply of the various woods required for the different parts of the vessel, the foreign demand for wood and wooden ships, the experience of the New England States and the seafaring powers of the native fishermen all played a part in the expansion of Maritime shipping. When shipbuilding spread from New Brunswick to Yarmouth, Windsor and other ports of Nova Scotia the industry came to maturity. For Nova Scotia worked the ships which it built, drawing its personnel from the fishermen who sailed from the south-west counties to the Banks. Between 1860 and 1869 the little town of Yarmouth added 105,000 tons to its fleet; and a number of marine insurance companies established themselves there. The youth of Yarmouth County fished, farmed, or went to sea, and often they did all three. Hard-driving Blue-nose skippers, unhampered by the labour regulations of the "Limejuice" (British Merchant Shipping) Act, commanded well disciplined, well paid, well fed crews and made substantial profits for the owners. They had merchandising as well as sailing duties to perform and received a share in the profits. Sometimes they retired with a modest fortune, which it was their delight to invest in a prettily situated farm.

As the volume and quality of shipping rose, the theatre of operation was extended. Nova Scotians no longer confined themselves to the traditional trade of freighting fish and lumber to the West Indies, with return cargoes of salt and West Indian products for North American ports. They pushed out on the high seas, securing the traffic from which their American rivals were retiring as the result of the Civil War and internal expansion. They took grain and petroleum to Europe and the Orient, coal from Cardiff to Rio de Janeiro and Montevideo, guano from the Chinchas (off Peru) to Europe, lumber from British North American ports to Great Britain in the summer and cotton from the Gulf ports in the winter. In 1874 wooden ship-building was at its height, but within five years machine industry had made fatal inroads upon it. Iron-hulled barques of British make, the forerunners of tramp steamers, secured the charters for perishable and easily damaged goods; and the "windjammers" were driven to distant seas with long voyages and low-class freights. By 1885 the victory of cheap iron and steel was complete and wooden vessels were sold to the Norwegian flag, some of them returning to be used as barges for hauling gypsum to American ports. Apart from a slight revival during the War the industry of wooden shipbuilding dis-appeared. The Hon. W. S. Fielding has said of this era:

> It may be only a dream, but I am willing to entertain the hope, even though it be a vision, that as a result of the iron and steel industry we shall see a revival of shipbuilding in the Maritime Provinces. Nothing that has occurred in this Province for the last half century has done more to create difficulty, has been a more serious blow to the development of that section of the Dominion than the decay of the industry of shipbuilding. It was the great industry throughout this Province, not only the industry of building its ships, but the business of owning and manning them. Not only did our people build the ships, but as the result of the building of them our young men all over our provinces grew up to be mariners and sailors of every sea, and no doubt to that fact is due to a very considerable degree the large measure of intelligence that is usually credited to the people of Nova Scotia, they were indeed people who went down to the sea in ships and did business in many waters.[1]

The competition of iron and steel destroyed a magnificent achieve-ment, an integration of capital and labour, of lumbering, fishing and agriculture, on which rested a progressive community life. The linch pin was broken, and industrialism continued its inroads upon the people of the Maritime Provinces.

Thrown back from the sea, the lumber industry had to find new uses for its products on land. One notable extension, the pulp and paper industry, has already been described. Under this adjustment the Canadian and American markets assumed a greater importance and a larger proportion of the lumber was taken out by railroads. Saw-mills were built inland and fewer logs were floated down to Saint John despite the ocean freights and market for by-products available at this port. Drying plants and planing mills were installed with a view to reducing the weight of the product and widening the market; and hardwood areas were tapped by the introduction of small portable mills. The Restigouche has steadily overtaken the Miramichi and the shift in areas of production continues. The general result of the changes in method of production and type of product has been to bring New Brunswick more directly within the sweep of the world

---

[1] Cited by Drummond, R., *Minerals and Mining*, Nova Scotia, pp. 233-4.

market. It has become increasingly sensitive to the secular and cyclical fluctuations in the building trades of North America and to changes in costs of transportation from rival sources of supply. As a protection the industry has endeavoured to diversify its production and develop by-products. Cutting regulations have been improved and an effective fire protective service has been installed, both in New Brunswick and Nova Scotia. Skill and self-reliance are still required of the lumberman, but the spread of the corporation has tended to break down the *esprit de corps* based on personal relations which was so marked when the industry was in family hands. With the increase in the practice of contracting for the delivery of logs the contact between the firm and the men in the bush has been weakened; while in the mills mass production has enlarged the field of routine. Since 1900 there have been several strikes in Saint John mills.

Like fishing and lumbering, mining began from the sea border and extended inland when transport improved. Gold, gypsum and coal have supplied the main mineral output of Nova Scotia since confederation. Gold was discovered in 1861 at points near the coast east of Halifax and production reached the maximum in 1898, after which date the predominance of low grade ore led to a permanent decline. On the other hand, the output of gypsum, the raw material for various plasters, has steadily increased in response to constructional activities in Canada and the United States. Growing output has been attended by concentration of quarries and shipping points and by the manufacture of some part of the semi-finished product within the province, but in the main the industry has been one of extracting a crude product for export to a foreign market. Neither gold nor gypsum can compare with coal in value of output or in influence on the life of the province.

Coal, being a heavy commodity and possessed in abundance by Great Britain and Europe, had to be sold in neighbouring markets to which there was cheap water transport, such as the New England States and Quebec. The most accessible mines lay along the west coast of Cape Breton, and during the period of the Reciprocity Treaty 1854–66 numerous small mines were opened. But the American coal duty of 1867 and a long period of depression in Canada had so serious an effect on the industry that by 1890 only the strongest mines survived. The provincial Government, as owner of the mines, assisted the reconstruction of the industry by the grant of favourable terms to lessees, looking to the Cape Breton coal industry to offset the decline in wooden shipbuilding; and thus facilitated an amalgamation of various mines under the direction of outside interests from Boston and Montreal, which formed in 1893 the Dominion Coal Company. With new capital resources modern mining equipment was installed, shipping piers were built, and the Black Diamond steamship line was established. Railway communication had been secured with the mainland in 1891 by the line from Point Tupper to Sydney, the centre of the Cape Breton mining area; and in 1896 a further line was opened from Sydney to the all-year port of Louisbourg. Increased output and the decline of the American demand, consequent upon the Boston "Smoke Nuisance" law of 1897 (which penalised the smoky coal of Nova Scotia) and the tariff increase of the same year, hastened the formation of the Dominion Iron and Steel Company and the erection of an iron and steel plant. Ore was obtained from Wabana, Newfoundland, by arrangement with the Company which, as noted below, was working that field. In 1901 the first furnaces were blown in and steel was produced in December of that year. A wire-rod mill was added in 1904 and a steel-rail mill in 1905. Difficulties over contracts made it expedient for the Coal Company and the Steel Company to unite as the Dominion Steel Corporation in 1910. All this was a case of development from without. Industrialism was late in its arrival, but once launched it developed rapidly by the aid of a technique perfected elsewhere. Community life, which depends on the control of natural resources, was weakened. In the exploitation of coal and iron outside capital met none of the resistance which fishing and lumbering with their natural diversity were able to offer. The resistance came, not from the industries as such, but from the workers to whom they gave employment.

This however was only one section of Nova Scotia's coal and iron industry. In the inland coal fields of Cumberland and Pictou development proceeded more evenly, and outside interests found it difficult to gain control. These fields had small resources and depended on a more expensive form of transport, the railroad. Some collieries close to water were in operation before confederation, but marked expansion did not come until the construction of the Intercolonial Railway in the 'seventies. To meet the demand for railway and foundry material the Nova Scotia Forge Company and the Nova Scotia Steel Company, which made steel ingots by the Siemens process, were established; and later the two united. Difficulties in procuring suitable local ore led in 1894 to the acquisition of a deposit at Wabana on Bell Island in Conception Bay, Newfoundland. This proved marvellously rich; and in order to be closer to the new ore and to take advantage of cheaper and better coking coal, properties were purchased in 1900 in Cape Breton adjacent to those of the Dominion Coal Company. They had belonged to the General Mining Association, which before 1858 had a monopoly of coal production in the province. The Steel Company now became the Nova Scotia Steel and Coal Company. Coke ovens and blast furnaces were erected in Cape Breton and the mainland plants were extended to handle the later stages of manufacture. In 1912 an ally, the Eastern Car Company, was formed to manufacture steel railway cars at New Glasgow. The Nova Scotia Steel and Coal Company in contrast with its rival developed slowly and in response to the demands of the province. It was managed on conservative lines by Maritime interests.

As the result of improved methods of coal mining and the increased demand of the iron and steel industry, the production of coal increased from 2·6 million tons in 1899 to 7·2 in 1913. With the War railroad construction ceased but munitions took its place. In 1920 the Nova Scotia Steel and Coal Company and the Dominion Steel Corporation were merged into the British Empire Steel Corporation ("Besco") and associated with them was Halifax Shipyards Limited, formed by officials of the Canada Steamship Company with a view to using Nova Scotia steel in shipbuilding. The coming of "Besco" meant the further loss of control by local interests, and in the post-war depression the conflict between native workers and outside control came to a head. The miners had been organised since 1879, when the "Provincial Workingmen's Association" was formed. For nearly forty years the union maintained an independent existence. Its record was conservative and constructive and it helped to secure for the industry adequate protective legislation. By its support of education, temperance and provident activities it gained the sympathy of the press and the public. In 1897 practically all the miners belonged to it, but in 1898 the American Knights of Labour entered its territory and created a schism. In 1908 it was exposed to a second invasion, this time from the United Mine Workers of America, who had become active in other coal fields of Canada. For a while it held its ground, but the War, with its rising cost of living, imposed a strain on the wage agreements under which it was working, and in 1917 it joined with its first rival in an amalgamation which soon afterwards affiliated with the United Mine Workers of America. The independence of forty years was at an end. The conclusion could not have been long delayed. When there was but one employer with head office at Montreal, the logical retort was membership in a strong international Union. After 1921 prolonged labour unrest accompanied by strikes and military repression lay like a storm-cloud over the province. It was part of the painful return to post-war conditions, but to Nova Scotians its bitterness was increased by the consciousness that the province had lost control of a leading industry, with absentee ownership on the one hand and foreign labour domination on the other.

The record of consumers' co-operation (co-operative stores) in Canada is a lean one, but to this there is one outstanding exception, the British Canadian Co-operative Society Limited of Sydney Mines and Glace Bay, established in 1906. It succeeded to two earlier ventures, the second of which failed with heavy losses to the miners in 1905. The new start was due to some immigrant Lancashire miners to whom co-operation was second nature and who resented the unscrupulous treatment by local merchants of the Old Country immigrants arriving at that time. In twenty-two years the Society has distributed $1,500,000 in patronage dividend, growing from strength to strength under the guidance of one man, its devoted secretary and general manager. It has been a centre of community life in a region of bleak industrialism, a camp of democracy and cash payment confronting the bondage of the outside merchants and the unpopular company store.

The sweep of industrialism and the rapid development of new agricultural areas in the western part of the continent have exerted a profound influence on the population and agriculture of the Maritime Provinces. Within their boundaries there has been a shift of population from agriculture and fishing to other occupations, but the internal redistribution is unimportant beside the movement to the continental mainland. The population indeed has not decreased, it has grown from three-quarters of a million in 1871 to one million in 1921, but there has been throughout the period a heavy drain of native-born to the United States and to other parts of Canada; and this has not been compensated by any substantial amount of new immigration. In 1921 at least 325,000 former Maritime residents were living elsewhere, about three-quarters of them in the United States. The result on the age distribution of the population has been that, while in Canada as a whole the youthful population has been growing very rapidly, in the Maritime Provinces it has been stationary or actually decreasing. In Prince Edward Island, an almost wholly rural province, the population reached its maximum at the census of 1891.

The intensive development of lumbering and mining in this group of provinces and the vast production of wheat and cattle in the continental West for export to Eastern America and to Europe made it difficult for their farmers to compete in the principal crops. They have therefore concentrated on products for which there was an adjacent industrial demand, such as dairy produce, or on specialities for which they had peculiar advantages of soil, climate and situation. This is most clearly seen in Prince Edward Island, which, apart from fishing and the canned lobster industry, is devoted wholly to agriculture. The Land Purchase Act of 1875 terminated the system of absentee landlordism which had disturbed the province for more than a century. Specialised agriculture began with the export of potatoes at a time when water transport by sailing ship was abundant. But the arrival of the Colorado beetle and the exhaustion of the soil through excessive cropping of potatoes and oats, the leading Maritime grain, turned attention to other opportunities. The production of factory cheese began in 1883 and of factory (creamery) butter in 1887. Progress was slow until in 1891 the Dominion Government sent down its Dairy Commissioner to organise cheese and butter factories on the co-operative method. After some years of pioneer effort the factories were strong enough to work independently on co-operative lines; and since then the range of co-operative marketing has been widened, notably in eggs and wool. The formation in 1912 of egg circles under Dominion guidance terminated a system of barter between the farmer and his local store which was incompatible with adequate returns and a high class of production. In the spring of 1914 the local circles were organised in a central sales agency, the Prince Edward Island Egg and Poultry Association. Improvement of the transport facilities between the island and mainland at the expense of the Dominion has made it possible to market perishable products on the mainland the whole year round. More recently the experience of the potato growers in the Aroostook Valley of Maine has been adapted to Prince Edward Island; and in addition to the large export trade in table potatoes a certified seed potato industry has been established to supply the demand of potato growers in the southern States for potatoes of high vitality and yield, such as Irish Cobblers and Green Mountains, the specialities of the island. But the most spectacular example of the ingenuity of the Maritime people in adapting themselves to changed conditions has been the creation of the Prince Edward Island silver fox industry. The depletion of the more valuable species of fur and the rise in the price of high grade furs stimulated an interest in the possibilities of fur farming. A long period of experiment, dating from the early 'eighties, solved the complicated problems connected with the improvement of strain, raising of young, feeding, nests and pens. Between 1900 and 1910 exceptional prices were realised in London. In 1910 the breeders who had founded the industry began to sell the live animals and in 1911 the first fox-breeding company was formed with a charter in the United States. A period of frenzied finance ensued. Options were taken on the unborn pups and the prices of breeding pairs rose to fantastic heights. The war arrested this extravagance and the industry has again settled down to more sober lines of growth. A system of registered pedigree has been introduced and measures have been taken to protect the industry from exploitation and fraud.

The agriculture of Nova Scotia has developed similarly. The foundations have been strengthened by the extension of dairying. Between 1881 and 1921 the output of butter increased by nearly 50 per cent. Though the number of milch cows declined, the smaller herd produced more and better milk. Cheese has been largely replaced by butter, ice-cream and fluid milk for local markets, and since 1901 there has also been a rapid increase in the production of poultry and eggs. There is no evidence for the view that the agriculture of these provinces has fallen of late years into stagnation.

The apple is Nova Scotia's speciality. The Annapolis-Cornwallis valley in which its cultivation is concentrated extends for 100 miles from Digby to Windsor, with Kentville as its centre. Commercial production began about 1880, since when a secondary crop grown for local consumption has become an important export industry, the average export rising from 30,000 barrels in 1880–5 to close on 1,000,000 in 1915–20. The apple came as a welcome substitute for the potato, the export crop on which the valley had relied until it was penalised by a heavy American duty in 1874. The climate, soil and conformation of the valley, with its well drained sandy slopes, proved excellent for apple growing; and the improvements in ocean transport consequent upon the introduction of the steel steamer provided profitable access to the British market, which takes the bulk of the crop. As the result of long experience and of experiment by individuals, aided by the counsels of the Nova Scotia Fruit Growers' Association, which has presided over the industry from the outset, a high technique has been achieved. Varieties have been reduced and standardised. Labour for picking and packing is obtained from Halifax and Lunenburg at the close of the fishing season. Since 1900 frost-proof warehouses have been in use for the packing and storage of fruit, some of them owned by the growers; since 1910 there has been a central sales organisation, the United Fruit Companies of Nova Scotia Limited, to which most of the local co-operative companies belong. The short haul from the valley to the ocean port of Halifax over the Dominion Atlantic Railway and the competition of liners for first-class freight, especially after the closing of the St Lawrence, placed the growers in a favourable position for reaching their leading market. And thus, with production, marketing and transportation improved, the industry has prospered. Furthermore, it illustrates well the way in which the activities of the three provinces are interlocked. Fertiliser comes from the Cape Breton mines, cooperage from the lumber industry, labour from the fisheries. And in its turn the beauty of the valley from blossom time to harvest has contributed to the profits of the tourist business.

The absorption of New Brunswick in its staple industry of lumbering has handicapped the growth of its agriculture. The timber trade set the pace of settlement. The timber ships brought back return cargoes of immigrants, who settled in the wild lands, selling the cleared lumber to the timber dealer and the field produce to the lumberman. Lumbering provided a cash market, as well as good wages for work in the bush during the winter season. It supplied revenue for provincial improvements, capital for industry and the means of purchasing requirements from abroad. On the other hand it took from the farms horses and crude products such as hay and oats, with the result that live-stock was reduced in quantity and deteriorated, and the general balance so essential to mixed farming was destroyed. Young men and immigrants were drawn from the farm and the persistent attention to detail which mixed farming demands became impossible. Moreover, the dependence on an industry so speculative as lumbering exposed farmers to serious fluctuations. Agriculture, therefore, has been largely confined to the dyked marsh lands, which skirt the Bay of Fundy and extend into Nova Scotia, and to the river valleys with their adjoining uplands, especially that of the St John. As roads and railways were pushed into the forest hinterland, new land has been brought under settlement and agriculture has improved along the lines of other provinces, with orchards in the lower St John valley and intensive potato raising in Carleton and Victoria counties. A market has been found for potatoes in the West Indies, Quebec and Ontario; and the success achieved is yet another proof of the skill with which the farmers have adjusted their agriculture to the demands of new markets in the face of intense competition in basic products and stiff tariffs in their natural market to the south. The ports of the Maritime Provinces have watched with concern the flow of wheat from the Canadian West through Montreal to the north of them and New York to the south. They cannot compete with Montreal in the summer because of the extra railway haul. In the winter Saint John handles a substantial volume, Halifax very little. New York offers to the shipper a varied mass of tonnage sailing regularly to all parts. The true interest of these provinces lies in the development of their own rich hinterland and the promotion of a trade of import and export between themselves and countries to the south.

The economic history of the three provinces since 1867 is one of prosperity so long as their face was towards the sea, and of struggle against adversity when the pull of the land increased, as happened very shortly after confederation. The completion of the Intercolonial Railway in 1876 and of the Canadian Pacific short line from Montreal to Saint John in 1890, the selection of Saint John as a winter terminus by the Allan and Canadian Pacific steamship lines soon after 1900, and the subsequent consolidation of the railways of the provinces under one or other of the two great systems were successive landmarks in the process. *Per se* they were highly advantageous, even though the railways chiefly brought western produce in and took eastern people out, but they were part of that larger evolution in which the "Maritimes" lost control over their economic destinies. The rent made in the fabric of life by the collapse of wooden shipbuilding intensified the strain under which they laboured, as the flower of their people moved west. Though Charlottetown was the cradle of confederation, the seat of the new Dominion was Ottawa. Nova Scotia has been a nursery of Cabinet ministers and of presidents and professors for the Universities of Canada and the United States of America. Business and finance took a similar toll. Of the numerous banks which flourished in the days of wooden ships only a few of the strongest survived; and these were forced by the policies which enabled them to survive to transfer their headquarters to the mainland. The Merchants Bank of Halifax became the Royal Bank of Canada in 1901 and changed its seat to Montreal in 1907. The Bank of Nova

Scotia moved its General Manager to Toronto in 1900; and its president, a Toronto financier, journeys annually to Halifax to present his address as a tribute to the days that were. In 1903 the Canadian Bank of Commerce absorbed the old Halifax Banking Company, which had been founded as far back as 1825. Such a development was doubtless requisite to a banking system which has branches from coast to coast. None the less the shock to local pride was considerable, and it contributed perhaps to a habit which has been observed in recent years, namely, tardiness to invest in local industrial enterprise.

The Dominion Government has endeavoured to join these provinces to the rest of Canada by devices which range from tariffs to the grant of "Better Terms" under the Confederation Agreement. Mention may be made of the duty placed on American coal in 1879; of the bounties to the iron and steel industry, which were granted in 1884 and continued by the Laurier Government for many years; and of the bounties paid to the fishing industry out of the moneys received from the United States under the Halifax Award of 1877. Consideration for them has been an incentive to the steps taken to increase the trade of Canada with the West Indies and Latin America. A preference was granted to the British West Indies in 1897 and agreements in 1912, 1920 and 1925 enlarged the preferences and provided subsidised steamship services. About 1900, Canadian banks, especially those of Maritime origin, began to open branches in the West Indies, including Cuba, and the chain has been extended to South America. Trade with these parts has grown rapidly since the war to the advantage of Halifax and Saint John.

The record of these provinces since confederation is on the whole a very remarkable one. Through the individuality of their people and the diversity of their resources they have stemmed a tide of industrialism which might have submerged a less sturdy stock. Where the opportunity has offered they have struck out along new lines, and they have made contributions to the cultural life of Canada which it is beyond the province of the economic historian to appraise.

CHAPTER XXVIII

NEWFOUNDLAND, 1867–1921

ALTHOUGH the final decision of Newfoundland not to enter the Dominion of Canada was deferred until 1869, still from 1867 onwards its history is that of a separate unit working out its own salvation, yet closely related to, and influenced by, its great neighbour. In 1867 the population was about 142,000, that of St John's and its suburbs being 22,000, and of Harbour Grace, the next town, 6,700: Carbonear had 4000 inhabitants, but generally the outports were but villages with population scattered over a deeply indented and broken coast-line of 6000 miles. In Labrador, the great dependency of the colony, there was a poor and small population of about 2500 known as liviers,[1] besides a few Indians and half-breeds: these by custom partitioned the hunting grounds far back from the coast. Under the care of the Moravian missions lived some 900 Eskimo.

The revenue of Newfoundland for three years ending with 1867 averaged £137,372 (say $686,860), and the expenditure £145,551 ($727,700). The imports in 1867 were valued at £1,156,460, and the exports at £1,055,959, representing a fair average, though there was an exceptional drop in the succeeding year.[2] The year 1867, marked by a serious gale on the Labrador coast which did widespread damage to the fishing schooners, has been called that of the "great fishery", but the exports of dried fish, though the highest since 1815, were beaten by nearly 60 per cent. seven years later.[3]

Charles F. Bennett, the great opponent of federation, became, as already stated,[4] Prime Minister of the colony in 1869. He held office for the ensuing four years, naturally making every effort to justify the ideal of independent progress: he had everything in his favour—good fisheries, good hay crops, good trade. The reorganisation of the police was one of his best achievements. At the general election of 1873 his Government was returned with a very small majority, which was shortly turned into a minority by political manœuvring. Mr (afterwards Sir) Frederick Carter was called upon to form an Administration, finished the session of 1874 by the help of the Speaker's casting vote, and then, going to the country, came back with a good working majority. A prosperous season gave him a start in endeavours to develop the colony, which later were aided by a windfall. The Treaty of Washington (8 May 1871) which came into operation on 1 July 1873 was designed to place on a satisfactory footing the recipro-

---

[1] This unusual term may have come from Dorset. *Oxf. Dict.* s.v. quotes Hardy's *Tess of the D'Urbervilles*.
[2] Figures taken from C.O. List, 1881: Prowse, p. 693, differs slightly.
[3] Sir W. Macgregor's *Report on Trade*, 1905, App. VI.   [4] *Vide supra*, p. 437.

cal fishing privileges enjoyed by the United States and the British possessions in each other's waters: it led up to an examination of the value of such privileges by a mixed tribunal, and resulted in the payment by the United States of a compensation of $5,500,000, of which nearly $1,000,000 went to Newfoundland:[1] ultimately this led to the denunciation of the treaty. Meanwhile the Government of the colony was facing in a practical way the difficulties raised by the French claims on the west shore of the island, where some assertion of their rights was overdue. A proposal to carry a railway across to St George's Bay got no further than a satisfactory reconnaissance survey in the summer of 1875. But in 1877 an attempt was made to establish practical administration in the West, when Commander Howorth was appointed magistrate at Curling in the Bay of Islands, and took up his residence in what is still counted the "Government House". Authority eventually arrived from home to make grants of land and issue mining licences on the west coast. This was characterised as "the boon for which the colony had been pleading in vain for many years, a virtual settlement of the vexed French shore question, and a removal of a serious and long-standing grievance", opening half of the island hitherto closed to settlement and industrial enterprise.[2]

For this credit is due to Mr (afterwards Sir) William Whiteway who in 1878 had become Prime Minister, and has left behind a reputation for sane enterprise. He first brought the question of a railway for the colony to a practical trial, with a project to carry a line from St John's northward by the great bays of the east coast to Hall's Bay on the north. Whiteway recommended the Government to build their own line:[3] but the Legislature granted a concession based on a subsidy and a land grant to the Newfoundland Railway Company. That concession and its successors bred continuous trouble. On 9 August 1881 the line was commenced; but not without a local riot, known as the "battle of Foxtrap". Expenditure on the railway stimulated business and seemed to inaugurate an era of prosperity: encouragement was given to other undertakings, particularly the construction of the dry dock at the end of the harbour of St John's, which for many years was large enough to admit the biggest ocean steamers afloat: begun in 1883, it was ready and formally opened in December 1884, when H.M.S. *Tenedos* was docked there. Already in 1882 the Colonial Cordage Company, established by Moses Monroe, had shown what private enterprise could effect. To-day, secured in its business by a protective duty, the factory supplies the twines, nets, and cordage which are required by the colony's fishermen. It was the prototype of other efforts.

Where debatable questions affecting the daily life and business of a people are left unsettled, they may at any moment become acute,

---

[1] Newfoundland actually received £203,873. See also chap. xxvi (ii).
[2] Speech at opening of Legislature, 1882 (*Journals of H. of Ass.* 1882).
[3] Prowse, p. 508.

and there are times when all crises seem to occur together. Such a period was opening for Newfoundland in regard to its fisheries. A resolution of the Congress of the United States in 1883 led to the denunciation of the Treaty of Washington, already mentioned, at the first possible moment. The Newfoundland Ministers, on being consulted as to their wishes, indicated that they were mainly concerned with the free entry of their fish into the States,[1] and ultimately made it a grievance that they were included in the *modus vivendi* arranged with the United States Government in 1888, after the breakdown of the Washington negotiations at which Sir James Winter represented Newfoundland, Mr Chamberlain and Sir Charles Tupper being the Commissioners for Great Britain and Canada respectively. The chief importance of this matter belongs to 1891: for the moment the French shore question dwarfed the claims of American fishermen.

French pressure had through various negotiations led to the conclusion of a draft convention in 1884 which seemed to Her Majesty's Government likely to clear up the disputes with France. Sir Clare Ford and Mr Pennell (of the Colonial Office) were sent to the colony to explain and commend it to the Legislature. The local political atmosphere was not at the time favourable to impartial consideration. At the end of 1883 a riot in Harbour Grace between Orangemen and Roman Catholics had seriously embittered party relations and weakened the Government. The two Commissioners, however, secured the concurrence of the Ministry subject to certain amendments. Negotiations were accordingly reopened, and on 14 November 1885 a new arrangement was concluded. But at this moment the general election in Newfoundland brought a change of Government, and a determination to take a stand against proposals for concessions to France. Mr (afterwards Sir Robert) Thorburn came into office as head of a so-called "Protestant" Administration, with a leaven of sound commercial principles. This Ministry left local monuments in the Thorburn road to the west of St John's and the Placentia railway; but these achievements were dwarfed by the international complications; for, rejecting the new convention on the ground that the French were, by the grant of large bounties, ruining the export trade of the colony, the new Assembly in their first session passed the Bait Act of 1886. This Act empowered the executive to prohibit the capture or sale of bait fishes, such as caplin, herring, etc., in Newfoundland waters except under a licence to be issued on the authority of the Governor in Council. On the urgent representation of the French the Crown disallowed the Act. This decision, announced to the Legislature early in the session of 1887, created profound dissatisfaction. The Assembly at once set aside all other business and passed a new Bait Act which was transmitted to the Home Government with an address again setting out their fears for the future of their fishing

---

[1] *Parl. Paper* C. 4937 (1887), p. 2.

industry, and urging that consideration be shown to the "loyal people of this colony struggling to maintain their position as an independent and honourable appendage of the British Crown".[1] They also sent to England as delegates the Premier and Sir Ambrose Shea. They could point to their recent Fisheries Commission as an earnest of their efforts to place the industry on a scientific basis.[2] The year was propitious: it was the year of jubilee, and of the first Colonial Conference. The support of their brothers overseas meant much to Newfoundland, though Canada for selfish reasons opposed the colony's demand. Eventually the Bait Act was allowed with the stipulation that it should not be put in force until the spring of 1888. In that year the French, looking round for a chance of reprisals, found an opening in the comparatively recent lobster fishery. Some Frenchmen had in 1886 erected a lobster factory at Port-aux-Choix in defiance of treaty obligations; they now alleged interference of the English factories with this and other fishing; a state of serious diplomatic tension was allayed late in 1889 by a compromise under which the French were allowed to establish lobster factories, if they did not in any way interfere with the native factories.

The arrangement was made without directly consulting the colonial Government. Its announcement coincided with the return of Sir William Whiteway to power in Newfoundland after the heavy defeat of the Thorburn Ministry. Local feeling was ripe for fresh excitement. The attitude of the French was certainly sufficient to inspire indignation. "The right of France", ran one of their arguments, "to the coast of Newfoundland reserved to her fishermen is only part of her ancient sovereignty over the island which she retained in ceding the soil to England":[3] and the Secretary of State himself had admitted that the object of France was to discourage the populating of the island.[4] A Patriotic Association was at once formed to fight the matter. A petition from the Legislature was followed by two deputations in the summer of 1890, one from the Government headed by the Premier, another from the Patriotic Association headed by Sir James Winter. The difficulties of the Imperial Government were fully explained: and further negotiations with France ensued. Meanwhile the compromise of 1889 had worked without special friction, though the closing of a factory controlled by Mr James Baird led to proceedings under which the action of the naval officer (Sir Baldwin Walker) was ultimately declared illegal by the Judicial Committee of the Privy Council.

A new cause of friction with the Home Government now arose. With their full knowledge Mr (afterwards Sir Robert) Bond proceeded from England in September 1890 to lay before the Government of the United States proposals from Newfoundland for a separate

---

[1] Prowse, pp. 517-19.   [2] *Ibid.* p. 647.
[3] *Ibid.* p. 541.   [4] *Parl. Paper* C. 4641, p. 18.

Reciprocity Treaty. Already in March the colonial Government had indicated their desire to act independently of Canada in regard to such matters.[1] How far the Colonial Office realised this is not clear: possibly Bond understood the Secretary of State as leaving him wider scope than was intended. But when the negotiations with the United States were coming to a satisfactory issue Canada protested violently, and the Home Government decided not to ratify the Blaine-Bond convention. Although it is wrong to suggest that the Imperial Government lent itself to an electioneering intrigue,[2] there is no question as to the indignation aroused, not only against Canada, but against the Mother Country.

The year 1891 so begun held still further trouble; for the Legislature was soon agitated by the news that imperial legislation would be introduced to regularise the *modus vivendi* with the French regarding the lobster fishery. Once more a joint delegation from both Houses was appointed to resist at the bar of the House of Lords the proposed "coercive legislation", and before the end of April the Premier and his colleagues were in England urging that they should be left to legislate for themselves in the direction required by the Imperial Government, that the measure proposed by the latter was opposed to the principles of responsible government, and that it was reverting to conditions now completely out of date.[3] After somewhat acrimonious discussions an agreement was reached under which imperial legislation was postponed until the colony had had the opportunity of passing an Act to confer the necessary authority on naval officers superintending the lobster fishery. When a bill for the purpose was brought before the Legislature on May 1892 it was rejected by 23 votes to 8.[4]

But now the colony was struck by a calamity which threw everything else into the shade. In July 1892 a great fire broke out in St John's which within 48 hours destroyed the greater part of the city, including some 2000 houses and stores besides the Church of England Cathedral (Gilbert Scott's beautiful building), together with other churches, public halls, government offices, and banks. The estimated damage was $20,000,000 of which not one-fourth was covered by insurance. Though the loss of life was not great, some 11,000 people were homeless, and distress was serious. As on other occasions, from Halifax and other parts of the Dominion of Canada relief and supplies poured in. The Governor, Sir Terence O'Brien, who was in London, cancelling all engagements, devoted himself to raising relief funds and hurried back to administer them in person. Yet the people of St John's were soon at work rebuilding their city and replacing the destroyed buildings by more substantial and finer structures. In

---

[1] *Parl. Paper* Cd. 6303 of 1891.　　　　[2] Prowse, p. 532.
[3] *Parl. Paper* Cd. 6365 of May 1891, especially pp. 6, 11.
[4] *Parl. Paper* Cd. 7129 of Aug. 1893, pp. 10, 79.

this, as in other crises, the pluck and determination of the New-foundlander rose admirably to the occasion.

When the Legislature met in 1893 there was a more reasonable spirit as to the French difficulties, and in the result the *modus vivendi* was continued, permanent legislation being postponed until after the coming general election. However, events arising out of that election (November 1893) led to a much longer postponement. The election was conducted with marked acerbity. The opposing parties were Whiteway's group and the so-called "Conservative" or mercantile party, combined with a strong section of the old Liberal or Roman Catholic party. Sir W. Whiteway by extreme manipulation of the government machinery came in with a substantial majority. The defeated side filed, under the Corrupt Practices Act, nine petitions affecting 17 members, and an extraordinary political fight followed. On 16 February 1894 the Legislature met. Within six weeks the two members for Bay de Verde were unseated. On 3 April the majority of Whiteway's party formed a deputation to the Governor and asked for a dissolution: the following day the Opposition as a deputation protested: the dissolution was not granted, Whiteway resigned and A. F. Goodridge became Premier. In the face of continued obstruction he endeavoured to carry on the business of the session. Prorogation followed prorogation—member after member was unseated as a result of the election petitions: representative government was reduced to a farce. Then came a blow affecting the entire commercial community. The death of a member of a firm in England caused the return of the bills drawn on that firm. A crisis followed. On 10 December, henceforth known as "Black Monday", the Commercial and Union Banks both closed their doors, and brought down with them several firms. The notes of the Union Bank had been practically the currency of the colony: its failure left everyone without any medium of exchange.

The fire of 1892, the bad fishery of 1893, culminating in this disastrous crisis of 1894, shook the community to its foundations. Two days afterwards Goodridge's Government resigned, and D. J. Greene became Premier: but only for a few months. In 1895 Whiteway was again at the head of the Government. The first necessity was to re-establish the finances. An appeal for assistance was made to the Home Government which pointed out that financial responsibility was the first attribute of responsible government,[1] but sent out a special commissioner, Sir Herbert Murray, to enquire into, and relieve the pressing distress. An approach was next made to Canada, and the possibility of entering the Dominion was very seriously considered. In April 1895 a conference was held in Ottawa, but after a month's deliberations proved abortive.[2] The Newfound-

---

[1] *Parl. Paper, H. of C.* CIV, 1895, p. 11.
[2] *Newf. Sess. Papers,* 1895 (Copy in Col. Office Lib. 10937).

land Ministers then set themselves resolutely to face their difficulties.

In some measure the perplexities of the time led up to the railway deal which soon became the most prominent factor both in the development and politics of the colony. Mr Robert G. Reid, a Scotsman who had made a reputation for good work in Canada had, in 1890, received a contract for the construction of railways in Newfoundland. In 1893 he entered into a further contract with the Government for extending the railway across the island and down the west coast to Port-aux-Basques, and maintaining and working it for ten years. Criticisms of this arrangement were dulled by the financial troubles following the crisis of 1894; and when the doubters came into power under Sir James Winter in October 1897, they contracted to sell the whole of the railway to Reid for $1,000,000 and a large land grant: also for a further cash payment the colony's telegraph lines, the dry dock, and other assets. There was strong opposition to the proposal, and the Governor, Sir Herbert Murray, declared himself against a scheme which placed the whole future of the colony under the control of a single individual.[1] The Ministry, however, persisted in the scheme as the only possible means of staving off serious financial embarrassment; and the Secretary of State explained in response to petitions that, though he condemned the scheme, it was a matter in which he could not interfere.[2]

The change gave a stimulus to enterprise. Reid took over the tram lines in St John's, and a concession for lighting the city with electricity, and introduced ideas and conditions already familiar in Canada. But many of the sounder merchants and politicians were opposed to the domination of a large contractor, and amongst them was Mr (soon Sir) Robert Bond, now recognised as a particularly independent and honest politician. In the general election of 1900 the attack on the Reid contract was prominent, and Bond, becoming Prime Minister, took immediate steps to modify it. In 1901 the railway, telegraph lines, and docks were bought back, and leased to a company known as the Reid Newfoundland Company, the directors of which were Reid and his sons. The colony thus became again the owner of its railway, but had little control over it, and Bond's arrangement was criticised as substituting, for a wealthy and substantial contractor, a company (with limited liability) which the Reids could interpose between them and any claims. The subsequent disputes and arbitrations became a dominant factor in Newfoundland finance and politics.

But the Bond Ministry had even more important business to face. The Imperial Government, having found a prospect of settling the French fishery questions, suggested a short special session in February 1901, in which the temporary French Treaties Act was extended: and delegates then proceeded to London for conference. The negotiations broke down because the colony declined to make concessions

[1] *Parl. Paper* C. 8867 of 1898 and C. 9137 of 1899. [2] *Parl. Paper* C. 9137, pp. 26, 28.

as to the sale of bait unless the French abandoned or materially modified their system of bounties on the export of fish. But in the following years, while the colonial Ministry was occupied with the railway question and other domestic matters (such as the arrangements for a Royal Naval Reserve depôt, 1901, the erection of Marconi stations on the Labrador coast, 1903, the development of the great iron deposits at Bell Island), the Home Government persevered with negotiations for the settlement of all Franco-British disputes, and within three years their efforts were rewarded. Although the questions of Egypt and Morocco took the first place in these negotiations, the Foreign Secretary dealt at length with the Newfoundland problem, insisting on the impossibility of developing the west shore with the French claims hanging over the settlers.[1] Under the new convention the French agreed to abandon for ever their rights of landing on the Treaty Shore under Article XIII of the Treaty of Utrecht, His Majesty's Government on their side arranging for compensation both to the persons engaged in the fishing industry and to the French nation at large. The national compensation was effected by territorial concessions in other parts of the world. The compensation to be paid to individuals was the subject of further conventions. When the colonial Legislature met on 31 March 1905 after a general election which sustained Sir Robert Bond's Ministry, the speech from the Throne announced that the conventions with France were ratified.[2] The long standing fester of the French claims had been completely removed, and on 7 April 1905 two naval officers, one from each nation, meeting at Paris as an Arbitral Tribunal, proceeded to settle within six months the whole of the private claims by awards amounting to £55,000.

In the same year (1905) began a new and well directed enterprise. The Anglo-Newfoundland Development Company promoted by Lord Northcliffe, who had decided to make his newspapers independent of outside supplies, obtained a large concession of land in the interior of Newfoundland, and proceeded to build on the Exploits River, 42 miles from the mouth, the mill and works soon to be known as Grand Falls. Backed by ample funds, Grand Falls soon became a flourishing settlement, and to-day is a considerable town, better laid out than any other in the island, with a well constructed railway to the port at Botwood. Thus, with a sound pulpwood enterprise inaugurated and the Bell Island iron mines fast developing, the colony made a fair start on activities which freed it from complete dependence on its fisheries, at the same time improving them by better arrangements for curing and marketing fish and refining oils.

[1] Lord Lansdowne, 8 Ap. 1904. Cd. 1952, pp. 5–7.
[2] On 8 Dec. 1904. *Parl. Paper, Treaty series*, no. 5 of 1905. See too Gooch, G. P. and Temperley, H. W. V., *British Documents on the Origins of the War* (1898–1914), vol. II, ch. 15, vol. III, ch. 16.

Yet a new and serious dispute now arose. In the session of 1905 the Legislature took steps to withhold from American fishermen the privilege of taking bait; and as soon as the new Act came into operation trouble began. On 12 October 1905 the United States formally complained that the Newfoundland steamer *Fiona* with the Minister of Marine and Fisheries on board had forbidden American vessels to fish on "the treaty coast where...they have fished un-molested since 1818".[1] They objected to such a question being raised without warning. Called upon by the Home Government for ex-planations, the colonial Ministry showed there had been no pro-hibition to fish, but merely new regulations. Pressed further, they urged that their regulations were solely for the protection of the fishery,[2] and that the failure to enforce them would amount to an abandonment of sovereignty over their own waters. The Imperial Government, however, looking to their treaty obligations, pressed a *modus vivendi*, which in effect freed United States fishermen from certain restrictions in return for general compliance with the disputed regulations.[3] In the ensuing discussions two special points became prominent—the use of purse-seines, and the practice of engaging Newfoundlanders on American vessels. The colonial Government objected strenuously to both, and urged that any concession was precluded by the result of the elections of 1904, and that proper control of American ships was essential.[4] Nevertheless the Home Government proceeded to arrange on 6 October 1906 a *modus vivendi* which was briefly as follows—United States ships were permitted to use purse-seines for the ensuing season, and to engage Newfoundlanders outside the 3-mile limit without interference or penalties; on the other hand they were not to fish on Sundays, were to pay light dues and as far as possible conform to customs regulations, provided that the colonial Government did not bring into force certain specified Acts or parts of Acts.[5] At the same time H.M.S. *Brilliant* was ordered to remain in Newfoundland waters till the end of the fishing season.

The action of the Home Government raised a storm of indignation and protest.[6] Ministers urged its reversal, characterising it as "sub-versive of the colony's constitutional right and calculated to work severe injury to the fisheries". The merchants in public meeting supported them. The Premier's organ in the press took the matter up on a note of almost hysterical indignation. On the other hand the press on the western side of the island attacked the Premier for a policy injurious to the west coast: and, moved by the west coast fishermen, the captain of the *Brilliant* arranged a satisfactory agree-ment as to the purse-seines. The Newfoundland Ministers were

[1] *Parl. Paper* Cd. 3262 of 1906, p. 1.   [2] *Ibid.* p. 20.
[3] *Ibid.* pp. 22, 26 *ad med.*, and p. 29 for details.
[4] *Ibid.* p. 41.   [5] *Ibid.* pp. 42–3.
[6] For the ensuing narrative see *Parl. Paper* C. 3765 of 1907, esp. pp. 21, 27, 61, 74, 90, 100.

greatly annoyed; actions were brought against fishermen for engaging with Americans. This only aggravated the bickering and irritation. Early in 1907 a bid for the sympathy of fellow colonists in Canada brought the question up in the Canadian House of Commons. This no doubt prepared the way for discussion at the Imperial Conference of 1907 at which Sir Robert Bond urged that the question was extremely serious, both as affecting relations with their great neighbour, and entailing a constitutional conflict with the Home Government. His suggestion to refer the matter to the new Hague Tribunal was accepted, but he resisted any temporary accommodation pending the preparation of the cases on both sides. Consequently an Imperial Order-in-Council was issued to ensure the observance of the *modus vivendi*. The colonial Government strongly protested, and in the speech from the Throne at the opening of the session of 1908 embodied their objections, thus placing the Governor, Sir William MacGregor, in an equivocal position, which called for the exercise of much tact and patience.

Bond's indignation with the Home Government was not endorsed by the colony. The elections in the autumn of 1908 indicated a loss of confidence which led to a political crisis of an extraordinary character, marked by the "tie election" of local notoriety, and a resultant deadlock. Edward P. Morris (now Lord Morris) became Prime Minister, advised a dissolution, and in the ensuing election was effectively supported. The Secretary of State complimented Sir William MacGregor on his handling of a situation "practically unprecedented in the history of Responsible Government in the Dominions".[1]

The new Ministry, aided by the large revenue of 1908, embarked on a somewhat spectacular series of improvements. A daily news bulletin was arranged for the post-offices throughout the colony. Taxation affecting the fishermen was reduced. Further grants were made for education. A more vigorous effort was made to combat tuberculosis. Old age pensions were introduced. A policy of branch railways was adopted with a view to linking Bonavista (*via* Trinity) Hearts Content, and Trepassey with the main line. Meanwhile the arbitration at the Hague was proceeding. The agreement on the reference between H.M. Government and that of the United States had been signed on 27 January 1909. Nearly eighteen months later the case was opened, and on 7 September 1910, the award was given largely in favour of Newfoundland, on the ground that certain contentions of the United States were inconsistent with any conception of territorial sovereignty.[2] Thus by 1911 fishery disputes were cleared away, and fresh opportunity was given for internal development, particularly for the progressive railway policy above mentioned, though how far the new branches were economically justified is very doubtful.

[1] *Newf. Sessional Papers*, 1909, App. p. 14.
[2] *North American Coast Fisheries Arbitration*, Printed Proceedings, pp. 1446 seqq.

But before the colony had time to find its feet again there came in 1914 the rupture with Germany, and, like the rest of the Empire, Newfoundland at once settled down to take its part in the fight. The depôt of the Royal Naval Reserve (H.M.S. *Briton*) sprang into full activity, and the Admiralty took steps to erect a powerful wireless telegraph station at Mount Pearl some 7 miles from St John's. Restrictive legislation on the Home model was adopted. Under the Governor, Sir W. Davidson, and his ministers, a Patriotic Association was formed, which decided to raise a separate Newfoundland Regiment. The three existing cadet corps formed the nucleus of a regiment, and on 12 October the first 500 men (the Blue Puttees) arrived in England. Concurrently the merchants and fishermen of the island were shipping their cargoes to Europe, taking advantage of the rise of prices. The detailed fortunes of the colony from 1914 to 1918 need not be followed. From the first the colonial Government adopted defensive measures similar to those of the Home authorities. An outstanding measure, indirectly due to the war, was the introduction in 1916 of the law prohibiting the use of intoxicating liquor. In 1916 Sir E. Morris arranged with the Opposition to form a Coalition Ministry, which swept away opposition to the Business Profits Tax by introducing in a special session (August 1917) legislation based on that of 1911 in Britain for curtailing the powers of the Upper House: also, though there was at no time serious anxiety as to supplies, it appointed a Food Controller. When, in January 1918, Morris resigned the Premiership and remained in England, Mr (soon to be Sir) William Lloyd became Prime Minister and was responsible for an Act to enforce compulsory service, which was accepted on the whole with good will. Lloyd eventually represented the colony at the Peace Conference at Paris.

There were at times alarms as to raids on the coast, and in 1917, when the German submarines made their short-lived raid into North American waters, the *Stephano* and other colonial vessels were destroyed. But to the colony itself war was distant. Yet it left a mark of which the community may well be proud. The seamen of Newfoundland had long been known in the navy as efficient and resourceful, but the end of the war left them with a greatly enhanced reputation. They readily undertook almost impossible boarding operations in wild seas which others would not face. Nothing but praise was accorded by the Fleet. Further, the men of the Newfoundland Regiment, when once their serjeant-major realised the way to handle them, rapidly showed their adaptability, and ultimately developed a battle discipline equal to that of the old British regiments and probably surpassing that of all the overseas troops. Newfoundland had preserved in its old west country stock those idiosyncrasies which gave the territorial regiments their dogged resistance. At Gallipoli they did well, but the test came to them at the action of Beaumont-Hamel

on 1 July 1916, when the regiment was set to take the village in face
of a murderous fire; they went into action 753 strong, only 68
answered the roll call next day. A few weeks later they were again
put to a supreme test against heavy odds at Gueudecourt. There out
of a strength of 383 they had 294 casualties, but carried out their task
without flinching, and earned themselves a lasting name in British
military records. On the field of Beaumont-Hamel now stands their
memorial in France. It was a proper compliment to them that on
the occupation of the German bridgeheads they were given a special
place, and marched into Cologne on 7 December 1918 under the
command of their own Major Bernard. The total number of men
enlisted or enrolled in the Newfoundland Regiment and Forestry
Corps during the years 1914–18 was 6859. Of these 5482 went
overseas: 1300 were killed, and 2314 wounded—a proportion which
greatly exceeded that of any other contingent. The regiment
thoroughly deserved their appellation of Royal granted in January
1918.

The war expenditure borne by the colony added $10,000,000 to
the public debt, besides the amounts raised privately. The after-care
of the disabled also threw a considerable charge on the revenues.
On the other hand, as soon as the first dislocation of business was
overcome, war conditions were favourable for the fishermen and
merchants and a wave of prosperity swept over the island. Prices of
fish were high, and the demand was steady. There was no hesitation
about shipping. A striking result of the demand for tonnage was the
reversion to the wooden local-built schooner: even hard-headed
business men prophesied a new era for the Newfoundland sailing
vessels: throughout the island, large fortunes were being made.
Unfortunately the high prices of war engendered extravagance: the
excitement of peace tempted men to think that prosperity would go
on for ever. In the course of 1920 a change came: prices dropped,
losses followed. It became difficult to raise revenue just when demands became insistent: the railway which had deteriorated during
the war was in a bad state, and unemployment was rife.

After the armistice the Coalition Government remained in power,
and on the whole handled matters well for the nine months which
were left to them: but gradually a rift appeared, and in May 1919
the Coalition was terminated by the revival of antagonism between
Mr (afterwards Sir W.) Coaker, with his followers the fishermen
members, and the other wing of the Coalition. Lloyd, essentially
loyal as a politician, found his position increasingly difficult and
midway through the session resigned, recommending Sir Michael
Cashin to succeed him. The reconstructed Government threw the
fishermen's party into opposition. The visit of the Prince of Wales, at
the start of his Empire tours, and the virtual settlement of the form of
reference to the Judicial Committee in the Labrador boundary dispute

marked Cashin's short administration. At the general election in the
autumn of 1919 Coaker joined forces with a comparatively young
politician, Mr William R. Warren, and the two agreed to place themselves under Mr (afterwards Sir Richard) Squires, whose adherents
were few, though his personal force was great. This rather heterogeneous Ministry came into power with promises of radical reform
and economy, and in particular of dealing faithfully with the Reid
Newfoundland Company. Yet, when public economy was vital, they
began by increasing expenditure in many directions. During 1920
and 1921 the outstanding question was the termination of the contract with the Reid Newfoundland Company, and the resumption
of complete responsibility for the railway, entailing heavy expenditure
at a moment when finances were overstrained by falling prices and
the aftermath of war. The guarantee for a large project, first initiated
by the Reids, then taken up by the Armstrong-Whitworth Company,
of utilising the water power of the Humber and erecting pulp mills
on a large scale was also mooted, but belongs to a later year. On
judicious handling of these questions the future of the colony largely
depended. In the years 1867–1921, while the population had increased
by only 66 per cent., revenue and expenditure had risen to fourteen
times the amounts of 1867, the average for three years ending with
1921 being $9,523,742 and $8,954,961, respectively. The debt was
forty times as great. Trade was but six or seven times more valuable.
The imports for 1921 were $28,909,727, the exports $22,441,267.

To sum up: the people of Newfoundland still conserve to an
unusual degree the characteristics of the earlier settlers. At the last
census there were 259,259 people: outside St John's with its 36,000
inhabitants, there are only three settlements of about 4000 inhabitants. Isolation, often in small coves with one or two houses,
where a man can keep to himself good fishing and plenty of wood,
fosters the old traditions: it also breeds a peculiarly self-reliant race,
but encourages strong prejudice, and hampers education. The colony
is still very largely unexplored. Less than four-fifths of England in
area, it has few main roads: the railway which follows the coast,
except where it crosses the island, leaves a vast portion of the country
without communication. Between the Gander and Conne Rivers
there is a track used by the Micmac Indians; during most summers
a few trappers go into the interior, but the area between the railway
on the north and Bay Despair on the south is almost unknown.
The long northern tongue of the island, though crossed by dog-
sleighs in the winter when the waters are frozen, has rarely been
traversed in summer, and remains sealed.

In such a country the primary factors in the life of the people are
simply their most pressing needs—livelihood, medical care, education
and spiritual aid. Work in the fisheries is hard, the return to agriculture is limited to potatoes, hay for cattle, and oats. Yet by demanding

the whitest flour, and rejecting more wholesome food, the islanders add to their physical difficulties. They are also, as a whole, too poor to support efficient medical practitioners. In St John's there is a full and competent staff of medical men; and at the chief outports there are resident doctors who, so far as physical strength permits, are available for the vast surrounding districts, by boat, or a rough trap, in all weathers. The Government, not having money to spare, has intervened very little. Until comparatively recently there was no hospital outside the capital: that has been most efficient, but the strain upon it has been far too severe. A wonderful impulse was given by Dr (now Sir) Wilfred Grenfell, who in 1892 came out to the colony as a medical missionary under the auspices of the Deep Sea Mission to Seamen, and, establishing himself at St Anthony on the north-east of the island, set up both there and on the Labrador a standard which has been a stimulus to the whole colony. Ancillary to the doctor is the nurse. A good deal had been done for the capital some years back by Miss Mary M. Southcott, but the first definite effort in the outports was made by Lady Harris's Committee in and after 1920 on a basis designed to be self-supporting. In the distant and less accessible outports the trained nurse is a godsend, and may prevent suffering and loss of life.

Education has only slowly made way through the colony. The religious organisations have been the chief instrument in spreading it, but their exclusiveness has wasted strength and diminished efficiency. Apart from the Roman Catholics, who everywhere guard their schools with peculiar jealousy, the Church of England and the Methodist body insist on separate schools, and of late years the Salvation Army has endeavoured to assert the same claim. Often within a few miles there are three or four struggling schools where one good one would be far more efficient. As regards secondary education, both Bishop Feild College and St Bonaventure's College maintain a fair standard: the Methodist College is not far behind. These reflect Canadian influence as well as that of the United States: this shows itself in pronunciation and manner as well as thought. The effect of English education is most marked in the older families, who aim at sending their boys and girls to the British Isles.

As with general education so with sport—there is a tendency to drop the English games. But the Newfoundlander is keen and competent in what he likes. Naturally so small a community cannot claim any great achievement in Literature, the Arts, Drama, or Music. Yet in the last two particularly the Newfoundlander, thrown very much on his own resources, reaches, chiefly with amateurs, a general level and enthusiasm exceeding those of many larger communities. And in the outer world Newfoundlanders have made their mark. The independence, self-reliance, and ingenuity which are striking features of their character, suggest great future possibilities.

CHAPTER XXIX

THE CONSTITUTION AND ITS WORKING,
1867–1921

THE Dominion of Canada is a Confederation of nine provinces working under a series of Acts known as the British North America Acts, 1867–1915, under Canadian legislation, depending for its constitutionality on those Acts, under the great landmarks of British constitutional development and under the common law except in so far as modified by Canada and its provinces. This complicated scheme prevents us on the one hand from thinking that Canada has a written constitution and on the other from believing that the casual study of a few documents can afford anything like an adequate view of the workings of Canadian political institutions. The British North America Acts are something like an institutional loom, in which for sixty years has been woven and rewoven a tapestry of law, custom, convention and tradition, as each generation has imaged the pattern and tried to express it in the web of constitutional life. Obviously, then, this chapter can present only a general conspectus of the working constitution, laying emphasis on characteristic and important features, and omitting so far as possible such procedure and rules as Canada and its provinces share with the United Kingdom.

The most fascinating and at the same time the most irritating problem of federalism clearly is the distribution of legislative powers. Many treatises have been written on this aspect of the Canadian constitution and year after year judicial decisions call for modifications and revisions. It is possible, however, to point out certain important features in this connection. First, there is in Canada no reserve of legislative power vested as in the United States of America in the people. All spheres of legislative action, all matters of Canadian legislative competency, are provided for whether in the federal Legislature or in the provincial Legislatures. "The whole area of self-government" is covered.[1] The expression, however, is one which must not be ridden to death.[2] It is obvious that there exists no Canadian legislative competency with regard to succession to the Crown, or the declaration of war or peace, and that no federal Act dissolving the union with the Empire would be constitutional. In addition, it is extremely doubtful whether extra-territorial legislation is possible[3]—

---

[1] *Attorney-General for Ontario* v. *Attorney-General for Canada* [1912], A.C. 571.
[2] Lord Haldane in *Attorney-General for British Columbia* v. *Attorney-General for Canada* [1914], A.C. 153.
[3] *Macleod* v. *Attorney-General for New South Wales* [1891], A.C. 455. Cf. *Journal of Comparative Legislation*, n.s. IX, 2, p. 210.

a doubt confirmed by the recent resolution of the Canadian Parliament to seek powers from the Imperial Parliament in this connection.[1] Secondly, the federal Legislature is not one of exclusive and defined powers as in the United States. To the provinces are granted sixteen enumerated and exclusive subjects and to the Confederation belong the general residuary power. However, in order to make that residuary power clearer and not to restrict its general nature, the federal Legislature is given control over twenty-nine enumerated subjects "notwithstanding anything in the Act". That is to say: the provinces possess certain defined and exclusive powers, and the Dominion possesses the residuum;[2] but the exclusive powers of the provinces may be modified or curtailed if judicial decision in definite suits draw any of them into the ambit of the enumerated subjects granted to the Confederation. The deduction, of course, follows that the Dominion cannot under its general authority trench on the subject-matters exclusively entrusted to the provinces. Thirdly, there is concurrent legislative power over agriculture and immigration, subject to the rule that in a clash of enactment that of the Dominion will prevail. Finally, the provinces possess exclusive control over education, with specially guaranteed protection for "denominational schools which any class of persons have by law in the province at the union". These schools must be recognised by law as denominational, and the protection cannot be construed to cover schools which were *de facto* denominational through such causes as the presence of a population professing one religion, or through the teaching of one faith.[3] The phrase "class of persons" must be interpreted to mean persons distinguished as a class by religious belief and not by race or language. Persons joined by "ties of faith" alone "form a class of persons within the meaning of the Act".[4]

At this point it is possible to discuss the nature and the rights and privileges of the various Legislatures in Canada which deal with this rather complicated distribution of legislative subject-matters. No Legislature is in any sense an agent or delegate—neither the Dominion from the British Legislature, nor the provincial from the British or Dominion Legislature. Every Legislature within its sphere is sovereign; its powers are "exclusive" and "supreme" and may be said to be "absolute".[5] It is a proper function of the courts to decide the respective limits of federal and provincial legislative powers, but when once these are settled no court can enquire whether they have been

---

[1] Keith, A. B., "Territorial Restrictions on Dominion Legislation", *ibid.* 3rd series, VII, I, pp. 103 ff.

[2] For an important modification see *Toronto Electric Commrs.* v. *Snider* [1925], A.C. 328.

[3] *Maher* v. *Town of Portland*, Wheeler, *Confederation Law*, pp. 362 ff.; *City of Winnipeg* v. *Barrett* [1892], A.C. 445.

[4] *Ottawa Separate Schools* v. *Mackell* [1917], A.C. 62.

[5] *Hodge* v. *The Queen* [1883], 9 App. Cas. 117; *The Liquidators of the Maritime Bank* v. *The Receiver-General of New Brunswick* [1892], A.C. 437; *Brophy* v. *Attorney-General of Manitoba* [1895], A.C. 202; *Attorney-General for Canada* v. *Cain and Gilhula* [1906], A.C. 542.

wisely exercised or in what manner they are exercised.[1] Legislative supremacy is the cardinal parliamentary doctrine throughout Canada. Canadian Legislatures within the limits assigned to them are supreme, and each may delegate to subordinate bodies coercive powers.

An interesting situation arises over the question of constituent powers. The Dominion cannot alter the British North America Acts in any vital manner, and all important changes must come from the British Parliament. These have always been forthcoming where a request has been made sufficiently and obviously covered by Canadian opinion; but the year 1867 has always been regarded as a covenanted occasion, Confederation as something of the nature of a treaty, and unless the wishes of the Canadian people are clear the British Government would be loth to act. Much discussion has taken place in Canada whether some plan could not be evolved by which Canada could obtain constituent powers. Nothing, however, has emerged. Quebec stands fairly solid for the *status quo*, and many who view with misgivings the developments of Canadian autonomy would support Quebec. The whole position must be purged from *a priori* reasoning such as that which claims that in this respect Canada is not only inferior to Australia, South Africa, and the Irish Free State, but even to its own provinces. There is indeed a growing demand for change; but it is well to remember that the Confederation is the child of serious and honourable obligations and that it has taken many years so to balance delicate and dangerous centrifugal and centripetal forces as to produce a corporate consciousness and the sense of nationhood. Sober realism seems to say that the granting of full constituent powers at present to the Dominion would be an exceedingly precarious experiment. No one who can think of the Dominion as a whole and apart from the pressure, often extreme in a vast territory, of his own local needs and aspirations, can soberly urge comprehensive imperial legislation. Constituent powers will undoubtedly come one day: but it is likely that they will come guarded by a "bill of rights"—covering clauses as in the Australian Commonwealth Act—beyond the legislative competence of the Dominion.

The provinces, however, possess full constituent powers—subject to the reservation that they must not touch the office of Lieutenant-Governor—and many changes have already taken place. Interest at present centres round procedure by the initiative and referendum in the western provinces. In 1919 the Judicial Committee of the Privy Council handed down an opinion that the Initiative and Referendum Act of Manitoba[2] was an interference with the office of Lieutenant-Governor and as such *ultra vires*.[3] Somewhat similar legislation took place in Saskatchewan and in Alberta. The Direct

---

[1] *Attorney-General for Ontario* v. *Attorney-General for Canada* [1912], A.C. 571.
[2] 6 Geo. V, c. 59 (Manitoba Act).
[3] *In re Initiative and Referendum Act* [1919], A.C. 935.

Legislation Act (1913) of the latter province laid down conditions on which a referendum could be asked for or the power of initiative exercised, and, while preserving the appearance of action by the Assembly, imposed on it a duty of repealing any measure disapproved by a referendum and of passing any measure (except a supply Act) originating through the initiative. In due course the Alberta Liquor Act passed into law by the process laid down by the Direct Legislation Act—a proper petition called for a referendum which itself declared in favour of the measure. The Legislature duly enacted it in substantially the same form. On a case arising under the liquor legislation appeal finally reached the Judicial Committee.[1] It was argued that the legislative procedure contravened the British North America Act of 1867 which gave to the Assembly alone power to make laws, and that the methods employed in Alberta substantially if not effectively destroyed that power. The Judicial Committee had not the point before them and were satisfied that the Liquor Act was an Act of the Legislature fully within its powers and duly assented to by the Crown. The opinion, however, appears to imply that a declaration by the electors outlining a bill was not essentially different from a general mandate by the electors to their representatives in the Assembly to pass any measure. If that be so—and of course the Direct Legislation Act was not under consideration—it would seem a logical deduction that a province can so change its constitution as to deprive effectively its Legislative Assembly of the traditional processes of building up and shaping a law by full discussion in committee and in the House, since a measure may practically come direct from the people and grave changes are not permitted. If this procedure obtains, it will mean vital changes and will give such broad and far-reaching interpretations to the constituent powers of the provinces as to alter fundamentally the well-known conventions of parliamentary Cabinet Government. It need hardly be added that no province has the constitutional right of secession from the Confederation.

The rights and privileges of the Canadian Legislatures are now fortunately settled. It is clear that the special form which they have assumed for the Parliament of the United Kingdom is part and parcel of the *lex et consuetudo parliamenti* and that a subordinate Legislature has no power to appropriate that law merely as a matter of appropriation.[2] On the other hand these privileges can be exercised under statute. For the Federal Parliament this has been done by the British North America Act of 1875 under which the Parliament of Canada can by law define its "privileges, immunities and powers" provided such definition does not include "privileges, immunities and powers" which are not enjoyed at the time of the passing of the law by the

[1] *Rex* v. *Nat Bell Liquors* [1922], 2 A.C. 128.
[2] Cf. *Landers* v. *Woodworth*, 2 S.C.R. 158; *Kielley* v. *Carson*, 4 Moo. P.C. 63; *Doyle* v. *Falconer*, 4 Moo. (N.S.), 203.

Parliament of the United Kingdom and its members.[1] In the provinces after 1867 a considerable struggle went on over the rights and privileges of the provincial Legislatures and statutes, and judicial decisions followed one another in an amazing round of controversy. In 1896 the Judicial Committee finally settled the matter in an opinion which stated that in the older provinces the right of definition was covered by the British North America Act of 1867 which continued save for the purposes of that Act the powers of the provincial Legislatures at federation. They also laid it down that the entire problem came within the exclusive power granted to a province to change its constitution.[2] To-day, all the provinces have defined by law the rights and privileges of their Legislatures.

Executive authority in both the federal and provincial areas is vested in the Crown, represented in the former by a Governor-General appointed for a term of years by the British Government, and in the latter by Lieutenant-Governors appointed for a term of years by the Dominion Government. The executive Government of the Dominion is carried on by a committee of the Privy Council—a Cabinet of ministers selected from the political party which may reasonably expect to command support in the House of Commons and appointed by the Governor-General on the advice of the Prime Minister. In the provinces similar conditions prevail. On the whole the executives, both federal and provincial, are modelled on traditional British types and normally follow the well-known lines of Cabinet Government. There is therefore no necessity to examine their organisation and working in detail. On the other hand, conventions and extra-legal rules have grown up in relation to the Crown and to the Crown in Council in Canada and its provinces to which special attention must be given later.

The Federal Parliament is bi-cameral, consisting of a Senate and a House of Commons. The former is a nominated House of ninety-six members appointed for life by the Governor-General in Council and distributed as follows: Ontario, 24; Quebec, 24; the Maritime Provinces and Prince Edward Island, 24 (i.e. Nova Scotia, 10; New Brunswick, 10; Prince Edward Island, 4); the Western Provinces, 24, six each. Senators from Quebec alone represent senatorial divisions. It is noteworthy that the Senate does not represent the constituent provinces—the federal idea as worked out in the United States and in Australia is not followed—but appointments are made in such a way as merely to represent grouped provinces. Women can be created senators.[3] There is no adequate provision for deadlock. The Governor-General can, it is true, recommend the Crown to add from

---

[1] 38 and 39 Vict. c. 38.

[2] *Fielding* v. *Thomas* [1896], A.C. 600. See too Riddell, W. R., *The Canadian Constitution in Form and in Fact*, p. 16.

[3] According to a decision of the Judicial Committee, overruling a unanimous judgment of the Supreme Court of Canada (46 "Times Law Reports", 4).

four to eight additional senators[1]—a provision which would appear to make the British Cabinet responsible. The request has been made only once, but the Colonial Secretary of the day firmly refused to act on it, stating that the exercise of the power depended on serious deadlock which actually held up the Administration and on its being shown that such addition of senators provided an adequate remedy.[2] As a matter of fact, as political issues have worked out, the possible number of additional senators would seldom if ever have balanced the party differences between the Houses. However that may be, the principles laid down by the Colonial Secretary are as old as 1877, and it is more than likely at the present time that not only would the Governor-General make the request, if advised by his ministers to do so, but that the Crown's action would be purely formal. The problem still remains, and Canada is thus left (unlike the United Kingdom, Australia, South Africa and the Irish Free State) without any adequate constitutional provision in a case of serious deadlock. It would be tedious to attempt any review of all the suggestions which have been made for changes. Difficulties and plans are most in evidence when a party after being in opposition for a long time at length takes office only to find a Senate overwhelmingly opposed to it—for no party has as yet ever sought to appoint senators of a different political creed. In such circumstances loud demands are made for change, rash promises are made and second Chambers are reviewed on the public platform, in the press and in Parliament with a diligence and vehemence worthy of the abbé Sieyès. The issues however lose interest and the problem becomes less serious as death thins the ranks of the Senate and loyal supporters of the Government soon fill them. "Senate reform" is apparently only an issue when the Houses are in pronounced party opposition. "Deadlock" and "reform" have never been prominently before the electorate apart from such conditions, and as these are resolved to the satisfaction of the Cabinet there arises a singular contentment with the *status quo*. Voices may be heard crying here and there in the wilderness of theory, but public interest sleeps until the party in power suffers defeat. Then the old speeches and the old arguments reappear once again to do their election duty, and in due course to be stored away to await the advent of the next political cycle.

The number of members of the House of Commons varies according to a redistribution of seats after every decennial census and is governed by a statutory constitutional principle. The representation of Quebec is fixed at sixty-five members, and to each province is assigned every ten years such a number of members as will bear the same proportion to its population as the number sixty-five bears to

[1] British North America Act, 1915 (5 and 6 Geo. V, c. 45).
[2] *Sessional Papers*, Canada (1877), no. 68; *Journals of the Senate*, Canada (1877), pp. 130, 174.

the population of Quebec. Any adult British subject can become a member subject to disqualifications analogous to those obtaining in Great Britain. All members receive a sessional indemnity for their services and enjoy certain privileges in travelling and in postal facilities. The leader of the Opposition is paid a statutory salary in addition to his sessional indemnity. The laws, regulations and rules governing the opening of the House, prorogations, adjournments and legislative procedure follow, *ceteris paribus*, British precedents, and any discussion of them would be superfluous. There are, however, certain points of historical and political interest to which attention may be drawn.

The electoral districts or constituencies are determined by the Federal Parliament. For many years after 1867 the exercise of this power led to bitter and disgraceful controversy, and "gerrymandering" the constituencies by means of a straight party vote proceeded on a considerable scale. In 1903, however, a more hopeful era began, and the Redistribution Bill of that year was introduced with no electoral schedules, the Prime Minister promising, if the Opposition would accept the measure, to refer it after second reading to a committee composed of seven members, of whom the Opposition should select three.[1] A similar plan was followed in 1914 by Sir Robert Borden.[2] Of course human nature is weak and party feelings are easily offended, but on the whole the constituencies are at present determined without wholesale attempts to beat the Opposition with the bludgeon of arbitrary legislation. The federal franchise has also figured prominently in party controversy. The power to determine it was left in 1867 to the Federal Parliament, but, until exercised, provision was made that the existing electoral laws of the provinces should hold good in the federal area. When the British North America Act was passed the franchise was granted to every male householder of full age in the territory of Algoma. On the other hand, in the five general elections held from 1867 to 1882 members were elected on the provincial franchises. Macdonald never liked this method and from the first deplored having the Federal House "at the mercy of a foreign body".[3] Before 1885 he introduced several abortive bills creating a federal franchise, but in that year he at length succeeded in carrying such a measure. The Act was at once the subject of merciless Liberal attack: it betrayed the federal principle, it was extravagant, it widened the ambit of patronage, it produced partisan revisions and so on.[4] Whatever the truth may have been, the fact remains that the Liberals were able on coming into power to return to the older plan which has been followed

[1] *Debates of H. of C., Canada*, 31 March 1903.
[2] *Ibid.* 10 Feb. 1914.
[3] Macdonald to Brown Chamberlin, 26 Oct. 1868, Pope, *Correspondence of Sir John Macdonald*, p. 75.
[4] Cf. *Official Report, Liberal Convention* (1893), p. 122.

substantially ever since. Under Dominion legislation the provincial voters' lists are now used, but the Dominion lays down the qualifications and disqualifications for electors. The combined provisions result in something approaching adult suffrage. Every House of Commons can continue for five years unless previously dissolved. The arrangements for a new election are in the hands of the chief electoral officer for the Dominion, who acts in each constituency through a returning officer. In addition to the general oversight of a particular contest, the latter is responsible for seeing that the candidates are qualified, have consented to nomination and have made deposits of two hundred dollars each, which are returned to them if successful. Those who fail to be elected forfeit their deposits unless they obtain such a percentage of the votes cast as Dominion legislation may from time to time determine. All official election expenses are a charge on the Dominion.[1]

In Ontario and British Columbia no second Chamber has ever existed, while Alberta and Saskatchewan were created provinces each with a single Chamber. New Brunswick abolished its second Chamber in 1892,[2] Manitoba in 1876,[3] while Prince Edward Island merged its second Chamber in the Assembly, whose members have been elected since 1893 partially on a property franchise and partially on adult suffrage.[4] The Legislative Council of Quebec consists of twenty-four members holding for life and appointed by the Lieutenant-Governor by instrument under the great seal of the province, each member representing one of the twenty-four divisions of the province. There is no provision for deadlock or for the adjustment of differences between the two Houses. As a matter of fact there has been no friction of consequence. The two Houses have co-ordinate legislative powers subject to the general rule covering proposals for taxation. The Legislative Council in Nova Scotia was apparently continued in 1867 as it existed at confederation—a nominated House of twenty-one members holding during pleasure and possessing legislative powers similar to those of the Council in Quebec. Years of friction followed. At length in 1925 the Liberal Government succeeded in reforming the Council's constitution to the extent that new members were appointed for ten year periods instead of for life and providing that legislation, with the single exception of legislation abolishing the Legislative Council, which passed the House of Assembly at three successive sessions could become law without the Council's concurrence.[5] When a Conservative Government took office attempts were made to bring pressure on the Council to vote itself out of existence. When these

[1] *Election Instructions*, 15 *August* 1925, Book A, (14)-8-25-35 M. (Ottawa, 1925.)
[2] 54 Vict. c. 9 (New Brunswick).
[3] 39 Vict. c. 28 (Manitoba).
[4] 56 Vict. c. 21 (Prince Edward Island).
[5] 15 and 16 Geo. V, c. 16 (Nova Scotia). For the debates see the *Morning Chronicle*, Halifax, 7, 16, 28, 29 April 1925.

failed, the Prime Minister requested his law officers to advise whether or not the Cabinet could request the Lieutenant-Governor to appoint members in excess of twenty-one. The provincial law officers believed that such power existed. On reference to Ottawa, the federal law officers expressed grave doubts about the matter, and, while generally opposed to the opinion of the provincial law officers, advised a reference to the supreme court of Nova Scotia before which four questions were argued in July 1926 covering the total membership; the powers to increase the number of members; where such powers, if legal, lay— with the Lieutenant-Governor in Council or with the King in Council; the terms of tenure, and, if during pleasure, whether that of the King or of the Lieutenant-Governor in Council. In the following October judgment was handed down.[1] On the vital issues the court was evenly divided. An appeal to the Judicial Committee followed, with the result that Nova Scotia abolished its Upper House which had been in existence 170 years.[2]

It is unnecessary to go into details in connection with the composition and procedure of the nine provincial Assemblies. In most provinces adult suffrage prevails. In Quebec and Nova Scotia there are small property, income or rental qualifications. The disqualifications for voting are similar to those in the federal area and follow British lines; but in Manitoba there are certain linguistic qualifications and in Saskatchewan and British Columbia there are racial disqualifications. The rules governing membership of the provincial Assemblies are on the whole similar. In addition to the traditional disqualifications no one who is a member of the Dominion Parliament or of another Legislative Assembly can sit, and clergymen are ineligible in Prince Edward Island. Members are paid in all the provinces and the procedure of the Houses follows almost entirely British precedents.

Canada does not possess a system of federal courts such as exists in the United States, although provision for such a system is made in the British North America Act of 1867. The provinces have exclusive powers to constitute and to organise courts for provincial purposes of both civil and criminal jurisdiction, and they can regulate procedure in civil matters. The Dominion Parliament may impose new duties on existing provincial courts and may give them new powers relating to subjects not assigned exclusively to the provinces. The British North America Act provides that the judges of the superior, district and county courts in the provinces must be paid by the Dominion, and their appointment must lie with the Governor-General in Council subject to certain regulations connected with the provincial bars. The provincial courts deal with all matters of

[1] See the *Morning Chronicle*, Halifax, 13, 14 July, 25 Oct. 1926.
[2] 44 "Times Law Reports", 1. Cf. Mackenzie, N., "Constitutional Questions in Nova Scotia", in *Journal of Comparative Legislation*, 3rd series, XI, 1, pp. 87 ff.

legislation whether under federal or provincial law, they also hear cases and petitions arising out of parliamentary elections. In addition it is their duty to give opinions on the constitutionality of bills for the guidance of the provincial Cabinets, and from their opinions appeal is possible to the supreme court of Canada, provided that such opinions are declared by provincial statutes to be judgments of the highest court of final resort in the province and that appeals shall be therefrom as from judgments in actions. Criminal law and criminal procedure are controlled exclusively by the Federal Government. The judges of the superior courts, of the supreme court of Canada and of the county courts hold office during good behaviour. Those of the first two classes can only be dismissed on a joint address from the Houses of the Canadian Parliament,[1] but county court judges may be removed by the Governor-General in Council for misdemeanour, ill-health, incapacity and the like, subject however to legal rules which guard against arbitrary procedure and lack of publicity in Parliament.

There are only two federal courts in Canada—the supreme court, consisting of a chief justice and five puisne judges, and the court of exchequer and admiralty. The latter deals with patents, trade marks and the like and with proceedings against the Crown in the federal area. The former has an appellate jurisdiction, criminal and civil, throughout Canada. There is no court of criminal appeal similar to that in England, but questions of law arising out of a criminal case may eventually reach the supreme court. To it may also come appeals in civil cases under rules laid down by federal legislation. No province can interfere with the legally constituted jurisdiction of the supreme court of Canada, or prevent appeals from its courts if federal legislation has not itself limited the right; and a province cannot grant powers of appeal where such are limited by federal law. The supreme court has also an appellate jurisdiction in cases of controverted elections, and from its decisions in such cases the Judicial Committee will not receive appeals.[2] The Governor-General in Council has authority to obtain opinions by direct answers from the supreme court on any questions of law or fact. The answers are not binding on the Governor-General in Council or on Canadian judges in any specific cases, but they are treated as final judgments for purposes of reference to the Judicial Committee.

The Crown has the undoubted right to hear appeals from all courts in Canada, and a Canadian Act purporting to bar the appeal in criminal cases is undoubtedly *ultra vires*.[3] Appeals lie direct to the Judicial Committee from the supreme court of Canada and from the higher provincial courts, but in the former cases appeals are allowed

[1] Provision has, however, been made for their retirement under certain statutory conditions (Judges Act, 1922).
[2] *Théberge* v. *Laudry*, 2 App. Cas. 102.
[3] *Nadan* v. *The King* [1926], 42 T.L.R. 356.

by special leave of the Judicial Committee and not as of right, while in the latter case they are regulated not only by special leave but by right under rules recognised in legal procedure. Within recent years there has been growing up a sentiment against appeals to the Judicial Committee. It is hard to form any idea of its strength, but of its existence and widening influence there can be no doubt. There is a certain implication of inferiority in status in the perpetuation of such appeals, and this is not in any degree modified by arguments emphasising on the one hand the calm aloofness of the Judicial Committee or on the other the "immemorial rights of British subjects". The former emphasis may cast grave aspersions on the whole Canadian judiciary while the latter may only serve to benefit rich corporations and not penurious suitors. Nor is it entirely just in this connection to base arguments on the peculiar religious and racial groupings within the Confederation, since from South Africa with somewhat similar conditions appeals only go to the Judicial Committee in cases of the greatest moment.[1] The problem is not a grave issue as yet in Canada, but it is of growing importance, and political wisdom would advise the anticipation of difficulties by the passing of a permissive British Act giving the Dominion complete control over the regulation of appeals. The burden would thus be thrown on Canada. It is extremely unlikely that any comprehensive action would be taken, but the permissive Act would at least rob theorists of fissiparous shafts and would above all eliminate dangerous criticisms connected with limitations on Dominion autonomy.

In concluding this division of the subject attention must be called to an anomalous situation which exists in connection with divorce. At confederation, the exclusive right of legislating on divorce was assigned to the Dominion, but the powers already belonging to certain of the provinces were not abrogated. As a consequence the courts of Nova Scotia, New Brunswick and British Columbia continued to possess their pre-federation jurisdiction in divorce.[2] There was, however, a general opinion that none of the other provinces possessed such rights. In order to eliminate apparent inequalities, it would seem reasonable that the federal Legislature should have created uniformity. Quebec, however, has proved hostile; or rather no Government has seemed prepared to risk antagonising that province, especially as there was a way out of the difficulty by granting divorces through federal legislation. The Senate investigates applications and divorce bills are first passed there. As a general rule they are accepted by the House of Commons in the form sent down by the Senate, but of course no rights to rejection or to amendment have been surrendered.[3] Recently this arrangement

[1] Cf. Whittaker v. The Mayor and Councillors of Durban [1920], 36 T.L.R. 734.
[2] See Watts v. Attorney-General for British Columbia [1908], A.C. 573.
[3] For procedure see Mackay, R. A., The Unreformed Senate of Canada, pp. 82 ff.; for the

has received a rude shock, for it now appears that the courts of Manitoba, Alberta and Saskatchewan possess a jurisdiction in divorce.[1] There thus arises the curious situation that citizens of Quebec, of Ontario, and possibly of Prince Edward Island who wish to begin divorce proceedings must resort to the cumbersome and somewhat expensive methods of federal legislation.[2] As matters stand the situation is undoubtedly irritating. Divorces within Canada have increased at a remarkable rate, while there is also a tendency to seek relief in the less strict States of the United States. The pressure of public opinion will undoubtedly make uniformity by judicial process inevitable.

The federal functions of the Crown are carried out by a Governor-General appointed by the King. His powers are specially defined powers, whereby he possesses sufficient executive authority to carry on the government of the Dominion. Provision is made for the carrying out of his functions by an administrator or deputy in case of absence, incapacity, removal or death. His person and office are guarded by well-known regulations, and as the personal representative of the monarch he commands national respect. His appointment has always called for the personal interest of the Crown, but responsibility for it of course lies with the British Cabinet and primarily with the Secretary of State for the Dominions. Canada shares in no official way in the appointment, and there is no evidence to show that there has ever been any deviation from the technical procedure to which in 1888 Macdonald gave unequivocal approval.[3] Responsibility is not shared, but the principle of consultation has long since been conceded. It is usual, when the office is about to become vacant, for the Canadian Cabinet to be asked whether the names of certain personages would meet with Canadian approval, and the Canadian Cabinet in turn allows certain names to leak out and there is wide discussion before the final appointment, as for example in the case of Lord Byng and his successor. This procedure is a common sense concession to ensure amicable working between the two Governments concerned, while at the same time it preserves the British Cabinet's responsibility. On the other hand there are growing up other signs of change. Until recently the Canadian Governments refused to make any requests that a Governor-General should be invited to enter on a new period of office. Former suggestions[4] that a

---

attitude of Quebec, Hall, H. R., "Divorce in Canada", *Annals of the American Academy of Political Science*, cvii, pp. 275 ff.; for the law, Evans, R. R., *The Law and Practice Relating to Divorce*, etc.

[1] *Board* v. *Board* [1919], A.C. 956; *Walker* v. *Walker* [1919], A.C. 947.

[2] The Lieutenant-Governor in Council in Prince Edward Island possesses under provincial statute, 5 William IV, c. 10 (1836), a long disused jurisdiction in all matters of marriage and divorce.

[3] Pope, J., *Correspondence of Sir John Macdonald*, p. 300.

[4] Cf. *Debates, H. of C., Canada* (21 Feb. 1883), p. 248; (3 May 1910), p. 8738.

Canadian should be appointed to the office have been revived. There is no public sentiment in favour of the idea, although parliamentary criticisms have not been wanting that, since the office is largely formal, some method must be found to curtail the growing expenditures. In this connection there is much public sympathy with proposals to cut down public charges, which are not inconsiderable.[1] These debates do not imply that the Governor-General is liable to parliamentary reference. The standing rule is that he is immune from adverse criticism and that members must not speak disrespectfully of him. Both Macdonald and Laurier, however, accepted the principle that the Cabinet is responsible if the Governor speaks or acts on any public question.[2] As a necessary corollary Speakers of the House of Commons have declared that they must refuse to make it a rule that all criticism of the Governor is debarred, for then ministers could shield themselves behind the Governor, for whose public actions and utterances there must always be a responsible minister on the floor of the House.[3] Tupper indeed in no very courteous terms discussed Lord Aberdeen's actions and Laurier himself was brought to book when he attempted to condone the same Governor's speeches.[4]

In each province the chief executive officer is a Lieutenant-Governor appointed by the Governor-General in Council. He can be dismissed by the Governor-General in Council for reasons assigned and disclosed to Parliament, but outside judicial review, and dismissals are not unknown in Canadian history. To-day a Lieutenant-Governor need not fear removal if he carries on his Government according to the honourable traditions of Cabinet government. Nor is he a mere creature of the Dominion. Once he is sworn in and as long as he holds office he is the representative of the Crown with complete powers to carry on the executive government of his province; he is as complete a representative of the Crown within his Government as the Governor-General is within his.[5] His position and functions cannot be touched by any federal or provincial legislation, but these limitations do not mean that the conferring on him of new powers would constitute an alteration of his office.[6] He is the normal channel of communication between his Government and that of the Dominion, and he has no power to correspond officially with the British Cabinet. Finally, he is not immune from parliamentary and public criticism, but, granted that he speaks and acts constitutionally, the Speaker of the Assembly will do his utmost to protect him from disrespectful

[1] *Debates, H. of C., Canada* (15 April 1890), pp. 4021 ff.; (29 June 1923), pp. 4627 ff.; (18 July 1924), pp. 4833 ff.

[2] *Ibid.* (1 March 1877), pp. 373 ff.; (8 Feb. 1898), p. 254.

[3] *Ibid.* (20 March 1890), pp. 4294 ff.; (7 Feb. 1898), pp. 176 ff.

[4] *Ibid.* (8 May 1899), pp. 2727 ff.; (7, 8 Feb. 1898), pp. 176, 254; *ibid.* (4 May 1898), p. 4838.

[5] *Liquidators of the Maritime Bank* v. *Receiver-General of New Brunswick* [1892], A.C. 437.

[6] *Attorney-General of Canada* v. *Attorney-General of Ontario*, 19 O.A.R. 31; 23 S.C.R. 458.

attack. That the path is by no means easy is illustrated from a courteous but none the less emphatic rebuke administered in 1920 to the Lieutenant-Governor by the Prime Minister of Ontario. The former had made a passing and really innocent reference in a speech to a matter at the moment before the public, and the latter at once drew his respectful attention to the courtesy necessary to avoid constitutional friction.[1]

* In the formation of a federal Cabinet through which the Governor-General carries on the executive government of the Dominion there have grown up certain conventions which have acquired almost the force of constitutional law. A Prime Minister is not a free man. Owing to the fact that the Senate is not truly federal, the Cabinet has from the earliest days assumed a federal aspect—a condition foretold in 1865[2]—and in most federal Cabinets the claims of the provinces have been recognised. In addition, the French Canadians, English-speaking Canadians in Quebec, and Roman Catholics in other provinces expect to have their peculiar groupings represented. A federal Cabinet thus tends to become a balancing of territorial, racial and religious interests rather than a body representing the party's "sagacity in council and administrative skill". The territorial limitation may lead to the inclusion of some singularly weak man who alone may represent his party in a province or group of provinces. The conventions based on race and religion are unfortunate. Federation ought to allay racial differences, and the national arena is not the place to allow a situation to prevail which in no small degree federation itself was accomplished to end. Though representation of an organised religion is not the function of a modern executive, yet the violation of the constitutional convention would involve political suicide, and no party seems in the least likely to court such a fate.[3]

There are important technical difficulties which may arise between a Governor-General and his Cabinet—he can legally and constitutionally dismiss them, ask for their resignation and refuse them a dissolution. The question of dismissal is illustrated by an episode in 1873. During the debate on a motion of want of confidence Lord Dufferin sent for Macdonald and asked him to resign. Tupper, to whom Macdonald gave his confidence, at once saw the Governor-General and told him respectfully, but firmly, that if he persisted in his request he would at once pass from general public respect to the headship of the Liberal party "denounced by the Conservatives for having violated every principle of constitutional Government". As a result, Macdonald was aroused from his bed in the small hours of the

---

[1] See *Ohio Law Bulletin*, vol. LXV, no. 9, pp. 103–4.
[2] *Parliamentary Debates on...Confederation, Province of Canada* (Dunkin, 27 Feb. 1865, p. 497).
[3] Cf. however, Macdonald to J. A. Chapleau, 6 June 1888, Pope, *Correspondence*, p. 414. For criticism of the situation see *Senate's Papers* (1919), 65427–1: *Report of the Special Committee on the Machinery of Government*, p. 8.

morning and told that Dufferin had recalled his decision.[1] The episode may be taken as having established a precedent and the issue has not again arisen. Another problem arose when Lord Aberdeen refused in 1896 to sanction many of Tupper's appointments when it became evident that the Prime Minister was on the eve of defeat at a general election. Aberdeen believed that he was acting in the public interests and he sought approval from the Colonial Secretary. There can be no doubt that Aberdeen lowered his office. The Governor-General is not called on to make straight the paths for an incoming Prime Minister, to separate the wheat from the chaff, or to seek support from England. It is his duty to follow ministerial advice and to throw the entire onus of praise or blame on his Cabinet. Tupper's actions were undoubtedly reprehensible, but ministerial responsibility ought to be left to work out its own destinies. The difficult problem of dissolution does not come within this survey, for no case occurs before Lord Byng's refusal to grant a dissolution in 1926.

Finally, in relation to the prerogatives of mercy and of honours, inherent and incidental difficulties between a Governor and his Cabinet have disappeared. The prerogative of mercy will be exercised under ministerial advice in cases of Canadian prisoners, and there is little danger of such friction arising as occurred in 1875 when Dufferin pardoned a prisoner on his own responsibility.[2] The prerogative of honours has of course never passed to the Governor-General, but a vague kind of responsibility existed, and informal advice, in which the Cabinet necessarily shared, was offered to him in relation to honours.[3] With the resolution in 1919 of the House of Commons against the conferring in future of titles of honour upon Canadians, whatever responsibility lay with the Governor or Governor in Council has ceased to exist.[4]

In each province the Lieutenant-Governor in Council carries out the executive Government, based on a system which follows *mutatis mutandis* the precedents and traditions in the federal area. Few important constitutional issues have arisen. In Manitoba, however, in 1915, a Lieutenant-Governor practically forced the resignation of his ministry when he insisted on the appointment of a commission to investigate reports of alleged widespread scandals.[5] In 1920 in the same province four groups were returned to the Legislature of which the Government's was the largest, but without a majority. The Lieutenant-Governor and the Prime Minister held a consultation and decided that the ordinary rule should not hold governing the resig-

---

[1] Tupper, Sir C., *Recollections of Sixty Years*, pp. 156–7.

[2] See *Sessional Papers, Canada* (1875), no. 11; (1879), no. 14; *Canada Gazette* (extra), 19 Jan. 1875; *Debates of H. of C., Canada* (1875), pp. 21 ff.; (1908), pp. 2915 ff.; (1896 sess. i), pp. 827 ff.; (sess. ii), p. 2279; Hansard, 3rd series, 223, pp. 1065 ff.; Hardinge, Sir A., *The Fourth Earl of Carnarvon*, II, pp. 117 ff.

[3] *Debates of H. of C., Canada* (6 June 1906), p. 7460; (5 Feb. 1914), p. 482.

[4] *Journals of H. of C., Canada* (22 May 1919), p. 295.

[5] *The Times*, 13 May 1915.

nation of a Cabinet without a clear majority. Accordingly it was agreed that the Cabinet should meet the House and they succeeded in carrying on the government until well on in the second session. On defeat the Prime Minister offered his resignation which the Lieutenant-Governor refused to accept. He urged that there was real need of a dissolution as the three parties were holding up the administrative machine, but that supply must be passed. An agreement was reached under which the Prime Minister pending an election withdrew his resignation, carried on the routine work of Government, passed supply and avoided anything likely to lead to another defeat. On an appeal to the electorate the air cleared and the progressive party gained a majority in the Assembly.[1] In Ontario in 1919 the Lieutenant-Governor on the defeat of Sir William Hearst's Ministry insisted on the Crown's discretion to choose and select someone to form a Ministry. Rejecting the suggestion that the official leader of the Opposition should necessarily be asked to do so, he requested Mr E. C. Drury of the Farmers' party (the largest group elected) to form an Administration, although Drury had at the moment no seat in the Legislature.

There remain for review the legal powers in the reservation and disallowance of bills. In the federal area the Governor-General can assent to, refuse assent to or reserve a bill for the Crown's pleasure, and the Crown in Council in Great Britain can within two years disallow any Act to which the Governor-General has given his assent.[2] Fortunately amicable arrangements have long since developed. Refusal of assent and reservation are simply impossible, and constitutional right governs at the expense of constitutional law. Nor does the British Cabinet disallow Canadian Acts: "a suspending clause is usually inserted in any measure, the provisions of which require negotiation with the British Government or further consideration or action by the Dominion Government before they may properly become operative".[3] The disallowance of provincial Acts is quite another problem. The constitution of Canada differs from that of Australia among other things in that the Governor-General in Council possesses an unqualified power to disallow any provincial statute within a year after assent has been given by the Lieutenant-Governor of a province. The power was doubtless inserted for two reasons. First, it was intended to correspond in some degree to the British power within the federal area, and secondly, Cartier laid it down in 1865 that it would be exercised "in case of unjust or unwise provincial legislation".[4] Whatever the reasons, the Confederation

---

[1] *The Western Municipal News* (Winnipeg), Dec. 1923, pp. 346 ff.
[2] For important changes in the prerogative instruments see *Sessional Papers, Canada* (1877), no. 13; and cf. *ibid.* (1867), no. 22.
[3] Borden, Sir R., *Canadian Constitutional Studies*, p. 66.
[4] *Parliamentary Debates on the Subject of Confederation, Province of Canada* (Cartier, 27 Feb. 1865), p. 502.

began with a disposition to treat the provinces as something analogous to municipalities and for a considerable period provincial legislation was disallowed as inequitable, unsound in principle or destructive of private or contractual rights: questions of constitutionality, however, were usually left to the courts. For many years we can trace through the reports of the federal Ministers of Justice almost a uniform purpose in advising the disallowance of provincial Acts as "contrary to reason and natural justice", as "flagrant violation of private rights", and this in relation to legislation otherwise *intra vires* of the provinces.

We have already noted that from at least 1892 onwards there was growing up a new conception of the nature of provincial rights based on the opinions of the Judicial Committee. The provincial legislative powers were defined as "exclusive", "absolute", "supreme", and the possibility of their abuse could not be asserted as a reason for limiting the absolute power of the legislation conferred.[1] The power to legislate might be abused but "the only remedy is an appeal to those by whom the Legislature is elected".[2] As a result, from 1894 to 1918, we see a new principle at work whose most clear-cut definitions were laid down by Sir Allen Aylesworth (Minister of Justice, 1906–11). He refused to advise disallowance no matter how "unjust" or "oppressive" or "outrageous" the provincial legislation might be, provided it was "within the power of the provincial Legislature to enact it". He refused to make decisions on questions which ought to be fought out at the provincial polls.[3] During these years these principles on the whole prevailed, although Mr C. J. Doherty in 1918 advised the disallowance of a British Columbia Act because it diminished substantially the consideration of a contract.[4] It is true that this disallowance might be justified from the fact that the Act in question annulled a contract to which the Federal Government was a party, but the Minister of Justice, while quoting for the Governor-General's benefit an opinion of the Judicial Committee, emasculated that opinion by deleting their important statement that the abuse of a power cannot be argued against its constitutional use.[5]

So matters stood down to 1923 when Sir Lomer Gouin advised the disallowance of a Nova Scotia Act, not as *ultra vires*, but as being of an extraordinary nature—which indeed it undoubtedly was—and as overriding a judgment of the supreme court of Canada.[6] The episode is outside our review, but it illustrates a singular recrudescence of the

---

[1] *Attorney-General for Canada* v. *Attorney-General for Ontario*, etc. (The Fisheries Case), 1898, A.C. 700. Cf. *Bank of Toronto* v. *Lambe*, 12 App. Cas. 575.
[2] Lord Herschell in the Fisheries Case. Cf. Chamberlain to Governor of Newfoundland, 5 Dec. 1898, *Parliamentary Papers*, Cd. 8137.
[3] *Debates of H. of C., Canada* (1909), pp. 1750 ff.
[4] 7 and 8 Geo. V, C. 31 (B.C. Act). See Mr Doherty's *Report*, P.C. (Canada), 1334 (30 May 1918).
[5] See *Bank of Toronto* v. *Lambe*, 12 App. Cas. 575.
[6] See his *Report*, P.C. (Canada), 2212 (21 Oct. 1922), and *Debates of H. of C., Canada* (1923), pp. 2436 ff.

idea that abuse of a legislative power fully constitutional is an argument against its use; and in addition it introduces a completely new conception—that a Legislature acting within the sphere of its acknowledged sovereignty ought not to reverse the judgment of a court—a conception completely opposed not merely to British but to Canadian constitutional law. It would seem then as though the whole problem were once more in the melting pot and that the battle over provincial legislative authority may once more have to be fought.[1] One point, however, appears to have been settled: the validity of a grant of a title to property made by a provincial Cabinet under the authority of an Act in the period before disallowance. The Judicial Committee has refused to accept the plea that disallowance would annul such a grant.[2]

It may be that Canada and its provinces have not made important contributions to political theory or to the science of government and that the oldest Dominion has been content to follow British developments, practices and customs. It is indeed true that Canadians walk oftenest by the still waters and along the quiet paths of tradition and that their historical origins do not favour creative politics. Be that as it may, they share with all organised communities in the fundamental facts that every nation gets the government which it deserves, that a study of comparative government is of purely intellectual interest, and that political institutions are of value in so far as they form a healthy framework for the highest community values. To claim that the British North America Acts are perfect would be folly, to deny that they provide for fundamental justice would be equally foolish. Under them, with a thousand traditions working through them, Canada has succeeded in establishing an equitable balance of exceedingly delicate centrifugal and centripetal forces. Canadians possess all the political problems peculiar to a nation, but are attempting to solve them with that sense of responsibility which belongs to a nation within an empire. Viewed from whatever standpoint, Canada's institutional problems are not as easy as those of an independent state. Yet there is no sentiment in Canada which would seek the easier road, to the rejection of a political conception whose grandeur and beneficent worth are accentuated because they call for the most vigilant citizenship and for the exercise of the most exacting public virtues. It is not without significance that the North America Acts are called *British*.

[1] Cf. Kennedy, W. P. M., "The Disallowance of Provincial Acts in the Dominion of Canada", *Journal of Comparative Legislation*, 3rd series, VI, Pt I, pp. 80 ff.
[2] *Wilson* v. *Esquimalt and Nanaimo Railway Co.* [1922], I A.C. 202.

CHAPTER XXX

CANADA AND THE EMPIRE, 1884–1921

IN 1884 Canada was a colony of the British Empire enjoying self-government in domestic affairs alone. In 1921 she was "a co-equal member of the community of nations forming the British Commonwealth of Nations". The story of this development constitutes one of the most interesting and important chapters in British and Canadian constitutional history. The change was brought about, not by any legislative enactment but by the gradual devolution of authority and responsibility for the conduct of Canada's external affairs from the British to the Canadian Government. Both in the United Kingdom and in Canada the executive authority is vested in His Majesty but is exercised by him only upon the advice of his constitutional advisers. At confederation the executive authority in and over Canada was exercised by Her Majesty, in respect of Canada's domestic affairs, through the Governor-General acting upon the advice of his constitutional advisers in Canada, and, in respect of Canada's external affairs, through her constitutional advisers in Great Britain. Since confederation in one important matter after another affecting Canada's external relations, Canada has requested, and the British Government has conceded, that the Crown should cease to act upon the advice of British Ministers and should act upon the advice of Canadian Ministers. And this process has continued until now the whole executive authority in and over Canada has passed from the Government of the United Kingdom to the Government of Canada. During this period the real ties which bind Canada to the Empire have been steadily strengthened and methods of co-operation have been established and developed to ensure the continued unity, strength and security of the whole.

These developments may conveniently be considered under two heads: Inter-Imperial Relations and Relations with Foreign Powers.

Under Inter-Imperial Relations will be included: (1) The development of an imperial organisation; (2) the improvement in imperial communications; (3) the changes in the commercial relations between Great Britain and Canada; and (4) the growth of a Canadian defence policy.

Relations with Foreign Powers will cover: (1) Canada's interest in foreign policy and diplomatic representation at foreign courts; (2) her participation in international conferences and in the negotiation and ratification of treaties; and (3) Canada's membership in international organisations, the most important of which are the League of Nations, the Permanent Court of International Justice and the International Labour Conference.

The Development of an Imperial Organisation. It was recognised by thoughtful students of imperial relations, both in Great Britain and in the self-governing colonies, that with the growth of population, of trade and of national sentiment in the colonies it was inevitable they should demand and receive a measure of control over their own external affairs. The problem was how to give this measure of control and at the same time preserve the strength and unity of the Empire. The ideal of imperial organisation which was most in men's thoughts during the first half of this forty-year period was the maintenance of power in one central government exercising authority in imperial affairs over the whole Empire. The Imperial Federation Movement was an expression of this ideal, and later the movement for the forma-tion of an Imperial Council with jurisdiction in defence and foreign affairs was another. The other ideal was the complete autonomy and self-government of the Dominions, maintaining the unity essential in matters of imperial concern, by consultation and co-operation. This ideal of autonomy and co-operation, not always clearly expressed but nevertheless steadily pursued, has gradually superseded the older ideal of centralised power and has now found expression in imperial organisation, through the Imperial Conference. It is for this ideal that Canadian political leaders on the whole have stood, and their opposition to a central authority exercising jurisdiction over the whole Empire—a position in which they were in the end supported by both Australia and South Africa—contributed to the abandonment of that policy and the triumph of the policy of autonomy and co-operation. The history of the development and organisation of the Imperial Conference is largely the history of the struggle between these two ideals and of the final triumph of the ideal of autonomy and co-operation.

The Development and Work of the Imperial Conference. In 1887 Her Majesty's advisers took advantage of Queen Victoria's Jubilee to invite the representatives of the colonies to meet in conference in London with representatives of the Imperial Government to consider matters of common concern. The opening address of Lord Salisbury was prophetic:

We all feel the gravity and the importance of this occasion. The decisions of this Conference may not be, for the moment, of vital importance; the business may seem prosaic, and may not issue in any great results at the moment. But we are all sensible that this meeting is the beginning of a state of things which is to have great results in the future. It will be the parent of a long progeniture, and distant Councils of the Empire may, in some far-off time, look back to the meeting in this room as the root from which all their greatness and all their beneficence sprang.[1]

The question of political relations was raised at this Conference but

---

[1] *Minutes of Proceedings of Colonial Conference*, 1887 (C. 5091), pp. 5–7.

not pressed. The Conference was more or less informal; the Canadian delegates were not even members of the Canadian Government. Its actual achievements were not great but its importance and significance lay in the fact that the Government of the Mother Country had called the representatives of the colonies into consultation on matters affecting their interests. This had never been done before and it was inevitable that such consultation should be repeated and its range widened.

It is not surprising, therefore, that in 1897 advantage was taken of Queen Victoria's Diamond Jubilee to summon another Colonial Conference, and on this occasion Canada and the other self-governing colonies were represented by their Prime Ministers. The occasion and the Conference made a deep impression throughout the Empire. The discussions covered such important questions as political, commercial and defence relations. Joseph Chamberlain, who had become Colonial Secretary, was chairman, and in his opening address he offered the suggestion

that it might be feasible to create a great council of the Empire to which the Colonies would send representative plenipotentiaries—not mere delegates who were unable to speak in their name, without further reference to their respective Governments, but persons who by their position in the Colonies, by their representative character, and by their close touch with colonial feeling, would be able upon all subjects submitted to them to give really effective and valuable advice. If such a council were created it would at once assume an immense importance, and it is perfectly evident that it might develop into something still greater. It might slowly grow to that Federal Council to which we must always look forward as our ultimate ideal.[1]

The Canadian view was that the existing political relations were satisfactory, and the decision of the Conference was "that the present political relations between the United Kingdom and the self-governing colonies are generally satisfactory under the existing conditions of things". Seddon (New Zealand) and Sir Edward Braddon (Tasmania) dissented. This Conference, however, marked a great advance over the Conference of 1887. It unanimously decided that it was desirable "to hold periodical conferences of representatives of the colonies and Great Britain, for the discussion of matters of common interest", and every five years was the period agreed upon.

The welcome accorded to Sir Wilfrid Laurier, the Canadian Prime Minister, in Great Britain made a deep impression on the Canadian people, and there can be no question that in his public addresses both in Great Britain and on his return to Canada he truly voiced the feelings and aspirations of the Canadian people. Speaking in England, he said: "The authority of the Queen does not rest on military force, but from the Pacific to the Atlantic rests on the cheerful allegiance of 5,000,000 people who feel themselves a nation. The feeling dominating Canada is one of pride in her local autonomy and

---

[1] *Proceedings, Colonial Conference,* 1897 (C. 8569), p. 5.

legislative liberty connected with imperial unity". Throughout his stay in Great Britain he consistently maintained that Canada had reached the status of a nation. When he returned to Montreal he stated that he had longed to live to see the day when Canada would no longer be a colony but would be a free nation within the Empire, and he was glad to be able to say he had lived to see that day. For this and similar public utterances he was criticised by some of his political opponents, but succeeding elections clearly demonstrated that he was expressing the real sentiments of the great majority of the Canadian people.

At the Conference of 1902, Chamberlain, who presided, again stressed the importance of the creation of an Imperial Council or some imperial organisation which should deal with matters of common concern to the whole Empire. He expressed his preference for a "real council of the Empire, to which all questions of imperial interest might be referred",[1] and his views in this respect were supported by representatives from Australia and New Zealand, but Canada opposed the creation of any new imperial organisation or an imperial council which would exercise any jurisdiction or control over the self-governing Dominions.

In a despatch of 20 April 1905, to the Dominion Government, Lyttelton, who had succeeded Chamberlain as Colonial Secretary, suggested that the title of the Colonial Conference should be changed to "Imperial Council" and that it should have a more permanent organisation, and outlined the form which this organisation should take. The Government of Canada, in a reasoned minute of council of 13 November 1905, opposed the change of name,

which they apprehend would be interpreted as marking a step distinctly in advance of the position hitherto attained in the discussion of the relations between the Mother Country and the Colonies. As the Committee understand the phrase, a Conference is a more or less unconventional gathering for informal discussion of public questions, continued, it may be, from time to time, as circumstances external to itself may render expedient, but possessing no faculty or power of binding action. The assembly of colonial ministers which met in 1887, 1897 and 1902 appear to the Committee to fulfil these conditions. The term Council, on the other hand, indicates, in the view of Your Excellency's Ministers, a more formal assemblage, possessing an advisory and deliberative character, and in conjunction with the word "Imperial" suggesting a permanent institution which, endowed with a continuous life, might eventually come to be regarded as an encroachment upon the full measure of autonomous legislative and administrative power now enjoyed by all the self-governing colonies.[2]

They then suggested that the title "Imperial Conference" would be less open to objection. In view of this despatch from the Canadian Government no further action was taken until the Conference of 1907.

At the Conference of 1907 the question of changing the name from Colonial Conference to Imperial Council was brought forward by the

---

[1] *Proceedings, Colonial Conference*, 1902 (Cd. 1299), p. 4.
[2] *Correspondence relating to future organisation of Colonial Conferences*, 1905 (Cd. 2785).

Prime Minister of Victoria, Sir Alfred Deakin, supported by New Zealand. Sir Alfred Deakin pointed out that it was not his desire to give the Council any legislative jurisdiction over the Dominions. Sir Wilfrid Laurier opposed the use of the word "council" as suggesting a body which did have some form of jurisdiction. Canada, however, concurred in and supported the proposal to change the Colonial Conference into an Imperial Conference, with a permanent secretariat and fixed periods for meeting. The important part of the resolution establishing the Imperial Conference declares:

> That it will be to the advantage of the Empire if a conference to be called the "Imperial Conference" is held every four years, at which questions of common interest may be discussed and considered as between His Majesty's Government and His Governments of the self-governing Dominions beyond the seas. The Prime Minister of the United Kingdom will be *ex-officio* President and the Prime Ministers of the self-governing Dominions *ex-officio* members of the Conference... that it is desirable to establish a system by which the several governments represented shall be kept informed during periods between the conferences in regard to matters which have been or may be subjects for discussion by means of a permanent secretarial staff charged under the direction of the Secretary of State for the Colonies with the duty of obtaining information for the use of the Conference, of attending to its resolutions, and of conducting correspondence on matters relating to its affairs.[1]

By the approval of this resolution by all the Governments concerned, the Conference ceased to be a conference between the Colonial Office and the Governments of the self-governing Colonies, with the Colonial Secretary presiding, and became a real Imperial Conference, a conference between His Majesty's Government and the Governments of the self-governing Dominions, presided over by the Prime Minister of the United Kingdom, who, at the Conference, was but *primus inter pares*. This resolution marked another great advance in imperial organisation. It not only gave form and permanence to a real imperial organisation, but it settled, and settled finally, so far as subsequent events have shown, that the basis of imperial organisation was to be co-operation between the self-governing nations of the Empire and not the centralisation of power in the hands of one Imperial Government. Sir Wilfrid Laurier, speaking in the House on the Imperial Conference of 1907, said: "There were many who believed that these relations should be based upon the principle that the young daughter communities should be simply satellites revolving around the parent State, but others there were who held—and in my estimation rightly held—that the proper basis of the British Empire was that it was to be composed of a galaxy of nations under the British Crown".[2] Later, on 3 February 1910, speaking on the Naval Service Bill, then before the House of Commons, he said: "This policy is in the best traditions of the Liberal party. This policy is the latest link in the long chain of events which, following the principles laid down by the Reformers of the old times, Baldwin and Lafontaine, step by step,

---

[1] *Minutes of Proceedings of Colonial Conference*, 1907 (Cd. 3523), p. v.
[2] *Debates of H. of C. (Canada)* (1907–8), p. 41.

stage by stage, have brought Canada to the position it now occupies, that is to say, the rank, dignity and status of a nation within the British Empire".[1]

The first Imperial Conference under the new constitution met in 1911, under the presidency of Mr Asquith, the Prime Minister of the United Kingdom. In his opening address he referred to

the combination of local autonomy—absolute, unfettered, complete—with loyalty to a common head, co-operation, spontaneous and unforced, for common interests and purposes, and, I may add, a common trusteeship, whether it be in India or in the Crown Colonies, or in the Protectorates, or within our own borders, of the interests and fortunes of fellow subjects who have not yet attained, or perhaps in some cases may never attain, to the full stature of self-government.... We each of us are, and we each of us intend to remain, master in our own household. This is, here at home and throughout the Dominions, the lifeblood of our polity. It is the "articulus stantis aut cadentis imperii". It is none the less true that we are, and intend to remain, units indeed, but units in a greater unity. And it is the primary object and governing purpose of these periodical conferences that we may take free counsel together in the matter which concerns us all.[2]

At the Conference of 1911 the formation of an Imperial Council was again brought forward, this time by New Zealand, but the Conference would not seriously entertain the proposal. This Conference was particularly notable in that for the first time the representatives of the Dominions were given a real insight into British foreign policy.

The Imperial Conference due in 1915 was postponed on account of the war and was not held until 1917. In the meantime the part which the Dominions had played in the war had changed the whole imperial situation. In 1917 Mr Lloyd George, the Prime Minister of the United Kingdom, invited the Prime Ministers of the Dominions to full and equal participation with him in the discussion of matters of foreign policy and of plans for the conduct of the war, and for this purpose constituted an Imperial War Cabinet, the functions of which he thus described (17 May 1917):

...that the responsible heads of the government of the Empire, with those ministers who are specially entrusted with the conduct of imperial policy, should meet together at regular intervals to confer about foreign policy and matters connected therewith, and come to decisions with regard to them which, subject to the control of their own Parliament, they will then severally execute. By this means they will be able to obtain full information about all aspects of imperial affairs, and to determine by consultation together the policy of the Empire in its most vital aspects, without infringing in any degree the autonomy which its parts at present enjoy.[3]

Sir Robert Borden, the Canadian Prime Minister, in his speeches in Great Britain during 1917 and 1918, emphasised the changed status. He pointed out that the British Prime Minister was only *primus inter pares* in the War Cabinet and each nation preserved in full its autonomy, its self-government and its ministerial responsibility. Prior to the organisation of the War Cabinet, he declared, Canada lacked full

---

[1] *Debates of H. of C. (Canada)* (1909–10), pp. 2953 f.
[2] *Minutes of Proceedings of Imperial Conference*, 1911 (Cd. 5745), p. 22.
[3] Hansard, XCIII, 1791.

national status, because the Imperial Government was the main factor in the foreign policy of the Empire. With the creation of the War Cabinet, inferiority of status had disappeared, as the Dominions had been admitted into equality of consultation. The report of the War Cabinet of 1918, referring to the creation of the Imperial War Cabinet, states:

> The common effort and sacrifice in the war have inevitably led to the recognition of an equality of status between the responsible Governments of the Empire. This equality has long been accepted in principle, and found its adequate expression in 1917 in the creation, or rather the natural coming into being, of the Imperial War Cabinet as an instrument for evolving a common imperial policy in the conduct of the war.[1]

The Imperial Conference of 1917, which was held at the same time as the Imperial War Cabinet of that year, on the motion of Sir Robert Borden adopted the following resolution:

> The Imperial War Conference are of opinion that the readjustment of the constitutional relations of the component parts of the Empire is too important and intricate a subject to be dealt with during the war, and that it should form the subject of a special Imperial Conference to be summoned as soon as possible after the cessation of hostilities. They deem it their duty, however, to place on record their view that any such readjustment, while thoroughly preserving all existing powers of self-government and complete control of domestic affairs, should be based upon a full recognition of the Dominions as autonomous nations of an Imperial Commonwealth and of India as an important portion of the same, should recognise the right of the Dominions and India to an adequate voice in the foreign policy and in foreign relations, and should provide effective arrangements for continuous consultation in all important matters of common imperial concern and for such necessary concerted action, founded on consultation, as the several Governments may determine.[2]

This declaration, together with the formation of the Imperial War Cabinet, was accepted as a formal recognition of the equality of status of the Dominions with the Mother Country in the Britannic Commonwealth, but it was recognised that such a change in status would involve certain constitutional readjustments, and it was desirable that a special Imperial Conference should be called after the war to consider these constitutional readjustments. It should be noted that in view of the part India had played in the war the Imperial Conference of 1917 recommended that India should be admitted to membership in the Conference. This was approved by all the Governments concerned and India took her place at the Imperial War Conference of 1918.

These constitutional developments continued throughout the war and in the negotiations and signature of the treaties of peace. The sessions of the Imperial War Cabinet and of the Imperial War Conference of 1918, the position accorded the Dominions at the Peace Conference and their membership in the League of Nations, which

---

[1] *The War Cabinet: Report for 1918* (Cd. 325), p. 7.
[2] *Minutes of Proceedings of Imperial War Conference*, 1917 (Cd. 8566), p. 5, Resolution ix.

will be dealt with later, all tended to support and confirm the equality of status of the Dominions in the Britannic family of nations.

With the conclusion of the Treaty of Peace, the Imperial War Cabinet, which was called into being for the purpose of the war, ceased to exist, but a Conference of Prime Ministers was called, in June 1921, the principal purpose of which was to make plans for the Constitutional Conference to be held pursuant to the resolution of 1917. The agenda of the Prime Ministers' Conference and the functions of the Constitutional Conference, when called, were the subject of a very important debate in the Canadian House of Commons in which the relation of the Dominions to the United Kingdom and to foreign affairs came under consideration and review. From this debate it is clear that so far as Canada was concerned it was recognised that one of the main purposes of the Constitutional Conference was to embody in a formal declaration the equality of status which had already been recognised and acted on, and to perfect plans for consultation and co-operation in major matters of foreign policy affecting the Empire as a whole.[1] The Conference concluded its deliberations without summoning a constitutional conference. Its reasons, as published, are set forth in a resolution adopted by the Conference, of which the following is the vital part: "Having regard to the constitutional developments since 1917 no advantage is to be gained by holding a Constitutional Conference".

Apparently the view of the Conference was that such progress had been made that it was unnecessary to summon a constitutional conference. This action was the subject of adverse comment in well-informed quarters in Canada.[2] It is clear that the acceptance of the principle of the equality of status of the Dominions with the Mother Country must involve certain administrative and legislative changes to make the forms correspond with the reality, and it is essential, in the interests of unity, that an understanding should be arrived at as to the conduct of foreign affairs. Without doubt subsequent conferences will be called upon to consider and agree upon these matters.

At the time of the American War of Independence, the prevailing conception of colonial relationship was that the only alternative to complete dependence was complete independence. Seventy years later this conception had been fundamentally changed, and far-seeing statesmen and political writers accepted the theory that there might be a division of governmental authority over the colonies, as between domestic and foreign affairs, and that the colonies might be granted full self-government in domestic affairs while the parent state retained full authority over foreign affairs, and this changed conception made the continued unity of the British Empire possible. Seventy

[1] *Debates of H. of C. (Canada)*, pp. 2626, 2634, 2647.
[2] Borden, Sir Robert, *Canadian Constitutional Studies*, p. 115.

years more brought a further and not less fundamental change, and far-seeing statesmen both in Great Britain and the Dominions recognised that the colonial status might be wholly abandoned and the Dominions become the equals of the Mother Country and still remain within the British Commonwealth of Nations.

Just as many British and colonial statesmen feared that the granting of complete self-government in domestic affairs would mean the separation of the colonies from the Mother Country, so some British and colonial statesmen have feared that the granting of equality of status to the Dominions would bring about this result, but past experience has shown that these fears have not been justified and that the larger the liberty enjoyed by the Dominions the greater the spirit of unity and of loyalty to the Crown and Empire.

Imperial Communications. In an Empire the parts of which are so widely separated, imperial communications are of vital importance, and from the standpoint of Canada this subject was one of the most outstanding discussed at the first Colonial Conference in 1887, and in some form or other this vital question has been discussed at most of the subsequent Conferences. At the Conference of 1887 Sir Alexander Campbell, the first delegate from Canada, drew attention to the completion of the Canadian Pacific Railway across Canada and to the fact that this had opened a new route to Australia and the East, and said: "We are here more in reference to that particular topic than any other". Sir Sandford Fleming, who had made this subject his own by his investigations and reports, stressed the urgency and importance as well as the feasibility of connecting the Australasian colonies with Great Britain by a new Pacific cable from Vancouver to Australia. The Eastern Extension Telegraph Company, with its headquarters in London, was strongly opposed, and the British Government at the time did not appear to be keenly interested. The Australasian colonies were divided on the issue, but after full discussion the Conference adopted the Canadian proposals that "the connection of Canada with Australasia by direct submarine telegraph across the Pacific is a project of high importance to the Empire".[1]

The special Colonial Conference in Ottawa in 1894 was called primarily to consider and further plans for this cable and for inter-imperial trade, though its work embraced the consideration of other imperial questions. This Conference declared in favour of immediate steps being taken to provide telegraphic communication by cable, free from foreign control, between Canada and Australia; and further that such cable should be extended from Australia to the Cape of Good Hope, and that the Canadian Government should make enquiries to ascertain the cost of the proposed Pacific cable and take steps to promote the undertaking in accordance with the views

---

[1] *Minutes of Colonial Conference*, 1887 (C. 5091), p. 514.

expressed at the Conference. Progress was reported at the Imperial Conference of 1897, but some of the Governments concerned requested further time for consideration. The opposition of the Eastern Extension Telegraph Company was strong and persistent and it detached some of the Australian colonies from the great enterprise, but in 1900 all obstacles were overcome and an agreement for the construction and operation of the Pacific cable was signed. The cable was completed and opened for use in 1902, and its success has exceeded the expectations of its promoters. Its great service during the war vindicated the courage and patriotism of the men who fought for its establishment.

The cheapening of imperial postage was another effort to promote imperial communications. At the Conference of 1887 it was rejected by the colonies as impracticable, but in 1898 the Canadian Government led the way by adopting imperial penny postage with the United Kingdom and thus demonstrated its practicability. In 1902 the Imperial Conference recommended the adoption of "the principle of cheap postage between the different parts of the British Empire on all newspapers and periodicals published therein", each Government being "allowed to determine the amount to which it may reduce such rate, and the time for such reduction going into effect".[1]

Improved steamship communications also occupied the attention of several conferences. That held at Ottawa in 1894 expressed its gratification at the successful efforts put forth by Canada and New South Wales to establish a regular monthly steamship service between Vancouver and Sydney and expressed the hope that all colonies interested would co-operate in securing the improvement and permanence of the same. It also expressed its interest in the steps being taken by Canada to secure a first-class mail and passenger service with all the modern appliances for storage and carrying perishable goods across the Atlantic, and affirmed the paramount importance of establishing "an uninterrupted through line of swift and superior communication between Australasia and Great Britain".[2]

The Conference of 1907 passed similar resolutions with regard to imperial communications, especially those between Great Britain and Canada, and through Canada with Australia and New Zealand, by the best service available within reasonable cost, the necessary financial support being contributed by them in equitable proportions.[3] The completion of an "all-red" route for telegraphic, mail, passenger and freight services on the most modern lines has drawn the separated parts of the Empire together, has helped imperial trade, and has greatly increased the knowledge of each part of the Empire of the other.

The next development will undoubtedly be the establishment of an

[1] Jebb, R., *The Imperial Conference*, II, 383; *The Colonial Conference*, 1902, p. xi.
[2] *Colonial Conference*, 1894 (C. 7553), p. 8.
[3] *Colonial Conference*, 1907 (Cd. 3523), p. x.

all-red Air Service. At the Prime Ministers' Conference of 1921 the matter received very careful consideration and definite steps were taken toward the development of an Imperial Air Service.

Commercial Relations. The most significant feature in the trade relations between Canada and the United Kingdom during the period under review was the granting of the British preference in the Canadian tariff of 1897, followed by the denunciation by the United Kingdom of the German and Belgian trade treaties which blocked the way to an effective preference. These treaties contained the following clauses:

Zollverein treaty, article 7: "In the colonies and possessions of Her Britannic Majesty the products of the states of the Zollverein shall not be subject to any other or higher import duties than the products of the United Kingdom of Great Britain and Ireland".

Belgian treaty, article 15: "Articles, the produce or manufacture of Belgium, shall not be subject in the British Colonies to other or higher duties than those which are, or may be, imposed upon similar articles of British origin".

So long as the treaties remained in force neither Canada nor any other self-governing colony could grant an effective tariff preference to the Mother Country.

Prior to the special Colonial Conference at Ottawa in 1894 Canada had made several efforts to have these treaties denounced, but without success. At the Conference of 1894 the subject of the treaties came up for discussion, and the following resolution was unanimously adopted:

That this Conference is of opinion that any provision in existing treaties between Great Britain and any foreign power which prevents the self-governing dependencies of the Empire from entering into agreements of commercial reciprocity with each other or with Great Britain should be removed.[1]

The Earl of Jersey, who represented the British Government at the Conference, in his despatch to the Marquess of Ripon, the Secretary of State for the Colonies, stated that all the colonial delegates desired "that the Colonies represented should make arrangements with one another, and, if possible, with Great Britain, which would give British an advantage over foreign products, and that for this purpose any statutory or treaty provisions which stand in the way should be removed"; also that "so far as might be possible, British subjects should take what they have to import from their own kindred rather than from foreign states".[2] But why did not the British Government respond to these repeated appeals of the colonies? Probably it was fearful of disarranging trade relations with continental neighbours.

In 1897 the Canadian Government brought in a revised tariff which granted a substantial preference to British goods, but it was contended that so long as the German and Belgian treaties remained in force these countries also were entitled to this preference and to this the Canadian Government was not prepared to agree. The

[1] *Report of Colonial Conference*, 1894 (C. 7553), p. 2.
[2] *Ibid.* p. 3.

Colonial Conference of 1897 followed, and the Canadian Prime Minister, Sir Wilfrid Laurier, lost no opportunity of expounding in England the policy and intentions of the Canadian Government. Speaking at Manchester, he assured his audience that Canada gave the preference gratuitously and did not expect England to depart from her traditional policy of free trade. But referring to the treaties, at Liverpool, he declared that if they were held to apply, then "either Canada will have to retreat or England will have to advance".[1] The Conference declared in favour of the denunciation of these treaties, and Canada's action settled the issue. On 30 July it was announced by the British Government that the necessary notice for the termination of these treaties had been given. The purpose of the Canadian Government in granting the preference was undoubtedly two-fold: (1) It was a step toward the fulfilment of the election pledges of the Liberal party that the tariff would be reduced; and (2) it was a real contribution to the cause of imperial unity. It certainly was a most practical and effective answer to the charge that the Liberals were less devoted to the cause of imperial unity than their political opponents.

The movement in favour of Imperial Preference in the Dominions, coupled with Chamberlain's failure at both the Colonial Conference of 1897 and that of 1902 to secure the adherence of the colonial statesmen to his policy of an Imperial Council, undoubtedly led him to seek, through Imperial Preference, a means of further cementing the bonds of empire and resulted in his great Imperial Preference Campaign in 1902 and 1903.

There has always existed a substantial body of opinion in the United Kingdom and in the Dominions in favour of an imperial preferential tariff whereby the Mother Country would grant the Dominions a preference in its markets in return for a preference in the markets of the Dominions, but so far the electorate of Great Britain has adhered to the policy of free trade and has not sanctioned the granting of a preference to the Dominions, though under the McKenna Duties, as amended in 1919, the Dominions were granted preferential rates one-third lower than the general rates. The result was a substantial increase in Canadian trade, particularly in motors and motor parts. The view, sometimes put forward in Great Britain in support of Imperial Preference, that, unless a preference were granted in the British markets in favour of Canadian products, political relations might be affected, is an entire misinterpretation of the Canadian attitude. The attitude of Canada has been that the question of a preference in the British market is one for the British electors and for the British electors alone to decide, and that while Canada would be glad to take advantage of any such preference, if given, her preference was not conditioned upon the giving of a preference by

[1] Skelton, O. D., *Life and Letters of Sir Wilfrid Laurier*, II, 73.

Great Britain, and the failure of Great Britain to give a preference will in no way affect political relations.

The British preference in Canada has always been the subject of criticism and occasionally of strong attack by the advocates of higher protection, on the ground that it is unfair to Canadian industry, and one form which this attack has taken and the one most difficult to answer is that Canada should not continue this preference unless Great Britain makes it reciprocal. Canada was the first nation in the Empire to bring Imperial Preference from the realm of discussion to that of practical commercial policy. The preference originally granted of 25 per cent. has been increased to $33\frac{1}{3}$ per cent. and has been extended to the other Dominions. Australia, New Zealand and South Africa have all followed Canada's example and have granted preferences in their markets to the Mother Country, the South African preference being on a limited list of commodities. New Zealand has granted a reciprocal preference to Canada. Australia and South Africa give Canada a preference on certain tariff items.

Canadian Defence Policy. To understand the Canadian point of view on questions of national and imperial defence it is essential to bear in mind the racial composition of Canada's population and her geographical position on the North American continent, with an unguarded frontier between her and the United States of over five thousand four hundred miles. Canada's population is drawn mainly from two great races—British and French. The latter, while devoted to Canada and to the maintenance of the British connection, looks upon Canada as its only home, and it is not reasonable to expect to find among Canadians of French origin the same ties of sentiment and affection to the Crown and Empire as are natural to those of British stock. For more than one hundred years no war has disturbed the relations between Canada and the United States. All disputes, and there have been many, have been settled by peaceable negotiations or by arbitration, and the Canadian people do not live in any apprehension of hostile attack either within their own borders or upon their coasts. Canada has also faced great problems of transportation and of settlement in the opening up and development of a territory larger than that of the United States. The statesmen of Canada have been compelled to take all these factors into account in considering questions of national and imperial defence.

The development of a Canadian Defence Policy falls conveniently into two divisions: Land Defence and Naval Defence. At a very early period the Canadian colonies formed militia forces to assist in their own defence, and in the war of 1812–14 demonstrated how important a part such forces could play when mobilised, even in a country with a very sparse and scattered population, but up to confederation the Imperial Government maintained regular troops in the North American colonies. At the pre-confederation Conference of 1865 between Canadian and British ministers, one of the most important questions discussed was the future defence of Canada. The Civil War in the United States, the disturbances on the frontier, and the notice given by the Government of the United States to terminate the convention restricting naval armaments on the Lakes all tended to create a feeling of insecurity and made the question of defence of vital concern both to Canada and to Great Britain. The Canadian ministers in their report of this Conference stated:

...The result arrived at was, that if the people of Canada undertook the works of defence at and west of Montreal, and agreed to expend in training their Militia, until the Union of all the Provinces was determined, a sum not less than is now expended annually for that service, Her Majesty's Government would complete the fortifications at Quebec, provide the whole armament for all the works, guarantee a loan for the sum necessary to construct the works undertaken by Canada, and in the event of war undertake the defence of every portion of Canada with all the resources of the Empire.

The report of the British ministers contained in a despatch from the Secretary of State for the Colonies to the Governor-General, dated 17 June 1865, after reciting the matters discussed relating to inland and naval defence, concludes:

On the last point, it seemed sufficient that Her Majesty's Government should accept the assurances given by the Canadian Ministers on the part of Canada, that that Province is ready to devote all her resources both in men and money to the maintenance of her connexion with the Mother Country, and should assure them in return that the Imperial Government fully acknowledged the reciprocal obligation of defending every portion of the Empire with all the resources at its command.[1]

After confederation the Canadian Government apparently interpreted this arrangement as committing the British Government to full responsibility for the whole naval defence of Canada. When, however, the Deputy Minister of the Department of Militia and Defence in 1870 put forward this point of view in a letter to the General Officer commanding troops in British North America, Cardwell, who in the meantime had become Secretary of State for War, communicated with the General Officer Commanding and laid down that the despatch "was not intended to exonerate the Government of the Dominions from any responsibility in taking a share in its own naval defence".

The new Parliament of Canada made provision for the continuance and development of a Canadian Militia Force and in 1883 provided for the organisation and maintenance of a small permanent force. By 1871 all British garrisons were withdrawn from Canada, and thereafter British troops remained only at the naval stations of Halifax and Esquimalt. In 1892 Canada entered into an agreement with the Imperial Government to contribute toward the cost of defence works and buildings and to meet the cost of maintaining a

[1] *Accounts and Papers, Colonies and British Possessions*, vol. XLVIII, Correspondence respecting the proposed union of the B.N.A. Provinces, no. 16254.

detachment of Royal Canadian Artillery or Royal Engineers at Esquimalt, and from 1893 up to 1905, when Canada took over the military station at Esquimalt, Canada contributed substantial sums annually for these purposes.

At the time of the South African War the Canadian Government raised a battalion to set free for active service the imperial battalion which was then doing garrison duty at Halifax, and at the Colonial Conference of 1902 a verbal pledge was given by the Canadian representatives to relieve the Imperial Government in perpetuity of the cost of garrisoning Halifax and Esquimalt. In 1905 this pledge was renewed in writing and accepted in the same year. In 1906 the last British soldiers left Canada, and in 1910 arrangements were completed whereby the Admiralty property at Halifax and Esquimalt was transferred to the control of the Canadian Government on the understanding that the necessary facilities for the docking and coaling of British warships would be given and that the naval docks would be efficiently maintained. Canada is now solely responsible for all military forces in Canada and for the maintenance of those naval stations.

The participation of Canadian military forces in the wars of the Empire has been a gradual development. Even prior to confederation the Canadian colonies had voluntarily offered assistance when the Empire was at war. During the Crimean War £20,000 was unanimously voted by the Canadian Parliament as a contribution to the Imperial Government "to show that Canada made common cause with England and with France in the Crimean War".[1] Further, the 100th Regiment, the Royal Canadians, was raised in 1858 in Canada for the regular army, and the War Office continued to maintain a recruiting depôt of the regiment in Canada until 1862. In 1884, when Lord Wolseley was appointed to command the expedition for the relief of Gordon at Khartoum, he remembered the exploits of the Canadian *voyageurs* on the Red River Expedition and sent for some of them to help him on the Nile. On this occasion 400 Canadians saw service in Egypt. When, in the course of that war, New South Wales offered the Imperial Government a body of troops, Lord Hartington, Secretary for War, put himself into communication with the other colonies; and Sir John Macdonald, the Canadian Prime Minister, who was opposed to Canada participating in the war,[2] replied to the intimation by offering to sanction recruiting in Canada for service in Egypt or elsewhere, but stipulated that the entire cost must fall on the Imperial Exchequer. This offer the Imperial Government did not accept.

The South African War brought up in a serious way the part which the Dominions should play in imperial defence. On 31 July 1899,

[1] *Debates of H. of C. (Canada)*, 1900, pp. 37, 38.
[2] Pope, Sir J., *Corresp. of Sir J. Macdonald*, p. 337.

Sir Wilfrid Laurier proposed and carried a motion in the Canadian House of Commons expressing sympathy with the efforts of the British Government to secure equal rights and liberties for British subjects in South Africa, but he held that Canada was not bound to take an active part in the war that seemed imminent. When war was declared, public opinion in Canada quickly developed in favour of sending a contingent to South Africa, and, due to this movement of opinion, the Laurier Government, in October 1899, decided to despatch volunteer troops. The arrangement with the Imperial Government was that Canada should pay the expense of raising and equipping the troops but that their pay while on service should be borne by the Imperial Government. Before the conclusion of the war Canada had contributed some 8000 men, involving an expenditure of approximately $2,000,000. The war was a striking expression of imperial sentiment in Canada, as elsewhere in the Empire. Mr Bourassa, one of the ablest of the younger Liberal members of the House of Commons from the province of Quebec, protested against the sending of Canadian troops to South Africa and resigned his seat in the House as a protest. He was re-elected by his constituency and thenceforth became the leader of an influential body of opinion in the province of Quebec against Canada participating in wars beyond her own borders. Sir Wilfrid Laurier maintained, both then and subsequently at the Colonial Conference of 1902, that Canada's participation in the war in South Africa could not be taken as a precedent for Canada's active participation in all future wars of the Empire.

From the conclusion of the South African War until the events of 1914 the problem of imperial defence and of the contribution of Canada and the other Dominions was discussed at the Imperial Conferences, and in intervening negotiations. Attention may be drawn to a few of the salient developments of this period. The Canadian Government co-operated with the Imperial Government in so fashioning the organisation of its militia as to enable it readily to become a part of the fighting force of the Empire. Lord Haldane, who became Secretary of State for War in 1905, was a strong advocate of uniformity in the equipment and training of the several forces of the Empire, so far as uniformity might be practicable, and he advocated this policy at the Imperial Conference of 1907. The plan was described by Asquith at the Subsidiary Defence Conference of 1909 as "a plan for so organising the forces of the Crown wherever they are that, while preserving the complete autonomy of each Dominion, should the Dominion desire to assist in the defence of the Empire in a real emergency, their forces could be rapidly combined into one homogeneous Imperial Army". At this conference the plan was approved and it was at once put into operation.

The Imperial Conference of 1907 adopted a resolution approving the principle of the creation of an Imperial General Staff selected from the forces of the Empire as a whole. In 1908 proposals were put forward through the Colonial Office to the Governments of the self-governing Dominions. These were accepted by the Governments concerned and the formation of the Imperial General Staff was then proceeded with. The Conference of 1907 also provided that the colonies might refer to the Committee of Imperial Defence for advice any local question in regard to which expert assistance was deemed desirable, and that whenever so desired a representative of the colony which wished for advice should be summoned to attend as a member of the committee during the discussion of the questions raised. Sir Frederick Borden had already attended meetings of the Committee of Imperial Defence shortly after its formation, when matters pertaining to the defence of Canada were discussed. The work of that committee was rendered more effective by two decisions reached at the Imperial Conference in 1911:

(1) That one or more representatives, appointed by the respective Governments of the Dominions, should be invited to attend meetings of the Committee of Imperial Defence when questions of naval and military defence affecting the Overseas Dominions are under consideration. (2) The proposal that a Defence Committee should be established in each Dominion is accepted in principle.[1]

In January 1914 Canada established a Defence Committee, shortly before the outbreak of war, which completed a War Book similar to the British War Book. Undoubtedly the plans for co-operation so worked out greatly facilitated effective co-operation by the Dominions during the Great War.

Canada's effort at that crisis is dealt with elsewhere, but it should be noted that the national status of Canada and her right to determine her own course in war, as in peace, was fully recognised by the Imperial Government. By the declaration of war on 4 August 1914, by the British Government, the whole Empire was at war, but the character and extent of Canada's participation in the war were determined solely by the action of the Government and Parliament of Canada. Not only did the Canadian Parliament pass the necessary war measures for levying taxation, raising troops and sending them overseas to fight, but it also controlled the administration of the Canadian forces in England and in France. In short, Canada joined with the United Kingdom in waging war against the enemy powers by the free action of her Government and Parliament, but such was the unity of sentiment throughout Canada on the grave issues raised by the war that the Canadian Government and Parliament acted with a promptness and unanimity equal to that of the Imperial Government and Parliament.

Towards the close of the year 1916 the Imperial Government

---

[1] Keith, *Selected Speeches and Documents on British Colonial Policy*, II, 340.

requisitioned a Canadian-owned and Canadian-registered vessel, and the Canadian Government asked for an explanation, which was to the effect that the Admiralty was aware that the registry of the vessel had been transferred to Canada recently, but as she was time-chartered to an English firm for employment between English and French ports my Lords did not consider Canadian interests were affected to such an extent that the Canadian ministers would wish to be consulted before the vessel was requisitioned. This view was not acceptable to the Government of Canada, which contended that the Admiralty had no constitutional right to requisition a vessel of Canadian ownership and registry.[1] The contention was accepted by the Imperial Government in a reply from the Colonial Secretary to the Governor-General of Canada, of May 1917, in which are set forth certain principles which should govern the methods of exercising the requisitioning authority as between His Majesty's Government and Dominion Governments.

Requisitioning authority should be regarded as vested in and only to be exercised on behalf of the Government of that part of the Empire in which the vessel's port of registry is situated, ports in Colonies not possessing responsible Government being treated as United Kingdom ports.

In 1916, by Order-in-Council under the Canadian War Measures Act, the office of Minister of Overseas Military Forces of Canada was created, and one of the King's Privy Councillors for Canada was duly appointed minister. In 1917 the Parliament approved this action by making provision by statute for the office and by this Act the minister was charged with the administration of the military affairs of Canada overseas. The Canadian forces in the field were placed by the Canadian Government under the Commander-in-Chief of the British army in France, for military operations, but in matters of organisation and administration the Canadian Government retained full responsibility for its own forces, and the Canadian troops in training in England as well as those in France came under the direction and supervision of the Canadian Overseas minister. As matters of organisation and administration had a direct bearing upon military operations and discipline, it was agreed between the British and Canadian authorities that these matters should be made the subject of conference between them, and in July 1918, to meet this situation, after full discussion and agreement with the imperial authorities, a Canadian Section of the General Headquarters of the British army in France was formed. In forming such a section it was not intended to interfere in any way with the responsibility of General Headquarters and the supreme command in relation to matters affecting military operations or discipline, but through this section

[1] Minute of the Can. Privy Council (30 Jan. 1917), in Borden, *Canadian Constitutional Studies*, pp. 121, 122.

46

the full control of the Canadian Government over matters concerning the organisation and administration of its forces could be realised.

Naval Defence. The question of naval defence has been considered in some form at every Colonial and Imperial Conference from 1887 to 1921. At the earlier conferences the question was, would the colonies assist in the naval defence of the Empire by contributions toward the expense of maintaining the British navy? The question, however, soon assumed a new character, viz. should there be but one navy for the whole Empire, under the control of the Admiralty in London, to which the Dominions should make contributions, or should each Dominion make its contribution to the naval defence of the Empire by establishing its own naval service, just as it had established its own military service? The policy of the Admiralty throughout has been a single navy and Dominion contributions. With the exception of the emergency contribution of Dreadnoughts proposed by the Canadian Government in 1913, to which further reference will be made, Canada has not favoured this policy, and since 1902 has definitely promoted the development of a Canadian Naval Service. Australia tried the policy of contribution, but abandoned it in favour of an Australian navy.

At the first Colonial Conference the principal subject for consideration was Imperial Defence, and an appeal was made to the colonies to assist in the defence of the Empire to the extent at least of maintaining the naval bases which served as an insurance of colonial property. Sir Alexander Campbell, the Canadian representative, referred to the promise of the British Government made during the negotiations preceding confederation to undertake the naval defence of the proposed Dominion, provided Canada spent not less than £200,000 a year on her land defence. He also pointed out that Canada had spent a very large sum on the construction of the Canadian Pacific Railway which would be of great strategic advantage to Great Britain in matters of Empire defence, and intimated that Canada considered that under the pre-confederation agreement the entire cost of naval defence should be borne by the Imperial Government.[1] Campbell also intimated that an attempt had been made a few years before to develop a naval school at Halifax, and that Lord Lorne, then Governor-General of Canada, had applied for and was given an old frigate by the Admiralty called *Charybdis*, "but she could not steam and she could not sail; so there was no use trying to do anything with her". That discouraged their efforts completely.

At the Imperial Conference of 1902 the representatives of Canada stated that Canada contemplated establishing her own naval service

----

[1] The published report of the pre-confederation agreement would hardly justify this statement.

and offered to take over the military stations at Halifax and Esquimalt, and, as already pointed out, these stations were subsequently taken over. At the Conference of 1907 no substantial progress was made on the question of naval defence, but there was a growing feeling in Canada and also in the other Dominions in favour of assisting in naval defence, and this movement in Canada found expression in 1909 in a resolution unanimously adopted by the House of Commons declaring Canada's readiness to assume her share in naval defence. Canada's request for a discussion of this question, so far as it affected her, led to the Special Defence Conference of 1909.[1] At the Conference of 1887 the Australian colonies had agreed to make a contribution toward the naval defence of the Empire and they entered into an agreement with the Admiralty covering the conditions of such contribution, but at the Colonial Conference of 1907 Australia intimated her desire to terminate this agreement, declaring that it was not satisfactory either to Australia or to Great Britain and that she intended to develop her own naval forces and police the Australian waters with her own ships. Australia's proposal was accepted by Great Britain and at the Subsidiary Defence Conference of 1909 the basis for the development by Canada and Australia of their own naval forces was agreed upon.

In 1910 the Canadian Naval Service Act was passed, which contains all the provisions necessary for developing as large a naval service as Canada may desire to maintain. Following the passage of this Act certain cruisers were purchased, a naval training school was established, and a real beginning was made toward the establishment of a Canadian navy. At the Imperial Conference of 1911 the representatives of Canada and Australia met the representatives of the United Kingdom and a plan was worked out for the co-operation of the naval forces of Canada and Australia with those of the United Kingdom, both in peace and war. This agreement recognised the autonomy of the Dominions and their right to control their own fleets. It delimited the sea areas in which Canada and Australia should fly the flag and protect the trade routes and commerce of the Empire. Under this agreement Canada was assigned the western half of the North Atlantic and the eastern half of the North Pacific Oceans. In 1911 the Canadian Government called for tenders for the construction of ships for the Canadian navy, but before the tenders were accepted the Government of Sir Wilfrid Laurier was defeated and the Government of Sir Robert Borden came into power. In the general election of 1911 the policy of developing a Canadian navy under the plans worked out at the Conferences of 1909 and 1911 was bitterly attacked by the opponents of the Government in the province of Quebec as being too imperialistic and as drawing Canada into imperial wars, while in Ontario and the English-speaking provinces

[1] *Report of the Special Defence Conference*, 1909 (Cd. 4948), pp. 5, 7.

it was attacked as not being imperial enough and as being separatist in its tendency. Notwithstanding the great popularity of Sir Wilfrid Laurier this issue cost his Government many seats in the province of Quebec. The principal issue in the other provinces was the Reciprocity Agreement with the United States, but the Government did not make any gains on the naval issue in those provinces.

The new Administration did not proceed with the naval programme worked out by their predecessors, and the tenders which had been received were not accepted. In 1912 Sir Robert Borden consulted the British Admiralty as to a Canadian naval contribution, and at the ensuing session of Parliament he introduced a bill providing for the immediate contribution of $35,000,000 to purchase three Dreadnoughts, stating that he believed the German rivalry had created a grave emergency which ought to be met in this way and that the question of a permanent naval policy could be settled in the future. His policy was largely fashioned on the recommendations of the British Admiralty which had become extremely anxious to add to the number of Dreadnoughts in the North Sea, then the crucial area. The Liberal Opposition, led by Sir Wilfrid Laurier, opposed the policy of direct contribution as tending to impair Canadian autonomy, and supported the policy outlined in the House of Commons' resolution of 1909 and embodied in the Naval Service Act of 1910 and in the agreement arrived at with Great Britain and Australia in 1911. Laurier moved an amendment to the Government's proposal providing for the construction of two fleet units, under the terms of the Naval Service Act of 1910, to be stationed on the Atlantic and Pacific coasts. The part which the naval issue had played in the general election of 1911 undoubtedly influenced the attitude of the parties and the people towards the Government's proposal. The issue in the House and the country developed into a conflict between the policy of a central Imperial navy, under the control of the Admiralty, to which Canada should contribute, and the policy of developing a Canadian Naval Service co-operating with the British Navy. The result was one of the most acute parliamentary controversies in Canadian history. The bill, however, passed the House of Commons but was rejected in the Senate, and before any further action was taken by the Government, war broke out and all controversy ceased. Pursuant to the provisions of the Canadian Naval Service Act the Canadian Naval Service, such as it was, was placed under the command of the Admiralty for the duration of the war.

At the Imperial Conference of 1918 the Admiralty brought forward a proposal for a single navy under one control for the whole Empire, and suggested contributions by the Dominions. This policy was definitely rejected by the Dominions, and in a most important memorandum signed by the Prime Ministers of the Dominions they disputed the practicability of a single navy under one control and affirmed both the practicability and the desirability of Dominion navies co-operating with the British navy in Empire defence:

The proposals set forth in the Admiralty Memorandum for a single navy at all times under a central naval authority are not considered practicable....The experience gained in this war has shown that in times of war a Dominion navy...can operate with the highest efficiency as part of a united navy, under one direction and command, established after the outbreak of war.[1]

Naval Defence was one of the subjects on the agenda of the Prime Ministers' Conference of 1921, and in the discussion on the agenda in the Canadian House of Commons the Prime Ministers' memorandum of 1918 appears to have been accepted by the Government and the House as embodying the policy which Canada would follow in naval defence. The view was expressed that Canada should strongly support the movement for limitation of armaments initiated by the League of Nations and that she might await the result of a conference on the limitation of armaments before deciding on the extent of her contribution to the naval defence of the Empire. The Washington Conference of 1921, in which Canada participated, reached an agreement on the limitation of naval armaments, and Canada is now in a position to determine the extent of the contribution she should fairly make to the naval defence of the Empire.

The principle of Dominion navies co-operating with the British navy embodied in the decisions of the Subsidiary Naval Conference of 1909, the Imperial Conference of 1911, and in the Prime Ministers' memorandum of 1918, will undoubtedly govern Canada's participation in the naval defence of the Empire.

Canada's Relation to Foreign Powers. The change in the relations of the Dominions to the Mother Country is in no way more strikingly illustrated than in the new methods adopted for dealing with questions of foreign policy affecting the Empire as a whole and the Dominions in particular. As has already been pointed out, it was inevitable that as the Dominions grew in population, in trade, and in national sentiment, their inhabitants should demand, and in the end should exercise, as large and complete control over their own destinies as those who resided in the Mother Land. It was therefore natural that the control by the Government and Parliament of the United Kingdom over the external relations of the Dominions should come to an end. The question was—when and how, and would this change involve separation from the Mother Country or larger co-operation with the Mother Country? The answer to these questions will be found in the developments of the past forty years.

Canada, as the oldest and most populous of the Dominions, faced the problems of external relations earlier than the others, and in a measure blazed the trail which the other Dominions have followed,

[1] *Debates of H. of C. (Canada)* (1920), IV, 3499.

with the full approval of the Mother Country. Canada's first direct participation in foreign affairs was in the negotiation of treaties affecting her own interests, particularly her commerce. In the year 1871 Sir John Macdonald, then Prime Minister of Canada, was appointed one of the plenipotentiaries for the negotiation of the Treaty of Washington. These negotiations dealt with matters that affected intimately Canada's interests, and it was on this ground that Macdonald was appointed. He was the first Canadian statesman to sign an international treaty, although he was not the first representative of the colony to assist in the negotiation of one. Macdonald, in accepting the appointment, made it a *sine qua non* that any arrangement relating to Canadian interests would be inoperative until ratified by the Canadian Parliament. As the negotiations proceeded, he felt that his colleagues were prepared to sacrifice Canadian interests to American demands and expected him to yield his opinions to theirs. On one occasion he wrote to Tupper, a member of his Government:

> You may imagine that my position was exceedingly embarrassing. In our separate caucuses my colleagues were continually pressing me to yield—in fact, I had no backer, and I was obliged to stand out, and, I am afraid, to make myself extremely disagreeable to them.[1]

Sir John Macdonald evidently believed that the interests of Canada were not being adequately safeguarded by the British plenipotentiaries, but none the less the part that he played in the negotiations at Washington was one of prime importance, because it gave recognition to Canada's right to participate in the negotiating of treaties affecting her interests, and it set a precedent that could not be ignored in subsequent negotiations. In 1874 the Hon. George Brown was appointed as one of two plenipotentiaries to negotiate a treaty with the United States, with reference to commerce, navigation and fisheries. This mode of representation was insisted on by the Mackenzie Government, in view of the negotiations of 1871 when Sir John Macdonald was but one commissioner out of six.[2]

On the appointment of the first Canadian High Commissioner in London, in 1879, the Canadian Government thus stated the position of Canada in reference to the negotiation of commercial treaties:

> ...that the very large, and rapidly augmenting commerce of Canada, and the increasing extent of her trade with foreign nations, is proving the absolute need of direct negotiation with them for the proper protection of her interests....The Canadian Government, therefore, submit that when occasion requires such negotiations to be undertaken, Her Majesty's Government should advise Her Majesty specially to accredit the representative of Canada to the foreign court, by association, for the special object, with the resident Minister or other Imperial negotiator.[3]

---

[1] Pope, *Memoirs of Sir J. Macdonald*, II, 94.
[2] Lewis, J., *Life of George Brown*, p. 227.
[3] Keith, II, 148.

In 1884 the Canadian Government desired to conduct negotiations for a reciprocity treaty with Spain, and Sir Charles Tupper, then Canadian High Commissioner in London, and the British Ambassador at Madrid were appointed plenipotentiaries. The Foreign Office communicated to the British Ambassador as follows: "If the Spanish Government are favourably disposed, the full power for these negotiations will be given to Sir Robert Morier and Sir Charles Tupper jointly. The actual negotiations would probably be conducted by Sir Charles Tupper, but the Convention, if concluded, must be signed by both plenipotentiaries".[1] This marks a great advance over 1871 and 1874. The negotiations, however, did not result in a treaty. Their significance was explained by Sir George Foster, then Minister of Finance: "We have also gained the recognition, so far as that goes, of our High Commissioner being given co-ordinate power with the British Minister resident of a foreign State, to negotiate a treaty, subject of course to the approval and sanction of the Queen".[2]

In 1893 Sir Charles Tupper and the Marquis of Dufferin, British Ambassador in Paris, negotiated the Franco-Canadian Commercial Treaty of that year. It was virtually Tupper's treaty and has the importance of being the first commercial treaty ever made by Canada or any other Dominion with a European power. Sir George Foster, in the Canadian House of Commons, described it as "one of the first results of the treaty-making power conferred upon us, or exercised by us, in conjunction with England, through our High Commissioner".[3] In the meantime the Liberal party in the Canadian House of Commons was demanding that Canada should have the right to enter into direct communication with foreign States for the purpose of negotiating commercial treaties. In 1882 this demand found expression in a resolution moved by the Hon. Edward Blake, then leader of the Liberal party:

That it is expedient to obtain all necessary powers to enable Her Majesty, through Her representative, the Governor-General of Canada, acting by and with the advice of the Queen's Privy Council for Canada, to enter by an agent or representative of Canada into direct communication with any British possession or foreign state, for the purpose of negotiating commercial arrangements tending to the advantage of Canada, subject to the prior consent or the subsequent approval of the Parliament of Canada, signified by Act.[4]

This resolution was opposed by Sir John Macdonald. He declared that a demand by Canada to enter into direct negotiations with foreign countries in the negotiation of commercial arrangements would mean "separation and independence".[5]

In 1892 the Liberal party in Parliament, through the Hon. David Mills, submitted a similar resolution demanding treaty-making power

[1] Tupper, Sir C., *Recollections*, p. 175.
[2] *H. of C. Debates (Canada)* (30 Sept. 1891), p. 6312.
[3] *Ibid.* (10 July 1894), II, 5577.   [4] *Ibid.* (1882), p. 1075.   [5] *Ibid.* (1882), pp. 1075 f.

in commercial matters. The relationship and proximity of Canada to the United States appeared to make some form of direct negotiation between them of the greatest importance to Canada, and for this direct negotiation the Liberal Opposition at Ottawa contended. These views, however, were not in accord with the views then entertained in the Colonial Office. The Marquess of Ripon (Colonial Secretary in the Rosebery Administration) in a despatch to the Governor-General, dated 28 June 1895, clearly and definitely rejected any claim of Canada or the other colonies to negotiate directly their own commercial treaties. Ripon declared that "to give the colonies the power of negotiating treaties for themselves without reference to Her Majesty's Government, would be to give them an international status as separate and sovereign States, and would be equivalent to breaking up the Empire into a number of independent States, a result which Her Majesty's Government are satisfied would be injurious equally to the colonies and to the Mother Country, and would be desired by neither".[1]

Ripon's views would have deprived Canada of some of the substantial advantages gained under the Conservative Administration, and they were not acted upon so far as Canada was concerned. When the Joint High Commission of 1898 was appointed to deal with outstanding questions between Canada and the United States, the Canadian members of the Commission, headed by Sir Wilfrid Laurier, the Canadian Prime Minister, had equal status with the British members of the Commission.

In the negotiation of the Franco-Canadian Commercial Treaty of 1907 the strict terms of Lord Ripon's despatch of 28 June 1895 were not insisted on, and the British Ambassador at Paris received the following instructions:

The selection of the negotiator is principally a matter of convenience, and in the present circumstances it will obviously be more practical that the negotiations should be left to Sir W. Laurier and to the Canadian Minister of Finance, who will doubtless keep you informed of their progress. If the negotiations are brought to a conclusion at Paris, you should sign the Agreement jointly with the Canadian negotiator, who would be given full powers for the purpose.[2]

The same policy was applied to the negotiation of the Boundary Waters Treaty between the United States and Canada in the years 1908 and 1909. This treaty not only covered questions relating to the utilisation of boundary waters but also made provision for dealing with "other questions or matters of difference arising between them (the United States and Canada) involving the rights, obligations or interests of either in relation to the other or to the inhabitants of the other along the common frontier between the United States and the Dominion of Canada".[3]

[1] Keith, II, pp. 159 f.   [2] Keith, II, 165, 166.
[3] Pope, Sir J., *Treaties with U.S. affecting Canada, 1814-1913*, p. 185.

The negotiation of this important treaty was carried on on behalf of Canada by Sir George Gibbons, under the direct supervision of Sir Wilfrid Laurier. Lord Bryce, British Ambassador at Washington, was kept fully informed of all the negotiations, co-operated with Sir George Gibbons, and signed the treaty on behalf of His Majesty. This treaty is notable in that it provides:

The High Contracting Parties agree to establish and maintain an International Joint Commission of the United States and Canada composed of six commissioners, three on the part of the United States appointed by the President thereof, and three on the part of the United Kingdom, appointed by His Majesty on the recommendation of the Governor in Council of the Dominion of Canada.[1]

This is the first time a provision appears in an international agreement that His Majesty should act on the advice of his Canadian constitutional advisers. It was prophetic of the future.

In the year 1909 the Canadian Parliament gave formal recognition to Canada's activity beyond her own borders by the establishment of the Department of External Affairs. Sir Wilfrid Laurier, in introducing the bill in the Canadian House of Commons, stated: "We have given this matter a good deal of consideration, and the conclusion we have arrived at is that the foreign affairs with which Canada has to deal are becoming of such absorbing moment as to necessitate special machinery".[2]

The negotiations for the reciprocity agreement between the United States and Canada in the year 1911 were conducted entirely by two members of the Canadian Government, and the British Ambassador took no part, although he was constantly in touch with the Canadian ministers.

At the Imperial Conference of 1911 the Dominion members were for the first time taken fully into the confidence of the British Government on matters of foreign policy. The Dominion members attended a meeting of the Committee of Imperial Defence when Sir Edward Grey reviewed the foreign policy of the Empire. Asquith, speaking at the close of the Conference on the importance and significance of this development and of the discussion "under the same veil of confidence in regard to co-operation for naval and military purposes", said:

Those, gentlemen, are matters as to which we cannot take the world into our confidence; we cannot even take our fellow subjects and our fellow citizens into our confidence in the full sense of the term, but we, who have gone into it with the frankness which such confidential discussions admit of, will agree that, even if the Conference had done no more than that, it would have been a landmark in the development of what I may call our imperial constitutional history.[3]

But the British Government was not at this time prepared to permit the Dominions to share in the responsibility for the conduct of foreign policy. Referring to the proposal of Sir Joseph Ward for the estab-

[1] Pope, *Treaties with U.S. affecting Canada*, p. 185, Art. 7.
[2] *Debates of H. of C. (Canada)* (1909), p. 1980.
[3] *Imperial Conference Report*, 1911 (Cd. 5745), p. 440.

lishment of an Imperial Council which should deal with foreign affairs, Asquith stated:

It would impair, if not altogether destroy, the authority of the Government of the United Kingdom in such grave matters as the conduct of foreign policy, the conclusion of treaties, the declaration and maintenance of peace, or the declaration of war, and, indeed, all those relations with foreign powers necessarily of the most delicate character, which are now in the hands of the Imperial Government, subject to its responsibility to the Imperial Parliament. That authority cannot be shared.[1]

It would appear from the proceedings of the Conference that the Canadian Prime Minister, Sir Wilfrid Laurier, agreed with this view. When in England in 1912 for conference with the British Government and the Admiralty, Sir Robert Borden sat as a member of the Committee of Imperial Defence and took part in the consideration of questions of foreign policy. On his return to Canada he advocated that Canada should share in the naval defence of the Empire and in the control of foreign policy. On 5 December 1912 he said:

Responsibility for the Empire's defence upon the high seas, in which is to be found the only effective guarantee of its existence, and which has hitherto been assumed by the United Kingdom, has necessarily carried with it responsibility for and control of foreign policy.... When Great Britain no longer assumes sole responsibility for defence upon the high seas, she can no longer undertake to assume sole responsibility for and sole control of foreign policy which is closely, vitally, and constantly associated with that defence in which the Dominions participate.[2]

The war, and the part the Dominions played in the war, changed the whole situation, and in 1917 Mr Lloyd George, who had become Prime Minister, invited the Prime Ministers of the Dominions to come to London for consultation in reference to the conduct of the war, and as has already been pointed out the Imperial War Cabinet was constituted. Thus the Dominions were introduced into active participation in the consideration of questions of foreign policy. The constitution of the War Cabinet was a fine stroke of imperial policy. The meetings in London, notwithstanding the submarine menace, of the Imperial War Cabinet in 1917 and again in 1918, to confer on plans for the continued prosecution of the war, were a splendid demonstration of the unity and determination of all parts of the Empire to see the war through to a successful conclusion. They were also striking evidence of the possibility of an Empire, founded not upon force but upon freedom, meeting the gravest national emergencies with a unity and energy unsurpassed in history. This, however, was but participation with members of the British Government in considering and deciding upon questions of foreign policy relating to the conduct of the war. A further advance was made when the Dominion members of the Imperial War Cabinet were invited to sit as members

---

[1] *Imperial Conference*, 1911, p. 71.
[2] Keith, II, 309 f.

of the Supreme War Council at Versailles at its session of 4 July 1918, and Sir Robert Borden and Mr Rowell attended the session representing Canada.

The Government of Canada was consulted as to the terms of the Armistice and gave its approval before the Armistice Agreement was signed. So soon as it appeared clear that an armistice was about to be agreed upon, the Prime Minister of Canada took up with the Prime Minister of the United Kingdom the question of Dominion representation at the Peace Conference. In a despatch of 19 October 1918, Sir Robert Borden stated:

> There is need of serious consideration as to representation of the Dominions in the peace negotiations. The press and people of this country take it for granted that Canada will be represented at the Peace Conference. I appreciate possible difficulties as to the representation of the Dominions, but hope you will keep in mind that certainly a very unfortunate impression would be created and possibly a dangerous feeling might be aroused if these difficulties are not overcome by some solution which will meet the national spirit of the Canadian people. We discussed the subject to-day in Council and I found among my colleagues a striking insistence which doubtless is indicative of the general opinion entertained in this country. In a word, they feel that new conditions must be met by new precedents.[1]

After the terms of the Armistice had been approved, but before it was actually signed, on the urgent request of the British Prime Minister the Canadian Prime Minister left for London, to consider the question of Dominion representation and other matters which would arise at the Peace Conference. The Canadian Government considered the direct representation of Canada at the Peace Conference of such importance that a despatch was sent to Sir Robert Borden, then in London, setting forth the considered views of the Government:

> Council to-day further considered Canadian representation at Peace Conference and is even more strongly of opinion than when you left, that Canada should be represented. Council is of opinion that in view of war efforts of Dominion other nations entitled to representation at Conference should recognize unique character of British Commonwealth composed of group of free nations under one Sovereign and that provision should be made for special representation of these nations at Conference even though it may be necessary that in any final decisions reached they should speak with one voice; that if this is not possible you should form one of whatever delegation represents British Commonwealth.[2]

The question of Dominion representation was taken up by Sir Robert Borden at the Imperial War Cabinet and subsequently at the Peace Conference in Paris, with the result that notwithstanding the opposition of certain powers the Dominions secured distinctive representation on the same basis as the smaller powers, and in addition Dominion representatives were chosen from time to time on the panel of five delegates representing the British Empire.[3]

[1] *Can. Sess. Pap.* 1919, Special Session, 41 j, p. 1.
[2] *Ibid.* p. 2.
[3] For details see Borden, *Constitutional Studies*, pp. 117 ff.

The Canadian plenipotentiaries received full powers from His Majesty to negotiate and sign the Treaties of Peace, on behalf of His Majesty, in respect of the Dominion of Canada, and they were so signed by them. The Canadian Government, however, refused to advise or agree to the ratification of the treaty though urged to do so, until it had been submitted to the Canadian Parliament for approval, and a special session was called for the sole purpose of considering the treaty, and after full debate the treaty was approved. His Majesty's Canadian ministers thereupon recommended the ratification of the treaty by His Majesty in respect of the Dominion of Canada, and a similar procedure was followed in the case of all the other peace treaties.

The system of communication between Prime Minister and Prime Minister, in reference to matters of Cabinet importance, approved by the Imperial War Cabinet of 1918, and the communications from the Foreign Office to the Dominions' Prime Ministers, through the Colonial Office, in reference to foreign affairs, is being continued. The Dominions are now receiving more or less continuous information in reference to foreign affairs affecting their interests.

At the Premiers' Conference of 1921 there was a very full review of foreign affairs by the Foreign Secretary and a thorough discussion of certain aspects of foreign policy affecting the Dominions, more particularly the question of the renewal of the Anglo-Japanese Alliance. On this question the Prime Minister of Canada, Mr Meighen, took a decided stand that, as the conditions which led to the establishment of the Alliance no longer existed and as its renewal might in the state of public opinion then existing in the United States lead to serious misunderstandings there, it was not wise to renew it, and that the United States should be invited to co-operate with Great Britain and Japan in any plans for the Pacific. This view, though at first strongly opposed, finally prevailed. The invitation of the United States to the Washington Conference provided the opportunity for the consideration of the matter, and the Four Power Pacific Pact between Great Britain, the United States, France and Japan, for preserving peace in the Pacific, was the result.

Diplomatic representation at a foreign court involves the recognition of a certain degree of sovereignty and international status of the State so represented. The question, therefore, of Canada sending a diplomatic representative to Washington involved important imperial and international considerations. To some the very suggestion foreboded disunion and the disruption of the Empire. To others it was but a natural and logical constitutional development within a co-operative British Commonwealth. The question, however, was not dealt with from a theoretical but from a practical point of view. The public men both of Canada and Great Britain were compelled to deal with actual conditions. These conditions were that the two peoples had a common boundary of over five thousand four hundred miles, and were in daily contact with each other on an ever-increasing scale, with questions of great importance and delicacy constantly arising between them, and according to diplomatic practice and the well-understood canons of international law they could not deal directly with each other, but must deal with all these questions through the British Ambassador at Washington, or the American Ambassador at London. The British Commonwealth, composed of a group of free self-governing nations united under a common Sovereign and pursuing in a large measure a common foreign policy, but each self-governing unit entitled to deal directly with foreign States in matters affecting its own interests, was not covered by existing diplomatic practice. The problem was—should the solution of Canadian problems be embarrassed and delayed and Canadian interests suffer, or should there be a development in international law and in diplomatic practice to meet these new conditions? The answer to this question was a characteristically British one, in which both the Governments of Canada and the United Kingdom concurred: International law and diplomatic usage should be modified to meet the conditions, and in 1920, with the approval of the Government of the United States, it was agreed that Canada should send her own minister to Washington to deal with Canadian affairs.

The question in one form or another had been before the Canadian people for nearly thirty years, but it was the developments during the war which led to its solution. The Canadian Government had found it desirable and necessary for the efficient conduct of business matters arising between the departments and administrative boards of the Canadian and American Governments to send a Canadian War Mission to Washington. This War Mission was established by Order-in-Council in January 1918, with authority to deal directly with the American administrative departments and boards. The results were so satisfactory that in 1918 and 1919 Sir Robert Borden discussed with the British Prime Minister, as well as with the Foreign and Colonial Secretaries, the importance and desirability of direct Canadian diplomatic representation at Washington. As a result of protracted conferences and correspondence between the two Governments the basis of Canadian representation was agreed upon, and, on 10 May 1920, the following announcement was made simultaneously in the British and Canadian Parliaments:

As a result of recent discussions an arrangement has been concluded between the British and Canadian Governments to provide more complete representation at Washington of Canadian interests than has hitherto existed. Accordingly it has been agreed that His Majesty, on advice of his Canadian ministers, shall appoint a Minister Plenipotentiary who will have charge of Canadian affairs and will at all times be the ordinary channel of communication with the United States Government in matters of purely Canadian concern, acting upon instructions from, and reporting direct to, the Canadian Government....

This new arrangement will not denote any departure either on the part of the British Government or of the Canadian Government from the principle of the diplomatic unity of the British Empire.[1]

The question of Canadian diplomatic representation at Washington was the subject of an important debate in the Canadian House of Commons in April 1921, and from this debate it appears clear that the Government believed that the appointment of a Canadian Minister to Washington would facilitate the amicable settlement of questions constantly arising between Canada and the United States; that it would strengthen rather than weaken the ties between Canada and Great Britain, and that through the Canadian Minister at Washington Canada might be able to render a real service to the Empire as a whole.

The League of Nations. Under the Covenant of the League of Nations the British Empire is one of the permanent members of the Council of the League. Before the Peace Treaty was finally approved by the Peace Conference a question was raised as to the eligibility of a Dominion for election to the Council. Sir Robert Borden contended that on the true construction of the Covenant the Dominions were entitled to exactly the same status and rights as other members, and as such to election to the Council, but he wished it made clear that this construction of the Covenant was accepted before the Treaty was finally approved by the Peace Conference. Accordingly M. Clemenceau, Mr Wilson and Mr Lloyd George signed the following memorandum:

The question having been raised as to the meaning of Article 4 of the League of Nations Covenant we have been requested by Sir Robert Borden to state whether we concur in his view that upon the true construction of the first and second paragraphs of that article representatives of the self-governing Dominions of the British Empire may be selected or named as members of the Council. We have no hesitation in expressing our entire concurrence in this view. If there were any doubt it would be entirely removed by the fact that the Articles of the Covenant are not subject to a narrow or technical construction.[2]

The organisation and work of the League of Nations made a strong appeal to the people of Canada and they have followed with deep interest the proceedings of the Assemblies of the League. Prior to the meeting of the first Assembly in November 1920 a series of conferences was held in London, between the delegations of the United Kingdom, the Dominions and India, in reference to the matters which were to come before the first Assembly. It was frankly recognised that, while each delegation must decide for itself the course which it would pursue in the Assembly, it was desirable that there should be as large a measure of co-operation as possible in all matters of major importance. During the Assembly the delegations frequently met for consultation, under the chairmanship of Mr (now

---

[1] *Debates of H. of C. (Canada)* (1920), p. 2178.
[2] *Can. Sess. Pap.* 1919, Special Session, 41 h, p. 19.

Lord) Balfour, the head of the British delegation, and these consultations were undoubtedly of very great benefit. On a number of questions that came before the Assembly the delegations did not vote the same way, but they did not differ on any vital matter. The fact that the different nations of the Empire could and did vote against each other came as a great surprise to the representatives of foreign States. It was clear they had not understood the genius and spirit of the British Empire, and the participation of the Dominions and India in the League has given to foreign States a much better understanding and appreciation of what the British Empire is. The participation of the representatives of Canada in the work of the League has given the Canadian people a new and closer interest in foreign affairs.

The Permanent Court of International Justice. The Covenant of the League makes provision for the establishment of a Permanent Court of International Justice, and one of the first acts of the League was to provide for the establishment of this Court. The statute for the constitution of the Court was submitted by the Council to the first Assembly, and the Canadian delegates took an active part in the discussion of the statute, and on their suggestion the committee to which the statute was referred for consideration inserted an amendment to make clear the right of each Dominion to nominate its own nationals for election as members of the Court. Canada signed the protocol establishing the Court, became one of the nations parties to it, and her Government submitted the names of two of its nationals for election, one of its nominees receiving a substantial vote at the election of the judges in the second Assembly of the League in 1921. Canada cordially supports the Permanent Court of International Justice. Its organisation marks a great advance in international co-operation for the settlement of juridical disputes by reason rather than the sword.

The International Labour Conference. Under the draft constitution of the International Labour Conference, as settled by the Committee of the Peace Conference and submitted to the Plenary Session of the Conference for approval, the Dominions would have been excluded from membership in the governing body. On the motion of Sir Robert Borden the report was referred to the drafting committee, with instructions to amend so as to make provision for Dominion representation in the International Labour Conference on the same basis as in the League of Nations. This resolution was adopted, the necessary changes were made, and at the first International Labour Conference held in Washington in the year 1919 Canada was elected a member of the governing body, a position which she continued to hold until a permanent seat on the governing body was awarded to her as one of the nations of principal industrial importance entitled to that right.

Reviewing the relations from 1884 to 1921, it is clear that vital changes have taken place not only in the status of Canada but in the organisation of the British Empire. Canada has acquired the right to a voice in foreign policy and to diplomatic representation at foreign courts. She has been received on the basis of full equality into the League of Nations, the Permanent Court of International Justice and the International Labour Conference. If she so desires she is entitled to representation at international conferences considering matters affecting her interests and to require that no treaty affecting her shall be ratified by His Majesty except upon the advice of his Canadian advisers. It was undoubtedly largely due to Canada's initiative that these rights have been secured, not only for Canada but for all the self-governing Dominions. These rights so accorded to the Dominions give them a position and status in international law.[1] It is quite true that their position cannot be defined under any existing categories, but new categories must be found to meet new conditions. The position once conceded to the Dominions cannot be withdrawn. It is true there still are limits to the legislative power of the Dominions in respect of amendments to their own constitutions and to external affairs. The legislative power for these purposes remains in the Imperial Parliament, but is held by it as trustee for the Dominions and is exercised only at their request.

Finally, it is difficult to say with any degree of certainty what Canadian public opinion was from time to time on the constitutional developments reviewed in this chapter, but it is reasonable to assume that on the whole the Canadian Government reflected the will of the people. The attitude of parties has been to some extent changeful. The Liberal party, under the leadership of Blake and Laurier, was jealous of Canadian autonomy and active in extending it, while the general attitude of the Conservative party was to lay greater stress on imperial unity. It was Sir Robert Borden, however, the leader of the Conservative party, who, as Prime Minister, took a leading part in the events of 1914 to 1920, and Mr Meighen, his successor, in the events of 1921 in which Canadian autonomy and Canadian status were so notably advanced. A Coalition or Union Government, composed of Conservatives and Liberals, under Sir Robert Borden, as Prime Minister, was in power from October 1917 until their retirement from office in July 1920, and the Liberal leaders in the Union Government were strong supporters of the policy pursued by that Government in reference to Canadian status and imperial co-operation. On the other hand, certain leading members of the Liberal party in the House of Commons opposed to the Union Government sharply criticised the events of the years 1918 to 1920, and expressed quite a different conception of the Empire from that taken by the Canadian delegates at the Peace Conference.

[1] Oppenheim, S., *International Law* (3rd ed. London, 1920), I, 170 f.

They claimed that under the British North America Act Canada was not and could not be a State, and that to seek representation in the matter of treaties and foreign affairs was not only undesirable but unnecessary.[1] No doubt these views represented a body of sentiment in the country, probably more in the Conservative party than in the Liberal. But the Liberal party, which came into office in 1921, guarded carefully all of the rights secured by their predecessors. And such has been the case since confederation; no right pertaining to self-government, once secured, has ever been surrendered.

[1] *Debates of H. of C. (Canada)* (1919), Second Session, pp. 77, 78.

They claimed that under the British North America Act Canada
was not and could not be a State, and that to seek representation in
the matter of treaties and ... ... was not only undesirable
but unnecessary. No doubt these views represented a body of
serious ... ... party
than in the Liberal, but the Liberal party, which came into office
in 1921, guarded carefully all of the rights secured by their

CHAPTER XXXI

CANADA IN THE WORLD WAR, 1914–1918

CANADA'S problem in the World War cannot be understood
without a preliminary glance at those post-Confederation years during
which her growth at last enabled her to take her place not only at the
foreign front but also at the Imperial War Cabinet in London, among
the Allied statesmen who made the Treaty of Versailles, and beside
the other autonomous peoples of the world in the League of Nations
at Geneva. Her population had not grown so fast as had been
expected; and barely eight millions met the war. The growth of
settled area was much greater; for, besides the new ground broken
in the Maritime Provinces, Quebec and Ontario, the whole ranching,
farming, and mining portions of the vast North-West and Pacific
areas were now first effectively used for settlement. In 1867 there was
no town west of southern Ontario; and Manitoba, which produced
the greatest number of volunteers in proportion to population, was
then in the far-off wilds. Even when the World War broke out,
Canada was still "fighting geography" all along the line.

Few Canadians saw any significance for their new Dominion
in the fact that the new German Empire was proclaimed at
Versailles in 1871; though that was the year in which all British
garrisons were withdrawn except from the naval bases of Halifax
and Esquimalt. Nor did Canadians see much significance in the
rapid growth of the German oversea possessions between 1884 and
1890. The Kaiser's "Krüger telegram" in 1896 naturally excited
sympathetic resentment in Canada, because it showed the new
German inclination to shake the mailed fist against the British both
at home and overseas. But two years later, when the American and
German fleets nearly came to blows at Manila, and the British
squadron prepared to side with the Americans, there was little, if any,
anticipation of a future world war. Nor did the German Navy Bill
of 1900 excite special interest in Canada, where expanding business,
a general election, and the South African contingents were the
questions then uppermost. The *Entente Cordiale* of 1904 with France
naturally interested a Dominion whose people came from the two
countries now drawing together against the rising German menace.
But even the "shining armour" speech which the Kaiser made in
favour of Austria in 1908, the very provocative Agadir incident in
1911, the Balkan War of 1912, and the practical doubling of the
German striking force in 1913, did not make the Canadian public
realise the gravity of the situation.

Yet in a very modest way Canada did prepare. But her active participation in any really great struggle beyond her own frontier depended on what her own public thought of it, and this public was far from being homogeneous in either race or language. Her barely eight millions included more than two million French Canadians, less than four million Anglo Canadians, less than one million "British-born", and about a million foreigners.[1] The French Canadians had by far the highest proportion of young married men with families. They and the Anglo Canadians had a fairly even balance of the sexes. The "British-born" had by far the highest proportion of young unmarried males. The foreigners included those whose mother countries were on opposing sides. A good half came from Germany and Austria, while very few indeed were Frenchmen born in France.

The French Canadians differ greatly from all the other inhabitants of Canada, and even from the French, for reasons we have already seen. Taken as a whole, though very French in certain racial ways, they are just as decidedly non-French in almost everything that would stimulate personal participation in a European war. It also happened that during 1913–14 the Manitoba school question was exciting acrimonious disputes which helped to fix French-Canadian thought even more than usual on internal questions.[2]

That any of his fundamental interests were at stake in the World War did not occur to the average French Canadian. He and his leaders knew that if they ceased to belong to the British Empire they would rapidly disappear in the "melting pot" of the United States; and therefore they were loyal to the Crown and Empire which guaranteed their own form of life. But their loyalty was subject to certain limitations when it came to spontaneous active service in a distant war which most of them considered as being rather the affair of the English-speaking majority, whose own Mother Country had the decision on peace or war in her hands. Moreover, the English-speaking majority was in far closer touch than the French-Canadian minority with imperial and world-wide affairs. A constant stream of immigration flows into English-speaking Canada. But the numbers of French Canadians are affected almost entirely by their birth-rate, not by immigration. Most Anglo Canadians have friends and relatives in the British Isles. Very few French Canadians have any such in France. Besides, more even than the parent French, they are landsmen, not seamen, and therefore less able to understand the decisive influence of sea-power. That a German victory at sea might ruin the British Empire, thereby ruining British Canada, in which they lived their French-Canadian lives, and that the only alternatives left would be submission to the Germans or absorption by the United States,

---

[1] "Anglo Canadian" is used here for all whose ancestors came from the British Isles. Those born in the British Isles were officially described as "British-born".

[2] *Vide supra*, chap. xxi.

scarcely dawned on the French-Canadian mind. Yet this very fact sheds all the more distinction on the unanimous vote of the French-Canadian members in both Dominion Houses in favour of Canadian participation in the war.

Until nearly the end of the nineteenth century Canadian preparation for war envisaged the United States as a possible invader; but the Spanish War (1898) made Americans and British better friends. Then the South African campaigns (1899–1902) led Canadians to think in terms of oversea contingents; and the alarming challenge of the new German fleet produced questions, debates, and a little decisive action. The premonitory German Navy Bill of 1900, the redistribution of the British navy, to face the North Sea danger, in and after 1904, and the general naval crisis of 1909, all at last combined to stimulate interest and cause the establishment of a small Canadian navy.[1] But Canada's own naval contribution to the World War was so small, while her other contributions were so much more important in every way, that no Canadian naval history need be recorded here; neither, still more regrettably, can the story of the 8000 Canadians who held commissions in the three imperial flying corps—naval, military, or Royal Air Force—because these, like many other Canadians, were serving in the British forces and on British charge.

Canadian war work was done mostly on the "Home Front" and the Western Front. But so complex were the correlations of the war that it would be unfair to concentrate attention on these two fronts alone without at least mentioning Canada's war finance, her connection with the inter-Allied Red Cross, and other diverse war activities. Local complexities and correlations may be imagined from the fact that in the city of Quebec alone the following numbers of war activities were officially surveyed: 56 military, 4 naval, 4 Air Forces, 3 civil, 20 semi-official, 7 unofficial, 6 imperial, 7 Allied, 1 provincial, and 1 municipal. There were French, Jugo-Slav and American activities of various kinds; while many Canadian activities interlocked with those of the Empire. But only the purely Canadian effort can be described here.

During the years 1871–96 Canada kept a permanent corps, of under 1000 men, stationed in tiny units to serve as schools for a militia which drilled for about a fortnight each year and never numbered one-hundredth part of the population. In the next fifteen years (1896–1911) great improvements were made under Sir Frederick Borden, an excellent Minister of Militia. Besides setting about the formation of something like the nucleus of a real army, he greatly increased the permanent corps, adding to it the branches of the service previously lacking. Further, he took a practical interest in staff work and the development of the Royal Military College, welcomed inter-

[1] See the naval debates in the Canadian House of Commons and Senate (1909–13).

imperial conferences, and envisaged oversea problems, facing a minor one during the Boer War. Moreover, he brought the militia into touch with the very few practical experiences its extremely short training allowed; and, above all, he learned the supremely important difference between civil control and civilian interference. Borden contemplated a permanent force of 5000, an active militia of 100,000, and a general reserve comprising all available able-bodied males— which reserve was no more than what the French, earlier British, and later Canadian laws had always reaffirmed. But practice fell short of theory; for, as has been seen, the country was not yet in earnest about the need of preparation. Only a year before the war a parliamentary return gave the following amounts as being the *per capita* expenditure on defence, according to the census of 1911: Canada $1.47, South Africa $1.49, New Zealand $2.43, Australia $5.11, British Isles $7.41. Most of the reasons for Canada's comparatively low expenditure have been given already; but these should be specially stressed: the continual "fight with geography" of barely 8,000,000 people spread out over a country the size of Europe, with many diverse parts—a population, moreover, of two distinct races and tongues, with a strong admixture of foreigners—all living within hail of a friendly, foreign, English-speaking country with fourteen times as many people, forty times as much wealth, and a Monroe Doctrine which seemed to shield Canada from any Old-World aggression.

Yet some good preparations were made. In 1907 Sir Percy Lake, as Canadian Chief of Staff, planned the central mobilisation camp at Valcartier, a few miles from Quebec. Five years later his successor, General Colin Mackenzie, brought these plans up to date for multiples of 10,000 men, up to a total of 200,000. Meanwhile, in 1908, at the Quebec Tercentenary, King George V, then Prince of Wales, reviewed the first assemblage of regular and militia units from every part of Canada. In the following year the naval crisis excited most attention. In 1910 Sir John French, the future commander of the original British Expeditionary Force, came out, on the invitation of the Laurier Government, and made excellent suggestions for a possible Canadian Expeditionary Force. The chief stress was laid on organisation, mobilisation, and the provision of a trained Staff able to do the double work of war, half at the home front (where General W. G. Gwatkin did so well in the war) and half at the fighting front. During all these years Borden and Lake kept in touch with the principal War Office experts concerned, especially Sir Douglas Haig, the British Commander-in-Chief in the later stages of the war.

On the change of Government in 1911 Sir Frederick Borden was replaced by Sir Sam Hughes. Hughes, an enthusiastic militiaman, threw himself into the crisis with devoted energy. Yet his extreme self-confidence, dislike for military experts, and disregard for the difference between civil control and civilian interference, all combined to make him assume a conglomerate authority which necessitated his resignation in 1916.

Early in 1914 the permanent heads of the departments which would be most affected by a sudden war had agreed on a combined plan of action; so that when, on 1 August, the crisis came, the governmental machinery worked both rapidly and well. Proclamations and Orders-in-Council regulated action concerning enemy subjects, the prohibition of exports, the internment of enemy vessels, the censorship of wireless and cables, the prevention of financial panics, etc. The Canadian Expeditionary Force sprang into life at the first official call for the one complete division which (in answer to Canada's question) the Imperial Government suggested as best for immediate use. But no sooner had this first division been authorised than other units were offered and accepted, among them the Princess Patricia's Canadian Light Infantry, raised mostly from ex-regulars. Two days after war began an Order-in-Council authorised the mobilisation of volunteers for oversea service "of such effective strength as may from time to time be determined". Four days later the exact composition of the first division was laid down, and immediate mobilisation ordered at Valcartier Camp, near Quebec. Meanwhile the little Canadian navy had been mobilised for use in co-operation with the Royal navy, for in this World War independent local squadrons were worse than useless. Indeed the British Grand Fleet in Scapa Flow was instantly recognised as the hub of the great Allied wheel.

There was a sudden financial panic. A run began on the banks while they were legally forced to pay either in Dominion notes or gold. But, even before war had been declared, an Order-in-Council authorised them to meet their obligations in their own notes, to increase their circulation within strictly responsible limits, and to draw on the Government for such Dominion notes as might be really needed. This Order ran counter to existing law. But it at once allayed the panic and was unanimously approved by Parliament. Another pre-sessional act that met with unanimous approval was the gift of a million bags of flour to the Mother Country, whose oversea communications were now menaced by the second strongest navy in the world. The Imperial Government, when cabling its thanks, laid stress on the special value of this gift "for the steadying of prices and the relief of distress". Government action was admirably matched by private benevolence of all kinds. The Canadian Red Cross and other existing societies faced the crisis with vastly expanded efforts and resources, while new associations were quickly started to meet the needs that soon arose. As time went on nearly all such associations, especially those connected with the Canadian Expeditionary Force, became at least semi-official, mostly to prevent overlapping and consequent waste.

Meanwhile Parliament held its first war session (18–22 August). The speech from the throne truly interpreted the general attitude of Canada: "The critical period into which we have just entered has aroused to the full the patriotism and loyalty which have always actuated the Canadian people. The spirit which thus animates Canada also inspires His Majesty's dominions throughout the world". The address in reply was moved by an Ontarian and seconded by a French Canadian, who laid special stress upon British sea-power as the guardian of freedom. Then Sir Wilfrid Laurier rose to support his old opponent, the Conservative Prime Minister, Sir Robert Borden, by declaring that

it is our duty, more pressing than all other duties, at once to let the friends and foes of Great Britain know, that there is in Canada but one mind and one heart, and that all Canadians stand behind the Mother Country, conscious and proud that she is engaged in this war, not from any selfish motive, not for any purpose of aggrandisement, but to maintain untarnished the honour of her name, to fulfil her obligations to her Allies, and to save civilisation from the unbridled lust of conquest and domination.... This war is for as noble a cause as ever impelled a nation to risk her all upon the arbitrament of the sword.... The allied nations are fighting for freedom against oppression, for democracy against autocracy, for civilisation against reversion to that state of barbarism in which the supreme law is the law of might.... It will go down on a still nobler page of history that England could have averted this war if she had been willing to forego the position which she has maintained for many centuries at the head of European civilisation; if she had been willing to desert her Allies, to sacrifice her obligations, to allow the German Emperor to bully heroic Belgium, to trample upon defenceless Luxembourg, to rush upon isolated France, and to put down his booted heel upon continental Europe. At that price England would have secured peace. But her answer to the German Emperor was "your proposals are infamous"...there is not to-day... a single man whose admiration for England is not greater by reason of this firm and noble attitude.

Sir Robert Borden cordially agreed with Sir Wilfrid Laurier that "nearly half a million of the very best citizens of Canada are of German origin" and promised that no Austrians or Germans would be molested unless they gave aid to the enemy or tried to leave Canada for enemy parts. His closing words were these:

In the awful dawn of the greatest war the world has ever known, in the hour when peril confronts us such as this Empire has not faced for a hundred years, every vain or unnecessary word seems a discord. As to our duty, we are all agreed: we stand shoulder to shoulder with Britain and the other British Dominions in this quarrel, and that duty we shall not fail to fulfil as the honour of Canada demands. ...In the very name of the peace that we sought at any cost, save that of dishonour, we have entered into this war; and, while gravely conscious of the tremendous issues involved, and of all the sacrifices that they may entail, we do not shrink from them, but with firm hearts we abide the event.

The veteran Sir George Foster sounded the note of the whole session thus: "That generosity which sometimes lies more or less concealed in partisan and racial disputes has burst all those ignoble bonds; and a feeling of pure patriotism, love of country, and devotion to what the flag symbolises, has come to the front disfigured by no mean or petty purpose".

In five days eight Acts were unanimously passed, including a War Appropriation of $50,000,000 and the authorisation of an Expeditionary Force of 25,000 men. A War Measures Act approved all executive orders given already, besides giving the Governor-General in Council full power to meet all emergencies by immediate Orders-in-Council. The Canadian Patriotic Fund, to help the dependents of the fighting men, was incorporated, with power to take over the assets and liabilities of its predecessor, which had been incorporated during the Boer War. The whole atmosphere of Ottawa seemed to be not only intensely patriotic but truly representative of the whole Dominion. A very practical imperial touch was added when the Imperial Government advanced £12,000,000 on precisely the same terms as those on which it could borrow for itself. The general public overwhelmingly approved of these combined efforts of the two great parties, and the press never reflected public opinion better than during these first momentous days.

Only one Canadian party opposed all participation in the war from first to last—the extreme *Nationalistes*, led by Henri Bourassa. An honest man, keen debater, and champion of extreme particularism, Bourassa had naturally thrown himself heart and soul into the fight for the official recognition of French as a medium of instruction in Ontario and Manitoba. Moreover, his appeal to "British fair play" had won much English-speaking sympathy. But he soon alienated it by exalting his provincial quarrels far above the issues vital to all French and British alike. His followers professed a narrowly conditioned loyalty, because their leaders knew that French Canadians could never have lived their own life outside the British Empire. But they resented the fact that to remain inside the Empire was a prime condition for their own survival. Their arguments about purely local defence were mere propaganda, when the fate of Canada might be settled thousands of miles away, and more especially at sea. Bourassa wrote and spoke as if he, as grandson of Papineau, the rebel orator of 1837, would be false to French Canadians unless he attacked all who took the British side. Yet another grandson, Talbot Papineau, died fighting as a captain in Princess Patricia's Light Infantry; 30,000 French Canadians volunteered;[1] a French Canadian, L. G. Desjardins, exposed Bourassa's arguments in *L'Angleterre, Le Canada et la Grande Guerre*; while, in a great mid-war debate (17 January 1916), Laurier himself spoke scathingly of "those who, blinded by passion and prejudice, would deny us the liberty of being humane". Happily for Canada, the followers of Bourassa, the enemy aliens, the out-and-out "pacifists", and the few other extreme opponents, all together, did not equal a tenth

[1] Estimate of Hist. Sect., General Staff, Ottawa.

of the loyal population whose representatives voted unanimously for Canada's participation in the war.[1]

Ten thousand more than the 25,000 needed for the First Division arrived at Valcartier, among them being units like the Fort Garry Horse, which chartered two special trains from Winnipeg to Quebec, entirely on its own account. The greatest single transport tonnage which had ever yet crossed the Atlantic in one convoyed fleet sailed from Gaspé Bay on 1 October. Three-fourths of the First Division came from the single million of the "British-born". But, besides having much the highest percentage of efficient males with the fewest family ties, this million naturally had the most insistent personal call to service near the old homeland. The Canadian-born proportion rose as time went on; and the country, as a whole, did its war work very well. Before the First Division landed for training on Salisbury Plain the Second was authorised and plans were laid for replacements: 8000 men were also raised for home defence, and garrisons were soon sent to Bermuda and St Lucia. Meanwhile the production of war supplies was greatly stimulated. Food, equipment and munitions were increasingly produced, not without troubles, nor yet without some scandals of the usual profiteering kind; but, on the whole, with a really patriotic energy that did honour to the home front all through. The worst failure was the Ross rifle, which had been the subject of debate for ten years before the war. The men at the front called it the "suicide rifle" and gladly threw it away in exchange for the British army rifle, with which they were presently armed.[2]

War finance was the chief topic when Parliament met in 1915. Revenue had fallen and expenditure risen; while war obligations had only just begun; for no Canadian troops had been in action yet. The War Appropriation Act authorised the borrowing of $100,000,000 from the Mother Country. Taxation was greatly increased and widely extended. The duties on tea, coffee, sugar, tobacco, and liquor had all been increased at the outbreak of war. Now a 5 per cent. flat increase was laid on every British, and $7\frac{1}{2}$ per cent. on every foreign, import. New taxes were imposed on sales of transportation tickets, telegrams, cheques, bank note circulation, Trust, Loan and Insurance Companies, as well as excess profits; while stamps were imposed on money orders, postal notes, patent medicines, perfumes, spirits and wines. The general situation was much aggravated by the results of the financial crisis in 1913 and by the great national expenditure on railways. The economic world crisis of 1913 had found Canada suffering from municipal over-expansion, especially in the West. Dominion, provincial and local taxation together reached $31.50 a head, or 60 cents more than in the United States and $6.87 more

[1] For the opponents' case see *Le Devoir* (Montreal) from 1914 on; also Ewart, J. S., *The Roots and Causes of the War*.

[2] See official documents in Hist. Sect. of General Staff and Ross Rifle, in *Debates, H. of Commons (Canada)* (1917), vol. CXXVI. See also Index: War, Supplies, Rifles, Ross.

than in the British Isles. Moreover, foreign investments were contracting, while imports were lessening and, with them, the very large share of revenue derived from customs. At the same time the Dominion was deeply committed both to the vast railway development which has resulted in the Canadian National system and to the beginning of the Hudson Bay line. Nearly $1,000,000,000 was spent by the Dominion on its railways during the war and reconstruction periods (1914–28): one-fifth on construction; four-fifths on what an economist[1] calls "bolstering up our system"—bonuses, loans, stock subscriptions, cash subsidies, bond guarantees, etc.

Two favouring circumstances on the economic side in 1915 were the "record" harvest and the domestic loan. The harvest steadied the Canadian market, helped New Zealand, whose harvest had been very bad, and enabled the Government to commandeer large supplies at reasonable rates. The Industrial Commission, which had just been appointed to stimulate agriculture, proved very useful in handling this harvest, because its powers included the allocation of suitable immigrants, the supervision of both raw materials and finished products, and all transportation. The 5 per cent. domestic war loan of $50,000,000 being subscribed twice over, its authorised total was doubled.

The darkest shadow of any kind was the profiteering which followed the first great rush of war supplies. The searching enquiry, conducted by Chief Justice Sir Charles Peers Davidson, revealed frauds in nearly every line, from shells to horses, and from submarines to drugs. But, on the whole, the country and Parliament were thoroughly sound. Leaders like Borden and Laurier were far above suspicion. Borden's remarks in the House forced two of his followers to resign. The scandals connected with the Shell Committee were exposed, and in May 1915 a War Purchasing Commission was appointed, under the chairmanship of Sir Edward Kemp, the future Minister of Militia. In that summer Lord Rhondda came out with other delegates to arrange for the establishment of an Imperial Munitions Board, which superseded the original Shell Committee, and was directly responsible to the Minister of Munitions in London, but was locally managed by Sir Joseph Flavelle, of Toronto, and locally financed by a Dominion loan of $100,000,000 besides the like amount from the Canadian banks. This Board, which included some good members of the former Shell Committee, did excellent work for the rest of the war.

Toward the close of the session Borden announced that over 100,000 men were already under arms. None had then been under fire, except the (mostly ex-regular) Princess Patricia's regiment, which formed part of the 27th Division of the British Expeditionary Force. Yet only twelve days later, on 22 April 1915, the First Canadian

---

[1] Prentice, J. S., "Canadian Federal Finance" in *Bulletin of Queen's University*, Kingston, Canada, no. 55, March 1928.

Division went into action under still more trying conditions, and emerged victorious after nearly four days of continual fighting against an outnumbering enemy who was following up the success of his first great poison-gas attack. Posted on the extreme British left, the Canadians were sharing the defence of the Ypres salient with the extreme French right, which was largely composed of Africans. Ypres, though hard to defend, was to be held at all costs, being of great importance, both as a point of Franco-British junction and as shielding vital positions in the rear. At five in the afternoon the Canadian 3rd Brigade saw the clouds of poison gas roll in on the French right, where the Africans broke in panic under the suffocating green fog, thus leaving a gap into which the Germans poured. The 3rd Brigade was threatened, front, left and rear. But, steadfast as when he won his South African V.C., its brigadier (now Sir Richard Turner) threw even his Field Engineers into the firing line, and held back the Germans. The future Canadian Corps Commander, General A. W. Currie, sent up some of his own brigade reserves; the British officer then commanding the Canadians, General E. A. H. Alderson, despatched his whole divisional reserve; and the Corps Commander, General Sir Hubert Plumer, sent forward a complete brigade to drive home the counter-attacks.

The Commander-in-Chief, Sir John French, thus described the action:

In spite of the danger to which they were exposed, the Canadians held their ground with a magnificent display of tenacity and courage; and it is not too much to say that the bearing and conduct of these splendid troops averted a disaster which might have been attended with the most serious consequences. They were supported with great promptitude by the reserves of the Divisions holding the salient and by a Brigade which had been resting in billets. Throughout the night the enemy's attacks were repulsed, effective counter-attacks were delivered, and at length touch was gained with the French right, and a new line was formed.

On 24 April the gas was used against the Canadians, who then had no means whatever of warding it off. Several units lost more than half their strength in the four-day fight. But the remainder held fast till relieved on the 25th. No wonder Canada thought that her First Division had most decidedly "made good". The First was again severely tried in May, this time at Festubert. In September the Second joined the First in forming a Canadian Corps under Alderson, with Currie and Sir Richard Turner as the new divisional commanders. Early in 1916 the Third Division joined under General M. S. Mercer, who had been promoted from the original 1st Brigade; while various cavalry, engineer, and other extra-divisional units kept on increasing the Canadian strength. The Fourth (and completing) Division reached the front at Ypres in August under General David Watson, who had previously won promotion from the 2nd Battalion to the 5th Brigade.

This year was a time of increasing anxiety. Everybody behind the scenes was convinced that much greater efforts, involving correspondingly greater sacrifices, would be required. The Government again led the way. Sir Thomas White, the Minister of Finance, did not exaggerate when he said, five years later, that "the Government of Canada, in the matter of raising men and in its attitude as to the extent of Canada's participation in the struggle, stood always decidedly in advance of public sentiment throughout the Dominion".[1] Though enlistments were 37,000 short of the 250,000 authorised up to the beginning of 1916, and though more than half still came from the single million of the "British-born", yet, on 12 January, an Order-in-Council raised the authorised total to 500,000. At the same time there was a corresponding increase of all the services that ministered to the Canadian Expeditionary Force. The Pensions Board in Canada was purely governmental. The Military Hospitals Commission in England administered both public and private funds. The Patriotic Fund was raised entirely by private subscription; but, like nearly all other war activities, became semi-official and under advisory control. National resources also were increasingly mobilised. Farms, mines, and factories alike rendered growing service to the cause. At the beginning of 1916, 250 factories were executing war orders, which now reached $500,000,000. Of course there still was the usual proportion of would-be profiteers, but most Canadians really wished to bear their share of the ever-growing burden, which resulted in a war debt seven times greater than all Canada's pre-war debts together. So heavy, too, was the loss of Canadian life that it almost equalled the loss incurred by the United States during the twenty months they were engaged in the war.[2]

The most significant precedent of 1916 was Borden's attendance at the meetings of the Imperial Cabinet, a precedent which led straight to Canadian representation in the Imperial War Cabinet and at the Imperial War Conferences of 1917–18. Borden also had the immense advantage of seeing the war with his own eyes. If, as some thought, all Opposition leaders (or those who were such in normal times) had come into personal touch with the war, there would probably have been fewer party divisions when fundamental issues were at stake. As to extending the life of Parliament for an extra year, there was no such division, since Laurier seconded what Borden proposed, and the House was unanimous. The session of 1916 was in most ways more harmonious than that of 1915, when the Opposition criticised some budget proposals rather severely, without, however, in any way opposing the whole sum required for the war. The new budget

---

[1] White, Sir T., *The Story of Canada's War Finance*.

[2] Canadian casualty report of 15 Jan. 1919. Killed, 35,684; died of wounds, 12,437; total, 48,121. U.S. report of 1 Sept. 1919 by General John J. Pershing (Washington: Gov. Printing Office, 1920, p. 77, par. 28). Killed, 35,556; died of wounds, 15,130; total, 50,686.

doubled the War Appropriation, allocated another $50,000,000 to defraying unpaid extra costs, and contemplated no reductions. The tone was buoyant, due chiefly to the 1915 harvest as well as to "the largest aggregate trade". Moreover, the next year's revenue was forecast at $200,000,000, an advance of over $50,000,000 on the pre-war forecast of 1914.

But 1916 ended ominously in the matter of enlistments. The authorised strength of 500,000 was 70,000 short, while another 70,000 had already become casualties. St Eloi, Mount Sorel and Courcelette took serious toll of the Canadian Corps, which, at the end of May, came under the admirable leadership of Lieut.-General Sir Julian (afterwards Lord) Byng. At St Eloi the Canadians had the supremely difficult task of holding an important position just wrested from a very powerful enemy, whose counter-strokes recovered the lost ground after a desperate fortnight. The battle of Mount Sorel began with the fight at Sanctuary Wood, which acquired additional importance from the fact that it was the first action in which the whole Canadian Corps fought as a single unit. The battle as a whole went through four fluctuations in which the Canadians did better than a bare recital of gains and losses would suggest. First, the far more numerous Germans carried the whole front line except the left at Hooge. Next day the Canadians countered without success. Then the Germans carried Hooge. But finally the Canadians re-captured their own original right. Leaving the salient in August the Canadians exchanged defensive work in the low ground near Ypres for offensive action in the rolling uplands of the Somme, where fighting had already been in progress for more than two months. The most memorable day was 15 September, because then, after making sure of their objective in the morning, the Canadians instantly organised another assault and took Courcelette. Long, exhausting, and apparently fruitless fighting went on during two months more of miserable weather, when the Canadians dug in for the winter. The Somme cost them nearly 27,000 casualties, while giving them only one complete victory, Courcelette. But the justification for British persistence lies in the fact that the Somme, despite its apparent stalemate, began the sapping of German *moral*, besides preventing the Germans from diverting overwhelming numbers against the hard-pressed French.

The Commander-in-Chief thus described the part played by the Canadians at Courcelette, where the 22nd Royal French Canadians did particularly well:

Our success made it possible to carry out during the afternoon that part of the plan which provided for the capture of Martinpuich and Courcelette, and by the end of the day both these villages were in our possession [taken respectively by the 15th Division, and 2nd Canadian Division, Major-General R. E. W. Turner].... The result of the fighting of 15 September and following days was a gain more considerable than any which had attended our arms in the course of a single operation since the commencement of the [Somme] offensive.[1]

Two very important changes of *personnel* marked the year 1916. The Duke of Connaught was to have left in 1914, but stayed to face the difficulties of the war. His work as Governor-General was extremely well done throughout, and Laurier's glowing tribute was well earned: "No Governor-General ever left our shores with so much of the blessings and affection of the people of Canada". His successor was the statesmanlike Duke of Devonshire. The other resignation was that of Sir Sam Hughes. Having created his own advisory council in England, he naturally resented the Cabinet appointment of a regular Minister of Oversea Military Forces in the person of Sir George Perley. Borden thereupon demanded his resignation, and Sir Edward Kemp succeeded him in Canada. Kemp and Perley did their best in circumstances which were particularly difficult in the case of Perley, who suddenly became the centre of an extremely complex organisation at the crisis of the war.

The year 1917 gave the enemy three great hopes of victory by land, and even one by sea. Bolshevist Russia deserted the Allies. France failed in the Nivelle offensive. Italy met disaster at Caporetto. And the "ruthless" submarine campaign threatened starvation to the British Isles. But the entry of the United States more than made up for the Bolshevist desertion. France and Italy recovered. The submarine sinkings were checked, though only just in time. And the various British armies, including the Canadians, more than held their own; the Canadians, in particular, opening their campaign with the most famous of all their victories—Vimy Ridge (soon to be described). This year likewise saw five Canadians among the six senior Canadian Corps generals, when General Byng, promoted to an Army command, was succeeded by General Sir Arthur Currie, who then had only one Briton, General L. J. Lipsett, commanding a division, the others being Sir Archibald Macdonell, Sir Henry Burstall and Sir David Watson. Sir Edward Morrison led the Corps Artillery. Next year a sixth Canadian, Sir Frederick Loomis, succeeded Lipsett, who shortly after fell at the head of a British division.

Equally important were events in the political field, for in 1917 Canada joined the Imperial War Cabinet in London, while at home she fought the sternest of all her elections, when the question of conscription divided the Liberals, united a Coalition, and aroused racial passions; but without changing the unanimity of Parliament in regard to the general prosecution of the war. Meanwhile, during the winter of 1916–17, a thorough reorganisation had been proceeding. Instead of raising new regiments which were bound to be broken up into replacements, certain units were raised simply as replacements.

---

[1] Haig, Sir Douglas, Field-Marshal, *Despatches* (*Dec. 1915–April 1919*), ed. Boraston, J. H.

This formed a far better system for keeping the Canadian Corps up to full strength, which, on Armistice Day, was 110,000 men at the front. Another change was the formation of all Canadians in England into a distinctively Canadian command under Sir Richard Turner. At the same time a great development took place in the Canadian railway troops, who, from April 1917 to the end of the war, did all light construction at the front and some of the broad-gauge work as well. Forestry also engaged a rapidly increasing number of Canadians in England and France, which eventually reached nearly 24,000. Corresponding increases occurred in all other auxiliary services. The *personnel* of the Canadian Army Medical Corps exceeded 15,000, with a bed capacity of 34,000. Voluntary associations, under full official recognition, worked harder than ever; none harder than the Canadian Red Cross, the Daughters of the Empire, and the servants of the Patriotic Fund. Everywhere the purely amateurish element had either to "get on or get out". True, the Canadian Expeditionary Force itself was composed mostly of amateurs. But these non-professionals had long ceased to be amateurish; and it must be remembered that in this war, as in the War of 1812, both the pre-viously keen militiamen and those who had never drilled before went through so intensive a training and so much actual experience that they became thoroughly seasoned veterans. Moreover, very many Canadian regulars held key positions, especially at first. The record of the Canadian Royal Military Cadets (who have a four-year course) is also worth special mention. The total number of ex-cadets on active service was 915. Of these 390 held Imperial or Indian com-missions. The remaining 525 served among the 22,592 officers of the Canadian Expeditionary Force. But, though these Royal Military Cadets together formed little more than 2 per cent. of the whole, they formed more than 20 per cent. of those holding staff appointments or unit commands, from battalions and batteries up.

The victory of Vimy Ridge now claims attention. Byng began organising it during the previous December. Every possible eventuality was carefully considered in the very elaborate plan; and many "key" officers, like Currie, were sent to study French methods at Verdun. On 1 March the Fourth Division carried out the great gas raid which was meant to be a full rehearsal. In itself this raid was a comparative failure. But it helped to reduce enemy *moral* and put the final touches on Canadian preparation. The regular attack began on Easter Monday, 9 April. The artillery barrage worked out to perfection. Three divisions assaulted and gained their assigned objectives with a combination of heroic dash and clockwork precision which left nothing to be desired. The Fourth was checked by the extremely strong defences of Hill 145. But next day, with the help of reinforce-ments, it won through. Four days more, and the whole German position was in Canadian hands; while the simultaneous advance of the British Divisions on the left combined to threaten the German hold on the very important mining town of Lens.

That summer witnessed desperate fighting round Hill 70, which was one key to Lens. But after long preparations against the next objective, Sallaumines Hill, the other key to Lens, a sudden call took the Canadians back to the area of Ypres, where they suffered 16,000 casualties and exhausting hardships in vile autumn weather, when working out their long and finally successful attacks on Passchendaele. In late November the Corps returned to their old Vimy front with mingled feelings: resentful over losses for what seemed hardly worth while, but exultant over work well done against a strong enemy and the worst of natural conditions. Had all ranks realised how necessary Passchendaele was to major operations elsewhere, there would have been less, perhaps no, resentment. In any case, Currie's own praise rang true and went home: "The greatest factor of success was the fighting spirit of the men, tempered by discipline, developed by training, and enhanced by the confidence in themselves and their officers created by a year of unbroken success".[1] The opinion of the supreme command is well expressed by Haig's own words in the Christmas despatch of 1917: "... the capture of Vimy Ridge had removed a constant menace to the security of our line"; "Canadian battalions found (5 May) Fresnoy full of German troops assembled for a hostile attack which was to have been delivered at a later hour. After hard fighting, in which the enemy lost heavily, the Canadians carried the village, thereby completing an unbroken series of successes". Again, on 23 August, after Hill 70 had been finally secured, he congratulated Currie "on the complete and important success with which your command of the Canadian Corps has been inaugurated".

Meanwhile the burning question of conscription was being fought out along the whole home front. The year 1917 had opened with a National Service week, the last attempt at volunteering; yet month by month the returns showed more casualties than recruits. The total authorised strength of 500,000 had never been reached. Conscription now seemed the only possible solution. But months were spent in negotiations with Laurier, whom Borden asked to join a Coalition Government, with a perfect balance of Liberals and Conservatives in the Cabinet. The crux of the argument was the interpretation of the Militia Act of 1904, which was passed by the Laurier Government, and which, as before, declared all male British subjects from 18 to 60, domiciled in Canada, as being liable for service "anywhere in Canada, and also beyond Canada for the defence thereof". Borden claimed that the Canadian Expeditionary Force was defending Canada in France. Laurier claimed that this was a misinterpretation of the Act.

---

[1] See Despatches, Hist. Sect., General Staff. Also *The Empire at War*, vol. II; *Canada in the Great World War*, vols. III-VI, etc.

On 11 June Borden introduced his Conscription Bill. A week later Laurier moved an amendment in favour of a referendum. This amendment was lost by 111 votes to 62. Then the second reading of the bill itself was carried by 118 to 55, while the third was carried by 102 to 44. As the debate proceeded, opinions divided more and more on racial lines, the overwhelming majority of English-speaking members voting for conscription, nearly all French Canadians against. The bill was very moderate. It limited the whole call to 100,000, though national registration had shown nearly 500,000 still available, if not more pressingly required, in certain cases, for other national work. The age-limits were 20–45; the youngest men without dependents were to be called first; and every possible care was taken to safeguard genuine exempts. But nothing could induce Laurier and those who stood by him to join any coalition or modify their case against conscription in any form whatever. Three-quarters of his followers were from the great majority of French Canadians, who, with the small minority of Anglo Canadians, claimed that the Canadian Expeditionary Force and the Canadian Militia were two quite different forces, that, in fact, there was one force in Canada in time of peace and quite a different force outside of Canada during this very distant war. Therefore, they argued, this could not be a case for a Canadian *levée en masse*. As for the French Canadians who had volunteered, the mass of home-staying French Canadians were proud enough of what these had done. But the home-stayers still regarded volunteers for oversea service as gallant adventurers, not as part of a national army defending their own form of life. Moreover, for reasons already stated, French Canadians could not feel the personal appeal that so profoundly moved most of their present opponents. Many of these opponents, again, only made antagonisms deeper by unjustly calling the French Canadians exasperating names. It was said that the more than 2,000,000 French Canadians had produced less than 20,000 volunteers. But, since all the "Canadian-born" were lumped together in the returns, this could not be proved in time. The Historical Section of the post-war General Staff at Ottawa thinks 30,000 nearer to the truth. This would strengthen the argument of those French Canadians who, favouring a voluntary participation in the war, claimed that certain sections of Anglo Canadians were no better than those whom they reviled.[1]

Another controversial point was the War-Time Elections Act, which, like the Military Voters Act, was designed to give votes to all engaged in actual war service. The latter Act enfranchised all British

[1] The difficulty of discriminating between the different kinds of "Canadian-born" is great. French Canadians cannot always be distinguished merely by their names. Many are descended from the Fraser Highlanders of the eighteenth century. Others bear English and Irish names; some even German (descendants of the "Brunswick Auxiliaries" of the American Revolution). On the other hand, many "Anglo Canadians" bear French names (Channel Islanders, Huguenots, etc.).

subjects connected with Canada who were actively engaged in war work, whether they were ordinarily resident in the Dominion or not, whether white or coloured, male or female, minors or adults. The former Act enfranchised all the womenfolk of past or present members of the forces overseas. Laurier accused the Coalition Government (which comprised thirteen Conservatives and ten Liberals) of having created "a special electorate in view of an impending election". The supporters of the "National Government" retorted that those who had made the greatest personal sacrifices for the cause, which even the Opposition thought just, should all have votes on the vital question of defence. In November the Government's prestige was greatly strengthened by the nearly four-fold over-subscription of the Victory War Loan. While $150,000,000 were asked for, nearly $550,000,000 were subscribed. The December election resulted in a sweeping general victory for the conscriptionists, among whom were nine-tenths of the whole Canadian Expeditionary Force. Borden had 153 votes in the new Parliament against only 82 for Laurier. Of these 82, moreover, only 20 came from outside the French-Canadian province of Quebec.

The year 1917 was also momentous in the matter of taxation; for it saw the imposition of the first Dominion Income Tax, which made a constitutional precedent, because direct taxation had hitherto been left to the provinces. The lowest exempted income was $2000 for those without dependents. This was reduced to $1000 in 1918; but the rate remained the same—4 per cent. The super-tax was raised on incomes of $6000 and upwards. But super-tax, surtax and general rates increased till 1920, when an income of $1,000,000 paid 65 per cent.

In the year 1918 came the greatest stress of the war. But both parties supported its prosecution; while the Canadian Corps was better organised, better supplied, stronger in numbers, and more successful than ever. Moreover, Canadian wheat, nickel, asbestos and wood for aircraft were never of greater value to the Allies than in this final year.

Reinforcements had to be rushed to point after point as the great German drive developed from March to July. The First Motor Machine-Gun Brigade lost three-fourths of its *personnel* in nineteen days on the Somme. Two divisions joined the First British Army, two others the Third. But they were not very heavily engaged; and on 15 July the reunited Canadian Corps entered the line in front of Arras quite ready for the final Allied offensive set in motion by Marshal Foch along the Marne only three days later. Replacements, reinforcements and reorganisation had not only brought the four divisions up to more than full strength but had given the Corps all the extra engineers and machine gunners so urgently needed for piercing the Hindenburg Line. On 20 July Currie was secretly warned that the Corps was to be the right wing and spear-head of the whole Fourth Army in the great surprise attack near Amiens. This meant crossing two army fronts and forwarding enormous supplies along a new line. But everything worked without a hitch; and such uniform victory was won by the Corps during the last hundred days of the war (4 August–11 November) that this period has ever since been known to Canadians as "Canada's Hundred Days".

So secret was the transfer that, except for the Allied generals concerned, neither friend nor foe knew what was about to happen, and 14 infantry and 3 cavalry divisions, with 450 tanks and 2000 guns, were concentrated on a 10-mile front just east of Amiens at the beginning of August. At dawn on the 8th the decisive blow was struck in what the Canadian Staff called the "L.C. Operation", because the Corps went into action to the cry of "Remember *Llandovery Castle!*"—the hospital ship which the Germans had just sunk with Canadian doctors and nurses on board. There was excellent co-operation all round: with the Australians and other British divisions who formed the rest of Lord Rawlinson's Fourth Army on the left; with the French on the right; and among all arms and branches of the Canadian Corps itself—infantry, cavalry, artillery, machine gunners, and field engineers; as well as with tanks from the British units in front, and the Canadians' own supply and medical branches close up in rear. The surprise was complete, the advance unprecedented, the result momentous. "The 8th of August", said Ludendorff, "is the black day of the German Army.... The war had to be ended". On the other hand, the Allied commanders found the results of the fortnight's battle so encouraging that they decided to continue the general offensive, instead of entrenching for the winter and waiting for American reinforcements next spring. The "spearhead" Canadians were therefore sent back to the First Army in front of Arras, whence they fought their way to the Canal du Nord. Here they paused before beginning six weeks of much more desperate fighting, over ground which the enemy had held all through the war, ground which was so vital to him now that he resisted to the very last. This long-drawn fight for Cambrai cost the Canadians over 30,000 killed and wounded. But these severe losses were due to no fault of Currie's; for one of his divisional commanders emphasised "the extraordinary skill with which our chief conducted these battles", adding: "We wish to place on record our appreciation of the care which he has evinced at all times for our lives and general well-being".[1]

Amiens, Arras, Cambrai, Mons: these are the battle honours of the Hundred Days; for throughout the final month that followed the fall of Cambrai the Canadians won fifty more miles of enemy ground—over the frontier and into Mons. Of Amiens Haig's final despatch,

[1] Livesay, W., *Canada's Hundred Days*, p. 115.

of 21 December 1918, reported that "The brilliant and predominating part taken by the Canadian and Australian Corps in this battle is worthy of the highest commendation. The skill and determination of these troops proved irresistible, and at all points met with rapid and complete success. The fine performance of the cavalry throughout all stages of the operation...rendered most valuable and gallant service".[1] Of Arras he wrote, with special reference to the Drocourt-Quéant Line, "this gallant feat of arms carried out by the Canadian Corps". Of Cambrai he expressed his "complete satisfaction" (as quoted in the Canadian Special Order of 3 October). This was particularly gratifying to the Corps Command, because Currie had acted entirely on his own initiative when choosing Inchy as the special point at which to attack the Canal du Nord. Haig's Armistice *communiqué* assigned a place of honour to the announcement that "The Canadian troops have captured Mons". And, at Mons itself, a crowning touch was given by that heroic soldier-statesman, King Albert of the Belgians, who publicly declared the Canadians to be "quite unsurpassed by any Corps in Europe".[2]

Canada's entire war effort is far too complex for any short summary here. But her general contribution in men and money may be fairly estimated from these two facts: first, that the men in her own forces comprised 8 per cent. of her own barely 8,000,000 people;[3] and secondly, that, as has already appeared, the sum the war cost her was seven times greater than the whole of her pre-war debt.[4] Of her 600,000 soldiers more than 400,000 went overseas; while two-thirds at the front were either killed or wounded. All things considered, therefore, her patriotic services were fully commensurate with her available resources. Nor were they rendered in vain. For in those fifty-two months of the war she won a greater, and far nobler, place, both within the Empire and in the world at large, than she could have gained in a whole century of peace bought by neutrality in this freeman's war.

---

[1] Haig, *Despatches*, p. 261.

[2] The late Major-General Sir David Watson, G.O.C., 4th Dn., stood beside the King at the time.

[3] The final figures at the A.G. Branch, Ottawa, are 619,636. These include Canadian-born, 318,705; "British-born", 237,644; Americans, 37,391; others, 25,896. The R.C.N. had over 10,000. (Some 20,000 more were in the three flying corps, the I.W.B. of R.E., etc.) For casualty details see *ante*, note on p. 748.

[4] See reports, by dates, of Minister of Finance. Also *Bulletins* 16 and 55 of Queen's Univ., Kingston. The 1914 debt was $385,000,000. "War, demobilization, Soldiers' Civil Re-establishment, and War Pensions", 1915–1927, were $2,088,000,000. The Interest-on-Debt tables do not discriminate between War debts and others. But since the total, 1915–1927, exceeds $1,200,000,000, and half must be due to the War, $600,000,000 may be added, making $2,688,000,000, or seven times $385,000,000. There is, however, a vast increase of the bonds held in Canada. In 1914 only $792,000 were so held. But at the peak of the debt, in 1920, while $135,000,000 were held in New York and $336,000,000 in London, the amount held in Canada was $2,066,000,000. (For a different estimate of War debts etc. see *supra*, pp. 636–8. Ed.)

CHAPTER XXXII

CANADA IN 1918–1921

THE Government in power at Ottawa when the World War came to an end with the Armistice of 11 November 1918, was the Unionist Government formed by Sir Robert Borden in 1917. In this Cabinet there was almost equal representation of Conservatives and of those Liberals who in 1917 had favoured the introduction of compulsory military service. Seldom have so many able and distinguished men sat together about the council board in Canada. Sir Robert Borden, the Prime Minister, had come through the period of the war with greatly enhanced reputation: his extraordinary patience, his dignity, his iron resolution had been just the qualities demanded by the crisis. Among Conservative-Unionists he had as colleagues Sir George Foster, Sir Thomas White, Sir Edward Kemp, Sir James Lougheed and Messrs Arthur Meighen, C. J. Doherty, J. D. Reid, Martin Burrell, and P. E. Blondin. Among Liberal-Unionists the Cabinet contained Messrs N. W. Rowell, T. A. Crerar, A. L. Sifton, C. C. Ballantyne, J. A. Calder, Frank Carvell, A. K. Maclean and General Mewburn. Labour was represented by Senator G. D. Robertson. The one conspicuous weakness of the Government was the absence of any adequate representation of French Canada: the only French Canadian in the Cabinet was Senator Blondin.

The Unionist Government had had a record of which any Government might have been proud. It had carried to a glorious conclusion Canada's war effort, and in doing so it had given an example of pure and patriotic administration of public affairs. During the earlier stages of the war there had been some unpleasant scandals in connection with contracts for war supplies awarded by the Canadian Government; but there had been no scandals in connection with the conduct of the war by the Unionist Administration. The Military Service Act had been administered with fairness and impartiality; generous provision had been made for pensions for disabled soldiers and their dependents; a department of soldiers' civil re-establishment had been created, as well as a soldiers' land settlement board; and Sir Thomas White's administration of the finances of the country, and especially his appeal in his Victory Loans to the Canadian investor, had been crowned with success. Prohibition of the manufacture or importation of intoxicating liquors had been enforced for the duration of the war, and one year afterward; and patronage had been completely abolished in the Civil Service and the purchasing of government supplies. On these and many other grounds the

Unionist Government was entitled to face the future with a clear conscience.[1]

It was natural to expect that the Government which had faced so successfully the problems of the war should continue to deal with the problems of reconstruction after the war. Long before the war ended, in fact, the Government had begun to make preparations for dealing with those problems. The harmony, moreover, which had existed in the Government suggested that the Unionist party should be made permanent. The crisis which had called it into existence in 1917 was past; but a new crisis had arisen which demanded in equal degree the subordination of party to patriotism.

These considerations had weight with the great majority of the members of the Cabinet and party; and for a time the Unionist Government presented an unbroken front to the Liberal Opposition. But gradually party spirit began to reassert itself. The first evidence of its recrudescence was seen, curiously enough, among an element in the Conservative ranks. Under the inspiration of Robert Rogers, formerly Minister of Public Works in the Borden Government, who had been dropped from the Unionist Cabinet of 1917, a demand sprang up for the return of straight Conservative rule. The movement gained support in Toronto, where it obtained the endorsement of the Central Conservative Association, and in Winnipeg, where it was approved by a Conservative provincial convention. At this convention the name of Sir Robert Borden was actually removed from the list of officers as honorary patron.

Almost at the same time restlessness began to be evident among the Liberal-Unionists. In the early summer of 1919 T. A. Crerar withdrew from the Cabinet, mainly because of disagreement with its tariff policy; and during the budget debate in 1919 W. S. Fielding, who had been Minister of Finance in the Laurier Government from 1896 to 1911, but who had supported the Unionists, went, with about twelve other Liberal-Unionists, back to the Opposition benches. These secessions were followed by others. In the beginning of 1920 A. K. Maclean, who, though only a minister without portfolio, had administered temporarily several important departments, resigned from the Government on the ground that, in his opinion, his mandate had expired; and at the end of 1919 "fighting Frank Carvell" took refuge in the post of chief commissioner of railways. At the beginning of 1919 General Mewburn had already resigned as Minister of Militia, for private reasons; and though he was succeeded by another Liberal-Unionist, Hugh Guthrie, this hardly added to the Liberal-Unionist representation in the Cabinet, since Guthrie had been Solicitor-General since 1917. These retirements took out of the Unionist Cabinet no less than four of the original Liberal members. It is true

[1] See the speech delivered by the Hon. N. W. Rowell at Bowmanville, Ont., on 17 December 1918, and republished as pamphlet *One Year of Union Government*.

that Rowell, Sifton, Calder, Ballantyne and Guthrie still remained; but these now constituted less than a third of the whole Cabinet. Just as the Coalition Government of Sir John Macdonald after 1867 became gradually a predominantly Conservative Administration, so the Unionist Government of Sir Robert Borden after 1918 gradually took on a predominantly Conservative complexion.

There were within the Government, however, elements of weakness more serious than any of these. On both Sir Robert Borden and Sir Thomas White, the two chief figures in the Administration, the strain of the war years had told heavily. In 1919 the health of both men broke down. During the summer Sir Thomas White was compelled, on grounds both of health and of the urgency of his personal affairs, to ask for release from office; and his resignation became effective on 2 August. Sir Robert Borden struggled against ill-health during almost the whole of 1919; but in December he suffered a breakdown, and his physicians advised him that his health "absolutely forbade him to continue at present the discharge of his official duties". He himself would have preferred to resign at once; but he was urged on all hands to continue in office, and to take a prolonged rest, in the hope that he might thereby recover his health. He therefore agreed to this course, and Sir George Foster took his place as acting Prime Minister.

A weakened Cabinet was thus left to deal with the difficult and dangerous problems of the reconstruction period. At no time in Canadian history has there been a situation which demanded statesmanship of a higher order. The demobilisation of the hundreds of thousands of Canadian troops had been accomplished with remarkable smoothness; but there remained the problem of the reabsorption in ordinary civilian life, not only of these troops, but of the vast numbers of those workers who had been engaged in the manufacture of munitions of war and in other war work. The country had been on a war basis; now it became necessary to put it back on a peace basis. The financial system of the world was in chaos, international trade was completely dislocated, and social unrest was universal. The times were out of joint, and it would have required a Government of supermen to set them right.

Curiously enough, the first serious revolt against the policies of the Government came from the farmers. The Canadian farmers as a class had suffered from the war less severely than many other classes in the community. They had obtained rising prices for their produce, and at the same time they had contributed *per capita* less in men and money to the war effort of the country than had the urban centres. They had had to pay rising prices for manufactured goods; but in this respect they were no worse off than anyone else. Unfortunately, in the spring of 1918, they had come into conflict with the Unionist Government over the question of the exemption of farmers' sons from military service. A monster deputation of five thousand farmers which waited on the Cabinet at Ottawa on 14 May 1918, was met by Sir Robert Borden with a flat refusal of their demands; and this incident undoubtedly coloured the attitude of the farmers toward the Unionist Government. Hardly had the Armistice of 11 November 1918 been signed when the Canadian Council of Agriculture, meeting at Winnipeg on 29 November, promulgated a political programme containing features so radical as to throw the farmers, almost of necessity, into direct opposition to the Government. Among the planks in this "National Farmers' Platform" were the following: an immediate and substantial all-round reduction of the customs tariff; free trade between Great Britain and Canada within five years; the revival and extension of the reciprocity agreement with the United States; the increase of direct taxes on unimproved land values, on incomes and on inherited estates; public ownership and control of railway, water, and aerial transportation, telephone, telegraph and express systems, all projects for the development of natural power, and the coal-mining industry; proportional representation; the opening of seats in Parliament to women; and the establishment of direct legislation through the initiative, the referendum and the recall. On this very advanced programme it was highly improbable that very many members of the Unionist Government would look with favour; and it was therefore almost a foregone conclusion that the farmers would soon be found entering the lists as opponents to the Government.

In several of the provinces the farmers had already organised for political action. In the Prairie Provinces the Grain Growers' organisations had been taking since 1910 an increasing interest in politics; and in Ontario the United Farmers had organised themselves in 1914. In the general elections in Ontario in 1919 the United Farmers had succeeded in sweeping the rural districts, and had captured a larger number of seats than either the Conservatives or the Liberals; with the result that E. C. Drury, one of their leaders, was invited to form a Farmers' Government, and became Prime Minister of the province. This success encouraged the farmers to enter the federal field as a political party; and at a conference held in Winnipeg in January 1920, at the call of the Canadian Council of Agriculture, the National Progressive Party was formed. When Parliament met in the spring, the party was able to muster eleven members in the House of Commons, and T. A. Crerar was elected its parliamentary leader.

The new party contained within it from the first two elements. There were those, led by H. W. Wood, the able organiser of the United Farmers of Alberta, and J. J. Morrison, the secretary of the United Farmers of Ontario, who frankly regarded the party as an occupational group, and rejoiced in the charge of "class-consciousness". On the other hand, there were those, led by T. A. Crerar, the new parliamentary chief of the party, and E. C. Drury, the Prime Minister of Ontario, who did not wish to confine the support of the party to agriculturists, but who wished to gather within its fold all those who subscribed to "progressive" principles. For the moment, however, this division of opinion was not pronounced; and the party was early recognised as constituting a serious threat to the supremacy, not only of the Unionist party, but hardly less of the Liberal party. When it is remembered that, in Canada, the rural constituencies outnumber the urban, the seriousness of the threat will be evident.

At the same time, there took place also a revival in strength of the Liberal party. On 17 February 1919, Sir Wilfrid Laurier died. Great as he was in personality and achievement, he had become in his later years somewhat embittered by the defeats of 1911 and 1917; but his death removed one of the greatest figures that have appeared in Canadian politics. Now the stage was set for a new and younger leader, whose appeal might be to the future rather than to the past. During the session of 1919 the Liberal leadership in the House was entrusted temporarily to D. D. McKenzie, of Cape Breton; but in the summer of 1919 a convention of the party was called at Ottawa to choose a permanent leader and to formulate a programme. There were several candidates for the leadership— W. S. Fielding, W. L. Mackenzie King, George P. Graham and D. D. McKenzie. Graham and McKenzie withdrew during the earlier stages of the balloting, and the final choice lay between Fielding and Mackenzie King. Fielding had the advantage of seniority: he had been a member of the Laurier Government in 1896. But he had given to the Unionist Government a general support during the last two years of the war, and for this reason he was not popular with the anti-conscriptionist Liberals, and especially with the French. Mackenzie King, on the other hand, had become a member of the Laurier Cabinet only in 1908. But he had the advantage of youth and vigour; he had remained faithful to Laurier during the elections of 1917; and he was the grandson of that somewhat mythical hero of the Liberal party, William Lyon Mackenzie, the "little rebel" of 1837. In the balloting Mackenzie King won the support of the Quebec votes, and he was elected leader by a small majority.

The convention—which was attended by no less than eight of the nine provincial Prime Ministers of Canada—proceeded to formulate a programme. This ran parallel in many respects to that of the Farmers' party: it pledged the Liberal party to lower tariffs, to the renewal of the reciprocity proposals of 1911, to proportional representation, and to other measures advocated by the Farmers. It lacked, however, many of the more radical features of the Farmers' platform, such as public ownership of all public utilities and the adoption of the referendum, the initiative and the recall. It contained also an expression of gratitude to the "valiant Canadian army for its splendid share in the great victory", of "devotion to the person and office of His Gracious Majesty King George the Fifth", and of "unalterable attachment to the British Empire"—expressions lacking in the pronunciamento of the agriculturists. But, even so, there were in the Liberal programme not a few rather rash promises which were a cause of embarrassment to the party when it later assumed power.

Faced with the opposition of the new Progressive party and of the reorganised and militant Liberal party, the Unionist Government seemed visibly to lose ground. It was the fate of war Governments in practically all countries to become, after the signing of peace, unpopular; and the Unionist Government in Canada was no exception to this rule. This was partly due to a natural reaction, to the restless and dissatisfied condition of men's minds; but it was due also in Canada to special causes. One of these was the continuance in peacetime of the practice, begun under the War Measures Act, of legislating by Order-in-Council; another was the semi-leaderless position of the Government during the prolonged absence of Sir Robert Borden, in 1919–20, in search of health.

Sir Robert Borden returned to Canada and resumed control of affairs in the early summer of 1920; but his health was no longer what it had been, and at a caucus held on 1 July he asked for his "honourable discharge". If ever statesman was entitled to such a discharge, it was Sir Robert Borden. During the long and painful years of the World War he had borne without murmuring unparalleled responsibilities; and now, with impaired health, he was as much justified in asking for demobilisation as the soldier who had fought in the trenches. Before submitting his resignation, however, to the Governor-General, the Duke of Devonshire, he took the precaution of ascertaining, by means of a mail vote, the views of his supporters as to his successor in the Premiership. It was understood that a majority favoured Sir Thomas White; but the latter resolutely declined the honour of forming a Government, and the choice of the party then fell on Arthur Meighen, the Minister of the Interior.

Meighen had many advantages. He was still, like Mackenzie King, a comparatively young man; the two had been fellow-students at the University of Toronto in the dying days of the nineteenth century. He was a master of parliamentary strategy, a keen and incisive speaker, and a man of high character. His chief defect was a somewhat melancholy manner and a mordant wit; and he was handicapped in Quebec by the fact that it had fallen to his lot, during the war, to introduce into Parliament the Military Service Act. He was unfortunate, at the outset, in losing the services of two of the Liberal-Unionists in the Cabinet, N. W. Rowell and A. K. Maclean, who now retired to private life; but he attacked with courage and resource the problem of forming a new Cabinet which should command the confidence of the country. In doing this, he was only moderately successful. He retained the services of Sir George Foster, Sir James Lougheed, Sir Edward Kemp, C. J. Doherty and J. D. Reid, among those Conservative-Unionists who had been members of the Cabinet of 1917, and also of Sir Henry Drayton, who had in 1919 succeeded Sir Thomas White as Minister of Finance. But among Liberal-Conservatives he was able to persuade only four to accept office—J. A. Calder, A. L. Sifton, C. C. Ballantyne and Hugh Guthrie. Only one French Canadian, moreover, entered the Cabinet, Senator Blondin. The rest of the ministers were new and comparatively untried men.

That the new Government was born under an evil star was clear to all who read the signs of politics. The tide had been flowing against the Borden regime; it now set in with redoubled force against the Meighen regime. Yet Meighen faced the situation with a stout heart. The party was reorganised, and was even rechristened—with singular infelicity—the National Liberal and Conservative party, in the vain expectation (apparently) that the new name would be a lode-star which would draw all men unto it. A new programme was formulated which, it was hoped, would be a rallying ground for moderate opinion. In this there was nothing new or startling. Emphasis was placed on the British connection, but also on Canadian autonomy; tariff revision was promised, but only after a thorough and scientific enquiry; direct taxation was advocated, but not to the exclusion of other means of raising revenue; immigration was to be encouraged, but only of settlers likely to be suitable. Inducements were held out to agriculture, to labour, to ex-service men; but these inducements were sane and reasonable. The programme was enlightened, but not spectacular. It contained nothing which the Government was not prepared to carry through to the letter. In some respects, it was merely a practical version of the policy of the Liberal and Progressive parties.

To moderate men the policies of the new Government were such as to make a strong appeal. But the times did not breed moderate men. The social unrest consequent on the war had given rise to all sorts of wild and radical ideas among even the most respectable members of society. The "man in the street" was, for the moment, off his balance. To him moderation made no appeal. Meighen made a gallant attempt to revive the fortunes of his Government; for eighteen months, indeed, he gave the country an honest, intelligent, and capable administration; but his best efforts were unavailing. By-election after by-election went against him; and by the end of 1921 the Government's majority, which had been seventy-one in 1917, had shrunk to twenty-one, with eight seats vacant.

By 1921 the thirteenth Parliament of the Dominion was approaching its legal termination; and it became necessary for the Government to submit its record to the country in a general election. The autumn of 1921 was consequently given over to a prolonged election campaign. Meighen covered the country from Regina to Halifax in a speaking tour in which he delivered over two hundred and fifty speeches, which for barbed wit and searching logic it would have been difficult to surpass. But Mackenzie King excelled him by covering the ground from Edmonton to Charlottetown, and in his speeches there was a vigour and aggressiveness which the Prime Minister perhaps lacked. It had been known that Mackenzie King was a fighter who did not use gloves; but in his electioneering campaign of 1921 he surpassed himself, as when he accused the Meighen Government of importing munitions of war into the country for warlike purposes. Crerar, the Progressive leader, did not speak so often, or in so many places, nor was his campaign so aggressive or so belligerent as that of the Liberal leader; but in many places it was just as effective.

As election day approached, it was clear that the Meighen Government was going to the polls with defeat staring it in the face. The Prime Minister made an attempt, at the last minute, to reorganise his Cabinet, in the hope of strengthening himself in Quebec and elsewhere; but his attempt merely served to illustrate the weakness of his position. At the beginning of the year he had lost by death one of the ablest of his Ministers, A. L. Sifton; and in the reorganisation he lost also Sir George Foster, C. J. Doherty, J. A. Calder, P. E. Blondin and J. D. Reid. He retained the services of Sir James Lougheed, Sir Edward Kemp, and C. C. Ballantyne; but these three men, with himself, were the only survivors of the Cabinet of 1917. Twelve of the twenty-two members of the Government were new to office, and of these there were four French Canadians without seats in the House. It is usual for a party in power to be able to appeal to the country on the ground that a Government formed by the Opposition would be a Government of untried men; but here was a Government appealing to the country which was itself composed mainly of untried men.

The elections took place on 6 December 1921; and the extent of the disaster which overtook the Meighen Government exceeded all expectations. Quebec returned, for the first time in history, a solid *bloc* of sixty-five Liberals; and every constituency in Nova Scotia and Prince Edward Island returned a Liberal. On the other hand, in the Prairie Provinces, the Progressives made an almost clean sweep. Meighen himself went down to defeat in his old constituency of Portage-la-Prairie. The only province in which the Conservatives had a majority was British Columbia; though in Ontario they had a plurality, winning thirty-seven seats, as against twenty-four for the Progressives and twenty-one for the Liberals. When the returns were in, it was found that the Liberals had captured one hundred and seventeen seats and the Progressives sixty-six, as against a total of only fifty for the Conservatives, with two seats held by Independents. In any case, Meighen was in a hopeless minority, and he lost no time in submitting his resignation to the new Governor-General, Lord Byng of Vimy. The Governor-General thereupon sent for Mackenzie King, and the Liberal leader accepted the invitation to form a Government.

The conspicuous part played by Canada in world politics during the Great War, at its termination and in the subsequent efforts for the organisation of peace, has already been described.[1] But we may note here the reactions of these events in Canadian politics.

Sir Robert Borden's fight, both at the Peace Conference and in the League of Nations, for the recognition of Canada's claims as a national unit within the British Empire was the result of considered policy. At the Imperial War Conference of 1917 he had moved a resolution asserting the "full recognition of the Dominions as autonomous nations of an Imperial Commonwealth", with "an adequate voice in foreign policy and foreign relations"; and at the very outset of the Peace Conference he had made an official statement to the effect that "the ideal of equal nationhood had impressed itself very powerfully upon the imagination of the people of the Dominions... and they are satisfied of like recognition in the greater League of Nations, to establish which the Peace Congress will forthwith bend its energies". He adopted, in fact, Sir Wilfrid Laurier's view that the British Empire was "a galaxy of free nations", and that the Canadian Cabinet were as much the advisers of His Majesty in regard to Canadian affairs as the British Cabinet were in regard to British affairs.

In the autumn of 1919 Sir Robert Borden submitted the Treaty of Versailles to the Canadian Parliament for ratification. Had the Liberal Opposition declined to vote for the ratification of the treaty on the ground that it was illiberal and impracticable, their course would have been intelligible and—as events have perhaps proved— justifiable. But they opposed its ratification, except in two or three instances, on no such grounds. They objected to ratification as unnecessary, and indeed as, in tendency, disruptive of the British Empire. "We are not a nation in the true sense of the term", objected D. D. McKenzie, the temporary leader of the party. "We are part of a great Empire of which we are proud, and we are nothing else". "We are a part of the British Empire, and I desire that we shall always remain so", exclaimed W. S. Fielding, "and I therefore regret the policy of Hon. gentlemen in pleading for separate recognition apart from the British Empire. By their demand for separate recognition apart from the British Empire they are beginning—they may not have meant it so—to break up the British Empire". That

[1] See chapter xxx.

leaders of the party of Sir Wilfrid Laurier should have advanced such views was an extraordinary illustration of the topsy-turvydom of Canadian politics when party considerations are at stake. In the sequel, the amendment offered by the Liberals was decisively negatived, and the treaty was approved. It was noticeable that Mackenzie King took no part in the fight against the ratification of the treaty; and since his accession to the leadership of the party shortly afterwards it is significant that the Liberals have never again come forward as the champions of the integrity of the British Empire against the separatist tendencies of the Conservative party.

Having established the principle that "in each Dominion the King acts only on the advice of his Ministers for that Dominion", the Government proceeded to carry this principle to its logical conclusion in regard to relations between Canada and the United States. During the Great War Canada had had a Canadian war mission at Washington, and this mission had achieved great success in obtaining for Canada United States business. In 1919 Sir Robert Borden had advanced the idea that the time was ripe for the establishment of separate representation for Canada at Washington; and Meighen, when he succeeded to the Premiership, inherited this idea. What was contemplated was not representation of a consular character, but the establishment of direct diplomatic relations. After triangular negotiations between London, Washington and Ottawa, an official statement to this effect was issued on 10 May 1920.[1]

Opposition to this proposal was expressed in the Canadian House of Commons by both Liberals and Conservatives; but the Government was able to rally a majority of the members of the House to its support, and opposition for the moment subsided. The Government's majority was, however, very small; and though an appropriation was placed in the estimates in 1921 for "Canadian representation in the United States", no representative was appointed, nor were any further steps taken. The reason given was that it had not been possible to make a suitable appointment. It remained for a Liberal Government over five years later to make the first appointment of a Canadian Minister at Washington. But the principle of the diplomatic representation of Canada at Washington was first enunciated by the Government of Sir Robert Borden, and first definitely established by the Government of Arthur Meighen.

At the Imperial War Conference of 1917 it had been recommended, that, at the earliest possible moment after the war, a special Imperial Conference should be called to deal with the constitutional relations between the various parts of the British Empire. It was hoped for a time that this Conference might be called in 1920, but it was found necessary to postpone calling it; and the Imperial Conference which was called for the summer of 1921 was understood to be a Conference

[1] See p. 733.

which might deal with anything but the constitutional question. The Constitutional Conference, in effect, was postponed *sine die*. The reasons for this were not far to seek. What had seemed logical and feasible amid the enthusiasm of the war years appeared difficult and dangerous amid the unrest and disillusionment of the years that followed. Not only in Canada, but in other Dominions as well, the fear of any rigid reorganisation of the Empire lay heavy on men's minds; and the danger of the failure of the Conference was, at the same time, too great and too serious to be contemplated. In four of the Dominions, moreover, general elections were imminent; and the representatives of these Dominions were not in a position to undertake binding agreements.

In these circumstances, the Imperial Conference of 1921 proved to be little more than a round-table discussion. As the result of pressure from Canada, amongst other reasons, Great Britain was persuaded not to renew the Japanese alliance; and out of the discussions of the Conference sprang the invitation of the President of the United States to the nations of the world to participate in the Washington Conference on disarmament, at which Canada was destined to be represented. But even in regard to the question of imperial defence the Imperial Conference came to no satisfactory or useful conclusions. Great Britain, staggering under a crushing burden of public debt, would obviously have been glad of assistance in providing for the naval and military defence of the Empire; and Australia was, apparently, willing and anxious to do her share. But Canada and South Africa, with their large French and Dutch populations, held back. Willing though the representatives of these Dominions may have been to come to the relief of the Mother Country, they knew that public opinion in their respective countries was not yet educated up to the point of accepting imperial responsibilities.

During the years 1918–21 Canada won the recognition of her status as an autonomous unit in the British Empire, and even as a unit in international politics. But she still desired to retain many of the advantages of membership in the British Empire—to avail herself on occasion, for instance, of the protection and prestige of the British navy and army, and of the services of British consular and diplomatic agents in Europe and Asia. In this there would have been nothing unusual, if Canada had at the same time shown a disposition to assist the Mother Country in carrying her heavy burden. But none of the political parties were at this time willing to espouse such a policy. A strong appeal to the pride and self-respect of Canadians might possibly have won for it considerable support in some of the provinces, and among those of the people who had some idea of what international politics meant. But in the province of Quebec, where the fear of "imperialism" had been sedulously cultivated by politicians of all parties, and in the Prairie Provinces, which were remote from the problems of world politics, the policy of contributing to the support of the British Empire had never probably a chance of success. It would have been bitterly denounced as derogating from Canada's new-born national dignity. One may regret that this was so; but political facts are stubborn things, and political parties neglect them at their peril.

In all countries the Great War was followed by a period of social and economic unrest, for which various causes were responsible. The dislocation of social and economic life which the war had brought about, and the consequent disillusionment when peace returned, were important factors; but a factor hardly less important was the triumph of communist principles in Russia during the war, and in other countries of continental Europe after the war. The labouring classes began to demand with growing insistence a share in the good things of this earth; and the fact that so many of them, during the war, had acquired a familiarity with fire-arms did not make their demand less dangerous.

In Canada, unrest began during demobilisation. While the Canadian troops were waiting in 1919 in Great Britain for transportation back to Canada, there occurred at Rhyl in Wales serious riots; and there was trouble in other camps as well. Once the Canadian troops were back in Canada, demobilisation was carried out with smoothness, and generous discharge allowances made easier the return to peace conditions. But the Rhyl riots were symptomatic of the restlessness of spirit which had infected some at least of the Canadian soldiers, and presaged no good for the future.

When trouble came, however, it was from another quarter. In the beginning of 1919 a movement obtained a foothold in Western Canada which looked toward the formation of "One Big Union" in Canada. The movement originated with the Industrial Workers of the World ("I.W.W." or—facetiously—"I won't work's"), whose headquarters were in Chicago; and its principles were pure Marxian Socialism. Its advocates were in favour of "direct action" as opposed to action by the various unions represented in the Trades and Labour Congress. The movement was frankly revolutionary, and was antagonistic to the existing labour organisations. Whether it would have obtained much support under ordinary conditions is doubtful; but, on 1 May 1919, there took place in Winnipeg a strike of the metal trades which gave the advocates of the One Big Union their opportunity.

The metal trades of Winnipeg, embracing nineteen unions, demanded of their employers the right of "collective bargaining". The employers were willing to accept this principle, but only as it was applicable to their individual shops. They were willing to negotiate with their own employees but not with a Metal Trades Council which represented all metal workers. Consequently, the metal workers "struck" on 1 May. With suspicious rapidity, the trouble spread.

On 7 May the Trades and Labour Council of Winnipeg called for a ballot on the question of a general sympathetic strike; and as a result of this ballot a general strike was called on 15 May. In the extent of this strike was seen the success of the movement toward One Big Union. Not only did the employees of private industries go on strike, but also the employees of many public services, including the firemen, the street-cleaners, the postmen, the telegraph and telephone operators, and even the police. A strike committee of five men was appointed by the Trades and Labour Council; and this committee became, to all intents and purposes, the temporary government of Winnipeg. The police and the waterworks employees, though technically on strike, were allowed to remain on duty "by permission of the strike committee"; and the moving-picture theatres were allowed to remain open. After a two-days' suspension, deliveries of milk and bread were resumed by order of the strike committee, which found that the children of strikers were suffering. But, so far as seemed feasible, an attempt was made to strangle and paralyse economic life in Winnipeg in order to assert the dominance of the labouring classes.

The strike lasted for nearly six weeks. For a time the strikers had complete control of Winnipeg, and not only suppressed the local newspapers, but attempted to censor despatches sent to newspapers elsewhere. At one time there was grave danger that the general strike would spread to other cities; and there were actually widespread "walk-outs", more or less sympathetic in nature, in Toronto, Vancouver, Edmonton, Calgary, Regina and Saskatoon. It was a critical period. Fortunately, the authorities—both Dominion, provincial and municipal—though refusing to abdicate their functions, displayed great self-restraint and moderation in dealing with the strikers. Though there were three thousand troops in barracks at Winnipeg, no attempt, fortunately, was made to crush the strike by force. It was only when the back of the strike had been broken, and the extremists among the strikers had grown desperate, that blood was shed. The strike was allowed to run its course; and the result was that revolutionists in Canada obtained a salutary lesson in the folly of attempting to browbeat the Canadian public.

Officially the general strike was called off on 26 June; but it had shown itself to be a failure long before. For this there were several causes. In the first place, the great international Labour unions, which were opposed to the One Big Union, steadfastly refused to countenance the strike; and for this reason the strikers were fortunately unable to persuade the railway employees to "down tools". Gradually, moreover, the more conservative element in the ranks of Labour began to return to work. In the second place, the authorities flatly declined to negotiate with the strikers until the general strike was called off. But the most important factor in the defeat of the strikers was the courageous and public-spirited attitude of the citizens of

Winnipeg. On 17 May a Citizens' Committee of One Thousand was organised which undertook to supply public and semi-public services. It supplied volunteers for fire-fighting, for food delivery, and, when the police force were dismissed, for police work; it forced the strike committee to withdraw the offensive "permit notices", and it undertook the publication of a newspaper, the *Citizen*. In a hundred different ways it strove successfully to counteract the strike; and if the strike failed, it was chiefly because the Citizens' Committee had demonstrated that it could not succeed. The people of Winnipeg could not be taken by the throat.

The ringleaders of the strike were arrested and tried on charges of sedition, and several of them were condemned to imprisonment in the penitentiary. The evidence adduced showed clearly that most of them had used language directly inciting to revolution; and there is no doubt that a widespread plot existed among the more extreme Labour leaders to upset the established order of things all over Canada. That the rank and file of the strikers saw whither the strike was leading is improbable; and though there continued for several months to be echoes of the disturbance, Labour men as a whole took to heart the lessons taught by the episode. Certainly, there have since then been in Canada no further outbursts of economic unrest at all comparable with that of the early summer of 1919.

Unrest, however, was not during this period confined to Labour. The farmers, as we have seen, were profoundly discontented; but their discontent found expression in political action, and in a strengthening of the organisations for the marketing of farm produce. Even the school-teachers organised in several provinces to enforce their will on unwilling school-trustees. But the most curious evidence of the prevailing unrest was seen in the movement which took place in the Canadian House of Commons itself for the abolition of titles of honour. During the later stages of the war a movement of this sort had arisen; but it had met with the opposition of Sir Robert Borden, and had temporarily died down. In 1919, however, it sprang up again with redoubled vigour; and, despite the opposition of some members of the Unionist Government, it resulted in the passing of an address praying the King that he would grant no "title of honour or titular distinction on any of your subjects...in Canada". The movement obtained the support of politicians in all parties, and was a striking illustration of the way in which the public mind was questioning all established institutions.

Beneath all the apparent unrest, however, there was a solid substratum of hard-headed common sense among the Canadian people, and a robust dislike of illegal and revolutionary methods. Within a comparatively short time, the signs of unrest had died down, and by the end of 1921 the country had returned to something resembling a normal peace basis.

CHAPTER XXXIII

CULTURAL DEVELOPMENT

(A) FRENCH

THE language of the French Canadians derives its origin from those parts of France where the purest French is spoken: the colonists almost all came from Normandy, Picardy and Aunis. True, the speech of these early settlers contained certain provincialisms; but dialect disappeared before the progress of standard French. To-day the French of Canada is the same as that of France, save only for a few archaisms and Anglicisms. But the French Canadians are jealous of their language and are continually working to free it from these faults and especially from any Anglicisms which have remained on its surface.[1]

In the seventeenth and eighteenth centuries Quebec and Montreal were centres of social life and genuine culture. As early as 1618, Marc Lescarbot, a Parisian barrister who had come to Acadia with Poutrincourt, published a volume of poems on Canadian subjects, entitled *Les Muses de la Nouvelle France*.[2] They were composed at Port Royal, where Lescarbot had founded the *Ordre du Bon Temps*, to amuse the colonists with literary diversions and scientific studies, during the long Canadian winter.[3] But it was at Quebec above all that French civilisation was to develop; and, in the first instance, through the education which young Canadians received from the colleges and convents. In 1666 we hear of the Jesuits' pupils defending literary and philosophical theses.[4] The *Lettres historiques* and *Lettres spirituelles* by Mother Marie of the Incarnation, an Ursuline nun, possess high literary value. The colonists themselves used to read, and several of them had libraries of which the bookplates have been discovered.[5] In 1664 Pierre Boucher published his *Histoire véritable de la Nouvelle France*, which has a charming *naïveté* of style. Historians of Canadian literature have omitted to speak either of Boucher or his book, on the ground that he was born in France. But if the name of Canadian can belong to one who had passed his life in Canada, had been Governor of Trois-Rivières, had founded Boucherville and had died there, then Boucher was a Canadian. Other Canadians of his

[1] See Roy, C., *Nos Origines littéraires*, p. 42; Maureau, *Dictionnaire des locutions vicieuses du Canada*; Rinfret, R., *Dictionnaire de nos fautes contre la langue française*, 1896; Lusignan, *Fautes à corriger*; Buies, A., *Anglicismes et canadienismes*, 1888; Clapin, S., *Dictionnaire canadien-français*; Caron, *Petit vocabulaire à l'usage des Canadiens-français*; *Dictionnaire des barbarismes et des solécismes les plus ordinaires de ce pays*, 1855; Blanchard, E., *En garde*, 1912.

[2] Perrier, A., 1618.   [3] Lescarbot, M., *Histoire de la Nouvelle France*, 1617.

[4] *Journal des Jésuites*, 1892.

[5] Gagnon, P., *Essai de bibliographie canadienne*, etc. (1895). One of the largest Canadian libraries in the eighteenth century belonged to Cugnet of Quebec. The inventory is in the *Archives Nationales* in Paris, under Colonies C ii A, vol. cxiv, ff. 144–204.

time had been born in France. His book was printed in Paris because under the French regime Canada had only one small printing-press, which belonged to the Bishop and was used to print his charges. The *Histoire véritable* is dated from Canada, which is enough to make it a Canadian book. Among many charming pages, it contains a lifelike eulogy of the Canadian winter. Life at Quebec, moreover, was often very courtly and polished, especially from 1750 to 1759. The refinements of society had penetrated to the manors of the country seigneurs. But this age, which saw the end of the French regime, has bequeathed us little but its songs. Some brought from France, others composed in Canada; military songs, love-songs, songs gay and melancholy, they betoken a race to which neither courage, cheerfulness nor poetry was foreign.[1]

French-Canadian political literature may be said to begin with the pamphlets which Pierre du Calvet wrote against General Haldimand, Governor of Quebec. Du Calvet was a Huguenot who had emigrated to Canada. He defended the Canadians vigorously, was thrown into prison, managed to obtain his release and went to England to defend his cause. His eloquent pamphlet, the *Appel à la Justice de l'État* (1784), gives a dark picture of life at Quebec under Haldimand's military rule. Eloquence developed after 1791, when Lower Canada received a first measure of parliamentary government. In 1792 Pierre Bédard, Antoine Panet and Joseph Papineau defended the French language in the Legislature against Richardson, the member who had proposed its abolition; and, as a result of the speech by Alain Chartier de Lotbinière on 21 January 1793, it was decided that both languages might be used in the Legislature.

The periodicals of the time contain a political literature not wanting in literary merit. Fleury-Mesplet founded the *Gazette littéraire* in 1778, with Valentin Jautard as editor.[2] It was suppressed in 1779 by General Haldimand; and Fleury-Mesplet and Jautard were arrested on account of an article by Jautard, entitled *Tant pis, tant mieux*. In 1785, Fleury-Mesplet started the *Gazette de Montréal*. In 1806 appeared the *Canadien*, founded as the organ of the French Canadians in the same way as the *Mercury* had been founded for the English Canadians. The articles are never signed, but their authors are known through a manuscript key, inserted at the end of the first volume of bound copies of the *Canadien*, which is preserved in the archives of the Seminary of Quebec.[3] After 1810 the *Canadien* was edited by Étienne Parent. The *Courrier de Québec*, founded in 1807, was more moderate. Finally De Bonne published the *Vrai Canadien*, representing the French opinion sympathetic to the English. To these orators and journalists must be added the name of L. J. Papineau, foremost

---

[1] See Barbeau, M. and Sapir, E., *Folk-Songs of French Canada*, 1926.

[2] McLachlan, R. W., "Fleury-Mesplet, the first printer at Montreal", in *Mémoires de la Société Royale*, 1906.

[3] See Roy, C., *Nos Origines littéraires*, p. 95.

French-Canadian leader in the "rebellion" of 1837, and the journalist Lemaître, who at that time directed the *Quotidienne*. These men did great service to the French language in Canada, writing and speaking it with talent and eloquence.

Despite political unrest, a concern for French culture persisted in high society. Literary clubs had been founded. At Montreal the *Gazette littéraire* had brought about the formation of a group "qui se préoccupait de devenir savant". A similar group was formed round the *Magasin de Québec* (1792). These two papers reprinted extracts from foreign literature and a few, unhappily anonymous, essays in Canadian literature. The group of the *Gazette littéraire* founded a small academy which modestly styled itself: "L'Académie naissante de Montréal". Its members held Voltairian and anticlerical views; and when Voltaire died, the *Gazette* published eulogies of the philosopher.

It is in these journals that we must look for the first essays in Canadian poetry. It was insipid enough at the outset, with its shepherds and ribbon-bedecked flocks, and was influenced by the court-poets, Bernis and Florian. The *Gazette littéraire* published fables, elegies and short poems, all anonymously. Joseph Quesnel is a good example of this light and amiable vein. Born at Saint-Malo in 1749, he had been a sailor, and in 1779 was in command of a vessel bringing arms to the American insurgents. His ship was captured by an English frigate and taken into Halifax. Quesnel settled in Canada, was naturalised and became store-keeper at Boucherville. He died in 1809. He was a musician and wrote an opera, *Lucas et Cécile*, which has been lost. The peasants in his comedy, *Colas et Colinette*, produced in 1790 at Montreal, have nothing Canadian about them. He wrote two other comedies, *L'Anglomanie ou le dîner à l'anglaise* and *Les Républicains français ou la Soirée du Cabaret*. His epistles, epigrams and songs were published in Huston's *Répertoire national* (1848–50).

Heroic poetry made its appearance with Joseph Mermet's *La Victoire de Châteauguay*, published in the Montreal *Spectateur* (25 November 1813). It enjoyed a moment of celebrity, and the drawing-rooms of Canada vied with each other in lionising the author, a lieutenant in the regiment of Watteville. The national enthusiasm had in fact been kindled by Colonel Charles M. de Salaberry's victory over the Americans in the Châteauguay woods, and Mermet gave expression to this feeling. He was born at Lyons in 1775 and lived only three years in Canada. The more peace-loving Michael Bibaud, born at Côte des Neiges near Montreal in 1782, wrote a volume of *Épîtres, Satires, Chansons, Épigrammes* (1830). A solemn classicist, without a spark of originality, he published numerous literary and political journals,[1] and composed a rather dull *Histoire du Canada* (3 vols. 1837–78). It

---

[1] *L'Aurore du Canada* (1815), *Le Courrier du Bas-Canada* (1819), *La Bibliothèque canadienne* (1825), *L'Observateur canadien* (1830), *Le Magasin du Bas-Canada* (1832), *L'Encyclopédie canadienne* (1842).

made people regret that by the impetuous Dr Labrie, of which the manuscript had been lost in the fire that destroyed the village of Saint-Benoît in 1837. Among other poets and writers of the time one may mention the magistrate Dominique Mondelet (1799–1863), whose *Chanson du Voyageur canadien* (1826) had a fair success, and who also left a *Traité sur la politique coloniale du Bas-Canada* (1835). Denis Benjamin Viger (1774–1861), one of the most energetic parliamentarians of this period, left occasional verse in periodicals, and numerous political works.[1] A. N. Morin (1803–65) owed the beginnings of his reputation to a political pamphlet, the *Lettre à l'honorable juge Bowen*. In 1826 he founded the *Minerve*. He offers less interest as a poet than Napoléon Aubin (1812–90), who published his verse in the *Fantasque*. Aubin had founded this journal in 1837, and it was responsible for his imprisonment at the time of the "rebellion". Joseph Lenoir-Rolland (1822–61) left poems which a bibliophile prepared for the press in 1916. Finally, George Etienne Cartier (1814–73) was one of the founders of the Canadian Confederation, and author of the song *Canada! mon pays! mes amours!* (1835), still famous in French Canada. The literature of this period, though not very remarkable, at least shows the presence of real culture among the French Canadians. The book-trade with France was organised in 1817, and the Canadians, who were great readers, came in contact with the romantic movement. Rousseau, Chateaubriand and Mme de Staël delighted them. In Mme de Staël they read that "les lettres fondent la liberté", and the idea pleased them.

Patriotic literature was heralded by F. X. Garneau. Born at Saint-Augustin in 1809, he studied in the notary Campbell's office at Quebec, where he was always ready to argue with his English companions. One of them told him that the French Canadians had no history. From that moment, Garneau determined to write the history of his country. In 1831 he stayed in Paris and London. D. B. Viger, whom the Canadians had sent to London to support their claims, engaged him as secretary, and Garneau found himself in a circle of Canadian patriots, like William Lyon Mackenzie, leader of the Radicals of Upper Canada, and Isidore Bédard, the representative of Quebec. Through them he made the acquaintance of Arthur Roebuck, an English M.P. who was Canadian-born and who supported the French Canadians in the Commons. These men were not without influence on his mind, and when, on his return to Canada, he began his great work, it was in a deeply liberal spirit. This *Histoire du Canada* (3 vols. 1845–8) was his great achievement, and he was still revising and correcting it in 1866 when he died. The most important contribution to the French-Canadian literature of

[1] *Considérations*, etc. (1809), *Analyse d'un entretien*, etc. (1826), *Considérations relatives à la dernière révolution de la Belgique* (1831), *Observations de l'hon. D. B. Viger contre la proposition faite dans le Conseil Législatif*, etc. (1835), *Mémoires relatifs à l'emprisonnement de l'hon. D. B. Viger* (1840), *La Crise ministérielle* (1844).

the age, it had the immense merit of creating a past for the Canadian people, of giving it a "local habitation" on this soil of America which it had cleared and made fruitful. The plan of Garneau's work is clear, the style sober. He is sometimes perhaps influenced by Michelet in his desire to write the history of the people, his ideas being very democratic. But he likes the philosophy of history, and does not limit himself to noting facts and dates. Garneau's *Histoire du Canada* had an enormous success among his fellow-countrymen, and its influence was felt on the whole of Canadian literature for more than fifty years.

Like all French Canadians, the abbé Henri Raymond Casgrain had been captivated by Garneau's book. He was an enthusiast, and something of a visionary. Born in 1831 at La Rivière-Ouelle, he had been brought up at the manor of Airvault, where tales and legends were interwoven with his education. He gathered knowledge from his father's library and read Chateaubriand with ardour. If Casgrain had the gift of making history live, he owed it to these impressionable years. Romanticism was invading Canada when he began to write, and he confesses in *Souvenances* that Romanticism exercised the greatest influence upon him. He tried to express, in his *Légendes*, the as yet dimly felt soul of Canada. Of his historical works, *Montcalm et Lévis* (1895) is written with enthusiasm; the others interest only the erudite. But his *Pélerinage au pays d'Évangéline* (1885) was crowned by the French Academy, which praised "le récit simple et clair, écrit en bon style et d'un sentiment tout français". Casgrain was above all an imaginative writer.

Several historical works have been published, which concern the specialist and possess no distinctly literary interest. One may, however, mention the abbé Ferland, who left a *Cours d'Histoire du Canada* (1861), and exercised some influence in person. He was a member of the group of the Crémazie bookshop, and one of the founders, in 1862, of the *Soirées canadiennes*. In 1863 he quarrelled with J. C. Taché and started the *Foyer canadien*. In what has been rather pompously called the "movement of 1860", he represents literary scepticism. In literature, "nous aurons ce que nous pourrons", he used to say. Mention must be made of M. Thomas Chapais' works: *L'Intendant Talon* (1905), *Montcalm* (1911), *Le Cours d'Histoire du Canada* (1919–21); of Ernest Gagnon's *Le Fort et le Château Saint-Louis* (1908) and *Louis Joliet* (1903); of Ernest Mayrand's *Frontenac et ses amis* (1903); of L. O. David's works on *Les Patriotes de 1837* (1884); and lastly of Benjamin Sulte, who has produced numerous volumes very rich and curious in historical learning.

With Philippe Aubert de Gaspé (1786–1869) it is still history, but history in the guise of anecdote and romance. Gaspé is a link between Canada under French, and Canada under British rule. He tells the history of manners at the end of the eighteenth century in his novel, *Les Anciens Canadiens* (which had first appeared in the *Soirées canadiennes*, 1862) and in his *Mémoires* (1885); works which are still the surest testimony on social life in Canada between 1763 and 1825. His novel is the story of the English conquest, it shows Canada as it appeared to him through the tales related by his father and mother. Gaspé depicts life in those colonial manors where French eighteenth-century civilisation still reigned. He shows how far removed were the Canadians of this period from the age of Indian warfare, how different was Champlain's age from that of the Marquis de Vaudreuil. Gaspé handled French with great ease and charm: he represented a refined and aristocratic Canada. The *Anciens Canadiens* enjoyed a great success: with Garneau's *Histoire du Canada*, it is the most popular book in French-Canadian literature.

In 1866 Napoléon Bourassa produced an Acadian novel, *Jacques et Marie*, which lacks any salient qualities. Joseph Marmette, Garneau's son-in-law, wished to "popularise by dramatising" the heroic part of the *Histoire du Canada*. To him we owe novels like *François de Bienville* and *Récits et Souvenirs* (1891). P. J. O. Chauveau (1820–90) wrote an uninteresting novel, *Charles Guérin*, and tales in verse—very bad verse—entitled *Souvenirs et Légendes* (1877). Antoine Gérin-Lajoie (1824–82) published in the *Soirées canadiennes* in 1862 his *Jean Rivard le défricheur*, and wrote a sequel called *Jean Rivard économiste* (1876). It is anything but a novel. Gérin-Lajoie thought it necessary to put his ideas on agriculture into novel-form, and *Jean Rivard* was written mainly to urge the French Canadians to remain on their farms. It contains thoughts such as the following, which summarises the book: *L'Agriculture est la mère de la prospérité nationale*. Less known, but far superior is John Lespérance's novel *Les Bostonnais* (1896). Laure Conan (Mlle Félicité Angers) first introduced the novel of analysis with *L'Oublié* and especially with *Angéline de Montbrun* (1881). In the very different genre of the newspaper-serial, Georges de Boucherville wrote a novel called *Une de perdue, deux de retrouvées*, a dramatic narrative revealing great powers of imagination.

Garneau's work had given such impetus to patriotism that all the poets in Canada were touched with national fervour. The best of this cycle of patriotic poetry is in Crémazie and Fréchette. These two poets rewrote the history of Canada; they put Garneau's book into verse. The house of Crémazie, who was a bookseller in Quebec, was the centre of a group of literary men. Crémazie (b. 1827) had read so much and so omnivorously that he was influenced excessively by his books. His work is contained in a single volume entitled: *Œuvres complètes d'Octave Crémazie*, published by the Canadian Institute of Quebec (1882). He had passed through a poetical period in which all the trash of Romanticism had served to compose his verses. It was Rome, Venice, Sorrento, Cordova and Milan which inspired this son of Quebec. Through Garneau he discovered Canada. In

1855 the visit of the French corvette, *La Capricieuse*, commanded by Captain de Belvèze, moved him deeply. The *Chant du vieux soldat canadien*, composed on this occasion, has remained famous; it has real eloquence and pathos, and it expresses one of the great feelings of the French Canadians, their love for France. Crémazie has, moreover, put into his poetry all that the Canadian soul revered with fervour at the time. He has sung of the missionaries, of the soldiers of the Papacy, of Catholicism. This harmony between his poetry and the sentiments of the French Canadians made him their national bard. But the scholar-poet was unsuccessful in business. He was obliged to live in exile in France, and died at Le Hâvre in 1879. From Paris he corresponded with the abbé Casgrain, and his letters, written in a clear and precise style, are of the greatest interest. They contain critical appreciations on Canadian literature. They have been collected in the *Œuvres complètes*.

The movement of which Crémazie's shop was the centre and Garneau's *Histoire du Canada* the guiding influence had been followed up by a young man named Louis Fréchette who, while studying law, was beginning to write poetry. Fréchette (b. 1839) became fascinated with literature in Crémazie's book-store. The result was a volume of verse, *Mes Loisirs* (1863), which had no success. Fréchette was writing for the *Journal de Lévis*, but his Liberalism led him to abandon it, and he went to Chicago where he founded *L'Observateur* (1866) and *L'Amérique* (1868–71). These papers were read by the French-Canadian colony, numerous at that time in Chicago. Fréchette held advanced views and was violent. In *La Voix d'un exilé* (1867) he showed that Victor Hugo was no stranger to him: in his poetry he demanded social reform. Returning to Canada, he sat from 1874 to 1878 on the benches of the Liberal Opposition in the Federal Parliament. In 1877 he published *Pêle-Mêle*, with which began his reputation. But it was *Fleurs boréales et Oiseaux de neige* (1880) that revealed him as a poet. When the French Academy crowned this volume, enthusiasm in Canada knew no bounds. *La Légende d'un peuple*, which appeared in Paris in 1887, also had a great success in Canada. But *Feuilles volantes* (1891) met with general indifference, and this deeply affected the poet. Violent attacks were launched against him, and he had to engage in polemics, especially with the poet Chapman. All this distressed him. His last volume, *Épaves poétiques*, appeared in 1908, the year of his death. Fréchette's verses sometimes possess greatness, but his taste for eloquence makes them turgid. He is too often inspired by indignation; he loves dramatic scenes. But Canadian manners and Canadian landscapes have inspired the poems of *Fleurs boréales* and *Feuilles volantes* with their imagery and harmony: it is here that his best poetry must be sought. His influence in Canada was great. He had introduced verbal romanticism, and the young poets long recognised him as their master.

A more modest fame fell to Pamphile Lemay (b. 1837), author of *Les Vengeances* and *Les Gouttelettes*: his gifts are for personal poetry. Basile Routhier (b. 1839), Judge of the High Court of Quebec, Knight Bachelor in 1911, has written *Les Échos* (1882), a volume of verse containing the national song of French Canada. Among other poets are Napoléon Legendre (1841–1907), Adolphe Poisson (b. 1849) and William Chapman, descended from a secretary of the Governor Sir George Prévost, and on his mother's side from the secretary of the Marquis de Tracy. His poetry is grandiloquent and redundant. But the best work of Fréchette's school is to be found in Nérée Beauchemin (b. 1850), whose *Floraisons matutinales* (1897) contains the famous poem *La Cloche de Louisbourg*. Finally Eudore Évanturel (1854–1919), who was the historian Parkman's secretary, has left a charming and little-known volume of verse: *Premières Poésies* (1878).

In the meantime, an art had been born, a little outside literature, or at least without literary pretensions. Gaspé had written popular tales, and may be considered as the creator of the genre in Canada. These stories are to be found only in certain journals, such as the *Soirées canadiennes*, *L'Opinion publique*, *Le Foyer canadien* and *L'Almanach du Peuple*. But Louis Fréchette was the master of the popular tale. Like Gaspé's, his stories are scattered in periodicals; but there is a collected volume, *La Noël au Canada* (1900); and *Originaux et Détraqués* is in the same vein. In *Forestiers et Voyageurs*, J. C. Taché (1821–95) created the popular type of the old trapper. Faucher de Saint-Maurice (1844–97) has also left a few tales among his essays and reminiscences of travel: *À la Brunante*, *De tribord à babord*, *Choses et autres*. He is picturesque but uneven. H. Beaugrand (b. 1848) published *La Chasse Galerie* (1899), one of the best collections of popular tales. He was also the founder of the journal *La Patrie*. In the enclosed, sentimental garden of Canadian literature there is yet a sunny corner where this vigorous plant has sprung up and flourished; and it is perhaps in these little stories that the best of French-Canadian literature is to be found.

In Montreal a movement had grown up around the library of the Canadian Institute. Founded in 1844, the Institute had had as its first presidents: A. C. Nelson (1844), Antoine Gérin-Lajoie (1845), J. Huston (1847), Francis Cassidy (1850), Joseph Doutre (1853) and Richard La Frenaie (1854). There were more than seven hundred members. The library possessed 4000 volumes in 1852 and the reading-room placed at the public disposal over one hundred papers. Occupying its own building, in the Rue Notre-Dame, the Canadian Institute became a centre of literary and scientific studies. Gifts were made to it in the form of books, maps, portraits, etc. A member of Parliament, Pierre Boucher de Boucherville, founded a literary prize. At fixed dates lectures were given, and there was a public course of lectures on history and literature. All this attracted a great many people. There were plans for establishing a museum, and Guillaume Barthe, who had been in Paris for many years past, acted as intermediary between the Canadian Institute and the learned societies of France. Already the Institute of France had made a present of two hundred volumes. Barthe was to receive mouldings and copies of works of art from French museums. Prince Napoleon Bonaparte, who had visited Canada and been received at the Canadian Institute, offered to send books. And in 1852 R. La Frenaie was able to say in his presidential address: "Thanks to the work of the Canadian Institute, the majority of our fellow-countrymen have been kept in touch with all the great mechanical, scientific or literary discoveries made in Europe or America, and have not remained strangers to the great questions which occupy the nations of to-day". But the Montreal clergy were afraid of the advanced views and liberal spirit of the Institute. Papineau belonged to it, and there were others whose ideas were suspect to the Bishop of Montreal. Many of the members had been involved in the affair of 1837, and this gave the society a vague odour of rebellion. Mgr Bourget fulminated interdicts against the library and the whole of the Institute, and so started a long quarrel. The Institute numbered men of great worth among its members. Etienne Parent, Gérin-Lajoie, Lusignan, Morin, Blanchet, Dorion, Lanctot, Arthur Buies, Wilfrid Laurier, L. A. Dessaules, president of the Institute in 1862, and especially Joseph Doutre, all joined issue with the Bishop. But the unfortunate Guibord case (1869) dealt the last blow to the Canadian Institute, which was dissolved in 1874. The library was dispersed.

From the literary point of view, no work of real importance had come from the Institute. *Les Fiancés de* 1812 is a rather weak novelette by Joseph Doutre, who had become the Institute's first laureate by winning the *Prix Boucherville*. Guillaume Barthe, who also belonged to the movement, lived for over thirty years in Paris. It was here, in 1855, that he published *Le Canada reconquis par la France* and *Souvenirs d'un demi-siècle*. He had made his début in 1837 by a poem against Lord Durham, *Les Exilés politiques*, published in Napoléon Aubin's paper, *Le Fantasque*. Barthe returned to Canada, where he died in 1893. Finally there was Arthur Buies who wrote brilliant *chroniques* in the Liberal papers of the time, and had begun by attacking the Catholic clergy. He then, however, became interested in colonial matters, and he devoted some moving pages to the curé Labelle, apostle of colonisation. His books on *Le Saguenay, L'Outaouais supérieur, La Matapédia* and *Le Portique des Laurentides* were written to reveal the beauty of Canada and to dissuade French Canadians from emigrating to the United States.

The various literary movements of French Canada had always had one or two guiding ideas, political or patriotic; but literary form, art for art's sake, had never been the sole aim of poet or prose-writer.

Towards 1895 a few young men of Montreal, who were fond of literature, founded a cenacle which they called the *École Littéraire*. Its one object was literature. In the manifesto of Wilfrid Larose, the president, we read that only literature interests him. "La littérature d'un peuple, c'est le résumé de ce qu'il signifie... Nous travaillerons donc d'un commun accord à développer la nôtre".[1] The great ambition of these young men was to put life into French-Canadian literature, which they judged a little dull. The leader of the school was Jean Charbonneau (b. 1875), who only published his first collection of poems, *Les Blessures*, in 1912 (Paris), and *L'Age de sang* quite recently. He is a disciple of the French Parnassians. M. Gonsalve Desaulniers figured as the doyen of these poets: his verses, very French in feeling, have not been published collectively.

The first meetings of the *École Littéraire* were held in the drawing-room of the Montigny family. Louvigny de Montigny and his brother Gaston were among the most fervent adepts of the movement. The verses and *chroniques* of Gaston de Montigny must be sought in the papers to which he contributed: *Le Journal*, *Les Débats*, *Le Pionnier*, and *Le Nationaliste*. M. Louvigny de Montigny has published a book on *La langue française au Canada*, and edited the Canadian edition of *Maria Chapdelaine* (1916). At the Montignys', too, one might see Joseph Melançon (b. 1877) who, under the pseudonym of Lucien Rainier, has published verses in *Le Nationaliste*, *Le Devoir* and *La Revue canadienne*; Gustave Comte, chronicler and journalist; Germain Beaulieu (b. 1870) whose verses appeared in *Le Terroir* (1909); Paul de Martigny, one of the founders of *Les Débats*; Albert Laberge, who has written a curious "regionalist" novel, *La Scouine*; E. Z. Massicotte (b. 1867) whose verses have not been collected and who has published only works of historical erudition; and Henri Desjardins (1874–1907), founder of an ephemeral paper, *La Voix du peuple* (1904). The members of the *École Littéraire* had in fact become too numerous for the Montigny drawing-room, and the elder M. de Montigny, who was Recorder of Montreal, lent the key of the Court-house to his sons' friends. In these precincts where the old Recorder "jugeait chaque matin les escarpes et les soulots... se tenaient les assises de l'idée; les rimes voletaient dans la salle où avaient retenti les objurgations et les amendes; et sur le siège du magistrat, la Poésie trônait, en gilet et en toque, dans la personne de Charles Gill".[2] The *École Littéraire* held its public meetings at the Château de Ramezay, once the palace of the French Governors and now converted into a historical museum. Louis Fréchette was called to preside over these assemblies which enjoyed a moment of fame in Montreal society. The *École Littéraire* produced a book entitled *Les Soirées du Château de Ramezay*, which is a sort of anthology of the movement. Charles Gill was one of the

---

[1] *Soirées du Château de Ramezay*, par l'École Littéraire de Montréal, p. xiii.
[2] Dantin, L., *Émile Nelligan et son Œuvre*, p. xxx.

most picturesque of these poets. He had lived in Paris, had studied
painting in Jérôme's studio and frequented the literary cafés; all this
gave him great prestige among the young poets of Montreal. His
work was collected and published after his death under the title
of *Le Cap Éternité* (1919). Albert Ferland (b. 1872) has written verses
of tender melancholy: *Mélodies poétiques* (1893), *Femmes rêvées* (1899)
and *Le Canada chanté* (1908); Hector Demers (1878–1917) has given
us *Les Voix champêtres* (1912). But two poets of the group, Émile
Nelligan and Albert Lozeau, have won renown in French Canada.
The son of an Irishman and a French Canadian, Nelligan is an
engaging figure. He was born in Montreal in 1882 and led the
Bohemian life as he imagined it was led in Paris. His great ambition
indeed was to go to Paris and have his verses printed there. He had
a complete contempt for everyday existence and its prosaic necessities. But he abandoned himself to melancholy, and this, complicated by his excesses, led to complete madness. Nevertheless he
has written some of the finest poems of which the French language
can boast in Canada. They have been collected by Louis Dantin in
Émile Nelligan et son Œuvre. What distinguishes his verses is their
profound originality; if at times one can detect in them influences
like that of Rodenbach, certain of his poems reveal a genius already
master of its thought and form: such are *Devant le feu*, *Clair de lune
intellectuel*, *Le Vaisseau d'or* and that tragic *Romance du vin*, which is
wonderfully moving. Albert Lozeau (b. 1878) has left several volumes
of poetry: *L'Âme solitaire* (1907); *Le Miroir des jours* (1912); *Lauriers et
feuilles d'érable* (1916). He possessed nothing like Nelligan's genius,
but his verses have a gentle and melancholy charm. He was a
cripple and round his long invalid's chair a small literary movement
had grown up. It must be observed that the *École Littéraire* was
almost entirely a poetical group, and produced no prose-writer of
interest.

Amédée Denault, founder of *Le Glaneur*, *L'Écrin littéraire* and *La
Croix*, has written *Lueurs d'aurore* (1893); Alphonse Beauregard (b.
1881), *Les Forces* (1912). Louis Joseph Doucet (b. 1874) has given us
La Chanson du passant (1908), *La Jonchée nouvelle* (1910), *Ode au Christ*
(1910), etc.; Albert Dreux (b. 1887) is the author of *Les Soirs* (1910).

This period also counts a few great journalists. J. Israel Tarte,
director of the Montreal *Patrie*, for which he wrote clear and vigorous
articles, has published a curious book entitled *Autour d'une carrière, 1880–
1897* (1897). We would also mention Paul Tardivel, a Catholic journalist and director of the Quebec *Vérité*; Godefroy Langlois; and Fernand
Rinfret, director of the Montreal *Canada*. Henri Bourassa, director of
the *Devoir*, has published several brochures of nationalist propaganda;
La Presse catholique et nationale is one of the most interesting. Olivar
Asselin was director of *Le Nationaliste*: of his manner one can judge
from the ironical *Souvenirs politiques de M. C. Langelier* (1909). Jules

Fournier (1884–1918) collaborated in *Le Nationaliste* and *Le Devoir* and directed *L'Action* (1911–16). With a vivid and original mind, he was a writer of the first rank and a judicious critic. His best work has been collected under the title of *Mon Encrier*.

Amongst women who have contributed to literature an interesting writer is Mme R. Dandurant, daughter of Gabriel Marchand and directress of the review *Le Coin du feu*. She has written *Contes de Noël* (1889) and *Nos Travers* (1901). Françoise (Mlle Robertine Barry) directs the *Journal de Françoise*, and has published *Fleurs champêtres* (1895). Mme Huguenin, under the pseudonym of Madeleine, is directress of the *Revue moderne*, and has written *Premier péché* and *Tout le long du chemin*. Michelle Le Normand (pseudonym of Mme Léo Paul Desrosiers) is the author of a novel, *Autour de la maison*, which is a charming and talented autobiography.

Essayists, historians and critics have a limited public. M. Édouard Montpetit, the economist, is secretary of the University of Montreal and a writer well known to French-Canadian readers. He is a member of the Belgian Academy and has published an essay entitled *Au Service de la tradition française*. The abbés Émile Chartier and Camille Roy are critics and historians of literature. The abbé Chartier has published *Pages de combat*. The abbé Roy, in *Nos Origines littéraires*, has written some remarkable studies on Canadian Letters. His last book is called *Les Érables en fleurs*. To Edmond de Nevers we owe a curious work entitled *L'Avenir du peuple canadien-français*; to Errol Bouchette, *L'Indépendance économique du Canada français* (1906). The abbé Lionel Groulx has written a book on *La Confédération canadienne* in good, clear French. M. Gustave Lanctot has published an admirably concise and living study on *F. X. Garneau*.

The single novelist of this period, M. Ernest Choquette, is the author of *Claude Paysan*, *Les Ribaud* and *La Terre*, novels of peasant-life in which the influences of Pierre Loti and René Bazin are visible. But M. Choquette was only the precursor of the École du Terroir. Under the patronage of *Le Devoir* and the review *L'Action française*, this well-intentioned movement has produced some interesting books, but too many that are stupid and wearisome. Engelbert Gallèze, Mlle Blanche Lamontagne and M. Alphonse Desislets are the best known poets of the movement. In this vein, M. Lionel Groulx has written the tales entitled *Les Rapaillages*, and M. Adjutor Rivard has given us *Chez nous* (1919). The appearance of *Maria Chapdelaine* confirmed the theories of the École du Terroir, which require Canadian writers and poets to restrict themselves to Canadian subjects. True, Marcel Dugas, in an article in *Le Nigog* (August 1918), showed that *Maria Chapdelaine* was an exotic work because its author, Louis Hémon, was a Breton who had passed only two or three years in Canada. Moreover, poets like Paul Morin (b. 1887) with *Le Paon d'émail* (1911); René Chopin (b. 1885) with *Le Cœur en exil* (1913);

Guy Delahaye (b. 1888) with *Les Phases* (1910); and Marcel Dugas with *Feux de Bengale à Verlaine glorieux*, *Versions* (1917) and *Apologies* (1919), all showed that independently of any "regionalism" one could be a good poet and a good writer. For the quarrel between the "regionalists" and the partisans of liberty in the choice of a subject, the pages of *Le Nigog* provided a duelling-ground. *Le Nigog* was a review of art and literature in which Léo Pol Morin published remarkable articles on music and F. Préfontaine studies on the plastic arts. This movement was created by a number of young men with an enthusiasm for liberty in art and letters, and it has been most useful. It caused much talk in Montreal in 1918; the abbé Olivier Maurault spoke of its results in a lecture on "regionalism" which he gave at the Institute of Ottawa in March 1920. "Les deux camps [he said] se saluèrent avec une certaine élégance". This campaign breathed a little movement into the literary life of French Canada.

We have now reached a period so recent that its results cannot yet be appreciated. What will be the future of French-Canadian literature? Dominated wholly by the literature of France, French-Canadian writers have not yet discovered their true originality. But one can well imagine a literature freed from any servile imitation and from any puerile "regionalism". Its character would be unequivocally Canadian, and its writers would bring into French literature a new element that might be called French Americanism.

Turning to the sphere of education, we note that, even from the time of the foundation of Quebec and Montreal, the anxiety for intellectual culture was evident. The *Jesuit Relations* reveal a touching desire for the real training of a people acquiring for themselves a new motherland. From 1635, the primary school and classical college are to be found in Quebec. That is the period when the New Englanders were laying the foundations of what was later to be Harvard University. The two civilisations are thus found to be at one in supporting education and linking with it their respective traditions. Later, at Montreal, the Sulpicians, soon after their arrival, gave their energetic attention to teaching. These are essential and illuminating facts which disclose the inner spirit of this first outlook on life in Canada and help us to discount the all too sweeping accusations of ignorance sometimes hurled at French Canadians of the past.

Recent historical research has traced out the geographical extension of education from 1635 to 1750; the movement accompanies closely the clearing of the land, and not infrequently the parish begins with the school. By the year 1750 there were fifteen primary schools for boys in the district of Quebec, ten at Montreal, seven at Three Rivers. In all Canada there were fifteen houses of education for girls under the direction of the Ursulines, the

Hospitallers, and the sisters of the Congregation of Notre-Dame founded by Marguerite Bourgeoys.[1] At Quebec there was a classical college and seminary, at Montreal the nucleus of a secondary school under the Jesuits. Even more striking was the provision for professional training. There were schools of hydrography and mathematics at Quebec and Montreal; schools of arts and crafts attached to the seminaries of Quebec and of St Joachim, and a similar effort at Montreal under the brothers Charon.

To meet the needs even of rudimentary education in that land of immense distances was a Herculean task. There were, naturally, outposts to which education could not reach, and this meant an inevitable renunciation of ideals. To supply, however, the education projected, there were, first, parish-priests who were teachers. Next there were sons of families settled in French Canada who took up school-mastering as a calling. Thirdly, there were itinerant teachers who visited scattered settlements and homes. Nor was private enterprise in several forms lacking as an adjunct to the established school system. There is indeed, on this point, ample indication of persistent co-operation and interest, a manifestation of that zeal for an educated life which affected in turn every class of society. The clergy, doubtless, were the great instigators; innumerable are the proofs which history records, revealing religious men and women busy at educational work. Ever since the first Recollet Fathers taught to savages the primary notions of French colonisation, effort of this kind never slackened. Monseigneur de Laval, first bishop of Quebec, was an educator and has had many followers. The administrative authorities begged on behalf of the Quebec Seminary, the professional and primary schools, help which the French monarchy did not always grant. Nor were those of the people at large who possessed some degree of culture indifferent. Many voices were joined to the cry of those who directed the colony's welfare in this matter; often, indeed, they were in advance of administrative opinion, and out of their own slender resources many people provided means for aiding the admirable work of the religious.

Though all was not perfect in so young and struggling a colony, yet it is necessary to insist on the above facts as a protest against certain historians who, commenting on accounts of travellers and administrators, have maintained that French Canada had no intellectual life. For schools existed; education in French Canada was real, and it worked. It transmitted to the people a French outlook on life, aided by a uniform language—French—the heritage of all; and, indeed, this systematic teaching of true French was the sole means of bringing about a common life which the patois of the provinces of old France would only have tended to disintegrate. The curriculum of the primary schools had the traditional simplicity: reading, writing

---

[1] Gosselin, A. (L'Abbé), *Education in Canada under the French Regime* (App.).

and arithmetic, and it sufficed for so small a population. The classical education kept closely to that of old France; while the more technical training prepared artisans, traders, sailors and discoverers for their calling. French-trained teachers coming into Canada brought with them special methods, and, above all, an unsurpassed discipline. All these influences contributed towards the unification of habits of life into a whole well-rounded culture at once French and yet Canadian. How vigorous and intense that culture was may be gleaned from the fact that the nation continued to live by it even after the fortunes of war in 1760 brought a definite separation from that old France whence it had been derived.

The conquest plunged the colony into difficult political problems, which were further complicated by the American Revolution. The evolution of Canadian institutions reflected the political troubles of the time. Down to 1824 the educational proposals of the Government were unacceptable to the great majority of French Canadians; and this fact tended to isolate the natural educational leaders from the political leaders. It would be a mistake, however, to regard this separation as a sign of irreconcileability. The abstention was demanded in some measure to protect the fixed resolve of those who were concerned to lose nothing of their national and religious traits. We can easily furnish proofs, moreover, of a real desire of the French in Canada to carry on more efficiently the work of education begun under the old regime. In 1801 the Government, under a change of policy, created the Royal Institution for the progress of education and the fostering of teaching under official guidance. Mgr Plessis, bishop of Quebec, immediately put on record his desire to co-operate, proposing, however, that the Institute should be duplicated and organised on a distinction of religion and language between the two sections. These ideas were not realised until much later; but their fruitfulness is well known to-day. In 1824 and again in 1829, when the laws authorised parochial or district schools, the clergy, although not finding in them all the advantages they desired, accepted them none the less for the good which they could and did accomplish. Besides, during that period of non-co-operation in the Government's educational projects, new schools were established, namely in Montreal; the presbyteries served again as schools and the travelling teachers pursued throughout the province their generous mission. After several tentative efforts[1] the situation was set right under the Union, when in 1846 decentralisation was agreed upon as the best and most promising policy. That initial cell, the parish, came at last into its own. Each parish, henceforth, had its independent school committee, directed solely by a superintendent. The parish school was restored to its parent religious and social stem and became "confessional" in fact by the presence of the curé on its committee. This basic

[1] Roy, E. M. (Father), *The Formation of the Educational System of French Canada.*

principle has never since been abandoned in the case of the Catholic elementary schools of Quebec. Thenceforth progress has taken place in every direction. A few years later, fuller educational machinery was supplied by the establishment of normal schools and a Council of Public Instruction for the province. On this council sat both Catholics and Protestants in proportionate numbers, and thus took place of necessity an open realisation of separateness where religious matters are concerned, just as Mgr Plessis had advocated years before.

Confederation crowned that principle by recognising the autonomy of the provinces in all matters affecting education. The Province of Quebec, henceforth, was free to initiate or to improve its educational machinery in its own way; and primary education has remained entirely faithful to its old "confessional" type as well as sharing fully in the spirit of the new constitution. In the management of the public schools power rests in the hands of a Council of Public Instruction, comprising two independent committees, Catholic and Protestant. The school commissions elected by the people express in the same way a scrupulous regard for religious beliefs. Under the direction of the Council, these local commissions nominate the teachers and concern themselves directly with the administration and welfare of the schools. This constitutes an educational regime of full liberty and mutual understanding to which, perhaps, full justice and sufficient homage have not yet been paid by public opinion.

From that time when, following immediately on confederation, the bitterness of political life steadily lessened and reforms revealed themselves in so many directions, the advance of education in Quebec has been continuous. There are to-day within its borders 7000 primary schools educating one-fifth of the population in English and French, history, geography, the elements of arithmetic and such sciences as are deemed necessary. There are also fifteen normal schools for the training of teachers.

In the light of these facts we can measure somewhat faithfully the amplitude of Quebec's contribution to the common life of the Dominion.

Outside the domain of the public educational system there is yet another evidence of educational zeal and interest in the foundation and maintenance—without state assistance—of an imposing array of classical colleges. After 1760 the Seminary of Quebec replaced the old college of the Jesuits. Afterwards in the height of those educational struggles when the people saw many of their traditions in peril, classical colleges were formed at Montreal, Nicolet, St Hyacinth, St Therese, St Anne de la Pocatière, l'Assomption, and elsewhere, which aimed to train an élite, particularly men who would ultimately engage in public life. Later on, as population increased, religious communities multiplied and other types of colleges were created in increasing numbers. At Montreal, under the care of the sisters of the Congregation of Notre-Dame, there is a large institution for the education of girls and the training of young women for the teaching profession. In few institutions of this kind, perhaps, have older and hallowed ideals been more closely wedded to the needs of to-day.

In all there are twenty-one classical colleges in the province. These institutions are especially noteworthy because they have jealously preserved for the Dominion so many characteristics of the colleges of old France, their models. The course of instruction is spread over eight years, six of which are allotted to the study of "letters"— Latin and Greek, both being obligatory—while English, French, history, geography and mathematics are included. The remaining two years are devoted to philosophy and the natural sciences. Still characterised by the principles of the old *Ratio Studiorum,* these colleges remain, in the midst of a world engrossed in practical matters, devotedly attached to a system which lays stress on general culture of a wide character.

University education by the logic of interior forces has developed independently of state control. In 1852 Laval University was founded at Quebec as a necessary development long desired. In 1876 a branch was organised at Montreal but became independent in 1919–20 under the name of the "Université de Montréal". To these two universities are affiliated the classical colleges which form their Faculties of Arts, and give them valuable points of contact throughout the province. The French-Canadian student, therefore, makes his "Humanity" at the classical college which corresponds to the American "college course"—taking his baccalaureate at about the age of twenty-one (after eight years of preparation). He then passes into the University for his professional training. This French type of higher education is unique in America, and gives, as it has ever desired to do, a special "formation" to an "élite".

While the French universities of Canada strictly speaking confined themselves to the four fundamental faculties of theology, law, medicine and arts, educated French Canadians have also given themselves to the wider public profession of service to the State. Further, when economic expansion opened up new fields of energy, technical training began and extended rapidly. Civil engineering, beaux-arts, industry, commerce, agriculture and similar avenues are now open to all who seek them. The more practical activities typical of North American life are thus provided for, without however renouncing the older scheme built on a desire for general culture. In several directions the province of Quebec has thrown itself heartily into enterprises of this kind, notably in 1907 when the school of higher commercial studies was founded at Montreal by the provincial Government. This and excellent technical colleges in the same city are undoubtedly models of their kind. Scholarships have also been founded for the furtherance of graduate studies and research abroad. The provincial Government by recent legislation, aided by different associations, sends each year to Europe or to the United States about twenty students of French-Canadian origin. Besides these, others go for similar purposes at their own charges. On their return many take up teaching of various kinds, and in fact at the present time almost half the Faculties in the French universities have been trained abroad.

The French group in Canada, so restricted in numbers on the morrow of the conquest, has survived and multiplied itself many times. It joins to its French characteristics—which include a filial affection to the land of its origin—a loyal attachment to the British Crown of which indeed it forms a powerful bulwark. In addition it flings against the encroachments of "Americanisation" the full force of energetic traditions. It has given proof many times of such virtues as courage, endurance and forethought. It has surmounted great difficulties and at times submitted chivalrously to reverses. It perseveres to contribute to the Dominion and to the British Empire a vigorous element of diversity in unity. Alone on the American continent it remains the guardian of that French civilisation to whose beauty the whole world is willing to bear witness.

(B) ENGLISH

To understand the development and character of the English-speaking portion of the Canadian people, we must take account of several factors which differentiate them from their kinsfolk across the sea. They live in a country of vast size and of varying economic conditions; within a century and a half all the provinces have gone through, and fringes of most are still in, the stage of the pioneer; they are an old people in a new environment which has modified the type. Those of the earliest stock are sprung from the English who came to the continent three centuries ago, and are as genuinely American as the New Englander or the Virginian; but they adopted from their French compatriots the term Canadian to signify a nationality in allegiance to the British throne; and without shadow of hesitation they have kept separate from, though of necessity they have been brought under the influence of, their powerful neighbour.

During the nineteenth century that neighbour itself underwent the experience of self-realisation through domestic war, the reception of diversified European immigration in unprecedented volume, and the rapid occupation of rich areas of territory. Until recently the United States had an established culture only along its eastern seaboard, and Canada on most of its frontier was faced by a civilisation unrestrained and dominated by the desire for material success. For spiritual ideals it had to look chiefly across the ocean, where rapid change, political and intellectual, was passing over the scene. From afar the echoing clash of old and new reached the scattered settlements; but on the outer rim of western civilisation, Canada, engrossed in supplying its primary wants, was less agitated by new ideas than determined to fashion its own democracy, with the result that to-day the English-speaking Canadian has a distinctive individuality. The cultural development of Canada may be dealt with in two periods separated by the confederation of the provinces as the Dominion in 1867. Before that event its phases were provincial: since then it has been shaping into a congruent whole.

For the present purpose the only two English-speaking sections of British North America to be considered are Upper Canada, with a small portion of Lower Canada, and the Maritime Provinces. They were not in pre-federation days so unequal, even in population, as they have since become, and in respect of culture the latter fully held their own with the Canadas. The Maritime Provinces, as they were the earliest to be developed, will be dealt with first.

What is commonly called the Annapolis valley in Nova Scotia is the oldest English-speaking region in the Dominion. Its farm lands, vacated by the expulsion of the Acadians in 1755, were occupied by settlers from New England, and this American element was reinforced both in the valley and in the near-lying portions of Nova Scotia and New Brunswick by a large inflow of Loyalists in 1783. Shortly before this immigrants from Scotland, the north of Ireland and in a lesser degree from England had begun to occupy other parts of the province, but by the time of confederation (1867) this inflow had practically ceased. Among the Loyalists were many families of good breeding drawn from the educated circles of the American colonies, who gave a character to such towns as Windsor, Annapolis Royal, Saint John and Fredericton; also since 1749 there had been in Halifax a succession of naval and military officers and officials who formed the *entourage* of the provincial Governors. There is, therefore, perhaps ground for the opinion that "in 1815 the society of Halifax and Quebec was as refined as that of Boston and Philadelphia".[1]

Appreciating the advantages of education these people took steps soon after their arrival to provide for the instruction of their sons. In 1780 the Government had offered £100 for the salary of the principal of a high school at Halifax, and, whenever there should be an attendance of forty pupils, £60 for that of an assistant. At Windsor and Fredericton academies soon followed, out of the former of which came King's College in 1790, the first colonial university to receive a charter after the American Revolution, and the earliest of the three King's Colleges of the British American provinces, the others being

---

[1] Baker, R. P., *A History of English-Canadian Literature to the Confederation*, p. 55. Cf. Chittick, V. L. O., *Thomas C. Haliburton*, pp. 20, 43.

at Toronto (1827) and Fredericton (1828). They were all supported by the state, but their old-world charters perpetuated in the young provinces the privileges of those who belonged to the Church of England as by law established. And chiefly for this reason they had stormy careers. Professing to promote loyalty, they fomented political discontent. The staff of King's College, Windsor, consisted of Anglican clergymen from English universities who endeavoured to mould the rising members of the governing classes in the principles of what they regarded as a liberal education. King's College, Fredericton (since 1860 the University of New Brunswick),[1] owed its origin to graduates of Harvard and other American colleges, but its type of teaching was the same as in Windsor, until Sir Howard Douglas (1823–31) raised what was virtually an academy to the status of a university with unusual freedom from ecclesiastical control.[2] By the middle of the nineteenth century two professors from Scotland, Dr Brydone-Jack and Dr Robb, brought to the province some of the scientific spirit that was stirring the Old Land.

The overwhelming majority of the people of the Maritime Provinces, however, was not connected with the Church of England. In the earliest immigration, and later among the Loyalists, were Congregationalist ministers, of whom there were in 1770 four Harvard graduates. These stimulated the education of their people. The settlers in central and eastern Nova Scotia were served by earnest clergymen from Scotland. Early in the nineteenth century Dr Thomas McCulloch, a graduate of Glasgow, took the lead in providing higher education for such youths as, being excluded by their religious convictions from entering King's College at Windsor, wished to prepare for the ministry or some other profession; and an academy of notable influence was established in Pictou, the centre of the Scottish community. But a brighter hope dawned when in 1818 the Earl of Dalhousie founded in Halifax the college which bears his name, to afford university training on the model of Edinburgh, untrammelled by ecclesiastical conditions. Politics, however, interfered with his plan and led to the establishment by the Baptists, in 1838, of Acadia College at Wolfville, Nova Scotia; and, as promising young men were often sent to the Scottish universities, it was not until the early 'sixties that Dalhousie renewed herself and entered into her days of promise and attainment. In 1862 the Methodists established Mount Allison College at Sackville, N.B., on the border between the two provinces, and the Roman Catholics St Francis Xavier's at Antigonish, N.S., in 1866. Sectarian and political influences have impaired the higher education of the Maritime Provinces, and recovery has been slow, though the situation has sensibly improved in recent years.

---

[1] In 1800–28 called "The College of New Brunswick".
[2] Harvey, E. L., in *Dalhousie Review*, vol. VI, pp. 341 ff.

In pursuance of the policy of supplying opportunities first for that class of the population from which the higher ranks are recruited, the Government of Nova Scotia in 1811 passed a Grammar School Act to provide grammar schools in seven counties and in three districts of that province. The common school lingered. The farmer and the shopkeeper in the nearer settlement got irregular attention; the fisherman and the lumberman were neglected. School attendance was very poor. A great forward step was taken in 1850 when the Hon. Joseph Howe induced J. W. Dawson (later Sir William), who had recently returned from Edinburgh University, to become the first Superintendent of Education. In his three years of indefatigable work he left a deep impress upon his native province, having insisted on the necessity for teachers trained in a normal school, the use of uniform text-books, and compulsory assessment for the support of schools. But it was not until 1864 that the last principle was put into effect when Dr (afterwards Sir Charles) Tupper as Premier with much courage carried the Free School Act. It was an immense boon to Nova Scotia, so varied in its educational attainments, and with more than one-quarter of its total population of five years old and upwards illiterate.

The progress of education in New Brunswick was even less favourable than in Nova Scotia, though in general it proceeded upon similar lines. The members of the governing class felt first the need for their own children and provided for them; the common people came afterwards. Sir Howard Douglas and Sir Edmund Walker Head (1847–54) deserve mention as having done much during their terms of office to improve both colleges and schools. By 1860, when immigration had ceased to be an important factor, there were in most counties grammar schools supported by subscription, fees and grants from the provincial Treasury, the Free School Act not being passed until 1871. Parish schools, supplied by teachers trained in a model or normal school and under the supervision of a Superintendent of Education, existed in every considerable community.

The settlement of Prince Edward Island was greatly retarded by the conditions under which the land was held by absentee proprietors and by its isolation, so that in the census of 1827 the population, nearly all farmers but some few fishermen, was only 23,500, of whom there were 1650 in the capital, Charlottetown. For years the Government, harassed by want of revenue, had given little or no encouragement to education, but by 1831 there were three district schools and three grammar schools. After 1830 immigration, good in quality and much of it intelligent, increased, and soon the rich soil of the island yielded prosperity to its inhabitants. In 1836 a central classical academy was opened in Charlottetown, which since 1860 has been known as Prince of Wales College, and has done much for the higher education of the Protestant section of the people. In 1831 the Roman Catholic bishop opened St Andrew's College, which under the changed name of St Dunstan's College (1855) has long been favourably known.

Politics and education were so interwoven in the web of the early life of all the provinces that the former, as it was the more alluring, provided the dominant pattern. Long before their arrival the Loyalists had found their chief interest in political discussion through the press or on the hustings. But the newspaper was also a medium of literary education. It contained selections from the latest European and American publications, together with some original prose and verse. In 1752, three years after its foundation, Halifax had its *Gazette*, the first paper of British North America, published by the son of the owner of the Boston *Newsletter*. Its European news was three months old, its readers were few, only seventy-two subscribers, but it carried a good deal of advertising. It still survives in the *Royal Gazette*. A much better known younger contemporary, also of American descent, was the *Halifax Journal*, published first in 1781 by John Howe, who left New England during the Revolutionary War. His famous son, Joseph Howe, after other journalistic ventures founded the *Novascotian* in 1828, and through it he fought and won the battle for the freedom of the press (1835) and became the most powerful advocate in the province for the introduction of responsible government. Saint John, N.B., also had its *Royal Gazette* with a Loyalist editor as early as 1783; and its advocate for responsible government in George E. Fenety, the editor of the *Commercial News* (1839), which was the first penny newspaper to be issued in the Maritime Provinces.

In the literature of Nova Scotia the most outstanding names were Thomas Chandler Haliburton and Joseph Howe, both men of Loyalist origin, and the former a product of the education given in King's College, Windsor. Haliburton's best work appeared first (1835) in the *Novascotian*. In the *Clockmaker*, one of the masterpieces of American humour, he depicted aspects of the life of his province with great vigour and originality, though with less restraint and finish than would have been demanded of him in a more fastidious environment. He also wrote the first description of the province in the form of history. Howe possessed fluency and imagination and has had few if any Canadian equals in oratory. He wrote occasional verse, but is best known as a writer for his influential letters to Lord John Russell in which his argumentative power shows to advantage.

The society of Nova Scotia as displayed in the fine government buildings at Halifax was gay rather than intellectual, its tone being set by the officers of the navy and army and enlivened by the occasional visit of a personage of distinction. Something similar was found at Fredericton, and even in Charlottetown in miniature. Here the best circle, a few families, "was allowed to be elegant and respectable"; there was in 1830 "a public subscription library on a liberal and respectable footing affording a variety of entertaining and standard works"; but it would appear that then and for years afterwards a liberally educated society was of the scantiest. The main Loyalist and Scottish stock of the provinces by the sea, nurtured by political, religious and educational leaders, tended towards Puritan democracy. At its best it was strong in character and intelligence.

On passing from the Maritime Provinces to the Canadas a different scene meets the eye; the stage is enlarged; newcomers enter so rapidly that by the time of confederation more than a million and a half people occupy what is now Ontario; towns, railways, canals are being constructed. But down to the middle of the century probably five out of six persons were engaged in farming or lumbering, and over large areas they were so isolated that they kept the characteristics and status of pioneers, except in so far as they were being slowly transformed by new conditions. Inasmuch as urban influence is a most important factor in cultural development, it may be observed how few and small were the cities of the provinces before confederation.

Halifax: (1800), 9000; (1817), 11,156; (1838), 14,422; (1851), 20,749; (1861), 25,000; (1871), 29,582.

Fredericton: (1824), 1849; (1851), 4500; (1861), 5652; (1871), 6000.

Saint John: (1824), 8488; (1851), 22,745; (1861), 27,000; (1871), 28,805.

Quebec: (1790), 14,000; (1825), 22,101; (1851), 42,052; (1861), 51,100; (1871), 59,700.

Montreal: (1790), 18,000; (1801), 22,000; (1825), 31,516; (1851), 57,715; (1861), 90,000; (1871), 107,000.

Toronto: (1805), 474; (1825), 1677; (1838), 12,570; (1844), 18,420; (1851), 30,775; (1861), 44,425; (1867), nearly 50,000.

Kingston: (1795), 376; (1817), 2250; (1829), 3628; (1845), 8000; (1851), 11,697; (1861), 13,700.

Hamilton: (1835), 2600; (1851), 14,112; (1861), 19,000.

In 1809 four mails were despatched during the winter from Quebec to York (Toronto) and took sixteen to eighteen days in transit.[1]

From the time of the conquest English-speaking officials and merchants had much influence in Quebec city, but they were so isolated by the French population of the province that they held slight communication with English-speaking Canada. Among them there was a sufficient nucleus of persons to form and maintain the Literary and Historical Society (1824) for which the Earl of Dalhousie secured a royal charter. Its "Transactions and Memoirs" contained contributions on local history and on scientific matters, often made by officers of the navy or army; encouragement also was given to literary talent by the offer of medals for original compositions. This society still survives. As early as 1785 a public library was opened

---

[1] Scadding, H., *Toronto of Old* (1873), pp. 533 ff.

and in 1822 it possessed 4000 volumes; in 1866 it became the property of the Literary and Historical Society.

In 1764 the *Quebec Gazette* in alternate columns of English and French was issued by a printer who had been apprenticed to a brother-in-law of Benjamin Franklin in Philadelphia. The advertisements spread before its 300 subscribers confirm the judgment that Quebec like Halifax at the end of the eighteenth century was a gay city. This paper earned much political influence and lived for more than a century, though a printer ran the risk of frequent summons before the Legislature. Its contemporary, the *Quebec Mercury*, founded in 1805 as the organ of the English-speaking population, likewise came into conflict from time to time with those in authority.

Montreal has always been the greatest distributing emporium of Canada, and the English portion of the population has by reason of its wealth possessed economic and social power. The Natural History Society of Montreal was established in 1829. It issued volumes of Transactions on the natural history of Canada and aided in the promotion of scientific surveys by the Government. The city's most famous son in science was Sir William Logan, born there of Scottish parents in 1789 and educated in her grammar school until he went to Edinburgh in 1814. "He gave the first great impulse to the systematic study of the geology of the older rocks and originated the Geological Survey of Canada".[1] From 1796 the city possessed a library which lives on, having been incorporated in 1885 in a free library established by the generosity of a few citizens and now known as the Fraser Institute.

The Montreal *Gazette*, still a leading newspaper, has had an interesting history. It was first issued in 1778 from the Château de Ramesay as a weekly in French, and its editor was used by Benjamin Franklin and two other delegates from the American Congress as an agent to detach the French population from their allegiance to Britain, but to no purpose. Ten years later it was printed in the two languages, then in English only; in 1847 it became a daily in summer, a tri-weekly in winter. Among its contributors have been several of the best known Canadian men-of-letters. The *Herald* also was an influential journal throughout this period. In Montreal also appeared a *Canadian Review* (1823–7), followed by the *Literary Garland* (1838–51), devoted to literature and supported among others by Mrs Moodie, Mrs Traill and Charles Sangster.

In 1801 the Legislature established the Royal Institution for the Advancement of Learning with the object of developing education through free schools and "foundations of a more comprehensive nature". In the trustees was vested all property that might be given or bequeathed for these purposes. But the Act proved ineffective,

---

[1] Dawson, Sir J. W., *Fifty Years of Work in Canada*, p. 50.

and its chief influence on higher education was through McGill University into which it was incorporated.

The most influential factor in the cultural development of the English population of both city and province was McGill University. Its charter dates from 1821, a medical school was incorporated into the University in 1829, and in 1843 teaching began in the Faculty of Arts. In 1811 a wealthy merchant, James McGill, acting on the suggestion of his friend the Rev. John Strachan, who will appear again, bequeathed his estate, Burnside, consisting of forty-six acres on the borders of Montreal, together with £10,000, to found a college bearing his name. In order to fulfil the terms of the will in respect of the date before which instruction was to begin, the Royal Institution for the Advancement of Learning, who were the trustees, in 1828 induced the Medical School, which had been opened in 1824 in connection with the Montreal General Hospital, to become the University Faculty of Medicine. Established on the model of Edinburgh it was not only the first medical school in Canada, but the first on the continent to furnish clinical facilities in a hospital similar to those in Edinburgh and elsewhere in Europe. The impulse to the Faculties of Arts and Science came with the appointment of John William Dawson as principal in 1855.

Since 1763 racial and religious differences had compelled the recognition of the principle of separate education for the two sections of the population. Education was therefore conducted in circumstances of more than usual difficulty, especially in the English-speaking communities outside the cities on the St Lawrence River and in the Eastern Townships. Frequent complaint was made of the evil influence of poor teachers from the United States. As in the other provinces, high schools were created first, two royal grammar schools having been established in 1816 in Montreal and Quebec, with teachers from England paid by the Imperial Government. It also attempted to provide in 1821, through the Royal Institution already mentioned, an elementary school in each parish and a model school in each county, but the plan failed, and for many years even secondary education, dependent as it was on private initiative, was very defective. The importance of the Education Act of 1846 has been explained above.[1]

The educational problems of Upper Canada were in general similar to those of Nova Scotia, though even more than there the determination of a minority to keep education under its own ecclesiastical control created a root of bitterness which it took long to eradicate. In that oligarchic society also an insistent demand arose for its own type of liberal education, which Lieutenant-Governor Simcoe had urged upon the Legislature of 1792 as being "indis-

---

[1] For English education in Quebec see *Canada and its Provinces*, xvi, 445–505, and *Education in the Province of Quebec*, Quebec Department of Public Instruction, 1914.

pensably necessary". Eventually, in 1798, as a result of Chief Justice Elmsley's report on education, grammar schools were established at four centres, from lands set aside partly for this purpose, but for years the needs of the people even in the higher branches were not supplied. Under the influence of Sir John Colborne, Upper Canada College (or the Minor College), still one of the strong schools of the Dominion, was opened in 1830 with a staff of masters drawn chiefly from Cambridge. Elementary schools were not instituted until 1816. An idea similar to that which, as we have seen, was developed in Lower Canada led Sir Peregrine Maitland in 1823 to recommend to Lord Bathurst the appointment of a General Board of Education to administer the school reserves and found a type of national education and a university, but with little result, though Dr Strachan made an effort to promote the common schools. In 1831 the Legislature was informed that "the minds of the youth of this province are left without due cultivation, or what is still worse, frequently with vulgar, low-bred, vicious and intemperate examples before them in the persons of their masters". Also in 1840 Lord Durham reported on the evidence of leading citizens that "The people [of a considerable portion of Upper Canada] may raise enough for their subsistence, and may even have a rude and comfortless plenty, but they can seldom acquire wealth; nor can even wealthy landowners prevent their children from growing up ignorant and boorish, and from occupying a far lower mental, moral and social position than they themselves fill". The same story is told partly by these figures: in 1838 out of a population of 450,000 in Upper Canada there were only about 300 children in the 13 district grammar schools, and only 24,000 in the 800 common schools; and in 1844 only 55 per cent. of the children of school age attended school.

The union of Lower and Upper Canada in 1841 made no essential change in the freedom of the latter in its educational affairs, except as regards the introduction of the separate school system. In 1854 Lord Elgin reported, with approval, of general schools that "Religion is left with municipalities, parents and managers of schools—the Government protecting the right of each parent and child". The Act of 1855 which widened the scope of separate schools was made to apply to the Upper Province by a political compromise to meet the demands of the Lower Province, and the principle became permanent in Ontario at confederation.

The foundation of a general system of national education was laid when the Legislature of 1841 voted an annual grant of £50,000 in support of common schools, aid therefrom to be confined to those districts which would tax themselves in an amount equal to what they would receive from the central fund. In 1844 Dr Egerton Ryerson was appointed second Superintendent of Education, which position he held until 1876. Fully awake to the needs of his native province, this forceful man put into effect ideas which had been in the air and others which he drew from the neighbouring States or Britain. In 1847 he persuaded the Legislature to recognise the principle of free schools supported by compulsory taxation levied upon the rateable property of the district and equal in amount to the legislative grant. This stimulated local initiative, though opposition to it came from the wealthier and childless classes and from denominational voluntary schools, and free schools were widely established on a local option basis from this time on, but they were not made universal until 1871. The principles of the earlier bill were developed and the functions of trustee boards enlarged by the bill of 1850 which has been called "The Charter of the Ontario school system".

By effecting in 1847 the creation of a provincial normal school, based largely on the model and normal schools of Dublin, Ryerson improved immeasurably the quality of the teachers, who up to that time had too often been incompetent and without character. Other important accomplishments of his were the authorisation in 1846, for general use, of the Irish public school text-books, which were not superseded until 1867, and the appropriation by the Legislature in 1850 of £3000 to supplement local support of public school libraries for the general advantage of their districts. Though the libraries were under the control of the local authorities, the books were to be purchased from a list recommended by the Department of Education in Toronto. Lord Elgin regarded this measure as having introduced "a new era in [the] educational and intellectual history of [Upper Canada]". In the latter half of the century "Mechanics' Institutes" became centres of popular education and were in many places the origin of the free public libraries. Not a few of those associated with Ryerson chiefly as inspectors of schools served the province well, but George Paxton Young, afterwards a professor in University College, may be singled out for the stimulus he gave through his reports to the teaching especially of English and Science in the grammar schools. Not the least important contribution to the moral and intellectual quality of the people was made by self-denying and often well educated ministers of religion who promoted the welfare of their communities, though, the immigration being overwhelmingly Protestant, the denominational rivalries of other lands and days took root only too easily in the fresh soil, and for many years retarded the healthy growth of higher education.

Of all the figures in the educational world of the Canadas during the first half of the nineteenth century the most arresting was Dr John Strachan. He was educated in Aberdeen and St Andrew's, but after coming to Canada he adopted the exclusive views that prevailed in a section of the Anglican Church, and became the protagonist of the party that demanded privileges for that communion in a provincial university. As far back as 1792 Lieutenant-Governor Simcoe had urged the endowment of such an institution, and in 1798 the Legislature set aside a grant of 500,000 acres of wild lands, the proceeds from the half of which were to provide for it. Under Strachan's influence the university was equipped with a Royal Charter in 1827 as King's College, Anglican in fact as in spirit. Tempestuous years followed, and the political waves were often driven across the academic preserve with such disturbing effect that no teaching was begun until 1843, Strachan being compelled to yield step by step. In 1849 King's College was secularised, in 1850 the name University of Toronto was given to it, and in 1853 it became University College in that University, the wider name being reserved, on the model of London University, for an examining body which should have in affiliation with it the arts colleges and professional schools. As a result of the exclusive character of King's College, the Methodists in 1842 secured a university charter for Victoria College at Cobourg, and about the same time the Church of Scotland in Canada created Queen's University at Kingston on the model of Edinburgh University. The situation was very difficult, and the attempt made under the Act of 1853 to co-ordinate the colleges within the University of Toronto proved premature. Thereupon the friends of University College, fearful lest the Government should disperse its endowment among its rivals, spent most of it on the erection of the Norman building which is one of the architectural ornaments of the province. What was left was devoted to the support of a strong staff in Arts drawn from British universities, reinforcing the original professors of King's College, who established the high standards in Arts which have ever since been maintained. Professional education suffered greatly by reason of the academic rivalries. By the Act of 1853 it received a setback from which it recovered but slowly. When his long cherished hopes were slain by the Legislature in 1849, Dr Strachan with astonishing tenacity of purpose went to England, secured a new charter for a university, raised an endowment and in 1852 founded the University of Trinity College in Toronto.

As early as 1800 there was at Niagara in Upper Canada a circulating library with "41 subscribers at 24s. each", and by 1812 it had 827 well selected volumes, but it was irretrievably damaged when the American troops occupied the village in 1813. Toronto, as the colonial capital, became also the cultural centre of the province because of its select circle of official persons who professed the refinements and amenities of an educated society, though their provincialism was not infrequently referred to by contemporary travellers. Thus Mrs Jameson, in 1837, "With an absolute want of the means of the most ordinary mental and moral development, we have here conventionalism in its most oppressive and ridiculous forms".[1] For

[1] Jameson, [Mrs] A., *Winter Studies and Summer Rambles* (ed. of 1923), p. 54.

the first third of the nineteenth century the settlements were isolated from one another by reason of the poor and often impassable roads, but Toronto drew from, and set the standards for, the most prosperous section of Upper Canada, becoming, as it has ever since remained, in a larger measure than any other provincial capital, representative of the life of its province.

The newspapers of Upper Canada were numerous, and "in the absence or scarcity of books [were] the principal medium of knowledge and communication".[1] In 1793 the *Upper Canada Gazette or American Oracle* appeared at Niagara or Newark, published by the Government, but it was transferred in 1800 under other direction to York (Toronto) and later became the *Weekly Register*. From 1824 the *Colonial Advocate*, a paper of greater historic interest, was issued by W. Lyon Mackenzie as the organ in his campaign which ended in the outbreak of 1837. Opposed to it were the *U.E. Loyalist*, the *Courier of Upper Canada* (1831), and the *Patriot* (1828) amalgamated later with the *Colonist* (1838–58). In 1838 Francis Hincks issued the *Examiner* and exercised much influence for some years. But a more powerful figure stepped upon the scene in 1844 when George Brown founded the *Globe* in Toronto, the policy of which he directed until his death in 1880, at the same time moulding and quickening the Liberal party. Influential though it was in political affairs its literary interests were narrow. By reason of the easy means of communication the press obtained news and opinion from the United States far earlier, more frequently and fuller than from Great Britain.[2]

Of interest in literature, widespread or concentrated, there was, owing to the conditions of settlement, little manifestation during the formative period of the Upper Province, though a *Canadian Literary Magazine* was issued in Toronto in 1833. But the gifted women of English birth and education, Mrs Moodie and Mrs Traill, described vividly certain aspects of frontier life, and there were writers of fiction, of whom John Richardson was the only one who earned a constituency much wider than his native province, and whose work is still read occasionally.

Conditions were even less favourable for the Fine Arts in a constituency without wealth, in which the cultivation of taste waited on the satisfaction of primary needs. At first amateurs sketched local scenes, but Paul Kane (1810–71) had the advantage of four years of study and wide travel in Europe before he was invited by Sir George Simpson to the territory of the Hudson's Bay Company, where he reproduced by pen and brush many scenes and types of Indian life. Other artists came to Canada in middle life, O. R. Jacobi from Prussia, Cornelius Krieghoff from Rotterdam, G. T. Berthon from France, and Daniel Fowler from England. They have left well

---

[1] *Ibid.* p. 68.
[2] Scadding, pp. 259–83.

executed landscapes and much of their portraiture is of historic value, but their work aroused no widespread interest. In 1834 an Art exhibition was held in the old Parliament Buildings, and in 1847 the Toronto Society of Arts was organised. It was a period when political struggles engrossed the attention of the few well educated persons, but even in the old American States Art was still in its infancy.

In 1849 the Canadian Institute, still flourishing as the Royal Canadian Institute, was founded in Toronto for "the encouragement of learning and the development of science and the arts throughout the province" by scientific discussions, the publication of Transactions, the establishment of a museum and the maintenance of a library for the use of its members and the public. It had a membership of upwards of 400 when in 1855 it absorbed the Toronto Athenaeum, a society founded earlier than the Institute for literary and historical entertainment as well as the support of a library.

Of the Far West before confederation little is to be said. Such education as the white settlers had was due mainly to the efforts of clergymen from Britain or Canada, who impelled by missionary zeal not only ministered to their spiritual needs but opened schools and sought to further the rudiments of civilisation. Permanent impressions were made by Dr Machray (afterwards Archbishop of Rupert's Land) and the Rev. John Black among the Selkirk settlers on the Red River; and by Bishop McLean, the Rev. James Nisbet and the McDougalls among the Indians of the Territories. Father Lacombe established schools in the 'sixties for whites at Edmonton and for Indians on the eastern slopes of the Rockies. Men such as these facilitated the establishment in the Canadian West of a community life in which law and order have been maintained with few discreditable episodes.

Since confederation a Canadian mind has come slowly into being. The realisation of the Dominion as it now is was due primarily to the settlers from Ontario, who were the first to develop Manitoba and the North West Territories, and to the people in British Columbia who were as strongly English in sentiment as any of the eastern provinces. The idealism of the old was therefore carried into the new, rooted in the conviction that there should be preserved on the northern half of this continent a British civilisation enriched by the Latin genius of Quebec. The fostering of this idealism and the unification of the country are to be laid in no small measure to the account of the common schools, the tone and type of which are similar throughout English-speaking Canada, though in the British North America Act education was left to the provinces, a prerogative which is jealously guarded by their Legislatures.

In the eastern English-speaking provinces the development of the schools has been for the most part on the lines which had been laid down before confederation. Changes have arisen through the shifting of population and industrial development. The former factor has created a serious problem for the rural school and has necessitated a constant enlargement of local school areas, consolidation having been so far only a partial solution. Urban centres have multiplied. Villages have become towns, towns small cities, and cities have reached far beyond their anticipated limits. Though there is not in this increase so large an alien element as in American cities, the foreigner has brought peculiar problems. Throughout these years the common public school has become the fertilising source of Canadian democracy, together with the high schools and more advanced collegiate institutes, which are virtually free to all, and are within the reach of those who live in well settled country parts or in towns. Instruction in the common school consists of eight grades; in the high schools, which pupils enter as a rule at fourteen and attend four years, it is given in English, history, classical and modern languages, mathematics, and the natural sciences and leads up to the normal schools and the universities. Technical, vocational, and night schools have been established and the adolescent manual worker is being cared for. Outwardly the prosperity of the country is reflected in the school buildings and their equipment. In most of the provinces the salaries of teachers also are good. Private schools on the model of the English Public School have increased, as with the growth of wealth the desire of many parents to have their children under more continuous supervision could be realised.

Along with the pioneers went teachers from the eastern provinces and through them the educational ideals of the East entered the prairies. On the opening of the West in the last quarter of the nineteenth century Manitoba in the nature of the case got a good start, and in the first decade of the twentieth Winnipeg became a city of first-rate importance. But its initial difficulties were greater than those of other Canadian cities as they were thrust upon it by the residuum of the foreigners crowding through to the new land. At the same time the French Canadians, having lived within the borders of the province from the early days of the fur trade, had in some localities become so large an element that for a time the separate school controversy was very acute, and "the Manitoba Schools Question" was made a Dominion political issue. As the province has now become settled, its system of education, elementary and secondary, is stable and similar to that of Ontario.

Under the regime of the Territorial Governments schools were provided for, but it was not until provincial status was given to Saskatchewan and Alberta in 1905 that they developed rapidly. Such unprecedented immigration as these provinces received in the years before the outbreak of the war in 1914 forced upon them three problems: those of the bilingual school for foreigners, of teaching facilities for the new settlers, and of the small rural school. These difficulties are being mitigated as the education of the alien is systematically promoted. French-speaking pupils may receive primary instruction in their native tongue, but English is the language of the province. Separate schools under ecclesiastical oversight are relatively few in number. The rural school will remain a problem as long as there is a frontier, or settlement on poor lands. The three Prairie Provinces form almost an educational unit. Organisation, text-books, standards of instruction and qualification for teachers are so similar that when children are moved, as is so frequently the case in a shifting population, from older to newer settlements, the educational waste both for them and their instructors is reduced to a minimum. The high schools of the prairie towns at once attract the attention of the visitor by their fine appearance.

The vastness of the territory of British Columbia, its settlements of farmers, miners and lumbermen separated in mountain valleys and on Vancouver Island, its rapidly growing city of Vancouver, and its small towns in which well educated newcomers from the Old Land have made their homes, explain the fact that "there is in this most English of the provinces every phase of cultural development from the pioneer stage to the highly educated gentleman".[1] In general, school organisation and the substance of the teaching approximate, especially in the cities, to what prevails beyond the mountains; but there is no system of separate schools, and there is a tendency to adopt the English ideals of class education in private schools.

In a new and sparsely settled country uniformity under central control is a necessity in order that the average teacher may receive guidance. But it is only too easy to protract the pioneer stage by detailed prescriptions of work, by the requirement of undue uniformity in text-books and by rigid inspection, and so to over-standardise even higher education in established communities which should have earned their right to a measure of freedom. Henceforth progress is to be made by eliciting the originality of those who are in charge of the best schools in cities and the developed portions of the provinces. Throughout Canada the average boy or girl is given a reasonably good preparation for life, but less opportunity is afforded the gifted, and, following American practice, the secondary stage of education begins too late. Few pupils enter on the study of classical or modern languages until fourteen years of age, and therefore at eighteen they are behind the best English and continental youth of the same age in humanistic studies. A survey of sixty years, however, justifies optimism. Nearly one-fifth of the population of the Dominion is at school, the daily attendance is good; notwithstanding a large foreign immigration the percentage of illiterates especially below

[1] Putman, J. H. and Weir, G. M., *Survey of the School System of British Columbia.*

fifty years of age has fallen at each of the last three census notably in the groups of earlier ages, and this rate of progress, if maintained, should soon result in the practical extinction of illiteracy.[1] The necessity of employing unqualified teachers has all but disappeared, and in respect of the character and training of its teachers Canada has no reason to take a secondary place. The present state of education is a triumph over difficulties and a challenge to the idealism of the people which will not be refused.

The progress of higher education in the Dominion since confederation can be paralleled only in the United States. There are six universities supported entirely by their provinces, New Brunswick, Toronto, Manitoba, Saskatchewan, Alberta and British Columbia. In Ontario Queen's and Western Universities receive provincial aid. Dalhousie in Halifax and McGill in Montreal are private foundations, the latter with a small measure of help from the Legislature. Others are supported by the Churches: King's, now in Halifax, Bishop's College in Lennoxville, Trinity in Toronto by the Anglicans; Mount Allison and Victoria by the Methodists (now the United Church of Canada), St Francis Xavier's in Antigonish, Nova Scotia, and St Michael's in Toronto by the Roman Catholics; Acadia in Nova Scotia and McMaster in Toronto by the Baptists. The universities and colleges in the provinces serving the French-speaking communities have been referred to above. In Ontario a most effective federation has been created of Victoria and Trinity Universities and St Michael's College with the University of Toronto, whereby the former two hold in abeyance their degree-conferring powers, except in Divinity, and all rank with the provincial University College in undergraduate work in Arts, enjoying the same privileges of university instruction, laboratories and library, and their students receiving the degrees in Arts from the Senate of the University of Toronto. Similar federations are being worked out in Winnipeg and Halifax. The present position of the universities of the western provinces is an indication of the lead that has been given in higher education and of the intelligent response on the part of the people.

In 1924–5 the total income of English-speaking universities was $9,619,503, of which $4,308,849 was government aid; their buildings and equipment also indicate the generosity of Legislatures and benefactors. Laboratories have been liberally equipped in the universities of the West as well as of the East, libraries are provided for regular work, some excellent museums are in process of development, and resources are being accumulated for research. As in the most advanced countries scientific methods prevail, and the Arts course has been greatly broadened, though conservatism has resisted the introduction of elective subjects on such a scale as prevails in the American

[1] *Illiteracy and School Attendance in Canada*, Dominion Bureau of Statistics, 1926, pp. 69 ff., 83 ff.

universities. But the honours system established at the beginning by teachers from Britain has been retained.

Professional standards are fairly uniform among the provinces. There is a Dominion Medical Council which issues a licence validating practice in all the provinces. The ordinary length of the medical course is six years, the final three of which are devoted to clinical instruction in well appointed hospitals. Some of the medical schools are of more than Canadian reputation. Dentistry, still a profession apart from medicine, has been reasonably provided for. Legal education has not advanced relatively as far as medical, though in all the provinces with universities except Ontario there are Faculties of Law. Theological training is conducted in denominational colleges in affiliation with or in faculties of universities. As might be expected in a country of such rapid expansion engineering schools are numerous and well equipped. Agriculture holds an honourable position in several of the larger universities and in separate colleges, as at Guelph in Ontario and at Truro in Nova Scotia. Of recent years attention has been given to adult education and extension work, especially in agriculture, the Labour organisations not having yet availed themselves of such facilities to the same extent as in England, perhaps because of the relatively less active participation of their members in public life.

The Canadian university cannot be understood apart from its history. Professors from the Old Land were the original source of its inspiration. These early teachers, often men of distinction and strong character, set high standards, and though Canada is now able to supply her own needs in large measure, many younger graduates still come from British universities to reinforce her intellectual life. But in the last three decades graduates of Canadian universities have in their turn been filling important academic positions in the United States, some even in Britain. Newcomb, Osler, and Schurman have adorned the country of their birth, though the first left it for his early training.

Through their graduates the old eastern universities have had much influence upon the public life of the Dominion, and of recent years there is a marked inclination on the part of the college man to enter business. The large attendance of students,[1] men and women, so great as to invite comparison with Scotland, drawn from all grades of society, but especially from families of old Canadian stock, makes the universities representative democracies. They are increasingly regarded as gateways to ampler spheres of opportunity. On this continent the complaint is often heard that "mass production" is

---

[1] In 1924–5 there were over 32,000 students registered in regular courses in universities and colleges, English-speaking and French. Of these 13,552 were in Arts and the pure Sciences, 2693 in Medicine, 2317 in Graduate Courses, 2202 in Engineering, 1690 in Theology, 1389 in Music, and so on. There was a teaching staff of 3864 professors and instructors. *Preliminary Report on the Combined Statistics of the Universities and Colleges of Canada*, 1925, Dominion Bureau of Statistics, Ottawa, 1926.

lowering the quality of higher education, and that democracy while cherishing the many is careless of the few. The remedy must be applied first in the schools where incipient aptitude should be recognised. In Canadian universities a process of selective education has been maintained through the operation of the system of pass and honour courses, and there is good reason for hoping that the development of the talented will neither impede nor be impeded by the equipment of the average.

From early days, as has been mentioned, local scientific societies, some of them still flourishing, were formed in provincial cities. These have their crown in the Royal Society of Canada, which was formally constituted in 1882 at Ottawa by the Marquess of Lorne, then Governor-General of the Dominion. The objects of the society were: "First, to encourage studies and investigations in literature and science; secondly, to publish transactions annually or semi-annually, containing the minutes of proceedings at meetings, records of the work performed, original papers and memoirs of merit and such other documents as may be deemed worthy of publication; thirdly, to offer prizes or other inducements for valuable papers on subjects related to Canada, and to aid researches already begun and carried so far as to render their ultimate value probable; fourthly, to assist in the collection of specimens with a view to the formation of a Canadian museum of archives, ethnology, archaeology and natural history". Several features of the constitution were drawn from the Institute of France, and the creation of the Literature and History sections—one for each language, French and English—was due to Quebec, which took more interest in these subjects than in science. There are now five sections: I and II, Literature, History, Archaeology and Sociology in French and in English; III, the Mathematical, Physical and Chemical Sciences; IV, the Geological Sciences; V, the Biological Sciences. The first list of fellows was composed of eighty of the leading scientists, historians and men-of-letters in Canada; to-day there are two hundred, an evidence of the rapid growth of the scientific spirit due especially to the work of the universities. The purpose of the society has been carried out in inducing the Federal Government to support geological, tidal and meteorological investigations; in the promotion of ethnological research, and, to take two other instances, in clarifying the early evidence for the voyages of Cartier and Champlain and for the boundaries of the provinces. Besides this, between forty and fifty literary and historical societies, dealing for the most part with local matters, are affiliated to the Royal Society and send delegates or report to its annual meeting. Thus the scientific and historical activities of the Dominion, apart from that of the universities, are brought under its review.

In line with similar movements in Great Britain and in the United States, the Federal Government established in 1917 the Advisory

Council for Scientific and Industrial Research which has conducted investigations of practical problems and has co-operated with the universities in the promotion of scientific research by the award of fellowships and bursaries.

In 1872 the Dominion Archives were founded in Ottawa by the Federal Government and their development has been unusually rapid. Originals and copies of documents relating to the history of Canada have been secured from the Record Office in London, from Paris and from many private sources. Not the least important of the acquisitions is a collection of pictures, some 1500 framed and 6000 unframed, together with prints and book illustrations. The Archives have proved to be an invaluable treasure-house for the investigations of the school of younger experts who are doing notable work in Canadian and colonial history. Reports and publications have been issued by the Dominion and the provincial Archives. Also the Champlain Society, with headquarters in Toronto, has re-edited and published in fine style over a series of years some of the rare documents and memoirs of explorations that shed light on early Canadian history.

Since confederation the establishment and maintenance of libraries by municipalities and Legislatures have proceeded apace. Of the latter that at Ottawa, which fell heir to that of the two Legislatures of 1841, is the most important, though it cannot be termed a national library. Under energetic leadership the libraries in the larger cities, and in some of the towns as well, have become important sources of education for young and old, and from them as community centres much cultural influence is widely diffused. There were in 1925, 608 free public libraries, of which 500 were in Ontario, containing about 3,600,000 volumes. The Province of Ontario maintains a very complete system of travelling libraries. Also the Universities of Saskatchewan and Alberta have endeavoured to extend some of their advantages through their provinces by means of libraries which are sent from place to place. In the last decade the use of public libraries has increased two-fold, and the improvement in the service is equally remarkable.

In regard to the character of the Canadian as a reader and the books of his preference statistics do not tell the whole tale. English publishers claim that, as far as they are concerned, Australians and New Zealanders are better readers than Canadians. Statistics seem to support this contention; but the contiguity to Canada of a populous country with the same language must be taken into account; and, to reduce the inequality of the comparison, it must be remarked that many English publishers in selling the rights of their books to the United States include those for Canada. Books and magazines of the higher order, including religious publications and university textbooks, are supplied in the main from Great Britain. In comparison with other peoples the reading quality of the Canadian public is difficult to estimate, though the relatively large number of university graduates who are found in all the provinces must be an important factor in leading to a favourable judgment.

Though the leading newspapers of the Dominion are not yet in the same class as the great journals of Britain either in the range of their foreign news or in their literary quality, they compare favourably with the better representatives of the press of the United States. Since confederation they have been broadening their interests, and now devote space to literature, the theatre, music and other fine arts; their news is as a rule presented without sensation, and their cable and telegraphic despatches involve large financial outlay. They are rarely now, as was formerly so often the case, the organs of outstanding persons who mould political opinion, but they still influence it greatly if the editorial columns are strong. University graduates are entering journalism in increasing numbers. The press of the large cities interferes with the dailies of the provincial towns, but the weekly newspaper fills a place of its own, and an important one, in the life of the community, bringing local news to a population scattered among hamlets and on farms, many of them still in pioneer conditions.

Canada lacks weekly journals of current politics, criticism and *belles lettres* such as are widely read in Britain, and somewhat in the United States, by the educated classes. The monthly review also is hardly known, though there has always been in the last twenty years one quarterly maintained by one or more of the universities which serves a similar purpose. The popular weekly and monthly have fair and improving constituencies, but they are seriously put to it by the competition of their American rivals with their strong financial support and immense circulation.

In Canadian literature also the growth of the national idea since confederation has had its effect.[1] Over poetry and the fine arts in general there moved a creative breath as the day of the new Dominion dawned. Impelled by the spirit of their own homeland a group of young men began to come into their power during the 'nineties, the best known of whom were Charles G. D. Roberts, Bliss Carman, Archibald Lampman, Wilfrid Campbell, and D. C. Scott. The solitary poetic note of Isabella Valancy Crawford awoke few echoes, but more recently the premature death of Marjorie Pickthall in 1922 has been lamented, as her poetry, of great ideality and charm, was only a partially realised possession. Fiction is relatively less noteworthy than poetry, but many writers have for years been choosing the Canadian environment for their stories, some with much originality and success, though unfortunately too often they themselves have

---

[1] For an account of English-Canadian Literature see the *Cambridge History of English Literature*, vol. XIV, chap. xi.

had to leave it. Young scholars and men-of-letters trained in the severe methods of modern literary appreciation and usually attached to a university are producing sincere work dealing with the literary, historical, economic, social and religious life of the Dominion.

In the latter half of the nineteenth century the artistic ideals of the country were fostered by a number of good painters, draughtsmen and decorative artists, such as Paul Peel, Blair Bruce, Edmund Morris and Robert Harris, who attained recognition abroad; in the twentieth century the late James Wilson Morrice and Horatio Walker have been well known in the great galleries of Britain and America. For years the ground had been preparing for the public appreciation of the artist. In 1872 the Ontario Society of Artists was founded and about the same time the Montreal Art Association. In 1880 the Royal Canadian Academy of Arts was established at Ottawa, under the patronage of Princess Louise, with a membership of painters, sculptors, architects, etchers and engravers, and this led to the creation of the National Gallery at Ottawa, maintained with funds placed by the Federal Government at the disposal of a Board of Trustees. They have endeavoured to secure representative Canadian paintings, in addition to those presented by the members of the Academy, and examples of European masters both early and modern; also to stimulate art throughout the Dominion by periodic exhibitions of selected pictures. In most of the larger cities there are small art galleries, but Montreal and recently Toronto are easily in the front, the latter with a fine building on "The Grange", long the home of Goldwin Smith. In Toronto also there is a Museum of Archaeology distinguished for its representative collections of Greek, American and especially Chinese art. The enthusiasm and support of a few leading citizens, such as the late Sir Edmund Walker of Toronto, aroused public interest in the arts and made possible the more recent developments. This has also been manifested, as commercial prosperity affected Canada at the opening of the twentieth century, in the acquisition of private collections.

The latest movement in painting is seen in a school of younger men called "The Seven", the most original of whom, Tom Thomson, an untutored artist, was drowned before he had reached the fulness of his powers. Looking with a fresh eye on Canadian scenery, its seasonal beauties of the wilderness, lakes and mountains, they have given it a bold and almost emotional interpretation in startling colour. They present, however, only one phase of the artistic promise of the country. Art schools are training teachers for the common schools and others who expect to earn their living by illustrating.

Two representatives of Canadian sculpture may be mentioned, Philippe Hébert, a French Canadian, and Walter S. Allward of Toronto. To the credit of the former are well grouped and executed historical figures in Quebec and Montreal; to the credit of the latter, in addition to work at home, is the inception of a colossal memorial to Canadian soldiers on Vimy Ridge. The work of A. Phimister Procter is so well known in the United States that he may be classed as an American. Also Dr Tait MacKenzie, though he has been for many years living in Philadelphia, is a Canadian, and his representations of athletic youth are found in Britain as well as in America. A work of fine design and execution, indeed one of the most impressive pieces of sculpture in the Dominion, is the Champlain monument, the work of an English sculptor, Vernon March, erected in 1924 at Orillia in Ontario to commemorate the first arrival of the explorer in this portion of the country.

A few impressive buildings erected before confederation show that the provinces were not without ideals in architecture, but it is only since wealth has made possible the construction of large public and business edifices and private mansions that architects have had full opportunities for their skill which is now being admirably displayed. As is general on this continent the residential quarters of a city shift so constantly that few family houses are transmitted from father to son, but in most cities better-class dwellings are of good domestic design and are in pleasing surroundings. Most typical of the civilisation of this continent are the great hotels which, in the judgment of a French architect, are the finest product of its architecture, and, serving as they do both the traveller and the civic community as a social centre, take the place of the town hall in the municipal civilisation of Europe.[1]

It can hardly be said that Canadians are a musical people, but the educational value of music in schools has received recognition, and conservatoires of music, some of them of high standing, are thronged with pupils. After discounting the desire for a conventional accomplishment, there remains a large constituency of persons with good musical taste, who appreciate not only the excellent choirs and orchestras but welcome with discrimination the artists of the world. Mention should be made of the Mendelssohn Choir of Toronto created by the late Dr A. S. Vogt. In the last decade annual festivals held in the four western provinces have proved to be an important development in musical appreciation.

The population of the older provinces is already distinguished by stability of character and uniformity of social life. Formerly there were but two strata, the small circles of official and professional people, especially lawyers, who maintained the English tradition and controlled government, over against whom were the shopkeepers and farmers, the latter by no means of the peasant order but independent owners of their homesteads, though wresting a hard living from land or forest, and frugal of necessity. But the common and high

---

[1] Hourticq, L., in *De Québec jusqu'à Vancouver*, pp. 13 ff.

school has been a great leveller, and there is now no class which through the transmission in families of higher education, social advantage and professional *ethos*, stands apart from and supplies the leaders of the community. From the farm indeed has come to the universities a great deal of their finest material, but too often to its own impoverishment, though the farmers by reason of their numbers have given the prevailing democratic tone to the provinces and are taking a more active interest in politics than ever. Especially in Ontario many of the more well-to-do spend their later life in modest comfort in villages or small towns, each of which with its brick cottages, verandahs, shade-trees and flower-gardens is almost a replica of its neighbour. There is no such diversified and refined society enjoying an established patrimony as the squires and gentlefolk who give interest to the English countryside. Geographical environment, involving as it does social change, has resulted in definite national types, English and French, which soon modify the characteristics of the newcomer, as happened to the Englishman in Ireland. A culture has been developed in continental conditions, interesting for comparison with that of the Australians and New Zealanders who are almost wholly of British origin.

The "National Policy" has wrought a change in the social life of Canada. With the creation of industries the manufacturer has become a new local magnate beside the banker and the corporation lawyer. While those who have made money may be without social or intellectual background, they often desire for their children a good education or at least a cultivated environment, but, enterprising though they are in business, the new rich are not sure of themselves in matters of taste, and therefore usually accept the conventional and are contented with the commonplace. As yet in Canada only a minority of the wealthy are competent to be genuinely critical. Those on this continent who are rapidly accumulating riches tend not only to conservatism in all things but to uniform tastes and standards. Moreover, along with this goes a sensitiveness to external opinion which is more obvious in adolescent countries than in those with an old civilisation. Originality is the outcome of culture broad and deep.

In older Canada, where the Anglo-Saxon element is strongest, the average educated person is mildly Puritan in sentiment. The drunkenness and loose manners of pioneer days have long since yielded to a developing culture, and Canadians are a people of marked sobriety. They are for the most part adherents of the Churches, which, indeed, conservative in their worship, their creeds and their moral standards, have both in town and country, along with the common schools, contributed much to the existing uniformity of mind in the English-speaking provinces. Difficult though it is to estimate the political morals of a people, inasmuch as money is not the only means of corruption, it may safely be said that almost without exception the political leaders of Canada have been men of high integrity, frequently indeed distinguished figures, and that suspicion of dishonesty in a politician is soon reflected at the polls.

But in the large cities of the East and in the West change is rapid. Here the older Canadian inheritance is being tested. Will the sap of two civilisations flowing strongly in the dominant British stock, rooted with the French in American soil, cause a new and diversified quality of fruit to appear? Within the last two decades Canada has had to meet peculiarly difficult problems arising from the great foreign immigration, the insistent economic and moral pressure of her neighbour and her experience in the Great War. She is set in the midst of the modern world with her gates open on the East to Europe, on the South to the United States, and on the Pacific to the Orient. Through her universities also the ideas of world-wide culture are being sown upon receptive soil. The probability, however, is that her civilisation will remain predominantly of the Anglo-Saxon type which she has inherited, but that it will slowly adjust itself to the forces of the world in which she is placed, yet distinguishable withal from that of her neighbour.

BIBLIOGRAPHY

PART I

THE MANUSCRIPT SOURCES OF CANADIAN HISTORY

By A. G. Doughty, G.M.G., Litt.D., LL.D.

Canada possesses an almost unbroken chain of material dealing with her history from her foundation to the present day. This material, with the exception of complementary papers, is found in three countries, France, England and Canada. The description attempted here is presented under the heading of each country. Owing to lack of space, it is restricted to the essential primary sources, omitting the collections in minor depositories.

For further and more detailed information, the following books will be found most useful: French sources: ROY, J. EDMOND, *Rapport sur les Archives de France relatives à l'histoire du Canada*, Publications des Archives du Canada, No. 6, Ottawa, Parmelee, 1911. English sources: GIUSEPPI, M. S., *A Guide to the Manuscripts preserved in the Public Record Office*, 2 vols. London, 1924. Canadian sources: PARKER, DAVID W., *A Guide to the Documents in the Manuscript Room at the Public Archives of Canada*, vol. 1, Publications of the Archives of Canada, No. 10, Ottawa, 1914. BIGGAR, H. P., "The Public Archives at Ottawa," in *Bulletin of the Institute of Historical Research*, vol. 11, No. 6, February 1925, vol. 111, No. 7, June 1925. In the *Annual Reports* of the Canadian Archives will be found lists of Canadian accessions as well as calendars of many series.

Though specifically concerned with the United States, the following publications will also be found useful: ANDREWS and DAVENPORT, *Guide to the Manuscript Materials for the History of the United States to 1783, in the British Museum, in minor London Archives, and in the Libraries of Oxford and Cambridge*, Washington, Carnegie Institution, 1908. ANDREWS, CHARLES M., *Guide to the Materials for American History to 1783, in the Public Record Office of Great Britain*, 2 vols. Washington, Carnegie Institution, 1912–14. PAULIN and PAXSON, *Guide to the Materials in London Archives for the History of the United States since 1783*, Washington, Carnegie Institution, 1914. PARKER, D. W., *Guide to the Materials for United States History in Canadian Archives*, Washington, Carnegie Institution, 1913.

The abbreviation T.O. stands for Transcripts preserved in Ottawa, and T.pt.O. for Transcripts in part in Ottawa, at the Canadian Archives. The word *Reports* means those issued by the Public Archives of Canada.

FRANCE

ARCHIVES NATIONALES

(*a*) RECORDS OF THE ARCHIVES NATIONALES

SERIES E. CONSEILS DU ROI. I. CONSEIL DES FINANCES. Contains important material concerning early fur-trading from 1603 to 1635 and other material. Calendared in the *Report for* 1883. (See Roy's *Rapport*, pp. 33–4.) (T.pt.O.)

SERIES F¹². COMMERCE ET INDUSTRIE, 1700–91. Consists of the minutes and papers of the Conseil du Commerce. Only a small portion dealing with duties, trade and fisheries relates to Canadian history. (See Roy's *Rapport*, pp. 37–42.) (T.pt.O.)

SERIES F¹⁵. HOSPICES, SECOURS. Documents concerning the pensions to the Acadian and Canadian families returning to France during the Seven Years' War: 1763–93. (T.pt.O.)

SERIES F⁵⁰. MARINE ET COLONIES. Relates to shipping and commerce with Canada and Louisiana. (See Roy's *Rapport*, pp. 42–3.) (T.pt.O.)

SERIES G. ADMINISTRATION FINANCIÈRE. A few sub-series of interest to Canada: G–1, Royal Dues, G–2, Domanial Dues, G–5, Admiralty, G–7, Financial Controller, G–8, Clergy. (See Roy's *Rapport*, pp. 42–5.)

SERIES H. ADMINISTRATION PROVINCIALE ET LOCALE. A few files concern Canada, specially H–4226 bearing on trade and administration. (See Roy's *Rapport*, pp. 46–8.)

SERIES J. TRÉSOR DES CHARTES. A few files contain Canadian material: J–246, 961 and 962 relate to Cartier and Roberval. (See Roy's *Rapport*, pp. 49–51.)

SERIES K. SECTION HISTORIQUE. A few files include material concerning Roberval, La Roche, La Salle, Hennepin, Le Borgne, church matters, western exploration and boundary claims, etc. (See Roy's *Rapport*, pp. 51–62, and *Report for 1910*, pp. 57–9.) (T.pt.O.)

SERIES M. MÉLANGES HISTORIQUES. A certain number of files concern Canada and relate mainly to church, trade and finance matters. (See Roy's *Rapport*, pp. 53–69.) (T.pt.O.)

SERIES N. CARTES ET PLANS. Eleven plans are of interest to Canada. (See Roy's *Rapport*, p. 69.)

SERIES O. ARCHIVES DE LA COURONNE. A few documents concern Canada, practically all included in other series. (See Roy's *Rapport*, pp. 70–1.)

SERIES P. CHAMBRE DES COMPTES. A few documents relate to Canadian paper-money. (See Roy's *Rapport*, pp. 72–3.)

SERIES S. BIENS DES CORPORATIONS SUPPRIMÉES. Composed of records of religious institutions. Carton 6847–8 relates to the Seminary of St Esprit; 7006–7041, to the Seminary of St Sulpice. (T.pt.O.)

SERIES T. SÉQUESTRÉ. Composed of papers seized during the Revolution. Carton T–776 contains the letters of Mother St Helena, published by Abbé Verreau; T–790, Papers of Bréard, one of Bigot's associates. (T.pt.O.)

SERIES V. GRANDES CHANCELLERIES ET CONSEILS. This series is composed of letters patent and judicial records. (See Roy's *Rapport*, pp. 77–9.) (T.pt.O.)

SERIES Y. CHÂTELET DE PARIS. This series contains the judicial records of the Prévôté of Paris. (T.pt.O.)

SERIES Z. JURIDICTIONS SPÉCIALES ET ORDINAIRES.

(b) ARCHIVES DES COLONIES

SERIES A. ACTES DU POUVOIR SOUVERAIN. This series consists of registers containing the King's orders and letters patent, and the arrêts of the Council of State. Registers 1 to 8, and 21 to 23, concern Canada. Most of the documents have been registered with the Sovereign Council. (T.O.)

SERIES B. CORRESPONDANCE MINISTÉRIELLE ET ORDRES ET DÉPÊCHES DU ROI. LETTRES ENVOYÉES. This series is mainly made up of the official despatches of the ministers to the governors and intendants, with letters from the same to ecclesiastics, officers and officials. It includes royal instructions and memoranda. The documents relate to all branches of the administration and to details of the military, economic, religious and social life of the colony.

The transcripts in the Canadian Archives are calendared as follows: vols. 1–42 in *Supplement* to the *Report for* 1899; vols. 42–74, in the *Report for* 1904; vols. 75–189, in the *Report for* 1905, vol. I, part VI. The last volumes, 190–213, are not calendared.

SERIES C¹¹. CANADA ET DÉPENDANCES, ACADIE, ÎLE SAINT-JEAN ET ÎLE ROYALE. This collection is composed of official and miscellaneous correspondence and various papers, sent to the French authorities by the governors, intendants, officers and officials of the Canadian colonies. The collection also contains numerous memoirs, reports, military plans and journals, grants, statistics, royal decrees and letters patent, returns relating to trade, industry, agriculture, fishing. This collection thus forms the complement of Series B. It covers the whole range of colonial life and is the basic material of early Canadian history. The collection is divided as follows:

C¹¹ A concerns New France and is calendared in the *Reports for* 1885, 1886 and 1887. (T.O.)

C¹¹ B concerns Île Royale and is calendared in the *Report for* 1887. (T.O.)

C¹¹ C concerns Newfoundland, Magdalen and St John's Islands, and is partly calendared in the *Report for* 1887. (T.O.)

C¹¹ D concerns Acadia and is calendared in the *Report for* 1887. (T.O.)

C¹¹ E concerns the whole of Canada. and is calendared in the *Report for* 1887. (T.O.)

C¹¹ G contains miscellaneous material and is calendared in the *Report for* 1887. (T.O.)

SERIES C¹² A and C¹² B. SAINT PIERRE ET MIQUELON. These series contain the official correspondence of that colony. (T.pt.O.)

SERIES D² C. TROUPES COLONIALES. This series is concerned with military records and is partly calendared in the *Report for* 1905. (T.pt.O.)

SERIES E. PERSONNEL COLONIAL. Consists of the colonial officers' and officials' files, including various documents. (T.pt.O.)

SERIES F¹ A. FONDS DES COLONIES. This series, 1670–1762, consists of the financial accounts and estimates of the colonies. (T.pt.O.)

SERIES F³ or COLLECTION MOREAU DE SAINT-MÉRY. A vast collection of original and transcript papers, made up of official correspondence between Versailles and the colonial authorities with miscellaneous documents. Complements Series B and C¹¹, and is partly calendared in the *Report for* 1899, *Supplement*, and *Report for* 1905. (T.O.)

SERIES F⁵ A. MISSIONS. Calendared in the *Report for* 1899. (T.O.)

SERIES G¹. ÉTAT CIVIL DES COLONIES. Consists of censuses, land records and registers of baptisms and burials. Summarised in Parker's *Guide*, pp. 253–4. (T.pt.O.)

(c) ARCHIVES DE LA MARINE

SERIES B¹. DÉCISIONS. Vols. 1–55 consist of the deliberations of the Council of Marine in charge of colonial matters from 1715 to 1721. Vols. 56–68 consist of the ministerial papers. The documents cover commerce, troops, finance, land grants, church matters, relations with English colonies and Indians, etc. (See Roy's *Rapport*, pp. 167–77.) (T.O.)

SERIES B². CORRESPONDANCE GÉNÉRALE: LETTRES ENVOYÉES. (T.O.)

SERIES B³. CORRESPONDANCE GÉNÉRALE: LETTRES REÇUES. (T.O.) These two series contain correspondence between the ministers and the seaport officials. (See Roy's *Rapport*, pp. 178–217.) (T.O.)

SERIES B⁴. CAMPAGNES. Consists of correspondence, journals and reports relating to voyages, naval engagements and expeditions. (See Roy's *Rapport*, pp. 217–27.) (T.O.)

SERIES C. PERSONNEL. This series includes correspondence, lists, returns, naval muster-rolls, as well as individual files of the personnel employed by the Department of Marine. (T.pt.O.)

SERIES E. COMPTABILITÉ. Consists of financial documents of the Department of Marine. (T.pt.O.)

MINISTÈRE DES COLONIES

DÉPÔT DES FORTIFICATIONS DES COLONIES. This collection is composed of technical memoirs, descriptions, maps and plans relating to colonial fortifications, but includes also numerous memoirs relating to economic and financial statements. Calendared in the *Report for* 1905, vol. 1. (T.pt.O.)

MINISTÈRE DE LA MARINE

The *Library* contains a certain number of manuscript materials (1629–1781) concerning Canada, relating mainly to troops, trade companies and fisheries. (See Roy's *Rapport*, pp. 243–6.)

The *Archives Office* contains documents (1669–1773) relating to colonial administration and naval operations.

DÉPÔT DES CARTES ET PLANS DE LA MARINE

Is very rich in early Canadian maps and plans. It also contains a large number of ships' journals and log-books, and some miscellaneous letters, journals and documents. (See Roy's *Rapport*, pp. 249–321.)

MINISTÈRE DES AFFAIRES ÉTRANGÈRES

MÉMOIRES ET DOCUMENTS, FRANCE. Contains a certain number of documents relating to trade and treaties affecting Canada. (See Roy's *Rapport*, pp. 569–71.) (T.O.)

MÉMOIRES ET DOCUMENTS, AMÉRIQUE. This series is mainly composed of memoirs and papers gathered for the information of the Department and relates to explorations, trade, colonisation, fisheries, finance, Indians, English colonies, land and church matters, etc. (See Roy's *Rapport*, pp. 571–8.) (T.O.)

MÉMOIRES ET DOCUMENTS, ANGLETERRE. Contains material relating to Acadians, Indian wars, finance. Calendared, but under different volume numbers, in the *Report for* 1883, pp. 122–38. (See Roy's *Rapport*, pp. 578–84.) (T.O.)

CORRESPONDANCE POLITIQUE, ANGLETERRE. This series is made up of the official correspondence exchanged with the French ambassador in England and contains material on the restoration of Quebec and Acadia, Hudson Bay and boundary claims, fishery and Nova Scotia and the Acadians. Vols. 43–5 are calendared in the *Report for* 1912, pp. 18–53. (See Roy's *Rapport*, pp. 585–648.) (T.O.)

ÉTATS-UNIS. This section contains the correspondence between France and her representatives in the United States relating to the War of Independence. Vols. 1–11 are calendared in the *Report for* 1912, pp. 162–214. (T.O.)

ROME. In this section are found a few documents concerning Canada.

HOLLANDE. Documents relating to the Treaty of Utrecht. (T.pt.O.)

PLANS ET CARTES. This collection contains but a few maps concerning Canada.

MINISTÈRE DE LA GUERRE

ARCHIVES HISTORIQUES. This collection embraces all military records down to 1790, correspondence, instructions, memoirs, journals and miscellaneous. Of slight import for the years 1637–1745, but extremely valuable for the years 1746–63. (T.O.)

BIBLIOTHÈQUE NATIONALE

DIVISION DES MANUSCRITS. This division contains numerous documents of importance to early Canadian history in its various sections: Fonds français, Nouvelles Acquisitions, Collection Clairambault, Mélanges Colbert. (T.O.)

COLLECTION LALLEMANT DE BETZ. Contains a certain number of maps relating to Canada. (See Roy's *Rapport*, pp. 787–802.)

At the Bibliothèque Nationale are also the *Département des Estampes* (see Roy's *Rapport*, pp. 803, etc.) and the *Cabinet des médailles*.

BIBLIOTHÈQUE DE L'ARSENAL

ARCHIVES DE LA BASTILLE. Gradis Papers: Documents relating to Lamothe Cadillac and Bigot's trial; Île Royale Papers.

BIBLIOTHÈQUE MAZARINE

HISTOIRE DE MONTRÉAL, by Dollier de Casson and a few memoirs. (T.pt.O.)

BIBLIOTHÈQUES PUBLIQUES DE FRANCE

The public libraries of France contain a certain number of interesting documents. Space forbids any summary. (See Roy's *Rapport*, pp. 897–923.)

ARCHIVES DES PORTS MARITIMES

Several of the Maritime Ports have extensive archives, containing much information on Canada's trade and shipping; specially La Rochelle, Dieppe, Honfleur and Rochefort. Part of the archives of the last-named port has been transcribed for the Canadian Archives. (See Roy's *Rapport*, pp. 925–72.)

SEMINAIRE DE SAINT-SULPICE

The Archives of the Seminary of Saint-Sulpice, which was the seigneurial owner of Montreal, is rich in Canadian material. (T.pt.O.)

ARCHEVÊCHÉ DE PARIS

Interesting material exists relating to missions. (T.pt.O.)

SEMINAIRE DU SAINT-ESPRIT

History of the Seminary of Saint-Esprit. (T.O.)

GREAT BRITAIN

BRITISH MUSEUM

The list here given is restricted to the most important collections.

ADDITIONAL MANUSCRIPTS. Among the many papers of this collection, only a few of the subjects are mentioned: Canadian maps; Acadian and Canadian boundary claims; Radisson's narrative; Siege of Louisbourg; Alexander and la Tour; Mascarene Papers and Acadian expulsion; Hardwicke Papers; Civil Government of Quebec; fur trade, 1761–5, etc. (T.O.)

BOUQUET PAPERS, 30 vols. 1756–65. Bouquet served in America and defeated Pontiac. Calendared in the *Report for* 1889, pp. 1–337. (T.O.)

HALDIMAND PAPERS, 232 vols. 1756–90. Papers of Governor Haldimand, most important for the period. Calendared in the *Reports for* 1884, 1885, 1886, 1887, 1888, 1889. (T.O.)

COTTONIAN MANUSCRIPTS. This collection contains a few documents relating to early navigation to Canada, and to the expedition of Argall. (T.O.)

EGERTON MANUSCRIPTS. This collection contains several papers relating to Nova Scotia, 1620–1747. (T.O.)

HARLEIAN COLLECTION. In this collection are found several papers on the North-West passage and Nova Scotia. (T.O.)

KING'S MANUSCRIPTS. The most important papers are the following: Reports on American Colonies, 1721–62; Gage and Burton's reports on Canada; Morse's description of Nova Scotia, 1784. (T.O.)

LANSDOWNE MANUSCRIPTS. They contain material relating to Anglo-French contentions concerning boundaries, fisheries and Indians; with French observations on the West Coast of America, 1721. (T.O.)

SLOANE MANUSCRIPTS. In this collection should be noted: Mackenzie's Journal to the Arctic Ocean; Relation du voyage de Radisson; and papers relating to the French in Hudson Bay. (T.O.)

STOWE MANUSCRIPTS. This collection includes Nelson's Voyage to Canada, 1682; Hearne's narrative of his voyage, 1770–2. (T.O.)

CHURCH BRIEFS, HARGRAVE MANUSCRIPTS, ROYAL MANUSCRIPTS. A few items of interest will be found in these collections. (T.pt.O.)

PUBLIC RECORD OFFICE
I. RECORDS OF THE CHANCERY AND PRIVY SEAL
(PATENT ROLLS)

In these two distinct offices, records concerning Canada will be found, which may be divided roughly into two classes: (a) Grants and charters; (b) Commissions, 1637–1864. (T.O.)

II. PRIVY COUNCIL

These records from 1540 to 1836 are now in the Public Record Office. Sales papers are at the Privy Council Office, Whitehall. Though as a rule the Privy Council acted in relation to the colonies only when special cases arose, still its records contain much of importance for Canadian history.

(a) Papers, etc. (P.C. 1):

COLONIAL PAPERS, 1677–1799. Papers relating to land grants in Maritime Provinces, 1765–7; reports on Acts of Quebec, Nova Scotia, 1767; Lake Superior Mines, 1771, etc. See *Acts of Privy Council of England, Colonial Series*.

(b) Registers (P.C. 2):

They contain the minutes of the proceedings of the Council and its orders, with reports of its committees, and reports and papers submitted. Papers to be mentioned, *inter alia*: Division of Nova Scotia, 1784; Canadian-American trade; John Meares and Nootka Sound, 1791; Division of Quebec, 1791; Indian trade; Emigrants for the Hudson's Bay Co.'s settlement, 1815–19; North West Co. vs. Hudson's Bay Co., 1820; Importations to New Brunswick, etc.

(c) Judicial Committee:

Records of the Judicial Committee of the Privy Council are preserved in the Privy Council Office, Whitehall.

III. STATE PAPERS

This collection consists of the papers which had accumulated from earliest times in the State Paper Office under the Secretaries of State, and which have not been transferred to more congenial series. As a rule, they do not go beyond the year 1782, but are continued in the papers of the three great departments, the Foreign Office, the Home Office and the Colonial Office.

The records of the Colonial Office now comprise the former State Papers Colonial, the America and West Indies papers, and Papers of the Board of Trade and Plantations, to which have been added the papers of the Colonial Office, since its creation as a distinct department of state. The records have been rearranged topographically under colonies.

(A) STATE PAPERS, DOMESTIC:

This division is almost entirely composed of papers formerly under the Secretary of State for the Southern Department, which included the colonies.

ELIZABETH TO GEORGE III (1558–1782). Only a few documents of interest to Canada remain in this series. Elizabeth, vols. 42–131, Frobisher's voyages; George III, vols. 8–10, Thurlow, Marriott and the Quebec Act. (See *Calendar of State Papers, Domestic*.)

ENTRY BOOKS. This series contains little about the colonies, but a few letters and commissions. Vol. 137, Lake Ontario; vol. 142, Hudson's Bay Co.; vol. 191, Louisbourg and Quebec expeditions; vol. 231, French-Canadian prisoners, 1759.

NAVAL. This series includes the correspondence with the Secretary of State relating to naval affairs, and is divided into several sections. Vols. 9–10, Rear-Adm. Walker's expedition; vols. 29, 31, 38, 41, 98, Canada, Louisbourg and Nova Scotia. (T.pt.O.)

MILITARY. Letters and documents to the Secretary of State from the War Office, not transferred to other series, 1702–82. Vol. 34, Walker's expedition; vols. 35, 38, 40, Nova Scotia.

(B) STATE PAPERS, FOREIGN AND FOREIGN OFFICE RECORDS:

This division is composed of the diplomatic correspondence. From 1547 to 1577 the State Papers Foreign are arranged chronologically and from July 1577 under the names of the various countries.

FRANCE. Important material exists here relating to Canadian history. Vols. 1–112, 1577–1640. (T.pt.O.)

TREATY PAPERS. These consist of the documents relating to the various negotiations conducted by Ministers and Plenipotentiaries, 1577–1780, as distinct from the regular correspondence. Of special interest are the papers relating to the restoration of Quebec, 1632, and the Treaty of Utrecht. Vols. 9 (1602–23), 11 (1632–7), 98–101 (1712), 117 (1754–5). (T.pt.O.)

TREATIES. Vols. 72–3, Treaty of Utrecht; vols. 117, 118, 123, 124, Treaty of Paris; vol. 127, Convention concerning Canadian paper-money; vol. 543, Peace between England and the United States, 1782.

VARIOUS. Vol. 77, 1766–7, Canadian paper-money and trade.

JACKSON PAPERS. Vol. 57, Three papers on Canada, 1807–10.

The records of the Foreign Office, with certain exceptions, date from 1782.

AMERICA, UNITED STATES OF, SERIES I (F.O. 4), 1780–92, AND SERIES II (F.O. 5), 1793–1905. These series contain much Canadian material, concerning boundary disputes, commercial relations, fisheries, extradition, French plans against Canada, Fenian raids, fugitive slaves, etc. (T.pt.O.)

FRANCE (F.O. 27), vol. 2. Negotiations of the Treaty of Versailles, 1782. (T.O.)

MISCELLANEA (F.O. 95), vol. 511. Same subject. (T.O.)

(C) STATE PAPERS, COLONIAL AND COLONIAL OFFICE RECORDS:

C.O. 1. COLONIAL PAPERS, GENERAL SERIES, 68 vols. 1574–1697. Contains occasional Canadian material. Calendared in *State Papers Colonial*. (T.O.)

C.O. 5. AMERICA AND WEST INDIES, vols. 1–187 (1689–1793), 207 (1771–84). For the Canadian historian this series is of special importance for its military material: Expedition to Canada, 1711, and the Seven Years' War, War of Independence; also Vancouver's despatches, 1791–3; Shirley's letters; and material dispersed among the New England papers. (T.O.)

C.O. 6. BRITISH NORTH AMERICA, vols. 1–16 and 19–20. Boundary Papers, United States, 1816–50. (T.O.)

C.O. 42. CANADA ORIGINAL CORRESPONDENCE, 1700–1894. This series consists of the correspondence of the Governors of Quebec (later Lower Canada), Upper Canada and Canada, with miscellaneous correspondence and papers. It forms the official basis of Canadian history. Transcripts under the title of the Q Series and original duplicate despatches from 1771 to 1840 are in Ottawa. Calendared in the *Reports for* 1890–3, 1896–1902 and 1909, but the first 23 volumes are calendared in the *Report for* 1921.

C.O. 43. ENTRY BOOKS, 1763–1873. These contain copies of despatches and instructions to be found in the Canadian G Series. (Transcripts in Ottawa, Series Q, where such volumes have a letter added to the volume number.) Printed in part in the *Report for* 1904, pp. 173–286, and in the *Report for* 1905, vol. 1, pp. 3–114.)

C.O. 44. ACTS, 1764–1899. Contains Imperial Acts relating to Canada.

C.O. 45. SESSIONAL PAPERS, 1764–1900. Includes Minutes of Council. (T.pt.O.)

C.O. 47. MISCELLANEA, 1764–1866. Includes among others: Paper-money, 1764; Lands in Roture, 1770; Quebec Code of Laws, 1773. (T.pt.O.)

C.O. 60. COLUMBIA, BRITISH. Original Correspondence (with the Home authorities), 1858–71. (But the Entry Books, 1858–71, are listed under C.O. 338.)

C.O. 61. COLUMBIA, BRITISH. Acts, 1858–67.

C.O. 62. COLUMBIA, BRITISH. Acts, Sessional Papers, 1864–1900.

C.O. 64. COLUMBIA, BRITISH. Acts, Miscellanea, 1860–70.

C.O. 134. HUDSON'S BAY. Original Correspondence, 1675–1759. Calendared in the *Report for* 1895. (T.O.)

C.O. 135. HUDSON'S BAY. Entry Books, 1770–89. (T.O.)

C.O. 164. MANITOBA. Acts, 1867–86.

C.O. 165. MANITOBA. Sessional Papers.

C.O. 188. NEW BRUNSWICK. Original Correspondence, 1784–1867. Official correspondence of the Governors with the Home authorities with draft replies. (Vols. 148–206 have been deposited in the Ottawa Archives.) Calendared in the *Report for* 1895. (T.O.)

C.O. 189. NEW BRUNSWICK. Entry Books, 1784–1867. (Out of 21 vols., vols. 6–9 have been presented to the Ottawa Archives.)

C.O. 190. NEW BRUNSWICK. Acts, 1786–1897.

C.O. 191. NEW BRUNSWICK. Sessional Papers, 1786–1900.

C.O. 193. MISCELLANEA, 1786–1865. (T.pt.O.)

C.O. 214. NORTH WEST TERRITORIES. Acts, 1877–98.

C.O. 215. NORTH WEST TERRITORIES. Sessional Papers, 1877–98.

C.O. 217. NOVA SCOTIA AND CAPE BRETON. Original Correspondence, 1702–1867. Official correspondence of the Governor with the Home authorities. Calendared with other papers in the *Report for* 1894, pp. 1–573. (T.O.)

C.O. 218. NOVA SCOTIA AND CAPE BRETON. Entry Books, 1710–1867. (T.O.)

C.O. 219. NOVA SCOTIA AND CAPE BRETON. Acts, 1725–1900.

C.O. 220. NOVA SCOTIA AND CAPE BRETON. Sessional Papers, 1725–1900.

C.O. 221. NOVA SCOTIA AND CAPE BRETON. Miscellanea, 1730–1860. (T.O.)

C.O. 226. PRINCE EDWARD ISLAND. Original Correspondence (with Home authorities), 1769–1873. Calendared in the *Report for* 1895. (T.pt.O.)

C.O. 227. PRINCE EDWARD ISLAND. Entry Books, 1769–1872. (T.O.)

C.O. 228. PRINCE EDWARD ISLAND. Acts.

C.O. 229. PRINCE EDWARD ISLAND. Sessional Papers, 1770–1800. (T.O.)

C.O. 231. PRINCE EDWARD ISLAND. Miscellanea, 1807–71.

C.O. 305. VANCOUVER ISLAND. Original Correspondence (with Home authorities), 1846–67. (Entry Books, 1849–67, listed under C.O. 410.)

C.O. 306. VANCOUVER ISLAND. Acts, 1852–66.

C.O. 307. VANCOUVER ISLAND. Sessional Papers, 1864–6.

C.O. 309. VICTORIA. Original Correspondence (with Home authorities), 1851–94. (Entry Books, 1851–77, listed under C.O. 411.)

C.O. 310. VICTORIA. Acts, 1851–98.

C.O. 311. VICTORIA. Sessional Papers, 1851–1900.

C.O. 313. VICTORIA, Miscellanea, 1838–1900.

C.O. 323. COLONIES (GENERAL), 1689–1894. (T.O.)

C.O. 324. COLONIES (GENERAL). Entry Books, 1662–1822. (T.O.)

C.O. 325. COLONIES (GENERAL). Miscellanea, 1744–1858. (T.O.)

C.O. 385. EMIGRATION ENTRY BOOKS, 1814–71. (T.O.)

C.O. 387. LORD AYLMER'S PAPERS, 1830–7.

IV. *TREASURY*

(*a*) In-letters:

T. 1. TREASURY BOARD PAPERS, 1557–1889. Original correspondence with occasional minutes, reports, accounts, etc.

(*b*) Out-letters:

T. 28. VARIOUS. America, 1763–1838. Includes Canadian correspondence.

(*c*) Minutes:

T. 29. MINUTE BOOKS, 1667–1870. Many Loyalist papers.

(*d*) Accounts:

T. 38. ACCOUNTS DEPARTMENTAL. Colonies, 1685–1838. Accounts of the Receivers General. Quebec.

(*e*) Miscellanea:

T. 50. AMERICAN, 1780–1835. Loyalist papers.
T. 64. VARIOUS. Colonies, 1680–1867. Shipping and trade returns, correspondence, despatches, etc.
COMMISSARIAT, 1689–1822. Accounts, correspondence, etc. relating to supply of provisions and the troops in Canada, etc.
CROWN LANDS, 1668–1803. Deeds, reports, etc.
LAW OPINIONS, 1763–1809. Material about Quebec.

EXPIRED COMMISSIONS

T. 79. AMERICAN LOYALIST CLAIMS COMMISSION, 1777–1812. Minute-books of the Commissioners, Reports on claims, etc.

TREASURY-SOLICITOR

PAPERS, 1584–1850. Of special Canadian interest are the following cases: 925, Finlay, Levy and others vs. Gov. Murray, 1768; 1127, Court-Martial on Captain Pring and others, 1815.
GENERAL SERIES. Bundle 4957, Court-Martial on Major Robert Rogers, 1768. Bundle 954, McBeath and Meldrum vs. Haldimand, 1779–87. (T.O.)

V. *EXCHEQUER AND AUDIT OFFICE*

The records now preserved under this division consist for the most part of public accounts from the Commissioners of Audit and various offices absorbed by the present Exchequer and Audit Office.

(*a*) Declared Accounts (A.O. 1):

ARMY. Accounts of paymasters-general of the forces in America, 1746–83.
BARRACK-MASTERS. Accounts of Lt.-Generals James Robertson, George Clarke and W. Crosbie, Barrack-Masters in North America, 1760–83, and their deputies, Murray and Brehm at Quebec, and Putnam in Nova Scotia, 1776–84.
CANADA AND NOVA SCOTIA. Accounts of public expenditure, 1775–1805.
COMMANDERS-IN-CHIEF, MILITARY GOVERNORS. Among other items, Haldimand, Governor at Three Rivers, 1762–5; Carleton, Commander in the Northern District, 1766–70; Massey, Commander in Nova Scotia, 1776–1828.
CONTRACTORS, PURVEYORS, ETC. (abroad). Accounts of Missing and Woodford, victual contractors for Annapolis, 1720–68; Rattan for Nova Scotia and Louisbourg, 1745–52; Stephenson and Blackburn for Nova Scotia, 1768–82, etc.
INDIANS IN NORTH AMERICA. Accounts of agents and superintendents of Indian Affairs, 1755–1802.

PAYMASTERS AND TREASURERS OF THE FORCES, ETC. Cramahé, paymaster in the Northern District of North America, 1774–80; Dunn, Quebec, 1774–84, etc.

QUARTERMASTERS. Lt. Col. Bradstreet, 1756–60; Lt. Col. Irving, 1760–5, Quebec; Major J. Maxwell, Montreal, 1770–2; Major J. Carden, Montreal, 1775–7; Major T. Campbell, Canada, 1775–9; Lt. Col. Handfield, Nova Scotia, 1776–83; Sir G. Carleton, Canada, 1778–82; Col. A. S. De Peyster, Upper Ports of Canada, 1775–84; Sir J. H. Craig, Halifax, 1779; Brig.-Gen. J. Campbell, Penobscot, 1779–81; Major-Gen. A. W. Powell, Canada, 1780–2.

GOVERNORS, AGENTS, ETC. Accounts of Gov. Knowles, of Cape Breton, 1746–7; Gov. Hopson, of Louisbourg, 1747–9; Governors Hopson, Arbuthnot and Parr, of Nova Scotia, 1752–92; Agents Kilby and Cumberland, Nova Scotia, 1758–85; Gov. Patterson of Prince Edward Island, 1780–7; Gov. Burton, of Three Rivers, 1760–3.

INDIANS, NORTH AMERICA. Sir John Johnson, Col. Guy Johnson, Lt. Col. Campbell, superintendents, 1755–85; Capt. Alexander Fraser and Daniel Claus, superintendent and agent, 1776–1802.

SETTLERS IN NOVA SCOTIA. Accounts for 1751–3.

WORKS AND FORTIFICATIONS. In North America and Canada.

(b) Accounts, Various (A.O. 3):

These consist for the most part of the particulars of accounts, subsidiary to the Declared Accounts and often contain more detailed information.

MISCELLANEOUS ACCOUNTS OF GOVERNORS AND OTHERS IN AMERICA, NOVA SCOTIA, NEW BRUNSWICK, ETC., with subsidiary documents. Vols. 126–8 (1711–1819). Among others: accounts of Governor Murray, Quebec, 1776; Sir Thomas Mills, Receiver-General of Quebec, 1778–90, and his deputy, William Grant, 1778–85; William Devaynes, Canada, 1781–2; Dr Hayes, Canada, 1776–83; Gen. Burton, Three Rivers, 1760–3; Guy Johnson and J. Campbell, Indian Dept. 1774–85; H. T. Cramahé, Quebec, 1774–80; Lt. Col. De Peyster, Upper Canada, 1775–84; Thomas Dunn, Canada, 1728–84; Robert Mathews, Gov. Haldimand's Secretary, Quebec, 1729–84; Lieut. Twiss, Comptroller of Works, Canada, 1779; Capt. Alex. Fraser, Indian Affairs, Quebec, 1726–81; Brig.-Gen. J. Campbell, Penobscot, 1779–81; Army Staff, Quebec, 1760; Col. Thomas Carleton, Quarter-Master General and his deputy, Major J. Carden, 1778–82.

COLONIES AND DEPENDENCIES. Vol. 396. Canada, 1772–1825; accounts of surveys of Samuel Holland, 1776–86. Vol. 400. Cape Breton and Prince Edward Island. Des Barres' administration.

(c) Claims, American Loyalists:

A.O. 12. 1726–1831. (T.pt.O.)
A.O. 13. 1780–1835. (T.pt.O.)

(d) Miscellanea:

A.O. 16. COLONIES AND DEPENDENCIES, 1764–1865. Warrants of establishments and appointments, instructions to officials, etc.

PIPE OFFICE

In the Pipe Office were kept duplicates on parchment of public accounts. These records consequently substantiate those of the Audit Office.

VI. CUSTOMS HOUSE

IMPORTS AND EXPORTS: AMERICA, 1762–73.

VII. *ADMIRALTY*

The departmental records of the Admiralty found here date only from Charles II. Papers of earlier date may exist scattered among other collections. The main divisions concerning Canada are the following:

Accountant General's Department:

ACCOUNTS: VARIOUS. Vols. 4 and 150, Quebec, Louisbourg and Halifax (1742–1808).

MISCELLANEA: VARIOUS. Vol. 8, Surveys in North America, 1783–94; Vol. 9, Papers and letters respecting Loyalists (no names) put on board transport ships.

ADMIRALS' JOURNALS, 1702–1855.
CAPTAINS' LOGS, 1669–1852.
MASTERS' LOGS, 1672–1840.
SHIPS' LOGS, 1799–1885.
} Transcripts in Ottawa of those relating to the Louisbourg and Quebec expeditions, 1745–59.

Secretary's Department (IN-LETTERS):

ADMIRALS' DESPATCHES, 1673–1867. (Arranged under stations.) Jamaica, vols. 230–41 (1713–79); Leeward Islands, vols. 305–15 (1745–95); North America, vols. 480–509 (1745–1815); Halifax, vols. 510–17 (1816–30), etc. (T.O.)
ADMIRALS UNEMPLOYED. Vol. 527 (1693–1742).
CAPTAINS' LETTERS, 1678–1792. (T.pt.O.)
LETTERS RELATING TO THE COLONIES, 1697–1839. (T.pt.O.)
SECRET LETTERS, 1756–1837. (T.pt.O.)
REPORTS OF COURTS-MARTIAL, 1680–1839. (T.pt.O.)

Secretary's Department (OUT-LETTERS):

SECRETARY'S LETTERS, 1679–1812. (T.pt.O.)
SECRET ORDERS AND LETTERS, 1745–1820. Of special interest is vol. 1331 (1745–61). (T.pt.O.)

VIII. *WAR OFFICE*

W.O. 1. IN-LETTERS, 1732–1868. Original correspondence relating to Canada, 1756–85. (T.O.)
W.O. 12. MUSTER BOOKS AND PAY LISTS. These are the chief means of tracing a man's services provided his regiment is known.
W.O. 28. HEADQUARTERS RECORDS. *America*, 1746–85. Muster-rolls, letters, memorials, etc. concerning troops in Canada. (T.O.)
W.O. 40. SELECTED UNNUMBERED PAPERS. Various papers relating to Canada. (T.O.)
W.O. 55. MISCELLANEA, 1684–1902. Various Ordnance correspondence relating to Nova Scotia and Canada. (T.O.)

IX. *BOARD OF TRADE*

These are the records of the new Board of Trade created in 1784. Down to 1839, they are in the Public Record Office; after that date, at the Board of Trade.

IN-LETTERS (B.T. 1). Original letters and papers communicated to the Board, 1791–1839.
MINUTES (B.T. 5). Daily proceedings of the Committee, 1783–1850. Material relating to Nova Scotia division, 1784; Quebec and Nova Scotia intercourse; American trade with Canada, Nova Scotia and New Brunswick; Labrador; Conditions in Canada, 1812; North West Fur Crop, etc.
MISCELLANEA (B.T. 6). Reports, accounts and returns; American intercourse with Nova Scotia (1783–1807).

X. *CHATHAM MSS. PAPERS*

Correspondence and papers of Lord Chatham, vols. 1–100, and of William Pitt, vols. 101–363. (T.O.)

XI. *GENERAL POST OFFICE*

The records relating to the colonial postal system will be found in the following divisions: *Treasury Letter-books*; *Orders of the Board*; *Commission Books*; *Instructions*; *General Accounts*; *American Letter Book*. (T.O.)

MANUSCRIPTS OF THE HOUSE OF LORDS

These manuscripts consist of two groups of papers: (*a*) Parliamentary and (*b*) non-Parliamentary papers. The first is composed of records of the proceedings of the committees, including particulars of proceedings of the House sitting in committee as well as notes of debate, evidence produced, legal opinions, records of votes, etc. Minutes of proceedings of select committees and proceedings of joint committees of House of Commons are also to be found there as well as resolutions, orders, motions, etc. The second group includes royal speeches and messages, treaties, petitions, memorials, etc. as well as papers presented as a result of orders of the House. (Papers relating to French encroachments, Treaty of Paris, Quebec Act, colonial ship lists, colonial trade reports, etc.)

The papers are calendared in *MSS. of the House of Lords,* to 1693 in *Rep. of Hist. MSS. Comm.* and for 1693–1710 in New series, Vols. I–VIII.

HUDSON'S BAY COMPANY

These records comprise several hundred memorial books, daily journals kept at forts, minute-books, out-letters and in-letters, stock books, account-books and maps. (T.pt.O.)

SOCIETY FOR THE PROPAGATION OF THE GOSPEL IN FOREIGN PARTS

The archives at Tufton St., Westminster, S.W., contain much Canadian material especially in the "Letters and reports of missionaries and other correspondents". (T.pt.O.)

LAMBETH PALACE LIBRARY

The archives of the Archbishop of Canterbury contain important material for the history of the Church of England in Canada.

CANADA

THE PUBLIC ARCHIVES, OTTAWA

(Original Official Collections)

SERIES C consists of the papers of the military secretary's office in Canada, from 1761 to 1879, and contains the correspondence with the War Office, the Admiralty and the Treasury, as well as with the Canadian officers, including a mass of reports, instructions, memorials, orderly books, journals, accounts, surveys, etc. See Cruikshank, *Inventory of the Military Documents in the Canadian Archives*, Ottawa, 1910.

SERIES E is composed of the original minute-books of the various Legislative and Executive Councils of Quebec, and Lower and Upper Canada from 1764 to 1867. It also includes about 900 portfolios of miscellaneous documents related to the council deliberations and consisting of letters, petitions, grants, Orders-in-Council, surveys, reports, etc. There is a summary of this series in Parker's *Guide*, pp. 31–3.

SERIES G. This series of 489 portfolios extends from 1771 to 1873, and is made up of the papers, mostly originals, from the Governor General's Office. It consists of original despatches from the Colonial Office to the Governors of Canada and the Lieutenant-Governors of some of the provinces; entry and letter-books; inter-provincial correspondence, instructions to governors, correspondence with the British ministers at Washington, and correspondence with the Treasury. The series relates to Lower Canada, 1787–1841; Upper Canada, 1796–1841; United Canada, 1841–67; Prince Edward Island, 1771–1867; Vancouver Island and British Columbia, 1849–67. A summary of this series will be found in Parker's *Guide*, pp. 7–67.

SERIES S. This collection of over 6000 volumes and portfolios consists of the correspondence of the Civil Secretary of the Governors and Lieutenant-Governors of Quebec and Lower and Upper Canada, from 1760 to 1867. The main divisions under subject matters include appointments, acts and bills, boundaries, commissions, Executive and Legislative Councils, courts and gaols, lands, licences, militia, public accounts, public works, churches and ecclesiastical affairs, customs, fisheries, Indian Affairs, rebellion 1837–8; schools, etc., etc.

C.O. 42. One hundred and twenty volumes of original duplicate despatches (1771–1866) of the Governors of Lower and Upper Canada to the Colonial Office, with sessional papers, were presented to the Archives in 1911.

C.O. 188. Vols. 148–206 (1784–1864) of this series containing the official correspondence of the Governors of New Brunswick, are now in the Canadian Archives.

INDIAN AFFAIRS. This series (1722–1867) consists of the administrative correspondence, departmental and local, relating to the administration of the Indians. It includes also minutes, land-books, entry books, accounts, reports, etc.

MILITIA PAPERS. This collection is made up of the old military records of Upper and Lower Canada and the departmental records of the Department of National Defence, and covers the period from 1770 to 1867. It consists of correspondence, returns, accounts, pay-lists, muster-rolls, abstracts and vouchers. It also includes the records of the Great War, now partly transferred to the Archives.

PRIVATE ORIGINAL COLLECTIONS
(IN THE PUBLIC ARCHIVES, OTTAWA)

Only the most important collections are here mentioned with a concise designation of their contents.

ASKIN PAPERS (1771–1860). Collection of correspondence and papers of John Askin and his descendants, mainly relating to commercial matters, fur trade, Indian tribes, the War of 1812 and the Rebellion of 1837. See Parker, *Guide to the Materials*, pp. 183–4.

ASSINIBOIA (1832–60). A volume of the Minutes of the Council of Assiniboia.

BAGOT PAPERS (1816–43). Official and miscellaneous correspondence and various documents of Sir Charles Bagot, when British Minister at Washington, 1816–18, and Governor of Canada, 1841–3. See Parker, *Guide to the Materials*, pp. 112–14.

BARING PAPERS (1819–71). Collection of the financial papers of the London bankers, Baring Bros., dealing with the great public works and enterprises in British North America, during the period from 1819 to 1871.

BAYFIELD PAPERS (1841–5). Surveys of the St Lawrence by Lieut. Henry Bayfield.

BEGG JOURNALS (1869–70). Journals of Alexander Begg of the Red River Expedition.

BELL-IRVINE JOURNAL (1870). Journal of the Red River Expedition.

BIGOT LETTERS (1746–56). Twenty-two personal letters of Intendant François Bigot.

BOURLAMAQUE COLLECTION (1756–63). Six volumes of military letters from Vaudreuil, Montcalm, Levis and others to Bourlamaque. Calendared in the *Report for* 1923.

BOWELL PAPERS (1870–1905). Correspondence of Sir Mackenzie Bowell, former Prime Minister of Canada.

BOYLE PAPERS (1899–1903). Papers of John Boyle, of Toronto, concerning Georgian Bay transportation. See *Report for* 1923, p. 9.

BREBŒUF NARRATIVES (1649). Narrative of the death of Fathers Brebœuf and Lalemant.

BRIDGES DIARIES (1806–11). Diaries of Samuel Bridges on his voyage from Portsmouth to Quebec and Montreal.

BUELL PAPERS (1836–85). Military papers relating mainly to the Riel Rebellion.

BULGER PAPERS (1810–70). Letters and papers of Captain Andrew Bulger relating chiefly to the Western posts and Indian Affairs during the War of 1812. See Parker, *Guide to the Materials*, pp. 111–12.

CANADA COMPANY (1824–90). Papers and books of records of the Canada Company relating to the settlement of Upper Canada.

CLAUS PAPERS (1716–1825). Correspondence and documents relating especially to the management of the Indians during the Seven Years' War and the War of Independence. See Parker, *Guide to the Materials*, pp. 106–10.

COWAN DIARIES (1856–67). Diaries of Dr William Cowan of Fort Garry.

CRESPEL NARRATIVE (1742). Voyage et naufrage du P. Emmanuel Crespel.

CROMWELL LETTER (1656). An order to Captain John Leverett to deliver the forts in Acadia to Thomas Temple. Printed in the *Report for* 1923.

DARTMOUTH PAPERS (1688–1798). Collection of official and miscellaneous correspondence and various documents relating to Canada, Newfoundland and Labrador. Calendared in the *Fourteenth Report of the Historical Commission*, London, 1895, the *Eleventh Report*, 1887, and the *Fifteenth Report*, 1896.

DELANCY-ROBINSON PAPERS (1825–40). Papers and letters relating to New Brunswick.

DESBARRES-ASHFIELD PAPERS (1784–1826). Papers of the first Governor of Cape Breton. Listed in the *Report for* 1923.

DEWDNEY PAPERS (1885). Relating to the second Riel Rebellion.

DURHAM PAPERS (1837–44). Original papers of Lord Durham during his Canadian administration. Calendared in the *Report for* 1923.

ERMATINGER PAPERS (1826–60). Papers of Judge Ermatinger relating to the Hudson's Bay questions and general correspondence.

FLEMING PAPERS (1827–1913). Correspondence and papers of Sir Sandford Fleming relating to the C.P.R., the Pacific Cable, etc.

FRANQUET JOURNAL (1751). Voyage du Sieur Franquet au Port St-Pierre, au Port des Trois-Rivières, de l'Île Saint-Jean.

HOWE PAPERS (1835–73). Collection of note-books, correspondence and speeches of Joseph Howe with miscellaneous papers.

JARVIS LETTERS (1792–1840). Correspondence of William Jarvis, the first Secretary of Upper Canada. See *Report for* 1910, p. 91.

JOHNSTON-HOWE PAPERS (1804–12). Some papers of Joseph Howe.

LAWRENCE PAPERS (1791–1843). Correspondence, reports and books of surveys of Joseph Lawrence, relating to the north-east New Brunswick boundary and Prince Edward Island. See Parker, *Guide to the Materials*, p. ix.

LOWE PAPERS (1850–91). Correspondence and papers of John Lowe with public men of the time on the C.P.R., Allan Line, exhibitions and administrative matters. See *Report for* 1913, pp. 43–4.

MACDONALD PAPERS (1856–91). Letters and papers of Sir John A. Macdonald, about 500 volumes.

MacDonnel Papers (1805–19). Papers relating to the Baldoon settlement.

MacDonnell Papers (Miles) (1811–62). Papers relating to the Selkirk settlement, 1811–12, La Prairie Council 1866–8, and other matters.

McGillivray Papers (1818–50). Papers of the McGillivray family and the Highland Society of Canada.

Mackenzie Letter-Books (1872–7). Letter-books of Alexander Mackenzie, the Prime Minister of Canada.

Maconochie-Wellwood Papers (1775). A few papers relating to the capture of St John's by the Americans. Printed in the *Report for* 1914.

Masson Collection (1790–1819). Consists mainly of correspondence and papers relating to the fur trade and the North West Co.

Muster-rolls of the Loyalists (1777–98). Original service lists. See *Report for* 1914, pp. 16–17, and *Report for* 1921, p. 10.

Neilson Collection (1733–1893). These are the papers of John Neilson and include his correspondence with Bédard and Papineau. Calendared in the *Report for* 1913, pp. 15–16, and pp. 99–151, and the *Report for* 1918, pp. 1–87.

Northcliffe Collection (1726–82). Papers and letters of General Robert Monckton, presented by Sir Leicester Harmsworth in memorial of his brother, Lord Northcliffe. Calendared in *The Northcliffe Collection*, Ottawa, 1926.

Paper-money (1764). Lists of holders of Canadian paper-money.

Papineau Letters (1819–56). Original and transcript letters of Papineau to Henry S. Chapman.

Pegasus (1786). Illustrated log-book of H.M.S. *Pegasus*.

Preston Collection (1799–1805). Letter-books of General Henry Bowyer, at Halifax.

Raymond Collection (1797–1840). Papers concerning the north-eastern boundary between Canada and the United States. See Parker, *Guide to the Materials*, pp. 186–7.

Salaberry Papers (1795–1829). Letters and commissions belonging to the Salaberry family. Calendared in the *Report for* 1912, pp. 289–91.

Selkirk Papers (1802–40). Correspondence and papers relating to the Selkirk Settlement and other matters.

Stefansson Papers (1914–18). Papers, notes and diaries of Vilhjalmur Stefansson's Arctic expedition.

Wolfe (1758–9). Order-book of Wolfe kept by Sir John Moore.

TRANSCRIPTS

From Quebec Archives:

Actes de Foy et Hommage (1667–1864).

Aveus, Dénombrements et Déclarations (1723–1831).

Cahiers d'Intendance. Titres présentés par les vassaux (1626–1750).

Insinuations du Conseil Souverain (1663–1758).

Jugements et Délibérations du Conseil Souverain (1717–60).

Ordonnances des Intendants (1705–60).

Papiers Terriers, Censive du Domaine du Roy (1723–1832).

Registres de la Prévôté de Québec (1689–1757).

Registres d'Intendance (Concessions en fief et en roture) (1672–1759). See Parker, *Guide to the Materials*, p. 104.

From Montreal:

Collection Judiciaire (1640–1760). Collection in the Montreal Court-House of ordinances, judgments, etc.

Ordonnances et Règlements pour le gouvernement de Montréal sous l'administration militaire du Canada (1760–4).

Saint-Sulpice Papers (1636–1830). Documents copied from the Archives of the Seminary of St-Sulpice and relating to the Island of Montreal seigneury, religious matters and different questions. See the *Report for* 1912, pp. 15–17.

Baby Collection (1701–1875). Collection of miscellaneous letters, in the course of transcription at the St-Sulpice Library.

MASSON PAPERS. Documents relating to the fur trade and the North West Company in McGill University Library.

From various sources:

BANCROFT COLLECTION (1787–1879). Transcripts of papers in the Bancroft Collection of the University of California, Berkeley, relating to the fur trade on the Western Coast.

BOUGAINVILLE PAPERS (1755–60). Journal and correspondence concerning Canada and the Seven Years' War.

CADILLAC PAPERS. Correspondence, memoirs and various papers relating to Canada and Acadia of Lamothe Cadillac.

DALHOUSIE PAPERS (1756–1831). Papers of Lord Dalhousie, Governor-General of Canada.

HARVEY CORRESPONDENCE (1829–42). Letter-books of Sir John Harvey, Governor of New Brunswick.

INGLIS PAPERS (1775–1849). Letters and journals of the two Nova Scotia bishops of that name. Calendared in the *Report for* 1912, pp. 215–88, and the *Report for* 1913, pp. 227–83.

LAFONTAINE PAPERS (1836–55). Correspondence and papers of Sir Louis H. Lafontaine.

LA PAUSE PAPERS (1756–60). Journals, papers and memoirs of Chevalier de la Pause, who served under Montcalm.

MARQUETTE INDIAN PRAYER BOOK (1668).

MORRIS (1748). A Brief Survey of Nova Scotia by Charles Morris.

MURRAY PAPERS (1759–86). Letters and papers of Governor James Murray. Calendared in the *Report for* 1912.

PAPINEAU AND PERRAULT LETTERS (1824–36). Miscellaneous correspondence.

PERKINS DIARIES (1766–1812). Diary of Simeon Perkins, Liverpool, N.S.

SHELBURNE COLLECTION (1663–1783). Documents and papers relating to Canada. Also known as Lansdowne Collection. Calendared in the *Report for* 1921, pp. 229–81.

SMITH LETTERS (1764–1835). Correspondence of William Smith, of New York, on Canadian affairs.

THOMSON (1759–88). Diaries of Sergeant-Major Thomson, who served during the siege of Quebec.

WASHINGTON LETTERS (1775–83). Correspondence of George Washington.

PROVINCIAL ARCHIVES

ALBERTA

The Archives of the Province are kept in the Provincial Library, Edmonton, the Librarian being also Provincial Archivist.

Most of the public records are kept in the various Departments, which were only created in 1905. The records before that date have remained in Winnipeg or Regina, the two successive administrative headquarters.

The Provincial Library, however, contains, among others, the following documents:

Warre and Vavasour expedition to Oregon Territory, 1845.

Minute Book of the Hudson's Bay Company's Council of the Northern department of Rupert's Land, from 1830 to 1843.

Journals of the Hudson's Bay Company and North West Company:

Journal, Rocky Mountain House, 1799.

Journal, Fort Edmonton, winters 1854–5 and 1855–6.

Journal, Dunvegan, Oct. 1839–Jan. 1842; 1828–9 and 1829–30.

Journal of Robert Terrill Rundle, Wesleyan missionary at Fort Edmonton, Oct. 7, 1840–8. (Copy.)

"Overland to Cariboo," by A. L. Fortune. Narrative of experiences of the overland expedition from Ontario to Cariboo, etc. B.C. (1862).

British Columbia

The Provincial Archives form part of the Provincial Library at Victoria, the official in charge holding the dual position of Librarian and Archivist.

The Archives include all departmental records prior to Confederation in 1871, and comprise Government despatches, Colonial Office records, departmental books and records, original letters of fur-traders and other Hudson's Bay Co. correspondence. They also include series of transcripts from the Public Record Office and the Admiralty, London.

Among the originals are the following:

British Columbia proclamations and ordinances, 1858–64.

House of Assembly, volume of Governor's messages, 1856–60.

Journal of Thompson's River Fort, by John Tod, 1841–3.

Report of the establishment of Fort Yukon, by Alex. H. Murray, 1847–8.

Letters of Simon Fraser, 1806–7.

Vancouver Island Exploring Expedition, by Robert Brown, Commander, 1864.

Manitoba

There is no distinct Archives Branch. Each Department of the Government retains its own records. In the Provincial Library at Winnipeg, however, will be found a collection of historical material, which is described in Appendix D, pp. 39–56, of the 33rd *Annual Report of the Library and Museum for the year ending 30th November* 1916, Winnipeg, King's Printer, 1919, the most important of which are the following:

Minutes of Council of Assiniboia, 1862–9; Records of Council of Assiniboia, 1835–69; Various administrative papers of Assiniboia Government, 1835–69; North West Territories, Minutes of Council, 1873–5; Papers relating to the Red River Rebellion, 1869–70.

New Brunswick

There is no special Archives Branch. Each Department keeps its own records. In the Office of the Clerk of the Executive Council at Fredericton will be found the following documents:

Correspondence and papers connected with the Executive Council; Minutes and rough minutes of Council; Executive Council Papers, 1787–1885.

Orders-in-Council, 1789–1847; Drafts of Commissions, 1784–1847; Opinions of Attorney and Solicitor General and Law Officials, 1785–1855; Maps and plans, 1760–1864; Miscellaneous papers.

In the Office of the Provincial Secretary:

Letter-books of the Governors of New Brunswick, 1784–1809; Letter-books of the Provincial Secretary, 1838–78; Journals of Proceedings respecting allotments of land, 1784–1840; Applications for land; letters and instructions relating to Loyalists; Lists of land grants, 1760–1850.

In the Legislative Library:

Legislative Papers, 1786–1858; Appendices to the Journals of Assembly, 1844–1906.

Nova Scotia

The Provincial Archives at Halifax form a branch under a Deputy-Keeper of Public Records and include, *inter alia*, the following documents:

Commission book at Annapolis Royal, 1720–41; Commission and letter-book, 1742–9; Original minutes of the Council at Annapolis Royal, 1720–42; Original despatches of the Board of Trade, 1745–99; Original letter-books of the Governors, 1763–6, 1778–9, 1783–9; Governor Wentworth's letter-books, 1783–1807; Letter-books of the Governors, 1808–10, 1811–13, 1852–67; Original or duplicate despatches of the Secretary of State to Lieutenant Governors, 1800–67.

Letters of Governor Lawrence to Colonial Governors and the French Governor of Cape Breton, 1753–6; Sir Jeffery Amherst's letters, 1760–84; Provincial Secretary's letter-books, 1803–69; Books of orders, commissions, instructions, warrants, etc. issued by the Governors, 1749–53; Books of warrants drawn by the Governors, 1760–1805; Minutes of Council of Nova Scotia, 1749–1870; Journals of the Legislative Council, 1763–83; Miscellaneous documents, 31 vols., 1748–1841; Miscellaneous documents, 26 vols., 1835–66; Miscellaneous documents, 4 vols., 1768–1870; Selected documents from the Legislative Council, 14 vols., 1760–1841; Papers from the House of Assembly, 14 vols., 1758–1841; Royal Warrants, Mandamus and Commissions, 1753–1840; Royal Instructions to Governors, 1729–1846; Orders of the King-in-Council relating to Nova Scotia, 1752–1852; Papers relating to settlement of Acadian districts, 1759–84; Casual and Territorial Revenue Papers, 1830–43; Correspondence with the British Minister at Washington, 1798–1800; Correspondence with the Provincial Governors, 1833–62; Public Accounts papers, 1758–1846.

Military Papers: 270 volumes of letter-books and order-books relating to Nova Scotia and New Brunswick.

Cape Breton Papers: Despatches from the Secretary of State to the Governors, 1784–1820; Minutes of Council, 1785–1820; Miscellaneous Papers, 1773–1841.

Tyrrell or Pichon Papers, 1754–5.

ONTARIO

The Provincial Archives at Toronto form a separate branch under a Provincial Archivist. The most important classes of its documents are:

Land Records: Correspondence, 1842–69; Heir and Devisee Commission Reports, 1812–72; Letter-books, land board registers, warrants, fiats, reports, returns. Crown and Clergy reserves, Canada Land Company papers, 1784–1867; Entry and letter-books of the Surveyor-General, Land surveys and patents; Sales and Free Land Grants, Field Notes, Lists of emigrants and settlers; Accounts Branch Papers; Registrar's Office Papers, 1792–1864.

Mines Branch Papers; Woods and Forest Branch Papers, from 1852.

Judicial Records: Minute-books, journals and record-books of various Courts and Quarter Sessions, including Rebellion Trial Commission records, 1802–58.

Osgoode Hall Papers: Record-books, Judgments, Docket books and records of proceedings of various courts, 1789–1850.

Private Papers:

Account-books, business ledgers, day-books, etc. kept at various places, 1802–75.

Baldwin Papers, 1806–56. Letters and papers.

Canniff Papers, 1812–98. Relate to medical service, War of 1812, Fenian Raid and N.W. Rebellion of 1885.

Hodgins Papers, 1836–74. Correspondence of Egerton Ryerson with Draper, Hincks and Sir John A. Macdonald. Miscellaneous letters and papers.

Irving Papers, 1870–1910. Relating to Schools, Lands, Boundaries, Fisheries, Indian Affairs, etc.

Jones Papers, 1799–1838. Miscellaneous family papers.

Kingsford Papers. Letters and scrap-books of the historian William Kingsford.

Macaulay Papers, mainly 1820–40. Correspondence and family papers of the Honourable John Macaulay.

McDonald Papers, 1819–40. Business correspondence of J. and C. McDonald, Gananoque.

Merritt Papers, 1780–1879. Miscellaneous papers, relating to the North West, War of 1812, Rebellion of 1837, Canals, Trade, Land Policy, Politics, etc.

Mowat Papers, 1872–80. Mainly relating to medical and Provincial matters.

Robinson Papers, 1812–51. Letters and papers of John Beverley Robinson relating to political affairs, War of 1812, Hudson's Bay Co. and Lord Selkirk, Canada Committee 1822, Rebellion of 1837, political papers, Head, Durham and Bagot.

Rogers Papers, 1783–1839. Military papers and family letters.

Russell Papers, 1725–1808. Family letters touching on the history of the period, Seven Years' War, American War; Account-books and papers of Peter Russell, Receiver-General, 1793–1808.

Strachan Papers, 1794–1867. Bishop Strachan's letter-books and papers relating to Church, Education, Clergy Reserves, Indian Affairs, War of 1812, etc.

Thompson Papers, 1790–1850. Journals, Field-books, surveys, etc. of the explorer David Thompson.

Miscellaneous manuscripts on various subjects.

Prince Edward Island

There is no regular system of public archives. The few records still extant are kept at Charlottetown in the various departments to which they are related, as follows:

Office of the Provincial Secretary:

Minutes of the Executive Council of Prince Edward Island, 1770–1870.
Proclamations and orders of the King-in-Council, etc. 1773–1876.
Commission Books: Books A to E, beginning in 1769.
Council Office, 1825: Containing the oaths of the various officials.

Land Office:

Complete set of books relating to land grants from 1769. Also maps and plans.

Government House:

Correspondence Books, October 1824 to August 1872.

Quebec

The Archives constitute a separate branch under a Provincial Archivist at Quebec. The most important series are the following:

Jugements et Délibérations du Conseil Souverain, 1663–1760.
Insinuations du Conseil Souverain, 1663–1758.
Ordonnances des intendants de la Nouvelle-France, 1705–60.
Registres d'intendance, concessions en fief et en roture, 1672–1759.
Actes de Foy et Hommage, 1667–1757.
Papiers terriers, censive du domaine du Roy, 1723–1832.
Aveux et dénombrements, 1723–81.
Procès-Verbaux des Grands Voyers, 1667–1767.
Terriers de la ville de Québec.
Registres de la Prévôté de Québec, 1666–1759.
Archives de la Justice seigneuriale de Notre-Dame des Anges.
Collection of autograph letters and documents (24 vols.).

Saskatchewan

The Provincial Archives are part of the Provincial Library at Regina, the same official holding the position of Provincial Librarian and Archivist; each department of the Government, however, retains its own records. But in the Provincial Library will be found, among printed material and transcripts, the following important originals:

Oaths of various officials, members of the Council or connected with the North West Council.

Minute Books of the Advisory Council, 1888–91.

Minute Books of the Executive Committee of the Assembly, 1892–8.

Eight volumes of proclamations and orders for the North West Territory, 1876–93.

Minutes of the Executive Committee which became Orders-in-Council, 1892–1905.

PART II

PRINTED WORKS

(Co-ordinated by Professor R. G. Trotter, M.A., Ph.D., in part from bibliographical lists selected by the contributors to this volume.)

A. GENERAL BIBLIOGRAPHY OF CANADIAN HISTORY

I. Bibliographies and Guides to Materials.

II. Printed Documents: (A) Official.
(B) Non-Official.

III. Historical Journals and Publications of Learned Societies.

IV. Newspapers.

V. Handbooks of Chronology, Lists of Office-Holders, Historical Tables, etc.

VI. Historical Atlases and Maps, and Works of General Description.

VII. General Works on Canadian History.

VIII. Works on Particular Regions or Special Topics:
(1) Quebec and Ontario.
(2) The Maritime Provinces.
(3) The West and the North.
(4) Relations with the United States.
(5) Special Topics.

IX. Biographical Works:
(1) Collections.
(2) Biographies and Memoirs.

B. SPECIAL SELECTED BIBLIOGRAPHIES

1. The Geographical and Ethnical Background.

2. The Old Regime.

3. The Struggle for Supremacy, 1682–1760.

4. British North America, 1760–1812.

5. The War of 1812–1814.

6. Lower and Upper Canada, 1815–1837.

7. The Mission of Lord Durham.

PART III

BIBLIOGRAPHY OF THE HISTORY OF NEWFOUNDLAND

A. GENERAL SELECTED BIBLIOGRAPHY

I. BIBLIOGRAPHIES AND GUIDES TO MATERIALS

(See also the Bibliographies referred to in volume I of this *History*, also in the *Cambridge Modern History*, vols. VII and IX–XII, and the *Cambridge History of British Foreign Policy*.)

ADAM, M. I., EWING, J. and MUNRO, J. (Compilers). *Guide to the Principal Parliamentary Papers Relating to the Dominions*, 1812–1911. Edinburgh, 1913.

BIGGAR, H. P. "Canada." *Histoire et historiens depuis cinquante ans...de 1876 à 1926*. Vol. II. Bibliothèque de la Revue Historique. Paris.
    A brief critical account of Canadian historical bibliography.

BURPEE, L. J. *Oxford Encyclopaedia of Canadian History*. (Makers of Canada.) Oxford, 1926.

Canadian Historical Review. Toronto, 1920– .
    A quarterly continuation of *Review of Historical Publications*, for which *v. infra*.

Contributions to Canadian Economics. Toronto, 1928– .

DIONNE, N. E. *Inventaire chronologique des livres...publiés...dans la province de Québec....* 5 vols. in *Trans. R.S.C.* 1904–11.

FARIBAULT, G. B. *Catalogue d'ouvrages sur l'histoire de l'Amérique, et en particulier sur celle...de Nouvelle-France*. Quebec, 1837.

FAUTEUX, A. *Bibliographie de l'histoire canadienne*. Montreal, 1926. Pamphlet.

GAGNON, P. *Essai de bibliographie canadienne....* Vol. I. Quebec, 1895. Vol. II. Montreal, 1913.

HARRISSE, H. *Notes pour servir à l'histoire, à la bibliographie et à la cartographie de la Nouvelle-France et des pays adjacents*, 1545–1700. Paris, 1872.

—— *Bibliotheca Americana vetustissima*: reprint with additions. Paris, 1872.

KINGSFORD, W. *Canadian Archaeology: an Essay*. Montreal, 1886.

—— *The Early Bibliography of the Province of Ontario*. Toronto, 1892.

LARNED, J. N. (Ed.). *The Literature of American History*. Boston, 1902.

MACFARLANE, W. G. *New Brunswick Bibliography*. Saint John, N.B., 1895.

MORGAN, H. J. *Bibliotheca Canadiensis: or A Manual of Canadian Literature*. Ottawa, 1867.

PUBLIC ARCHIVES OF CANADA. *Catalogue of Pamphlets, Journals, and Reports in the Public Archives of Canada*, 1611–1867. Prepared by N. Fee. 2nd edn. Ottawa, 1916.
    A further catalogue is in preparation including pamphlets published since 1867.

Review of Historical Publications relating to Canada, 1895 and 1896, etc. Ed. by G. M. Wrong, H. H. Langton and W. S. Wallace. 22 vols. and 2 general index vols. University of Toronto, 1897–1918.

ROYAL EMPIRE SOCIETY (formerly Royal Colonial Institute). *Catalogue of the Library....* London, 1930.

—— *Overseas Official Publications. A Quarterly Bulletin*. London, 1927– .

SHORTT, A. and DOUGHTY, A. G. (Editors). *Canada and its Provinces*. Vol. XXIII. Toronto, 1917.

TORONTO PUBLIC LIBRARY. *Books and Pamphlets Published in Canada up to the Year Eighteen Hundred and Thirty-Seven, Copies of which are in the Public Reference Library*. Toronto, 1916. Supplements: No. 1, 1919; No. 2, 1926.

—— *The Canadian Catalogue of Books Published in Canada, Books about Canada, as well as Those Written by Canadians, during 1921 and 1922*. Toronto, 1923. Continued annually.

—— *The Rebellion of 1837–38: a Bibliography of the Sources of Information in the Public Reference Library*. Toronto, 1924.

—— *Material concerning the Hudson's Bay Territories, North-West Passage, Fur Trade, etc.*, in the Toronto Reference Library. (In the press.)

—— *Canadian Books: a Study Outline for the People*. Toronto, 1923.

TROTTER, R. G. *Canadian History: A Syllabus and Guide to Reading*. Toronto, 1926.

WALLACE, W. S. "The Bibliography of Canadiana." *Canadian Historical Review*, vol. v, 1924.
  A critical discussion of some of the principal bibliographies, and of bibliographical needs.
WICKERSHAM, J. *A Bibliography of Alaskan Literature*, 1724–1924. Cordova, Alaska, 1928. Useful concerning British Columbia.

II. PRINTED DOCUMENTS

(See also the information concerning printed versions and calendars of documents described above in "The Manuscript Sources of Canadian History".)

A. *OFFICIAL*

On several topics documentary information of the highest importance which is not noticed here is to be found in the various series mentioned below. The *Canada Year Book* gives annually a list of publications of the Dominion Government (1913–) and of the Provincial Governments (1914–). A detailed list of bibliographies and indexes of printed government documents may be found in *An Account of Government Document Bibliography in the United States and Elsewhere*, by J. B. CHILDS, Chief, Division of Documents, Library of Congress, Government Printing Office, Washington, 1927. Also *v. supra*, p. 834; Adam, Ewing and Munro's *Guide* and the *Bulletin* of the Royal Empire Society.

Acts of the British and Dominion Parliaments, and of Provincial Legislatures before and after Confederation.
Canada Gazette.
Canada Year Book. 1867–71, 1905– . Second series. Ottawa, 1906– .
Census of Canada. Decennial beginning with 1871. Vol. IV of the first census, 1876, contains an extensive compilation of all available census statistics from 1665.
Debates of the British Parliament of the Canadian House of Commons, 1870–2, 1875– ; and of the Senate, 1876– . Before Confederation debates were printed with some irregularity in the Maritime Provinces, and in the Province of Canada for brief periods in an unofficial *Mirror of Parliament*. Debates of the Legislature of Quebec were printed first in 1879. In general the debates of the Provincial Legislatures since 1867 are not printed.
Journals and *Sessional Papers* of the Dominion Parliament, and of the Provincial Legislatures before and after Confederation, and of the Legislature of the North West Territories. The *Journals* of the Assembly of Upper Canada were not printed contemporaneously before 1825 but are printed in *Reports* of the Ontario Archives.
Labour Gazette. Ottawa, 1900– .
Reports and *Publications* of the Public Archives of Canada and the Provincial Archives of Nova Scotia, Quebec, Ontario, and British Columbia.
Current lists of publications of the Dominion Government are issued by the King's Printer, Ottawa. Among the special lists issued by separate departments those of the Geological Survey and the Natural Resources Intelligence Service are the most generally useful.
QUEBEC, PROVINCE OF. *Statistical Year Book.* Quebec, 1914– .

B. *NON-OFFICIAL*

BELL, K. and MORRELL, W. P. (Editors). *Select Documents on British Colonial Policy*, 1830–60. Oxford, 1928.
EGERTON, H. E. and GRANT, W. L. (Editors). *Canadian Constitutional Development, Shown by Selected Speeches and Despatches, with Introductions and Explanatory Notes.* London, 1907.
HOUSTON, W. (Editor). *Documents Illustrative of the Canadian Constitution. With Notes and Appendices.* Toronto, 1891.
INNIS, H. A. and LOWER, A. R. M. *Select Documents in Canadian Economic History.* Toronto University Press. (In the press.)

KEITH, A. B. *Selected Speeches and Documents on British Colonial Policy*, 1763–1917. 2 vols. Oxford, 1918.

KENNEDY, W. P. M. (Editor). *Statutes, Treaties, and Documents of the Canadian Constitution*, 1713–1926. New and rev. edn. Oxford, 1929.

TREATIES. *Indian Treaties and Surrenders from* 1680 *to* 1890. 2 vols. Ottawa, 1891.

Treaties and Agreements Affecting Canada in Force between His Majesty and the United States of America, with Subsidiary Documents, 1814–1925. Ottawa, 1927.

III. HISTORICAL JOURNALS AND PUBLICATIONS OF LEARNED SOCIETIES

For a full list see *Union List of Serials in the Libraries of the United States and Canada*, edited by W. Gregory, New York, 1927. This indicates all important periodicals available in some two hundred libraries. It can be supplemented by Library of Congress cards for new sets of periodicals received in these libraries. See also *A Catalogue of the Periodicals (in which are Included the Publications and Transactions of Learned Societies) to be found in the Libraries of the City of Toronto.* 3rd edn. Toronto Public Library, 1924.

The *Handbook of American Historical Societies*, prepared by the Committee on Handbook of the Conference of Historical Societies [Madison, 1926], gives full data concerning societies in the U.S.A. but is inadequate for Canada. In the *Reports* of the Canadian Historical Association, however, are current lists of affiliated societies.

For British journals and publications of learned societies important for the study of Imperial History see the Bibliographies in vols. I–III of this series.

A selected list of periodicals—British, Canadian, and American—may be found in R. G. Trotter, *Canadian History: A Syllabus and Guide*, pp. 15–18. Only the most important Canadian publications are given below:

Acadiensis...a Quarterly. Saint John, 1901–8.
Bulletin des recherches historiques. Levis, 1895– . Index, 4 vols. 1925.
Canadian Defence Quarterly. Ottawa, 1923– .
CANADIAN HISTORICAL ASSOCIATION. *Reports.* Ottawa, 1922– .
Canadian Historical Review. Toronto, 1920– .
CHAMPLAIN SOCIETY. *Publications.* Toronto, 1907– .
Dalhousie Review. Halifax, 1921– .
GEOGRAPHICAL SOCIETY OF QUEBEC. *Transactions*, 1880– .
HISTORICAL AND SCIENTIFIC SOCIETY OF MANITOBA. *Transactions*, 1883– .
NEW BRUNSWICK HISTORICAL SOCIETY. *Collections.* Saint John, 1894– .
NOVA SCOTIA HISTORICAL SOCIETY. *Collections*, 1879– .
    Vol. XXI contains a list of papers read before the Society, 1878–1927.
ONTARIO HISTORICAL SOCIETY. *Reports* and *Papers*, 1898– .
QUEBEC LITERARY AND HISTORICAL SOCIETY. *Transactions*, etc., 1829– . An Index of Papers, etc., 1829–91, is in *Transactions*, No. 20, 1891. *Index to Archival Publications of the Society*, 1824–1924.
Queen's Quarterly. Kingston, 1893– . Selected articles, beginning in 1911, reprinted as *Bulletins of the Departments of History and of Political and Economic Science of Queen's University.*
Revue Canadienne. Montreal, 1863–1923. Comprehensive Index for 1863–1907.
ROYAL CANADIAN INSTITUTE. *Publications....* Toronto, 1852– .
ROYAL SOCIETY OF CANADA. *Proceedings and Transactions*, 1883– .

IV. NEWSPAPERS

For a list of "Principal Newspapers Founded" between 1752 and 1914, with dates of founding, see SHORTT, A. and DOUGHTY, A. G. (Editors), *Canada and its Provinces*, vol. XXIII, Toronto, 1917, pp. 361–2. See also *Newspaper Reference Book of Canada*, 1903. The articles on journalism in HOPKINS, *Canada: an Encyclopaedia*, vol. V (*v. infra*, p. 838), are informing. The following are useful:

Canadian News, The. London. 11 June 1856 to 16 March 1876; 19 Oct. 1912 to 26 Sept. 1918.

Canadian Newspaper Directory. A. McKim, Ltd., Montreal. The issue for 1892 contains a sketch of Canadian journalism by E. B. Biggar.

Desbarat's Newspaper Directory, 1912. Desbarat's Advertising Agency, Ltd., Montreal and Toronto.

Directory of Canadian Newspapers, 1900. Central Press Advertising Agency, Toronto.

A History of Canadian Journalism.... Toronto, 1908.

V. HANDBOOKS OF CHRONOLOGY, LISTS OF OFFICE-HOLDERS, HISTORICAL TABLES, ETC.

AUDET, F. J. *Canadian Historical Dates and Events.* Ottawa, 1917.

Canadian Almanac. Toronto, 1847– .

Canadian Parliamentary Companion, later *Canadian Parliamentary Guide.* 1862– .

Canadian Trade Index. Canadian Manufacturers Association, Toronto. Annual, 1925– . Published irregularly and in various forms prior to 1925.

COTÉ, J. O. *Political Appointments and Elections in the Province of Canada from 1841 to 1865.* 2nd edn. enlarged. Ottawa, 1866. With an Appendix from 1 January 1866 to 30 June 1867 and Index by his son, N. O. Coté. Ottawa, 1918.

COTÉ, N. O. *Political Appointments, Parliament, and the Judicial Bench in the Dominion of Canada, 1867 to 1895.* Ottawa, 1896. The same, 1896 to 1917. Ottawa, 1917.

DESJARDINS, J. *Guide parlementaire historique de la Province de Québec 1792 à 1902.* Quebec, 1902.

Heaton's Annual: the Commercial Handbook of Canada. Toronto, 1905.

SHORTT, A. and DOUGHTY, A. G. (Editors). *Canada and its Provinces.* Vol. XXIII. Toronto, 1917.

TANGUAY, Mgr C. *Répertoire général du clergé Canadien par ordre chronologique depuis la fondation de la colonie jusqu'à nos jours.* Montreal, 1893.

VI. HISTORICAL ATLASES AND MAPS, AND WORKS OF GENERAL DESCRIPTION

In addition to the following works the student will find of great value numerous publications of the Bureau of Statistics, the Conservation Commission, the Geographic Board, the Geological Survey, and the Natural Resources Intelligence Service of the Dominion Government, as well as the Departments of Lands, Forests, Mines, etc., of the several Provinces.

AMI, H. M. (Editor). *North America.* Vol. I. *Canada and Newfoundland.* 2nd edn. revised. (*Stanford's Compendium of Geography and Travel.* New Issue.) London, 1915.

Atlas of Canada. Department of the Interior. Ottawa, 1915.

BOUCHETTE, J. *The British Dominions in North America.* 3 vols. London, 1832.

BURPEE, L. J. (Editor). *An Historical Atlas of Canada.* Toronto, 1928.

FITE, E. D. and FREEMAN, A. (Compilers and editors). *A Book of Old Maps: Delineating American History from the Earliest Days down to the Close of the Revolutionary War.* Cambridge, Mass., 1926.

HAMMOND, M. O. *Canadian Footprints.* Toronto, 1926.

Handbook of Canada. Issued...[for] the Meeting of the British Association for the Advancement of Science at Toronto, August 1924. Toronto, 1924.

HERBERTSON, A. J. and HOWARTH, O. J. R. (Editors). *Oxford Survey of the British Empire.* Vol. IV. *America.* Oxford, 1914.

Lovell's Gazetteer of...Canada. Ed. G. M. Adam. Montreal.

PUBLIC ARCHIVES OF CANADA. *Catalogue of Maps, Plans and Charts in the Map Room of the Dominion Archives.* Ottawa, 1912.

The collection has greatly increased and a new catalogue is in preparation.

—— *Catalogue of Pictures...in the Public Archives of Canada.* With introduction and notes by J. F. KENNEY. Part I, Section I. Ottawa, 1925.

ROGERS, J. D. *Historical Geography of the British Colonies. Canada.* Part III. *Geographical.* Oxford, 1911. Ed. by Sir C. P. Lucas.

TORONTO PUBLIC LIBRARY. ...*A Guide to the J. Ross Robertson Historical Collection in the Public Reference Library.* 2 vols. Toronto, 1917–21.
    A notable pictorial collection.

—— *Map Collection of the Public Reference Library of the City of Toronto, Canada.* Toronto, 1923.

VII. GENERAL WORKS ON CANADIAN HISTORY

Contributions dealing specifically with Canada are to be found in the principal co-operative American histories: *The American Nation,* ed. by A. B. HART, 26 vols. New York, 1904–18; *Chronicles of America,* ed. by A. JOHNSON, 50 vols. New Haven, 1918–21; *History of North America,* ed. by G. C. LEE, 20 vols. Philadelphia, 1903–7; *Narrative and Critical History of America,* ed. by J. WINSOR, 8 vols. Boston and New York, 1886–9.

BENGOUGH, J. W. *A Caricature History of Canadian Politics...from the Union of* 1841.... 2 vols. Toronto, 1886.

BOURINOT, Sir J. G. *Canada under British Rule,* 1760–1905. Rev. edn. London, 1922.

BRYCE, G. *Short History of the Canadian People.* Rev. edn. Toronto, 1914.

BURPEE, L. J. *The Oxford Encyclopaedia of Canadian History.* (Makers of Canada.) Oxford, 1926.

COCKBURN, A. P. *Political Annals of Canada.* Toronto, 1905.

EGERTON, H. E. *A short History of British Colonial Policy.* 2nd edn. 1905.

GRANT, W. L. (Editor). *Makers of Canada.* Revised and enlarged edn. 2 vols. Oxford, 1928.

HOPKINS, J. C. (Editor). *Canada: An Encyclopaedia of the Country.* 6 vols. Toronto, 1898–9.

—— (Editor). *Canadian Annual Review of Public Affairs.* Toronto, 1901– . (Proceeding.) Continued from 1926 by the Canadian Annual Review Company.

KENNEDY, W. P. M. *The Constitution of Canada: an Introduction to its Development and Law.* Oxford, 1922.

KINGSFORD, W. *History of Canada.* 10 vols. Toronto, 1887–98.
    Extends to the Union of 1841.

LUCAS, Sir C. P. (Editor). *Historical Geography of the British Dominions.* Oxford. Vol. V, comprising four Parts bound separately:

    LUCAS, Sir C. P. *Canada: Part I, Historical, to* 1763. 2nd edn. 1916.
    EGERTON, H. E. *Canada: Part II, Historical,* 1763–1921. 3rd edn. 1923.
    ROGERS, J. D. *Canada: Part III* (*v. supra,* p. 837).

MARTIN, C. *Empire and Commonwealth: Studies in Governance and Self-Government in Canada.* Oxford, 1929.

MORGAN, H. J. (Editor). *Dominion Annual Register and Review,* 1878–1886. Ottawa, 1879–87.

PARKMAN, F. *V. infra,* pp. 847, 851, 854.

SHORTT, A. and DOUGHTY, A. G. (Editors). *Canada and its Provinces.* 23 vols. Toronto, 1914. (Vol. XXIII, Index, etc., 1917.)
    A series of the first importance for the study of the history, institutions and culture of Canada.

TODD, A. *Parliamentary Government in the British Colonies.* London, 1880.

WITTKE, C. *A History of Canada.* New York, 1928.

WRONG, G. M. and LANGTON, H. H. (Editors). *Chronicles of Canada.* 32 vols. Toronto, 1914–16.

WRONG, G. M. *The Rise and Fall of New France.* 2 vols. Toronto, 1928.

ZIMMERMANN, A. *Kolonialpolitik Grossbritanniens.* 2 vols. Berlin, 1898.

VIII. WORKS ON PARTICULAR REGIONS OR SPECIAL TOPICS

(1) QUEBEC AND ONTARIO

(Also *v. infra*, pp. 856–60.)

BIBAUD, M. *Histoire du Canada*. Vol. I. Montreal, 1837. Vol. II. 1844. Vol. III. 1878.

BOUCHETTE, J. *Topography of Canada*. London, 1815.

—— *A Topographical Dictionary of the Province of Lower Canada*. London, 1832.

BROWN, G. W. "The St Lawrence Waterway in the Nineteenth Century." *Queen's Quarterly*, vol. XXXV, 1928.

CHAPAIS, T. *Cours d'histoire du Canada*, 1760–1841. 4 vols. Quebec, 1919–23.

CHRISTIE, R. *A History of the Late Province of Lower Canada*. 6 vols. Quebec, 1848–55.

DAWSON, S. E. *The St Lawrence, its Basin and Borderlands*. Toronto, 1905.

DOUGHTY, A. G. and DIONNE, N. E. *Quebec under Two Flags....* 2 vols. Quebec, 1903.

GARNEAU, F. X. *Histoire du Canada*. 5th edn. Annotated by H. GARNEAU. 2 vols. Paris, 1913–20.

MIDDLETON, J. E. and LANDON, F. *The Province of Ontario: a History*, 1615–1927. 4 vols. Toronto, 1927.

NEWBIGIN, MARION I. *Canada: the Great River, the Lands and the Men*. London, 1926.

ROBERTSON, J. R. *Landmarks of Toronto*. 6 vols. Toronto, 1894–1914.

SMITH, W. H. *Canada: Past and Present: Being a Historical, Geographical and Statistical Account of Canada West*. 2 vols. Toronto, 1851.

SULTE, B. *Histoire des Canadiens-Français*, 1608–1880. 8 vols. Montreal, 1882–4.

VATTIER, G. *Esquisse historique de la colonisation de la province de Québec*. Paris, 1928.

WILLSON, H. BECKLES. *Quebec, the Laurentian Province*. Toronto, 1912.

WRONG, G. M. *A Canadian Manor and its Seigneurs*. Toronto, 1908.

(2) THE MARITIME PROVINCES

(Also *v. infra*, pp. 860, 866.)

BIRD, W. R. *A Century at Chignecto*. Toronto, 1928.

BREBNER, J. B. *New England's Outpost: Acadia before the Conquest of Canada*. New York, 1927.

BROWN, R. *History of...Cape Breton*. London, 1869.

CAMPBELL, D. *History of Prince Edward Island*. Charlottetown, 1875.

—— *Nova Scotia in its Historical, Mercantile and Industrial Relations*. Montreal, 1873.

DAWSON, J. W. *Acadian Geology*. London, 1868.

FLEMING, S. *The Intercolonial: An Historical Sketch*, 1832–1876. Montreal, 1876.

GESNER, A. *The Industrial Resources of Nova Scotia, its Physical Geography...Natural History* [etc.]. Halifax, 1849.

—— *New Brunswick, with Notes for Emigrants...History....* London, 1847.

HANNAY, J. *The History of New Brunswick*. 2 vols. Saint John, 1909.

HARVEY, D. C. *The French Régime in Prince Edward Island*. New Haven, 1926.

JOHNSON, J. F. W. *Report on the Agricultural Capabilities of...New Brunswick*. Fredericton, 1850.

MACMECHAN, A. *The Book of Ultima Thule*. Toronto, 1927.

MACPHAIL, A. *History of Prince Edward Island* (in *Canada and its Provinces*, vol. XIII). Toronto, 1914.

MURDOCH, B. *A History of Nova Scotia or Acadie*. 3 vols. Halifax, 1865–7. A chronicle extending to 1828.

RAYMOND, W. O. *The River St John...*1604–1784. Rev. edn. Saint John, 1909.

VERNON, C. W. *Cape Breton*. Toronto, 1903.

WARBURTON, A. B. *A History of Prince Edward Island*. Saint John, N.B., 1923. Extends to 1831.

WILLSON, H. BECKLES. *Nova Scotia: the Province that has been passed by*. London, 1912.

(3) THE WEST AND THE NORTH

(Also *v. infra*, pp. 861–5, 867–9.)

ADAM, G. M. *The Canadian North West*. Toronto, 1885.

BANCROFT, H. H. *History of British Columbia*. San Francisco, 1887.

BEGG, ALEX. *History of British Columbia.* Toronto, 1894.

BEGG, ALEX. *History of the North West.* 3 vols. Toronto, 1894–5.

BROWN, R. N. R. *The Polar Regions: A Physical and Economic Geography of the Arctic and Antarctic.* New York, 1927.

BRYCE, G. *A History of Manitoba.* Toronto, 1906.

CHAMBERS, E. J. *The Unexploited West.* Dept. of Interior, Ottawa, 1914.

HOWAY, F. W. *British Columbia: the Making of a Province.* Toronto, 1928.

MARKHAM, Sir C. R. *The Lands of Silence: A History of Arctic and Antarctic Exploration.* Cambridge, 1921.

MORICE, Father A. G. *History of the Catholic Church in Western Canada.* 2 vols. Toronto, 1910.

—— *History of the Northern Interior of British Columbia,* 1660–1880. Toronto, 1904.

OLIVER, E. H. *The Canadian North-West....* 2 vols. Ottawa, 1914.

SCHOLEFIELD, E. O. S. and HOWAY, F. W. *British Columbia from the Earliest Times to the Present.* 4 vols. Vancouver, 1914.

SCHOOLING, Sir W. *V. infra,* p. 862.

STEFANSSON, V. *The Friendly Arctic.* New York, 1921.

(4) RELATIONS WITH THE UNITED STATES

(Also *v. supra,* pp. 819–22, 826–8, *v. infra,* pp. 848–56, 859, 863–6, 874–6, and the *Cambridge History of British Foreign Policy.*)

ADAMS, R. G. *A History of the Foreign Policy of the United States.* New York, 1924.

ALVORD, C. W. *The Mississippi Valley in British Politics.* 2 vols. Cleveland, 1917.

BALCH, T. W. *The Alaska Canadian Frontier.* Philadelphia, 1902.

BEMIS, S. F. (Editor). *The American Secretaries of State and their Diplomacy.* New York, 1927, etc.

CALLAHAN, J. M. "American-Canadian Relations concerning Annexation, 1846–1871." *Studies in American History.* Bloomington, Indiana, 1926. Pp. 187–214.

—— *The Neutrality of the American Lakes and Anglo-American Relations.* (Johns Hopkins Univ. Studies.) Baltimore, 1898.

DUNNING, W. A. *The British Empire and the United States.* New York, 1914.

FALCONER, Sir R. A. *The United States as a Neighbour: from a Canadian Point of View.* Cambridge, 1926.

FISH, C. R. *American Diplomacy...with Sixteen Maps.* New York, 1915.

HILL, C. E. *Leading American Treaties.* New York, 1922.

HODGINS, T. *British and American Diplomacy Affecting Canada,* 1782–1899. Toronto, 1900. Strongly tendencious.

KEENLEYSIDE, H. L. *Canada and the United States.* New York, 1929.

MACDONALD, JAMES A. *...The North American Idea.* Toronto, 1917.

MACKAY, R. A. *Papers relating to...the International Joint Commission.* Ottawa, 1929.

McELROY, R. *The Pathway of Peace.* Cambridge, 1927.

MOFFETT, S. E. *The Americanization of Canada.* Columbia University, New York, 1907.

MOORE, J. B. (Editor). *History and Digest of the International Arbitrations to which the United States has been a Party.* 6 vols. Washington, 1898.

MOWAT, R. B. *The Diplomatic Relations of Great Britain and the United States.* London, 1925.

MUNRO, W. B. *American Influences on Canadian Government: The Marfleet Lectures, delivered at the University of Toronto,* 1929. Toronto, 1929.

SEARS, L. M. *A History of American Foreign Relations.* New York, 1927.

WRONG, G. M. *The United States and Canada: A Political Study.* Cincinnati, 1921.

(5) WORKS RELATING TO SPECIAL TOPICS

ANDREWS, I. D. *Report on Trade and Commerce of British North American Colonies... since 1829.* Washington, 1851.

Canada: A Memorial Volume: A General Reference Work on Canada. Montreal, 1889.

CARROTHERS, W. A. *Emigration from the British Isles....* London, 1929.

COLBY, C. C. *Source Book for the Economic Geography of North America.* Chicago, 1923.
COWAN, HELEN I. *British Emigration to British North America, 1783–1837.* (University of Toronto Studies.) 1928.
ENGLAND, R. *The Central European Immigrant in Canada.* Toronto, 1929.
HAWKES, A. *The Birthright. A Search for the Canadian Canadian and the larger Loyalty.* Toronto, 1919.
HEAGERTY, J. J. *Four Centuries of Medical History in Canada: And a Sketch of the Medical History of Newfoundland.* 2 vols. Toronto, 1928.
HIND, N. Y. *et al. Eighty Years' Progress of British North America.* Toronto, 1863.
INNIS, H. A. *An Introduction to Canadian Economic History: Being a History of the Fur Trade in Canada.* New Haven, 1929.
JOHNSON, S. C. *History of Emigration to North America.* London, 1913.
LAUT, AGNES. *The Fur Trade of America.* New York, 1921.
LE MOINE, Sir J. M. *Les Pêcheries du Canada.* Quebec, 1863.
MOORE, E. S. *Canada's Mineral Resources.* Toronto, 1929.
MOORE, W. H. *The Clash: A Study in Nationalities.* Toronto, 1918.
MORLEY, P. T. *Bridging the Chasm.* Toronto, 1919.
MYERS, G. *History of Canadian Wealth.* Chicago, 1914.
NICHOLSON, B. *The French Canadian: a Sketch of his more prominent Characteristics.* Toronto, 1902.
PORRITT, E. *Sixty Years of Protection in Canada, 1846–1907.* London, 1908.
ROBERTSON, J. R. *History of Freemasonry in Canada.* 2 vols. Toronto, 1900.
ROY, P. G. *Les petites choses de notre histoire.* 2 vols. Levis, 1919.
SELLAR, R. *The Tragedy of Quebec: the Expulsion of its Protestant Farmers.* Huntingdon, Quebec, 1907. 4th edn. Toronto, 1916.
SIEGFRIED, A. *The Race Question in Canada.* London, 1907.
SKELTON, ISABEL. *The Backwoodswoman: a Chronicle of Pioneer Home Life in Upper and Lower Canada.* Toronto, 1924.
SKELTON, O. D. *The Railway Builders.* (Chronicles of Canada.) Toronto, 1916.
—— *The Language Issue in Canada.* Queen's University, *Bulletin*, April 1917.
SMITH, W. *History of the Post Office in British North America, 1639–1870.* Cambridge, 1920.
WALLACE, F. W. *In the Wake of the Windships.* Toronto, 1927.
—— *Wooden Ships and Iron Men.* London, 1924.

IX. BIOGRAPHICAL WORKS

(1) COLLECTIONS

(Also *v. supra*, pp. 837, 838.)
BUCHANAN, A. W. P. *The Bench and Bar of Lower Canada down to 1850.* Montreal, 1925.
CAMPBELL, W. *The Scotsman in Canada.* 2 vols. London, n.d.
CANNIFF, W. *The Medical Profession in Upper Canada, 1783–1850.* Toronto, 1894.
DAVIN, N. F. *The Irishman in Canada.* 1887.
DENT, J. C. *The Canadian Portrait Gallery.* 4 vols. Toronto, 1880–1.
GRANT, W. L. (Editor). *Makers of Canada.* Revised and enlarged edn. 12 vols. Oxford, 1926.
RATTRAY, W. J. *The Scot in Canada.* 1880–4.
RIDDELL, W. R. *The Legal Profession in Upper Canada.* Toronto, 1916.
TANGUAY, Abbé C. *Dictionnaire généalogique des familles canadiennes.* 7 vols. Montreal, 1871–90.
WALLACE, W. S. *The Dictionary of Canadian Biography.* Toronto, 1926.
    Replaces many older compendia.
Who's Who in Canada, 1925–26. Edited by B. C. Greene. Toronto. 18th edn.
    Title and editor various for earlier years.

(2) Biographies and Memoirs

(This section includes only works with an important bearing upon more than one chapter or group of chapters. For additional biographies *v. infra, passim*.)

BETHUNE, Bishop A. N. *Memoir of Bishop Strachan.* Toronto, 1870.

BIGGAR, C. R. W. *Sir Oliver Mowat: A Biographical Sketch.* 2 vols. Toronto, 1905.

BOYD, J. *Sir George Etienne Cartier, Bart.: His Life and Times.* Toronto, 1914.

BRADY, A. *Thomas D'Arcy McGee.* (Canadian Statesmen.) Toronto, 1925.

BURPEE, L. J. *Sandford Fleming: Empire Builder.* London, 1915.

BURWASH, N. *Egerton Ryerson.* Revised by C. B. SISSIONS. (Makers of Canada.) Oxford, 1926.

CARTWRIGHT, Sir R. J. *Reminiscences.* Toronto, 1912.

CHISHOLM, J. A. (Editor). *Speeches and Public Letters of Joseph Howe.* 2 vols. Halifax, 1909.

DAFOE, J. W. *Laurier: A Study in Canadian Politics.* Toronto, 1922.

DAVID, L. O. *Laurier, sa vie, ses œuvres.* Beauceville, 1919.

DECELLES, A. D. *Cartier et son temps.* Montreal, 1907. See also Makers of Canada.
—— *Laurier et son temps.* Montreal, 1920.

GRANT, W. L. *The Tribune of Nova Scotia.* (Chronicles of Canada.) Toronto, 1914.
    A study of Joseph Howe, embodying articles by Principal G. M. GRANT in the *Canadian Monthly*, 1875.

HANNAY, J. *Sir Leonard Tilley.* (Makers of Canada.) Oxford, 1926.

HINCKS, Sir F. *Reminiscences of his Public Life.* Montreal, 1884.

LEWIS, J. *George Brown.* (Makers of Canada.) Oxford, 1926.

LONGLEY, J. W. *Joseph Howe.* (Makers of Canada.) Oxford, 1926.
—— *Sir Charles Tupper.* (Makers of Canada.) Oxford, 1926.

LYALL, Sir A. *Life of the Marquis of Dufferin and Ava.* 2 vols. London, 1905.

MACKENZIE, A. *The Life and Speeches of Hon. George Brown.* Toronto, 1882.

MACNAUGHTON, J. *Lord Strathcona.* (Makers of Canada.) Oxford, 1926.

MERRITT, J. P. *Biography of the Hon. W. H. Merritt, M.P.* St Catherine's, 1875.

PARKIN, G. R. *Sir John A. Macdonald.* (Makers of Canada.) Oxford, 1926.

POPE, Sir J. *Correspondence of Sir John Macdonald.* Toronto, 1921.
—— *The Day of Sir John Macdonald.* (Chronicles of Canada.) Toronto, 1915.
—— *Memoirs of Sir John A. Macdonald.* 2 vols. Ottawa, 1894.
—— *Sir John A. Macdonald Vindicated: A Review of the Rt Hon. Sir Richard Cartwright's Reminiscences.* Toronto, 1912. Pamphlet.

PRESTON, W. T. R. *The Life and Times of Lord Strathcona.* Toronto, 1914.

ROBINSON, Major Gen. Sir C. W. *Life of John Beverley Robinson.* London, 1904.

RYERSON, E. *Story of My Life.* Ed. by J. G. HODGINS. Toronto, 1883.

SAUNDERS, E. M. *Life and Letters of Sir Charles Tupper.* 2 vols. London, 1916.

SKELTON, ISABEL. *The Life of Thomas D'Arcy McGee.* Gardenvale, 1925.

SKELTON, O. D. *The Day of Sir Wilfrid Laurier.* (Chronicles of Canada.) Toronto, 1916.
—— *The Life and Times of Sir Alexander Tilloch Galt.* Toronto, 1920.
—— *Life and Letters of Sir Wilfrid Laurier.* 2 vols. Toronto, 1921.

TUPPER, Sir C. *Recollections of Sixty Years in Canada.* London, 1914.

TUPPER, Sir C. H. (Editor). *Supplement to the Life and Letters of Sir Charles Tupper.* Toronto, 1926.

VAUGHAN, W. *The Life and Work of Sir William Van Horne.* New York, 1920. (Republished in Makers of Canada.) Oxford, 1926.

WALLACE, W. S. *Sir John Macdonald.* (Canadian Statesmen.) Toronto, 1924.

WILLISON, Sir J. S. *Sir Wilfrid Laurier and the Liberal Party.* 2 vols. Toronto, 1903. (Republished, with three new chapters, in Makers of Canada.) Oxford, 1926.

WILLSON, H. BECKLES. *The Life of Lord Strathcona and Mount Royal.* London, 1915.

YOUNG, J. *Public Men and Public Life in Canada: The Story of the Canadian Confederacy.* 2 vols. Toronto, 1912.

B. SPECIAL SELECTED BIBLIOGRAPHIES

CHAPTER I

SECTION 1. THE GEOGRAPHICAL AND ETHNICAL BACKGROUND

(Also *v. supra*, pp. 837–9, and *infra*, pp. 844–51.)

(1) THE GEOGRAPHICAL BACKGROUND

COLLINS, W. H., Director of the Geological Survey of Canada. "The Geology and Physical Geography of Canada"; in *Handbook of Canada*, prepared as a guide book for the meeting of the British Association for the Advancement of Science in Canada, Toronto, 1924, pp. 346–74.

DAWSON, G. M., Director of the Geological Survey of Canada. "Physical Geography and Geology"; in *Handbook of Canada*, prepared as a guide book for the meeting of the British Association for the Advancement of Science in Canada, ? 1897, part I, chapter I.

DOWLING, D. B. *An Outline of the Physical Geography of Canada.* Reprinted from the 13th *Report* of the Geographic Board of Canada. *Sess. Pap.* No. 25 d, 1915.

HUNTINGTON, E. *The Red Man's Continent.* (Chronicles of America.) New Haven, 1918.

NEWBIGIN, MARION I. *V. supra*, p. 839.

(2) THE ETHNICAL BACKGROUND

The greater part of the voluminous scattered literature, down to 1910, is condensed in *Handbook of American Indians North of Mexico*, Bulletin 30, Bureau of American Ethnology, ed. by F. W. Hodge, 2 vols. Washington, 1910. Those portions of the work relating to Canada were reprinted, with a few minor changes, under the direction of JAMES WHITE as *Handbook of Indians of Canada*, Appendix to the 10th *Report* of the Geographic Board of Canada, Ottawa, 1913. For a guide to the many books and articles that have appeared since 1910 consult the critical lists published periodically in the *Canadian Historical Review*. Only a few of the most important are given below. For Indian treaties *v. supra*, p. 836.

BLAIR, E. H. *The Indian Tribes of the Upper Mississippi and the Region of the Great Lakes....* 2 vols. Cleveland, 1911–12.

BOAS, F. "Ethnology of the Kwakiutl." In 35th *Annual Report of the Bureau of American Ethnology*, 1913–14. 2 vols. Washington, 1921.

EMMONS, G. T. "Tahltan Indians." University of Pennsylvania, *The Museum, Anthropological Publications*, vol. IV, no. 1, 1911.

GODDARD, P. E. "The Beaver Indians." *Anthropological Papers, American Museum of Natural History*, vol. X, part IV, pp. 201–93. New York, 1916.

HAWKES, E. W. *The Labrador Eskimo.* Memoir 91, Geological Survey, Department of Mines. Ottawa, 1916.

JENNESS, D. "The Copper Eskimos." *Report of the Canadian Arctic Expedition*, 1913–1918, vol. XII. Ottawa, 1922.

—— *The People of the Twilight.* New York, 1928.

MOOREHEAD, W. K. *The Stone Age in North America.* 2 vols. Boston and New York, 1910.

—— *Stone Ornaments Used by the Indians in the United States and Canada.* Andover, 1917.

MORICE, Father A. "The Great Déné Race." *Anthropos*, vol. I, pp. 229–77, 483–508, 695–730; vol. II, pp. 1–34, 181–96; vol. IV, pp. 582–606; vol. V, pp. 113–42, 419–43, 643–53, 969–90.

RADIN, P. "Genetic Relationship of the North American Indian Languages."
　　University of California Publications in American Archaeology and Ethnology, vol. XIV,
　　pp. 489–502. Berkeley, California, 1919.
—— *The Story of the American Indian.* New York, 1928.
SAPIR, E. "Na-Dene Languages: A Preliminary Report." *American Anthropologist*,
　　vol. XVII, July 1915, pp. 534–58.
SKINNER, A. "Notes on the Eastern Cree and Northern Saulteaux." *Anthropo-
　　logical Papers, American Museum of Natural History*, vol. IX, part I, pp. 1–177.
　　New York, 1911.
—— "Political Organization, Cults and Ceremonies of the Plains Ojibway and
　　Plains Cree Indians." *Anthropological Papers, American Museum of Natural
　　History*, vol. II, part VI, pp. 475–542. New York, 1913.
SMITH, H. I. *The Archaeological Collection from the Southern Interior of British Columbia.*
　　Museum of the Geological Survey, Canada. Ottawa, 1912.
—— *An Album of Prehistoric Canadian Art.* Bulletin No. 37. Anthropological Series
　　No. 8, Department of Mines. Ottawa, 1923.
SPECK, F. "Beothuk and Micmac." *Indian Notes and Monographs, Museum of the
　　American Indian, Heye Foundation.* New York, 1922.
STEENSBY, H. P. "An Anthropological Study of the Origin of the Eskimo Culture."
　　Meddelelser om Gronland, vol. LIII, pp. 39–228. Copenhagen, 1917.
STEFANSSON, V. "The Stefansson-Anderson Arctic Expedition." *Anthropological
　　Papers, American Museum of Natural History*, vol. XIV, part I. New York, 1914.
—— *My Life with the Eskimo.* New York, 1913.
WAUGH, F. W. *Iroquois Foods and Food Preparation.* Memoir 86, Geological Survey,
　　Department of Mines. Ottawa, 1916.
WISSLER, C. *The American Indian: An Introduction to the Anthropology of the New World.*
　　New York, 1917.

CHAPTERS II AND III

SECTION 2. THE OLD REGIME

(For additional authorities, unprinted and printed, see vol. I, pp. 847–50; also
supra, pp. 811–19, 821, 826–8, 834.)

(1) CONTEMPORARY AND EARLY WORKS AND COLLECTIONS OF EARLY MATERIAL

BELMONT, Abbé DE. *Histoire du Canada.* (Collection de Mémoires et de Relations
　　sur l'histoire ancienne du Canada, publiés sous la direction de la Société
　　littéraire et historique de Québec. Quebec, 1840. Pp. 36.)
BIGGAR, H. P. (Editor). *The Precursors of Jacques Cartier, 1497–1534....* Canadian
　　Archives. Ottawa, 1911.
—— *The Voyages of Jacques Cartier, published from the originals with translations, notes
　　and appendices.* Public Archives of Canada. Ottawa, 1924.
BOUCHER, P. *Histoire véritable et naturelle des mœurs et productions du pays de la Nouvelle-
　　France....* Paris, 1664.
BRÉARD, C. et P. *Documents relatifs à la Marine Normande et à ses armements aux
　　XVIème et XVIIème siècles pour la Canada, l'Afrique, les Antilles, le Brésil et les Indes.*
　　Rouen, 1889.
CASGRAIN, Abbé H. R. (Editor). *Collection des manuscrits du Maréchal de Lévis.*
　　12 vols. Montreal and Quebec, 1889–95. (For details see *C.M.H.* VII, p. 773.)
CAYET, P. *Chronologie septénaire contenant l'histoire de la paix entre les rois de France
　　et d'Espagne, et les choses les plus mémorables advenues...jusques à la fin de l'an* 1604.
　　(Nouvelle Collection des Mémoires pour servir à l'histoire de France, 2e
　　partie, vol. 12. Paris, 1838.)
　　Contains a narrative of a voyage of Pont-Gravé to Tadousac and of De
　　Monts to Acadia in 1603.
CHAMPLAIN, S. DE. *Œuvres de Champlain.* Publiés par l'abbé C. H. Laverdière. 2e
　　édition. Tomes I–VI. Quebec, 1870. The Works of Champlain are partly re-
　　printed, with translations and notes, by the Champlain Society, vols. XV, XVI.

CHARLEVOIX, Le Père F. X. *Histoire et description générale de la Nouvelle-France....* 3 vols. Paris, 1744.

CLÉMENT, P. (Editor). *Lettres, instructions et mémoires de Colbert.* Paris, 1865.

COLDEN, C. *The history of the five Indian nations of Canada, which are dependent on the Province of New York in America....* 2 vols. London, 1755.

Collection de Manuscrits contenant lettres, mémoires, et autres documents historiques relatifs à la Nouvelle-France.... 4 vols. Quebec, 1883-5.

CUGNET, F. J. *Traité de la Loi des Fiefs, qui a toujours été suivie en Canada depuis son établissement....* Quebec, 1775.

DENYS, N. *Description and Natural History of Acadia....* Champlain Society *Publications,* vol. II.

—— *Description géographique et historique des costes de l'Amérique Septentrionale. Avec l'histoire naturelle du Païs.* 2 vols. Paris, 1672.

DOLLIER DE CASSON, F. *A History of Montreal 1640-72.* Edited and translated... with a Life of the Author by RALPH FLENLEY. London, 1928.

Édits, Ordonnances Royaux, Déclarations et Arrêts du Conseil d'État du Roi concernant le Canada [1627-1756]. Quebec, 1854-6. (For details see *C.M.H.* VII, p. 767.)

HAKLUYT, R. *Divers Voyages touching the discoverie of America and Lands adjacent unto the same, made first of all by our Englishmen and afterwards by the Frenchmen and Britons.* London, 1582.

—— *The Principall Navigations,...and Discoveries of the English Nation....* 1st edn. London, 1589. 2nd edn. enlarged. 3 vols. 1598-1600. New edn. published for the Hakluyt Society in 12 vols. Glasgow, 1903-5. Another edn. in 8 vols. London, 1907. Reprinted with additions, 1926-8.

Jugements et délibérations du Conseil Souverain de la Nouvelle-France. 6 vols. Quebec, 1885-91.

Prints the documents only as far as 1716.

LAËT, J. DE. *L'Histoire du Nouveau Monde ou description des Indes Occidentales.* Leyde, 1640.

LA POTHERIE (M. de Bacqueville de). *Histoire de l'Amérique Septentrionale.* 4 vols. Paris, 1753.

(LA TOUR.) *Mémoires sur la vie de M. de Laval, Premier évêque de Québec.* Cologne, 1741.

LE CLERCQ, C. *First Establishment of the Faith in New France....* Translated with notes by J. G. Shea. 2 vols. New York, 1881.

LESCARBOT, M. *History of New France....* Champlain Society *Publications,* vols. I, VII, XI.

LITERARY AND HISTORICAL SOCIETY OF QUEBEC. *Historical Documents,* or *Mémoires sur le Canada.* 9e série. Quebec, 1838-1915.

MARGRY, P. *Mémoires et documents....Découvertes et établissements des Français dans l'Ouest et dans le sud de l'Amérique Septentrionale.* 6 vols. Paris, 1879-88.

—— *Relations et mémoires inédits, pour servir à l'histoire de la France dans les pays d'outre-mer....* Paris, 1865.

Marie de l'Incarnation, Lettres de la Révérende Mère. (Édition Richaudeau.) 3 vols. Tournai, 1876.

MARTYR, P. *De Orbe Novo.* Translated from the Latin with Notes and Introduction. By T. A. MacNutt. 2 vols. New York, 1912.

Contains passages relating to Cabot and Gomez.

Mémoires des Commissaires du Roi et de ceux de Sa Majesté Britannique sur les possessions et les droits respectifs des deux Couronnes en Amérique.... 7 vols. Paris, 1755-7.

Memorials of the English and French Commissaries Concerning the limits of Nova Scotia or Acadia. London, 1755.

Mercure François (Le), ou la suite de l'histoire de la paix, commençant à l'année 1605. 25 vols. Paris, 1605-43.

MICHELANT et RAMÉ. *Voyage de Jacques Cartier au Canada en* 1534. *Nouvelle édition, publiée d'après l'édition de 1598 et d'après Ramusio, par H. M. Michelant avec deux cartes. Documents inédits sur Jacques Cartier et le Canada, communiqués par M. Alfred Ramé.* Paris, 1865.

MICHELANT et RAMÉ. *Relation Originale du Voyage de Jacques Cartier au Canada en 1534. Documents inédits sur Jacques Cartier et le Canada.* (Nouvelle série.) Paris, 1867.

MUNRO, W. B. *Documents relating to the Seigniorial Tenure in Canada, 1598–1854.* Champlain Society, *Publications,* vol. III. Toronto, 1908.

MURPHY, H. C. *The Voyage of Verazzano.* New York, 1875.
  Though its conclusions have been discredited, it is useful for its appendix of original documents.

Nouvelle-France, documents historiques; correspondance étrangère entre les autorités françaises et les gouverneurs et intendants. Vol. I. Quebec, 1893.
  The plan of this collection is defective.

O'CALLAGHAN, E. B. (Editor). *Documents relative to the Colonial History of the State of New York.* 15 vols. Vols. III, IX, X. Albany, 1856–87.

OLSON, J. E. and BOURNE, E. G. (Editors). *The Northmen, Columbus and Cabot, 985–1503.* New York, 1906. (*Original Narratives of Early American History.*)

Pièces et documents relatifs à la tenure seigneuriale. Quebec, 1852.

PUBLIC ARCHIVES OF CANADA. BOARD OF HISTORICAL PUBLICATIONS. *Documents relating to Canadian Currency, Exchange and Finance during the French Period.* Selected and edited with notes and introduction by ADAM SHORTT. 2 vols. Ottawa, 1925.

PURCHAS, S. *Purchas His Pilgrimage....* 4 vols. London, 1625. Reprinted in 20 vols. Glasgow, 1905–7.

SAGARD, G. *Le grand voyage du pays des Hurons....* 2 vols. Paris, 1865. A reprint of edn. of 1632.

—— *Histoire du Canada et voyages que les frères mineurs Récollects y ont faicts pour la conversion des infidelles depuis l'an 1615.* 4 vols. Paris, 1866. A reprint of edn. of 1636.

SOCIÉTÉ HISTORIQUE DE MONTRÉAL. *Mémoires et Documents relatifs à l'Histoire du Canada.* 12 series, 1856–1921: "Ordonnances de M. de Maisonneuve". "Histoire de Montréal, par H. Dollier de Casson", "Les véritables motifs de Messieurs et dames de la Société de Notre Dame de Montréal".

THEVET, A. *Les singularitez de la France Antartique. Nouvelle édition avec notes et commentaires par Paul Gaffarel.* Paris, 1878. Published in 1558, contains details on Cartier's voyages, the Indians and the country.

THWAITES, R. G. (Editor). *Jesuit Relations and Allied Documents.* 73 vols. Cleveland, 1894–1907.

WINTHROP, J. *The History of New England from 1630 to 1649.* New edn. by James Savage. 2 vols. Boston, 1853.

(2) LATER WORKS

BAXTER, J. P. *A Memoir of Jacques Cartier.* New York and London, 1906.

BIBAUD, M. *Histoire du Canada sous la domination française.* 2 vols. Montreal, 1843–4.

BIGGAR, H. P. *The Early Trading Companies of New France....* Toronto, 1901.

—— "Voyages of the Cabots and Corte-Reals to Newfoundland and Greenland, 1497–1503." *Revue Hispanique,* vol. X.

BOURINOT, Sir J. G. "Hist....Account of the I. of Cape Breton." *Trans. R. Soc. Can.* sect. II, 1891. Montreal, 1891.

BREVOORT, J. C. *Verazzano the Navigator.* New York, 1874.

CHAPAIS, T. *Jean Talon.* Quebec, 1904. (See also p. 839.)

CLEMENT, P. *Histoire de Colbert.* 2 vols. Paris, 1892.

COLBY, C. W. *Canadian Types of the Old Regime, 1608–98.* New York, 1910.

COUILLARD-DESPRÉS, Abbé. *En marge de la "Tragédie d'un peuple" de M. Émile Lauvrière.* Bruges, 1925. (*V. infra,* p. 847.)

—— *Observations sur l'Histoire de l'Acadie Françoise de M. Moreau.* Paris, 1873; Montreal, 1919.

DE COSTA, B. F. *Verazzano: the Explorer.* New York, 1881.

DIONNE, N. E. *La Nouvelle France de Cartier à Champlain, 1540–1607.* Quebec, 1891.

—— *Samuel Champlain.* 2 vols. Quebec, 1891, 1906. Appendix of documents.

DOUGLAS, J. *Old France in the New World: Quebec in the 17th Century.* Cleveland and London, 1905.

DUSSIEUX, L. E. *Le Canada sous la domination française.* Paris, 1855.

EASTMAN, M. *Church and State in early Canada.* Edinburgh, 1915.

FAILLON, Abbé. *Histoire de la colonie française en Canada.* 3 vols. Villemarie, 1865–6.

—— *Vie de la Sœur Bourgeoys.* 2 vols. Villemarie, 1853.

—— *Vie de Mademoiselle Mance.* 2 vols. Villemarie, 1854.

FAUTEUX, J. N. *Essai sur l'industrie au Canada sous le régime français.* 2 vols. Quebec, 1927.

FERLAND, Abbé J. B. *Cours d'histoire du Canada.* 2 vols. Quebec, 1861–5.

GAFFAREL, P. *Histoire de la découverte de l'Amérique.* Vol. II. Paris, 1892.

GOSSELIN, Mgr AMÉDÉE. *L'instruction sous le régime français.* Quebec, 1911.

GOSSELIN, Abbé AUGUSTE. *Vie de Mgr de Laval.* 2 vols. Quebec, 1891.

HARRISSE, H. *Les Corte-Real et leurs Voyages au Nouveau-Monde.* Paris, 1883.

—— *Découverte et évolution cartographique de Terre-Neuve et des pays circonvoisins.* Paris, 1900.

—— *The Discovery of North America.* London, 1892.

—— *John Cabot, the Discoverer of North-America and Sebastian his Son.* London, 1896.

HUTCHINSON, T. *The History of the Colony of Massachusett's Bay.* Vols. I and II. London, 1765–7.

INSH, G. P. *Scottish Colonial Schemes, 1620–1688.* Glasgow, 1922.

KELLOGG, LOUISE P. *The French Régime in Wisconsin.* Madison, 1925.

KIRKE, H. *The First English Conquest of Canada.* London, 1871. 2nd edn. 1908.

KOHL, J. G. *A History of the Discovery of the East Coast of North America.* (Collections of the Maine Historical Society, second series.) Portland, 1869.

KUNTSMAN, F. *Die Entdeckung America's-Atlas.* München, 1859.

LANCTOT, G. *L'Administration de la Nouvelle France....* Paris, 1929.

LA RONCIÈRE, C. DE. *Histoire de la Marine Française.* Vols. III and IV. Paris, 1906, 1910.

LARSEN, S. "La découverte de l'Amérique vingt ans avant Christophe Colomb." *Journal de la Société des Américanistes de Paris*, Nouvelle série, Tome XVIII, pp. 75–89. Paris, 1926.
    Contains a critical examination of the expedition of John Scolp, a Dane, to America in 1472.

LAUVRIÈRE, E. *La Tragédie d'un peuple. Histoire du peuple acadien, de ses origines à nos jours.* 2 vols. Paris, 1922. (*V. supra*, Couillard-Després.)

LAVERDIÈRE et CASGRAIN, Abbés (Editors). *Le Journal des Jésuites....* Quebec, 1871.

LEROY-BEAULIEU, J. *De la colonisation chez les peuples modernes.* Paris, 1898.

LOCKHART, E. *Narrative of the Oppressive Law Proceedings....Also a genealogical account of the family of Alexander, Earl of Stirling...followed by an Historical View of their hereditary possession in Nova Scotia, Canada....* Edinburgh, 1856.

LORIN, H. *Le comte de Frontenac.* Paris, 1895.

MARCEL, G. *Cartographie de la Nouvelle-France.* Paris, 1885.

MOREAU, M. *Histoire de l'Acadie Françoise....* Paris, 1873.

MOREL, Abbé E. "Jean-François de la Roque, seigneur de Roberval, Vice-Roi du Canada." *Société Historique de Compiègne*, 1892, pp. 15–58.

MUNRO, W. B. *Crusaders of New France....* (Chronicles of America.) New Haven, 1918.

—— *The Seigneurs of Old Canada.* (Chronicles of Canada.) Toronto, 1914.

—— *The Seigniorial System in Canada.* New York, 1927.

PARKMAN, F. *Pioneers of France in the New World.* 2 vols. Boston, 1897.

—— *The Jesuits in North America.* 20th edn. 1885.

—— *La Salle and the discovery of the Great West.* Boston, 1878.

—— *The old Régime in Canada.* Boston, 1880. 2 vols. Boston, 1897.

—— *Count Frontenac and New France under Louis XIV.* Boston, 1877.

—— *A Half Century of Conflict.* 2 vols. Boston, 1892.

—— *Montcalm and Wolfe.* 2 vols. Boston, 1884.

POPE, J. *Jacques Cartier. His Life and Voyages.* Ottawa, 1890.

RAMEAU DE SAINT-PÈRE, E. *La France aux colonies.* Paris, 1859.
RICHAUDEAU, Abbé. *Vie de la Mère Marie de l'Incarnation.* Tournai, 1873.
ROCHEMONTEIX, P. C. DE. *Les Jésuites et la Nouvelle-France au XVII° siècle.* 3 vols. Paris, 1896.
ROGERS, C. *Memorials of the Earl of Stirling and of the House of Alexander.* 2 vols. Edinburgh, 1877.
ROY, J. E. *Histoire de la seigneurie de Lauzon.* 6 vols. Levis, 1897–1904.
SAINTOYANT, J. *La colonisation française sous l'ancien régime*, vol. I. Paris, 1929.
SALONE, E. *La Colonisation de la Nouvelle-France.* Paris, 1906.
STEVENS, H. *Historical and Geographical Notes on the Earliest Discoveries in America, 1453–1530.* New Haven, 1869.
    Valuable for its facsimiles of ancient maps.
WEISE, A. J. *The Discoveries of America.* New York, 1884.
WILLIAMSON, J. A. *The Voyages of the Cabots....* London, 1929.
WINSHIP, G. P. *Cabot Bibliography, with an Introductory Essay on the Careers of the Cabots, Based upon an Independent Examination of the Sources of Information.* London, 1900.
WINSOR, J. *Cartier to Frontenac: Geographical Discovery in the Interior of North America, 1534–1700.* Boston, 1894.
WRONG, G. M. *The Canadian Manor and its Seigneurs.* Toronto, 1908.

CHAPTER IV

SECTION 3. THE STRUGGLE FOR SUPREMACY, 1682–1760

(For additional authorities, unprinted and printed, *v. supra*, pp. 824–8, 837–40, and Bibliography of chapters II and III; also vol. I, pp. 852–5, and *C.M.H.* VII, 772.)

(1) DOCUMENTS AND CONTEMPORARY WORKS

ACADIA. *Relation de ce qui s'est passé en Acadie au sujet de neuf mille Français neutres.* (Paris? 1775.)
AMHERST PAPERS. P.R.O. London. W.O. XXXIV.
BEATSON, R. *Naval and Military Memoirs of Great Britain*, 1727–90. 6 vols. London, 1804.
Belknap Papers, The. In *Collections* of the Mass. Hist. Soc., 5th series, vols. II and III. Boston, 1877.
BOUGAINVILLE, LOUIS ANTOINE, Comte de. *Mémoire sur l'état de la Nouvelle France à l'époque de la guerre de sept ans. Relations et mémoires inédits.* Paris, 1867.
BOUQUET, H. Letters and Papers relating to military Events in America, 1757–1765. Brit. Mus. Add. MSS.
BRADSTREET, Col. *Impartial account of Col. Bradstreet's Expedition.* By a volunteer in the expedition. London, 1859.
BURCHETT, J. *Memoirs of Transactions at sea...* (1688–1697). London, 1703.
CANADA. "Jugement impartial sur les opérations militaires de la campagne en Canada," 1759. (Quebec Lit. and Hist. Soc. *Collection de mémoires....* Quebec, 1840.)
—— *Mémoires sur le C., depuis 1749 jusqu'à 1760.* Quebec Lit. and Hist. Soc. Quebec, 1838.
—— "Recueil de ce qui s'est passé en Canada...depuis l'année 1682." *Trans. of Lit. and Hist. Soc. of Quebec.* Quebec, 1871.
—— *Relation de ce qui s'est passé cette année en Canada....* Paris (?), 1756 (?).
CASGRAIN, H. R. (Editor). *Extraits des archives des Ministères de la Marine et de la Guerre à Paris.... Canada. Correspondance générale*, 1755–1760. Quebec, 1890.
—— *Collection des manuscrits du Maréchal de Lévis.* 12 vols. Montreal and Quebec, 1889–95. *V. supra*, section 2.
—— *Documents inédits sur l'Acadie, 1710–1815.* Quebec, 1888–91.
CÉLORON, *Journal de M. de.* Archives de la Marine. Paris.
Dinwiddie Papers, The. Vols. I and II. Virginia Historical Collections. New series, vols. III and IV. Richmond, Virginia, 1883–4.

DURELL, P. (Capt. R.N.). *A Particular Account of the taking of Cape Breton*. London, 1745.

ENTICK, J. *The general history of the late War*.... 5 vols. London, 1763–4.

FRASER, Col. M. *MS. journal relating to the siege of Quebec in 1759*. Quebec Lit. and Hist. Soc. *Historical Documents*. 2nd series. Quebec, 1867.

"General Orders in Wolfe's Army during the Expedition up the River St Lawrence, 1759." Quebec Lit. and Hist. Soc. *Historical Documents*. 4th series. Quebec, 1875.

Gentleman's Magazine, 1755–60. Various accounts and letters.

"Gordon's Journal of the siege of Louisbourg, 1758." *Collections* of Nova Scotia Hist. Soc. Vol. v. Halifax, N.S., 1887.

Grenville Papers. Ed. with notes, by W. J. SMITH. 4 vols. London, 1852–3.

HALDIMAND, Sir F. Official Correspondence when Commander-in-Chief in North America and Governor of Quebec. Brit. Mus. Add. MSS. 21661–21666, 21682, 21686–7.

HARDWICKE PAPERS. Brit. Mus. Add. MSS. 35349–36278.

IBERVILLE, Sieur d', *Mémoire du, sur Boston et ses Dépendances*. 1701?.

JOHNSON, Sir WILLIAM, *Papers of*. Ed. by J. SULLIVAN. Vols. I, II, III. Albany, N.Y., 1921–2.

JOHNSTONE, Chevalier de, *Mémoires du*. Quebec Lit. and Hist. Soc. *Hist. Documents*. 9th series. Quebec, 1915.

KNOX, Captain J. *An Historical Journal of the Campaigns in North America for the years 1757–1760*. 2 vols. London, 1769. 2nd edn. Edited by A. G. DOUGHTY for the Champlain Soc. 3 vols. Toronto, 1914.

LÉVIS, F. G. DE, Duc. *Recueil des pièces relatives à la Publication des manuscrits du Maréchal de Lévis sur la guerre du Canada*, 1755–1760. Rennes, 1888.

LIVINGSTON, W. *A Review of the Military Operations in North America*, 1753–1756. London, 1757. 2nd edn. (with additional papers). Dublin, 1757.

LOUDOUN, Earl of. *The conduct of a Noble Commander in America impartially reviewed*. London, 1758.

—— *An answer vindicating the character of a Noble Lord*. London, 1760.

LOUISBOURG, *Lettre d'un Habitant de*. (1745.) Eng. transl. Ed. G. M. WRONG, 1897.

—— Two journals of the siege of. Anon. 1758. Archives de la Marine, Paris.

MALARTIC, Le Comte GABRIEL DE MAURÈS DE and GEFFERAT, P. *Journal des campagnes au Canada de 1755 à 1760*. Dijon, 1890.

MANTE, T. *History of the late war in North America*. London, 1772.

MARGRY, P. *V. supra*, p. 845.

MATHER, COTTON. *Magnalia Christi Americana*, 1620–98. London, 1702. Vol. II contains a *Life of Sir W. Phipps*.

MICHEL, J. *The Contest in America between France and Great Britain*.... By an impartial hand. London, 1757.

MONTCALM, *Journal du Marquis de*, 1756–1759. Ed. by H. R. CASGRAIN. Quebec, 1895.

MONTRESOR. *Journals of Col. James* (1757–9) *and Captain John Montresor* (1757–1758). New York Hist. Soc., 1881.

MURRAY, J. "Journal of the Siege of Quebec, 1759–60." Quebec Lit. and Hist. Soc. *Historical Documents*. 3rd series. Quebec, 1871.

NEWCASTLE PAPERS. Brit. Mus. Add. MSS.

NOVA SCOTIA ARCHIVES. Vol. I. *Selections from the Public Documents of the Province of Nova Scotia*. Ed. by T. B. AKINS, 1869. Vol. III. *Original Minutes of H.M.'s Council of Annapolis Royal*, 1720–39. Halifax, 1908.

ORME, Captain R. "Journal" [of an expedition against Fort du Quesne]. Hist. Society of Pennsylvania, *Memoirs*. Vol. v. Philadelphia, 1855.

PANET, J. C. *Journal du siège de Québec en 1759*. Montreal, 1866.

PARSONS, U. *Life of William Pepperell*. 3rd edn. Boston, 1856.

PENHALLOW, S. *History of the Wars of New England with the Eastern Indians*. Boston, 1726. New edn. 1859.

PEPPERELL PAPERS, THE. In *Collections* of the Massachusetts Hist. Soc. Vols. I and x. Boston.

PITT, WILLIAM (Earl of CHATHAM), *Correspondence of, with Colonial Governors*. Ed. by GERTRUDE S. KIMBALL. 2 vols. New York, 1906.

POUCHOT, M. *Memoir upon the late War in North America, between the French and the English, 1755–1760*. Transl. and ed. by F. B. HOUGH. Roxbury, Mass., 1866.

POULLIN DE LUMINA, É. J. *Histoire de la Guerre contre les Anglais depuis 1745*. 2 vols. Geneva, 1759–60.

QUEBEC. *Journal du siège de Québec déposé à la bibliothèque de Hartwell*. Quebec, 1836.
—— *Relation du siège de Québec en* 1759. Quebec Lit. and Hist. Soc. Quebec, 1840.
—— *Journal of the expedition up the River St Lawrence*. Quebec Lit. and Hist. Soc. Quebec, 1866.

RAMEZAY, *Mémoire du Sieur de*. Quebec Lit. and Hist. Soc. Quebec, 1861.

REED, C. B. *The first great Canadian...d'Iberville*. Chicago, 1910.

ROGERS, R. *Journals of Major R. Rogers*. London, 1765. Ed. by F. B. HOUGH. Albany, 1883.
—— *Reminiscences of the French War....* Concord, New Hampshire, 1831.

SARGENT, W. (Editor). *The history of the Expedition against fort du Quesne in* 1755. Hist. Society of Pennsylvania. Philadelphia, 1826.

SAVAGE, T. *Account of the late Action of the New Englanders*. London, 1691. Reprinted in Mass. Hist. Soc. Coll. vol. XIII.

SHIRLEY, W. *The conduct of Major General W. Shirley, briefly stated*. London, 1758.

SHIRLEY, W. *Correspondence, 1731–1760*. Ed. by C. H. LINCOLN. 2 vols. New York, 1912.

STARK, General J., *Memoirs and official Correspondence of*. Ed. by C. STARK. Concord, 1860.

STOBO, Major R., *Memoirs of*. London, 1800. Another edn., ed. by M. B. C. Pittsburgh, 1854.

Stopford Sackville MSS. Hist. MSS. Commission. Vol. II, pp. 257–71. London, 1910.

THOMAS, J., *Diary of* (1755). *Collections* of Nova Scotia Hist. Soc. Vol. I. Halifax, 1879.

Townshend MSS. Hist. MSS. Comm. XIITH *Report*, App. 4. London, 1887.

VAUDREUIL, Comte de. "Voyage to Canada." *New York Col. Doc.* X, 297.

VETCH, SAMUEL. "Journal." *Collections* of Nova Scotia Hist. Soc. Vol. IV. Halifax, 1885.

WALKER, Sir H. (Admiral). *A Journal...of the Late Expedition to Canada*. London, 1720.

WALPOLE, HORACE (Earl of Orford). *Memoirs of the reign of King George the Second*. London, 1847.

WASHINGTON, GEORGE. *Journal*. Ed. by J. M. TONER. Albany, 1893.
—— *Writings of*. Ed. by J. SPARKS. 12 vols. Vol. II. Boston, 1837.

WINSLOW, Colonel J. *Journal of the expulsion of the Acadians in* 1755. *Collections* of Nova Scotia Hist. Soc. Vol. III. Halifax, 1883.
—— *Journal of the siege of Fort Beauséjour*, 1755. *Ibid*. Vol. IV. 1885.

WOOD, W. (Colonel) (Editor). *Logs of the Conquest of Canada*. Champlain Soc. Toronto, 1909.

(2) LATER WORKS

ADAMS, J. T. *Revolutionary New England* (1691–1776). Boston, 1923.

ARCHIBALD, Sir A. G. "The Expulsion of the Acadians." *Trans. of Nova Scotia Hist. Soc.* vol. V. Halifax, 1887.

BEER, G. L. *British Colonial Policy, 1754–65*. London, 1907.

BONNECHOSE, C. DE. *Montcalm et le Canada français*. 5th edn. Paris, 1882.

BRADLEY, A. G. *The Fight with France for North America*. London, 1900.

BROGLIE, ALBERT (Duc de). *La Paix d'Aix la Chapelle*. Paris, 1892.

BUTLER, Col. L. *History of the King's Royal Rifle Corps*. Vol. I. *The Royal Americans*. London, 1913.

CASGRAIN, H. R. *Guerre du Canada, 1756–1760. Montcalm et Lévis*. 2 vols. Quebec, 1891.
—— *Wolfe and Montcalm*. Toronto, 1905. Revised by A. G. DOUGHTY. Toronto, 1926.

CAUVAIN, H. *Dernière Campagne du Marquis de Montcalm*. Paris, 1885.

CHARTERIS, Hon. E. *William Augustus, Duke of Cumberland, and the Seven Years' War.* London, 1925.

CLOWES, W. LAIRD. *The Royal Navy.* 6 vols. Vol. III. London, 1897–1901.

CORBETT, Sir J. S. *England and the Seven Years' War.* 2 vols. London, 1907.

DOUGHTY, A. G. *The Acadian Exiles....* (Chronicles of Canada.) Toronto, 1916.

—— *The Siege of Quebec and the Battle of the Plains of Abraham.* 6 vols. Quebec, 1902. Vol. VI contains a full bibliography.

DU BOSCQ DE BEAUMONT, G. *Les derniers jours de l'Acadie.* London, 1899.

DUSSIEUX, L. E. *Le Canada sous la domination française, d'après les archives de la Marine et de la Guerre.* Paris, 1855.

EDWARDS, J. P. *Louisbourg: an historical sketch.* Nova Scotia Hist. Soc. Vol. IX. Halifax, N.S., 1895.

FAILLON, l'Abbé. *Histoire de la colonie française en Canada.* 3 vols. Paris, 1865–6.

FEYROL, J. *Les Français en Amérique.* Paris, 1886.

FORTESCUE, Hon. Sir J. W. *A History of the British Army.* Vol. II. London, 1899.

GABRIEL, C. N. *La Guerre du Canada, 1756–1760.* Verdun, 1887.

HART, G. E. *The Fall of New France, 1755–1760.* Montreal, 1888.

HULBERT, A. B. *The Historic Highways of America.* (III, *Washington's Road.* IV, *Braddock's Road.*) Cleveland, 1903.

KÉRALLAIN, R. DE. *Les Français au Canada: la jeunesse de Bougainville et la guerre de sept ans.* Paris, 1896.

LACOUR-GAYET, G. *La Marine militaire de la France sous le règne de Louis XV.* Paris, 1902.

McLENNAN, J. S. *Louisbourg from its Foundation to its Fall, 1713–1758.* London, 1918.

MAHON, Major-General R. H. *General James Murray.* London, 1921.

MAYO, L. S. *Jeffery Amherst, a Biography.* New York, 1916.

MORGAN, W. T. "Some Attempts at imperial co-operation during the Reign of Queen Anne." *Trans. of R. Hist. Soc.* London, 1927.

MYRAND, J. E. *William Phipps devant Québec.* Quebec, 1893. Montreal, 1925.

OSGOOD, H. L. *The American Colonies in the Eighteenth Century.* Vol. IV. New York, 1924.

PAJOL, Comte C. P. V. *Les Guerres sous Louis XV.* Vol. VI. Paris, 1888.

PARKMAN, F. *A Half Century of Conflict.* 2 vols. 1st edn. Boston, 1892. (Often reprinted.)

—— *Montcalm and Wolfe.* 2 vols. 1st edn. Boston, 1884. (Often reprinted.)

PURDON, Major H. G. *A History of the 47th Foot [The Loyal Regiment (North Lancashire)].*

RIKER, T. W. "The Politics behind Braddock's Expedition." *Amer. Hist. Rev.* vol. XIII, July 1908.

RUVILLE, A. von. *William Pitt, Earl of Chatham.* (English transl.) 3 vols. London, 1907.

SCHÖNE, L. *La politique coloniale sous Louis XV.* Paris, 1907.

SEVERANCE, F. H. *An old Frontier of France.* New York, 1917.

SHIPPEN, E. *Memoir of Henry Bouquet, 1719–1765.* Philadelphia, 1900.

STONE, W. L. *Life and Times of Sir W. Johnson, Bart.* Albany, 1865.

TOWNSHEND, Major-General Sir C. V. F. *Military Life of Field-Marshal George, first Marquess Townshend, 1724–1807.* London, 1901.

WADDINGTON, R. *Louis XV et le Renversement des Alliances.* Paris, 1896.

—— *La Guerre de Sept Ans.* 5 vols. Paris, 1899 ff.

WAUGH, W. T. *James Wolfe: Man and Soldier.* Montreal and New York, 1928.

WHITTON, F. E. *Wolfe and North America.* London, 1928.

WILLIAMS, BASIL. *William Pitt, Earl of Chatham.* 2 vols. London, 1913.

WILLSON, H. BECKLES. *Life and Letters of James Wolfe.* London, 1909.

WINSOR, J. *Rival claimants for North America, 1497–1755.* Worcester, Mass., 1895.

WOOD, G. A. *The struggle in America between England and France, 1697–1763.* London, 1895.

—— *William Shirley, Governor of Massachusetts.* New York, 1920.

WOOD, W. *The Fight for Canada.* London, 1904. 2nd ed. 1905.

WRONG, G. M. *The Fall of Canada, 1759–60.* Oxford, 1914.

—— *The Conquest of New France....* New Haven, 1918.

—— *The Rise and Fall o New France.* 2 vols. London, 1928.

CHAPTER V

For bibliography to this chapter see pp. 880–5.

CHAPTERS VI, VII AND VIII

SECTION 4. BRITISH NORTH AMERICA, 1760–1812

(For additional authorities, unprinted and printed, *v. supra*, pp. 817–31, 837–40, and for the American Revolution vol. 1, pp. 876–88.)

(1) CONTEMPORARY MATERIALS

ADAMS, J. *The Works of John Adams....With a Life of the Author...by C. F. Adams.* 10 vols. Boston, 1850–6.

ALLEN, E. *Ethan Allen's Narrative of the Capture of Ticonderoga, and of His Captivity....* Written by Himself. Burlington, 1849.

CAVENDISH, Sir HENRY. *Debates of the House of Commons in the year* 1774, *on the Bill for making more effectual provision for the Government of the Province of Quebec.* Ed. by J. Wright. London, 1839.
 From shorthand notes taken by Cavendish.

CRUIKSHANK, E. A. (Editor). *The Correspondence of Lieutenant-Governor John Graves Simcoe, with allied Documents.* 4 vols. Ontario Hist. Soc. Toronto, 1923–6.

CUGNET, F. J. *An abstract of the Several Royal Edicts and Declarations, and Provincial Regulations and Ordinances....* London, 1772.

—— *Extraits des Édits, Déclarations, Ordonnances et Règlements, de sa Majesté Très Chrétienne.* Quebec, 1775.
 Much fuller than the above.

—— *Traité de la Loi des Fiefs.* Quebec, 1775.

—— *Traité de la Police.* Quebec, 1775.

—— *Traité abrégé des anciennes Loix, Coutumes, et Usages de la Colonie du Canada.* Quebec, 1775.
 The fullest. Cugnet was French Secretary to the Government in Canada after the conquest. His compilations probably played an important part in preserving the old laws of Canada.

FLICK, A. C. (Editor). *The Papers of Sir William Johnson.* Vols. IV–VI. Albany, 1925–8.

FORCE, PETER. *American Archives...a Documentary History of...the North American Colonies.* Fourth series. Vols. I, II, III. Washington, 1837.

FORD, W. C. (Editor). *Journals of the Continental Congress,* 1774–89. Washington, 1904.

GANONG, W. F. "...Documents relating to New Brunswick," in N.B. Hist. Soc. *Coll.* vols. II, III.

GRAY, H. *Letters from Canada....* London, 1809.

HERIOT, G. *Travels through the Canadas.* London, 1807.

JACKSON, J. M. *View of the Political situation of the Province of Upper Canada.* London, 1809.

[KNOX, WILLIAM.] *The Justice and Policy of the Late Act of Parliament for making More Effectual Provision for the Government of the Province of Quebec....* London, 1774. Pamphlet.
 A defence of the Quebec Act by the Under Secretary of State for the Colonies.

—— *Extra Official State Papers. By a Late Under Secretary of State.* 2 vols. London, 1789.

LA ROCHEFOUCAULT-LIANCOURT, Duc de. *Travels through the U.S. and Upper Canada in* 1795–97, *with an authentic Account of Lower Canada.* Eng. transl. 4 vols. 2nd edn. London, 1800.

Lower Canada Jurist. Vol. I. Quebec, 1857.

Masères, Baron Francis. *An Account of the Proceedings of the British and Other Protestants of the Province of Quebeck....* London, 1775. *Additional Papers concerning the Province of Quebeck.* London, 1776. An appendix to *An Account of the Proceedings.*

—— *The Canadian Freeholder*, a Dialogue shewing the sentiments of the bulk of the Freeholders on the late Quebec Act. 3 vols. London, 1776–9.

—— *A Collection of Several Commissions, and Other Public Instruments....*London, 1772.

—— *Draught of an Act of Parliament for investing the Governour and Council of the Province of Quebec, without an Assembly...with a Power of Making Laws and Ordinances... during the Space of Fourteen Years.* Two pamphlets under this title, 1772 or 1773.

—— *Draught of an Act of Parliament for settling the Laws of the Province of Quebec.* 1772. Pamphlet.

Another pamphlet under the same title was published shortly afterwards.

—— *Mémoire à la Défense d'un Plan d'Acte de Parlement pour l'Établissement des Loix de la Province de Québec.* London, 1773. Pamphlet.

—— *Occasional Essays on Various Subjects, chiefly Political and Historical.* London, 1809.

Meigs, Major R. J. *Journal of the Expedition Against Quebec.* Mass. Hist. Soc. *Coll.*, Second series, vol. II.

O'Callaghan, E. B. (Editor). Documents. *V. supra.*

Ordinances made for the Province of Quebec by the Governor and Council of the said Province since the Establishment of the Civil Government. Quebec, 1767. Reprinted by Pub. Arch. Can. *V. infra.*

Pub. Arch. Can. *Documents relating to the Constitutional History of Canada, 1759–1791,* selected and edited with notes by A. Shortt and A. G. Doughty. 2nd edn. 2 vols. Ottawa, 1918.

—— *Documents relating to the Constitutional History of Canada, 1791–1818,* ed. by A. G. Doughty and D. A. McArthur. Ottawa, 1914.

—— *Report,* 1918. *Ordinances and Proclamations of the Règne Militaire,* and *Proclamations issued by Government from 1764 until 1791.* The former are not complete for the district of Quebec because the journal of the military government of Quebec is lost. The latter are complete.

—— *Reports,* 1913 and 1914–1915. *Ordinances made for the Province of Quebec by the Governor and Council of the said Province since the Establishment of the Civil Government.* This collection does not include some of the ordinances which were disallowed.

—— *Reports,* 1882, 1884, 1885, 1886, 1888, 1889, 1890, 1891, 1892, 1919–21. Miscellaneous documents in appendices.

Quebec Gazette, published weekly from 21 June 1764, except during the period of the imposition of the Stamp Tax. The sole Canadian paper of this period. Though the official medium for the publication of public documents, it was not otherwise a government organ.

Raymond, W. O. (Ed.). *V. infra*, p. 860.

Selkirk, Lord. *Sketch of the British fur trade in North America....* London, 1816.

Senter, I. *The Journal of Isaac Senter.* Philadelphia, 1846.

Senter was physician and surgeon to Arnold's invading army.

Simcoe, Mrs John G., *Diary of* (ed. J. R. Robertson). Toronto, 1912.

Wallace, W. S. (Editor). *The Masères Letters,* 1766–68. Toronto, 1919.

Weld, I. *Travels through...Upper and Lower Canada,* 1795–97. London, 1799.

Wilmot, John E. *Historical View of the Commission for Enquiring into the Losses, Services and Claims of the American Loyalists.* London, 1815.

Young, A. H. (Editor). *The Parish Register of Kingston, Upper Canada,* 1785–1811. Kingston Historical Society, 1921.

(2) Later Works

Alvord, C. W. *V. supra*, p. 840.

—— "The Genesis of the Proclamation of 1763." Michigan Hist. Soc. *Coll.* vol. XXXVI, 1908.

Bemis, S. F. *Jay's Treaty: A Study in Diplomacy and Commerce.* New York, 1923.

BRADLEY, A. G. *Lord Dorchester*. (Makers of Canada.) 2nd edn. Oxford, 1926.
BROWN, G. W. "The St Lawrence in the Boundary Settlement of 1783." *C.H.R.* vol. IX, September 1928.
BURT, A. L. "The Mystery of Walker's Ear." *C.H.R.* vol. III, September 1922.
—— "Sir Guy Carleton and his First Council." *C.H.R.* vol. IV, December 1923.
—— "Who was the 'Com[man]d[ant] de la Troupe dans Chaque Coste'?" *C.H.R.* vol. VII, September 1926.
CANNIFF, W. *History of the Settlement of Upper Canada*. Toronto, 1869.
CARTER, C. E. *Great Britain and the Illinois Country, 1763–1774*. Washington, 1910.
CODMAN, J. *Arnold's Expedition to Quebec*. New York, 1901.
COFFIN, V. *The Province of Quebec and the Early American Revolution*. University of Wisconsin, Madison, 1896.
    Based upon extensive research, but somewhat controversial.
COUPLAND, R. *The Quebec Act*. Oxford, 1925. A strong defence of the Quebec Act.
DIONNE, N. E. "Pierre Bédard et son Temps." *Trans. R.S.C.* 2nd ser. vol. IV, 1898.
EGERTON, H. E. (Editor). *The Royal Commission on...American Loyalists, 1783–5*. (Notes of D. P. Coke.) Oxford, 1915.
FITZMAURICE, Lord EDMOND. *Life of Shelburne*. 2 vols. London, 1912.
FLICK, A. C. *Loyalism in New York during the American Revolution*. New York, 1901.
GANONG, W. F. "...Origins of Settlements in New Brunswick." *Trans. R.S.C.* 1904.
GILBERT, G. A. "The Connecticut Loyalists." *A.H.R.* vol. IV, p. 273.
GROULX, Abbé L. *Lendemains de conquête*. Montreal, 1920.
    A full discussion of the few years after the conquest by a strong "nationalist".
HARRELL, I. S. *Loyalism in Virginia*. Philadelphia, 1926.
LUCAS, Sir C. *A History of Canada, 1763–1912*. Oxford, 1909.
MCILWRAITH, JEAN N. *Sir Frederick Haldimand*. (Makers of Canada.) 2nd edn. Toronto, 1926.
MACKINTOSH, W. A. "Canada and Vermont...." *C.H.R.* VII, 1926.
MCLAUGHLIN, A. C. "The Western Posts and the British Debts." *Report of the Am. Hist. Ass.* 1894.
MAHON, R. H. *Life of General the Hon. James Murray....* London, 1921.
PARKMAN, F. *The Conspiracy of Pontiac*. 2 vols. Boston, 1857.
PATERSON, G. C. *Land Settlement in Upper Canada, 1783–1840*. Ontario Archives Report for 1920. Toronto, 1921.
"Le Règne Militaire en Canada." *Mémoires de la Société Historique de Montréal*. Montreal, 1870. Along with Pub. Arch. Can. *Report*, 1918 (cf. *supra*, p. 853), the chief authority for the period of military government.
REID, MARJORIE G. "The Quebec Fur-traders and Western Policy, 1763–1774." *C.H.R.* vol. VI, March 1925.
RIDDELL, W. R. *The Life of John Graves Simcoe....* Toronto, 1926.
RYERSON, E. *The Loyalists of America and their Times*. 2 vols. Toronto, 1880.
    Lacks discrimination.
SABINE, L. *The Loyalists of the American Revolution*. 2 vols. Boston, 1864.
SAWTELLE, W. O. "Acadia: the Pre-Loyalist Migration and the Philadelphia Plantation." *Penn. Magazine of Hist. and Biog.* Philadelphia, 1927.
SCOTT, D. C. *John Graves Simcoe*. (Makers of Canada.) 2nd edn. Toronto, 1926.
SCOTT, S. M. "Civil and Military Authority in Canada, 1764–1766." *C.H.R.* vol. IX, June 1928.
SHORTT, A. *Life of the Settler in W. Canada before...1812*. Queen's University *Bulletin*, 1914.
SIEBERT, W. H. *The Loyalists of Pennsylvania*. Ohio State University Studies. Columbus, 1920.
SIEBERT, W. H. and GILLIAM, FLORENCE E. "The Loyalists in Prince Edward Island." *Trans. R.S.C.* 3rd ser. vol. IV, 1910.
SMITH, J. H. *Arnold's March from Cambridge to Quebec...with a Reprint of Arnold's Journal*. New York and London, 1903.
—— *Our Struggle for the Fourteenth Colony*. New York and London, 1907.
    The most complete account of the military operations against Canada.

SMITH, WILLIAM. *History of Canada, from its first discovery to the year* 1791. 2 vols. Quebec, 1815.
By the son of Chief Justice Smith who arrived in Canada in 1786.
—— *First Days of British Rule in Canada.* Queen's University *Bulletin*, No. 42.
—— "The Struggle over the Laws of Canada, 1763–1783." *C.H.R.* vol. I, June 1920.
STARK, J. H. *The Loyalists of Massachusetts....* Boston, 1910.
STEVENS, W. E. *The Northwest Fur Trade,* 1763–1800. Univ. of Illinois Studies. Urbana, 1928.
The "Northwest" dealt with is the "Old Northwest" of the United States.
STONE, E. M. *The Invasion of Canada in* 1775, *including the Journal of Captain Simeon Thayer....* Providence, 1867.
SULTE, M. B. "Le Régime Militaire, 1760–1764." *Trans. R.S.C.* 2nd ser. vol. XI.
Largely a reworking of the material in the *Mémoires de la Société Historique de Montréal.*
TYLER, M. C. *The Literary History of the American Revolution.* 2 vols. New York, 1897.
VAN TYNE, C. H. *The Loyalists in the American Revolution.* New York, 1902.
—— *England and America.* Cambridge, 1927.
WALLACE, W. S. "The Beginnings of British Rule in Canada." *C.H.R.* vol. VI, September 1925. A short summary.
—— *The United Empire Loyalists.* (Chronicles of Canada.) Toronto, 1914.
WITTKE, C. "Canadian Refugees in the American Revolution." *C.H.R.* vol. III, 1922.

CHAPTER IX

SECTION 5. THE WAR OF 1812–1814

(For additional authorities, unprinted and printed, *v. supra,* pp. 819–22, 825–8, 830–1, 840. *C.M.H.* vol. VII, 797–9 and *C.H.B.F.P.* I, 609.)

(1) CONTEMPORARY MATERIALS

ADAMS, J. Q., *The Diary of, 1794–1845.* London, 1928.
American State Papers. Documents, Legislative and Executive, of the Congress of the United States. [1789–1838.] 38 vols. Washington, 1832–61. The following volumes are important here: *Foreign Relations,* vols. II and III; *Commerce and Navigation,* vol. I; *Finance,* vol. I; *Military Affairs,* vol. I; *Naval Affairs,* vol. I.
Annals of the Congress of the United States. 42 vols. Washington, 1834–56. [From 1st Cong. through 18th Cong., 1st Session.]
Annual Register. London, 1812–15.
BARING, A. *Inquiry into the Causes and Consequences of the Orders-in-Council, etc.* London, 1808.
BATHURST, Earl, *Report on the MSS. of* (Hist. MSS. Comm.). London, 1923.
CASTLEREAGH, Viscount. *Memoirs and Corresp. of Robert Stewart, Viscount Castlereagh.* Ed. C. W. Vane. (Vols. VIII–X.) 12 vols. London, 1851–3.
CHRISTIE, R. *The Military and Naval Operations in the Canadas during the late War.* Quebec, 1818.
CRUIKSHANK, E. A. (Ed.). *Documentary History of the Campaigns on the Niagara Frontier....* 9 vols. Lundy's Lane Hist. Soc., Welland, 1896–1908.
—— (Ed.). *Documents relating to the Invasion of Canada and the Surrender of Detroit, 1812.* Publications of Can. Archives. No. 7. Ottawa, 1913.
EDGAR, MATILDA (Lady) (Ed.). *Ten Years in Upper Canada in Peace and War, 1805–1815....* Toronto, 1890.
GALLATIN, J. *A Great Peace Maker; The Diary of,* ed. Count Gallatin. London, 1914.
"In Anticipation of the War of 1812." Canadian Archives *Report,* 1896.
JAMES, W. *A Full and Correct Account of the Military Occurrences of the Late War....* 2 vols. London, 1818. Biassed, but containing important official documents.
MICHIGAN PIONEER AND HISTORICAL SOCIETY. *Historical Collections,* vol. XV. Lansing, 1890. Copies of papers in the Canadian Archives concerning British-United States Relations during the War of 1812.

Naval Chronicle, The. London, 1812–15.

Niles' Register. 76 vols. Baltimore, 1811–49.

RICHARDSON, J. *War of 1812.* Brockville, 1842. With notes and a life by A. C. CASSELMAN. Toronto, 1902.

WELLINGTON, 1st Duke of, *Supplementary Despatches of.* 15 vols. Vol. IX. London, 1858–72.

WOOD, W. (Ed.). *Select British Documents of the Canadian War of 1812.* 3 vols. Champlain Soc., Toronto, 1920–8.

(2) LATER WORKS

ADAMS, H. *History of the United States* [1800–17]. 9 vols. New York, 1889–91.

ANON. *Some Account of the Public Life of the late Lieut.-General Sir George Prevost....* London, 1823.

BABCOCK, L. L. *The War of 1812 on the Niagara Frontier.* Buffalo Hist. Soc., 1927.

CLARKE, J. F. *History of the Campaign of 1812 and the Surrender of the Post of Detroit.* New York, 1848.

COFFIN, W. F. *1812: the War and Its Moral, a Canadian Chronicle.* Montreal, 1864.

COX, I. J. *The Indian as a Diplomatic Factor in the History of the Old North West.* Chicago Hist. Soc., 1910.

CRUIKSHANK, E. A. "A Study of Disaffection in Upper Canada in 1812–1815." *Trans. Roy. Soc. Can.*, 1912.

DRAKE, B. *Life of Tecumseh and of his brother.* Cincinnati, 1841.

EDGAR, MATILDA (Lady). *General Brock.* Revised by Brig.-Gen. E. A. CRUIKSHANK. (Makers of Canada.) Oxford, 1926.

FITZGIBBON, M. A. *A Veteran of 1812. The Life of James Fitzgibbon.* Toronto, 1898.

HACKER, LOUISE M. "Western Land Hunger and the War of 1812: a Conjecture." *Mississippi Valley Hist. Rev.*, March 1924.

HANNAY, J. *History of the War of 1812.* Toronto, 1905.

LUCAS, Sir C. P. *The Canadian War of 1812.* Oxford, 1906.

LYMAN, T. *The Diplomacy of the United States, 1778–1828.* 2 vols. Boston, 1828.

McLAUGHLIN, A. C. "Western Posts and British Debts." *American Hist. Assoc. Report*, 1894.

MAHAN, A. T. *Sea Power in its Relation to the War of 1812.* 2 vols. Boston, 1905.

MILLS, DUDLEY. "The Duke of Wellington and the Peace Negotiations at Ghent in 1814." *Can. Hist. Rev.*, March 1921.

PRATT, J. W. *Expansionists of 1812.* New York, 1925.

ROOSEVELT, T. *The Naval War of 1812.* New York, 1882.

SLOCUM, C. E. *The Ohio Country between the Years 1783 and 1815.* New York, 1910.

SMYTH, Sir J. CARMICHAEL. *Précis of the Wars in Canada from 1755 to...1814.* London, 1826. 2nd ed. Ed. by his son. London, 1862.

SNIDER, C. H. J. *Under the Red Jack: Privateers of the Maritime Provinces of Canada in the War of 1812.* Toronto, 1928.

TUPPER, F. BROCK. *Life and Corresp. of Major-Gen. Sir Isaac Brock.* 2nd ed. London, 1847.

UPDYKE, F. A. *The Diplomacy of the War of 1812.* Baltimore, 1915.

WOOD, W. *The War with the United States.* Toronto, 1921.

CHAPTER X (i) AND (ii)

SECTION 6. LOWER AND UPPER CANADA, 1815–1837

(For additional authorities, unprinted and printed, *v. supra*, pp. 819–28, 830, 831, 835–9, 842.)

(1) CONTEMPORARY WORKS

BELL, Rev. W. *Hints to Emigrants.* Edinburgh, 1824.

—— *Counsel for Emigrants...* Aberdeen, 1834.

DUNLOP, W. *Statistical Sketches of U.C.* London, 1833.

GALT, JOHN. *Autobiography.* 2 vols. London, 1833.

GOURLAY, R. *Statistical Account of Upper Canada.* 2 vols. and General Introduction. London, 1822.

HALL, Lieut. F. *Travels in Canada and the U.S. in 1816 and 1817.* London, 1818.

HEAD, Sir F. B., Bt. *The Emigrant.* London, 1846.

—— *A Narrative.* 2nd edn. London, 1839.

HORTON, Sir R. J. WILMOT. *Exposition and Defence of Earl Bathurst's administration of the Affairs of Canada 1822 to 1827.* London, 1838.

HOWISON, J. *Sketches of Upper Canada.* Edinburgh, 1821.

JAMESON, ANNA. *Winter Studies and Summer Rambles in Canada.* 3 vols. London, 1838.

M'GREGOR, J. *British America.* 2 vols. London, 1832.

MACKENZIE, W. L. *Sketches of Canada and the United States.* London, 1833.

MACTAGGART, J. *Three years in Canada.* 2 vols. London, 1829.

PAPINEAU, L. J. *Speech of L. J. Papineau on the hustings at the opening of the election for the West Ward of the City of Montreal.* Montreal, 1927. Pamphlet, McGill University Library.

PRESTON, T. R. *Three years' residence in Canada.* 2 vols. London, 1840.

ROEBUCK, J. A. *The Canadian Portfolio.* London, 1838.

STRACHAN, JAMES. *Visit to the Province of Upper Canada—1819.* Aberdeen, 1820.

—— *Remarks on Emigration from the United Kingdom.* London, 1827.

STRICKLAND, Major S. *Twenty-seven Years in Canada West.* 2 vols. London, 1853.

TALBOT, E. A. *Five Years' Residence in the Canadas....* 2 vols. London, 1824.

TALBOT PAPERS, THE. Ed. J. H. Coyne. *Trans. R.S.C.,* 1907, 1909.

TRAILL, CATHERINE PARR. ... *The Backwoods of Canada: Being Letters from the Wife of an Emigrant Officer.* London, 1836.

(2) LATER WORKS

CARRIER, L. N. *Les Évènements de 1837.* Quebec, 1857.

CARTWRIGHT, C. E. *Life and Letters of the Hon. Richard Cartwright.* Toronto, 1876.

CIRCÉ-COTÉ, Mme E. *Papineau: Son Influence sur la Pensée Canadienne.* Montreal, 1924.

DAVID, L. O. *Les Deux Papineau.* Montreal, 1896. Pamphlet.

—— *Les Patriotes de 1837–38.* Montreal, 1884.

DECELLES, A. D. *Papineau.* (Makers of Canada.) Oxford, 1926.

—— *The Patriotes of '37.* (Chronicles of Canada.) Toronto, 1916.

DENT, J. C. *Story of the Upper Canadian Rebellion.* 2 vols. Toronto, 1885.

DUNHAM, AILEEN. *Political Unrest in Upper Canada, 1815–36.* London, 1927.

EGERTON, H. E. and GRANT, W. L. *V. supra,* p. 835.

ERMATINGER, C. O. *The Talbot Régime,* 1791–1840. St Thomas, 1904.

EWART, ALISON and JARVIS, JULIA. "The Personnel of the Family Compact, 1791–1841." *C.H.R.* vol. VII, 1926.

GLOBENSKY, C. A. M. *La Rébellion de 1837.* Quebec, 1883.

HAIGHT, C. *Life in Canada fifty years ago.* Toronto, 1885.

HERRINGTON, W. S. *History of the County of Lennox and Addington.* Toronto, 1913.

LANGTON, W. A. (Editor). *Early Days in Upper Canada: Letters of John Langton....* Toronto, 1926.

LEADER, R. E. *Life and Letters of J. A. Roebuck.* London, 1897.

LINDSAY, C. *Life and Times of William Lyon Mackenzie.* 2 vols. Toronto, 1862.

MACHAR. *Memorials of the Rev. John Machar, D.D.* Toronto, 1873.

MERRITT, J. P. *Biography of the Hon. W. H. Merritt, M.P.* St Catharine's, 1875.

MOORE-SMITH, G. C. *Life of Sir John Colborne, Field Marshal Lord Seaton.* London, 1903.

Papineau et Nelson: Blanc et Noir. Montreal, 1848. Pamphlet.

PUTNAM, J. H. *Egerton Ryerson in Upper Canada.* Toronto, 1912.

RIDDELL, W. R. *The Life of William Dummer Powell.* Michigan Hist. Soc. Lansing, 1925.

—— *Robert Gourlay....* Toronto, 1916.

SHORTT, A. "The Economic Effect of the War of 1812 on Upper Canada." Ont. Hist. Soc. *Papers,* X (1913).

SMITH, W. "Robert Gourlay." Queen's University *Bulletin.* Kingston, 1926.

WALLACE, W. S. *The Family Compact.* (Chronicles of Canada.) Toronto, 1915.

YOUNG, A. H. "John Strachan." *Queen's Quarterly.* Kingston, 1928.

CHAPTER XI

SECTION 7. THE MISSION OF LORD DURHAM

(For additional authorities, unprinted and printed, *v. supra*, pp. 819, 820, 826, and *infra*, sections 8, 9.)

(1) CONTEMPORARY WORKS AND SOURCES

BULLER, C. *Responsible Government for the Colonies.* London, 1840. Reprinted in E. M. Wrong, *Charles Buller...* (*v. infra*, p. 858).

DURHAM, Earl of. *Report on the Affairs of British North America*, with appendices, 1839. The edition cited in the narrative is that edited by Sir C. P. Lucas, 3 vols. Oxford, 1912. It contains an introduction, the *Report*, the *Appendices* without minutes of evidence, some despatches, and a *Sketch of Lord Durham's Mission*, written by Charles Buller in 1840.

FRY, A. A. *Report of the Case of the Canadian Prisoners.* London and Dublin, 1839. Pamphlet.

HALIBURTON, T. C. *A Reply to the Report of the Earl of Durham.* London, 1839.

—— *The Bubbles of Canada.* London, 1839.

HINCKS, F. *Brief Review of the Report of the House of Assembly on Lord Durham's Report.* Toronto, 1839.

Journals of the Special Council, Lower Canada, 1838–40.

MELBOURNE, Viscount. *Lord Melbourne's Papers.* Ed. by L. C. Sanders. London, 1890.

PRESTON, T. R. *Three Years' Residence in Canada*, 1837–9. 2 vols. London, 1840.

PUB. ARCH. CAN. *Report for* 1928. Appendices A (Catalogue of J. A. Roebuck Papers) and F (Charles Buller to John Stuart Mill, 13 October 1838).

Report from the Select Committee of the House of Assembly of U. C. on the State of the Province. Toronto, 1839.

Report from the Select Committee of the Legislative Council of U. C. on the Report of the Earl of Durham. Toronto, 1839.

RICHARDSON, Major J. *Eight Years in Canada.* Montreal, 1847.

ROBINSON, J. B. *Canada and the Canada Bill. By the Hon....C.J. of Upper Canada.* London, 1840. Pamphlet.

ROEBUCK, J. A. *The Colonies of England....* London, 1849.

VICTORIA, Queen. *Letters of Queen Victoria*, 1837–61. Ed. by A. C. Benson and Viscount Esher. Popular edn. 3 vols. London, 1908.

YOUNG, G. R. *Statement of the Escheat Question in P. E. I.* London, 1838.

(2) LATER WORKS

BRADSHAW, F. *Self-Government in Canada...the story of Lord Durham's Report.* London, 1903.

BROUGHAM, Lord. *Life and Times of Henry, Lord Brougham.* 3 vols. Edinburgh, 1871.

DENT, J. C. *Story of the Upper Canadian Rebellion.* 2 vols. Toronto, 1885.

GARNETT, R. *Edward Gibbon Wakefield.* London, 1898.

LEADER, R. E. *Life and Letters of J. A. Roebuck.* London, 1897.

MILLS, R. C. *The Colonisation of Australia* (1829–42). London, 1915.

NEW, C. W. *Lord Durham. A Biography.* Oxford, 1929.

O'CONNOR, IRMA. *Edward Gibbon Wakefield.* London, 1929.

PARKER, C. S. *Life and Letters of Sir James Graham.* 2 vols. London, 1907.

—— *Sir Robert Peel from his Private Papers.* 3 vols. London, 1891–9.

REID, S. *Life and Letters of Lord Durham.* 2 vols. London, 1906.

SHORTRIDGE, W. P. "The Canadian-American Frontier during...1837–8." *C.H.R.*, March 1926.

SMITH, WM. "Lord Durham's Administration." *C.H.R.* vol. VIII, September 1927.

STEPHEN, C. *The Rt Hon. Sir James Stephen.* London, 1906.

TORRENS, W. M. *Memoirs of William, Viscount Melbourne.* 2 vols. London, 1878.

TREVELYAN, G. M. *Lord Grey of the Reform Bill.* London, 1920.

TREVELYAN, Sir G. O. *Life and Letters of Lord Macaulay.* London, 1908.

WALPOLE, S. *Life of Lord John Russell.* 2 vols. London, 1889.

WRONG, E. M. *Charles Buller and Responsible Government.* Oxford, 1926.

CHAPTERS XII, XIII AND XV

SECTION 8. CANADA UNDER RESPONSIBLE GOVERNMENT, 1840–1867

(For additional authorities, unprinted and printed, *v. supra*, pp. 819, 820, 825–7, 856–8, and *infra*, pp. 863–5.)

(1) CONTEMPORARY WORKS

ADDERLEY, C. B. *Review of "The Colonial Policy of Lord John Russell's Administration" by Earl Grey, 1853: and of Subsequent Colonial History.* London, 1869.

BONNYCASTLE, Sir R. H. *The Canadas in 1841.* 2 vols. London, 1842.

—— *Canada and the Canadians in 1846.* 2 vols. London, 1846.

Canada, the Land of Hope. By the Editor of *The Canadian News.* London, 1857.

DAWSON, S. J. *Report on the Exploration of the Country between Lake Superior and the Red River Settlement, and between the Latter Place and the Assiniboine and Saskatchewan.* Toronto, 1859.

ELGIN, JAMES, eighth Earl of. *Extracts from the Letters of James, Earl of Elgin to Mary Louisa, Countess of Elgin, 1847–62.* Privately printed, 1864.

GALT, A. T. *Canada, 1849–1859.* Quebec, 1860. Pamphlet.

GREY, HENRY, third Earl. *Colonial Policy of Lord J. Russell's administration.* 2 vols. London, 1853.

HINCKS, F. *Canada: its Financial Position and Resources.* London, 1849.

HIND, H. Y. *North-West Territory. Reports of Progress: together with a Preliminary and General Report....* Toronto, 1859.

KAYE, Sir J. W. *Life and Correspondence of Charles, Lord Metcalfe.* Revised edn. 2 vols. London, 1858.

—— *Selections from the Papers of Lord Metcalfe.* London, 1855.

KEEFER, T. G. *Sketch of the Rise and Progress of the Reciprocity Treaty....* Toronto, 1860.

KINGSFORD, W. *The Canadian Canals: their History and Cost....* Toronto, 1865.

MONCK, FRANCES E. O. *My Canadian Leaves, 1864–5.* London, 1891.

MONRO, A. *History...of Brit. N. America.* Montreal, 1864.

MOODIE, Mrs S. *Roughing it in the Bush.* 2 vols. London, 1852.

RICHARDSON, Major J. *Eight Years in Canada.* Montreal, 1847.

SCROPE, G. P. *Memoir of the Life of the Right Honorable Charles, Lord Sydenham....* London, 1843.

STRICKLAND, Major J. *Twenty-seven Years in Canada West.* 2 vols. London, 1854.

TREMENHEERE, H. S. *Notes on Public Subjects, made during a Tour in the United States and Canada.* London, 1852.

WAKEFIELD, E. G. *Art of Colonization.* London, 1849.

—— *A View of Sir Charles Metcalfe's Government of Canada. By a member of the Provincial Parliament.* London, 1844. Reprinted in E. M. Wrong, *Charles Buller.*

WALROND, T. *Letters and Journals of James, Eighth Earl of Elgin.* London, 1872.

WIDDER, F. *Information for Intending Immigrants of All Classes to Upper Canada.* Toronto, 1855.

(2) LATER WORKS

ALLIN, C. D. and JONES, G. M. *Annexation, Preferential Trade and Reciprocity....* Toronto, 1911.

BURN, D. L. "Canada and the Repeal of the Corn Laws." *Camb. Hist. Journ.* vol. II, 1928.

CALLAHAN, J. M. "American Canadian Relations concerning Annexation, 1846–71." *Studies in American History.* Bloomington, Indiana, 1926.

DAVID, L.-O. *L'Union des deux Canadas, 1841–1867.* Montreal, 1898.

GÉRIN-LAJORIE, A. *Dix Ans au Canada, 1840–50.* Quebec, 1888.

GLAZEBROOK, G. P. DE T. *Sir Charles Bagot in Canada.* Oxford, 1929.

HATCH, I. T. *The Reciprocity Treaty: a Report to Congress.* Washington, 1860.

HAYNES, F. E. *The Reciprocity Treaty with Canada of 1854.* Baltimore, 1892.

HINCKS, Sir F. *The Political History of Canada between* 1840 *and* 1855. Montreal, 1877.
KEEFER, T. C. *Canals of Canada*. Montreal, 1894.
KENNEDY, W. P. M. *Lord Elgin*. (Makers of Canada.) Oxford, 1926.
KNAPLUND, P. "The Buller-Peel Correspondence regarding Canada, 1841." *C.H.R.* vol. VIII, March 1927.
—— "Sir James Stephen and British North American Problems, 1840–1847." *C.H.R.* vol. V, 1924.
LEACOCK, S. B. *Mackenzie, Baldwin, Lafontaine, Hincks*. (Makers of Canada.) Oxford, 1926.
MACDONNELL, U. N. "Gibbon Wakefield and Canada subsequent to the Durham Mission." Queen's University *Bulletin*, No. 49, 1924–5.
MOREHOUSE, FRANCES. "Canadian Migration in the Forties." *C.H.R.* vol. IX, December 1928.
MORISON, J. L. *British Supremacy and Canadian Self-Government*, 1839–54. Glasgow, 1919.
—— *Life of the Eighth Earl of Elgin*. London, 1927.
OLIPHANT, L. *Episodes in a Life of Adventure*. London, 1887.
OLIPHANT, Mrs M. *Life of Laurence Oliphant*. 2 vols. London, 1891.
ROBINSON, C. *History of the Reciprocity Treaty of* 1854 *with Canada*. (U.S. Senate Document, 62nd Congress, 1st session, No. 17.)
SHORTT, A. *Lord Sydenham*. (Makers of Canada.) Oxford, 1926.
—— *Railroad Construction and National Prosperity: an Historic Parallel*. Ottawa, 1914.
TANSILL, C. C. *Canadian Reciprocity Treaty of* 1854. Johns Hopkins University Studies. Baltimore, 1922.
TURCOTTE, L. P. *Le Canada sous l'Union*, 1841–67. 2 vols. Quebec, 1871.
WRONG, G. M. *The Earl of Elgin*. London, 1905.

CHAPTERS X (iii) AND XIV

SECTION 9. THE MARITIME PROVINCES, 1815–1867

(For additional authorities, unprinted and printed, *v. supra*, pp. 819–29, 840–2, 849, and *infra*, pp. 866, 867.)

(1) CONTEMPORARY WORKS

The Acadian Recorder. Halifax.
ATKINSON, W. C. *Historical...Account of New Brunswick...* 3rd edn. Edinburgh, 1844.
Constitutions of Cape Breton, Nova Scotia, New Brunswick, British Columbia, and Vancouver Island. Can. Sess. Papers, 1883, vol. 12, No. 70.
HALIBURTON, T. C. *Sam Slick*. New edn. Ed. R. P. Baker. Toronto, 1923.
HOWE, J., *Speeches...of. V. supra*, p. 842.
MARTIN, C. (Editor). "The Correspondence between Joseph Howe and Charles Buller, 1845–1848." *C.H.R.* vol. VI, December 1925.
MOORSOM, W. *Letters from Nova Scotia*. London, 1830.
The Novascotian. Halifax.
PERLEY, M. H. *Reports on the Sea and River Fisheries of New Brunswick*. Fredericton, 1852.
RAYMOND, W. O. (Editor). *The Winslow Papers*, 1776–1826. Saint John, 1901.

(2) LATER WORKS

BOURINOT, Sir J. G. *Builders of Nova Scotia*. Toronto, 1900.
    A valuable survey of settlement, religious history, biography, etc.
CHITTICK, V. L. O. *Thomas Chandler Haliburton: A Study in Provincial Toryism*. New York, 1924.
GANONG, W. F. "Cartography of New Brunswick." *Trans. R.S.C.*
HANNAY, J. *Lemuel Allan Wilmot*. (Makers of Canada.) Oxford, 1926.
    This edition has corrections, by G. E. Wilson, of the edition of 1907.
—— *Sir Leonard Tilley*. (Makers of Canada.) Oxford, 1926.

LIVINGSTON, W. R. *The Evolution of Responsible Government in Nova Scotia.* Madison, Wisconsin, 1927.

LONGLEY, J. W. *V. supra,* p. 842.

MACMECHAN, A. *Old Province Tales.* Toronto, 1924.

—— *Sagas of the Sea.* London, 1923.

—— *There go the Ships.* Toronto, 1928.

PAYNE, A. M. "Life of Sir S. Cunard." Nova Scotia Hist. Soc. *Coll.* 1918.

SAUNDERS, E. M. *Three Premiers of Nova Scotia.* Toronto, 1909.
    Biographies of Howe, Johnstone, and Tupper.

CHAPTER XVI

SECTION 10. THE OPENING OF THE WEST, TO 1867

(For additional authorities, unprinted and printed, *v. supra,* pp. 818, 820, 824–9, 834–40, 843–8, and *infra,* sections 11, 12, 14.)

(1) CONTEMPORARY WORKS

BACK, Sir GEORGE. *Journal of the Arctic Land Expedition.* London, 1836.

BAFFIN, WM. *Voyages of William Baffin,* 1612–22. Ed. by Sir C. R. Markham. London, 1880.

BALLANTYNE, R. M. *Hudson's Bay.* Edinburgh, 1848.

CARVER, J. *Travels...* 1766–68. London, 1781.

CHRISTY, M. (Editor). *The Voyages of Captain Luke Fox and Captain Thomas James,* 1631–2.... 2 vols. Hakluyt Society. London, 1894.

COCKING, M. *Journal of Matthew Cocking,* 1772–73. Ed. by L. J. Burpee. *Trans R.S.C.* 1908.

COOK, JAMES. *A Voyage to the Pacific Ocean in* 1776–80. 3 vols. London, 1884.

DOBBS, A. *Account of the Countries adjoining Hudson's Bay....* London, 1744.

FRANKLIN, Sir JOHN. *Narrative of a Journey to the Shores of the Polar Sea in* 1819–22. London, 1823.

—— *Narrative of a Second Expedition to the Shores of the Polar Sea,* 1825–7. London, 1828.

HARGRAVE, J. J. *Red River.* Montreal, 1871.

HARMON, D. W. *...Travels in the Interior of North America.* Andover, Mass., 1820.

HEARNE, SAMUEL. *Journey from Prince of Wales Fort in Hudson's Bay to the Northern Ocean,* 1769–72. London, 1795.

HENDRY, A. *Journal of Anthony Hendry,* 1754–55. Ed. by L. J. Burpee. *Trans. R.S.C.* 1907.

HENRY, ALEXANDER. *Travels and Adventures in Canada and the Indian Territories.* Ed. by J. Bain. Toronto, 1901.

KELSEY, HENRY. *The Kelsey Papers.* With an introduction by A. G. Doughty and C. Martin. Pub. Arch. Ottawa, 1929.

LA VÉRENDRYE. *The Journals of La Vérendrye.* Ed. by L. J. Burpee. Champlain Society. Toronto, 1927.

LONG, J. *Voyages and Travels,* 1768–1782. Chicago, 1922.

MACDONALD, D. G. F. *British Columbia and Vancouver I.* London, 1862.

M'GILLIVRAY, D. *The Journal of Duncan M'Gillivray.* Ed. by A. S. Morton. Toronto, 1929.

MACKENZIE, Sir ALEXANDER. *Voyages from Montreal through the Continent of North America,* 1789 *and* 1793. London, 1801.

—— *Alexander Mackenzie's Voyages.* Ed. by J. W. Garvin. Toronto, 1928.

MARGRY, P. *Découvertes et établissements des Français dans l'ouest.* 6 vols. Paris, 1879–88.

MARTIN, R. M. *The Hudson's Bay Territories and Vancouver's I....* London, 1849.

MAYNE, R. C. *Four Years in British Columbia....* London, 1862.

MEARES, J. *Voyages...in* 1788–9 *from China to N.W. America....* London, 1790.

OLDMIXON, J. *The British Empire in America.* London, 1741.

PORTLOCK, N. *A Voyage...to the North-West Coast of America in* 1785–8. London, 1789.

PUB. ARCH. CAN. *The Canadian North-West, its Early Development and Legislative Records*. Ed. by E. H. Oliver. 2 vols. Ottawa, 1914.
—— *Report for* 1928. Appendix E (Some Account of the Trade Carried on by the North West Company).
RADISSON, P. E. *Voyages of Pierre Esprit Radisson*. Ed. by G. D. Scull. Prince Society. Boston, 1885.
RAE, JOHN. *Narrative of an Expedition to the Shores of the Arctic Sea*. London, 1850.
RICHARDSON, Sir JOHN. *Arctic Searching Expedition*. London, 1851.
ROSS, A. *The Red River Settlement....* London, 1856.
SELKIRK, Earl of. Memorial to...Duke of Richmond. Montreal, 1819.
SIMPSON, THOMAS. *Narrative of the Discoveries on the North Coast of America*. London, 1843.
SOUTHESK, Earl of. *Saskatchewan and the Rocky Mts....* Toronto, 1875.
THOMPSON, D. *David Thompson's Narrative of his Explorations in Western America, 1784–1812*. Ed. by J. B. Tyrrell. Champlain Society. Toronto, 1916.
VANCOUVER, GEORGE. *Voyage of Discovery to the North Pacific Ocean....* London, 1798.

(2) LATER WORKS

ASHER, G. M. *Henry Hudson the Navigator*. London, 1860.
BANCROFT, H. H. *History of the Northwest Coast*. San Francisco, 1884.
BRYCE, G. *Mackenzie, Selkirk, Simpson*. (Makers of Canada.) Oxford, 1926.
—— *The Remarkable History of the Hudson's Bay Company*. 3rd edn. London, 1910.
BURPEE, L. J. *The Search for the Western Sea*. London, 1808.
COATS, R. H. and GOSNELL, R. E. *Sir James Douglas*. (Makers of Canada.) Oxford, 1926.
COUES, ELLIOTT. *New Light on the Early History of the Greater North-West*. 3 vols. New York, 1897.
DAVIDSON, G. C. *The North West Company*. University of California Publications in History, vol. VII. Berkeley, 1918.
DUGAS, G. *The Canadian West down to the year* 1822. Montreal, 1905.
—— *Histoire de l'Ouest Canadien de* 1822 *à* 1869. Montreal, 1906.
FLEMING, R. H. "The Origin of Sir Alexander Mackenzie and Company." *C.H.R.* vol. IX, June 1928.
INNIS, H. A. "The North West Company." *C.H.R.* vol. VIII, December 1927.
—— *Peter Pond*. Toronto, 1929.
KELLOGG, LOUISE P. *The French Régime in Wisconsin and the North West*. Publications of the State Historical Society of Wisconsin. Madison, 1925.
LAUT, A. C. *The Conquest of the Great Northwest*. 2 vols. New York, 1908.
MANNING, W. R. *The Nootka Sound Controversy*. Washington, 1905.
MARTIN, C. *Lord Selkirk's Work in Canada*. Oxford, 1916.
MASSON, L. R. *Les Bourgeois de la Compagnie du Nord-Ouest*. 2 vols. Quebec, 1889–90.
MERK, F. "The Oregon Pioneers and the Boundary." *A.H.R.*, July 1924.
MILLS, L. "The Real Significance of the Nootka Sound Incident." *C.H.R.*, 1925.
MORTON, A. S. "La Vérendrye: Commandant, Fur-Trader, and Explorer." *C.H.R.* vol. IX, December 1928.
PRITCHETT, J. P. "Some Red River Fur-Trade Activities." *Minnesota History Bulletin*, vol. V, May 1924.
SAGE, W. N. *Life of Sir James Douglas*. University of Toronto. (In the press.)
SCHAFER, J. *Hist. of the Pacific Northwest*. New York, 1905.
SCHOOLING, Sir W. *The Governor and Company of Adventurers of England trading into Hudson Bay during* 250 *years*. London, 1920.
WADE, M. S. *Mackenzie of Canada*. Edinburgh and London, 1927.
WILLSON, H. BECKLES. *The Great Company*. Toronto, 1899.
WINSOR, J. *The Mississippi Basin: the Struggle in America between England and France, 1697–1763*. Boston, 1895.
WRONG, H. *Sir Alexander Mackenzie, Explorer and Fur Trader*. Toronto, 1927.

CHAPTER XVII

For bibliography to this chapter see pp. 880–5.

CHAPTERS XVIII, XIX AND XXIV

SECTION 11. CONFEDERATION AND THE EXPANSION OF THE DOMINION

(For additional authorities, unprinted and printed, *v. supra*, pp. 841–2, sections 8, 9, 10, and *infra*, pp. 865–9.)

(1) CONTEMPORARY AND NEARLY CONTEMPORARY WORKS

BEGG, ALEXANDER. *The Creation of Manitoba: or A History of the Red River Troubles.* Toronto, 1871.

BENJAMIN, L. N. (Ed.). *The St Albans Raid....* Boston, 1865.

BOLTON, E. C. and WEBBER, H. H. *The Confederation of British North America.* London, 1866.

BRITISH COLUMBIA, LEGISLATIVE COUNCIL. *Debate on the Subject of Confederation with Canada.* Reported by W. S. Sebright Green. Victoria, 1912. Reprinted from original edn. Victoria, 1870.

BRITISH NORTH AMERICAN ASSOCIATION. *Confederation...being Extracts from Speeches Recently Delivered...in Canada, Nova Scotia, and New Brunswick, by...Members of the Confederation Conference held at Quebec on the 10th Oct., 1864.* London, 1865.

BUTLER, W. F. *The Great Lone Land.* London, 1873.

CANADA (Province). *Parliamentary Debates on the Subject of the Confederation of the British North American Provinces....* Quebec, 1865.

CARNARVON, HENRY HOWARD MOLYNEUX, 4th Earl of. *Speeches on Canadian Affairs.* Ed. by Sir Robert Herbert. London, 1902.

CAUCHON, J. *L'Union des provinces de l'Amérique Britannique du Nord.* Quebec, 1865. Also an edition in English, translated by G. H. Macauley. Quebec, 1865.

DENISON, G. T. *The Fenian Raid at Fort Erie.* Toronto, 1866.

DUFFERIN and AVA, Marquis of. *Speeches and Addresses.* London, 1882.

DUFFERIN and AVA, Marchioness of. *My Canadian Journal.* London, 1891.

GALT, A. T. *Speech on the Proposed Union of the British North American Provinces, delivered at Sherbrooke, C.E., 23 November, 1864.* Montreal, 1864. Pamphlet.

GRAY, J. H. *Confederation: or the Political and Parliamentary History of Canada....* 2 vols. (Only the first published.) Toronto, 1872.

HAMILTON, P. S. *Union of the Colonies of British North America: Being Three Papers upon this Subject, Originally published in 1854.* Montreal, 1864. With introduction.

HUYSHE, G. L. *The Red River Expedition.* London, 1871.

MACDONALD, A. A. "Notes on the Quebec Conference." Ed. by A. G. Doughty. *C.H.R.* vol. 1, March 1920.

MCDOUGALL, W. *The Red River Rebellion: Eight Letters to the Hon. Joseph Howe.* Toronto, 1870. Pamphlet.

MCGEE, T. D. *Notes on Federal Governments, Past and Present. With an Appendix, containing the Federal Constitution of the New Zealand Colonies.* Montreal, 1865. Pamphlet.

—— *Speeches and Addresses, Chiefly on the Subject of British-American Union.* London, 1865.

MORRIS, ALEX. *Nova Britannia: or Our New Dominion fore-shadowed....* Ed. by J. C. Dent. Toronto, 1884.

PENNY, E. G. (Editor of the Montreal *Herald*). *The Proposed...Confederation: Why it should not be imposed...by Imperial Legislation.* Montreal, 1867. Pamphlet.

POPE, Sir J. (Editor). *Confederation: being a Series of hitherto unpublished documents....* Toronto, 1895.

The Proposed B.N.A. Federation: a Reply to Mr Penny's Reasons why it should not be imposed...by Imperial Legislation. From the Montreal "Daily News". Montreal, 1867. Pamphlet.

RAWLINGS, T. *The Confederation of the British North American Provinces, their Past History and Future Prospects....* London, 1865.

RUSSELL, A. J. *The Red River Country, Hudson's Bay and Northwest Territories, considered in relation to Canada....* 3rd edn. Montreal, 1870. 1st edn. was in 1869.

RUSSELL, W. H. *Canada: its Defences, Condition, and Resources.* (The last volume of his *Diary, North and South.*) London, 1865.

TACHÉ, J. C. *Des provinces de l'Amérique du Nord....* Quebec, 1858.

TAYLOR, J. W. *Relations between the United States and the Northwest British America.* U.S. Docs. 37th Cong. 2nd Sess. House Exec. Docs. vol. 10, No. 146, Serial 1138. Pamphlet.

WATKIN, Sir E. W. *Canada and the States: Recollections, 1851–1886.* London, 1887.

WHELAN, E. *The Union of the British Provinces: a Brief Account of the Several Conferences held...in Sept. and Oct. 1864....* Charlottetown, 1865. New edn., with introd. by D. C. Harvey. Gardenvale, 1927.

WOLSELEY, Sir G. *The Story of a Soldier's Life.* London, 1903.

(2) LATER WORKS

ADAMS, E. D. *Great Britain and the American Civil War.* 2 vols. London, 1925.

BLEGEN, T. C. "A Plan for the Union of British North America and the United States, 1866." *Mississippi Valley Historical Review,* vol. IV, March 1918.

BOVEY, W. "Confederate Agents in Canada during the American Civil War." *C.H.R.* vol. II, March 1921.

BURPEE, L. J. "Joseph Howe and the Anti-Confederation League." *Trans. R.S.C.* 3rd ser. vol. x.

CALLAHAN, J. M. *The Alaska Purchase and Americo-Canadian Relations.* West Virginia University Studies in American History. Ser. 1, Diplomatic History, Nos. 2 and 3. Morgantown.

CANADIAN HISTORICAL ASSOCIATION. *Report for 1927.* A group of papers on various aspects of the federation movement.

CARTWRIGHT, Sir R. J. *Memories of Confederation.* Ottawa, 1906.

COLQUHOUN, A. H. U. *The Fathers of Confederation.* (Chronicles of Canada.) Toronto, 1916.

EGERTON, H. E. *Federations and Unions within the British Empire.* Oxford, 1911.

FOLWELL, W. W. *A History of Minnesota.* 4 vols. St Paul, 1921–6.

GRANT, Rev. G. M. *Ocean to Ocean: Sandford Fleming's Expedition through Canada in 1872.* Toronto, 1873.

GROULX, Abbé L. *La confédération canadienne, ses origines.* Montreal, 1918. A French-nationalist interpretation.

HAMMOND, M. O. *Confederation and its Leaders.* Toronto, 1917.

HARDINGE, Rt Hon. Sir ARTHUR. *The Life of Henry Howard Molyneux Herbert, Fourth Earl of Carnarvon.* Ed. by Elizabeth, Countess of Carnarvon. 3 vols. Oxford, 1925.

HARTSOUGH, MILDRED LUCILE. *The Twin Cities as a Metropolitan Market. A Regional Study of the Economic Development of Minneapolis and St Paul.* University of Minnesota. Studies in the Social Sciences, No. 18. Minneapolis, 1925.

HOWAY, F. W. "Attitude of Governor Seymour toward Confederation," and "Governor Musgrave and Confederation." *Trans. R.S.C.* 3rd ser. vols. XIV and XV.

HUGHES, KATHERINE. *Father Lacombe: the black-robe Voyageur.* Toronto, 1911.

KNAPLUND, P. *Gladstone and Britain's Imperial Policy.* London, 1927.

LABILLIÈRE, F. P. DE. *Federal Britain.* London, 1894.

LANDON, F. "The *Trent* Affair of 1861." *C.H.R.* vol. III, March 1922.

LANGTON, W. A. (Editor). *Early Days in Canada: Letters of John Langton.* Toronto, 1926.

MACDONALD, HELEN G. *Canadian Public Opinion on the American Civil War.* Columbia University. New York, 1926.

MACDONALD, Capt. J. B. A. *Troublous Times in Canada: A History of the Fenian Raids of 1866 and 1870.* Toronto, 1910.

McDOUGALL, Rev. J. *In the Days of the Red River Rebellion.* Toronto, 1903.

MACLEAN, J. *McDougall of Alberta.* Toronto, 1927.

MACNAUGHTON, J. *Lord Strathcona.* (Makers of Canada.) Oxford, 1926.

MARTIN, C. "The First 'New Province' of the Dominion." *C.H.R.* vol. I, December 1920.

MAURICE, Sir F. and ARTHUR, Sir G. *Life of Lord Wolseley*. London, 1924.

MORICE, Rev. A. G. *History of the Catholic Church in Western Canada from Lake Superior to the Pacific*. 2 vols. Toronto, 1910.

PAYNE, E. J. *Colonies and Colonial Federations*. 1904.

POPE, Sir J. *V. supra*, p. 842.

PRITCHETT, J. P. "The Origin of the So-Called Fenian Raid on Manitoba in 1871." *C.H.R.* vol. x, March 1929.

Quebec and Confederation: A Record of the Debate of the Legislative Assembly of Quebec on the Motion Proposed by J. N. Francœur. Ottawa, 1918.

RANEY, W. F. "Recruiting and Crimping in Canada for the Northern Forces, 1861–1865." *Mississippi Valley Hist. Rev.*, June 1923.

RIDDELL, W. R. "Some Origins of the B. N. A. Act, 1867." *Trans. R.S.C.*, 1917.

ROBERTS, M. *The Western Avernus, or Toil and Travel in Western North America....* New edn. Westminster, 1896.

ROGERS, N. McL. "The Confederate Council of Trade." *C.H.R.* vol. VII, December 1926.

SAGE, W. N. "The Annexationist Movement in British Columbia." *Trans. R.S.C.* 3rd ser. vol. XXI.

SKELTON, O. D. *V. supra*, p. 842, and *infra*, pp. 871, 873.

SQUAIR, J. *The Townships of Darlington and Clarke, Ontario*. Toronto, 1927.

STRICKLAND, Major. *Twenty-seven Years in Canada West*. 2 vols. London, 1853.

TROTTER, R. G. "An Early Proposal for the Federation of British North America." *C.H.R.* vol. VI, June 1925.

—— *Canadian Federation: its Origins and Achievement*. Toronto and London, 1924.

—— "Lord Monck and the Great Coalition of 1864." *C.H.R.* vol. III, June 1922.

—— "Some American Influences upon the Canadian Federation Movement." *C.H.R.* vol. v, September 1924.

TUPPER, Sir C. *V. supra*, p. 842.

VAUGHAN, W. *Sir William Van Horne*. (Makers of Canada.) Oxford, 1926.

WHITELAW, W. M. *Maritime Union and the Charlottetown Conference*. (In preparation.)

WILSON, G. E. "New Brunswick's Entrance into Confederation." *C.H.R.* vol. IX, March 1928.

WRONG, G. M., WILLISON, Sir J., LASH, Z. A., FALCONER, Sir R. A. *The Federation of Canada, 1867–1917: Four Lectures Delivered in the University of Toronto, in March, 1917*. Toronto, 1917.

YOUNG, J. *Public Men and Public Life in Canada, being Recollections of Parliament and the Press....* 2 vols. 2nd edn. Toronto, 1912.

CHAPTERS XX, XXI AND XXXII

SECTION 12. CANADIAN NATIONAL POLITICS, 1867–1921

(For additional authorities, unprinted and printed, *v. supra*, pp. 825–7, 841–2.)

(1) BIOGRAPHIES, AND COLLECTIONS OF SPEECHES

ABERDEEN, Lord and Lady. *"We twa": Reminiscences*. 2 vols. London, 1925.

ARGYLL, JOHN GEORGE, 9th Duke of. *Memories of Canada....* London, 1884.

BARTHE, U. (Compiler). *Wilfrid Laurier on the platform*. Quebec, 1890.

BEGBIE, H. A. *The fourth Earl Grey*. London, 1918.

BIGGAR, C. R. W. *Sir Oliver Mowat*. 2 vols. Toronto, 1905.

BLACK, C. E. D. *The Marquess of Dufferin and Ava*. London, 1903.

BONNETERRE, A. DE. *L'hon. J. A. Chapleau, sa biographie, ses discours*. Montreal, 1887.

BRYCE, G. "The real Strathcona." *Canadian Magazine*, 1915.

BUCHAN, JOHN. *Lord Minto: A memoir*. London, 1924.

BUCKINGHAM, W. and ROSS, G. W. *The Hon. Alexander Mackenzie, his life and times.* Toronto, 1892.
CAMPBELL, Sir A. *Speeches on divers occasions.* Ottawa, 1885.
CHARLTON, J. *Speeches and addresses.* Toronto, 1912.
COLQUHOUN, A. H. U. "Our eight prime ministers." *Canadian Magazine*, 1917.
DUFFERIN AND AVA. *V. supra*, p. 863.
HAM, G. H. *Reminiscences of a raconteur.* Toronto, 1921.
HOPKINS, J. C. *The life and work of the Right Hon. Sir John Thompson.* Brantford, 1895.
KING, Rt Hon. W. L. M. *The Message of the Carillon.* Toronto, 1927.
LANGELIER, C. *Souvenirs politiques.* 2 vols. Quebec, 1909–12.
LAURIER, Sir W. *Discours à l'étranger et au Canada.* Montreal, 1910.
LYALL, Sir ALFRED. *Life of the Marquis of Dufferin and Ava.* 2 vols. London, 1905.
McGILLICUDDY, O. E. *The making of a Premier: An outline of the life story of the Right Hon. W. L. Mackenzie King.* Toronto, 1922.
MEIGHEN, Rt Hon. A. *Oversea Addresses.* Toronto, 1921.
NEWTON, Lord. *Lord Lansdowne: a Biography.* London, 1929.
ROSS, Sir GEORGE W. *Getting into parliament and after.* Toronto, 1913.
RUSSELL, Mr Justice. "The career of Sir John Thompson." *Dalhousie Review*, July 1921.
SMITH, GOLDWIN. *Reminiscences.* Toronto, 1912.
TASSE, J. *Le 38me fauteuil.* Montreal, 1891.
WILLISON, Sir J. *Reminiscences, political and personal.* Toronto, 1919.

(2) SPECIAL STUDIES

AMES, Sir H. B. "The organization of political parties in Canada." Supplement to the *American Political Science Review*, February 1912, pp. 181–8.
Canada first: A memorial of the late William A. Foster, Q.C., with introduction by Goldwin Smith. Toronto, 1890.
COLLINS, J. E. *Canada under the administration of Lord Lorne.* Toronto, 1884.
DAVID, L. O. *Histoire du Canada depuis la confédération.* Montreal, 1909.
—— *Souvenirs et biographies*, 1870–1910. Montreal, 1911.
DENISON, Col. G. T. *The struggle for imperial unity.* Toronto, 1909.
HANNA, D. B. *Trains of recollection.* Toronto, 1924.
IRVINE, W. *The Farmers in Politics.* Toronto, 1921.
LAUT, AGNES C. *Canada at the cross-roads.* Toronto, 1921.
PARKIN, G. R. *The Great Dominion: Studies of Canada.* London, 1895.
STEWART, G. *Canada under the Administration of the Earl of Dufferin.* London, 1878.
WALLACE, W. S. "Canada a nation," in F. H. Hooper (Ed.), *These eventful years: the twentieth century in the making.* New York, 1924.
—— "The growth of Canadian national feeling." *C.H.R.* vol. I, 1920. Separately published in enlarged form, Toronto, 1927.
[WILLISON, Sir J.] *The new Canada: A survey of the conditions and problems of the Dominion.* London, 1912.

CHAPTER XXVII

SECTION 13. ECONOMIC DEVELOPMENT OF
THE MARITIME PROVINCES, 1867–1921

(*V. supra*, section 9.)

BIOLOGICAL BOARD OF CANADA. *Publications.*
BROWN, R. *The coal fields and coal trade of the Island of Cape Breton.* London, 1871.
COMMISSION OF CONSERVATION REPORTS. Fernow, B. E. *Forest Conditions of Nova Scotia.* Ottawa, 1912. Stafford, S. *The Canadian Oyster.* Ottawa, 1913. Idem. *Sea Fisheries of Eastern Canada.* Ottawa, 1913.
DAWSON, S. J. *Report on the Navigation of R. St John....* Ottawa, 1870.
DES BRISAY, M. B. *History of the Country of Lunenburg.* Toronto, 1895.

DRUMMOND, R. *Minerals and Mining Nova Scotia*. Stellarton, 1918.
Economic Geography. Stelgenbauer, F. A. "Geographic Aspects of the Prince Edward Island Fur Industry," January 1927, pp. 110–25. Colby, C. "An analysis of the Apple Industry of the Annapolis-Cornwallis Valley," vol. I, pp. 173–97, 337–55.
FORSEY, F. *Economic and Social Aspects of the Nova Scotia Coal Industry*. Toronto, 1926.
GILPIN, E. *Minerals of Nova Scotia*. Halifax, 1901.
Halifax Commission, 1877, Proceedings of. 3 vols. Washington, 1878.
History of the Bank of Nova Scotia, 1832–1900. n.d.
INNIS, H. A. *The Fur Trade of Canada*. Toronto, 1927.
KNIGHT, T. F. *Shore and deep sea Fisheries of Nova Scotia*. Halifax, 1867.
LEWIS, R. G. and BOYCE, G. H. *Wood-Using Industries of the Maritime Provinces*. Forestry Branch Bulletin, No. 44. Ottawa.
The Maritime Provinces since Confederation. Dominion Bureau of Statistics. Ottawa, 1926.
MARR, G. J. *The Effect of Confederation on the Trade of the Maritime Provinces of Canada*. A MS. thesis of which the original is in the Library of the University of Toronto.
MINING SOCIETY OF NOVA SCOTIA. *Transactions*.
NOVA SCOTIA, PROVINCE OF. *A submission of its claims with respect to Maritime disabilities within Confederation as presented to the Royal Commission*. Halifax, 1926.
PORRITT, E. "Canada's National Policy." *Political Science Quarterly*, vol. XXXII.
Report of the Dominion shad fishery Commission, 1908–1910. Ottawa, 1910.
Report of Proceedings of the Canada-West Indies Conference, 1920. Ottawa, 1920.
Report of the Royal Commission investigating the Fisheries of the Maritime Provinces and the Magdalen Islands. Ottawa, 1928.
Reports of Department of Marine and Fisheries of Canada.
Reports of Department of Mines of Nova Scotia.
Royal Commission on the natural resources, trade and legislation of certain portions of His Majesty's Dominions, Minutes of Evidence taken in the Maritime Provinces of Canada in 1914. London, 1915.
SELEKMAN, B. M. *Postponing Strikes*. New York, 1927.
WHITBECK, R. H. "A geographical study of Nova Scotia." *Bulletin of the American Geographical Society*, June 1914.

CHAPTER XXVIII (NEWFOUNDLAND)

For bibliography to this chapter see pp. 880–5.

CHAPTER XXII

SECTION 14. THE PRAIRIE PROVINCES, 1867–1921

(For additional authorities, *v. supra*, pp. 820, 826, 861–6, and sections 10, 11, and *infra*, pp. 869–71.)

ANDERSON, J. T. M. *The Education of the New Canadian*. Toronto, 1918.
ARCHER, S. A. (Ed.). *Mems. of Charlotte S. Bompas, 1830–1917*. London, 1929.
BEGG, A. *The Creation of Manitoba*. Toronto, 1871.
BEGG, A. and NURSEY, W. *Ten Years in Winnipeg*. Winnipeg, 1879.
BENOIT, Dom P. *Vie de Mgr Taché*. 2 vols. Montreal, 1904.
BLACK, N. F. *History of Saskatchewan and the North West Territories*. 2 vols. Regina, 1913.
BOULTON, Major C. A. *Reminiscences of the North West Rebellions*. Toronto, 1886.
BUTLER, Capt. W. F. *The Wild North Land*. London, 1873.
Canada in 1880. Reports of Tenant Farmers' Delegates on the Dominion of Canada as a Field for Settlement. Ottawa, 1881.
CHAPLEAU, J. A. *Speech of Hon. J. A. Chapleau—Execution of Louis Riel*. Montreal, 1886.

COWIE, I. *The Company of Adventurers...Seven Years in the Service of the...Company...* 1867–1874. Toronto, 1913.

EWART, J. *The Manitoba School Question.* Toronto, 1894.

GILBERT, LOUIS. *La Saskatchewan.* Paris, n.d.

GORDON, Rev. C. W. *The Life of James Robertson.* Toronto, 1908.

GRANT, G. M. *Ocean to Ocean: Sandford Fleming's Expedition through Canada in 1872.* Toronto, 1873.

GREELEY, A. W. *The Polar Regions in the Twentieth Century.* London, 1929.

GUNN, D. and TUTTLE, C. R. *History of Manitoba.* Ottawa, 1880.

HAYDON, A. L. *The Riders of the Plains.* London, 1910.

HEALY, W. J. *Women of Red River.* Winnipeg, 1923.

HEILPRIN, A. *Alaska and the Klondike.* New York, 1899.

Journals of the Council of the North-West Territories, 1877–1887.

LONGSTRETH, T. M. *The Silent Force.* London, 1927.

MACBETH, R. G. *The Making of the Canadian West.* 2nd edn. Toronto, 1905.

—— *Policing the Plains.* Toronto, 1922.

McCORMICK, J. H. *Lloydminster or 5000 miles with the Barr Colonists.* n.d.

McDOUGALL, Rev. J. *Pathfinding on Plain and Prairie.* Toronto, 1898.

MACHRAY, Rev. R. *Life of Archbishop Machray.* Toronto, 1909.

MACKENZIE, N. M. W. J. *The Men of the Hudson's Bay Company*, 1670–1920. Fort William, 1921.

MACOUN, J. *Manitoba and the Great North-West.* Guelph, 1882.

The Manitoba School Case, 1894. Edited for the Canadian Government by the Appellants' Solicitors in London. London, 1895.

MARTIN, CHESTER. *The Natural Resources Question.* Winnipeg, 1920.

MAVOR, J. *Report to the Board of Trade on the North-West of Canada.* London, 1904.

MOBERLY, H. J. *When Fur was King.* Toronto, 1929. Autobiographical.

MORRIS, A. *The Treaties of Canada with the Indians of Manitoba and the North-West Territories.* Toronto, 1880.

OLIVER, E. H. "The Contest between Lieutenant-Governor Royal and the Legislative Assembly of the North-West Territories, 1888–1893." *Trans. R.S.C.*, 1923.

—— "The Beginnings of White Settlement in Northern Saskatchewan." *Trans. R.S.C.*, 1925.

PRUD'HOMME, L. A. *L'Élément Français au Nord-Ouest.* Montreal, 1904.

The Queen vs. Louis Riel. Report of Trial at Regina. Ottawa, 1886.

Report of the Agricultural Credit Commission of the Province of Saskatchewan, 1913.

Reports of Department of the Interior.

SOUTHESK, Earl of. *Saskatchewan and the Rocky Mountains.* Edinburgh, 1875.

STEELE, S. B. *Forty Years in Canada: Reminiscences of the Great North-West.* Toronto, 1918.

STEFANSSON, V. *The Northward Course of Empire.* New York, 1922.

TACHÉ, Bishop A. A. *The Amnesty Question with regard to the Northwest Difficulty.* St Boniface, 1893.

WALLACE, J. N. *The wintering Partners on Peace River.* Ottawa, 1929.

WOODSWORTH, J. S. *Strangers within Our Gates.* Toronto, 1908.

CHAPTER XXIII

SECTION 15. BRITISH COLUMBIA, 1871–1921

(For additional authorities *v. supra*, pp. 820, 828–30, and sections 10, 11, 16.)

ALASKAN BOUNDARY TRIBUNAL. *Proceedings of the Alaskan Boundary Tribunal.* 10 vols. Washington, 1904.

COATS, R. H. and GOSNELL, R. E. *Sir James Douglas.* Oxford, 1926.

COWAN, G. H. *British Columbia's Claim for Better Terms.* Vancouver, 1904.

EGERTON, Mrs FRED. *Admiral Sir Geoffrey Phipps Hornby: A Biography*. London, 1896.
  Gives information regarding San Juan.
FOSTER, J. W. *Diplomatic Memoirs*. 2 vols. London, 1910.
  Acted for the United States in the Bering Sea and Alaskan Boundary
  Arbitration. Strongly pro-American.
FUR SEAL ARBITRATION. *Proceedings of the Tribunal of Arbitration at Paris*, 1893.
  16 vols. Washington, 1895.
GOSNELL, R. E. *Sixty Years of Progress: British Columbia*. n.p., n.d. Contains a reliable
  sketch of late political history by one who was in touch with events.
—— *Year Book of British Columbia*. Victoria, 1911– . Issued by the Government of
  British Columbia, compiled from official sources.
KERR, J. B. *Biographical Dictionary of well-known British Columbians*. Vancouver, 1890.
Message of the President of the United States, December 21, 1866. House of Represen-
  tatives, 39th Congress, 2nd Session, Executive Document No. 24.
  Containing correspondence and reports on San Juan trouble.
MILTON, Viscount. *A History of the San Juan Water Boundary Question*. London, 1869.
  An accurate and succinct account of the origin and progress of the dispute,
  compiled from and largely composed of official reports.
PROCTER, F. J. *The Financial Crisis in British Columbia*. Vancouver, n.d. (*c*. 1900).
Report of the British Columbia Fishery Commission, 1892. Ottawa, 1893.
Report of the Royal Commission on Chinese Immigration. Ottawa, 1885.
Report of the Royal Commission on Chinese and Japanese Immigration. Ottawa, 1902.
[STOCK, EUGENE.] *Metlakahtla and the North Pacific Mission*. London, 1881.
  The official account of the foundation and development of Metlakahtla,
  but ending before the trouble.
WELLCOME, H. S. *The Story of Metlakahtla*. London, 1887. An account of the
  Metlakahtla mission and its disruption, biassed against the Church authorities.

CHAPTERS XXV AND XXVI

SECTION 16. THE ECONOMIC DEVELOPMENT
OF THE DOMINION OF CANADA, 1867–1921

I. *GENERAL WORKS*

BRADLEY, A. G. *Canada in the Twentieth Century*. London, 1925.
Canada under the National Policy: Arts and Manufactures. Montreal, 1883.
Canada Year Book. Ed. by S. A. Cudmore. Ottawa, 1867– . (Proceeding.)
  The official statistical abstract of the Dominion, each edition containing
  statistics of current trade, with summaries extending back to Confederation.
*Canadian Economics, Papers prepared for reading before the Economical Section of the
  British Association, Montreal Meeting*. Montreal, 1885.
CHALMERS, R. *A History of Currency in the British Colonies*. London, 1893.
CHOMLEY, C. H. *Protection in Canada and Australia*. London, 1904.
COGHLAN, T. A. *Report on Immigration, with special reference to Canada*. Intelligence
  Dept. New South Wales, Bulletin 13. Sydney, 1905.
FUCHS, C. J. *The Trade Policy of Great Britain and her Colonies since* 1860. Translated
  by C. H. M. Archibald. London, 1905.
JEANS, J. S. *Canada's Resources and Possibilities*. London, 1904.
JOHNSON, G. *Canada, its History. . . and Natural Resources*. Ottawa and London, 1886.
MCLEAN, S. J. *Tariff History of Canada*. (Univ. of Toronto Studies in History
  and Economics.) Toronto, 1895.
MORGAN, H. J. (Editor). *The Dominion Annual Register and Review*, 1878–86.
  8 vols. Ottawa, 1879–87.
ROOT, J. W. *Colonial Tariffs*. Liverpool, 1906.
—— *Trade Relations of the British Empire*. 2nd edn. Liverpool, 1904.

II. *WORKS ON SPECIAL SUBJECTS*

(1) COMMUNICATIONS

(For additional authorities *v. supra*, pp. 859–68. Among biographies, *supra*, pp. 841, 842, see especially those of Van Horne, Strathcona, John A. Macdonald and Laurier.)

Highways.

CANADIAN GOOD ROADS ASSOCIATION. *Annual Reports*, 1913– .

Commissioner of Highways, Department of Railways and Canals, Ottawa. *Annual Reports* and special *Bulletins*.

ONTARIO GOOD ROADS ASSOCIATION. *Annual Reports*, 1902– .

PROVINCIAL DEPARTMENTS OF HIGHWAYS. *Annual Reports*.

PUBLIC ROADS AND HIGHWAYS COMMISSION OF ONTARIO. *Report*. Toronto, 1914.

Inland Waterways.

CORPS OF ENGINEERS, UNITED STATES ARMY, in collaboration with the United States Shipping Board. *Report on Transportation on the Great Lakes*. Washington, 1926. Dealing with historical development of all important trades, both bulk and package freight.

DEPARTMENT OF RAILWAYS AND CANALS. *Annual Reports*.

DOMINION MARINE ASSOCIATION. *Annual Reports*.

Great Inland Water-way Projects in the United States. Annals of the Amer. Acad. of Political and Social Science. January 1928.

INTERNATIONAL JOINT WATERWAYS COMMISSION. ST LAWRENCE WATERWAY. 67th Cong. 2nd Sess. Sen. Doc. No. 114, 1922.
    Commission advocated deepening of canals along the St Lawrence route, with reasons.

KEEFER, T. C. *V. supra*, p. 860.

MACELWEE, R. S. and RITTER, A. H. *Economic Aspects of the Great Lakes—St Lawrence Ship Channel*. New York, 1921. With strong support for it.

MACGIBBON, D. A. "Aspects of the proposed St Lawrence Shipway." *Queen's University Quarterly*, 1929.

RITTER, A. H. *Transportation Economics of the Great Lakes—St Lawrence Ship Channel*. Washington, 1925.

ROYAL COMMISSION ON LAKE GRAIN RATES. *Report*. Sessional Papers, No. 211, 1923.

Railways.

CANADIAN PACIFIC AND CANADIAN NATIONAL RAILWAYS. *Annual Reports*.

Correspondence regarding Grand Trunk Railway Company Acquisition and Memoranda respecting the same. Sessional Papers, No. 90, 1919.

DEPARTMENT OF RAILWAYS AND CANALS. *Annual Reports*.

FLAVELLE, Sir JOSEPH. "A Plan Aimed to Solve the Railway Tangle." *The Globe*, Toronto, 25 August 1921.

FLEMING, Sir SANDFORD. *The Intercolonial. A Historical Sketch of the Inception, Location, Construction and Completion of the Line of Railway uniting the Inland and Atlantic Provinces of the Dominion*. Montreal, 1876.

Grand Trunk Arbitration. The Award and Reasons for Award. Ottawa, 1921.
    Gives decisions of majority and minority of the Board of Arbitration.

INNIS, H. A. *History of the Canadian Pacific Railway*. London, 1923.

JACKMAN, W. T. *Economics of Transportation*. Toronto and Chicago, 1926.
    Includes the historical development so far as required as a basis for a study of the economic principles of transportation.

—— Articles in *The Monetary Times*, Toronto, 27 April, 4, 11 May 1917; 2 May, 19 December 1919; 12 August to 13 October 1921; in *Traffic World*, Chicago, 29 June, 6 July 1918; in *The Monetary Times Annual*, Toronto, 1919–26; in *Queen's Quarterly*, Kingston, January–March 1922; in *The Railway Age*, New York, 11, 18 March 1922.
    These deal with current developments and problems.

LOVETT, H. A. *Canada and the Grand Trunk*, 1829–1924. Montreal, 1924.

MACGIBBON, D. A. *Railway Rates and the Canadian Railway Commission*. Boston, 1917. Early part gives carefully documented history of railway development.

PAYNE, J. L. Articles in *Railway Age Gazette*, New York, vol. 61, p. 589, and vol. 62, p. 181; in *The Railway Age*, New York, vol. 64, p. 36; vol. 66, pp. 31, 1555; vol. 68, p. 141; vol. 70, pp. 109, 787, 883, 929; vol. 71, pp. 107, 294. Shows the recent changes in railway conditions in Canada and the losses due to government ownership.

RAILWAY INQUIRY COMMISSION. *Report*. Sessional Papers, No. 20 g, 1917.

RAILWAY RATES COMMISSION, 1895. *Report*. Sessional Papers, No. 29, 1895.

Report on "Railway Commissions," by S. J. McLean. Sessional Papers, No. 20 a, 1902.

Report on "Rate Grievances on Canadian Railways," by S. J. McLean. Sessional Papers, No. 20 a, 1902.

ROYAL COMMISSION ON RAILWAYS, 1888. *Report*. Sessional Papers, No. 8 a, 1888.

SHAUGHNESSY, Lord. "Plan for Solving the Railway Problem", in *The Globe*, Toronto, 25 April 1921.

SKELTON, O. D. *The Railway Builders. A Chronicle of Overland Highways*. (Chronicles of Canada.) Toronto, 1916.

TROUT, J. M. and EDWARD. *The Railways of Canada*. Toronto, 1871.

(2) AGRICULTURE

(For additional authorities *v. supra*, pp. 861–5, and the articles in *Canada and its Provinces* on "General Economic History", "Agriculture", "The Dairy Industry".)

Annual Report of the Canadian Cooperative Wool Growers, Ltd. Toronto, 1918– .

BOOTH, J. F. *Cooperative Marketing of Grain in Western Canada*. United States Department of Agriculture. Technical Bulletin No. 63. Washington, 1928.

BULLER, A. H. R. *Essays on Wheat...in W. Canada*. New York, 1919.

CLARK, W. C. *The Country Elevator in the Canadian West*. Queen's University *Bulletin*. Kingston, 1916.

Dairy Factories Report, 1920. Dominion Bureau of Statistics. Ottawa.

DRYDEN, W. A. and RITCH, W. T. *The Sheep Industry in Canada, United States and Great Britain*. Ottawa, 1911.

FAIR, LOUISA M. *The Transportation of Canadian Wheat to the Sea*. McGill Univ. Econ. Studies. Toronto, 1925.

FAY, C. R. *Cooperation in the Canadian West*. London, 1925.

FOOD RESEARCH INSTITUTE, Stanford Univ., U.S.A. Vols. I–III. 1925–6.

HOPKINS, E. S. and NEWMAN, L. H. *The Organization, Achievements and Present Work of the Experimental Farms*. Ottawa, 1924.

MACKINTOSH, W. A. *Agricultural Cooperation in Western Canada*. Toronto, 1924.

Massey-Harris, An Historical Sketch, 1846–1926. Toronto, 1927.

MOOREHOUSE, HOPKINS. *Deep Furrows*. Toronto, 1918.

Ontario Agricultural Commission Report, 1881. Toronto.

PATTON, H. S. *Grain Growers' Cooperation in Western Canada*. Harvard Economic Studies. Cambridge, Mass., 1928.

Royal Grain Inquiry Commission Report, 1925. Ottawa, 1925.

RUTHERFORD, J. G. *The Cattle Trade of Western Canada*. Special Report to the Dominion Department of Agriculture. Ottawa, 1909.

Slaughtering and Meat Packing, and Allied Industries. Dominion Bureau of Statistics. Ottawa, 1921.

The Western Producer. Saskatoon, 1925– .

TODD, S. E. "Making our Live Stock Industry." *Farmer's Advocate*, 30 June 1927.

WOOD, L. A. *A History of Farmers' Movements in Canada*. Toronto, 1924.

ZAVITZ, C. A. *Alfalfa*. Ontario Department of Agriculture, Bulletin No. 280. Toronto, 1920.

—— *Forty Years' Experiments with Grain Crops*. Ontario Department of Agriculture, Bulletin No. 332. Toronto, 1927.

(3) Industrial Development

(For additional authorities *v. supra*, pp. 863–9, and *infra*, p. 874.)

A. General and Special Works.

ADNEY, T. *The Klondike Stampede.* New York, 1900.

BIGGAR, E. B. *Hydro-Electric Development in Ontario.* Toronto, 1920.
A brief and uncritical sketch of the Hydro-Electric Commission.

CARNEGIE, D. *The History of the Munitions Supply in Canada, 1914–1918.* London, 1925.

Census of Canada. The census of industries, like that of population, has been taken every ten years since 1870–1, with an intercensal inquiry every five years since 1905. The intercensal inquiry, being made through the post, is necessarily less detailed than the decennial census. The facts in the industrial census have reference to the location of the works, the capital employed, the number of employees, their salaries or wages, and the class and value of the products. In addition to the general census reports, many bulletins and publications, monthly, annual, and occasional on industry have been issued by the Dominion Bureau of Statistics, established in 1918, and previous to that date by the Census and Statistics Office.

DONALD, W. J. A. *The Canadian Iron and Steel Industry.* Cambridge, Mass., 1915.

FORSEY, E. *Economic and Social Aspects of the Nova Scotia Coal Industry.* McGill Economic Studies. Toronto, 1926.

HALIBURTON, R. G. *The Coal Trade of the New Dominion.* Halifax, 1868. Pamphlet.

INNIS, H. A. *The Fur Trade of Canada.* Toronto, 1927.

LANGEVIN, Hon. H. S. *Report on British Columbia.* Ottawa, Sess. Papers, 1872, No. 10.

LOGAN, H. A. *The history of Trade-Union Organization in Canada.* Chicago, 1928.

MAVOR, J. *Niagara in Politics.* New York, 1925.
Marked by a bias against public ownership of water powers.

Minutes of Evidence Taken in the Central and Western Provinces of Canada in 1916 before the Royal Commission on the Natural Resources, Trade, and Legislation of Certain Portions of His Majesty's Dominions. British Parliamentary Papers. Cd. 8458. London, 1917.

MOORE, E. S. *Canada's Mineral Resources.* Toronto, 1929.

Proceedings of the Special Committee appointed for Inquiry into the Cost of Living. Ottawa, 1919.

REICH, N. *The Pulp and Paper Industry in Canada, With Special Reference to the Export of Pulpwood.* McGill Economic Studies. Toronto, 1921.

Report of the Board of Inquiry into Cost of Living. Ottawa, 1915.

Report of the Royal Commission on Relations of Capital and Labour in Canada. Ottawa, 1889.

Report of the Royal Commission on the Coal Mining Industry in Nova Scotia. Halifax, 1926.

Report of Royal Commission on Mineral Resources of Ontario. Toronto, 1890.

Report of the Royal Commission on Pulpwood. Ottawa, 1924.

Report of the Royal Ontario Nickel Commission. Toronto, 1917.

"Report of the Select Committee Appointed to Inquire into the Manufacturing Interests of the Dominion." *Appendix to Journals, House of Commons, Canada,* 1874, No. 3.

"Report of the Select Committee on the Causes of the Present Depression of the Manufacturing, Mining, Commercial, Shipping, Lumber, and Fishing Interests." *Appendix to Journals, House of Commons, Canada,* 1876, No. 3.

"Report of Select Committee on Combinations." *Appendix to Journals, House of Commons, Canada,* 1888, No. 4.

Reports of the Commission of Conservation. Ottawa, 1910–1919.

Reports of the Mines Branch. Ottawa.

Reports of the Mines Departments in the Provinces, particularly the Bureau of Mines of Ontario.

Reports of the Ontario Hydro-Electric Commission. Toronto, 1906– .
ROSS, V. *Petroleum in Canada.* Toronto, 1917.
SELEKMAN, B. M. *Postponing Strikes.* New York, 1927.
SHORTT, A. *Early Economic Effects of the European War upon Canada.* Carnegie
 Endowment for International Peace, Preliminary Economic Studies of the
 War. New York, 1918.
SMALL, H. B. *The Products and Manufactures of the New Dominion.* Ottawa, 1868.
STAPELLS, H. G. *The Recent Consolidation Movement in Canadian Industry.* (Un-
 published thesis in the Library of the University of Toronto, 1922.)
   A careful study of the consolidation movement between 1909 and 1921.
STEWART, B. M. *Canadian Labour Laws and the Treaty.* New York, 1926.

B. Principal Periodicals relating to Industry.

Canada Lumberman and Woodworker. Toronto, 1880– . *Canadian Engineer.* Toronto,
 1893– . *Canadian Machinery and Manufacturing News.* Toronto, 1905– .
 Canadian Manufacturer. Toronto, 1880– . *Canadian Mining Journal,* with which
 is incorporated the *Canadian Mining Review.* Gardenvale, Quebec, 1907– .
 Canadian Mining Review, established 1879. *Canadian Textile Journal,* Garden-
 vale, Quebec, 1883– . *Financial Post of Canada.* Toronto, 1907– . *The
 Financial Times.* Montreal, 1912– . *Hardware and Metal.* Toronto, 1888– .
 Industrial Canada. Toronto, 1900– . *Labour Gazette.* Department of Labour,
 Ottawa, 1900– . *Monetary Times.* Toronto, 1867– . *Pulp and Paper Magazine.*
 Gardenvale, Quebec, 1903– .

(4) FINANCE AND BANKING

Note: The subject of this section is mainly contemporary history, and information has been obtained chiefly from private and confidential sources.

Automotive Industries of Canada. Facts and Figures of the Automobile Industry in Canada.
 Toronto, 1925.
BRECKENRIDGE, R. M. *History of Banking in Canada.* United States National
 Monetary Commission. Washington, 1910.
CLARK, A. B. *An Outline of provincial and municipal Taxation in Brit. Col., Alberta,
 Saskatchewan and Manitoba.* Winnipeg, 1920.
FIELD, F. W. *Capital Investments in Canada. The Monetary Times of Canada.* Montreal,
 1914.
Fiftieth Anniversary of the Royal Bank of Canada. Montreal, 1919.
MACLEAN, A. K. *Budget Speech in* 1918. Ottawa, 1918.
PAISH, Sir GEORGE. *The Export of Capital and the Cost of Living.* Manchester Statis-
 tical Society. Manchester, n.d.
PERRY, J. R. *Public Debts in Canada.* Univ. of Toronto Studies in History and
 Economics. Vol. 1. Toronto, 1901.
Report of Assessment and Taxation Commission, Province of Manitoba. Winnipeg, 1919.
ROSS, V. A. *History of the Canadian Bank of Commerce.* Toronto, 1920.
SKELTON, O. D. *Canadian Federal Finance.* Queen's Univ. *Bulletin,* July 1915, Oct.
 1918.
VINEBERG, S. *Provincial and Local Taxation in Canada.* New York, 1912.
VINER, JACOB. *Canada's Balance of International Indebtedness.* Harvard Economic
 Studies, vol. 26. Cambridge, Mass., 1924.
WHITE, Sir W. THOMAS. *Budget Speeches in* 1914, 1915, 1916, 1917, 1919. Ottawa,
 1914– .
—— *The Story of Canada's War Finance.* Montreal, 1921.
WILLIS, H. P. and BECKHART, B. H. (Editors). *Foreign Banking Systems.* New
 York, 1929.

(5) COMMERCIAL POLICY AND THE DEVELOPMENT OF COMMERCE

(For additional authorities *v. supra*, pp. 863–9, 872.)

ADAM, G. M. (Editor). *Handbook of Commercial Union.* With an introduction by Goldwin Smith. Toronto, 1888.

Correspondence between the British Ambassador at Washington and the Government of Canada in connection with Negotiations for a Reciprocity Treaty between Canada and the United States. Sessional Papers, Canada, 1912, No. 82 a.
Contains the important material relating to the reciprocity agreement of 1911.

DAVIDSON, J. *Commercial Federation and Colonial Trade Policy.* London, 1900.

DOMINION BUREAU OF STATISTICS. *Annual Report on the Trade of Canada.*
The historical summaries extend back to Confederation. See especially the annual report for the year ended 31 March 1926.

FLECK, A. A. *Kanada: volkswirtschaftliche Grundlagen und weltwirtschaftliche Beziehungen.* Jena, 1912.

LAUREYS, H. *La conquête des marchés extérieurs.* Montreal, 1927.

McLEAN, S. J. *The Tariff History of Canada.* University of Toronto Studies. Toronto, 1895.

NASMITH, G. G. *Timothy Eaton.* Toronto, 1923.

PORRITT, E. *Sixty Years of Protection in Canada,* 1846–1912. 2nd edn. Winnipeg, 1913.

—— *The Revolt in Canada against the New Feudalism.* London, 1911.
The latter covers the years from 1907 in greater detail than the former. Both are strongly free trade.

Report of the Board of Inquiry into the Cost of Living in Canada. 2 vols. (especially vol. 2). Ottawa, 1915.
An analytical study of the economic history of Canada from 1900 to 1913, with special emphasis on the importation of capital and labour in this period.

SHORTT, A. *Imperial Preferential Trade from a Canadian Point of View.* Toronto, 1904.

SMITH, GOLDWIN. *Canada and the Canadian Question.* London, 1891.

UNITED STATES TARIFF COMMISSION. *Colonial Tariff Policies.* Chap. xiii—"The preferential policy in Canada." Washington, 1922. From the U.S. official point of view.

—— *Reciprocity and Commercial Treaties.* Washington, 1919. Pp. 61–100, 363–81.
An account of the working of the Reciprocity Treaty of 1854–66 and the subsequent efforts to restore it.

CHAPTER XXIX

SECTION 17. THE CONSTITUTION AND ITS WORKING, 1867–1914

(For additional authorities *v. supra*, pp. 863–6, and *infra*, section 18. Among biographies and collections of correspondence those of Macdonald, Mowat, and Laurier, q.v., throw light on political movements connected with constitutional developments.)

Appeal Cases. Privy Council. London.

BORDEN, Sir R. *Canadian Constitutional Studies.* Toronto, 1922.

BOURINOT, Sir J. *Parliamentary Procedure and Practice in the Dominion of Canada.* Ed. by Flint. Toronto, 1916.

British North America Acts, 1867–1916.

BRYCE, Viscount. *Modern Democracies.* Vol. 1. London, 1921.

The Canadian Bar Review. Toronto.

The Canadian Law Times. Toronto.

CAMERON, E. R. *The Canadian Constitution.* Winnipeg, 1915.

CARTWRIGHT, J. R. *Cases Decided on the B.N.A. Act.* Toronto, 1887 ff.

CLEMENT, W. H. P. *The Law of the Canadian Constitution.* Toronto, 1916.
DAWSON, R. M. *The Principles of Political Independence.* London, 1922.
Imperial War Cabinet: Report for 1917 (Cd. 9005); *Report for* 1918 (Cmd. 325).
The Journal of Comparative Legislation. London, 1896– . (Proceeding.)
KEITH, A. B. *Responsible Government in the Dominions.* 3 vols. Oxford, 1912. Revised edn. 2 vols. 1927.
—— "The Development of colonial Self-Government in the Nineteenth Century." *Journal of R. Soc. of Arts,* vol. LVI.
—— *Imperial Unity and the Dominions.* Oxford, 1916.
—— *War Government in the Dominions.* Oxford, 1921.
—— *The Constitution, Administration and Laws of the Empire.* London, 1924.
KENNEDY, W. P. M. *Documents of the Canadian Constitution,* 1759–1915. Oxford, 1918. New and enlarged edition. Oxford, 1930.
—— *The Nature of Canadian Federalism.* Toronto, 1921.
—— *The Constitution of Canada—an Introduction to its Development and Law.* Oxford, 1922.
LEFROY, A. H. F. *Legislative Power in Canada.* Toronto, 1898.
—— *Canada's Federal System.* Toronto, 1913.
—— *Leading Cases in Canadian Constitutional Law.* Toronto, 1920.
—— (with W. P. M. KENNEDY). *Short Treatise on Canadian Constitutional Law.* Toronto, 1918.
MACKAY, R. A. *The Unreformed Senate of Canada.* Oxford, 1926.
The Report of Sir George Murray on the Public Business of Canada. Ottawa, 1912.
Reports of the Ministers of Justice and Orders in Council upon the Subject of Dominion and Provincial Legislation. Ottawa, 1867– . (Proceeding.)
Reports of the Supreme Court and of the Provincial Courts. Ottawa and Provincial Capitals.
RIDDELL, W. R. *The Constitution of Canada in its History and Practical Working.* New Haven, 1917.
—— *The Canadian Constitution in Form and in Fact.* New York, 1923.
Rules of the House of Commons, and of the *Senate.*
The Senate's Report on the Machinery of Government. Ottawa, 1919.
SINCLAIR, R. V. *Rules and Practice before the Senate of Canada upon Bills of Divorce.* Toronto, 1915.
SMITH, H. A. *Federalism in North America.* Boston, 1923.
The Times Law Reports. London.
WHEELER, E. J. *Confederation Law of Canada.* London, 1896.

CHAPTER XXX

SECTION 18. CANADA AND THE EMPIRE, 1884–1921

ARGYLL, JOHN GEORGE, 9th Duke of. *Imperial Federation.* London, 1885.
BOURASSA, H. "The French-Canadian in the British Empire." *Monthly Review,* 1902.
—— *Le problème de l'Empire....* Montreal, 1916.
CAPPON, J. "Canada's Relation to the Empire." *Queen's Quarterly,* vol. XIX, 1911.
CORBETT, P. E. and SMITH, H. A. *Canada and World Politics: A Study of the Constitutional and International Relations of the British Empire.* Toronto, 1928.
COURTHOPE, W. J. "The Cabinet and the Empire." *Nat. Rev.* vol. LXIII.
CRAIK, Sir HENRY. "The Cabinet Secretariat." *Nineteenth Century,* vol. XCI.
DEWEY, A. G. *The Dominions and Diplomacy.* 2 vols. London, 1929.
DILKE, Sir C. W. *Problems of Greater Britain.* 2 vols. London, 1890.
EGERTON, H. E. *British Colonial Policy in the Twentieth Century.* London, 1922.
EWART, J. S. *The Kingdom of Canada, Imperial Federation, the Colonial Conferences, the Alaska Boundary, and Other Essays.* Toronto, 1908.
—— *The Kingdom Papers.* Ottawa, 1912– .
—— *The Independence Papers.* Ottawa, 1925– .

FALCONER, Sir ROBERT A. "The New Imperial Allegiance." *University Magazine*, vol. XV.

Great Britain and the Dominions: Lectures on the Harris Foundation, 1927. University of Chicago. n.d.

HALL, D. *The British Commonwealth of Nations*. London, 1920.

HALL, W. P. *Empire to Commonwealth: Thirty Years of British Imperial History*. New York, 1928.

HUGHES, Rt Hon. W. M. *The Splendid Adventure: a Review of Empire Relations*. London, 1929.

JEBB, R. *The Britannic Question*. London, 1913.

—— "Conference or Cabinet." *United Empire*, vol. XI, 1920.

—— *The Empire in Eclipse*. London, 1926.

—— *The Imperial Conference*. 2 vols. London, 1911.

—— *Studies in Colonial Nationalism*. London, 1905.

Journal of the Parliaments of the Empire. 1920– .

KEITH, A. B. "The Canadian Constitution and External Relations." *Journal Comp. Legis.* 1919.

—— "The War Government of the British Empire; the Imperial War Cabinet. *Times Hist. of the War*, vol. XII.

—— *The Sovereignty of the British Dominions*. London, 1929.

KENNEDY, W. P. M. "Canada's National Status." *North American Review*, vol. CCXVI, 1922. See also an article in the same volume by J. S. Ewart and an article by W. P. M. Kennedy in vol. CCXVII; also *Edinburgh Review*, April 1924; *Contemporary Review*, November 1924.

LABILLIÈRE, F. P. DE. *Federal Britain*. London, 1894.

LEE, R. W. "Canada and the Empire." *University Magazine*, vol. XV, April 1916.

LOW, Sir SIDNEY. "The Coming of the Empire Cabinet." *Nineteenth Century*, vol. LXXXI.

—— "The Problem of an Imperial Executive." *King's College Lectures*, London, 1913.

LUCAS, Sir C. P. *The Empire at War*. Vol. I. Oxford, 1921.

MACKENZIE, N. A. M. "The Treaty Making Power in Canada." *Amer. Journ. of International Law*, July 1925.

Minutes and Proceedings of the Colonial and the Imperial Conferences.

MOUSLEY, E. "The Cabinet Secretariat and Empire Government." *Fortnightly Review*, vol. CXIII.

PARKIN, G. R. *Imperial Federation*. London, 1892.

POLEY, A. T. "The Privy Council and Problems of closer union of the Empire." *Journ. Comp. Legis.* No. 37, 1916.

PORRITT, E. *The Fiscal and Diplomatic Freedom of the British Dominions*. Oxford, 1923.

ROWELL, Hon. N. W. *The British Empire and World Peace*. Toronto, 1922.

SCHUYLER, R. L. *Parliament and the British Empire*. Cambridge, 1929.

SIEGFRIED, A. *The Race Question in Canada*. London, 1907.

Part IV deals with Canada's external relations, and is interesting as an outsider's point of view.

SKELTON, O. D. "Canada and the Most Favoured Nation Treaties." *Queen's Quarterly*, January 1912.

SMITH, GOLDWIN. *Canada and the Canadian Question*. London, 1891.

WADE, Sir C. G. "The Dominions and the Colonial Office." *Empire Review*, vol. XXII, 1918.

WILLISON, Sir J. *The Life of Sir George Parkin*. London, 1929.

WRONG, G. M. "Canada and the Imperial War Cabinet." *C.H.R.* vol. I, March 1920.

—— "The Evolution of the Foreign Relations of Canada." *C.H.R.* vol. XI, 1925.

ZIMMERN, A. *The Third British Empire*. London, 1926.

CHAPTER XXXI

SECTION 19. CANADA IN THE WORLD WAR

There are still very few authoritative books on the war, and much of the enormous mass of Records still lies in the Departments concerned, though much is already in the Public Archives, which contain a War Archives Survey.

BEAVERBROOK, Lord (Sir MAX AITKEN). *Canada in Flanders.* 2 vols. London and Toronto, 1916, 1917. Vol. III, by C. G. D. Roberts, 1918.

Canada in the Great World War...by Various Authorities. 6 vols. Toronto, 1917–21.

Canadian Defence Quarterly. Ottawa, 1923– .

CARNEGIE, D. *The History of Munitions Supply in Canada, 1914–1918.* London, 1925.

Copies of Proclamations, Orders in Council and Documents Relating to the European War. Compiled by the Department of the Secretary of State of Canada. Ottawa, 1915. With 4 supplements, 1915–17.

DESJARDINS, L. C. *England, Canada and the Great War.* 2nd edn. Quebec, 1918.

FETHERSTONHAUGH, R. C. (Editor and Compiler). *The Royal Montreal Regiment: 14th Battalion, C.E.F., 1914–1925.* Montreal, 1927.

HAHN, J. E. *The Intelligence Service within the Canadian Corps.* Toronto. (In the press.)

HAIG, Sir D. *The Despatches of Sir Douglas Haig.* Ed. J. H. B. Boraston. 2 vols. London, 1919.

HOPKINS, J. C. *Canada at War.* New York, 1919.

LIVESAY, J. F. B. *Canada's Hundred Days.* Amiens to Mons, August 8 to November 11, 1918. Toronto, 1919.

LUCAS, Sir C. P. (Editor). *The Empire at War.* 5 vols. Vol. II. London, 1921–6.

MACPHAIL, Sir ANDREW. *History of the Canadian Forces, 1914–1918: Medical Services.* Ottawa, 1925.
The Historical Section of the General Staff are issuing an official history, of which this is the first volume.

NASMITH, G. G. *On the Fringe of the Great Fight.* Toronto, 1917.

SCOTT, Canon F. G. *The Great War as I Saw It.* Toronto, 1922. A chaplain's view.

SEELY, J. E. B., Maj.-Gen. *Adventure.* London, 1930.

SEGSWORTH, W. E. *Retraining Canada's Disabled Soldiers.* Dept. of Soldiers' Civil Re-Establishment. Ottawa, 1920.

SKELTON, O. D. "Canadian War Finance," in *Amer. Econ. Rev.,* Dec. 1917.

WHITE, Sir THOS. *The Story of Canada's War Finance.* Canadian Bank of Commerce. Montreal, 1921.

WILLIAMS, R. H. *Princess Patricia's Canadian Light Infantry, 1914–1919.* 2 vols. Toronto, 1923.

CHAPTER XXXII

For bibliography to this chapter see pp. 880–5.

CHAPTER XXXIII

SECTION 20. CULTURAL DEVELOPMENT

(For English-Canadian literature *v. The Cambridge History of English Literature*; but a few important titles on this subject, published since that work appeared, are included here. For additional authorities for this chapter *v. supra*, sections 8–12.)

(1) GENERAL

ARGYLL, JOHN GEORGE, 9th Duke of. *Canadian Pictures, drawn with pen and pencil.* London, 1884.

BOURINOT, Sir J. G. *Intellectual Development of the Canadian People.* Toronto, 1881.

—— *Canada's Intellectual Strength and Weakness.* Montreal and London, 1893.

BRADLEY, A. G. *Canada in the Twentieth Century*. London, 1925.
BROADUS, E. K. and E. H. *A Book of Canadian Prose and Verse*. Toronto, 1923.
CASWELL, E. S. (Editor). *Canadian Singers and their Songs*. Toronto, 1925.
DAWSON, Sir J. W. *Fifty Years of Work in Canada. Scientific and Educational, Being Autobiographical Notes*. Ed. by R. Dawson. London, 1901.
Education in the Province of Quebec. Department of Public Instruction of Quebec. Quebec, 1914.
GIBBON, J. M. (Editor and Translator). *Canadian Folk Songs (Old and New)*. London, 1927.
HOUSSER, F. B. *A Canadian Art Movement. The Story of the Group of Seven*. Toronto, 1926.
JARAY, G. L. et HOURTICQ, L. *De Québec à Vancouver*. Paris, 1924.
    Two keen French observers.
MACMECHAN, A. *Headwaters of Canadian Literature*. Toronto, 1924.
MACTAVISH, N. *The Fine Arts in Canada*. Toronto, 1925.
PIERCE, L. A. *An Outline of Canadian Literature*. Toronto, 1927.
PIERCE, L. A. and MORIN, V. (Editors). *Makers of Canadian Literature*. More than 40 vols. projected. Toronto, 1924– .
ROYAL SOCIETY OF CANADA. *Proceedings and Transactions*. Ottawa.
SANDIFORD, P. *Comparative Education: Studies of the Educational Systems of Six Modern Nations*. London, 1918.
SISSONS, C. B. *Bi-Lingual Schools in Canada*. Toronto, 1917.

(2) FRENCH

D'ARLES, HENRI (pseud.) (Abbé Henri Beaudé). *Nos Historiens*. Montreal, 1921.
ARNOULD, LOUIS. *Nos Amis les Canadiens*. Paris, 1913.
BERTHELOT-BRUNET. *Canada dans Vingt-cinq ans de Littérature française, publié sous la direction d'Eugène Montfort*. Paris, 1925.
BRACQ, J. C. *The Evolution of French Canada*. New York, 1924.
CASGRAIN, Abbé HENRI-R. "Biographie de P. A. de Gaspé." Tome II des *Œuvres complètes*, 1885.
—— *Un Contemporain: F.-X. Garneau*. Quebec.
—— "Le Mouvement littéraire au Canada." *Œuvres complètes*. Montreal, 1896.
CHARBONNEAU, JEAN. *Les Influences françaises au Canada*. 2 vols. Montreal, 1915.
CHARTIER, Abbé ÉMILE. *Au Canada. Supplément au Manuel illustré de la Littérature française*. Paris, 1923.
CREMAZIE, OCTAVE. *Œuvres complètes, précédées d'une Étude de l'abbé Casgrain*. Montreal, 1882.
DANTIN, LOUIS. *Émile Nelligan et son Œuvre*. Montreal, 1903.
DARVEAU, L. M. *Nos Hommes de Lettres*. Montreal, 1873.
DESSAULLES, L. A. *Discours sur l'Institut canadien*. Des Presses du journal *Le Pays*. Montreal, 1863.
—— *La Grande Guerre ecclésiastique pour la suprématie ecclésiastique dans l'ordre temporel*. Montreal, 1873.
—— *Réponse honnête à une circulaire assez peu chrétienne*. Montreal, 1873.
DIONNE, N. E. *Le Parler populaire des Canadiens-français*. Quebec, 1909.
DUGAS, MARCEL. *Apologies*. Montreal, 1919.
ÉCOLE LITTÉRAIRE DE MONTRÉAL. *Les Soirées du Château de Ramezay*. Montreal, 1900.
FOURNIER, JULES. *Mon Encrier*. 2 vols. (Préface d'Olivar Asselin.) Montreal, 1922.
FOURNIER, J. et ASSELIN, O. *Anthologie des Poètes canadiens*. Montreal, 1920.
Foyer canadien, Le. Quebec, 1863–6.
GAGNON, ERNEST. *Chansons populaires du Canada*. Quebec, 1865.
GAUTHERON, RENÉ. *Au Canada. Histoire de la Littérature française illustrée, publiée par Joseph Bédier et Paul Hazard*. Paris, 1923.
GOSSELIN, AMÉDÉE. "L'instruction primaire au Canada." *Bulletin du Parler français*, V, 281–300.
GOURMONT, RÉMY DE. *La Langue française au Canada. Esthétique de la langue française*. Paris, 1907.

HALDEN, CHARLES ABDER. *Études de Littérature canadienne-française*, précédées d'une introduction: "La Langue et la Littérature française au Canada, la famille française et la nation canadienne," par Louis Herbette. Paris, 1904.
—— *Nouvelles Études, de Littérature canadienne-française*. Paris, 1907.
HONRIER, P. *La langue française au Canada*. Montreal, 1913.
HUSTON, J. *Répertoire national ou Recueil de Littérature canadienne*. 4 vols. Montreal, 1848–50.
LAFONTAINE, J. L. *L'Institut canadien en 1855*. Montreal, 1855.
LANCTOT, GUSTAVE. *François-Xavier Garneau*. In *Makers of Canadian Literature*. Toronto.
LAREAU, EDMOND. *Histoire de la Littérature canadienne*. Montreal, 1874.
LARUE, HUBERT. *Chansons Historiques*. Le Foyer canadien, Quebec, 1865.
LEFAIVRE, A. *Conférence sur la Littérature canadienne*. Versailles, 1877.
MASSICOTTE, E. Z. *Conteurs canadiens-français du XIXe siècle*. Montreal, 1908.
Nigog, Le. (Revue mensuelle.) Montreal, 1918.
RIVARD, A. *L'origine et le Parler des Canadiens-français*. Quebec, 1903.
ROQUEBRUNE, R. La Roque de. "Les Mouvements de la Littérature canadienne-française." *Revue de l'Amérique latine*. Paris, Nov. 1923.
—— "Les Contes populaires du Canada." *Le Monde Nouveau*. Paris, 1923.
ROSSEL, VIRGILE. *Histoire de la Littérature française hors de France*. Lausanne, 1895.
ROY, Abbé CAMILLE. *Manuel d'Histoire de la Littérature canadienne-française*. Quebec, 1915.
—— *Soirées canadiennes*. (Revue mensuelle.) 5 vols. Quebec, 1861–5.
SULTE, BENJAMIN. *La Langue française au Canada*. Levis, 1898.
TÊTU, H. *Historique des journaux de Québec*. Quebec, 1889.
VATTIER, G. *Essai sur la mentalité canadienne-française*. Paris, 1928.

(3) ENGLISH

BAKER, R. P. *A History of English-Canadian Literature to the Confederation: its Relation to the Literature of Great Britain and the United States*. Cambridge, Mass., 1920.
CHITTICK, V. L. O. *Thomas Chandler Haliburton ("Sam Slick"). A Study in Provincial Toryism*. New York, 1924.
GARVIN, J. W. (Editor). *Canadian Poems of the Great War*. Toronto, 1918.
HIND, H. Y. *The University of King's College, Windsor, Nova Scotia, 1790–1890*. New York, 1890.
HODGINS, J. G. *The Establishment of Schools and Colleges in Ontario, 1792–1910*. 3 vols. Toronto, 1910.
—— *Historical and Other Papers and Documents Illustrative of the Educational System of Ontario, 1792–1872*. 4 vols. Toronto, 1911–12.
JAMESON, ANNA. *Winter Studies and Summer Rambles in Canada*. Ed. by P. A. W. Wallace. Toronto, 1923.
LOGAN, J. D. and FRENCH, D. G. *Highways of Canadian Literature*. Toronto, 1924.
MACMILLAN, C. *McGill and its Story, 1821–1921*. London, 1921.
MOODIE, SUSANNA. *Roughing it in the Bush, or Forest Life in Canada: with an Introductory Chapter in which Canada of the Present is Compared with Canada of Forty Years Ago*. Toronto, 1871.
PUTMAN, J. H. *Egerton Ryerson and Education in Upper Canada*. Toronto, 1912.
RAYMOND, W. O. *The Genesis of the University of New Brunswick. With a Sketch of the Life of William Brydone-Jack, A.M., D.C.L., President 1861–85*. Saint John, N.B., 1919.
SCADDING, HENRY. *Toronto of Old, Collections and Recollections Illustrative of Settlement and Social Life of the Capital of Ontario*. Toronto, 1873.
STEVENSON, L. *Appraisals of Canadian Literature*. Toronto, 1926.
Toronto, The University of, and its Colleges, 1827–1906. Toronto, 1906.
WALLACE, W. S. *A Centenary History of the University of Toronto*. Toronto, 1927.

PART III

NEWFOUNDLAND

(CHAPTERS V, XVII AND XXVIII)

A. *MANUSCRIPT MATERIALS*

The manuscript materials for the history of Newfoundland and the fisheries during the sixteenth and early seventeenth centuries are too widely scattered to admit of systematic description. They must be sought in the usual sources of British maritime and colonial history for which reference should be made to the Bibliography attached to vol. I of this work and the notes to Chaps. ii, iii and v of that volume. The records of the High Court of Admiralty and of other Courts dealing with maritime and commercial causes, especially the Court of Chancery and the King's Bench, also afford data of great value concerning fishery cases. But these voluminous records have not been calendared, and the relevant matter is not easily found.

For the period after 1660 the main source is to be found in the State Papers, Colonial, which have been calendared to 1715, but many papers of importance are also to be found in the State Papers, Domestic. The records of the Admiralty are of value for the history of Newfoundland during the period of the Naval Governors. Papers relating to the long diplomatic controversies concerning the fisheries will be found scattered through the State Papers, Foreign and the Foreign Office Records, especially in the correspondence with France and Spain.

The principal records relating to the modern colony are collected in the Public Record Office, Series C.O. 194, 195, etc. The archives preserved in Newfoundland are very imperfect before the nineteenth century, but from 1818 onwards they are comparable with those of any other colony (e.g. Canada), though they are not so systematically arranged as those at Ottawa.

There has been no systematic exploration for material relating to Newfoundland in the British Museum and other important collections of MSS., but incidental mention of particular items may be found in Andrews' and Davenport's *Guide* (*v. supra*, p. 813). Probably the records of the western ports of England contain valuable material concerning the Newfoundland fishery; but they have been little explored save those of Poole, which throw light on that industry in the late seventeenth century.

B. *PARLIAMENTARY AND OTHER OFFICIAL PUBLICATIONS*

These provide an unusually important mass of material. See especially:

Three *Reports from the Select Committee on the State of the Trade to Newfoundland*, 1793. *Reports of H. of C., First Series*, 1696–1800, vol. x, pp. 392, 409, 433.

Report from the Select Committee on the Newfoundland Trade, 1817; *Second Series*, Sess. 1817 (436), vol. VI, p. 465 [66].

Convention... with the U.S. of America respecting the Newfoundland Fishery, 20 Oct. 1818; Sess. 1819, CXII, 67 or XVIII, 421; 1830 (350), XXI, 223; 1831–2 (515 and 704), XXXII, 255 and 261; 1839 (525), XXXIV, 565; *Changes in Constitution*, 1842 (362), XXVIII, 143; *Roman Catholic Bishopric*, 1851 (169), XXXVI, 619; *Halifax Fisheries Commission*, 1878 (C. 2056), LXXX, 1; 1879 (C. 2183, 2186), LXXVII, 35, 59.

Negotiations between Great Britain and U.S. respecting Newfoundland Fisheries.

1884 (C. 3848), LXXXVII, 15; 1887 (C. 4937, 4995), XCI, 637, 829; 1888 (C. 5262), CIX, 583; 1906 (Cd. 3262), CXXXVII, 389; 1908 (Cd. 3734), CXXV, 939 (Cd. 3754), CXXV, 943; *Arbitration*, 1909 (Cd. 4528 and 4815), CV, 1091 and 1099; *Award*, 1910 (Cd. 5896), LXXIV, 385; *Interpretation of Treaty of 1818*, 1912–13 (Cd. 6450), CXXII, 639.

Negotiations between Great Britain and France respecting Newfoundland.

Convention, 1857, XVIII, 7; 1886, XLVI, 521; 1887, LVIII, 353; 1886 (C. 4641), XLVI, 521; 1890 (C. 6044), LXXXI, 37; 1890–1 (C. 6256), XCVI, 203, (C. 6365), XCVI, 631, (C. 6488), LVII, 97; 1893–4 (C. 7129), CIX, 189, (C. 7215), LX, 833; *Modus Vivendi*, 1892 (C. 6637), XCV, 627; *Fisheries on Grand Bank*, 1889 (C. 9045[20]); *Treaty*, 1905 (Cd. 2383), CIII, 241; 1906 (Cd. 2737), CXXXVI, 203.

British Documents on the Origins of the War, 1898–1914. Ed. by G. P. Gooch and H. W. V. Temperley. Vols. II and III. H.M. Stationery Office, 1927–8.

Labrador Boundary Case. Proceedings before the Privy Council. (1925.) Vols. I–IV; especially IV. (See also the DARTMOUTH PAPERS, p. 826.)

C. *SELECT LIST OF PRINTED WORKS*

(1) GENERAL WORKS

Most of the works on the history of Newfoundland are uncritical compilations from earlier writers, where they are not biassed propaganda to support one side or another in the diplomatic controversies that have raged round the island and its fisheries. There is no comprehensive and scholarly history of the colony.

ANON. *Newfoundland. A view of its Rise and Progress.* Poole, 1828.

ANSPACH, L. A. *History of Newfoundland.* London, 1819.
> Untrustworthy as history, but of value for its description of the island and the Banks from first-hand knowledge.

BIRKENHEAD, Earl of, see SMITH, F. E.

BROWN, R. *History of Cape Breton with some account of the Discovery and Settlement of Newfoundland.* London, 1869.

DOUGLASS, W. D. *A Summary, Historical and Political, of the First Planting, Progressive Improvements, and Present State of the British Settlements in North America.* Boston, 1749–50. London, 1755–60.

GOSLING, W. G. *Labrador: its Discovery...and Development.* New York, 1911.

HARRISSE, H. *V. supra*, pp. 834, 847.

HARVEY, Rev. M. *Short History of Newfoundland.* London, 1890.

HOWLEY, M. F., Bishop. *Ecclesiastical History of Newfoundland.* Boston, 1888.

ISHAM, C. *The Fishery Question, its Origin, History and Present Situation.* New York, 1878.

LANGTRY, J. *History of the Church in Eastern Canada and Newfoundland.* (Colonial Church Histories.) London, 1892.

MACFARLAND, R. *History of the New England Fisheries.* New York, 1911.
> A clear and valuable account.

MONTGOMERY, R. M. *History of Nova Scotia and Newfoundland.* London, 1837.

MOORE, J. B. *Digest of International Law.* 8 vols. Washington, 1906.
> Vol. I, pp. 767–875, contains a discussion of the Fishery Question.

PAGE, F. R. *History and Description of Newfoundland.* London, 1860.

PASCOE, C. F. *Digest of the Records of the Society for the Propagation of the Gospel.* London, 1893.

PEDLEY, Rev. C. *History of Newfoundland from the earliest times to 1860.* London, 1863.
> A valuable survey of the usual sources.

PINSENT, Sir R. "Our Oldest Colony." *Proceedings* of the Roy. Col. Inst. 1884–5. Vol. XVI.

PROWSE, D. W. *History of Newfoundland from English, Colonial and Foreign Records.* London, 1895.
> The most comprehensive and best documented chronicle of the colony yet written. But the references are very imperfect and the historical judgments unreliable.

REEVES, J. *History of the Government of Newfoundland.* London, 1793.
> A valuable and reliable work, based upon official papers to which the writer had access as Chief Justice.

ROGERS, J. D. *Newfoundland.* In Sir C. Lucas' *Hist. Geog. of the British Colonies*, vol. V, pt IV. Oxford, 1911.
> The best and most scholarly account of the history of the colony within a comparatively narrow compass.

ST JOHN, W. C. *Catechism of the History of Newfoundland.* St John's, 1835.

SMITH, F. E. (later Earl of BIRKENHEAD). *Newfoundland.* (Story of the Empire Series.) London, 1901. New edn. 1920.
> A slight compilation from the most accessible sources.

WILSON, Rev. W. *Newfoundland and its Missionaries: History of Wesleyan Church.* Cambridge, Mass., 1866.

(2) WORKS RELATING TO PARTICULAR PERIODS

(a) *Contemporary Works*

Period i. To 1713:

BEAUDOIN, Abbé J. *Journal d'une expédition de d'Iberville en Acadie et à Terre-Neuve*, 1697.
> Publié avec une introduction et des notes par l'Abbé Gosselin. Evreux, 1900.

BIGGAR, H. P. *The Precursors of Jacques Cartier.* Ottawa, 1917.

CARTIER, J. *Voyages.* Translated with notes and appendices by H. P. Biggar. Ottawa, 1924.
> The best edition.

CHAMPLAIN, S. DE. *Works.* Translated with notes and appendices by H. P. Biggar. Champlain Society. Toronto, 1922.
> The best edition.

CHARLEVOIX, LE PÈRE DE. *Histoire et Description de la Nouvelle France.* Paris, 1744.
> Many other editions.

CHILD, Sir J. *A new Discourse of Trade.* Enlarged edn. London, 1694.

CLEIRAC, E. *Les Us et Coutumes de la Mer.* Bordeaux, 1671.

COLLIBER, S. *Columna Rostrata, or a Critical History of English Sea Affairs.* London, 1727.

CORDEYRO, P. ANTONIO. *Historia insulana das ilhas a Portugal sugeytas no Oceano Occidental.* Lisbon, 1717.

DESBOROW, C. *The Humble Address of the Lords Spiritual and Temporal to His Majesty in relation to the Petition of Charles Desborow.* Also *An Act to Encourage Trade to Newfoundland.* London, 1699.

EBURNE, R. *A Plaine Pathway to Plantations.* London, 1624.
> Chiefly in Newfoundland.

GEARE, A. *Ebenezer, or a Monument of Thankfulness—The miraculous Preservation of 9 Men on a Voyage from Plymouth to Newfoundland.* London, 1708.

HAKLUYT, R. *V. supra*, p. 845. See especially vols. VII and VIII of Maclehose edition.

HAYMAN, R. *Quodlibets lately come from New Britaniola, old Newfoundland.* London, 1628.

HOYARSABAL, M. DE. *Les Voyages aventureux du Capitaine Martin de Hoyarsabal.* Bordeaux, 1579. 2nd edn. 1633.

LECLERCQ, C. *Nouvelle Relation de la Gaspesie.* Paris, 1691.
> Account of Indians on the west coast of Newfoundland.

MARTIN, Captain STEPHEN, R.N., *Life of.* Ed. by C. R. Markham. (*N.R.S.* 1895.)

MASON, J. *A Briefe Discourse of the New-Found-Land....* Edinburgh, 1620.

MONSON, Sir WILLIAM, *The Naval Tracts of.* Ed. by M. Oppenheim. 5 vols. (*N.R.S.* 1902–14.) Several references to Newfoundland.

OLDMIXON, J. *The British Empire in America.* 3rd edn. London, 1741.
> A chapter on Newfoundland.

PHILANGLUS. *Britannia Languens, or A Discourse of Trade.* London, 1680.

PURCHAS, S. *V. supra*, p. 846 (especially vols. I, XIV, XVIII, XIX of Maclehose edition).

VAUGHAN, Sir W. (Orpheus Junior). *Cambrensium Caroleia*, etc. London, 1625.

—— *The Golden Fleece.* London, 1626.

—— *The Newlanders Cure—published for the Weale of Great Brittaine.* London, 1630.

WEST INDIA MERCHANT. *A Letter…concerning the Treaty about Newfoundland.* London, 1712.

—— *Extract from Lord Oxford's Impeachment relating to the Newfoundland Fishery.* London, 1713.

WHITBOURNE, Capt. Sir R. *A Discourse and Discovery of Newfoundland.* London, 1622.

YOUNG, F. *Remarks on the Debate on the Newfoundland Fishery.* London, 1670.

Period ii. 1713–1818:

ANON. *The True Interest of Great Britain as to the Trade and Government of Canada, Newfoundland and Labrador.…* London, 1767.

ANON. *Papers relating to the Rupture with Spain.* London, 1762.

ANON. "The French View of the Treaty of Peace." *Scots Magazine*, December 1762.

ANSPACH, L. A. *Summary of Laws of Commerce and Navigation, adapted to the Present State, Government and Trade of the Island of Newfoundland.* London, 1809.

AUCHMUTY, R. *The Importance of Cape Breton to the British Nation.* London, 1745.

BOLLAN, W. *Coloniae Anglicanae Illustratae, or the Acquest of Dominion and the Plantation of Colonies made bv the English in America.* London, 1762.

—— *The Ancient Rights of the English People to the American Fishery and its various Diminutions examined and stated.* London, 1764.

CARSON, W. *Reasons for Colonising Newfoundland.* St John's, 1813.

CARTWRIGHT, G. "Manner of determining Disputes among the Fishermen, and the Quantity of Fish annually shipped from Newfoundland." *Monthly Review*, XIII, 276, 1784.

CHAPPELL, E. *The Voyage of H.M.S. Rosamund to Newfoundland.* London, 1818.

CHOISEUL, E. *Mémoire historique sur la négociation de la France…avec les pièces justificatives.* Leipzig, 1761.

DOUGLASS, W. *Considerations on the State of British Fisheries in America.* London, 1749.

EARNSHAW, J. *Abstracts of Acts of Parliament concerning the Greenland and Newfoundland Fishery.* London, 1793.

HARLEIAN COLLECTION OF VOYAGES. *Considerations on the Trade of Newfoundland.* London, 1745.

HEATHCOTE, G. *Letter to the Lord Mayor of London concerning Peace between Great Britain and France.* London, 1762.
    Against allowing French rights in Newfoundland.

"AN HONEST MAN." *A Reply to Heathcote's Letter.* London, 1762.

KNAPTON, J. and P. *The Importance and Advantage of Cape Breton truly and impartially considered.* London, 1757.

LE ROY, C. C., Sieur de B. DE LA POTHERIE. *Histoire de l'Amérique Septentrionale.* 4 vols. Paris, 1722.

MASSIE, J. *Historical Account of the Naval Power of France. The State of English Fisheries in Newfoundland.* London, 1762.
    Shows the importance attached to the Newfoundland fisheries by both competitors.

MILES, W. A. *Remarks on the Act… for the Encouragement of the Newfoundland Fisheries.* [The Act of 1775.] London, 1779.

(PITT, WM.) *Address to the Right Hon. Wm. Pitt. Considerations on the Importance of the American Fisheries*, etc. London, 1759.

ROGERS, Colonel R. *A Concise Account of North America.* London, 1765.
    Includes an interesting description of Newfoundland.

SABINE, Rev. J. *A View of the Moral State of Newfoundland.* Boston, Mass., 1818.

SCHULTES, H. P. *A Dissertation on the Public Fisheries of Great Britain.* London, 1813.

WILLIAMS, Capt. G. *Account of the Island of Newfoundland.* London, 1765.
    A valuable authority as the writer had served in the island for fourteen years; affords material for testing the accuracy of official accounts.

Period iii. 1818–1874:

BONNYCASTLE, Sir R. H. *Newfoundland in 1842.* London, 1842.

BROWNE, C. A. *Letters and Extracts from the Addresses and Occasional Writings of J. B. Jukes.* London, 1871.
    Includes letters from Newfoundland to Mr Jukes' family.
CARTWRIGHT, F. D. *Life and Correspondence of Major Cartwright.* London, 1826.
CORMACK, W. E. *Narrative of a Journey across Newfoundland in 1822.* Ed. by F. A. Bruton. London, 1928.
FIELD, C. W. *A Statement of Advantages upon making St John's a Port of Call.* London, 1856.
HOWARTH, Commr. R.N. *Report on Newfoundland and the Labrador Fisheries.* St John's, 1874.
HOWLEY, R. *Letters on the present State of Newfoundland and Confederation.* St John's, 1869.
HUNT, R. M. *Life of Sir H. Palliser.* London, 1844.
JUKES, J. B. *Excursions in and about Newfoundland during the years 1839 and 1840.* 2 vols. London, 1842.
MORRIS, Hon. P. (1) *Observations on the Present State of Newfoundland.* 1823.
    (2) *Remarks on the State of Society, Religion, Morality and Education at Newfoundland.* 1827.
    (3) *Arguments to prove the policy and necessity of granting to Newfoundland a Constitutional Government. A Letter to the Rt Hon. William Huskisson, M.P.* London, 1828.
    These are bound together in a single volume in the Library of the Colonial Office.
—— *Review of the History, Government, Constitutions, [etc.] of Newfoundland in a series of Letters...to Earl Grey.* St John's, 1847.
SCORESBY, W. *The Northern Whale Fishery.* Edinburgh, 1820.
SYDENHAM, J. *History of the Town and County of Poole [Dorset].* Poole, 1839.
    See pp. 396–401.
VITET, L. *Histoire de Dieppe.* Paris, 1847.
[WINTON, H.?] *A Chapter in the History of Newfoundland for the year 1861.* St John's, 1861.
WIX, Rev. E. *A Retrospect of the Operations of the S.P.G. in North America. A Sermon.* St John's, 1832. 2nd edn. 1833.
—— *Six Months of a Newfoundland Missionary's Journal.* London, 1836.

(b) *Later Works*

ANON. "Les Pêcheries et les Traités." *Revue des Deux Mondes,* 1874.
"ASSADA." "La découverte de l'Amérique par les Normands." *La Géographie,* 1912. (Tome XXIV.)
AVEZAC, MACAYA M. DE. *Les Navigations Terreneuviennes de Jean et Sébastien Cabot.* Paris, 1869.
    In the extensive literature relating to the Cabot voyages and the controversies connected with them there are many references to Newfoundland and the fisheries. For a select list of the more important works see vol. I, pp. 847–8, and Williamson, J. A. *The Cabots.* London, 1929. See also Winship, G. P. p. 848.
BELLET, A. *Les Français à Terre-Neuve et sur les côtes de l'Amérique du Nord. La Grande Pêche de la Morue à Terre-Neuve, depuis la découverte du Nouveau Monde par les Basques au XIVe siècle.* Paris, 1902.
BLAKE, EDITH. "The Beothuks of Newfoundland." *Nineteenth Century,* vol. XXIV, 1888.
BOURGEOIS, E. "Nos Droits à Terre-Neuve." *Annales des Sciences Politiques,* 1899.
BROWN, VERA L. "Spanish Claims to the Newfoundland Fisheries." *Report of Canadian Historical Association* (1925), pp. 64–82.
CAIX, R. DE. *Terre-Neuve, St Pierre et le French Shore.* Paris, 1904.
CORDEIRO, L. *De la Part prise par les Portugais dans la Découverte de l'Amérique.* Lisbon, 1876.
COUGHLAN, F. *Account of early History of Wesleyanism in Newfoundland.* London, 1876.
DAUBIGNY, E. *Choiseul et la France d'outre-mer...avec une appendice sur les origines de la question de Terre-Neuve.* Paris, 1892.

Ducéré, A. *Recherches historiques sur la Pêche de la Morue et la Découverte de Terre-Neuve par les Basques et les Bayonnais.* Pau, 1893.

Gosse, Sir E. *Life of Philip H. Gosse.* London, 1890.

Grenfell, Sir W. T. *A Labrador Doctor: an Autobiography.* Boston, 1919.

Guichard, L. *The French Shore.* A thesis in the University of Paris. 1901–2.

Harrisse, H. *Les Corte-Real et leurs Voyages au Nouveau Monde.* Paris, 1883.

—— *Découverte et évolution cartographique de Terre-Neuve et des pays circonvoisins.* Paris, 1900.

See also article in *Revue de Géographie*, 1900.

Harvey, M. and Hatton, J. *Newfoundland.* London, 1883.

Harvut, T. *Les Malouins à Terre-Neuve et les Droits de la France sur cette isle, d'après des documents authentiques.* Rennes, 1895.

Heagerty, J. J. *Four Centuries of Medical History in Canada and a Sketch of the Medical History of Newfoundland.* 2 vols. Toronto, 1928.

Howley, J. P. *The Beothucks or Red Indians, the aboriginal inhabitants of Newfoundland.* Cambridge, 1915.

Kirke, H. *The First English Conquest of Canada with some account of the earliest Settlements in Nova Scotia and Newfoundland.* London, 1871. 2nd edn. 1908.

Le Mesurier, H. W. "The early Relations between Newfoundland and the Channel Islands." *Geographical Review*, 1916. Vol. ii.

McGrath, Sir P. T. "Will Newfoundland join Canada?" *Queen's Quarterly*, 1929.

Musset, G. *Les Rochellais à Terre-Neuve.* La Rochelle, 1899.

Perret, R. *La Géographie de Terre-Neuve.* Paris, 1913.

A very useful book with much historical material.

Ricci, J. H. de. *The Fisheries Dispute and Annexation of Canada.* London, 1888.

Roncière, C. de la. *Histoire de la Marine Française.* Vols. iii and iv. Paris, 1900– .

Much valuable material on the early period that is not accessible elsewhere.

—— *La Question de Terre-Neuve.* Paris, 1904.

Sabine, F. *Report on the Principal Fisheries of the American Seas.* Washington, 1853.

Siddall, E. J. *The Origin of Nonconformity in St John's.* St John's, 1895.

Tucker, H. W. *Memoir of the Life and Episcopate of Ed. Feild, Bishop of Newfoundland, 1844–76.* London, 1877.

—— *Newfoundland as it was and as it is in 1877.* London, 1877.

Tuttle, J. *John Mason (including a reprint of his Tract on Newfoundland).* Prince Society, Boston, 1887.

Weeden, W. B. *Economic and Social History of New England, 1620–1789.* 2 vols. Boston, 1890.

Williamson, J. A. *Maritime Enterprise, 1485–1558.* Oxford, 1913.

—— *The Cabots and the Discovery of North America.* London, 1929.

Woodbury, C. L. *Relation of the Fisheries to the Discovery of North America.* Boston, 1880.

INDEX

CAMBRIDGE: PRINTED BY
W. LEWIS, M.A.
AT THE UNIVERSITY PRESS